THE INTERNATIONAL BIBLIOGRAPHY OF SOCIOLOGY

This bibliography, with its sister publications, Anthropology, Economics, and Political Science (known together as the *International Bibliography of the Social Sciences* (*IBSS*)) is an essential tool for librarians, academics and researchers wishing to keep up to date with the published literature in the social sciences.

The *IBSS* lists journal articles and monographs from all over the world and in over 70 languages, all with English title translations where needed.

From 1991, users already familiar with the bibliography will notice major improvements in contents and currency. There is greater coverage of monographs as well as journals, with continued emphasis on international publications, especially those from the developing world and Eastern Europe. Indexing techniques have been refined: the *IBSS* now offers more specific subject and geographical indexes together with an author index. A subject index in French continues to be provided.

Prepared until 1989 at the Fondation nationale des sciences politiques in Paris, the *IBSS* is now compiled and edited by the British Library of Political and Economic Science at the London School of Economics. The International Committee for Social Science Information and Documentation and UNESCO continue to support the publication. The new *International Bibliography* not only maintains its traditional extensive coverage of periodical literature, but considerably extends its coverage of monographic material by incorporating most of that which would previously have been included in the *London Bibliography of the Social Sciences*, publication of which has now been discontinued.

Also available from Routledge

Copies of the *International Bibliography of the Social Sciences* for previous years.

Thematic Lists of Descriptors. Four subject volumes published in 1989, following the classification and index terms of the relevant volume of the *IBSS*.

Copies of the *London Bibliography of the Social Sciences* for previous years are available from Schmidt Periodicals, Dettendorf, D-8201 Bad Feilnbach 2, Germany.

INTERNATIONAL BIBLIOGRAPHY OF THE SOCIAL SCIENCES

BIBLIOGRAPHIE INTERNATIONALE DES SCIENCES SOCIALES

published annually in four parts since 1961: UNESCO, Paris
paraissant chaque année en quatre parties jusqu'en 1961: UNESCO, Paris

International bibliography of sociology / Bibliographie internationale de sociologie [red cover / couverture rouge] Vol.1:1951 (publ. 1952)

International bibliography of political science / Bibliographie internationale de science politique [grey cover / couverture grise] Vol.1:1952 (publ. 1954)

International bibliography of economics / Bibliographie internationale de sciences économiques [yellow cover / couverture jaune] Vol.1:1952 (publ. 1955)

International bibliography of social and cultural anthropology / Bibliographie internationale d'anthropologie sociale et culturelle [green cover / couverture verte] Vol.1:1955 (publ. 1958)

Prepared by

THE BRITISH LIBRARY OF POLITICAL AND ECONOMIC SCIENCE

with the support of the International Committee for Social Science Information
and Documentation with the assistance of UNESCO

Editor
Jean Sykes
Librarian, British Library of Political and Economic Science

Editorial Manager
Csanád Siklós

Assistant Editorial Manager
Liam Earney

Database Design
Robert H. Browne

Editorial Assistants
Michelle Brattle Mary Bispham
Kath Farrell Deborah Harrower Rebecca Ursell
Anna Vaughan Kim Wilson

INTERNATIONAL BIBLIOGRAPHY OF THE SOCIAL SCIENCES

2000

INTERNATIONAL BIBLIOGRAPHY OF SOCIOLOGY

VOLUME L

BIBLIOGRAPHIE INTERNATIONALE DES SCIENCES SOCIALES

BIBLIOGRAPHIE INTERNATIONALE DE SOCIOLOGIE

Prepared with the support of the International Committee for Social Science Information and Documentation with the assistance of UNESCO

Établie avec le concours du Comité international pour l'information et la documentation en sciences sociales avec l'assistance de l'UNESCO

London and New York

First published in 2001 by
Routledge
(on behalf of The British Library of Political and Economic Science)

11 New Fetter Lane
London EC4P 4EE
&
29 West 35th Street
New York, NY 10001

Routledge is an imprint of the Taylor & Francis Group

©2001, British Library of Political and Economic Science

Printed in Great Britain by
Biddles Ltd, Guildford and King's Lynn

All rights reserved. No part of this book may be reprinted or reproduced or utilized in any form or by any electronic, mechanical, or other means, now known or hereafter invented, including photocopying and recording, or in any information storage or retrieval system, without permission in writing from the publishers.

British Library Cataloguing in Publication Data

A CIP catalogue record for this book is available from the British Library.
ISBN 0-415-26238-0
ISSN 0085-2074

Editorial Correspondence should be sent to:

International Bibliography of the Social Sciences
British Library of Political and Economic Science
London School of Economics
10 Portugal Street
London WC2A 2HD
United Kingdom

Telephone: (U.K.) 020-7955-7455
Fax: (U.K.) 020-7955-6923
email: ibss@lse.ac.uk
http://www.lse.ac.uk/ibss/

CONTENTS

International Committee for Social Science
    Information and Documentation   vi

Preface   vii

Selection criteria   ix

List of periodicals consulted   xi

List of abbreviations   lxvii

Classification scheme   cvii

Bibliography for 2000   1

Author index   305

Placename index   411

Subject index   421

Index des matières   515

INTERNATIONAL COMMITTEE FOR SOCIAL SCIENCE INFORMATION AND DOCUMENTATION

LE COMITÉ INTERNATIONAL POUR L'INFORMATION ET LA DOCUMENTATION EN SCIENCES SOCIALES

Krishna G. Tyagi, National Social Science Documentation Centre, New Delhi (President)

Arnaud Marks, SWIDOC/KNAW, Amsterdam (Secretary General)

ACKNOWLEDGEMENTS

The Editor would like to thank the members of the International Committee, and all those who have contributed to the production of these volumes, particularly: Kaarlo Mäkelä of Eduskunnan Kirjasto, the Library of Parliament at Helsinki; Dr Csaba Nagy of the Library of the Hungarian Parliament, Budapest; Ekkehart Seusing of the Zentralbibliothek der Wirtschaftswissenschaften, Bibliothek des Instituts für Weltwirtschaft, Kiel; and, Yusuke Iijima and the Database Committee of the Japan Sociological Society.

PREFACE

The **International Bibliography of the Social Sciences** is an annual four volume publication covering Economics, Political Science, Sociology and Anthropology. It is compiled by the British Library of Political and Economic Science under the auspices of the International Committee for Social Science Information and Documentation. Until recently UNESCO gave financial support for the preparation of the IBSS volumes, but in consultation with the ICSSD it was decided that UNESCO's support should be transferred to the distribution of the IBSS volumes. This has greatly benefitted a number of information and documentation centres in developing countries.

Some 100,000 articles (from over 2,500 journals) and 20,000 books are scanned each year in the process of compiling the **International Bibliography**. Coverage is international with publications in over 70 languages from more than 60 countries. All titles are given in their original language and in English translation.

The selection policy (criteria appear on page ix) is designed to provide a tool for retrospective search rather than current awareness. Each volume represents the most significant new material published in that discipline in a given year.

With the increase in interdisciplinary material published in the social sciences, some items will be listed in more than one of the four volumes. It is nonetheless advisable to check other disciplines in the series to avoid missing relevant items which may for some reason be cited in only one volume.

Production of the **International Bibliography** is computerized. The database from which it is extracted is available on CD-ROM, providing access to a broader range of material than is cited in these volumes, and updated quarterly. There is also an online service available in the United Kingdom.

PRÉFACE

La **Bibliographie internationale des sciences sociales** est un ouvrage annuel en 4 volumes couvrant la science économique, la science politique, la sociologie et l'anthropologie. Elle est préparée par la British Library of Political and Economic Science sous les auspices du Comité international pour l'information et la documentation en sciences sociales. Jusqu'ici l'assistance financière de l'UNESCO était consacrée à la préparation des volumes de la Bibliographie internationale des sciences sociales. Cependant, et en consultation avec le CIDSS, il a été décidé de transférer cette assistance financière à la distribution de la BISS, ce dont bénéficient un certain nombre de centres d'information et de documentation dans les pays en voie de développement.

Chaque année, quelques 100,000 articles (provenant de 2,500 périodiques) et 20,000 livres sont analysés et indexés en vue de la préparation de la **Bibliographie internationale**. Il s'agit d'une bibliographie véritablement internationale puisqu'elle comprend des publications en plus de 70 langues, provenant de plus de 60 pays. Tous les titres sont présentés dans la langue originale avec une traduction en anglais.

Dans le choix des références, on a davantage cherché à fournir un instrument de recherche retrospective plutôt qu'un service d'information courante. Chaque volume présente les publications les plus significatives parues dans cette discipline au cours d'une année donnée.

Du fait du nombre croissant de publications de nature interdisciplinaire dans les sciences sociales, certains éléments peuvent apparaître dans plus d'un des 4 volumes. Il est cependant conseillé de se reporter aux autres volumes disciplinaires de la série, au cas où des références importantes ne figuraient que dans un seul volume.

La préparation de la **Bibliographie internationale** est informatisée. La base de données dont elle est issue est disponible sur CD-ROM. Elle donne accès à une plus large sélection de publications que celles citées dans ces volumes, et sera mise à jour 4 fois par an. En Grande Bretagne il existe aussi un service en ligne.

SELECTION CRITERIA

1. Subject.

Documents relevant to sociology.

2. Nature and form.

Publications of known authorship and lasting significance to sociology, whether in serial or monographic form, typically works with a theoretical component intending to communicate new knowledge, new ideas or making use of new materials.

Previously published materials in all formats are omitted, including most translations. Also excluded are textbooks, materials from newspapers or news magazines, popular or purely informative papers, presentations of predominantly primary data and legislative or judicial texts and items of parochial relevance only.

LIST OF PERIODICALS CONSULTED
LISTE DES PERIODIQUES CONSULTÉS

Abacus: Journal of accounting, finance and business studies. (0001-3072). Oxford.
Aboriginal history. (0314-8769). Canberra.
Academy of Management review. (0363-7425). Ada OH.
Acadiensis: Journal of the history of the Atlantic Region. (0044-5851). Fredericton.
Accounting and business research. (0001-4788). London.
Accounting review. (0001-4826). Sarasota FL.
Accounting, auditing and accountability journal. (0951-3574). Bradford.
Accounting, business and financial history. (0958-5206). London.
Accounting, organizations and society. (0361-3682). Oxford.
Acta asiatica. (0567-7254). Tokyo.
Acta baltica. (0567-7289). Taunus.
Acta ethnographica. (1216-9803). Budapest.
Acta juridica hungarica. (1216-2574). Budapest.
Acta oeconomica. (0001-6373). Budapest.
Acta orientalia. (0001-6438). Copenhagen.
Acta politica. (0001-6810). Meppel.
Acta sociologica [Mexico]. (0186-6028). Mexico City.
Acta sociologica [Norway]. (0001-6993). Oslo.
Acta Universitatis Łódziensis: Folia oeconomica. (0208-6018). Łódz.
Acta Universitatis Łódziensis: Folia sociologica. (0208-600X). Łódz.
Actualité économique. (0001-771X). Montreal.
Addiction. (0965-2140). Abingdon.
Administration. (0001-8325). Dublin.
Administration [Kumamoto]. Kumamoto.
Administration and society. (0095-3997). Thousand Oaks CA.
Administration for development. (0311-4511). Boroko.
Administrative science quarterly. (0001-8392). Ithaca NY.
Affari sociali internazionali. Milan.
Africa [Edinburgh]. (0001-9720). Edinburgh.
Africa [Rome]. Rome.
Africa development = Afrique & développement. (0850-3907). Dakar.
Africa insight. (0256-2804). Pretoria.
Africa perspective. Witwatersrand.
Africa quarterly. (0001-9828). New Delhi.
Africa today. (0001-9887). Denver CO.
African affairs. (0001-9909). Oxford.
African anthropology = Anthropologie africaine. (1024-0969). Yaounde.
African arts. (0001-9933). Los Angeles CA.
African development review = Revue africaine de développement. Abidjan.
African economic history. (0145-2258). Madison WI.
African journal of international and comparative law = Revue africaine de droit international et comparé. (0954-8890). London.

LIST OF PERIODICALS CONSULTED

African music. (0065-4019). Grahamstown.
African notes. (0002-0087). Ibadan.
African review. (0856-0056). Dar es Salaam.
African sociological review = Revue Africaine de sociologie. (1027-4332). Grahamstown.
African studies. (0002-0184). Witwatersrand.
African studies review. (0002-0206). New Brunswick, NJ.
African study monographs. (0285-1601). Kyoto.
African study monographs. Supplementary issues. (0286-9667). Kyoto.
African urban quarterly. (0747-6108). Nairobi.
Africana. (0871-2336). Porto.
Africana gandensia. Ghent.
Africana Marburgensia. (0174-5603). Berlin.
Africana research bulletin. Freetown.
Afrika Spectrum. (0002-0397). Hamburg.
Afrika Zamani: An annual journal of African history. (0850-3079). Dakar.
Afrique 2000. (1017-0952). Brussels.
Afrique contemporaine. (0002-0478). Paris.
Afrique et l'Asie modernes. (0399-0370). Paris.
Ageing and society. (0144-686X). Cambridge.
Agenda. (1013-0950). Dalbridge.
Agrekon. (0303-1853). Pretoria.
Agricultura y sociedad. (0211-8394). Madrid.
Agricultural history. (0002-1482). Berkeley CA.
Agriculture and resources quarterly. (1032-9722). Canberra.
Al Muntaka. (0753-9894). France.
Al-Abhath. Beirut.
Al-Qantara. (0211-3589). Madrid.
Aletheia. (1413-0394). Canoas.
Allgemeines statistisches Archiv. (0002-6018). Göttingen.
Alternatives. (0304-3754). Boulder CO.
Amazonia peruana. (0252-886X). Lima.
América indígena. (0002-7081). Mexico City.
American anthropologist. (0002-7294). Arlington VA.
American behavioral scientist. (0002-7642). Thousand Oaks CA.
American economic review. (0002-8282). Nashville TN.
American education studies review. Osaka.
American ethnologist. (0094-0496). Arlington VA.
American historical review. (0002-8762). Washington DC.
American journal of agricultural economics. (0002-9092). Ames IA.
American journal of comparative law. (0002-919X). Berkeley CA.
American journal of economics and sociology. (0002-9246). New York NY.
American journal of international law. (0002-9300). Washington DC.
American journal of Islamic social sciences. (0742-6763). Herndon VA.
American journal of orthopsychiatry. (0002-9432). New York NY.
American journal of physical anthropology. (0002-9483). New York NY.
American journal of political science. (0092-5853). Madison WI.
American journal of primatology. (0275-2565). New York NY.
American journal of sociology. (0002-9602). Chicago IL.
American philosophical quarterly. (0003-0481). Bowling Green OH.
American political science review. (0003-0554). Washington DC.
American psychologist. (0003-066X). Washington DC.

LISTE DES PERIODIQUES CONSULTÉS

American review of Canadian studies. (0272-2011). Washington DC.
American sociological review. (0003-1224). Washington DC.
American sociologist. (0003-1232). New Brunswick NJ.
Amerindia. (0221-8852). Paris.
Análise social. (0003-2573). Lisbon.
Analysis. (0003-2638). Oxford.
Anarchist studies. (0967-3393). Cambridge.
Anatolian studies. (0066-1546). London.
Ancient Nepal. Kathmandu.
ANEMOS. Hasekô Sôgôkenkyusho.
Annales æquatoria. (0254-4296). Lovenjoel.
Annales d'économie et de statistique. (0769-489X). Paris.
Annales d'études internationales = Annals of international studies. (0066-2135). Brussels.
Annales de géographie. (0003-4010). Paris.
Annales de l'économie publique sociale et coopérative = Annals of public and cooperative economics. (1370-4788). Brussels.
Annales internationales de criminologie = International annals of criminology = Anales internacionales de criminología. (0003-4452). Paris.
Annales universitatis Mariae Curie-Skłodowska: Sectio H. Oeconomia. (0459-9586). Lublin.
Annales: Économies, sociétés, civilisations. (0395-2649). Paris.
Annales: Histoire, sciences sociales. Paris.
Annali della fondazione Luigi Einaudi. Turin.
Annali di ca'foscari. Venice.
Annals of family studies. Tokyo.
Annals of human biology. (0301-4460). London.
Annals of regional science. (0570-1864). Heidelberg.
Annals of the American Academy of Political and Social Science. (0002-7162). Thousand Oaks CA.
Annals of the Association of American Geographers. (0004-5608). Washington DC.
Annals of the Institite of Statistical Mathematics. Tokyo.
Année africaine. (0570-1937). Paris.
Année sociologique. (0066-2399). Paris.
Annuaire des pays de l'Ocean indien. (0247-400X). Paris.
Annuaire français de droit international. (0066-3085). Paris.
Annual bulletin. Kobe.
Annual bulletin of the Faculty of Humanities Matsuyama Shinonome College. Matsuyama.
Annual journal of the Japanese Association of Labor Sociology. Tokyo.
Annual of economic jurisprudence. Tokyo.
Annual of Institute Kanazawa Economical College. Kanazawa City.
Annual of the Department of Antiquities of Jordan. Amman.
Annual of the Institute of Economic Research Chuo University. Tokyo.
Annual of the Society of Economic Sociology. Kobe.
Annual report of Shizuoka Kenritsu Daigaku. Hamamatsu.
Annual report of studies in humanities and social sciences. Nara City.
Annual report of University of Shizuoka, Hamamatsu College. Shizuoka.
Annual reports of the Faculty of Arts and Letters Tohoku University. Tohoku.
Annual research report of Education Department of Rikkyo University. Tokyo.
Annual review of anthropology. (0084-6570). Palo Alto CA.
Annual review of energy and the environment. (0362-1626). Palo Alto CA.
Annual review of psychology. (0066-4308). Palo Alto CA.
Annual review of public health. (0163-7525). Palo Alto CA.
Annual review of Shukutoku University. Shukutoku.

LIST OF PERIODICALS CONSULTED

Annual review of sociology. (0360-0572). Palo Alto CA.
Annual review of sociology [Japan]. Tokyo.
Annuals of Japan Association for Urban Sociology. Japan.
Annuals of sociology. Tokyo.
Anthropological forum. (0066-4677). Nedlands WA.
Anthropological linguistics. (0003-5483). Bloomington IN.
Anthropological papers of the American Museum of Natural History. (0065-9452). New York NY.
Anthropological quarterly. (0003-5491). Washington DC.
Anthropological science. (0918-7960). Tokyo.
Anthropological theory. (1463-4996). London.
Anthropologie [Paris]. (0003-5521). Paris.
Anthropologie visuelle. Paris.
Anthropology and aesthetics. (0277-1322). Santa Monica CA.
Anthropology and humanism. (0193-5615). Arlington VA.
Anthropology today. (0268-540X). London.
Anthropos [Athens]. (1105-2155). Athens.
Anthropos [St. Augustin]. (0257-9774). Sankt Augustin.
Antipode. (0066-4812). Oxford.
Antiquités africaines. (0066-4871). Paris.
Antiquity. (0003-598X). Cambridge.
Antropologia portuguesa. (0870-0990). Coimbra.
Antropologica. (0003-6110). Caracas.
Antropologiska studier. (0003-6129). Stockholm.
Anuario de estudios centroamericanos. (0377-7316). San José.
Anuario de eusko folklore. (0210-7732). San Sebastián.
Anuario indigenista. (0185-5441). Colonia Florida.
Anuarul arhivei de folclor. (0255-4895). Bucharest.
Anuarul Institutului de Etnografie și Folclor „Constantin Brăiloiu". (1220-5230). Bucharest.
Applied economics. (0003-6846). London.
Applied economics letters. (1350-4851). London.
Applied financial economics. (0960-3107). London.
Appropriate technology. (0305-0920). London.
Apuntes. (0252-1865). Lima.
Arab affairs. (0950-0731). London.
Arab studies journal. (1083-4753). Washington DC.
Arab studies quarterly. (0271-3519). Belmont MA.
Arabica. (0570-5398). Leiden.
Archaeologia polona. (0066-5924). Warsaw.
Archaeology in Oceania. (0003-8121). Sydney.
Archeologia. (0066-605X). Warsaw.
Archeologia polski. (0003-8180). Warsaw.
Archipel. (0044-8613). Paris.
Archiv des öffentlichen Rechts. (0003-8911). Tübingen.
Archiv des Völkerrechts. (0003-892X). Tübingen.
Archiv für Kommunalwissenschaften. (0003-9209). Stuttgart.
Archiv für Rechts- und Sozialphilosophie = Archives de philosophie du droit et de philosophie sociale = Archives for philosophy of law and social philosophy = Archivo de filosofía jurídica y social. (0001-2343). Stuttgart.
Archiv für Sozialgeschichte. (0066-6505). Bonn.
Archív orientální. (0044-8699). Prague.

LISTE DES PÉRIODIQUES CONSULTÉS

Archives européennes de sociologie = European journal of sociology = Europäisches Archiv für Soziologie. (0003-9756). Cambridge.
Archives of economic history. Athens.
Archives of suicide research. (1381-1118). Dordrecht.
Area. (0004-0894). London.
Argumentation. (0920-427X). Dordrecht.
Armed forces and society. (0095-327X). New Brunswick NJ.
Arquivo. Maputo.
Artha vijñāna. (0971-586X). Pune.
Artibus asiae. (0004-3648). Ascona.
ASEAN economic bulletin. (0217-4472). Singapore.
Asia journal of theology. (0218-0812). Bangalore.
Asia major. (0004-4482). Princeton NJ.
Asia Pacific business review. (1360-2381). London.
Asia Pacific journal of anthropology. (1444-2213). Canberra.
Asia Pacific journal on environment and development. (1023-7895). Dhaka.
Asian and Pacific migration journal. (0117-1968). Quezon City.
Asian culture (Asian-Pacific culture) quarterly. (0378-8911). Taipei.
Asian Development Bank Occasional Papers. Manila.
Asian economic journal. Hong Kong.
Asian economic review. (0004-4555). Hyderabad.
Asian economies. (0304-260X). Seoul.
Asian folklore studies. (0385-2342). Nagoya.
Asian journal of political science. Singapore.
Asian journal of public administration. (0259-8272). Hong Kong.
Asian music. (0044-9202). Ithaca NY.
Asian Pacific communication. (0957-6851). Clevedon.
Asian perspective [S. Korea]. (0258-9184). Seoul.
Asian perspectives [Hawaii]. (0066-8435). Honolulu HI.
Asian profile. (0304-8675). Hong Kong.
Asian research trends. (0917-1479). Tokyo.
Asian studies review. (0314-7533). Sydney.
Asian survey. (0004-4687). Berkeley CA.
Asian thought and society. (0361-3968). New York NY.
Asian-Pacific economic literature. (0818-9935). Oxford.
Atlal. The journal of Saudi Arabian archaeology. Riyadh.
Aus der Südosteuropa-Forschung. Munich.
Aussenpolitik. (0587-3835). Bielefeld.
Aussenwirtschaft. (0004-8216). Zurich.
Australian Aboriginal studies. (0729-4352). Canberra.
Australian and New Zealand journal of sociology. (0004-8690). Bundoora.
Australian and New Zealand journal of statistics. (1369-1473). Oxford.
Australian cultural history. (0728-8433). Kensington NSW.
Australian economic history review. (0004-8992). Oxford.
Australian economic papers. (0004-900X). Adelaide.
Australian economic review. (0004-9018). Oxford.
Australian geographer. (0004-9182). Gladesville NSW.
Australian geographical studies. (0004-9190). Campbell.
Australian historical studies. (1031-461X). Carlton.
Australian journal of agricultural economics. (0004-9395). East Melbourne.
Australian journal of anthropology. (1035-8811). Sydney.

LIST OF PERIODICALS CONSULTED

Australian journal of Chinese affairs. (0156-7365). Canberra.
Australian journal of international affairs. (0004-9913). Canberra.
Australian journal of linguistics. (0726-8602). Cambridge.
Australian journal of political science. (1036-1146). Oxford.
Australian journal of politics and history. (0004-9522). Queensland.
Australian journal of public administration. (0313-6647). Sydney.
Australian journal of social issues. (0157-6321). Sydney.
Australian quarterly. (0005-0091). Balmain.
Australian studies. (0954-0954). Stirling.
Australian year book of international law. (0084-7658). Canberra.
Australian-Canadian studies. (0810-1906). Nathan QLD.
Austrian history yearbook. (0667-2378). Minneapolis MN.
AWR Bulletin. (0014-2492). Vienna.
Azania. (0067-270X). Nairobi.
Aziia i Afrika segodnia. Moscow.
Baessler-Archiv. (0005-3856). Berlin.
Baishin. Osaka.
Balkanologie. (1279-7952). Paris.
Banca Nazionale del Lavoro quarterly review. (0005-4607). Rome.
Bancaria. (0005-4623). Rome.
Bangladesh development studies. (0304-095X). Dhaka.
Bangladesh journal of political economy. Dhaka.
Bangladesh journal of public administration. Dhaka.
Bank of England quarterly bulletin. (0005-5166). London.
BC studies. (0005-2949). Vancouver.
Behavioral and brain sciences. (0140-525X). New York NY.
Beiträge zur Japanologie. (0522-6759). Vienna.
Belizean studies. (0250-6831). Belize City.
Benelux. Brussels.
Berkeley journal of sociology. (0067-5830). Berkeley CA.
Berkeley technology law journal. (0885 2715). Berkeley CA.
Berliner indologische Studien. Reinbek.
Berliner Journal für Soziologie. (0863-1808). Berlin.
Bevolking en gezin. (0772-764X). Brussels.
Biblical archaeologist. (0006-0895). Baltimore MD.
Biblioteka etnografii polskiej. (0067-7655). Warsaw.
BIISS journal. (1010-9356). Dhaka.
Bijdragen tot de taal-, land- en volkenkunde. (0006-2294). Leiden.
Bilig. (1301-0549). Ankara.
Bioethics. (0269-9702). Oxford.
Biography. (0162-4962). Honolulu HI.
Biométrie humaine et anthropologie. (1279-7863). Paris.
Body and society. (1357-034X). London.
Boekmancahier: kwartaalschrift voor kunst, onderzoek en beleid. (0925-0239). Amsterdam.
BOFIT discussion papers. (1456-4564). Helsinki.
Boletim do Museu Paraense Emílio Goeldi: Série antropologia. (0522-7291). Belém.
Boletín de antropología americana. (0252-841X). Mexico City.
Boletin de la Asociación Española de Orientalistas. (0571-3692). Madrid.
Boletín. Centro de estudios monetarios latinoamericanos. (0186-7229). Mexico City.
Borneo research bulletin. (0006-7806). Williamsburg VA.
Borneo review. Sabah.

LISTE DES PERIODIQUES CONSULTÉS

Botswana notes and records. (0525-5059). Gaborone.
Boundary and security bulletin. (0967-411X). Durham.
British accounting review. (0890-8389). London.
British elections and parties review. (1368-9886). Ilford.
British journal for the history of science. (0007-0874). Cambridge.
British journal of Canadian studies. (0269-9222). London.
British journal of clinical psychology. (0144-6657). Leicester.
British journal of criminology. (0007-0955). London.
British journal of developmental psychology. (0261-510X). Leicester.
British journal of educational studies. (0007-1005). Oxford.
British journal of ethnomusicology. (0968-1221). London.
British journal of industrial relations. (0007-1080). Oxford.
British journal of management. (1045-3172). Chichester.
British journal of Middle Eastern studies. (1353-0194). Durham.
British journal of political science. (0007-1234). Cambridge.
British journal of psychology. (0007-1269). Leicester.
British journal of social psychology. (0144-6665). Leicester.
British journal of social work. (0045-3102). Oxford.
British journal of sociology. (0007-1315). London.
British review of New Zealand studies. (0951-6204). Edinburgh.
British year book of international law. (0068-2691). Oxford.
Brookings papers on economic activity. (0007-2303). Washington DC.
Brookings review. (0745-1253). Washington DC.
Bulletin. Yokohama.
Bulletin d'études indiennes. (0761-3156). Paris.
Bulletin de l'École française d'Extrême-Orient. (0336-1519). Paris.
Bulletin de la Société d'archéologie copte. Cairo.
Bulletin de la Société des études océaniennes. Papeete.
Bulletin des études africaines de l'INALCO. Paris.
Bulletin du Centre genevois d'Anthropologie. Louvain.
Bulletin for international fiscal documentation. (0007-4624). Amsterdam.
Bulletin of Aichi University of Education. Aichi.
Bulletin of Chukyo Gakuin University. Gifu.
Bulletin of comparative labour relations. The Hague.
Bulletin of Eastern Caribbean affairs. (0254-7406). Cave Hill.
Bulletin of economic research. (0307-3378). Oxford.
Bulletin of education. Tokyo.
Bulletin of Faculty of Education, Okayama University. Okayama.
Bulletin of graduate studies. Tokyo.
Bulletin of Hirosaki Gakuin College. Hirosaki.
Bulletin of Hokkaido Tokai University. Sapporo.
Bulletin of Holy Cross College. Mie.
Bulletin of Indonesian economic studies. (0007-4918). Canberra.
Bulletin of International Research Center for Japanese Studies. Kyoto.
Bulletin of Ishinomaki Senshu University. Ishinomaki.
Bulletin of Joetsu University education. Japan.
Bulletin of Kanto Gakuin University. Yokohama.
Bulletin of Latin American research. (0261-3050). Oxford.
Bulletin of liberal arts and sciences of the National Defense Medical College. Tokyo.
Bulletin of Musashino Women's College. Tokyo.
Bulletin of Sakuyo Music College. Okayama.

LIST OF PERIODICALS CONSULTED

Bulletin of Shiga Junior College of Cultural Studies. Shiga.
Bulletin of Shukugawa Gakuin Junior College. Nishinomiya.
Bulletin of sociology. Tokyo.
Bulletin of Tanzanian affairs. (0952-2948). London.
Bulletin of the Akita Prefectural College of Agriculture. Akita City.
Bulletin of the American Schools of Oriental Research. (0003-097X). Baltimore MD.
Bulletin of the Bihar Tribal Welfare Research Institute. Ranchi.
Bulletin of the Department of Management and Information Science Jôbu University. Gunma.
Bulletin of the doctoral research course in human culture. Tokyo.
Bulletin of The Faculty of Education. Tokyo.
Bulletin of the Faculty of Education [Sapporo]. Sapporo.
Bulletin of the Faculty of Education [Wakayama]. Wakayama.
Bulletin of the Faculty of Education Hokkaido University. Hokkaido.
Bulletin of the Faculty of Education, Chiba University. Chiba.
Bulletin of the Faculty of General Education of Utsunomiya University. Tochigi.
Bulletin of the Faculty of Humanities and Social Science. Tsu.
Bulletin of the Faculty of Humanities of Aichi Gakuin University. Aichi.
Bulletin of the Faculty of Literature Aichi Prefectural University. Aichi.
Bulletin of the Faculty of Sociology. Kyoto.
Bulletin of the Faculty of Sociology [Ôtsu]. Ôtsu.
Bulletin of the Graduate Division of Literature. Tokyo.
Bulletin of the Indian Institute of History of Medicine. (0304-9558). New Delhi.
Bulletin of the Institute of Ethnology, Academia Sinica. (0001-3935). Taipei.
Bulletin of the Institute of Oriental Philosophy. Tokyo.
Bulletin of the Institute of Socio-Information and Communication Studies. Tokyo.
Bulletin of the International Committee on Urgent Anthropological and Ethnological Research. (0538-5865). Vienna.
Bulletin of the Japan Society for the Study of Adult Education. Tokyo.
Bulletin of the Museum of Far Eastern Antiquities. (0081-5691). Stockholm.
Bulletin of the Nanzan Institute for Religion and Culture. (0386-720X). Nagoya.
Bulletin of the Polytechnic University. Tokyo.
Bulletin of the Research Institute Chuo-Gakuin University. Tokyo.
Bulletin of the School of Education. Nagoya.
Bulletin of the School of Oriental and African Studies. (0041-977X). London.
Bulletin of the Shizuoko Institute of Science and Technology. Fukuroi.
Bulletin of Tibetology. (0007-5159). Gangtok.
Bulletin of Tohoku Fukushi University. Sendai.
Bulletin, Yokohama City University. Yokohama.
Bulletin. Bank of Finland. (0784-6509). Helsinki.
Bulletin. Committee for Middle East Trade. London.
Bulletin. Kagawa University. Takamatsu.
Bulletin. Oita University, Faculty of Education. Oita City.
Bulletin. Tokyo University, Graduate School. Tokyo.
Bulletin. University of the Ryukyus, College of Law and Letters. Okinawa.
Bulletin: Bank of Botswana. Gabarone.
Bungaku-kenkyuka Kiyo (Journal of the Waseda Graduate School). Waseda.
Bungakubu ronshu (Journal of the Aichi Prefectural University). Aichi.
Business economist. (0306-5049). Watford.
Business ethics quarterly. (1052-150X). Bowling Green OH.
Business ethics: a European review. (0962-8770). Oxford.
Business history. (0007-6791). Ilford.

LISTE DES PERIODIQUES CONSULTÉS

Business history review. (0007-6805). Boston MA.
Business library review. (1045-7798). Reading.
Cahiers africains d'administration publique = African administrative studies. (0007-9588). Tangiers.
Cahiers d'études africaines. (0008-0055). Paris.
Cahiers d'études arabes. (0985-1909). Paris.
Cahiers d'études sur la Méditerranée orientale et le monde turco-iranien. (0764-9878). Paris.
Cahiers d'histoire de l'Institut de recherches marxistes. (0246-9731). Paris.
Cahiers d'outre-mer. (0373-5843). Bordeaux.
Cahiers de l'Asie du Sud-Est. (0399-1652). Paris.
Cahiers de l'homme. (0068-5046). Paris.
Cahiers de l'ISSP. Neuchâtel.
Cahiers de linguistique asie orientale. (0153-3320). Paris.
Cahiers de Tunisie. (0008-0012). Tunis.
Cahiers des Amériques latines. (0008-0020). Paris.
Cahiers des sciences humaines. (0768-9829). Paris.
Cahiers du CEDAF = ASDOC-studies. (0250-1619). Brussels.
Cahiers du monde russe. (1252-6576). Paris.
Cahiers économiques et monétaires. (0396-4701). Paris.
Cahiers internationaux de sociologie. (0008-0276). Paris.
Cahiers ivoiriens de recherche linguistique. (0252-9386). Abidjan.
Cakalele: Maluku research journal. (1053-2285). Honolulu HI.
California management review. (0008-1256). Berkeley CA.
Cambridge anthropology. Cambridge.
Cambridge journal of economics. (0309-166X). London.
Cambridge law journal. (0008-1973). Cambridge.
Cambridge review of international affairs. (0955-7571). Cambridge.
Canadian Association of African Studies newsletter = Association canadienne des études africaines bulletin. (0228-8397). Ottawa.
Canadian ethnic studies = Études ethniques au Canada. (0008-3496). Montréal.
Canadian geographer. (0008-3658). Montreal.
Canadian historical review. (0008-3755). Toronto.
Canadian journal of African studies = Revue canadienne des études africaines. (0008-3968). Ottawa.
Canadian journal of agricultural economics = Revue canadienne d'économie rurale. (0008-3976). Ottawa.
Canadian journal of economics = Revue canadienne d'économique. (0008-4085). Downsview.
Canadian journal of human sexuality. (1188-4517). Ontario.
Canadian journal of philosophy. (0045-5091). Calgary.
Canadian journal of political and social theory. (0380-9420). Montreal.
Canadian journal of political science = Revue canadienne de science politique. (0008-4239). Ottawa.
Canadian journal of sociology = Cahiers canadiens de sociologie. (0318-6431). Edmonton.
Canadian journal of statistics = Revue canadienne de statistiques. (0319-5724). Ottawa.
Canadian public administration = Administration publique du Canada. (0008-4840). Toronto.
Canadian review of sociology and anthropology = Revue canadienne de sociologie et d'anthropologie. (0008-4948). Montréal.
Canadian review of studies in nationalism = Revue canadienne des études sur le nationalisme. (0317-7904). Charlottetown.
Canadian yearbook of international law = Annuaire canadien de droit international. (0069-0058). Vancouver.
Canberra anthropology. (0314-9099). Canberra.
Capital and class. (0309-8168). London.
Capitalism, nature, socialism. (1045-5752). New York NY.

LIST OF PERIODICALS CONSULTED

Caravelle. (0008-0152). Toulouse.
Caribbean quarterly. (0008-6495). Kingston.
Caribbean studies = Estudios del Caribe = Études des Caraïbes. (0008-6533). Puerto Rico.
Caribe contemporáneo. (0185-2426). Mexico City.
Cato journal. (0273-3072). Washington DC.
Central Asian survey. (0263-4937). Abingdon.
Central Asiatic journal. (0008-9192). Wiesbaden.
Central European history. (0008-9389). Boston.
CEPAL review. (0251-2920). Santiago.
Challenge. (0577-5132). Armonk NY.
Child abuse and neglect. (0145-2134). Denver CO.
Child care in practice. (1357-5279). Belfast.
Child development. (0009-3920). Chicago IL.
Child welfare. (0009-4021). Washington DC.
Children and society. (0951-0605). London.
China city planning review. (1002-8447). Beijing.
China information. (0920-203X). Leiden.
China journal. Canberra.
China law reporter. Chicago IL.
China quarterly. (0009-4439). London.
China report. (0009-4455). New Delhi.
China review international. (1069-5834). Honolulu HI.
Chinese culture. (0009-4544). Taiwan.
Chinese economic studies. (0009-4552). Armonk NY.
Chinese sociology and anthropology. (0009-4625). Armonk NY.
Ching feng. (0009-4668). Hong Kong.
Chukyo daigkau shakaigaku kiyo. Aichi.
Ciclos. (0327-4063). Buenos Aires.
Ciências sociais hoje. São Paulo.
Cities. (0264-2751). London.
City. (1360-4813). London.
Civilisations. (0009-8140). Brussels.
Civilization study. Japan.
Civitas. (0009-8191). Rome.
Cognition. (0010-0277). Amsterdam.
Cognitive linguistics. (0936-5907). Berlin.
Cognitive science. (0364-0213). Norwood NJ.
Cold war history. (1468-2745). Ilford.
Collection. Purusārtha. (0339-1744). Paris.
Collegium antropologicum. (0350-6134). Zagreb.
Columbia journal of transnational law. (0010-1931). New York NY.
Columbia journal of world business. (0022-5428). New York NY.
Columbia law review. (0010-1958). New York NY.
Commonwealth and comparative politics. (1466-2043). Ilford.
Communicateur. Paris.
Communication & society. Nagareyama.
Communication research. (0093-6502). Thousand Oaks CA.
Communication review. (1071-4421). New York NY.
Communication theory. (1050-3293). New York NY.
Communist and post-communist studies. (0967-067X). Exeter.
Community development in Japan. Japan.

LISTE DES PERIODIQUES CONSULTÉS

Community development journal. (0010-3802). Oxford.
Community welfare study. Osaka.
Comparative and international law journal of Southern Africa. (0010-4051). Pretoria.
Comparative political studies. (0010-4140). Thousand Oaks CA.
Comparative politics. (0010-4159). New York NY.
Comparative social research. (0195-6310). Greenwich CT.
Comparative studies in society and history. (0010-4175). New York NY.
Comparative studies of South Asia, Africa and the Middle East. (1089-201X). Durham NC.
Complutum. (1131-6993). Madrid.
Comprehensive urban studies. (0386-3506). Tokyo.
Computational and mathematical organization theory. (1381-298X). Dordrecht.
Computational economics. (0927-7099). Dordrecht.
Comunicación y sociedad. (0214-0039). Navarre.
Comunidades y culturas peruanas. Lima.
Comunità internazionale. (0010-5066). Padua.
Cono sur. (0716-8713). Santiago.
Constitutional political economy. (1043-4062). Dordrecht.
Contemporary accounting research. (0823-9150). Toronto.
Contemporary British history. (1361-9462). Ilford.
Contemporary economic policy. (0735 0007). Oxford.
Contemporary economic problems. (0732-4308). Washington DC.
Contemporary Pacific. (1043-898X). Honolulu HI.
Contemporary policy issues. (0735-0007). Huntington Beach CA.
Contemporary security policy. (1352-3260). Ilford.
Contemporary sociological studies. Hokkaido.
Contemporary sociology - a journal of reviews. (0094-3061). Washington DC.
Contemporary South Asia. (0958-4935). Abingdon.
Contemporary Southeast Asia: A journal of international and strategic affairs. (0129-797X). Singapore.
Contention: Debates in society, culture, and science. (1056-1072). Bloomington IN.
Continuity and change. (0268-4160). Cambridge.
Contributions to Indian sociology. (0069-9667). New Delhi.
Contributions to Nepalese studies. Kirtipur.
Contributions to political economy. (0277-5921). London.
Cooperation and conflict. (0010-8367). London.
Coyuntura económica. (0120-3576). Bogota.
Coyuntura social. (0121-2532). Bogotá.
Crime and delinquency. (0011-1287). Thousand Oaks CA.
Crime and delinquency. Tokyo.
Crime and justice. (0192-3234). Chicago IL.
Crime, law and social change. (0925-4994). Dordrecht.
Criminal justice: the international journal of policy and practice. (1466-8025). London.
Criminology. (0011-1384). Columbus OH.
Critica marxista. (0011-152X). Rome.
Critica sociologica. (0011-1546). Rome.
Critical Asian studies. (1467-2715). London.
Critical perspectives on accounting. (1045-2354). London.
Critical review. (0891-3811). Chicago IL.
Critical social policy. (0261-0183). London.
Critical sociology. (0896-9205). Eugene OR.
Critique of anthropology. (0308-275X). London.
Croatian economic survey. (1330-4860). Zagreb.

LIST OF PERIODICALS CONSULTED

Cross-cultural research. (1069-3971). Thousand Oaks CA.
Crossroads. (0741-2037). DeKalb IL.
Cuadernos americanos. (0185-156X). Mexico City.
Cuadernos de administracion. (0120-3592). Bogota.
Cuadernos de nuestra América. Havana.
Cuadernos de sección antropologia-etnografia. (0213-0297). San Sebastián.
Cuadernos del sur. (1405-1966). Oaxaca.
Cuestiones políticas. Maracaibo.
Cultural anthropology. (0886-7356). Arlington VA.
Cultural dynamics. (0921-3740). London.
Cultural studies. (0950-2386). London.
Cultural values. (1362-5179). Oxford.
Culture & psychology. (1354-067X). London.
Culture, health and sexuality. (1369-1058). London.
Culture, medicine and psychiatry. (0165-005X). Dordrecht.
Curare. (0344-8622). Heidelberg.
Curator. (0011-3069). New York NY.
Current anthropology. (0011-3204). Washington DC.
Current English studies. Tokyo.
Current history. (0011-3530). Philadelphia PA.
Current issues in language and society. (1352 0520). Clevedon.
Current research on peace and violence. (0356-7893). Tampere.
Current sociology. (0011-3921). London.
Current world leaders. (0192-6802). Santa Barbara CA.
Cyprus review. (1015-2881). Nicosia.
Czech sociological review. (1210-3861). Prague.
Dædalus. (0011-5266). Cambridge MA.
Daigaku jiho. Japan.
Daigaku ronshu. Hiroshima.
De Economist. (0013-063X). Dordrecht.
Debates de coyuntura económica. (0120-8969). Bogota.
Defence and peace economics. (1043-0717). Yverdon.
Delhi law review. Delhi.
Democracy & nature. (1085-5661). Basingstoke.
Democratization. (1351-0347). Ilford.
Demografie. (0011-8265). Prague.
Demography. (0070-3370). Washington DC.
Derechos humanos. (0327-1846). Buenos Aires.
Desarrollo económico. (0046-001X). Buenos Aires.
Desarrollo y sociedad. (0120-3584). Bogota.
Deutschland Archiv: Zeitschrift für das vereinigte Deutschland. (0012-1428). Cologne.
Developing economies. (0012-1533). Tokyo.
Developing world bioethics. (1471-8731). Oxford.
Development. (1011-6370). Rome.
Development & socio-economic progress. Cairo.
Development and change. (0012-155X). London.
Development anthropologist. (1087-9900). Binghamton NY.
Development dialogue. (0345-2328). Uppsala.
Development in practice. (0961-4524). Oxford.
Development policy review. (0950-6764). Oxford.
Development Southern Africa. (0376-835X). Halfway House.

LISTE DES PERIODIQUES CONSULTÉS

Developmental psychology. (0012-1649). Washington.
Diachronica. (0176-4225). Amsterdam.
Dialectical anthropology. (0304-4092). Dordrecht.
Diaspora. (1044-2057). Toronto.
Die Welt des Orients. Göttingen.
Diplomacy and statecraft. (0959-2296). Ilford.
Diplomatic history. (0145-2096). Wilmington, DE.
Dirasat: Administrative Sciences. (1026-373X). Amman.
Dirasat: Educational Sciences. (1026-3713). Amman.
Dirasat: Human and Social Sciences. (1026-3721). Amman.
Dirasat: the humanities. (0255-8033). Amman.
Disability and society. (0968-7599). Abingdon.
Disasters: Journal of disaster studies, policy and management. (0361-3666). Oxford.
Discourse & society. (0957-9265). London.
Discourse studies. (1461-4456). London.
Discussion papers. Nagoya.
Documents. (0151-0827). Paris.
Dohodaigaku ronso. Nagoya.
Dokumente. (0012-5172). Bonn.
Dor ledor. Tel Aviv.
Douwa mondai kenkyu. Osaka.
Dreptul. Bucharest.
Druzhba narodov. Moscow.
Early China. (0362-5028). Berkeley CA.
East Asian review. Seoul.
East European Jewish affairs. (1350-1674). London.
East European meetings in ethnomusicology. (1221-9711). Bucharest.
East European politics and societies. (0888-3254). Berkeley CA.
East European quarterly. (0012-8449). Boulder CO.
Eastern Africa economic review. (0012-866X). Nairobi.
Eastern Africa social science research review. Addis Ababa.
Eastern anthropologist. (0012-8686). Lucknow.
Eastern Buddhist. (0012-8708). Kyoto.
Ecological economics. (0921-8009). Amsterdam.
Ecology of food and nutrition. (0367-0244). New York NY.
Econometric reviews. (0747-4938). New York NY.
Econometric theory. (0266-4666). New York NY.
Econometrica. (0012-9682). Evanston IL.
Economia & lavoro. (0012-978X). Rome.
Economia [Lisbon]. (0870-3531). Lisbon.
Economia [Quito]. (0012-9704). Quito.
Economia chilena. (0717-3830). Santiago.
Economia e banca. (0393-9243). Trento.
Economia internazionale. (0012-981X). Genoa.
Economía y administración. (0716-0100). Concepción.
Economia y desarrollo. (0252-8584). Havana.
Economic affairs [Calcutta]. (0424-2513). Calcutta.
Economic and business review for Central and South-Eastern Europe. (1580-0466). Ljubljana.
Economic and industrial democracy. (0143-831X). London.
Economic and social review. (0012-9984). Dublin.
Economic bulletin. Norges bank. (0029-1676). Oslo.

LIST OF PERIODICALS CONSULTED

Economic development and cultural change. (0013-0079). Chicago IL.
Economic development quarterly. (0891-2424). Thousand Oaks CA.
Economic eye. (0389-0503). Tokyo.
Economic geography. (0013-0095). Worcester MA.
Economic history review. (0013-0117). Oxford.
Economic inquiry. (0095-2583). Oxford.
Economic issues. (1363-7029). Stoke-on-Trent.
Economic journal. (0013-0133). Oxford.
Economic modelling. (0264-9993). Guildford.
Economic notes. (0391-5026). Siena.
Economic papers [Australia]. (0812-0439). East Hawthorn.
Economic papers. Bank of Korea. Seoul.
Economic policy. (0266-4658). Oxford.
Economic record. (0013-0249). Sydney.
Economic systems. (0939-3625). Heidelberg.
Economic systems research. (0953-5314). Abingdon.
Economic theory. (0938-2259). Heidelberg.
Económica [Argentina]. (0013-0419). La Plata.
Economica [London]. (0013-0427). London.
Economics and philosophy. (0266-2671). New York NY.
Economics and politics. (0954-1985). Oxford.
Economics letters. (0165-1765). Amsterdam.
Economics of planning. (0013-0451). Dordrecht.
Économie appliquée. (0013-0494). Paris.
Économie et statistique. (0336-1454). Paris.
Économie internationale. (1240-8093). Paris.
Économies et sociétés. (0013-0567). Paris.
Economisch en sociaal tijdschrift. (0013-0575). Antwerp.
Economy and society. (0308-5147). London.
Economy and society [Japan]. Tokyo.
Edinburgh anthropology. (0953-2919). Edinburgh.
Education and urban society. (0013-1245). Thousand Oaks CA.
Educational gerontology. (0360-1277). London.
Educational research. (0013-1881). London.
Ekistics. (0013-2942). Athens.
Ekonomia. Nicosia.
Ekonomisk debatt. (0345-2646). Stockholm.
Ekonomist. (0869-4672). Moscow.
Ekonomski pregled. (0424-7558). Zagreb.
Electoral studies. (0261-3794). Kidlington.
Electronic markets: The international journal of electronic commerce & business media. (1019-6781). London.
Elementa: Journal of Slavic studies and comparative cultural semiotics. (1064-6663). New York NY.
Empirica. (0340-8744). Dordrecht.
Empirical economics. (0377-7332). Heidelberg.
Employee relations. (0142-5455). Bradford.
Energy economics. (0140-9883). Oxford.
Energy policy. (0301-4215). Guildford.
English in Africa. (0376-8902). Grahamstown.
English world-wide. (0172-8865). Amsterdam.
Ensayos sobre política económica. (0120-4483). Bogota.

LISTE DES PERIODIQUES CONSULTÉS

Enterprise & innovation management studies. (1463-2446). London.
Entrepreneurship & regional development. (0898-5626). London.
Entrepreneurship, innovation, and change. (1059-0137). New York NY.
Entrepreneurship: Theory and practice. (1042-2587). Waco TX.
Entreprises et histoire. (1161-2770). Paris.
Environment. (0013-9157). Washington DC.
Environment and behavior. (0013-9165). Thousand Oaks CA.
Environment and planning A: International journal of urban and regional research. (0308-518X). London.
Environment and planning B: Planning and design. (0265-8135). London.
Environment and planning C: Government and policy. (0263-774X). London.
Environment and planning D: Society and space. (0263-7758). London.
Environment and urbanization. (0956-2478). London.
Environmental & resource economics. (0924-6460). Dordrecht.
Environmental impact assessment review. (0195-9255). New York NY.
Environmental information science. Tokyo.
Environmental law. (0046-2276). Portland OR.
Environmental politics. (0964-4016). Ilford.
Environmental values. (0963-2719). Cambridge.
ESP. Tokyo.
Espace géographique. (0046-2497). Paris.
Espace populations sociétés. (0755-7809). Villeneuve d'Ascq.
Esprit. (0014-0759). Paris.
Estrategia económica y financiera. (0121-4802). Bogota.
Estudios de Asia y Africa. (0185-0164). Mexico City.
Estudios de economía. (0304-2758). Santiago.
Estudios demográficos y urbanos. (0186-7210). Mexico City.
Estudios económicos. Mexico City.
Estudios internacionales. (0716-0240). Santiago.
Estudios latinoamericanos. (0187-1811). Mexico City.
Estudios políticos. (0185-1616). Mexico City.
Estudos de antropologia cultural e social. (0870-4457). Lisbon.
Ethical theory and moral practice. (1386-2820). Dordrecht.
Ethics. (0014-1704). Chicago IL.
Ethnic and racial studies. (0141-9870). London.
Ethnic studies report. (1010-5832). Kandy.
Ethnicities. (1468-7968). London.
Ethnographisch archäologische Zeitschrift. (0012-7477). Berlin.
Ethnography. (1466-1381). London.
Ethnologia Polona. (0137-4079). Warsaw.
Ethnologica helvetica. Bern.
Ethnologie française. (0046-2616). Paris.
Ethnologies. (1481-5974). Quebec.
Ethnology. (0014-1828). Pittsburgh PA.
Ethnomusicology. (0014-1836). Bloomington IN.
Ethnos. (0014-1844). Stockholm.
Etnografia polska. (0071-1861). Warsaw.
Etnograficheskoe obozrenie. Moscow.
Etnologiska studier. (0374 7530). Gothenburg.
Etnoloska tribina. (0351-1944). Zagreb.
Études Æquatoria. Mbandaka.

LIST OF PERIODICALS CONSULTED

Études balkaniques. Sofia.
Études canadiennes = Canadian studies. (0153-1700). Talence.
Études et documents. (0182-788X). Paris.
Études et documents berbères. (0295-5245). Paris.
Études inter-ethniques. (0761-7291). Lille.
Études internationales. (0014-2123). Quebec.
Études maliennes. Bamako.
Études mésoaméricaines. (0378-5726). Mexico City.
Études mongoles et sibériennes. (0766-507S). Nanterre.
Études rurales. (0014-2182). Paris.
Études sociales. Paris.
Eurasian studies. (1300-1604). Ankara.
Eurasian studies yearbook. (0042-0786). Bloomington IN.
Eure: Revista latinoamericana de estudios urbanos regionales. (0250-7161). Santiago.
Eurobalkans. Aegina.
Euromoney. (0014-2433). London.
Europa ethnica. Vienna.
Europe-Asia studies. (0966-8136). Abingdon.
European accounting review. (0963-8180). London.
European business organization law review. (1566-7529). The Hague.
European economic review. (0014-2921). Amsterdam.
European financial management. (1354-7798). Oxford.
European foreign affairs review. (1384-6299). The Hague.
European history quarterly. (0265-6914). London.
European journal of archaeology. (1461-9571). London.
European journal of communication. (0267-3231). London.
European journal of crime, criminal law and criminal justice. (0928-9569). Deventer.
European journal of cultural studies. (1367-5494). London.
European journal of development research. (0957-8811). Ilford.
European journal of finance. (1351-847X). London.
European journal of industrial relations. (0959-6801). London.
European journal of international relations. (1354-0661). London.
European journal of law and economics. (0929-1261). Dordrecht.
European journal of philosophy. (0966-8373). Oxford.
European journal of political research. (0304-4130). Dordrecht.
European journal of population = Revue européenne de démographie. (0168-6577). Amsterdam.
European journal of social psychology. (0046-2772). Chichester.
European journal of social theory. (1368-4310). London.
European journal of the history of economic thought. (0967-2567). London.
European journal of women's studies. (1350-5068). London.
European journal on criminal policy and research. (0928-1371). Dordrecht.
European law journal. (1351-5993). Oxford.
European review of agricultural economics. (0165-1587). Berlin.
European review of history = Revue européenne d'histoire. (1350-7486). Abingdon.
European review of Latin American and Caribbean studies = Revista europea de estudios latinoamericanos y del Caribe. (0924-0608). Amsterdam.
European security. (0966-2839). Ilford.
European societies. (1461-6696). London.
European sociological review. (0266-7215). Oxford.
European Union politics. (1465-1165). London.
European urban and regional studies. (0969-7764). London.

LISTE DES PERIODIQUES CONSULTÉS

Evaluation. (1356-3890). London.
Evaluation review. (0193-841X). Thousand Oaks CA.
Evolution and human behavior. (1090-5138). New York NY.
Evolutionary anthropology. (1060-1538). New York NY.
Explorations in economic history. (0014-4983). Duluth MN.
Extrême-orient, extrême-occident: Cahiers de recherches comparatives. (0754-5010). Paris.
Fabula. (0014-6242). Berlin.
Faculty bulletin humanity and science. Kobe.
Family and community history. (1463-1180). Leeds.
Family studies. Kobe.
Far Eastern affairs. (0206-149X). Moscow.
Fasciculi archaeologiae historicae. (0860-0007). Warsaw.
Fashion theory. (1362-704X). Oxford.
Federal Reserve Bank of New York economic policy review. New York NY.
Federal Reserve bulletin. (0014-9209). Washington DC.
Federalist. (0393-1358). Pavia.
Feminism & psychology. (0959-3535). London.
Feminist economics. (1354-5701). London.
Feminist legal studies. (0966-3622). Liverpool.
Feminist review. (0141-7789). London.
Feminist studies. (0046-3663). College Park MD.
Feminist theory. (1464-7001). London.
Field methods. (1525-822X). Thousand Oaks CA.
Finance & development. (0015-1947). Washington DC.
Finance India. (0970-3772). Delhi.
Financial analysts journal. (0015-198X). Charlottesville VA.
Financial history review. (0968-5650). Cambridge.
Financial management. (0046-3892). Tampa FL.
Financial markets, institutions and instruments. (0963-8008). Malden MA.
Financial news analysis. Dakar.
Finansy. (0869-446X). Moscow.
Finanzarchiv. (0015-2218). Tübingen.
Finnish economic papers. (0784-5197). Helsinki.
Finnish review of East European studies. Helsinki.
Finsk tidskrift. (0015-248X). Turku.
First language. (0142-7237). Chalfont St Giles.
Fiscal studies. (0143-5671). London.
Folia linguistica. (0165-4004). Berlin.
Folia primatologica. (0015-5713). Basle.
Folk. (0085-0756). Copenhagen.
Folklore [Calcutta]. (0015-5896). Calcutta.
Folklore [London]. (0015-587X). London.
Food and foodways. (0740-9710). New York NY.
Food policy. (0306-9192). Oxford.
For new sociology. Tokyo.
Foreign affairs. (0015-7120). New York NY.
Foreign policy. (0015-7228). Washington DC.
Foreign trade review. New Delhi.
Forensic linguistics. (1350-1771). Birmingham.
Forschungen und Berichte. (0863-0739). Berlin.
Forschungsjournal neue soziale Bewegungen. (0933-9361). Wiesbaden.

LIST OF PERIODICALS CONSULTED

Forum. Tokyo.
Forum for development studies. (0803-9410). Oslo.
French cultural studies. (0957-1558). Chalfont St Giles.
French politics, culture, and society. (0882-1267). Oxford.
French studies. (0016-1128). Belfast.
Games and economic behavior. (0899-8256). Orlando FL.
Garcia de Orta: série de antropobiologia. (0870-0168). Lisbon.
Gendai no Esupuri. Japan.
Gendai shakairion kenkyu. Tokyo.
Gendaishakaigaku kenkyu. Sapporo.
Gender and development. (1355-2074). Oxford.
Gender and history. (0953-5233). Oxford.
Gender and Japanese history. Tokyo.
Gender and society. (0891-2432). Thousand Oaks CA.
Gender, place and culture: A journal of feminist geography. (0966-369X). Abingdon.
Gender, technology and development. (0971-8524). New Delhi.
Gender, work and organization. (0968-6673). Manchester.
Genèses. (1135-3219). France.
Geneva papers on risk and insurance theory. (0926-4957). Dordrecht.
Genus. (0016-6987). Rome.
Geoforum. (0016-7185). Oxford.
Geografiska annaler: Series B — Human geography. (0435-3684). Uppsala.
Geographia polonica. (0016-7282). Warsaw.
Geographical analysis. (0016-7363). Columbus OH.
Geographical journal. (0016-7398). London.
Geographical review. (0016-7428). New York NY.
Geographical review of India. (0375-6386). Calcutta.
Geographical review of Japan. (0016-7444). Tokyo.
Geographische Rundschau. (0016-7460). Braunschweig.
Geography. Sheffield.
Geojournal. (0343-2521). Dordrecht.
Geopolitics. (1465-0045). Ilford.
Geopolitique. (0752-1693). Paris.
George Washington international law review. (0748-4305). Washington DC.
Georgica. (0232-4490). Konstanz.
German history: the journal of the German history society. (0266-3554). London.
German politics. (0964-4008). London.
Gerontologist. Washington DC.
Geschichte und Gesellschaft. (0340-613X). Göttingen.
Gewerkschaftliche Monatshefte. (0016-9447). Düsseldorf.
Giornale degli economisti e annali di economia. (0017-0097). Milan.
Glasnik Slovenskega etnološkega društva = Bulletin of the Slovene ethnological society. Ljubljana.
Global dialogue. (1450-0590). Nicosia.
Global environmental change. (0959-3780). Oxford.
Global governance. (1075-2846). Boulder CO.
Global social policy: an interdisciplinary journal of public policy and social development. (1468-0181). London.
Global society. (1360-0826). Abingdon.
Gospodarka narodowa. (0867-0005). Warsaw.
Gospodarka planowa. (0017-2421). Warsaw.
Gosudarstvo i pravo. (0132-0769). Moscow.

LISTE DES PERIODIQUES CONSULTÉS

Göteborgs etnografiska museum årstryck. (0280-3887). Gothenburg.
Gothenburg studies in social anthropology. (0348-4076). Gothenburg.
Governance. (0952-1895). Oxford.
Government and opposition. (0017-257X). London.
Gradhiva. (0764-8928). Paris.
Grassroots development. (0733-6608). Rosslyn VA.
Greek economic review. Athens.
Green globe yearbook. Oxford.
Greener management international. (0966-9671). Sheffield.
Group analysis: The journal of group analytic psychotherapy. (0533-3164). London.
Group decision and negotiation. (0926-2644). Dordrecht.
Group processes and intergroup relations. (1368-4302). London.
Groupwork. (0951-824X). London.
Growth and change. (0017-4815). Oxford.
Gyosei shakai ronshu. Fukushima.
Habitat international. (0197-3975). Oxford.
Hacienda pública española. (0210-1173). Madrid.
Hallinnon tutkimus. Tampere.
Hamburger Jahrbuch für Wirtschafts- und Gesellschaftspolitik. Tübingen.
Hannan ronshu. Osaka.
Harsunan Nijeriya. Kano.
Harvard journal of Asiatic studies. (0073-0548). Cambridge MA.
Harvard law review. (0017-811X). Cambridge MA.
Health and human rights. (1079-0969). Cambridge MA.
Health and social work. (0360-7283). Washington DC.
Health care for women international. (0739-9332). London.
Health policy. (0168-8510). Shannon.
Health policy and planning. (0268-1080). Oxford.
Health sciences. Tokyo.
Health transition review. (1036-4005). Canberra.
Health, risk & society. (1369-8575). Oxford.
Hebrew annual review. Columbus OH.
Hebrew studies. (0146-4094). Madison WI.
Hemispheres. (0239-8818). Warsaw.
Heritage of Zimbabwe. (0556-9605). Harare.
Hespëris Tamuda. Rabat.
Hessische Blätter für Volks- und Kulturforschung. (1075-3479). Marburg.
Hevrah u-revahah = Society and welfare. Jerusalem.
Higher education. (0018-1560). Dordrecht.
Hikone ronso. Shiga.
Himal. (1012-9804). Lalitpur.
Himalayan research bulletin. (0891-4834). New York NY.
Hiroshima Hogaku. Hiroshima.
Hispanic American historical review. (0018-2168). Durham NC.
Historical archaeology. (0440-9213). Tucson AZ.
Historical journal. (0018-246X). Cambridge.
Historical social research = Historische Sozialforschung. (0172-6404). Cologne.
History. (0018-2648). London.
History and anthropology. (0275-7206). Reading.
History and technology. (0734-1512). Reading.
History and theory. (0018-2656). Middletown CT.

LIST OF PERIODICALS CONSULTED

History in Africa. (0361-5413). New Jersey.
History of political economy. (0018-2702). Durham NC.
History of political thought. (0143-781X). Thorverton.
History of psychiatry. (0957-154X). Chalfont St Giles.
History of religions. (0018-2710). Chicago IL.
History of the family. (1081-602X). Greenwich CT.
History of the human sciences. (0952-6951). London.
Hitotsubashi journal of commerce and management. (0018-2796). Tokyo.
Hitotsubashi journal of economics. (0018-280X). Tokyo.
Hitotsubashi journal of law and politics. (0073-2796). Tokyo.
Hitotsubashi journal of social studies. (0073-280X). Tokyo.
Hitotsubashi ronsô. Tokyo.
Hogaku (Bulletin of Kokugakuin University). Kokugakuin.
Hogaku (Journal. Surugadai University). Surugadai.
Hogaku kenkyu. Tokyo.
Hogaku kenyū. Tokyo.
Hogaku ronshu. Yamanashi.
Hogaku seijigaku ronkyu. Tokyo.
Hokuriku hogaku. Kanazawa.
Homines. (0252-8908). Hato Rey.
Homme. (0439-4216). Paris.
Homme et la société. (0018-4306). Paris.
Hong Kong anthropologist. Hong Kong.
Hong Kong economic papers. (0018-4578). Hong Kong.
Hong Kong law journal. (0378-0600). Hong Kong.
Horizontes antropológicos. (0104-7183). Porto Alegre.
Hosei Kenkyu. Fukuoka.
Hosogaku kenkyu. Tokyo.
Housing policy debate. (1051-1482). Washington DC.
Housing, theory and society. (1403-6096). Stockholm.
Howard journal of criminal justice. (0265-5527). Oxford.
Hudai keizai ronshû. Toyama.
Human communication studies. Tokyo.
Human development. (0018-716X). Basel.
Human ethology bulletin. (0739-2036). Orono ME.
Human nature. (1045-6767). Hawthorne NY.
Human organization. (0018-7259). Temple Terrace FL.
Human relations. (0018-7267). London.
Human rights quarterly. (0275-0392). Baltimore MD.
Human studies. (0163-8548). Dordrecht.
Humor. (0933-1719). Berlin.
Hyogo University of Teacher Education journal. Hyogo.
Identities: global studies in culture and power. (1070-289X). Newark NJ.
IDS bulletin. (0265-5012). Brighton.
Ifo-Studien. (0018-9731). Berlin.
IFRA: Les cahiers. Nairobi.
Immigrants and minorities. (0261-9288). Ilford.
Impact assessment and project appraisal. Guildford.
Impact of science on society. (0019-2872). Paris.
Ind-Africana. Delhi.
India quarterly. (0019-4220). New Delhi.

LISTE DES PERIODIQUES CONSULTÉS

Indian economic and social history review. (0019-4646). New Delhi.
Indian economic journal. (0019-4662). Bombay.
Indian economic review. (0019-4671). Delhi.
Indian geographical journal. (0019-4824). Madras.
Indian journal of agricultural economics. (0019-5014). Bombay.
Indian journal of economics. (0019-5170). Allahabad.
Indian journal of gender studies. (0971-5215). New Delhi.
Indian journal of industrial relations. (0019-5286). New Delhi.
Indian journal of labour economics. (0971-7927). Patna.
Indian journal of political science. (0019-5510). Madras.
Indian journal of public administration. (0019-5561). New Delhi.
Indian journal of regional science. (0046-9017). Calcutta.
Indian journal of social science. New Delhi.
Indian journal of social work. (0019-5634). Bombay.
Indian labour journal. (0019-5723). Shimla.
Indian psychological abstracts and reviews. (0971-524X). New Delhi.
Indiana journal of global legal studies. (1080-0727). Bloomington IN.
Indigenous affairs. (1024-3283). Copenhagen.
Indigenous world. (1024-0217). Copenhagen.
Indo Asia. (0019-719X). Sachsenheim-Hohenhaslach.
Indo-Iranian journal. (0019-7246). Dordrecht.
Indonesia. Ithaca NY.
Indonesia and the Malay world. (1363-9811). Oxford.
Indonesian quarterly. (0304-2170). Jakarta.
Industria. Bologna.
Industrial and corporate change. (0960-6491). Oxford.
Industrial and labor relations review. (0019-7939). Ithaca NY.
Industrial and social relations. (0258-7181). Bellville.
Industrial archaeology review. (0309-0728). Leicester.
Industrial relations. (0019-8676). eng.
Industrial relations journal. (0019-8692). Oxford.
Industrielle Beziehungen. (0943-2779). Mering.
Industry and innovation. (1366-2716). Abingdon.
Industry of free China. (0019-946X). Taipei.
Información comercial española. (0019-977X). Madrid.
Information & society. Tokyo.
Information economics and policy. (0167-6245). Amsterdam.
Information, communication & society. (1369-118X). London.
Informationen zur Raumentwicklung. (0303-2493). Bonn.
Informations sociales. (0046-9459). Paris.
Inner Asia. (1464-8172). Cambridge.
Innovation: the European journal of social sciences. (1351-1610). Oxford.
Inquiry. (0020-174X). Oslo.
Institut d'histoire du temps present bulletin. (0247-0101). Paris.
Instructional science. (0020-4277). Dordrecht.
Insurance mathematics & economics. (0167-6687). Amsterdam.
Integración latinoamericana. (0325-1675). Buenos Aires.
Intelligence and national security. (0268-4527). Ilford.
Inter-Asia cultural studies. (1464-9373). London.
Interchange. (0826-4805). Dordrecht.
Intercultural communication studies. (1057-7769). San Antonio TX.

LIST OF PERIODICALS CONSULTED

Intereconomics. (0020-5346). Hamburg.
Interfaces. (0092-2102). Providence RI.
Internasjonal politikk. (0020-577X). Oslo.
International affairs [London]. (0020-5850). London.
International affairs [Moscow]. (0130-9641). Minneapolis, MN.
International and comparative law quarterly. (0020-5893). London.
International business and management forum. Japan.
International contributions to labour studies. (1052-9187). San Diego CA.
International economic journal. (1016-8737). Seoul.
International economic outlook. Oxford.
International economic review. (0020-6598). Philadelphia PA.
International feminist journal of politics. (1461-6742). London.
International history review. (0707-5332). Burnaby, British Columbia.
International interactions. (0305-0629). Reading.
International journal. (0020-7020). Toronto.
International journal for philosophy of religion. (0020-7047). Dordrecht.
International journal for the semiotics of law = Revue internationale de sémiotique juridique. (0952-8059). Liverpool.
International journal of accounting. (0020-7063). Heidelberg.
International journal of African historical studies. (0361-7882). Boston MA.
International journal of American linguistics. (0020-7071). Chicago IL.
International journal of children's rights. (0927-5568). The Hague.
International journal of comparative and applied criminal justice. Wichita KS.
International journal of comparative labour law and industrial relations. (0952-617X). The Hague.
International journal of comparative sociology. (0020-7152). Leiden.
International journal of cross cultural management. (1470-5958). London.
International journal of cultural studies. (1367-8779). London.
International journal of Dravidian linguistics. Trivandrum.
International journal of entrepreneurship and innovation. (1465-7503). London.
International journal of forecasting. (0169-2070). Amsterdam.
International journal of game theory. (0020-7276). Heidelberg.
International journal of health services. (0020-7314). Amityville NY.
International journal of human resource management. (0958-5192). London.
International journal of industrial organization. (0167-7187). Amsterdam.
International journal of Japanese sociology. (0918-7545). Tokyo.
International journal of Kurdish studies. (0885-386X). New York NY.
International journal of law, policy, and the family. (1360-9939). Oxford.
International journal of Middle East studies. (0020-7438). New York NY.
International journal of offender therapy and comparative criminology. (0306-624X). New York NY.
International journal of organizational analysis. (1055-3185). Bowling Green KY.
International journal of pharmacy practice. (0961-7671). London.
International journal of philosophical studies. (0967-2559). London.
International journal of politics, culture and society. (0891-4486). New York NY.
International journal of primatology. (0164-0291). New York NY.
International journal of psychoanalysis. (0020-7578). London.
International journal of public opinion research. (0954-2892). Oxford.
International journal of Punjab studies. (0971-5223). New Delhi.
International journal of social economics. (0306-8293). Bradford.
International journal of social psychiatry. (0020-7640). London.
International journal of social research methodology: theory & practice. (1364-5579). London.
International journal of sustainable development. (0960-1406). Geneva.

LISTE DES PERIODIQUES CONSULTÉS

International journal of the economics of business. (1357-1516). Abingdon.
International journal of the history of sport. (0952-3367). Ilford.
International journal of the sociology of language. (0165-2516). Berlin.
International journal of the sociology of law. (0194-6595). London.
International journal of transport economics. (0391-8440). Rome.
International journal of urban and regional research. (0309-1317). Sevenoaks.
International journal on minority and group rights. (1385-4879). Dordrecht.
International labour review. (0020-7780). Geneva.
International migration = Migrations internationales = Migraciones internacionales. (0020-7985). Geneva.
International migration review. (0197-9183). New York NY.
International minds. (0957-1299). London.
International negotiation: a journal of theory and practice. (1382-340X). The Hague.
International organization. (0020-8183). Cambridge MA.
International peacekeeping. (1353-3312). Ilford.
International perspectives. (0381-4874). Ottawa.
International political science review = Revue internationale de science politique. (0192-5121). London.
International politics. (1384-5748). The Hague.
International regional science review. (0160-0176). Thousand Oaks CA.
International relations. (0047-1178). London.
International relations [Japan]. Japan.
International review of administrative sciences. (0020-8523). London.
International review of applied economics. (0269-2171). Abingdon.
International review of education. (0020-8566). The Hague.
International review of law and economics. (0144-8188). New York NY.
International review of retail, distribution and consumer research. (0959-3969). London.
International review of social history. (0020-8590). Cambridge.
International review of the Red Cross. (1560-7755). Geneva.
International security. (0162-2889). Cambridge MA.
International small business journal. (0266-2426). Macclesfield.
International social science journal. (0020-8701). Oxford.
International social work. (0020-8728). London.
International sociology. (0268-5809). London.
International spectator. (0393-2729). Rome.
International studies. (0020-8817). New Delhi.
International studies in the philosophy of science. (0269-8595). Abingdon.
International studies quarterly. (0020-8833). Malden MA.
International studies review. (1521-9488). Malden MA.
International tax and public finance. (0927-5940). Dordrecht.
Internationale Politik. (0014 2476). Bonn.
Internationale Politik und Gesellschaft. (0945-2419). Bonn.
Internationales Asienforum. (0020-9449). Cologne.
Internet archaeology. (1363-5387). York.
Investigaciones economicas. (0210-1521). Madrid.
IPW Berichte. (0046-970X). Frankfurt-am-Main.
IPW-Forschungshefte. (0323-3901). Berlin.
IRAL. (0019-042X). Heidelberg.
Iran nameh. Bethesda MD.
Iranian journal of international affairs. (1016-6130). Tehran.
Iranica antiqua. (0021-0870). Louvain.

LIST OF PERIODICALS CONSULTED

Iraq. (0021-0889). London.
Irian. (0304-2189). Jayapura.
Irish banking review. (0021-1060). Dublin.
Irish journal of sociology. (0791-6035). Maynooth.
Irish political studies. (0790-7184). Limerick.
Irish review. (0790-7850). Cork.
Isis. (0021-1753). Chicago IL.
ISLA: Journal of Micronesian studies. Mangiloa.
Islam et sociétés au sud du Sahara. (0984-7685). Paris.
Islamic law and society. Leiden.
Israel affairs. (1353-7121). Ilford.
Israel exploration journal. (0021-2059). Jerusalem.
Israel law review. (0021-2237). Jerusalem.
Israel oriental studies. (0334-4401). Tel Aviv.
Israel yearbook on human rights. (0333-5925). Dordrecht.
Issue. (0047-1607). Emory GA.
Issues & studies. (1013-2511). Taipei.
Italia contemporanea. (0392-3568). Milan.
IWK: Internationale wissenschaftliche Korrespondenz zur Geschichte der deutschen Arbeiterbewegung. (0046-8428). Berlin.
Iyu Machi. Okinawa.
Iztapalapa. (0185-4259). Mexico City.
Jahrbuch des öffentlichen Rechts der Gegenwart. (0075-2517). Tübingen.
Jahrbuch Extremismus & Demokratie. Bonn.
Jahrbuch für Antisemitismusforschung. (0941-8563). Frankfurt.
Jahrbuch für christliche Sozialwissenschaften. (0075-2584). Münster.
Jahrbuch für Ethnomedizin und Bewußtseinsforschung = Yearbook for ethnomedicine and the study of consciousness. (0942-1408). Berlin.
Jahrbuch für Geschichte von Staat, Wirtschaft und Gesellschaft Lateinamerikas. (0075-2673). Cologne.
Jahrbuch für musikalische Volks- und Völkerkunde. Eisenach.
Jahrbuch für Soziologiegeschichte. Leverkusen.
Jahrbuch für Wirtschaftsgeschichte. (0075-2800). Berlin.
Jahrbuch für Wirtschaftswissenschaften: Review of Economics. (0948-5139). Göttingen.
Jahrbücher für Geschichte Osteuropas. (0021-4019). Stuttgart.
Jahrbücher für Nationalökonomie und Statistik. (0021-4027). Stuttgart.
Jain journal. (0021-4043). Calcutta.
Jamaica journal. (0021-4124). Kingston.
Japan and the world economy. (0922-1425). Amsterdam.
Japan Christian review. Tokyo.
Japan digest. (0960-1473). Folkestone.
Japan echo. (0388-0435). Tokyo.
Japan election studies. Tokyo.
Japan journal of sport sociology. Tsukuba.
Japan labor bulletin. Tokyo.
Japan marketing journal. Tokyo.
Japan quarterly. (0021-4590). Tokyo.
Japan review of international affairs. (0913-8773). Tokyo.
Japanese annual of international law. (0448-8806). Tokyo.
Japanese economic review. (1352-4739). Tokyo.
Japanese journal of administrative behavior. Nagoya.
Japanese journal of educational research. Tokyo.

LISTE DES PERIODIQUES CONSULTÉS

Japanese journal of family sociology. Tokyo.
Japanese journal of gerontology. Tokyo.
Japanese journal of nursing science. Tokyo.
Japanese journal of religious studies. (0304-1042). Nagoya.
Japanese journal of sociological criminology. Tokyo.
Japanese journal of women's studies. Tokyo.
Japanese journalism review. Tokyo.
Japanese religions. (0448-8954). Kyoto City.
Japanese scientific review. Tokyo.
Japanese sociological review. Tokyo.
Javnost = Public. (1318-3222). Ljubljana.
Jewish journal of sociology. (0021-6534). London.
Jewish quarterly review. (0021-6682). Philadelphia PA.
Jewish social studies. (0021-6704). New York NY.
Jimbun ronsō. Osaka.
Jinbun gakuho. Tokyo.
Jinbun-ronkyu. Nishinomiya.
Jinbun: Journal of Kyoto University. Kyoto.
Jinbungakubu kiyo. Toyama.
Jinko mondai kenkyu. Tokyo.
Jinko to Kaihatsu. Tokyo.
Jogtudományi közlöny. (0021-7166). Budapest.
Joho to shakai (Journal of Edogawa University). Nagareyama.
Jomin bunka. Tokyo.
Josei kukan. Tokyo.
Journal de la Société de Statistique de Paris. (0037-914X). Paris.
Journal de la Société des américanistes. (0037-9174). Paris.
Journal de la Société des Océanistes. (0300-953X). Paris.
Journal des Africanistes. (0399-0346). Paris.
Journal du droit international. (0021-8170). Paris.
Journal for East European management studies. (0949-6181). Mering.
Journal for the scientific study of religion. (0021-8294). Provo UT.
Journal for the theory of social behaviour. (0021-8308). Oxford.
Journal für Entwicklungspolitik. (0258-2384). Frankfurt.
Journal Japan Women's University Faculty of Integrated Arts and Social Sciences. Kawasaki.
Journal of accounting and economics. (0165-4101). Amsterdam.
Journal of accounting and public policy. (0278-4254). New York NY.
Journal of accounting research. (0021-8456). Chicago IL.
Journal of African economies. (0963-8024). Oxford.
Journal of African history. (0021-8537). Cambridge.
Journal of African languages and linguistics. (0167-6164). Berlin.
Journal of African law. (0221-8553). London.
Journal of African Marxists. (0263-2268). London.
Journal of African religion and philosophy. Kampala.
Journal of agricultural economics. (0021-857X). Reading.
Journal of agricultural economics research. Washington DC.
Journal of American studies. (0021-8758). Cambridge.
Journal of American-East Asian relations. (1058-3947). Chicago IL.
Journal of anthropological archaeology. (0278-4165). San Diego CA.
Journal of anthropological research. (0091-7710). Albuquerque NM.
Journal of applied behavioral science. (0021-8863). Thousand Oaks.

LIST OF PERIODICALS CONSULTED

Journal of applied econometrics. (0883-7252). Chichester.
Journal of applied economics. (1514-0326). Buenos Aires.
Journal of applied psychoanalytic studies. (1521-1401). New York.
Journal of applied psychology. (0021-9010). Washington DC.
Journal of applied social psychology. (0021-9029). Silver Spring MD.
Journal of architectural and planning research. (0738-0895). Chicago IL.
Journal of Asian and African affairs. (1044-2979). Washington DC.
Journal of Asian and African studies [Leiden]. (0021-9096). Leiden.
Journal of Asian business. (1068-0055). Ann Arbor MI.
Journal of Asian history. (0021-910X). Wiesbaden.
Journal of Asian studies. (0021-9118). Ann Arbor MI.
Journal of Australian political economy. (0156-5826). Sydney.
Journal of Australian studies. Bundoora.
Journal of banking and finance. (0378-4266). Amsterdam.
Journal of BARD. Comilla.
Journal of behavioral education. (1053-0819). New York NY.
Journal of biosocial science. (0021-9320). Cambridge.
Journal of black psychology. (0095-7984). Thousand Oaks CA.
Journal of black studies. (0021-9347). Thousand Oaks CA.
Journal of British studies. (0021-9371). Chicago IL.
Journal of business. (0021-9398). Chicago IL.
Journal of business & economic statistics. (0735-0015). Alexandria VA.
Journal of business and society. (1012-2591). Nicosia.
Journal of business ethics. (0167-4544). Dordrecht.
Journal of business finance and accounting. (0306-686X). Oxford.
Journal of Canadian studies = Revue d'études canadiennes. (0021-9495). Peterborough.
Journal of Caribbean studies. (0190-2008). Lexington KY.
Journal of child and family studies. (1062-1024). New York NY.
Journal of Chinese law. (1041-7567). Lincoln NE.
Journal of Chinese philosophy. Honolulu HI.
Journal of church and state. (0021-969X). Waco TX.
Journal of common market studies. (0021-9886). Oxford.
Journal of communication. (0021-9916). New York NY.
Journal of communist studies and transition politics. (1352-3279). Ilford.
Journal of community and applied social psychology. (1052-9284). Chichester.
Journal of comparative economics. (0147-5967). Duluth MN.
Journal of comparative family studies. (0047-2328). Calgary.
Journal of comparative policy analysis: research and practice. (1387-6988). Dordrecht.
Journal of conflict resolution. (0022-0027). Thousand Oaks CA.
Journal of conflict studies. (1198-8614). New Brunswick.
Journal of constitutional and parliamentary studies. New Delhi.
Journal of consumer affairs. (0022-0078). Madison WI.
Journal of consumer policy. (0342-5843). Dordrecht.
Journal of contemporary African studies. (0258-9001). Abingdon.
Journal of contemporary Asia. (0047-2336). Manila.
Journal of contemporary ethnography. (0891-2416). Thousand Oaks CA.
Journal of contemporary history. (0022-0094). London.
Journal of contingencies and crisis management. (0966-0879). Oxford.
Journal of cooperative studies. (0961-5784). Buxton.
Journal of cost management. (0899-5141). Boston MA.
Journal of criminal law. (0022-0183). London.

LISTE DES PERIODIQUES CONSULTÉS

Journal of criminal law and criminology. (0091-4169). Chicago IL.
Journal of cross-cultural gerontology. (0169-3816). Dordrecht.
Journal of democracy. (1045-5736). Baltimore MD.
Journal of developing areas. (0022-037X). Macomb IL.
Journal of developing societies. (0169-796X). Leiden.
Journal of development assistance. (1341-3953). Tokyo.
Journal of development economics. (0304-3878). Amsterdam.
Journal of development planning. (0085-2392). New York NY.
Journal of development studies. (0022-0388). Ilford.
Journal of East and West studies. Seoul.
Journal of East Asian affairs. (1010-1608). Seoul.
Journal of Eastern African research & development. (0251-0405). Nairobi.
Journal of econometrics. (0304-4076). Amsterdam.
Journal of economic and social measurement. (0747-9662). Amsterdam.
Journal of economic behavior and organization. (0167-2681). Amsterdam.
Journal of economic cooperation among Islamic countries. (0252-953X). Ankara.
Journal of economic dynamics and control. (0165-1889). Amsterdam.
Journal of economic growth. (1381-4338). Dordrecht.
Journal of economic history. (0022-0507). New York NY.
Journal of economic issues. (0021-3624). Lewisburg PA.
Journal of economic literature. (0022-0515). Nashville TN.
Journal of economic methodology. (1350-178X). London.
Journal of economic perspectives. (0895-3309). Nashville TN.
Journal of economic psychology. (0167-4870). Amsterdam.
Journal of economic studies. (0144-3585). Bradford.
Journal of economic surveys. (0950-0804). Oxford.
Journal of economic theory. (0022-0531). Bruges.
Journal of economics & management strategy. (1058-6407). Cambridge MA.
Journal of economics [Austria] = Zeitschrift für Nationalökonomie. (0931-8658). Vienna.
Journal of educational sociology. Tokyo.
Journal of environment and development. (1070-4965). Thousand Oaks CA.
Journal of environmental economics and management. (0095-0696). Duluth MN.
Journal of environmental law. (0952-8873). Oxford.
Journal of environmental management. (0301-4797). London.
Journal of environmental planning and management. (0964-0568). Abingdon.
Journal of environmental sociology. Tokyo.
Journal of ethnic and migration studies. (1369-183X). Abingdon.
Journal of European economic history. (0391-5115). Rome.
Journal of European integration history = Revue d'histoire de l'intégration européenne = Zeitschrift für Geschichte der europäischen Integration. (0947-9511). Baden-Baden.
Journal of European public policy. (1350-1763). London.
Journal of European social policy. (0958-9287). London.
Journal of evolutionary economics. (0936-9937). Berlin.
Journal of experimental child psychology. (0022-0965). Duluth MN.
Journal of experimental social psychology. (0022-1031). Duluth MN.
Journal of Family Education Center. Yokohama.
Journal of family history. (0363-1990). Thousand Oaks, CA.
Journal of family therapy. (0163-4445). Oxford.
Journal of family violence. (0885-7482). New York NY.
Journal of finance. (0022-1082). New York NY.
Journal of financial and quantitative analysis. (0022-1090). Seattle WA.

LIST OF PERIODICALS CONSULTED

Journal of financial economics. (0304-405X). Amsterdam.
Journal of financial intermediation. (1042-9573). Orlando FL.
Journal of financial services research. (0920-8550). Dordrecht.
Journal of forecasting. (0277-6693). Chichester.
Journal of foreign exchange and international finance. (0970-3632). Pune.
Journal of forensic economics. (0898-5510). Kansas City KS.
Journal of forensic psychiatry. (0958-5184). London.
Journal of forest economics. Tokyo.
Journal of futures markets. (0270-7314). New York NY.
Journal of gender studies. (0958-9236). Abingdon.
Journal of health economics. (0167-6296). Amsterdam.
Journal of health politics, policy and law. (0361-6878). Durham NC.
Journal of Himeji Gakuin Women's Junior College. Himeji.
Journal of historical sociology. (0952-1909). Oxford.
Journal of home economics of Japan. Tokyo.
Journal of housing and the built environment. (1566-4910). Dordrecht.
Journal of housing economics. (1051-1377). Orlando FL.
Journal of housing research. (1052-7001). Washington DC.
Journal of human development. (1464-9888). Basingstoke.
Journal of human evolution. (0047-2484). London.
Journal of human resources. (0022-166X). Madison WI.
Journal of human sciences [Osaka]. Osaka.
Journal of human sciences [Tokyo]. Tokyo.
Journal of humanities and natural sciences. (0495-8012). Tokyo.
Journal of Hyogo Educational University. Yashiro.
Journal of Imperial and Commonwealth history. (0308-6534). Ilford.
Journal of Indian philosophy. (0022-1791). Dordrecht.
Journal of Indo-European studies. (0092-2323). Washington DC.
Journal of industrial economics. (0022-1821). Oxford.
Journal of industrial relations. (0022-1856). Sydney.
Journal of industry and management. Osaka.
Journal of inquiry and research. Osaka.
Journal of institutional and theoretical economics = Zeitschrift für die gesamte Staatswissenschaft. (0932-4569). Tübingen.
Journal of interdisciplinary economics. (0260-1079). Bicester.
Journal of interdisciplinary history. (0022-1953). Cambridge MA.
Journal of interdisciplinary studies: An international journal of interdisciplinary and interfaith dialogue. (0890-0132). Santa Monica CA.
Journal of international accounting auditing and taxation. (1061-9518). Greenwich CT.
Journal of international affairs. (0022-197X). New York NY.
Journal of international business studies. (0047-2506). New Orleans LA.
Journal of international development. (0954-1748). Chichester.
Journal of international economic law. (1369-3034). Oxford.
Journal of international economics. (0022-1996). Amsterdam.
Journal of international financial management and accounting. (0954-1314). Oxford.
Journal of international financial markets, institutions & money. (1042-4431). Binghampton NY.
Journal of international money and finance. (0261-5606). Guildford.
Journal of international politics and economics. Tokyo.
Journal of international relations. Tokyo.
Journal of international relations and development. (1408-6980). Ljubljana.
Journal of international studies. Tokyo.

LISTE DES PERIODIQUES CONSULTÉS

Journal of international trade and economic development. (0963-8199). London.
Journal of Islamic economics. (0128-0066). Selangor.
Journal of Israeli history: studies in Zionism and statehood. (1353-1042). Ilford.
Journal of Japanese studies. (0095-6848). Seattle WA.
Journal of Jewish studies. (0022-2097). Oxford.
Journal of Kibi International University. Okayama.
Journal of Kobe Yamate College. Japan.
Journal of Korean studies. Los Angeles CA.
Journal of Kyoto Medical Association. Kyoto.
Journal of labor economics. (0734-306X). Chicago IL.
Journal of labor research. (0195-3613). Fairfax VA.
Journal of Laboratory Institute. Tokyo.
Journal of language and social psychology. (0261-927X). Clevedon.
Journal of Latin American studies. (0022-216X). Cambridge.
Journal of law. Tokyo.
Journal of law and economics. (0022-2186). Chicago IL.
Journal of law and political studies. Tokyo.
Journal of law and society. (0263-323X). Oxford.
Journal of law, economics, & organization. (8756-6222). Cary NC.
Journal of legal pluralism and unofficial law. (0732-9113). Birmingham.
Journal of legal studies. (0047-2530). Chicago IL.
Journal of leisure research. (0022-2216). Alexandria VA.
Journal of libertarian studies. (0363-2873). Burlingame CA.
Journal of linguistics. (0022-2267). Cambridge.
Journal of Literary Society of Yamaguchi University. Yamaguchi.
Journal of macroeconomics. (0164-0704). Baton Rouge LA.
Journal of management and governance. (1385-3457). Dordrecht.
Journal of management studies. (0022-2380). Oxford.
Journal of market history. Kumamoto.
Journal of marriage and the family. (0022-2445). Minneapolis MN.
Journal of mass communication studies. Tokyo.
Journal of material culture. (1359-1835). London.
Journal of mathematical economics. (0304-4068). Amsterdam.
Journal of mathematical sociology. (0022-250X). New York NY.
Journal of Mauritian studies. Moka.
Journal of medicine and philosophy. (0360-5310). SZ Lisse.
Journal of Mediterranean studies. (1016-3476). Msida.
Journal of modern African studies. (0022-278X). Cambridge.
Journal of modern history. (0022-2801). Chicago IL.
Journal of modern Italian studies. (1354-571X). London.
Journal of modern Korean studies. Fredericksburg VA.
Journal of monetary economics. (0304-3932). Amsterdam.
Journal of money, credit and banking. (0022-2879). Columbus OH.
Journal of multilingual and multicultural development. (0143-4632). Clevedon.
Journal of multinational financial management. (1042-444X). Oxford, U.K.
Journal of Natal and Zulu history. Durban.
Journal of Near Eastern studies. (0022-2968). Chicago IL.
Journal of Nigerian languages and literatures. (0943-1640). Munich.
Journal of North African studies. (1362-9387). Ilford.
Journal of Northeast Asian studies. (0738-7997). Washington DC.
Journal of northwest semitic languages. (0259-0131). Stellenbosch.

LIST OF PERIODICALS CONSULTED

Journal of occupational and organizational psychology. (0963-1798). Leicester.
Journal of occupational rehabilitation. (1053-0487). New York NY.
Journal of Okazaki College of Foreign Studies. Okinawa.
Journal of Osaka Sangyo University social sciences. Osaka.
Journal of Pacific Asia. Tokyo.
Journal of Pacific history. (0022-3344). Canberra.
Journal of Pacific studies. (1011-3029). Suva.
Journal of Palestine studies. (0377-919X). Berkeley CA.
Journal of peace research. (0022-3433). London.
Journal of peasant studies. (0306-6150). Ilford.
Journal of personality. (0022-3506). Malden MA.
Journal of personality and social psychology. (0022-3514). Washington DC.
Journal of philosophy. (0022-362X). New York NY.
Journal of pidgin and creole languages. (0920-9034). Amsterdam.
Journal of planning literature. (0885-4122). Thousand Oaks CA.
Journal of policy analysis and management. (0276-8739). New York NY.
Journal of policy history. (0898-0306). University Park PA.
Journal of policy modeling. (0161-8938). New York NY.
Journal of political economy. (0022-3808). Chicago IL.
Journal of political ideologies. (1356-9317). Abingdon.
Journal of political philosophy. (0963-8016). Oxford.
Journal of politics. (0022-3816). Austin TX.
Journal of popular culture. (0022-3840). Bowling Green OH.
Journal of population economics. (0933-1433). Heidelberg.
Journal of population research. Canberra.
Journal of post Keynesian economics. (0160-3477). Armonk NY.
Journal of pragmatics. (0378-2166). Amsterdam.
Journal of psychology. (0022-3980). Washington DC.
Journal of public administration research and theory. (1053-1858). New Brunswick NJ.
Journal of public economics. (0047-2727). Amsterdam.
Journal of public policy. (0143-814X). Cambridge.
Journal of quantitative anthropology. (0922-2995). Dordrecht.
Journal of real estate finance and economics. (0895-5638). Dordrecht.
Journal of real estate literature. Grand Forks ND.
Journal of real estate portfolio management. (1083-5547). Grand Forks ND.
Journal of real estate research. (0896-5803). Grand Forks ND.
Journal of refugee studies. (0951-6328). Oxford.
Journal of regional policy. Naples.
Journal of regional science. (0022-4146). Malden MA.
Journal of regulatory economics. (0922-680X). Dordrecht.
Journal of religion in Africa. (0022-4200). Leiden.
Journal of research in crime and delinquency. (0022-4278). Thousand Oaks CA.
Journal of risk and uncertainty. (0895-5646). Dordrecht.
Journal of risk research. (1366-9877). London.
Journal of ritual studies. (0890-1112). Pittsburgh PA.
Journal of rural development and administration. (0047-2751). Peshawar.
Journal of rural problem. Tokyo.
Journal of rural studies. (0743-0167). Oxford.
Journal of rural studies [Japan]. Tokyo.
Journal of semantics. (0167-5133). Oxford.
Journal of Slavic military studies. (1351-8046). Ilford.

LISTE DES PERIODIQUES CONSULTÉS

Journal of social and biological structures. (0140-1750). Greenwich CT.
Journal of social and clinical psychology. (0736-7236). New York NY.
Journal of social and evolutionary systems. (1061-7361). Stamford CT.
Journal of social and personal relationships. (0265-4075). London.
Journal of social development in Africa. (1012-1080). Harare.
Journal of social distress and the homeless. (1053-0789). New York NY.
Journal of social history. (0022-4529). Pittsburgh PA.
Journal of social issues. (0022-4537). New York NY.
Journal of social policy. (0047-2794). Cambridge.
Journal of social problems. Tokyo.
Journal of social psychology. (0022-4545). Washington DC.
Journal of social science. Zomba.
Journal of social sciences and humanities. (0023-4044). Seoul.
Journal of social studies. Dhaka.
Journal of social studies. Japan.
Journal of social work. (1468-0173). London.
Journal of social work practice. (0265-0533). Abingdon.
Journal of social, political and economic studies. (0193-5941). Washington DC.
Journal of Southeast Asian studies. (0022-4634). Singapore.
Journal of Southern African studies. (0305-7070). Abingdon.
Journal of strategic studies. (0140-2390). Ilford.
Journal of structural learning and intelligent systems. (1027-1015). Newark NJ.
Journal of studies in contemporary social theory. Tokyo.
Journal of Sugiyama Jogakuen University. Japan.
Journal of the American Oriental Society. (0003-0279). Ann Arbor MI.
Journal of the American Statistical Association. (0162-1459). Alexandria VA.
Journal of the Anthropological Society of Oxford. (0044-8370). Oxford.
Journal of the Asia Pacific economy. (1354-7860). London.
Journal of the Asiatic Society. (0368-3303). Calcutta.
Journal of the Asiatic Society of Bangladesh. Dhaka.
Journal of the Assam Research Society. Guwahati.
Journal of the Australian Population Association. (0814-5725). Canberra.
Journal of the Center for Women's Studies. Tokyo.
Journal of the College of Business Administration and Information Science. Japan.
Journal of the Culture Research Institute. Tokyo.
Journal of the economic and social history of the orient. (0022-4995). Leiden.
Journal of the history of ideas. (0022-5037). Baltimore MD.
Journal of the history of philosophy. (0022-5053). St. Louis MO.
Journal of the history of sexuality. (1043-4070). Chicago IL.
Journal of the history of the behavioral sciences. (0022-5061). New York NY.
Journal of the Institute of International Sociology. Japan.
Journal of the International Phonetic Association. Los Angeles CA.
Journal of the Japanese and international economies. (0889-1583). Duluth MN.
Journal of the Madras University: Section A — Humanities. Madras.
Journal of the Maharaja Sayajirao University of Baroda. (social science number). Baroda.
Journal of the Malaysian branch of the Royal Asiatic Society. (0126-7353). Kuala Lumpur.
Journal of the Mysore University: Section A-Arts. Mysore.
Journal of the Oriental Institute. (0030-5324). Baroda.
Journal of the Pakistan Historical Society. Karachi.
Journal of the Polynesian Society. (0032-4000). Auckland.
Journal of the Research Society of Buddhism and Cultural Heritage. Japan.

LIST OF PERIODICALS CONSULTED

Journal of the Research Society of Pakistan. Lahore.
Journal of the Royal Asiatic Society (Sri Lanka branch). Colombo.
Journal of the Royal Statistical Society: Series A (statistics in society). (0964-1998). London.
Journal of the Royal Statistical Society: Series B (statistical methodology). (1369-7412). London.
Journal of the Royal Statistical Society: Series C (applied statistics). (0035-9254). Oxford.
Journal of the Royal Statistical Society: Series D (the statistician). (00390526). London.
Journal of the Rural Life Society of Japan. Tsukuba.
Journal of the Siam Society. (0857-7099). Bangkok.
Journal of the study of human rights. Tokyo.
Journal of the Third World spectrum. (1072-5040). Washington DC.
Journal of the Walter Roth Museum of Anthropology. (0256-4653). Georgetown DC.
Journal of theoretical politics. London.
Journal of Third World studies. (8755-3449). Americus GA.
Journal of time series analysis. (0143-9782). Oxford.
Journal of Tokyo Keizai University. (0493-4091). Tokyo.
Journal of transport economics and policy. (0022-5258). Bath.
Journal of urban economics. (0094-1190). Duluth MN.
Journal of urban history. (0096-1442). Thousand Oaks CA.
Journal of West African languages. (0022-5401). Dallas TX.
Journal of women's education. Tokyo.
Journal of women's history. (1042-7961). Bloomington IN.
Journal of world business. (1090-9516). Stamford CT.
Journal of world history. (1045-6007). Honolulu HI.
Journal of world trade. (1011-6702). London.
Journal of Yasuda Women's University. Hiroshima.
Journal. Institute of Muslim Minority Affairs. (0266-6952). London.
Journal. Konan University, Faculty of Letters. Kobe.
Journal. Okayama University, School of General Education. Okayama.
Journal. Yamaguchi University, Literary Society. Yamaguchi.
Jurnal antropologi dan sosiologi. (0126-9518). Selangor.
Kabar seberang. (0314-5786). Townsville.
Kagoshima keizai daigaku shakaigakubu ronshu. Kagoshima.
Kagoshima law review. Kagoshima.
Kaiho shakaigaku kenkyu. Tokyo.
Kailash: A journal of Himalayan studies. Kathmandu.
Kajian Malaysia. (0127-4082). Penang.
Kanagawa University review. Kanagawa.
Kano studies. Kano.
Kansai University review of law and politics. Osaka.
Kansaneläkelaitoksen julkaisuja. (0355-4821). Helsinki.
Kanto toshigakkai ronshû. Tokyo.
Kasarinlan. Quezon City.
Kazoku shakaigaku kenkyu. Tokyo.
Keiei Johogakubu Kiyo (Bulletin of Jobu University). Gumma.
Keieisenryaku kiso koza. Tokyo.
Keio business review. (0453-4557). Tokyo.
Keio communication review. Tokyo.
Keio economic studies. (0022-9709). Tokyo.
Keizai orai. Japan.
Keizai ronshu: Journal of Toyama University. Toyama.
Keizaigaku ronshû. Kagoshima.

LISTE DES PERIODIQUES CONSULTÉS

Keizaigaku zasshi (Journal of Osaka Municipal University). Osaka.
Keizaigaku-ronshu of Kagoshima University. Kagoshima.
Kenkyu kiyo (Bulletin of Hyogo Kyoiku University). Nishiwaki.
Kenkyu kiyo (Journal of Aomori University). Aomori.
Kenkyu kiyo (Journal of Kibi Kokusai University). Takahashi.
Kenkyu kiyo (Journal. Tamagwa Fukushi University). Sendai.
Kenkyu-kiyo. Tokyo.
Kenkyu-kiyo (Bulletin of Osaka Kyoiku University). Osaka.
Kenkyunenpo (Bulletin of Rissho University). Tokyo.
Kenmin Katsudo kenkyu. Saitama.
Kesu Kenkyu. Tokyo.
Kigyo-kenkyusho Nenpo. Nagoya.
Kikan fukushi rodo. Tokyo.
Kikan Tomorrow. Amagasaki.
Kindai. Kobe.
Kindai Fudo. Osaka.
Kinki daigaku kyouyou gakuba kenkyū kiyou. Osaka.
Kiyo (Bulletin of Tyukyo University). Nagoya.
Kiyo (Journal of Seitoku College). Tokyo.
Kiyo shakaigakka. Tokyo.
Knowledge, technology & policy. (0897-1986). New Jersey.
Kobe economic and business review. (0075-6407). Kobe.
Kobe International University review. Kobe.
Kobe journal of higher education. Kobe.
Kokugakuin daigaku nihonbunka kenkyushoho. Tokyo.
Kokugakuin hougaku. Tokyo.
Kokumin Seikatsu Kenkyu. Tokyo.
Kölner Zeitschrift für Soziologie und Sozialpsychologie. (0340-0425). Wiesbaden.
Komodo Science. Tokyo.
Konjunkturpolitik. (0023-3498). Berlin.
Korea and world affairs. Seoul.
Korea economic report. Seoul.
Korea focus. (1225-8113). Seoul.
Korea journal. (0023-3900). Seoul.
Korea observer. (0023-3919). Seoul.
Korean culture. (0270-1618). Los Angeles CA.
Korean financial review. Seoul.
Korean social science journal. Seoul.
Korean studies. (0145-840X). Honolulu HI.
Közgazdasági szemle. (0023-4346). Budapest.
Kredit und Kapital. (0023-4591). Berlin.
Kroeber anthropological society papers. (0023-4869). Berkeley CA.
Kumamoto journal of culture and humanities. Kumamoto.
Kunnallistieteellinen aikakauskirja. Finland.
Kwansai Gakuin University annual studies. Hyogo.
Kwansei Gakuin daigaku shakaigakubu kiyo. Hyogo.
Kwansei Gakuin law review. (0452-9480). Nishinomiya.
Kwartalnik historii kultury materialnej. (0023-5881). Warsaw.
Kyklos. (0023-5962). Basle.
Kyoiku-shakaigaku kenkyu. Tokyo.
Kyoikugakubu kenkyu hokoku (Bulletin of Yamanashi University). Kohu.

LIST OF PERIODICALS CONSULTED

Kyoto journal of sociology. Kyoto.
Kyoto University economic review. (0023-6055). Kyoto.
Kyoto University research studies in education. Kyoto.
Kyoyobu kiyo (Bulletin of Rissho University). Tokyo.
L.S.E. quarterly. (0269-9710). Oxford.
Labour [Canada] = Travail. (0700-3862). St. John's.
Labour [Italy]. (1121-7081). Oxford.
Labour, capital and society = Travail, capital et société. (0706-1706). Montreal.
Laissez-faire. (0963-6633). London.
Lakimies. Helsinki.
Lalit kalā. New Delhi.
Land economics. (0023-7639). Madison WI.
Land reform, land settlement and cooperatives. (0251-1894). Rome.
Language. (0097-8507). Baltimore MD.
Language & communication. (0271-5309). New York NY.
Language in society. (0047-4045). New York NY.
Language problems and language planning. (0272-2690). Amsterdam.
Latin American business review. (1097-8526). Binghampton NY.
Latin American Indian literatures journal. (0888-5613). McKeesport PA.
Latin American perspectives. (0094-582X). Thousand Oaks CA.
Latin American politics and society. (1531-426X). Coral Gables FL.
Latin American research review. (0023-8791). Albuquerque NM.
Law and contemporary problems. (0023-9186). Durham NC.
Law and critique. (0957-8536). Liverpool.
Law and philosophy. (0167-5249). Dordrecht.
Law and policy. (0265-8240). Oxford.
Law and society review. (0023-9216). Amherst MA.
Ledelse og Erhvervsøkonomi. (0902-3704). Copenhagen.
Legislative studies. (0816-9152). Canberra.
Legislative studies quarterly. (0362-9805). Iowa City IA.
Leiden journal of international law. (0922-1565). The Hague.
Leisure sciences. (0149 0400). London.
Levante. (0024-1504). Rome.
Leviatán. (0210-6337). Madrid.
Liberian studies journal. (0024-1989). Bloomington IL.
Libyan studies. (0263-7189). London.
Linguistic inquiry. (0024-3892). Cambridge MA.
Linguistic review. (0167-6318). Hawthorne NY.
Linguistics. (0024-3949). Berlin.
Linguistics and philosophy. (0165-0157). Dordrecht.
Linguistics of the Tibeto-Burman area. (0731-3500). Berkeley CA.
Linguistique africaine. Paris.
Links. (0024-404X). Offenbach.
Literatura ludowa. (0024-4708). Wroclaw.
Littérature orale arabo-berbère. (0336-5654). Paris.
Local economy. (0269-0942). London.
Local economy quarterly. Luton.
Local environment. (1354-9839). Abingdon.
Local government review in Japan. (0288-7622). Tokyo.
Local government studies. (0300-3930). Ilford.
Lokayan bulletin. (0970-5406). New Delhi.

LISTE DES PERIODIQUES CONSULTÉS

Lotus. Shiga.
Low intensity conflict and law enforcement. (0966-2847). Ilford.
Lud. (0076-1435). Wroclaw.
Maandschrift economie. (0013-0486). Tilburg.
Macedonian review. Skopje.
Magyar jog. (0025-0147). Budapest.
Magyar közigazgatás. (0865-736X). Budapest.
Magyar tudomány. (0025-0325). Budapest.
Malaysian journal of tropical geography. (0127-1474). Kuala Lumpur.
Man in India. (0025-1569). Ranchi.
Management accounting research. (1044-5005). London.
Management science. (0025-1909). Providence RI.
Managerial and decision economics. (0143-6570). Chichester.
Manchester School. (1463-6786). Oxford.
Mandenkan. (0752-5443). Paris.
Mankind quarterly. (0025-2344). Washington DC.
Manusia dan Masyarakat. (0126-8678). Kuala Lumpur.
Marga. Colombo.
Marine policy. (0308-597X). Guildford.
Marketing letters. (0923-0645). Dordrecht.
Marx-Engels Jahrbuch. (0232-6132). Berlin.
Marxistische Blätter. (0542-7770). Essen.
Masculinities. (1072-8538). New York NY.
Mathematical finance. (0960-1627). Oxford.
Mathematical social sciences. (0165-4896). Amsterdam.
Media culture and society. (0163-4437). London.
Mediation quarterly. (0739-4098). San Francisco CA.
Medical anthropology. (0145-9740). Reading.
Medical anthropology quarterly. (0745-5194). Arlington VA.
Medicine, conflict and survival. (1362-3699). Ilford.
Medina, mimshal vihasim benleumiyim. (0334-2514). Jerusalem.
Mediterranean politics. (1362-9395). Ilford.
Mediterranean quarterly: A journal of global issues. (1047-4552). Durham NC.
Medizin Mensch Gesellschaft. (0340-8183). Stuttgart.
Megamot. (0025-8679). Jerusalem.
Meiji daigaku kyouyou ronshuu. Tokyo.
Meiji gakuin ronso. Tokyo.
Melanesian law journal. Papua New Guinea.
Melbourne journal of politics. (0085-3224). Melbourne.
Memoirs of Osaka Kyoiku University. Osaka.
Memoirs of Taisho University. Tokyo.
Memoirs. Bukkyo University, Postgraduate Research Institute. Kyoto.
Memoria. Mexico City.
Men and masculinities. (1097-184X). Thousand Oaks CA.
Mens en maatschappij. (0025-9454). Houten.
Mesoamérica. (0252-9963). Guatemala.
Mesopotamia. (0076-6615). Florence.
Metapolítica. (1405-4558). Mexico City.
Method and theory in the study of religion. (0943-3058). New York NY.
Metroeconomica. (0026-1386). Bologna.
Mezinárodní vztahy. (0323-1844). Prague.

LIST OF PERIODICALS CONSULTED

Middle East business and economic review. Australia.
Middle East journal. (0026-3141). Bloomington IN.
Middle East policy. (1061-1924). Washington DC.
Middle East quarterly. (1073-9467). Lawrence KS.
Middle East report. (0899-0328). Washington DC.
Middle East Studies Association bulletin. (0026-3184). Tucson AZ.
Middle Eastern studies. (0026-3206). Ilford.
Migracijske teme. (0352-5600). Zagreb.
Milbank quarterly. (0887-378X). New York NY.
Millennium. (0305-8298). London.
Mind. (0026-4423). Oxford.
Mind and language. (0268-1064). Oxford.
Minerva. (0026-4695). Dordrecht.
Mirovaia ekonomika i mezhdunarodnye otnosheniia. (0131-2227). Moscow.
Mitologicas. (0326-5676). Buenos Aires.
Mitteilungen der Deutschen Orient-Gesellschaft zu Berlin. (0342-118X). Berlin.
Mitteilungen. S.W.A. Wissenschaftliche Gesellschaft = Journal SWA Scientific Society. Windhoek.
Mittelforum - rivista nord est. (1123-7597). Venice.
Mobilization. (1086-671X). San Diego CA.
Moct-Most: Economic policy in transitional economies. (1120-7388). Dordrecht.
Modern Asian studies. (0026-749X). Cambridge.
Modern China. (0097-7004). Thousand Oaks CA.
Modern law review. (0026-7961). Oxford.
Monatsberichte der Deutschen Bundesbank. (0012-0006). Frankfurt am Main.
Monatsberichte. Österreichisches Institut für Wirtschaftsforschung. (0029-9898). Vienna.
Monde arabe maghreb machrek. (1241-5294). Paris.
Monde copte. (0399-905X). Limoges.
Mondes en développement. (0302-3052). Paris.
Monetaria. (0185-1136). Mexico City.
Monetary and economic studies. (0288-8432). Tokyo.
Money affairs. (0187-7615). Mexico City.
Mongolia survey. (1081-5082). Bloomington IN.
Mongolian studies. (0190-3667). Bloomington IN.
Monthly report of the Deutsche Bundesbank. (0418-8292). Frankfurt am Main.
Monthly review: State Bank of India, Economic Research Department. (0039-0003). Bombay.
Monumenta Nipponica. (0027-0741). Tokyo.
Monumenta serica. (0254-9948). St. Augustin.
Morocco: The journal of the society for Moroccan studies. London.
Most: Economic journal on Eastern Europe and the former Soviet Union. Bologna.
Mouvement social. (0027-2671). Paris.
Multilingua. (0167-8507). Berlin.
Municipal problems. Tokyo.
Nagoya daigaku shakaigaku ronshu. Nagoya.
Nampo-bunka. Tenri.
Nanzan shûkyô bunka kenkyûjo kenkyûjohô. Nagoya.
Nara Women's University sociological studies. Nara.
Narodna tvorchist' ta etnografiia. Kiev.
Národní hospodářství. (0032-0749). Prague.
National Institute economic review. (0027-9501). London.
National interest. (0884-9382). Washington DC.
National tax journal. (0028-0283). Columbus OH.

LISTE DES PERIODIQUES CONSULTÉS

Nationalism and ethnic politics. (1353-7113). Ilford.
Nationalities papers. (0090-5992). Omaha NE.
Nations and nationalism. (1354-5078). Cambridge.
Natural resources forum. (0165-0203). Guildford.
Natural resources journal. (0028-0739). Albuquerque NM.
Nature and resources. (0028-0844). Carnforth.
Negotiation journal. (0748-4526). New York NY.
NEHA-bulletin. (0920-9875). Amsterdam.
NEHA-jaarboek voor economische, bedrijfs- en techniekgeschiedenis. (1380-5517). Amsterdam.
Nenpo shakaigaku ronshu. Tokyo.
Netherlands international law review. (0165-070X). Dordrecht.
Netherlands journal of social sciences = Sociologia Neerlandica. (0038-0172). Assen.
Netherlands quarterly of human rights. (0169-3441). Dordrecht.
Netherlands yearbook of international law. (0167-6768). Dordrecht.
Neue Gesellschaft / Frankfurter Hefte. (0177-6738). Bonn.
Neue politische literatur. (0028-3320). Frankfurt am Main.
New economy. (1070-3535). London.
New England economic review. Boston MA.
New European. (0953-1432). Bradford.
New formations. (0950-2378). London.
New left review. (0028-6060). London.
New media & society. (1461-4448). London.
New perspectives on Turkey. (0896-6346). Great Barrington MA.
New political economy. (1356-3467). Abingdon.
New politics. (0028-6494). Brooklyn NY.
New quest. (0258-0381). Pune.
New technology, work and employment. (0268-1072). Oxford.
New Vico studies. (0733-9542). New York NY.
New York University journal of international law and politics. (0028-7873). New York NY.
New Zealand economic papers. (0077-9954). Wellington.
New Zealand international review. (0110-0262). Wellington.
New Zealand journal of history. (0028-8322). Auckland.
New Zealand sociology. (0112-921X). Palmerston.
Newsletter of Baluchistan studies. Naples.
NIAS. (0904-597X). Copenhagen.
Nieuwe West-Indische gids = New West Indian guide. (0028-9930). Dordrecht.
Nigerian field. (0029-0076). Ibadan.
Nigerian forum. (0189-0816). Lagos.
Nigerian journal of economic and social studies. (0029-0092). Ibadan.
Nigerian journal of international affairs. (0331-3646). Lagos.
Nigerian journal of policy and strategy. Kuru.
Nigerian journal of political science. (0031-8524). Zaria.
Nigerian journal of public administration and local government. Nsukka.
Nihon Keizaiseisaku Gakkai Nenpo. Tokyo.
Nihon rôdô shakai gakkai nenpô. Tokyo.
Nilo-Ethiopian studies. (1340-329X). Kyoto.
Nilo-Ethiopian studies newsletter. (0919-8210). Kyoto.
Nineteenth-century contexts. (0890-5495). Basle.
Ningen kagaku kenkyu (Journal of Waseda University). Tokyo.
Nogyo mondai kenkyu. Tokyo.
Nogyo sogo kenkyu. Tokyo.

LIST OF PERIODICALS CONSULTED

Nonprofit management and leadership. (1048-6682). San Francisco CA.
NORA: Nordic journal of women's studies. (0803-8740). Oslo.
Nord nytt. (0008-1345). Copenhagen.
Nordic journal of African studies. (1235-4481). Helsinki.
Nordic journal of linguistics. (0332-5865). Oslo.
Norsk økonomisk tidsskrift. (0039-0720). Oslo.
North Korea quarterly. (0340-104X). Hamburg.
Noson seikatsu kenkyu. Tsukuba.
Notas mesoamericanas. Puebla.
Noticario de historia agraria. (1132-1261). Zaragoza.
Nougyo shijo kenkyu. Sapporo.
Nueva sociedad. (0251-3552). Caracas.
Numen. (0029-5973). Leiden.
Nuova antologia. Florence.
Obshchestvennye nauki i sovremennost'. (0869-0499). Moscow.
Ocean development and international law. (0090-8320). London.
Oceania. (0029-8077). Sydney.
Oceanic linguistics. (0029-8115). Honolulu HI.
OECD economic studies. (0255-0822). Paris.
Omni-management. Japan.
OPEC review. (0277-0180). Oxford.
Open economies review. (0923-7992). Dordrecht.
Opinião pública. (0104-6276). São Paulo.
Oral history. (0143-0955). Colchester.
Orbis. (0030-4387). Philadelphia PA.
Ordo. (0048-2129). Stuttgart.
Organization and environment. (1086-0266). Thousand Oaks CA.
Organization science. (1047-7039). Linthicum MD.
Organization studies. (0170-8406). Berlin.
Organization: the interdisciplinary journal of organization, theory and society. (1350-5084). London.
Organizational behavior and human decision processes. (0749-5978). Duluth MN.
Oriens Extremus. (0030-5197). Wiesbaden.
Orient. (0030-5227). Leverkusen.
Orientalia. (0030-5367). Rome.
Orissa historical research journal. Orissa.
Orita. (0030-5596). Ibadan.
Osaka daigaku ningenkagakubu kiyō. Osaka.
Osaka economic papers. (0473-4548). Osaka.
Osaka shogyo daigaku ronshu. Osaka.
Osaka studies in sociology of education. Osaka.
Österreichische Zeitschrift für Politikwissenschaft. (1615-5548). Vienna.
Osteuropa. (0030-6428). Stuttgart.
Osteuropa Wirtschaft. (0030-6460). Stuttgart.
Otemon economic studies. (0475-0756). Osaka.
Overseas social security news. Tokyo.
Oxford agrarian studies. (0264-5491). Abingdon.
Oxford bulletin of economics and statistics. (0305-9049). Oxford.
Oxford development studies. (1360-0818). Abingdon.
Oxford economic papers. (0030-7653). Oxford.
Oxford international review. (0966 0054). Oxford.
Oxford journal of archaeology. (0262-5253). Oxford.

LISTE DES PERIODIQUES CONSULTÉS

Oxford review of economic policy. (0266-903X). Oxford.
Oyo-shakaigaku kenkyu (Journal of Rikkyo University). Tokyo.
Pacific affairs. (0030-851X). Vancouver.
Pacific economic bulletin. (0817-8038). Canberra.
Pacific historical review. (0030-8684). Berkeley CA.
Pacific perspective. (0379-626X). Suva.
Pacific review. (0951-2748). London.
Pacific Rim law and policy journal. (1066-8632). Seattle WA.
Pacific studies. (0275-3596). Laie HI.
Pacific viewpoint. (0030-8978). Wellington.
Paideuma. (0078-7809). Stuttgart.
Pakistan development review. (0030-9729). Islamabad.
Pakistan economic and social review. (1011-002X). Lahore.
Pakistan horizon. (0030-980X). Karachi.
Pakistan journal of applied economics. (0254-9204). Karachi.
Pakistan journal of history and culture. (1012-7682). Islamabad.
Palaeoslavica: International journal for the study of Slavic medieval literature, history, language and ethnology. (1070-5465). Cambridge MA.
Palestine-Israel journal of politics, economics and culture. (0793-1395). Jerusalem.
Państwo i prawo. (0031-0980). Warsaw.
Papeles de economía española. (0210-9107). Madrid.
Papers in regional science. (0486-2902). Urbana IL.
Papers: revista de sociologia. (0210-2862). Barcelona.
Parliamentary affairs. (0031-2290). Oxford.
Party politics. (1354-0688). London.
Past and present. (0031-2746). Oxford.
Patterns of prejudice. (0031-322X). London.
Peace and conflict. (1078-1919). Mahwah NJ.
Peasant studies. Salt Lake City UT.
Penant. (0336-1551). Le Vésinet.
Péninsule. Paris.
Pensamiento iberoamericano. (0212-0208). Madrid.
Pensée. (0031-4773). Paris.
Pensiero politico. (0031-4846). Florence.
Pénzügyi szemle. (0031-496X). Budapest.
Peripherie. (0173-184X). Berlin.
Perspectiva económica. (0100-039X). São Leopoldo.
Perspectives on science. (1063-6145). Chicago IL.
Perspectives on social problems. Greenwich CT.
Pesquisa e planejamento econômico. (0100-0551). Rio de Janeiro.
Petersburg journal of cultural studies. (0136-0159). St. Petersburg.
Peuples méditerranéens = Mediterranean peoples. (0399-1253). Paris.
Philippine economic journal. Quezon City.
Philippine journal of public administration. (0031-7675). Quezon City.
Philippine quarterly of culture and society. (0115-0243). Cebu City.
Philippine studies. (0031-7837). Quezon City.
Philosophical quarterly. (0031-8094). Oxford.
Philosophie politique. Paris.
Philosophy. Tokyo.
Philosophy & public affairs. (0048-3915). Princeton NJ.
Philosophy & social criticism. (0191-4537). London.

LIST OF PERIODICALS CONSULTED

Philosophy east and west. (0031-8221). Honolulu HI.
Philosophy of the social sciences. (0048-3931). Thousand Oaks CA.
Planeación y desarrollo. (0034 8686). Colombia.
Planning and administration. (0304-117X). The Hague.
Planning practice and research. (0269-7459). London.
Planning theory & practice. (1464-9357). London.
Police studies. (0141-2949). Bradford.
Policing and society. (1043-9463). New York NY.
Policy and politics. (0305-5736). Bristol.
Policy sciences. (0032-2687). Dordrecht.
Policy studies. (0144-2872). London.
Polis [Bologna]. Bologna.
Polis [Moscow]. (0321-2017). Moscow.
Polis [York]. (0412-257X). Thorverton.
Polish quarterly of international affairs. (1230-4999). Warsaw.
Política internacional. (0873-6650). Lisbon.
Politica: tiddskrift for politisk videnskab. (0105-0710). Aarhus.
Political communication. (1058-4609). London.
Political economy journal of India. (0971-2097). Chandigarh.
Political geography. (0962-6298). Oxford.
Political power and social theory. Greenwich CT.
Political psychology. (0162-895X). Malden MA.
Political quarterly. (0032-3179). Oxford.
Political research quarterly. (1065-9129). Salt Lake City UT.
Political science. (0032-3187). Wellington.
Political science and politics. (1049-0965). Washington DC.
Political science quarterly. (0032-3195). New York NY.
Political studies. (0032-3217). Oxford.
Political theory. (0090-5917). Thousand Oaks CA.
Politička misao. (0032-3241). Zagreb.
Politico. (0032-325X). Milan.
Politics. (0263-3957). London.
Politics and society. (0032-3292). Thousand Oaks, CA.
Politics and the individual: International journal of political socialization and political psychology. (0939-6071). Hamburg.
Politics and the life sciences. (0730-9384). Guildford, Surrey.
Politics, groups and the individual: International journal of political psychology and political socialization. (1430-0230). Norderstedt.
Politiikka. Tampere.
Politikon. (0258-9346). Stellenbosch.
Politique africaine. (0244-7827). Paris.
Politique et sociétés. (1203-9438). Montreal.
Politique étrangère. (0032-342X). Paris.
Politique internationale. (0221-2781). Paris.
Politiques et management public. (0758-1726). Paris.
Politische Vierteljahresschrift. (0032-3470). Wiesbaden.
Politisches Denken Jahrbuch. (0942-2307). Stuttgart.
Politix. (0295-2319). Paris.
Population. (0032-4663). Paris.
Population and development review. (0098-7921). New York NY.
Population and environment. (0199-0039). New York NY.

LISTE DES PERIODIQUES CONSULTÉS

Population research and policy review. (0167-5923). Dordrecht.
Population review. (0032-471X). La Jolla CA.
Population studies [London]. (0032-4728). London.
Population studies [New York]. (0082-805X). New York NY.
Post-communist economies. (1463-1377). Abingdon.
Post-Soviet affairs. (1060-586X). Silver Spring MD.
Postgraduate Research Institute Bukkyo University. Kyoto.
Pouvoirs. (0152-0768). Paris.
Praca i zabezpieczenie społeczne. (0032-6186). Warsaw.
Practice. (0950-3153). Birmingham.
Praxis international. (0260-8448). Oxford.
Présence africaine. (0032-7638). Paris.
Presidential studies quarterly. (0360-4918). New York NY.
Primates. (0032-8332). Aichi.
Problèmes d'Amérique latine. (0765-1333). Paris.
Problèmes politiques et sociaux. (0015-9743). Paris.
Problems of communism. (0032-941X). Washington DC.
Probus. (0921-4771). Berlin.
Proceedings for Annual Conference of Japan Institute of Tourism Research. Tokyo.
Proceedings of the Academy of Political Science. (0065-0684). New York NY.
Proceedings. American Statistical Association. Alexandria VA.
Professional geographer. (0033-0124). Washington DC.
Progress in human geography. (0309-1325). Sevenoaks.
Progress in planning. (0305-9006). Oxford.
Projet. (0033-0884). Paris.
Prokla: Zeitschrift für kritische Sozialwissenschaft. (0342-8176). Berlin.
Przegląd archeologiczny. (0079-7138). Warsaw.
Przegląd orientalistyczny. (0033-2283). Warsaw.
Przegląd polonijny. (0137-303X). Wroclaw.
Przegląd socjologiczny. (0033-2356). Lódz.
Przegląd statystyczny. (0033-2372). Warsaw.
Psychoanalytic studies. (1460-8952). Oxford.
Psychological bulletin. (0033-2909). Washington DC.
Psychological review. (0033-295X). Washington DC.
Psychology and developing societies. New Delhi.
Psychology of women quarterly. (0361-6843). New York NY.
Psychology, evolution & gender. (1461-6661). London.
Public administration. (0033-3298). Oxford.
Public administration and development. (0271-2075). Chichester.
Public administration and policy. (1022-0275). Hong Kong.
Public administration review. (0033-3352). Washington DC.
Public affairs quarterly. (0887-0373). Bowling Green OH.
Public choice. (0048-5829). Dordrecht.
Public culture. (0899-2363). Durham NC.
Public enterprise. (0351-3564). Ljubljana.
Public finance = Finances publiques. (0033-3476). Frankfurt am Main.
Public finance review. (1091-1421). Thousand Oaks CA.
Public interest. (0033-3557). Washington DC.
Public law. (0033-3565). London.
Public money and management. (0954-0962). Oxford.
Public opinion quarterly. (0033-362X). Chicago IL.

LIST OF PERIODICALS CONSULTED

Publius: the journal of federalism. (0048-5950). Easton PA.
Publizistik. (0033-4006). Konstanz.
Punishment & society. (1462-4745). London.
Quaderni del Dipartimento di studi glottoantropologici. Rome.
Quaderni dell'osservatorio elettorale. Florence.
Quaderni della rivista di economia agraria. Bologna.
Quaderni di sociologia. (0033-4952). Turin.
Quaderni di studi arabi. Venice.
Quaderni storici. (0301-6307). Bologna.
Qualitative inquiry. (1077-8004). Thousand Oaks CA.
Qualitative research. (1468-7941). London.
Quarterly bulletin. Central Bank of Ireland. (0069-1542). Dublin.
Quarterly economic bulletin. (0952-0724). Liverpool.
Quarterly economic commentary. (0306-7866). Glasgow.
Quarterly economic review. Bank of Korea. Seoul.
Quarterly ethnology. Osaka.
Quarterly journal of administration. (0001-8333). Ile-Ife.
Quarterly journal of economics. (0033-5533). Cambridge MA.
Quarterly of social research. Tokyo.
Quarterly of social security research. Tokyo.
Quarterly review of economics and finance. (0033-5797). Champaign IL.
Quarterly review. Federal Reserve Bank of New York. (0147-6580). New York NY.
Quest. (1011-226X). Lusaka.
Race and class. (0306-3968). London.
Radical history review. (0163-6545). New York NY.
Rand journal of economics. (0741-6261). Santa Monica CA.
Rassegna economica. Naples.
Rassegna italiana di sociologia. (0486-0349). Bologna.
Rassegna parlamentare. Rome.
Rationality and society. (1043-4631). London.
Recherches contemporaines. (1251-2419). Paris.
Recherches économiques de Louvain. (0770-4518). Louvanin-la-Neuve.
Recherches sociographiques. (0034-1282). Quebec.
Recherches sociologiques. (0771-677X). Leuven.
Refuge. (0229-5113). Toronto.
Regards sur l'actualité. (0337-7091). Paris.
Region and community studies bulletin. Kobe.
Regional and federal studies. (1359-7566). Ilford.
Regional science and urban economics. (0166-0462). Amsterdam.
Regional studies. (0034-3404). Abingdon.
Rekishi to shakai. Tokyo.
Relaciones internacionales. (0185-0814). Mexico City.
Relations internationales. (0335-2013). Paris.
Religion. (0048-721X). London.
Religion, state and society. (0963-7494). Abingdon.
Report of the Institute of Social Sciences. Tokyo.
Report of the Sociology & Social Work Institute. Tokyo.
Reports of the Research Institute for Japanese Culture. Sendai.
Reproductive health matters. (0968-8080). London.
Res publica [Brussels]. (0486-4700). Brussels.
Res publica [Liverpool]. (1356-4765). Liverpool.

LISTE DES PERIODIQUES CONSULTÉS

Resarun. Itanagar.
Research bulletin. Kyushu.
Research bulletin of Kagoshima Women's College. Kagoshima.
Research bulletin of sociology. Tokyo.
Research bulletin. Meisei University. Tokyo.
Research bulletin. Tokyo University, Graduate School of Sociology. Tokyo.
Research evaluation. (0958-2029). Guildford.
Research in African literatures. (0034-5210). Bloomington IN.
Research in economic anthropology. (0190-1281). Greenwich CT.
Research in education. (0034-5237). Manchester.
Research in law and economics. Greenwich CT.
Research in Melanesia. (0254-0665). Port Moresby.
Research in political economy. (0161-7230). Greenwich CT.
Research in population economics. (0163-7878). Greenwich CT.
Research in social movements, conflicts and change. (0163-786X). Greenwich CT.
Research in social psychology. Tokyo.
Research in social stratification and mobility. (0276-5624). Greenwich CT.
Research in the sociology of work. (0277-2833). Greenwich CT.
Research papers in education — policy and practice. (0267-1522). London.
Research report. National Institute for Educational Research. Tokyo.
Reserve Bank of India bulletin. (0034-5512). Bombay.
Resources policy. (0301-4207). Oxford.
Rethinking Marxism. (0893-5696). New York NY.
Review. Suva.
Review of African political economy. (0305-6244). Abingdon.
Review of Association of Region and Community Studies. Tokyo.
Review of Austrian economics. (0889-3047). Dordrecht.
Review of black political economy. (0034-6446). New Brunswick NJ.
Review of Central and East European law. (0925-9880). Dordrecht.
Review of contemporary ideas. Tokyo.
Review of economic conditions in Italy. (0034-6799). Rome.
Review of economic studies. (0034-6527). Oxford.
Review of economics and statistics. (0034-6535). Cambridge.
Review of economies in transition. (1235-7405). Helsinki.
Review of financial studies. (0893-9454). Cary NC.
Review of income and wealth. (0034-6586). New York NY.
Review of Indonesian and Malaysian affairs. (0034-6594). Sydney.
Review of industrial organization. (0889-938X). Dordrecht.
Review of international economics. (0965-7576). Oxford.
Review of international political economy. (0969-2290). London.
Review of international studies. (0260-2105). Cambridge.
Review of Islamic economics. (0962-2055). Leicester.
Review of Middle East studies. Buckhurst Hill.
Review of modern thought. Tokyo.
Review of Osaka University of Commerce. Osaka.
Review of policy issues. (1355-6223). Sheffield.
Review of political economy. (0953-8259). Abingdon.
Review of politics. (0034-6705). Notre Dame IN.
Review of population and social policy. (0918-788X). Tokyo.
Review of quantitative finance and accounting. (0924-865X). Dordrecht.
Review of radical political economics. (0486-6134). Stamford CT.

LIST OF PERIODICALS CONSULTED

Review of rural and urban planning in Southern and Eastern Africa. Harare.
Review of social economy. (0034-6764). London.
Review of the Osaka University of Commerce. Osaka.
Review of urban and regional development studies. (0917-0553). Tokyo.
Review. Federal Reserve Bank of St. Louis. (0014-9187). St. Louis MO.
Review. Fernand Braudel Center. (0147-9032). Binghamton NY.
Reviews in anthropology. (0093-8157). Newark NJ.
Revista Andina. (0259-9600). Cusco.
Revista brasileira de ciência política. (0103-3352). Brasilia.
Revista brasileira de ciências sociais. (0102-6909). São Paulo.
Revista brasileira de economia. (0034-7140). Rio de Janeiro.
Revista brasileira de estudos de população. (0102-3098). Brazil.
Revista brasileira de estudos políticos. (0034-7191). Belo Horizonte.
Revista colombiana de antropología. (0486-6525). Bogota.
Revista de administración pública. (0034-7639). Madrid.
Revista de antropología. (0120-6613). Bogota.
Revista de ciência política. (0034-8023). Rio de Janeiro.
Revista de ciências sociais. (0041-8862). Ceará.
Revista de ciencias sociales. (0034-7817). Puerto Rico.
Revista de economía y estadística. (0034-8066). Córdoba.
Revista de estudios políticos. (0048-7694). Madrid.
Revista de etnografie şi folclor. (0034-8198). Bucharest.
Revista de fomento social. (0015-6043). Madrid.
Revista de historia económica. (0212-6109). Madrid.
Revista de planeación y desarrollo. (0034-8686). Bogota.
Revista de sociologia e politíca. (0104-4478). Curtiba.
Revista del Centro de Estudios Constitucionales. (0214-6185). Madrid.
Revista econômica do nordeste. (0100-4956). Fortaleza.
Revista interamericana de planificación. (1390-0315). Guatemala.
Revista internacional de estudos africanos. (0871-2344). Lisbon.
Revista latinoamericana de estudios avanzados. (1316-0486). Caracas.
Revista mexicana de ciencias politicas y sociales. Mexico City.
Revista mexicana de sociología. (0035-0087). Mexico City.
Revista mexicana del Caribe. (1405-2962). Chetumal, Quintana Roo.
Revista occidental. Tijuana.
Revista paraguaya de sociología. Asunción.
Revista Universidad EAFIT. (0120-033X). Medellín.
Revue belge de droit international = Belgian review of international law = Belgisch tijdschrift voor internationaal recht. (0035-0788). Brussels.
Revue canadienne d'études de développement = Canadian journal of development studies. (0225-5189). Ottawa.
Revue d'assyriologie et d'archéologie orientale. Paris.
Revue d'économie politique. (0373-2630). Paris.
Revue d'économie régionale et urbaine. (0180-7307). Paris.
Revue d'études comparatives est-ouest. (0338-0599). Paris.
Revue d'études palestiniennes. (0252-8290). Paris.
Revue d'histoire moderne et contemporaine. (0048-8003). Paris.
Revue de Corée. Seoul.
Revue de l'économie meridionale. (0987-3813). Montpellier.
Revue de l'histoire des religions. (0035-1423). Paris.
Revue de l'Institut de sociologie. (0770-1055). Brussels.

LISTE DES PERIODIQUES CONSULTÉS

Revue de l'Institut des bellos-lettres arabes. (0018-862X). Tunis Bab Meuara.
Revue de l'OFCE: Observations et diagnostics économiques. (0751-6614). Paris.
Revue de science criminelle et de droit pénal comparé. (0035-1733). Paris.
Revue de statistique appliquée. (0035 175X). Paris.
Revue des mondes musulmans et de la Méditerranée. (0997-1327). Aix-en-Provence.
Revue diplomatique. Tokyo.
Revue du droit public: et de la science politique en France et à l'étranger. (0035-2578). Paris.
Revue du travail. (0035-2705). Brussels.
Revue économique. (0035-2764). Paris.
Revue économique et sociale. (0035-2772). Lausanne-Dorigny.
Revue européenne de droit public = European review of public law = Europäische Zeitschrift des öffentlichen Rechts = Rivista europea di diritto pubblico. (1105-1590). London.
Revue européenne des sciences sociales: Cahiers Vilfredo Pareto. (0048-8046). Geneva.
Revue française d'administration publique. (0152-7401). Paris.
Revue française d'histoire d'outre-mer. (0300-9513). Paris.
Revue française d'histoire des idées politiques. (1266-7862). Paris.
Revue française de science politique. (0035-2950). Paris.
Revue française de sociologie. (0035-2969). Gap.
Revue générale de droit international public. (0035-3094). Paris.
Revue hellénique de droit international. (0035-3256). Athens.
Revue internationale de droit comparé. (0035-3337). Paris.
Revue internationale de droit penal = International review of penal law. (0223-5404). Ramonville St. Agne.
Revue juridique, politique et économique du Maroc. (0251-4761). Rabat.
Revue politique et parlementaire. (0035-385X). Paris.
Revue roumaine des sciences économiques = Romanian economic review. (1220-5397). Bucharest.
Revue Tiers-Monde. (0040-7356). Paris.
Revue trimestrielle de droit européen. (0035-4317). Paris.
Revue tunisienne des sciences sociales. (0035-4333). Tunis.
Rig. (0035-5267). Stockholm.
Rinrigaku Nenpo. Tokyo.
Riron to hoho = Sociological theory and methods. (0913-1442). Sapporo.
Risk, decision and policy. (1357-5309). Cambridge.
Risparmio. (0035-5615). Milan.
Ritsumeikan kokusaikankei kenkyu. Kyoto.
Ritsumeikan review of industrial society. Kyoto.
Ritsumeikan sangyoshakai ronsyu. Kyoto.
Rivista di diritto finanziario e scienza delle finanze. (0035-6131). Milan.
Rivista di economia agraria. (0035-6190). Bologna.
Rivista di politica economica. (0391-6170). Rome.
Rivista di storia economica. (0393-3415). Turin.
Rivista di studi politici internazionali. (0035-6611). Florence.
Rivista internazionale di scienze economiche e commerciali. (0035-6751). Padua.
Rivista internazionale di scienze sociali. (0035-676X). Milan.
Rivista italiana di scienza politica. (0048-8402). Bologna.
Rivista storica italiana. (0035-7073). Naples.
Rivista trimestrale di diritto pubblico. (0557-1464). Milan.
Rock art research. (0813-0426). Melbourne.
Roma. Chandigarh.
Romani studies. (1528-0748). Cheverly MD.
Ronshu (Bulletin of Tohoku Gakuin University). Sendai.

LIST OF PERIODICALS CONSULTED

Ronshu (Bulletin of Tokyo Women's University). Tokyo.
Ronshu (Journal of Komatsu College). Komatsu.
Ronshu (Journal of Matsuyama University). Matsuyama.
Ronso. Mizunami.
Ronso. Japan.
Ronso Shinrigaku Kiyo (Journal of Meiji Gakuin University). Tokyo.
Rosei jiho. Tokyo.
Round table. (0035-8533). Abingdon.
Royal Bank of Scotland review. (0267-1190). Edinburgh.
Rural africana. (0085-5839). East Lansing MI.
Rural development in Nigeria. Ibadan.
Rural history: Economy, society, culture. (0956-7933). Cambridge.
Rural sociology. (0036-0112). College Station TX.
Russian politics and law. (1061-1940). Armonk NY.
RWI-Mitteilungen. (0933-0089). Berlin.
Ryudai law review. Okinawa.
Ryukoku Kiyo. Kyoto.
Saeculum. (0080-5319). Freiburg.
SAIS review. (0036-0777). Washington DC.
Sangeet natak. New Delhi.
Santé mentale au Québec. (0383-6320). Montreal.
Sapientia. Amagasaki.
Sarawak gazette. (0036-4762). Kuching.
Sarawak Museum journal. (0375-3050). Kuching.
Sari. (0127-2721). Selangor.
Sarjana. Kuala Lumpur.
Savanna. (0331-0523). Zaria.
Savings and development. (0393-4551). Milan.
Scandinavian economic history review. (0358-5522). Lund.
Scandinavian journal of development alternatives and area studies. (0280-2791). Stockholm.
Scandinavian journal of economics. (0347-0520). Oxford.
Scandinavian journal of social welfare. (0907-2055). Copenhagen.
Scandinavian journal of the Old Testament. (0901-8328). Aarhus.
Scandinavian political studies. (0080-6757). Oxford.
School field. (0353-6807). Ljubljana.
Schweizerische Zeitschrift für Soziologie = Revue suisse de sociologie. (0379-3664). Zurich.
Schweizerische Zeitschrift für Volkswirtschaft und Statistik = Revue suisse d'économie politique et de statistique. (0303-9692). Basel.
Science and education. (0926-7220). Dordrecht.
Science and public policy. (0302-3427). Guildford.
Science and society. (0036-8237). New York NY.
Science as culture. (0959-5431). London.
Science, technology & development. (0950-0707). Ilford.
Scottish journal of political economy. (0036-9292). Oxford.
Scripta ethnologica. (0325-6669). Buenos Aires.
Searchlight South Africa. (0954-3384). London.
Security dialogue. (0967-0106). London.
Security studies. (0963-6412). Ilford.
Seguridad estratégica regional. Buenos Aires.
Seijo communication review. Tokyo.
Seijo University economic papers. Tokyo.

LISTE DES PERIODIQUES CONSULTÉS

Seikatsubunkakenkyû. Nagoya.
Selected reports in ethnomusicology. Los Angeles CA.
Semiotica. (0037-1998). Berlin.
Senri ethnological studies. Osaka.
Senriyama bungaku-ronshu. Osaka.
Senshu sociology. Kanagawa.
Shakai bunseki. Tokyo.
Shakai-kagaku Tokyu. Tokyo.
Shakai-undo. Tokyo.
Shakaibunka kenkyu. Hiroshima.
Shakaigaku hyoron. Tokyo.
Shakaigaku kenkyuka kiyo (Bulletin of Keio-Gijuku Graduate School). Tokyo.
Shakaigaku nenpō. Sendai.
Shakaigaku ronko. Tokyo.
Shakaigaku ronshu (Bulletin of Momoyama University). Osaka.
Shakaigaku ronshu [Nagoya]. Nagoya.
Shakaigaku ronso. Tokyo.
Shakaigaku-nenshi. Tokyo.
Shakaigaku-senko kiyo. Tokyo.
Shakaigaku-zasshi. Kobe.
Shakaigakubu kiyo (Bulletin of Ryukoku University). Otsu.
Shakaigakubu kiyo (Journal of Kansai University). Osaka.
Shakaigakubu ronso. Ibaraki.
Shakaijinruigaku nenpo. Tokyo.
Shakaishinrigaku kenkyu. Tokyo.
Shaman. (1216-7827). Szeged.
Shimbun kenkyu. Tokyo.
Shinbungaku hyoron. Japan.
Shisei. Tokyo.
Shiseikenkyu. Osaka.
Shizen, ningen, shakai. Yokohama.
Shnaton. Tel-Aviv.
SIER Bulletin. Kwaluseni.
Signs. (0097-9740). Chicago IL.
Sikh review. (0037-5123). Calcutta.
Simmei shakaigaku kenkyu. Kawasaki.
Simulation and gaming. (0037-5500). Thousand Oaks CA.
Singapore economic review. (0217-5908). Singapore.
Singapore journal of tropical geography. (0129-7619). Singapore.
Sino-American relations. Taiwan.
Siso no Kagaku. Tokyo.
Sistema. (0210-0223). Madrid.
Slavic review. (0037-6779). Stanford CA.
Slavonic and East European review. (0037-6795). London.
Slovo. (0954-6839). London.
Small business economics. (0921-898X). Dordrecht.
Small enterprise development. (0957-1329). London.
Small wars and insurgencies. (0959-2318). Ilford.
Smithsonian contributions to anthropology. (0081-0223). Washington DC.
Social & cultural geography. (1464-9365). London.
Social action [New Delhi]. (0037-7627). New Delhi.

LIST OF PERIODICALS CONSULTED

Social analysis [Adelaide]. (0155-977X). Adelaide.
Social analysis [Fukuoka]. Fukuoka.
Social and economic studies. (0037-7651). Kingston.
Social and legal studies. (0964-6639). London.
Social anthropology. (0964-0282). Cambridge.
Social behaviour. (0885-6249). Chichester.
Social biology. (0037-766X). New York NY.
Social choice and welfare. (0176-1714). Heidelberg.
Social cognition. (0278-016X). New York NY.
Social compass. (0037-7686). London.
Social dynamics. (0253-3952). Rondebosch.
Social forces. (0037-7732). Chapel Hill NC.
Social history. (0307-1022). London.
Social identities: Journal for the study of race, nation and culture. (1350-4630). Abingdon.
Social indicators research. (0303-8300). Dordrecht.
Social information. Sapporo.
Social justice. (0094-7571). San Francisco CA.
Social networks. (0378-8733). Amsterdam.
Social philosophy & policy. (0265-0525). Cambridge.
Social policy. (0037-7783). New York NY.
Social policy and administration. (0144-5596). Oxford.
Social politics: international studies in gender, state and society. (1072-4745). Cary NC.
Social problems. (0037-7791). Berkeley CA.
Social psychology quarterly. (0190-2725). Washington DC.
Social research. (0037-783X). New York NY.
Social science & medicine. (0277-9536). Exeter.
Social science history. (0145-5532). Durham NC.
Social science information. (0539-0184). London.
Social science Japan. (1340-7155). Tokyo.
Social science Japan journal. (1369-1465). Oxford.
Social science Japan review. Tokyo.
Social science quarterly. (0038-4941). Austin TX.
Social science research. (0049-089X). Orlando FL.
Social science review of Kagoshima University. Kagoshima.
Social sciences [Kyoto]. Kyoto.
Social sciences [Moscow]. (0134-5486). Minneapolis MN.
Social sciences in China. (0252-9203). Beijing.
Social sciences review. Tokyo.
Social sciences review. Tokyo.
Social scientist. (0970-0293). New Delhi.
Social security: Journal of welfare and social security studies. (0334-231X). Jerusalem.
Social semiotics. (1035-0330). Queensland.
Social service review. (0037-7961). Chicago IL.
Social studies of science. (0306-3127). London.
Social work and social sciences review. (0953-5225). London.
Social work education. (0261-5479). London.
Socialism and democracy. New York NY.
Socialismo y participación. Lima.
Socialist alternatives. Quebec.
Socialist history. (0969-4331). London.
Sociedad. (0327-7712). Buenos Aires.

LISTE DES PERIODIQUES CONSULTÉS

Sociétés contemporaines. (1150-1944). Paris.
Society. (0147-2011). New Brunswick NJ.
Society & Animals. (1063-1119). Cambridge.
Society of Malawi journal. (0037-993X). Blantyre.
Socio-economic planning sciences. (0038-0121). Exeter.
Sociolinguistics. (0257-7135). Dordrecht.
Sociologia [Bratislava] = Sociology [Bratislava]. (0049-1225). Bratislava.
Sociologia [Rome]. (0038-0156). Rome.
Sociologia internationalis. (0038-0164). Berlin.
Sociologia ruralis. (0038-0199). Oxford.
Sociologia urbana e rurale. (0392-4939). Bologna.
Sociologica. Tokyo.
Sociological bulletin. (0038-0229). New Delhi.
Sociological forum. (0884-8971). New York NY.
Sociological methodology. (0081-1750). Oxford.
Sociological methods and research. (0049-1241). Thousand Oaks CA.
Sociological perspectives. (0731-1214). Las Vegas NV.
Sociological practice: a journal of clinical and applied psychology. (1522-3442). New York.
Sociological quarterly. (0038-0253). Greenwich CT.
Sociological research online. (1360-7804). Guildford.
Sociological review. (0038-0261). London.
Sociological review [Kobe]. Kobe.
Sociological review of Ryukoku University. Kyoto.
Sociological spectrum. (0273-2173). Washington DC.
Sociological theory. (0735-2751). Malden MA.
Sociologický časopis. (0038-0288). Prague.
Sociologie du travail. (0038-0296). Paris.
Sociologische gids. (0038-0334). Meppel.
Sociologos. Tokyo.
Sociologus. (0038-0377). Berlin.
Sociology [U.K.]. (0038-0385). Cambridge.
Sociology and social research. (0038-0393). Los Angeles CA.
Sociology of health and illness. (0141-9889). Oxford.
Sociology of health care. Hampton Hill.
Sociology of law. Tokyo.
Sociology of religion. (0038-0210). Holiday FL.
Sociology of the sciences. Dordrecht.
Sociology today. Tokyo.
Sôgô toshi kenkyû. Tokyo.
Sogokagakubu-kiyo. Hiroshima.
SOJOURN: Journal of social issues in Southeast Asia. (0217-9520). Singapore.
Sophia. Tokyo.
Sophia University studies in sociology. Tokyo.
Soshiolojika. Tokyo.
Soshioroji. Kyoto.
Sotsial'no-gumanitarnye Znaniia. (0869-8120). Moscow.
Sotsiologicheskie issledovaniia (sotsis). (0132-1625). Moscow.
South African archaeological bulletin. (0038-1969). Vlaeberg.
South African Archaeological Society: Goodwin series. (0304-3460). Vlaeberg.
South African geographical journal = Suid-Afrikaanse geografiese tydskrif. (0373-6245). Wits.
South African historical journal = Suid-Afrikaanse historiese joernaal. (0258-2473). Pretoria.

LIST OF PERIODICALS CONSULTED

South African journal of African languages = Suid-Afrikaanse tydskrif vir Afrikatale. (0257-2117). Pretoria.
South African journal of economic history. Pretoria.
South African journal of economics = Suid-Afrikaanse tydskrif vir ekonomie. (0038-2280). Pretoria.
South African journal of ethnology = Suid-Afrikaanse tydskrif vir etnologie. (0379-8860). Pretoria.
South African journal of international affairs. (1022-0461). Johannesburg.
South African journal of sociology = Suid-Afrikaanse tydskrif vir sosiologie. Pretoria.
South African labour bulletin. Johannesburg.
South African law journal. (0258-2503). Kenwyn.
South Asia. (0085-6401). Armidale.
South Asia research. (0262-7280). New Delhi.
South Asian anthropologist. (0257-7348). Ranchi.
South Asian studies. (0266-6030). London.
South Asian survey. (0971-5231). New Delhi.
South East Asia research. (0967-828X). London.
South East Asian review. Gaya.
South European society & politics. (1360-8746). Ilford.
Southeast Asia: history and culture. Tokyo.
Southeast Asian affairs. (0377-5437). Singapore.
Southeast Asian research materials group newsletter. (0311-290X). Canberra.
Southeast Asian studies. Kyoto.
Southern Africa record. (0377-5445). Braamfontein.
Southern economic journal. (0038-4038). Stillwater OK.
Soziale Welt. (0038-6073). Baden Baden.
Soziologie. (0340-918X). Stuttgart.
Space & polity. (1356-2576). Abingdon.
Space commerce. (1043-934X). Reading.
Spanish economic review. (1435-5469). Heidelberg.
Spoudai. Piraeus.
Sprawozdania archeologiczne. (0081-3834). Warsaw.
Sri Lanka journal of social sciences. (0258-9710). Colombo.
Sri Lanka journal of the humanities. Peradeniya.
St. Andrew's University sociological review. Osaka.
Staat und Recht. (0038-8858). Berlin.
Staff papers.International Monetary Fund. (0020-8027). Washington DC.
State politics & policy quarterly. (1532-4400). Illinois.
Statistica. (0039-0380). Bologna.
Statistical papers = Statistische Hefte. (0932-5026). Heidelberg.
Statistics in transition. (1234-7655). Warsaw.
Statsvetenskaplig tidskrift. (0039-0747). Lund.
Statute law review. (0144-3593). Oxford.
Storia contemporanea. (0039-1875). Bologna.
Storia politica società. Turin.
Strategic management journal. (0143-2095). Chichester.
Studi bresciani. (1121-6557). Brescia.
Studi storici. (0039-3037). Rome.
Studia africana. (1130-5703). Barcelona.
Studia demograficzne. (0039-3134). Warsaw.
Studia diplomatica. (0770-2965). Brussels.
Studia ethnica. (1427-0110). Warsaw.
Studia fennica. (0085-6835). Helsinki.

LISTE DES PERIODIQUES CONSULTÉS

Studia fennica: Folkloristica. (1235-1946). Helsinki.
Studia iranica. (0772-7852). Lésigny.
Studia orientalia. (0039-3282). Helsinki.
Studia prawno-ekonomiczne. (0081-6841). Łódź.
Studia rosenthaliana. (0039-3347). Amsterdam.
Studia socjologiczne. (0039-3371). Warsaw.
Studies and essays — behavioral sciences and philosophy. (1342-4262). Kanazawa.
Studies in American political development. (0898-588X). New York NY.
Studies in comparative culture. Tokyo.
Studies in comparative history of circum-Japan Sea areas. Niigata.
Studies in comparative international development. (0039-3606). New Brunswick NJ.
Studies in conflict and terrorism. (1057-610X). London.
Studies in East European thought. (0925-9392). Dordrecht.
Studies in family planning. (0039-3665). New York NY.
Studies in history. (0257-6430). New Delhi.
Studies in history and philosophy of modern physics. (1355-2198). Oxford.
Studies in history and philosophy of science. (0039-3681). Oxford.
Studies in human sciences. Tokyo.
Studies in language and culture. Hiroshima.
Studies in law, politics, and society. London.
Studies in philosophy and education. (0039-3746). Dordrecht.
Studies in political economy. (0707-8552). Ottawa.
Studies in social science. Fukuoka.
Studies in social sciences. Hiroshima.
Studies in sociology, psychology and education. Tokyo.
Studies in the humanities. Matsumoto.
Studies in the humanities and sciences. Hiroshima.
Studies in the linguistic sciences. Urbana IL.
Studies in Third World societies. (1056-9189). Williamsburg VA.
Studies in Western Australian history. Nedlands WA.
Studies in Western history. Osaka.
Studies of broadcasting. Tokyo.
Studies of The Japan Institute of Labour. Tokyo.
Studies on the history of sociology. Tokyo.
Studies. Kwansei Gakuin university, Sociology Department. Hyogo.
Studii şi comunicări etnologie. (1221-6518). Bucharest.
Study for the history of social services. Japan.
Study of sociology. Sendai.
Südosteuropa Aktuell. Munich.
Südosteuropa Mitteilungen. (0340-174X). Munich.
Südosteuropa-Jahrbuch. Munich.
Südosteuropa-Schriften. (1430-8770). Munich.
Südosteuropa-Studie. Munich.
SUGIA: Sprache und Geschichte in Afrika. (0170-5946). Cologne.
Suomalais-Ugrilaisen Seuran Aikakauskirja. (0355-0214). Helsinki.
Suomalais-Ugrilaisen Seuran kansatieteellisiä julkaisuja. (0359-7679). Helsinki.
Surugadai University studies. Japan.
Survey of Jewish affairs. (0741-6571). Oxford.
Survival. (0039-6338). Oxford.
Svobodnaia mysl'. (0869-4435). Moscow.
Swedish economic policy review. (1400-1829). Stockholm.

LIST OF PERIODICALS CONSULTED

Symbolon. (0082-0660). Frankfurt am Main.
Systems research and behavioral science. (1092-7026). Chichester.
Tama Gakkai. Tokyo.
Tamkang journal of area studies. Taipei.
Tantara. Antananavivo.
Tanzanian economic trends. (0856-3373). Dar es Salaam.
Tareas. (0494-7061). Panama City.
Társadalmi szemle. (0039-971X). Budapest.
Társadalomkutatás. (0580-4795). Budapest.
Te reo. (0494-8440). Auckland.
Technology and culture. (0040-165X). Baltimore MD.
Technology and development. (0914-918X). Tokyo.
Teikyo journal of sociology. Tokyo.
Tel Aviv: Journal of the Institute of Archaeology of Tel Aviv University. (0334-4355). Tel Aviv.
Telecommunications policy. (0308-5961). Amsterdam.
Telos. (0090-6514). New York NY.
Temas de economía mundial. Havana.
Tempo social. (0103-2070). São Paulo.
Temps modernes. (0040-3075). Paris.
Teoria politica. (0394-1248). Milan.
Terra. Helsinki.
Terrain. (0760-5668). Paris.
Terrorism and political violence. (0954-6553). Ilford.
Text. (0165-4888). Berlin.
Theory and decision. (0040-5833). Dordrecht.
Theory and psychology. (0959-3543). London.
Theory and society. (0304-2421). Dordrecht.
Theory culture and society. (0263-2764). London.
Thesis eleven. (0725-5136). London.
Third World planning review. (0142-7849). Liverpool.
Third World quarterly. (0143-6597). Abingdon.
Tibet journal. (0970-5368). Dharamshala.
Tidsskriftet antropologi. (0906-3021). Copenhagen.
Tijdschrift voor economie en management. (0772-7664). Louvain.
Tijdschrift voor economische en sociale geografie = Journal of economic and social geography. (0040-747X). Oxford.
Time & society. (0961-463X). London.
Tochi-seido shigaku. Tokyo.
Tohoku daigaku bungakuba nenpo. Sendai.
Tohoku daigaku kyoyobu kiyo. Miyagi.
Tokai law review. Tokyo.
Tokiwa journal of human science. Mita.
Toledo journal of Great Lakes' law, science & policy. (1097-9328). Toledo.
Toshi mondai. Tokyo.
Toshi-mondai kenkyu. Osaka.
Totalitarian movements and political religions. (1469-0764). Ilford.
Toukei. Tokyo.
Tourism geographies. (1461-6688). London.
Town planning review. (0041-0020). Liverpool.
Toyama daigaku keizai ronshu. Toyama City.
Transactions of the Asiatic Society of Japan. Tokyo.

LISTE DES PERIODIQUES CONSULTÉS

Transactions of the Institute of British Geographers: New series. London.
Transactions of the Institute of Humanities. Yokohama.
Transactions of the Philological Society. (0079-1636). Oxford.
Transafrican journal of history. (0251-0391). Nairobi.
Transfer: European review of labour and research. (1024-2589). Antwerp.
Transformation. (0258-7696). Durban.
Transit: Europäische Revue. (0938-2062). Frankfurt am Main.
Transition. (1012-8263). Georgetown.
Transitions. (1211-0205). Prague.
Translator: Studies in intercultural communication. (1355-6509). Manchester.
Transnational organized crime. (1357-7387). Ilford.
Transportation. (0049-4488). Dordrecht.
Transportation research. (0191-2615). Tarrytown NY.
Transportation science. (0041-1655). Linthicum MD.
Tri-view. Tokyo.
Tribus. (0082-6413). Stuttgart.
Trimestre económico. (0041-3011). Mexico City.
Tsukuba annals of sociology. Tsukuba.
Tsukuba journal of sociology. Tsukuba.
Turcica: revue d'études turques. (0082-6847). Louvain.
Türk halk kültürü araştirmalari. Ankara.
Turkish review of Balkan studies. Istanbul.
Turkish review of Middle East studies. Istanbul.
Turkish studies. (1468-3849). Ilford.
Turkish yearbook of international relations = Milletlerarasi münasebetler Türk yilli&gi. (0544-1943). Ankara.
Twentieth century British history. (0955-2359). Oxford.
Tyuo tyosa ho. Tokyo.
Ufahamu. (0041-5715). Los Angeles CA.
Ukrainian economic review. (1080-725X). Philadelphia PA.
Ulkopolitiikka. (0501-0659). Helsinki.
Unisa Latin American report. (0256-6060). Pretoria.
Uniswa research journal. Kwaluseni.
Universitas. (0049-5530). Legon.
University of Western Australia Anthropological Research Museum occasional papers. (0810-8536). Perth.
University studies. Ibaruki-Ken.
Uomo. Rome.
Uomo & cultura. Palermo.
Urban advance. Nagoya.
Urban affairs annual reviews. (0083-4688). Thousand Oaks CA.
Urban affairs review. (1078-0874). Thousand Oaks CA.
Urban anthropology. (0894-6019). Brockport NY.
Urban forum. (1015-3802). Johannesburg.
Urban geography. (0272-3638). Silver Spring MD.
Urban studies. (0042-0980). Abingdon.
US-Japan women's journal. (0898-8900). Palo Alto CA.
Utilitas. (0953-8208). Edinburgh.
Utilities policy. (0957-1787). Oxford.
Valóság. (0324-7228). Budapest.
Venture capital. (1369-1066). London.

LIST OF PERIODICALS CONSULTED

Verfassung und Recht in Übersee = Law and politics in Africa, Asia and Latin America. (0506-7286). Baden-Baden.
Vestnik Moskovskogo universiteta. Seriia 12 Politicheskie nauki. (0201-7385). Moscow.
Vestnik Moskovskogo universiteta. Seriia 5 Geografiia. Moscow.
Vestnik Moskovskogo universiteta. Seriia 6 Ekonomika. (0130-0105). Moscow.
Vestnik Moskovskogo universiteta. Seriia 9 Filologiia. (0130-0075). Moscow.
Vestnik Sankt-Peterburgskogo universiteta. Seriia 5 Ekonomika. (0233-755X). St. Petersburg.
Vestnik Sankt-Peterburgskogo universiteta. Seriia 6 Filosofiia, politologiia, sotsiolgiia, psikhologiia, pravo. St. Petersburg.
Vestsi natsyianalnai akademii navuk Belarusi: Seryia gumanitarnykh navuk. (0321-1649). Minsk.
Vierteljahrschrift für Sozial- und Wirtschaftsgeschichte. (0340-8728). Stuttgart.
Vierteljahrshefte für Zeitgeschichte. (0042-5702). Munich.
Vierteljahrshefte zur Wirtschaftsforschung. (0340-1707). Berlin.
Vietnam social sciences. (1013-4328). Hanoi.
Vietnamese studies. (0085-7823). Hanoi.
Visual anthropology. (0894-9468). New York NY.
Visual anthropology review. (1058-7187). Arlington VA.
Volkskundig bulletin. (0166-0667). Amsterdam.
Volonta. (0392-5013). Milan.
Voluntas. (0957-8765). New York NY.
Voprosy ekonomiki. (0042-8736). Moscow.
Wage & social security. Tokyo.
WAMP: West African Museums Programme bulletin. London.
War studies journal. (1363-1225). London.
Waseda bulletin of comparative law. (0285-9211). Tokyo.
Waseda economic papers. (0511-1943). Tokyo.
Waseda koto gakuin kennkyu nenshi. Tokyo.
Waseda shogaku. Tokyo.
Washington quarterly. (0163-660X). Cambridge MA.
Welsh history review = Cylchgrawn hanes Cymru. (0083-792X). Cardiff.
Welt des Islams. (0043-2539). Leiden.
Welt Trends: internationale Politik und vergleichende Studien. (0944-8101). Potsdam.
Weltwirtschaft. (0043-2652). Tübingen.
Weltwirtschaftliches Archiv. (0043-2636). Tübingen.
Werkdocumenten over etnische kunst = Working papers in ethnic art. Ghent.
West African journal of archaeology. (0331-3158). Ibadan.
West European politics. (0140-2382). Ilford.
Wirtschaftsdienst. (0043-6275). Hamburg.
Wirtschaftspolitische Blätter. (0043-6291). Vienna.
Wirtschaftswissenschaft. (0043-633X). Berlin.
Women's studies. (0049-7878). Reading.
Women's studies international forum. (0277-5395). Oxford.
Work and occupations. (0730-8884). Thousand Oaks CA.
Work, employment and society. (0950-0170). Cambridge.
Working papers in linguistics. Columbus OH.
World archaeology. (0043-8243). London.
World Bank economic review. (0258-6770). Washington DC.
World Bank research observer. (0257-3032). Washington DC.
World development. (0305-750X). Oxford.
World economy. (0378-5920). Oxford.
World futures. (0260-4027). New York NY.

LISTE DES PERIODIQUES CONSULTÉS

World in Slavic society. Kobundo.
World of music. (0043-8774). Bamberg.
World politics. (0043-8871). Baltimore MD.
World review. Indooroophilly QLD.
World today. (0043-9134). London.
WSI Mitteilungen. (0342-300X). Frankfurt am Main.
Wuqûf. (0930-9306). Hamburg.
XXI secolo. Turin.
Yagl-Ambu. (0254-0681). Papua New Guinea.
Yale journal on regulation. (0741-9457). New Haven CT.
Yale law journal. (0044-0094). New Haven CT.
Yamaguchi daigaku kyoikugakuba ronsoh. Yamaguchi.
Yapi kredi economic review. (1019-1232). Istanbul.
Yearbook of co-operative enterprise. (0952-5556). Oxford.
Yearbook of Finnish foreign policy. (0355-0079). Helsinki.
Yhtyneet kuvalehdet oy. (0355-0303). Helsinki.
York papers in linguistics. (0307-3238). York.
Yoron. Tokyo.
Youth problems study. Osaka.
Yugoslav law = Droit yougoslave. (0350-2252). Belgrade.
Zagreb journal of economics. (1331-4599). Zagreb.
Zaïre-Afrique. (0049-8513). Kinshasa.
Zambezia. (0379-0622). Harare.
Zambia journal of history. Lusaka.
Zeitschrift für ausländisches öffentliches Recht und Völkerrecht. (0044-2348). Stuttgart.
Zeitschrift für Balkanologie. (0044-2356). Wiesbaden.
Zeitschrift für Energie Wirtschaft. (0343-5377). Wiesbaden.
Zeitschrift für Ethnologie. (0044-2666). Berlin.
Zeitschrift für öffentliches recht. (0948-4396). Vienna.
Zeitschrift für Parlamentsfragen. (0340-1758). Wiesbaden.
Zeitschrift für Politik. (0044-3360). Cologne.
Zeitschrift für Recht und Wirtschaft: Betriebs-Berater. Heidelberg.
Zeitschrift für Sexualforschung. (0932-8114). Stuttgart.
Zeitschrift für Soziologie. (0340-1804). Stuttgart.
Zeitschrift für Unternehmensgeschichte. (0342-2852). Stuttgart.
Zeitschrift für vergleichende Rechtswissenschaft [Heidelberg]. (0044-3638). Heidelberg.
Zeitschrift für Verkehrswissenschaft. (0044-3670). Düsseldorf.
Zeitschrift für Wirtschafts- und Sozialwissenschaften. (0342-1783). Berlin.
Zeitschrift für Wirtschaftspolitik. (0721-3808). Stuttgart.
Zimbabwe journal of economics. Harare.
Zyouhou to shakai. Chiba.

LIST OF ABBREVIATIONS USED
LISTE DES ABRÉVIATIONS UTILISÉES

Acad. Man. Rev. Academy of Management review. (0363-7425). Academy of Management: Pace University, P.O. Box 3020, 235 Elm Road, Briarcliff Manor, NY 10510-8020, U.S.A.

Acad. Manag. J. Academy of Management journal. (0001-4273). Academy of Management: Pace University, P.O. Box 3020, 235 Elm Road, Briarcliff Manor, NY 10510-8020, U.S.A.

Acadiensis Acadiensis: Journal of the history of the Atlantic Region. (0044-5851). University of New Brunswick: Fredericton, New Brunswick, E3B 5A3, Canada.

Acc. Aud. Accountab. J. Accounting, auditing and accountability journal. (0951-3574). MCB University Press: 60/62 Toller Lane, Bradford, West Yorkshire BD8 9BY, U.K.

Acc. Bus. Res. Accounting and business research. (0001-4788). Institute of Chartered Accountants in England and Wales: Chartered Accountants' Hall, Moorgate Place, London EC24 6EQ, U.K.

Acta Asia. Acta asiatica. (0567-7254). Institute of Eastern Culture: 4-1 Nishi-kanda 2 Chōme, Chiyoda, Tokyo, Japan.

Acta Sociol. Acta sociologica [Norway]. (0001-6993). Scandinavian University Press: P.O. Box 2959, Tøyen, N-0608 Oslo, Norway, in association with Scandinavian Sociological Association.

Acta Sociol. [Mexico] Acta sociologica [Mexico]. (0186-6028). Universidad Nacional Autónoma de México, Facultad de Ciencias Políticas y Sociales: Ciudad Universitaria, Coyoacán, 04510 México D.F., Mexico.

Addiction Addiction. (0965 2140). Carfax Publishing: P.O. Box 25, Abingdon, Oxfordshire OX14 3UE, U.K.

Adm. Sci. Qua. Administrative science quarterly. (0001-8392). Cornell University, Johnson Graduate School of Management: Caldwell Hall, Cornell University, Ithaca, NY 14853, U.S.A.

Admin. Soc. Administration and society. (0095-3997). Sage Publications: 2455 Teller Road, Newbury Park, Thousand Oaks, CA 91320, U.S.A.

Administration Administration. (0001-8325). Institute of Public Administration of Ireland: 57-61 Lansdowne Road, Dublin 4, Ireland.

Af. Spec. Afrika Spectrum. (0002-0397). Institut für Afrika-Kunde: Neuer Jungfernstieg 21, D-20354 Hamburg, Germany.

Afr. Affairs African affairs. (0001-9909). Oxford University Press: Great Clarendon Street, Oxford OX2 6DP, U.K., in association with Royal African Society: 18 Northumberland Avenue, London WC2N 5BJ, U.K.

Afr. Cont. Afrique contemporaine. (0002-0478). Documentation Française: 29-31 quai Voltaire, 75340 Paris Cedex 07, France.

Afr. Devel. Africa development = Afrique & développement. (0850-3907). Council for the Development of Social Science Research in Africa / Conseil pour le développement de la recherche en sciences sociales en Afrique: B.P. 3304, Dakar, Senegal.

Afr. Insight Africa insight. (0256-2804). Africa Institute of South Africa: P.O. Box 630, Pretoria 0001, South Africa.

Afr. Q. Africa quarterly. (0001-9828). Indian Council for Cultural Relations: Azad Bhavan, Indraprastha Estate, New Delhi 110 002, India.

LIST OF ABBREVIATIONS USED

Afr. Stud. R. African studies review. (0002-0206). African Studies Association: Rutgers, State University of New Jersey, Douglass Campus, 132 George Street, New Brunswick, NJ 08901-1400, U.S.A.

Africa [Edinburgh] Africa [Edinburgh]. (0001-9720). Edinburgh University Press: 22 George Square, Edinburgh EH8 9LF, U.K., in association with International African Institute: Connaught House, Aldwych, London WC2A 2AE, U.K.

Age. Soc. Ageing and society. (0144-686X). Cambridge University Press: The Edinburgh Building, Shaftesbury Road, Cambridge CB2 2RU, U.K., in association with Centre for Policy on Ageing / British Society of Gerontology.

A.J.S. American journal of sociology. (0002-9602). University of Chicago Press: 5720 S. Woodlawn Avenue, Chicago, IL 60637, U.S.A.

Al-Abhath Al-Abhath.. American University of Beirut, Faculty of Arts and Sciences: Beirut, Lebanon.

Aletheia Aletheia. (1413-0394). Revista Aletheia: Editora da ULBRA, Rua Miguel Tostes, 101, CEP: 92420-280 - Canoas/RS - Brasil, in association with Universidade Luterana do Brasil.

All. Stat. A. Allgemeines statistisches Archiv. (0002-6018). Physica-Verlag: Tiergartenstrasse 17, 69121 Heidelberg, Germany, in association with Deutsche Statistische Gesellschaft.

Alternatives Alternatives. (0304-3754). Lynne Rienner Publishers: 1800 30th Street, Boulder, CO 80301, U.S.A.

Am. Anthrop. American anthropologist. (0002-7294). American Anthropological Association: 4350 North Fairfax Drive, Suite 640, Arlington, VA 22203-1620, U.S.A.

Am. Behav. Sc. American behavioral scientist. (0002-7642). Sage Publications: 2455 Teller Road, Newbury Park, Thousand Oaks, CA 91320, U.S.A.

Am. Econ. Rev. American economic review. (0002-8282). American Economic Association: 2014 Broadway, Suite 305, Nashville, TN 37203, U.S.A.

Am. Ethn. American ethnologist. (0094-0496). American Anthropological Association: 4350 North Fairfax Drive, Suite 640, Arlington VA 22203-1620, U.S.A.

Am. J. Econ. S. American journal of economics and sociology. (0002-9246). American Journal of Economics and Sociology.

Am. J. Islam. Soc. Sci. American journal of Islamic social sciences. (0742-6763) Association of Muslim Social Scientists / International Institute of Islamic Thought: P.O. Box 669, Herndon VA 22070, U.S.A.

Am. J. Orthopsy. American journal of orthopsychiatry. (0002-9432). American Orthopsychiatric Association.

Am. J. Pol. Sc. American journal of political science. (0092-5853). University of Wisconsin Press: 2537 Daniels Street, Madison, WI 53718-6772, U.S.A., in association with Midwest Political Science Association.

Am. Phil. Q. American philosophical quarterly. (0003-0481). Philosophy Documentation Center: Bowling Green State University, Bowling Green, OH 43403-0189, U.S.A.

Am. Psychol. American psychologist. (0003-066X). American Psychological Association: 750 First Street, NE Washington, DC 20002-4242.

Am. Sociol. American sociologist. (0003-1232). Transaction Publishers: Rutgers University, New Brunswick, NJ 08903, U.S.A.

Am. Sociol. R. American sociological review. (0003-1224). American Sociological Association: 1307 New York Avenue NW, Suite 700, Washington, DC 20005-4701, U.S.A.

Anál. Soc. Análise social. (0003-2573). Instituto de Ciências Sociais da Universidade de Lisboa: Avenida das Forças Armadas, Edificio I.S.C.T.E., Ala Sul, 1º andar, 1600 Lisbon, Portugal, in association with Junta Nacional de Investigação Científica e Tecnológia / Instituto Nacional de Investigação Científica.

Anarch. St. Anarchist studies. (0967-3393). White Horse Press: 10 High Street, Knapwell, Cambridge CB3 8NR, U.K.

LISTE DES ABRÉVIATIONS UTILISÉES

Ann. Am. Poli. Annals of the American Academy of Political and Social Science. (0002-7162). Sage Publications: 2455 Teller Road, Newbury Park, Thousand Oaks, CA 91320, U.S.A., in association with American Academy of Political and Social Science.

Ann. As. Am. G. Annals of the Association of American Geographers. (0004-5608). Association of American Geographers: 1710 16th Street N.W., Washington DC 20009, U.S.A.

Ann. Géogr. Annales de géographie. (0003-4010). Armand Colin: 34 bis rue de l'Université, 75007 Paris, France.

Ann. R. Anthr. Annual review of anthropology. (0084-6570). Annual Reviews: 4139 El Camino Way, P.O. Box 10139, Palo Alto, CA 94303-0139, U.S.A.

Ann. Sociol. Année sociologique. (0066-2399). Presses Universitaires de France: 108 boulevard Saint-Germain, 75006 Paris, France.

Annales Annales: Économies, sociétés, civilisations. (0395-2649). Armand Colin: 34 bis rue de l'Université, 75007 Paris, France, in association with C.N.R.S. / École des hautes études en sciences sociales.

Anth. Th. Anthropological theory. (1463-4996). Sage Publications: 6 Bonhill Street, London EC2A 4PU, U.K.

Anthr. Quart. Anthropological quarterly. (0003-5491). Catholic University of America Press: 620 Michigan Avenue, N.E., Administration Building Room 303, Washington DC 20064, U.S.A., in association with Catholic University of America, Department of Anthropology: Washington, DC 20064, U.S.A.

Apuntes Apuntes. (0252-1865). Revista Apuntes: Apartado Postal 4683, Lima 1, Peru.

Arc. Kommunal. Archiv für Kommunalwissenschaften. (0003-9209). Verlag W. Kohlhammer: Heßbrühlstraße 69, Postfach 80 04 30, 70549 Stuttgart 80, Germany, in association with Deutsches Institut für Urbanistik: Straße des 17. Juni 112, Postfach 12 62 24, 1000 Berlin 12, Germany.

Arc. Recht. Soz. Archiv für Rechts- und Sozialphilosophie = Archives de philosophie du droit et de philosophie sociale = Archives for philosophy of law and social philosophy = Archivo de filosofía jurídica y social. (0001-2343). Franz Steiner Verlag: Birkenwaldstraße 44, Postfach 10 15 26, D-7000 Stuttgart 1, Germany, in association with Internationale Vereinigung für Rechts- und Sozialphilosophie.

Area Area. (0004-0894). Royal Grographical Society (with IBG): 1 Kensington Gore, London SW7 2AR, U.K.

Argumentation Argumentation. (0920-427X). Kluwer Academic Publishers: P.O. Box 322, 3300 AH Dordrecht, The Netherlands, in association with European Centre for the Study of Argumentation: Unversité Libre de Bruxelles, Institut de Philosophie, 143 avenue A.-Buyl, C.P. 188, B-1050 Brussels, Belgium.

Arm. Forces Soc. Armed forces and society. (0095-327X). Transaction Publishers: Rutgers University, New Brunswick, NJ 08903, U.S.A., in association with Inter-University Seminar on Armed Forces and Society: Box 46, 1126 East 59th Street, Chicago, IL 60637, U.S.A.

Asia J. Theol. Asia journal of theology. (0218-0812). Association for Theological Education in South East Asia: P.O. Box 3167, 1099 Manila, Philippines.

Asia Pac. Bus. Rev. Asia Pacific business review. (1360-2381). Frank Cass: Newbury House, 890-900 Eastern Avenue, Newbury Park, Ilford, Essex IG2 7HH, U.K., in association with Frank Cass: 5804 NE Hassalo Street, Portland, OR 97213-3644, U.S.A.

Asian Cult. (Asian-Pac. Cult.) Q. Asian culture (Asian-Pacific culture) quarterly. (0378-8911). Asian-Pacific Cultural Center: Asian-Pacific Parliamentarians' Union, 6F, 66 Aikuo East Road, Taipei, Taiwan 10726.

Asian Dev. R. Asian development review. (0116-1105). Asian Development Bank: P.O. Box 789, 0980 Manila, Philippines.

Asian J. Pub. Admin. Asian journal of public administration. (0259-8272). University of Hong Kong, Department of Political Science: Pokfulam Road, Hong Kong.

LIST OF ABBREVIATIONS USED

Asian Mus. Asian music. (0044-9202). Society for Asian Music: Department of Asian Music, Lincoln Hall, Cornell University, Ithaca, NY 14853, U.S.A.

Asian Pacif. Migrat. J. Asian and Pacific migration journal. (0117-1968). Scalabrini Migration Center: P.O. Box 10541 Broadway Centrum, 1113 Quezon City, Philippines.

Asian Persp. [S. Korea] Asian perspective [S. Korea]. (0258-9184). Kyungnam University, Institute for Far Eastern Studies: 28-42 Samchung-dong, Chongro-ku, Seoul 110-230, South Korea.

Asian Prof. Asian profile. (0304-8675). Asian Research Service: Rm. 704, Federal Building, 369 Lockhart Road, Hong Kong.

Asian Res. Trends Asian research trends. (0917-1479). Centre for East Asian Cultural Studies for Unesco: The Toyo Bunko, Honkomagome 2-28-21, Bunkyo-ku, Tokyo 113-0021, Japan.

Aus. J. Anth. Australian journal of anthropology. (1035-8811). Australian Anthropological Society: University of Sydney, Department of Anthropology, Sydney, NSW 2006, Australia.

Aust. Abor. S. Australian Aboriginal studies. (0729-4352). Australian Institute of Aboriginal and Torres Strait Islander Studies: G.P.O. Box 553, Canberra ACT 2601, Australia.

Aust. & N.Z. J. Statist. Australian and New Zealand journal of statistics. (1369-1473). Blackwell Publishers: 108 Cowley Road, Oxford OX4 1JF, U.K.

Aust. Geogr. Australian geographer. (0004-9182). Carfax Publishing: P.O. Box 25, Abingdon, Oxfordshire OX14 3UE, U.K.

Aust. Geogr. Stud. Australian geographical studies. (0004-9190). Blackwell Publishers: 108 Cowley Road, Oxford OX4 1JF, U.K., in association with Australian Defence Force Academy, Campbell, ACT 2600, Australia.

Aust. J. Pol. Sci Australian journal of political science. (1036-1146). Carfax Publishing: P.O. Box 25, Abingdon, Oxfordshire OX14 3UE, U.K., in association with Australasian Political Studies Association.

B. Éc. Fr. Ex.-Or. Bulletin de l'École française d'Extrême-Orient. (0336-1519). École française d'Extrême-Orient: 22 avenue du Président Wilson, 75116 Paris, France.

B. Lat. Am. Res. Bulletin of Latin American research. (0261-3050). Elsevier Science: PO Box 211, 1000 AE Amsterdam, The Netherlands, in association with Society for Latin American Studies.

Beit. Japan. Beiträge zur Japanologie. (0522-6759). Universität Wien, Institut für Japanologie: AAKH-Campus, Spitalgasse 2-4, 1090 Vienna, Austria.

Berl. J. Soziol. Berliner Journal für Soziologie. (0863-1808). Leske & Budrich: Gerhart-Hauptmann-Straße 27, 51379 Leverkusen, Germany, in association with Institut für Soziologie der Humbodt-Universität zu Berlin: Hans-Loch-Str. 349, O-1136 Berlin, Germany.

Bilig Bilig. (1301-0549). Foundation of Ahmet Yesevi University: Bilig Editörlügü, Ahmet Yesevi Üniversitesi, Mütevelli Heyet Baskanligi, Tashkent Caddesi, 10.sok. No:30, 06430 Bahçelievler, Anakara, Turkey.

Bioethics Bioethics. (0269-9702). Blackwell Publishers: 108 Cowley Road, Oxford OX4 1JF, U.K.

Biography Biography. (0162-4962). University of Hawaii Press: 2840 Kolowalu Street, Honolulu, HI 96822-1888, U.S.A., in association with Center for Biographical Research: Varsity College, University of Hawaii, Honolulu, HI. 96822, U.S.A.

Bod. Soc. Body and society. (1357-034X). Sage Publications: 6 Bonhill Street, London EC2A 4PU, U.K., in association with School of Human Studies, University of Teesside.

Boekmancahier Boekmancahier: kwartaalschrift voor kunst, onderzoek en beleid. (0925-0239). Boekman Foundation: Herengracht 415, 1017 BP Amsterdam, The Netherlands.

Br. J. Addict. British journal of addiction. (0952-0481). Carfax Publishing: P.O. Box 25, Abingdon, Oxfordshire OX14 3UE, U.K., in association with Society for the Study of Addiction to Alcohol and Other Drugs: Addiction Reseach Unit, National Addiction Centre, 101 Denmark Hill, London SE5 8AF, U.K.

Br. J. Clin. Psycho. British journal of clinical psychology. (0144-6657). British Psychological Society: St. Andrews House, 48 Princess Road East, Leicester LE1 7DR, U.K.

LISTE DES ABRÉVIATIONS UTILISÉES

Br. J. Crimin. British journal of criminology. (0007-0955). Oxford University Press: Great Clarendon Street, Oxford OX2 6DP, U.K., in association with Institute for the Study and Treatment of Delinquency.

Br. J. Educ. S. British journal of educational studies. (0007-1005). Blackwell Publishers: 108 Cowley Road, Oxford OX4 1JF, U.K.

Br. J. Hist. Sci. British journal for the history of science. (0007-0874). Cambridge University Press: The Edinburgh Building, Shaftsbury Road, Cambridge, CB2 2RU., in association with British Society for the History of Science.

Br. J. Ind. R. British journal of industrial relations. (0007-1080). Blackwell Publishers: 108 Cowley Road, Oxford OX4 1JF, U.K., in association with London School of Economics: Houghton Street, London WC2A 2AE, U.K.

Br. J. Manag. British journal of management. (1045-3172). Blackwell Publishers Ltd: 108 Cowley Road, Oxford OX4 1JF, U.K., in association with British Academy of Management.

Br. J. Psy. British journal of psychology. (0007-1269). British Psychological Society: St. Andrews House, 48 Princess Road East, Leicester LE1 7DR, U.K.

Br. J. Soc. British journal of sociology. (0007-1315). Routledge: 11 New Fetter Lane, London EC4P 4EE, U.K., in association with London School of Economics and Political Science: Houghton Street, London WC2A 2AE, U.K.

Br. J. Soc. P. British journal of social psychology. (0144-6665). British Psychological Society: St. Andrews House, 48 Princess Road East, Leicester LE1 7DR, U.K.

Br. J. Soc. W. British journal of social work. (0045-3102). Oxford University Press: Great Clarendon Street, Oxford OX2 6DP, U.K., in association with British Association of Social Workers.

Bull. Ét. Indien. Bulletin d'études indiennes. (0761-3156). Association Française pour les Études Sanskrites: 52 rue du Cardinal Lemoine, F-75231 Paris Cedex 05, France.

Bus. Eth. Eur. Rev. Business ethics: a European review. (0962-8770). Blackwell Publishers: 108 Cowley Road, Oxford, OX4 1JF, U.K.

C. Asian Sur. Central Asian survey. (0263-4937). Carfax Publishing: P.O. Box 25, Abingdon, Oxfordshire OX14 3UE, U.K., in association with Society for Central Asian Studies: Unit 8, 92 Lots Road, London SW10 4BQ, U.K.

Cah. Amer. Lat. Cahiers des Amériques latines. (0008-0020). Université de la Sorbonne Nouvelle (Paris III), Institut des hautes études de l'Amérique latine: 28 rue Saint-Guillaume, 75007 Paris, France.

Cah. Ét. Afr. Cahiers d'études africaines. (0008-0055). Éditions de l'École des hautes études en sciences sociales: 54 boulevard Raspail, 75006 Paris, France.

Cah. Int. Soc. Cahiers internationaux de sociologie. (0008-0276). Presses Universitaires de France: 108 boulevard Saint-Germain, 75006 Paris, France.

Cah. Mon. Russe Cahiers du monde russe. (1252-6576). Éditions de l'École des hautes études en sciences sociales: 54 boulevard Raspail, 75006 Paris, France.

Cah. Outre-mer Cahiers d'outre-mer. (0373-5843). Université de Bordeaux III, Institut de géographie: Domaine Universitaire, 33405 Talence, France.

Calif. Manag. R. California management review. (0008-1256). University of California, Walter A. Haas School of Business: 350 Barrows Hall. University of California, Berkeley, CA 94720, U.S.A.

Cam. R. Int. Aff. Cambridge review of international affairs. (0955-7571). University of Cambridge, Centre of International Studies: Fitzwilliam House, 32 Trumpington Street, Cambridge CB2 1QY, U.K.

Camb. Law J. Cambridge law journal. (0008-1973). Cambridge University Press: The Edinburgh Building, Shaftesbury Road, Cambridge CB2 2RU, U.K., in association with University of Cambridge, Faculty of Law.

LIST OF ABBREVIATIONS USED

Can. Ethn. Stud. Canadian ethnic studies = Études ethniques au Canada. (0008-3496). Canadian Ethnic Studies Journal: Department of History, University of Calgary, 2500 University Drive N.W., Calgary AB, Canada, T2N 1N4.

Can. Geogr. Canadian geographer. (0008-3658). Canadian Association of Geographers: Burnside Hall, Rm 425, McGill University, 805 Sherbrooke Street West, Montreal, Quebec, H3A 2K6 Canada.

Can. Hist. R. Canadian historical review. (0008-3755). University of Toronto Press: 5201 Dufferin Street, Downsview, Ontario M3H 5T8, Canada.

Can. J. Afr. St. Canadian journal of African studies = Revue canadienne des études africaines. (0008-3968). Canadian Association of African Studies = Association canadienne des études africaines: Innis College, University of Toronto, 2 Sussex Avenue, Toronto, Ontario M5S IAI, Canada.

Can. J. Phil. Canadian journal of philosophy. (0045-5091). University of Calgary Press: 2500 University Drive N.W., Calgary, Alberta T2N 1N4, Canada.

Can. J. Soc. Canadian journal of sociology = Cahiers canadiens de sociologie. (0318-6431). University of Alberta, Department of Sociology: Edmonton, Alberta T6G 2H4, Canada.

Can. Publ. Ad. Canadian public administration = Administration publique du Canada. (0008-4840). , in association with Institute of Public Administration of Canada/Institut d'administration public du Canada: 1075 rue Bay Street, Suite 401, Toronto, Ontario, Canada, M5S 2B1.

Can. R. Soc. A. Canadian review of sociology and anthropology = Revue canadienne de sociologie et d'anthropologie. (0008-4948). Canadian Sociology and Anthropology Association: Concordia University, 1455 boulevard de Maisonneuve W., Montréal, Québec H3G 1M8, Canada.

Can. Yb. Int. Law Canadian yearbook of international law = Annuaire canadien de droit international. (0069-0058). University of British Columbia: Vancouver BC, V6T 1W5, Canada, in association with International Law Association, Canadian Branch.

Canad. J. Human Sex. Canadian journal of human sexuality. (1188-4517). Sex Information and Education Council of Cananda (SIECCAN): 850 Coxwell Avenue, East York, Ontario M4C 5RI, Canada.

Cap. Class Capital and class. (0309-8168). Conference of Socialist Economists: 25 Horsell Road, London N5 1XL, U.K.

Cap. Nat. Social. Capitalism, nature, socialism. (1045-5752). Guilford Publications: 72 Spring Street, New York, NY 10012, U.S.A.

Caravelle Caravelle. (0008-0152). Presses Universitaires du Mirail: Université de Toulouse - Le Mirail, 5 allée Antonio Machado, 31058 Toulouse Cedex 1, France, in association with Institut pluridisciplinaire d'études sur l'Amérique latine à Toulouse: 56 rue du Taur, 31069 Toulouse Cedex, France.

CEPAL R. CEPAL review. (0251-2920). United Nations Economic Commission for Latin America and the Caribbean: Casilla 179-D, Santiago, Chile.

Ch. Feng Ching feng. (0009-4668). Christian Study Centre on Chinese Religion and Culture: 6/F Kiu Kin Mansion, No.566 Nathan Road, Kowloon, Hong Kong.

Chi. Inform. China information. (0920-203X). Documentation and Research Centre for Contemporary China, Sinologisch Instituut: Postbus 9515, 2300 RA Leiden, The Netherlands.

Child C. Pract. Child care in practice. (1357-5279). Child Care in Practice Group: School of Social Work, 7 Lennoxvale, Belfast, BT9 5BY.

Child. Devel. Child development. (0009-3920). University of Chicago Press: 5720 S. Woodlawn Avenue, Chicago, IL 60637, U.S.A., in association with Society for Research in Child Development: 5720 South Woodlawn Avenue, Chicago, IL 60637, U.S.A.

Child. Soc. Children and society. (0951-0605). John Wiley & Sons: Baffins Lane, Chichester, West Sussex PO19 1UD, U.K., in association with National Children's Bureau of the United Kingdom.

Child Wel. Child welfare. (0009-4021). Child Welfare League of America: 440 1st Street N.W., Washington DC 20001-2085, U.S.A.

LISTE DES ABRÉVIATIONS UTILISÉES

Chin. Soc. Anth. Chinese sociology and anthropology. (0009-4625). M.E. Sharpe, Inc: 80 Business Park Drive, Armonk, NY 10504, U.S.A.

China J. China journal. Contemporary China Centre: Australian National University, Research School of Pacific and Asian Studies, Canberra ACT 0200, Australia.

China Quart. China quarterly. (0009-4439). Cambridge University Press: The Edinburgh Building, Shaftesbury Road, Cambridge CB2 2RU, U.K., in association with School of Oriental and African Studies: Thornhaugh Street, Russell Square, London WC1H 0XG, U.K.

China R. China report. (0009-4455). Sage Publications India: 32 M-Block Market, Greater Kailash I, New Delhi 110 048, India.

Cities Cities. (0264-2751). Elsevier Science: PO Box 211, 1000 AE Amsterdam, The Netherlands.

City City. (1360-4813). City: 5 Dryden Street, Covent Garden, London, WC2E 9NB, U.K.

Cogn. Ling. Cognitive linguistics. (0936-5907). Walter de Gruyter: Genthiner Strasse 13, D-10785 Berlin, Germany.

Cognition Cognition. (0010-0277). Elsevier Science: PO Box 211, 1000 AE Amsterdam, The Netherlands.

Comm. Dev. J. Community development journal. (0010-3802). Oxford University Press: Great Clarendon Street, Oxford OX2 6DP, U.K.

Comm. Post-Comm. Stud. Communist and post-communist studies. (0967-067X). Elsevier Science: PO Box 211, 1000 AE Amsterdam, The Netherlands.

Commun. Theory Communication theory. (1050-3293). Guilford Publications: 72 Spring Street, New York, NY 10012, U.S.A., in association with International Communication Association: 8140 Burnet Road, P.O. Box 9589, Austin, TX. 78766-9589, U.S.A.

Comp. Int. Law J. S. Afr. Comparative and international law journal of Southern Africa. (0010-4051). University of South Africa, Institute of Foreign and Comparative Law: P.O. Box 392, Pretoria, South Africa.

Comp. Stud. S. Comparative studies in society and history. (0010-4175). Cambridge University Press: 40 West 20th Street, New York, NY 10011-4211, U.S.A., in association with Society for the Comparative Study of Society and History.

Comp. Stud. S. As. Af. Mid. East Comparative studies of South Asia, Africa and the Middle East. (1089-201X). Duke University Press: Box 90660, Durham, NC 27708-0660, U.S.A., in association with Comparative studies of South Asia, Africa and the Middle East: Department of History, Box 90719, 226 Carr, Duke University, Durham, NC 27708-0719.

Confl. Resolut. Journal of conflict resolution. (0022-0027). Sage Publications: 2455 Teller Road, Newbury Park, Thousand Oaks, CA 91320, U.S.A., in association with Peace Science Society (International).

Constit. Pol. Econ. Constitutional political economy. (1043-4062). Kluwer Academic Publishers: P.O. Box 17, 3300 AA Dordrecht, The Netherlands, in association with Center for Study of Public Choice.

Cont. Pac. Contemporary Pacific. (1043-898X). University of Hawaii Press: 2840 Kolowalu Street, Honolulu, HI 96822-1888, U.S.A., in association with Center for Pacific Islands Studies: University of Hawaii at Manoa, 1890 East-West Road, 215 Moore Hall, Honolulu, HI 96822, U.S.A.

Contemp. Br. Hist. Contemporary British history. (1361-9462). Frank Cass: Newbury House, 890-900 Eastern Avenue, Newbury Park, Ilford, Essex IG2 7HH, U.K.

Contr. I. Soc. Contributions to Indian sociology. (0069-9667). Sage Publications India: 32 M-Block Market, Greater Kailash I, New Delhi 110 048, India, in association with Institute of Economic Growth: University of Delhi, Delhi 110007, India.

Contrib. Nepal. Stud. Contributions to Nepalese studies. Centre for Nepal and Asian Studies, in association with Tribhuvan University.

LIST OF ABBREVIATIONS USED

Coop. Conflict Cooperation and conflict. (0010-8367). Sage Publications Ltd.: 6 Bonhill Street, London, EC2A 4PU, U.K., in association with Nordic Cooperation Committee for International Politics.
Cr. Law Soc. Chan. Crime, law and social change. (0925-4994). Kluwer Academic Publishers: P.O. Box 322, 3300 AH Dordrecht, The Netherlands.
Crime Delin. Crime and delinquency. (0011-1287). Sage Publications: 2455 Teller Road, Newbury Park, Thousand Oaks, CA 91320, U.S.A.
Criminology Criminology. (0011-1384). American Society of Criminology: 1314 Kinnear Road Suite 212, Columbus, OH 43212, U.S.A.
Crit. Anthr. Critique of anthropology. (0308-275X). Sage Publications: 6 Bonhill Street, London EC2A 4PU, U.K.
Crit. Marx. Critica marxista. (0011-152X). Editori Riuniti Riviste: Via Serchio 9, 00198 Rome, Italy.
Crit. Persp. Acc. Critical perspectives on accounting. (1045-2354). Academic Press: 24-28 Oval Road, London NW1 7DX, U.K.
Crit. Rev. Critical review. (0891-3811). Critical Review: P.O. Box 14528, Chicago, IL 60614, U.S.A., in association with Center for Independent Thought: 942 Howard Street, Room 109, San Francisco, CA 94103, U.S.A.
Crit. Soc. Pol. Critical social policy. (0261-0183). Sage Publications Ltd: 6 Bonhill Street, London, EC2A 4PU, U.K.
Crit. Sociol. Critical sociology. (0896-9205). Humanities Press, Inc: 112 Water Street, Suite 400, Boston MA, 02109 U.S.A.
Critica Sociol. Critica sociologica. (0011-1546). S.I.A.R.E.S.: Corso Vittorio Emanuele 24, 00186 Rome, Italy.
Cuad. Am. Cuadernos americanos. (0185-156X). Universidad Nacional Autónoma de México, Facultad de Ciencias Políticas y Sociales: Ciudad Universitaria, Coyoacán, 04510 México D.F., Mexico.
Cuad. Nues. Am. Cuadernos de nuestra América. Centro de Estudios Sobre America: Ave. 3ra no. 1805 e/ 18 y 20, Playa Zona Postal 13, Havana, Cuba.
Cult. Anthro. Cultural anthropology. (0886-7356). American Anthropological Association: 4350 North Fairfax Drive, Suite 640, Arlington, VA 22203-1620, U.S.A., in association with Society for Cultural Anthropology.
Cult. Dyn. Cultural dynamics. (0921-3740). Sage Publications: 6 Bonhill Street, London EC2A 4PU, U.K.
Cult. Health. Sex. Culture, health and sexuality. (1369-1058). Taylor & Francis Ltd: 1 Gunpowder Square, London, EC4A 3DF, U.K.., in association with International Association for Study of Sexuality, Culture and Society.
Cult. Medic. Psych. Culture, medicine and psychiatry. (0165-005X). Kluwer Academic Publishers: P.O. Box 322, 3300 AH Dordrecht, The Netherlands.
Cult. Psyc. Culture & psychology. (1354-067X). Sage Publications: 6 Bonhill Street, London EC2A 4PU, U.K.
Cult. St. Cultural studies. (0950-2386). Routledge: 11 New Fetter Lane, London EC4P 4EE, U.K.
Cult. Val. Cultural values. (1362-5179). Blackwell Publishers Ltd: 108 Cowley Road, Oxford, OX4 1JF, U.K., in association with Institute for Cultural Research, Lancaster University.
Curr. Anthr. Current anthropology. (0011-3204). University of Chicago Press: 5720 S. Woodlawn Avenue, Chicago, IL 60637, U.S.A., in association with Wenner-Gren Foundation for Anthropological Research.
Curr. Sociol. Current sociology. (0011-3921). Sage Publications: 6 Bonhill Street, London EC2A 4PU, U.K., in association with International Sociological Association.
Czech Soc. Rev. Czech sociological review. (1210-3861). Institute of Sociology of the Czech Academy of Sciences: Jilská 1, 110 00 Praha 1, Czech Republic.

LISTE DES ABRÉVIATIONS UTILISÉES

Dædalus Dædalus. (0011-5266). American Academy of Arts and Sciences: 136 Irving Street, Cambridge, MA 02138, U.S.A.

Demo. & Nat. Democracy & nature. (1085-5661). Carfax Publishing: P.O. Box 25, Abingdon, Oxfordshire, OX14 3UE, U.K.

Demografie Demografie. (0011-8265). Český statistický úř, Demografie: Sokolovská č. n. 142, 18604 Praha 8-Karlín, vchod z budovy A, místnost A, 215., in association with Federální Statistický Úřad.

Demography Demography. (0070-3370). Population Association of America: 1722 N. Street N.W., Washington DC 20036, U.S.A.

Desar. Econ. Desarrollo económico. (0046-001X). Instituto de Desarrollo Económico y Social: Aráoz 2838, 1425 Buenos Aires, Argentina.

Desar. Soc. Desarrollo y sociedad. (0120-3584). Universidad de los Andes, Facultad de Economía, Centro de Estudios sobre Desarrollo Económico: Carrera 1E no. 18/A-10, Apartado Aereo 4976, Bogota D.E., Colombia.

Deut. Arch. Deutschland Archiv: Zeitschrift für das vereinigte Deutschland. (0012-1428). Leske & Budrich: Gerhart-Hauptmann-Straße 27, 51379 Leverkusen, Germany.

Dirasat Ad. Sc. Dirasat: Administrative Sciences. (1026-373X). Deanship of Academic Research: University of Jordan, Amman, Jordan.

Dirasat Ed. Dirasat: Educational Sciences. (1026-3713). Deanship of Academic Research: University of Jordan, Amman, Jordan.

Dirasat Hum. Soc. Sc. Dirasat: Human and Social Sciences. (1026-3721). Deanship of Academic Research: University of Jordan, Amman, Jordan.

Dis. and Soc. Disability and society. (0968-7599). Carfax Publishing: P.O. Box 25, Abingdon, Oxfordshire OX14 3UE, U.K.

Disasters Disasters: Journal of disaster studies, policy and management. (0361-3666). Blackwell Publishers: 108 Cowley Road, Oxford OX4 1JF, U.K.

Disc. Soc. Discourse & society. (0957-9265). Sage Publications: 6 Bonhill Street, London EC2A 4PU, U.K.

Disc. St. Discourse studies. (1461-4456). Sage Publications: 6 Bonhill Street, London EC2A 4PU, U.K.

Documents Documents. (0151-0827). Documents: 50 rue de Laborde, 75008 Paris, France.

Dokumente Dokumente. (0012-5172). Europa Union Verlag: Bachstraße 32, 53115 Bonn, Germany, in association with Gesellschaft für übernationale Zusammenarbeit: Bachstraße 32, 53005 Bonn, Germany.

E. Eur. Pol. Soc. East European politics and societies. (0888-3254). University of California Press Journals: 2120 Berkeley Way, Berkeley, CA 94720-5812, U.S.A.

E. Eur. Quart. East European quarterly. (0012-8449). University of Colorado: Box 29 Regent Hall, Boulder, CO 80309-0029, U.S.A.

Ec. Lav. Economia & lavoro. (0012-978X). Fondazione Giacomo Brodolini: Via Torino 122, 00184 Rome, Italy.

Ec. Sociét. Économies et sociétés. (0013-0567). Presses de l'Institut de Sciences Mathematiques et Économiques Appliquées: 14 rue Corvisart, 75013 Paris, France.

Econ. Dev. Cult. Change Economic development and cultural change. (0013-0079). University of Chicago Press: 5720 S. Woodlawn Avenue, Chicago, IL 60637, U.S.A.

Econ. Devel. Q. Economic development quarterly. (0891-2424). Sage Publications: 2455 Teller Road, Newbury Park, Thousand Oaks, CA 91320, U.S.A.

Econ. Ind. Dem. Economic and industrial democracy. (0143-831X). Sage Publications: 6 Bonhill Street, London EC2A 4PU, U.K., in association with Arbetslivscentrum (The Swedish Center for Working Life): Box 5606, S-114 86 Stockholm, Sweden.

LIST OF ABBREVIATIONS USED

Econ. J. Economic journal. (0013-0133). Blackwell Publishers: 108 Cowley Road, Oxford OX4 1JF, U.K., in association with Royal Economic Society: Imperial College of Science and Technology, London SW7 2AZ, U.K.
Econ. Philos. Economics and philosophy. (0266-2671). Cambridge University Press: 40 West 20th Street, New York, NY 10011-4211, U.S.A.
Econ. Polit. Economics and politics. (0954-1985). Blackwell Publishers: 108 Cowley Road, Oxford OX4 1JF, U.K.
Econ. Soc. Economy and society. (0308-5147). Routledge: 11 New Fetter Lane, London EC4P 4EE, U.K.
Econ. Soc. R. Economic and social review. (0012-9984). 4 Burlington Road, Dublin 4, Ireland.
Econ. Soc. Tijd. Economisch en sociaal tijdschrift. (0013-0575). UFSIA (Antwerp University): Venusstraat 35, 2000 Antwerp, Belgium.
Écon. Stat. Économie et statistique. (0336-1454). Institut national de la statistique et des études économiques: 18 boulevard Adolphe Pinard, 75675 Paris Cedex 14, France.
Economica Economica [London]. (0013-0427). Blackwell Publishers: 108 Cowley Road, Oxford OX4 1JF, U.K., in association with London School of Economics and Political Science: Houghton Street, London WC2A 2AE, U.K.
Educ. Urban. Soc. Education and urban society. (0013-1245). Sage Publications: 2455 Teller Road, Newbury Park, Thousand Oaks, CA 91320, U.S.A.
Educat. Res. Educational research. (0013-1881). Routledge: 11 New Fetter Lane, London EC4P 4EE, U.K., in association with National Foundation for Educational Research: The Mere, Upton Park, Slough, Berkshire SL1 2DQ, U.K.
Ekistics Ekistics. (0013-2942). Athens Technological Organization, Athens Center of Ekistics: 24 Strat. Syndesmou St., 10673 Athens, Greece.
Entr. Hist. Entreprises et histoire. (1161-2770). Éditions ESKA: 27 rue Dunois, 75013 Paris, France.
Envir. Behav. Environment and behavior. (0013-9165). Sage Publications: 2455 Teller Road, Newbury Park, Thousand Oaks, CA 91320, U.S.A., in association with Environmental Design Research Association.
Envir. Imp. Assess. Rev. Environmental impact assessment review. (0195-9255). Elsevier Science: PO Box 211, 1000 AE Amsterdam, The Netherlands, in association with Department of Urban Studies and Planning, MIT.
Envir. Plan. A. Environment and planning A: International journal of urban and regional research. (0308-518X). Pion: 207 Brondesbury Park, London NW2 5JN, U.K.
Envir. Plan. D. Environment and planning D: Society and space. (0263-7758). Pion: 207 Brondesbury Park, London NW2 5JN, U.K.
Environ. Urban. Environment and urbanization. (0956-2478). International Institute for Environment and Development: 3 Endsleigh Street, London WC1H 0DD, U.K.
Environ. Values Environmental values. (0963-2719). White Horse Press: 10 High Street, Knapwell, Cambridge CB3 8NR, U.K.
Environment Environment. (0013-9157). Heldref Publications: 1319 Eighteenth Street N.W., Washington, DC 20036-1802, U.S.A.
Espace Géogr. Espace géographique. (0046-2497). Éditions BELIN: 8 rue Férou, 75006 Paris, France.
Espace Pop. Soc. Espace populations sociétés. (0755-7809). Université des Sciences et Techniques de Lille-Flandres-Artois: 59655 Villeneuve d'Ascq Cedex, France.
Esprit Esprit. (0014-0759). Esprit: 212 rue Saint-Martin, 75003 Paris, France.
Est. Latinam. Estudios latinoamericanos. (0187-1811). Universidad Nacional Autónoma de México, Facultad de Ciencias Políticas y Sociales: Ciudad Universitaria, Coyoacán, 04510 México D.F., Mexico.

LISTE DES ABRÉVIATIONS UTILISÉES

Est. Polí. Estudios políticos. (0185-1616). Universidad Nacional Autónoma de México, Facultad de Ciencias Políticas y Sociales: Ciudad Universitaria, Coyoacán, 04510 México D.F., Mexico.

Ét. Int. Études internationales. (0014-2123). Centre québécois de relations internationales: Faculté des sciences sociales, Université Laval, Québec G1K 7P4, Canada.

Ethic. Theory Moral P. Ethical theory and moral practice. (1386-2820). Kluwer Academic Publishers: P.O. Box 322, 3300 AH Dordrecht, The Netherlands, in association with Societas Ethica European Society for Research in Ethics.

Ethics Ethics. (0014-1704). University of Chicago Press: 5720 S. Woodlawn Avenue, Chicago, IL 60637, U.S.A.

Ethn. Fr. Ethnologie française. (0046-2616). Armand Colin: 34 bis rue de l'Université, 75007 Paris, France.

Ethn. Racial Ethnic and racial studies. (0141-9870). Routledge: 11 New Fetter Lane, London EC4P 4EE, U.K.

Ethnog. Ethnography. (1466-1381). Sage Publications: 6 Bonhill Street, London EC2A 4PU, U.K.

Ethnologies Ethnologies. (1481-5974). Folklore Studies Association of Canada / L'Association canadienne d'ethnologie et de folklore: CÉLAT, Université Laval, Québec, Canada G1K 7P4.

Ethnology Ethnology. (0014-1828). University of Pittsburgh: Department of Anthropology, Pittsburgh, PA 15260, U.S.A.

Ethnos Ethnos. (0014-1844). Routledge: 11 New Fetter Lane, London EC4P 4EE, U.K.

Ethos Ethos. (0091-2131). American Anthropological Association: 4350 North Fairfax Drive, Suite 640, Arlington, VA 22203-1620, U.S.A.

Etn. Polska Etnografia polska. (0071-1861). Instytut Archeologii i etnologii: Polskiej Akademii Nauk, Al. Solidarnosci 105, 00-140 Warszawa, Poland.

Eur. Econ. R. European economic review. (0014-2921). Elsevier Science: PO Box 211, 1000 AE Amsterdam, The Netherlands, in association with European Economic Association: 34 Voie du Roman Pays, B-1348 Louvain-la-Neuve, Belgium.

Eur. Ethn. Europa ethnica. Wilhelm Braumüller: A-1092 Vienna, Servitengasse 5, Austria.

Eur. J. Comm. European journal of communication. (0267-3231). Sage Publications: 6 Bonhill Street, London EC2A 4PU, U.K.

Eur. J. Crim. Pol. Res. European journal on criminal policy and research. (0928-1371). Kluwer Academic Publishers: P.O. Box 17, 3300 AA Dordrecht, The Netherlands, in association with Research and Documentation Centre (WODC) of the Ministry of Justice.

Eur. J. Crime Crim. Law Crim. Just. European journal of crime, criminal law and criminal justice. (0928-9569). Kluwer Law and Taxation Publishers: P.O. Box 23, 7400 GA Deventer, The Netherlands.

Eur. J. Law Econ. European journal of law and economics. (0929-1261). Kluwer Academic Publishers: P.O. Box 322, 3300 AH Dordrecht, The Netherlands.

Eur. J. Phil. European journal of philosophy. (0966-8373). Blackwell Publishers: 108 Cowley Road, Oxford OX4 1JF, U.K.

Eur. J. Pop. European journal of population = Revue européenne de démographie. (0168-6577). Kluwer Academic Publishers: P.O. Box 322, 3300 AH Dordrecht, The Netherlands.

Eur. J. Soc. Archives européennes de sociologie = European journal of sociology = Europäisches Archiv für Soziologie. (0003-9756). Cambridge University Press: The Edinburgh Building, Shaftesbury Road, Cambridge CB2 2RU, U.K.

Eur. J. Soc. Psychol. European journal of social psychology. (0046-2772). John Wiley & Sons: Baffins Lane, Chichester, West Sussex PO19 1UD, U.K., in association with European Association of Experimental Social Psychology.

Eur. J. Soc. Theory European journal of social theory. (1368-4310). SAGE Publications: 6 Bonhill Street, London EC2A 4PU, United Kingdom.

LIST OF ABBREVIATIONS USED

Eur. J. Wom. Stud. European journal of women's studies. (1350-5068). Sage Publications: 6 Bonhill Street, London EC2A 4PU, U.K., in association with European Women's Studies Association: Heidelberglaan 2, 3584 CS Utrecht, Netherlands.

Eur. Sociol. R. European sociological review. (0266-7215). Oxford University Press: Great Clarendon Street, Oxford OX2 6DP, U.K.

Eur. Urban Reg. Stud. European urban and regional studies. (0969-7764). Sage Publications: 6 Bonhill Street, London EC2A 4PU, U.K.

Eur.-Asia Stud. Europe-Asia studies. (0966-8136). Carfax Publishing: P.O. Box 25, Abingdon, Oxfordshire OX14 3UE, U.K.

Euro. J. Dev. Res. European journal of development research. (0957-8811). Frank Cass: Newbury House, 890-900 Eastern Avenue, Newbury Park, Ilford, Essex IG2 7HH, U.K.

Euro. Journ. Cult. Stud. European journal of cultural studies. (1367-5494). Sage Publications Ltd: 6 Bonhill Street, London, EC2A 4PU, U.K.

Euro. Soc. European societies. (1461-6696). Routledge: 11 New Fetter Lane, London EC4P 4EE, U.K.

Eval. Rev. Evaluation review. (0193-841X). Sage Publications: 2455 Teller Road, Newbury Park, Thousand Oaks, CA 91320, U.S.A.

Evaluation Evaluation. (1356-3890). Sage Publications: 6 Bonhill Street, London EC2A 4PU, U.K., in association with Tavistock Institute.

Evol. Hum. Behav. Evolution and human behavior. (1090-5138). Elsevier Science: PO Box 211, 1000 AE Amsterdam, The Netherlands.

Fash. Theory Fashion theory. (1362-704X). Berg Publishers: 150 Cowley Road, Oxford OX4 1JJ, U.K.

Fem. Econ. Feminist economics. (1354-5701). Routledge: 11 New Fetter Lane, London EC4P 4EE, U.K.

Fem. Stud. Feminist studies. (0046-3663). Feminist Studies: University of Maryland, Women's Studies Program, College Park, MD 20742, U.S.A.

Fem. Theo. Feminist theory. (1464-7001). Sage Publications: 6 Bonhill Street, London EC2A 4PU, U.K.

Feminist R. Feminist review. (0141-7789). Routledge: 11 New Fetter Lane, London EC4P 4EE, U.K., in association with Feminist Review: 11 Carleton Gardens, Brecknock Road, London N19 5AQ, U.K.

Fie. Meth. Field methods. (1525-822X). Sage Publications: 2455 Teller Road, Thousand Oaks, CA, 91320 U.S.A.

Folklore [London] Folklore [London]. (0015-587X). Routledge: 11 New Fetter Lane, London EC4P 4EE, U.K., in association with Folklore society.

Food Food. Food and foodways. (0740-9710). Harwood Academic Publishers: 270 8th Avenue, New York, NY 10011, U.S.A.

Food Pol. Food policy. (0306-9192). Elsevier Science: PO Box 211, 1000 AE Amsterdam, The Netherlands.

Foreign Aff. Foreign affairs. (0015-7120). Council on Foreign Relations: 58 East 68th Street, New York, NY 10021, U.S.A.

Foreign Pol. Foreign policy. (0015-7228). Carnegie Endowment for International Peace.

Fors. Jour. Soz. Beweg. Forschungsjournal neue soziale Bewegungen. (0933-9361). Westdeutscher Verlag: Postfach 5829, D-65048 Wiesbaden, Germany, in association with Forschungsgruppe Neue Soziale Bewegungen.

Fr. Cult. Stud. French cultural studies. (0957-1558). Alpha Academic: Halfpenny Furze, Mill Lane, Chalfont St. Giles, Buckinghamshire HP8 4NR, U.K.

Fr. Stud. French studies. (0016-1128). Society for French Studies.

LISTE DES ABRÉVIATIONS UTILISÉES

Fre. Pol. Cult. Soc. French politics, culture, and society. (0882-1267). Berghahn Books: 3, Newtec Place, Magdalen Road, Oxford OX4 1RE, U.K.
Fst. Lang. First language. (0142-7237). Alpha Academic: Halfpenny Furze, Mill Lane, Chalfont St. Giles, Buckinghamshire, HP8 4NR, U.K.
Gen. Dev. Gender and development. (1355-2074). Oxfam Publishing: 274 Banbury Road, Oxford OX2 7DZ, U.K.
Gen. Tech. Dev. Gender, technology and development. (0971-8524). Sage Publications India: 32 M-Block Market, Greater Kailash I, New Delhi 110 048, India, in association with Asian Institute of Technology, Thailand.
Gend. Hist. Gender and history. (0953-5233). Blackwell Publishers: 108 Cowley Road, Oxford OX4 1JF, U.K.
Gend. Place Cult. Gender, place and culture: A journal of feminist geography. (0966-369X). Carfax Publishing: P.O. Box 25, Abingdon, Oxfordshire OX14 3UE, U.K.
Gend. Work & Org. Gender, work and organization. (0968-6673). Blackwell Publishers: 108 Cowley Road, Oxford OX4 1JF, U.K., in association with UMIST.
Gender Soc. Gender and society. (0891-2432). Sage Publications: 2455 Teller Road, Newbury Park, Thousand Oaks, CA 91320, U.S.A., in association with Sociologists for Women in Society.
Genèses Genèses. (1135-3219). Calman-Lévy.
Geoforum Geoforum. (0016-7185). Elsevier Science: PO Box 211, 1001 AE Amsterdam, The Netherlands.
Geogr. Anal. Geographical analysis. (0016-7363). Ohio State University Press: 1070 Carmack Road, Columbus, OH 43210, U.S.A.
Geogr. Ann. B. Geografiska annaler: Series B — Human geography. (0435-3684). Svenska Sällskapet för Antropologi och Geografi: University of Uppsala, Department of Physical Geography, Box 554, S-751 22 Uppsala, Sweden.
Geogr. J. Geographical journal. (0016-7398). Royal Geographical Society (with IBG): 1 Kensington Gore, London SW7 2AR, U.K.
Geogr. Pol. Geographia polonica. (0016-7282). Institute of Geography and Spatial Organization, Polish Academy of Sciences: Twarda 51/55, 00-818 Warsaw, Poland.
Geogr. Rev. Geographical review. (0016-7428). American Geographical Society: 120 Wall Street, Suite 100; New York; NY 10005; U.S.A.
Geogr. Rund. Geographische Rundschau. (0016-7460). Westermann Schulbuchverlag: Georg-Westermann-Allee 66, 3300 Braunschweig, Germany.
Geojournal Geojournal. (0343-2521). Kluwer Academic Publishers: P.O. Box 17, 3300 AA Dordrecht, The Netherlands.
Ger. Hist. German history: the journal of the German history society. (0266-3554). Arnold Publishers: Journals Department, 338 Euston Road, London, NW1 3BH, U.K., in association with German History Society.
Gesch. Ges. Geschichte und Gesellschaft. (0340-613X). Vandenhoeck & Ruprecht: Theaterstraße 13, 37073 Göttingen, Germany.
Gewerk. Monat. Gewerkschaftliche Monatshefte. (0016-9447). Bund-Verlag: Hansestraße 63 a, Postfach 90 08 40, 51118 Cologne, Germany, in association with Bundesvorstand des DGB: Hans-Böckler-Straße 39, 4000 Düsseldorf 30, Germany.
Glob. Dial. Global dialogue. (1450-0590). Centre for World Dialogue: 39 Rega Fereou Street, CY-1087 Nicosia, Cyprus.
Gos. Pravo Gosudarstvo i pravo. (0132-0769). Nauka: Profsoiuznaia ul. 90, 117864 Moscow, Russia.
Green. Mgt. Int. Greener management international. (0966-9671). Greenleaf Publishing Ltd: Aizlewood Business Center, Aizlewood's Mill, Nursery Street, Sheffield S3 8GG, U.K.
Group Decis. Negot. Group decision and negotiation. (0926-2644). Kluwer Academic Publishers: P.O. Box 17, 3300 AA Dordrecht, The Netherlands.

LIST OF ABBREVIATIONS USED

Groupwork Groupwork. (0951-824X). Whiting and Birch: P.O. Box 872, Forest Hill, London SE23 8HL, U.K.
Hab. Int. Habitat international. (0197-3975). Elsevier Science: PO Box 211, 1000 AE Amsterdam, The Netherlands, in association with Centre for Development Planning Studies, University of Sheffield.
Harv. Law Rev. Harvard law review. (0017-811X). Harvard Law Review Association: Gannett House, 1511 Massachusetts Avenue, Cambridge, MA 02138, U.S.A.
Health Hum. Rights Health and human rights. (1079-0969). Harvard School of Public Health: 8 Story Street, 5th Floor, Cambridge, MA 02138, U.S.A.
Health Pol. Health policy. (0168-8510). Elsevier Science: PO Box 211, 1000 AE Amsterdam, The Netherlands.
Health Pol. Plan. Health policy and planning. (0268-1080). Oxford University Press: Great Clarendon Street, Oxford OX2 6DP, U.K., in association with London School of Hygiene and Tropical Medicine: Keppel (Gower) Street, London WC1E 7HT, U.K.
Health Soc. Work Health and social work. (0360-7283). National Association of Social Workers: 750 First Street N.E., Suite 700, Washington DC 20002-4241, U.S.A.
Hemispheres Hemispheres. (0239-8818). Polish Academy of Sciences, Centre for Studies on non-European Countries: Rynek 9, 50-106 Wroclaw, Poland.
High. Educ. Higher education. (0018-1560). Kluwer Academic Publishers: P.O. Box 17, 3300 AA Dordrecht, The Netherlands.
Hisp. Am. Hist. Rev. Hispanic American historical review. (0018-2168). Duke University Press: Box 90660, Durham, NC 27708-0660, U.S.A., in association with American Historical Association, Conference on Latin American History.
Hist. Fam. History of the family. (1081-602X). JAI Press: 100 Prospect Street, P.O. Box 811, Stamford, CT 06904-0811, U.S.A.
Hist. Human Sci. History of the human sciences. (0952-6951). Sage Publications: 6 Bonhill Street, London EC2A 4PU, U.K.
Hist. J. Historical journal. (0018-246X). Cambridge University Press: The Edinburgh Building, Shaftesbury Road, Cambridge CB2 2RU, U.K.
Hist. Polit. Thou. History of political thought. (0143-781X). Imprint Academic: P.O. Box 1, Thorverton, Devon, EX5 5YX, U.K.
Hist. Psychiat. History of psychiatry. (0957-154X). Alpha Academic: Halfpenny Furze, Mill Lane, Chalfont St Giles, Buckinghamshire HP8 4NR, U.K.
Hist. Soc. R. Historical social research = Historische Sozialforschung. (0172-6404). Zentrum für Historische Sozialforschung: Zentralarchiv für Empirische Sozialforschung, Universität zu Köln, Bachemerstr. 40, D-5000 Cologne, Germany, in association with Arbeitsgemeinschaft für Quantifizierung und Methoden in der historisch sozialwissenschaftlichen Forschung.
Hist. Theory History and theory. (0018-2656). History and Theory, Wesleyan University: 287 High Street, Middletown, CT 06457-0507, U.S.A.
Hito. J. Soc. Stud. Hitotsubashi journal of social studies. (0073-280X). Hitotsubashi University: 2-1 Naka, Kunitachi, Tokyo 186, Japan.
Hom. Soc. Homme et la société. (0018-4306). Editions l'Harmattan: 5-7 rue de l'École-Polytechnique, 75005 Paris, France, in association with Centre National des Lettres / Centre National de la Recherche Scientifique.
Homme Homme. (0439-4216). Éditions de l'École des hautes études en sciences sociales: 54 boulevard Raspail, 75006 Paris, France, in association with Laboratoire d'anthropologie sociale: Collège de France, 52 rue du Cardinal-Lemoine, 75005 Paris, France.
Hous. Pol. Deb. Housing policy debate. (1051-1482). Fannie Mae Foundation: 4000 Wisconsin Avenue N.W., North Tower Suite One, Washington DC 20016-2804, U.S.A.

LISTE DES ABRÉVIATIONS UTILISÉES

Hous. Th. Soc. Housing, theory and society. (1403-6096). Scandinavian University Press: P.O. Box 3255, S-103 65 Stockholm, Sweden.

Howard J. Crim. Just. Howard journal of criminal justice. (0265-5527). Blackwell Publishers: 108 Cowley Road, Oxford OX4 1JF, U.K., in association with the Howard League: 708 Holloway Road, London N19 3NL, U.K.

Hum. Nature Human nature. (1045-6767). Aldine de Gruyter: 200 Saw Mill River Road, Hawthorne, NY 10532, U.S.A.

Hum. Rights Q. Human rights quarterly. (0275-0392). Johns Hopkins University Press: 2715 North Charles Street, Baltimore, MD 21218-4363, U.S.A.

Human. Org. Human organization. (0018-7259). Society for Applied Anthropology: 5205 E.Flowler Avenue, Suite 310, Temple Terrace, FL 33617, U.S.A.

Human Relat. Human relations. (0018-7267). Sage Publications: 6 Bonhill Street, London EC2A 4PU, U.K., in association with Tavistock Institute.

Human St. Human studies. (0163-8548). Kluwer Academic Publishers: P.O. Box 322, 3300 AH Dordrecht, The Netherlands.

Humor Humor. (0933-1719). Mouton de Gruyter: Postfach 303421, 10728 Berlin, Germany.

Identities Identities: global studies in culture and power. (1070-289X). Gordon and Breach Science Publishers SA: P.O. Box 20029, Riverfront Plaza Station, Newark, NJ 07102-0301, U.S.A.

Ind. J. Gend. Stud. Indian journal of gender studies. (0971-5215). Sage Publications India: 32 M-Block Market, Greater Kailash I, New Delhi 110 048, India, in association with Centre for Women's Development Studies: New Delhi, India.

Ind. J. Glob. Legal Stud. Indiana journal of global legal studies. (1080-0727). Indiana Journal of Global Legal Studies: Indiana University School of Law - Bloomington, Third Street and Indiana Avenue, Bloomington, IN 47405-1001, U.S.A.

Ind. J. Ind. Rel. Indian journal of industrial relations. (0019-5286). Shri Ram Centre for Industrial Relations and Human Resources: 4E/16 Jhandewalan Extension, New Delhi 110015, India.

Ind. J. Reg. Sci. Indian journal of regional science. (0046-9017). Regional Science Association India: CK-134, Sector 11, Saltlake City, Calcutta 700091, India.

Ind. Lab. Rel. Industrial and labor relations review. (0019-7939). Cornell University, New York State School of Industrial and Labor Relations: 201 ILR Research Building, Cornell University, Ithaca, NY 14853-3901, U.S.A.

Ind. Psych. Abs. Rev. Indian psychological abstracts and reviews. (0971-524X). Sage Publications India: 32 M-Block Market, Greater Kailash I, New Delhi 110 048, India, in association with Indian Council of Social Science Research: New Delhi, India.

Ind. Relat. Industrial relations. (0019-8676). Blackwell Publishers: 108 Cowley Road, Oxford OX4 1JF, U.K., in association with University of California, Berkeley, Institute of Industrial Relations: Berkeley, CA 94720, U.S.A.

Ind. Relat. J. Industrial relations journal. (0019-8692). Blackwell Publishers: 108 Cowley Road, Oxford OX4 1JF, U.K.

Indian Ec. Soc. His. R. Indian economic and social history review. (0019-4646). Sage Publications India: 32 M-Block Market, Greater Kailash I, New Delhi 110 048, India, in association with Indian Economic and Social History Association.

Indian J. Soc. W. Indian journal of social work. (0019-5634). Tata Institute of Social Sciences: PB No. 8313 Deonar, Bombay 400 088, India.

Indust. Bezieh. Industrielle Beziehungen. (0943-2779). Rainer Hampp Verlag: Indbez, Meringerzeller Str. 16, D-86415 Mering, Germany.

Inf. Raum. Informationen zur Raumentwicklung. (0303-2493). Bundesamt für Bauwesen und Raumordnung: Am Michaelshof 8, Postfach 20 01 30, 53177 Bonn, Germany.

Inf. Soc. Informations sociales. (0046-9459). Caisse Nationale des Allocations Familiales: 23 rue Daviel, 75634 Paris Cedex 13, France.

LIST OF ABBREVIATIONS USED

Info. Comm. Soc. Information, communication & society. (1369-118X). Routledge: 11 New Fetter Lane, London EC4P 4EE, U.K.
Inquiry Inquiry. (0020-174X). Scandinavian University Press: P.O. Box 2959, Tøyen, N-0608 Oslo 6, Norway.
Int. Asien. Internationales Asienforum. (0020-9449). Weltform Verlag: Marienburger Straße 22, 5000 Cologne 51, Germany, in association with Europäisches Institut für Politische, Wirtschaftliche und Soziale Fragen.
Int. Fem. J. Pol. International feminist journal of politics. (1461-6742). Routledge: 11 New Fetter Lane, London EC4P 4EE, U.K.
Int. J. International journal. (0020-7020). Canadian Institute of International Affairs: 15 Kings College Circle, Toronto, Ontario, Canada M5S 2V9.
Int. J. Afr. H. S. International journal of African historical studies. (0361-7882). Boston University, African Studies Center: 270 Bay State Road, Boston, MA 02215, U.S.A.
Int. J. Child. Rig. International journal of children's rights. (0927-5568). Kluwer Law International: P.O. Box 85889, 2508 CN The Hague, The Netherlands.
Int. J. Comp. L. L. I. R. International journal of comparative labour law and industrial relations. (0952-617X). Kluwer Law International: P.O. Box 85889, 2508 CN The Hague, The Netherlands.
Int. J. Comp. Soc International journal of comparative sociology. (0020-7152). E.J. Brill: P.O. Box 9000, 2300 PA Leiden, The Netherlands.
Int. J. Health. Ser. International journal of health services. (0020-7314). Baywood Publishing: 26 Austin Avenue, P.O. Box 337, Amityville, NY 11701, U.S.A.
Int. J. Hist. Sport International journal of the history of sport. (0952-3367). Frank Cass: Newbury House, 890-900 Eastern Avenue, Newbury Park, Ilford, Essex IG2 7HH, U.K.
Int. J. Hum. Res. Man. International journal of human resource management. (0958-5192). Routledge: 11 New Fetter Lane, London EC4P 4EE, U.K.
Int. J. Jap. Sociol. International journal of Japanese sociology. (0918-7545). Japan Sociological Society: Department of Sociology, Tokyo University, 7-3-1 Hongo, Bunkyo-ku, Tokyo 113-8654, Japan.
Int. J. Law Policy Fam. International journal of law, policy, and the family. (1360-9939). Oxford University Press: Great Clarendon Street, Oxford OX2 6DP, U.K.
Int. J. M. E. Stud. International journal of Middle East studies. (0020-7438). Cambridge University Press: 40 West 20th Street, New York, NY 10011-4211, U.S.A., in association with Middle East Studies Association of North America: University of Arizona, 1232 North Cherry, Tuscon, AZ 85721, U.S.A.
Int. J. Min. Gr. Rights International journal on minority and group rights. (1385-4879). Kluwer Academic Publishers / Martinus Nijhoff: P.O. Box 17, 3300 AA Dordrecht, The Netherlands.
Int. J. Pharm. Prac. International journal of pharmacy practice. (0961-7671). Royal Pharmaceutical Society of Great Britain: 1 Lambeth High Street, London SE1 7JN, U.K.
Int. J. Phil. Stud. International journal of philosophical studies. (0967-2559). Routledge: 11 New Fetter Lane, London EC4P 4EE, U.K.
Int. J. Philos. Relig. International journal for philosophy of religion. (0020-7047). Kluwer Academic Publishers: P.O. Box 17, 3300 AA Dordrecht, The Netherlands.
Int. J. Pub. Op. Res. International journal of public opinion research. (0954-2892). Oxford University Press: Great Clarendon Street, Oxford OX2 6DP, U.K., in association with World Association for Public Opinion Research.
Int. J. S. Lang. International journal of the sociology of language. (0165-2516). Mouton de Gruyter: Postfach 303421, 10728 Berlin, Germany.
Int. J. S. Law International journal of the sociology of law. (0194-6595). Academic Press: 24-28 Oval Road, London NW1 7DX, U.K.

LISTE DES ABRÉVIATIONS UTILISÉES

Int. J. Soc. Psyc. International journal of social psychiatry. (0020-7640). Avenue Publishing: 55 Woodstock Avenue, London NW11 9RG, U.K.

Int. J. Urban Reg. Res. International journal of urban and regional research. (0309-1317). Edward Arnold: Mill Road, Dunton Green, Sevenoaks, Kent TN13 2YA, U.K.

Int. Jour. Cult. Stud. International journal of cultural studies. (1367-8779). Sage Publications: 6 Bonhill Street, London EC2A 4PU, U.K.

Int. Journ. Sust. Dev. International journal of sustainable development. (0960-1406). Inderscience Enterprises Ltd: World TRade Centre Building, 110 Avenue Louis Casai, Casa Postale 306, CH-1215 Geneva Airport, Switzerland.

Int. J.Psy. International journal of psychoanalysis. (0020-7578). Institute of Psychoanalysis: 63 New Cavendish Street, London W1M 7RD, U.K.

Int. Migr. International migration = Migrations internationales = Migraciones internacionales. (0020-7985). International Organization for Migration: P.O. Box 71, 1211 Geneva 19, Switzerland.

Int. Migr. Rev. International migration review. (0197-9183). Center for Migration Studies: 209 Flagg Place, Staten Island, NY 10304-1199, U.S.A.

Int. Phil. Sci. International studies in the philosophy of science. (0269-8595). Carfax Publishing: P.O. Box 25, Abingdon, Oxfordshire OX14 3UE, U.K.

Int. Pol. Internasjonal politikk. (0020-577X). Norwegian Institute of International Affairs: Postboks 8159 Dep., 0033 Oslo 1, Norway.

Int. Pol. Sci Rev. International political science review = Revue internationale de science politique. (0192-5121). Sage Publications: 6 Bonhill Street, London EC2A 4PU, U.K., in association with International Political Science Association.

Int. Politics International politics. (1384-5748). Kluwer Law International: P.O. Box 85889, 2508 CN The Hague, The Netherlands.

Int. R. Applied Ec. International review of applied economics. (0269-2171). Carfax Publishing: P.O. Box 25, Abingdon, Oxfordshire OX14 3UE, U.K.

Int. R. Educat. International review of education. (0020-8566). Kluwer Academic Publishers: P.O. Box 322, 3300 AH Dordrecht, The Netherlands.

Int. R. Law Econ. International review of law and economics. (0144-8188). Butterworth-Heinemann: Elsevier Science Inc, 655 Avenue of the Americas, New York, NY 10010, U.S.A.

Int. R. Red Cross International review of the Red Cross. (1560-7755). International Review of the Red Cross: 19 avenue de la Paix, 1202 Geneva, Switzerland, in association with International Committee of the Red Cross and Red Crescent Movement.

Int. R. Ret. Dist. Cons. Res. International review of retail, distribution and consumer research. (0959-3969). Routledge: 11 New Fetter Lane, London EC4P 4EE, U.K.

Int. Reg. Sci. R. International regional science review. (0160-0176). Sage Publications: 2455 Teller Road, Thousand Oaks, CA 91320, U.S.A.

Int. Rev. Admin. Sci. International review of administrative sciences. (0020-8523). Sage Publications: 6 Bonhill Street, London EC2A 4PU, U.K., in association with International Institute of Administrative Sciences, European Group of Public Administration: rue Defacqz 1, Box 11, B-1050 Brussels, Belgium.

Int. Rev. S. H. International review of social history. (0020-8590). Cambridge University Press: The Edinburgh Building, Shaftesbury Road, Cambridge, CB2 2RU, in association with International Institute for Social History: Cruquiusweg 31, 1019 AT Amsterdam, The Netherlands.

Int. Soc. Work International social work. (0020-8728). Sage Publications Ltd: 6 Bonhill Street, London, EC2A 4PU, U.K., in association with International Association of Schools of Social Work.

Int. Sociol. International sociology. (0268-5809). Sage Publications: 6 Bonhill Street, London EC2A 4PU, U.K., in association with International Sociological Association: Consejo Superior de Investigaciones Cientificas. Pinar 25, 28006 Madrid, Spain.

LIST OF ABBREVIATIONS USED

Inter-Asia Cult. St. Inter-Asia cultural studies. (1464-9373). Routledge, Taylor and Francis Ltd: 11 New Fetter Lane, London, EC4P 4EE, U.K., in association with Center for Asia/Pacific/Cultural studies, National Tsing Hua University, 101, Sec. 2 Kuang Fu Road, Hsinchuy 30043, Taiwan.
Interchange Interchange. (0826-4805). Kluwer Academic Publishers: P.O. Box 322, 3300 AH Dordrecht, The Netherlands.
Intern. J. Organiz. Anal. International journal of organizational analysis. (1055-3185). 3-R Executive Systems.
Irish J. Soc. Irish journal of sociology. (0791-6035). Irish Journal of Sociology: Department of Political Science and Sociology, University College, Galway, Ireland, in association with Sociological Association of Ireland.
Irish Rev. Irish review. (0790-7850). Cork University Press: Crawford Business Park, Crosses Green, Cork, Republic of Ireland.
Islam Soc. S. Sah. Islam et sociétés au sud du Sahara. (0984-7685). Editions de la Maison des Sciences de l'Homme: Secrétariat scientifique, 54 boulevard Raspail, 75270 Paris Cedex 06, France.
Isr. Aff. Israel affairs. (1353-7121). Frank Cass: Newbury House, 890-900 Eastern Avenue, Newbury Park, Ilford, Essex IG2 7HH, U.K.
Isr. Y.book. Hum. Rig. Israel yearbook on human rights. (0333-5925). Martinus Nijhoff: Spuiboulevard 50, 3311 GR Dordrecht, The Netherlands, in association with Tel Aviv University, Faculty of Law.
Iss. Stud. Issues & studies. (1013-2511). National Chengchi University, Institute of International Relations: 64 Wan Shou Road, Wenshan 116, Taipei, Taiwan.
J. Afr. Econ. Journal of African economies. (0963-8024). Oxford University Press: Great Clarendon Street, Oxford OX2 6DP, U.K.
J. Afr. Hist. Journal of African history. (0021-8537). Cambridge University Press: The Edinburgh Building, Shaftesbury Road, Cambridge CB2 2RU, U.K.
J. Afr. Law Journal of African law. (0221-8553). University of London, School of Oriental and African Studies: Thornhaugh Street, Russell Square, London WC1H 0XG, U.K.
J. Am. Stat. Ass. Journal of the American Statistical Association. (0162-1459). American Statistical Association: 1429 Duke Street, Alexandria, VA 22314-3415, U.S.A.
J. Am. Stud. Journal of American studies. (0021-8758). Cambridge University Press: The Edinburgh Building, Shaftesbury Road, Cambridge CB2 2RU, U.K.
J. App. Behav. Sc. Journal of applied behavioral science. (0021-8863). Sage Publications: 2455 Teller Road, Thousand Oaks, CA 91320, U.S.A., in association with NTL Institute.
J. App. Psy. Stud. Journal of applied psychoanalytic studies. (1521-1401). Kluwer Academic/Human Science Press: 233 Spring Street, New York, N.Y. 10013-1578, U.S.A.
J. Appl. Econ. Journal of applied econometrics. (0883-7252). John Wiley & Sons: Baffins Lane, Chichester, West Sussex PO19 1UD, U.K.
J. Appl. Psychol. Journal of applied psychology. (0021-9010). American Psychological Association: 750 First Street N.E., Washington DC 20002-4242, U.S.A.
J. Arch. Plan. Res. Journal of architectural and planning research. (0738-0895). Locke Science Publishing: P.O. Box 146413, Chicago, IL 60614, U.S.A.
J. As. Afr. S. Journal of Asian and African studies [Leiden]. (0021-9096). E.J. Brill: P.O. Box 9000, 2300 PA Leiden, The Netherlands.
J. As. Bus. Journal of Asian business. (1068-0055). Journal of Asian Business: Center for International Business Education, 914 Hill Street, University of Michigan Business School, Ann Arbor MI 48109-1234, U.S.A.
J. Behav. Educat. Journal of behavioral education. (1053-0819). Human Sciences Press: 233 Spring Street, New York, NY 10013-1578, U.S.A.

LISTE DES ABRÉVIATIONS UTILISÉES

J. Biosoc. Sc. Journal of biosocial science. (0021-9320). Biosocial Society: Department of Biological Anthropology, Downing Street, Cambridge CB2 3DZ, U.K.

J. Black Psychol. Journal of black psychology. (0095-7984). Sage Publications: 2455 Teller Road, Newbury Park, Thousand Oaks, CA 91320, U.S.A., in association with Association of Black Psychologists.

J. Busin. Ethics Journal of business ethics. (0167-4544). Kluwer Academic Publishers: P.O. Box 322, 3300 AH Dordrecht, The Netherlands / P.O. Box 358, Accord Station, Hingham, MA 02018-0358, U.S.A.

J. Ch. Philos. Journal of Chinese philosophy. Dialogue Publishing: P.O. Box 11071, Honolulu, HI 96826, U.S.A.

J. Child Fam. Stud. Journal of child and family studies. (1062-1024). Kluwer Academic/Human Sciences Press: 233 Spring Street, New York, NY 10013-1578, U.S.A.

J. Comm. Journal of communication. (0021-9916). Oxford University Press: 200 Madison Avenue, New York, NY 10016, U.S.A.

J. Comm. App. Soc. Psychol. Journal of community and applied social psychology. (1052-9284). John Wiley & Sons: Baffins Lane, Chichester, West Sussex PO19 1UD, U.K.

J. Comp. Fam. Stud. Journal of comparative family studies. (0047-2328). Journal of comparative family studies: Department of Sociology, University of Calgary, Calgary, Alberta, T2N 1N4 Canada.

J. Consum. Pol. Journal of consumer policy. (0342-5843). Kluwer Academic Publishers: P.O. Box 17, 3300 AA Dordrecht, The Netherlands.

J. Cont. Asia Journal of contemporary Asia. (0047-2336). Journal of Contemporary Asia Publishers: P.O. Box 592, Manila 1099, Philippines.

J. Contemp. Afr. St. Journal of contemporary African studies. (0258-9001). Carfax Publishing: P.O. Box 25, Abingdon, Oxfordshire OX14 3UE, U.K.

J. Contemp. Ethnog. Journal of contemporary ethnography. (0891-2416). Sage Publications: 2455 Teller Road, Newbury Park, Thousand Oaks, CA 91320, U.S.A.

J. Co-op. St. Journal of cooperative studies. (0961-5784). Society for Co-operative Studies: 18 Macclesfield Road, Buxton, Derbyshire SK17 9AH, U.K.

J. Cr-Cult. Gerontol. Journal of cross-cultural gerontology. (0169-3816). Kluwer Academic Publishers: P.O. Box 17, 3300 AA Dordrecht, The Netherlands.

J. Crim. Law Criminol. Journal of criminal law and criminology. (0091-4169). Northwestern University School of Law: 357 East Chicago Avenue, Chicago, IL 60611, U.S.A.

J. Dev. Econ. Journal of development economics. (0304-3878). Elsevier Science: PO Box 211, 1000 AE Amsterdam, The Netherlands.

J. Dev. Soc. Journal of developing societies. (0169-796X). E.J. Brill: P.O. Box 9000, 2300 PA Leiden, The Netherlands.

J. Dev. Stud. Journal of development studies. (0022-0388). Frank Cass: Newbury House, 890-900 Eastern Avenue, Newbury Park, Ilford, Essex IG2 7HH, U.K.

J. E. Eur. Man. Stud. Journal for East European management studies. (0949-6181). Rainer Hampp Verlag: Indbez, Meringerzeller Str. 16, D-86415 Mering, Germany.

J. Econ. Beh. Journal of economic behavior and organization. (0167-2681). Elsevier Science: PO Box 211, 1000 AE Amsterdam, The Netherlands.

J. Econ. Pers. Journal of economic perspectives. (0895-3309). American Economic Association: 2014 Broadway, Suite 305, Nashville, TN 37203, U.S.A.

J. Econ. Psyc. Journal of economic psychology. (0167-4870). Elsevier Science: PO Box 211, 1000 AE Amsterdam, The Netherlands, in association with International Association for Research in Economic Psychology: Egmontstraat 13, 1050 Brussels, Belgium.

J. Econ. Soc. Journal of economic and social measurement. (0747-9662). IOS Press: Van Diemenstraat 94, 1013 CN Amsterdam, The Netherlands.

LIST OF ABBREVIATIONS USED

J. Econ. Sur. Journal of economic surveys. (0950-0804). Blackwell Publishers: 108 Cowley Road, Oxford OX4 1JF, U.K.

J. Econ. Theo. Journal of economic theory. (0022-0531). Academic Press: 41 Tempelhof, B-8000 Brugge, Belgium.

J. Environ. Manag. Journal of environmental management. (0301-4797). Academic Press: 24-28 Oval Road, London NW1 7DX, U.K.

J. Environ. Plan. Manag. Journal of environmental planning and management. (0964-0568). Carfax Publishing: P.O. Box 25, Abingdon, Oxfordshire OX14 3UE, U.K.

J. Eth. Migr. St. Journal of ethnic and migration studies. (1369-183X). Carfax Publishing: P.O. Box 25, Abingdon, Oxfordshire OX14 3UE, U.K., in association with JEMS, CEMES: P.O. Box 4, Torpoint PL11 3YN, U.K.

J. Europe. Soc. Pol. Journal of European social policy. (0958-9287). Sage Publications: 6 Bonhill Street, London EC2A 4PU, U.K., in association with Journal of European Social Policy.

J. Exp. S. Psychol. Journal of experimental social psychology. (0022-1031). Academic Press: 1 East First Street, Duluth, MN 55802, U.S.A.

J. Fam. Hist. Journal of family history. (0363-1990). Sage Publications Inc.: 2455 Teller Road, Newbury Park, Thousand Oaks, CA 91320, U.S.A., in association with National Council on Family Relations.

J. Fam. Ther. Journal of family therapy. (0163-4445). Blackwell Publishers: 108 Cowley Road, Oxford OX4 1JF, U.K., in association with Association for Family Therapy: 6 Ileol, Seddon, Danescourt, Llandaff, Cardiff CF5 2QX, U.K.

J. Fam. Viol. Journal of family violence. (0885-7482). Plenum Publishing: 233 Spring Street, New York, NY 10013-1578, U.S.A.

J. Folk. Res. Journal of folklore research. (0737-7037). Indiana University Folklore Institute: 504 North Fess, Bloomington, IN 47405, U.S.A., in association with Folklore Institute.

J. For. Psy. Journal of forensic psychiatry. (0958-5184). Routledge: 11 New Fetter Lane, London EC4P 4EE, U.K.

J. Gender St. Journal of gender studies. (0958-9236). Carfax Publishing: P.O. Box 25, Abingdon, Oxfordshire OX14 3UE, U.K., in association with Hull Centre for Gender Studies, University of Hull: HU6 7RX, U.K.

J. Health Econ. Journal of health economics. (0167-6296). Elsevier Science: PO Box 211, 1000 AE Amsterdam, The Netherlands.

J. Health Polit. Pol. Law Journal of health politics, policy and law. (0361-6878). Duke University Press: Box 90660, Durham, NC 27708-0660, U.S.A.

J. Hist. Beh. Sci. Journal of the history of the behavioral sciences. (0022-5061). John Wiley & Sons: 605 Third Avenue, New York, NY 10158-0012, U.S.A.

J. Hist. Ideas. Journal of the history of ideas. (0022-5037). Johns Hopkins University Press: 2715 North Charles Street, Baltimore, MD 21218-4363, U.S.A.

J. Hist. Philos. Journal of the history of philosophy. (0022-5053). Journal of the History of Philosophy: Emory Univeristy, Department of Philosophy, Atlanta, GA 30322, U.S.A.

J. Hous. Ec. Journal of housing economics. (1051-1377). Academic Press: 6277 Sea Harbor Drive, Orlando, FL 32887-4900, U.S.A.

J. Hous. Res. Journal of housing research. (1052-7001). Fannie Mae Foundation: 4000 Wisconsin Avenue N.W., North Tower Suite One, Washington DC 20016-2804, U.S.A.

J. Hum. Dev. Journal of human development. (1464-9888). Carfax Publishing, Taylor & Francis Ltd: Rankine Road, Basingstoke, Hants, RG24 8PR, U.K., in association with United Nations Development Programme.

J. Hum. Nat. Sci. Journal of humanities and natural sciences. (0495-8012). Tokyo Keizai University: 1-7 Minami-cho, Kokubunji-shi, Tokyo 185-8502, Japan.

LISTE DES ABRÉVIATIONS UTILISÉES

J. Hum. Res. Journal of human resources. (0022-166X). University of Wisconsin Press: 2537 Daniels Street, Madison, WI 53718-6772, U.S.A.

J. Ind. Phil. Journal of Indian philosophy. (0022-1791). Kluwer Academic Publishers: P.O. Box 17, 3300 AA Dordrecht, The Netherlands.

J. Ind. Relat. Journal of industrial relations. (0022-1856). Journal of Industrial Relations: G.P.O. Box 4479, Sydney, NSW 2001, Australia.

J. Int. Bus. Stud. Journal of international business studies. (0047-2506). Academy of International Business: Tulane University, A.B. Freeman School of Business, New Orleans, LA 70118, U.S.A., in association with Georgetown University School of Business: 3240 Prospect Street, NW, Washington DC 20007, U.S.A.

J. Int. Dev. Journal of international development. (0954-1748). John Wiley & Sons: Baffins Lane, Chichester, West Sussex PO19 1UD, U.K., in association with Institute for Development Policy and Management: University of Manchester, Precinct Centre, Oxford Road, Manchester M13 9QS, U.K.

J. Interd. Stud. Journal of interdisciplinary studies: An international journal of interdisciplinary and interfaith dialogue. (0890-0132). Institute for Interdisciplinary Research: 2828 Third Street, Suite 11, Santa Monica, CA 90405-4150, U.S.A., in association with International Christian Studies Association.

J. Jap. Int. Ec. Journal of the Japanese and international economies. (0889-1583). Academic Press: 1 East First Street, Duluth, MN 55802, U.S.A., in association with Tokyo Center for Economic Research.

J. Labor Ec. Journal of labor economics. (0734-306X). University of Chicago Press: 5720 S. Woodlawn Avenue, Chicago, IL 60637, U.S.A., in association with Economics Research Center / NORC.

J. Labor Res. Journal of labor research. (0195-3613). George Mason University, Department of Economics: MSN 3G4, Fairfax, VA 22030-4444, U.S.A.

J. Lang. Soc. Psychol. Journal of language and social psychology. (0261-927X). Multilingual Matters: Bank House, 8a Hill Road, Clevedon, Avon BS21 7HH, U.K.

J. Lat. Am. St. Journal of Latin American studies. (0022-216X). Cambridge University Press: The Edinburgh Building, Shaftesbury Road, Cambridge CB2 2RU, U.K.

J. Law Soc. Journal of law and society. (0263-323X). Blackwell Publishers: 108 Cowley Road, Oxford OX4 1JF, U.K.

J. Man. Gov. Journal of management and governance. (1385-3457). Kluwer Academic Publishers: P.O. Box 322, 3300 AH Dordrecht, The Netherlands, in association with Academia Italiana di Economia Aziendale.

J. Manag. Stu. Journal of management studies. (0022-2380). Blackwell Publishers: 108 Cowley Road, Oxford OX4 1JF, U.K.

J. Marriage Fam. Journal of marriage and the family. (0022-2445). National Council on Family Relations: 3989 Central Avenue Northeast, Suite 550, Minneapolis, MN 55421-3921, U.S.A.

J. Math. Sociol. Journal of mathematical sociology. (0022-250X). Gordon and Breach Science Publishers: P.O. Box 786, Cooper Station, New York, NY 10276, U.S.A.

J. Medic. Philos. Journal of medicine and philosophy. (0360-5310). Swets & Zeitlinger Publishers: P.O. Box 825, 2160 SZ Lisse, The Netherlands.

J. Mod. Afr. S. Journal of modern African studies. (0022-278X). Cambridge University Press: The Edinburgh Building, Shaftesbury Road, Cambridge CB2 2RU, U.K.

J. Multiling. Journal of multilingual and multicultural development. (0143-4632). Multilingual Matters: Bank House, 8a Hill Road, Clevedon, Avon BS21 7HH, U.K.

J. N. African Stud. Journal of North African studies. (1362-9387). Frank Cass: Newbury House, 890-900 Eastern Avenue, Newbury Park, Ilford, Essex IG2 7HH, U.K.

LIST OF ABBREVIATIONS USED

J. N.W. Sem. Lang. Journal of northwest semitic languages. (0259-0131). University of Stellenbosch, Department of Ancient Studies: Stellenbosch 7600, South Africa.

J. Occup. Organ. Psychol. Journal of occupational and organizational psychology. (0963-1798). British Psychological Society: St. Andrews House, 48 Princess Road East, Leicester LE1 7DR, U.K.

J. Occupat. Rehabil. Journal of occupational rehabilitation. (1053-0487). Plenum Publishing: 233 Spring Street, New York, NY 10013-1578, U.S.A.

J. Peace Res. Journal of peace research. (0022-3433). Sage Publications: 6 Bonhill Street, London EC2A 4PU, U.K., in association with International Peace Research Institute, (PRIO): Fuglehauggata 11, 0260 Oslo 2, Norway.

J. Peasant Stud. Journal of peasant studies. (0306-6150). Frank Cass: Newbury House, 890-900 Eastern Avenue, Newbury Park, Ilford, Essex IG2 7HH, U.K.

J. Pers. Soc. Psychol. Journal of personality and social psychology. (0022-3514). American Psychological Association: 750 First Street N.E., Washington DC 20002-4242, U.S.A.

J. Personal. Journal of personality. (0022-3506). Blackwell Publishers: 350 Main Street, Malden, MA 02148, U.S.A.

J. Phil. Journal of philosophy. (0022-362X). Journal of Philosophy: 709 Philosophy Hall, Columbia University, New York, NY 10027, U.S.A.

J. Plan. Lit. Journal of planning literature. (0885-4122). Sage Publications: 2455 Teller Road, Newbury Park, Thousand Oaks, CA 91320, U.S.A.

J. Policy An. Journal of policy analysis and management. (0276-8739). John Wiley & Sons: 605 Third Avenue, New York, NY 10158-0012, U.S.A., in association with Association for Public Policy Analysis and Management.

J. Polit. Ec. Journal of political economy. (0022-3808). University of Chicago Press: 5720 S. Woodlawn Avenue, Chicago, IL 60637, U.S.A.

J. Polit. Phil. Journal of political philosophy. (0963-8016). Blackwell Publishers: 108 Cowley Road, Oxford OX4 1JF, U.K.

J. Pop. Cult. Journal of popular culture. (0022-3840). Popular Press: Bowling Green State University, Bowling Green, OH 43402, U.S.A., in association with Modern Language Association of America, Popular Literature Section / Midwest Modern Language Association, Folklore Section.

J. Pop. Ec. Journal of population economics. (0933-1433). Springer-Verlag: Tiergartenstrasse 17, D-69121 Heidelberg, Germany.

J. Prag. Journal of pragmatics. (0378-2166). Elsevier Science: PO Box 211, 1000 AE Amsterdam, The Netherlands.

J. Psychol. Journal of psychology. (0022-3980). Heldref Publications: 1319 Eighteenth Street N.W., Washington, DC 20036-1802, U.S.A.

J. R. Stat. Soc. Journal of the Royal Statistical Society: Series C (applied statistics). (0035-9254). Blackwell Publishers: 108 Cowley Road, Oxford OX4 1JF, U.K., in association with Royal Statistical Society: 25 Enford Street, London W1H 2BH, U.K.

J. Real Est. Finan. Econ. Journal of real estate finance and economics. (0895-5638). Kluwer Academic Publishers: P.O. Box 17, 3300 AA Dordrecht, The Netherlands.

J. Refug. S. Journal of refugee studies. (0951-6328). Oxford University Press: Great Clarendon Street, Oxford OX2 6DP, U.K., in association with University of Oxford, Refugee Studies Programme: Queen Elizabeth House, 21 St. Giles, Oxford OX1 3LA, U.K.

J. Reg. Sc. Journal of regional science. (0022-4146). Blackwell Publishers: 350 Main Street, Malden, MA 02148, U.S.A., in association with Department of Geography and Regional Development, University of Arizona: Harvill Building, Box 2, Tucson, AZ 85721, U.S.A.

J. Relig. Afr. Journal of religion in Africa. (0022-4200). E.J. Brill: P.O. Box 9000, 2300 PA Leiden, The Netherlands.

LISTE DES ABRÉVIATIONS UTILISÉES

J. Res. Crim. Delin. Journal of research in crime and delinquency. (0022-4278). Sage Publications: 2455 Teller Road, Newbury Park, Thousand Oaks, CA 91320, U.S.A., in association with National Council on Crime and Delinquency: 685 Market Street, Suite 620, San Francisco, CA. 94105, U.S.A.

J. Roy. Stat. Soc. A. Journal of the Royal Statistical Society: Series A (statistics in society). (0964-1998). Blackwell Publishers: 108 Cowley Road, Oxford OX4 1JF, U.K., in association with Royal Statistical Society: 12 Errol Street, London EC1Y 8LX, U.K.

J. Royal Anth. Inst. Journal of the Royal Anthropological Institute. (0025 1496). Royal Anthropological Institute of Great Britain and Ireland: 50 Fitzroy Street, London W1P 5HS, U.K.

J. S. Afr. Stud. Journal of Southern African studies. (0305-7070). Carfax Publishing: P.O. Box 25, Abingdon, Oxfordshire OX14 3UE, U.K.

J. Sci. S. Relig. Journal for the scientific study of religion. (0021-8294). Society for the Scientific Study of Religion: Brigham Young University, Department of Sociology, 875 SWKT, Provo, UT 84602, U.S.A.

J. SE. As. Stud. Journal of Southeast Asian studies. (0022-4634). Singapore University Press: Yusof Ishak House, 10 Kent Ridge Crescent, Singapore 119260.

J. Slav. Mil. Stud. Journal of Slavic military studies. (1351-8046). Frank Cass: Newbury House, 890-900 Eastern Avenue, Newbury Park, Ilford, Essex IG2 7HH, U.K.

J. Soc. Clin. Psychol. Journal of social and clinical psychology. (0736-7236). Guilford Publications: 72 Spring Street, New York, NY 10012, U.S.A.

J. Soc. Distr. Home. Journal of social distress and the homeless. (1053-0789). Human Sciences Press: 233 Spring Street, New York, NY 10013-1578, U.S.A.

J. Soc. Evol. Sys. Journal of social and evolutionary systems. (1061-7361). JAI Press: 100 Prospect Street, P.O. Box 811, Stamford, CT 06904-0811, U.S.A.

J. Soc. Issues Journal of social issues. (0022-4537). Plenum Publishing: 233 Spring Street, New York, NY 10013-1578, U.S.A., in association with Society for the Psychological Study of Social Issues.

J. Soc. Océan. Journal de la Société des Océanistes. (0300-953X). Société des oceanistes: Musée de l'homme, 75116 Paris, France.

J. Soc. Pol. Journal of social policy. (0047-2794). Cambridge University Press: The Edinburgh Building, Shaftesbury Road, Cambridge CB2 2RU, U.K., in association with Social Policy Association.

J. Soc. Work. Practice Journal of social work practice. (0265-0533). Carfax Publishing: P.O. Box 25, Abingdon, Oxfordshire OX14 3UE, U.K.

J. Strat. Stud. Journal of strategic studies. (0140-2390). Frank Cass: Newbury House, 890-900 Eastern Avenue, Newbury Park, Ilford, Essex IG2 7HH, U.K.

J. Struct. Learn. Int. Syst. Journal of structural learning and intelligent systems. (1027-1015). Gordon and Breach Publishers: P.O. Box 32160, Newark NJ 07102, U.S.A.

J. Theor. Pol. Journal of theoretical politics. (0951-6928) Sage Publications: 6 Bonhill Street, London EC2A 4PU, U.K.

J. Theory Soc. Behav. Journal for the theory of social behaviour. (0021-8308). Blackwell Publishers: 108 Cowley Road, Oxford OX4 1JF, U.K.

J. Third World Spect. Journal of the Third World spectrum. (1072-5040). Journal of the Third World spectrum: P.O. Box 44843, Washington DC 20026, U.S.A.

J. Third World St. Journal of Third World studies. (8755-3449). Association of Third World Studies: P.O. Box 1232, Americus, GA 31709, U.S.A.

J. Tokyo Keizai Uni. Journal of Tokyo Keizai University. (0493-4091). Tokyo Keizai Academy of Business Administration: Kokubunji-shi, Tokyo, Japan.

J. Urban Ec. Journal of urban economics. (0094-1190). Academic Press: 1 East First Street, Duluth, MN 55802, U.S.A.

LIST OF ABBREVIATIONS USED

J. Urban Hist. Journal of urban history. (0096-1442). Sage Publications: 2455 Teller Road, Newbury Park, Thousand Oaks, CA 91320, U.S.A.
J. W. Bus. Journal of world business. (1090-9516). JAI Press: 100 Prospect Street, P.O. Box 811, Stamford, CT 06904-0811, U.S.A.
J. World Hist. Journal of world history. (1045-6007). University of Hawaii Press: 2840 Kolowalu Street, Honolulu, HI 96822-1888, U.S.A., in association with World History Association: Department of History and Politics, Drexel University, Philadephia, PA 19104, U.S.A.
Jahr. Christ. Sozialwiss. Jahrbuch für christliche Sozialwissenschaften. (0075-2584). Verlag Regensberg: Daimlerweg 58, Postfach 6748-6749, 4400 Münster, Germany, in association with Universität Münster, Institut für Christliche Sozialwissenschaften.
Jahrb. N. St. Jahrbücher für Nationalökonomie und Statistik. (0021-4027). Lucius & Lucius Verlagsgesellschaft: Gerokstraße 51, 70184 Stuttgart, Germany.
Jahrb. Wirt. Gesch. Jahrbuch für Wirtschaftsgeschichte. (0075-2800). Akademie-Verlag Berlin.
Javnost Javnost = Public. (1318-3222). European Institute for Communication and Culture: P.O. Box 2511, 1001 Ljubljana, Slovenia.
Jew. Soc. Stud. Jewish social studies. (0021-6704). Conference on Jewish Social Studies.
Journ. Mod. Italian Studs. Journal of modern Italian studies. (1354-571X). Routledge: 11 New Fetter Lane, London EC4P 4EE, U.K.
Journ. Pol. Ideol. Journal of political ideologies. (1356-9317). Carfax Publishing: P.O. Box 25, Abingdon, Oxfordshire OX14 3UE, U.K.
Jpn. Forum Japan forum. (0955-5803). Routledge: 11 New Fetter Lane, London EC4P 4EE, U.K., in association with British Association for Japanese Studies.
Know. Tech. Pol. Knowledge, technology & policy. (0897-1986). Transaction Periodicals Consortium: Rutgers University, 35 Berrue Circle, Piscataway, NJ 08854-8042, U.S.A.
Kölner Z. Soz. Soz. Psy. Kölner Zeitschrift für Soziologie und Sozialpsychologie. (0340-0425). Westdeutscher Verlag: Postfach 5829, D-65048 Wiesbaden, Germany.
Kor. Foc. Korea focus. (1225-8113). Korea Foundation: Seocho P.O. Box 227, Seoul, South Korea.
Korea J. Korea journal. (0023-3900). Korean National Commission for Unesco: C.P.O. Box 64, Seoul, 100-022 Korea.
Korea Obs. Korea observer. (0023-3919). Institute of Korean Studies: C.P.O. Box 3410, Seoul 100-643, South Korea.
Labour Cap. Soc. Labour, capital and society = Travail, capital et société. (0706-1706). McGill University, Centre for Developing Area Studies: 3715 rue Peel, Montréal, Québec H3A 1X1, Canada.
Labour [Italy] Labour [Italy]. (1121-7081). Blackwell Publishers: 108 Cowley Road, Oxford OX4 1JF, U.K., in association with Fondazione Giacomo Brodolini: Via Torino 122, 00184 Rome, Italy.
Land Ref. Land Sett. Coop. Land reform, land settlement and cooperatives. (0251-1894). Food and Agriculture Organization: Viale delle Terme di Caracalla, 00100 Rome, Italy.
Lang. Prob. Lang. Plan. Language problems and language planning. (0272-2690). John Benjamins Publishing: P.O. Box 75577, Amsteldijk 44, 1070 Amsterdam, The Netherlands.
Lang. Soc. Language in society. (0047-4045). Cambridge University Press: 40 West 20th Street, New York, NY 10011-4211, U.S.A.
Lat. Am. Pers. Latin American perspectives. (0094-582X). Sage Publications: 2455 Teller Road, Newbury Park, Thousand Oaks, CA 91320, U.S.A.
Lat. Am. Res. R. Latin American research review. (0023-8791). Latin American Studies Association: Latin American Institute, 801 Yale NE, University of New Mexico, Albuquerque, NM 87131-1016, U.S.A.
Law Cont. Pr. Law and contemporary problems. (0023-9186). Duke University, School of Law: Room 006, Durham, NC 27706, U.S.A.

LISTE DES ABRÉVIATIONS UTILISÉES

Law Philos. Law and philosophy. (0167-5249). Kluwer Academic Publishers: P.O. Box 322, 3300 AH Dordrecht, The Netherlands.

Law Soc. Rev. Law and society review. (0023-9216). Law and Society Association: Hampshire House Box 33615, University of Massachusetts at Amherst, Amherst, MA 01003-3615, U.S.A.

Led. Erhv. Ledelse og Erhvervsøkonomi. (0902-3704). Foreningen af Danske Civiløkonomer (FDC).

Leviatán Leviatán. (0210-6337). Editorial Pablo Iglesias: Monte Esquinza 30, 28010 Madrid, Spain.

Loc. Env. Local environment. (1354-9839). Carfax Publishing: P.O. Box 25, Abingdon, Oxfordshire OX14 3UE, U.K.

Loc. Govt. St. Local government studies. (0300-3930). Frank Cass: Newbury House, 890-900 Eastern Avenue, Newbury Park, Ilford, Essex IG2 7HH, U.K.

Local. Ec. Local economy. (0269-0942). Routledge: 11 New Fetter Lane, London EC4P 4EE, in association with Local Economy Policy Unit: South Bank University, 103 Borough Road, London SE1 0AA, U.K.

Lud Lud. (0076-1435). Polskie Towarzystwo Ludoznawcze: ul. Szewska 36, 50-139 Wroclaw, Poland.

Maan. Econ. Maandschrift economie. (0013-0486). Maandschrift Economie: Postbus 90153, 5000 LE Tilburg, The Netherlands.

Mag. Tud. Magyar tudomány. (0025-0325). Akadémiai Kiadó: P.O. Box 245, H-1519 Budapest, Hungary, in association with Magyar Tudományos Akadémia: Roosevelt-tér 9, 1051 Budapest, Hungary.

Malay. J. Trop. Geogr. Malaysian journal of tropical geography. (0127-1474). University of Malaya: Kuala Lumpur, Malaysia.

Man India Man in India. (0025-1569). Sudarshan Press: Church Road, Ranchi 834 001 Bihar, India.

Mankind Q. Mankind quarterly. (0025-2344). Council for Social and Economic Studies: Suite C-2, 1133 13th Street N.W., Washington DC 20005-4297, U.S.A.

Market. Lett. Marketing letters. (0923-0645). Kluwer Academic Publishers: P.O. Box 322, 3300 AH Dordrecht, The Netherlands.

Marx. Blät Marxistische Blätter. (0542-7770). Neue Impulse Verlag: Hoffnungstraße 18, 45127 Essen, Germany.

Math. Soc. Sc. Mathematical social sciences. (0165-4896). Elsevier Science: PO Box 211, 1000 AE Amsterdam, The Netherlands.

Med. Anthr. Q. Medical anthropology quarterly. (0745-5194). American Anthropological Association: 4350 North Fairfax Drive, Suite 640, Arlington, VA 22203-1620, U.S.A., in association with Society for Medical Anthropology.

Med. Anthrop. Medical anthropology. (0145-9740). Harwood Academic Publishers: P.O. Box 90, Reading, Berkshire RG1 8JL, U.K.

Med. Conf. Surv. Medicine, conflict and survival. (1362-3699). Frank Cass: Newbury House, 890-900 Eastern Avenue, Newbury Park, Ilford, Essex IG2 7HH, U.K.

Med. Q. Mediation quarterly. (0739-4098). Jossey-Bass: 350 Sansome Street, 5th Floor, San Francisco, CA 94104, U.S.A.

Media Cult. Soc. Media culture and society. (0163-4437). Sage Publications: 6 Bonhill Street, London EC2A 4PU, U.K.

Megamot Megamot. (0025-8679). National Institute for Research in the Behavioural Sciences, Henrietta Szold Institute: 9 Colombia Street, Kiryat Menachem, Jerusalem 96583, Israel.

Men. Masc. Men and masculinities. (1097-184X). Sage Publications: 2455 Teller Road, Thousand Oaks, CA 91320, U.S.A.

Mens Maat. Mens en maatschappij. (0025-9454). Amsterdam University Press: Prinsengracht 747-751, 1017 JX Amsterdam.

Metapolítica Metapolítica. (1405-4558). Centro de Estudios de Política Comparada: Playa Eréndira 19, Barrio Santiago Sur, México D.F. 08800, Mexico.

LIST OF ABBREVIATIONS USED

Meth. Theo. Stud. Rel. Method and theory in the study of religion. (0943-3058). Mouton de Gruyter: Postfach 303421, 10728 Berlin, Germany, in association with North American Association for the Study of Religion.
Middle E. Stud. Middle Eastern studies. (0026-3206). Frank Cass: Newbury House, 890-900 Eastern Avenue, Newbury Park, Ilford, Essex IG2 7HH, U.K.
Migrac. Teme Migracijske teme. (0352-5600). Institute for Migration and Nationalities Studies: Trg Stjepana Radića 3, 10000 Zagreb, Croatia.
Milbank Q. Milbank quarterly. (0887-378X). Blackwell Publishers: 108 Cowley Road, Oxford OX4 1JF, U.K., in association with Milbank Memorial Fund.
Millennium Millennium. (0305-8298). Millennium Publishing Group: London School of Economics and Political Science, Houghton Street, London WC2A 2AE, U.K.
Mind Lang. Mind and language. (0268-1064). Blackwell Publishers: 108 Cowley Road, Oxford OX4 1JF, U.K.
Minerva Minerva. (0026-4695). Kluwer Academic Publishers: P.O. Box 17, 3300 AA Dordrecht, The Netherlands.
Mobilization Mobilization. (1086-671X). San Diego State University, Department of Sociology: San Diego, CA 92182-4423, U.S.A.
Mod. Asian S. Modern Asian studies. (0026-749X). Cambridge University Press: The Edinburgh Building, Shaftesbury Road, Cambridge CB2 2RU, U.K.
Mod. Chi. Modern China. (0097-7004). Sage Publications: 2455 Teller Road, Newbury Park, Thousand Oaks, CA 91320, U.S.A.
Mon. Ar. Mag. Mack. Monde arabe maghreb machrek. (1241-5294). Documentation Française: 29-31 quai Voltaire, 75340 Paris Cedex 07, France, in association with Fondation Nationale des Sciences Politiques, Centre d'Études et de Recherches Internationales, Section Monde arabe / Université de Paris, Centre d'Études de l'Orient, Paris, France.
Multilingua Multilingua. (0167-8507). Mouton de Gruyter: Postfach 303421, 10728 Berlin, Germany.
Nat. Inter. National interest. (0884-9382). National Affairs: 1112 16th Street N.W., Suite 530, Washington DC 20036, U.S.A.
Nat. Nat. Nations and nationalism. (1354-5078). Cambridge University Press: The Edinburgh Building, Shaftesbury Road, Cambridge CB2 2RU, U.K., in association with Association for the Study of Ethnicity and Nationalism.
Nat. Pap. Nationalities papers. (0090-5992). Carfax Publishing: P.O.Box 25, Abingdon, Oxfordshire OX14 3UE, U.K.
Nat. Resour. Nature and resources. (0028-0844). Parthenon Publishing Group: Casterton Hall, Carnforth, Lancashire LA6 2LA, U.K., in association with UNESCO: 7 place de Fontenoy, 75700 Paris, France.
Natl. Inst. Econ. R. National Institute economic review. (0027-9501). National Institute of Economic and Social Research: 2 Dean Trench Street, Smith Square, London SW1P 3HE, U.K.
Negot. J. Negotiation journal. (0748-4526). Plenum Publishing: 233 Spring Street, New York, NY 10013-1578, U.S.A.
Neth. J. Soc. Sci. Netherlands journal of social sciences = Sociologia Neerlandica. (0038-0172). Van Gorcum: P.O. Box 43, 9400 AA Assen, The Netherlands, in association with Netherlands' Sociological and Anthropological Society.
New Left R. New left review. (0028-6060). 6 Meard Street, London W1V 3HR, U.K.
New Med. & Soc. New media & society. (1461-4448). Sage Publications: 6 Bonhill Street, London EC2A 4PU, U.K.
New Persp. Turk. New perspectives on Turkey. (0896-6346). Simon's Rock College of Bard: 84 Alford Road, Great Barrington, MA 01230-9702, U.S.A.

LISTE DES ABRÉVIATIONS UTILISÉES

New Polit. New politics. (0028-6494). New Politics Associates: P.O. Box 98, Brooklyn, NY 11231, U.S.A.
New Tech. Work. Empl. New technology, work and employment. (0268-1072). Blackwell Publishers: 108 Cowley Road, Oxford OX4 1JF, U.K.
Nig. J. Econ. Soc. Stud. Nigerian journal of economic and social studies. (0029-0092). Nigerian Economic Society: University of Ibadan, Department of Economics, Ibadan, Nigeria.
Non. Manag. Leader. Nonprofit management and leadership. (1048-6682). Jossey-Bass: 350 Sansome Street, 5th Floor, San Francisco, CA 94104, U.S.A.
NORA NORA: Nordic journal of women's studies. (0803-8740). Taylor & Francis Ltd: PO Box 2562 Solli, N-0202 Oslo, Norway, in association with NORA, Department of Human Work Sciences, Division: Gender and Technology, Luleå University of Technology.
Nord. J. Afr. St. Nordic journal of African studies. (1235-4481). Helsinki University Press: Helsinki, Finland, in association with Nordic Association of African Studies: Uppsala, Sweden.
Nord. Ny. Nord nytt. (0008-1345). NEFA-Norden: Astrid Caspersen Institutfor Arkæologi og Etnologi, Københavns Universitetet Vandkunsten 5, DK-1470 Køvenhavn K.
N.Z. J. Hist. New Zealand journal of history. (0028-8322). University of Auckland, History Department: Private Bag 92019 Auckland, New Zealand.
Obshch. Nauki Sovrem. Obshchestvennye nauki i sovremennost'. (0869-0499). Nauka Publishers: Profsoiuznaia ul. 90, 117864 Moscow, Russia.
OECD Ec. Stud. OECD economic studies. (0255-0822). OECD: 2 rue André-Pascal, 75775 Paris Cedex 16, France.
Oral Hist. Oral history. (0143-0955). Oral History Society: Colchester, U.K.
Org. Environ. Organization and environment. (1086-0266). Sage Publications: P.O. Box 5084, Thousand Oaks, CA 91359, U.S.A.
Organ. Stud. Organization studies. (0170-8406). Walter de Gruyter GmbH + Co. KG: Genthiner Strasse 13, D-10785 Berlin, Germany, in association with European Group for Organizational Studies.
Organiz. Sci. Organization science. (1047-7039). Institute for Operations Research and the Management Sciences: 901 Elkridge Landing Road, Suite 400, Linthicum, MD 21090, U.S.A.
Organization Organization: the interdisciplinary journal of organization, theory and society. (1350-5084). Sage Publications: 6 Bonhill Street, London EC2A 4PU, U.K.
Orita Orita. (0030-5596). University of Ibadan: Department of Religious Studies, Ibadan, Nigeria.
Osteuropa Osteuropa. (0030-6428). Deutsche Verlags-Anstalt: Neckarstraße 121, Postfach 1060 12, D70190 Stuttgart, Germany, in association with Deutsche Gesellschaft für Osteuropakunde: Schaperstraße 30, 1000 Berlin 15, Germany.
Ox. Dev. Stud. Oxford development studies. (1360-0818). Carfax Publishing: P.O. Box 25, Abingdon, Oxfordshire OX14 3UE, U.K.
Ox. Econ. Pap. Oxford economic papers. (0030-7653). Oxford University Press: Great Clarendon Street, Oxford OX2 6DP, U.K.
Ox. R. Econ. Pol. Oxford review of economic policy. (0266-903X). Oxford University Press: Great Clarendon Street, Oxford OX2 6DP, U.K.
Pac. Stud. Pacific studies. (0275-3596). Institute for Polynesian Studies: Brigham Young University-Hawaii, 55-220 Kulanui Street, Box 1979, Laie, HI 96762, U.S.A.
Paideuma Paideuma. (0078-7809). Franz Steiner Verlag: Birkenwaldstraße 44, Postfach 10 15 26, D-7000 Stuttgart 1, Germany, in association with Frobenius Institut: Liebigstrasse 41, 6000 Frankfurt am Main, Germany.
Pak. Dev. R. Pakistan development review. (0030-9729). Pakistan Institute of Development Economics: P.O. Box 1091, Islamabad, Pakistan.

LIST OF ABBREVIATIONS USED

Pap. Reg. Sci. Papers in regional science. (0486-2902). Regional Science Association International: University of Illinois at Urbana-Champaign, 1-3 Observatory, 901 South Mathews Avenue, Urbana, IL 61801-3682, U.S.A.

Past Pres. Past and present. (0031-2746). Oxford University Press: Great Clarendon Street, Oxford OX2 6DP, U.K.

Patt. Prej. Patterns of prejudice. (0031-322X). Sage Publications: 6 Bonhill Street, London EC2A 4PU, U.K., in association with Institute of Jewish Affairs: 11 Hertford Street, London W1Y 7DX, U.K.

Peace Con. Peace and conflict. (1078-1919). Lawrence Erlbaum Associates Inc. Publishers: 10 Industrial Avenue, Mahwah NJ 07430-2262, U.S.A.

Péninsule Péninsule. Association Péninsule: 30 rue Boissière, 75116 Paris, France.

Pensée Pensée. (0031-4773). Institut de recherches marxistes: 64, boulevard Auguste-Blanqui, 75013 Paris, France.

Phil. Q. Cult. Soc. Philippine quarterly of culture and society. (0115-0243). University of San Carlos: Publications Office, Cebu City 6000, Philippines.

Phil. Stud. Philippine studies. (0031-7837). Ateneo de Manila University Press: P.O. Box 154, Manila 1099, Philippines.

Philos. E.W. Philosophy east and west. (0031-8221). University of Hawaii Press: 2840 Kolowalu Street, Honolulu, HI 96822-1888, U.S.A.

Philos. Pub. Philosophy & public affairs. (0048-3915). Princeton University Press: 41 William Street, Princeton, NJ 08540, U.S.A.

Philos. S. Sc. Philosophy of the social sciences. (0048-3931). Sage Publications: 2455 Teller Road, Newbury Park, Thousand Oaks, CA 91320, U.S.A.

Philos. Soc. Crit. Philosophy & social criticism. (0191-4537). Sage Publications: 6 Bonhill Street, London EC2A 4PU, U.K.

Plan. Pract. Res. Planning practice and research. (0269-7459). Carfax Publishing: P.O. Box 25, Abingdon, Oxfordshire OX14 3UE, U.K.

Plan. Th. Pract. Planning theory & practice. (1464-9357). Routledge, Taylor and Francis Ltd: 11 New Fetter Lane, London, EC4P 4EE, U.K., in association with Royal Town Planning Institute, 26 Portland Place, London, W1N 4BE.

Pol. et Soc. Politique et sociétés. (1203-9438). Société québécoise de science politique, Département de science politique: Université du Québec à Montréal, C.P. 8888, succ. A, Montreal, Quebec H3C 3P8, Canada.

Pol. Geogr. Political geography. (0962-6298). Elsevier Science: PO Box 211, 1000 AE Amsterdam, The Netherlands.

Pol. Misao Politička misao. (0032-3241). Fakultet političkih znanosti u Zagrebu: 10000 Zagreb, Lepušićeva 6, Croatia.

Pol. Res. Q. Political research quarterly. (1065-9129). University of Utah: Salt Lake City, UT 84112, U.S.A., in association with Western Political Science Association / Pacific Northwest Political Science Association / Southern California Political Science Association / Northern California Political Science Association.

Pol. Sci. Q. Political science quarterly. (0032-3195). Academy of Political Science: 475 Riverside Drive, Suite 1274, New York, NY 10115-1274, U.S.A.

Poli. Soc. Policing and society. (1043-9463). Harwood Academic Publishers: 270 8th Avenue, New York, NY 10011, U.S.A.

Policy Pol. Policy and politics. (0305-5736). The Policy Press, University of Bristol: 34 Tyndalls Park Road, Bristol BS8 1PY, U.K.

Policy St. Policy studies. (0144-2872). Carfax Publishing: P.O. Box 25, Abingdon, Oxfordshire OX14 3UE, U.K., in association with Policy Studies Institute.

Polis [Moscow] Polis [Moscow]. (0321-2017). Polis: Kolpachnyi per. 9a, 101831, Moscow, Russia.

LISTE DES ABRÉVIATIONS UTILISÉES

Polit. Int. Politique internationale. (0221-2781). Politique Internationale: 11 rue du Bois de Boulogne, 75116 Paris, France.
Polit. Life Sci. Politics and the life sciences. (0730-9384). Beech Tree Publishing: 10 Watford Close, Guildford, Surrey GU1 2EP, U.K., in association with Association for Politics and the Life Sciences: Lake Superior State University, 650 West Easterday Ave., Sault Ste Marie, MI 49783-1699, U.S.A.
Polit. Psych. Political psychology. (0162-895X). Blackwell Publishers: 350 Main Street, Malden, MA 02148, U.S.A., in association with International Society of Political Psychology.
Polit. Soc. Politics and society. (0032-3292). Sage Publications: 2455 Teller Road, Thousand Oaks, CA 91320, U.S.A.
Polit. Stud. Political studies. (0032-3217). Blackwell Publishers: 108 Cowley Road, Oxford OX4 1JF, U.K., in association with Political Studies Association of the United Kingdom: c/o Jack Hayward, Department of Politics, The University, Hull HU6 7RX, U.K.
Polit. Theory Political theory. (0090-5917). Sage Publications: 2455 Teller Road, Newbury Park, Thousand Oaks, CA 91320, U.S.A.
Politikon Politikon. (0258-9346). Political Science Association of South Africa / Staatkundige Vereniging van Suid-Afrika: Box 1041, Florida 1710, South Africa.
Politix Politix. (0295-2319). Presses de la Fondation nationale des sciences politiques: 44 rue du Four, 75006 Paris, France.
Pop. Dev. Rev. Population and development review. (0098-7921). Population Council: One Dag Hammarskjold Plaza, New York, NY 10017, U.S.A.
Pop. Res. Pol. R. Population research and policy review. (0167-5923). Kluwer Academic Publishers: P.O. Box 17, 3300 AA Dordrecht, The Netherlands.
Pop. Stud. Population studies [London]. (0032-4728). London School of Economics: Houghton Street, London WC2A 2AE, U.K.
Population Population. (0032-4663). Éditions de l'Institut national d'études démographiques: 133 boulevard Davout, 75980 Paris Cedex 20, France.
Post-Sov. Aff. Post-Soviet affairs. (1060-586X). V.H. Winston & Sons: 7961 Eastern Avenue, Silver Spring, MD 20910, U.S.A., in association with Joint Committee on Soviet Studies of the American Council of Learned Societies and the Social Science Research Council.
Prob. Am. Lat. Problèmes d'Amérique latine. (0765-1333). Documentation Française: 29-31 quai Voltaire, 75340 Paris Cedex 07, France.
Prof. Geogr. Professional geographer. (0033-0124). Association of American Geographers: 1710 16th Street N.W., Washington DC 20009, U.S.A.
Prog. H. Geog. Progress in human geography. (0309-1325). Edward Arnold: Mill Road, Dunton Green, Sevenoaks, Kent TN13 2YA, U.K.
Prog. Plan. Progress in planning. (0305-9006). Elsevier Science: PO Box 211, 1000 AE Amsterdam, The Netherlands.
Projet Projet. (0033-0884). Assas Éditions: 14 rue d'Assas, 75006 Paris, France.
Prokla Zeit. Krit. Soz. Prokla: Zeitschrift für kritische Sozialwissenschaft. (0342-8176). Verlag Westfälisches Dampfboot: Dorotheenstrasse 26a, D-48145 Münster, Germany, in association with Vereinigung zur Kritik der politischen Ökonomie e.V.: Postfach 100 529, D-10565 Berlin, Germany.
Prz. Pol. Przegląd polonijny. (0137-303X). Ossolineum, Publishing House of the Polish Academy of Sciences: Rynek 9, 50-106 Wroclaw, Poland, in association with Polska Akademia Nauk, Komitet Badania Polonii.
Prz. Soc. Przegląd socjologiczny. (0033-2356). Zakład Narodowy Imienia Ossolińskich: ul. Rynek 9, Wroclaw, Poland, in association with Łódzkie towarzystwo naukowe: ul Rewolucji 1905 roku 41/43, Łódz, Poland.
Przeg. Orient. Przegląd orientalistyczny. (0033-2283). Komitetu Badad'n Naukowych.

LIST OF ABBREVIATIONS USED

Psychol. B. Psychological bulletin. (0033-2909). American Psychological Association: 750 First Street N.E., Washington DC 20002-4242, U.S.A.
Psychol. Devel. Soc. Psychology and developing societies. (0971-3336). Sage Publications India: 32 M-Block Market, Greater Kailash I, New Delhi 110 048, India.
Psychol. Rev. Psychological review. (0033-295X). American Psychological Association: 750 First Street, NE, Washington, DC 20002-4242, U.S.A.
Psychol. Wom. Quart. Psychology of women quarterly. (0361-6843). Cambridge University Press: 40 West 20th Street, New York, NY 10011-4211, U.S.A., in association with American Psychological Association.
Publ. Adm. D. Public administration and development. (0271-2075). John Wiley & Sons: Baffins Lane, Chichester, West Sussex PO19 1UD, U.K., in association with Royal Institute of Public Administration: Regent's College, Inner Circle, Regent's Park, London NW1 4NS, U.K.
Publ. Admin. Public administration. (0033-3298). Blackwell Publishers: 108 Cowley Road, Oxford OX4 1JF, U.K., in association with Royal Institute for Public Administration: 3 Birdcage Walk, London SW1H 9JH, U.K.
Publ. Aff. Q. Public affairs quarterly. (0887-0373). Philosophy Documentation Center: Bowling Green State University, Bowling Green, OH 43403-0189, U.S.A.
Publ. Cult. Public culture. (0899-2363). Duke University Press: Box 90660, Durham, NC 27708-0660, S.A.
Publ. Inter. Public interest. (0033-3557). National Affairs: 1112 16th Street N.W., Suite 530, Washington DC 20036, U.S.A.
Publ. Opin. Q. Public opinion quarterly. (0033-362X). University of Chicago Press: 5720 S. Woodlawn Avenue, Chicago, IL 60637, U.S.A., in association with American Association for Public Opinion Research.
Publizistik Publizistik. (0033-4006). Westdeutscher Verlag: Postfach 5829, D-65048 Wiesbaden, Germany, in association with Deutsche Gesellschaft für Publizistik- und Kommunikationswissenschaft / Österreichische Gesellschaft für Publizistik- und Kommunikationswissenschaft / Schweizerische Gesellschaft für Kommunikations- und Medienwissenschaft: Martin-Legros-Straße 53, D-5300 Bonn 1, Germany.
Pun. & Soc. Punishment & society. (1462-4745). Sage Publications: 6 Bonhill Street, London EC2A 4PU, U.K.
Q. J. Econ. Quarterly journal of economics. (0033-5533). MIT Press: 55 Hayward Street, Cambridge, MA 02142, U.S.A., in association with Harvard University.
Quad. Sociol. Quaderni di sociologia. (0033-4952). Edizioni di Comunità: 20090 Segrate, Milan, Italy.
Qual. Inq. Qualitative inquiry. (1077-8004). Sage Publications: 2455 Teller Road, Newbury Park, Thousand Oaks, CA 91320, U.S.A.
R. African Lit. Research in African literatures. (0034-5210). Indiana University Press: 601 N. Morton, Bloomington, IN 47404-3797, U.S.A.
R. Droit Pub. Revue du droit public: et de la science politique en France et à l'étranger. (0035-2578). Librairie Générale de Droit et de Jurisprudence: Editions juridiques associées, 14 rue Pierre et Marie Curie, 75005 Paris, France.
R. Ec. Reg. Urb. Revue d'économie régionale et urbaine. (0180-7307). ADICUEER (Association des directeurs d'instituts et des centres universitaires d'études économiques régionales): 4 rue Michelet, 75006 Paris, France.
R. Econ. S. Review of economic studies. (0034-6527). Blackwell Publishers: 108 Cowley Road, Oxford OX4 1JF, U.K.
R. Econ. Soc. Revue économique et sociale. (0035-2772). Société d'études économiques et sociales: Bâtiment des facultés des sciences humaines (BFSH1), CH-1015 Lausanne-Dorigny, Switzerland.

LISTE DES ABRÉVIATIONS UTILISÉES

R. Et. Palest. Revue d'études palestiniennes. (0252-8290). Editions de Minuit: 7 rue Bernard-Palissy, 75006 Paris, France, in association with Institut des études palestiniennes / Fondation Diana Tamari Sabbagh.

R. Eur. Lat.am. Caribe European review of Latin American and Caribbean studies = Revista europea de estudios latinoamericanos y del Caribe. (0924-0608). CEDLA Edita: Keizersgracht 395-397, 1016 EK Amsterdam, The Netherlands, in association with CEDLA (Interuniversitair Centrum voor Studie en Documentatie van Latijns Amerika) / RILA (Royal Institute of Linguistics and Anthropology): Keizersgracht 395-397, 1016 Amsterdam, The Netherlands.

R. Fr. Sci. Pol. Revue française de science politique. (0035-2950). Fondation nationale des sciences politiques / Association française de science politique: 27 rue Saint-Guillaume, 75341 Paris, France.

R. Ind. Malay. Aff. Review of Indonesian and Malaysian affairs. (0034-6594). RIMA, University of Sydney, Department of Southeast Asian Studies: Sydney, NSW 2006, Australia.

R. Pol. Econ. Review of political economy. (0953-8259). Routledge, Taylor & Francis Ltd: 11 New Fetter Lane, London EC4P 4EE, U.K.

R. Soc. Econ. Review of social economy. (0034-6764). Routledge: 11 New Fetter Lane, London EC4P 4EE, U.K., in association with Association for Social Economics.

R. T-Monde Revue Tiers-Monde. (0040-7356). Presses Universitaires de France: 108 boulevard Saint-Germain, 75006 Paris, France, in association with Université de Paris, Institut d'étude du développement économique et social: 58 boulevard Arago, 75013 Paris, France.

R. Tun. Sci. Soc. Revue tunisienne des sciences sociales. (0035-4333). Université de Tunis, Centre d'Études et de Recherches Économiques et Sociales: 23 rue d'Espagne, 1000 Tunis, Tunisia.

Race Class Race and class. (0306-3968). Sage Publications Ltd: 6 Bonhill Street, London EC2A 4PU, U.K., in association with Institute of Race Relations: 2-6 Leeke Street, King's Cross Road, London WC1X 9HS, U.K.

Rad. Hist. R. Radical history review. (0163-6545). Cambridge University Press: 40 West 20th Street, New York, NY 10011-4211, U.S.A.

Rass. It. Soc. Rassegna italiana di sociologia. (0486-0349). Società editrice il Mulino: Strada Maggiore 37, 40125 Bologna, Italy.

Rat. Soc. Rationality and society. (1043-4631). Sage Publications: 6 Bonhill Street, London EC2A 4PU, U.K.

Rech. Cont. Recherches contemporaines. (1251-2419). Centre d'histoire de la France contemporaine: Département d'histoire, Université de paris X - Nanterre, 200, avenue de la République 92000 Nanterre Cedex, France.

Rech. Sociogr. Recherches sociographiques. (0034-1282). Recherches sociographiques: Département de Sociologie, Université Laval, Québec G1K 7P4, Canada.

Recher. Sociolog. Recherches sociologiques. (0771-677X). Université Catholique de Louvain: Place Montesquieu 1/1, B-1348 Louvain-la-Neuve, Belgium.

Reg. Stud. Regional studies. (0034-3404). Carfax Publishing: P.O. Box 25, Abingdon, Oxfordshire OX14 3UE, U.K., in association with Regional Studies Association.

Regio Regio. (0865 557X).

Relat. Int. Relations internationales. (0335-2013). Société d'études historiques des relations internationales contemporaines: Université de Paris I, Institut Pierre-Renouvin, 11 cité Véron, F 75018 Paris, France, in association with Institut universitaire de hautes études internationales: Geneva, Switzerland.

Religion Religion. (0048-721X). Academic Press: 24-28 Oval Road, London NW1 7DX, U.K.

R.E.M. Revue de l'économie meridionale. (0987-3813). Centre national de la recherche scientifique: 1 place Aristide Briand, 92195 Meudon Cedex, France, in association with Université de Montpellier, Faculté de droit et des sciences économiques, Centre regional de la productivité et des études économiques: 39 rue de l'Université, 34060 Montpellier Cedex, France.

LIST OF ABBREVIATIONS USED

Reprod. Health Mat. Reproductive health matters. (0968-8080). Blackwell Science Ltd: Osney Mead, Oxford OX2 0EL, U.K.

Res. Educ. Research in education. (0034-5237). Manchester University Press: Oxford Road, Manchester M13 9NR, U.K.

Res. Soc. Work Research in the sociology of work. (0277-2833). JAI Press: 100 Prospect Street, P.O. Box 811, Stamford, CT 06904-0811, U.S.A.

Rethink. Marx. Rethinking Marxism. (0893-5696). Guilford Publications: 72 Spring Street, New York, NY 10012, U.S.A., in association with Association for Economic and Social Analysis: University of Massachusetts at Amhurst, Amhurst, MA, U.S.A.

Rev. Afr. Pol. Ec. Review of African political economy. (0305-6244). Carfax Publishing: P.O. Box 25, Abingdon, Oxfordshire OX14 3UE, U.K., in association with ROAPE: Regency House, 75-77 St. Mary's Road, Sheffield S2 4AN, U.K.

Rev. Bl. Pol. Ec. Review of black political economy. (0034-6446). Transaction Publishers: Rutgers University, New Brunswick, NJ 08903, U.S.A., in association with National Economic Association / Clark Atlanta University, Southern Center for Studies in Public Policy: 240 Brawley Drive S.W., Atlanta, GA 30314, U.S.A.

Rev. Bras. Ciên. Soc. Revista brasileira de ciências sociais. (0102-6909). Editora Revista dos Tribunais: Rua Conde do Pinhal 78, 01501 São Paulo, SP. Brazil, in association with Associação Nacional de Pós-Graduação e Pesquisa em Ciências Sociais: Largo de São Francisco, 01-4° andar, s/408 Centro, Rio de Janeiro RJ., Cep 20051, Brazil.

Rev. Cien. Soc. Revista de ciencias sociales. (0034-7817). Universidad de Puerto Rico, Facultad de Ciencias Sociales, Centro de Investigaciones Sociales: Rio Piedras, Puerto Rico 00931.

Rev. de l'OFCE Revue de l'OFCE: Observations et diagnostics économiques. (0751-6614). Observatoire Français des Conjonctures Économiques: 69 quai d'Orsay, 75007 Paris, France.

Rev. Econ. St. Review of economics and statistics. (0034-6535). MIT Press: Cambridge, Massachusetts 02142, U.S.A., in association with Harvard University.

Rev. Ét. Comp. Est-Ouest Revue d'études comparatives est-ouest. (0338-0599). Centre national de la recherche scientifique: 1 place Aristide Briand, 92195 Meudon Cedex, France, in association with Institut de recherches juridiques comparatives du C.N.R.S., Centre d'études des pays socialistes / Économie et techniques de planification des pays de l'est.

Rev. Fom. Soc. Revista de fomento social. (0015-6043). CESI-JESPRE: Pablo Aranda 3, 28006 Madrid, Spain, in association with INSA-ETEA: Escritor Castilla Aguayo 4, Apartado 439, 14004 Cordoba, Spain.

Rev. Fr. Soc. Revue française de sociologie. (0035-2969). Éditions Ophrys: B.P. 87, 05003 Gap Cx, France, in association with Institut de recherche sur les sociétés contemporaines: 59-61 rue Pouchet, 75017 Paris, France.

Rev. Int. Droit C. Revue internationale de droit comparé. (0035-3337). Société de legislation comparée: 28 rue Saint-Guillaume, 75007 Paris, France.

Rev. Int. Sci. Ec. Com. Rivista internazionale di scienze economiche e commerciali. (0035-6751). Casa Editrice Dott. Antonio Milani: Via Jappelli 5, 315121 Padua, Italy, in association with Università Commerciale Luigi Bocconi.

Rev. Int. Stud. Review of international studies. (0260-2105). Cambridge University Press: The Edinburgh Building, Shaftesbury Road, Cambridge CB2 2RU, U.K., in association with British International Studies Association.

Rev. Latin. Estud. Avanz. Revista latinoamericana de estudios avanzados. (1316-0486). RELEA: Aparado de Correo 50520, Caracas 1050-A, Venezuela.

Rev. Mexicana Cien. Pol. Revista mexicana de ciencias politicas y sociales. (0185-1918). Universidad Nacional Autónoma de México, Facultad de Ciencias Políticas y Sociales: Ciudad Universitaria, Coyoacán, 04510 México D.F., Mexico.

Rev. Parag. Sociol. Revista paraguaya de sociología. Centro Paraguayo de Estudios Sociológicos: Eligio Ayala 973, Casilla no.2.157, Asunción, Paraguay.

LISTE DES ABRÉVIATIONS UTILISÉES

Rev. Plan. Desar. Revista de planeación y desarrollo. (0034-8686). Departamento Nacional de Planeación: Calle 26 No. 13-19 Piso 16 Biblioteca, Bogotá, Colombia.

Rev. Sci. Crim. D. P. Revue de science criminelle et de droit pénal comparé. (0035-1733). Éditions Sirey: 22 rue Soufflot, 75005 Paris, France, in association with Université Panthéon-Assas (Paris 2), Institut de Droit Comparé, Section de Science Criminelle.

Rev. Soc. Polit. Revista de sociologia e politíca. (0104-4478). Universidade Federal do Paraná, Departamento de Ciencias Sociais: Rua General Carneiro 460 sala 912, 80060-150, Curitiba PR, Brazil.

Rev. Univ. EAFIT Revista Universidad EAFIT. (0120-033X). Universidad EAFIT: Escuela de Administración y Finanzas y Tecnologias, Carrera 49 no. 7 Sur-50, Apartado Aéreo 3300, Medellín, Colombia.

Rig Rig. (0035-5267). Föreningen för svensk kulturhistoria: Nordiska museet, 11521 Stockholm, Sweden.

Rir. To Ho. Riron to hoho = Sociological theory and methods. (0913-1442). Japanese Association for Mathematical Sociology: c/o Yukio Shirakura, Hokkaido University, Faculty of Literature, Sapporo 060, Japan.

Riv. Dir. Finan. Sci. Fin. Rivista di diritto finanziario e scienza delle finanze. (0035-6131). A. Giuffrè Editore: Via Busto Arsizio 40, Milan 20151, Italy, in association with Dipartimento di Economia pubblica territoriale dell'Università / Camera di Commercio di Pavia / Università di Roma, Facoltà di Giurisprudenza, Istituto di diritto pubblico: Strada Nuova 65, 27100 Pavia, Italy.

Riv. Int. Sci. Soc. Rivista internazionale di scienze sociali. (0035-676X). Università Cattolica del Sacro Cuore: Vita e Pensiero, Largo A. Gemelli, 1-1 20123 Milan, Italy.

Rom. Stud. Romani studies. (1528-0748). Gypsy Lore Society: 5607 Greenleaf Road, Cheverly, MD 20785, U.S.A.

Rural Hist. Rural history: Economy, society, culture. (0956-7933). Cambridge University Press: The Edinburgh Building, Shaftesbury Road, Cambridge CB2 2RU, U.K.

Rural Sociol. Rural sociology. (0036-0112). Department of Sociology: Wilson Hall, Montana State University, Bozeman, MT 59715, U.S.A., in association with Rural Sociological Society: Texas A & M University, College Station, TX, U.S.A.

Rural Stud. Études rurales. (0014-2182). Éditions de l'École des hautes études en sciences sociales: 54 boulevard Raspail, 75006 Paris, France, in association with Laboratoire d'anthropologie sociale: Collège de France, 52 rue du Cardinal Lemoine, 75005 Paris, France.

Rus. Pol. Law Russian politics and law. (1061-1940). M.E. Sharpe: 80 Business Park Drive, Armonk, NY 10504, U.S.A.

S. Afr. Geogr. J. South African geographical journal = Suid-Afrikaanse geografiese tydskrif. (0373-6245). South African Geographical Society = Suid-Afrikaanse Geografiese Vereniging: Department of Geography and Environmental Studies, University of the Witwatersrand, P.O. Wits 2050, South Africa.

S. Afr. J. Int. Affairs South African journal of international affairs. (1022-0461). South African Institute of International Affairs: P.O. Box 31596, Braamfontein, 2017 Johannesburg, South Africa.

S. Asian Surv. South Asian survey. (0971-5231). Sage Publications India: 32 M-Block Market, Greater Kailash I, New Delhi 110 048, India, in association with Indian Council for South Asian Cooperation.

S. E. Asian R. South East Asian review. Centre for Southeast Asian Studies.

S. Econ. J. Southern economic journal. (0038-4038). Southern Economic Association: College of Business Administration, Oklahoma State University, Stillwater, OK 74078, U.S.A.

S. Euro. Soc. Pol. South European society & politics. (1360-8746). Frank Cass: Newbury House, 890-900 Eastern Avenue, Newbury Park, Ilford, Essex IG2 7HH, U.K.

SAIS R. SAIS review. (0036-0777). Johns Hopkins University, Paul H. Nitze School of Advanced International Studies: 1619 Massachusetts Avenue N.W., Washington DC 20036, U.S.A.

LIST OF ABBREVIATIONS USED

San. Ment. Qué Santé mentale au Québec. (0383-6320). Revue Santé mentale au Québec: C.P. 548, Succ. Places d'Armes, Montréal, Québec H2Y 3H3, Canada.

Sav. Develop. Savings and development. (0393-4551). Giordano Dell'Amore Foundation: Via S. Vigilio 10, 20142 Milan, Italy.

Scan. J. Old. Test. Scandinavian journal of the Old Testament. (0901-8328). DK-8000 Aarhus C., Denmark: Aarhus University Press, in association with University of Aarhus, Department of Old Testament Studies.

Scand. J. Dev. Alt. A. Stud. Scandinavian journal of development alternatives and area studies. (0280-2791). Scandinavian Journal of Development Alternatives: P.O. Box 7444, 103 91 Stockholm, Sweden.

Sch. Field School field. (0353-6807). Slovene Society of Researchers in the School Field: Editorial Office, The School Field, Mestni trg 17, 1000 Ljubljana, Slovenia.

Schweiz. Z. Soziologie Schweizerische Zeitschrift für Soziologie = Revue suisse de sociologie. (0379-3664). Seismo Press: P.O. Box 313, CH-8028 Zürich, Switzerland, in association with Université de Genève.

Sci. Pub. Pol. Science and public policy. (0302-3427). Beech Tree Publishing: 10 Watford Close, Guildford, Surrey GU1 2EP, U.K., in association with International Science Policy Foundation: 12 Whitehall, London SW1Y 2DY, U.K.

Sci. Soc. Science and society. (0036-8237). Guilford Publications: 72 Spring Street, New York, NY 10012, U.S.A.

Scot. J. Poli. Econ. Scottish journal of political economy. (0036-9292). Blackwell Publishers: 108 Cowley Road, Oxford OX4 1JF, U.K., in association with Scottish Economic Society: Division of Economics, University of Stirling, Stirling FK9 4LA, U.K.

Scr. Ethn. Scripta ethnologica. (0325-6669). Centro Argentino de Etnología Americana: Consejo Nacional de Investigaciones Cientificas y Tecnicas, Av. de Mayo 1437 1 "A" (1085), Buenos Aires, Argentina.

S.E. Asia Res. South East Asia research. (0967-828X). In Print, in association with School of Oriental and African Studies.

Secur. Dial. Security dialogue. (0967-0106). Sage Publications: 6 Bonhill Street, London EC2A 4PU, U.K.

Semiotica Semiotica. (0037-1998). Walter de Gruyter: Genthiner Strasse 13, D-10785 Berlin, Germany, in association with International Association for Semiotic Studies.

Signs Signs. (0097-9740). University of Chicago Press: 5720 S. Woodlawn Avenue, Chicago, IL 60637, U.S.A.

Sikh Rev. Sikh review. (0037-5123). Sikh Cultural Centre: 116 Karnani Mansion, 25A Park Street, Calcutta 700 016, India.

Sing. J. Trop. Geogr. Singapore journal of tropical geography. (0129-7619). Blackwell Publishers: 108 Cowley Road, Oxford OX4 1JF, U.K., in association with National University of Singapore: Department of Geography, Kent Ridge, Republic of Singapore 0511.

Slavic R. Slavic review. (0037-6779). American Association for the Advancement of Slavic Studies: 128 Encina Commons, Stanford University, Stanford, CA 94305, U.S.A.

Slov. Národop. Slovensky národopis. (0037-7023). Slovak Academic Press: P.O. Box 57, Nám. Svobody 6, 81005 Bratislava, Slovakia, in association with Slovenska Akademia Vied, Narodopisny Ustav.

Slovo Slovo. (0954-6839). University of London, School of Slavonic and East European Studies: Senate House, Malet Street, London WC1E 7HU, U.K.

Soc. Act. Social action [New Delhi]. (0037-7627). Indian Social Institute, Social Action Trust: Lodi Road, New Delhi 130003, India.

Soc. Anal. [Adelaide] Social analysis [Adelaide]. (0155-977X). University of Adelaide, Department of Anthropology: G.P.O. Box 498, Adelaide 5A 5001, Australia.

LISTE DES ABRÉVIATIONS UTILISÉES

Soc. and. Anim. Society & Animals. (1063-1119). White Horse Press: 10 High Street, Knapwell, Cambridge, CB3 8NR, U.K.

Soc. Anthrop. Social anthropology. (0964-0282). Cambridge University Press: The Edinburgh Building, Shaftesbury Road, Cambridge CB2 2RU, U.K.

Soc. Čas. Sociologický časopis. (0038-0288). Institute of Sociology of the Czech Academy of Sciences: Jilská 1, 110 00 Praha 1, Czech Republic.

Soc. Cogn. Social cognition. (0278-016X). Guilford Publications: 72 Spring Street, New York, NY 10012, U.S.A.

Soc. Compass Social compass. (0037-7686). Sage Publications: 6 Bonhill Street, London EC2A 4PU, U.K., in association with International Federation of Institutes for Social and Socio-Religious Research (FERES) / Centre de Recherches Socio-Religieuses: Université Catholique de Louvain, Belgium.

Soc. Econ. S. Social and economic studies. (0037-7651). University of the West Indies, Institute of Social and Economic Research: Mona, Kingston 7, Jamaica.

Soc. Forc. Social forces. (0037-7732). University of North Carolina Press: P.O. Box 2288, Chapel Hill, NC 27515-2288, U.S.A., in association with University of North Carolina, Department of Sociology: 168 Hamilton Hall, University of North Carolina, Chapel Hill, NC 27599-3210, U.S.A.

Soc. Hist. Social history. (0307-1022). Routledge: 11 New Fetter Lane, London EC4P 4EE, U.K.

Soc. Ident. Social identities: Journal for the study of race, nation and culture. (1350-4630). Carfax Publishing: P.O. Box 25, Abingdon, Oxfordshire OX14 3UE, U.K.

Soc. Just. Social justice. (0094-7571). Global Options: P.O. Box 40601, San Francisco, CA 94140, U.S.A.

Soc. Leg. Stud. Social and legal studies. (0964-6639). Sage Publications: 6 Bonhill Street, London EC2A 4PU, U.K.

Soc. Networks Social networks. (0378-8733). Elsevier Science: PO Box 211, 1000 AE Amsterdam, The Netherlands, in association with International Network for Social Network Analysis (INSNA).

Soc. Philos. Pol. Social philosophy & policy. (0265-0525). Cambridge University Press: The Edinburgh Building, Shaftesbury Road, Cambridge CB2 2RU, U.K.

Soc. Pol. Admin. Social policy and administration. (0144-5596). Blackwell Publishers: 108 Cowley Road, Oxford OX4 1JF, U.K.

Soc. Polit. Social politics: international studies in gender, state and society. (1072-4745). Oxford University Press, 2001 Evans Rd. Cary, NC 27513.

Soc. Prob. Social problems. (0037-7791). University of California Press Journals: 2120 Berkeley Way, Berkeley, CA 94720-5812, U.S.A., in association with Society for the Study of Social Problems.

Soc. Sci. China Social sciences in China. (0252-9203). China Social Sciences Publishing House: Jia 158 Gulouxidajie, Beijing 100720, China, in association with Chinese Academy of Social Science.

Soc. Sci. Hist. Social science history. (0145-5532). Duke University Press: Box 90660, Durham, NC 27708-0660, U.S.A., in association with Social Science History Association.

Soc. Sci. Info. Social science information. (0539-0184). Sage Publications: 6 Bonhill Street, London EC2A 4PU, U.K., in association with Maison des sciences de l'homme / École des hautes études en sciences sociales.

Soc. Sci. Jap. J. Social science Japan journal. (1369-1465). Oxford University Press: Great Clarendon Street, Oxford OX2 6DP, U.K., in association with Institute of Social Science, University of Tokyo.

Soc. Sci. Med. Social science & medicine. (0277-9536). Elsevier Science: PO Box 211, 1000 AE Amsterdam, The Netherlands.

Soc. Sci. Q. Social science quarterly. (0038-4941). University of Texas Press: P.O. Box 7819, Austin, TX 78713-7819, U.S.A., in association with Southwestern Social Science Association: W.C. Hogg Building, The University of Texas at Austin, Austin, TX 78713, U.S.A.

LIST OF ABBREVIATIONS USED

Soc. Sci. R. Social science research. (0049-089X). Academic Press: 6277 Sea Harbor Drive, Orlando, FL 32887-4900.
Soc. Sec. Social security: Journal of welfare and social security studies. (0334-231X). National Insurance Institute: 13 Weizman Avenue, Jerusalem 91909, Israel.
Soc. Sem. Social semiotics. (1035-0330). Carfax Publishing: P.O. Box 25, Abingdon, Oxfordshire OX14 3UE, U.K.
Soc. Stud. Sci. Social studies of science. (0306-3127). Sage Publications: 6 Bonhill Street, London EC2A 4PU, U.K.
Social. Int. Sociologia internationalis. (0038-0164). Duncker & Humblot: Postfach 410329, Dietrich-Schäfer-Weg 9, 1000 Berlin 41, Germany.
Society Society. (0147-2011). Transaction Publishers: Rutgers University, New Brunswick, NJ 08903, U.S.A.
Socio. Econ. Socio-economic planning sciences. (0038-0121). Elsevier Science: PO Box 211, 1000 AE Amsterdam, The Netherlands.
Sociol. Bul. Sociological bulletin. (0038-0229). Indian Sociological Society: Institute of Social Sciences, 8 Nelson Mandela Road, Vasant Kunj, New Delhi 110070, India.
Sociol. For. Sociological forum. (0884-8971). Plenum Publishing: 233 Spring Street, New York, NY 10013-1578, U.S.A.
Sociol. Gids Sociologische gids. (0038-0334). Boom: Postbus 1058, 7940 KB Meppel, The Netherlands.
Sociol. Lav. Sociologia del lavoro. Franco Angeli Editore: Viale Monza 106, 20127 Milan, Italy, in association with Università di Bologna, Centro Internazionale di Documentazione e Studi Sociologico Sui Problemi del Lavoro: Casella postale 413, 40100 Bologna, Italy.
Sociol. Meth. Sociological methods and research. (0049-1241). Sage Publications: 2455 Teller Road, Newbury Park, Thousand Oaks, CA 91320, U.S.A.
Sociol. Q. Sociological quarterly. (0038-0253). JAI Press: 100 Prospect Street, P.O. Box 811, Stamford, CT 06904-0811, U.S.A.
Sociol. Res. Online Sociological research online. (1360-7804). University of Surrey: Guildford, U.K.
Sociol. Rev. Sociological review. (0038-0261). Blackwell Publishers: 108 Cowley Road, Oxford OX4 1JF, U.K., in association with University of Keele: Keele, Staffordshire ST5 5BG, U.K.
Sociol. Rur. Sociologia ruralis. (0038-0199). Blackwell Publishers Ltd: 108 Cowley Road, Oxford, OX4 IJF, U.K., in association with European Society for Rural Sociology / Société Européenne de Sociologie Rurale / Europäischen Gesellschaft für Land- und Agrarsoziologie: c/o Pavel Uttitz (Secretary Treasurer), Forschungsgesellschaft für Agrarpolitik und Agrarsoziologie e.V., Meckenheimer Allee 125, 5300 Bonn 1, Germany.
Sociol. Theory Sociological theory. (0735-2751). Blackwell Publishers: 350 Main Street, Malden, MA 02148, U.S.A., in association with American Sociological Association: 1722 N. Street, N.W., Washington DC 20036, U.S.A.
Sociol. Trav. Sociologie du travail. (0038-0296). Dunod.
Sociologia [Brat.] Sociologia [Bratislava] = Sociology [Bratislava]. (0049-1225). Redakcia Časopisu Sociológia: Klemensova 19, 813 64 Bratislava 1, Slovakia, in association with Slovak Academy of Sciences, Institute of Sociology.
Sociologia [Rome] Sociologia [Rome]. (0038-0156). Istituto Luigi Sturzo: Via delle Coppelle 35, 00186 Rome, Italy.
Sociologus Sociologus. (0038-0377). Duncker & Humblot: Postfach 410329, Dietrich-Schäfer-Weg 9, 1000 Berlin 41, Germany.
Sociology Sociology [U.K.]. (0038-0385). Cambridge University Press: The Edinburgh Building, Shaftesbury Road, Cambridge CB2 2RU, U.K.
SOJOURN SOJOURN: Journal of social issues in Southeast Asia. (0217-9520). Institute of Southeast Asian Studies: 30 Heng Mui Keng Terrace, Pasir Panjang, Singapore 119614, Singapore.

LISTE DES ABRÉVIATIONS UTILISÉES

Sot. Issle. Sotsiologicheskie issledovaniia (sotsis). (0132-1625). Nauka Publishers: 121099 Moscow, G-99, Shubinskii per., 6, Russia.
Soz. Welt. Soziale Welt. (0038-6073). Nomos Verlagsgesellschaft: Waldseestraße 3-5, 76530 Baden-Baden, Germany, in association with Arbeitsgemeinschaft sozialwissenschaftlicher Institute: Universität Bamberg, Feldkirchenstraße 21, 8600 Bamberg, Germany.
Spa. & Pol. Space & polity. (1356-2576). Carfax Publishing: P.O. Box 25, Abingdon, Oxfordshire OX14.
Sri Lanka J. Soc. Sci. Sri Lanka journal of social sciences. (0258-9710). Natural Resources, Energy & Science Authority of Sri Lanka: 47/5 Maitland Place, Colombo 7, Sri Lanka.
St. Ess. Beh. Sc. Phil. Studies and essays — behavioral sciences and philosophy. (1342-4262). The Faculty of Letters, Kanazawa University, Kanazawa, 920-1192 Japan.
St. Philos. Educ. Studies in philosophy and education. (0039-3746). Kluwer Academic Publishers: P.O. Box 322, 3300 AH Dordrecht, The Netherlands.
St. Pol. Soc. Storia politica società. Associazione Storia Politica Società: Via Principe Amedeo, 12, 10123, Torino, Italy.
Statistica Statistica. (0039-0380). Cooperitiva Libraria Universitaria Editrice.
Strat. Manage. J. Strategic management journal. (0143-2095). John Wiley & Sons: Baffins Lane, Chichester, West Sussex PO19 1UD, U.K.
Stud. Afr. Studia africana. (1130-5703). Centre d'Estudis Africans: Barcelona, Spain.
Stud. Comp. Int. Dev. Studies in comparative international development. (0039-3606). Transaction Publishers: Rutgers University, New Brunswick, NJ 08903, U.S.A.
Stud. Demogr. Studia demograficzne. (0039-3134). Panstwowe Wydawnictwo Naukowe: Miodowa 10, 00-251 Warsaw, Poland, in association with Polska Akademia Nauk, Komitet Nauk Demograficznych.
Stud. East. Eur. Th. Studies in East European thought. (0925-9392). Kluwer Academic Publishers: P.O. Box 17, 3300 AA Dordrecht, The Netherlands.
Stud. Hist. Phil. Mod. Phys. Studies in history and philosophy of modern physics. (1355-2198). Elsevier Science: PO Box 211, 1000 AE Amsterdam, The Netherlands.
Stud. Hist. Phil. Sci. Studies in history and philosophy of science. (0039-3681). Elsevier Science: PO Box 211, 1000 AE Amsterdam, The Netherlands.
Stud. Ling. Sci. Studies in the linguistic sciences. (0049-2388) University of Illinois at Urbana-Champaign, Department of Linguistics: 4088 Foreign Languages Building MC-168, 707 S. Mathews Avenue, Urbana, IL 61801-3625, U.S.A.
Stud. Pol. Ec. Studies in political economy. (0707-8552). Studies in Political Economy: P.O. Box 4729, Station E, Ottawa, Ontario K1S 5H9, Canada.
Stud. Socj. Studia socjologiczne. (0039-3371). Wydawnictwo Instytut Filozofii i Socjologii PAN: pok 233 (Palac Staszica), Nowy Swiat 72, 00-330, Warsaw, Poland.
Svobod. Mysl' Svobodnaia mysl'. (0869-4435). Izdatel'stvo "Press": ul. Pravdy 24, 125865 Moscow, Russia.
Syst. Res. Behav. Sci. Systems research and behavioral science. (1092-7026). John Wiley & Sons: Baffins Lane, Chichester, West Sussex PO19 1UD, U.K., in association with International Federation for Systems Research.
Tareas Tareas. (0494-7061). Centro de Estudios Latinoamericanos "Justo Arosemena".
Te reo Te reo. (0494-8440). Linguistic Society of New Zealand: c/o University of Auckland, Private Bag, Auckland, New Zealand.
Technol. Cul. Technology and culture. (0040-165X). Johns Hopkins University Press: 2715 North Charles Street, Baltimore, MD 21218-4363, U.S.A., in association with Society for the History of Technology.
Telos Telos. (0090-6514). Telos Press: 431 E. 12th Street, New York, NY 10009, U.S.A.

LIST OF ABBREVIATIONS USED

Tempo Soc. Tempo social. (0103-2070). Universidade de São Paulo, Departamento de Sociologia: Av. Prof. Luciano Gualberto, 315, 05508-900 São Paulo, Brazil.
Temps Mod. Temps modernes. (0040-3075). Gallimard: 4 rue Férou, Paris 6, France.
Text Text. (0165-4888). Mouton de Gruyter: Postfach 303421, 10728 Berlin, Germany.
Theory Cult. Soc. Theory culture and society. (0263-2764). Sage Publications: 6 Bonhill Street, London EC2A 4PU, U.K.
Theory Decis. Theory and decision. (0040-5833). Kluwer Academic Publishers: P.O. Box 17, 3300 AA Dordrecht, The Netherlands.
Theory Soc. Theory and society. (0304-2421). Kluwer Academic Publishers: P.O. Box 17, 3300 AA Dordrecht, The Netherlands.
Thes. Elev. Thesis eleven. (0725-5136). Sage Publications: 6 Bonhill Street, London EC2A 4PU, U.K.
Third World Plan. R. Third World planning review. (0142-7849). Liverpool University Press: 4 Cambridge Street, Liverpool L69 7ZU, U.K.
Tijds. Econ. Manag. Tijdschrift voor economie en management. (0772-7664). Katholieke Universiteit Te Leuven: Redactiesecretariaat, Naamsestraat 69, 3000 Leuven, Belgium.
Time Soc. Time & society. (0961-463X). Sage Publications: 6 Bonhill Street, London EC2A 4PU, U.K.
Tour. Geogr. Tourism geographies. (1461-6688). Routledge: 11 New Fetter Lane, London EC4P 4EE, U.K.
Town Plan. R. Town planning review. (0041-0020). Liverpool University Press: Senate House, Abercromby Square, Liverpool L69 3BX, U.K., in association with University of Liverpool, Department of Civic Design (Town and Regional Planning).
Transfer Transfer: European review of labour and research. (1024-2589). Keesing Publishers: Keesinglaan 2-20, B-2100 Antwerp, Belgium.
Turk. Year. Int. Rel. Turkish yearbook of international relations = Milletlerarasi münasebetler Türk yilli&gi. (0544-1943). Research center for international political and economic relations: Ankara University, Faculty of Political Science, 06590-Cebeci, Ankara, Turkey.
Ufahamu Ufahamu. (0041-5715). African Activist Association: James S. Coleman African Studies Centre, University of California, Los Angeles, CA 90024-1130, U.S.A.
Urban Aff. Rev. Urban affairs review. (1078-0874). Sage Publications: 2455 Teller Road, Newbury Park, Thousand Oaks, CA 91320, U.S.A.
Urban Geogr. Urban geography. (0272-3638). V.H. Winston & Sons: 7961 Eastern Avenue, Silver Spring, MD 20910, U.S.A.
Urban Stud. Urban studies. (0042-0980). Carfax Publishing: P.O. Box 25, Abingdon, Oxfordshire OX14 3UE, U.K., in association with University of Glasgow, Centre for Urban and Regional Research: Adam Smith Building, University of Glasgow, Glasgow G12 8RT, U.K.
US-Jap. Wom. J. US-Japan women's journal. (0898-8900). US-Japan Women's Center.
Valóság Valóság. (0324-7228). Hirlapkiadó Vállalat: Blaha Lujza ter 3, 1959 Budapest 8, Hungary, in association with Tudományos Ismeretterjesztő Társulat.
Verf. Rec. Über. Verfassung und Recht in Übersee = Law and politics in Africa, Asia and Latin America. (0506-7286). Nomos Verlagsgesellschaft: Waldseestraße 3-5, 76530 Baden-Baden, Germany, in association with Hamburger Gesellschaft für Völkerrecht und Auswärtige Politik: Rothenbaumchaussee 21-23, D-20148 Hamburg, Germany.
Vest. Lenin. Univ. 6 Vestnik Leningradskogo universiteta. Seriia 6 Istoriia kpss, nauchnyi kommunizm, filosofiia pravo. (0132-4624). Universiteta Nab. 7/9, 199034 Leningrad, Russia.
Vest. Mosk. Univ. Ser. 9 Filol. Vestnik Moskovskogo universiteta. Seriia 9 Filologiia. (0130-0075). Izdatel'stvo Moskovskogo Universiteta: ul. B. Nikitskaia, 5-7, 103009 Moscow, Russia.

LISTE DES ABRÉVIATIONS UTILISÉES

Vest. San.-Peter. Univ. Vestnik Sankt-Peterburgskogo universiteta. Seriia 6 Filosofiia, politologiia, sotsiolgiia, psikhologiia, pravo. Izdatel'stvo Sankt-Peterburgskogo Universiteta: Universitetskaia nab. 7/9, 199034 St. Petersburg, Russia.

Vier. Wirt.schung Vierteljahrshefte zur Wirtschaftsforschung. (0340-1707). Duncker & Humblot: Postfach 410329, Dietrich-Schäfer-Weg 9, 1000 Berlin 41, Germany, in association with Deutsches Institut für Wirtschaftsforschung: Königin-Luise-Straße 5, D-1000 Berlin 33, Germany.

Viet. Soc. Sci. Vietnam social sciences. (1013-4328). Hanoi University: Hanoi, Vietnam, in association with National Centre for Social Sciences and the Humanities.

Viet. Stud. Vietnamese studies. (0085-7823). Vietnamese Studies: 46 Tran Hung Dao Street, Hanoi, Vietnam.

Vis. Anthrop. Visual anthropology. (0894-9468). Harwood Academic Publishers: 270 8th Avenue, New York, NY 10011, U.S.A.

Voluntas Voluntas. (0957-8765). Kluwer academic/Plenum publishers: P.O. Box 17, 3300 AA Dordrecht, The Netherlands, in association with Charities Aid Foundation.

Vop. Ekon. Voprosy ekonomiki. (0042-8736). Izdatel'stvo Pravda: ul. Pravdy 24, 125865 Moscow, Russia, in association with Rossiiskaia Akademiia Nauk, Institut Ekonomiki.

Welt Islams Welt des Islams. (0043-2539). E.J. Brill: P.O. Box 9000, 2300 PA Leiden, The Netherlands.

Wom. St. Inter. For. Women's studies international forum. (0277-5395). Elsevier Science: PO Box 211, 1000 AE Amsterdam, The Netherlands.

Wom. Stud. Women's studies. (0049-7878). Gordon and Breach Science Publishers: P.O. Box 90, Reading, Berkshire RG1 8JL, U.K.

Wor. Futur. World futures. (0260-4027). Harwood Academic Publishers: 270 8th Avenue, New York, NY 10011, U.S.A.

Work Occup. Work and occupations. (0730-8884). Sage Publications: 2455 Teller Road, Newbury Park, Thousand Oaks, CA 91320, U.S.A.

World Dev. World development. (0305-750X). Elsevier Science: PO Box 211, 1000 AE Amsterdam, The Netherlands.

World of Mus. World of music. (0043-8774). Otto-Friedrich-Universität Bamberg: D-96045 Bamberg, Germany.

Yale Law J. Yale law journal. (0044-0094). Yale Law Journal Co.: P.O. Box 208215, New Haven, CT 06520-8215, U.S.A.

Z. Balkan. Zeitschrift für Balkanologie. (0044-2356). Otto Harrassowitz: Wiesbaden, Germany, in association with Friedrich-Schiller-Universität Jena, Institut für Slawistik: Grietgasse 6, 07743 Jena.

Z. Polit. Zeitschrift für Politik. (0044-3360). Carl Heymanns Verlag: Luxemburger Straße 449, 5000 Cologne 41, Germany, in association with Hochschule für Politik München: Ludwigstraße 8, 8000 Munich, Germany.

Z. Soziol. Zeitschrift für Soziologie. (0340-1804). Lucius & Lucius Verlagsgesellschaft mbH: Gerokstraße 51, D-70184, Stuttgart, Germany.

Z. Verkehr. Zeitschrift für Verkehrswissenschaft. (0044-3670). Verkehrs-Verlag J. Fischer: Paulusstraße 1, 40237 Düsseldorf, Germany.

CLASSIFICATION SCHEME
PLAN DE CLASSIFICATION

A.	**General studies / Études générales.**
A.1.	Sociology and the social sciences / Sociologie et sciences sociales.
A.2.	Sociological research / Recherche sociologique.
A.3.	Reference works, information services and documents / Ouvrages de référence, services d'information et documents.
B.	**Theory and methodology / Théorie et méthodologie.**
B.1.	Theory / Théorie.
	Epistemology / Epistémologie; Historiography / Historographie; Philosophy / Philosophie; Sociological theory / Théorie sociologique
B.2.	Research methods / Méthodes de recherche.
	Data analysis / Analyse des données; Data collection / Rassemblement des données
C.	**Individuals. Groups. Organizations / Individus. Groupes. Organisations.**
C.1.	Psychology / Psychologie.
	Cognition / Cognition; Personality and emotions / Personnalité et émotions
C.2.	Clinical psychology / Psychologie clinique.
C.3.	Social psychology / Psychologie sociale.
C.4.	Interpersonal relations / Relations interpersonnelles.
C.5.	Groups and group dynamics / Groupes et dynamique de groupe.
	Collective identity and memory / Identité et mémoire collective; Conflict and conflict resolution / Conflit and résolution des conflits; Group dynamics / Dynamique de groupe;

CLASSIFICATION SCHEME

C.6. Organizations / Organisations.

D. Culture / Culture.

D.1. Culture / Culture.
Cultural studies / Études culturelles; Modernity and post-modernity / Modernité et postmodernité

D.2. Everyday life / Vie quotidienne.
Popular culture / Culture populaire

D.3. Religion / Religion.
Buddhism / Bouddhisme; Christianity / Christianisme; Islam / Islam; Judaism / Judaïsme

D.4. Science and knowledge / Science et connaissance.

D.5. Language, communication and media / Langage, communication et médias.
Communications technology / Technologies de communication; Media / Médias; Sociolinguistics / Sociolinguistique

D.6. Art / Art.
Cinema / Cinéma; Literature / Littérature; Music / Musique

D.7. Education / Éducation.
Academic access and achievement / Accès a l'éducation et la réussite éducationnelle; Academic staff / Personnel enseignant; Education systems / Systèmes d'enseignement; Pedagogy / Pédagogie; Primary education / Enseignement primaire; Secondary education / Enseignement secondaire; Tertiary education / Enseignement post-scolaire

E. Social structure / Structure sociale.

E.1. Social process and organization / Processus et organisation sociale.
Power relations / Rapports de pouvoir; Social norms / Normes sociales

E.2. Social stratification / Stratification sociale.
Disability / Invalidité

E.3. Social change / Changement social.
Globalization / Mondialisation

F. Population. Family. Gender. Ethnic groups / Population. Famille. Sexe. Groupe ethnique.

F.1. Age groups / Groupes d'âges.
Children / Enfants; Youth / Jeunesse; Older persons / Personnes âgées

PLAN DE CLASSIFICATION

F.2. Demography / Démographie.

F.3. Demographic trends and population policy / Tendances démographiques et politique démographique.
    Family planning / Planning familial; Fertility / Fécondité; Morbidity / Morbidité; Mortality / Mortalité

F.4. Marriage and family / Mariage et famille.
    Divorce / Divorce; Domestic violence / Violence dans la famille; Family relations / Liens de famille; Marriage and cohabitation / Mariage et concubinage; One-parent families / Famille monoparentale; Parenthood / Paternité-maternité

F.5. Gender and gender relations / Sexe et relations des sexes.
    Feminism / Féminisme; Gender differentiation / Différenciation sexuelle; Gender roles / Rôles de sexe; Sex discrimination / Discrimination sexuelle

F.6. Sexual behaviour / Comportement sexuelle.
    Homosexuality / Homosexualité

F.7. Race and ethnicity / Race et ethnicité.
    Ethnicity / Ethnicité; Interethnic relations / Relations interethniques

F.8. Migration / Migration.
    Immigrant adaptation / Adaptation des immigrants; Internal migration / Migration interne; International migration / Migration internationale

G. **Environment. Community. Rural. Urban / Environnement. Communauté. Rural. Urbain.**

G.1. Environment. Ecology. Geography. Human settlements / Environnement. Écologie. Géographie. Établissements humains.
    Ecology / Écologie; Human geography / Géographie humaine; Sustainable development / Développement soutenable

G.2. Local community / Collectivités locales.

G.3. Rural and urban relations / Rapports rurale et urbaine.

G.3.1. Rural sociology / Sociologie rurale.
    Rural development / Développement rural

G.3.2. Urban sociology / Sociologie urbaine.
    Housing / Logement; Social differentiation and segregation / Différenciation et ségrégation urbaine; Urban planning and infrastructure / Aménagement et infrastructure urbaine; Urban space / Espace urbain; Urbanization and development / Urbanisation et développement urbain

CLASSIFICATION SCHEME

H.	**Economic life / Vie économique.**
H.1.	Economic sociology / Sociologie économique.
H.2.	Economic and production systems / Systèmes économiques et de production.
H.3.	Economic conditions and living standards / Conditions économiques et niveau de vie. *Income / Revenu*
H.4.	Markets and consumption / Marchés et consommation. *Consumerism / Consumérisme*
H.5.	Finance / Finance.
I.	**Labour / Travail.**
I.1.	Sociology of industry and work / Sociologie de l'industrie et du travail. *Business ethics / Déontologie commerciale*
I.2.	Employment and labour market / Emploi et marché du travail. *Employment discrimination / Discrimination dans l'emploi; Gender issues / Questions de sexe; Unemployment / Chômage*
I.3.	Personnel management and working conditions / Administration du personnel et conditions de travail. *Human resources / Ressources humaines; Management / Gestion; Working conditions / Conditions de travail*
I.4.	Vocational training, occupations and careers / Formation professionnelle, professions et carrières. *Career development / Déroulement de carrière; Occupations / Professions; Training / Formation*
I.5.	Labour relations / Relations du travail. *Labour disputes / Conflits du travail; Trade unions / Syndicats*
J.	**Politics. State. International relations / Politique. État. Relations internationales.**
J.1.	Political sociology / Sociologie politique.
J.2.	Political thought / Pensée politique.
J.3.	Political systems / Systèmes politique.
J.4.	Social control / Régulation sociale. *Criminal justice / Justice pénale; Criminology / Criminologie; Police / Police*

PLAN DE CLASSIFICATION

J.5. Law / Loi.

J.6. Public administration / Administration publique.

J.7. Political parties, pressure groups and political movements / Partis politiques, groupes de pression et mouvements politiques.
Social movements / Mouvements sociaux

J.8. Political behaviour and elections / Comportement politique et élections.
Elections / Élections

J.9. International relations / Relations internationales.
Military sociology / Sociologie militaire

K. Social problems. Social welfare. Social work / Problèmes sociaux. Bien-être social. Travail social.

K.1. Social problems / Problèmes sociaux.
Addiction / Dépendance; Homelessness / Les sans-abri; Suicide / Suicide; Violence / Violence

K.2. Social welfare / Bien-être social.
Care of the aged / Aide aux personnes âgées; Child welfare / Bien-être des enfants; Disability support / Invalidité support; Welfare state / État-providence

K.3. Social work / Travail social.

K.4. Health care / Soins médicaux.
Community care / Soins en dehors du milieu hospitalier; Health care services / Services de santé; Medical personnel / Personnel médical; Medical sociology / Sociologie médicale; Mental health / Santé mentale; Public health / Santé publique

BIBLIOGRAPHY FOR 2000

BIBLIOGRAPHIE POUR 2000

A: GENERAL STUDIES
ÉTUDES GÉNÉRALES

A.1: Sociology and the social sciences
Sociologie et sciences sociales

1. Akademicheskaia traditsiia v istorii sotsiologii Rossii. *[In Russian]*; (The academic tradition in the history of sociology in Russia.) *[Summary]*. E.I. Kukushkina. **Sot. Issle.** 4 2000 pp.97-107.
2. Analytic narratives. Daniel Carpenter; Theda Skocpol; Sunita Parikh; Robert Bates; Avner Grief; Margaret Levi; Jean-Laurent Rosenthal; Barry Weingast; Silvia Pedraza; Christopher Chase-Dunn; Thomas D. Hall; E. Susan Manning. **Soc. Sci. Hist.** 24:4 Winter:2000 pp.653-696. *Collection of 4 articles*.
3. Between sociology and theology: the spirit of capitalism debate. Keith Tester. **Sociol. Rev.** 48:1 2:2000 pp.43-57.
4. The circumstances of the development of sociology in Central European countries — Slovak sociology in the 20th century. L'udovít Turčan. **Sociologia [Brat.]** 32:6 Fall:2000 pp.507-520.
5. Cumulative knowledge, credit and memory. Jonathan H. Turner; Kyung-man Kim; Stephan Fuchs; Joseph H. Spear; Randall Collins; R.S. Smith; Peter I. Rose; Eric A. Kincanon. **Am. Sociol.** 30:2 Summer:1999 pp.5-77. *Collection of 4 articles*.
6. De totalidades y parcelas. Las ciencias sociales ante la unidad de la realidad social. *[In Spanish]*; [Totality and parts. Social sciences faced with the unity of social reality]. Jaime Osorio. **Acta Sociol. [Mexico]** 24 9-12:1998 pp.153-180.
7. Decorative sociology: towards a critique of the cultural turn. Chris Rojek; Bryan Turner. **Sociol. Rev.** 48:4 11:2000 pp.629-648.
8. Ethnography, belief ascription, and epistemological barriers. Todd Edwin Jones; John R. Weeks [Comments by]. **Human Relat.** 53:1 1:2000 pp.117-176.
9. Etnosotsiologiia: proidennoe i novye gorizonty. *[In Russian]*; (Ethnosociology: past achievements, new horizons.) *[Summary]*. Iu.V. Aroutiunian; L.M. Drobizheva. **Sot. Issle.** 4 2000 pp.11-21.
10. Extending the rational choice model from the economy to society. Milan Zafirovski. **Econ. Soc.** 29:2 5:2000 pp.181-206.
11. Heeft de sociologie een toekomst? Over de hardnekkige onvolledigheid van de sociologische beroepsopvatting. *[In Dutch]*; [Does sociology have a future? The sociologist's incomplete professional identity] *[Summary]*. Arie Glebbeek; Henk de Vos. **Mens Maat.** 75:4 12:2000 pp.277-297.
12. The historical imagination in the human sciences. Tony Burns; Paul Cocks; P.H. Clarke; Robin Williams; James Good; Roger Smith; Graham Richards; Arthur Still; John C. Burnham. **Hist. Human Sci.** 13:4 11:2000 pp.97-124. *Collection of 4 articles*.

A: GENERAL STUDIES

13 Interactive social science. Michael Gibbons; Steve Woolgar; Elizabeth Shove; Arie Rip; Sally Baldwin; Peter Simmons; Gordon Walker; Tony J. Watson; Joan Orme; Chris Caswill. **Sci. Pub. Pol.** 27:3 6:2000 pp.159-221. *Collection of 8 articles.*
14 Is social anthropology still worth the trouble? A response to some echoes from America. Maurice Godelier. **Ethnos** 65:3 2000 pp.301-316.
15 Melanchthon's rhetoric and the practical origins of reformation human science. Daniel M. Gross. **Hist. Human Sci.** 13:3 8:2000 pp.5-22.
16 Nouvelles sociologies, anthropologies et éthique de l'émancipation. Pistes programmatiques. *[In French]*; (New sociologies, anthropologies and the ethic of emancipation: programmatic paths.) Philippe Corcuff. **Hom. Soc.** 136-137 2-3:2000 pp.157-170.
17 On writing: on writing sociology. Zygmunt Bauman. **Theory Cult. Soc.** 17:1 2:2000 pp.79-90.
18 The organic ethnologist of Algerian migration. Pierre Bourdieu; Loïc Wacquant. **Ethnog.** 1:2 12:2000 pp.173-182.
19 Postmodernity. David Lyon. Buckingham: Open University Press, 1999. 131p. *ISBN: 033520144X, 0335201458. Includes index. (Series:* Concepts in the social sciences).
20 Qualitative sociology in rural studies. Gilbert W. Gillespie, Jr.; Peter R. Sinclair; Nancy A. Naples; Carolyn Sachs; Gregory Peter; Michael Mayerfeld Bell; Susan Jarnagin; Donna Bauer; Suzanne E. Tallichet; Peter Leigh Taylor; J.D. Wulfhorst; Peter Howden; Frank Vanclay; Curtis W. Stofferahn. **Rural Sociol.** 65:2 6:2000 pp.180-330. *Collection of 8 articles.*
21 Realism and social science. R. Andrew Sayer. Thousand Oaks CA, London: Sage Publications, 1999. 240p. *ISBN: 0761961232, 0761961240.*
22 Reduction, supervenience, and the autonomy of social scientific laws. Lee C. McIntyre. **Theory Decis.** 48:2 3:2000 pp.101-122.
23 Rossiiskaia sotsiologiia shestidesiatykh godov: v vospominaniiakh i dokumentakh. *[In Russian]*; [Russian sociology in the 1960s: memoirs and documents]. Institut sotsiologii. St. Petersburg: Russkogo Khristianskogo gumanitarnogo instituta, 1999. 684p. *ISBN: 5875162465. Includes bibliographical references.*
24 Sciences sociales et postcommunisme. La sociologie polonaise des élites politiques (1990-2000). *[In French]*; (Social sciences and post-communism: Polish sociology on political elites (1990-2000).) *[Summary]*. Jérome Heurtaux. **Rev. Ét. Comp. Est-Ouest** 31:2 6:2000 pp.49-100.
25 The social sciences in the Philippines: reflections on trends and developments. Maria Cynthia Rose Banzon Bautista. **Phil. Stud.** 48:2 2000 pp.175-208.
26 Social theory: a historical introduction. Alex Callinicos. Cambridge: Polity Press, 1999. viii, 339p. *ISBN: 0745616445, 0745616453. Includes bibliographical references (p. [319]-326) and index.*
27 Sociobiológ na ľadovci. *[In Slovak]*; (A sociobiologist on the iceberg.) Martin Kanovský. **Sociologia [Brat.]** 32:5 2000 pp.483-498.
28 Sociological enlightenment — for whom, about what? Zygmunt Bauman. **Theory Cult. Soc.** 17:2 4:2000 pp.71-82.
29 Sociology after humanism: a lesson from contemporary science studies. Daniel Breslau. **Sociol. Theory** 18:2 7:2000 pp.289-307.
30 Sociology and aesthetics. Eduardo de la Fuente. **Eur. J. Soc. Theory** 3:2 5:2000 pp.235-248.
31 Sociology and the vernacular voice: text, context and the sociological imagination. Robin Williams. **Hist. Human Sci.** 13:4 11:2000 pp.73-95.
32 Sociology facing the next millennium. Manuel Castells; Immanuel Wallerstein; Göran Therborn; Gosta Esping-Andersen; Ulrich Beck; Bruno Latour; Barbara Adam; Saskia Sassen; Mike Featherstone; John Urry. **Br. J. Soc.** 51:1 1-3:2000 pp.5-201. *Collection of 10 articles.*
33 Sociology: themes and perspectives. Michael Haralambos; Martin Holborn. London: HarperCollins, 2000. 1152p. *ISBN: 0003275078. Includes bibliographical references.*

A: ÉTUDES GÉNÉRALES

34 Sociology's Eurocentrism and the 'rise of the West' revisited. Gregor McLennan. **Eur. J. Soc. Theory** 3:3 8:2000 pp.275-291.
35 Sotsiokul'turnie determinanty razvitiia gendernoi teorii v Rossii i na Zapade. *[In Russian]*; [Socio-cultural patterns of the development of gender theory in Russia and Western countries]. O. Voronina. **Obshch. Nauki Sovrem.** 4 2000 pp.9-20.
36 Sotsiologi Rossii i SNG XIX-XX vv. Biobibliograficheskii spravochnik. *[In Russian]*; [CIS and Russian sociology, 19th-20th centuries: a bio-bibliographical guide]. Zhan Terent'evich. Toshchenko [Ed.]; et al. Moscow: Editorial URSS, 1999. 367p. *ISBN: 5836000042. Includes bibliographical references.*
37 Subalterns of technopoly: brokering techno-power in academic sociology. William Keenan. **Br. J. Soc.** 51:2 6:2000 pp.321-338.
38 Taking stock of the discipline: some reflections on the state of American sociology. Bruce Keith. **Am. Sociol.** 31:1 Spring:2000 pp.5-14.
39 Toward spatially integrated social science. Michael F. Goodchild; Luc Anselin; Richard P. Appelbaum; Barbara Herr Harthorn. **Int. Reg. Sci. R.** 23:2 4:2000 pp.139-159.
40 (The tradition and possibility of rational choice theory in sociology.) *[Summary]*; *[Text in Japanese]*. Hiroshi Tarohmaru. **Rir. To Ho.** 15:2 10:2000 pp.287-298.

A.2: **Sociological research**
Recherche sociologique

41 Anthony Giddens: an introduction to a social theorist. Lars Bo Kaspersen. Oxford: Blackwell Publishers, 2000. viii, 226p. *ISBN: 0631207333, 0631207341. Includes bibliographical references and index.*
42 Budgets for social and behavioral science research: 2001. Howard Silver. **Society** 38:1 11-12:2000 pp.47-85.
43 The business of research: issues of politics and practice. Janet Lewis; Jessica A. Ogden; John D.H. Porter; Elizabeth Ettorre; Dawn Chatty; Gillian Lewando Hundt; Catherine Jones Finer; Hilary Third; Hazel Kemshall; Paul Bate; Jan Waterson. **Soc. Pol. Admin.** 34:4 12:2000 pp.365-508. *Collection of 10 articles*
44 Can what is right with sociology fix what is wrong with sociology? A view from the 'come-back' generation. Michael Woolcock; Joshua Kim. **Am. Sociol.** 31:1 Spring:2000 pp.15-31.
45 Causal attribution and Mill's methods of experimental inquiry: past, present and prospect. Peter A. White. **Br. J. Soc. P.** 39:3 9:2000 pp.429-448.
46 Challenges for research ethics and moral knowledge construction in the applied social sciences. Stephen L. Payne. **J. Busin. Ethics** 26:4 8:2000 pp.307-318.
47 The cloud — lecturing on feminist research. Anna Wahl. **NORA** 7:2-3 1999 pp.97-108.
48 Danger in the field: risk and ethics in social research. Geraldine Lee-Treweek [Ed.]; Stephanie Linkogle [Ed.]. London: Routledge, 2000. 212p. *ISBN: 0415193222, 0415193214. Includes bibliographical references and index.*
49 The dynamics of resource allocation in research organizations. D. Filson. **J. Econ. Beh.** 43:2 10:2000 pp.263-277.
50 Encounters with Asia: contemporary Japan. Makoto Hogetsu; Jun Ayukawa; Hisaya Nonoyama; Hidenori Fujita; Yasushi Matsumoto. **Am. Sociol.** 31:3 Fall:2000 pp.3-71. *Collection of 5 articles.*
51 Estudio de casos. *[In Spanish]*; [Case studies]. Xavier Coller. Madrid: Centro de Investigaciones Sociológicas, 2000. 139p. *ISBN: 8474762952. Includes bibliographical references (p. [135]-139).*
52 Grassroots globalization and the research imagination. Arjun Appadurai. **Publ. Cult.** 12:1 Winter:2000 pp.1-20.
53 In the vineyard: working in African American studies. Perry A. Hall. Knoxville TN: University of Tennessee Press, 1999. xii, 247p. *ISBN: 1572330546. Includes bibliographical references (p. [231]-237) and index.*

A: GENERAL STUDIES

54 Korean studies at the crossroads. Seung-hwan Lee; Yonung Kwon; Kwang-ok Kim; Hyunchin Lim; Hong-woo Kim; Chung-un Chan; Yee-heum Yoon; Young-hee Shim; Eun-yeong Na; Jae-ho Cha; Jaeyeol Yee; Kyung-koo Han; Jaehyuck Lee. **Korea J.** 40:1 Spring:2000 pp.8-393. *Collection of 12 articles.*

55 Middle-range realism; *[Summary in French]; [Summary in German].* Ray Pawson. **Eur. J. Soc.** XLI:2 2000 pp.283-325.

56 Moving forward by looking back: a half-century of the SSSR, RRA, and social scientific research on religion. David O. Moberg; Charles Y. Glock; James E. Dittes; William V. D'Antonio; Karel Dobbelaere; Armand L. Mauss; Stacy A. Hammons; William H. Swatos, Jr.; James A. Beckford; Ruth A. Wallace; Mary Jo Neitz; Thomas Robbins; Peter Beyer; Ralph W. Hood, Jr.; Jackson W. Carroll. **J. Sci. S. Relig.** 39:4 12:2000 pp.401-557. *Collection of 14 articles.*

57 'New wine into old bottles': literature on Israel in 2000. Neill Lochery. **Middle E. Stud.** 36:3 7:2000 pp.209-230.

58 Redécouvrir le Brésil. *[In French];* [Rediscovering Brazil]. Georges Couffignal; Martine Droulers; Laurent Vidal; Enali Leca de Biaggi; Licia Valladares; Jean Duvignaud; Dominique Vidal; Paulo César Da Costa Gomes. **Cah. Amer. Lat.** 34 2000 pp.13-98. *Collection of 7 articles.*

59 Research and social action. Ricardo Falla. **Lat. Am. Pers.** 27:1 1:2000 pp.45-55.

60 Research performances. Geraldine Pratt. **Envir. Plan. D.** 18:5 10:2000 pp.639-653.

61 Researching volunteer associations and other nonprofits: an emergent interdisciplinary field and possible new discipline. David Horton Smith. **Am. Sociol.** 30:4 Winter:1999 pp.5-35.

62 Rozhovor s R. Roškom na prelome milénia o našej sociológii a sociológoch. *[In Slovak];* (Millennium interview with R. Roško about Slovak sociology and sociologists.) L. Macháček. **Sociologia [Brat.]** 32:1 2000 pp.5-30.

63 Social and human capital: the search for appropriate technomethodology. Tom Schuller. **Policy St.** 21:1 3:2000 pp.25-36.

64 Social environmental research in the European Union: research networks and new agendas. Michael Redclift; et al. Northampton MA: Edward Elgar Publishing, 2000. 142p. *ISBN: 1840642114. Includes bibliographical references and index.*

65 Sociological encounters in Asia. William J. Buxton; Lawrence T. Nichols; Marion J. Levy, Jr.; Talcott Parsons; Ken'ichi Tominaga; Gary T. Marx. **Am. Sociol.** 31:2 Summer:2000 pp.3-100. *Collection of 5 articles.*

66 La sociologie française contemporaine. *[In French];* [Contemporary French sociology]. Jean-Michel Berthelot [Ed.]. Paris: Presses Universitaires de France, 2000. 274p. *ISBN: 2130503020. Includes bibliographical references.*

67 Sociologies inactuelles, sociologies actuelles? *[In French];* [Sociologies, past and present?] Michel Wieviorka; Cecilia Montero Casassus; Philippe Steiner; Éric Letonturier; Lise Demailly. **Cah. Int. Soc.** CVIII 1-6:2000 pp.5-124. *Collection of 5 articles.*

68 Un sociologue dans le monde. *[In French];* [A sociologist at large]. Catherine Levy [Interviewer]; Farouk Hasdam Bey; Elias Sanbar; Pierre Bourdieu. **R. Et. Palest.** 74:22 Winter:2000 pp.3-13.

69 Some meanings of 'the private' in sociological thought. Joe Bailey. **Sociology** 34:3 8:2000 pp.381-401.

70 Sorting things out: classification and its consequences. Geoffrey C. Bowker; Susan Leigh Star. Cambridge MA: MIT Press, 1999. xii, 377p. *ISBN: 0262024616. Includes bibliographical references (p. [335]-365) and indexes.*

71 Symbols and social activism: an agenda for African studies and the ASA for the 21st century; *[Summary in French].* Sandra E. Greene. **Afr. Stud. R.** 42:2 9:1999 pp.1-14.

72 Toward a more perfect union: the career and contributions of Robin M. Williams, Jr. Peter I. Rose. **Am. Sociol.** 30:2 Summer:1999 pp.78-91.

73 Towards a collaborative environment research agenda. Alyson Warhurst [Ed.]. Basingstoke: Macmillan, 1999. 208p. *ISBN: 0333674790.*

A: ÉTUDES GÉNÉRALES

74 The turn to biographical methods in social science: comparative issues and examples. Prue Chamberlayne [Ed.]; Joanna Bornat [Ed.]; Tom Wengraf [Ed.]. New York: Routledge, 2000. 346p. *ISBN: 0415228379, 0415228387. Includes bibliographical references and index. (Series:* Social research today).

75 A very qualified success, indeed: the case of Anthony Giddens and British sociology. Steve Fuller. **Can. J. Soc.** 25:4 Fall:2000 pp.507-516.

76 What's sexy in New Zealand sociolinguistics? Janet Holmes. **Te reo** 41 6:1998 pp.28-44.

77 Zamyšlení nad českou sociologií výchovy, vzdělávání a mládeže v 90. letech. *[In Czech]*; (Reflections on Czech sociology of education and youth in the 1990s.) *[Summary]*. Radomír Havlík; Jaroslav Kota. **Soc. Čas.** 36:1 2000 pp.87-96.

A.3: Reference works, information services and documents
Ouvrages de référence, services d'information et documents

78 The academic library and its users. Peter Jordan. Aldershot, Brookfield VT: Gower, 1998. viii, 157p. *ISBN: 0566079399. Includes bibliographical references and index.*

79 The ASLIB directory of information sources in the United Kingdom. ASLIB. London: ASLIB, 1999. *ISBN: 0851424090. Includes index.*

80 The ASLIB directory of information sources in the United Kingdom. ASLIB. London: ASLIB, 2000. *ISBN: 0851424317. Includes index.*

81 The Blackwell dictionary of sociology: a user's guide to sociological language. Allan G. Johnson. Malden MA, Oxford: Blackwell Publishers, 2000. xii, 413p. *ISBN: 0631216804, 0631216812. Includes bibliographical references and index.*

82 Collins English dictionary and thesaurus. Glasgow: HarperCollins, 2000. 1397p. *ISBN: 0004725026.*

83 Concise Routledge encyclopedia of philosophy. Routledge. London, New York: Routledge, 2000. xxxiv, 1030p. *ISBN: 0415223644. Includes bibliographical references and index.*

84 The dictionary of human geography. R.J. Johnston [Ed.]; David Smith [Ed.]; et al. Oxford, Malden MA: Blackwell Publishers, 2000. xvii, 958p. *ISBN: 0631205608, 0631205616. Includes bibliographical references and index.*

85 The directory of university libraries in Europe. Europa Publications Limited. London: Europa Publications Limited, 2000. x, 413p. *ISBN: 1857430719. Includes indexes.*

86 Encyclopedia of contemporary French culture. Keith Reader [Ed.]; Alex Hughes [Ed.]. London: Routledge, 1998. xxii, 618p. *ISBN: 0415131863. Includes bibliographical references and index.*

87 The Europa directory of international organizations 2000. Europa Publications Limited. London: Europa, 2000. xiv, 578p. *ISBN: 1857430921. Includes index.*

88 Handbook of research methods in social and personality psychology. Harry T. Reis [Ed.]; Charles M. Judd [Ed.]. New York: Cambridge University Press, 2000. xii, 558p. *ISBN: 0521551285. Includes bibliographical references and indexes.*

89 Handbook of social theory. George Ritzer [Ed.]; Barry Smart [Ed.]. London: Sage Publications, 2000. 640p. *ISBN: 0761958401. Includes bibliographical references and index.*

90 Handbuch der Demographie. *[In German]*; [The demography handbook]. Ulrich Mueller [Ed.]; Andreas Diekmann [Ed.]; Bernhard Nauck [Ed.]. Berlin, New York: Springer-Verlag, 2000. xiv, 1426p. *ISBN: 3540661069, 3540661085.* 2 volumes. *Includes bibliographical references (p. [1250]-1387) and indexes.*

91 Historical atlas of south-west England. Roger Kain [Ed.]; William Ravenhill [Ed.]; Helen Jones. Exeter: University of Exeter Press, 1999. xxii, 564p. *ISBN: 0859894347.*

92 Information sources in development studies. Sheila Allcock [Ed.]. London, New Providence NJ: Bowker-Saur, 1999. xiii, 239p. *ISBN: 1857392760, 1857392817. Includes bibliographical references and index. (Series:* Guides to information sources).

A: GENERAL STUDIES

93 The international dictionary of adult and continuing education. Peter Jarvis; Arthur L. Wilson. London: Kogan Page, 1999. vi, 202p. *ISBN: 0749426713.*
94 Maps for historians. Paul Hindle. Chichester: Phillimore, 1998. 148p. *ISBN: 0850339240.*
95 Mental Health Act manual. Richard M. Jones [Ed.]. London: Sweet & Maxwell, 1999. xix, 697p. *ISBN: 0421674806. Includes index.*
96 The new Penguin dictionary of modern quotations. Robert Andrews. London: Penguin Books, 2000. viii, 588p. *ISBN: 0140293078.*
97 The new Penguin thesaurus. Rosalind Fergusson [Ed.]; David Pickering [Ed.]; Martin H. Manser [Ed.]. London: Penguin, 2000. 666p. *ISBN: 0140293116.*
98 The Oxford dictionary of thematic quotations. Susan Ratcliffe [Ed.]. Oxford, New York: Oxford University Press, 2000. 584p. *ISBN: 0198602189.*
99 The Penguin dictionary of literary terms and literary theory. J.A. Cuddon. London: Penguin, 1999. 1024p. *ISBN: 0140513639.*
100 The Penguin dictionary of sociology. Nicholas Abercrombie; Stephen Hill; Bryan S. Turner. London: Penguin, 2000. x, 449p. *ISBN: 0140513809. Includes bibliographical references.*
101 Statistical sources for social research on Western Europe 1945-1995: a guide to social statistics. Franz Rothenbacher. Opladen: Leske + Budrich, 1998. 399p. *ISBN: 3810020478.* (*Series:* Europe in comparison - 6).
102 The Virgin alternative guide to British universities 2001. Piers Dudgeon. London: Virgin, 2000. 512p. *ISBN: 0753504723.*
103 Who's who in 2000 years of British history. Juliet Gardiner. London: Collins & Brown, 2000. 864p. *ISBN: 1855857715.*
104 The Women's Library in Istanbul. Asli Davaz-Mardin. **Gend. Hist.** 12:2 7:2000 pp.448-466.
105 World directory of peace research and training institutions. UNESCO. Oxford, Cambridge MA: Blackwell Publishers, 2000. 300p. *ISBN: 9230037265. Includes index.* (*Series:* World social science information directories).

B: THEORY AND METHODOLOGY
THÉORIE ET MÉTHODOLOGIE

B.1: Theory
Théorie

Epistemology
Epistémologie

106   Antoine Arnauld (1612-1694). John Woods. **Argumentation** 14:1 2:2000 pp.31-44.
107   The causal-doxastic theory of the basing relation. Keith Allen Korcz. **Can. J. Phil.** 30:4 12:2000 pp.525-550.
108   Causalità come congiunzione probabile. *[In Italian]*; [Causality as a likely conjunction]. M. Chiara Barlucchi. **Quad. Sociol.** XLIV:22 2000 pp.81-104.
109   Causation and the postmodern critique of objectivity. J. Tim O'Meara. **Anth. Th.** 1:1 3:2001 pp.31-56.
110   Collingwood on re-enactment and the identity of thought. Giuseppina D'Oro. **J. Hist. Philos.** XXXVIII:1 1:2000 pp.87-102.
111   Consequential evaluation and practical reason. Amartya Sen. **J. Phil.** XCVII:9 9:2000 pp.477-502.
112   A critique of methodological reason. Stanley Aronowitz; Robert Ausch. **Sociol. Q.** 41:4 Fall:2000 pp.699-719.
113   Critique of pure reason. Immanuel Kant; Allen W. Wood [Ed.]; Paul Guyer [Ed.]. Cambridge: Cambridge University Press, 1998. xi, 785p. *ISBN: 0521354021. Translated from the German Kritik der reinen Vernunft. Includes bibliographical references (p. 77-80) and index. (Series:* The Cambridge edition of the works of Immanuel Kant).
114   Davidson on meaning normativity: public or social. John Fennell. **Eur. J. Phil.** 8:2 8:2000 pp.139-154.
115   Elección racional. *[In Spanish]*; [Rational choice]. Pau Marí-Klose. Madrid: Centro de Investigaciones Sociológicas, 2000. 197p. *ISBN: 8474762928.*
116   Formal rationality and its pernicious effects on the social sciences. Harold Kincaid. **Philos. S. Sc.** 30:1 3:2000 pp.67-88.
117   Habermas and Kant: judgement and communicative experience. Ståle R.S. Finke. **Philos. Soc. Crit.** 26:6 11:2000 pp.21-46.
118   Identity is simple. Ken Akiba. **Am. Phil. Q.** 37:4 10:2000 pp.389-404.
119   Interpretative Soziologien. *[In German]*; [Interpretative sociology]. Thomas Eberle; Ronald Hitzler; Albert Ogien; Rodney Watson. **Schweiz. Z. Soziologie** 26:3 12:2000 pp.449-529. *Collection of 4 articles.*
120   Judgment and truth in Frege. Michael Kremer. **J. Hist. Philos.** XXXVIII:4 10:2000 pp.549-581.
121   Kant and the reach of reason: studies in Kant's theory of rational systematization. Nicholas Rescher. New York: Cambridge University Press, 1999. 258p. *ISBN: 0521661005, 0521667917. Includes bibliographical references and index.*
122   Lenguaje y cultura o lo imaginario y la razón. Una aproximación a la hermenéutica simbólica. *[In Spanish]*; [Language and culture or the imaginary and rationality: an approximation of symbolic hermeneutics] *[Summary]*. Blanca Solares. **Rev. Mexicana Cien. Pol.** XLIII:174 10-12:1998 pp.61-80.
123   Lo global y lo local: una forma de arqueología. *[In Spanish]*; [Global and local knowledge: a form of archaeology]. Olga del Pilar López. **Rev. Univ. EAFIT** 115 7-9:1999 pp.71-80.

B: THEORY AND METHODOLOGY

124 Made for each other: the interdependence of deconstruction and philosophical hermeneutics. Stephen M. Feldman. **Philos. Soc. Crit.** 26:1 1:2000 pp.51-70.
125 Minding the world: Adorno's critique of idealism. Espen Hammer. **Philos. Soc. Crit.** 26:1 1:2000 pp.71-92.
126 Objectivism in hermeneutics? Gadamer, Habermas, Dilthey. Austin Harrington. **Philos. S. Sc.** 30:4 12:2000 pp.491-507.
127 On sources and narratives in historical social science: a realist critique of positivist and postmodernist epistemologies. Joseph M. Bryant. **Br. J. Soc.** 51:3 9:2000 pp.489-524.
128 On why the best should always meet. Tor Sandqvist. **Econ. Philos.** 16:2 10:2000 pp.287-313.
129 Outline of a theory of reasonable deliberation. Anthony Simon Laden. **Can. J. Phil.** 30:4 12:2000 pp.551-579.
130 Pascalian meditations. Pierre Bourdieu; Richard Nice [Tr.]. Cambridge: Polity Press, 2000. vii, 256p. *ISBN: 074562054X, 0745620558. Translated from the French. Includes bibliographical references and indexes.*
131 Practical rationality, morality, and purely justificatory reasons. Joshua Gert. **Am. Phil. Q.** 37:3 7:2000 pp.227-243.
132 Le *Pramāṇaratna* de Raghunātha, traité de gnoséologie bhatta-mīmāṃsaka. *[In French]*; [Raghunātha's *Pramāṇaratn*, treatise on the bhatta-mīmāṃsaka theory of knowledge] *[Summary]*. Gerdi Gerschheimer. **Bull. Ét. Indien.** 16 1998 pp.51-82.
133 The problem of intuition. Steven D. Hales. **Am. Phil. Q.** 37:2 4:2000 pp.135-147.
134 La raison, l'Orient et l'Occident. *[In French]*; [Reason, East and West]. Amartya Sen. **Esprit** 270 12:2000 pp.80-98.
135 La réalité et/de la nature. *[In French]*; [Reality and/of nature]. Robert Cresswell. **Homme** 157 1-3:2001 pp.175-195.
136 Reason without freedom: the problem of epistemic normativity. David Owens. London, New York: Routledge, 2000. 199p. *ISBN: 0415223881, 041522389X. Includes bibliographical references and index. (Series:* International library of philosophy).
137 Resisting explanation. G.R. Mayes. **Argumentation** 14:4 11:2000 pp.361-380.
138 The role of contexts in understanding and explanation. Mark Bevir. **Human St.** 23:4 10:2000 pp.395-411.
139 So we need something else for reason to mean. Nikolas Kompridis. **Int. J. Phil. Stud.** 8:3 10:2000 pp.271-296.
140 The truth of the matter: Roy Bhaskar's critical realism and the concept of alethic truth. Ruth Groff. **Philos. S. Sc.** 30:3 9:2000 pp.407-435.
141 Two dogmas of belief reason. Hans Rott. **J. Phil.** XCVII:9 9:2000 pp.503-522.
142 Wanderung zwischen den Welten. Erkenntnistheoretische Voraussetzungen des Eigen- und Fremdverstehens am Beispiel der afrikanischen Philosophie. *[In German]*; [Travelling between two worlds: assumptions in knowledge theory about self-understanding and understanding others in African philosophy]. Erika Dettmar. **Paideuma** 45 1999 pp.161-180.

Historiography
Historiographie

143 After the *Nueva Historia*: recent trends in Peruvian historiography. Paulo Drinot. **R. Eur. Lat.am. Caribe** 68 4:2000 pp.65-76.
144 Alexander Hirner — a historian of Slovak sociology. Robert Klobucký. **Sociologia [Brat.]** 32:6 Fall:2000 pp.555-576.
145 Amos Funkenstein's perceptions of Jewish history: an evaluation of his work by his students. David Biale; Abraham P. Socher; Peter Eli Gordon; Nina Caputo; Stephen D. Benin; David Sorkin; David Engel; Steven J. Zipperstein. **Jew. Soc. Stud.** 6:1 Fall:1999 pp.1-149. *Collection of 9 articles.*

B: THÉORIE ET MÉTHODOLOGIE

146 The autonomy of history: truth and method from Erasmus to Gibbon. Joseph M. Levine. Chicago IL, London: University of Chicago Press, 1999. xviii, 249p. *ISBN: 0226475417*. *Includes bibliographical references and index.*

147 L'avenir du Canada: par rapport à quelle histoire? *[In French]*; [Canada's future: in relation to which history?] Jocelyn Létourneau. **Can. Hist. R.** 81:2 6:2000 pp.230-259.

148 Bias in historical description, interpretation, and explanation. C. Behan McCullagh. **Hist. Theory** 39:1 2000 pp.39-66.

149 Competing master narratives on post-war Canada. Alvin Finkel. **Acadiensis** XXIX:2 Spring:2000 pp.188-204.

150 Competing memories of the nation: liberal historians and the reconstruction of the Swiss past 1870-1900. Oliver Zimmer. **Past Pres.** 168 8:2000 pp.194-226.

151 De l'abus de l'historiographie. Approches de l'histoire Russe de Herberstein à Custine. *[In French]*; (Historiographical abuse. Approaches to the history of Russia from Herberstein to Custine.) Francine-Dominique Liechtenhan. **Cah. Mon. Russe** 41:1 1-3:2000 pp.135-150.

152 Eight Eurocentric historians. James M. Blaut. New York, London: Guilford Press, 2000. 228p. *ISBN: 1572305916, 1572305908. Includes index.*

153 The English idea of history from Coleridge to Collingwood. Christopher Parker. Aldershot: Ashgate, 2000. vii, 244p. *ISBN: 1840142545. Includes bibliographical references (p. [231]-240) and index.*

154 Explaining large-scale historical change. Daniel Little. **Philos. S. Sc.** 30:1 3:2000 pp.89-112.

155 A fiction of the past: the sixties in American history. Dominick Cavallo. New York: St. Martin's Press, 1999. 282p. *ISBN: 031221930X. Includes bibliographical references (p. [257]-278) and index.*

156 Francesco Patrizi in the 'time-sack': history and rhetorical philosophy. Paul Richard Blum. **J. Hist. Ideas.** 61:1 1:2000 pp.59-74.

157 German childhoods: the making of a historiography. Nicholas Stargardt. **Ger. Hist.** 16:1 1998 pp.1-15.

158 Geschichtstheorie zwischen postmoderner Philosophie und geschichtswissenschaftlicher Praxis. *[In German]*; [Historical theory between postmodern philosophy and historical practice]. Georg G. Iggers. **Gesch. Ges.** 26:2 4-6:2000 pp.335-346.

159 Historia y ensayo en Germán Arciniegas. *[In Spanish]*; [History and essay in the work of Germán Arciniegas]. Roberto Machuca Becerra. **Cuad. Am.** 82:4 7-8:2000 pp.22-39.

160 Historians and social values. Joseph Th. Leerssen [Ed.]; Ann Rigney [Ed.]. Amsterdam: Amsterdam University Press, 2000. 243p. *ISBN: 9053564586. Huizinga Institute (Dutch National Research Institute of Cultural History).*

161 Les historiens et le travail de mémoire. *[In French]*; [Historians and the work of memory]. Olivier Mongin; Emmanuel Macron; Paul Ricœur; Olivier Abel; Benjamin Stora; Thierry Maurice; Henry Laurens; Rony Brauman; Stephen Smith; Claudine Vidal; Marc Le Pape; Jean-Pierre Chrétien. **Esprit** 266-267 8-9:2000 pp.6-189. *Collection of 9 articles.*

162 History and subjectivity. Geoffrey M. White; James V. Wertsch; Keiko Matsuki; Regina M. Feldman; John Eidson; Charlotte Linde. **Ethos** 28:4 12:2000 pp.493-632. *Collection of 6 articles.*

163 History by the numbers: an introduction to quantitative approaches. Pat Hudson. London, New York: Arnold Publishing Ltd., 2000. xxi, 278p. *ISBN: 0340663227, 0340614684. Includes bibliographical references and index.*

164 'I riro i te hoko': problems in cross-cultural historical scholarship. Angela Ballara. **N.Z. J. Hist.** 34:1 4:2000 pp.20-33.

165 La investigación histórica del 'tiempo presente' en Alemania. *[In Spanish]*; [The historical investigation of the 'present' in Germany] *[Summary]*. Walther L. Bernecker. **Rev. Mexicana Cien. Pol.** XLIII:174 10-12:1998 pp.17-37.

166 Istoricheskaia sotsiologiia v strukture sotsiologicheskogo znaniia. *[In Russian]*; (Historical sociology in the structure of sociological knowledge.) *[Summary]*. N.V. Romanovskii. **Sot. Issle.** 6 2000 pp.10-20.

B: THEORY AND METHODOLOGY

167 Istorizm sotsial'no-politicheskogo iavleniia (otnoshenie sotsiologii i istoriografii v svete problemy istorizma). *[In Russian]*; [The historicism of a socio-political phenomenon (the relationship of sociology to historigraphy in the light of the historicism problem]. A.G. Nikitina. **Polis [Moscow]** 5(58) 2000 pp.167-177.

168 «L'Acadie, c'est un détail»: les représentations de l'Acadie dans le récit national Canadien. *[In French]*; ['Acadia? A mere detail'. Representations of Acadia in the Canadian national narrative]. Jacques Paul Couturier. **Acadiensis** XXIX:2 Spring:2000 pp.102-119.

169 Lester Grabbe and historiography: an apologia. Thomas L. Thompson. **Scan. J. Old. Test.** 14:1 2000 pp.140-161.

170 The liberal order framework: a prospectus for a reconnaissance of Canadian history. Ian McKay. **Can. Hist. R.** 81:4 12:2000 pp.617-645.

171 Melodrama and the historians. Rohan McWilliam. **Rad. Hist. R.** 78 Fall:2000 pp.57-84.

172 Mythes et archives: l'historiographie indonésienne vue de Bima. *[In French]*; (Myths and archives: Indonesian historiography seen from Bima.) *[Summary]*. Henri Chambert-Loir. **B. Éc. Fr. Ex.-Or.** 87:1 2000 pp.215-246.

173 Die neueste deutsche Geschichte aus skandinavischer Sicht. Das Deutschland-Bild in Skandinavien und die skandinavische Deutschland-Forschung. *[In German]*; [Recent German history from a Scandinavian perspective. The image of Germany in Scandinavia and Scandinavian research on Germany]. Karl Christian Lammers. **Gesch. Ges.** 26:2 4-6:2000 pp.347-366.

174 New developments in history in the 1950s and 1960s. Jim Obelkevich. **Contemp. Br. Hist.** 14:4 Winter:2000 pp.125-167.

175 New historicism: postmodern historiography between narrativism and heterology. Jürgen Pieters. **Hist. Theory** 39:1 2000 pp.21-38.

176 New methods for social history. Larry J. Griffin [Ed.]; Marcel van der Linden [Ed.]. Cambridge, New York: Cambridge University Press, 1998. 165p. *ISBN: 0521655994.* (*Series:* International review of social history. Supplement - 6).

177 New perspectives on the modern history of Korea. Cho Songgu. **Asian Res. Trends** 9 1999 pp.63-80.

178 On the case: explorations in social history. Mariana Valverde; J.R. Miller; Doug Owram; Shirley Tillotson; Bryan D. Palmer; Franca Iacovetta [Comments by]; Wendy Mitchinson [Comments by]. **Can. Hist. R.** 81:2 6:2000 pp.266-294.

179 Oral history: a handbook. Ken Howarth. Stroud: Sutton Publishing, 1998. ix, 214p. *ISBN: 0750917563. Includes bibliographical references (p. 209) and index.*

180 Path dependence in historical sociology. James Mahoney. **Theory Soc.** 29:4 8:2000 pp.507-548.

181 A place for memory: the interface between individual and collective history. Michael G. Kenny. **Comp. Stud. S.** 41:3 7:1999 pp.420-437.

182 The pursuit of history: aims, methods and new directions in the study of modern history. John Tosh. Harlow, New York: Longman, 2000. x, 227p. *ISBN: 0582304717. Includes bibliographical references (p. 215-218) and index.* (*Series:* The silver library).

183 Reflektierte Archivarbeit — der „Königsweg" osteuropäischer Zeitgeschichte. Die übersichtliche „Welt der Modelle" und die „konstitutive Widersprüchlichkeit" des Sowjetsystems. *[In German]*; [Reflexive archival research - the ideal method for contemporary Eastern European history. The 'clear view' provided by a 'world of models' and the 'constitutive inconsistency' of the Soviet system]. Klaus Gestwa. **Osteuropa** 50:5 5:2000 pp.549-561.

184 (Re)imag(in)ing other[2]ness: a postmortem for the postmodern in India. Richard M. Eaton. **J. World Hist.** II:1 Spring:2000 pp.57-78.

185 A retrospective of historiography in China at the turn of the century and a look at its future. Dai Yi. **Soc. Sci. China** XXI:1 Spring:2000 pp.157-170.

186 O sangue da terra. Novas perspectivas da historiografia Brasileira. *[In Portuguese]*; [The blood of the earth: new perspectives on Brazilian historiography] *[Summary]*; *[Summary in French]*. Antonio Torres Montenegro. **Caravelle** 75 2000 pp.77-92.

B: THÉORIE ET MÉTHODOLOGIE

187 Should Korean historians abandon nationalism? Chan-Seung Park. **Korea J.** 39:2 Summer:1999 pp.318-342.
188 Thinking beyond the boundaries: empire, feminism and the domains of history. Antoinette Burton. **Soc. Hist.** 26:1 1:2001 pp.60-71.
189 Today's view of the Third Reich and the Second World War in German historiographical discourse. Ulrich Schlie. **Hist. J.** 43:2 6:2000 pp.543-564.
190 Toward the Islamization of history: a historical survey. M.M.M. Mahroof. **Am. J. Islam. Soc. Sci.** 17:1 Spring:2000 pp.65-83.
191 Trends in Western historiography on Korea. Sung-gi Hong. **Korea J.** 39:3 Autumn:1999 pp.338-350.
192 Truth's other: ethics, the history of the Holocaust, and historiographical theory after the linguistic turn. Michael Dintenfass. **Hist. Theory** 39:1 2000 pp.1-20.
193 Ubiquity: the science of history - or why the world is simpler than we think. Mark Buchanan. London: Weidenfeld & Nicolson, 2000. 224p. *ISBN: 0297643762*.
194 Voice of the past: oral history. Paul Richard Thompson. New York: Oxford University Press, 2000. *ISBN: 0192893173. Includes bibliographical references and index.*
195 Von der Historischen Sozialwissenschaft zur Historischen Anthropologie? *[In German]*; [From historical social science to historical anthropology?] *[Summary]*. Michael Mitterauer. **Hist. Soc. R.** 25:2 2000 pp.139-177.
196 Who matters? Public history and the invention of the Canadian past. Frits Pannekoek. **Acadiensis** XXIX:2 Spring:2000 pp.205-217.
197 Word *and* deed: why a *post*-poststructural history is needed, and how it might look. Adrian Jones. **Hist. J.** 43:2 6:2000 pp.517-541.
198 Writing First Nations into Canadian history: a review of recent scholarly works. Ken Coates. **Can. Hist. R.** 81:1 3:2000 pp.99-114.

Philosophy
Philosophie

199 African theory of mind-body: an Esan cultural paradigm. Godwin Azenabor. **Afr. Q.** 39:4 1999 pp.121-134.
200 Approaching the *Dao*: from Lao Zi to Zhuang Zi. Wenyu Xie. **J. Ch. Philos.** 27:4 12:2000 pp.469-488.
201 Aristotle's ethics: critical essays. Nancy Sherman [Ed.]. Lanham MD, Oxford: Rowman & Littlefield, 1999. xviii, 331p. *ISBN: 0847689158, 084768914X. Includes bibliographical references. (Series:* Critical essays on the classics).
202 Art, language, and truth in Heidegger's radical zen. Archie S. Graham. **J. Ch. Philos.** 27:4 12:2000 pp.503-544.
203 Autonomy unbound. Paul Barry Clarke. Aldershot: Ashgate, 1999. vii, 384p. *ISBN: 1840147989. Includes bibliographical references and index.*
204 Bodies and eternity: Nietzsche's relation to the feminine. Katrin Froese. **Philos. Soc. Crit.** 26:1 1:2000 pp.25-50.
205 Broken imperatives: the ethical dimension of Nancy's thought. James Gilbert-Walsh. **Philos. Soc. Crit.** 26:2 3:2000 pp.29-50.
206 Charles Taylor on overcoming incommensurability. Neil Levy. **Philos. Soc. Crit.** 26:5 9:2000 pp.47-61.
207 Charles Taylor's *Sources of the Self*: a transcendental apologetic? D.P. Baker. **Int. J. Philos. Relig.** 47:3 6:2000 pp.155-174.
208 Christian Thomasius and the desacralization of philosophy. Ian Hunter. **J. Hist. Ideas.** 61:4 10:2000 pp.595-616.
209 A common humanity: thinking about love and truth and justice. Raimond Gaita. London: Routledge, 2000. 293p. *ISBN: 0415241138.*
210 Conditions for understanding the meaning of a sentence: the *Nyāya* and the *Advaita Vedānta*. J.L. Shaw. **J. Ind. Phil.** 28:3 6:2000 pp.273-294.

B: THEORY AND METHODOLOGY

211 Confucius and act-centered morality. Hsei-yung Hsu. **J. Ch. Philos.** 27:3 9:2000 pp.331-344.

212 Contingency and the 'time of the dream': Kuki Shūz and French pre-war philosophy. Thorsten Botz-Bornstein. **Philos. E.W.** 50:4 10:2000 pp.481-506.

213 Correlations, constellations and the truth: Adorno's ontology of redemption. David Kaufmann. **Philos. Soc. Crit.** 26:5 9:2000 pp.62-80.

214 The crisis of reason: European thought, 1848-1914. J.W. Burrow. New Haven CT: Yale University Press, 2000. 271p. *ISBN: 0300083904. Includes bibliographical references and index. (Series:* Yale intellectual history of the West).

215 La critique de l'objectivisme et le problème de la psychologie phénoménologique chez Sartre et Merleau-Ponty. *[In French]*; [The critique of objectivism and the problem of phenomenological psychology in Sartre and Merleau-Ponty]. Jan Patočka. **Temps Mod.** 55:608 3-5:2000 pp.223-234.

216 Cultivating ethos through the body. Seamus Carey. **Human St.** 23:1 1:2000 pp.23-42.

217 Currents in contemporary French intellectual life. Nick Hewlett [Ed.]; Christopher Flood [Ed.]. Basingstoke: Macmillan, 2000. 248p. *ISBN: 0333714318. Includes index.*

218 Deleuze et Sartre: idée d'une conscience impersonnelle. *[In French]*; [Deleuze and Sartre: the idea of an impersonal conscience]. Jean Khalfa. **Temps Mod.** 55:608 3-5:2000 pp.189-222.

219 [Desire and the other: comments on Hegel's concept of self-awareness]; *[Text in Japanese]*. Eiyoshi Kikuchi. **St. Ess. Beh. Sc. Phil.** 20 3:2000 pp.113-134.

220 Developing the modern concept of the self: the trial of Meister Eckhart. Ben Morgan. **Telos** 116 Summer:1999 pp.56-80.

221 Does continuous creation entail occasionalism? Malebranche (and Descartes). Andrew Pessin. **Can. J. Phil.** 30:3 9:2000 pp.413-440.

222 Dummett's antirealism and time. Yuval Dolev. **Eur. J. Phil.** 8:3 12:2000 pp.253-276.

223 Durkheimian time. William Watts Miller. **Time Soc.** 9:1 3:2000 pp.5-20.

224 The early intellectual careers of Bakhtin and Herzen: towards a philosophy of the act. Ruth Coates. **Stud. East. Eur. Th.** 52:4 12:2000 pp.239-258.

225 Education, ecology, and science: an international symposium on Whitehead's process philosophy. Jack G. Priestley; Howard Woodhouse; Elspeth Crawford; Brian Hendley; Alan Peacock; Pete A.Y. Gunter; Paul Ernest; Mark Flynn; Mary Elizabeth Moore; J.M. Breuvart; Ian Winchester; Sandra Fidyk; Jan Van der Veken. **Interchange** 31:2-3 2000 pp.117-334. *Collection of 13 articles.*

226 Emotional reason: how to deliberate about value. Bennett Helm. **Am. Phil. Q.** 37:1 1:2000 pp.1-22.

227 Ethical explorations. John Skorupski. Oxford, New York: Oxford University Press, 1999. viii, 300p. *ISBN: 0198238304. Includes bibliographical references.*

228 Expressivism, projectivism and Santayana. Glenn Tiller. **J. Hist. Philos.** 38:2 4:2000 pp.239-258.

229 La felicidad en la obra de Schopenhauer. *[In Spanish]*; (Happiness in the work of Schopenhauer.) Enrique Suárez-Íñiguez. **Est. Polí.** 21 5-8:1999 pp.219-234.

230 Fifty Eastern thinkers. Diané Collinson; Kathryn Plant; Robert Wilkinson. London: Routledge, 2000. xvii, 425p. *ISBN: 0415202841. Includes bibliographical references and index. (Series:* Routledge key guides).

231 Fodor on concepts: philosophical aspects. Christopher Peacocke. **Mind Lang.** 15:2-3 4-6:2000 pp.327-340.

232 Freedom and fatefulness: Augustine, Arendt and the journey of memory. Dean Hammer. **Theory Cult. Soc.** 17:2 4:2000 pp.83-104.

233 From Gangeśa's *Tattvacintāmani*: discourse on perceptual presentation of something as other than what it is. Stephen H. Phillips; N.S. Ramanuja Tatacharya. **J. Ind. Phil.** 28:5-6 12:2000 pp.567-650.

234 German philosophy since Kant. Anthony O'Hear [Ed.]. Cambridge, New York: Cambridge University Press, 1999. vi, 445p. *ISBN: 0521667828. Includes bibliographical references and index. (Series:* Royal Institute of Philosophy supplement - 44).

B: THÉORIE ET MÉTHODOLOGIE

235 Hegel, les juifs et nous. *[In French]*; [Hegel, the Jews and us]. Joseph Cohen; Raphaël Zagury-Orly. **Temps Mod.** 55:608 3-5:2000 pp.279-295.

236 Heidegger and *Dasein*'s 'bodily nature': what is the hidden problematic? David R. Cerbone. **Int. J. Phil. Stud.** 8:2 6:2000 pp.209-230.

237 Humanism and early modern philosophy. Jill Kraye [Ed.]; M.W.F. Stone [Ed.]. New York: Routledge, 2000. 288p. *ISBN: 0415186161. Includes bibliographical references and index.* (*Series:* London studies in the history of philosophy).

238 An intelligent person's guide to ethics. Mary Warnock. London: Duckworth, 1998. 128p. *ISBN: 0715628410. Includes index.*

239 Internal and external opposition to the Bodhisattva's gift of his body. Reiko Ohnuma. **J. Ind. Phil.** 28:1 2:2000 pp.43-76.

240 José Gaos. *[In Spanish]*; [José Gaos]. Leopoldo Zea. **Cuad. Am.** 79:1 1-2:2000 pp.13-63.

241 K 100-letiiu so dnia smerti F. Nietzsche. *[In Russian]*; (The 100th anniversary of F. Nietzsche's death.) B.V. Markov; W. Stegmaier; P.G. Vyzhletsov; A.G. Pogoniailo; I.I. Evlampiev; Iu.F. Voropaev; M.M. Pozdnev. **Vest. Lenin. Univ.** 6 3(22) 12:2000 pp.3-57. *Collection of 7 articles.*

242 Kant trouble: the obscurities of the enlightened. Diane Morgan. New York: Routledge, 2000. 224p. *ISBN: 0415183529, 0415183537. Includes bibliographical references and index.* (*Series:* Warwick studies in European philosophy).

243 Khabermas i Fuko - teoretiki grazhdanskogo obshchestva. *[In Russian]*; (Habermas and Foucault: thinkers for civil society.) *[Summary]*. B. Flyvbjerg. **Sot. Issle.** 2 2000 pp.127-136.

244 Kierkegaard and what we mean by 'philosophy'. Alastair Hannay. **Int. J. Phil. Stud.** 8:1 3:2000 pp.1-22.

245 Knowledge and action I: means to the human end in *Bhātta Mīmāmsā* and *Advaita Vedānta*. C. Ram-Prasad. **J. Ind. Phil.** 28:1 2:2000 pp.1-24.

246 Knowledge and action II: attaining liberation in *Bhātta Mīmāmsā* and *Advaita Vedānta*. C. Ram-Prasad. **J. Ind. Phil.** 28:1 2:2000 pp.25-42.

247 Korean thought in the 20th century. Young-bae Song; Sang-ik Lee; Woo-sung Huh; Jae-hyun Kim; Jae-soon Park; Yun-gi Hong. **Korea J.** 40:2 Summer:2000 pp.5-194. *Collection of 6 articles.*

248 The limits of irony: Rorty and the China challenge. Randall Peerenboom; Richard Rorty [Comments by]. **Philos. E.W.** 50:1 1:2000 pp.56-96.

249 Losev i Chekhov: k postanovke problemy. *[In Russian]*; (Losev and Chekhov: some ideas.) E.A. Takho-Godi. **Vest. Mosk. Univ. Ser. 9 Filol.** 2 3-4:2000 pp.92-105.

250 Metaphysics in Dōgen. Kevin Schilbrack. **Philos. E.W.** 50:1 1:2000 pp.34-55.

251 Metaphysics to metafictions: Hegel, Nietzsche, and the end of philosophy. Paul S. Miklowitz. Albany NY: State University of New York Press, 1998. xxv, 221p. *ISBN: 0791438783, 0791438775. Includes bibliographical references (p. 193-209) and index.* (*Series:* SUNY series in Hegelian studies).

252 Michel Foucault: materialism and education. Mark Olssen. Westport CT, London: Bergin & Garvey, 1999. xii, 201p. *ISBN: 0897895878. Includes bibliographical references and index.* (*Series:* Critical studies in education and culture).

253 Mind the gap: the philosophy of Gillian Rose. Nigel Tubbs. **Thes. Elev.** 60 2:2000 pp.42-60.

254 The mind's eternity in Spinoza's *Ethics*. Steven Parchment. **J. Hist. Philos.** XXXVIII:3 7:2000 pp.349-382.

255 Moral disagreements: classic and contemporary readings. Christopher W. Gowans [Ed.]. New York: Routledge, 2000. 264p. *ISBN: 0415217113, 0415217121. Includes bibliographical references and index.*

256 The mystery of truth: Louis-Claude de Saint-Martin's enlightened mysticism. David Bates. **J. Hist. Ideas.** 61:4 10:2000 pp.635-656.

257 Naturalism: a critical analysis. J.P. Moreland [Ed.]; William Lane Craig [Ed.]. London: Routledge, 2000. 286p. *ISBN: 0415235243. Includes bibliographical references and index.* (*Series:* Routledge studies in twentieth century philosophy - 5).

B: THEORY AND METHODOLOGY

258 The nature of properties: nominalism, realism, and trope theory. Michael Tooley [Ed.]. New York: Garland Publishing, 1999. xvi, 374p. *ISBN: 0815330669. Includes bibliographical references. (Series:* Analytical metaphysics - 3).

259 Necesidad y azar. *[In Spanish]*; (Necessity and fate.) Fernando Ayala Blanco. **Est. Polí.** 21 5-8:1999 pp.235-246.

260 Necessity and possibility: the metaphysics of modality. Michael Tooley [Ed.]. New York: Garland Publishing, 1999. xxiv, 394p. *ISBN: 081533382X. Includes bibliographical references. (Series:* Analytical metaphysics - 5).

261 The need for philosophical analysis in a postmodern era. Robin Barrow. **Interchange** 30:4 1999 pp.415-432.

262 The new Wittgenstein. Alice Marguerite Crary [Ed.]; Rupert J. Read [Ed.]. New York: Routledge, 2000. 403p. *ISBN: 0415173183, 0415173191. Includes bibliographical references and index.*

263 Nietzsche on nobility and the affirmation of life. Christopher Hamilton. **Ethic. Theory Moral P.** 3:2 6:2000 pp.169-193.

264 Nietzsche's metaethics: against the privilege readings. Brian Leiter. **Eur. J. Phil.** 8:3 12:2000 pp.277-297.

265 Non-I and thou: Nishida, Buber, and the moral consequences of self-actualization. James W. Heisig. **Philos. E.W.** 50:2 2000 pp.179-207.

266 Onto-hermeneutics and Confucian hermeneutics. Francis Schüssler Fiorenza; Chung-ying Cheng; Yong Huang; Jane Geaney; Xunwu Chen; Warren G. Frisina. **J. Ch. Philos.** 27:1 3:2000 pp.1-125. *Collection of 6 articles.*

267 Ontotheology? Understanding Heidegger's *destruktion* of metaphysics. Iain Thomson. **Int. J. Phil. Stud.** 8:3 10:2000 pp.297-328.

268 Peter Winch and 'the idea of a social science'. Steven Lukes; John Horton; Vincent Descombes; Brian Fay; Philip Pettit; Nigel Pleasants; Theodore R. Schatzki; Frank Cioffi; Peter Lassman; Michael Lynch. **Hist. Human Sci.** 13:1 2:2000 pp.3-156. *Collection of 10 articles.*

269 The philosophy of social science: new perspectives. Garry Potter. New York: Prentice Hall, 2000. ix, 256p. *ISBN: 0582369746. Includes bibliographical references and index.*

270 Piety, justice, and the unity of virtue. Mark L. McPherran. **J. Hist. Philos.** XXXVIII:3 7:2000 pp.299-328.

271 Plenitude, possibility, and the limits of reason: a medieval Arabic debate on the metaphysics of nature. Taneli Kukkonen. **J. Hist. Ideas.** 61:4 10:2000 pp.539-560.

272 Possible worlds in the *Tahâfut al-tahâfut*: Averroes on plenitude and possibility. Taneli Kukkonen. **J. Hist. Philos.** XXXVIII:3 7:2000 pp.329-347.

273 Problems of Chinese moral philosophy. A.S. Cua. **J. Ch. Philos.** 27:3 9:2000 pp.269-286.

274 Problems of moral philosophy. Theodor W. Adorno; Thomas Schröder [Ed.]; Rodney Livingstone [Tr.]. Oxford: Polity Press, 2000. viii, 224p. *ISBN: 074561941X. Translated from the German Probleme der Moralphilosophie. Includes index.*

275 Realism detranscendentalized. José L. Zalabardo. **Eur. J. Phil.** 8:1 4:2000 pp.63-88.

276 Reductionist contractualism: moral motivation and the expanding self. David W. Shoemaker. **Can. J. Phil.** 30:3 9:2000 pp.343-370.

277 Repetition and ethics in late Foucault. Michael Schwartz. **Telos** 117 Fall:2000 pp.113-132.

278 Resentment and the 'feminine' in Nietzsche's politico-aesthetics. Caroline Joan Picart. University Park PA: Pennsylvania State University Press, 1999. viii, 206p. *ISBN: 0271018887, 0271018895. Includes bibliographical references (p. [181]-186) and index.*

279 La revolución kantiana de Luhmann. *[In Spanish]*; [Luhmann's Kantian revolution]. Javier Torres Nafarrate. **Acta Sociol. [Mexico]** 25 1-4:1999 pp.69-80.

280 Rôle historique de la philosophie arabo-musulmane dans l'évolution des tendances matérialistes mondiales. *[In French]*; [The historical role of Arab-Muslim philosophy in the development of global materialist trends]. Hussein M'Roué. **Pensée** 323 7-9:2000 pp.143-158.

281 «Siècles, voici mon siècle, solitaire...» réflexions sur: *Le Siècle de Sartre* de Bernard-Henri Lévy. *[In French]*; ['Centuries, here is my century, alone...'. Reflections on *Le Siècle*

de Sartre by Bernard-Henri Lévy]. Juliette Simont. **Temps Mod.** 55:608 3-5:2000 pp.153-182.

282 The significance of Jewishness for Wittgenstein's philosophy. David G. Stern. **Inquiry** 43:4 12:2000 pp.383-401.

283 Simone de Beauvoir writing the self: philosophy becomes autobiography. Jo-Ann Pilardi. Westport CT, London: Greenwood Press, 1999. 133p. *ISBN: 0275963349, 0313302537. Includes bibliographical references and index. (Series:* Contributions in philosophy - 60).

284 The social bearing of nature. Theodore R. Schatzki. **Inquiry** 43:1 3:2000 pp.21-38.

285 The structure of the social. Jonathan Joseph; Simon Kennedy. **Philos. S. Sc.** 30:4 12:2000 pp.508-527.

286 Synergy of complements and the exclusivity of opposites. György G. János. **Wor. Futur.** 56:1 2000 pp.1-19.

287 Ten modes of individualism — none of which works — and their alternatives. Mario Bunge. **Philos. S. Sc.** 30:3 9:2000 pp.384-406.

288 *The sociology of philosophies: a global theory of intellectual change* by Randall Collins. Peter Munz; Mario Bunge; Steve Fuller; Brian Baigrie; I.C. Jarvie; Jagdish Hattiangadi; Randall Collins. **Philos. S. Sc.** 30:2 6:2000 pp.157-325. *Collection of 8 articles.*

289 Theories of concepts: a wider task. Christopher Peacocke. **Eur. J. Phil.** 8:3 12:2000 pp.298-321.

290 Time and causation. Michael Tooley [Ed.]. New York: Garland Publishing, 1999. xvi, 392p. *ISBN: 0815330650. Includes bibliographical references. (Series:* Analytical metaphysics - 2).

291 Time and space reunited. Zygmunt Bauman. **Time Soc.** 9:2-3 6-9:2000 pp.171-186.

292 Too-blue: colour-patch for an expanded empiricism. Brian Massumi. **Cult. St.** 14:2 4:2000 pp.177-226.

293 Towards an ethics of love: Arendt on the will and St. Augustine. Lauren Swayne Barthold. **Philos. Soc. Crit.** 26:6 11:2000 pp.1-20.

294 Understanding Foucault. Geoff Danaher; Jen Webb; Tony Schirato. London: Sage Publications, 2000. xv, 172p. *ISBN: 0761968164, 0761968156. Includes bibliographical references and index.*

295 Utopie ou idéologie? *[In French]*; (Utopia or Ideology?) Nestor Capdevila. **Hom. Soc.** 136-137 2-3:2000 pp.77-94.

296 La vérité dans l'effectivité social-historique. *[In French]*; [The truth in socio-historical effectiveness]. Cornelius Castoriadis. **Temps Mod.** 55:609 6-8:2000 pp.41-70.

297 The very idea of sameness of extension across time. Gary Ebbs. **Am. Phil. Q.** 37:3 7:2000 pp.245-268.

298 Vrolijke wetenschap: Nietzsche als vriend. *[In Dutch]*; [Merry science: Nietzsche as a friend]. Niels Helsloot. Agora, 1999. 343p. *ISBN: 9039107521.*

299 Walter Benjamin: overpowering conformism. Esther Leslie. Sterling VA: Pluto Press, 2000. 298p. *ISBN: 0745315739. Includes bibliographical references. (Series:* Modern European thinkers).

300 What is claimed in a Kantian judgment of taste? Miles Rind. **J. Hist. Philos.** XXXVIII:1 1:2000 pp.63-86.

301 What philosophy might be about: some socio-philosophical speculations. Stan Godlovitch. **Inquiry** 43:1 3:2000 pp.3-20.

302 What we owe to each other. Thomas Scanlon. Cambridge MA, London: Belknap Press, 1998. 420p. *ISBN: 0674950895.*

303 Winch and Wittgenstein on understanding ourselves critically: descriptive not metaphysical. Nigel Pleasants. **Inquiry** 43:3 9:2000 pp.289-317.

304 Wittgenstein and the social sciences: critical reflections concerning Peter Winch's interpretations and appropriations of Wittgenstein's thought. Richard E. Flathman. **Hist. Human Sci.** 13:2 5:2000 pp.1-15.

305 Zygmunt Bauman: prophet of postmodernity. Dennis Smith. Cambridge; Malden MA: Polity Press; Blackwell Publishers, 1999. xi, 250p. *ISBN: 0745618987, 0745618995.*

B: THEORY AND METHODOLOGY

Includes bibliographical references (p. [221]-238) and index. (Series: Key contemporary thinkers).

Sociological theory
Théorie sociologique

306   The 'actors' of modern society: the cultural construction of social agency. John W. Meyer; Ronald L. Jepperson. **Sociol. Theory** 18:1 3:2000 pp.100-120.

307   The Adorno reader. Theodor W. Adorno; Brian O'Connor [Ed.]. Oxford, Malden MA: Blackwell Publishers, 2000. *ISBN: 0631210768, 0631210776. Includes bibliographical references and index. (Series:* Blackwell readers).

308   Advances in generative structuralism: structured agency and multilevel dynamics. T.J. Fararo; C.T. Butts. **J. Math. Sociol.** 24:1 1999 pp.1-65.

309   Against reflexivity as an academic virtue and source of privileged knowledge. Michael Lynch. **Theory Cult. Soc.** 17:3 6:2000 pp.26-54.

310   Alfred Schutz and the 'objectifying attitude'. Austin Harrington. **Sociology** 34:4 11:2000 pp.727-740.

311   André Gorz and the Sartrean legacy: arguments for a person-centered social theory. Finn Bowring. New York: St. Martin's Press, 2000. 218p. *ISBN: 0312231032. Includes bibliographical references and index.*

312   Antecedentes teóricos de la etnometodología y el interaccionismo simbólico. *[In Spanish]*; [Theoretical antecedents of ethnomethodology and symbolic interactionism] *[Summary]*. Cecilia Rodríguez Dorantes. **Rev. Mexicana Cien. Pol.** XLIII:174 10-12:1998 pp.39-60.

313   Anti-reductionist sociology. Roger Sibeon. **Sociology** 33:2 5:1999 pp.317-334.

314   *Beruf*, rationality and emotion in Max Weber's sociology; *[Summary in French]*; *[Summary in German]*. J.M. Barbalet. **Eur. J. Soc.** XLI:2 2000 pp.329-351.

315   Beyond the 'French fries and the Frankfurter': an agenda for critical theory. Lorraine Y. Landry. **Philos. Soc. Crit.** 26:2 3:2000 pp.99-129.

316   The Blackwell companion to major social theorists. George Ritzer [Ed.]. Malden MA: Blackwell Publishers, 2000. 800p. *ISBN: 0631207104. Includes bibliographical references and index. (Series:* Blackwell companions to sociology).

317   The Blackwell companion to social theory. Bryan S. Turner [Ed.]. Oxford, Cambridge MA: Blackwell Publishers, 2000. 570p. *ISBN: 063121366X. Includes bibliographical references and index.*

318   The Cambridge companion to Weber. Stephen P. Turner. Cambridge, New York: Cambridge University Press, 2000. xx, 288p. *ISBN: 0521561493, 052156753X. Includes bibliographical references (p. 272-278) and index.*

319   Can there be a Nietzschean sociology? W.G. Runciman. **Eur. J. Soc.** XLI:1 2000 pp.3-21.

320   Celebrating and advocating the personalisation of the world: a reply to Don Gardner. Nigel Rapport. **Aus. J. Anth.** 11:2 8:2000 pp.223-233.

321   Chinese relationalism: theoretical construction and methodological considerations. Kwang-Kuo Hwang. **J. Theory Soc. Behav.** 30:2 6:2000 pp.155-178.

322   Cidadania e multiculturalismo: a teoria social no Brasil contemporâneo. *[In Portuguese]*; [Citizenship and multiculturalism: social theory in contemporary Brazil]. Ilse Scherer-Warren; et al. Lisbon: Editora da UFSC, 2000. 202p.

323   A comparative analysis of theories of collective actions. Youngjae Jin. **Korea Obs.** 31:1 Spring:2000 pp.123-148.

324   Creativity and master trends in contemporary sociological theory. José Maurício Domingues. **Eur. J. Soc. Theory** 3:4 11:2000 pp.467-498.

325   Critical theory, politics, and society: an introduction. Peter M.R. Stirk. New York: Pinter, 1999. 246p. *ISBN: 1855675587, 1855675595. Includes bibliographical references and index.*

326   Culture and charisma: outline of a theory. Philip Smith. **Acta Sociol.** 43:2 2000 pp.101-112.

327 Death. So what? Sociology, sequestration and emancipation. Hugh Willmott. **Sociol. Rev.** 48:4 11:2000 pp.649-665.
328 Dekonstrukce jako politické jednání. *[In Czech]*; (Deconstruction as political action: two trends of deconstruction in contemporary social theory.) *[Summary]*. Ondřej Císař. **Soc. Čas.** 36:1 2000 pp.97-110.
329 Del funcionalismo al neofuncionalismo: creando una posición en el campo de la teoría social. *[In Spanish]*; [From functionalism to neofunctionalism: creating a position in the social theory camp]. Jeffrey C. Alexander; Adriana Murguía Lores. **Acta Sociol. [Mexico]** 25 1-4:1999 pp.105-128.
330 The development of Durkheim's social realism. Robert Alun Jones. Cambridge, New York: Cambridge University Press, 1999. xi, 324p. *ISBN: 0521650453. Includes bibliographical references (p. 309-316) and index. (Series:* Ideas in context - 55).
331 A difusão do limiar: margens, hegemonias e contradições. *[In Portuguese]*; (The diffusion of the threshold: fringes, hegemonies and contradictions.) João De Pina Cabral. **Anál. Soc.** XXXIV:153 Spring:2000 pp.865-892.
332 The dilemma of determinism: Qu Qiubai and the origins of Marxist philosophy in China. Nick Knight. **Chi. Inform.** XIII:4 Spring:1999 pp.1-26.
333 (Dis)figurations: discourse/critique/ethics. Ian H. Angus. London, New York: Verso, 2000. 269p. *ISBN: 1859847595, 1859842771. Includes index.*
334 Dreams of pure sociology. Donald Black. **Sociol. Theory** 18:3 11:2000 pp.343-367.
335 Esistenza e incolumità: una nota sulle recenti opere di Zygmunt Bauman. *[In Italian]*; [Existence and security: the recent works of Zygmunt Bauman]. Alessandro Dal Lago. **Rass. It. Soc.** XLI:1 1-3:2000 pp.131-142.
336 The essential Wallerstein. Immanuel Maurice Wallerstein. New York: New Press, 2000. 476p. *ISBN: 1565845854. Includes bibliographical references and index.*
337 ¿Está la experiencia aún en crisis? Reflexiones sobre un lamento de la escuela de Francfort. *[In Spanish]*; [Still in crisis? Lamenting the Frankfurt School]. Martin Jay. **Rev. Mexicana Cien. Pol.** XLIV:176 5-8:1999 pp.15-36.
338 The ethnological counter-current in sociology. Fuyuki Kurasawa. **Int. Sociol.** 15:1 3:2000 pp.11-32.
339 L'étrange carrière de la notion de classe sociale dans la tradition de Chicago en sociologie. *[In French]*; [The strange career of the notion of social class in the Chicago School]. Jean-Michel Chapoulie. **Eur. J. Soc.** XLI:1 2000 pp.53-70.
340 Explorations in critical social science. Michael Dillon; Kwok Wei Leng; Lisa Blackman; David Gartman; Serguei Alex Oushakine; Elizabeth Wilson; John Marks. **Theory Cult. Soc.** 17:5 10:2000 pp.1-151. *Collection of 7 articles.*
341 For Bourdieu, against Alexander: reality and reduction. Garry Potter. **J. Theory Soc. Behav.** 30:2 6:2000 pp.229-246.
342 From commodity production to sign production: a triple triangle model for Marx's semiotics and Peirce's economics. Joohan Kim. **Semiotica** 132:1-2 2000 pp.75-100.
343 From Kant to Weber: freedom and culture in classical German social theory. Paul. Kamolnick [Ed.]; Thomas M. Powers [Ed.]. Malabar FL: Krieger Publishing Company, 1999. xv, 202p. *ISBN: 0894649922. Includes bibliographical references and index. (Series:* Open forum series).
344 Gilles Deleuze, Félix Guattari and the total system. Mohamed Zayani. **Philos. Soc. Crit.** 26:1 1:2000 pp.93-114.
345 Handlungs- und Strukturtheorie nach Max Weber. *[In German]*; [A theory of agency and structure following Max Weber] *[Summary]*; *[Summary in French]*. Wolfgang Schluchter. **Berl. J. Soziol.** 10:1 2000 pp.125-136.
346 Hans Morgenthau's anti-Machiavellian Machiavellianism. Benjamin Wong. **Millennium** 29:2 2000 pp.389-409.
347 The hidden abode: sociology as analysis of the unexpected. Alejandro Portes [Speech by]. **Am. Sociol. R.** 65:1 2:2000 pp.1-18.
348 L'humanisme interminable de Claude Lévi-Strauss. *[In French]*; [The infinite humanism of Claude Lévi-Strauss]. Patrice Maniglier. **Temps Mod.** 55:609 6-8:2000 pp.216-241.

B: THEORY AND METHODOLOGY

349 The ideal of equality. Andrew Williams [Ed.]; Matthew Clayton [Ed.]. New York: St. Martin's Press, 2000. *ISBN: 0312230176. Includes bibliographical references and index.*

350 Identidad, tolerancia e intolerancia: un horizonte abierto a la investigación desde la teoría de los sistemas de Niklas Luhmann. *[In Spanish]*; [Identity, tolerance and intolerance: Niklas Luhmann's systems theory]. Silvia Molina y Vedia. **Rev. Mexicana Cien. Pol.** XLIV:176 5-8:1999 pp.37-60.

351 Ideology, the state, and the aesthetic level of practice. Gary Tedman. **Rethink. Marx.** 11:4 Winter:1999 pp.57-73.

352 The implications of scepticism. Petr Lom. **Eur. J. Soc. Theory** 3:3 8:2000 pp.325-338.

353 Intervenir dans le processus historique. *[In French]*; (Intervening in the historical process.) Zellig Harris. **Hom. Soc.** 136-137 2-3:2000 pp.29-56.

354 Introduction to sociology. Theodor W. Adorno; Christoph Gödde [Ed.]; Edmund Jephcott [Tr.]. Stanford CA: Stanford University Press, 2000. ix, 198p. *ISBN: 0804739331. Translated from the German Einleitung in die Soziologie. Includes bibliographical references (p. [155]-189) and index.*

355 L'invention de la paysannerie: un moment de l'histoire de la sociologie française d'après-guerre. *[In French]*; (The invention of peasantry. A moment in the post-war history of French sociology.) *[Summary]*; *[Summary in German]*; *[Summary in Spanish]*. Henri Mendras. **Rev. Fr. Soc.** 41:3 7-9:2000 pp.539-552.

356 Is the case for social science laws strengthening? Clive Beed; Cara Beed. **J. Theory Soc. Behav.** 30:2 6:2000 pp.131-153.

357 Jean Baudrillard: in radical uncertainty. Mike Gane. London, Sterling VA: Pluto Press, 2000. 118p. *ISBN: 0745316360, 0745316352. Includes bibliographical references. (Series: Modern European thinkers).*

358 Jeden sociologický přelud: „sociální konstrukce skutečnosti". *[In Czech]*; (A sociological mirage: 'the social construction of reality'.) *[Summary]*. Philippe de Lara. **Soc. Čas.** 36:3 2000 pp.259-274.

359 Luhmann, Habermas, and the theory of communication. Loet Leydesdorff. **Syst. Res. Behav. Sci.** 17:3 5-6:2000 pp.273-288.

360 Marx and justice. James Daly. **Int. J. Phil. Stud.** 8:3 10:2000 pp.351-400.

361 Marx and the figure of desire. Bradley J. MacDonald. **Rethink. Marx.** 11:4 Winter:1999 pp.21-37.

362 Marx, nature, and the ethics of nonidentity. Michelle Mawhinney. **Rethink. Marx.** 12:1 Spring:2000 pp.47-64.

363 Marxist axioms as self-contradictory Parsonian statements in sociology. Jan Ajzner. **Human St.** 23:2 4:2000 pp.157-178.

364 Max Weber's interpretive sociology and rational choice approach. Zenonas Norkus. **Rat. Soc.** 12:3 8:2000 pp.259-282.

365 Max Weber's methodology: an ideal-type. Sven Eliaeson. **J. Hist. Beh. Sci.** XXXVI:3 Summer:2000 pp.241-263.

366 Meeting halfway between Rochester and Frankfurt: generative salience, focal points, and strategic interaction. John W. Schiemann. **Am. J. Pol. Sc.** 44:1 1:2000 pp.1-16.

367 Modernity and morality in Habermas's discourse ethics. James Gordon Finlayson. **Inquiry** 43:3 9:2000 pp.319-340.

368 Necessarily contingent, equally different, and relatively universal: the antinomies of Ernesto Laclau's social logic of hegemony. Beverley Best. **Rethink. Marx.** 12:3 Fall:2000 pp.38-57.

369 (New knowledge toward society.); *[Text in Japanese]*. Masachi Osawa; Toshiki Satou; Tomomi Endo; Aug Nishizaka; Kimio Ito; Kazue Sakamoto; Shin'ya Tateiwa; Gaku Doba. **Rir. To Ho.** 15:1 6:2000 pp.21-134. *Collection of 8 articles.*

370 (Newcomb's problem and backward causality: the formalization of Weber's Protestant ethic.) *[Summary]*; *[Text in Japanese]*. Yuzuru Suzuki. **Rir. To Ho.** 15:2 10:2000 pp.331-344.

371 Niklas Luhman. Roar Hagen; Rudolf Stichweh; Dag Østerberg; Niels Åkerstrøm Andersen; Jean Clam. **Acta Sociol.** 43:1 2000 pp.3-79. *Collection of 6 articles.*

B: THÉORIE ET MÉTHODOLOGIE

372 An offer one might prefer to refuse: the systems theoretical legacy of Niklas Luhmann. Ingolfur Blühdorn. **Eur. J. Soc. Theory** 3:3 8:2000 pp.339-354.

373 On the critique of 'utilitarian' theories of action: newly identified convergences among Simmel, Weber and Parsons. Donald N. Levine. **Theory Cult. Soc.** 17:1 2:2000 pp.63-78.

374 Opyt gymanitarnogo izucheniia tvorchestva (Evoliutsiia vzgliadov M. Fuko). *[In Russian]*; [Experiencing the humanitarian study of creativity: the evolution of Foucault's views]. V. Rozin. **Obshch. Nauki Sovrem.** 3 2000 pp.131-141.

375 Parsons' emergent Durkheims. Edward A. Tiryakian. **Sociol. Theory** 18:1 3:2000 pp.60-83.

376 Peter Checkland at 70: a review of soft systems thinking. Mike C. Jackson [Ed.]; Peter Checkland. **Syst. Res. Behav. Sci.** 17:S1 11:2000 pp.3-81. *Collection of 4 articles*.

377 Pierre Bourdieu: a critical introduction. Jeremy F. Lane. London, Sterling VA: Pluto Press, 2000. viii, 228p. *ISBN: 0745315062, 0745315011. Includes bibliographical references (p. 202-224) and index. (Series:* Modern European thinkers).

378 Plurality in dialogue: a comment on Bakhtin. Zali Gurevitch. **Sociology** 34:2 5:2000 pp.243-264.

379 A political economy of new times? Critical reflections on the network society and the ethos of informational capitalism. Barry Smart. **Eur. J. Soc. Theory** 3:1 2:2000 pp.51-66.

380 Problems of form. Michael Irmscher [Tr.]; Leah Edwards [Tr.]; Dirk Baecker [Ed.]. Stanford CA: Stanford University Press, 1999. x, 248p. *ISBN: 0804734232, 0804734240. Includes bibliographical references (p. [201]-248). (Series:* Writing science).

381 La production du social: autour de Maurice Godelier. *[In French]*; [The production of the social: on Maurice Godelier]. Philippe Descola [Ed.]; Jacques Hamel [Ed.]; Pierre Lemonnier [Ed.]; Maurice Godelier. Paris: Fayard, 1999. 515p. *ISBN: 2213603804. Includes bibliographical references*.

382 Rationality, ethics, and space: on situated universalism and the self-interested acknowledgement of 'difference'. Gary Bridge. **Envir. Plan. D.** 18:4 8:2000 pp.519-535.

383 A realist theory of hegemony. Jonathan Joseph. **J. Theory Soc. Behav.** 30:2 6:2000 pp.179-202.

384 Reflexivity: one step up. Dick Pels. **Theory Cult. Soc.** 17:3 6:2000 pp.1-25.

385 Rethinking the postmodern perspective: excavating the Kantian system to rebuild social theory. Michael Roberts. **Sociol. Q.** 41:4 Fall:2000 pp.681-698.

386 Das Risiko der Unsicherheitsabsorption. Ein Vergleich konstruktivistischer Beobachtungsweisen des BSE-Risikos. *[In German]*; (Uncertainty absorption in risk-taking. Comparing constructivist observations of risks from BSE.) *[Summary]*. Veronika Tacke. **Z. Soziol.** 29:2 4:2000 pp.83-102.

387 A sense of time: temporality and historicity in sociological inquiry. Harry H. Bash. **Time Soc.** 9:2-3 6-9:2000 pp.187-204.

388 Shame and the social bond: a sociological theory. Thomas J. Scheff. **Sociol. Theory** 18:1 3:2000 pp.84-99.

389 The social construction of equality in everyday life. Scott R. Harris. **Human St.** 23:4 10:2000 pp.371-393.

390 Social Darwinism: linking evolutionary thought to social theory. Peter Dickens. Buckingham: Open University Press, 2000. 135p. *ISBN: 0335202187, 0335202195. Includes bibliographical references and index. (Series:* Concepts in the social sciences).

391 Social integration, system integration and collective subjectivity. José Maurício Domingues. **Sociology** 34:2 5:2000 pp.225-242.

392 Social mechanisms: an analytical approach to social theory. Peter Hedström [Ed.]; Richard Swedberg [Ed.]. Cambridge: Cambridge University Press, 1998. viii, 340p. *ISBN: 0521593190, 0521596874. Includes bibliographical references and indexes. (Series:* Studies in rationality and social change).

393 La «sociedad mundial» y la carencia de reflexiones normativas en las teorías sociales de Niklas Luhmann y Norbert Elias. *[In Spanish]*; ['Global society' and the lack of normative reflection in the social theory of Niklas Luhmann and Norbert Elias] *[Summary]*. Oliver Kozlarek. **Rev. Mexicana Cien. Pol.** XLIV:177-178 9-4:1999-2000 pp.19-48.

B: THEORY AND METHODOLOGY

394   The society of society: the grand finale of Niklas Luhmann. Daniel Lee. **Sociol. Theory** 18:2 7:2000 pp.320-330.
395   Sociological theory. George Ritzer. New York: McGraw-Hill, 2000. xviii, 769p. *ISBN: 0072296054. Includes bibliographical references (p. 641-749) and indexes.*
396   La sociologie d'inspiration biologique au XIXe siècle: une science de l'«organisation» sociale. *[In French]*; (Sociology of biological inspiration in the XIXth century: a science of social 'organization'.) *[Summary]*. Dominique Guillo. **Rev. Fr. Soc.** 41:2 4-6:2000 pp.241-276.
397   The stranger and social theory. Vince Marotta. **Thes. Elev.** 62 8:2000 pp.121-134.
398   The structure of sociological theory. Jonathan H. Turner; P.R. Turner; et al. Belmont CA: Wadsworth, 1998. xxiv, 632p. *ISBN: 0534513530. Includes bibliographical references and indexes.*
399   The subjectivist-objectivist divide: against transcendence. Nicos Mouzelis. **Sociology** 34:4 11:2000 pp.741-762.
400   The Talcott Parsons reader. Talcott Parsons; Bryan S. Turner [Ed.]. Malden MA: Blackwell Publishers, 1999. vii, 360p. *ISBN: 1557865434, 1557865442. Includes bibliographical references and index. (Series: Blackwell readers).*
401   Thematizing embeddedness: reflexive sociology as interpretation. Joseph D. Lewandowski. **Philos. S. Sc.** 30:1 3:2000 pp.49-66.
402   A theoretical frame of reference for family systems therapy? An introduction to Luhmann's theory of social systems. Tannelie Blom; Leo Van Dijk. **J. Fam. Ther.** 21:2 5:1999 pp.195-216.
403   Theorie: Niklas Luhmann. *[In Spanish]*; [Niklas Luhmann's theory]. Niklas Luhmann; José Luis Hoyo Arana [Tr.]; Josetxo Beriain; Rosa Ma. Lince Campillo; Javier Torres Nafarrate; Rodrigo Jokisch. **Est. Polí.** 21 5-8:1999 pp.7-112. *Collection of 6 articles.*
404   Theorizing classical sociology. Larry J. Ray. Buckingham: Open University Press, 1999. ix, 218p. *ISBN: 033519866X, 0335198651. Includes bibliographical references (p. [203]-215) and index.*
405   Theorizing the good society: hermeneutic, normative and empirical discourses; *[Summary in French]*. Jeffrey Alexander. **Can. J. Soc.** 25:3 Summer:2000 pp.271-309.
406   Thinking with Bourdieu and against Bourdieu: a 'practical' critique of the *habitus*. Anthony King. **Sociol. Theory** 18:3 11:2000 pp.417-433.
407   Understanding agency: social theory and responsible action. Barry Barnes. London: Sage Publications, 2000. xii, 163p. *ISBN: 0761963677, 0761963685. Includes bibliographical references and index.*
408   „Vergemeinschaftung" und „Vergesellschaftung" bei Max Weber. Eine Rekonstruktion seines Sprachgebrauchs. *[In German]*; ('Communal relationships' and 'associative relationships': a reconstruction of Max Weber's terminology.) *[Summary]*. Klaus Lichtblau. **Z. Soziol.** 29:6 12:2000 pp.423-443.
409   A Weberian theory of time. Sandro Segre. **Time Soc.** 9:2-3 6-9:2000 pp.147-170.
410   The willingness of the executioners: a Foucauldian critique of Goldhagen. Karen Vintges; Eric Tjong Tjin Tai. **Euro. Journ. Cult. Stud.** 3:2 5:2000 pp.147-172.

B.2:   **Research methods**
       Méthodes de recherche

411   Accountability in action? Program evaluation in nonprofit human service agencies. Richard Hoefer. **Non. Manag. Leader.** 11:2 Winter:2000 pp.167-178.
412   Approccio biografico e *grounded theory*: una proposta metodologica per l'analisi delle nuove forme di debolezza sociale. *[In Italian]*; (Biographical approach and grounded theory: a methodological proposal to analyze the new occupational weakness.) *[Summary]*. Federico Chicchi. **Sociol. Lav.** 78-79 2000 pp.28-56.
413   Comments on neural networks. Haejung Paik. **Sociol. Meth.** 28:4 5:2000 pp.425-453.

B: THÉORIE ET MÉTHODOLOGIE

414 A critical review of research on immigrant entrepreneurship. Jan Rath; Robert Kloosterman. **Int. Migr. Rev.** 34:3 Fall:2000 pp.657-681.
415 Developing effective research proposals. Keith F. Punch. London: Sage Publications, 2000. vii, 125p. *ISBN: 0761963553. Includes bibliographical references and index.* (*Series:* Essential resources for social research).
416 Doing critical management research. Mats Alvesson; Stanley A. Deetz. Thousand Oaks CA, London: Sage Publications, 2000. 232p. *ISBN: 0761953337, 0761953329. Includes bibliographical references and index.*
417 Doing research with children. Anne Greig; Jayne Taylor. London: Sage Publications, 1999. ix, 175p. *ISBN: 0761955909, 0761955895. Includes bibliographical references (p. [161]-170) and index.*
418 Doing your research project: a guide for first-time researchers in education and social science. Judith Bell. Buckingham, Philadelphia PA: Open University Press, 1999. xiv, 230p. *ISBN: 0335203884, 0335203892. Includes bibliographical references (p. [216]-225) and index.*
419 Evaluating WIC. Douglas J. Besharov; Peter Germanis. **Eval. Rev.** 24:2 4:2000 pp.123-190.
420 (Evolution of evaluating strategy during consensus makings.); *[Text in Japanese]*. Jun Kobayashi. **Rir. To Ho.** 15:1 6:2000 pp.181-196.
421 First steps in research and statistics: a practical workbook for psychology students. Dennis Howitt; Duncan Cramer. London, New York: Routledge, 2000. 272p. *ISBN: 0415201012. Includes bibliographical references and index.*
422 Foundations of behavioral research. Fred N. Kerlinger; Howard B. Lee. Fort Worth TX: Harcourt College Publishers, 2000. 890p. *ISBN: 0155078976.*
423 In search of structure: essays in social science and methodology. M. Fennema [Ed.]; Cees van der Eijk [Ed.]; Huibert Schijf [Ed.]. Amsterdam: Het Spinhuis, 1998. 277p. *ISBN: 9055891142. Includes bibliographical references (p. 255-277).*
424 Introduction to research methods. Robert B. Burns. Frenchs Forest: Pearson Education, 2000. ix, 613p. *ISBN: 0733909124. Includes bibliographical references and index.*
425 Media research methods: measuring audiences, reactions and impact. Barrie Gunter. Thousand Oaks CA, London: Sage Publications, 1999. 272p. *ISBN: 0761956581, 076195659X.*
426 The need for experimental research in criminal justice settings. Lynette Feder; Robert F. Boruch; James F. Short, Jr.; Margaret A. Zahn; David P. Farrington; Lawrence W. Sherman; Ann Oakley; Timothy Victor; Joe S. Cecil; Anthony Petrosino; Carolyn Turpin-Petrosino; James O. Finckenauer; Annette Jolin; William Feyerherm; David S. Cordray; Franklyn W. Dunford. **Crime Delin.** 46:3 7:2000 pp.291-434. *Collection of 9 articles.*
427 Participatory diagramming: deploying qualitative methods through an action research epistemology. Mike Kesby. **Area** 32:4 12:2000 pp.423-436.
428 Personalizing evaluation. Saville Kushner. London: Sage Publications, 2000. xv, 223p. *ISBN: 0761963626, 0761963618. Includes bibliographical references and index.*
429 The practice of social research. Earl R. Babbie. Belmont CA: Wadsworth, 1998. *ISBN: 053450468X. Includes bibliographical references and index.*
430 Producing possible Hannahs: theory and the subject of research. Eileen Honan; Michele Knobel; Carolyn Baker; Bronwyn Davies. **Qual. Inq.** 6:1 3:2000 pp.9-32.
431 Promises fulfilled? A review of 20 years of life course research; *[Summary in French]*; *[Summary in German]*. Karl Ulrich Mayer. **Eur. J. Soc.** XLI:2 2000 pp.259-282.
432 Reflexive methodology: new vistas for qualitative research. Mats Alvesson; Kaj Skoldberg. Thousand Oaks CA, London: Sage Publications, 1999. 352p. *ISBN: 0803977069, 0803977077.*
433 Reliability in experimental sociology. Shane R. Thye. **Soc. Forc.** 78:4 6:2000 pp.1277-1310.
434 Reporting unethical research behaviour. Neil S. Wenger; Stanley G. Korenman; Richard Berk; Honghu Liu. **Eval. Rev.** 23:5 10:1999 pp.553-570.
435 Research as relationship. Deborah Ceglowski. **Qual. Inq.** 6:1 3:2000 pp.88-103.

B: THEORY AND METHODOLOGY

436 Research design: successful designs for social and economic research. C. Hakim. London: Routledge, 2000. xvi, 256p. *ISBN: 0415223121, 041522313X. Includes bibliographical references and index. (Series:* Social research today).

437 Research methods in education. Louis Cohen; Lawrence Manion; Keith Morrison. London, New York: Routledge, Falmer Press, 2000. xvi, 446p. *ISBN: 0415195411. Includes bibliographical references (p. 407-437) and index.*

438 Research training for social scientists: a handbook for postgraduate researchers. Dawn Burton [Ed.]. London: Sage Publications, 2000. xv, 503p. *ISBN: 0761963510, 0761963502. Includes bibliographical references and index.*

439 Samoorganizatsionnyi podkhod k izucheniiu obshchestva: metodologicheskii aspekt. *[In Russian]*; [A self-organizational approach to the study of society: a methodological aspect] *[Summary]*. R.A. Zobov; V.N. Kelasev. **Vest. San.-Peter. Univ.** 2(13) 6:1999 pp.40-50.

440 Sequence analysis and optimal matching methods in sociology: review and prospect. Andrew Abbott; Angela Tsay; Joel H. Levine [Comments by]; Lawrence L. Wu [Comments by]. **Sociol. Meth.** 29:1 8:2000 pp.3-76.

441 Stabilität subjektorientierter Strukturen. Das Lebensstilmodell von Schulze im Zeitvergleich. *[In German]*; [The stability of subject-centered structures. A time-related comparison of the lifestyle model of Schulze] *[Summary]*. Thomas Müller-Schneider. **Z. Soziol.** 29:5 10:2000 pp.361-374.

442 Theoretical perspectives in environment-behavior research: underlying assumptions, research problems, and methodologies. Seymour Wappner [Ed.]; et al. New York: Kluwer Academic/Plenum Publishers, 2000. xiii, 320p. *ISBN: 0306461927. Includes bibliographical references and indexes.*

443 Theory-based evaluation in practice: what do we learn? Johanna D. Birckmayer; Carol Hirschon Weiss. **Eval. Rev.** 24:4 8:2000 pp.407-431.

444 We've been framed: visualising methodology. Ruth Holliday. **Sociol. Rev.** 48:4 11:2000 pp.503-521.

Data analysis
Analyse des données

445 Análisis dinámico. *[In Spanish]*; [Dynamic analysis]. Emilio J. Castilla. Madrid: Centro de Investigaciones Sociológicas, 1998. 199p. *ISBN: 8474762693. Includes bibliographical references (p. 191-199).*

446 Analyses of infectious disease data from household outbreaks by Markov chain Monte Carlo methods. Philip D. O'Neill; David J. Balding; Niels G. Becker; Mervi Eerola; Denis Mollison. **J. R. Stat. Soc.** 49:4 2000 pp.517-542.

447 Analysis of census microdata. Angela Dale; Clare Holdsworth; Ed Fieldhouse. London: Arnold Publishing Ltd., 1998. 320p. *ISBN: 0340692286.*

448 (An analysis of missing data in contingency tables: a case of intergenerational mobility in education.); *[Text in Japanese]*. Tokio Yasuda. **Rir. To Ho.** 15:1 6:2000 pp.165-180.

449 Assessing qualitative television audience research: incorporating feminist and anthropological theoretical innovation. Amanda D. Lotz. **Commun. Theory** 10:4 11:2000 pp.447-467.

450 Bancos de datos. *[In Spanish]*; [Databases]. Magdalena Cordero Valdavida. Madrid: Centro de Investigaciones Sociológicas, 1998. 199p. *ISBN: 8474762561. Includes bibliographical references (p. 193-196).*

451 A Bayesian approach to combining information from a census, a coverage measurement survey, and demographic analysis. Michael R. Elliott; Roderick J.A. Little. **J. Am. Stat. Ass.** 95:450 6:2000 pp.351-362.

452 The bearing correlogram: a new method of analyzing directional spatial autocorrelation. Michael S. Rosenberg. **Geogr. Anal.** 32:3 7:2000 pp.267-278.

453 Bias in meta-analysis due to outcome variable selection within studies. J.L. Hutton; Paula R. Williamson. **J. R. Stat. Soc.** 49:3 2000 pp.359-370.

B: THÉORIE ET MÉTHODOLOGIE

454 Case studies as spurious evaluations: the example of research on educational inequalities. Peter Foster; Roger Gomm; Martyn Hammersley. **Br. J. Educ. S.** 48:3 9:2000 pp.215-230.

455 'Clinton faces nation': a case study in the construction of focus group data as public opinion. Sue Wilkinson; Celia Kitzinger. **Sociol. Rev.** 48:3 8:2000 pp.408-424.

456 Development of a structural hazard rate model in sociological research. Xian Liu. **Sociol. Meth.** 29:1 8:2000 pp.77-117.

457 Diseño de investigación o protocolo de tesis para licenciatura en ciencias sociales. *[In Spanish]*; [Investigation design or thesis protocol for social science degrees]. Isabel Horcasitas. **Acta Sociol. [Mexico]** 25 1-4:1999 pp.141-152.

458 Dreamscape: Simulation der Entstehung von Normen im Naturzustand mittels eines computerbasierten Modells des Rational-Choice-Ansatzes. *[In German]*; (Dreamscape: a simulation of the emergence of norms out of the state of nature using a computer-based rational choice model.) *[Summary]*. Niels Lepperhoff. **Z. Soziol.** 29:6 12:2000 pp.463-484.

459 A dynamic optimization model for school network planning. António Antunes; Dominique Peeters. **Socio. Econ.** 34:2 6:2000 pp.101-120.

460 Een vertekend beeld van de maatschappij? Een onderzoek naar selectieve uitval in een telefonische enquête ten gevolge van onderdekking en nonrespons. *[In Dutch]*; (A distorted image of society? A study of bias in a telephone questionnaire due to undercoverage and nonresponse.) *[Summary]*. Sonja Rispens; Henk van Goor. **Sociol. Gids** XLVII:6 11-12:2000 pp.448-474.

461 An equity model for locating environmentally hazardous facilities. Anthony Falit-Baiamonte; Jeffrey P. Osleeb. **Geogr. Anal.** 32:4 10:2000 pp.351-368.

462 Ethnography and experiment in social psychological theory building: tactics for integrating qualitative field data with quantitative lab data. Gary Alan Fine; Kimberly D. Elsbach. **J. Exp. S. Psychol.** 36:1 1:2000 pp.51-76.

463 Evolutionary game theory. Kazunori Araki; Hamish Low; Ilan Eshel; Dorothea K. Herreiner; Larry Samuelson; Emilia Sansone; Avner Shaked; Ben Cooper; Chris Wallace. **Sociol. Meth.** 28:3 2:2000 pp.310-381. *Collection of 3 articles.*

464 Expected utility and case-based reasoning. Akihiko Matsui. **Math. Soc. Sc.** 39:1 1:2000 pp.1-12.

465 Explicit form of neutral social decision rules for basic rationality conditions. Lev A. Sholomov. **Math. Soc. Sc.** 39:1 1:2000 pp.81-107.

466 Exploring dynamic networks: hypotheses and conjectures. Robb Willer; David Willer. **Soc. Networks** 22:3 7:2000 pp.251-272.

467 A finite population ESS and a long run equilibrium in an n players coordination game. Yasuhito Tanaka. **Math. Soc. Sc.** 39:2 3:2000 pp.195-206.

468 Fitting population dynamics models to count and cull data using sequential importance sampling. Verena M. Trenkel; David A. Elston; Stephen T. Buckland. **J. Am. Stat. Ass.** 95:450 6:2000 pp.363-374.

469 From interview transcript to interpretive story: Part 1 — viewing the transcript through multiple lenses. Coralie McCormack. **Fie. Meth.** 12:4 11:2000 pp.282-297.

470 From interview transcript to interpretive story: Part 2 — developing an interpretive story. Coralie McCormack. **Fie. Meth.** 12:4 11:2000 pp.298-315.

471 The generalizability of multilevel models of burglary victimization: a cross-city comparison. Pamela Wilcox Rountree; Kenneth C. Land. **Soc. Sci. R.** 29:2 6:2000 pp.284-305.

472 A heteroscedastic generalized extreme value discrete choice model. Langche Zeng. **Sociol. Meth.** 29:1 8:2000 pp.118-144.

473 Interpreting forensic DNA mixtures: allowing for uncertainty in population substructure and dependence. Wing K. Fung; Yue-Qing Hu. **J. Roy. Stat. Soc. A.** 163:2 2000 pp.241-254.

474 Interpretivism and generalisation. Malcolm Williams. **Sociology** 34:2 5:2000 pp.209-224.

475 An introduction to statistics in psychology: a complete guide for students. Dennis Howitt; Duncan Cramer. Harlow: Prentice Hall, 2000. xii, 482p. *ISBN: 0130173142. Includes bibliographical references and index.*

B: THEORY AND METHODOLOGY

476 Is causal induction based on causal power? Critique of Cheng (1997). Klaus Lober; David R. Shanks. **Psychol. Rev.** 107:1 1:2000 pp.195-212.

477 Je česká společnost „postmaterialistická"? *[In Czech]*; (Is Czech society 'post-materialist'?) *[Summary]*. Ladislav Rabušic. **Soc. Čas.** 36:1 2000 pp.3-22.

478 Lo studio della mortalità in coorti di lavoratori attraverso modelli per dati raggruppati. *[In Italian]*; (Using models for grouped data to analyse occupational mortality data.) *[Summary]*. Carlo Trivisano. **Statistica** LX:2 4-6:2000 pp.297-314.

479 Meta-analysis using multilevel models with an application to the study of class size effects. Harvey Goldstein; Min Yang; Rumana Omar; Rebecca Turner; Simon Thompson. **J. R. Stat. Soc.** 49:3 2000 pp.399-412.

480 Methods for density estimation in thick-slice versions of Wicksell's problem. Andrey Feuerverger; Peter Hall. **J. Am. Stat. Ass.** 95:450 6:2000 pp.535-546.

481 Un metodo di intelligenza artificiale per l'estrazione di informazione da dati statistici. *[In Italian]*; (An artificial intelligence method for extracting information from statistical data.) *[Summary]*. A.O. Arigoni; L. Governatori; A. Rossi. **Statistica** LX:2 4-6:2000 pp.215-242.

482 Modelle zur Aufdeckung unbeobachteter Heterogenität bei der Erklärung von Lebenszufriedenheit. *[In German]*; (Models for discovering unobserved heterogeneity in the analysis of life satisfaction.) *[Summary]*. Petra Stein. **Z. Soziol.** 29:2 4:2000 pp.138-159.

483 Modelling exposure opportunities: estimating relative risk for motor neurone disease in Finland. Clive E. Sabel; Anthony C. Gatrell; Markku Löytönen; Paula Maasilta; Matti Jokelainen. **Soc. Sci. Med.** 50:7-8 4:2000 pp.1121-1138.

484 Modified innovation diffusion - a way to explain the diffusion of cholera in Linköping in 1866? A study in methods. Nicklas Skillnäs. **Geogr. Ann. B.** 81(B):4 1999 pp.243-260.

485 Multinomial logit latent-class regression models: an analysis of the predictors of gender-role attitudes among Japanese women. Kazuo Yamaguchi. **A.J.S.** 105:6 5:2000 pp.1702-1740.

486 Potential maximizers and network formation. Marco Slikker; Bhaskar Dutta; Anne van den Nouweland; Stef Tijs. **Math. Soc. Sc.** 39:1 1:2000 pp.55-70.

487 A primer in longitudinal data analysis. Toon W. Taris. London: Sage Publications, 2000. ix, 163p. *ISBN: 0761960260, 0761960279. Includes bibliographical references and index.*

488 Principles of research design in the social sciences. Frank Bechhofer; Lindsay Paterson. London: Routledge, 2000. ix, 172p. *ISBN: 0415214424, 0415214432. Includes bibliographical references and index.* (*Series:* Social research today).

489 Proportional hazards models: a latent competing risk approach. Alan E. Gelfand; Sujit K. Ghosh; Cindy Christiansen; Stephen B. Soumerai; Thomas J. McLaughlin. **J. R. Stat. Soc.** 49:3 2000 pp.385-397.

490 Providing space for time: the impact of temporality on life course research. Melinda Mills. **Time Soc.** 9:1 3:2000 pp.91-127.

491 Sampling distributions of segregation indexes. Michael R. Ransom. **Sociol. Meth.** 28:4 5:2000 pp.454-475.

492 Simple methods for simulating sociomatrices with given marginal totals. John M. Roberts, Jr. **Soc. Networks** 22:3 7:2000 pp.273-283.

493 Some analyses of Erdős collaboration graph. Vladimir Batagelj; Andrej Mrvar. **Soc. Networks** 22:2 5:2000 pp.173-186.

494 Statistical method and the Peircean account of truth. Andrew Reynolds. **Can. J. Phil.** 30:2 6:2000 pp.287-314.

495 Statistics: a tool for social research. Joseph F. Healey. Belmont CA: Wadsworth, 1999. xviii, 540p. *ISBN: 0534552609. Includes index.*

496 Statistics of ordinal variation. Julian Blair; Michael G. Lacy. **Sociol. Meth.** 28:3 2:2000 pp.251-280.

497 Strategies of causal inference in small-N analysis. James Mahoney. **Sociol. Meth.** 28:4 5:2000 pp.387-424.

B: THÉORIE ET MÉTHODOLOGIE

498 Towards a sociology of measurement: the meaning of measurement error in the case of DNA profiling. Linda Derksen. **Soc. Stud. Sci.** 30:6 12:2000 pp.803-845.
499 Understanding social statistics. Jane L. Fielding; G. Nigel Gilbert. London: Sage Publications, 2000. v, 329p. *ISBN: 0803979827, 0803979835. Includes bibliographical references (p. [322]-323) and index).*
500 Using multilevel models to model heterogeneity: potential and pitfalls. Craig Duncan; Kelvyn Jones. **Geogr. Anal.** 32:4 10:2000 pp.279-305.
501 Die Zuverlässigkeit retrospektiv erhobener Lebensverlaufsdaten. Analysen zur Partnerschaftsbiografie des Familiensurvey. *[In German];* (Reliability issues of retrospective life course data: an analysis of partnership biographies in the *Familiensurvey.) [Summary].* David Fischer-Kerli; Thomas Klein. **Z. Soziol.** 29:4 8:2000 pp.294-312.

Data collection
Rassemblement des données

502 The accessibility and applicability of knowledge: predicting context effects in national surveys. Alexander Todorov. **Publ. Opin. Q.** 64:4 Winter:2000 pp.429-451.
503 Adapting the cognitive interview to enhance long-term (35 years) recall of physical activities. Ronald P. Fisher; Karen L. Falkner; Maurizio Trevisan; Michelle R. McCauley. **J. Appl. Psychol.** 85:2 4:2000 pp.180-189.
504 Approaches to sampling and case selection in qualitative research: examples in the geography of health. Sarah Curtis; Wil Gesler; Glenn Smith; Sarah Washburn. **Soc. Sci. Med.** 50:7-8 4:2000 pp.1001-1014.
505 Beginning anew: doing qualitative research; *[Summary in French].* B. Gail Frankel Perry. **Can. J. Soc.** 25:1 Winter:2000 pp.97-107.
506 Between voice and discourse: quilting interviews on anorexia. Paula Saukko. **Qual. Inq.** 6:3 9:2000 pp.299-336.
507 Beyond bias? The promise and limits of Q method in human geography. Paul Robbins; Rob Krueger. **Prof. Geogr.** 52:4 11:2000 pp.636-648.
508 The biographical illusion: constructing meaning in qualitative interviews. Margaretha Järvinen. **Qual. Inq.** 6:3 9:2000 pp.370-391.
509 Clarifying question meaning in a household telephone survey. Frederick G. Conrad; Michael F. Schober. **Publ. Opin. Q.** 64:1 Spring:2000 pp.1-28.
510 A comparison of randomized response, computer-assisted self-interview, and face-to-face direct questioning: eliciting sensitive information in the context of welfare and unemployment benefit. Peter G.M. van der Heijden; Ger van Gils; Jan Bouts; Joop J. Hox. **Sociol. Meth.** 28:4 5:2000 pp.505-537.
511 Computer-mediated focus groups. Jill T. Walston; Robert W. Lissitz. **Eval. Rev.** 24:5 10:2000 pp.457-483.
512 Consequences of reducing nonresponse in a national telephone survey. Scott Keeter; Carolyn Miller; Andrew Kohut; Robert M. Groves; Stanley Presser. **Publ. Opin. Q.** 64:2 Summer:2000 pp.125-148.
513 Counting women's work in the agricultural census of Nepal: a report. Sona Joshi. **Gen. Tech. Dev.** 4:2 5-8:2000 pp.255-270.
514 Data as representations: contextualizing qualitative and quantitative research strategies. Jaan Valsiner. **Soc. Sci. Info.** 39:1 3:2000 pp.99-114.
515 Decisions and strategies in a sequential search experiment. Joep Sonnemans. **J. Econ. Psyc.** 21:1 2:2000 pp.91-102.
516 Doing qualitative research differently: free association, narrative and the interview method. Wendy Hollway; Tony Jefferson. London: Sage Publications, 2000. 192p. *ISBN: 0761964266, 0761964258.*

B: THEORY AND METHODOLOGY

517   Dynamic inquiry relationships: ways of creating, sustaining, and improving the inquiry process through the recognition and management of conflicts. Tineke A. Abma. **Qual. Inq.** 6:1 3:2000 pp.133-151.
518   An evaluation of a large-scale CATI household survey using random digit dialling. Don J. Bennett; David Steel. **Aust. & N.Z. J. Statist.** 42:3 9:2000 pp.255-270.
519   Experiments with incentives in telephone surveys. Eleanor Singer; John Van Hoewyk; Mary P. Maher. **Publ. Opin. Q.** 64:2 Summer:2000 pp.171-188.
520   Exporting social survey research. Martin Bulmer; Roger Jowell; Manfred Kuechler; Mark Orkin; Cynthia J. Buckley; Agustín Escobar; Bryan Roberts; Margaret Newby; Sajeda Amin; Ian Diamond; Ruchira T. Naved; Carmi Schooler; Chiaka Diakite; Jerome Vogel; Pierre Mounkoro; Leslie Caplan. **Am. Behav. Sc.** 42:2 10:1998 pp.151-284. *Collection of 8 articles.*
521   Interviewing children: a guide for child care and forensic practitioners. Michelle Aldridge; Joanne Wood. Chichester: John Wiley & Sons, 1998. xvi, 229p. *ISBN: 0471970522, 0471982075. Includes bibliographical references and index. (Series:* Wiley series in child care and protection).
522   Kiss and tell: surveying sex in the twentieth century. Julia A. Ericksen; Sally A. Steffen. Cambridge MA: Harvard University Press, 1999. ix, 270p. *ISBN: 0674505352. Includes bibliographical references (p. [231]-260) and index.*
523   The management of 'safe' and 'unsafe' complaint sequences in research interviews. Kathryn J. Roulston. **Text** 20:3 2000 pp.307-345.
524   The measurement of personal values in survey research: a test of alternative rating procedures. John A. McCarty; L.J. Shrum. **Publ. Opin. Q.** 64:3 Fall:2000 pp.271-298.
525   Nonresponse and other sources of survey error. S.B. Cohen; S.R. Machlin; T.M. Ezzati-Rice; M.R. Frankel; D.C. Hoaglin; J.D. Loft; V.G. Coronado; R.A. Wright; W.W. Yu; M. Winglee; R. Valliant; J.M. Brick; J.W. Cohen; J.M. Thorpe. **J. Econ. Soc.** 26:2 2000 pp.83-151. *Collection of 5 articles.*
526   Le note etnografiche: raccolta e analisi. *[In Italian];* [Ethnographic data: collection and analysis]. Giampietro Gobo. **Quad. Sociol.** XLIII:21 1999 pp.144-167.
527   Oprosnye metody sbora dannykh: predpochteniia respondentov. *[In Russian];* (Respondents' preferences regarding methods of data collection in surveys.) *[Summary].* A.Iu. Miagkov. **Sot. Issle.** 8 2000 pp.98-108.
528   'Placing' interviews: location and scales of power in qualitative research. Sarah A. Elwood; Deborah G. Martin. **Prof. Geogr.** 52:4 11:2000 pp.649-659.
529   Qualitative research in criminology. Fiona Brookman [Ed.]; Lesley Noaks [Ed.]; Emma Wincup [Ed.]. Aldershot, Brookfield VT: Ashgate, 1999. vii, 184p. *ISBN: 1840145714. Includes bibliographical references. (Series:* Cardiff papers in qualitative research).
530   Qualitative researching with text, image and sound: a practical handbook for social research. Martin Bauer [Ed.]; George Gaskell [Ed.]. London: Sage Publications, 2000. 384p. *ISBN: 0761964819. Includes bibliographical references.*
531   The quality and comparability of child care data in U.S. surveys. R. Kelly Raley; Kathleen Mullan Harris; Ronald R. Rindfuss. **Soc. Sci. R.** 29:3 9:2000 pp.356-381.
532   The relative costs and benefits of telephone interviews versus self-administered diaries for daily data collection. Marilyn J. Hoppe; Mary Rogers Gillmore; Danny L. Valadez; Diane Civic; Jane Hartway; Diane M. Morrison. **Eval. Rev.** 24:1 2:2000 pp.102-116.
533   Research design: an intricacy of data collection. Ranu Jain. **Indian J. Soc. W.** 60:4 10:1999 pp.525-537.
534   Response rate trends in Japanese surveys. Nicolaos E. Synodinos; Shigeru Yamada. **Int. J. Pub. Op. Res.** 12:1 Spring:2000 pp.48-72.
535   Telescoping of landmark events: implications for survey research. George D. Gaskell; Daniel B. Wright; Colm A. O'Muircheartaigh. **Publ. Opin. Q.** 64:1 Spring:2000 pp.77-89.
536   A validation of the ethnosurvey: the case of Mexico-U.S. migration. Douglas S. Massey; Rene Zenteno. **Int. Migr. Rev.** 34:3 Fall:2000 pp.766-793.
537   Web surveys: a review of issues and approaches. Mick P. Couper. **Publ. Opin. Q.** 64:4 Winter:2000 pp.464-494.

538 What I didn't know about working in an endangered language community: some fieldwork issues. Naomi Nagy. **Int. J. S. Lang.** 144 2000 pp.143-160.
539 You got a problem with that? Exploring evaluators' disagreements about ethics. Michael Morris; Lynette R. Jacobs. **Eval. Rev.** 24:4 8:2000 pp.384-406.

C: INDIVIDUALS. GROUPS. ORGANIZATIONS
INDIVIDUS. GROUPES. ORGANISATIONS

C.1: Psychology
Psychologie

540   The ability to detect unseen staring: a literature review and empirical tests. John Colwell; Sadi Schröder; David Sladen. **Br. J. Psy.** 91:1 2:2000 pp.71-86.
541   African self-consciousness and health-promoting behaviors among African American college students. Shawn N. Thompson; John W. Chambers, Jr. **J. Black Psychol.** 26:3 8:2000 pp.330-345.
542   Behavior modification: what it is and how to do it. Garry Martin; Joseph Pear. Upper Saddle River NJ: Prentice Hall, 1999. xx, 444p. *ISBN: 0130807427. Includes bibliographical references (p. 401-432) and indexes.*
543   Between the modern and the postmodern: the possibility of self and progressive understanding in psychology. Jack Martin; Jeff Sugarman. **Am. Psychol.** 55:4 4:2000 pp.397-406.
544   Child development and evolutionary psychology. David F. Bjorklund; Anthony D. Pellegrini. **Child. Devel.** 71:6 11-12:2000 pp.1687-1708.
545   Child psychology. Agnès Florin; Khanh Lê; Kim Cúc Thi Văn; Hoi Loan Nguyen; Dai Ngoc Ho; Khanh Nguyen; Frédérique F. Berger; Đuc Minh Nguyen; Hong Thuý Thi Nguyen; Thuý Minh Quách; Phuong Kiet Đang; Câm Tú Hoàng; Phú Ngoc Nguyen; Minh Đuc Thi Tran; Thu Huong Tran; Thuc Xuan Nguyen. **Viet. Stud.** 36:3(137) 2000 pp.5-96. *Collection of 12 articles.*
546   Child psychology: a handbook of contemporary issues. Lawrence Balter [Ed.]; Catherine Tamis-LeMonda [Ed.]. Philadelphia PA: Psychology Press, 1999. xviii, 542p. *ISBN: 1841690007. Includes bibliographical references and index.*
547   Children's language: consensus and controversy. N.R. Cattell. London: Cassell, 2000. x, 276p. *ISBN: 0304701289, 0304706817. Includes bibliographical references and index.*
548   Codependent forevermore: the invention of self in a twelve step group. Leslie Irvine. Chicago IL: University of Chicago Press, 1999. vii, 210p. *ISBN: 0226384713, 0226384721. Includes bibliographical references (p. 193-206) and index.*
549   The cognitive impact of past behavior: influences on beliefs, attitudes, and future behavioral decisions. Dolores Albarracín; Robert S. Wyer, Jr. **J. Pers. Soc. Psychol.** 79:1 7:2000 pp.5-22.
550   Collective efficacy versus self-efficacy in coping responses to stressors and control: a cross-cultural study. John Schaubroeck; Simon S.K. Lam; Jia Lin Xie. **J. Appl. Psychol.** 85:4 8:2000 pp.512-525.
551   The development of infant intersensory perception: advantages of a comparative convergent-operations approach. Robert Lickliter; Lorraine E. Bahrick. **Psychol. B.** 126:2 3:2000 pp.260-280.
552   The development of intersensory temporal perception: an epigenetic systems/limitations view. David J. Lewkowicz. **Psychol. B.** 126:2 3:2000 pp.281-308.
553   Developmental psychology: achievements and prospects. Mark Bennett [Ed.]. Philadelphia PA: Psychology Press, 1999. xvi, 338p. *ISBN: 0863775772, 0863775780. Includes bibliographical references and indexes.*
554   Developmental psychology: childhood and adolescence. David R. Shaffer. Pacific Grove CA: Brooks/Cole Publishing, 1999. *ISBN: 053436361X. Includes bibliographical references and indexes.*
555   The diagnosis of schizophrenia in the borderline learning-disabled forensic population: six case-reports. Ernest Gralton; Adrian James; Julie Crocombe. **J. For. Psy.** 11:1 4:2000 pp.185-197.

C: INDIVIDUS. GROUPES. ORGANISATIONS

556 The dictionary of psychology. Raymond J. Corsini. Philadelphia PA: Brunner/Mazel, 1999. xv, 1156p. *ISBN: 158391028X.*

557 (Differences in self concept among students: emotionally disturbed, learning disabled, educable mentally retarded and non-disabled.); *[Text in Arabic].* Khawlah Yahya. **Dirasat Ed.** 26:2 9:1999 pp.369-396.

558 The ecological self: metaphor and developmental experience? Marianne Spitzform. **J. App. Psy. Stud.** 2:3 7:2000 pp.265-285.

559 Effects of indoor lighting, gender, and age on mood and cognitive performance. Igor Knez; Christina Kers. **Envir. Behav.** 32:6 11:2000 pp.817-831.

560 Evolutionary psychology: a critical introduction. C.R. Badcock. London: Polity, 2000. 304p. *ISBN: 0745622054.*

561 Evolutionary psychology: potential and limits of a Darwinian framework for the behavioral sciences. Pascal Boyer; Jutta Heckhausen; Catrin Rode; Xt Wang; Peter M. Todd; Heidi Keller; Paul Rozin; Daniel Cervone; Peter Hammerstein. **Am. Behav. Sc.** 43:6 3:2000 pp.917-1041. *Collection of 9 articles.*

562 The frequency of temporal-self and social comparisons in people's personal appraisals. Anne E. Wilson; Michael Ross. **J. Pers. Soc. Psychol.** 78:5 5:2000 pp.928-942.

563 Functionalism and self-consciousness. Mark McCullagh. **Mind Lang.** 15:5 11:2000 pp.481-499.

564 Gestalt psychology in Italy. Ian Verstegen. **J. Hist. Beh. Sci.** XXXVI:1 Winter:2000 pp.31-42.

565 Hilgard's introduction to psychology. Rita L. Atkinson; et al. Fort Worth TX: Harcourt College Publishers, 1999. 768p. *ISBN: 015508044X.*

566 International handbook of psychology. Mark R. Rosenzweig [Ed.]; Kurt Pawlik [Ed.]. London: Sage Publications, 2000. 629p. *ISBN: 0761953299.*

567 International research in Antarctic psychology. Peter Suedfeld; Karine Weiss; Elisabeth Rosnet; Christine Le Scanff; Marc-Simon Sagal; Robin Burns; Peter Sullivan; Antonio Peri; Cristina Scarlata; Marta Barbarito; JoAnna Wood; Sylvia J. Hysong; Desmond J. Lugg; Deborah L. Harm; R. Bhargava; S. Mukerji; Usha Sachdeva; Lawrence A. Palinkas; Matt Houseal; G. Daniel Steel; Masafumi Tanaka. **Envir. Behav.** 32:1 1:2000 pp.7-156. *Collection of 8 articles.*

568 Interpretation, truth and correspondence. Pentti Moilanen. **J. Theory Soc. Behav.** 30:4 12:2000 pp.377-390.

569 Is acculturation unidimensional or bidimensional? A head-to-head comparison in the prediction of personality, self-identity, and adjustment. Andrew G. Ryder; Lynn E. Alden; Delroy L. Paulhus. **J. Pers. Soc. Psychol.** 79:1 7:2000 pp.49-65.

570 Issues in the psychology of women. Maryka Biaggio [Ed.]; Michel Hersen [Ed.]. New York, London: Kluwer Academic/Plenum Publishers, 2000. xii, 303p. *ISBN: 0306463210. Includes bibliographical references and index.*

571 Lingua ex machina : reconciling Darwin and Chomsky with the human brain. William H. Calvin; Derek Bickerton. Cambridge MA, London: MIT Press, 2000. 298p. *ISBN: 0262032732. Includes bibliographical references and index.*

572 Lives in time and place: the problems and promises of developmental science. Richard A. Settersten. Amityville NY: Baywood, 1999. vi, 318p. *ISBN: 0895032007. Includes bibliographical references (p. 257-296) and indexes. (Series:* Society and aging).

573 Maxims or myths of beauty? A meta-analytic and theoretical review. Judith H. Langlois; Lisa Kalakanis; Adam J. Rubenstein; Andrea Larson; Monica Hallam; Monica Smoot. **Psychol. B.** 126:3 5:2000 pp.390-423.

574 Mindfulness theory and social issues. Ellen J. Langer; Mihnea Moldoveanu; Robert J. Sternberg; Ron Ritchhart; David N. Perkins; Christine Kawakami; Judith B. White; Steven Reiss; Clifford Nass; Youngme Moon; Judee K. Burgoon; Charles R. Berger; Vincent R. Waldron; Jack Demick. **J. Soc. Issues** 56:1 Spring:2000 pp.1-159. *Collection of 9 articles.*

575 The nature-nurture debate: the essential readings. Wendy M. Williams [Ed.]; Stephen J. Ceci [Ed.]. Malden MA: Blackwell Publishers, 1999. 294p. *ISBN: 063121738X,*

C: INDIVIDUALS. GROUPS. ORGANIZATIONS

0631217398. Includes bibliographical references and index. (Series: Essential readings in developmental psychology).

576 Negative correlates of computer game play in adolescents. John Colwell; Jo Payne. **Br. J. Psy.** 91:3 8:2000 pp.295-310.

577 The neighborhoods they live in: the effects of neighborhood residence on child and adolescent outcomes. Tama Leventhal; Jeanne Brooks-Gunn. **Psychol. B.** 126:2 3:2000 pp.309-337.

578 A new age of personality: an essay on the psychology of our times. Marcel Gauchet. **Thes. Elev.** 60 2:2000 pp.23-41.

579 Oedipus Rex at *Eve's Bayou* or the little Black girl who left Sigmund Freud in the swamp. D. Soyini Madison. **Cult. St.** 14:2 4:2000 pp.311-340.

580 On inferring one's beliefs from one's attempt and consequences for subsequent compliance. Dariusz Dolinski. **J. Pers. Soc. Psychol.** 78:2 2:2000 pp.260-272.

581 Perceiving benefits in adversity: stress-related growth in women living with HIV/AIDS. Karolynn Siegel; Eric W. Schrimshaw. **Soc. Sci. Med.** 51:10 11:2000 pp.1543-1554.

582 Portraits of successful entrepreneurs and high-flyers: a psychological perspective. Syrine Kit Sum Lam. Aldershot: Ashgate, 1999. 270p. *ISBN: 1840147911.*

583 Predictors of moral reasoning among African American children: a preliminary study. Marisha L. Humphries; Bonita L. Parker; Robert J. Jagers. **J. Black Psychol.** 26:1 2:2000 pp.51-64.

584 The primary process and the unconscious: experimental evidence supporting two psychoanalytic presuppositions; *[Summary in French]; [Summary in German]; [Summary in Spanish].* Linda A.W. Brakel; Shasha Kleinsorge; Michael Snodgrass; Howard Shevrin. **Int. J.Psy.** 81:3 6:2000 pp.553-569.

585 A psychological analysis of a psychological phenomenon: the dialogical construction of meaning. Ingrid E. Josephs. **Soc. Sci. Info.** 39:1 3:2000 pp.115-130.

586 The psychological appeal of Bill Watterson's *Calvin*. Diana L. Mahony. **Humor** 13:1 2000 pp.19-40.

587 Psychological testing and assessment. Lewis R. Aiken. Boston MA: Allyn & Bacon, 2000. ix, 501p. *ISBN: 0205295673. Includes bibliographical references (p. 456-483) and indexes.*

588 The psychological trade-offs of goal investment. Eva M. Pomerantz; Jill L. Saxon; Shigehiro Oishi. **J. Pers. Soc. Psychol.** 79:4 10:2000 pp.617-630.

589 Psychology. Henry. Gleitman; Alan J. Fridlund; Daniel. Reisberg. New York: W.W. Norton & Company, 1999. *ISBN: 0393973646. Includes bibliographical references (p. 32-90) and index.*

590 Psychology and the media: a second look. Lita Linzer Schwartz [Ed.]. Washington DC, London: American Psychological Association, 1999. xii, 223p. *ISBN: 1557985782. Includes bibliographical references and index.*

591 Psychology in the 21st century. Robert Plomin; John Crabbe; John T. Cacioppo; Gary G. Berntson; John F. Sheridan; Martha K. McClintock; Harry T. Reis; W. Andrew Collins; Ellen Berscheid; Michael I. Posner; Gregory J. DiGirolamo; Richard J. Davidson; Daren C. Jackson; Ned H. Kalin; Barbara A. Mellers; John A. Bargh; Melissa J. Ferguson; Thomas A. Widiger; Lee Anna Clark; Peter E. Nathan; Scott P. Stuart; Sara L. Dolan. **Psychol. B.** 126:6 11:2000 pp.806-981. *Collection of 9 articles.*

592 Re-examining psychology: critical perspectives and African insights. T.L. Holdstock. London, New York: Routledge, 2000. 255p. *ISBN: 0415187923. Includes bibliographical references and index.*

593 A scandal in Salzburg or Freud's surreptitious role in the 1908 Abraham-Jung dispute. Philip Kuhn. **Int. J.Psy.** 81:4 8:2000 pp.705-732.

594 A science of meaning: can behaviorism bring meaning to psychological science? Richard J. DeGrandpre. **Am. Psychol.** 55:7 7:2000 pp.721-739.

595 Simple heuristics that make us smart. Gerd Gigerenzer; Peter M. Todd; ABC Research Group. New York: Oxford University Press, 1999. xv, 416p. *ISBN: 0195121562. Includes bibliographical references (p. 367-396) and indexes.*

C: INDIVIDUS. GROUPES. ORGANISATIONS

596 The six faces of the cube: the mechanism that guarantees survival described by six scientific disciplines. Guenter Greiner. **J. Soc. Evol. Sys.** 21:3 1998 pp.243-258.

597 Der Status des 'Mentalen' in kulturtheoretischen Handlungserklärungen. Zum Problem der Relation von Verhalten und Wissen nach Stephen Turner und Theodore Schatzki. *[In German]*; (The status of mind in culturalist explanations of action. On the issue of the relationship between behaviour and knowledge according to Stephen Turner and Theodore Schatzki.) *[Summary]*. Andreas Reckwitz. **Z. Soziol.** 29:3 6:2000 pp.167-185.

598 Theoretical foundations and biological bases of development in adolescence. Richard M. Lerner [Intro.]; Jacqueline V. Lerner [Ed.]. New York, London: Garland Publishing, 1999. xvii, 339p. *ISBN: 0815332904. Includes bibliographical references.* (*Series:* Adolescence: development, diversity, and context - 1).

599 Three psychologies: perspectives from Freud, Skinner, and Rogers. Robert D. Nye. Pacific Grove CA: Brooks/Cole, 2000. x, 181p. *ISBN: 053436845X. Includes bibliographical references and index.*

600 Toward a feminist developmental psychology. Patricia H. Miller [Ed.]; Ellin Kofsky Scholnick [Ed.]. New York: Routledge, 2000. 309p. *ISBN: 0415921783, 0415921775. Includes bibliographical references and index.*

601 Unto others: the evolution and psychology of unselfish behavior. Elliott Sober; David Sloan Wilson. Cambridge MA: Harvard University Press, 1998. 394p. *ISBN: 0674930460. Includes bibliographical references (p. 363-386) and index.*

602 Western rationality and the angel of dreams: self, psyche, dreaming. Murray Lionel Wax. Lanham MD, Oxford: Rowman & Littlefield, 1999. ix, 171p. *ISBN: 0847693740, 0847693759. Includes bibliographical references (p. 151-166) and index.*

603 What anthropology can do for psychology: facing physics envy, ethnocentrism, and a belief in 'race'. Jefferson M. Fish. **Am. Anthrop.** 102:3 9:2000 pp.552-563.

604 What is psychology? Andrew M. Colman. London, New York: Routledge, 1999. xii, 204p. *ISBN: 0415169011, 041516902X. Includes bibliographical references and index.*

605 What psychology can do for anthropology, or why anthropology took postmodernism on the chin. Patricia M. Greenfield. **Am. Anthrop.** 102:3 9:2000 pp.564-610.

606 When choice is demotivating: can one desire too much of a good thing? Sheena S. Iyengar; Mark R. Lepper. **J. Pers. Soc. Psychol.** 79:6 12:2000 pp.995-1006.

Cognition
Cognition

607 Across the great divide: bridging the gap between understanding of toddlers' and older children's thinking. Zhe Chen; Marvin W. Dachler; Robert S. Siegler. Chicago IL: University of Chicago Press, 2000. vii, 108p. *Includes bibliographical references.* (*Series:* Monographs of the Society for Research in Child Development).

608 At home with nature: effects of 'greenness' on children's cognitive functioning. Nancy M. Wells. **Envir. Behav.** 32:6 11:2000 pp.775-795.

609 Behavioral and cognitive correlates of exercise self-schemata. Zenong Yin; Michael P. Boyd. **J. Psychol.** 134:3 5:2000 pp.269-282.

610 Bilingual acquisition: theoretical implications of a case study. Margaret Deuchar; Suzanne Quay. Oxford, New York: Oxford University Press, 2000. 163p. *ISBN: 0198236859. Includes bibliographical references.*

611 Caricaturing facial expressions. Andrew J. Calder; Duncan Rowland; Andrew W. Young; Ian Nimmo-Smith; Jill Keane; David I. Perret. **Cognition** 76:2 8:2000 pp.105-146.

612 Cognitive aging: a primer. Denise C. Park [Ed.]; Norbert Schwarz [Ed.]. Philadelphia PA: Psychology Press, 2000. xiii, 292p. *ISBN: 0863776922. Includes bibliographical references and indexes.*

613 Cognitive mapping: past, present, and future. Rob Kitchin; Scott Freundschuh. New York: Routledge, 2000. 256p. *ISBN: 0415208068. Includes bibliographical references and index.*

C: INDIVIDUALS, GROUPS, ORGANIZATIONS

614 Cognitive psychology. John B. Best. Belmont CA: Brooks/Cole Wadsworth, 1999. xx, 524p. *ISBN: 0534354173. Includes bibliographical references (p. 471-488) and indexes.*
615 Cognitive psychology: a student's handbook. Michael W. Eysenck; Mark T. Keane. London: Routledge, 2000. *ISBN: 0863773753.*
616 Cognitive psychology and its implications. John R. Anderson. New York: W.H. Freeman, 2000. 531p. *ISBN: 0716736780. Includes bibliographical references (p. 464-502) and indexes.*
617 A connectionist defence of the inscrutability thesis. Francisco Calvo Garzón. **Mind Lang.** 15:5 11:2000 pp.465-480.
618 The content of intentions. Elisabeth Pacherie. **Mind Lang.** 15:4 9:2000 pp.400-432.
619 Core knowledge. Elizabeth S. Spelke. **Am. Psychol.** 55:11 11:2000 pp.1233-1243.
620 Counterfactuals as self-generated primes: the effect of prior counterfactual activation on person perception judgments. Adam D. Galinsky; Gordon B. Moskowitz; Ian Skurnik. **Soc. Cogn.** 18:3 Fall:2000 pp.252-280.
621 Creativity as an extension of intelligence: faceted definition and structural hypotheses. Samuel Shye; Gil Goldzweig. **Megamot** XL:1 11:1999 pp.31-53.
622 The development of language. Martyn Barrett [Ed.]. London: Routledge, 2000. 432p. *ISBN: 086377847X.*
623 Do young children have adult syntactic competence? Michael Tomasello. **Cognition** 74:3 3:2000 pp.209-254.
624 Early lexical acquisition: the role of cross-situational learning. Nameera Akhtar; Lisa Montague. **Fst. Lang.** 19(3):57 9:1999 pp.347-358.
625 The effects of cigarette consumption on the Sternberg visual memory search paradigm. Robert Tait; Mathew Martin-Iverson; Patricia T. Michie; Leon Dusci. **Addiction** 95:3 3:2000 pp.437-448.
626 Essentials of cognitive psychology. Alan J. Parkin. Hove: Psychology Press, 2000. 320p. *ISBN: 0863776728, 0863776736.*
627 Examination of relationships among trait-like individual differences, state-like individual differences, and learning performance. Gilad Chen; Stanley M. Gully; Jon-Andrew Whiteman; Robert N. Kilcullen. **J. Appl. Psychol.** 85:6 12:2000 pp.835-847.
628 Eye and brain: the psychology of seeing. R.L. Gregory. Princeton NJ: Princeton University Press, 1998. ix, 277p. *ISBN: 0198524234, 0691048401, 0198524129, 0691048371. Includes bibliographical references (p. [256]-268) and index. (Series:* Princeton science library).
629 Factor structure of the Everyday Memory Questionnaire. Ian M. Cornish. **Br. J. Psy.** 91:3 8:2000 pp.427-438.
630 Foundations of spatial vision: from retinal images to perceived shapes. Joseph S. Lappin; Warren D. Craft. **Psychol. Rev.** 107:1 1:2000 pp.6-38.
631 Frequency versus probability formats in statistical word problems. Johnathon St.B.T. Evans; Simon J. Handley; Nick Perham; David E. Over; Valerie A. Thompson. **Cognition** 77:3 12:2000 pp.197-214.
632 Freud's different versions of forgetting 'Signorelli': rhetoric and repression; *[Summary in French]; [Summary in German]; [Summary in Spanish].* Michael Billig. **Int. J.Psy.** 81:3 6:2000 pp.483-498.
633 How important are the cognitive skills of teenagers in predicting subsequent earnings? Richard J. Murnane; John B. Willett; Yves Duhaldeborde; John H. Tyler. **J. Policy An.** 19:4 Fall:2000 pp.547-568.
634 Human and machine perception 2: emergence, attention and creativity. Virginio Cantoni [Ed.]; et al. New York, London: Kluwer Academic/Plenum Publishers, 1999. xiv, 222p. *ISBN: 0306462915. Papers presented at the Third International Workshop on Human and Machine Perception, September 1998, Pavia. Includes bibliographical references and index.*
635 Inferring children's categorizations from sequential touching behaviors: an analytical model. Hoben Thomas; Michael P. Dahlin. **Psychol. Rev.** 107:1 1:2000 pp.182-194.

C: INDIVIDUS. GROUPES. ORGANISATIONS

636 Language acquisition. Victoria Southgate; Kerstin Meints; Chris Sinha; Kristine Jensen de López; David McNeill; Michael Tomasello; Ewa Dąbrowska; Michael Israel; Christopher Johnson; Patricia J. Brooks; Holger Diessel. **Cogn. Ling.** 11:1-2 2000 pp.5-151. *Collection of 7 articles.*

637 Learning strategies, learning anxiety and knowledge acquisition. Peter Warr; Jonathon Downing. **Br. J. Psy.** 91:3 8:2000 pp.311-334.

638 Making a good decision: value from fit. E. Tory Higgins. **Am. Psychol.** 55:11 11:2000 pp.1217-1230.

639 Making judgments about ability: the role of implicit theories of ability in moderating inferences from temporal and social comparison information. Ruth Butler. **J. Pers. Soc. Psychol.** 78:5 5:2000 pp.965-978.

640 Memory, consciousness, and the brain: the Tallinn conference. Endel Tulving [Ed.]. Philadelphia PA: Psychology Press, 2000. xviii, 397p. *ISBN: 1841690155. Includes bibliographical references and indexes.*

641 Mental representation and the spatial structure of virtual environments. Loïc Belingard; Patrick Péruch. **Envir. Behav.** 32:3 5:2000 pp.427-442.

642 Metaphoric structuring: understanding time through spatial metaphors. Lera Boroditsky. **Cognition** 75:1 4:2000 pp.1-28.

643 Multicultural minds: a dynamic constructivist approach to culture and cognition. Ying-yi Hong; Michael W. Morris; Chi-yue Chiu; Verónica Benet-Martínez. **Am. Psychol.** 55:7 7:2000 pp.709-720.

644 Oscillator-based memory for serial order. Gordon D.A. Brown; Tim Preece; Charles Hulme. **Psychol. Rev.** 107:1 1:2000 pp.127-181.

645 The particularity of visual perception. Matthew Soteriou. **Eur. J. Phil.** 8:2 8:2000 pp.173-189.

646 Perception: theory, development, and organisation. Paul Rookes; Jane Willson. London, New York: Routledge, 2000. *ISBN: 0415190932, 0415190940. Includes bibliographical references and index. (Series:* Routledge modular psychology).

647 Preconditions for active transfer in learning processes. Tiina Soini. Helsinki: Finnish Society of Sciences and Letters; Finnish Academy of Sciences and Letters, 1999. 165p. *ISBN: 9516533027. (Series:* Commentationes Scientarium Socialium - 55).

648 Predicting and understanding behavioral volitions: the interplay between goals and behaviors. Marco Perugini; Mark Conner. **Eur. J. Soc. Psychol.** 30:5 9-10:2000 pp.705-731.

649 The psychology of social chess and the evolution of attribution mechanisms: explaining the fundamental attribution error. Paul W. Andrews. **Evol. Hum. Behav.** 22:1 1:2001 pp.11-29.

650 The psychology of the unthinkable: taboo trade-offs, forbidden base rates, and heretical counterfactuals. Philip E. Tetlock; Orie V. Kristel; S. Beth Elson; Melanie C. Green; Jennifer S. Lerner. **J. Pers. Soc. Psychol.** 78:5 5:2000 pp.853-870.

651 Quantity and quality of musical practice as predictors of performance quality. Aaron Williamon; Elizabeth Valentine. **Br. J. Psy.** 91:3 8:2000 pp.353-376.

652 The reinstatement of dissonance and psychological discomfort following failed affirmations. Adam D. Galinsky; Jeff Stone; Joel Cooper. **Eur. J. Soc. Psychol.** 30:1 1-2:2000 pp.123-147.

653 Resolving the debate over birth order, family size, and intelligence. Joseph Lee Rodgers; H. Harrington Cleveland; Edwin van den Oord; David C. Rowe. **Am. Psychol.** 55:6 6:2000 pp.599-612.

654 The role of background knowledge in speeded perceptual categorization. Thomas J. Palmeri; Celina Blalock. **Cognition** 77:2 11:2000 pp.B45-B57.

655 Running shared mental models as a distributed cognitive process. Adrian P. Banks; Lynne J. Millward. **Br. J. Psy.** 91:4 11:2000 pp.513-531.

656 Social exchange and reciprocity: confusion or a heuristic? Toko Kiyonari; Shigehito Tanida; Toshio Yamagishi. **Evol. Hum. Behav.** 21:6 11:2000 pp.411-428.

C: INDIVIDUALS. GROUPS. ORGANIZATIONS

657   Social ignition: the interplay of motivation and social cognition. Gabriele Oettingen; Roy F. Baumeister; Mark Muraven; Dianne M. Tice; Gordon B. Moskowitz; Amanda R. Salomon; Constance M. Taylor; Jens Förster; E. Tory Higgins; Fritz Strack; David Dunning; Keith S. Beauregard. **Soc. Cogn.** 18:2 Summer:2000 pp.101-222. *Collection of 5 articles.*

658   Some shortcomings of long-term working memory. Fernand Gobet. **Br. J. Psy.** 91:4 11:2000 pp.551-570.

659   Spoken word recognition and lexical representation in very young children. Daniel Swingley; Richard N. Aslin. **Cognition** 76:2 8:2000 pp.147-166.

660   Talent in context: historical and social perspectives on giftedness. Karen B. Rogers [Ed.]; Reva C. Friedman [Ed.]. Washington DC, London: American Psychological Association, 1998. xxiv, 218p. *ISBN: 155798493X. Includes bibliographical references and index.*

661   Toward an understanding of adult intellectual development: investigating within-individual convergence of interest and knowledge profiles. Charlie L. Reeve; Milton D. Hakel. **J. Appl. Psychol.** 85:6 12:2000 pp.897-908.

662   Using neural network analysis to uncover the trace effects of national culture. John F. Veiga; Michael Lubatkin; Roland Calori; Philippe Very; Y. Alex Tung. **J. Int. Bus. Stud.** 31:2 2000 pp.223-238.

663   Validity of measures of cognitive processes and general ability for learning and performance on highly complex computerized tutors: is the g factor of intelligence even more general? Mary Roznowski; David N. Dickter; Sehee Hong; Linda L. Sawin; Valerie J. Shute. **J. Appl. Psychol.** 85:6 12:2000 pp.940-955.

664   Verbal and visual causal arguments. Uwe Oestermeier; Friedrich W. Hesse. **Cognition** 75:1 4:2000 pp.65-104.

665   Wanting to have vs. wanting to be: the effect of perceived instrumentality on goal orientation. Joke Simons; Siegfried Dewitte; Willy Lens. **Br. J. Psy.** 91:3 8:2000 pp.335-352.

666   When further learning fails: stability and change following repeated presentation of text. Catherine O. Fritz; Peter E. Morris; Robert A. Bjork; Rochel Gelman; Thomas D. Wickens. **Br. J. Psy.** 91:4 11:2000 pp.493-511.

667   Why do we think? Consequences of regarding thinking as behavior. Geir Overskeid. **J. Psychol.** 134:4 7:2000 pp.357-374.

668   Wisdom as a classical source of human strength: conceptualization and empirical inquiry. Deirdre A. Kramer. **J. Soc. Clin. Psychol.** 19:1 Spring:2000 pp.83-101.

Personality and emotions
Personnalité et émotions

669   Adrienne Rich, location and the body. Mary Eagleton. **J. Gender St.** 9:3 11:2000 pp.299-312.

670   Adult attachment and the defensive regulation of attention and memory: examining the role of preemptive and postemptive defensive processes. R. Chris Fraley; Joseph P. Garner; Phillip R. Shaver. **J. Pers. Soc. Psychol.** 79:5 11:2000 pp.816-826.

671   Analyzing emotions as culturally constructed scripts. Usha Menon. **Cult. Psyc.** 6:1 3:2000 pp.40-50.

672   Behind the mask: destruction and creativity in women's aggression. Dana Crowley Jack. Cambridge MA, London: Harvard University Press, 1999. 321p. *ISBN: 0674064852. Includes bibliographical references (p. 285-310) and index.*

673   Character and well-being: towards an ethics of character. Michele Mangini. **Philos. Soc. Crit.** 26:2 3:2000 pp.79-98.

674   La contribution des émotions à l'impartialité des décisions. *[In French]*; [The contribution of emotions to impartial decisions]. Patricia Paperman. **Soc. Sci. Info.** 39:1 3:2000 pp.29-73.

C: INDIVIDUS. GROUPES. ORGANISATIONS

675 Coping-related expectancies and dispositions as prospective predictors of coping responses and symptoms. Salvatore J. Catanzaro; Heidi H. Wasch; Irving Kirsch; Jack Mearns. **J. Personal.** 68:4 8:2000 pp.757-788.

676 Cultural psychology of surprise: holistic theories and recognition of contradiction. Incheol Choi; Richard E. Nisbett. **J. Pers. Soc. Psychol.** 79:6 12:2000 pp.890-905.

677 A cultural-psychological analysis of emotions. Carl Ratner. **Cult. Psyc.** 6:1 3:2000 pp.5-39.

678 Culture and personality: toward an integrated cultural trait psychology. A. Timothy Church. **J. Personal.** 68:4 8:2000 pp.651-704.

679 The development of personality, self, and ego in adolescence. Richard M. Lerner [Intro.]; Laura E. Hess [Ed.]. New York, London: Garland Publishing, 1999. xiii, 357p. *ISBN: 0815332920. Includes bibliographical references. (Series:* Adolescence: development, diversity, and context - 3).

680 Downward comparison in everyday life: reconciling self-enhancement models with the mood-cognition priming model. Joanne V. Wood; John L. Michela; Caterina Giordano. **J. Pers. Soc. Psychol.** 79:4 10:2000 pp.563-579.

681 The effectiveness of a culture- and gender-specific intervention for increasing resiliency among African American preadolescent females. Faye Z. Belgrave; Gretchen Chase-Vaughn; Famebridge Gray; Jerveada Dixon Addison; Valerie R. Cherry. **J. Black Psychol.** 26:2 5:2000 pp.133-147.

682 Emotional experience in everyday life across the adult life span. Laura L. Carstensen; Monisha Pasupathi; Ulrich Mayr; John R. Nesselroade. **J. Pers. Soc. Psychol.** 79:4 10:2000 pp.644-655.

683 Emotional state and the detection of change in facial expression of emotion. P.M. Niedenthal; J.B. Halberstadt; J. Margolin; A.H. Innes-Ker. **Eur. J. Soc. Psychol.** 30:2 3-4:2000 pp.211-222.

684 Emotions and leadership: the role of emotional intelligence. Jennifer M. George. **Human Relat.** 53:8 8:2000 pp.1027-1056.

685 Exploring individual differences in reactions to mortality salience: does attachment style regulate terror management mechanisms? Mario Mikulincer; Victor Florian. **J. Pers. Soc. Psychol.** 79:2 8:2000 pp.260-273.

686 Exposure to humor before and after an unpleasant stimulus: humor as a preventative or a cure. Arnie Cann; Lawrence G. Calhoun; Jamey T. Nance. **Humor** 13:2 2000 pp.177-191.

687 Factors influencing the relation between extraversion and pleasant affect. Richard E. Lucas; Frank Fujita. **J. Pers. Soc. Psychol.** 79:6 12:2000 pp.1039-1056.

688 Focalism: a source of durability bias in affective forecasting. Timothy D. Wilson; Thalia Wheatley; Jonathan M. Meyers; Daniel T. Gilbert; Danny Axsom. **J. Pers. Soc. Psychol.** 78:5 5:2000 pp.821-836.

689 Gender and emotion: social psychological perspectives. Agneta Fischer [Ed.]. Cambridge, New York; Paris: Cambridge University Press; Editions de la Maison des Sciences de l'Homme, 2000. xi, 331p. *ISBN: 0521630150, 0521639867. Includes bibliographical references and index. (Series:* Studies in emotion and social interaction - 2).

690 Handbook of emotions. Jeannette M. Haviland-Jones [Ed.]; Michael Lewis [Ed.]. New York: Guilford Press, 2000. xvi, 720p. *ISBN: 1572305290. Includes bibliographical references and indexes.*

691 Hope and dysphoria: the moderating role of defense mechanisms. Paul Kwon. **J. Personal.** 68:2 4:2000 pp.199-224.

692 How emotions work. Jack Katz. Chicago IL: University of Chicago Press, 1999. xii, 407p. *ISBN: 0226425991. Includes bibliographical references (p. 381-392) and index.*

693 Humility: theoretical perspectives, empirical findings and directions for future research. June Price Tangney. **J. Soc. Clin. Psychol.** 19:1 Spring:2000 pp.70-82.

694 Hypochondriacal concerns and the five factor model of personality. Eamonn Ferguson. **J. Personal.** 68:4 8:2000 pp.705-724.

695 Hysteria. Christopher Bollas. London, New York: Routledge, 1999. 208p. *ISBN: 0415220327, 0415220335. Includes bibliographical references and index.*

C: INDIVIDUALS. GROUPS. ORGANIZATIONS

696 'I only have eyes for you': the partiality of positive emotions. Aaron Ben-Ze'ev. **J. Theory Soc. Behav.** 30:3 9:2000 pp.341-351.

697 The impostor phenomenon: self-perceptions, reflected appraisals, and interpersonal strategies. Mark R. Leary; Katharine M. Patton; Amy E. Orlando; Wendy Wagoner Funk. **J. Personal.** 68:4 8:2000 pp.725-756.

698 The influence of rearing order on personality development within two adoption cohorts. Jeremy M. Beer; Joseph M. Horn. **J. Personal.** 68:4 8:2000 pp.789-819.

699 An introduction to theories of personality. Robert B. Ewen. Mahwah NJ: Lawrence Erlbaum Associates, 1998. 598p. *ISBN: 0805827196. Includes bibliographical references (p. 559-582) and index.*

700 Linking childhood personality with adaptation: evidence for continuity and change across time into late adolescence. Rebecca L. Shiner. **J. Pers. Soc. Psychol.** 78:2 2:2000 pp.310-325.

701 Loneliness. Leroy S. Rouner [Ed.]. Notre Dame IN: University of Notre Dame Press, 1998. xviii, 301p. *ISBN: 0268013187. Includes bibliographical references and index. (Series:* Boston University studies in philosophy and religion - 19).

702 Modesty as a virtue. Michael Ridge. **Am. Phil. Q.** 37:3 7:2000 pp.269-283.

703 'Mood contagion': the automatic transfer of mood between persons. Roland Neumann; Fritz Strack. **J. Pers. Soc. Psychol.** 79:2 8:2000 pp.211-223.

704 Motivation and self-regulation across the life span. Jutta Heckhausen [Ed.]; Carol S. Dweck [Ed.]. Cambridge: Cambridge University Press, 1998. ix, 461p. *ISBN: 0521591767. Includes bibliographical references and index.*

705 A multimodal cognitive-behavioural approach to anger reduction in an occupational sample. Mark A. Gerzina; Peter Drummond. **J. Occup. Organ. Psychol.** 73:2 6:2000 pp.181-194.

706 Nothing more than feelings? The role of emotions in moral judgement. David Pizarro. **J. Theory Soc. Behav.** 30:4 12:2000 pp.355-376.

707 Personality and job performance: the big five revisited. Gregory M. Hurtz; John J. Donovan. **J. Appl. Psychol.** 85:6 12:2000 pp.869-879.

708 Personality, emotional experience, and efforts to control emotions. Renée M. Tobin; William G. Graziano; Eric J. Vanman; Louis G. Tassinary. **J. Pers. Soc. Psychol.** 79:4 10:2000 pp.656-669.

709 Personality processes and problem behavior. Rick H. Hoyle; Robert F. Krueger; Avshalom Caspi; Terrie E. Moffitt; Marvin Zuckerman; D. Michael Kuhlman; Vicki S. Helgeson; Heidi L. Fritz; M. Lynne Cooper; V. Bede Agocha; Melanie S. Sheldon; Howard S. Friedman; Thomas J. Dishion; Thomas A. Wills; James M. Sandy; Alison Yaeger; Alexandra Loukas; Jennifer L. Krull; Laurie Chassin; Adam C. Carle; Meg Gerrard; Frederick X. Gibbons; Monica Reis-Bergan; Daniel W. Russell; Michele C. Fejfar; Joshua D. Miller; Krista K. Trobst; Jerry S. Wiggins; Paul T. Costa, Jr.; Jeffrey H. Herbst; Robert R. McCrae; Henry L. Masters, III. **J. Personal.** 68:6 12:2000 pp.953-1252. *Collection of 12 articles.*

710 Personality traits and culture: new perspectives on some classic issues. Robert R. McCrae; Philip K. Bock; Anthony J. Marsella; Joan Dubanoski; Winter C. Hamada; Heather Morse; Michael Harris Bond; A. Timothy Church; Marcia S. Katigbak; Khairul A. Mastor; Putai Jin; Martin Cooper; J.W.P. Heuchert; Wayne D. Parker; Heinrich Stumpf; Chris P.H. Myburgh; Juris G. Draguns; Anna V. Krylova; Valery E. Oryol; Alexey A. Rukavishnikov; Thomas A. Martin; Verónica Benet-Martínez; Oliver P. John. **Am. Behav. Sc.** 44:1 9:2000 pp.10-157. *Collection of 9 articles.*

711 Perspectives on personality: the relative accuracy of self versus others for the predication of emotion and behavior. Jana S. Spain; Leslie G. Eaton; David C. Funder. **J. Personal.** 68:5 10:2000 pp.837-868.

712 Phenotypic, genetic, and nonshared environmental parallels in the structure of personality: a view from the multidimensional personality questionnaire. Robert F. Krueger. **J. Pers. Soc. Psychol.** 79:6 12:2000 pp.1057-1067.

C: INDIVIDUS. GROUPES. ORGANISATIONS

713   Reexamining the circumplex model of affect. Nancy A. Remington; Leandre R. Fabrigar; Penny S. Visser. **J. Pers. Soc. Psychol.** 79:2 8:2000 pp.286-300.

714   Risk. Deborah Lupton. London, New York: Routledge, 1999. vi, 184p. *ISBN: 0415183332, 0415183340. Includes bibliographical references (p. [173]-180) and index. (Series:* Key ideas).

715   The role of job control as a moderator of emotional dissonance and emotional intelligence-outcome relationships. Rebecca Abraham. **J. Psychol.** 134:2 3:2000 pp.169-184.

716   The role of stressful events in the relationship between positive and negative affects: evidence from field and experimental studies. Alex J. Zautra; John W. Reich; Mary C. Davis; Phillip T. Potter; Nancy A. Nicolson. **J. Personal.** 68:5 10:2000 pp.927-951.

717   Self-control, morality, and human strength. Roy F. Baumeister; Julie Juola Exline. **J. Soc. Clin. Psychol.** 19:1 Spring:2000 pp.29-42.

718   Self-regulation and depletion of limited resources: does self-control resemble a muscle? Mark Muraven; Roy F. Baumeister. **Psychol. B.** 126:2 3:2000 pp.247-259.

719   Spirituality: description, measurement, and relation to the five factor model of personality. Douglas A. MacDonald. **J. Personal.** 68:1 2:2000 pp.153-197.

720   Stalking the perfect measure of implicit self-esteem: the blind men and the elephant revisited? Jennifer K. Bosson; William B. Swann, Jr.; James W. Pennebaker. **J. Pers. Soc. Psychol.** 79:4 10:2000 pp.631-643.

721   Stress and accessibility of proximity-related thoughts: exploring the normative and intraindividual components of attachment theory. Mario Mikulincer; Gurit Birnbaum; David Woddis; Orit Nachmias. **J. Pers. Soc. Psychol.** 78:3 3:2000 pp.509-523.

722   Stress and alcohol use: a daily process examination of the stressor-vulnerability model. Stephen Armeli; Margaret Anne Carney; Howard Tennen; Glenn Affleck; Timothy P. O'Neil. **J. Pers. Soc. Psychol.** 78:5 5:2000 pp.979-994.

723   Strong feelings: emotion, addiction, and human behavior. Jon Elster. Cambridge MA, London: MIT Press, 1999. xii, 252p. *ISBN: 0262050560. Includes bibliographical references and index. (Series:* Jean Nicod lectures. A Bradford book).

724   A student dies, a school mourns: dealing with death and loss in the school community. Ralph L. Klicker. Philadelphia PA: Accelerated Development, 2000. 145p. *ISBN: 1560327421. Includes bibliographical references (p. 131-135) and indexes.*

725   Subjective overachievement: individual differences in self-doubt and concern with performance. Kathryn C. Oleson; Kirsten M. Poehlmann; John H. Yost; Molly E. Lynch; Robert M. Arkin. **J. Personal.** 68:3 6:2000 pp.491-524.

726   Theories of personality. Calvin S. Hall; Gardner Lindzey; John B. Campbell. New York: John Wiley & Sons, 1998. xxvii, 740p. *ISBN: 0471303429. Includes bibliographical references (p. 652-722) and index.*

727   A three-factor model of trait anger: dimensions of affect, behavior, and cognition. René Martin; David Watson; Choi K. Wan. **J. Personal.** 68:5 10:2000 pp.869-898.

728   La tiédeur. *[In French]*; [Warmth]. Philippe Garnier. Paris: Presses universitaires de France, 2000. 148p. *ISBN: 2130503187.*

729   Tracing the origin of humor. Daniel D. Perlmutter. **Humor** 13:4 2000 pp.457-468.

730   The uncertain mind: individual differences in facing the unknown. Richard M. Sorrentino; Christopher R.J. Roney. Philadelphia PA: Psychology Press, 2000. x, 194p. *ISBN: 0863776914. Includes bibliographical references (p. [173]-186) and index. (Series:* Essays in social psychology).

731   Unraveling the mysteries of anxiety and its disorders from the perspective of emotion theory. David H. Barlow. **Am. Psychol.** 55:11 11:2000 pp.1247-1263.

732   Using the implicit association test to measure self-esteem and self-concept. Anthony G. Greenwald; Shelly D. Farnham. **J. Pers. Soc. Psychol.** 79:6 12:2000 pp.1022-1038.

733   Virtue ethics and situationist personality psychology. Maria Merritt. **Ethic. Theory Moral P.** 3:4 12:2000 pp.365-383.

734   Volunteering as a lifestyle choice: negotiating self-identities in Japan. Lynne Y. Nakano. **Ethnology** XXXIX:2 Spring:2000 pp.93-108.

C: INDIVIDUALS. GROUPS. ORGANIZATIONS

735   What is beyond the big five? Plenty! Sampo V. Paunonen; Douglas N. Jackson. **J. Personal.** 68:5 10:2000 pp.821-836.

736   Women's anger: clinical and developmental perspectives. Deborah L. Cox; Sally D. Stabb; Karin H. Bruckner. Philadelphia PA, London: Brunner/Mazel, 1999. xviii, 254p. *ISBN: 0876309465. Includes bibliographical references (p. 223-240) and index.*

C.2: Clinical psychology
Psychologie clinique

737   Acceptance and commitment therapy: an experiential approach to behavior change. Steven C. Hayes; Kirk Strosahl; Kelly G. Wilson. New York, London: Guilford Press, 1999. xvi, 304p. *ISBN: 1572304812. Includes bibliographical references (p. 289-297) and index.*

738   Adult psychological problems: an introduction. Michael J. Power [Ed.]; Lorna A. Champion [Ed.]. Hove: Psychology Press, 2000. xii, 242p. *ISBN: 0863776418, 0863776426. Includes bibliographical references and index. (Series:* Contemporary psychology).

739   Affective style, psychopathology, and resilience: brain mechanisms and plasticity. Richard J. Davidson. **Am. Psychol.** 55:11 11:2000 pp.1196-1214.

740   Algumas considerações sobre psicodrama e psicoterapia-técnica mista. *[In Portuguese]*; [Some reflections about psychodrama and mixed technique-psychotherapy] *[Summary]*. Luisa Branco Vicente. **Aletheia** 10 1999 pp.75-86.

741   Associations between primary appraisals and life-events while controlling for depression. Eamonn Ferguson; Claire Lawrence; Gerald Matthews. **Br. J. Clin. Psycho.** 39:2 6:2000 pp.143-156.

742   Attitudes to emotional expression and personality in predicting post-traumatic stress disorder. J. Nightingale; R.M. Williams. **Br. J. Clin. Psycho.** 39:3 9:2000 pp.243-254.

743   Autistic devices in small children in mourning; *[Summary in French]*; *[Summary in German]*; *[Summary in Spanish]*. Mario Gomberoff; Liliana Pualuan de Gomberoff. **Int. J.Psy.** 81:5 10:2000 pp.907-920.

744   Becoming a subject: some theoretical and clinical issues; *[Summary in French]*; *[Summary in German]*; *[Summary in Spanish]*. Roger Kennedy. **Int. J.Psy.** 81:5 10:2000 pp.875-892.

745   Being mentally ill: a sociological theory. Thomas J. Scheff. New York: Aldine de Gruyter, 1999. xiv, 220p. *ISBN: 0202305864, 0202305872. Includes bibliographical references (p. 203-211) and index.*

746   The Berlin Wall on the therapist's couch. Christine Leuenberger. **Human St.** 23:2 4:2000 pp.99-121.

747   Beyond empathy: a therapy of contact-in-relationship. Richard G. Erskine; Janet Moursund; Rebecca Trautmann. Philadelphia PA, London: Brunner/Mazel, 1999. xiii, 380p. *ISBN: 0876309635. Includes bibliographical references and index.*

748   Can we do psychoanalytic outcome research? A feasibility study; *[Summary in French]*; *[Summary in German]*; *[Summary in Spanish]*. Susan C. Vaughan; Randall D. Marshall; Roger A. MacKinnon; Roger Vaughan; Lisa Mellman; Steven P. Roose. **Int. J.Psy.** 81:3 6:2000 pp.513-527.

749   Carers' attributions for challenging behaviour. Brian Stanley; Penny J. Standen. **Br. J. Clin. Psycho.** 39:2 6:2000 pp.157-168.

750   Case analyses for abnormal psychology: learning to look beyond the symptoms. Randall E. Osborne; Joan Lafuze; David V. Perkins. Philadelphia PA: Psychology Press, 2000. xxi, 200p. *ISBN: 0863775837, 0863775845. Includes bibliographical references (p. 195-197) and index.*

751   Causal uncertainty and depressive symptoms: appraisals and coping as mediating variables. Edward C. Chang. **J. Soc. Clin. Psychol.** 19:3 Fall:2000 pp.420-436.

752   The central phobic position: a new formulation of the free association method; *[Summary in French]*; *[Summary in German]*; *[Summary in Spanish]*. André Green. **Int. J.Psy.** 81:3 6:2000 pp.429-451.

C: INDIVIDUS. GROUPES. ORGANISATIONS

753 Child mental health problems in Arab children: application of the strengths and difficulties questionnaire. A.A. Thabet; D. Stretch; P. Vostanis. **Int. J. Soc. Psyc.** 46:4 Winter:2000 pp.266-280.
754 Childhood disorders. Philip C. Kendall. Hove: Psychology Press, 2000. ix, 229p. *ISBN: 0863776086, 0863776094. Includes bibliographical references and index.* (*Series:* Clinical psychology: a modular course).
755 Children of depressed mothers: from early childhood to maturity. Marian Radke-Yarrow; Pedro Martinez; Anne Mayfield; Donna Ronsaville. Cambridge: Cambridge University Press, 1998. xv, 216p. *ISBN: 0521551315. Includes bibliographical references and index.*
756 Children's emotional and behavioral disorders: attributions of parental responsibility by professionals. Harriette C. Johnson; David E. Cournoyer; Gene A. Fisher; Brenda E. McQuillan; Sheila Moriarty; Audra L. Richert; Edward J. Stanek; Cheryl L. Stockford; Beverly R. Yirigian. **Am. J. Orthopsy.** 70:3 7:2000 pp.327-339.
757 A confirmatory factor analysis of the hospital anxiety and depression scale: comparing empirically and theoretically derived structures. Martin Dunbar; Graeme Ford; Kate Hunt; Geoff Der. **Br. J. Clin. Psycho.** 39:1 3:2000 pp.79-94.
758 Coping with psychotic symptoms in the early phases of schizophrenia. Steve Boschi; Richard E. Adams; Evelyn J. Bromet; Janet E. Lavelle; Elyse Everett; Nora Galambos. **Am. J. Orthopsy.** 70:2 4:2000 pp.242-252.
759 The counselor and the group: integrating theory, training, and practice. James P. Trotzer. Philadelphia PA: Accelerated Development, 1999. xxx, 574p. *ISBN: 1560326999. Includes bibliographical references (p. 471-490) and index.*
760 Counteractive self-control in overcoming temptation. Yaacov Trope; Ayelet Fishbach. **J. Pers. Soc. Psychol.** 79:4 10:2000 pp.493-506.
761 The countertransference: a Latin American view. Beatriz de León de Bernardi. **Int. J.Psy.** 81:2 4:2000 pp.331-351.
762 Critical perspectives on mental health. Vicki Coppock; John Hopton. New York: Routledge, 2000. 224p. *ISBN: 1857288793, 1857288807. Includes bibliographical references and index.*
763 A cross-cultural comparison of British and Japanese lay theories of schizophrenia. Adrian Furnham; Masako Murao. **Int. J. Soc. Psyc.** 46:1 Spring:2000 pp.4-20.
764 Culture and the mental health consequences of trauma. Vikram Patel. **Indian J. Soc. W.** 61:4 10:2000 pp.619-630.
765 A Delphi approach to characterising 'relapse' as used in UK clinical practice. Tom Burns; Matthew Fiander; Bernard Audini. **Int. J. Soc. Psyc.** 46:3 Autumn:2000 pp.220-235.
766 Depression among Latina cervical cancer patients. Beth E. Meyerowitz; Silvia C. Formenti; Kathleen O. Ell; Beth Leedham. **J. Soc. Clin. Psychol.** 19:3 Fall:2000 pp.352-371.
767 Les désastres naturels. *[In French];* (Natural disasters.) Yvon Lefebvre [Ed.]; Claude Martel; Danielle Maltais; Suzie Robichaud; Anne Simard; Gilles Lalande; Lise Lachance; Martin Fortin; Christophe Fortin; Johanne Charbonneau; Françoise-Romaine Ouellette; Stéphanie Gaudet; Suzanne King; Ronald G. Barr; Alain Brunet; Jean-François Saucier; Michael Meaney; Shannon Woo; Cheryl Chanson; Louise Lemyre; Yaniv Benzimra; Ginette B. Pouliot. **San. Ment. Qué** XXV:1 Spring:2000 pp.7-216. *Collection of 9 articles.*
768 Development and validation of the Workshop Behavior Checklist: a scale for assessing work performance of people with severe mental illness. Hector Tsang; Ip Yee Chiu. **Int. J. Soc. Psyc.** 46:2 Summer:2000 pp.110-121.
769 Differential environmental factors in anorexia nervosa: a sibling pair study. Fay Murphy; Nicholas A. Troop; Janet L. Treasure. **Br. J. Clin. Psycho.** 39:2 6:2000 pp.193-204.
770 The dove that returns, the dove that vanishes. Michael Parsons. New York: Routledge, 2000. 226p. *ISBN: 0415211824, 0415211816. Includes bibliographical references and index.* (*Series:* New library of psychoanalysis - 39).

C: INDIVIDUALS. GROUPS. ORGANIZATIONS

771 The effect of extended family living on the mental health of three generations within two Asian communities. Edmund J.S. Sonuga-Barke; Minal Mistry. **Br. J. Clin. Psycho.** 39:2 6:2000 pp.129-142.

772 Employment outcomes in family-aided assertive community treatment. William R. McFarlane; Robert A. Dushay; Susan M. Deakins; Peter Stastny; Ellen P. Lukens; Joanne Toran; Bruce Link. **Am. J. Orthopsy.** 70:2 4:2000 pp.203-214.

773 Evolutionary psychiatry: a new beginning. Anthony Stevens; John Price. London: Routledge, 2000. 310p. *ISBN: 0415219787.*

774 Factor analysis of three standardized tests of memory in a clinical population. N.M. Hunkin; J.V. Stone; C.L. Isaac; J.S. Holdstock; R. Butterfield; L.I. Wallis; A.R. Mayes. **Br. J. Clin. Psycho.** 39:2 6:2000 pp.169-180.

775 Fifty years after the Boulder model. Ludy T. Benjamin, Jr.; David B. Baker; Donald K. Routh; George W. Albee; Cynthia D. Belar; Peter E. Nathan; Donald R. Peterson; George Stricker. **Am. Psychol.** 55:2 2:2000 pp.233-254. *Collection of 8 articles.*

776 Gender differences in adolescent depressive symptomatology: towards an integrated social-developmental model. Jennifer Aubé; Laura Fichman; Christina Saltaris; Richard Koestner. **J. Soc. Clin. Psychol.** 19:3 Fall:2000 pp.297-313.

777 Harassed bodies: an examination of the relationships among women's experiences of sexual harassment, body image, and eating disturbances. Melanie S. Harned. **Psychol. Wom. Quart.** 24:4 12:2000 pp.336-348.

778 How much is enough? endings in psychotherapy and counselling. Lesley Murdin. London, New York: Routledge, 2000. viii, 176p. *ISBN: 041518892X, 0415188938. Includes bibliographical references and index.*

779 How to predict the past: from trauma to depression. Mikkel Borch-Jacobsen; Douglas Brick [Tr.]. **Hist. Psychiat.** 11:1(41) 3:2000 pp.15-35.

780 Hypochondria: a tentative approach. Bernd Nissen. **Int. J.Psy.** 81:4 8:2000 pp.651-666.

781 Illness disclosure and mental health among women with HIV/AIDS. Lisa K. Comer; Barbara Henker; Margaret Kemeny; Gail Wyatt. **J. Comm. App. Soc. Psychol.** 10:6 11-12:2000 pp.449-464.

782 Insight and the nature of therapeutic action in the psychoanalysis of 4- and 5-year-old children. Angela Joyce; Jenny Stoker. **Int. J.Psy.** 81:6 12:2000 pp.1139-1154.

783 Intensive interaction and autism: some theoretical concerns. Melanie Nind; Stuart Powell. **Child. Soc.** 14:2 4:2000 pp.98-109.

784 Interpretation and containment; *[Summary in French]*; *[Summary in German]*; *[Summary in Spanish].* Lucy LaFarge. **Int. J.Psy.** 81:1 2:2000 pp.67-84.

785 Intimacy and alienation: memory, trauma and personal being. Thomas Ogden [Foreword]; Russell Meares. New York: Routledge, 2000. 190p. *ISBN: 0415220300. Includes bibliographical references and index.*

786 Issues in therapy with lesbian, gay, bisexual and transgendered clients. Dominic Davies [Ed.]; Charles Neal [Ed.]. Buckingham: Open University Press, 2000. 224p. *ISBN: 0335203310, 0335203329. Includes index.*

787 The looming maladaptive style: anxiety, danger, and schematic processing. John H. Riskind; Nathan L. Williams; Theodore L. Gessner; Linda D. Chrosniak; Jose M. Cortina. **J. Pers. Soc. Psychol.** 79:5 11:2000 pp.837-852.

788 Mental disorders in India: an analysis of epidemiological studies. H.C. Ganguli. **Indian J. Soc. W.** 61:3 7:2000 pp.394-419.

789 Mental illness in Jiri, Nepal. Mark Tausig; Sree Subedi; Janardan Subedi; James Ross; Chris L. Broughton; Robin Singh; J. Blangero; S. Williams-Blangero. **Contrib. Nepal. Stud.** 27:1 1:2000 pp.105-115.

790 On inhibition/disinhibition in developmental psychopathology: views from cognitive and personality psychology and a working inhibition taxonomy. Joel T. Nigg. **Psychol. B.** 126:2 3:2000 pp.220-246.

791 O padrão alimentar anormal em estudantes de Porto Alegre: levantamento epidemiológico medido pelo EAT-26. *[In Portuguese]*; [Eating disorder levels among Porto Alegre

C: INDIVIDUS. GROUPES. ORGANISATIONS

students: an epidemiological survey measured by EAT-26] *[Summary]*. Carlos Alberto Sampaio Martins de Barros; Cíntia Leite Nahra. **Aletheia** 9 1999 pp.27-38.

792 Parenting among mothers with a serious mental illness. Daphna Oyserman; Carol T. Mowbray; Paula Allen Meares; Kirsten B. Firminger. **Am. J. Orthopsy.** 70:3 7:2000 pp.296-315.

793 The past and possible futures of hope. C.R. Snyder. **J. Soc. Clin. Psychol.** 19:1 Spring:2000 pp.11-28.

794 Patient-rated therapeutic relationship and outcome in general practitioner treatment of psychological problems. John Cape. **Br. J. Clin. Psycho.** 39:4 11:2000 pp.383-395.

795 Post-traumatic stress theory: research and application. Brian G. Pauwels [Ed.]; John H. Harvey [Ed.]. Philadelphia PA: Brunner/Mazel, 2000. xvi, 225p. *ISBN: 158391014X. Includes bibliographical references and index.*

796 Prevalence and predictors of post-traumatic stress symptoms following childbirth. Jo Czarnocka; Pauline Slade. **Br. J. Clin. Psycho.** 39:1 3:2000 pp.35-51.

797 The prevalence of *nervios* and associated symptomatology among inhabitants of Mexican rural communities. V. Nelly Salgado de Snyder; María de Jesús Diaz-Perez; Victoria D. Ojeda. **Cult. Medic. Psych.** 24:4 12:2000 pp.453-470.

798 Principles and practice of behavioral assessment. Stephen N. Haynes; William Hayes O'Brien. New York: Kluwer Academic/Plenum Publishers, 1999. 348p. *ISBN: 0306462214. Includes bibliographical references and index. (Series:* Applied clinical psychology).

799 The professional is political: an interpretation of the problem of the past in solution-focused therapy. Amy Rossiter. **Am. J. Orthopsy.** 70:2 4:2000 pp.150-161.

800 Promoting mental health after childbirth: a controlled trial of primary prevention of postnatal depression. Sandra A. Elliott; Teresa J. Leverton; Marion Sanjack; Helen Turner; Pauline Cowmeadow; Jane Hopkins; Diane Bushnell. **Br. J. Clin. Psycho.** 39:3 9:2000 pp.223-241.

801 Psy et société. *[In French]*; [Psychoanalysis and society]. Monique Selim; Michèle Bertrand; Bernard Doray; Olivier Douville; Richard Rechtman; Eugène Enriquez; Jean-Pierre Lebrun; Fabrice Müller; Laurent Bazin. **Hom. Soc.** 138 10-12:2000 pp.3-128. *Collection of 8 articles.*

802 Psychoanalysis, the anxiety of influence, and the sadomasochism of everyday life. John Munder Ross. **J. App. Psy. Stud.** 1:1 1:1999 pp.57-78.

803 The psychoanalyst and the transsexual patient; *[Summary in French]*; *[Summary in German]*; *[Summary in Spanish]*. Colette Chiland. **Int. J.Psy.** 81:1 2:2000 pp.21-35.

804 Psychological management of post-stroke depression. Ian I. Kneebone; Emma Dunmore. **Br. J. Clin. Psycho.** 39:1 3:2000 pp.53-65.

805 Psychosocial predictors of acculturative stress in Mexican immigrants. Joseph D. Hovey. **J. Psychol.** 134:5 9:2000 pp.490-502.

806 Repositioning cross-cultural counseling in a multicultural society. Miu Chung Yan; Ching Man Lam. **Int. Soc. Work** 43:4 10:2000 pp.481-494.

807 The role of cognitive vulnerability and stress in the prediction of postpartum depressive symptomatology. Rachel Grazioli; Deborah J. Terry. **Br. J. Clin. Psycho.** 39:4 11:2000 pp.329-347.

808 Social and environmental predictors of maternal depression in current and recent welfare recipients. Kristine Siefert; Phillip J. Bowman; Colleen M. Heflin; Sheldon Danziger; David R. Williams. **Am. J. Orthopsy.** 70:4 10:2000 pp.510-522.

809 Some views on the manifestation of the death instinct in clinical work; *[Summary in French]*; *[Summary in German]*; *[Summary in Spanish]*. Michael Feldman. **Int. J.Psy.** 81:1 2:2000 pp.53-65.

810 Symbols and their function in managing the anxiety of change: an intersubjective approach; *[Summary in French]*; *[Summary in German]*; *[Summary in Spanish]*. James Rose. **Int. J.Psy.** 81:3 6:2000 pp.453-470.

811 The three-year persistence of depressive symptoms in men and women. Piet Bracke. **Soc. Sci. Med.** 51:1 7:2000 pp.51-64.

C: INDIVIDUALS. GROUPS. ORGANIZATIONS

812 The timing, triggers and qualities of recovered memories in therapy. Bernice Andrews; Chris R. Brewin; Jenny Ochera; John Morton; Debra A. Bekerian; Graham M. Davies; Phil Mollon. **Br. J. Clin. Psycho.** 39:1 3:2000 pp.11-26.

813 The transtheoretical stages of change as a predictor of premature termination, attendance and alliance in psychotherapy. Jo Derisley; Shirley Reynolds. **Br. J. Clin. Psycho.** 39:4 11:2000 pp.371-382.

814 Traumatic migrations and their psychic vicissitudes. Salman Akhtar; Maurice Apprey; Ira Brenner; W. Nathaniel Howell; Vamık D. Volkan. **J. App. Psy. Stud.** 1:2 4:1999 pp.123-179. *Collection of 5 articles.*

815 Using workshops on loss for adults with learning disabilities. Sue Read; Vicky Papakosta-Harvey; Sal Bower. **Groupwork** 12:2 2000 pp.6-26.

816 Varieties of long-term outcome among patients in psychoanalysis and long-term psychotherapy: a review of findings in the Stockholm Outcome of Psychoanalysis and Psychotherapy Project (STOPPP); *[Summary in French]*; *[Summary in German]*; *[Summary in Spanish].* Rolf Sandell; Johan Blomberg; Anna Lazar; Jan Carlsson; Jeanette Broberg; Johan Schubert. **Int. J.Psy.** 81:5 10:2000 pp.921-942.

817 Viljan att begära och tvånget att försaka. Ett köns- och kulturvetenskapligt perspektiv på anorexi. *[In Swedish]*; [Wanting to have and the compulsion to go without: a gender and cultural perspective on anorexia]. Birgitta Meurling. **Nord. Ny.** 79 11:2000 pp.93-103.

818 Voices of reason, voices of insanity: studies of verbal hallucinations. Ivan Leudar; Philip Thomas. New York: Routledge, 2000. 240p. *ISBN: 0415147867, 0415147875.*

819 When father kills mother: guiding children through trauma and grief. Jean Harris-Hendriks; Tony Kaplan; Dora Black. New York, London: Routledge, 2000. 281p. *ISBN: 0415196272, 0415196280. Includes bibliographical references and indexes. Royal College of Psychiatrists.*

820 When she was bad: borderline personality disorder in a posttraumatic age. Dana Becker. **Am. J. Orthopsy.** 70:4 10:2000 pp.422-432.

C.3: **Social psychology**
Psychologie sociale

821 After Eden: envy and the defences against anxiety paradigm. Mark Stein. **Human Relat.** 53:2 2:2000 pp.193-212.

822 AGENDA 2000 — social judgment and attitudes: warmer, more social, and less conscious. N. Schwarz. **Eur. J. Soc. Psychol.** 30:2 3-4:2000 pp.149-176.

823 AGENDA 2000 — stereotyping, prejudice, and discrimination at the seam between the centuries: evolution, culture, mind and brain. Susan T. Fiske. **Eur. J. Soc. Psychol.** 30:3 5-6:2000 pp.299-322.

824 Assessing perceived social inequity: a relative deprivation framework. Alexandra F. Corning. **J. Pers. Soc. Psychol.** 78:3 3:2000 pp.463-477.

825 Assimilation and contrast in social comparisons as a consequence of self-construal activation. U. Kühnen; B. Hannover. **Eur. J. Soc. Psychol.** 30:6 11-12:2000 pp.799-812.

826 Automatic preference for White Americans: eliminating the familiarity explanation. Nilanjana Dasgupta; Debbie E. McGhee; Anthony G. Greenwald; Mahzarin R. Banaji. **J. Exp. S. Psychol.** 36:3 5:2000 pp.316-328.

827 Automatic vigilance: the attention-grabbing power of approach- and avoidance-related social information. Dirk Wentura; Klaus Rothermund; Peter Bak. **J. Pers. Soc. Psychol.** 78:6 6:2000 pp.1024-1037.

828 'But I'm different to them': constructing contrasts between self and others in talk-in-interaction. Paul Dickerson. **Br. J. Soc. P.** 39:3 9:2000 pp.381-398.

829 Collective action and psychological change: the emergence of new social identities. John Drury; Steve Reicher. **Br. J. Soc. P.** 39:4 12:2000 pp.579-604.

830 Communication context, explanation, and social judgment. A. Todorov; M. Lalljee; W. Hirst. **Eur. J. Soc. Psychol.** 30:2 3-4:2000 pp.199-210.

C: INDIVIDUS. GROUPES. ORGANISATIONS

831 Comparison based satisfaction: contrast and empathy. Eduard Brandstätter. **Eur. J. Soc. Psychol.** 30:5 9-10:2000 pp.673-703.
832 The consequences of communicating social stereotypes. Micah S. Thompson; Charles M. Judd; Bernadette Park. **J. Exp. S. Psychol.** 36:6 11:2000 pp.567-599.
833 Constraints on equifinality: goals are good explanations only for controllable outcomes. John McClure; Lisa Densley; James H. Liu; Michael Allen. **Br. J. Soc. P.** 40:1 3:2001 pp.99-116.
834 Context effects on Scottish national and European self-categorization: the importance of category accessibility, fragility and relations. Adam Rutland; Marco Cinnirella. **Br. J. Soc. P.** 39:4 12:2000 pp.495-519.
835 Converging interracial consequences of exposure to violent rap music on stereotypical attributions of Blacks. James D. Johnson; Sophie Trawalter; John F. Dovidio. **J. Exp. S. Psychol.** 36:3 5:2000 pp.233-251.
836 Conversation as a resource for influence: evidence for prototypical arguments and social identification processes. Scott A. Reid; Sik Hung Ng. **Eur. J. Soc. Psychol.** 30:1 1-2:2000 pp.83-100.
837 Decategorization and the reduction of bias in the crossed categorization paradigm. N. Ensari; N. Miller. **Eur. J. Soc. Psychol.** 31:2 3-4:2001 pp.193-216.
838 Direct and moderating effects of community context on the psychological well-being of African American women. Carolyn E. Cutrona; Daniel W. Russell; Robert M. Hessling; P. Adama Brown; Velma Murry. **J. Pers. Soc. Psychol.** 79:6 12:2000 pp.1088-1101.
839 Displacing place-identity: a discursive approach to locating self and other. John Dixon; Kevin Durrheim. **Br. J. Soc. P.** 39:1 3:2000 pp.27-44.
840 Distinctness of others, mutability of selves: their impact on self-evaluations. Diederik A. Stapel; Willem Koomen. **J. Pers. Soc. Psychol.** 79:6 12:2000 pp.1068-1087.
841 Doing social psychology. Dorothy Miell [Ed.]; Margaret Wetherell [Ed.]. London, Thousand Oaks CA: Sage Publications, 1998. 330p. *ISBN: 076196049X, 0761960503. Includes bibliographical references and index. Open University.*
842 Effects of contact and personality on intergroup attitudes of different professionals. K. Liebkind; J. Haaramo; I. Jasinskaja-Lahti. **J. Comm. App. Soc. Psychol.** 10:3 5-6:2000 pp.171-182.
843 The effects of in-group versus out-group social comparison on self-esteem in the context of a negative stereotype. Hart Blanton; Jennifer Crocker; Dale T. Miller. **J. Exp. S. Psychol.** 36:5 9:2000 pp.519-530.
844 Effects of perceived group variability on the gathering of information about individual group members. Carey S. Ryan; Laura M. Bogart; Joshua P. Vender. **J. Exp. S. Psychol.** 36:1 1:2000 pp.90-101.
845 The effects of social context, source fairness, and perceived self-source similarity on social influence: a self-categorisation analysis. Michael J. Platow; Duncan Mills; Dianne Morrison. **Eur. J. Soc. Psychol.** 30:1 1-2:2000 pp.69-81.
846 The encoding and transfer of stereotype-driven inferences. Paul R. D'Agostino. **Soc. Cogn.** 18:3 Fall:2000 pp.281-291.
847 Essentialist beliefs about social categories. Nick Haslam; Louis Rothschild; Donald Ernst. **Br. J. Soc. P.** 39:1 3:2000 pp.113-128.
848 Evidence for implicit evaluative in-group bias: affect-biased spontaneous trait inference in a minimal group paradigm. Sabine Otten; Gordon B. Moskowitz. **J. Exp. S. Psychol.** 36:1 1:2000 pp.77-89.
849 An examination of the Association of African American Mothers' perceptions of their neighborhoods with their parenting and adolescent adjustment. Ronald D. Taylor. **J. Black Psychol.** 26:3 8:2000 pp.267-287.
850 Feeling and thinking: the role of affect in social cognition. Joseph P. Forgas [Ed.]. Paris; Cambridge, New York: Éditions de la Maison des Sciences de l'Homme; Cambridge University Press, 2000. xvi, 421p. *ISBN: 052164223X. Includes bibliographical references and indexes. (Series:* Studies in emotion and social interaction).

C: INDIVIDUALS. GROUPS. ORGANIZATIONS

851 Feeling 'holier than thou': are self-serving assessments produced by errors in self- or social prediction? Nicholas Epley; David Dunning. **J. Pers. Soc. Psychol.** 79:6 12:2000 pp.861-875.

852 Group-based dominance and opposition to equality as independent predictors of self-esteem, ethnocentrism, and social policy attitudes among African Americans and European Americans. John T. Jost; Erik P. Thompson. **J. Exp. S. Psychol.** 36:3 5:2000 pp.209-232.

853 How do we communicate stereotypes? Linguistic bases and inferential consequences. Daniël H.J. Wigboldus; Gün R. Semin; Russell Spears. **J. Pers. Soc. Psychol.** 78:1 1:2000 pp.5-18.

854 How we explain depends on whom we explain: the impact of social category on the selection of causal comparisons and causal explanations. Sonya A. Grier; Ann L. McGill. **J. Exp. S. Psychol.** 36:6 11:2000 pp.545-566.

855 The impact of opposites: implications of trait inferences and their antonyms for person judgment. Diederik A. Stapel; Willem Koomen. **J. Exp. S. Psychol.** 36:5 9:2000 pp.439-464.

856 The impact of positive mood and category importance on crossed categorization effects. Darren I. Urada; Norman Miller. **J. Pers. Soc. Psychol.** 78:3 3:2000 pp.417-433.

857 In what sense are prejudicial beliefs personal? The importance of an in-group's shared stereotypes. S. Alexander Haslam; Angeline Wilson. **Br. J. Soc. P.** 39:1 3:2000 pp.45-64.

858 Intergroup discrimination in the minimal group paradigm: categorization, reciprocation, or fear? Lowell Gaertner; Chester A. Insko. **J. Pers. Soc. Psychol.** 79:1 7:2000 pp.77-94.

859 An investigation of the link between attributional judgments and stereotype-based judgments. Lucy Johnston; Michael Bristow; Nicholas Love. **Eur. J. Soc. Psychol.** 30:4 7-8:2000 pp.551-568.

860 Isms and the structure of social attitudes. Gerard Saucier. **J. Pers. Soc. Psychol.** 78:2 2:2000 pp.366-385.

861 Just say no (to stereotyping): effects of training in the negation of stereotypic associations on stereotype activation. Kerry Kawakami; John F. Dovidio; Jasper Moll; Sander Hermsen; Abby Russin. **J. Pers. Soc. Psychol.** 78:5 5:2000 pp.871-888.

862 Longitudinal multilevel models of the big-fish-little-pond effect on academic self-concept: counterbalancing contrast and reflected-glory effects in Hong Kong schools. Herbert W. Marsh; Chit-Kwong Kong; Kit-Tai Hau. **J. Pers. Soc. Psychol.** 78:2 2:2000 pp.337-349.

863 Mood and heuristics: the influence of happy and sad states on sensitivity and bias in stereotyping. Jaihyun Park; Mahzarin R. Banaji. **J. Pers. Soc. Psychol.** 78:6 6:2000 pp.1005-1023.

864 Motivated cultural cognition: the impact of implicit cultural theories on dispositional attribution varies as a function of need for closure. Chi-yue Chiu; Michael W. Morris; Ying-yi Hong; Tanya Menon. **J. Pers. Soc. Psychol.** 78:2 2:2000 pp.247-259.

865 Pattern of disconfirming information and processing instructions as determinants of stereotype change. Miles Hewstone; Manfred Hassebrauck; Andrea Wirth; Michaela Waenke. **Br. J. Soc. P.** 39:3 9:2000 pp.399-412.

866 Perceived variability and stereotype change. Miles Hewstone; Jürgen Hamberger. **J. Exp. S. Psychol.** 36:2 3:2000 pp.103-124.

867 The primacy of self-referent information in perceptions of social consensus. Russell W. Clement; Joachim Krueger. **Br. J. Soc. P.** 39:2 6:2000 pp.279-300.

868 Recovering Bartlett's social psychology of cultural dynamics. Yoshihisa Kashima. **Eur. J. Soc. Psychol.** 30:3 5-6:2000 pp.383-404.

869 Recruitment of exemplars as reference points in social judgments. Jerzy J. Karylowski; Krzysztof Konarzewski; Michael A. Motes. **J. Exp. S. Psychol.** 36:3 5:2000 pp.275-303.

870 Re-engaging the history of social psychology. Ian Lubek; Kurt Danziger; Clare MacMartin; Andrew S. Winston; Henderikus J. Stam; H. Lorraine Radtke; James M.M. Good; Erika Apfelbaum; Sam Parkovnick; John D. Greenwood; Man Cheung Chung; Ian A.M. Nicholson; Nicole B. Barenbaum; Frances Cherry; Franz Samelson. **J. Hist. Beh. Sci.** XXXVI:4 Fall:2000 pp.319-506. *Collection of 13 articles.*

C: INDIVIDUS. GROUPES. ORGANISATIONS

871 The 'relative self': informational and judgmental consequences of comparative self-evaluation. Thomas Mussweiler; Fritz Strack. **J. Pers. Soc. Psychol.** 79:1 7:2000 pp.23-38.

872 Running from the shadow: psychological distancing from others to deny characteristics people fear in themselves. Jeff Schimel; Tom Pyszczynski; Jeff Greenberg; Heather O'Mahen; Jamie Arndt. **J. Pers. Soc. Psychol.** 78:3 3:2000 pp.446-462.

873 The self in social psychology. Roy F. Baumeister [Ed.]. Philadelphia PA, Hove: Psychology Press, 1999. ix, 492p. *ISBN: 0863775721, 086377573X. Includes bibliographical references and indexes.* (*Series:* Key readings in social psychology).

874 Self-evaluation maintenance in a larger social context. Constance J. Pilkington; Karen A. Smith. **Br. J. Soc. P.** 39:2 6:2000 pp.213-228.

875 The social animal. Elliot Aronson. New York: Worth Publishers; W.H. Freeman, 1999. xviii, 548p. *ISBN: 0716733129. Includes bibliographical references (p. [463]-530) and indexes.*

876 Social appraisal as correlate, antecedent, and consequence of mental and physical health outcomes. Thomas E. Joiner, Jr.; Kathleen D. Vohs; Norman B. Schmidt. **J. Soc. Clin. Psychol.** 19:3 Fall:2000 pp.336-351.

877 Social categorization and stereotyping: 'you mean I'm one of 'them'?' Craig Johnson; Mark Schaller; Brian Mullen. **Br. J. Soc. P.** 39:1 3:2000 pp.1-26.

878 Social categorizations, social comparisons and stigma: presentations of self in people with learning difficulties. W.M.L. Finlay; E. Lyons. **Br. J. Soc. P.** 39:1 3:2000 pp.129-146.

879 Social dominance: an intergroup theory of social hierarchy and oppression. Jim Sidanius; Felicia Pratto. Cambridge: Cambridge University Press, 1999. x, 403p. *ISBN: 0521622905. Includes bibliographical references and index.*

880 Social identity and the true believer: responses to threatened self-stereotypes among the intrinsically religious. Christopher T. Burris; Lynne M. Jackson. **Br. J. Soc. P.** 39:2 6:2000 pp.257-278.

881 Social identity theory: past achievements, current problems and future challenges. R. Brown. **Eur. J. Soc. Psychol.** 30:6 11-12:2000 pp.745-778.

882 Social psychology. Eliot R. Smith; Diane M. Mackie. Philadelphia PA: Psychology Press, 1999. 673p. *ISBN: 086377587X. Includes bibliographical references and index.*

883 Social psychology. Sharon S. Brehm; Saul M. Kassin; Steven Fein. Boston MA: Houghton Mifflin, 1999. *ISBN: 0395909228. Includes bibliographical references and indexes.*

884 Social psychology. Robert A. Baron. Boston MA, London: Allyn & Bacon, 1999. 650p. *ISBN: 0205311318.*

885 Social psychology. Robert S. Feldman. Upper Saddle River NJ; London: Prentice Hall; Prentice Hall International, 1998. xxii,p614p. *ISBN: 013660739X. Includes bibliographical references (p. 537-590) and index.*

886 Social psychology: an applied perspective. P. Wesley Schultz; Stuart Oskamp. Upper Saddle River NJ: Prentice Hall, 2000. x, 246p. *ISBN: 0130962481. Includes bibliographical references (p. 213-239) and indexes.*

887 Social psychology and health. Wolfgang Stroebe. Buckingham: Open University Press, 2000. x, 342p. *ISBN: 0335199224, 0335199216. Includes bibliographical references and index.* (*Series:* Mapping social psychology).

888 Social psychology: exploring universals across cultures. Fathali M. Moghaddam. New York: W.H. Freeman, 1998. xxiii, 610p. *ISBN: 0716728494. Includes bibliographical references (p. 550-588) and indexes.*

889 The spotlight effect in social judgment: an egocentric bias in estimates of the salience of one's own actions and appearance. Thomas Gilovich; Victoria Husted Medvec; Kenneth Savitsky. **J. Pers. Soc. Psychol.** 78:2 2:2000 pp.211-222.

890 The structure of attitudes: attribute importance, accessibility and judgment. Frenk van Harreveld; Joop van der Pligt; Nanne K. de Vries; Silke Andreas. **Br. J. Soc. P.** 39:3 9:2000 pp.363-380.

891 Toward a narrative conceptualization of stereotypes: contextualizing perceptions of public housing residents. M.S. Salzer. **J. Comm. App. Soc. Psychol.** 10:2 3-4:2000 pp.123-138.

C: INDIVIDUALS. GROUPS. ORGANIZATIONS

892 Value priorities and subjective well-being: direct relations and congruity effects. L. Sagiv; S.H. Schwartz. **Eur. J. Soc. Psychol.** 30:2 3-4:2000 pp.177-198.
893 Voices from the South: the construction of Brazilian community social psychology. Maria de Fátima Quintal de Freitas. **J. Comm. App. Soc. Psychol.** 10:4 7-8:2000 pp.315-326.
894 When are we better than them and they worse than us? A closer look at social discrimination in positive and negative domains. Katherine J. Reynolds; John C. Turner; S. Alexander Haslam. **J. Pers. Soc. Psychol.** 78:1 1:2000 pp.64-80.
895 Why do superiors attend to negative stereotypic information about their subordinates? Effects of power legitimacy on social perception. Rosa Rodríguez-Bailón; Miguel Moya; Vincent Yzerbyt. **Eur. J. Soc. Psychol.** 30:5 9-10:2000 pp.651-671.

C.4: **Interpersonal relations**
Relations interpersonnelles

896 Among friends? An examination of friendship and the self-serving bias. W. Keith Campbell; Constantine Sedikides; Glenn D. Reeder; Andrew J. Elliott. **Br. J. Soc. P.** 39:2 6:2000 pp.229-240.
897 Attachment to the missing object: infidelity and obsessive love. Lucinda Mitchell. **J. App. Psy. Stud.** 2:4 10:2000 pp.383-398.
898 Attitudes and attraction: a new test of the attraction, repulsion and similarity-dissimilarity asymmetry hypotheses. Ramadhar Singh; Soo Yan Ho. **Br. J. Soc. P.** 39:2 6:2000 pp.197-212.
899 Communicating emotion: social, moral, and cultural processes. Sally Planalp. Cambridge; Paris: Cambridge University Press; Editions de la Maison des Sciences de l'Homme, 1999. xv, 295p. *ISBN: 2735107957, 2735108163, 0521553156, 0521557410. Includes bibliographical references and index. (Series: Studies in emotion and social interaction).*
900 Competence in early adult romantic relationships: a developmental perspective on family influences. Rand D. Conger; Ming Cui; Chalandra M. Bryant; Glen H. Elder, Jr. **J. Pers. Soc. Psychol.** 79:2 8:2000 pp.224-237.
901 Conversation analysis: principles, practices, and applications. Ian Hutchby; Robin Wooffitt. Cambridge: Polity Press, 1998. vii, 273p. *ISBN: 0745615481, 0745615481, 074561549X. Includes bibliographical references and index.*
902 Couples' shared participation in novel and arousing activities and experienced relationship quality. Arthur Aron; Christina C. Norman; Elaine N. Aron; Colin McKenna; Richard E. Heyman. **J. Pers. Soc. Psychol.** 78:2 2:2000 pp.273-284.
903 Determinants of friendship choices in multiethnic society. Eric Fong; Wsevolod W. Isajiw. **Sociol. For.** 15:2 6:2000 pp.249-271.
904 Dialogic civility in a cynical age: community, hope, and interpersonal relationships. Julia T. Wood [Foreword]; Ronald C. Arnett; Pat Arneson. Albany NY: State University of New York Press, 1999. xvii, 331p. *ISBN: 0791443256, 0791443264. Includes bibliographical references (p. 305-322) and index. (Series: SUNY series in communication studies).*
905 Egocentric empathy gaps between owners and buyers: misperceptions of the endowment effect. Leaf Van Boven; David Dunning; George Loewenstein. **J. Pers. Soc. Psychol.** 79:1 7:2000 pp.66-76.
906 Empathy. Nancy Snow. **Am. Phil. Q.** 37:1 1:2000 pp.65-78.
907 Empathy as a communication strategy in the pharmacy — a study based on cognitive and behavioural analysis. J. Lilja; S. Larsson; D. Hamilton; J. Issakainen. **Int. J. Pharm. Prac.** 8:3 9:2000 pp.176-187.
908 An experimental test of the role of alcohol in relationship conflict. Geoff MacDonald; Mark P. Zanna; John G. Holmes. **J. Exp. S. Psychol.** 36:2 3:2000 pp.182-193.
909 Friendship and moral danger. Dean Cocking; Jeanette Kennett. **J. Phil.** XLVII:5 5:2000 pp.278-296.

C: INDIVIDUS. GROUPES. ORGANISATIONS

910 General traits of personality and affectivity as predictors of satisfaction in intimate relationships: evidence from self- and partner-ratings. David Watson; Brock Hubbard; David Wiese. **J. Personal.** 68:3 6:2000 pp.413-450.

911 Group problem-solving processes: social interactions and individual actions. Ming Ming Chiu. **J. Theory Soc. Behav.** 30:1 3:2000 pp.27-49.

912 Grovelling and other vices: the sociology of sycophancy. Alphons Silbermann. London: Athlone Press, 2000. 212p. *ISBN: 0485115441. Includes index. Translated from the German.*

913 How do I love thee? Let me count the properties. Simon Keller. **Am. Phil. Q.** 37:2 4:2000 pp.163-173.

914 The impact of past relationships on interpersonal behavior: behavioral confirmation in the social-cognitive process of transference. Michele S. Berk; Susan M. Andersen. **J. Pers. Soc. Psychol.** 79:4 10:2000 pp.546-562.

915 Including the other in self: implications for judgments of equity and satisfaction in close relationships. Louis J. Medvene; Cayla R. Teal; Susan Slavich. **J. Soc. Clin. Psychol.** 19:3 Fall:2000 pp.396-419.

916 The influence of argumentative role (initiator vs. resistor) on perceptions of serial argument resolvability and relational harm. Kristen Linnea Johnson; Michael E. Roloff. **Argumentation** 14:1 2:2000 pp.1-16.

917 Interpersonal relationships. Diana Dwyer. London, New York: Routledge, 2000. 160p. *ISBN: 041519623X, 0415196248. Includes bibliographical references and index.*

918 An item response theory analysis of self-report measures of adult attachment. R. Chris Fraley; Niels G. Waller; Kelly A. Brennan. **J. Pers. Soc. Psychol.** 78:2 2:2000 pp.350-365.

919 Listeners as co-narrators. Janet B. Bavelas; Linda Coates; Trudy Johnson. **J. Pers. Soc. Psychol.** 79:6 12:2000 pp.941-952.

920 Love and anger in romantic relationships: a discrete systems model. Bruce J. Ellis; Neil M. Malamuth. **J. Personal.** 68:3 6:2000 pp.525-558.

921 Making sense of humor in young romantic relationships: understanding partners' perceptions. Amy M. Bippus. **Humor** 13:4 2000 pp.395-417.

922 The management and production of risk in romantic relationships: a postmodern paradox. Richard Bulcroft; Kris Bulcroft; Karen Bradley; Carl Simpson. **J. Fam. Hist.** 25:1 1:2000 pp.63-92.

923 The management of matches: a research program on solidarity in durable social relations. Werner Raub; Jeroen Weesie. **Neth. J. Soc. Sci.** 36:1 2000 pp.71-88.

924 Minding the close relationship: a theory of relationship enhancement. John H. Harvey; Julia Omarzu. Cambridge: Cambridge University Press, 1999. x, 225p. *ISBN: 0521633184. Includes bibliographical references and index.*

925 The moderating effect of trivial triggering provocation on displaced aggression. William C. Pedersen; Candace Gonzales; Norman Miller. **J. Pers. Soc. Psychol.** 78:5 5:2000 pp.913-927.

926 Moderní partnerské vztahy a jejich proměny v době pozdní modernity. *[In Czech]*; (Modern partner relationships and their transformation in the age of late modernity.) *[Summary]*. Tomáš Katrňák. **Soc. Čas.** 36:3 2000 pp.307-316.

927 Overcoming mistrust. Andrew Kydd. **Rat. Soc.** 12:4 11:2000 pp.397-424.

928 Perceived superiority in close relationships: why it exists and persists. Caryl E. Rusbult; Paul A.M. Van Lange; Tim Wildschut; Nancy A. Yovetich; Julie Verette. **J. Pers. Soc. Psychol.** 79:4 10:2000 pp.521-545.

929 Perspectives on solidarity. Aafke Komter. **Neth. J. Soc. Sci.** 36:1 2000 pp.3-14.

930 Power, severity, and context in disagreement. J. Rees-Miller. **J. Prag.** 32:8 2000 pp.1087-1112.

931 Proximal paradox: friends and relatives in the era of globalization. Josepa Cucó i Giner. **Eur. J. Soc. Theory** 3:3 8:2000 pp.313-324.

932 Reconcilable differences. Andrew Christensen; Neil S. Jacobson. New York: Guilford Press, 2000. xv, 333p. *ISBN: 1572302615. Includes bibliographical references (p. 317-319) and index.*

C: INDIVIDUALS. GROUPS. ORGANIZATIONS

933 Regulating the interpersonal self: strategic self-regulation for coping with rejection sensitivity. Ozlem Ayduk; Rodolfo Mendoza-Denton; Walter Mischel; Geraldine Downey; Philip K. Peake; Monica Rodriguez. **J. Pers. Soc. Psychol.** 79:5 11:2000 pp.776-792.

934 Responsiveness as responsibility: Cavell's reading of Wittgenstein and King Lear as a source for an ethics of interpersonal relationships. Davide Sparti. **Philos. Soc. Crit.** 26:5 9:2000 pp.81-107.

935 A safe haven: an attachment theory perspective on support seeking and caregiving in intimate relationships. Nancy L. Collins; Brooke C. Feeney. **J. Pers. Soc. Psychol.** 78:6 6:2000 pp.1053-1073.

936 Self-esteem and the quest for felt security: how perceived regard regulates attachment processes. Sandra L. Murray; John G. Holmes; Dale W. Griffin. **J. Pers. Soc. Psychol.** 78:3 3:2000 pp.478-498.

937 Self-other agreement in personality and affectivity: the role of acquaintanceship, trait visibility, and assumed similarity. David Watson; Brock Hubbard; David Wiese. **J. Pers. Soc. Psychol.** 78:3 3:2000 pp.546-558.

938 Sex-typicality and attractiveness: are supermale and superfemale faces super-attractive? Gillian Rhodes; Catherine Hickford; Linda Jeffery. **Br. J. Psy.** 91:1 2:2000 pp.125-140.

939 Social relationships: the nature and function of relational schemas. John G. Holmes. **Eur. J. Soc. Psychol.** 30:4 7-8:2000 pp.447-495.

940 State-of-the-art: the structure of argumentation. A. Francisca Snoeck Henkemans. **Argumentation** 14:4 11:2000 pp.447-473.

941 Temporal stability as a moderator of relationships in the theory of planned behaviour. Mark Conner; Paschal Sheeran; Paul Norman; Christopher J. Armitage. **Br. J. Soc. P.** 39:4 12:2000 pp.469-493.

942 The three faces of love: college students' perception of the spouse, date and cross-sex friend. Jayanti Basu; Rajyasri Ray. **Psychol. Devel. Soc.** 12:2 7-12:2000 pp.177-213.

943 Trust: a sociological theory. Piotr Sztompka. Cambridge, New York: Cambridge University Press, 1999. xii, 214p. *ISBN: 0521591449, 0521598508. Includes bibliographical references (p. 201-210) and index. (Series:* Cambridge cultural social studies).

944 Understanding misunderstanding in the Ammani bargaining event: pragmatic failure or instrumental rudeness? *[Summary in Arabic].* Russell E. Arent. **Dirasat Hum. Soc. Sc.** 27:1 2:2000 pp.222-243.

945 Visible acts of meaning: an integrated message model of language in face-to-face dialogue. Janet Beavin Bavelas; Nicole Chovil. **J. Lang. Soc. Psychol.** 19:2 6:2000 pp.163-194.

946 What the motivated mind sees: comparing friends' perspectives to married partners' views of each other. Sandra L. Murray; John G. Holmes; Dan Dolderman; Dale W. Griffin. **J. Exp. S. Psychol.** 36:6 11:2000 pp.600-620.

947 What's the point in discussion? Donald Bligh. Exeter: Intellect, 2000. viii, 312p. *ISBN: 1871516692. Includes bibliographical references and index.*

948 When experience counts most: effects of experiential similarity on men's and women's receipt of support during bereavement. J. Jill Suitor; Karl Pillemer. **Soc. Networks** 22:4 10:2000 pp.299-312.

949 When pretence can be beneficial. Nava Kahana; Tikva Lecker. **Theory Decis.** 48:1 2:2000 pp.85-99.

950 Wing to wing, oar to oar: readings on courting and marrying. Amy A. Kass; Leon Kass. Notre Dame IN: University of Notre Dame Press, 2000. xv, 636p. *ISBN: 0268019592, 0268019606. Includes bibliographical references. (Series:* The ethics of everyday life).

C: INDIVIDUS. GROUPES. ORGANISATIONS

C.5: Groups and group dynamics
      Groupes et dynamique de groupe

Collective identity and memory
Identité et mémoire collective

951 Abolition, independence, and soccer: premillennial dilemmas of Martinican identity. William F.S. Miles. **Fre. Pol. Cult. Soc.** 17:2 Spring:1999 pp.23-33.
952 Ancestor worship and identity: ritual, interpretation, and social normalization in the Malaysian Chinese community. Ian Clarke. **SOJOURN** 15:2 10:2000 pp.273-295.
953 The battlegrounds of European identity. Martin Kohli. **Euro. Soc.** 2:2 2000 pp.113-137.
954 Becoming Canadian: problems of an emerging identity. Madeline A. Kalbach; Warren E. Kalbach. **Can. Ethn. Stud.** XXXI:2 1999 pp.1-16.
955 British identity and 'the people's princess'. Jim McGuiran. **Sociol. Rev.** 48:1 2:2000 pp.1-18.
956 Le Canada français: entre mythe et utopie. *[In French]*; [French Canada: between myth and utopia]. Roger Bernard. Ottawa: Le Nordir, 1998. 238p. *ISBN: 292136574X. Includes bibliographical references (p. [233]-236) and index.*
957 Commemorating the Anglo-Boer war in post-apartheid South Africa. Bill Nasson. **Rad. Hist. R.** 78 Fall:2000 pp.149-165.
958 Crucible of the millennium? The Clovis affair in contemporary France. Susan J. Terrio. **Comp. Stud. S.** 41:3 7:1999 pp.438-457.
959 The discursive construction of national identity. Ruth Wodak. Edinburgh: Edinburgh University Press, 1999. 240p. *ISBN: 0748610804. Translated from the German. (Series: Critical discourse analysis).*
960 Długie trwanie narodu. Sens Polskości w dziesięć lat później. *[In Polish]*; [The duration of the nation — Polish national traits ten years on] *[Summary]*. Ewa Nowicka. **Prz. Soc.** XLVIII:2 1999 pp.111-125.
961 Dreams come untrue. José Murilo de Carvalho. **Dædalus** 129.2 Spring:2000 pp.57-82.
962 Eighty minute patriots? National identity and sport in modern Wales. Martin Johnes. **Int. J. Hist. Sport** 17:4 12:2000 pp.93-110.
963 The emergence of a regional identity in the Kaliningrad oblast. Ingmar Oldberg. **Coop. Conflict** 35:3 9:2000 pp.269-288.
964 The emergence of new identities in the Western Cape. Simon Bekker; Anne Leildé; Scarlett Cornelissen; Steffen Horstmeier. **Politikon** 27:2 11:2000 pp.221-238.
965 Entre invention et construction des traditions: l'héritage historique et culturel des Albanais. *[In French]*; [Between the invention and construction of tradition: Albanian historical and cultural heritage]. Albert Doja. **Nat. Pap.** 28:3 9:2000 pp.417-448.
966 Entre steppes et stèles. Territoires et identités au Bachkortostan. *[In French]*; (Between steppes and stelas. Territories and cultural identities in Bashkortostan.) *[Summary]*. Xavier Le Torrivellec. **Cah. Mon. Russe** 41:2-3 4-9:2000 pp.369-400.
967 Etnopsihologijski okvir Hrvatske i Srpske nacije. *[In Croatian]*; (The ethnopsychological framework of the Croatian and Serbian nations.) *[Summary]*; *[Summary in Russian]*. Ivo Rendić-Miočević. **Migrac. Teme** 16:1-2 2000 pp.141-166.
968 Expliquer le nationalisme: les contradictions d'Ernest Gellner. *[In French]*; [Explaining nationalism: the contradictions of Ernest Gellner] *[Summary]*; *[Summary in German]*. Antoine Roger. **Eur. J. Soc.** XLI:2 2000 pp.189-226.
969 Football fandom and post-national identity in the new Europe. Anthony King. **Br. J. Soc.** 51:3 9:2000 pp.419-442.
970 Frida Kahlo remaps the nation. Steven S. Volk. **Soc. Ident.** 6:2 6:2000 pp.165-188.
971 The grimace of Macho Ratón: artisans, identity, and nation in late twentieth-century western Nicaragua. Les W. Field. Durham NC, London: Duke University Press, 1999. xxi, 282p. *ISBN: 0822322889, 0822322552. Includes bibliographical references and index.*

C: INDIVIDUALS. GROUPS. ORGANIZATIONS

972 Group-identity based self-protective strategies: the stigma of race, gender, and garlic. Christian S. Crandall; Jo-Ann Tsang; Richard D. Harvey; Thomas W. Britt. **Eur. J. Soc. Psychol.** 30:3 5-6:2000 pp.355-382.

973 Gruppi ed identità sociali nell'Italia di età moderna: percorsi di ricerca. *[In Italian]*; [Groups and social identity in modern Italy: research paths]. Biagio Salvemini [Ed.]. Bari: Edipuglia, 1998. 382p. *ISBN: 8872282071. Includes bibliographical references.*

974 Histoire vs mémoire en France aujourd'hui. *[In French]*; [History vs memory in France today]. Jacques Revel. **Fre. Pol. Cult. Soc.** 18:1 Spring:2000 pp.1-12.

975 History and memory in Vietnam today: the journal *Xua & Nay*. David G. Marr. **J. SE. As. Stud.** 31:1 3:2000 pp.1-25.

976 Holocaust som erindringssted — en introduksjon. *[In Norwegian]*; [The Holocaust as a place of remembrance - an introduction]. Kyrre Kverndokk. **Nord. Ny.** 81 12:2000 pp.5-16.

977 Human sciences and national identity in modern Japan: who defined the 'Japanese tradition'? Oguma Eiji. **China R.** 36:2 4-6:2000 pp.239-251.

978 La identidad nacional de los jóvenes y el Estado de las Autonomías. *[In Spanish]*; [National identity among youths in Spain]. Félix Moral; Araceli Mateos. Madrid: Centro de Investigaciones Sociológicas, 1999. 127p. *ISBN: 8474762871. Includes bibliographical references (p. 93-94).*

979 'If you don't speak French, you're out': Don Cherry, the Alberta Francophone Games, and the discursive construction of Canada's francophones; *[Summary in French]*. Christine Dallaire; Claude Denis. **Can. J. Soc.** 25:4 Fall:2000 pp.415-440.

980 The immemorial Iranian nation? School textbooks and historical memory in post-revolutionary Iran. Haggay Ram. **Nat. Nat.** 6:1 1:2000 pp.67-90.

981 Je n'ai pas toujours eu une certaine idée de la France. *[In French]*; [I haven't always had a definite idea of France]. Claude Sicre. **Temps Mod.** 55:608 3-5:2000 pp.76-99.

982 «Land of east wind»: mise en forme d'une mémoire *mi'gmaq*. *[In French]*; [Land of east wind: the formation of a *mi'gmaq* memory]. P.D. Clarke. **Can. R. Soc. A.** 37:2 5:2000 pp.167-196.

983 Moderná slovenská národná identita a postoje Slovákov voči Európe. *[In Slovak]*; [The modern national identity of Slovaks and their attitude towards Europe]. Ján Bunčák; Magdaléna Piscová. **Sociologia [Brat.]** 32:3 Spring:2000 pp.289-310.

984 Národná identita ako naratívna konštrukcia. *[In Slovak]*; (National identity as narrative construction.) Andrej Findor. **Sociologia [Brat.]** 32:1 2000 pp.57-79.

985 National, ethnic or civic? Contesting paradigms of memory, identity and culture in Israel. Uri Ram. **St. Philos. Educ.** 19:5-6 11:2000 pp.405-422.

986 Negotiations of memory: rethinking 1798 commemoration. Guy Beiner. **Irish Rev.** 26 Autumn:2000 pp.60-70.

987 Nekateri razmisleki ob preučevanju domačinskih razumevanj nacije v dolini zgornje Kolpe po vzpostavitvi Slovensko-Hrvaške državne meje. *[In Croatian]*; (Some thoughts regarding research on local notions of the nation in the valley of the upper Kolpa/Kupa after establishment of the Slovenian-Croatian state border.) *[Summary]*; *[Summary in French]*. Duška Knežević-Hočevar. **Migrac. Teme** 16:1-2 2000 pp.29-46.

988 Northern identities: historical interpretations of 'the North' and 'Northernness'. Neville Kirk [Ed.]. Brookfield VT: Ashgate, 2000. xiv, 227p. *ISBN: 0754600394. Includes bibliographical references and index.*

989 On the sedimentation and accreditation of social knowledges of difference: mass media, journalism, and the reproduction of East/West alterities in unified Germany. Dominic C. Boyer. **Cult. Anthro.** 15:4 11:2000 pp.459-491.

990 Performativity and belonging. Vikki Bell [Ed.]. London: Sage Publications, 1999. 250p. *ISBN: 076196522X, 0761965238. (Series:* Theory, culture & society).

991 Political Zionism and the *'nebeski narodniks'*: towards an understanding of the Serbian national self. David MacDonald. **Slovo** 10:1-2 1998 pp.91-114.

992 Les politiques de la tradition. Identités culturelles et identités nationales dans le Pacifique. *[In French]*; [The politics of tradition: cultural identity and national identity in the

C: INDIVIDUS. GROUPES. ORGANISATIONS

Pacific]. Alain Babadzan; Stephanie Lawson; Toon van Meijl; Brigitte Derlon; Patrick Pillon; Caroline Graille; Marc Tabani; Robert Tonkinson. **J. Soc. Océan.** 109:2 1999 pp.7-147. *Collection of 9 articles.*

993 Posztkommunista társadalom és kollektív emlékezet. *[In Hungarian]*; [Postcommunist society and collective memory]. Richárd László. **Valóság** 42:2 1999 pp.1-18.

994 Present pasts: media, politics, amnesia. Andreas Huyssen. **Publ. Cult.** 12:1 Winter:2000 pp.21-38.

995 Le processus de l'indépendance et la notion de Patrie dans l'imaginaire paraguayen. *[In French]*; [The process of independence and the notion of homeland in the Paraguayan imaginary]. Ana María Díaz. **Cah. Amer. Lat.** 31-32 1999 pp.261-276.

996 The public representation of culture and history. Neil J. Smelser; Jeffrey C. Alexander; David Tyack; Martha Farnsworth Riche; Barry Schwartz; Todd Bayma; Robert McC. Adams; Kenneth Prewitt; Sheldon Hackney; Michael Schudson; Howard Gardner; Kathleen Anne Ross; M.R.C. Greenwood; Karen Kovacs North; Judith Dollenmayer; Donald M. Stewart; William M. Chace; Eugene E. García. **Am. Behav. Sc.** 42:6 3:1999 pp.913-1091. *Collection of 14 articles.*

997 Rewindykacje regionalne a proces dekompozycji tradycyjnej tożsamości narodowej Polaków. Przykład górnego Śląska. *[In Polish]*; (Regional revindications and the decomposition process of Poles' national identity. The case of Upper Silesia.) *[Summary]*. Kazimiera Wódz; Jacek Wódz. **Prz. Soc.** XLVIII:2 1999 pp.95-110.

998 Sacred place, chosen people: land and national identity in Welsh spirituality. Dorian Llywelyn. Cardiff: University of Wales Press, 1999. xii, 210p. *ISBN: 0708315194, 0708315208. Includes bibliographical references and index.*

999 Should we create a niche or fall in line? Identity negotiation and small group effectiveness. William B. Swann, Jr.; Laurie P. Milton; Jeffrey T. Polzer. **J. Pers. Soc. Psychol.** 79:2 8:2000 pp.238-250.

1000 Territorial change and national identities in Eastern and Western Europe. Dennis G. Pringle [Ed.]; Vladimir Kolossov; Joni Virkkunen; Katariina Kosonen; Fabrizio Eva; Jan Mansvelt Beck; Damir Magaš; Virginie Mamadouh. **Geojournal** 48:2 1999 pp.67-144. *Collection of 8 articles.*

1001 To have a culture of our own: on Israeliness and its variants. Motti Regev. **Ethn. Racial** 23:2 3:2000 pp.223-247.

1002 Tradition, pluralism and identity: in honour of T.N. Madan. Veena Das [Ed.]; Dipankar Gupta [Ed.]; Patricia Uberoi [Ed.]; T.N. Madan [Dedicatee]. Thousand Oaks CA: Sage Publications, 1999. 476p. *ISBN: 0761993819. Includes bibliographical references and index. (Series:* Contributions to Indian Sociology. Occasional studies - 8).

1003 Typisch deutsch: Wie deutsch sind die Deutschen. *[In German]*; [Typically German: how German are the Germans?] Hermann Bausinger. Munich: C.H. Beck, 2000. 175p. *ISBN: 3406421482. Includes bibliographical references (p. 162-[171]) and index.*

Conflict and conflict resolution
Conflit et résolution des conflits

1004 L'Allemagne et l'Europe centrale à l'heure de la réconciliation. *[In French]*; [Reconciliation between Germany and Central Europe]. Anne Bazin [Ed.]; Catherine Perron [Ed.]; Brigitte Rauschenbach; Jerzy Holzer; Piotr Madajczyk; Tomas Kafka. **Rev. Ét. Comp. Est-Ouest** 31:1 3:2000 pp.5-108. *Collection of 5 articles.*

1005 Bias as a research strategy in participant observation: the case of intergroup conflict. John Drury; Clifford Stott. **Fie. Meth.** 13:1 2:2001 pp.47-67.

1006 Bowen Systems Theory and mediation. Wayne Regina. **Med. Q.** 18:2 Winter:2000 pp.111-128.

1007 Bringing peace into the room: the personal qualities of the mediator and their impact on the mediation. Daniel Bowling; David Hoffman. **Negot. J.** 16:1 1:2000 pp.5-28.

C: INDIVIDUALS. GROUPS. ORGANIZATIONS

1008 Brücken schlagen. Lokale Versöhnungsarbeit nach gewaltsamen Konflikten. *[In German]*; [Building bridges: local reconciliation after violent conflict]. Katharina Gajdukowa. **Deut. Arch.** 33:5 9-10:2000 pp.821-836.

1009 Civilians versus police: mediation can help to bridge the divide. Vivian Berger. **Negot. J.** 16:3 7:2000 pp.211-235.

1010 Community mediation: past and future. Scott Bradley; Melinda Smith; Liz O'Brien; Betty McManus; Cheryl Cutrona; Harry M. Boertzel; Raymond Shonholtz; Andrew M. Sachs; Timothy Hedeen; Patrick G. Coy; Elizabeth Ellen Gordon; Susan L. Senecah. **Med. Q.** 17:4 Summer:2000 pp.315-407. *Collection of 8 articles.*

1011 Creating the conditions for peacemaking: theories of practice in ethnic conflict resolution. Marc Howard Ross. **Ethn. Racial** 23:6 11:2000 pp.1002-1034.

1012 Discrepant values and measures of negotiator performance. Dana R. Clyman; Thomas M. Tripp. **Group Decis. Negot.** 9:4 7:2000 pp.251-274.

1013 Emotional reactions to conflict: do dependence and legitimacy matter? Cathryn Johnson; Rebecca Ford; Joanne Kaufman. **Soc. Forc.** 79:1 9:2000 pp.101-137.

1014 An experiment in peace: reconciliation-aimed workshops of Jewish-Israeli and Palestinian youth. Ifat Maoz. **J. Peace Res.** 37:6 11:2000 pp.721-736.

1015 An experimental investigation of virtual negotiations with dynamic plots. Giampiero E.G. Beroggi. **Group Decis. Negot.** 9:5 9:2000 pp.415-429.

1016 Facilitating 'perspectival reciprocity' in mediation: some reflections on a failed case. Calvin Smith. **Human St.** 23:1 1:2000 pp.1-21.

1017 Facing the decisions one should make and the decisions one wants to make. Donald E. Conlon; Henry Moon. **Negot. J.** 16:3 7:2000 pp.269-280.

1018 Hewlett conference 2000: focus on negotiation pedagogy. Sara Cobb; Howard Gardner; Ron S. Fortgang; Kevin Avruch; Deborah M. Kolb; Carrie Menkel-Meadow; Robert C. Bordone; Keith G. Allred; Jeffrey Loewenstein; Leigh Thompson; Daniel L. Shapiro. **Negot. J.** 16:4 10:2000 pp.315-420. *Collection of 10 articles.*

1019 Hybrid forms of third-party dispute resolution: theoretical implications of combining mediation and arbitration. William H. Ross; Donald E. Conlon. **Acad. Man. Rev.** 25:2 4:2000 pp.416-427.

1020 Identitätskonstruktionen und Parteinahme: Überlegungen zur Konflikttheorie. *[In German]*; (Taking sides and constructing identities: reflections on conflict theory.) *[Summary]*. Günther Schlee. **Sociologus** 50:1 2000 pp.64-89.

1021 Influence of social motives on integrative negotiation: a meta-analytic review and test of two theories. Carsten K.W. De Dreu; Laurie R. Weingart; Seungwoo Kwon. **J. Pers. Soc. Psychol.** 78:5 5:2000 pp.889-905.

1022 Interdependence in negotiation: effects of exit options and social motive on distributive and integrative negotiation. Ellen Giebels; Carsten K.W. De Dreu; Evert Van de Vliert. **Eur. J. Soc. Psychol.** 30:2 3-4:2000 pp.255-272.

1023 International crisis decisionmaking as a two-level process. Peter F. Trumbore; Mark A. Boyer. **J. Peace Res.** 37:6 11:2000 pp.679-698.

1024 Mediation as parallel seminars: lessons from the student takeover of Columbia University's Hamilton Hall. Carol B. Liebman. **Negot. J.** 16:2 4:2000 pp.157-182.

1025 The mediator as nonviolent advocate: revisiting the question of mediator neutrality. David Dyck. **Med. Q.** 18:2 Winter:2000 pp.129-150.

1026 Multiple conflicts and competing agendas: a framework for conceptualizing structured encounters between groups in conflict — the case of a coexistence project of Jews and Palestinians in Israel. Ifat Maoz. **J. Man. Gov.** 6:2 2000 pp.135-156.

1027 Rapport in conflict resolution: accounting for how face-to-face contact fosters mutual cooperation in mixed-motive conflicts. Aimee L. Drolet; Michael W. Morris. **J. Exp. S. Psychol.** 36:1 1:2000 pp.26-50.

1028 Reconnecting systems maintenance with social justice: a critical role for conflict resolution. Mara Schoeny; Wallace Warfield. **Negot. J.** 16:3 7:2000 pp.253-268.

1029 Rhetorical power, accountability and conflict in committees: an argumentation approach. John A.A. Sillince. **J. Manag. Stu.** 37:8 12:2000 pp.1125-1156.

1030 The role of mediation in the settlement of planning disputes at appeal: the debate and research agenda. Barry Pearce; Michael Stubbs. **Envir. Plan. A.** 32:8 8:2000 pp.1335-1358.
1031 Theorizing the standoff: contingency in action. Robin Erica Wagner-Pacifici. Cambridge, New York: Cambridge University Press, 2000. xiv, 276p. *ISBN: 0521652448. Includes bibliographical references (p. 258-267) and index. (Series:* Cambridge cultural social studies).

Group dynamics
Dynamique de groupe

1032 Ambiguity, complexity and dynamics in the membership of collaboration. Chris Huxham; Siv Vangen. **Human Relat.** 53:6 6:2000 pp.771-806.
1033 Assessing concertive control in the term environment. Brett M. Wright; James R. Barker. **J. Occup. Organ. Psychol.** 73:3 9:2000 pp.345-361.
1034 Attitude-behaviour relations: the role of in-group norms and mode of behavioural decision-making. Deborah J. Terry; Michael A. Hogg; Blake M. McKimmie. **Br. J. Soc. P.** 39:3 9:2000 pp.337-362.
1035 Church-related groups in Quebec. Networks or quasi-networks? Suzie Robichaud; Vincent Lemieux; Myriam Duplain. **Schweiz. Z. Soziologie** 26:1 3:2000 pp.149-168.
1036 A cognitive three-process model of computer-mediated group interaction. Brian Whitworth; Brent Gallupe; Robert McQueen. **Group Decis. Negot.** 9:5 9:2000 pp.431-456.
1037 The collective construction of work group moods. Caroline A. Bartel; Richard Saavedra. **Adm. Sci. Qua.** 45:2 6:2000 pp.197-231.
1038 Communication and coordination in social networks. Michael Suk-Young Chwe. **R. Econ. S.** 67(1):230 1:2000 pp.1-16.
1039 The Condorcet's jury theorem in a bioethical context: the dynamics of group decision making. Tom Koch; Mark Ridgley. **Group Decis. Negot.** 9:5 9:2000 pp.379-392.
1040 The COOP 98 conference. Regine Teulier-Bourgine; Pascale Zaraté; Kristin Braa; Tone Irene Sandahl; H. Ulrich Hoppe; Katrin Gaßner; Martin Mühlenbrock; Frank Tewissen; Oliver Stiemerling; Volker Wulf; Jakob E. Bardram. **Group Decis. Negot.** 9:3 5:2000 pp.185-250. *Collection of 5 articles.*
1041 Crossed categorization and intergroup bias: the moderating roles of intergroup and affective context. Richard J. Crisp; Miles Hewstone. **J. Exp. S. Psychol.** 36:4 7:2000 pp.357-383.
1042 Crowds, context and identity: dynamic categorization processes in the 'poll tax riot'. Clifford Stott; John Drury. **Human Relat.** 53:2 2:2000 pp.247-274.
1043 Determining groups from the clique structure in large social networks. Lucia Falzon. **Soc. Networks** 22:2 5:2000 pp.159-172.
1044 Discrimination constrained and justified: variable effects of group variability and in-group identification. Jolanda Jetten; Russell Spears; Michael A. Hogg; Antony S.R. Manstead. **J. Exp. S. Psychol.** 36:4 7:2000 pp.329-356.
1045 Dynamical systems to define centrality in social networks. R. Poulin; M.-C. Boily; B.R. Mâsse. **Soc. Networks** 22:3 7:2000 pp.187-220.
1046 Effects of individual versus mixed individual and group experience in rule induction on group member learning and group performance. Felix C. Brodbeck; Tobias Greitemeyer. **J. Exp. S. Psychol.** 36:6 11:2000 pp.621-648.
1047 Emotion and group cohesion in productive exchange. Edward J. Lawler; Shane R. Thye; Jeongkoo Yoon. **A.J.S.** 106:3 11:2000 pp.616-657.
1048 An examination of organizational and team commitment in a self-directed team environment. James W. Bishop; K. Dow Scott. **J. Appl. Psychol.** 85:3 6:2000 pp.439-450.
1049 Extending the reach of collective decision support systems: provisions for disciplining judgment-driven exercises. John W. Sutherland. **Theory Decis.** 48:1 2:2000 pp.1-46.

C: INDIVIDUALS. GROUPS. ORGANIZATIONS

1050   Family group decision making: protecting children and women. Joan Pennell; Gale Burford. **Child Wel.** LXXIX:2 3-4:2000 pp.131-158.
1051   Group processes: dynamics within and between groups. Rupert Brown. Oxford, Malden MA: Blackwell Publishers, 2000. xxiii, 417p. *ISBN: 0631218521, 0631184961. Includes bibliographical references (p. 361-409) and index.*
1052   Group socialization and prejudice: the social transmission of intergroup attitudes and beliefs. Serge Guimond. **Eur. J. Soc. Psychol.** 30:3 5-6:2000 pp.335-354.
1053   Groupwork across the disciplines I. John Rowan; Linda Finlay; Oded Manor; Mark Doel; Catherine Sawdon; Jacky Drysdale; Rod Purcell; Mark Harrison; Dave Ward. **Groupwork** 11:3 1999 pp.6-103. *Collection of 6 articles.*
1054   The impact of role training in a user-driven group support system environment. Chelley Vician; Gerardine Desanctis. **Group Decis. Negot.** 9:4 7:2000 pp.275-296.
1055   The impact of time pressure and information on negotiation process and decisions. Alice F. Stuhlmacher; Matthew V. Champagne. **Group Decis. Negot.** 9:6 11:2000 pp.471-491.
1056   The influence of shared mental models on team process and performance. John E. Mathieu; Tonia S. Heffner; Gerald F. Goodwin; Eduardo Salas; Janis A. Cannon-Bowers. **J. Appl. Psychol.** 85:2 4:2000 pp.273-283.
1057   Intergroup emotions: explaining offensive action tendencies in an intergroup context. Diane M. Mackie; Thierry Devos; Eliot R. Smith. **J. Pers. Soc. Psychol.** 79:4 10:2000 pp.602-616.
1058   Intergroup relations in a changing political context: the case of veiled and unveiled university students in Turkey. Nuran Hortaçsu. **Eur. J. Soc. Psychol.** 30:5 9-10:2000 pp.733-744.
1059   Majority-minority influence: identifying argumentative patterns and predicting argument-outcome links. Renée A. Meyers; Dale E. Brashers; Jennifer Hanner. **J. Comm.** 50:4 Autumn:2000 pp.3-30.
1060   Measuring domination in directed networks. René van den Brink; Robert P. Gilles. **Soc. Networks** 22:2 5:2000 pp.141-157.
1061   Motivation gains in performance groups: paradigmatic and theoretical developments on the Köhler effect. Guido Hertel; Norbert L. Kerr; Lawrence A. Messé. **J. Pers. Soc. Psychol.** 79:4 10:2000 pp.580-601.
1062   Network exchange theory. David Willer [Ed.]. Westport CT: Praeger, 1999. 336p. *ISBN: 0275953777, 0275953785. Includes bibliographical references (p. [309]-321) and indexes.*
1063   Overlapping mental representations of self and in-group: reaction time evidence and its relationship with explicit measures of group identification. Susan Coats; Eliot R. Smith; Heather M. Claypool; Michele J. Banner. **J. Exp. S. Psychol.** 36:3 5:2000 pp.304-315.
1064   Performance and satisfaction in conflicted interdependent groups: when and how does self-esteem make a difference? Michelle K. Duffy; Jason D. Shaw; Eric M. Stark. **Acad. Manag. J.** 43:4 8:2000 pp.772-782.
1065   Performance implications of leader briefings and team-interaction training for team adaptation to novel environments. Michelle A. Marks; Stephen J. Zaccaro; John E. Mathieu. **J. Appl. Psychol.** 85:6 12:2000 pp.971-986.
1066   Performance-based reward distribution methods for anonymous decision-making groups. B. Gavis; J.H. Gerdes, Jr.; J. Kalvenes. **Group Decis. Negot.** 9:5 9:2000 pp.393-413.
1067   The personal-group discrepancy: is there a common information basis for personal and group judgment? Thomas Kessler; Amélie Mummendey; Utta-Kristin Leisse. **J. Pers. Soc. Psychol.** 79:1 7:2000 pp.95-109.
1068   Le phénomène collégial: une théorie structurale de l'action collective entre pairs. *[In French]*; (The collegial phenomenon: a structural theory of collective action among peers.) Emmanuel Lazega. **Rev. Fr. Soc.** XL:4 10-12:1999 pp.639-670.
1069   Power in mixed exchange networks: a rational choice model. Kazuo Yamaguchi. **Soc. Networks** 22:2 5:2000 pp.93-121.
1070   Power through appointment. Joseph M. Whitmeyer. **Soc. Sci. R.** 29:4 12:2000 pp.535-555.

C: INDIVIDUS. GROUPES. ORGANISATIONS

1071 Pragmatic use of stereotyping in teamwork: social loafing and compensation as a function of inferred partner-situation fit. Jason E. Plaks; E. Tory Higgins. **J. Pers. Soc. Psychol.** 79:6 12:2000 pp.962-974.

1072 Prinzipien einer deutsch-tschechischen Teamentwicklung. *[In German]*; [Principles of German-Czech team development]. Christian Eberhardt. **J. E. Eur. Man. Stud.** 5:4 2000 pp.377-391.

1073 Prosocial values and group assortation within an N-person prisoner's dilemma game. Kennon M. Sheldon; Melanie Skaggs Sheldon; Richard Osbaldiston. **Hum. Nature** 11:4 2000 pp.387-404.

1074 Reproducing social structure in task groups: the role of structural ritualization. Jane Sell; J. David Knottnerus; Christopher Ellison; Heather Mundt. **Soc. Forc.** 79:2 12:2000 pp.453-475.

1075 The role of empathy in improving intergroup relations. Walter G. Stephan; Krystina Finlay. **J. Soc. Issues** 55:4 Winter:1999 pp.729-743.

1076 Self-categorization, affective commitment and group self-esteem as distinct aspects of social identity in the organization. Massimo Bergami; Richard P. Bagozzi. **Br. J. Soc. P.** 39:4 12:2000 pp.555-577.

1077 Social identity and inter-group dynamics: the case of Palestinian children in Jordan; *[Summary in Arabic]*. Nadia Monacelli; Helmi Sari; Felice Carugati. **Dirasat Hum. Soc. Sc.** 27:1 2:2000 pp.205-221.

1078 Social identity and intergroup relations within the hospital. Dan LaTendresse. **J. Soc. Distr. Home.** 9:1 1:2000 pp.51-69.

1079 (The structuring of trust relations in groups and the transition of within-group order.); *[Text in Japanese]*. Ryuhei Tsuji. **Rir. To Ho.** 15:1 6:2000 pp.197-208.

1080 Teamworking. Stephen J. Procter [Ed.]; Frank Mueller [Ed.]. Basingstoke, New York: Macmillan, St. Martin's Press, 1999. 284p. *ISBN: 0333760034, 0312229011. Papers presented at the Second International Workshop on Teamworking, University of South Australia, 1998. Includes bibliographical references and index.*

1081 Terror management and the vicissitudes of sports fan affiliation: the effects of mortality salience on optimism and fan identification. M. Dechesne; J. Greenberg; J. Arndt; J. Schimel. **Eur. J. Soc. Psychol.** 30:6 11-12:2000 pp.813-836.

1082 Tongued with fire: groups in experience. W. Gordon Lawrence. London: Karnac Books, 2000. 254p. *ISBN: 1855752247.*

1083 The typical student as an in-group member: eliminating optimistic bias by reducing social distance. Peter Harris; Wendy Middleton; Richard Joiner. **Eur. J. Soc. Psychol.** 30:2 3-4:2000 pp.235-253.

1084 Unfixing the fixed pie: a motivated information-processing approach to integrative negotiation. Carsten K.W. de Dreu; Sander L. Koole; Wolfgang Steinel. **J. Pers. Soc. Psychol.** 79:6 12:2000 pp.975-987.

1085 Utility and dynamic social networks. Norman P. Hummon. **Soc. Networks** 22:3 7:2000 pp.221-249.

1086 Varieties of groups and the perception of group entitativity. Brian Lickel; David L. Hamilton; Grazyna Wieczorkowska; Amy Lewis; Steven J. Sherman; A. Neville Uhles. **J. Pers. Soc. Psychol.** 78:2 2:2000 pp.223-246.

C.6: **Organizations**
Organisations

1087 Agency and social networks: strategies of action in a social structure of position, opposition, and opportunity. William B. Stevenson; Danna Greenberg. **Adm. Sci. Qua.** 45:4 12:2000 pp.651-678.

1088 Die Anforderungen an die interne Unternehmenskommunikation in neuen Organisationskonzepten. *[In German]*; (The demands for corporate communications in

C: INDIVIDUALS, GROUPS, ORGANIZATIONS

	new organizational concepts.) *[Summary]*. Uwe Wilkesmann. **Publizistik** 45:4 12:2000 pp.476-495.
1089	Behavioral science foundations of organization development: a critique from the Islamic perspective. Syed Abdul Hamid al-Junaid; Syed Aziz Anwar. **Am. J. Islam. Soc. Sci.** 17:1 Spring:2000 pp.1-19.
1090	Body and organization. Ruth Holliday [Ed.]; Hugh Willmott [Ed.]; John Hassard [Ed.]. London: Sage Publications, 2000. ix, 254p. *ISBN: 0761959181, 0761959173. Includes bibliographical references and index.*
1091	Boundary activities in 'boundaryless' organizations: a case study of a transformation to a team-based structure. Robert L. Cross; Aimin Yan; Meryl Reis Louis. **Human Relat.** 53:6 6:2000 pp.841-868.
1092	Business psychology and organisational behaviour. Eugene McKenna. London: Routledge, 2000. 698p.
1093	The challenges of eco-leadership: green Machiavellianism. Dallas Hanson; Stuart Middleton. **Green. Mgt. Int.** 29 Spring:2000 pp.95-107.
1094	Change management: a guide to effective implementation. James McCalman; Rob Paton. London: Paul Chapman, 2000. 280p. *ISBN: 0761964983.*
1095	Chic, mystique, and misconception: Argyris and Schön and the rhetoric of organizational learning. Raanan Lipshitz. **J. App. Behav. Sc.** 36:4 12:2000 pp.456-473.
1096	Climate quality and climate consensus as mediators of the relationship between organizational antecedents and outcomes. Michael K. Lindell; Christina J. Brandt. **J. Appl. Psychol.** 85:3 6:2000 pp.331-348.
1097	Consistent questions of ambiguity in organizational crisis communication: Jack in the Box as a case study. Robert R. Ulmer; Timothy L. Sellnow. **J. Busin. Ethics** 25:2 5:2000 pp.143-156.
1098	Conventions: an interpretation of deep structure in organizations. Pierre-Yves Gomez; Brittany C. Jones. **Organiz. Sci.** 11:6 11-12:2000 pp.696-708.
1099	Creating a hybrid organizational form from parental blueprints: the emergence and evolution of knowledge firms. Amalya L. Oliver; Kathleen Montgomery. **Human Relat.** 53:1 1:2000 pp.33-56.
1100	Cultural industries: learning from evolving organizational practices. Joseph Lampel; Theresa Lant; Jamal Shamsie; N. Anand; Richard A. Peterson; Mary Ann Glynn; Ken Starkey; Christopher Barnatt; Sue Tempest; John M. Mezias; Stephen J. Mezias; Nachoem M. Wijnberg; Gerda Gemser; Glenn B. Voss; Daniel M. Cable; Zannie Giraud Voss; Thomas R. Eisenmann; Joseph L. Bower; Paul M. Hirsch. **Organiz. Sci.** 11:3 5-6:2000 pp.236-361. *Collection of 9 articles.*
1101	Discourse and organization. David Grant [Ed.]; Tom Keenoy [Ed.]; Cliff Oswick [Ed.]. London, Thousand Oaks CA: Sage Publications, 1998. viii, 248p. *ISBN: 0761956719, 0761956700. Includes bibliographical references (p. [222]-243) and index.*
1102	Discourse and the study of organization: toward a structurational perspective. Loizos Heracleous; John Hendry. **Human Relat.** 53:10 10:2000 pp.1251-1286.
1103	Discourse, organizations and national cultures. Britt-Louise Gunnarsson. **Disc. St.** 2:1 2:2000 pp.5-34.
1104	Discourses of organizing. Tom Keenoy; Robert J. Marshak; Cliff Oswick; David Grant; Mats Alvesson; Dan Kärreman; Barbara Schneider; Ellen S. O'Connor; Bradley G. Jackson; Nic Beech; Michael K. Mauws. **J. App. Behav. Sc.** 36:2 6:2000 pp.133-258. *Collection of 8 articles.*
1105	Dyadic communication relationships in organizations: an attribution/expectancy approach. Bruce Barry; J. Michael Crant. **Organiz. Sci.** 11:6 11-12:2000 pp.648-664.
1106	The effect of organizational structure on perceptions of procedural fairness. Marshall Schminke; Maureen L. Ambrose; Russell S. Cropanzano. **J. Appl. Psychol.** 85:2 4:2000 pp.294-304.
1107	The emergence of organizational forms: a community ecology approach. Martin Ruef. **A.J.S.** 106:3 11:2000 pp.658-714.

C: INDIVIDUS. GROUPES. ORGANISATIONS

1108 The emergent organization: communication as its site and surface. James R. Taylor; Elizabeth J. Van Every. Mahwah NJ: Lawrence Erlbaum Associates, 2000. xii, 351p. *ISBN: 0805821937, 0805821945. Includes bibliographical references (p. 327-340) and indexes.*

1109 Emotion in organizations. Stephen Fineman [Ed.]. London: Sage Publications, 2000. 288p. *ISBN: 0761966250, 0761966242.*

1110 Ethnographic fiction science: making sense of managerial work and organizational research processes with Caroline and Terry. Tony J. Watson. **Organization** 7:3 8:2000 pp.489-510.

1111 Foci and correlates of organizational identification. Daan van Knippenberg; Els C.M. van Schie. **J. Occup. Organ. Psychol.** 73:2 6:2000 pp.137-148.

1112 The impact of person and organizational values on organizational commitment. Joan E. Finegan. **J. Occup. Organ. Psychol.** 73:2 6:2000 pp.149-170.

1113 Interaction and transformation in SSM. Lars Mathiassen; Peter Axel Nielsen. **Syst. Res. Behav. Sci.** 17:3 5-6:2000 pp.243-254.

1114 Kaizen strategies for supporting organisational change: evolution and revolution in the organisation. Michael Colenso. London: Financial Times Management, 1999. 256p. *ISBN: 0273639854.*

1115 Knowing in practice. Silvia Gherardi [Ed.]; Etienne Wenger; Dvora Yanow; Alessia Contu; Hugh Willmott; Frank Blackler; Norman Crump; Seonaidh McDonald; Yrjö Engeström [Comments by]; Lucy Suchman; Davide Nicolini; John Law. **Organization** 7:2 5:2000 pp.211-354. *Collection of 9 articles.*

1116 The knowing organization: how organizations use information to construct meaning, create knowledge, and make decisions. Chun Wei Choo. New York: Oxford University Press, 1998. xviii, 298p. *ISBN: 0195110129, 0195110110. Includes bibliographical references (p. 275-290) and index.*

1117 Managing organizational behavior. Henry L. Tosi; John R. Rizzo; Neal P. Mero. Malden MA: Blackwell Publishers, 1999. 560p. *ISBN: 0631212574, 0631208836. Includes bibliographical references and index.*

1118 A meta-analytic review of occupational commitment: relations with person- and work-related variables. Kibeom Lee; Julie J. Carswell; Natalie J. Allen. **J. Appl. Psychol.** 85:5 10:2000 pp.799-811.

1119 Mixed results, lousy process: the management experience of organizational change. Mike Doyle; Tim Claydon; Dave Buchanan. **Br. J. Manag.** 11:Special 9:2000 pp.59-80.

1120 On the context sensitivity of institutional interaction. Ilkka Arminen. **Disc. Soc.** 11:4 10:2000 pp.435-458.

1121 Order, complexity and benefits in social organizations and other organized structures. J.S. Shiner. **Wor. Futur.** 55:4 2000 pp.329-340.

1122 Organisational climate and dual commitment in private and public sector enterprises. T. Chandramohan Reddy; M. Gajendran; S. Gayathri. **Ind. J. Ind. Rel.** 36:1 7:2000 pp.53-66.

1123 Organisational culture and organisational commitment. Sangeeta Tripathi; Alka Kapoor; Nachiketa Tripathi. **Ind. J. Ind. Rel.** 36:1 7:2000 pp.24-40.

1124 Organization and aesthetics. Antonio Strati. London, Thousand Oaks CA: Sage Publications, 1999. 216p. *ISBN: 0761952381, 076195239X. Includes bibliographical references (p. [195]-207) and index.*

1125 Organization development: behavioral science interventions for organization improvement. Wendell L. French; Cecil Bell, Jr. Upper Saddle River NJ: Prentice Hall, 1999. xv, 343p. *ISBN: 013242231X. Includes bibliographical references and indexes.*

1126 Organizational commitment as a mediator of the relationship between Islamic work ethic and attitudes toward organizational change. Darwish A. Yousef. **Human Relat.** 53:4 4:2000 pp.513-538.

1127 Organizational discourse(s): significations, stakeholders and strategy. Cliff Oswick; Tom W. Keenoy; David Grant; Mats Alvesson; Dan Karreman; Fiona Anderson-Gough; Christopher Grey; Keith Robson; Stephanie A. Welcomer; Dennis A. Gioia; Martin

C: INDIVIDUALS. GROUPS. ORGANIZATIONS

Kilduff; Richard Dunford; Deborah Jones; Cynthia Hardy; Ian Palmer; Nelson Phillips. **Human Relat.** 53:9 9:2000 pp.1115-1248. *Collection of 6 articles.*

1128 Organizational learning and the learning organization: developments in theory and practice. Mark Easterby-Smith [Ed.]; Luis Araujo [Ed.]; John Burgoyne [Ed.]. London, Thousand Oaks CA: Sage Publications, 1999. viii, 247p. *ISBN: 0761959165. Includes bibliographical references and index.*

1129 Organizational learning and the transfer of knowledge: an investigation of quality improvement. Daniel Z. Levin. **Organiz. Sci.** 11:6 11-12:2000 pp.630-647.

1130 Organizational routines as a source of continuous change. Martha S. Feldman. **Organiz. Sci.** 11:6 11-12:2000 pp.611-629.

1131 Organizational socialization in two cultures: results from the United States and Hong Kong. Robert J. Taormina; Talya N. Bauer. **Intern. J. Organiz. Anal.** 8:3 2000 pp.262-289.

1132 Organizations: rational, natural, and open systems. W. Richard Scott. Upper Saddle River NJ: Prentice Hall, 1998. xvi, 416p. *ISBN: 0132663546. Includes bibliographical references (p. 364-400) and indexes.*

1133 Organizing bodies: policy, institutions and work. Nick Watson [Ed.]; Linda McKie [Ed.]. Basingstoke: Macmillan, 2000. 230p. *ISBN: 0333774477, 0333774469. Includes index.*

1134 Partnering across borders: negotiating organizational culture in a German-Japanese joint venture. Mary Yoko Brannen; Jane E. Salk. **Human Relat.** 53:4 4:2000 pp.451-488.

1135 Perceptions of organizational readiness for change: factors related to employees' reactions to the implementation of team-based selling. Lillian T. Eby; Danielle M. Adams; Joyce E.A. Russell; Stephen H. Gaby. **Human Relat.** 53:3 3:2000 pp.419-441.

1136 The place of culture in organization theory: introducing the morphogenetic approach. Robert Willmott. **Organization** 7:1 2:2000 pp.95-128.

1137 Power, control and computer-based performance monitoring: repertoires, resistance and subjectivities. Kirstie Ball; David C. Wilson. **Organ. Stud.** 21:3 2000 pp.539-565.

1138 Principles of organizational behaviour. Robin Fincham; Peter S. Rhodes. New York: Oxford University Press, 1999. *ISBN: 0198775784, 0198775776. Includes bibliographical references.*

1139 The project of rationalization: a critique and reappraisal of neo-institutionalism in organization studies. Hans Hasselbladh; Jannis Kallinikos. **Organ. Stud.** 21:4 2000 pp.697-720.

1140 Reading and writing organizational lives. Carl Rhodes. **Organization** 7:1 2:2000 pp.7-30.

1141 Redirecting critique in postmodern organization studies: the perspective of Foucault. Andrew Chan. **Organ. Stud.** 21:6 2000 pp.1059-1075.

1142 Relational demography and relationship quality in two cultures. Lisa Hope Pelled; Katherine R. Xin. **Organ. Stud.** 21:6 2000 pp.1077-1094.

1143 Self-assessment accuracy and assessment centre decisions. Raymond Randall; Eammon Ferguson; Fiona Patterson. **J. Occup. Organ. Psychol.** 73:4 12:2000 pp.443-459.

1144 Shopfloor innovation: facilitating the suggestion and implementation of ideas. C.M. Axtell; D.J. Holman; K.L. Unsworth; T.D. Wall; P.E. Waterson; E. Harrington. **J. Occup. Organ. Psychol.** 73:3 9:2000 pp.265-285.

1145 The socially constructed organization. John Shotter [Foreword]; David Campbell. London: Karnac Books, 2000. 116p. *ISBN: 1855750340, 185575245X. Includes bibliographical references (p. 107-112) and index.* (Series: Systemic thinking and practice series. Work with organizations).

1146 A structural perspective on the impact of network organizations. C.M. Topper; K.M. Carley. **J. Math. Sociol.** 24:1 1999 pp.67-96.

1147 A study of individual differences and self-awareness in the context of multi-source feedback. Clive Fletcher; Caroline Baldry. **J. Occup. Organ. Psychol.** 73:3 9:2000 pp.303-319.

1148 Studying organization: theory and method. Stewart R. Clegg [Ed.]; Cynthia Hardy [Ed.]. London, Thousand Oaks CA: Sage Publications, 1999. xv, 464p. *ISBN: 0761960457. Includes bibliographical references and index.*

C: INDIVIDUS. GROUPES. ORGANISATIONS

1149 Tacit knowledge, organizational learning and societal institutions: an integrated framework. Alice Lam. **Organ. Stud.** 21:3 2000 pp.487-513.

1150 Taking science out of organization science: how would postmodernism reconstruct the analysis of organizations? Richard M. Weiss. **Organiz. Sci.** 11:6 11-12:2000 pp.709-731.

1151 Teaming up and out? Getting durable cooperation in a collegial organization. Emmanuel Lazega. **Eur. Sociol. R.** 16:3 9:2000 pp.245-266.

1152 Termites and champions: case comparisons by metaphor. E.E. Liz Walley; Mark Stubbs. **Green. Mgt. Int.** 29 Spring:2000 pp.41-54.

1153 The threat of failure, the perils of success and CEO character: sources of strategic persistence. Veronika Kisfalvi. **Organ. Stud.** 21:3 2000 pp.611-639.

1154 Transforming the organization: a socio-technical approach. Howard W. Oden. Westport CT: Quorum, 1999. xiii, 346p. *ISBN: 1567202268. Includes bibliographical references and index.*

1155 Trust and inter-organizational networking. Sue Newell; Jacky Swan. **Human Relat.** 53:10 10:2000 pp.1287-1328.

1156 Trust, confidence and voluntary organisations: between values and institutions. Fran Tonkiss; Andrew Passey. **Sociology** 33:2 5:1999 pp.257-274.

1157 Vision revisited: telling the story of the future. Ira M. Levin. **J. App. Behav. Sc.** 36:1 3:2000 pp.91-107.

D: CULTURE
CULTURE

D.1: Culture
Culture

1158 América Latina: postcolonial, neobarroca, postmoderna. *[In Spanish]*; [Latin America: postcolonial, neobaroque, postmodern]. Rigoberto Lanz; George Yúdice; Neil Larsen; Hermann Herlinghaus; Roberto A. Follari; Gustavo Luis Gutiérrez; Afrânio Mendes Catani; Ángel Orcajo. **Rev. Latin. Estud. Avanz.** 10 1-4:2000 pp.15-136. *Collection of 6 articles.*

1159 Approaching Byzantium: identity, predicament and afterlife. Johann P. Arnason. **Thes. Elev.** 62 8:2000 pp.39-70.

1160 Being and cultural difference: (mis)understanding otherness in early modernity. John Mandalios. **Thes. Elev.** 62 8:2000 pp.91-108.

1161 Changing times: reflections on the development of self and culture. Cynthia Lightfoot; Maria C.D.P. Lyra; Andrew J. Lock; E. Sue Savage-Rumbaugh; William M. Fields; Peter Damerow; F. Francis Strayer; Cláudia De Lemos; Katherine Nelson; Chris Sinha; Michael Chandler; John Shotter; Theodore R. Sarbin; Geoffrey M. White; Donald E. Polkinghorne. **Cult. Psyc.** 6:2 6:2000 pp.99-272. *Collection of 13 articles.*

1162 The civilizational dimension in sociological analysis. S.N. Eisenstadt. **Thes. Elev.** 62 8:2000 pp.1-22.

1163 The clash of civilizations: a model of historical development? Gregory Melleuish. **Thes. Elev.** 62 8:2000 pp.109-120.

1164 Classical humanism and modern societies. Athena S. Leoussi. **Society** 37:5 7-8:2000 pp.70-84.

1165 Colonial and post-colonial encounters. Niaz Ali Zaman [Ed.]; Firdous Azim [Ed.]; Shawkat Hussain [Ed.]. New Delhi: Manohar, 2000. x, 227p. *Includes bibliographical references and index. The University Press Limited, Dhaka, Bangladesh.*

1166 Complex life: nonmodernity and the emergence of cognition and culture. Alan Dean. Aldershot: Ashgate, 2000. vi, 149p. *ISBN: 0754610497. Includes bibliographical references.*

1167 Cuba: island of dreams. Antoni Kapcia. Oxford: Berg Publishers, 2000. 256p. *ISBN: 185973331X, 1859733263. Includes bibliographical references.*

1168 The cultural economy of cities: essays on the geography of image-producing industries. Allen John Scott. London: Sage Publications, 2000. 245p. *ISBN: 0761954546, 0761954554.*

1169 Cultural politics in Latin America. Ronnie Munck [Ed.]; Anny Brooksbank Jones [Ed.]. Basingstoke: Macmillan, 2000. 200p. *ISBN: 0333802063. Includes index.*

1170 Cultural revitalization and tourism at the Morería Nima' K'iche'. Matthew Krystal. **Ethnology** XXXIX:2 Spring:2000 pp.149-162.

1171 Culture and achievement. Nathan Glazer. **Publ. Inter.** 140 Summer:2000 pp.49-63.

1172 La culture et le capital. *[In French]*; [Culture and capital]. Olivier Abel. **Esprit** 265 7:2000 pp.119-139.

1173 The culture of fear: why Americans are afraid of the wrong things. Barry Glassner. New York: Basic Books, 1999. xxviii, 276p. *ISBN: 0465014895, 0465014909. Includes bibliographical references (p. 211-257) and index.*

1174 The cultures of the American New West. Neil Campbell. Edinburgh: Edinburgh University Press, 2000. *ISBN: 0748611762.*

1175 Cultuur van zijn voetstuk de secularisering van het cultuurbegrip. *[In Dutch]*; (Culture toppled from its pedestal: the secularization of the cultural understanding.) *[Summary]*. Sjaak Koenis. **Boekmancahier** 12:43 3:2000 pp.47-65.

D: CULTURE

1176 Desiring nature: identity and becoming in narratives of travel. Simone Fullagar. **Cult. Val.** 4:1 1:2000 pp.58-76.
1177 Dollars and lipstick: the United States through the eyes of African women. Yvette Djachechi Monga. **Africa [Edinburgh]** 70:2 2000 pp.192-208.
1178 Encyclopedia of contemporary British culture. Peter Childs [Ed.]; Mike Storry [Ed.]. London: Routledge, 1999. xxvii, 628p. *ISBN: 0415147263. Includes bibliographical references and index.*
1179 Encyclopedia of contemporary German culture. John Sandford [Ed.]. London: Routledge, 1999. xxx, 696p. *ISBN: 0415124484. Includes bibliographical references and index.*
1180 Encyclopedia of contemporary Italian culture. Gino Moliterno [Ed.]. London: Routledge, 2000. xxiv, 677p. *ISBN: 0415145848. Includes bibliographical references and index.*
1181 The English sense of humor? Antony Easthope. **Humor** 13:1 2000 pp.59-76.
1182 Les Français face au français. *[In French]*; [The French and French]. Jean-Luc Giribone. **Esprit** 262 3-4:2000 pp.246-293.
1183 Gilberto Freyre e a singularidade cultural brasileira. *[In Portuguese]*; (Gilberto Freyre and the singularity of Brazilian culture.) *[Summary]*. Jessé Souza. **Tempo Soc.** 12:1 5:2000 pp.69-100.
1184 Global citizenship and cultural identities. Keiko Seki. **Hito. J. Soc. Stud.** 31:2 12:1999 pp.85-95.
1185 Great revolutions of the 20th century in a civilizational perspective. Jaroslav Krejčí. **Thes. Elev.** 62 8:2000 pp.71-90.
1186 In China's image: Chinese self-perception in Western thought. Rupert Hodder. Basingstoke: Macmillan, 2000. 224p. *ISBN: 0333917952. Includes index.*
1187 In search of American Jewish culture. Stephen J. Whitfield. Hanover NH: University Press of New England, 1999. xvi, 307p. *ISBN: 0874517540. Includes bibliographical references and index. (Series:* Brandeis series in American Jewish history, culture, and life).
1188 The liberal foundations of cultural nationalism. Chaim Gans. **Can. J. Phil.** 30:3 9:2000 pp.441-466.
1189 Making the body beautiful: a cultural history of aesthetic surgery. Sander L. Gilman. Princeton NJ: Princeton University Press, 1999. *ISBN: 0691026726. Includes bibliographical references and index.*
1190 Der Müll in der Öffentlichkeit. Reflexive Modernisierung als kulturelle Transformation. Ein deutsch-französischer Vergleich. *[In German]*; (Waste in the public sphere. Reflexive modernization as cultural transformation — a comparison of France and Germany.) *[Summary]*. Reiner Keller. **Soz. Welt.** 51:3 2000 pp.245-266.
1191 Of irritation, texts and men: feminist audience studies and cultural citizenship. Joke Hermes. **Int. Jour. Cult. Stud.** 3:3 12:2000 pp.351-367.
1192 One nation, two cultures. Gertrude Himmelfarb. New York: Knopf, 1999. xii, 179p. *ISBN: 0375404554. Includes bibliographical references (p. [147]-175) and index.*
1193 Polish culture as the nation's own culture and as a foreign culture. Janusz Mucha. **E. Eur. Quart.** XXXIV:2 Summer:2000 pp.217-242.
1194 Politics, culture, and postmodernism. Ronaldo Munck; Jesús Martín-Barbero; Atilio A. Boron; Hernán Vidal; Catherine Davies; Tânia Pellegrini. **Lat. Am. Pers.** 27:4 7:2000 pp.11-143. *Collection of 6 articles.*
1195 Problematizing 'Asia'. Ge Sun; Shiu-Lun Hui [Tr.]; Kinchi Lau [Tr.]; Haejoang Cho Han; Michael Shin [Tr.]; Kohei Hanasaki; Ichiyo Muto [Tr.]; Ghassan Hage; Tejaswini Niranjana; Melani Budianta; C.J.W.L. Wee; Vinod Raina; Hee-yeon Cho. **Inter-Asia Cult. St.** 1:1 4:2000 pp.13-143. *Collection of 7 articles.*
1196 Public pedagogy as cultural politics: Stuart Hall and the 'crisis' of culture. Henry A. Giroux. **Cult. St.** 14:2 4:2000 pp.341-360.
1197 Romántica legitimación y dominación en nuestra visión de la cultura: notas sobre las fuentes culturales de nuestras opciones paradigmáticas. *[In Spanish]*; [Romantic legitimation and domination in our vision of culture: notes on the cultural origins of our paradigmatic options]. Miguel Alvarado Borgoño. **Rev. Parag. Sociol.** 36:104 1-4:1999 pp.31-48.

D: CULTURE

1198 Self-other relations and the rationality of cultures. Paul Healy. **Philos. Soc. Crit.** 26:6 11:2000 pp.61-84.
1199 Siglo XXI: continuidades y rupturas. *[In Spanish]*; [21st century: continuity and rupture]. Christian Graf von Krockow; Renato Ortiz; Jesus Martín-Barbero; Octavio Ianni; Rossana Reguillo; César Cansino; Renée De La Torre. **Metapolítica** 5:17 1-3:2001 pp.36-117. *Collection of 6 articles.*
1200 Speed and social life. Giovanni Gasparini; Pierre Lantz; Jean Chesneaux; Hanns-Georg Brose. **Soc. Sci. Info.** 39:3 9:2000 pp.383-438. *Collection of 4 articles.*
1201 Spengler's theory of civilization. John Farrenkopf. **Thes. Elev.** 62 8:2000 pp.23-38.
1202 Społeczny świat górnośląskiego racjonalizmu: kulturowe przemiany i ich konteksty. *[In Polish]*; (The social world of Upper-Silesian regionalism: cultural transformations and their contexts.) *[Summary]*. Wojciech Świątkiewicz. **Prz. Soc.** XLVIII:2 1999 pp.77-94.
1203 Studio universitario, orientamenti valoriali, consumi culturali. *[In Italian]*; (University study, value orientations, cultural consumption.) *[Summary]*. Giancarlo Gasperoni. **Rass. It. Soc.** XLI:1 1-3:2000 pp.109-129.
1204 Survival and modernization - Ethiopia's enigmatic present: a philosophical discourse. Messay Kebede. Lawrenceville NJ: Red Sea Press, 1999. xxiii, 460p. *ISBN: 1569020841, 156902085X. Includes bibliographical references (p. [437]-447) and index.*
1205 Transformace kulturní identity v souvislosti s procesy evropské integrace. *[In Slovak]*; (The transformation of cultural identity within the process of European integration (the problem of cultural and social changes in Czech local communities).) Martin Matejů. **Sociologia [Brat.]** 32:1 2000 pp.43-56.
1206 Traveling theory: France and the United States. Ieme van der Poel [Ed.]; Sophie Bertho [Ed.]. Madison WI; London: Fairleigh Dickinson University Press; Associated University Presses, 1999. 77p. *ISBN: 0838637817. Includes bibliographical references (p. 157-168) and index.*
1207 Twenty years of *Sinlapa watthanatham*: cultural politics in Thailand in the 1980s and 1990s. Hong Lysa. **J. SE. As. Stud.** 31:1 3:2000 pp.26-47.
1208 The universality of culture: reflection, interaction and the logic of identity. Martin Fuchs. **Thes. Elev.** 60 2:2000 pp.11-22.
1209 Which road to the South? Revisionists revisit the Mezzogiorno. Lucy Riall. **Journ. Mod. Italian Studs.** 5:1 Spring:2000 pp.89-100.

Cultural studies
Études culturelles

1210 Activity theory is a dead end for cultural-historical psychology. Aaro Toomela. **Cult. Psyc.** 6:3 9:2000 pp.353-364.
1211 Banality for cultural studies. Gregory J. Seigworth. **Cult. St.** 14:2 4:2000 pp.227-268.
1212 Bourdieu and culture. Derek Robbins. London: Sage Publications, 2000. xxviii, 156p. *ISBN: 0761960430, 0761960449. Includes bibliographical references and index.*
1213 A companion to postcolonial studies. Henry Schwarz [Ed.]; Sangeeta Ray [Ed.]. Malden MA: Blackwell Publishers, 2000. xxiv, 598p. *ISBN: 0631206620. Includes bibliographical references and index. (Series:* Blackwell companions in cultural studies).
1214 Cosmetics and the female body: a critical appraisal of poststructuralist theories of masquerade. Llewellyn Negrin. **Euro. Journ. Cult. Stud.** 3:1 1:2000 pp.83-102.
1215 The crucial in between: the centrality of mediation in cultural studies. Johan Fornäs. **Euro. Journ. Cult. Stud.** 3:1 1:2000 pp.45-66.
1216 Cultural evolution, reductionism in the social sciences, and explanatory pluralism. Jean Lachapelle. **Philos. S. Sc.** 30:3 9:2000 pp.331-361.
1217 Cultural studies and academic stardom. Joe Moran. **Int. Jour. Cult. Stud.** 1:1 4:1998 pp.67-82.
1218 Cultural studies in Japan. Takeshi Satô. **Int. Jour. Cult. Stud.** 3:1 4:2000 pp.11-25.

D: CULTURE

1219 Culture and development: a critical introduction. Susanne Schech; Jane Haggis. Oxford, Malden MA: Blackwell Publishers, 2000. xviii, 226p. *ISBN: 0631209506, 0631209514*. Includes bibliographical references and index.

1220 Culture, government and spatiality: reassessing the 'Foucault effect' in cultural-policy studies. Clive Barnett. **Int. Jour. Cult. Stud.** 2:3 12:1999 pp.369-397.

1221 El debate posmoderno y los estudios culturales II. *[In Spanish]*; [The postmodern debate and cultural studies II]. Atilio A. Boron; Denis Goulet; Héctor Meléndez. **Rev. Cien. Soc.** 6 1:1999 pp.1-98. *Collection of 3 articles*.

1222 Detraditionalization of society and the rise of cultural studies in South Korea. Keehyeung Lee. **Inter-Asia Cult. St.** 1:3 12:2000 pp.477-490.

1223 Forty years of cultural studies: an interview with Richard Hoggart, October 1997. Mark Gibson [Interviewer]; John Hartley [Interviewer]; Richard Hoggart. **Int. Jour. Cult. Stud.** 1:1 4:1998 pp.11-24.

1224 Hacia unos estudios culturales Latinoamericanos: algunas notas sobre el impacto en la enseñanza. *[In Spanish]*; [Towards Latin American cultural studies: some notes on the impact on education] *[Summary]*. Yolanda Martínez-San Miguel. **Rev. Cien. Soc.** 5 6:1998 pp.113-136.

1225 The idea of culture. Terry Eagleton. Oxford: Blackwell Publishers, 2000. 156p. *ISBN: 0631219668, 063121965X*. *Includes bibliographical references and index. (Series:* Blackwell manifestos).

1226 Impure acts: the practical politics of cultural studies. Henry A. Giroux. New York, London: Routledge, 2000. x, 166p. *ISBN: 0415926556, 0415926564*. *Includes bibliographical references (p. 142-160) and index*.

1227 Irish cultural studies. Spurgeon Thompson; David Lloyd; Clair Wills; Colin Graham; Diane Negra; Katie Kane; Kathryn Conrad; Karen Steele; Anthony Hale; Margot Gaylor Backus; James Doan. **Cult. St.** 15:1 1:2001 pp.1-191. *Collection of 9 articles*.

1228 Is Elvis a God? Cult, culture, questions of method. John Frow. **Int. Jour. Cult. Stud.** 1:2 8:1998 pp.197-210.

1229 The Jameson reader. Fredric Jameson; Kathi Weeks [Ed.]; Michael Hardt [Ed.]. Oxford, Malden MA: Blackwell Publishers, 2000. 408p. *ISBN: 0631202692, 0631202706*. *Includes bibliographical references and index. (Series:* Blackwell readers).

1230 The Japanese and Europe: images and perceptions. Bert Edström [Ed.]. Richmond: Japan Library, 1999. 272p. *ISBN: 1873410867*.

1231 Kulturrelativismus und die Übersetzbarkeit des kulturell Fremden in der Sicht von Quine und Davidson. Eine Beobachtung aus sozialwissenschaftlicher Perspektive. *[In German]*; (Cultural relativism and the translatability of the culturally strange in the views of Quine and Davidson: an observation from the point of view of the social sciences.) *[Summary]*. Gabriele Cappai. **Z. Soziol.** 29:4 8:2000 pp.253-274.

1232 Performativity in practice: some recent work in cultural geography. Catherine Nash. **Prog. H. Geog.** 24:4 12:2000 pp.653-669.

1233 Policing the borders of Birmingham: cultural studies, semiotics, and the politics of repackaging theory. Jeffrey R. Di Leo. **Semiotica** 130:3-4 2000 pp.201-215.

1234 Regarding the biology of machines: gendered cultural studies of the internet. Sarah Kember. **Euro. Journ. Cult. Stud.** 3:1 1:2000 pp.103-116.

1235 Richard Hoggart's grandmother's ironing: some questions about 'power' in international cultural studies. Mark Gibson. **Int. Jour. Cult. Stud.** 1:1 4:1998 pp.25-44.

1236 Studying culture: a practical introduction. Judy Giles; Tim Middleton. Malden MA: Blackwell Publishers, 1999. xi, 280p. *ISBN: 0631206213, 0631206221*. *Includes bibliographical references (p. 262-277) and index*.

1237 The theory of cultural logic: how individuals combine social intelligence with semiotics to create and maintain cultural meaning. Nick J. Enfield. **Cult. Dyn.** 12:1 3:2000 pp.35-64.

1238 Three approaches to cultural psychology: a critique. Carl Ratner. **Cult. Dyn.** 11:1 3:1999 pp.7-32.

1239 Transforming poetry: the allegory of cultural studies. Claudia Nadine. **Fr. Cult. Stud.** 11(2):2 6:2000 pp.219-234.

D: CULTURE

1240 Transnational cultural studies: what price globalisation? David Birch. **Soc. Sem.** 10:2 8:2000 pp.141-156.
1241 Új kultúraelmélet felé. *[In Hungarian]*; (Towards a new theory of culture.) Péter Kolin. **Mag. Tud.** 44:11 1999 pp.1296-1309.
1242 Under construction: cultural studies in cyberspace. Will Brooker. **Int. Jour. Cult. Stud.** 1:3 12:1998 pp.415-424.
1243 Virtual Eden: *Lolita*, pornography, and the perversions of American studies. Paul Giles. **J. Am. Stud.** 34:1 4:2000 pp.41-66.
1244 Die Wahrnehmung der Cultural Studies. Cultural Studies zwischen hilfswissenschaftlicher Vereinnahmung und radikaler Kontextualität. *[In German]*; [The perception of cultural studies: cultural studies between reception as auxiliary science and radical contextualism] *[Summary]*. Udo Göttlich. **Social. Int.** 37:2 1999 pp.189-220.
1245 What are the duties of a cultural theory of duties? Gilberto Pérez Campos. **Cult. Psyc.** 6:3 9:2000 pp.317-332.

Modernity and post-modernity
Modernité et postmodernité

1246 La 'communauté' des modernes. Étude comparative d'une idée-valeur polysémique en Russie et en Occident. *[In French]*; [The 'community' of the modern. A comparative study of a polysemic value-idea in Russia and the West] *[Summary]*; *[Summary in German]*; *[Summary in Spanish]*. Stephane Vibert. **Soc. Anthrop.** 8:3 10:2000 pp.263-294.
1247 La crisis de la crítica. *[In Spanish]*; [The crisis of criticism] *[Summary]*. Francisco José Ramos. **Rev. Cien. Soc.** 5 6:1998 pp.96-112.
1248 The Enlightenment and modernity. Norman Geras [Ed.]; Robert Wokler [Ed.]. New York; Basingstoke: St. Martin's Press; Macmillan, 2000. xv, 232p. *ISBN: 0312223854, 0333716507. Includes bibliographical references and index.*
1249 Evil spirits: nihilism and the fate of modernity. Gary Banham [Ed.]; Charlie Blake [Ed.]. Manchester: Manchester University Press, 2000. 228p. *ISBN: 071905642X, 0719056438.* (*Series:* Angelaki humanities).
1250 Gramsci's critical modernity. Esteve Morera. **Rethink. Marx.** 12:1 Spring:2000 pp.16-46.
1251 Hans Blumenberg and Hannah Arendt on the 'unworldly worldliness' of the modern age. Elizabeth Brient. **J. Hist. Ideas.** 61:3 7:2000 pp.513-530.
1252 Home territories: media, mobility, and identity. Dave Morley. London: Routledge, 2000. 340p. *ISBN: 041515765X, 0415157641. Includes bibliographical references and index.*
1253 In praise of philosophy: Johann P. Arnason's long but successful journey towards a theory of modernity. Wolfgang Knöbl. **Thes. Elev.** 61 5:2000 pp.1-24.
1254 In the eye of the storm: Oxford Circus and the fashioning of modernity. Christopher Breward. **Fash. Theory** 4:1 3:2000 pp.3-26.
1255 Jung and the postmodern: the interpretation of realities. Christopher Hauke. New York: Routledge, 2000. 204p. *ISBN: 0415163854, 0415163862. Includes bibliographical references and index.*
1256 Liquid modernity. Zygmunt Bauman. Cambridge: Polity, 2000. vi, 228p. *ISBN: 074562409X, 0745624103. Includes bibliographical references and index.*
1257 Mediating modernity in Bali. Carol Warren. **Int. Jour. Cult. Stud.** 1:1 4:1998 pp.83-108.
1258 Missionary positions: Christian, modernist, postmodernist. Robert J. Priest; Jonathan Benthall [Comments by]; Kenelm Burridge [Comments by]; James Clifford [Comments by]; Michèle D. Dominy [Comments by]; Alan Dundes [Comments by]; James D. Faubion [Comments by]; Neville Hoad [Comments by]; Sjoerd R. Jaarsma [Comments by]; Lothar Käser [Comments by]; Rita Smith Kipp [Comments by]; Tanya Luhrmann [Comments by]; Peter Pels [Comments by]; Judith Shapiro [Comments by]; Sjaak Van Der Geest [Comments by]. **Curr. Anthr.** 42:1 2:2001 pp.29-68.
1259 Modern morals in postmodernity: a critical reflection on professional codes of ethics. Toon van Meijl. **Cult. Dyn.** 12:1 3:2000 pp.65-84.

D: CULTURE

1260 Modern times, modern places. Peter Conrad. London: Thames & Hudson, 1999. 752p. *ISBN: 0500281513. Includes index.*

1261 Modernity and postmodern culture. Jim McGuigan. Buckingham, Philadelphia PA: Open University Press, 1999. x, 177p. *ISBN: 033519916X, 0335199151. Includes bibliographical references (p. [155]-164) and index. (Series:* Issues in cultural and media studies).

1262 Mourning Korean modernity in the memory of the Cheju April 3rd Incident. Seong-nae Kim. **Inter-Asia Cult. St.** 1:3 12:2000 pp.461-476.

1263 Multiple modernities. S.N. Eisenstadt; Björn Wittrock; Johann P. Arnason; Nilüfer Göle; Dale F. Eickelman; Sudipta Kaviraj; Stanley J. Tambiah; Tu Weiming; Jürgen Heideking; Renato Ortiz. **Dædalus** 129:1 Winter:2000 pp.1-260. *Collection of 10 articles.*

1264 Narratives of modernization: the student movement and social and cultural change in West Germany. David Roberts. **Thes. Elev.** 63 11:2000 pp.38-52.

1265 Negotiating the 'double bind': Heller's theory of modernity. John Grumley. **Eur. J. Soc. Theory** 3:4 11:2000 pp.429-447.

1266 Origins of the present crisis. T.J. Clark. **New Left R.** 2 3-4:2000 pp.85-96.

1267 Particularism and the modernization process in southern Italy. Antonio Mutti. **Int. Sociol.** 15:4 12:2000 pp.579-590.

1268 Postmodernity, post-coloniality and globalisation: a Chinese perspective. Wang Ning. **Soc. Sem.** 10:2 8:2000 pp.221-234.

1269 The problematics of postmodernism for feminist media studies. Natalie Fenton. **Media Cult. Soc.** 22:6 11:2000 pp.723-742.

1270 The real problem for postmodernism. David Pilgrim; Sigurd Reimers [Comments by]. **J. Fam. Ther.** 22:1 2:2000 pp.6-28.

1271 The rise of postmodernisms and the 'end of science'. Gerald Holton. **J. Hist. Ideas.** 61:2 4:2000 pp.327-341.

1272 Social psychology and modernity. Thomas Johansson. Buckingham: Open University Press, 2000. vi, 176p. *ISBN: 0335201105, 0335201040. Includes bibliographical references and index.*

1273 Social theory and modernity. Nigel Dodd. Malden MA: Polity Press, 1999. vi, 279p. *ISBN: 0745613136, 0745613144. Includes bibliographical references (p. [249]-262) and index.*

1274 Style and socialism: modernity and material culture in post-war Eastern Europe. David Crowley [Ed.]; Susan Reid [Ed.]. Oxford: Berg Publishers, 1999. 256p. *ISBN: 1859732348, 1859732399.*

1275 Text and context: narrative, postmodernism and cybernetics. Paolo Bertrando. **J. Fam. Ther.** 22:1 2:2000 pp.83-103.

1276 A theory of modernity. Agnes Heller. Malden MA: Blackwell Publishers, 1999. 313p. *ISBN: 0631216138, 063121612X. Includes bibliographical references and index.*

1277 Toiletry time: defecation, temporal strategies and the dilemmas of modernity. David Inglis; Mary Holmes. **Time Soc.** 9:2-3 6-9:2000 pp.223-246.

1278 Transgressing boundaries: postmodernism and cultural criticism. Shelley Walia. **Sociol. Bul.** 49:1 3:2000 pp.97-110.

1279 Transgressing the modern: explorations in the Western experience of otherness. John Jervis. Oxford: Blackwell Publishers, 1999. 232p. *ISBN: 0631211101, 0631211098. Includes index.*

1280 When 'the light of the great cultural problems moves on': on the possibility of a cultural theory of modernity. Heidrun Friese; Peter Wagner. **Thes. Elev.** 61 5:2000 pp.25-40.

1281 Zygmunt Bauman: dialectic of modernity. Peter Beilharz. London: Sage Publications, 2000. xi, 180p. *ISBN: 0761967346. Includes bibliographical references (p. [174]-176) and index.*

D: CULTURE

D.2: Everyday life
Vie quotidienne

1282 The 24 hour society: transforming time in our lives. Leon Kreitzman. London: Profile, 1999. 260p. *ISBN: 1861971044*.

1283 Le coeur à l'ouvrage: théorie de l'action ménagère. *[In French]*; [One's heart in one work: a theory of housework]. Jean-Claude Kaufmann. Paris: Pocket, 2000. 351p. *ISBN: 2266100068. Includes bibliographical references (p. 335-345)*.

1284 Co-residence of mid-life children with their elderly parents in England and Wales: changes between 1981 and 1991. Emily Grundy. **Pop. Stud.** 54:2 7:2000 pp.193-206.

1285 The extra-professional life: leisure, retirement and unemployment. Robert A. Stebbins. **Curr. Sociol.** 48:1 1:2000 pp.1-23.

1286 Future notes: the meal-in-a-pill. Warren Belasco. **Food Food.** 8:4 2000 pp.253-271.

1287 Hitting the jackpot: lives of lottery millionaires. Pasi Falk; Pasi Mäenpää. Oxford: Berg Publishers, 1999. 224p. *ISBN: 185973300X, 1859733050. Includes bibliographical references*.

1288 Home: territory and identity. J. Macgregor Wise. **Cult. St.** 14:2 4:2000 pp.295-310.

1289 Intersubjectivity and contemporary social theory: the everyday as critique. Howard Feather. Aldershot: Ashgate, 2000. 176p. *ISBN: 1859722814. Includes bibliographical references*.

1290 The labor of Sisyphus? Women's and men's reactions to housework. Glenna Spitze; Karyn A. Loscocco. **Soc. Sci. Q.** 81:4 12:2000 pp.1087-1100.

1291 Leisure and culture. Chris Rojek. Basingstoke; New York: Macmillan; St. Martin's Press, 2000. ix, 234p. *ISBN: 0333680006, 0333680014, 0312225911. Includes bibliographical references (p. 215-226) and index*.

1292 Leisure, time and space: meanings and values in people's lives. Sheila Scraton [Ed.]. Eastbourne: Leisure Studies Association, 1998. 198p. *ISBN: 0906337682. Includes bibliographical references*.

1293 'Once you know something, you can't not know it': an empirical look at becoming vegan. Barbara McDonald. **Soc. and. Anim.** 8:1 2000 pp.1 23.

1294 Performing culture: understanding expertise in everyday life. John Tulloch. Thousand Oaks CA, London: Sage Publications, 1999. 240p. *ISBN: 0761956077, 0761956085*.

1295 Praktiken und Strategien der Bewältigung des Alltagslebens in einem Dorf im sozialistischen Bulgarien. *[In German]*; [Coping practices and strategies in everyday life in a village in socialist Bulgaria]. Klaus Roth. **Z. Balkan.** 35:1 1999 pp.63-77.

1296 The sexual politics of meat: a feminist-vegetarian critical theory. Carol J. Adams. New York: Continuum, 2000. 272p. *ISBN: 0826411843. Includes bibliographical references (p. [243]-260) and index*.

1297 Social psychological and structural influences on vegetarian beliefs. Linda Kalof; Thomas Dietz; Paul C. Stern; Gregory A. Guagnano. **Rural Sociol.** 64:3 9:1999 pp.500-511.

1298 Speed and social life. Marc Bessin; Giovanni Gasparini; Harald Weinrich; William Grossin; Javier Santiso; Francis Jauréguiberry; Jean-Marc Ramos. **Soc. Sci. Info.** 39:2 6:2000 pp.195-285. *Collection of 6 articles*.

1299 Strukturell-situationale Gegebenheiten als Bestimmungsfaktoren der Verkehrsmittelwahl. *[In German]*; (Structural and situational factors as determinants of the choice of means of transport.) *[Summary]*. Peter Preisendörfer. **Soz. Welt.** 51:4 2000 pp.487-501.

1300 Sustaining identities? Prolegomena for inquiry into contemporary foodways. Mira Crouch; Grant O'Neill. **Soc. Sci. Info.** 39:1 3:2000 pp.181-192.

1301 Svobodnoe vremia: k optimal'nomu stiliu dosuga (vzgliad iz Kanady). *[In Russian]*; (Free time: towards optimal leisure (a view from Canada).) R.A. Stebbins. **Sot. Issle.** 7 2000 pp.64-82.

1302 Verkehr und/oder Telekommunikation? — Eine Untersuchung zu physischen und virtuellen Raumüberwindungsprozessen. *[In German]*; [Traffic and/or telecommunication? - An investigation into physical and virtual spatial behaviour] *[Summary]*. Dirk Vallée; Stefan Köhler. **Z. Verkehr.** 71:4 2000 pp.305-332.

D: CULTURE

1303 What's eating us? Food, sex, identities. Elspeth Probyn. London: Routledge, 2000. 192p. *ISBN: 0415223059, 0415223040. Includes bibliographical references and index.*

1304 Work-lifestyle choices in the 21st century: preference theory. C. Hakim. Oxford: Oxford University Press, 2000. 280p. *ISBN: 0199242100, 0199242097.*

Popular culture
Culture populaire

1305 Amateurs and professionals in post-war British sport. Dilwyn Porter; Stephen Wagg; Ray Physick; Richard Holt; Martin Polley; Wray Vamplew; Adrian Smith. **Contemp. Br. Hist.** 14:2 Summer:2000 pp.1-188. *Collection of 6 articles.*

1306 L'analisi sociologica dello sport. *[In Italian]*; [The sociological analysis of sport]. Pippo Russo. **Rass. It. Soc.** XLI:2 4-6:2000 pp.303-313.

1307 Artificial paradises: a drugs reader. Mike Jay [Ed.]. London, New York: Penguin, 1999. xx, 384p. *ISBN: 014118115X. Includes bibliographical references.*

1308 Baseball in the global era: economic, legal, and cultural perspectives. David P. Fidler; Samuel O. Regalado; Angel Vargas; Samuel R. Hill; Masaru Ikei; Leonard Koppett; William B. Gould IV; Mark S. Rosentraub; Roberto González Echevarría. **Ind. J. Glob. Legal Stud.** 8:1 Fall:2000 pp.1-165. *Collection of 9 articles.*

1309 Bleep! Censoring rock and rap music. Sandra Davidson [Ed.]; Betty Houchin Winfield [Ed.]. Westport CT, London: Greenwood Press, 1999. ix, 132p. *ISBN: 0313307059. Selected papers from the 1993 international conference, "On the Beat: Rock 'n' Rap, Mass Media and Society", held at the University of Missouri. Includes bibliographical references (p. [115]-121) and index. (Series:* Contributions to the study of popular culture - 68).

1310 Bluegrass and 'White trash': a case study concerning the name 'folklore' and class bias. Jeannie B. Thomas; Doug Enders. **J. Folk. Res.** 37:1 1-4:2000 pp.23-52.

1311 The bohemianization of mass culture. Elizabeth Wilson. **Int. Jour. Cult. Stud.** 2:1 4:1999 pp.11-32.

1312 The British seaside: holidays and resorts in the twentieth century. John K. Walton. Manchester; New York: Manchester University Press; St. Martin's Press, 2000. 216p. *ISBN: 071905169X, 0719051703. Includes bibliographical references and index. (Series:* Studies in popular culture).

1313 Cannabis culture: a journey through disputed territory. Patrick Matthews. London: Bloomsbury, 1999. 256p. *ISBN: 0747542813.*

1314 Circuits of tourism: stepping beyond the 'production/consumption' dichotomy. Irena Ateljevic. **Tour. Geog.** 2:4 11:2000 pp.369-388.

1315 Class, ethnicity, and color in the making of Brazilian football. José Sergio Leite Lopes. **Dædalus** 129:2 Spring:2000 pp.239-270.

1316 Clothes at rest: elements for a sociology of the wardrobe. Saulo B. Cwerner. **Fash. Theory** 5:1 3:2001 pp.79-92.

1317 Constructing tourism landscapes — gender, sexuality and space; *[Summary in French].* Annette Pritchard; Nigel J. Morgan. **Tour. Geog.** 2:2 5:2000 pp.115-139.

1318 Consuming fantasies: mediated stardom in Hong Kong Cantonese opera and cinema. Kevin Latham. **Mod. Chi.** 26:3 7:2000 pp.309-347.

1319 Desi music vibes: the performance of Indian youth culture in Chicago. Gregory Diethrich. **Asian Mus.** XXXI:1 Fall-Winter:1999-2000 pp.35-62.

1320 Domesticating Disney: onstage strategies of adaptation in Tokyo Disneyland. Aviad E. Raz. **J. Pop. Cult.** 33:4 Spring:2000 pp.77-100.

1321 Dress, gender and cultural change: Asian American and African American rites of passage. Annette Lynch. Oxford, New York: Berg Publishers, 1999. xi, 126p. *ISBN: 1859739792, 1859739741. Includes bibliographical references (p. 117-122) and index. (Series:* Dress, body, culture).

D: CULTURE

1322 Eating out: social differentiation, consumption, and pleasure. Alan Warde; Lydia Martens. Cambridge, New York: Cambridge University Press, 2000. xi, 246p. *ISBN: 0521590442, 0521599695. Includes bibliographical references (p. 234-242) and index.*

1323 Édition et grand public. *[In French]*; [Publishing and the general public]. Alban Cerisier; Françoise Geoffroy-Bernard; Francis Lacassin; Jean-Philippe Mazaud; Jacques Michon; Pascal Fouché; Bertrand Legendre; Bernard Valentini; Jean-Claude Zylberstein. **Entr. Hist.** 24 6:2000 pp.10-116. *Collection of 6 articles.*

1324 Embeddedness and the tourism industry in the Polish southern uplands: social processes as an explanatory framework. Ray Riley. **Eur. Urban Reg. Stud.** 7:3 7:2000 pp.195-210.

1325 The fashioned body: fashion, dress, and modern social theory. Joanne Entwistle. Malden MA: Polity Press, 2000. 258p. *ISBN: 074562006X, 0745620078. Includes bibliographical references and index.*

1326 French beach sports culture in the twentieth century. Michel Rainis. **Int. J. Hist. Sport** 17:1 3:2000 pp.144-158.

1327 The gathering storm: Manchester Storm supporter survey 1998. Garry Crawford. Salford: Institute for Social Research, University of Salford, 1998. 61p. *ISBN: 0904483274. Includes bibliographical references.* (*Series:* Salford papers in sociology - no. 25).

1328 Gazing on communism: heritage tourism and post-communist identities in Germany, Hungary and Romania; *[Summary in French]*. Duncan Light. **Tour. Geog.** 2:2 5:2000 pp.157-176.

1329 German travel cultures. Rudy Koshar. Oxford: Berg Publishers, 2000. 256p. *ISBN: 1859734510, 1859734464.*

1330 Global sport: identities, societies, civilizations. Joseph A. Maguire. Cambridge, Malden MA: Polity Press, Blackwell Publishers, 1999. x, 239p. *ISBN: 0745615317, 0745615325. Includes bibliographical references (p. [217]-232) and index.*

1331 Gothic, metal, rap, and rave - youth culture and its educational dimensions. Martina Claus-Bachmann; Ansgar Jerrentrup; Friedrich Neumann; Bettina Roccor; Stefanie Rhein; Gunther Diehl; Susanne Binas; Tamara Kurz. **World of Mus.** 42:1 2000 pp.13-148. *Collection of 9 articles.*

1332 Heroes and heroin: from True Romance to Pulp Fiction. Caroline Jewers. **J. Pop. Cult.** 33:4 Spring:2000 pp.39-62.

1333 *Homo videns*: la sociedad teledirigida. *[In Spanish]*; [*Homo videns*: the remote-controlled society]. Giovanni Sartori; Ana Díaz Soler. Madrid: Taurus, 1998. 159p. *ISBN: 8430602739. Includes bibliographical references (p. 155-159).*

1334 (The impact of television programs on drug users.); *[Text in Arabic]*. M.F. Al Qudah. **Dirasat Hum. Soc. Sc.** 26:Supp. 12:1999 pp.686-717.

1335 Inside subculture: the postmodern meaning of style. David Muggleton. Oxford, New York: Berg Publishers, 2000. viii, 198p. *ISBN: 1859733476, 1859733522. Includes bibliographical references (p. 175-190) and indexes.* (*Series:* Dress, body, culture).

1336 Intellectuals and popular television in China: *Expectations* as a cultural phenomenon. Wang Yi. **Int. Jour. Cult. Stud.** 2:2 8:1999 pp.222-245.

1337 An introduction to studying popular culture. Dominic Strinati. London: Routledge, 2000. xvi, 288p. *ISBN: 0415157668, 0415157676. Includes bibliographical references and index.*

1338 Looking for style: reconstructing acquisition of style in youth cultures; *[Summary in German]*. Burkhard Schäffer. **Sociologus** 49:2 1999 pp.160-179.

1339 Nerd nation: images of nerds in US popular culture. Lori Kendall. **Int. Jour. Cult. Stud.** 2:2 8:1999 pp.260-283.

1340 New age travellers: vanloads of uproarious humanity. Kevin Hetherington. London: Cassell, 2000. x, 191p. *ISBN: 0304339784, 0304339776. Includes bibliographical references and index.*

1341 'No one likes us, we don't care': the myth and reality of Millwall fandom. Garry Robson. Oxford: Berg Publishers, 2000. 203p. *ISBN: 1859733727, 1859733670. Includes index.*

1342 On the beaten track: tourism, art and place. Lucy R. Lippard. New York: New Press, 1999. 192p. *ISBN: 1565844548.*

D: CULTURE

1343 The Orange arch: creating tradition in Ulster. Neil Jarman. **Folklore [London]** 112:1 4:2001 pp.1-22.
1344 Performance-enhancing drugs in sport: response by the international sports community. Richard W. Pound. **Int. J.** LV:3 Summer:2000 pp.485-495.
1345 Performances, discourses, and trial balloons: negotiating change at special events. Evelyn Payne Hatcher. **Cult. Dyn.** 10:3 11:1998 pp.307-323.
1346 Photography, tourism and the Kodak Hula Show. Joyce D. Hammond. **Vis. Anthrop.** 14:1 2001 pp.1-32.
1347 Playing symbolically with death in extreme sports. David Le Breton. **Bod. Soc.** 6:1 3:2000 pp.1-12.
1348 Reisen til landet uten navn: countrykulturens rom. *[In Norwegian]*; (The space of country culture.) *[Summary]*. Synnøve Bøgeberg. **Nord. Ny.** 81 12:2000 pp.41-53.
1349 Risk functions for frequency of alcohol-related negative consequences: New Zealand survey data. Allan Wyllie; Jia-Fang Zhang; Sally Casswell. **Addiction** 95:12 12:2000 pp.1821-1832.
1350 Le sable et l'argile: à propos des pratiques ludiques et spectaculaires dans les Landes. *[In French]*; (Sand and clay: about play and show practices in the Landes.) Sébastien Darbon; Frédéric Saumade. **Ethn. Fr.** XXX:3 7-9:2000 pp.445-458.
1351 The social ageing of *Les Inrockuptibles*. Chris Andrews. **Fr. Cult. Stud.** 11(2):2 6:2000 pp.235-248.
1352 The social organization of sexuality and gender in alternative hard rock: an analysis of intersectionality. Mimi Schippers. **Gender Soc.** 14:6 12:2000 pp.747-764.
1353 Die soziale Konstruktion des japanischen Alpinismus. Kultur, Ideologie und Sport im modernen Bergsteigen. *[In German]*; (The social construction of Japanese alpinism. Culture, ideology and sports in modern mountaineering.) *[Summary]*. Wolfram Manzenreiter. **Beit. Japan.** 36 2000 pp.1-246.
1354 Sport as story: form and content in athletics. Joseph R. Gusfield. **Society** 37:4 5-6:2000 pp.63-80.
1355 Sport, health and drugs: a critical sociological perspective. Ivan Waddington. New York: Routledge, 2000. 200p. *ISBN: 0419251901, 0419252002.* Includes bibliographical references and index.
1356 Sport in Europe: politics, class, gender. J.A. Mangan [Ed.]. London: Frank Cass, 1999. ix, 268p. *ISBN: 0714649465, 0714680052.* Includes bibliographical references and index. (*Series:* The European sports history review - 1).
1357 Sportcult. Toby Miller [Ed.]; Randy Martin [Ed.]. Minneapolis MN, London: University of Minnesota Press, 1999. vii, 294p. *ISBN: 0816631840, 0816631832.* Includes bibliographical references. (*Series:* Cultural politics - 16).
1358 Sporting bodies: dynamics of shame and pride. Elspeth Probyn. **Bod. Soc.** 6:1 3:2000 pp.13-28.
1359 A telenovela brasileira: do nacionalismo à exportação. *[In Portuguese]*; [Brazilian soap operas: from nationalism to exports] *[Summary]*; *[Summary in French]*. Lidia Santos. **Caravelle** 75 2000 pp.137-150.
1360 Television and civilization: the unity of opposites? Michael Keane. **Int. Jour. Cult. Stud.** 2:2 8:1999 pp.246-259.
1361 'That shadowy realm of the interior': Oprah Winfrey and Hamlet's glass. Eva Illouz. **Int. Jour. Cult. Stud.** 2:1 4:1999 pp.109-131.
1362 'The Bali syndrome': the explosion and implosion of 'exotic' tourist spaces. Claudio Minca. **Tour. Geog.** 2:4 11:2000 pp.389-403.
1363 'The largest popular culture movement in the Western World': intellectuals and Gaúcho traditionalism in Brazil. Ruben George Oliven. **Am. Ethn.** 27:1 2:2000 pp.128-146.
1364 'This is not a rebel song': the Irish conflict and popular music. Bill Rolston. **Race Class** 42:3 1-3:2001 pp.49-67.
1365 The time race and time signification in the reform era: a study of changing movie theaters in urban China. Julia Lui Chu; Zhongdang Pan. **Int. Jour. Cult. Stud.** 2:1 4:1999 pp.33-57.

D: CULTURE

1366 Tourism and modernity: a sociological analysis. Ning Wang. Oxford: Pergamon, 2000. viii, 271p. *ISBN: 0080434460. Includes bibliographical references (p. 227-254) and indexes.* (*Series:* Tourism social science series).

1367 Le tourisme francophone en Louisiane: un enjeu identitaire. *[In French]*; [French speaking tourism in Louisiana: an issue of identity] *[Summary]*. Sara Le Menestrel. **Ethnologies** 21:1 1999 pp.133-162.

1368 Understanding sport and body culture in Japan. John Horne. **Bod. Soc.** 6:2 6:2000 pp.73-86.

1369 Values in sport: elitism, nationalism, gender equality, and the scientific manufacturing of winners. Claudio Marcello Tamburrini [Ed.]; Torbjörn Tännsjö [Ed.]. London, New York: E & FN Spon, 2000. 256p. *ISBN: 0419253602, 041925370X. Includes bibliographical references and index.* (*Series:* Ethics and sport book series).

1370 'Who's the mack?' The performativity and politics of the pimp figure in gangsta rap. Eithne Quinn. **J. Am. Stud.** 34:1 4:2000 pp.115-136.

1371 Zoos: public places to view private lives. S.M.P. Benbow. **J. Pop. Cult.** 33:4 Spring:2000 pp.13-24.

D.3: Religion
Religion

1372 African American women's definitions of spirituality and religiosity. Jacqueline S. Mattis. **J. Black Psychol.** 26:1 2:2000 pp.101-122.

1373 After atheism: religion and ethnicity in Russia and Central Asia. David C. Lewis. Richmond VA: Curzon, 2000. 320p. *ISBN: 0700711643. Includes bibliographical references (p. 311-316) and index.* (*Series:* Caucasus world).

1374 The being that knew too much. Patrick Grim. **Int. J. Philos. Relig.** 47:3 6:2000 pp.141-154.

1375 Beyond unbelief: religious uncertainty and religious indifference in countries with self-induced and enforced secularization. Heiner Meulemann. **Euro. Soc.** 2:2 2000 pp.167-194.

1376 Caste among Sikhs: dichotomy between belief & practice. Bhai Harbans Lal. **Sikh Rev.** 48:4(556) 4:2000 pp.47-60.

1377 Choice and religion: a critique of rational choice theory. Steve Bruce. Oxford, New York: Oxford University Press, 1999. ix, 247p. *ISBN: 0198295847. Includes bibliographical references.*

1378 The Church of Scientology. J. Gordon Melton. Salt Lake City UT: Signature Books, CESNUR, 2000. vi, 80p. *ISBN: 1560851392. Translated from the Italian Chiesa di Scientology. Includes bibliographical references (p. 79-80).* (*Series:* Studies in contemporary religions - 1).

1379 Cities of God. Graham Ward. London: Routledge, 2000. 368p. *ISBN: 0415202566, 0415202558.*

1380 Comparing religions through law: Judaism and Islam. Jacob Neusner; Tamara Sonn. London: Routledge, 1999. xii, 263p. *ISBN: 0415194865, 0415194873. Includes bibliographical references and index.*

1381 Conceptualizing religion and spirituality: points of commonality, points of departure. Peter C. Hill; Kenneth I. Pargament; Ralph W. Hood, Jr.; Michael E. McCullough; James P. Swyers; David B. Larson; Brian J. Zinnbauer. **J. Theory Soc. Behav.** 30:1 3:2000 pp.51-77.

1382 The Dao of ethics: from the writings of Levinas to the Daodejing. A.T. Nuyen. **J. Ch. Philos.** 27:3 9:2000 pp.287-298.

1383 Deux générations face à la mort. Acteurs de recompositions symboliques contemporaines. *[In French]*; (Two generations facing death: actors of symbolic reconstructions.) *[Summary]*. Jean-Pierre Hiernaux; Florence Vandendorpe; Edmond Legros. **Recher. Sociolog.** XXXI:1 2000 pp.111-122.

D: CULTURE

1384 The dynamics and destiny of Indian spirituality in the West: Hare Krishna. Arnaldo Nesti; Kim Knott; E. Burke Rochford, Jr.; Finn Madsen; Nurit Zaidman; István Kamarás; Silas Guerriero; Federico Squarcini. **Soc. Compass** 47:2 6:2000 pp.147-271. *Collection of 8 articles.*

1385 The dynamics of religious organizations: The extravasation of the sacred and other essays. Phillip E. Hammond. Oxford: Oxford University Press, 2000. 197p. *ISBN: 0198297629. Includes bibliographical references and index.*

1386 Edward Said and the religious effects of culture. William D. Hart. Cambridge, New York: Cambridge University Press, 2000. xiii, 236p. *ISBN: 0521770521, 0521778107. Includes bibliographical references (p. 228-234) and index. (Series:* Cambridge studies in religion and critical thought - 8).

1387 The enforcement of morality. John Kekes. **Am. Phil. Q.** 37:1 1:2000 pp.23-36.

1388 Ethics and faith: the reality of absolutes. Robert K. Garcia; Pamela Werrbach Proietti; Bradley N. Seeman; Peter Schotten; Oskar Gruenwald; Jesse J. Thomas; John E. Stapleford; Albert F. Spencer; David A. Grandy. **J. Interd. Stud.** XII:1-2 2000 pp.1-177. *Collection of 9 articles.*

1389 Evidential arguments from evil. Richard Otte. **Int. J. Philos. Relig.** 48:1 8:2000 pp.1-10.

1390 From Comte to Baudrillard: socio-theology after the end of the social. Andrew Wernick. **Theory Cult. Soc.** 17:6 12:2000 pp.55-75.

1391 From facts to God: an onto-cosmological argument. William F. Vallicella. **Int. J. Philos. Relig.** 48:3 12:2000 pp.157-182.

1392 From 'pagan' Muslims to 'baptized' communists: religious conversion and ethnic particularity in Russia's eastern provinces. Paul W. Werth. **Comp. Stud. S.** 42:3 7:2000 pp.497-523.

1393 From religious conformity to innovation: new ideas of religious journey and holy places. Nobutaka Inoue. **Soc. Compass** 47:1 3:2000 pp.21-32.

1394 Fundamentalism, sectarianism, and revolution: the Jacobin dimension of modernity. Shmuel Noah Eisenstadt. Cambridge, New York: Cambridge University Press, 1999. 280p. *ISBN: 0521641845, 0521645867. Includes bibliographical references and index. (Series:* Cambridge cultural studies).

1395 Georges Dumézil: theories, critiques and theoretical extensions. Dean A. Miller. **Religion** 30:1 1:2000 pp.27-40.

1396 Global perspectives on methodology in the study of religion. Armin W. Geertz. **Meth. Theo. Stud. Rel.** 12:1-2 2000 pp.49-73.

1397 Globalización y reconversión religiosa: ¿un reto a la identidad latinoamericana? *[In Spanish]*; (Globalization and religious reconversion: a challenge to the Latin American identity?) Silvio Platero. **Cuad. Nues. Am.** XIII:25 1-6:2000 pp.113-133.

1398 Les hindous croient-ils en la réincarnation? *[In French]*; [Do Hindus believe in reincarnation?] *[Summary]*. Robert Deliège. **Ann. Sociol.** 50:1 2000 pp.217-234.

1399 Hindu Varanasi. Wilbert M. Gesler; Margaret Pierce. **Geogr. Rev.** 90:2 4:2000 pp.222-237.

1400 The history of religion and the study of religion in Mexico. Yolotl González Torres. **Meth. Theo. Stud. Rel.** 12:1-2 2000 pp.38-48.

1401 Holistic revolution: the essential reader. William Bloom [Ed.]. London: Allen Lane, 2000. xix, 408p. *ISBN: 0713994215. Includes bibliographical references and index.*

1402 The idea of human dignity in classical Chinese philosophy: a reconstruction of Confucianism. Qianfan Zhang. **J. Ch. Philos.** 27:3 9:2000 pp.299-330.

1403 The integral paradigm: the truth of faith and the social sciences. Vincent Jeffries. **Am. Sociol.** 30:4 Winter:1999 pp.36-55.

1404 Is 'God exists' a 'hinge proposition' of religious belief? Duncan Pritchard. **Int. J. Philos. Relig.** 47:3 6:2000 pp.129-140.

1405 Jesus in Disneyland: religion in postmodern times. David Lyon. Cambridge, Malden MA: Blackwell Publishers, 2000. 188p. *ISBN: 0745614892, 0745614884. Includes bibliographical references and index.*

D: CULTURE

1406 „Kampf der Götter" — „Polytheismus der Werte": Variationen zu einem Thema von Max Weber. *[In German]*; ('Struggle of the gods' — 'polytheism of values': variations on Max Weber's theme.) *[Summary]*. Hartmann Tyrell. **Social. Int.** 37:2 1999 pp.157-187.

1407 A magyar vallási helyzet öt dimenziója. *[In Hungarian]*; (Five dimensions of Hungary's religious situation.) Miklós Tomka. **Mag. Tud.** 44:5 1999 pp.549-559.

1408 The measure of American religion: toward improving the state-of-the-art. Brian Steensland; Jerry Z. Park; Mark D. Regnerus; Lynn D. Robinson; W. Bradford Wilcox; Robert D. Woodberry. **Soc. Forc.** 79:1 9:2000 pp.291-318.

1409 Mediascape missionaries? Notes on religion as identity in a local African setting. Knut Lundby; Daniel Dayan. **Int. Jour. Cult. Stud.** 2:3 12:1999 pp.398-417.

1410 The middle way: theology, politics and economics in the later thought of R.H.Preston. R. John Elford [Ed.]; Ian S. Markham [Ed.]. London: SCM Press, 2000. 303p. *ISBN: 0334027934.*

1411 Moderner Fundamentalismus. *[In German]*; (Modern fundamentalism.) *[Summary]*; *[Summary in French]*. Stefan Breuer. **Berl. J. Soziol.** 10:1 2000 pp.5-20.

1412 Molinism and compatibilism. Kenneth J. Perszyk. **Int. J. Philos. Relig.** 48:1 8:2000 pp.11-34.

1413 Negative theology in Heidegger's *Beiträge zur Philosophie*. David R. Law. **Int. J. Philos. Relig.** 48:3 12:2000 pp.139-156.

1414 A népi vallásosságról. *[In Hungarian]*; (Folk religion.) Tamás Mohay. **Mag. Tud.** 44:5 1999 pp.535-548.

1415 Neue Geistliche Gemeinschaften und Bewegungen — Prototypen einer Kirche als sozialem Netzwerk. *[In German]*; [New religious communitites and movements - prototypes of a church as social network]. Michael Hochschild. **Social. Int.** 38:1 2000 pp.115-140.

1416 The New Age: a survey and critique. George D. Chryssides. **Glob. Dial.** 2:1 Winter:2000 pp.109-119.

1417 The new cult phenomenon in Philippine society. Gerry Lanuza. **Phil. Stud.** 47:4 1999 pp.492-514.

1418 New religious movements as indicators of the de-structuring of religion and of mutations in the symbolic field. Françoise Champion. **Social. Int.** 38:1 2000 pp.47-62.

1419 Ninian Smart and the phenomenological approach to religious education. L. Philip Barnes. **Religion** 30:4 10:2000 pp.315-332.

1420 Nivison and the 'problem' in Xunzi's ethics. James Behuniak; David S. Nivison [Comments by]. **Philos. E.W.** 50:1 1:2000 pp.97-118.

1421 Novaiazychestvo v sovremennoi kul'ture. *[In Russian]*; (Neopaganism in modern culture.) V. Krutous. **Svobod. Mysl'** 7 2000 pp.78-89.

1422 Observations on the scholarly study of religions as pursued in some Muslim countries. Jacques Waardenburg. **Meth. Theo. Stud. Rel.** 12:1-2 2000 pp.91-109.

1423 On Huang Tsung-hsi's understanding of the *Mencius*. Shu-Hsien Liu. **J. Ch. Philos.** 27:3 9:2000 pp.251-268.

1424 On polytropy: or the natural condition of spiritual cosmopolitanism in India: the Digambar Jain case. Michael Carrithers. **Mod. Asian S.** 34:4 10:2000 pp.831-862.

1425 Ostdeutschland — Ein weites Feld für „neue religiöse Bewegungen"? *[In German]*; [East Germany - a wide sphere for 'new religious movements']. Klaus Hartmann. **Social. Int.** 38:1 2000 pp.73-86.

1426 Philosophy of change and the deconstruction of self in the *Zhuangzi*. Youru Wang. **J. Ch. Philos.** 27:3 9:2000 pp.345-360.

1427 Race, immorality and money in the American Baha'i community: impeaching the Los Angeles spiritual assembly. Juan R.I. Cole. **Religion** 30:2 4:2000 pp.109-148.

1428 'Reference' to D. Z. Phillips. Randy Ramal. **Int. J. Philos. Relig.** 48:1 8:2000 pp.35-56.

1429 Regional religions? Extending the 'semi-involuntary' thesis of African-American religious participation. Matthew O. Hunt; Larry L. Hunt. **Sociol. For.** 15:4 12:2000 pp.569-594.

D: CULTURE

1430 Religion and community. Keith Ward. Oxford; New York: Clarendon Press; Oxford University Press, 2000. 366p. *ISBN: 019875258X*. *Includes bibliographical references and indexes.*

1431 Religion and race in Latin America. Antonio Mutti; Roberto J. Blancarte; Ari Pedro Oro; Pablo Semán; Antônio Flávio Pierucci; Reginaldo Prandi; Roberto Motta. **Int. Sociol.** 15:4 12:2000 pp.591-682. *Collection of 5 articles.*

1432 Religion and society in modern Europe. René Rémond. Oxford, Malden MA: Blackwell Publishers, 1999. viii, 237p. *ISBN: 0631208186, 0631208178. Translated from the French Religion et société en Europe. Includes bibliographical references and index. (Series:* The making of Europe).

1433 Religion et religiosité en Amérique Latine. *[In French]*; [Religion and religiosity in Latin America]. Thomas Calvo; Christophe Guidicelli; Pierre Ragon; Thérèse Bouysse-Cassagne; Virginie de Véricourt; Philippe Waniez; Violette Brustlein. **Cah. Amer. Lat.** 33 2000 pp.13-123. *Collection of 6 articles.*

1434 Religion in modern Europe: a memory mutates. Grace Davie. New York: Oxford University Press, 2000. 218p. *ISBN: 0198280653. Includes bibliographical references and index. (Series:* European societies).

1435 Religion in the contemporary world: a sociological introduction. Alan Aldridge. Malden MA; Cambridge: Blackwell Publishers; Polity Press, 2000. vii, 232p. *ISBN: 0745620825, 0745620833. Includes bibliographical references (p. [216]-226) and index.*

1436 Religiöse Wiedergeburt und Entstehung einer neuen „konfessionellen Landschaft" in Rußland. *[In German]*; [Religious renaissance and the creation of a new 'confessional landscape' in Russia]. Aleksej Krindač. **Osteuropa** 50:2 2:2000 pp.161-175.

1437 Religiosity and agency and communion: their relationship to religious judgmentalism. Richard Beck; C. Dewayne Miller. **J. Psychol.** 134:3 5:2000 pp.315-324.

1438 Religious attributions and proximity of influence: an investigation of direct interventions and distal explanations. Matthew Weeks; Michael B. Lupfer. **J. Sci. S. Relig.** 39:3 9:2000 pp.348-362.

1439 Religious brand loyalty and political loyalties. Paul Djupe. **J. Sci. S. Relig.** 39:1 3:2000 pp.78-89.

1440 Religious diversity: where exclusivists often go wrong. David Basinger. **Int. J. Philos. Relig.** 47:1 2:2000 pp.43-56.

1441 Religious minorities in Iran. Eliz Sanasarian. New York: Cambridge University Press, 2000. 229p. *ISBN: 0521770734. Includes bibliographical references and index. (Series:* Cambridge Middle East studies).

1442 Repentance in civic and religious traditions. Amitai Etzioni; Gordon Bazemore; Estelle Frankel; Patrick Glynn; John O. Haley. **Am. Behav. Sc.** 41:6 3:1998 pp.764-867. *Collection of 5 articles.*

1443 Resources, race, and female-headed congregations in the United States. Mary Ellen Konieczny; Mark Chaves. **J. Sci. S. Relig.** 39:3 9:2000 pp.261-271.

1444 Revolutionizing spirituality: reflections on Marxism and religion. John Brentlinger. **Sci. Soc.** 64:2 Summer:2000 pp.171-193.

1445 The role of method and theory in the IAHR. Armin W. Geertz; Russell T. McCutcheon. **Meth. Theo. Stud. Rel.** 12:1-2 2000 pp.3-37.

1446 Seeking the seekers in the sociology of religion; *[Summary in French]*. Margit Warburg. **Soc. Compass** 48:1 3:2001 pp.91-102.

1447 The Sikh identity in contemporary world. Ujagar Singh Bawa. **Sikh Rev.** 48:4(556) 4:2000 pp.82-92.

1448 Sinnsuche und das Phänomen der neuen religiösen Bewegung. *[In German]*; [The search for meaning and the phenomenon of the new religious movement]. Christel Gärtner. **Social. Int.** 38:1 2000 pp.87-114.

1449 The sociology of religion. Gerry Lanuza. **Phil. Stud.** 47:3 1999 pp.351-379.

1450 The sociology of religion in Britain. A hybrid case. Grace Davie. **Schweiz. Z. Soziologie** 26:1 3:2000 pp.193-218.

D: CULTURE

1451 Stalemate and strategy: rethinking the evidential argument from evil. J.L. Schellenberg. **Am. Phil. Q.** 37:4 10:2000 pp.405-419.
1452 The supply-side model of religion: the Nordic and Baltic states. Steve Bruce. **J. Sci. S. Relig.** 39:1 3:2000 pp.32-46.
1453 Szabadkőművesség és természetes vallás. *[In Hungarian]*; [Freemasonry and natural religion]. Róbert Péter. **Valóság** 42:9 1999 pp.18-35.
1454 Tecnologie del sé e industria della coscienza. *[In Italian]*; [Technologies of self and industry of conscience]. Marcello Tarì. **Critica Sociol.** 133 Spring:2000 pp.73-84.
1455 Theologizing in Asia: pluralism, relativism and subjectivism. Vimal Tirimanna. **Asia J. Theol.** 14:1 4:2000 pp.57-67.
1456 *Tongbian*: a Chinese strand of thought. Chenshan Tian. **J. Ch. Philos.** 27:4 12:2000 pp.441-468.
1457 Tra *New Age* e *Next Age*. *[In Italian]*; (Between New Age and Next Age: the Movement of Spiritual Inner Awareness.) *[Summary]*. Massimo Introvigne. **Critica Sociol.** 133 Spring:2000 pp.2-19.
1458 Ultimate concern and language engagement: a reexamination of the opening message of the *Dao-De-Jing*. Bo Mou. **J. Ch. Philos.** 27:4 12:2000 pp.429-440.
1459 The varieties of sacred experience: finding the sacred in a secular grove. N.J. Demerath, III. **J. Sci. S. Relig.** 39:1 3:2000 pp.1-11.
1460 When psychotherapy replaces religion. James Davison Hunter. **Publ. Inter.** 139 Spring:2000 pp.5-21.
1461 Wiederkehr des Religiösen? *[In German]*; [The retreat of religion?] Detlef Pollack. **Social. Int.** 38:1 2000 pp.13-46.
1462 William Johnson's contemplation approach to Buddhist-Christian dialogue. Yuen-tai So. **Ch. Feng** 42:1-2 3-6:1999 pp.83-110.
1463 Women and religion. Majella Franzmann. New York: Oxford University Press, 1999. 192p. *ISBN: 019510773X. Includes bibliographical references and index.*

Buddhism
Bouddhisme

1464 Le bouddhisme en Occident: approches sociologique et anthropologique. *[In French]*; [Buddhism in the Western World: sociological and anthropological approaches]. Lionel Obadia; Martin Baumann; Michelle Spuler; Elke Hahlbohm-Helmus; Norbert Chelli; Louis Hourmant; Éric Rommeluère. **Recher. Sociolog.** XXXI:3 2000 pp.1-132. *Collection of 8 articles.*
1465 Buddhism in East Asia. D. P. Singhal. New Delhi: Books & Books, 2000. xi, 216p. *ISBN: 8185016569. Includes bibliographical references (p. [199]-210) and index.*
1466 Dramatic intervention: human rights from a Buddhist perspective. Peter D. Hershock. **Philos. E.W.** 50:1 1:2000 pp.9-33.
1467 Dynamics of the Buddhist revival movement in south China: state, society and transnationalism. Yoshiko Ashiwa. **Hito. J. Soc. Stud.** 32:1 7:2000 pp.15-31.
1468 Folk Buddhism in Lao rural environment. Georges Condominas. **S. E. Asian R.** XXIV:1-2 1-12:1999 pp.21-52.
1469 How the swans came to Lake Michigan: the social organization of Buddhist Chicago. Paul David Numrich. **J. Sci. S. Relig.** 39:2 6:2000 pp.189-203.
1470 Odrodzenie buddyzmu w Mongolii po 1990 roku. *[In Polish]*; (The revival of Buddhism in Mongolia after 1990.) Agata Bareja-Starzyńska; Thupten Kunga Chashab; Marek Mejor. **Przeg. Orient.** 3-4 1999 pp.213-238.
1471 The scrambling of the sacred and the profane by the contemporary Sinhalese Buddhist traders in the city of Kandy, Sri Lanka: a case study. Desmond Mallikarachchi. **Sri Lanka J. Soc. Sci.** 21:1-2 6-12:1998 pp.135-166.
1472 William James and Buddhism: American pragmatism and the Orient. David Scott. **Religion** 30:4 10:2000 pp.333-352.

1473 Zhuangzi's fishnet allegory: a text-critical analysis. Hans-Georg Möller. **J. Ch. Philos.** 27:4 12:2000 pp.489-502.

Christianity
Christianisme

1474 The British Black Pentecostal 'revival': identity and belief in the 'new' Nigerian churches. Stephen Hunt; Nicola Lightly. **Ethn. Racial** 24:1 1:2001 pp.104-130.
1475 Catholicism, politics and society in twentieth-century France. Kay Chadwick [Ed.]. Liverpool: Liverpool University Press, 2000. 295p. *ISBN: 0853239843, 0853239746.*
1476 (Christian culture and the African peasantry in 20th century Western Kenya.); *[Text in Japanese]*. Nobuhiro Nakabayashi. **St. Ess. Beh. Sc. Phil.** 20 3:2000 pp.29-64.
1477 The Christian understanding of God as transcendence and immanence: a response to Liu Shu-hsien's understanding of the 'pure transcendence of God'. Benedict Hung-biu Kwok. **Ch. Feng** 42:1-2 3-6:1999 pp.35-58.
1478 Christianisme(s). *[In French]*; [Christianity/-ies]. Ernest-Marie Laperrousaz; François Vouga; Jean-Daniel Dubois; Bernard Cottret; Émile Poulat; Michael Löwy; Frei Betto; Antoine Casanova. **Pensée** 322 4-6:2000 pp.5-115. *Collection of 8 articles.*
1479 Church-based community activism: a comparison of Black and White Catholic congregations. James C. Cavendish. **J. Sci. S. Relig.** 39:1 3:2000 pp.64-77.
1480 Claiming the social passion: the role of the United Church of Canada in creating a culture of social well-being in Canadian society. Ted Reeve. Toronto: Moderator's Consultation on Faith and the Economy, 1999. 120p. *ISBN: 1551341123. Includes bibliographical references.*
1481 Credentialism across creeds: clergy education and stratification in Protestant denominations. Paul Perl; Patricia M.Y. Chang. **J. Sci. S. Relig.** 39:2 6:2000 pp.171-188.
1482 The dead hand of human rights: contrasting Christianities in post-transition Malawi. Harri Englund. **J. Mod. Afr. S.** 38:4 12:2000 pp.579-603.
1483 Developing Christian characters in multi-cultural Asian societies: problems, goals and suggestions. Shun-hing Chan. **Asia J. Theol.** 14:1 4:2000 pp.154-169.
1484 Drumcree: a struggle for recognition. Peter Mulholland. **Irish J. Soc.** 9 1999 pp.5-30.
1485 En torno a la crisis de Manos Unidas. *[In Spanish]*; (Apropos the *Manos Unidas* crisis.) Revista de Fomento Social. **Rev. Fom. Soc.** 55:219 7-9:2000 pp.311-339.
1486 The evolution of Western individualism. Andreas Buss. **Religion** 30:1 1:2000 pp.1-25.
1487 A finite God reconsidered. Frank B. Dilley. **Int. J. Philos. Relig.** 47:1 2:2000 pp.29-42.
1488 Gay and lesbian Christians: homosexual and religious identity integration in the members and participants of a gay-positive church. Eric M. Rodriguez; Suzanne C. Ouellette. **J. Sci. S. Relig.** 39:3 9:2000 pp.333-347.
1489 A hermeneutical proposal for the interpretation of Korean Christianity: fusion of horizons, paradigm shifts, and conversion experience. Jiwhang Lew. **Ch. Feng** 42:1-2 3-6:1999 pp.59-82.
1490 History, opposition, and salvation in Agarabi Adventism. George Westermark. **Pac. Stud.** 21:3 9:1998 pp.51-71.
1491 Hit és tudomány a katolikus teológia szemszögéből. A keresztény teológia tudomány jellege. *[In Hungarian]*; (Belief and scholarship viewed from the angle of Catholic theology.) Béla Weissmahr. **Mag. Tud.** 44:5 1999 pp.514-526.
1492 Introduction to the sociology of missions. Robert L. Montgomery. Westport CT: Praeger, 2000. xxi, 183p. *ISBN: 0275966917. Includes bibliographical references and index.*
1493 Jubileo del año 2000: ¿centralidad de la Iglesia o de los pueblos oprimidos? *[In Spanish]*; (Jubilee 2000: centrality of the church or of the oppressed people?) Giulio Girardi. **Cuad. Nues. Am.** XIII:25 1-6:2000 pp.76-88.
1494 Levensloop en kerkverlating: een nieuwe en overkoepelende verklaring voor enkele empirische regelmatigheden. *[In Dutch]*; (Life course and leaving the church: a new and

D: CULTURE

comprehensive explanation for some empirical regularities.) Nan Dirk de Graaf; Ariana Need; Wout Ultee. **Mens Maat.** 75:3 9:2000 pp.229-257.

1495 Life in a Hutterite colony: an outsider's experience and reflections on a forgotten people in our midst. Donald W. Huffman. **Am. J. Econ. S.** 59:4 10:2000 pp.549-571.

1496 The Mormons of Malaybalay. Lucita G. Tilanduca. **Phil. Stud.** 47:3 1999 pp.380-392.

1497 Muscular Christianity. Stuart J. Smyth. **Asia J. Theol.** 14:1 4:2000 pp.68-81.

1498 Native evangelism in Central Mexico. Hugo G. Nutini. **Ethnology** XXXIX:1 Winter:2000 pp.39-54.

1499 On the road to Częstochowa: rhetoric and experience on a Polish pilgrimage. Marysia Galbraith. **Anthr. Quart.** 73:2 4:2000 pp.61-73.

1500 Organizational revival from within: explaining revivalism and reform in the Roman Catholic Church. Roger Finke; Patricia Wittberg. **J. Sci. S. Relig.** 39:2 6:2000 pp.154-170.

1501 Il paradigma esoterico e un modello di applicazione. Note sul movimento gnostico di Samael Aun Weor. *[In Italian]*; [The esoteric paradigm and an application model: notes on the Gnostic movement of Samael Aun Weor]. Pierluigi Zoccatelli. **Critica Sociol.** 135 Autumn:2000 pp.33-49.

1502 Parrocchie romane: in vista del Giubileo. *[In Italian]*; [Roman parishes: in view of the millennium]. Diletta Belardinelli. **Critica Sociol.** 133 Spring:2000 pp.133-150.

1503 The politics of evangelism: masculinity and religious conversion among Gitanos. Paloma Gay y Blasco. **Rom. Stud.** 10:1 6:2000 pp.1-22.

1504 Post i abstynencja w ortodoksyjnym kościele koptyjskim. *[In Polish]*; (Fasting and abstinency in the orthodox Coptic church.) Iza Elżbieta Smolińska. **Przeg. Orient.** 3-4 1999 pp.247-258.

1505 Pravoslavnyi fundamentalizm. *[In Russian]*; (Orthodox fundamentalism.) K.N. Kostiuk. **Polis [Moscow]** 5(58) 2000 pp.133-154.

1506 Relational trinity and its conceptual implications for Asian community. Salai Hla Aung. **Asia J. Theol.** 14:1 4:2000 pp.82-92.

1507 Religion as a source of social change in the new South Africa. Robert C. Garner. **J. Relig. Afr.** XXX:3 2000 pp.310-343.

1508 Religious market share and intensity of church involvement in five denominations. Paul Perl; Daniel V.A. Olson. **J. Sci. S. Relig.** 39:1 3:2000 pp.12-31.

1509 La renovación Carismática Católica en la Argentina: ¿religiosidad popular, comunidad emocional o nuevo movimiento religioso? *[In Spanish]*; [The Catholic Charismatic Renewal in Argentina: popular religiosity, emotional community or a new religious movement?] Abelardo Jorge Soneira. **Scr. Ethn.** XXII 2000 pp.149-161.

1510 Scotland's shame? bigotry and sectarianism in modern Scotland. T. M. Devine [Ed.]. Edinburgh: Mainstream, 2000. 281p. *ISBN: 1840183306. Includes bibliographical references (p. 273-281).*

1511 Šetření ISSP 1998 — náboženství. *[In Czech]*; (International social survey program 1998 — religion.) *[Summary]*. Dana Hamplová. **Soc. Čas.** 36:4 2000 pp.431-440.

1512 'To whom much has been given...': religious capital and community voluntarism among churchgoing Protestants. Jerry Z. Park; Christian Smith. **J. Sci. S. Relig.** 39:3 9:2000 pp.272-286.

1513 Understanding anti-Catholicism in Northern Ireland. John D. Brewer; Gareth I. Higgins. **Sociology** 33:2 5:1999 pp.235-255.

1514 Whatever happened to what used to be the largest Catholic country in the world? Patrícia Birman; Márcia Pereira Leite. **Dædalus** 129:2 Spring:2000 pp.271-290.

1515 What's God got to do with the American experiment? John J. DiIulio, Jr. [Ed.]; E.J. Dionne [Ed.]. Washington DC: Brookings Institution Press, 2000. xvii, 188p. *ISBN: 0815718691. Includes bibliographical references (p. 171-176) and index.*

1516 Why angels fall: a portrait of Orthodox Europe from Byzantium to Kosovo. Victoria Clark. London: Macmillan, 2000. xviii, 460p. *ISBN: 033375185X. Includes bibliographical references and index.*

Islam
Islam

1517 Alevi politics in contemporary Turkey. Tahire Erman; Emrah Göker. **Middle E. Stud.** 36:4 10:2000 pp.99-118.

1518 (*Am* in language and the holy Qur'an.); *[Text in Arabic]*. Mahmoud A. Jaffal. **Dirasat Hum. Soc. Sc.** 26:Supp. 12:1999 pp.895-912.

1519 Fluid identities: Muslims and Western Europe's nation states. Jorgen S. Nielsen. **Cam. R. Int. Aff.** XIII:2 Spring-Summer:2000 pp.212-227.

1520 Getting God's ear: women, Islam, and healing in Saudi Arabia and the Gulf. Eleanor Abdella Doumato. New York: Columbia University Press, 2000. xii, 312p. *ISBN: 0231116667, 0231116675. Includes bibliographical references (p. 285-303) and index.*

1521 I sentieri di Allah: aspetti della diffusione dell'Islam delle confraternite in Italia. *[In Italian]*; [The ways of Allah: aspects of the diffusion of Islam from Italian communities] *[Summary]*. Fabrizio Speziale. **Critica Sociol.** 135 Autumn:2000 pp.10-32.

1522 In the house of the law: gender and Islamic law in Ottoman Syria and Palestine. Judith E. Tucker. Berkeley CA: University of California Press, 1998. xi, 221p. *ISBN: 0520210395. Includes bibliographical references (p. 211-216) and index.*

1523 Islam and modernism in Egypt. Charles C. Adams. New York: Routledge, 2000. 283p. *ISBN: 0415209080. Includes bibliographical references.* (*Series:* Orientalism - 10).

1524 Islam and society in Turkey. David Shankland. Huntingdon: Eothen, 1999. x, 240p. *ISBN: 0906719275, 0906719267. Includes bibliographical references (p. [215]-228) and index.*

1525 Islam and the challenge of religious pluralism. Mahmoud M. Ayoub. **Glob. Dial.** 2:1 Winter:2000 pp.53-64.

1526 Islam as 'the middle path'. Larry Poston. **Am. J. Islam. Soc. Sci.** 17:1 Spring:2000 pp.85-99.

1527 L'islam dans la culture des Qazaqs de Sibérie occidentale. *[In French]*; (The place of Islam in western Siberia's Kazakh culture.) *[Summary]*. Šulpan K. Ahmetova. **Cah. Mon. Russe** 41:2-3 4-9:2000 pp.357-368.

1528 L'islam et la fin du voyage: comment l'autre est devenu occident. *[In French]*; [Islam and the end of the journey: how the other became the West]. Tahar Labib. **Soc. Compass** 47:1 3:2000 pp.11-20.

1529 The Islamic factor in Dagestan. Robert Bruce Ware; Enver Kisriev. **C. Asian Sur.** 19:2 6:2000 pp.235-252.

1530 The Islamization of Ottoman cities. Marc David Baer. **New Persp. Turk.** 20 Spring:1999 pp.132-142.

1531 Minorities in contemporary Islamist discourse. Uriah Furman. **Middle E. Stud.** 36:4 10:2000 pp.1-20.

1532 The Muslim family in Europe. Fatima Husain; Margaret O'Brien; Christiane Timmerman; Zafar Khan; Saeed Zokaei; David Phillips; Edien Bartels; Trees Pels; Mustafa Hussain. **Curr. Sociol.** 48:4 10:2000 pp.1-116. *Collection of 7 articles.*

1533 Muslim women and Islamic tradition: studies in modernisation. Mariam Allana [Ed.]. New Delhi: Kanishka Publishers, 2000. vi, 270p. *ISBN: 8173913447. Includes bibliographical references and index.*

1534 La passion pour le Prophète aux Comores et en Afrique de l'Est, ou l'épopée du *Maulid al-Barzandji*. *[In French]*; [Passion for the Prophet in the Comoros and in East Africa, or the saga of *Maulid al-Barzandji*]. Abdallah Chanfi Ahmed. **Islam Soc. S. Sah.** 13 12:1999 pp.65-90.

1535 La place des musulmans dans le multiculturalisme laïc en Grande-Bretagne. *[In French]*; [A place for Muslims in the secular multiculturalism of Great Britain]. Tariq Modood; Albert Bastenier [Comments by]. **Soc. Compass** 47:1 3:2000 pp.41-60.

1536 Praxis of *taqiyya*: the perseverance of the Pashaye Ismaili enclave, Nangarhar, Afghanistan. Hafizullah Emadi. **C. Asian Sur.** 19:2 6:2000 pp.253-264.

1537 The rise of Sunni militancy in Pakistan: the changing role of Islamism and the Ulama in society and politics. S.V.R. Nasr. **Mod. Asian S.** 34:1 2:2000 pp.139-180.

D: CULTURE

1538   The Salafi movement in Jordan. Quintan Wiktorowicz. **Int. J. M. E. Stud.** 32:2 5:2000 pp.219-240.

1539   Le syncrétisme islam-paganisme chez les peuples türks de Sibérie occidentale. *[In French]*; (The Islam/paganism syncretism among West Siberia's Turkic peoples.) *[Summary]*. Aleksandr G. Seleznev. **Cah. Mon. Russe** 41:2-3 4-9:2000 pp.341-356.

1540   Tendances actuelles de l'islam au Cameroun: état des lieux et perspectives. *[In French]*; [Current trends in Islam in Cameroon]. Gilbert L. Taguem Fah. **Afr. Cont.** 194 4-6:2000 pp.53-66.

1541   Visible Islam in modern Turkey. Adil Özdemir; Kenneth Frank. Basingstoke: Macmillan, 2000. 259p. *ISBN: 0333776704, 0312234791. Includes bibliographical references.*

1542   'Where East meets West': the development of Qur'anic education in Darfur. Rüdiger Seeseman. **Islam Soc. S. Sah.** 13 12:1999 pp.41-64.

1543   Whither Islam? A survey of modern movements in the Moslem world. H.A.R. Gibb [Ed.]. New York: Routledge, 2000. 384p. *ISBN: 0415209072. (Series:* Orientalism - 9).

Judaism
Judaïsme

1544   Death rests a while: holy day and Sabbath effects on Jewish mortality in Israel. J. Anson; O. Anson. **Soc. Sci. Med.** 52:1 1:2001 pp.83-98.

1545   Defenders of the faith: inside ultra-Orthodox Jewry. Samuel C. Heilman. Berkeley CA: University of California Press, 2000. xxi, 400p. *ISBN: 0520221125. Includes bibliographical references (p. [371]-389) and index.*

1546   Jewish fundamentalism in Israel. Israël Shahak; Norton Mezvinsky. London, Sterling VA: Pluto Press, 1999. xvi, 176p. *ISBN: 0745312810. Includes bibliographical references and index. (Series:* Pluto Middle Eastern).

1547   Judaism and the Copernican shift in the universe of faiths. Dan Cohn-Sherbok. **Glob. Dial.** 2:1 Winter:2000 pp.25-36.

1548   Promoting injury or freedom: radical pluralism and Orthodox Jewish symbolism. Davina Cooper. **Ethn. Racial** 23:6 11:2000 pp.1062-1085.

1549   Sifting through tradition: the creation of Jewish feminist identities. Lynn Resnick Dufour. **J. Sci. S. Relig.** 39:1 3:2000 pp.90-106.

1550   Sir Sidney Hamburger and Manchester Jewry: religion, city, and community. Bill Williams. Portland OR: Valentine Mitchell, 1999. 306p. *ISBN: 0853033633, 0853033706. Includes bibliographical references and index. (Series:* Parkes-Wiener series on Jewish studies).

1551   The spiritual self-in-relation: empathy and the construction of spirituality among modern descendants of the Spanish Crypto-Jews. Janet Liebman Jacobs. **J. Sci. S. Relig.** 39:1 3:2000 pp.53-63.

1552   What is scepticism and can it be found in the Hebrew Bible? William H.U. Anderson. **Scan. J. Old. Test.** 13:2 1999 pp.225-257.

D.4:   **Science and knowledge**
       Science et connaissance

1553   Aleksandr Bogdanov's history, sociology and philosophy of science. Arran Gare. **Stud. Hist. Phil. Sci.** 31A:2 6:2000 pp.231-248.

1554   'All that is solid melts into air': historians of technology in the information revolution. Rosalind Williams. **Technol. Cul.** 41:4 10:2000 pp.641-668.

1555   Aspects of Aristotelian statics in Galileo's dynamics. J. De Groot. **Stud. Hist. Phil. Sci.** 31A:4 12:2000 pp.645-664.

1556   L'aventure des disciplines: trois thèses dans les études de la science contemporaine. *[In French]*; [The adventure of disciplines: three theses in the study of contemporary science]. Gilles Klein. **Cah. Int. Soc.** CIX 7-12:2000 pp.393-414.

D: CULTURE

1557 Book history and the sciences. Jonathan R. Topham; Adrian Johns; Leslie Howsam; Nicolaas Rupke. **Br. J. Hist. Sci.** 33:2(116) 6:2000 pp.155-222. *Collection of 4 articles.*

1558 Cataloguing power: delineating 'competent naturalists' and the meaning of species in the British Museum. Gordon McOuat. **Br. J. Hist. Sci.** 34:1(120) 3:2001 pp.1-28.

1559 Cleavage: technology, controversy, and the ironies of the man-made breast. Nora Jacobson. New Brunswick NJ, London: Rutgers University Press, 2000. vii, 302p. *ISBN: 0813527155, 0813527147. Includes bibliographical references and index.*

1560 A companion to the philosophy of science. W.H. Newton-Smith [Ed.]. Malden MA: Blackwell Publishers, 2000. xvi, 576p. *ISBN: 0631170243. Includes bibliographical references and index. (Series:* Blackwell companions to philosophy - 18).

1561 La construction du savoir dans les discussions scientifiques. Apports de la linguistique interactionnelle et de l'analyse conversationnelle à la sociologie des sciences. *[In French]*; (The construction of knowledge within scientific discussions.) *[Summary]*; *[Summary in German]*. Lorenza Mondada. **Schweiz. Z. Soziologie** 26:3 12:2000 pp.615-636.

1562 Constructive tensions in feminist technology studies. Maria Lohan. **Soc. Stud. Sci.** 30:6 12:2000 pp.895-916.

1563 Constructuing rBST in Canada: biotechnology, instability and the management of nature; *[Summary in French]*. Kevin Edson Jones. **Can. J. Soc.** 25:3 Summer:2000 pp.311-341.

1564 Controlling our destinies: historical, philosophical, ethical, and theological perspectives on the Human Genome Project. Phillip R. Sloan [Ed.]. Notre Dame IN: University of Notre Dame Press, 1999. xxx, 535p. *ISBN: 0268008205, 0268008183. Includes bibliographical references and index. (Series:* Studies in science and the humanities from the Reilly Center for Science, Technology, and Values - 5).

1565 Coordination des connaissances spécialisées et expertise: théorie et application empirique. *[In French]*; (Co-ordination of specialised knowledge and expertise: theory and empirical application.) *[Summary]*. F. Munier; K. Nanopoulos. **Ec. Sociét.** XXXIV:5 5:2000 pp.79-94.

1566 The cultural dynamics of science. Sal Restivo; Julia Loughlin; Isabel Licha; Dhirendra Sharma; Assata Zerai; Jennifer L. Croissant; Wenda K. Bauchspies. **Cult. Dyn.** 12:2 7:2000 pp.135-260. *Collection of 6 articles.*

1567 Defenders of the truth: the battle for science in the sociobiology debate and beyond. Ullica Christina Olofsdotter Segerstråle. Oxford: Oxford University Press, 2000. 493p. *ISBN: 0198505051.*

1568 Democratizing philosophy of science for local knowledge movements: issues and challenges. Sandra Harding. **Gen. Tech. Dev.** 4:1 1-4:2000 pp.1-24.

1569 Drei Argumente für die Freiheit der Wissenschaft. *[In German]*; [Three arguments for the freedom of science] *[Summary]*. Kurt Bayertz. **Arc. Recht. Soz.** 86:3 2000 pp.303-326.

1570 Explaining theory choice: an assessment of the critical realist contribution to explanation in science. Mark S. Peacock. **J. Theory Soc. Behav.** 30:3 9:2000 pp.319-339.

1571 The extent of the present. William Craig. **Int. Phil. Sci.** 14:2 7:2000 pp.165-186.

1572 Femmes en sciences: obstacles, défits et enjeux. *[In French]*; [Women in science: obstacles, challenges and issues]. O.K. Ben Hassine. **R. Tun. Sci. Soc.** 36:118 1999 pp.11-26.

1573 For an aesthetics of knowing: twenty conjectures on the responsiveness to connections in science practices. Sergio Manghi. **Wor. Futur.** 55:3 2000 pp.277-292.

1574 Fundamental and accidental symmetries. Peter Kosso. **Int. Phil. Sci.** 14:2 7:2000 pp.109-122.

1575 Für einen moderaten Relativismus in der Wissenschaftssoziologie: Zur Debatte um die philosophischen Voraussetzungen und Konsequenzen der neueren Wissenschaftssoziologie. *[In German]*; (For a moderate relativism in the sociology of science: on the philosophical presuppositions and consequences of the new sociology of science.) Bernd Schofer. **Kölner Z. Soz. Soz. Psy.** 52:4 12:2000 pp.696-719.

1576 The golem: between the technological and the divine. Lisa Nocks. **J. Soc. Evol. Sys.** 21:3 1998 pp.281-304.

D: CULTURE

1577 The governance of science: ideology and the future of the open society. Steve Fuller. Philadelphia PA: Open University Press, 2000. 167p. *ISBN: 0335202357, 0335202349. Includes bibliographical references and index. (Series:* Issues in society).

1578 Have biologists wrapped up philosophy? Stephen R.L. Clark. **Inquiry** 43:2 6:2000 pp.143-166.

1579 Holism and the understanding of science: integrating the analytical, historical and sociological. Louis Caruana. Aldershot, Burlington VT: Ashgate, 2000. viii, 173p. *ISBN: 0754613143. Includes bibliographical references and index.*

1580 How science takes stock: the story of meta-analysis. Morton Hunt. New York: Russell Sage Foundation, 1999. 256p. *ISBN: 0871543982.*

1581 „In der Mathematik ist ein Streit mit Sicherheit zu entscheiden" — Perspektiven einer Soziologie der Mathematik. *[In German]*; ['In mathematics, disputes can be decided with certainty' — towards a sociology of mathematics] *[Summary]*. Bettina Heintz. **Z. Soziol.** 29:5 10:2000 pp.339-360.

1582 Incommensurability and translation: Kuhnian perspectives on scientific communication and theory change. Rema Rossini Favretti [Ed.]; Giorgio Sandri [Ed.]; Roberto Scazzieri [Ed.]. Cheltenham, Northampton MA: Edward Elgar Publishing, 1999. xiii, 507p. *ISBN: 1858989434. Includes bibliographical references and index.*

1583 Informational Darwinism. Arthur B. Cody. **Inquiry** 43:2 6:2000 pp.167-180.

1584 Introductory readings in the philosophy of science. E.D. Klemke [Ed.]; Robert Hollinger [Ed.]; David Wÿss Rudge [Ed.]; A. David Kline [Ed.]. Amherst NY: Prometheus Books, 1998. 579p. *ISBN: 1573922404. Includes bibliographical references.*

1585 Intuitionism as a (failed) Kuhnian revolution in mathematics. Bruce Pourciau. **Stud. Hist. Phil. Sci.** 31A:2 6:2000 pp.297-330.

1586 Kant's hands and Earman's pions: chirality arguments for substantival space. Carl Hoefer. **Int. Phil. Sci.** 14:3 10:2000 pp.237-256.

1587 Knowledge and the social sciences: theory, method, practice. David Goldblatt [Ed.]. London: Routledge, 2000. 192p. *ISBN: 0415222850.*

1588 The knowledge web: from electronic agents to Stonehenge and back - and other journeys through knowledge. James Burke. New York: Simon & Schuster, 1999. 285p. *ISBN: 0684859343. Includes bibliographical references.*

1589 Landscape and postcolonial science. Itty Abraham. **Contr. I. Soc.** 34:2 5-8:2000 pp.163-188.

1590 Limits of change: cognitive constraints on 'postmodernization' and the political redirection of science. Jochen Gläser. **Soc. Sci. Info.** 39:3 9:2000 pp.439-465.

1591 *Machina ex deo*: William Harvey and the meaning of instrument. Don Bates. **J. Hist. Ideas.** 61:4 10:2000 pp.577-594.

1592 Multiculturalismo y enseñanza de la ciencia. *[In Spanish]*; [Multiculturalism and the teaching of science]. Steve Fuller. **Leviatán** 81 Autumn:2000 pp.49-58.

1593 Narrow versus wide mechanism: including a re-examination of Turing's views on the mind-machine issue. B. Jack Copeland. **J. Phil.** XCVII:1 1:2000 pp.5-32.

1594 Nauka v Vostochnoi Evrope. *[In Russian]*; (Science in Eastern Europe.) E. Vodopianova. **Svobod. Mysl'** 3 2000 pp.87-98.

1595 On ambivalence and risk: reflexive modernity and the new human genetics. Anne Kerr; Sarah Cunningham-Burley. **Sociology** 34:2 5:2000 pp.283-304.

1596 Pandora's hope: essays on the reality of science studies. Bruno Latour. Cambridge MA, London: Harvard University Press, 1999. x, 324p. *ISBN: 0674653351, 067465336X. Includes bibliographical references (p. 312-316) and index.*

1597 Peaceful nuclear explosions and the geography of scientific authority. Scott Kirsch. **Prof. Geogr.** 52:2 5:2000 pp.179-192.

1598 Performing technology's stories: on social constructivism, performance, and performativity. John Law; Vicky Singleton. **Technol. Cul.** 41:4 10:2000 pp.765-775.

1599 Philosophical concepts in physics: the historical relation between philosophy and scientific theories. James T. Cushing. Cambridge, New York: Cambridge University Press, 1998.

xix, 424p. *ISBN: 0521570719, 052157823X. Includes bibliographical references (p. 400-411) and indexes.*

1600 Philosophy of science: a contemporary introduction. Alexander Rosenberg. London: Routledge, 2000. 191p. *ISBN: 041515281X, 0415152801. Includes bibliographical references and index. (Series:* Routledge contemporary introductions to philosophy).

1601 Playing safe: science and the environment. Jonathon Porritt. London: Thames & Hudson, 2000. 143p. *ISBN: 0500280738. Includes bibliographical references and index. (Series:* Prospects for tomorrow).

1602 Printsip krasoty v teorii elementarnykh chastits (matematicheskie nachala «natural'noi folosofii» fiziki elementarnykh chastits). *[In Russian];* (The principle of beauty in the theory of elementary particles (mathematical origin of 'natural philosophy' in particle physics).) *[Summary].* V.P. Branskii. **Vest. San.-Peter. Univ.** 3(20) 9:1999 pp.19-30.

1603 Profiles of the future: an inquiry into the limits of the possible. Arthur C. Clarke. London: Gollancz, 1999. 256p. *ISBN: 057506790X.*

1604 Quality control and validation boundaries in a triple helix of university-industry-government: 'Mode 2' and the future of university research. Yuko Fujigaki; Loet Leydesdorff. **Soc. Sci. Info.** 39:4 12:2000 pp.635-656.

1605 Relativity: history and interpretations. Craig Callender; John D. Norton; Roberto Torretti; Carl Hoefer; Jonathan Bain; Robert Weingard. **Stud. Hist. Phil. Mod. Phys.** 31B:2 6:2000 pp.129-246. *Collection of 6 articles.*

1606 Robert Rosen: the well-posed question and its answer — why are organisms different from machines? Donald C. Mikulecky. **Syst. Res. Behav. Sci.** 17:5 9-10:2000 pp.419-432.

1607 Savoir et responsabilité. *[In French];* [Knowledge and responsibility]. Michel de Sève [Ed.]; Simon Langlois [Ed.]; Bernard Arcand; et al. Quebec: Editions Nota bene, 1999. x, 315p. *ISBN: 2895180199. Includes bibliographical references.*

1608 Science, technology and democracy. Jean-Jacques Salomon. **Minerva** XXXVIII:1 2000 pp.33-52.

1609 Science, technology and modernity: Beck and Derrida on the politics of risk. Ross Abbinnett. **Cult. Val.** 4:1 1:2000 pp.101-126.

1610 Les sciences institutions, pratiques, discours. *[In French];* [Scientific institutions, practices, discourses]. Jean-Michel Berthelot; Yves Gingras; Antonio Firmino da Costa; Patrícia Ávila; Margarida Senna Martinez; David Pontille; Pascal Ragouet; Claude Rosental; Olivier Martin. **Cah. Int. Soc.** CIX 7-12:2000 pp.221-392. *Collection of 7 articles.*

1611 The semiosis of Francis Bacon's scientific empiricism. Harvey Wheeler. **Semiotica** 133:1-4 2001 pp.45-67.

1612 Setting up a discipline: conflicting agendas of the Cambridge History of Science Committee, 1936-1950. Anna K. Mayer. **Stud. Hist. Phil. Sci.** 31A:4 12:2000 pp.665-690.

1613 Le sexe du savoir. *[In French];* [The sex of knowledge]. Michèle Le Doeuff. Paris: Flammarion, 2000. 378p. *ISBN: 2080814613.*

1614 Sexed equations and vexed physicists: the 'two cultures' revisited. Christopher Norris. **Int. Jour. Cult. Stud.** 2:1 4:1999 pp.77-107.

1615 Social constructivism and the philosophy of science. André Kukla. New York: Routledge, 2000. 170p. *ISBN: 0415234182, 0415234190. Includes bibliographical references and index. (Series:* Philosophical issues in science).

1616 The sociological roots of science. Edgar Zilsel. **Soc. Stud. Sci.** 30:6 12:2000 pp.935-949.

1617 La sociologie des sciences au prisme de ses manuels. *[In French];* [The sociology of science through the prism of its handbooks]. Olivier Martin. **Cah. Int. Soc.** CIX 7-12:2000 pp.415-428.

1618 Sotsial'no-ekonomicheskie problemy rossiiskoi nauki: dolgosrochnye aspekty razvitiia. *[In Russian];* (Social and economic problems of Russian science: long-term aspects of development.) A. Varshavskii. **Vop. Ekon.** 12 12:1998 pp.67-86.

1619 Surviving closure: post-rejection adaptation and plurality in science. H.M. Collins. **Am. Sociol. R.** 65:6 12:2000 pp.824-845.

D: CULTURE

1620 Symposium: the Human Genome Diversity Project. Joseph S. Alper; Jon Beckwith; James E. Bowman; Batsheva Bonné-Tamir; Frank C. Dukepoo; Henry T. Greely; Fatimah L.C. Jackson; Michael Harkin; Debra Harry; Jonathan Marks; Nils Holtug; Trefor Jenkins; Y. Edward Hsia; Kenneth K. Kidd; Judith R. Kidd; Felix I.D. Konotey-Ahulu; Margaret Lock; Darryl R.J. Macer; Hilary Rose; Francisco M. Salzano; Udo Schüklenk; Kenneth M. Weiss; Dorothy C. Wertz; David B. Resnik. **Polit. Life Sci.** 18:2 9:1999 pp.285-340. *Collection of 21 articles.*

1621 The technical substrates of unconscious memory: rereading Derrida's Freud in the age of teletechnology. Patricia Ticineto Clough. **Sociol. Theory** 18:3 11:2000 pp.383-398.

1622 Technology as magic: the triumph of the irrational. Richard Stivers. New York: Continuum, 1999. viii, 240p. *ISBN: 0826412114. Includes bibliographical references (p. [212]-236) and index.*

1623 Theoretical chemistry in the making: appropriating concepts and legitimising techniques. Helge Kragh; B.S. Park; Mary Jo Nye; Andreas Karachalios; Ana Simões; Kostas Gavroglu; Jeffry Ramsey; Valeria Mosini; Sam Schweber; Matthias Wächter. **Stud. Hist. Phil. Mod. Phys.** 31B:4 12:2000 pp.435-609. *Collection of 8 articles.*

1624 Theoretical terms and the principle of the benefit of doubt. Igor Douvan. **Int. Phil. Sci.** 14:2 7:2000 pp.135-146.

1625 Theory versions instead of articulations of a paradigm. Ruey-lin Chen. **Stud. Hist. Phil. Sci.** 31A:3 6:2000 pp.449-472.

1626 ¿Tienen sexo las ciencias? *[In Spanish]*; [Do the sciences have a gender?] Cristina Santamarina. **Leviatán** 82 Winter:2000 pp.69-88.

1627 Time, tense and special relativity. Joshua M. Mozersky. **Int. Phil. Sci.** 14:3 10:2000 pp.221-236.

1628 Trans-scientific frameworks of knowing: complementarity views of the different types of human knowledge. Søren Brier. **Syst. Res. Behav. Sci.** 17:5 9-10:2000 pp.433-458.

1629 The underdetermination of theory by data and the 'strong programme' in the sociology of knowledge. Samir Okasha. **Int. Phil. Sci.** 14:3 10:2000 pp.283-297.

1630 Van Fraassen's critique of inference to the best explanation. Samir Okasha. **Stud. Hist. Phil. Sci.** 31A:4 12:2000 pp.691-710.

1631 Wissenschaftliche Kontrolle und Kontrolle der Wissenschaft. Deutungen eines Professors der Biowissenschaften. *[In German]*; [Scientific control and control of science. The interpretations of a life sciences professor] *[Summary]; [Summary in French]*. Ursula Streckeisen. **Schweiz. Z. Soziologie** 26:3 12:2000 pp.663-683.

D.5: **Language, communication and media**
Langage, communication et médias

1632 Accuracy, stability and reciprocity in informal conversational networks in rural Kenya. Kevin White; Susan Cotts Watkins. **Soc. Networks** 22:4 10:2000 pp.337-355.

1633 Answering questions requesting scientific explanations for communication. Charles Pavitt. **Commun. Theory** 10:4 11:2000 pp.379-404.

1634 Building a theory of multi-media CMC: an analysis, critique and integration of computer-mediated communication theory and research. Charles Soukup. **New Med. & Soc.** 2:4 12:2000 pp.407-426.

1635 Communication: an introduction. Karl Erik Rosengren. Thousand Oaks CA, London: Sage Publications, 2000. xii, 219p. *ISBN: 0803978367, 0803978375. Includes bibliographical references and index.*

1636 Deciphering information technologies: modern societies as networks. Nico Stehr. **Eur. J. Soc. Theory** 3:1 2:2000 pp.83-94.

1637 L'écrit et la lecture dans un monde de communication. *[In French]*; [Reading and writing in a world of communication]. Hervé Bourges. **Projet** 262 6:2000 pp.16-26.

1638 Evolution of communication in perfect and imperfect worlds. Patrick Grim; Trina Kokalis; Ali Tafti; Nicholas Kilb. **Wor. Futur.** 56:2 2000 pp.179-197.

D: CULTURE

1639 Examining frame formation in peer group conversations. Philip Kretsedemas. **Sociol. Q.** 41:4 Fall:2000 pp.639-656.

1640 Extending the theory of the coordinated management of meaning (CMM) through a community dialogue process. W. Barnett Pearce; Kimberly A. Pearce. **Commun. Theory** 10:4 11:2000 pp.405-423.

1641 Good to talk: living and working in a communication culture. Deborah Cameron. London: Sage Publications, 2000. 272p. *ISBN: 0761957707.*

1642 Humor as a double-edged sword: four functions of humor in communication. John C. Meyer. **Commun. Theory** 10:3 8:2000 pp.310-331.

1643 Ihminen tietoyhteiskunnassa: kansalaisten viestintävalmiudet kansalaisyhteiskunnan mahdollistajana. *[In Finnish]*; [People and information society: the citizens' communication skills and the opening of new prospects for civil society]. Marja-Liisa Viherä. Turku: Turun kauppakorkeakoulu, 1999. 365p. *ISBN: 9517389388.*

1644 Information society as theory or ideology: a critical perspective on technology, education and employment in the information age. Nicholas Graham. **Info. Comm. Soc.** 3:2 2000 pp.139-152.

1645 The information society in Europe: work and life in an age of globalization. Werner M. Herrmann [Ed.]; Ken Ducatel [Ed.]; Juliet Webster [Ed.]. Lanham MD, Oxford: Rowman & Littlefield, 2000. 320p. *ISBN: 0847695905, 0847695891.*

1646 The information society: study of continuity and change. John Feather. London: Library Association Publishing, 2000. 212p. *ISBN: 1856043614.*

1647 Message production: progress, challenges and prospects. Steven R. Wilson; John O. Greene; James Price Dillard; Charles R. Berger; Denise Haunani Solomon; Janet R. Meyer; Linda J. Marshall; Jon F. Nussbaum; Doreen K. Baringer; Brant B. Burleson; Sally Planalp. **Commun. Theory** 10:2 5:2000 pp.135-250. *Collection of 9 articles.*

1648 The organization of discussion in university settings. Helen Basturkmen. **Text** 20:3 2000 pp.249-270.

1649 Rappresentazioni sociali e senso comune. Due itinerari possibili per lo studio della comunicazione quotidiana. *[In Italian]*; [Social representations and common sense: two possible paths in the study of everyday communication] *[Summary]*. Pina Lalli. **Rass. It. Soc.** XLI:1 1-3:2000 pp.53-79.

1650 The relation between dialectic and rhetoric. Eric C.W. Krabbe; M. Van Der Poel [Comments by]; Hanns Hohmann; Eveline Feteris [Comments by]; Michael Leff; M.A. Van Rees [Comments by]; Scott Jacobs; Jean Goodwin [Comments by]; Frans H. Van Eemeren; Peter Houtlosser; Eugene Garver [Comments by]; Edward Schiappa; A. Francisca Snoeck Henkemans [Comments by]. **Argumentation** 14:3 8:2000 pp.205-338. *Collection of 12 articles.*

1651 Seizing the moment: the problem of conversational agency. David R. Gibson. **Sociol. Theory** 18:3 11:2000 pp.368-382.

1652 The sequential production of social acts in conversation. Wolfgang Ludwig Schneider. **Human St.** 23:2 4:2000 pp.123-144.

1653 The social psychology of communication impairment. Shelagh Brumfitt. London: Whurr, 1999. ix, 126p. *ISBN: 1861560958. Includes bibliographical references and index.*

1654 Teacher and student gender and peer group gender composition in German foreign language classroom discourse: an exploratory study. M. Chavez. **J. Prag.** 32:7 2000 pp.1019-1058.

1655 Theories of human communication. Stephen W. Littlejohn. Belmont CA: Wadsworth, 1999. xiv, 409p. *ISBN: 0534548199. Includes bibliographical references (p. 365-396) and indexes.*

1656 Virtual communities: a new social structure? Edna Granit; Liron Nathan. **Megamot** XL:2 3:2000 pp.298-315.

D: CULTURE

Communications technology
Technologies de communication

1657 An approach to representing the spatial structure of the information society. Qing Shen. **Urban Geogr.** 21:6 8-9:2000 pp.543-560.
1658 Bases para una etnografia de los multimedios de comunicacion en la Argentina. *[In Spanish]*; [Foundations for an ethnography of multimedia communication in Argentina]. Mario Roberto Pitluk. **Scr. Ethn.** XXII 2000 pp.113-130.
1659 Come back public/private; (almost) all is forgiven: using feminist methodologies in researching information communication technologies. Maria Lohan. **Wom. St. Inter. For.** 23:1 1-2:2000 pp.107-118.
1660 Communication processes for virtual organizations. Gerardine DeSanctis; Peter Monge; Martha Grabowski; Karlene H. Roberts; Robert Kraut; Charles Steinfield; Alice P. Chan; Brian Butler; Anne Hoag; Manju K. Ahuja; Kathleen M. Carley; D. Sandy Staples; John S. Hulland; Christopher A. Higgins; Batia M. Wiesenfeld; Sumita Raghuram; Raghu Garud; Sirkka L. Jarvenpaa; Dorothy E. Leidner. **Organiz. Sci.** 10:6 11-12:1999 pp.693-818. *Collection of 7 articles.*
1661 Community, place and cyberspace. D.J. Walmsley. **Aust. Geogr.** 31:1 3:2000 pp.5-20.
1662 A cultural project based on multiple temporary consensus: identity and community in *Wired*. Divina Frau-Meigs. **New Med. & Soc.** 2:2 6:2000 pp.227-244.
1663 Culture and technology in modern Japan. Ian Inkster [Ed.]; Fumihiko Satofuka [Ed.]. London: I.B. Tauris, 2000. xii, 169p. *ISBN: 1860643256. Includes bibliographical references and index.*
1664 The cybercultures reader. David Bell [Ed.]; Barbara M. Kennedy [Ed.]. London: Routledge, 2000. 688p. *ISBN: 0415183782, 0415183790. Includes bibliographical references.*
1665 Cyberethics: morality and law in cyberspace. Richard A. Spinello. Boston MA: Jones and Bartlett, 2000. xiv, 165p. *ISBN: 0763712698. Includes bibliographical references (p. 157-160) and index.*
1666 Cyberostracism: effects of being ignored over the Internet. Kipling D. Williams; Christopher K.T. Cheung; Wilma Choi. **J. Pers. Soc. Psychol.** 79:5 11:2000 pp.748-762.
1667 (Cyber)space ... 'the final frontier'. The future of ancient studies in the digital world. Sakkie Cornelius; Pierre J. Venter. **J. N.W. Sem. Lang.** 26:1 2000 pp.153-170.
1668 Defending community: difference and Utopia online. Cati Coe. **Int. Jour. Cult. Stud.** 1:3 12:1998 pp.391-414.
1669 Digitopians: transculturalism, computers and the politics of hope. Jeff Lewis. **Int. Jour. Cult. Stud.** 1:3 12:1998 pp.373-389.
1670 Does the internet make us lonely? Axel Franzen. **Eur. Sociol. R.** 16:4 12:2000 pp.427-438.
1671 Global medium — local tool? How readers and media companies use the Web. Lóa Aldísardóttir. **Eur. J. Comm.** 15:2 6:2000 pp.241-251.
1672 Information and communication technologies and the network organization: a critical analysis. Gillian Symon. **J. Occup. Organ. Psychol.** 73:4 12:2000 pp.389-414.
1673 Information and communication technologies: reshaping voluntary organizations? Eleanor Burt; John A. Taylor. **Non. Manag. Leader.** 11:2 Winter:2000 pp.131-144.
1674 The information society as mega-machine: the continuing relevance of Lewis Mumford. Christopher May. **Info. Comm. Soc.** 3:2 2000 pp.241-265.
1675 'Information society' in Eastern Europe? Chances, possibilities, tasks and programs. Bálint Magyar; László Z. Karvalics. **E. Eur. Quart.** XXXIV:4 Winter:2000 pp.509-522.
1676 The Internet and society. James Slevin. Malden MA: Polity Press, 2000. 266p. *ISBN: 0745620868, 0745620876. Includes index.*
1677 La Internet, ¿comunicación o información? (usos y abusos). *[In Spanish]*; (The Internet: communication or information? (Uses and abuses).) Rosa Ma. Lince Campillo. **Est. Polí.** 22 9-12:1999 pp.75-112.

D: CULTURE

1678 The Internet edge: social, legal and technological challenges for a networked world. Mark Stefik. Cambridge MA: MIT Press, 1999. xviii, 320p. *ISBN: 026219418X. Includes bibliographical references and index.*

1679 IT in Western culture: a new technology with ancient roots. Athena Leoussi. **Know. Tech. Pol.** 13:2 Summer:2000 pp.14-29.

1680 Online communities: supporting sociability, designing usability. Jenny Preece. New York: John Wiley & Sons, 2000. 439p. *ISBN: 0471805998. Includes bibliographical references and index.*

1681 Online personal networks: size, composition and media use among distance learners. Caroline Haythornthwaite. **New Med. & Soc.** 2:2 6:2000 pp.195-226.

1682 Places in the net: experiencing cyberspace. Clinton R. Hicks. **Cult. Dyn.** 10:1 3:1998 pp.49-90.

1683 Post-EDSA communication media. Florangel Rosario-Braid; Ramon R. Tuazon. **Phil. Stud.** 48:1 2000 pp.3-25.

1684 The psychology of the Internet. Patricia M. Wallace. Cambridge, New York: Cambridge University Press, 1999. xi, 264p. *ISBN: 0521632943. Includes bibliographical references and index.*

1685 Regenerating communities in the UK: getting plugged into the information society? Gordon Dabinett. **Comm. Dev. J.** 35:2 4:2000 pp.157-166.

1686 Les réseaux de sociabilité téléphonique. *[In French]*; (Telephone sociability networks.) *[Summary]*. Carole Rivière. **Rev. Fr. Soc.** 41:4 10-12:2000 pp.685-718.

1687 Social exclusion and information and communication technologies: lessons from studies of single parents and the young elderly. Leslie Haddon. **New Med. & Soc.** 2:4 12:2000 pp.387-406.

1688 Telematics in the East End of London: new media as a cultural form. Bridgette Wessels. **New Med. & Soc.** 2:4 12:2000 pp.427-444.

1689 The Tower of Babel vs the power of babble: future political, economic and cultural consequences of synchronous, automated translation systems (SATS). Sam Lehman-Wilzig. **New Med. & Soc.** 2:4 12:2000 pp.467-494.

1690 TV and the Internet: pitfalls in forecasting the future. Robert Kubey. **Know. Tech. Pol.** 13:2 Summer:2000 pp.63-85.

1691 The use of the Internet among academic gay communities in Taiwan: an exploratory study. Chung-Chuan Yang. **Info. Comm. Soc.** 3:2 2000 pp.153-172.

1692 The virtual university: the Internet and resource-based learning. Steve Ryan. London; Sterling VA: Kogan Page; Stylus Publishing Inc, 2000. xiii, 204p. *ISBN: 0749425083. Includes bibliographical references (p. 190-197) and indexes.*

1693 The World Wide Web and contemporary cultural theory. Andrew Herman [Ed.]; Thomas Swiss [Ed.]. New York: Routledge, 2000. 312p. *ISBN: 0415925010, 0415925029. Includes bibliographical references (p. [277]-296) and index.*

Media
Médias

1694 Approaches to media literacy: a handbook. Art Silverblatt; Jane Ferry; Barbara Finan. Armonk NY: M.E. Sharpe, 1999. xii, 280p. *ISBN: 0765601842, 0765601850. Includes bibliographical references (p. 251-270) and index.*

1695 Being a part of the family? Genre, gender and production in a Japanese TV drama. Katja Valaskivi. **Media Cult. Soc.** 22:3 5:2000 pp.309-326.

1696 The big chill: investigative reporting in the current media environment. Joseph Bernt [Ed.]; Marilyn S. Greenwald [Ed.]. Ames IA: Iowa State University Press, 2000. ix, 244p. *ISBN: 0813828058. Includes bibliographical references and index.*

1697 Broadcasting in a new media-landscape. B. De Graeve. **Tijds. Econ. Manag.** XLV:4 12:2000 pp.499-518.

D: CULTURE

1698   Building bridges: media for migrants and the public-service mission in Germany. Kira Kosnick. **Euro. Journ. Cult. Stud.** 3:3 9:2000 pp.319-342.

1699   Caught in the cross-fire: Tibet, media and promotional culture. Peter Bishop. **Media Cult. Soc.** 22:5 9:2000 pp.645-664.

1700   Communicating unreality: modern media and the reconstruction of reality. Gabriel Weimann. Thousand Oaks CA: Sage Publications, 2000. xiii, 441p. *ISBN: 0761919856, 0761919864. Includes bibliographical references (p. 391-425) and index.*

1701   Culture formation in a new television station: a multi-perspective analysis. Christine Daymon. **Br. J. Manag.** 11:2 6:2000 pp.121-136.

1702   De-Westernizing media studies. Myung-Jin Park [Ed.]; James Curran [Ed.]. London: Routledge, 2000. ix, 342p. *ISBN: 041519394X, 0415193958. Includes bibliographical references and index.* (*Series:* Communication and society).

1703   A dictionary of communication and media studies. James Watson; Anne Hill. New York; London: St. Martin's Press; Arnold Publishing Ltd., 2000. 364p. *ISBN: 0340676353.*

1704   The effects of media and task on user performance: a test of the task-media fit hypothesis. Brian E. Mennecke; Joseph S. Valacich; Bradley C. Wheeler. **Group Decis. Negot.** 9:6 11:2000 pp.507-529.

1705   „Einfach typisch für einen ahnungslosen Besser-Wessi...": Rezipientenbriefe als Reaktion auf einen massenmedialen Reiz. *[In German]*; ('Just typical of an ignorant *Besser-Wessi...*': recipients' letters as a reaction to a mass media stimulus.) Thomas Ohlemacher; Jörg Jerusel. **Publizistik** 45:3 9:2000 pp.330-345.

1706   Emancipation, the media and modernity: arguments about the media and social theory. Nicholas Garnham. Oxford: Oxford University Press, 2000. 272p. *ISBN: 0198742258, 019874224X. Includes bibliographical references.*

1707   The end of the world news: television and a problem of articulation in Bali. Mark Hobart. **Int. Jour. Cult. Stud.** 3:1 4:2000 pp.79-102.

1708   Entertainment-education and social change: an analysis of parasocial interaction, social learning, collective efficacy, and paradoxical communication. Michael J. Papa; Arvind Singhal; Sweety Law; Saumya Pant; Suruchi Sood; Everett M. Rogers; Corinne L. Shefner-Rogers. **J. Comm.** 50:4 Autumn:2000 pp.31-55.

1709   L'essor des médias: l'exemple de la Tanzanie. *[In French]*; (The soaring of media: a Tanzanian example.) *[Summary]*. Odile Racine-Issa. **Afr. Cont.** 196 10-12:2000 pp.36-48.

1710   Extending a contrast resolution model of humor in television advertising: the role of surprise. Dana L. Alden; Ashesh Mukherjee; Wayne D. Hoyer. **Humor** 13:2 2000 pp.193-217.

1711   The 'face at the window' study: a fresh approach to media influence and to investigating the influence of television and videos on children's imagination. Teresa Belton. **Media Cult. Soc.** 22:5 9:2000 pp.629-644.

1712   Framing friction: media and social conflict. Mary S. Mander [Ed.]. Urbana IL: University of Illinois Press, 1999. 290p. *ISBN: 0252067339, 0252024265. Includes bibliographical references and index.*

1713   The future of public media cultures: cosmopolitan democracy and ambivalence. Nicholas Stevenson. **Info. Comm. Soc.** 3:2 2000 pp.192-214.

1714   Gotcha: life in a tabloid world. Catherine Lumby. St. Leonards: Allen & Unwin, 1999. 280p. *ISBN: 186508073X. Includes bibliographical references and index.*

1715   Im Osten was Neues? Ein Beitrag zur Standortbestimmung der Kommunikations- und Medienwissenschaft. *[In German]*; (All quiet on the Eastern Front? A contribution to defining the situation of communication and media science.) Georg Ruhrmann; Matthias Kohring; Alexander Görke; Michaela Maier; Jens Woelke. **Publizistik** 45:3 9:2000 pp.283-309.

1716   In the worst possible taste: children, television and cultural value. Hannah Davies; David Buckingham; Peter Kelley. **Euro. Journ. Cult. Stud.** 3:1 1:2000 pp.5-26.

1717   Information, storytelling and attractions: TV journalism in three modes of communication. Mats Ekström. **Media Cult. Soc.** 22:4 7:2000 pp.465-518.

D: CULTURE

1718　Inside the BBC and CNN: managing media organisations. Lucy Küng-Shankleman. London, New York: Routledge, 2000. viii, 245p. *ISBN: 0415213215, 0415213223. Includes bibliographical references (p. [233]-238) and index.*

1719　Interpreting Diana: television audiences and the death of a princess. Robert Turnock. London: British Film Institute, 2000. 138p. *ISBN: 0851707890, 0851707882. Includes bibliographical references and index.*

1720　Investigative journalism: context and practice. Hugo de Burgh [Ed.]. London, New York: Routledge, 2000. 264p. *ISBN: 0415190533, 0415190541. Includes bibliographical references and index.*

1721　Koudwatervrees bij de publieke omroepen: over multiculturele diversiteit en de rol van allochtonen in de media. *[In Dutch]*; [Public broadcasters have cold feet about multicultural diversity and the role of ethnic minorities in the media] *[Summary]*. Carmelita Serkei. **Boekmancahier** 12:44 6:2000 pp.111-122.

1722　The language of magazines. Linda McLoughlin. London, New York: Routledge, 2000. 115p. *ISBN: 0415214246. Includes bibliographical references and index. (Series: Intertext).*

1723　The liberalization of the mass media in Africa and its impact on indigenous languages: the case of Kiswahili in Kenya. Paul M. Musau. **Ufahamu** XXVI:II-III 1998 pp.4-17.

1724　'Lifting the veil': the arts, broadcasting and Irish society. Brian O'Neill. **Media Cult. Soc.** 22:6 11:2000 pp.763-785.

1725　Live television is still alive: on television as an unfulfilled promise. Jérôme Bourdon. **Media Cult. Soc.** 22:5 9:2000 pp.531-556.

1726　The magazines handbook. Jenny McKay. London: Routledge, 2000. 288p. *ISBN: 0415170354, 0415170346. Includes bibliographical references and index.*

1727　Making sense of audience discourses: towards a multidimensional model of mass media reception. Kim Christian Schrøder. **Euro. Journ. Cult. Stud.** 3:2 5:2000 pp.233-258.

1728　Media and everyday life in modern society. Shaun Moores. Edinburgh: Edinburgh University Press, 2000. viii, 168p. *ISBN: 0748611797. Includes bibliographical references (p. 151-162) and index.*

1729　Media and social change: the modernizing influences of television in rural India. Kirk Johnson. **Media Cult. Soc.** 23:2 3:2001 pp.147-169.

1730　The media and the Kosovo conflict. Reiner Grundmann; Dennis Smith; Sue Wright; Richard C. Vincent; Daya Kishan Thussu; Rossella Savarese; Stig A. Nohrstedt; Sophia Kaitatzi-Whitlock; Rune Ottosen; Kristina Riegert; Piers Robinson; Christiane Eilders; Albrecht Lüter. **Eur. J. Comm.** 15:3 9:2000 pp.291-428. *Collection of 7 articles.*

1731　Media (and) war. Daya Kishan Thussu; Philip Hammond; Elena Koltsova; Richard A. Brody; Will Barton Catmur; Sandra B. Hrvatin; Martina Trampuž; Richard Keeble. **Javnost** VII:3 2000 pp.5-97. *Collection of 7 articles.*

1732　The media at war: communication and conflict in the twentieth century. Susan L. Carruthers. Basingstoke: Macmillan, 2000. xii, 321p. *ISBN: 0333691423, 0333691431, 0312228007, 0312228015. Includes bibliographical references (p. 281-305) and index.*

1733　Media imperialism revisited: some findings from the Asian case. Kalyani Chadha; Anandam Kavoori. **Media Cult. Soc.** 22:4 7:2000 pp.415-432.

1734　Media regulation, public interest, and the law. Mike Feintuck. Edinburgh: Edinburgh University Press, 1999. ix, 230p. *ISBN: 0748609970. Includes bibliographical references (p. 217-223) and index.*

1735　A mídia e a construção do biográfico o sensacionalismo da morte em cena. *[In Portuguese]*; [The media and the construction of the biographical: the sensationalism of death on the air] *[Summary]*. Elizabeth Rondelli; Micael Herschmann. **Tempo Soc.** 12:1 5:2000 pp.201-218.

1736　Minority languages, nationalism and broadcasting: the British and Irish examples. Mike Cormack. **Nat. Nat.** 6:3 7:2000 pp.383-398.

1737　The misuse value of the TV set: reading media objects in transnational urban spaces. Anna McCarthy. **Int. Jour. Cult. Stud.** 3:3 12:2000 pp.307-330.

D: CULTURE

1738 Mouthpiece or money-spinner? The double life of Chinese television in the late 1990s. Zhao Bin. **Int. Jour. Cult. Stud.** 2:3 12:1999 pp.291-305.

1739 Narrative and genre: key concepts in media studies. Nick Lacey. Basingstoke; New York: Macmillan; St. Martin's Press, 2000. ix, 268p. *ISBN: 033365871X. Includes bibliographical references (p. 256-263) and index.*

1740 New documentary: a critical introduction. Stella Bruzzi. London: Routledge, 2000. 208p. *ISBN: 0415182956. Includes index.*

1741 News culture. Stuart Allan. Buckingham, Philadelphia PA: Open University Press, 1999. ix, 229p. *ISBN: 0335199569. Includes bibliographical references (p. [199]-217) and index. (Series: Issues in cultural and media studies).*

1742 News in my backyard: media and democracy in an 'all American' city. Tawnya Adkins-Covert; Denise P. Ferguson; Selene Phillips; Philo C. Wasburn. **Sociol. Q.** 41:2 Spring:2000 pp.227-244.

1743 The place of media power: pilgrims and witnesses of the media age. Nick Couldry. London: Routledge, 2000. xii, 238p. *ISBN: 0415213142, 0415213150. Includes bibliographical references and index.*

1744 The politics of 'new' men's lifestyle magazines. Nick Stevenson; Peter Jackson; Kate Brooks. **Euro. Journ. Cult. Stud.** 3:3 9:2000 pp.366-385.

1745 Pop music radio in the public service: BBC Radio 1 and new music in the 1990s. David Hendy. **Media Cult. Soc.** 22:6 11:2000 pp.743-761.

1746 Popular journalism with Chinese characteristics: from revolutionary modernity to popular modernity. Li Zhurun. **Int. Jour. Cult. Stud.** 1:3 12:1998 pp.307-328.

1747 Poverty as we know it: media portrayals of the poor. Rosalee A. Clawson; Rakuya Trice. **Publ. Opin. Q.** 64:1 Spring:2000 pp.53-64.

1748 Presentations of Romanies in the Czech media: on category work in television debates. Ivan Leudar; Jiří Nekvapil. **Disc. Soc.** 11:4 10:2000 pp.487-514.

1749 Prikaz rezultata analize programskih sadržaja radijskih postaja na području Zagreba i Zagrebačke županije. *[In Croatian]*; (An overview of the analysis of the program content of the radio-stations in Zagreb and the Zagreb county.) *[Summary].* Marina Mučalo. **Pol. Misao** 37:4 2000 pp.113-128.

1750 Prime suspects: the influence of local television news on the viewing public. Franklin D. Gilliam, Jr.; Shanto Iyengar. **Am. J. Pol. Sc.** 44:3 7:2000 pp.560-573.

1751 'Probably the most public occasion the world has ever known': 'public' and 'private' in press coverage of the death and funeral of Diana, Princess of Wales. Elizabeth Frazer. **Journ. Pol. Ideol.** 5:2 6:2000 pp.201-223.

1752 The public and private dialogue about the American family on television. Kelly Fudge Albada. **J. Comm.** 50:4 Autumn:2000 pp.79-110.

1753 Public television in America. Eli M. Noam [Ed.]; Jens Waltermann [Ed.]. Gütersloh: Bertelsmann Foundation, 1998. 181p. *ISBN: 3892043884. Includes bibliographical references.*

1754 Qualität auf dem Anzeigenmarkt und ihre publizistischen Implikationen. *[In German]*; (Quality in the advertising market and its implications for journalism.) Michaela Pieler. **Publizistik** 45:3 9:2000 pp.346-361.

1755 Radio Onde Furlane, mezzo di comunicazione locale in un contesto globale. *[In Italian]*; (*Radio Onde Furlane*: a local medium in a global context.) Cinzia Sut. **Rass. It. Soc.** 41:4 2000 pp.571-586.

1756 Radiocracy — radio, democracy and development. John Hartley; Peter M. Lewis; Tony Stoller; Lumko Mtimde; Steve Buckley; Geraint Ellis; Zane Ibrahim; Elaine Windrich; Susana Villaran; Nick Caistor; Yesudhasan Thomas Jayaprakash; Max Easterman; Graeme Turner; Kevin Howley; Martin Spinelli; Kate Lacey; Jo Tacchi. **Int. Jour. Cult. Stud.** 3:2 8:2000 pp.153-298. *Collection of 16 articles.*

1757 Reference, image, text in German and Australian advertising posters. R. Gardner; Sigrid Luchtenberg. **J. Prag.** 32:12 2000 pp.1807-1822.

1758 Reinventing Hong Kong: memory, identity and television. Eric Kit-wai Ma. **Int. Jour. Cult. Stud.** 1:3 12:1998 pp.329-349.

D: CULTURE

1759 Reklamnye tekhnologii gendera. *[In Russian]*; [Gender in technology advertising]. I.V. Groshev. **Obshch. Nauki Sovrem.** 4 2000 pp.172-187.

1760 Reporting gender in Southern Africa: a media guide. Barbara Lopi [Comp.]. Harare, Lusaka: Southern African Research and Documentation Centre, 1999. vi, 168p. *ISBN: 1779100043. Papers presented at a workshop, Lusaka, November 1998. Includes bibliographical references (p. 69-72). Zambia Institute of Mass Communication Educational Trust.*

1761 Representations of familialism in the British popular media. Deborah Chambers. **Euro. Journ. Cult. Stud.** 3:2 5:2000 pp.195-214.

1762 Reproducing the nation: 'banal nationalism' in the Turkish press. Arus Yumul; Umut Özkırımlı. **Media Cult. Soc.** 22:6 11:2000 pp.787-804.

1763 Rethinking the media audience: the new agenda. Pertti Alasuutari [Ed.]. London: Sage Publications, 1999. viii, 212p. *ISBN: 0761950702, 0761950710. Includes bibliographical references and index.*

1764 Rozvoj lokálnej televízie na Slovensku. *[In Slovak]*; (The development of local television in Slovakia.) Roman Ivantyšyn. **Sociologia [Brat.]** 32:1 2000 pp.111-122.

1765 Scheduling: the last creative act in television? John Ellis. **Media Cult. Soc.** 22:1 1:2000 pp.25-38.

1766 Seeing things: television in the age of uncertainty. John Ellis. London: I.B. Tauris, 2000. 193p. *ISBN: 1860641253. Includes bibliographical references and index.*

1767 Seeing White — female Whiteness and the purity of children in Australian, Chinese and British visual culture. Stephanie Hemelryk Donald. **Soc. Sem.** 10:2 8:2000 pp.157-172.

1768 'SHARP!' Lurking incoherence in a television portrayal of an older adult. Jake Harwood. **J. Lang. Soc. Psychol.** 19:1 3:2000 pp.110-140.

1769 Silences of the media: whiting out Aboriginality in making news and making history. Subhabrata Bobby Banerjee; Goldie Osuri. **Media Cult. Soc.** 22:3 5:2000 pp.263-284.

1770 Something completely different: British television and American culture. Jeffrey S. Miller. Minneapolis MN, London: University of Minnesota Press, 2000. xvii, 250p. *ISBN: 0816632413, 0816632405. Includes bibliographical references and index.*

1771 Tabloidization, journalism and the possibility of critique. Graeme Turner. **Int. Jour. Cult. Stud.** 2:1 4:1999 pp.59-76.

1772 Television. Annette Hamilton; Helen Creese; Stephen Atkinson; Pam Nilan. **R. Ind. Malay. Aff.** 34:1 Winter:2000 pp.11-154. *Collection of 4 articles.*

1773 Television across Europe: a comparative introduction. Graham Murdock [Ed.]; Peter Dahlgren [Ed.]; Jan Wieten [Ed.]. London: Sage Publications, 2000. 288p. *ISBN: 0761968857, 0761968849.*

1774 Television and new media audiences. Ellen Seiter. Oxford, New York: Clarendon Press, 1998. 154p. *ISBN: 0198711425, 0198711417. Includes bibliographical references (p. [141]-148) and index. (Series: Oxford television studies).*

1775 Thinking across spaces: transnational television from Turkey. Asu Aksoy; Kevin Robins. **Euro. Journ. Cult. Stud.** 3:3 9:2000 pp.343-365.

1776 Third-person perception of television-viewing behavior. Wolfram Peiser; Jochen Peter. **J. Comm.** 50:1 Winter:2000 pp.25-45.

1777 Turkish (television) culture is ordinary. Ayşe Öncü; Kira Kosnick; Asu Aksoy; Kevin Robins. **Euro. Journ. Cult. Stud.** 3:3 9:2000 pp.296-365. *Collection of 3 articles.*

1778 Turning a way of life into a business: an account and critique of the transformation of British television from public service to commercial enterprise. G. Ursell. **Crit. Persp. Acc.** 11:6 12:2000 pp.741-764.

1779 Visual digital culture: surface play and spectacle in new media genres. Andrew Darley. London, New York: Routledge, 2000. x, 225p. *ISBN: 0415165555, 0415165547. Includes bibliographical references (p. 207-215) and index. (Series: Sussex studies in culture and communication).*

1780 The voice from the void: wireless, modernity and the distant dead. Jeffrey Sconce. **Int. Jour. Cult. Stud.** 1:2 8:1998 pp.211-232.

D: CULTURE

1781   The Western media and the Algerian crisis. Fouzi Slisli. **Race Class** 41:3 1-3:2000 pp.43-58.

1782   Women outdoors: advertising, controversy and disputing feminism in the 1990s. Janice Winship. **Int. Jour. Cult. Stud.** 3:1 4:2000 pp.27-55.

1783   Zur Qualität der Medienkontrolle: Ergebnisse einer Befragung deutscher Rundfunk- und Medienräte. *[In German]*; (Quality criteria in supervising the media: results of a survey of German broadcasting supervisors.) *[Summary]*. Hans-Bernd Brosius; Patrick Rössler; Claudia Schulte zur Hausen. **Publizistik** 45:4 12:2000 pp.417-441.

Sociolinguistics
Sociolinguistique

1784   An analysis of comic discourses: how language mediates problems of human communication and unattachment. Wai King Tsang. **Semiotica** 131:1-2 2000 pp.155-184.

1785   At war with diversity: US language policy in an age of anxiety. James Crawford. Clevedon, Buffalo NY: Multilingual Matters, 2000. vii, 143p. *ISBN: 1853595055, 1853595063. Includes bibliographical references (p. 128-137) and index. (Series:* Bilingual education and bilingualism - 25).

1786   Beyond the mother tongue: learning the meaning of Yiddish in America. Jeffrey Shandler. **Jew. Soc. Stud.** 6:3 Spring-Summer:2000 pp.97-123.

1787   Can instructions to nonverbal IQ tests be given in pantomime? Additional applications of a general theory of signs. John W. Oller, Jr.; Kunok Kim; Yongjae Choe. **Semiotica** 133:1-4 2001 pp.15-44.

1788   Childly language: children, language, and the social world. Alison Sealey. New York: Longman, 2000. 229p. *ISBN: 0582307791. Includes bibliographical references and index. (Series:* Real language).

1789   'Codeswitching'. G. Bensimon-Choukroun; Carol Myers-Scotton; Cyril Aslanov; Steven Gross; Penelope Gardner-Chloros; Reeva Charles; Jenny Cheshire; Sarah Lawson; Itesh Sachdev; Harriet Jisa; Marlene Dolitsky; Agnes Yu; Bruce Bain. **J. Prag.** 32:9 2000 pp.1253-1411. *Collection of 10 articles.*

1790   The construction of units in conversational talk. Margret Selting. **Lang. Soc.** 29:4 12:2000 pp.477-518.

1791   Conversational interruptions in Israeli-Palestinian 'dialogue' events. Yael-Janette Zupnik. **Disc. St.** 2:1 2:2000 pp.85-110.

1792   Critical discourse analysis. Jan Blommaert; Chris Bulcaen. **Ann. R. Anthr.** 29 2000 pp.447-466.

1793   Croatian dialects in the United States: sociolinguistic conditions for the maintenance of a dialect. Rudolf Filipović. **Int. J. S. Lang.** 147 2001 pp.51-63.

1794   Croatian linguistic loyalty. Radoslav Katičić. **Int. J. S. Lang.** 147 2001 pp.17-29.

1795   Crossing the line in Quebec and Catalonia: the consequences of the linguistically 'mixed' marriage. Paul E. O'Donnell. **Lang. Prob. Lang. Plan.** 24:3 Fall:2000 pp.233-247.

1796   The cultural analysis of texts. Mikko Lehtonen. London: Sage Publications, 2000. 174p. *ISBN: 0761965513, 0761965505.*

1797   An der Schnittstelle zweier „Weltsprachen" — die Kanalinseln zwischen Anglo- und Frankophonie. *[In German]*; [At the interface of two 'world languages' - the Channel Islands between French and English]. Hellmut Losch. **Eur. Ethn.** 56:1-2 2000 pp.51-63.

1798   Dialect convergence and divergence across European borders. Frans Hinskens [Ed.]; Jeffrey L. Kallen [Ed.]; Johan Taeldeman [Ed.]; Beat Glauser; Hugo Ryckeboer; Hubert Klausmann; Inge Lise Pedersen; Anneli Sarhimaa; Hans Goebl. **Int. J. S. Lang.** 145 2000 pp.1-215. *Collection of 8 articles.*

1799   The end of a semiotic fallacy. Inna R. Semetsky. **Semiotica** 130:3-4 2000 pp.283-300.

1800   Ethnomethodology, conversation analysis, and 'institutional talk'. Stephen Hester; David Francis. **Text** 20:3 2000 pp.391-413.

D: CULTURE

1801 Evaluations of Hawaii Creole English and Standard English. Mary Lynn Fiore Ohama; Carolyn C. Gotay; Ian S. Pagano; Larry Boles; Dorothy D. Craven. **J. Lang. Soc. Psychol.** 19:3 9:2000 pp.357-377.

1802 Form and ideology: Arabic sociolinguistics and beyond. Niloofar Haeri. **Ann. R. Anthr.** 29 2000 pp.61-87.

1803 A global model of communication. Alexandros Ph. Lagopoulos. **Semiotica** 131:1-2 2000 pp.45-78.

1804 Globalisation and the theorisation of language. Horst Ruthrof. **Soc. Sem.** 10:2 8:2000 pp.187-200.

1805 Grassroots English in a communication paradigm. Lachman M. Khubchandani; Priya Hosali. **Lang. Prob. Lang. Plan.** 23:3 Fall:1999 pp.251-272.

1806 The ground floor of the world: on the socio-economic consequences of linguistic globalization. Philippe Van Parijs. **Int. Pol. Sci Rev.** 21:2 4:2000 pp.217-233.

1807 If my complaints could passions move: an interlanguage study of aggression. D.H. Tatsuki. **J. Prag.** 32:7 2000 pp.1003-1018.

1808 'I'm just saying ...': discourse markers of standpoint continuity. Robert T. Craig; Alena L. Sanusi. **Argumentation** 14:4 11:2000 pp.425-445.

1809 L'intégration linguistique à l'école et les conséquences sur la langue parlée en famille. Le cas des élèves allophones en Suisse. *[In French]*; [Linguistic integration at school and its consequences on the language spoken at home. Allophone pupils in Switzerland] *[Summary]*. Christine Blaser. **Can. Ethn. Stud.** XXXI:1 1999 pp.139-158.

1810 Inviting collaborations in stories about a woman. Wayne A. Beach. **Lang. Soc.** 29:3 9:2000 pp.379-407.

1811 Islands and identity in sociolinguistics: Hong Kong, Singapore and Taiwan. Tope Omoniyi; John E. Joseph; Rodney H. Jones; Angel Mei Yi Lin; Anna Kwan-Terry; Anthea Fraser Gupta; Phyllis Ghim-lian Chew; Shuanfan Huang; John Kwock-ping Tse; Chao-chih Liao. **Int. J. S. Lang.** 143 2000 pp.1-188. *Collection of 11 articles.*

1812 A kisebbségi nyelv sorsa a vegyes házasságokban. *[In Hungarian]*; [The fate of the minority language in mixed marriages]. Anna Sándor. **Valóság** 42:8 1999 pp.87-97.

1813 Language and ethnicity in the new South Africa. Nkonko M. Kamwangamalu [Ed.]; Ernst Kotzé; Vic Webb; Mariana Kriel; Barbara Bosch; Elizabeth de Kadt; Gary Barkhuizen; Vivian de Klerk; Sarah Slabbert; Rosalie Finlayson. **Int. J. S. Lang.** 144 2000 pp.7-160. *Collection of 8 articles.*

1814 Language and gender. Angela Goddard; Lindsey Meân Patterson. London, New York: Routledge, 2000. 122p. *ISBN: 0415201772. Includes bibliographical references and index.* (*Series:* Intertext).

1815 Language and negotiation of ethnic/racial identity among Dominican Americans. Benjamin Bailey. **Lang. Soc.** 29:4 12:2000 pp.555-582.

1816 Language contact in East-Central Europe. Dubravko Škiljan; Milorad Radovanović; Jiří Nekvapil; Juliet Langman; István Lanstyák; Szabolcs Simon; Miklós Kontra; István Csemicskó; Anna Fenyvesi; Csaba Pléh; Péter Bodor; Klára Sándor. **Multilingua** 19:1-2 2000 pp.3-168. *Collection of 8 articles.*

1817 Language planning for the 'other Jewish languages' in Israel: an agenda for the beginning of the 21st century. Joshua A. Fishman. **Lang. Prob. Lang. Plan.** 24:3 Fall:2000 pp.215-231.

1818 Language use in Fiji and Aotearoa/NZ: trends and implications for Fiji Hindi. Nikhat Shameem. **Te reo** 41 6:1998 pp.126-136.

1819 Languages of former colonial powers and former colonies: the case of Puerto Rico. Jorge A. Vélez; Sharon Clampitt-Dunlap; Amparo Morales; C. William Schweers, Jr.; Madeleine Hudders; Joan M. Fayer; Alicia Pousada; Miriam Eisenstein Ebsworth; Timothy Ebsworth; José Solis Jordán. **Int. J. S. Lang.** 142 2000 pp.5-173. *Collection of 8 articles.*

1820 Linguistic competence and regional identity in Brittany: attitudes and perceptions of identity. Rachel Hoare. **J. Multiling.** 21:4 2000 pp.324-346.

1821 The management of heterosexist talk: conversational resources and prejudiced claims. Susan A. Speer; Jonathan Potter. **Disc. Soc.** 11:4 10:2000 pp.543-572.

D: CULTURE

1822 La mémoire des mots. *[In French]*; [The memory of words]. André Roman; Leila Messaoudi; Mohamed Lazhar Abbès; Hassan Hamzé; Habiba Naffati; Joseph Dichy; Karim Chibout; Anne Vilnat; Douglas Skuce; Ingrid Meyer; Judy Kavanagh; Sofia Benyahia; Abdelhamid Camoun; Miloud Taifi; Ismail Timimi; Geneviève Boidin; Christian Boitet; Alpha Mamadou Diallo; Ibra Diene; Zachée Denis Bitjaa Kody; Sylvie Porhiel; Pierre Lerat; Hussein Habaili; Slim Ben Hazez; Gaha Kamel; Raphaël Rajaspera; Ambroise Queffélec; Lina Sader Feghali; Antoine Noujaim. **R. Tun. Sci. Soc.** 35:117 1998 pp.11-404. *Collection of 24 articles.*

1823 Minoritisation, identity and ethnolinguistic vitality in Catalonia. David Atkinson. **J. Multiling.** 21:3 2000 pp.185-197.

1824 The organization of justificatory discourse in interaction: a comparison within and across cultures. Barbara Warnick; Valerie Manusov. **Argumentation** 14:4 11:2000 pp.381-404.

1825 Peculiar sociolinguistic features of the Slavic world. Dalibor Brozović. **Int. J. S. Lang.** 147 2001 pp.5-15.

1826 Political unity and linguistic diversity in Europe. Peter A. Kraus. **Eur. J. Soc.** XLI:1 2000 pp.138-163.

1827 The politics of visual language: deafness, language choice, and political socialization. James Roots. Ottawa: Carleton University Press, 1999. 106p. *ISBN: 0886293456. Includes bibliographical references.*

1828 A presuppositional account of reference fixing. Manuel García-Carpintero. **J. Phil.** XCVII:3 3:2000 pp.109-148.

1829 Proximal and distal deixis in negotiation talk. K.D. Glover. **J. Prag.** 32:7 2000 pp.915-926.

1830 Public and private self as two aspects of the speaker: a contrastive study of Japanese and English. Yukio Hirose. **J. Prag.** 32:11 2000 pp.1623-1656.

1831 The question of Chinese indirectness: a comparison of Chinese and English participative decision-making discourse. Lorrita Ngor-to Yeung. **Multilingua** 19:3 2000 pp.221-264.

1832 The real as limit to interpretation. Ruth Ronen. **Semiotica** 132:1-2 2000 pp.121-136.

1833 Recontextualization and communicative styles in job interviews. Jann Scheuer. **Disc. St.** 3:2 5:2001 pp.223-248.

1834 The relationship between ethnolinguistic identity and English language achievement for native Russian speakers and native Hebrew speakers in Israel. Bonnie Ellinger. **J. Multiling.** 21:4 2000 pp.292-307.

1835 A repair mechanism in Turkish conversation: the case of *Estagfurullah*. Arın Bayraktaroglu. **Multilingua** 19:3 2000 pp.281-310.

1836 The Russian diaspora in Latvia and Estonia: predicting language outcomes. Artemi Romanov. **J. Multiling.** 21:1 2000 pp.58-71.

1837 Sociolinguistics: an introduction to language and society. Peter Trudgill. London: Penguin, 2000. 256p. *ISBN: 0140289216.*

1838 South Africa's system of official languages. Klavs Skovsholm. **Verf. Rec. Über.** 33:1 2000 pp.5-25.

1839 Speech acts in conversation. José Luis Blas Arroyo; Andrea Golato; Helga Kotthoff; Zhu Hua; Li Wei; Qian Yuan; Joanne Scheibman. **J. Prag.** 32:1 2000 pp.1-124. *Collection of 5 articles.*

1840 Swimming against the tide: language planning on Jersey. Mari C. Jones. **Lang. Prob. Lang. Plan.** 24:2 Summer:2000 pp.167-196.

1841 To be Xhosa or not to be Xhosa ... that is the question. Vivian de Klerk. **J. Multiling.** 21:3 2000 pp.198-215.

1842 Types of process in action. Radan Martinec. **Semiotica** 130:3-4 2000 pp.243-268.

1843 Unilingual past, multilingual present, uncertain future: the case of Yaounde. Gisele Tchoungui. **J. Multiling.** 21:2 2000 pp.113-128.

1844 Unspeakable emotion: a discursive analysis of police talk about reactions to trauma. Christina Howard; Keith Tuffin; Christine Stephens. **J. Lang. Soc. Psychol.** 19:3 9:2000 pp.295-314.

1845 What is a language community? David D. Laitin. **Am. J. Pol. Sc.** 44:1 1:2000 pp.142-155.

1846 Wittgenstein and Davidson on the sociality of language. Meredith Williams. **J. Theory Soc. Behav.** 30:3 9:2000 pp.299-318.
1847 Women and language change in NZE: the case for considering individual as well as group data. Margaret A. Maclagan. **Te reo** 41 6:1998 pp.69-79.

D.6: Art
Art

1848 The aesthetics of Thorstein Veblen revisited. Rick Tilman; Robert Griffin. **Cult. Dyn.** 10:3 11:1998 pp.325-340.
1849 Les architectes et la commande publique. *[In French]*; [Architects and state commissions]. Florent Champy. Paris: Presses Universitaires de France, 1998. xiii, 397p. *ISBN: 2130493661. Includes bibliographical references (p. [373]-383) and index.*
1850 Art and ethical criticism: an overview of recent directions of research. Noël Carroll. **Ethics** 110:2 1:2000 pp.350-404.
1851 The arts of the motorcycle: biology, culture, and aesthetics in technological choice. Steven L. Thompson. **Technol. Cul.** 41:1 1:2000 pp.99-115.
1852 Artysta i publiczność — dyskurs o sztuce i sprawach polskich. O malarstwie Jerzego Dudy-Gracza. *[In Polish]*; (An artist and his audience — discourse concerning art and problems of Polish society. On the paintings by Jerzy Duda-Gracz.) *[Summary]*. Anna Matuchniak-Krasuska. **Prz. Soc.** XLVIII:2 1999 pp.189-217.
1853 Authenticity and impersonality in Adorno's aesthetics. Susan Hahn. **Telos** 117 Fall:2000 pp.60-78.
1854 Beyond art and beauty: in search of the object of philosophical aesthetics. Andreas Speer. **Int. J. Phil. Stud.** 8:1 3:2000 pp.73-88.
1855 Bilder der Moderne: Studien zu einer Soziologie der Kunst- und Kulturinhalte. *[In German]*; [Pictures of the modern age: studies towards a sociology of art and cultural content]. Werner Gephart. Opladen: Leske + Budrich, 1998. 260p. *ISBN: 381002032X. Includes bibliographical references.*
1856 But is it art? Decision making and discursive resources in the field of cultural production. Michael K. Mauws. **J. App. Behav. Sc.** 36:2 6:2000 pp.229-244.
1857 Commande publique d'architecture et segmentation de la profession d'architecte les effets de l'organisation administrative sur la répartition du travail entre architectes. *[In French]*; (Architectural commissions in the public sphere and the segmentation of the architectural profession: the effects of administrative organisation on the division of labour among architects.) Florent Champy. **Genèses** 37 12:1999 pp.93-113.
1858 Dire et (d')écrire les pratiques de danse. Opposition entre pratiques discursives et non discursives. *[In French]*; [Speaking and writing about dancing techniques. The opposition of discursive and non-discursive practices] *[Summary]*. Sylvia Faure. **Cah. Int. Soc.** CVIII 1-6:2000 pp.161-178.
1859 Economic engagements with art. Neil De Marchi [Ed.]; Craufurd D.W. Goodwin [Ed.]. Durham NC, London: Duke University Press, 1999. vii, 506p. *ISBN: 0822326329, 082232489X. Includes bibliographical references and index.*
1860 The feminine in modern art: Benjamin, Simmel and the gender of modernity. Janet Wolff. **Theory Cult. Soc.** 17:6 12:2000 pp.33-53.
1861 Human bodies in Chinese and European painting: an economic analysis. Nachoem M. Wijnberg. **Cult. Dyn.** 11:1 3:1999 pp.89-104.
1862 Identité du personnage théâtral: de l'anonymat à l'autoréférence. *[In French]*; [The identity of stage characters: from anonymity to self-reference]. Tadeusz Kowzan. **Semiotica** 130:3-4 2000 pp.269-282.
1863 Machian epistemology and its part in František Kupka's painterly cognition of reality. John G. Hatch. **Slovo** 12 2000 pp.51-69.
1864 Modernist misapprehensions of Foucault's aesthetics. Jon Simons. **Cult. Val.** 4:1 1:2000 pp.40-57.

D: CULTURE

1865 Multicultural Iberia: language, literature, and music. Dru Dougherty [Ed.]; Milton Mariano Azevedo [Ed.]. Berkeley CA: University of California at Berkeley, 1999. vii, 258p. *ISBN: 0877250030*. Includes bibliographical references. (*Series:* Research series - 103).

1866 Nathalie Heinich, sociologist of the arts: a critical appraisal. Rudi Laermans. **Boekmancahier** 12:46 12:2000 pp.389-403.

1867 Of art and blasphemy. Anthony Fisher; Hayden Ramsay. **Ethic. Theory Moral P.** 3:2 6:2000 pp.137-167.

1868 Performing the absolute. Marina Abramovic organizing the unfinished business of Arthur Schopenhauer. Pierre Guillet de Monthoux. **Organ. Stud.** 21:0 2000 pp.29-52.

1869 The primal scene and Picasso's *Guernica*; *[Summary in French]*; *[Summary in German]*; *[Summary in Spanish]*. Raul Hartke. **Int. J.Psy.** 81:1 2:2000 pp.121-139.

1870 Researching the visual: images, objects, contexts and interactions in social and cultural inquiry. Michael Emmison; Philip Smith. London: Sage Publications, 2000. xiv, 242p. *ISBN: 0761958452, 0761958460*. Includes bibliographical references (p. *[231]-238*) and index. (*Series:* Introducing qualitative methods).

1871 Sellars without homogeneity. Eric M. Rubenstein. **Int. J. Phil. Stud.** 8:1 3:2000 pp.47-71.

1872 Speech act metaphor in theatre. Eli Rozik. **J. Prag.** 32:2 2000 pp.203-218.

1873 Subject, commodity, marketplace: the American Artists Group and the mass production of distinction. Barry Shank. **Rad. Hist. R.** 76 Winter:2000 pp.25-52.

1874 Teatral'naia germenevtika i analiz teatral'nogo teksta. *[In Russian]*; (Theatrical hermeneutics and the analysis of texts.) I. Tsunskii. **Obshch. Nauki Sovrem.** 3 2000 pp.161-171.

1875 Theater is niet cool: *the do's and don'ts* van jongerenmarketing in het theater. *[In Dutch]*; (Theatre is not cool: the do's and don'ts of theatre marketing for young people.) *[Summary]*. Lobke Buenen; Marieke Peters. **Boekmancahier** 12:44 6:2000 pp.148-158.

1876 The true judge of beauty and the paradox of taste. Jason Gaiger. **Eur. J. Phil.** 8:1 4:2000 pp.1-19.

1877 'What makes you think you exist?' A speech move schematic and its application to Pinter's *The Birthday Party*. Michael Toolan. **J. Prag.** 32:2 2000 pp.177-201.

1878 Why did Adorno 'hate' jazz? Robert W. Witkin. **Sociol. Theory** 18:1 3:2000 pp.145-170.

Cinema
Cinéma

1879 'A nightmare on the brain of the living': messianic historicity, alienations, and *Independence Day*. Phillip E. Wegner. **Rethink. Marx.** 12:1 Spring:2000 pp.65-86.

1880 African cinema/critical configurations. N. Frank Ukadike; Peter Hitchcock; Girma Negash; Sheila Petty; Arnold Shepperson; Keyan G. Tomaselli; Jude G. Akudinobi; Mweze Ngangura. **Soc. Ident.** 6:3 9:2000 pp.243-395. *Collection of 7 articles*.

1881 The archeology of origin: transnational visions of Africa in a borderless cinema; *[Summary in French]*. Sheila Petty. **Afr. Stud. R.** 42:2 9:1999 pp.73-86.

1882 The biopic. Glenn Man [Ed.]; Sue Tweg; Thomas Doherty; Clifford Marks; Robert Torry; T. Hugh Crawford; Margaret D. Stetz; James Burns; George F. Custen; Mikita Brottman; Audrey Levasseur; Lucy Fischer. **Biography** 23:1 Winter:2000 pp.1-211. *Collection of 10 articles*.

1883 Blue. Peter Wollen. **New Left R.** 6 11-12:2000 pp.120-133.

1884 British cinema in documents. Sarah Street. London: Routledge, 2000. x, 194p. *ISBN: 0415168015, 0415168007*. Includes bibliographical references and index.

1885 Chinese cinema at the 1999 international Rotterdam film festival. Woei Lien Chong; Anne Sytske Keijser. **Chi. Inform.** XIII:4 Spring:1999 pp.97-129.

1886 Death and the maiden: the feminine and the nation in recent New Zealand films. Maureen Molloy. **Signs** 25:1 Autumn:1999 pp.153-170.

1887 Effects of humorous heroes and villains in violent action films. Cynthia M. King. **J. Comm.** 50:1 Winter:2000 pp.5-24.

1888 L'ethnographe et le cinéaste: un «véloportrait» des origines. *[In French]*; (Ethnographer and filmmaker: a *véloportrait* from the origins.) *[Summary]*. Jean Rouch. **Afr. Cont.** 196 10-12:2000 pp.5-16.
1889 Film swapping in the public sphere: youth audiences and alternative cultural publicities. Göran Bolin. **Javnost** VII:2 2000 pp.57-74.
1890 Filmkultúra és filmművészet. *[In Hungarian]*; [Film culture and film art]. Károly Nemes. **Valóság** 42:3 1999 pp.42-52.
1891 Flexible films? Helen Blair; Al Rainnie. **Media Cult. Soc.** 22:2 3:2000 pp.187-204.
1892 French cinema: economy, policy and place in the making of a cultural-products industry. Allen J. Scott. **Theory Cult. Soc.** 17:1 2:2000 pp.1-38.
1893 Genet, projet de scénario. *[In French]*; [Genet, screenplay]. Richard Dindo. **R. Et. Palest.** 74:22 Winter:2000 pp.84-98.
1894 Hollywood films and Chinese domestic films in China (Part I). Stanley Rosen; Wang Yongzhi; Ren Yi; Xing Ying; Special Task Group for 1998 Front-Line; Lu Shaoyang; Gao Du; Mao Qiang; Guo Fengtong; Zhang Yan; He Wenjin; Zhan Shibang; Weng Li; Ji Wen; Duan Mu; Zhang Xin; Wang Anyi; Li Yiming. **Chin. Soc. Anth.** 32:1 Fall:1999 pp.3-90. *Collection of 17 articles.*
1895 Hollywood films and Chinese domestic films in China (Part II). Shao Peng; Li Fei; Zhu Yi; He Zhongshun; Chen Ken; Zhang Yang; Xiang Jing; Zhang Renjie; Song Quanzhong; Jin Zhongqiang; Hu Jun; Ji Hua; Zeng Yabo; Zhang Yimou; Da Lan; Ya Zi; Niu Jingmei; Wu Guanping; Wu Xiaodong; Zhang Boqing; Tang Jiqun; Wang Jinyue; Shao Yangeng. **Chin. Soc. Anth.** 32:2 Winter:1999-2000 pp.11-99. *Collection of 24 articles.*
1896 Loin d'Auschwitz, Roberto Benigni, bouffon malin. *[In French]*; [Far from Auschwitz, Roberto Benigni, cunning clown]. Michel Henochsberg. **Temps Mod.** 55:608 3-5:2000 pp.42-59.
1897 Male Hindi filmgoers' gaze: an ethnographic interpretation. Steve Derné; Lisa Jadwin. **Contr. I. Soc.** 34:2 5-8:2000 pp.243-272.
1898 Mental retardation in American film: a semiotic analysis. Patrick J. Devlieger; Tal Baz; Carlos Drazen. **Semiotica** 129:1 4:2000 pp.1-28.
1899 Le Mexique, lieu symbolique et fantasmatique dans le cinéma Américain. *[In French]*; [Mexico: a symbolic place in American cinema] *[Summary]*; *[Summary in Spanish]*. Sabine Coudassot-Ramirez; Quitterie Duhurt. **Caravelle** 74 6:2000 pp.227-240.
1900 The movies as history: visions of the twentieth century. David W. Ellwood [Ed.]. Stroud: Sutton, 2000. x, 214p. *ISBN: 0750923318. Includes bibliographical references and index.*
1901 Moving still life: Jean-Daniel Pollet's Francis Ponge. Shirley Ann Jordan. **Fr. Stud.** LIV:4 10:2000 pp.479-492.
1902 Oh *Les derniers jours*. *[In French]*; [Oh *The Last Days*]. Gérard Wacjman. **Temps Mod.** 55:608 3-5:2000 pp.2-29.
1903 The returns of Cleopatra Jones. Jennifer De Vere Brody. **Signs** 25:1 Autumn:1999 pp.91-122.
1904 Robert Bresson toujours vivant. *[In French]*; [The living legacy of Robert Bresson]. Jean Sémolué. **Esprit** 261 2:2000 pp.6-17.
1905 Savage theory: cinema as modern magic. Rachel O. Moore. Durham NC: Duke University Press, 2000. 199p. *ISBN: 0822323885, 0822323540.*
1906 *Shoah*: histoire et mémoire. *[In French]*; [*Shoah*: history and memory]. Jean-François Forges. **Temps Mod.** 55:608 3-5:2000 pp.30-41.
1907 *Short cuts* and long shots: Raymond Carver's stories and Robert Altman's film. Kasia Boddy. **J. Am. Stud.** 34:1 4:2000 pp.1-22.
1908 Social class, cultural repertoires, and popular culture: the case of film. Lisa A. Barnett; Michael Patrick Allen. **Sociol. For.** 15:1 3:2000 pp.145-163.
1909 Struggles for representation: African American documentary film and video. Janet K. Cutler [Ed.]; Phyllis Rauch Klotman [Ed.]. Bloomington IN: Indiana University Press, 1999. xxxiii, 483p. *ISBN: 0253335957, 0253213479. Includes bibliographical references (p. [457]-472) and indexes.*

D: CULTURE

1910 The three father figures in Tian Zhuangzhuang's film *The Blue Kite*: the emasculation of males by the Communist Party. Hanna Bøje Nielsen. **Chi. Inform.** XIII:4 Spring:1999 pp.83-96.
1911 Transcultural cinema. David MacDougall; Lucien Taylor [Ed.]. Princeton NJ: Princeton University Press, 1998. x, 318p. *ISBN: 0691012342, 0691012350.*
1912 'You don't have to be filmish' the Toronto Jewish film festival. Mikel J. Koven. **Ethnologies** 21:1 1999 pp.115-132.

Literature
Littérature

1913 Amadou Hampaté Bâ. Ralph A. Austen; Kenneth W. Harrow; Moradewun Adejunmobi. **R. African Lit.** 31:3 Fall:2000 pp.1-36. *Collection of 3 articles.*
1914 Arabic Canadian literature: overview and preliminary bibliography. Elizabeth Dahab. **Can. Ethn. Stud.** XXXI:2 1999 pp.100-114.
1915 Being here and writing there: gender and the politics of translation in a Brazilian landscape. Claudia de Lima Costa. **Signs** 25:3 Spring:2000 pp.727-760.
1916 Biography and historiography: the case of David Ben-Gurion. Michael Keren. **Biography** 23:2 Spring:2000 pp.332-351.
1917 'Black and 'cause I'm Black I'm blue': transverse racial geographies in Toni Morrison's *The Bluest Eye*. Katherine McKittrick. **Gend. Place Cult.** 7:2 6:2000 pp.125-142.
1918 The Cambridge guide to women's writing in English. Lorna Sage; Germaine Greer; Elaine Showalter. Cambridge: Cambridge University Press, 1999. viii, 696p. *ISBN: 0521495253, 0521668131.*
1919 Conjectures on world literature. Franco Moretti. **New Left R.** 1 1-2:2000 pp.54-68.
1920 Consuming spaces: Clive Barker, William Gibson and the cultural poetics of postmodern fantasy. Robbie B.H. Goh. **Soc. Sem.** 10:1 4:2000 pp.21-40.
1921 Cultural citizenship and crime fiction: politics and the interpretive community. Joke Hermes; Cindy Stello. **Euro. Journ. Cult. Stud.** 3:2 5:2000 pp.215-232.
1922 De «*nepantla*» à Ithaque: l'écriture sans limites de Tomás Segovia. *[In French]*; [From '*nepantla*' to Ithaca: Tomás Segovia's literature without limits] *[Summary]*. Bernard Sicot. **Caravelle** 74 6:2000 pp.211-226.
1923 Development and quality of life: a critique of Amartya Sen's *Development as Freedom*. Vicente Navarro. **Int. J. Health. Ser.** 30:4 2000 pp.661-674.
1924 L'écrit en révolution. *[In French]*; [Writing in revolt]. Richard Robert. **Esprit** 262 3-4:2000 pp.205-223.
1925 La escritura de mujeres: ¿otra visión del continente africano? *[In Spanish]*; [Women's writing: another view of the African continent?] Inmaculada Díaz Narbona. **Stud. Afr.** 11 3:2000 pp.70-83.
1926 Exotic reminiscences: the feminime other in French fiction on South East Asia. Srilata Ravi. **Fr. Cult. Stud.** 11(1):31 2:2000 pp.53-74.
1927 From big sticks to talking sticks: family, work, and masculinity in Stephen King's *The Shining*. Stephen Davenport. **Men. Masc.** 2:3 1:2000 pp.308-352.
1928 From garden to gardener: the cultivation of little girls in Carroll's *Alice* books and Ruskin's *Of Queen's Gardens*. Joanna Tapp Pierce. **Wom. Stud.** 29:6 2000 pp.741-762.
1929 Gender and sexuality in Asian American literature. Sau-ling C. Wong; Jeffrey J. Santa Ana. **Signs** 25:1 Autumn:1999 pp.171-230.
1930 Gender in Taiwan's postmodern literature. Shu-chen Chiang. **Asian Cult. (Asian-Pac. Cult.) Q.** XXVIII:1 Spring:2000 pp.9-28.
1931 La généalogie imaginaire de la littérature algérienne francophone. *[In French]*; [The imaginary genealogy of francophone Algerian literature] *[Summary]*. Farid Laroussi. **Can. J. Afr. St.** 33:1 1999 pp.53-63.
1932 Gibran and the Arabic literary movement in America. Nadeem Naimy. **Al-Abhath** XLVII 1999 pp.5-22.

D: CULTURE

1933 'Homosapiens A' and 'Homosapiens Z': love, resignation, and cultural disorientation in Pham Thi Hoài's novel, *Thiên sú*. Dana Healy. **S.E. Asia Res.** 8:2 7:2000 pp.185-203.

1934 How Polish is Polishness: about Mickiewicz's *Grażyna*. Irena Grudzińka Gross. **E. Eur. Pol. Soc.** 14:1 Winter:2000 pp.1-11.

1935 Ideology, identity and language in modern Hebrew literature. Risa Domb. **Isr. Aff.** 7:1 Autumn:2000 pp.71-86.

1936 Irish women writing. Maureen O'Connor; Karen Steele; Eileen Morgan; Helen V. Emmitt; Kim McMullen; Jeanette Roberts Shumaker; Vona Groarke; Siobhán Campbell. **Wom. Stud.** 29:4 2000 pp.415-542. *Collection of 8 articles*.

1937 James Joyce's *The Dead*. Morris L. Peltz; Alice Jones; Stanley J. Coen; Jay Martin; Paul Schwaber. **J. App. Psy. Stud.** 2:2 4:2000 pp.101-145. *Collection of 5 articles*.

1938 Kak pisat' memuary, ili dvoinoi avtoritet. *[In Russian]*; [How to write memoirs]. N. Bikkeinin. **Svobod. Mysl'** 6 2000 pp.95-108.

1939 Ken Saro-Wiwa: (a bio-critical study). Femi Ojo-Ade. Brooklyn NY: Africana Legacy Press, 1999. 300p. *ISBN: 0966383710. Includes bibliographical references (p. 294-300)*.

1940 The linguistic representation of femininity and masculinity in Jean Genet's *Notre-Dame des Fleurs*. Barbara E. Bullock; Denis M. Provencher. **Fr. Cult. Stud.** 12(1):34 2:2001 pp.43-58.

1941 Literary geography: Joyce, Woolf and the city. Jeri Johnson. **City** 4:2 7:2000 pp.199-214.

1942 Literature across boundaries: the perception and impact of francophone African literatures in South Africa; *[Summary in French]*. Pius Adesanmi. **Cah. Ét. Afr.** XL(2):158 2000 pp.241-256.

1943 Literature in English by Filipino women. Edna Zapanta Manlapaz. **Fem. Stud.** 26:1 Spring:2000 pp.187-230.

1944 Littérature, sociologie et sociologie de la littérature: à propos de lectures sociologiques de *À la recherche du temps perdu*. *[In French]*; (Literature, sociology, and literature sociology. In relation to sociological readings of *À la recherche du temps perdu*.) *[Summary]*. Florent Champy. **Rev. Fr. Soc.** 41:2 4-6:2000 pp.345-364.

1945 Making friends? Contemporary women poets' difficulties with friendship. Vicki Bertram. **Wom. St. Inter. For.** 23:5 9-10:2000 pp.629-643.

1946 Man writing: gender in late twentieth-century Irish poetry. Joseph Lennon. **Wom. Stud.** 29:5 2000 pp.619-649.

1947 Mental pain and the cultural ointment of poetry; *[Summary in French]*; *[Summary in German]*; *[Summary in Spanish]*. Salman Akhtar. **Int. J.Psy.** 81:2 4:2000 pp.229-243.

1948 Modern Japanese literature and Christian writers. Yamagata Kazumi. **Acta Asia.** 79 2000 pp.21-37.

1949 Mounsi: from oblivion to remembrance of the self through writing. Kathryn Lay-Chenchabi; Bernadette Dejean de la Batie. **Fr. Cult. Stud.** 11(2):2 6:2000 pp.249-268.

1950 Not really prostitution: the political economy of sexual tourism in Gide's *Si le grain ne meurt*. Judith Still. **Fr. Stud.** LIV:1 1:2000 pp.17-34.

1951 On the nation's margins: the social place of literature in Singapore. Philip Holden. **SOJOURN** 15:1 4:2000 pp.30-51.

1952 Open book: one publisher's war. Steve MacDonogh. Dingle: Brandon, 1999. 255p. *ISBN: 0863222633*.

1953 O osobliwościach uprawiania socjologii literatury. *[In Polish]*; (On the peculiarities of the sociology of literature studies.) *[Summary]*. Bogusław Sułkowski. **Prz. Soc.** XLVIII:2 1999 pp.127-149.

1954 Ot zhenskoi literatury k 'zhenskomu romanu'? *[In Russian]*; (From female literature to the 'female novel'?) V.G. Ivanitskii. **Obshch. Nauki Sovrem.** 4 2000 pp.151-163.

1955 Passion's fortune: the story of Mills & Boon. Joseph McAleer. Oxford: Oxford University Press, 1999. 320p. *ISBN: 0198204558*.

1956 Postwar literature and the Asian experience: with reference to three writers. Kawamura Minato. **Acta Asia.** 79 2000 pp.38-54.

D: CULTURE

1957 Reflections on fiction, representation, and organization studies: an essay with special reference to the work of Jorge Luis Borges. Christian De Cock. **Organ. Stud.** 21:3 2000 pp.589-609.

1958 Rompols not of the Bailey: Fred Vargas and the *polar* as *mini-proto-mythe*. Sara Poole. **Fr. Cult. Stud.** 12(1):34 2:2001 pp.95-108.

1959 Scattered felicity in Philippine poetry. L.M. Grow. **Phil. Stud.** 47:3 1999 pp.393-406.

1960 Self-writing, literary traditions, and post-emancipation identity: the case of Mary Seacole. Evelyn J. Hawthorne. **Biography** 23:2 Spring:2000 pp.309-331.

1961 Society in fiction. Niels Mulder. **Phil. Stud.** 48:2 2000 pp.235-264.

1962 A sociological analysis of the *Satanic verses* affair. Bridget Fowler. **Theory Cult. Soc.** 17:1 2:2000 pp.39-62.

1963 Svengali's web: the alien enchanter in modern culture. Daniel Pick. New Haven CT: Yale University Press, 2000. 290p. *ISBN: 0300082045. Includes bibliographical references and index.*

1964 'The bright bone of a dream': drama, performativity, ritual, and community in Michael Ondaatje's *Running in the family*. S. Leigh Matthews. **Biography** 23:2 Spring:2000 pp.352-371.

1965 'The past is infinite': history and myth in Toni Morrison's trilogy. Suzette Spencer [Intro.]; Barbara Christian. **Soc. Ident.** 6:4 12:2000 pp.409-423.

1966 The tyranny of time in the fiction of Najib Mahfouz. Fadia Suyoufie. **Al-Abhath** XLVII 1999 pp.59-84.

1967 Varieties of risible experience: grades of laughter in modern American literature. D.G. Kehl. **Humor** 13:4 2000 pp.379-393.

1968 Vyzov romantizmu v postmodernistskom britanskom romane. *[In Russian]*; (Romanticism challenged in the postmodernist British novel.) N.A. Solov'eva. **Vest. Mosk. Univ. Ser. 9 Filol.** 1 1-2:2000 pp.53-67.

1969 When Helen awakens: revisionary myth in Judy Grahn's *The Queen of Wands*. Sylvia B. Henneberg. **Wom. Stud.** 29:3 2000 pp.285-308.

1970 'You must create a female': republican order and its natural base in *Frankenstein*. Margit Stange. **Wom. Stud.** 29:3 2000 pp.309-331.

Music
Musique

1971 Boogie opera: Eddie, Douzi, and artistic convention. Tom Simmons. **J. Pop. Cult.** 33:4 Spring:2000 pp.101-122.

1972 Folk song genres and their melodies in India: music use and genre process. Edward O. Henry. **Asian Mus.** XXXI:2 Spring-Summer:2000 pp.71-106.

1973 The 'folk-song' competition: an aspect of the search for an English national music. John Francmanis. **Rural Hist.** 11:2 10:2000 pp.181-205.

1974 'Hard and heavy': gender and power in a heavy metal music subculture. Leigh Krenske; Jim McKay. **Gend. Place Cult.** 7:3 9:2000 pp.287-304.

1975 Immaginario musicale e cultura di massa nella nuova era. *[In Italian]*; [Musical imagination and mass culture in the New Age]. Enrica Tedeschi. **Critica Sociol.** 133 Spring:2000 pp.48-72.

1976 Liberatory, nationalising and moralising by ellipsis: reading and listening to Lhussein Slaoui's song *Lmirikan*. Jamila Bargach. **J. N. African Stud.** 4:4 Winter:1999 pp.61-88.

1977 Les mondes de l'art à l'épreuve du salariat: le cas des musiciens de jazz français. *[In French]*; (The art world faced with becoming a group of salaried workers. The case of jazz musicians in France.) Philippe Coulangeon. **Rev. Fr. Soc.** XL:4 10-12:1999 pp.689-714.

1978 Music & politics. John Hutnyk; Sanjay Sharma; Koushik Banerjea; Virinder S. Kalra; Ashwani Sharma; Steve Wright; Raminder Kaur; Partha Banerjea. **Theory Cult. Soc.** 17:3 6:2000 pp.55-180. *Collection of 7 articles.*

D: CULTURE

1979 Music and the politics of sound: nationalism, citizenship, and auditory space. George Revill. **Envir. Plan. D.** 18:5 10:2000 pp.597-614.
1980 Music: the business. Ann Harrison. London: Virgin, 2000. 288p. *ISBN: 0753504332.*
1981 The mystery of samba: popular music and national identity in Brazil. Hermano Vianna; John Charles Chasteen. Chapel Hill NC: University of North Carolina Press, 1999. xx, 147p. *ISBN: 080782464X, 0807847666. Translated from the Portuguese Mistério do samba. Includes bibliographical references and index. (Series:* Latin America in translation/en traducción/em tradução).
1982 La nuova sociologia della musica. *[In Italian]*; [The new sociology of music]. Tia DeNora; Marco Santoro; Timothy J. Dowd; Antoine Hennion; Maria Teresa Torti. **Rass. It. Soc.** XLI:2 4-6:2000 pp.165-302. *Collection of 5 articles.*
1983 Per una sociologia della musica New Age. *[In Italian]*; (Towards a sociology of New Age music.) *[Summary].* Federico Del Sordo. **Critica Sociol.** 133 Spring:2000 pp.30-47.
1984 Performing the (sound) world. Susan J. Smith. **Envir. Plan. D.** 18:5 10:2000 pp.615-638.
1985 Popular culture, marginality and institutional incorporation: German-Turkish rap and Turkish pop in Berlin. Ayse S. Caglar. **Cult. Dyn.** 10:3 11:1998 pp.243-261.
1986 Regionalist accents of global music: the Occitan rap of *Les Fabulous Trobadors.* Joan Gross; Vera Mark. **Fr. Cult. Stud.** 12(1):34 2:2001 pp.77-94.
1987 Songs of the caged, songs of the free: music and the Vietnamese refugee experience. Adelaida Reyes. Philadelphia PA: Temple University Press, 1999. xix, 218p. *ISBN: 1566396859, 1566396867. Includes bibliographical references (p. 201-209) and index.*
1988 Sounding autonomy: Adorno, Coltrane and jazz. Nick Nesbitt. **Telos** 116 Summer:1999 pp.81-98.
1989 Subliminalité et sémantique: la construction du sens dans la chanson. *[In French]*; [Subliminality and semantics: the construction of meaning in song]. Louis Jean Calvet. **Semiotica** 132:1-2 2000 pp.137-150.

D.7: **Education**
Éducation

1990 Le choix d'un espace scolaire pour les parents de la diaspora arménienne: un choix religieux, un choix politique, un choix social. *[In French]*; [Choice of school for parents of the Armenian diaspora: a religious choice, a political choice, a social choice]. Annick Lenoir-Achdjian. **Can. Ethn. Stud.** XXXI:2 1999 pp.115-128.
1991 The crisis in urban adult basic education. Donna D. Amstutz; Vanessa Sheared; Jennifer McCabe; Donna Umeki; Alan K. Ferguson; Doris A. Flowers; David R.M. Beck; E. Frances Rees. **Educ. Urban. Soc.** 32:2 2:2000 pp.155-276. *Collection of 7 articles.*
1992 Critical thinking in education: a review. R.T. Pithers; Rebecca Soden. **Educat. Res.** 42:3 Winter:2000 pp.237-249.
1993 Désinstitutionnalisation et transformation du rapport aux normes scolaires. *[In French]*; (The disinstitutionalisation and transformation of educational norms.) *[Summary].* Marie Verhoeven. **Recher. Sociolog.** XXXI:1 2000 pp.197-210.
1994 Educación y pobreza: políticas, estrategias y desafíos. *[In Spanish]*; [Education and poverty: policies, strategies and challenges]. José Rivero. **Rev. Parag. Sociol.** 36:106 9-12:1999 pp.107-144.
1995 Education and human survival: the relevance of the global security framework to international education; *[Summary in French]; [Summary in German]; [Summary in Spanish]; [Summary in Russian].* Christopher Williams. **Int. R. Educat.** 46:3-4 7:2000 pp.183-204.
1996 Education: way behind but trying to catch up. Claudio de Moura Castro. **Dædalus** 129:2 Spring:2000 pp.291-314.
1997 Educational research: language and content. Lessons in publication policies from the low countries. Paul Smeyers; Bas Levering. **Br. J. Educ. S.** 48:1 3:2000 pp.70-81.

D: CULTURE

1998   Factors influencing post-school choice: some data from India. Autar S. Dhesi. **Rev. Int. Sci. Ec. Com.** XLVII:3 9:2000 pp.451-472.

1999   Generic research designs in the study of education: a systemic typology. James Steve Counelis. **Syst. Res. Behav. Sci.** 17:1 1-2:2000 pp.51-63.

2000   Handbook of the sociology of education. Maureen T. Hallinan [Ed.]. New York, London: Kluwer Academic/Plenum Publishers, 2000. xv, 588p. *ISBN: 0306462389. Includes bibliographical references and index. (Series:* Handbooks of sociology and social research).

2001   Hermeneutical evaluation of ethical praxis: the search for a moral basis of education. John H. Durnin; Richard M. Jacobs. **J. Struct. Learn. Int. Syst.** 14:3 2000 pp.199-228.

2002   Identity and education: the links for mature women students. Janet Parr. Aldershot: Ashgate, 2000. 141p. *ISBN: 1840149973. Includes bibliographical references.*

2003   Identity and language learning: social processes and educational practice. Bonny Norton. New York: Longman, 2000. 173p. *ISBN: 0582382254, 0582382246. Includes bibliographical references and index. (Series:* Language in social life).

2004   Lifeworlds and learning: essays in the theory, philosophy and practice of lifelong learning. Bill Williamson. Leicester: NIACE, 1998. 220p. *ISBN: 1862010447. Includes bibliographical references (p. [207]-214) and index. National Institute of Adult Continuing Education.*

2005   Literacy and the new work order: an international literature review. Chris Holland; Tony Cooke; Fiona Frank. Leicester: National Institute of Adult Continuing Education, 1998. 140p. *ISBN: 1862010188, 1862010080. Includes bibliographical references (p. 129-140).*

2006   Literacy in the age of information — knowledge, power or domination? An assessment of the International Adult Literacy Survey. Jean-Paul Hautecoeur; Nancy Darcovich; Mary Hamilton; David Barton; Nathalie Druine; Danny Wildemeersch; Daniele Manesse; Sofia Valdivielso Gomez; Peter Roberts; Allan B.I. Bernardo. **Int. R. Educat.** 46:5 9:2000 pp.357-465. *Collection of 8 articles.*

2007   Maternal education and child health: a feminist dilemma. Sonalde Desai. **Fem. Stud.** 26:2 Summer:2000 pp.425-446.

2008   Misconceptions about the learning approaches, motivation and study practices of Asian students. David Kember. **High. Educ.** 40:1 7:2000 pp.99-121.

2009   Obcokrajowców uczenie Polski. «Studia Polskie» i rozwój edukacji międzynarodowej we współczesnym świecie. *[In Polish];* [Polish studies in an international context: contemporary international education]. Jarosław Rokicki; Janusz Mucha; Jadwiga Kowalikowa; Władysław T. Miodunka; Maria Elżbieta Sajenczuk; Stanisław Blejwas; Cheong Byung Kwon; Aleksander Kiklewicz; Jolanta Żurawska; Anna Dąbrowska; Urszula Dobesz; Małgorzata Pasieka; Bożena Gojawiczyńska; Marzena Kupczyk; Anna Omulecka; Piotr H. Lewiński; Grażyna Zarzycka; Małgorzata Gaszyńska-Magiera; Mirosław Jelonkiewicz; Elżbieta Wierzbicka; Wojciech Minicz; Alicja Skalska; Waldemar Martyniuk. **Prz. Pol.** XXVI:1(95) 2000 pp.5-200. *Collection of 21 articles.*

2010   Popular education and social movements in Scotland today. Ian Martin [Ed.]; Mae Shaw [Ed.]; Jim Crowther [Ed.]. Leicester: National Institute of Adult Continuing Education, 1999. 312p. *ISBN: 1862010412. Includes bibliographical references and index.*

2011   Racism and education. Theresa Richardson; Benjamin Baez; Aristotelis Santas. **St. Philos. Educ.** 19:4 7:2000 pp.297-361. *Collection of 3 articles.*

2012   Realism and educational research: new perspectives and possibilities. David Scott. London, New York: Falmer Press, 2000. 165p. *ISBN: 0750709197, 0750709189. Includes bibliographical references and indexes. (Series:* Social research and educational studies - 19).

2013   Socio-economic differences in foundation-level literacy. Lynne G. Duncan; Philip H.K. Seymour. **Br. J. Psy.** 91:2 5:2000 pp.145-166.

2014   Sociologie de l'éducation. *[In French];* [Sociology of education]. D. Martuccelli; M. Duru-Bellat; P. Merle; J.O. Jonsson; R. Erikson; F. Dubet; A. van Zanten; J. Perroton; A. Barrère; F. Ropé; L. Tanguy; Ch. Musselin; D. Meuret. **Ann. Sociol.** 50:2 2000 pp.297-554. *Collection of 10 articles.*

D: CULTURE

Academic access and achievement
Accès à l'éducation et la réussite éducationnelle

2015 Accessibility of women to science, technology and mathematics (STM) education in Nigeria. A.M. Oyeneyin; M.O. Salau; E.A. Ayodele. Ibadan: Development Policy Centre, 1999. ix, 109p. *ISBN: 9783481991. Includes bibliographical references (p. 101-109). (Series:* Research report - 20).
2016 Adult learning in England: a review. J. Hillage. Brighton: IES, 2000. 118p. *ISBN: 1851842993. (Series:* IES Report - 369).
2017 After affirmative action? Richard F. Tomasson; Caroline Hodges Persell; Linda S. Gottfredson; Barbara L. McCombs; Curtis Crawford; Abigail Thernstrom. **Society** 37:5 7-8:2000 pp.9-46. *Collection of 6 articles.*
2018 Alienation, class and enclosure in UK universities. David Harvie. **Cap. Class** 71 Summer:2000 pp.103-132.
2019 Anything to declare? The struggle for inclusive education and children's rights. John Kenworthy; Joe Whittaker. **Dis. and Soc.** 15:2 3:2000 pp.219-231.
2020 Behavior problems, academic skill delays and school failure among school-aged children in foster care: their relationship to placement characteristics. Bonnie T. Zima; Regina Bussing; Stephanny Freeman; Xiaowei Yang; Thomas R. Belin; Steven R. Forness. **J. Child Fam. Stud.** 9:1 3:2000 pp.87-104.
2021 The best of the brightest: definitions of the ideal self among prize-winning students. Michèle Lamont; Jason Kaufman; Michael Moody. **Sociol. For.** 15:2 6:2000 pp.187-224.
2022 Child health and school enrollment: a longitudinal analysis. Harold Alderman; Jere R. Behrman; Victor Lavy; Rekha Menon. **J. Hum. Res.** 36:1 Winter:2001 pp.185-205.
2023 Community college enrollment, college major, and the gender wage gap. Andrew M. Gill; Duane E. Leigh. **Ind. Lab. Rel.** 54:1 10:2000 pp.163-181.
2024 Desegregation update: equity and accountability in urban schools. Carolyn Talbert-Johnson; Ellen Goldring; Claire Smrekar; Ralph D. Mawdsley; Beverly A. Tillman; Lessie L. Cochran; Barbara Wilson Farmer; Edgar I. Farmer; Ralph Gardner; Loretta F. Meeks; Wendell A. Meeks; Claudia A. Warren. **Educ. Urban. Soc.** 33:1 11:2000 pp.8-101. *Collection of 7 articles.*
2025 Les disparités d'alphabétisation et de scolarisation en Turquie. *[In French]*; [Literacy and schooling disparities in Turkey] *[Summary]*. Ali Arayıcı. **Int. R. Educat.** 46:1-2 5:2000 pp.117-146.
2026 Disproportionate representation in special education: a synthesis and recommendations. Martha J. Coutinho; Donald P. Oswald. **J. Child Fam. Stud.** 9:2 6:2000 pp.135-156.
2027 The effects of class size on student achievement: new evidence from population variation. Caroline M. Hoxby. **Q. J. Econ.** CXV:4 11:2000 pp.1239-1285.
2028 Effects of cross-age peer tutoring networks among students with autism and general education students. Debra M. Kamps; Erin Dugan; Jessica Potucek; Angelia Collins. **J. Behav. Educat.** 9:2 6:1999 pp.97-115.
2029 En debatt om en muslimsk friskola. *[In Danish]*; (A debate about a private Muslim school.) *[Summary]*. Kristina Gustafsson. **Nord. Ny.** 78 8:2000 pp.5-26.
2030 Equality issues for the new millennium. Sneh Shah [Ed.]. Aldershot: Ashgate, 2000. xiv, 165p. *ISBN: 0754612511. Includes bibliographical references and index.*
2031 Excluded men: men who are missing from education and training. Veronica McGivney. Leicester: National Institute of Adult Continuing Education, 1999. 157p. *ISBN: 1862020390.*
2032 (Factors determining the academic achievement of the highest and lowest achievers on the general secondary exams in Jordan.); *[Text in Arabic].* S. Al Tall; A. Owaidat; K. Olayyan; R. Shraim. **Dirasat Ed.** 26:2 9:1999 pp.296-325.
2033 Factors influencing early dropout: the case of Russian immigrant students attending an Israeli University. Shifra Sagy. **J. App. Behav. Sc.** 36:3 9:2000 pp.362-375.

D: CULTURE

2034 Families or schools? Explaining the convergence in White and Black academic performance. Michael D. Cook; William N. Evans. **J. Labor Ec.** 18:4 10:2000 pp.729-754.

2035 Family structure, parental perceptions, and child labor in Kenya: what factors determine who is enrolled in school? Claudia Buchmann. **Soc. Forc.** 78:4 6:2000 pp.1349-1378.

2036 Family/school inequality and African-American/Hispanic achievement. Vincent J. Roscigno. **Soc. Prob.** 47:2 5:2000 pp.266-290.

2037 Fermate la scuola. Voglio scendere. *[In Italian]*; [Stop school, let me out] *[Summary]*. Adriana Luciano. **Sociol. Lav.** 78-79 2000 pp.86-105.

2038 Forecasting enrollments for immigrant entry-port school districts. Peter A. Morrison. **Demography** 37:4 11:2000 pp.499-510.

2039 From the woman question in technology to the technology question in feminism: rethinking gender equality in IT education. Flis Henwood. **Eur. J. Wom. Stud.** 7:2 5:2000 pp.209-228.

2040 Functional literacy of young Guyanese adults. Zellyne Jennings. **Int. R. Educat.** 46:1-2 5:2000 pp.93-116.

2041 Gender and education in Tanzanian schools. M. Mboya; S. Bendera. Dar es Salaam: Dar es Salaam University Press, 1999. ix, 153p. *ISBN: 9976603061. Includes bibliographical references.*

2042 Gender, 'race', and class in schooling: a new introduction. Chris Gaine; Rosalyn George. London, Philadelphia PA: Falmer Press, 1999. vii, 171p. *ISBN: 0750707585, 0750707577. Includes bibliographical references (p. 153-165) and index.*

2043 Higher education demand in Spain: the influence of labour market signals and family background. Cecilia Albert. **High. Educ.** 40:2 9:2000 pp.147-162.

2044 The inclusion of pupils with a chronic health condition in mainstream schools: what does it mean for teachers? Suzanne Mukherjee; Jane Lightfoot; Patricia Sloper. **Educat. Res.** 42:1 Spring:2000 pp.59-72.

2045 An investigation of academic self-concept and its relationship to academic achievement in African American college students. Kevin Cokley. **J. Black Psychol.** 26:2 5:2000 pp.148-164.

2046 Is education a priority for scheduled castes? A study of three districts of Bihar. S.K. Pant. **Indian J. Soc. W.** 61:1 1:2000 pp.66-88.

2047 Jeunes, familles et écoles: un monde en transformation. *[In French]*; (Youth, families and schools: a changing world.) Marie McAndrew; Michel Pagé; Mathieu Jodoin; Francine Lemire; Adaõ Do Nascimento; Marie-Louise Lefebvre; Maryse Potvin; Pia Carrasco; Damaris Rose; Johanne Charbonneau; Monique Lebrun; Janine Hohl; Margalit Cohen-Émerique; Gladys L. Symons. **Can. Ethn. Stud.** XXXI:1 1999 pp.5-138. *Collection of 7 articles.*

2048 Klassenlage und Bildungsentscheidungen: Eine empirische Anwendung der Wert-Erwartungstheorie. *[In German]*; (Social class and the choice of education: an empirical application of the subjective expected utility theory.) *[Summary]*. Rolf Becker. **Kölner Z. Soz. Soz. Psy.** 52:3 9:2000 pp.450-474.

2049 Learning in social action: a contribution to understanding informal education. Griff Foley. Bonn; Leicester; London: IIZ-DVV; NIACE; Zed Books, 1999. x, 163p. *ISBN: 1862010676, 1856496848, 185649683X. Includes bibliographical references and index. (Series: Global perspectives on adult education and training).*

2050 Literacy, power and social justice. Adrian Blackledge. Stoke-on-Trent: Trentham, 2000. v, 159p. *ISBN: 1858561582, 1858561574. Includes bibliographical references and index.*

2051 Magnet schools and the pursuit of racial balance. Ellen Goldring; Claire Smrekar. **Educ. Urban. Soc.** 33:1 11:2000 pp.17-35.

2052 A meta-analysis of the predictive validity of the selection process used by universities in Israel. Tamar Kennet-Cohen; Shmuel Bronner; Carmel Oren. **Megamot** XL:1 11:1999 pp.54-71.

2053 Motivation to commit oneself as a determinant of achievement in problem-based learning. Henk J.M. van Berkel; Henk G. Schmidt. **High. Educ.** 40:2 9:2000 pp.231-242.

D: CULTURE

2054 Negev Bedouin parents' views on the reasons for school drop-out. Ron Hoz; Anat Kainan; Ivan Reid. **Res. Educ.** 63 5:2000 pp.68-80.

2055 The new affirmative action: socioeconomic preference criteria in college admissions. Stanley B. Malos. **J. App. Behav. Sc.** 36:1 3:2000 pp.5-22.

2056 Not just for men: a case study of the teaching and learning of information technology in higher education. Sue Clegg; Deborah Trayhurn; Andrea Johnson. **High. Educ.** 40:2 9:2000 pp.123-146.

2057 Les «nouveaux acteurs» de la sélection universitaire: les bacheliers technologiques en question. *[In French]*; (The new 'actors' of university selection: French 'bac' technology graduates.) *[Summary]*. Thierry Blöss; Valérie Erlich. **Rev. Fr. Soc.** 41:4 10-12:2000 pp.747-776.

2058 L'origine sociale des collégiens et des lycéens en France: une analyse des conditions sociales de production de la statistique. *[In French]*; (The social origins of pupils in France: an analysis of the social conditions producing the statistics.) Charles Soulié. **Population** 55:1 1-2:2000 pp.169-180.

2059 Peer effects in private and public schools across countries. Ron W. Zimmer; Eugenia F. Toma. **J. Policy An.** 19:1 Winter:2000 pp.75-92.

2060 Profiles of African American college students' educational utility and performance: a cluster analysis. Stephanie J. Rowley. **J. Black Psychol.** 26:1 2:2000 pp.3-26.

2061 Putting the 'affirm' into affirmative action: preferential selection and academic performance. Ryan P. Brown; Tonyamas Charnsangavej; Kelli A. Keough; Matthew L. Newman; Peter J. Rentfrow. **J. Pers. Soc. Psychol.** 79:5 11:2000 pp.736-747.

2062 Racial desegregation: magnet schools, vouchers, privatization, and home schooling. Loretta F. Meeks; Wendell A. Meeks; Claudia A. Warren. **Educ. Urban. Soc.** 33:1 11:2000 pp.88-101.

2063 Racism in education and the construction of citizenship in Ecuador. Carlos de la Torre. **Race Class** 42:2 10-12:2000 pp.33-45.

2064 La réduction des inégalités sociales devant l'école depuis le début du siècle. *[In French]*; (A reduction in social inequalities in education since the beginning of the century.) *[Summary]*. Claude Thélot; Louis-André Vallet. **Écon. Stat.** 334 4:2000 pp.3-32.

2065 (The relationship of school behavior to parental practices, and achievement of 6th, 7th, and 8th grade students in Jordanian schools.) *[Summary]*; *[Text in Arabic]*. N. Dawoud. **Dirasat Ed.** 26:1 3:1999 pp.33-49.

2066 School, family, community: mapping school inclusion in the UK. Alan Dyson; Elaine Robson. Leicester: Youth Work Press, 1999. vii, 68p. *ISBN: 086155213X*.

2067 School provision for ethnic minorities: the Gypsy paradigm. Jean-Pierre Liégeois [Ed.]. Hatfield: University of Hertfordshire Press, 1998. 310p. *ISBN: 0900458887*. (Series: Interface collection - 11).

2068 School quality and the longer-term effects of Head Start. Janet Currie; Duncan Thomas. **J. Hum. Res.** 35:4 Fall:2000 pp.755-774.

2069 School reform and desegregation: the real deal or more of the same? Ralph Gardner; Carolyn Talbert-Johnson. **Educ. Urban. Soc.** 33:1 11:2000 pp.74-87.

2070 Sibling similarity in high school graduation outcomes: causal interdependency or unobserved heterogeneity? Gerald S. Oettinger. **S. Econ. J.** 66:3 1:2000 pp.631-648.

2071 Sibship sex composition: effects on educational attainment. Dalton Conley. **Soc. Sci. R.** 29:3 9:2000 pp.441-457.

2072 (Students' acceptance standards in accounting departments and their effects on their performance during the undergraduate study.) *[Summary]*; *[Text in Arabic]*. Majeed A. Hatef. **Dirasat Ad. Sc.** 27:2 7:2000 pp.310-320.

2073 Tears and laughter in the margins. Tuula Gordon. **NORA** 8:3 2000 pp.149-159.

2074 Teenage pregnancy and female educational underachievement: a prospective study of a New Zealand birth cohort. David M. Fergusson; Lianne J. Woodward. **J. Marriage Fam.** 62:1 2:2000 pp.147-161.

2075 (The tutorial lessons as perceived by Jordanian people.); *[Text in Arabic]*. Moh'd Batsh. **Dirasat Ed.** 26:2 9:1999 pp.342-368.

D: CULTURE

2076 Whatever happened to equal opportunities in schools? Kate Myers [Ed.]. Buckingham, Philadelphia PA: Open University Press, 1999. 241p. *ISBN: 0335203043, 0335203035. Includes bibliographical references and index.*

2077 White enrollment in nonpublic schools, public school racial composition, and student performance. Carl L. Bankston, III; Stephen J. Caldas. **Sociol. Q.** 41:4 Fall:2000 pp.539-550.

2078 Women's education and career opportunities in Kenya. Marylene C. Barngetuny. Nairobi: Creative Publishing, 1999. ix, 106p. *ISBN: 9966999205. Includes bibliographical references (p. 101-103) and index.*

Academic staff
Personnel enseignant

2079 Conflicting missions? Teachers' unions and educational reform. Tom Loveless [Ed.]. Washington DC: Brookings Institution Press, 2000. vi, 328p. *ISBN: 0815753047, 0815753039. Includes bibliographical references and index.*

2080 Desegregating urban school administration: a pursuit of equity for Black women superintendents. Beverly A. Tillman; Lessie L. Cochran. **Educ. Urban. Soc.** 33:1 11:2000 pp.44-59.

2081 The educational experiences of Jordanian teachers of English: implications for teacher education; *[Summary in Arabic]*. Turki Diab. **Dirasat Ed.** 26:1 3:1999 pp.255-266.

2082 Les enseignants face à la redéfinition normative de leur métier. *[In French]*; (Teachers and the normative redefinition of the profession.) *[Summary]*. Branka Cattonar; Éric Mangez. **Recher. Sociolog.** XXXI:1 2000 pp.185-196.

2083 Ethnic studies and foreign language teacher education in the United States: a response to population shifts. Flore Zéphir. **J. Multiling.** 21:3 2000 pp.230-246.

2084 Intention vs. abilities — the ethical dilemmas facing Israeli teachers in the 90s. Liron Dushnik; Naama Sabar Ben-Yehoshua. **Megamot** XL:3 8:2000 pp.442-465.

2085 Job insecurity of Israeli secondary school teachers: a multidimensional approach. Zehava Rosenblatt; Ayalla Ruvio. **Megamot** XL:3 8:2000 pp.486-511.

2086 Learning how to fish: issues for teachers engaging in self-evaluation and reflective enquiry in school. Keith Humphreys; Ziva Susak. **Res. Educ.** 64 11:2000 pp.78-90.

2087 Learning to teach grammar in the modern foreign languages classroom: some implications for Initial Teacher Education. Gee Macrory. **Res. Educ.** 64 11:2000 pp.1-11.

2088 Networks, identity, and (in)action: a comparison between Russian and Finnish teachers. Risto Alapuro; Markku Lonkila. **Euro. Soc.** pp.65-90.

2089 The next generation of faculty. Lorraine Mwenifumbo; K. Edward Renner. **Interchange** 31:1 2000 pp.61-78.

2090 Predictors of the academic performance of teacher education students. Kathy Hall; Paul Marchant. **Res. Educ.** 63 5:2000 pp.89-99.

2091 Professeur du secondaire: une profession féminine? Éléments pour une approche socio-historique. *[In French]*; [Secondary teacher: a feminine profession? Contributions to a socio-historical approach]. Marlaine Cacouault-Bitaud. **Genèses** 36 9:1999 pp.92-115.

2092 Recruitment, access and retention: some issues for secondary Initial Teacher Education in the current social context. Joan Whitehead; Keith Postlethwaite. **Res. Educ.** 64 11:2000 pp.44-55.

2093 (The relationships of principals' interpersonal orientations and teachers' perceptions, feelings, and satisfaction with the school climate.) *[Summary]*; *[Text in Arabic]*. Y. Haddad; M. Samarneh. **Dirasat Ed.** 26:1 3:1999 pp.202-222.

2094 Representing teachers: professional construction as reflected in employment ads. Vered Tzur; Amalya Oliver-Lumerman. **Megamot** XL:2 3:2000 pp.244-261.

2095 Research and the challenges of contemporary school leadership: the contribution of critical scholarship. Gerald Grace. **Br. J. Educ. S.** 48:3 9:2000 pp.231-247.

2096 Role pressures in school principals' work as predictors of burnout. Isaac A. Friedman. **Megamot** XL:2 3:2000 pp.218-243.
2097 School marks and teachers' accountability to colleagues. Maykel Verkuyten. **Disc. St.** 2:4 11:2000 pp.452-472.
2098 Superteachers: from policy towards practice. Alan Sutton; Angela Wortley; Jenny Harrison; Christine Wise. **Br. J. Educ. S.** 48:4 12:2000 pp.413-428.
2099 Target setting in the induction of newly qualified teachers: emerging colleagueship in a context of performance management. John Spindler; Colin Biott. **Educat. Res.** 42:3 Winter:2000 pp.275-285.
2100 Teachers and the myth of modernisation. Martin Merson. **Br. J. Educ. S.** 48:2 6:2000 pp.155-169.
2101 Teachers facing the confusion and conflicts in today's Japan. Yoshiyuki Kudomi. **Hito. J. Soc. Stud.** 31:2 12:1999 pp.69-83.
2102 Teaching as a mode of friendship. William K. Rawlins. **Commun. Theory** 10:1 2:2000 pp.5-26.
2103 Trainee teachers' perception of their knowledge about expert teaching. Olugbemiro Jegede; Margaret Taplin; Sing-lai Chan. **Educat. Res.** 42:3 Winter:2000 pp.287-308.
2104 The urban school principalship: changes and challenges. Peter J. Cistone; Joseph M. Stevenson; Van E. Cooley; Jianping Shen; Zhixin Su; Jeanne P. Adams; Elliot Mininberg; Liliana Rodriguez-Campos; Rigoberto Rincones-Gomez; Bradley S. Portin; Lourdes Zaragoza Mitchel; Gary L. Wegenke; Kathy Kimball; Kenneth A. Sirotnik. **Educ. Urban. Soc.** 32:4 8:2000 pp.435-543. *Collection of 8 articles.*
2105 (Urgent training needs of Arabic language teachers in Jordan.); *[Text in Arabic].* Hamdan A. Nasur. **Dirasat Ed.** 27:2 9:2000 pp.240-260.
2106 Worship in the primary school: a survey of head teachers' attitudes in rural west Wales. Geraint Davies. **Res. Educ.** 64 11:2000 pp.20-35.

Education systems
Systèmes d'enseignement

2107 African languages, English, and educational policy in Namibia. Joyce B.G. Sukumane. **Stud. Ling. Sci.** 28:1 Spring:1998 pp.207-220.
2108 Analyzing educational careers: a multinomial transition model. Richard Breen; Jan O. Jonsson. **Am. Sociol. R.** 65:5 10:2000 pp.754-772.
2109 Can effective schools be inclusive schools? Ingrid Lunt; Brahm Norwich. London: Institute of Education, University of London, 1999. 93p. *ISBN: 0854735887. Includes bibliographical references. (Series:* Perspectives on education policy).
2110 Collaborating to desegregate a 'Black' school: how can a low-power stakeholder gain voice? Maddy Janssens; Katrien Seynaeve. **J. App. Behav. Sc.** 36:1 3:2000 pp.70-90.
2111 Le concept de démocratisation de l'institution scolaire: une typologie et sa mise à l'épreuve. *[In French]*; (The concept of democratization of the school system: elaboration and application of a typology.) *[Summary]*; *[Summary in Spanish].* P. Merle. **Population** 55:1 1-2:2000 pp.15-50.
2112 Constraints to implementing educational innovations: the case of multigrade schools. Luis A. Benveniste; Patrick J. McEwan. **Int. R. Educat.** 46:1-2 5:2000 pp.31-48.
2113 Cultural transfer in adult education: the case of the folk development colleges in Tanzania. Alan Rogers. **Int. R. Educat.** 46:1-2 5:2000 pp.67-92.
2114 La démocratie condamne-t-elle l'école à la crise? *[In French]*; [Does democracy push schools into crisis?] Guy Coq. **Esprit** 268 10:2000 pp.39-51.
2115 La démocratisation de l'enseignement en France: polémiques autour d'une question d'actualité. *[In French]*; (The democratization of education in France: controversy over a topical question.) *[Summary]*; *[Summary in Spanish].* M. Duru-Bellat; A. Kieffer. **Population** 55:1 1-2:2000 pp.51-80.

D: CULTURE

2116 Démocratisation de l'enseignement: une comparaison Européene. *[In French]*; (Democratization of teaching: a European comparison.) *[Summary]*. Marie Duru-Bellat; Annick Kieffer. **Rev. de l'OFCE** 73 4:2000 pp.243-258.

2117 Dewey and European education: general problems and case studies. Jürgen Oelkers; Gert J.J. Biesta; Siebren Miedema; John Darling; John Nisbet; Cristina Allemann-Ghionda; Jan H. Schneider; Stefan Bittner; Irina Mchitarjan; Barbara Sörensen Criblez; Philipp Gonon; Daniel Tröhler; Roswitha Lehmann-Rommel. **St. Philos. Educ.** 19:1-2 3:2000 pp.1-218. *Collection of 11 articles*.

2118 Dilemmas in leadership: women of colour in the academy. Philomena Essed. **Ethn. Racial** 23:5 9:2000 pp.888-904.

2119 Disciplinary practices in Nebraska's public schools. Beth Winbinger; Antonis Katsiyannis; Teara Archwamety. **J. Child Fam. Stud.** 9:3 9:2000 pp.389-400.

2120 Diversity, choice and markets in education: benefits and costs. Geoff Whitty. **Hito. J. Soc. Stud.** 31:2 12:1999 pp.53-68.

2121 L'ecole et les langues nationales au Mali. *[In French]*; [Education and national languages in Mali]. Drissa Diakité; Samba Traoré; Mamadou L. Haïdara; Soumana Kané; Mamadou L. Kanouté; Amadou T. Doumbia; Ingse Skattum; Demba Pamanta; Marianne Opheim; Gérard Dumestre. **Nord. J. Afr. St.** 9:3 2000 pp.6-186. *Collection of 10 articles*.

2122 L'école et l'exigence éthique. *[In French]*; [Schools and ethical behaviour]. Jacqueline Costa-Lascoux. **Projet** 261 3:2000 pp.21-34.

2123 L'égalité en Russie: mythes et réalités. *[In French]*; (Equality in Russia: myth and reality.) *[Summary]*. David Konstantinovskij. **Rev. Ét. Comp. Est-Ouest** 31:3 9:2000 pp.69-97.

2124 The enduring nature of the tripartite system of secondary schooling in Germany: some explanations. Hubert Ertl; David Phillips. **Br. J. Educ. S.** 48:4 12:2000 pp.391-412.

2125 Les enjeux pédagogiques et institutionnels du partenariat dans l'enseignement technique et professionnel. *[In French]*; [Pedagogic and institutional challenges of partnership in the area of technical and professional education] *[Summary]*. Kouadio Aska. **Int. R. Educat.** 46:1-2 5:2000 pp.147-168.

2126 L'enseignement privé islamique dans le Nord-Cameroun. *[In French]*; [Private Islamic education in north Cameroon]. Hamadou Adama. **Islam Soc. S. Sah.** 13 12:1999 pp.7-40.

2127 Evolving the curriculum: groupwork and community based learning. Lynne Muir. **Groupwork** 12:1 2000 pp.72-82.

2128 Experiential learning around the world: employability and the global economy. Norman Evans [Ed.]. London, Philadelphia PA: Jessica Kingsley Publishers, 2000. 222p. *ISBN: 1853027367. Includes bibliographical references and indexes. (Series:* Higher education policy - 52).

2129 From mass higher education to universal access: the American advantage. Martin Trow. **Minerva** XXXVII:4 Winter:1999 pp.303-328.

2130 The grammar school question: a review of research on comprehensive and selective education. David Crook; Geoff Whitty; Sally Power. London: Institute of Education, University of London, 1999. viii, 72p. *ISBN: 0854736085. Includes bibliographical references. (Series:* Perspectives on education policy).

2131 Hackney Downs: the school that dared to fight. Maureen O'Connor; et al. London: Cassell, 1999. xix, 266p. *ISBN: 0304707104. Includes bibliographical references and index.*

2132 Higher education reformed. Peter Scott [Ed.]. London, New York: Falmer Press, 2000. 256p. *ISBN: 0750709774, 0750709782. Includes bibliographical references and index. (Series:* New millennium).

2133 Implementation of school-based management: a multi-perspective analysis of the case of Hong Kong; *[Summary in French]*; *[Summary in German]*; *[Summary in Spanish]*; *[Summary in Russian]*. Yin Cheong Cheng; Man Tak Chan. **Int. R. Educat.** 46:3-4 7:2000 pp.205-232.

2134 Importing organizational reform: the case of lay boards in Hungary. Anthony W. Morgan; Amy Aldous Bergerson. **High. Educ.** 40:4 12:2000 pp.423-448.

2135 In pursuit of school ethos. Caitlin Donnelly. **Br. J. Educ. S.** 48:2 6:2000 pp.134-154.

D: CULTURE

2136 In the frame. Integrated education in Northern Ireland: the implications of expansion. Grace Fraser; Valerie Morgan. Coleraine: University of Ulster, Centre for the Study of Conflict, 1999. vi, 118p. *ISBN: 1859231330. Includes bibliographical references.*

2137 Issues of educational administration in the Arab Gulf region. Mohammed Al-Saeed; K.E. Shaw; Alan Wakelam. **Middle E. Stud.** 36:4 10:2000 pp.63-74.

2138 It takes a city: getting serious about urban school reform. Paul Thomas Hill; Christine Campbell; James Harvey. Washington DC: Brookings Institution Press, 2000. xvii, 205p. *ISBN: 0815736398. Includes bibliographical references (p. 193-198) and index.*

2139 Knowledge links: innovation in university-business partnerships. Steve Lissenburgh; Rebecca Harding. London: Institute for Public Policy Research, 2000. xvi, 133p. *Includes bibliographical references (p. 129-133).*

2140 Konserwatyzm i rewolucje w systemach oświatowych. Polska reforma oświaty. *[In Polish]*; (Conservatism and revolutions in education systems. The Polish reform of education.) *[Summary]*. Zdzisława Kawka. **Prz. Soc.** XLIX:1 2000 pp.147-168.

2141 Korea's obsession with private tutoring. Heung-ju Kim. **Kor. Foc.** 8:5 9-10:2000 pp.76-89.

2142 A legacy of learning: your stake in standards and new kinds of public schools. David T. Kearns; James Harvey. Washington DC: Brookings Institution Press, 2000. xii, 226p. *ISBN: 0815748949. Includes bibliographical references and index.*

2143 Must liberal support for separate schools be subject to a condition of individual autonomy? Neil Burtonwood. **Br. J. Educ. S.** 48:3 9:2000 pp.269-284.

2144 Nonformal education, distance education and the restructuring of schooling: challenges for a new basic education policy. Wim Hoppers. **Int. R. Educat.** 46:1-2 5:2000 pp.5-30.

2145 Open learning system in APEC member economies. Kwan-chun Lee; Eun Soon Baik; Young Hwa Kee; Sung Jung Park; Sharan B. Merriam; Marquis Bureau. **Korea Obs.** 31:2 Summer:2000 pp.149-316. *Collection of 5 articles.*

2146 Organizational structures of teachers in traditional and magnet schools in a large urban school district. Barbara Wilson Farmer; Edgar I. Farmer. **Educ. Urban. Soc.** 33:1 11:2000 pp.60-73.

2147 Las políticas de diversificación y diferenciación superior en el Brasil: alteraciones en el sistema y en las universidades públicas. *[In Spanish]*; [Politics of diversification and discrimination in higher education in Brazil. changes to the education system and public universities]. Afrânio Mendes Catani; João Ferreira de Oliveira. **Cuad. Am.** XIV:6(84) 11-12:2000 pp.77-94.

2148 The post-colonial state and educational reform: Zimbabwe, Zambia and Botswana. Rugano Jonas Zvobgo. Harare: Zimbabwe Publishing House, 1998. 214p. *ISBN: 1779050259.* (*Series:* Progressive teaching).

2149 Quel avenir pour nos deux langues? *[In French]*; [What's the future for our two languages?] Bertrand Girod de l'Ain. **Documents** 55:1 1-3:2000 pp.83-93.

2150 Reclaiming education. James Tooley. London: Cassell, 2000. 258p. *ISBN: 0304705667.*

2151 A reform for troubled times: takeovers of urban schools. Robert L. Green; Bradley R. Carl. **Ann. Am. Poli.** 569 5:2000 pp.56-70.

2152 Réseau des écoles et nouvelles pratiques du territoire montagnard. L'exemple des hautes terres du Puy-de-Dôme. *[In French]*; (School networks and new ways of life in mountain areas. The Puy-de-Dôme highlands as a case study.) *[Summary]*. M. Lacouture. **Ann. Géogr.** 109:616 11-12:2000 pp.613-630.

2153 The role of Turkish schools in the educational system and social transformation of Central Asian countries: the case of Turkmenistan and Kyrgyzstan. Cennet Engin Demir; Ayse Balci; Fusun Akkok. **C. Asian Sur.** 19:1 3:2000 pp.141-155.

2154 The school and community study: characteristics of students who have emotional and behavioral disabilities served in restructuring public schools. Krista Kutash; Albert J. Duchnowski; Vestena Robbins; Pamela K. Calvanese; Brian Oliveira; Marsha Black; Deloris Vaughn. **J. Child Fam. Stud.** 9:2 6:2000 pp.175-190.

2155 School choice and social justice. Harry Brighouse. Oxford, New York: Oxford University Press, 2000. *ISBN: 0198295863. Includes bibliographical references and index.*

D: CULTURE

2156   School, reform and society in the new Russia. Anthony Jones [Foreword]; Stephen L. Webber. Basingstoke; New York: Macmillan; St. Martin's Press, 2000. xx, 252p. *ISBN: 0333733967, 0312224133. Includes bibliographical references (p. 227-244) and indexes. Centre for Russian and East European Studies, University of Birmingham. (Series:* Studies in Russian and East European history and society).

2157   School students' views on school councils and daily life at school. Priscilla Alderson. **Child. Soc.** 14:2 4:2000 pp.121-134.

2158   Schools making a difference: lets be realistic! School mix, school effectiveness, and the social limits of reform. Martin Thrupp. Buckingham, Philadelphia PA: Open University Press, 1999. ix, 225p. *ISBN: 0335202136, 0335202128. Includes bibliographical references and index.*

2159   Schul- und Hochschulorganisation. *[In German]*; [Organization of schools and colleges]. Robert K. von Weizsäcker [Ed.]. Berlin: Duncker & Humblot, 2000. 291p.

2160   Sexual ideology and schooling: towards democratic sexuality education. Alexander McKay. Albany NY: State University of New York Press, 1999. x, 214p. *ISBN: 0791445232, 0791445240. Includes bibliographical references (p. 195-209) and index.*

2161   Spaces and places of Black educational desire: rethinking Black supplementary schools as a new social movement. Heidi Safia Mirza; Diane Reay. **Sociology** 34:3 8:2000 pp.521-544.

2162   Stemming the tide of rising school exclusions: problems and possibilities. Graham Vulliamy; Rosemary Webb. **Br. J. Educ. S.** 48:2 6:2000 pp.119-133.

2163   Uneducating South Africa: the failure to address the 1910-1993 legacy; *[Summary in German]*; *[Summary in French]*; *[Summary in Spanish]*; *[Summary in Russian]*. Johannes W. Fedderke; Raphael de Kadt; John M. Luiz. **Int. R. Educat.** 46:3-4 7:2000 pp.257-282.

2164   Virtue, vice and vacancy in educational policy and practice. Pádraig Hogan. **Br. J. Educ. S.** 48:4 12:2000 pp.371-390.

2165   What works in school improvement? Lessons from the field and future directions. Alma Harris. **Educat. Res.** 42:1 Spring:2000 pp.1-12.

2166   When schools compete: a cautionary tale. Edward B. Fiske; Helen F. Ladd. Washington DC: Brookings Institution Press, 2000. xvii, 342p. *ISBN: 0815728360, 0815728352. Includes bibliographical references (p. 323-328) and index.*

2167   Whose education for all? Recolonization of the African mind. Birgit Brock-Utne. New York: Falmer Press, 1999. 368p. *ISBN: 0815334788. Includes bibliographical references.*

Pedagogy
Pédagogie

2168   Are learning approaches and thinking styles related? A study in two Chinese populations. Li-fang Zhang; Robert J. Sternberg. **J. Psychol.** 134:5 9:2000 pp.469-489.

2169   Le christianisme à l'école. *[In French]*; [Christianity at school]. René Nouailhat. **Pensée** 322 4-6:2000 pp.123-135.

2170   Citizenship and school history: in defence of, or as a protection against the state? Terry Haydn. **Sch. Field** X:3-4 Autumn-Winter:1999 pp.33-46.

2171   Citizenship education in the curriculum: an international review. David Kerr. **Sch. Field** X:3-4 Autumn-Winter:1999 pp.5-31.

2172   Classrooms with a difference: facilitating learning on the information highway. Elizabeth J. Burge; Judith M. Roberts. Montreal: Chenelière, McGraw-Hill, 1998. x, 142p. *ISBN: 2894611609. Includes bibliographical references. (Series:* Lifelong learning on the information highway).

2173   (The communicative approach as practised by teachers of English for the basic stage in Jordan: an analytical study.) *[Summary]*; *[Text in Arabic]*. M. Tahbub; T. Diab. **Dirasat Ed.** 26:1 3:1999 pp.128-141.

D: CULTURE

2174   The comparative influence of individual, peer tutoring, and communal learning contexts on the text recall of African American children. Ebony M. Dill; A. Wade Boykin. **J. Black Psychol.** 26:1 2:2000 pp.65-78.

2175   Compressed video learning: creating active learners. Judith M. Roberts. Montreal: Chenelière, McGraw-Hill, 1998. xii, 133p. *ISBN: 289461196X. Includes bibliographical references.* (*Series:* Lifelong learning on the information highway).

2176   Conexiones: ambientes de aprendizaje colaborativos, una respuesta a los nuevos retos de la educación. *[In Spanish]*; ['Connections': collaborative learning envriroments, a response to new education challenges]. Claudia María Zea; María Del Rosario Atuesta; Miguel Ángel González; Jorge Ignacio Montoya; Irma Urrego. **Rev. Univ. EAFIT** 118 4-6:2000 pp.47-57.

2177   Conflicting philosophies of education in Israel/Palestine. Ilan Gur-Ze'ev; Adam Tenenbaum; Denise Asaad; Uri Ram; Yossi Dahan; Gal Levy; Yossi Yonah; Aharon Aviram; H.A. Alexander. **St. Philos. Educ.** 19:5-6 11:2000 pp.363-507. *Collection of 8 articles.*

2178   La construction européenne dans l'enseignement de l'histoire en France et en Allemagne. *[In French]*; [The European slant on the teaching of history in France and Germany]. Annick Bolmont-Couval. **Documents** 55:1 1-3:2000 pp.111-121.

2179   A critical examination of three factors in the decline of proof. Gila Hanna. **Interchange** 31:1 2000 pp.21-34.

2180   The curriculum: theory and practice. A.V. Kelly. London: Paul Chapman, 1999. xi, 244p. *ISBN: 1853963844, 1853964301. Includes bibliographical references and index.*

2181   Democracy, education, and the moral life. Donald Arnstine; William L. Blizek; Arthur Brown; Barbara Arnstine; Ronald David Glass. **St. Philos. Educ.** 19:3 5:2000 pp.255-296. *Collection of 5 articles.*

2182   Democratic social education: social studies for social change. David W. Hursh; E. Wayne Ross. London, New York: Falmer Press, 2000. vii, 263p. *ISBN: 0815337280, 0815328559. Includes bibliographical references and indexes.* (*Series:* Garland reference library of social science - volume 1156).

2183   (Determining the level of teaching effectiveness of the faculty members at Mu'tah University from their students' point of view.); *[Text in Arabic]*. A. Battah; R. Sa'ud. **Dirasat Ed.** 26:2 9:1999 pp.472-482.

2184   (Developing and evaluating an instructional model in designing and producing instructional materials according to system approach.) *[Summary]*; *[Text in Arabic]*. Narjes Hamdi. **Dirasat Ed.** 26:1 3:1999 pp.70-91.

2185   Developmentally appropriate practice and a national literacy strategy. Ros Fisher. **Br. J. Educ. S.** 48:1 3:2000 pp.58-69.

2186   An ecological inventory approach to developing curricula for rural areas of developing countries. David Baine; Biranchi Puhan; Gautam Puhan; Siba Puhan. **Int. R. Educat.** 46:1-2 5:2000 pp.49-66.

2187   Educated for the 21st century? John Tomlinson; Vivienne Little; Susan Tomlinson; Emily Bower. **Child. Soc.** 14:4 9:2000 pp.243-253.

2188   Educating citizens for a pluralistic society. Rosa Bruno-Jofré [Ed.]; Natalia Aponiuk [Ed.]; Ken Osborne; Dick Henley; Eric W. Stockden; Jamie-Lynn Magnusson; Romulo Magsino; John C. Long; Raymond G. Théberge; Beryle Mae Jones; Beverley Bailey; Jon Young; Robert J. Graham; Antonio Tony J. Tavares; Helen Bochonko; Chris Dooley. **Can. Ethn. Stud.** XXXII:1 2000 pp.1-187. *Collection of 11 articles.*

2189   Feminism and the classroom teacher: research, praxis, and pedagogy. Amanda Coffey; Sara Delamont. London: Falmer Press, 2000. 176p. *ISBN: 0750707496. Includes bibliographical references and index.*

2190   Genre effects on higher education students' text reading for understanding. Hazel Francis; Susan Hallam. **High. Educ.** 39:3 4:2000 pp.279-296.

2191   Globalisation and pedagogy: space, place, and identity. Richard Edwards; Robin Usher. London, New York: Routledge, 2000. 216p. *ISBN: 0415191149. Includes bibliographical references and index.*

D: CULTURE

2192 Homeschooling comes of age. Patricia M. Lines. **Publ. Inter.** 140 Summer:2000 pp.74-85.
2193 Homogeneity in students' conceptions about the efficiency of instructional interventions: origins and consequences for instructional design. Jan Elen; Joost Lowyck. **J. Struct. Learn. Int. Syst.** 14:3 2000 pp.253-265.
2194 How a qualitative approach to concept map analysis can be used to aid learning by illustrating patterns of conceptual development. Ian M. Kinchin; David B. Hay; Alan Adams. **Educat. Res.** 42:1 Spring:2000 pp.43-58.
2195 Implications for evaluation from a study of students' perceptions of good and poor teaching. David Kember; Anthony Wong. **High. Educ.** 40:1 7:2000 pp.69-98.
2196 L'insegnamento del diritto finanziario. *[In Italian]*; [The teaching of financial law]. Andrea Amatucci. **Riv. Dir. Finan. Sci. Fin.** LVIII:4 12:1999 pp.492-525.
2197 Instructional and cognitive impacts of Web-based education. Beverly Abbey [Ed.]. Hershey PA: Idea Group Publishing, 2000. 250p. *ISBN: 1878289594. Includes bibliographical references and index.*
2198 The interplay of a biology teacher's beliefs, teaching practices and gender-based student-teacher classroom interaction. Hsiao-Ching She. **Educat. Res.** 42:1 Spring:2000 pp.100-112.
2199 Learning beyond the classroom: a role for groupwork? Marion Silverlock. **Groupwork** 12:1 2000 pp.58-71.
2200 The mass class and teaching assistants: a case for discussion exercises. Marina Karides; Joya Misra. **Am. Sociol.** 30:4 Winter:1999 pp.72-85.
2201 Networked learning: the pedagogy of the Internet. Margaret Haughey; Terry Anderson. Montreal: Chenelière, McGraw-Hill, 1998. xii, 155p. *ISBN: 2894611587. Includes bibliographical references. (Series:* Lifelong learning on the information highway).
2202 Norms and niches: voices in higher education. Susanne V. Knudsen. **NORA** 8:3 2000 pp.137-148.
2203 Notes on school-based crime fighting: international lessons in moral education. Wendy Hall Maloney; Robert J. Kelly. **J. Soc. Distr. Home.** 9:2 4:2000 pp.71-90.
2204 'Our history syllabus has us gasping': history in Canadian schools — past, present, and future. Ken Osborne. **Can. Hist. R.** 81:3 9:2000 pp.404-435.
2205 El Paraguay y la Argentina en los textos escolares: una perspectiva bilateral de las representaciones del otro. *[In Spanish]*; [Paraguay and Argentina in school textbooks: a bilateral perspective of representations of the other]. Liliana María Brezzo. **Rev. Parag. Sociol.** 36:104 1-4:1999 pp.49-80.
2206 Peer tutoring: teaching students with learning disabilities to deliver time delay instruction. Brenda L. Telecsan; Deborah Bott Slaton; Kay B. Stevens. **J. Behav. Educat.** 9:2 6:1999 pp.133-154.
2207 The practice of university history teaching. Alan Booth [Ed.]; Paul Hyland [Ed.]. Manchester: Manchester University Press, 2000. 256p. *ISBN: 0719054915.*
2208 The regulation of argumentative reasoning in pedagogic discourse. Kristina Love. **Disc. St.** 2:4 11:2000 pp.420-451.
2209 Relationships between student scientific epistemological beliefs and perceptions of constructivist learning environments. Chin-Chung Tsai. **Educat. Res.** 42:2 Summer:2000 pp.193-205.
2210 (Reorganization of education by promoting the curriculum about computer networks.) *[Summary]; [Text in Japanese].* Akiyuki Ando. **J. Hum. Nat. Sci.** 108 10:1999 pp.123-138.
2211 Representación e inclusión del Caribe en los libros de texto de las escuelas primarias en los Estados Unidos. *[In Spanish]*; [Representation and inclusion of the Caribbean in primary school textbooks in the United States] *[Summary].* Bárbara C. Cruz. **Rev. Cien. Soc.** 6 1:1999 pp.123-140.
2212 Rupture politique et enseignement de l'histoire en Afrique du Sud: les manuels de l'enseignement primaire. *[In French]*; [Political breakdown and the teaching of history in South Africa: primary school textbooks] *[Summary]; [Summary in German]; [Summary in*

D: CULTURE

Spanish]; [Summary in Russian]. Claude Carpentier. **Int. R. Educat.** 46:3-4 7:2000 pp.283-304.

2213 Service-learning pedagogy as universities' response to troubled times. Sam Marullo; Bob Edwards; John Wallace; Kelly Ward; Lisa Wolf-Wendel; Robert Gronski; Kenneth Pigg; Andrew Schamess; Rene Wallis; Ronald David; Keith Eiche; Maria da Gloria Miotto Wright; Christopher J. Koliba; Anne R. Roschelle; Jennifer Turpin; Robert Elias; Melissa Aberle-Grasse; Sara Grusky; Shelly Schaefer Hinck; Mary Ellen Brandell; Robert G. Bringle; Richard Games; Catherine Ludlum Foos; Robert Osgood; Randall Osborne. **Am. Behav. Sc.** 43:5 2:2000 pp.746-900. *Collection of 13 articles.*

2214 Standardized minds: the high price of America's testing culture and what we can do about it. Peter Sacks. Cambridge MA: Perseus Books, 2000. xii, 351p. *ISBN: 0738202436.*

2215 Teachers' conceptions of education: a practical knowledge perspective on 'good' teaching. Yvonne de Vries; Douwe Beijaard. **Interchange** 30:4 1999 pp.371-398.

2216 Teaching economics in the 21st century. William E. Becker. **J. Econ. Pers.** 14:1 Winter:2000 pp.109-120.

2217 'Telling our way of life': modes of mediating social life in German and Polish primary-school textbooks. Kristina Bennert; Dariusz Galasiński. **Soc. Sem.** 10:3 12:2000 pp.293-312.

2218 Theorizing citizenship education III. Alistair Ross; Joel Westheimer; Joseph Kahne; Tope Omoniyi; Helen Walkington; Chris Wilkins; Dieter Lenzen; Michael F. Shaughnessy [Interviewer]; Mitja Sardoč [Interviewer]; Cathie Holden; Paul Naylor; Helen Cowie. **Sch. Field** XI:1-2 Spring-Summer:2000 pp.7-142. *Collection of 8 articles.*

2219 A third grade teacher in a technocratic school system asks a dangerous question: what is learning? Paul De Witt. **Interchange** 30:4 1999 pp.399-414.

2220 Tomorrow's citizens: critical debates in citizenship and education. Nick Pearce [Ed.]; Joe Hallgarten [Ed.]. London: Institute for Public Policy Research, 2000. 110p. *ISBN: 1860300960.*

2221 Understanding Paulo Freire: reflections on the origins, concepts, and possible pitfalls of his educational approach. James Blackburn. **Comm. Dev. J.** 35:1 1:2000 pp.3-15.

2222 University knowledge in an age of supercomplexity. Ronald Barnett. **High. Educ.** 40:4 12:2000 pp.409-422.

2223 Using computer listserves to achieve a more diverse classroom: the 'virtual salon'. Thomas L. Steiger; Rhonda F. Levine. **Crit. Sociol.** 25:1 1999 pp.36-58.

2224 Versions of Vygotsky. Julia Gillen. **Br. J. Educ. S.** 48:2 6:2000 pp.183-198.

2225 What's so special? Teachers' models and their realisation in practice in segregated schools. Joan Adams; John Swain; Jim Clark. **Dis. and Soc.** 15:2 3:2000 pp.233-245.

2226 Why Johnny can't think and neither can his local journalist, doctor, architect, or teacher. David Clarke. **Know. Tech. Pol.** 12:4 Winter:2000 pp.44-71.

2227 Yabancılara Türkçe öğretimi ve gramer-tercüme metodu. *[In Turkish];* (Teaching Turkish as a foreign language and grammar translation method.) *[Summary]; [Summary in Russian].* M. Sani Adigüzel. **Bilig** 16 Winter:2001 pp.25-46.

2228 Zum Fremdsprachenunterricht in Mittel-und Osteuropa. Neuere Tendenzen. *[In German];* [The teaching of foreign languages in Central and Eastern Europe: new trends]. Mona Selten-Eisenhardt. **Osteuropa** 50:1 1:2000 pp.77-87.

Primary education
Enseignement primaire

2229 Children's views of the primary classroom as an environment for working and learning. Ruth Kershner; Pam Pointon. **Res. Educ.** 64 11:2000 pp.64-77.

2230 Fælles ansvar for folkeskolen. *[In Danish];* (Joint responsibility for primary schools.) *[Summary].* Kirsten Egholk. **Nord. Ny.** 78 8:2000 pp.61-94.

D: CULTURE

2231 Perceived crowding in Indian classrooms: the effects of age, gender and household density. Janak Pandey; Meera Verma; R. Barry Ruback. **Psychol. Devel. Soc.** 12:2 7-12:2000 pp.139-154.

2232 Prácticas de aceptación y rechazo de estudiantes dominicanos(as) en una escuela elemental en Puerto Rico. *[In Spanish]*; [Acceptance and rejection practices concerning Dominican students in a Puerto Rican elementary school] *[Summary]*. Alberto López Carrasquillo. **Rev. Cien. Soc.** 6 1:1999 pp.141-164.

2233 (Pre-school education in the Hashemite Kingdom of Jordan: field study.); *[Text in Arabic]*. N. Al Surour. **Dirasat Ed.** 26:2 9:1999 pp.267-295.

2234 Urban and rural differences in primary school attendance: an empirical study for Tanzania. Samer Al-Samarrai; Barry Reilly. **J. Afr. Econ.** 9:4 12:2000 pp.430-474.

Secondary education
Enseignement secondaire

2235 Bullying in 25 secondary schools: incidence, impact and intervention. Derek Glover; Gerry Gough; Michael Johnson; Netta Cartwright. **Educat. Res.** 42:2 Summer:2000 pp.141-156.

2236 Cognitive style and behaviour in secondary school pupils in Kuwait. Richard J. Riding; Jamal Al Hajji. **Educat. Res.** 42:1 Spring:2000 pp.29-42.

2237 Departmental characteristics and the experience of secondary science teaching. James Donnelly. **Educat. Res.** 42:3 Winter:2000 pp.261-273.

2238 L'école secondaire russe en mutation (d'après la situation à Moscou). *[In French]*; (Secondary education in the throes of change during the reform: a view from Moscow.) *[Summary]*. Galina Čerednichenko. **Rev. Ét. Comp. Est-Ouest** 31:3 9:2000 pp.99-125.

2239 Functionele gemeenschappen, godsdienstigheid en prestaties in het voortgezet onderwijs. *[In Dutch]*; (Functional communities, religiosity and achievement in secondary education.) Anne Bert Dijkstra; René Veenstra. **Mens Maat.** 75:2 6:2000 pp.129-150.

2240 Leadership on race in a changing suburban high school. Patrick I. Connelly. **J. App. Bchav. Sc.** 36:4 12:2000 pp.407-424.

2241 The shared management role of the head of department in English secondary schools. Marie Brown; Bill Boyle; Trudy Boyle. **Res. Educ.** 63 5:2000 pp.33-47.

Tertiary education
Enseignement post-scolaire

2242 Academia y democracia en la universidad pública mexicana. *[In Spanish]*; [Academia and democracy in Mexican public universities] *[Summary]*. Daniel Cazés. **Rev. Mexicana Cien. Pol.** XLIV:177-178 9-4:1999-2000 pp.83-100.

2243 Academic restructuring: organizational change and institutional imperatives. Patricia J. Gumport. **High. Educ.** 39:1 1:2000 pp.67-92.

2244 Akkreditierung und Evaluation an deutschen Hochschulen: Ein Königsweg für die Reform deutscher Hochschulen? *[In German]*; (Accreditation and evaluation of German universities — an ideal method for the transformation of German universities?) *[Summary]*. Thomas Heimer; Johann Schneider. **Vier. Wirt.schung** 69:3 2000 pp.468-480.

2245 (The attitudes of Jordan University students toward a number of variables related to university life.) *[Summary]*; *[Text in Arabic]*. F. al Hadidi. **Dirasat Ed.** 26:1 3:1999 pp.50-69.

2246 (Attitudes of student teachers towards the practical education programme at the University of Jordan: an evaluative study.) *[Summary]*; *[Text in Arabic]*. Turki Diab. **Dirasat Ed.** 26:1 3:1999 pp.142-164.

2247 Benchmarking for higher education. Norman Jackson [Ed.]; Helen S. Lund [Ed.]. Philadelphia PA: Open University Press, 2000. *ISBN: 0335204538, 0335204546. Includes bibliographical references and index.*

D: CULTURE

2248 Co/extra-curricular activities: a reserve potential for youth development on university campuses. Gurmeet Hans. **Indian J. Soc. W.** 60:4 10:1999 pp.587-605.

2249 Comparability of postgraduate academic qualifications: some issues, challenges and experiences. George Gordon. **High. Educ.** 40:4 12:2000 pp.377-388.

2250 El conflicto universitario (1999-2000) a la luz del discurso escrito. *[In Spanish]*; [The university conflict (1999-2000) in the light of the written media] *[Summary]*. Georgina Paulín Pérez. **Rev. Mexicana Cien. Pol.** XLIV:177-178 9-4:1999-2000 pp.361-402.

2251 La crisis en la UNAM. *[In Spanish]*; [The crisis in UNAM] *[Summary]*. Heriberta Castaños Lomnitz. **Rev. Mexicana Cien. Pol.** XLIV:177-178 9-4:1999-2000 pp.295-312.

2252 The cultural role of universities in the community: revisiting the university — community debate. Paul Chatterton. **Envir. Plan. A.** 32:1 1:2000 pp.165-182.

2253 Determinants of college completion: school quality or student ability? Audrey Light; Wayne Strayer. **J. Hum. Res.** 35:2 Spring:2000 pp.299-332.

2254 Differences of degrees: higher education in the American states and Canadian provinces. G.W. Boychuk. **Can. Publ. Ad.** 43:4 Winter:2000 pp.453-478.

2255 Disciplinary cultures and the moral order of studying — a case study of four Finnish university departments. Oili-Helena Ylijoki. **High. Educ.** 39:3 4:2000 pp.339-362.

2256 (Entrance examination and choice in education — what attracts applicants for national and public universities in Japan?) *[Summary]*; *[Text in Japanese]*. Takeyoshi Iwamoto; Atsushi Hoshi. **St. Ess. Beh. Sc. Phil.** 20 3:2000 pp.21-38.

2257 Factors affecting departmental peer collaboration for faculty development: two cases in context. Kathleen M. Quinlan; Gerlese S. Åkerlind. **High. Educ.** 40:1 7:2000 pp.23-52.

2258 Faculty autonomy: perspectives from Taiwan. Jay R. Dee; Alan B. Henkin; Jessica Hsin-Hwa Chen. **High. Educ.** 40:2 9:2000 pp.203-216.

2259 The financing of higher education in Sub-Saharan Africa. Ben Jongbloed [Ed.]; Hanneke Teekens [Ed.]. Utrecht: Lemma, 2000. 127p. *ISBN: 9051894562.*

2260 The future of knowledge production in the academy. Tomas Hellström [Ed.]; Merle Jacob [Ed.]. Philadelphia PA: Society for Research into Higher Education & Open University Press, 2000. 163p. *ISBN: 0335206166, 0335206174. Includes bibliographical references and index.*

2261 The future of the liberal university in the era of the global knowledge grab. Claire Polster. **High. Educ.** 39:1 1:2000 pp.19-42.

2262 Global magnets: science and technology disciplines and departments in the United Kingdom. Sami Mahroum. **Minerva** XXXVII:4 Winter:1999 pp.379-390.

2263 Globalization, neo-liberalism and the changing face of corporate hegemony in higher education. William Carroll; James Beaton. **Stud. Pol. Ec.** 62 Summer:2000 pp.71-98.

2264 Gown and town: the university and the city in Europe, 1200-2000. Laurence Brockliss. **Minerva** XXXVIII:2 2000 pp.147-170.

2265 Higher education research: its relationship to policy and practice. Ulrich Teichler [Ed.]; Jan Sadlak [Ed.]. Oxford: Pergamon, 2000. xvi, 192p. *ISBN: 0080434525. Includes bibliographical references (p. 175-187) and index. (Series:* Issues in higher education).

2266 Higher education today: the impact of state politics and policies on access and economic development. Marilyn Gittell; Neil Scott Kleiman; Ross Gittell; Norman Sedgley; J. Phillip Thompson; Sarah Tobias; David E. Lavin; Cathy J. Cohen; Claire E. Nee. **Am. Behav. Sc.** 43:7 4:2000 pp.1053-1206. *Collection of 6 articles.*

2267 How well can we measure graduate over-education and its effects? H. Battu; C.R. Belfield; P.J. Sloane. **Natl. Inst. Econ. R.** 171 1:2000 pp.82-93.

2268 Individual differences in undergraduate essay-writing strategies: a longitudinal study. Mark Torrance; Glyn V. Thomas; Elizabeth J. Robinson. **High. Educ.** 39:2 3:2000 pp.181-200.

2269 International research orientation of Swiss universities: self-regulated or politically imposed? Franz Horváth; Karl Weber; Martin Wicki. **High. Educ.** 40:4 12:2000 pp.389-408.

2270 International trends in the quantity and quality of entrants to computer science courses in higher education; *[Summary in German]*. Christine Bruniaux; Kirstine Hansen; Hilary Steedman; Anna Vignoles; Karin Wagner. **Vier. Wirt.schung** 4:69 2000 pp.527-543.

D: CULTURE

2271 The irony of globalization: the experience of Japanese women in British higher education. Toshie Habu. **High. Educ.** 39:1 1:2000 pp.43-66.
2272 Learning through the distance mode: challenges for Canadian women in higher education. M.D. Ushadevi. **S. Asian Surv.** 7:1 1-6:2000 pp.33-48.
2273 Managing equal opportunities in higher education: guide to understanding and action. Diana Woodward; Karen Ross; John Bird; Graham Upton. Buckingham: Open University Press, 2000. ix, 174p. *ISBN: 033519561X, 0335195601. Includes bibliographical references and index. Society for Research into Higher Education.*
2274 Managing international students: recruitment to graduation. Christine Humfrey. Philadelphia PA: Open University Press, 1999. xv, 164p. *ISBN: 0335203086, 0335203078. Includes bibliographical references and index. Society for Research into Higher Education.* (*Series:* Managing colleges and universities).
2275 Managing quality in higher education: an international perspective on institutional assessment and change. John Brennan; Tarla Shah. Philadelphia PA: Open University Press, 2000. 159p. *ISBN: 0335206735, 0335206743. Includes bibliographical references and index.*
2276 Measurement of the socio-economic status of Australian higher education students. Julie McMillan; John Western. **High. Educ.** 39:2 3:2000 pp.223-248.
2277 Monash: remaking the university. Simon Marginson. St. Leonards: Allen & Unwin, 2000. xvi, 280p. *ISBN: 1865082686. Includes index.*
2278 A new world of knowledge: Canadian universities and globalization. Sheryl Bond [Ed.]; Jean-Pierre Lemasson [Ed.]. Ottawa: International Development Research Centre, 1999. xii, 294p. *ISBN: 0889368937.*
2279 Policing the subject: learning outcomes, managerialism and research in PCET. James Avis. **Br. J. Educ. S.** 48:1 3:2000 pp.38-57.
2280 The politics of governance in higher education: the case of quality assurance. Brian Salter; Ted Tapper. **Polit. Stud.** 48:1 3:2000 pp.66-87.
2281 El programa de mejoramiento del profesorado (PROMEP) y sus críticas. *[In Spanish]*; [The Faculty Improvement Programme (PROMEP) and its critics] *[Summary].* Elena Zogaib Achcar. **Rev. Mexicana Cien. Pol.** XLIV:177-178 9-4:1999-2000 pp.135-158.
2282 Proposals that work: a guide for planning dissertations and grant proposals. Lawrence F. Locke; Waneen Wyrick Spirduso; Stephen J. Silverman. Thousand Oaks CA: Sage Publications, 2000. xvi, 350p. *ISBN: 0761917063, 0761917071. Includes bibliographical references (p. 339-344) and index.*
2283 Quality assessment in diverse disciplinary settings. Jouni Kekäle. **High. Educ.** 40:4 12:2000 pp.465-488.
2284 A questão da universidade e da formação em ciências sociais. *[In Portuguese]*; (The question of the university and education in social sciences.) *[Summary].* Sylvia Gemignani Garcia. **Tempo Soc.** 12:1 5:2000 pp.123-140.
2285 Research and teaching at a research university. Robert C. Serow. **High. Educ.** 40:4 12:2000 pp.449-464.
2286 Rethinking faculty development. Lanthan D. Camblin, Jr.; Joseph A. Steger. **High. Educ.** 39:1 1:2000 pp.1-18.
2287 The returns to higher education in Britain: evidence from a British cohort. R. Blundell; L. Dearden; A. Goodman; H. Reed. **Econ. J.** 110:461 2:2000 pp.82-99.
2288 Selection as contract to teach at the student's level: experiences from a South African mathematics and science foundation year. Hermien Zaaiman; Henk van der Flier; Gerard D. Thijs. **High. Educ.** 40:1 7:2000 pp.1-22.
2289 Similarities and differences: measuring diversity and selecting peers in higher education. Daniel W. Lang. **High. Educ.** 39:1 1:2000 pp.93-129.
2290 The stratification of Israeli universities: implications for higher education policy. Abraham Yogev. **High. Educ.** 40:2 9:2000 pp.183-202.
2291 The teaching and research relationship within an institutional evaluation. Javier Vidal; Miguel A. Quintanilla. **High. Educ.** 40:2 9:2000 pp.217-230.

2292 UNAM. Escenarios sincréticos de un conflicto. *[In Spanish]*; [UNAM: syncretic aspects of a conflict] *[Summary]*. Guillermina Baena Paz. **Rev. Mexicana Cien. Pol.** XLIV:177-178 9-4:1999-2000 pp.313-342.

2293 La UNAM, su gratuidad y su autonomía: elementos para un debate. *[In Spanish]*; [UNAM's cost-free status and autonomy: themes for a debate] *[Summary]*. Octavio Rodríguez Araujo. **Rev. Mexicana Cien. Pol.** XLIV:177-178 9-4:1999-2000 pp.343-360.

2294 La universidad hoy. *[In Spanish]*; [Today's university]. Juan Ramón de la Fuente; Leopoldo Zea; Hugo Casanova Cardiel; Roberto Rodríguez Gómez; Raúl Domínguez Martínez; José Enrique Pérez Cruz; Bernardino Montejano; Mario Magallón Anaya; Héctor Castañeda Ibarra; Axel Ramírez; Jean-Pierre Lavaud; J. Jesús María Serna Moreno; Anna M. Fernández Poncela; Carlos Arroyo Reyes; José Antonio Rico Ferrer; Silvia Nagy-Zekmi; Laura Llull; Alberto Enríquez Perea. **Cuad. Am.** 81:3 5-6:2000 pp.11-244. *Collection of 8 articles.*

2295 La universidad pública: esencia, misión y crisis. *[In Spanish]*; [Public university: core, mission and crisis] *[Summary]*. Marcos Kaplan. **Rev. Mexicana Cien. Pol.** XLIV:177-178 9-4:1999-2000 pp.101-134.

2296 University in transition. Detlef Müller-Böling [Ed.]. Gütersloh: Bertelsmann Foundation, 1998. 309p. *ISBN: 3892043663. Includes bibliographical references.*

2297 Vallástudományok és felsőoktatás. *[In Hungarian]*; (Religious studies in higher education.) András Máté-Tóth. **Mag. Tud.** 44:5 1999 pp.569-580.

2298 Vida universitaria. *[In Spanish]*; [University life]. Manuel Bernardo Rojas López [Interviewer]; Bruno Mazzoldi; Jesús Martín-Barrero; Oscar González [Interviewer]; Freddy Tellez. **Rev. Univ. EAFIT** 117 1-3:2000 pp.69-81.

2299 Widening the circle: faculty-student support groups as innovative practice in higher education. Carol A. Mullen; April Whatley; William A. Kealy. **Interchange** 31:1 2000 pp.35-60.

E: SOCIAL STRUCTURE
STRUCTURE SOCIALE

E.1: Social process and organization
Processus et organisation sociale

2300 The accidental derogation of the lay actor: a critique of Giddens's concept of structure. Anthony King. **Philos. S. Sc.** 30:3 9:2000 pp.362-383.
2301 Acquisition of the algorithms of social life: a domain-based approach. Daphne Blunt Bugental. **Psychol. B.** 126:2 3:2000 pp.187-219.
2302 Alexander Hirner on social system problems. Juraj Schenk. **Sociologia [Brat.]** 32:6 Fall:2000 pp.521-538.
2303 Autonomy beyond voluntarism: in defense of hierarchy. Stefaan E. Cuypers. **Can. J. Phil.** 30:2 6:2000 pp.225-256.
2304 A behavioral genetic analysis of the relationship between the socialization scale and self-reported delinquency. Jeanette Taylor; Matt McGue; William G. Iacono; David T. Lykken. **J. Personal.** 68:1 2:2000 pp.29-50.
2305 Contemporary British society. Nicholas Abercrombie; Alan Warde; Rosemary Deem; et al. Malden MA: Polity Press, 2000. *ISBN: 0745622968, 0745622976. Includes bibliographical references and index.*
2306 Contemporary Northern Irish society: an introduction. Colin Coulter. London: Pluto Press, 1999. ix, 286p. *ISBN: 0745312543, 0745312446. Includes bibliographical references (p. 258-273) and index. (Series:* Contemporary Irish studies).
2307 Cooperation in modern society: promoting the welfare of communities, states, and organizations. Mark Van Vugt; et al. New York: Routledge, 2000. 256p. *ISBN: 041521758X. Includes bibliographical references and index.*
2308 The cost of the game: a taxonomy of social interactions. Francesco Parisi. **Eur. J. Law Econ.** 9:2 3:2000 pp.99-114.
2309 Distinguishing non-knowledge; *[Summary in French].* Klaus P. Japp. **Can. J. Soc.** 25:2 Spring:2000 pp.225-238.
2310 L'émancipation sociale: ce qu'on en dit, ce qu'on en fait. *[In French];* [Social emancipation: what is said, and what is done about it]. Roland Lew. **Hom. Soc.** 136-137 2-3:2000 pp.9-28.
2311 L'être solitaire. La solitude dans l'opinion publique. *[In French];* (The solitary being. Solitude in public opinion.) *[Summary].* Judith Lazar. **Recher. Sociolog.** XXXI:2 2000 pp.157-175.
2312 Historische versus moderne Milieus. Die Rezeption des Milieukonzepts von M. Rainer Lepsius in der deutschen Geschichtsschreibung und Soziologie. *[In German];* [Historical versus modern milieus: the milieu-concept of M. Rainer Lepsius in German historiography and sociology] *[Summary].* Dieter Rink. **Social. Int.** 37:2 1999 pp.245-276.
2313 L'hospitalité. *[In French];* [Hospitality]. Anne Gotman; Jacques Barou; Michel Reeber; René Schérer; Louis Assier-Andrieu; Marianne Modak; Claude Spielmann; Joëlle Garbarini; Julien Damon; Claire de Galembert; Nikola Tietze; Christophe Robert. **Inf. Soc.** 85 2000 pp.4-118. *Collection of 17 articles.*
2314 Invisible ties: from patronage to networks. Bruce Mazlish. **Theory Cult. Soc.** 17:2 4:2000 pp.1-20.
2315 Order with things? Humans, artifacts, and the sociological problem of rule-following. Alex Preda. **J. Theory Soc. Behav.** 30:3 9:2000 pp.269-298.
2316 (Patterns of socialization in school as perceived by teachers of official basic schools in Madaba district.) *[Summary]; [Text in Arabic].* N. Ja'nini. **Dirasat Ed.** 26:1 3:1999 pp.108-127.
2317 Le processus de sublimation dans la société. *[In French];* [The process of sublimation in society]. Eugène Enriquez. **Temps Mod.** 55:609 6-8:2000 pp.104-130.

E: STRUCTURE SOCIALE

2318 Proposal of a four-dimensional model of social response. Paul R. Nail; Geoff MacDonald; David A. Levy. **Psychol. B.** 126:3 5:2000 pp.454-470.
2319 Realism, causality and the problem of social structure. Paul Lewis. **J. Theory Soc. Behav.** 30:3 9:2000 pp.249-268.
2320 A reconstrução do Estado social na Europa meridional. *[In Portuguese]*; (The reconstruction of the social state in Southern Europe.) *[Summary]*. Maurizio Ferrera. **Anál. Soc.** XXXIV:151-152 Winter:2000 pp.457-476.
2321 Shaping a settler elite: students, competition and leadership at South African College, 1829-95. Wayne K. Durrill. **J. Afr. Hist.** 41:2 2000 pp.221-239.
2322 Smoothing machines and the constitution of society. William Bogard. **Cult. St.** 14:2 4:2000 pp.269-294.
2323 Some problems and possibilities in the study of dynamical social processes. John E. Puddifoot. **J. Theory Soc. Behav.** 30:1 3:2000 pp.79-97.
2324 Soziale Lagen in der Schweiz. *[In German]*; (Social structures ('*soziale lagen*') in Switzerland.) *[Summary]*. Markus Lamprecht; Hanspeter Stamm. **Schweiz. Z. Soziologie** 26:2 7:2000 pp.261-295.
2325 Spatiality and the new social studies of childhood. Sarah Holloway; Gill Valentine. **Sociology** 34:4 11:2000 pp.763-784.
2326 Stuart Hall and the antinomian tradition. Chris Rojek. **Int. Jour. Cult. Stud.** 1:1 4:1998 pp.45-66.
2327 The subject of ideals. Lior Barshack. **Cult. Val.** 4:1 1:2000 pp.77-100.
2328 Tantalizing times: an examination of discontent and disconnects in contemporary American society. V. Barry Dauphin. **J. App. Psy. Stud.** 2:3 7:2000 pp.219-245.
2329 'The synergism hypothesis': on the concept of synergy and its role in the evolution of complex systems. Peter A. Corning. **J. Soc. Evol. Sys.** 21:2 1998 pp.133-172.
2330 Toward a theory of public ritual. Amitai Etzioni. **Sociol. Theory** 18:1 3:2000 pp.44-59.
2331 Understanding contemporary society: understanding the present. Gary Browning; Abigail Halci; Frank Webster. Thousand Oaks CA, London: Sage Publications, 1999. 400p. *ISBN: 0761959254, 0761959262*.
2332 Unraveling three of a kind: cohesion, community and solidarity. Talja Blokland. **Neth. J. Soc. Sci.** 36:1 2000 pp.56-70.
2333 Uses of social capital in Russia: modern, pre-modern and anti-modern. R. Rose. **Post-Sov. Aff.** 16:1 1-3:2000 pp.33-57.
2334 The web of group affiliations revisited: social life, postmodernism, and sociology. Bernice A. Pescosolido; Beth A. Rubin. **Am. Sociol. R.** 65:1 2:2000 pp.52-76.

Power relations
Rapports de pouvoir

2335 Empowerment and continuous improvement in the United States, Mexico, Poland, and India: predicting fit on the basis of the dimensions of power distance and individualism. Christopher Robert; Tahira M. Probst; Joseph J. Martocchio; Fritz Drasgow; John J. Lawler. **J. Appl. Psychol.** 85:5 10:2000 pp.643-658.
2336 Importance et signification de l'esclavage pour dettes. *[In French]*; (The importance and meaning of enslavement through debt.) *[Summary]*. Alain Testart. **Rev. Fr. Soc.** 41:4 10-12:2000 pp.609-642.
2337 Non-disciplinary power and the network society. Iain Munro. **Organization** 7:4 11:2000 pp.679-695.
2338 The power structure of rural grassroots units and its operational mechanisms: a case study of the situation in Changwuzhen in Heilongjiang province. Wang Yalin. **Soc. Sci. China** XXI:2 Summer:2000 pp.5-23.
2339 Resistance and the arts of domination: miners and the Bolivian state. Harry Sanabria. **Lat. Am. Pers.** 27:1 1:2000 pp.56-81.

E: SOCIAL STRUCTURE

2340 The sexual games of the body politic: fantasy and state violence in Northern Ireland. Begoña Aretxaga. **Cult. Medic. Psych.** 25:1 3:2001 pp.1-27.

2341 A status value theory of power in exchange relations. Shane R. Thye. **Am. Sociol. R.** 65:3 6:2000 pp.407-432.

Social norms
Normes sociales

2342 Animal rights and wrongs. Roger Scruton. London: Metro, 2000. xi, 206p. *Includes bibliographical references (p. 191-197) and index. Demos.*

2343 Auf der Suche mach einer öffentlichen Moral: Deutschland vor dem neuen Jahrhundert. *[In German]*; [The search for a public morality: Germany at the start of a new century]. Helmut Schmidt. Munich: Goldmann, 2000. 268p. *ISBN: 344215071X.*

2344 Beyond regulations: ethics in human subjects research. Nancy M.P. King [Ed.]; Gail E. Henderson [Ed.]; Jane S. Stein [Ed.]. Chapel Hill NC, London: University of North Carolina Press, 1999. xii, 279p. *ISBN: 0807847704, 0807824682. Includes bibliographical references and index. (Series:* Studies in social medicine).

2345 Building community social capital. John Durston. **CEPAL R.** 69 12:1999 pp.103-118.

2346 Can we return to the concept of duty in a culture of rights? Implications for morality and identity. Sunil Bhatia. **Cult. Psyc.** 6:3 9:2000 pp.303-316.

2347 Class, gender, and parental values in the 1990s. Hong Xiao. **Gender Soc.** 14:6 12:2000 pp.785-803.

2348 Cosmopolitanism and the banality of geographical evils. David Harvey. **Publ. Cult.** 12:2 Spring:2000 pp.529-564.

2349 Cultural relativism. John J. Tilley. **Hum. Rights Q.** 22:2 5:2000 pp.501-547.

2350 De l'être au devoir être: réflexions sur les rapports entre science et philosophie morale. *[In French]*; [From the being to the ought-to-be: the relationship between science and moral philosophy]. Caroline Eggli. Geneva: Université de Genève, 1999. 100p. *Includes bibliographical references (p. 97-100).*

2351 Defending the moral moderate: contractualism and common sense. Rahul Kumar. **Philos. Pub.** 28:4 Fall:1999 pp.275-309.

2352 Folk conceptions of fairness and unfairness. Michael B. Lupfer; Kelly P. Weeks; Kelly A. Doan; David A. Houston. **Eur. J. Soc. Psychol.** 30:3 5-6:2000 pp.405-428.

2353 For common things: irony, trust, and commitment in America today. Jedediah Purdy. New York: Alfred A. Knopf, 1999. xxiii, 226p. *ISBN: 0375407081. Includes bibliographical references (p. [211]-215) and index.*

2354 From cultural diversity to universal ethics: three models. Samuel Fleischacker. **Cult. Dyn.** 11:1 3:1999 pp.105-128.

2355 Globalization and the need for universal ethics. Karl-Otto Apel. **Eur. J. Soc. Theory** 3:2 5:2000 pp.137-156.

2356 Governing morals: a social history of moral regulation. Alan Hunt. Cambridge: Cambridge University Press, 1999. x, 273p. *ISBN: 0521646898, 0521640717. (Series:* Cambridge studies in law and society).

2357 Homogénéisation ou diversification des systèmes de valeurs en Europe occidentale. *[In French]*; (The convergence and divergence of value systems in Western Europe.) *[Summary]*. Henri Mendras. **Rev. de l'OFCE** 71 10:1999 pp.299-312.

2358 Infracção e censura — representações e percursos da sociologia do desvio. *[In Portuguese]*; (Infringement and censorship — representations and paths in the sociology of deviance.) *[Summary]*. Pedro Moura Ferreira. **Anál. Soc.** XXXIV:151-152 Winter:2000 pp.639-672.

2359 Intrinsic moral value and racial differences. Stephen Kershnar. **Publ. Aff. Q.** 14:3 7:2000 pp.205-224.

2360 Is it a different world to when you were growing up? Generational effects on social representations and child-rearing values. Jacqueline Scott. **Br. J. Soc.** 51:2 6:2000 pp.355-376.

2361 John Rawls's law of peoples. Charles R. Beitz; Allen Buchanan; Justin D'Arms; Daniel Jacobson; David McCarthy; Connie S. Rosati; William A. Galston. **Ethics** 110:4 7:2000 pp.669-822. *Collection of 6 articles.*

2362 A man can be made human: understanding and enhancing morality, values, and ethical behaviour. D. Suar. **Ind. Psych. Abs. Rev.** 7:1 1-6:2000 pp.1-39.

2363 Ménages et normes sociales en Belgique: vers une plus grande diversité? *[In French]*; (Households and social norms in Belgium — towards greater diversity?) *[Summary]*. Pau Baizan Munoz; Josianne Duchêne. **Recher. Sociolog.** XXXI:1 2000 pp.123-134.

2364 Modernizácia a anómia. Je teória anómie aktuálna i v súčasnej Slovenskej spoločnosti? *[In Slovak]*; (Modernization and anomie. Is the theory of anomie topical in the present Slovak society?) *[Summary]*. Peter Ondrejkovič. **Sociologia [Brat.]** 32:4 2000 pp.343-360.

2365 Moral compromises, moral integrity and the indeterminacy of value rankings. Theo Van Willigenburg. **Ethic. Theory Moral P.** 3:4 12:2000 pp.385-404.

2366 Moral conflict and legal reasoning. Scott Veitch. Oxford: Hart Publishing, 1999. viii, 219p. *ISBN: 1841131083*. (*Series:* European Academy of Legal Theory series).

2367 Moral geographies: ethics in a world of difference. David M. Smith. Edinburgh: Edinburgh University Press, 2000. xi, 244p. *ISBN: 0748612793, 0748612785. Includes bibliographical references (p. 215-234) and index.*

2368 New directions in ethics: naturalisms, reasons and virtue. Soran Reader. **Ethic. Theory Moral P.** 3:4 12:2000 pp.341-364.

2369 Penser la violation. Relations morales et protection publique. *[In French]*; [Thinking about violation. Moral relations and public protection]. Frédéric Worms. **Esprit** 261 2:2000 pp.66-85.

2370 Platonic ethics, old and new. Julia Annas. Ithaca NY, London: Cornell University Press, 1999. viii, 196p. *ISBN: 0801435188, 0801485177. Includes bibliographical references and index.* (*Series:* Cornell studies in classical philology - 57).

2371 Producing and consuming trust. Eric M. Uslaner. **Pol. Sci. Q.** 115:4 Winter:2000-2001 pp.569-590.

2372 Transformatsiia tsennostei Rossiiskogo obshchestva. *[In Russian]*; (The transformation of values in Russian society.) E.I. Bashkirova. **Polis [Moscow]** 6(59) 2000 pp.51-65.

2373 The virtue of civility. Cheshire Calhoun. **Philos. Pub.** 29:3 Summer:2000 pp.251-275.

E.2: **Social stratification**
Stratification sociale

2374 À propos de la *service class*: les classes moyennes dans la sociologie britannique. *[In French]*; (The service class: middle classes in British sociology.) *[Summary]*. Catherine Bidou-Zachariasen. **Rev. Fr. Soc.** 41:4 10-12:2000 pp.777-796.

2375 Actors in processes of inclusion and exclusion: towards a dynamic approach. Georg Vobruba. **Soc. Pol. Admin.** 34:5 12:2000 pp.601-613.

2376 Der avancierende Fremde. Zur Genese von Unsicherheitserfahrungen und Konflikten in einem ethnisch polarisierten und sozialräumlich benachteiligten Stadtteil. *[In German]*; [The advancing stranger. On the genesis of experiences of danger and conflict in an ethnically polarised and socio-spatially segregated district] *[Summary]*. Jörg Hüttermann. **Z. Soziol.** 29:4 8:2000 pp.275-293.

2377 The best of times for some and the worst of times for others? Gender and class divisions in urban Britain today. L. Bondi; H. Christie. **Geoforum** 31:3 8:2000 pp.329-343.

2378 Bildungssysteme, soziale Ungleichheit und subjektive Schichteinstufung. Die institutionelle Basis von Individualisierungsprozessen im internationalen Vergleich. *[In German]*; (Educational systems, social inequality and the self-evaluation of inequality. The

E: SOCIAL STRUCTURE

institutional base of individualization in international comparison.) *[Summary]*. Martin Groß. **Z. Soziol.** 29:5 10:2000 pp.375-396.

2379 The bushman myth: the making of a Namibian underclass. Robert Gordon. Boulder CO, Oxford: Westview Press, 1999. 336p. *ISBN: 0813335817*.

2380 Can we live together? Equality and difference. Alain Touraine. Cambridge: Polity Press, 2000. ix, 326p. *ISBN: 0745622119, 0745622127. Translated from the French Pourrons-nous vivre ensemble? Egaux et différents. Includes bibliographical references and index.*

2381 Caste as census category: implications for sociology. Nandini Sundar. **Curr. Sociol.** 48:3 7:2000 pp.111-126.

2382 Les catégories socioprofessionnelles. *[In French]*; [Socioprofessional categories]. Alain Desrosières; Laurent Thévenot. Paris: La Découverte, 2000. 122p. *ISBN: 2707132217. Includes bibliographical references (p. 115-[120]).*

2383 Celeb-reliance: intellectuals, celebrity and upward mobility. Bruce Robbins. **Rad. Hist. R.** 76 Winter:2000 pp.3-14.

2384 Charles Tilly's *Durable Inequality*. Erik Olin Wright; Barbara Laslett; Aldon Morris; Charles Tilly. **Comp. Stud. S.** 42:2 4:2000 pp.458-493. *Collection of 4 articles.*

2385 Chudoba, marginalizace, sociální vyloučení. *[In Czech]*; (Poverty, marginalization, social exclusion.) *[Summary]*. Petr Mareš. **Soc. Čas.** 36:3 2000 pp.285-298.

2386 Citizenship and inequality: historical and global perspectives. Evelyn Glenn. **Soc. Prob.** 47:1 2:2000 pp.1-20.

2387 Class and the conceptualization of citizenship in twentieth-century Britain. Eugenia Low. **Hist. Polit. Thou.** XXI:1 Spring:2000 pp.114-131.

2388 Class and the customary: the ambiguous legacy of the *indigenato* in Mozambique. Bridget O'Laughlin. **Afr. Affairs** 99:394 1:2000 pp.5-42.

2389 Class cleavages in party preferences in the new democracies in Eastern Europe: a comparison with Western democracies. Mérove Gijsberts; Paul Nieuwbeerta. **Euro. Soc.** 2:4 2000 pp.397-430.

2390 Class struggle and social welfare. Michael Lavalette [Ed.]; Gerry Mooney [Ed.]. New York: Routledge, 2000. 256p. *ISBN: 0415201047, 0415201055. Includes bibliographical references and index. (Series:* State of welfare).

2391 Class-specific *habitus* and the social reproduction of the business elite in Germany and France. Michael Hartman. **Sociol. Rev.** 48:2 5:2000 pp.241-261.

2392 Crafting society: ethnicity, class, and communication theory. Donald G. Ellis. Mahwah NJ: Lawrence Erlbaum Associates, 1999. xvi, 229p. *ISBN: 0805832734. Includes bibliographical references (p. 209-219) and indexes. (Series:* LEA's communication series).

2393 Creating and spreading status beliefs. Cecilia L. Ridgeway; Kristan Glasgow Erickson. **A.J.S.** 106:3 11:2000 pp.579-615.

2394 Dalit identity and culture. Valerian Rodrigues; Raj Kumar; Y. Chinna Rao; Suguna Ramanathan; Ravindra Patil; P.L. Mimroth. **Soc. Act.** 50:1 1-3:2000 pp.1-86. *Collection of 6 articles.*

2395 Égalité et hiérarchie: Célestin Bouglé et Louis Dumont face aux systèmes des castes. *[In French]*; [Equality and hierarchy: Célestin Bouglé and Louis Dumont tackle caste systems]. Alain Policar. **Esprit** 271 1:2001 pp.43-62.

2396 Einstellungen zur sozialen Ungleichheit in Ostdeutschland: Plädoyer für eine doppelte Vergleichsperspektive. *[In German]*; (Attitudes towards social inequality in East Germany: argumentation for an expanded perspective.) *[Summary]*. Stefan Liebig; Roland Verwiebe. **Z. Soziol.** 29:1 2:2000 pp.3-26.

2397 Elite perceptions of the poor: reflections for a comparative research project. Abram de Swaan; James Manor; Else Øyen; Elisa Reis. **Curr. Sociol.** 48:1 1:2000 pp.43-54.

2398 Elites: choice, leadership and succession. Antónia Pedroso de Lima [Ed.]; João de Pina-Cabral [Ed.]. Oxford: Berg Publishers, 2000. 256p. *ISBN: 1859733999, 1859733948. Includes index.*

E: STRUCTURE SOCIALE

2399 La exclusión social de los indios chankas en una economía globalizada. *[In Spanish]*; [Social exclusion of Chankas Indians in a globalized economy]. Carlos Junquera Rubio. **Cuad. Am.** 79:1 1-2:2000 pp.172-188.

2400 The exclusive society: social exclusion, crime and difference in late modernity. Jock Young. London: Sage Publications, 1999. vii, 216p. *ISBN: 0803981511, 0803981503. Includes bibliographical references and index.*

2401 Gangland: cultural elites and the new generationalism. Mark Davis. St. Leonards: Allen & Unwin, 1999. xx, 398p. *ISBN: 186508106X. Includes bibliographical references (p. 352-382) and index.*

2402 Generic processes in the reproduction of inequality: an interactionist analysis. Michael Schwalbe; Sandra Godwin; Daphne Holden; Douglas Schrock; Shealy Thompson; Michelle Wolkomir. **Soc. Forc.** 79:2 12:2000 pp.419-452.

2403 Geographies of welfare and social exclusion. John Mohan. **Prog. H. Geog.** 24:2 6:2000 pp.291-300.

2404 Gesellschaftliche Integrationsprobleme im Spiegel soziologischer Gegenwartsdiagnosen. *[In German]*; (Societal problems of integration in the light of sociological diagnoses of our time.) *[Summary]*. Uwe Schimank. **Berl. J. Soziol.** 10:4 2000 pp.449-469.

2405 Hereditary stratification in middle-range societies; *[Summary in French]*. Jérôme Rousseau. **J. Royal Anth. Inst.** 7:1 3:2001 pp.117-132.

2406 Hierarchy. Paul H. Rubin. **Hum. Nature** 11:3 2000 pp.259-280.

2407 Housing and its influence on the development of social inequalities in the post-communist Czech Republic. Tomáš Kostelecký. **Czech Soc. Rev.** VIII:2 Fall:2000 pp.177-193.

2408 Indicators of women's social status as determinants of the marital timing of women in Hong Kong. Odalia M.H. Wong. **Asian Prof.** 27:5 10:1999 pp.389-400.

2409 Inklusion und soziale Ungleichheit. *[In German]*; (Inclusion and social inequality.) *[Summary]*. Thomas Schwinn. **Berl. J. Soziol.** 10:4 2000 pp.471-483.

2410 IQ and stratification: an empirical evaluation of Herrnstein and Murray's social change argument. Charles R. Tittle; Thomas Rotolo. **Soc. Forc.** 79:1 9:2000 pp.1-28.

2411 The issue of social differentiation in the work of Alexander Hirner. Silvia Heřmanová. **Sociologia [Brat.]** 32:6 Fall:2000 pp.577-592.

2412 "Klass intellektualov" v postindustrial'nom obshchestve. *[In Russian]*; ('Intellectual class' in postindustrial society.) V.L. Inozemtsev. **Sot. Issle.** 6 2000 pp.67-77.

2413 Klasse und Geschlecht als Kategorien sozialer Ungleichheit. *[In German]*; (Class and gender as categories of social inequality.) *[Summary]*. Petra Frerichs. **Kölner Z. Soz. Soz. Psy.** 52:1 3:2000 pp.36-59.

2414 Los límites de la igualdad de oportunidades. *[In Spanish]*; [The limitations of equal opportunities]. Ángel Puyol González. **Leviatán** 80 Summer:2000 pp.63-84.

2415 The logic of affirmative action: caste, class and quotas in India. Frank de Zwart. **Acta Sociol.** 43:3 2000 pp.235-250.

2416 Marxian questions, working-class struggles, socialist aspirations. Harvey J. Kaye. **Crit. Sociol.** 25:1 1999 pp.16-29.

2417 Müssen soziale Vorurteile falsch sein? *[In German]*; (Are social prejudices necessarily wrong?) Gregor Reichelt. **Soz. Welt.** 51:1 2000 pp.111-120.

2418 The new class society. Robert Perrucci; Earl Wysong. Lanham MD: Rowman & Littlefield, 1999. xiii, 299p. *ISBN: 0847691721, 084769173X. Includes bibliographical references (p. 277-292) and index.*

2419 'Now you see 'em, now you don't': Jewish visibility and the problem of citizenship in the British telecom 'Beattie' campaign. Linda Rozmovits. **Media Cult. Soc.** 22:6 11:2000 pp.707-722.

2420 Old debate, new evidence. Meir Yaish. **Eur. Sociol. R.** 16:2 6:2000 pp.159-183.

2421 Permeable homes: domestic service, household space, and the vulnerability of class boundaries in urban India. Sara Dickey. **Am. Ethn.** 27:2 5:2000 pp.462-489.

2422 A phenomenology of working class experience. Simon J. Charlesworth. Cambridge, New York: Cambridge University Press, 2000. 312p. *ISBN: 0521650666, 0521659159. Includes bibliographical references.*

E: SOCIAL STRUCTURE

2423 Policy responses to social exclusion: towards inclusion. Janie Percy-Smith [Ed.]. Buckingham: Open University Press, 2000. viii, 244p. *ISBN: 0335204732, 0335204740*. *Includes index.*

2424 Quelle politique contre les inégalités? *[In French]*; [Which policy against inequality?] Catherine Grémion. **Esprit** 261 2:2000 pp.55-65.

2425 Reconsidering worlds of pain: life in the working class(es). Thomas J. Gorman. **Sociol. For.** 15:4 12:2000 pp.693-717.

2426 Relatedness, class, and social organization in a village in southern Thailand. Emanuel Polioudakis. **Evol. Hum. Behav.** 21:5 9:2000 pp.297-316.

2427 Renewing class analysis. Rosemary Crompton [Ed.]; et al. Oxford: Blackwell Publishers, 2000. 207p. *ISBN: 0631221875. Includes bibliographical references and index. (Series:* Sociological Review monographs).

2428 Die Restrukturierung der Klassengesellschaft: Elemente einer zeitgenössischen Ungleichheitstheorie. *[In German]*; (Restructuring class society: elements of a contemporary theory of social inequality.) *[Summary]*; *[Summary in French]*. Hermann Strasser; Andrea Maria Dederichs. **Berl. J. Soziol.** 10:1 2000 pp.79-98.

2429 The settler phenomenon in the Middle Belt and the problem of national integration in Nigeria. Ibrahim James [Ed.]. Jos: Midland Press, 1999. 286p. *ISBN: 9783481169*. *Includes bibliographical references.*

2430 Situational stratification: a micro-macro theory of inequality. Randall Collins. **Sociol. Theory** 18:1 3:2000 pp.17-43.

2431 Social divisions. Geoff Payne [Ed.]. Basingstoke: Macmillan, 2000. xvii, 286p. *ISBN: 033376336X, 0333763351*.

2432 Social exclusion: a review and assessment of its relevance to developing countries. Emma Grant; Ilona Blue; Trudy Harpham. **J. Dev. Soc.** XVI:2 2000 pp.201-221.

2433 Social inclusion: possibilities and tensions. Angus Stewart [Ed.]; Peter Askonas [Ed.]. Basingstoke: Macmillan, 2000. 270p. *ISBN: 0333918355, 0333791983. Includes bibliographical references and index.*

2434 Social stratification and social mobility. Kazuo Seiyama; Hiroyuki Kondo; Junsuke Hara; Takatoshi Imada. **Int. J. Jap. Sociol.** 9 9:2000 pp.3-63. *Collection of 4 articles*.

2435 Sociálna mobilita: pojmy, teórie, hypotézy. *[In Slovak]*; (Social mobility: concepts, theories and hypotheses.) *[Summary]*. Ján Sopóci. **Sociologia [Brat.]** 32:2 2000 pp.139-152.

2436 The sociological conundrum of the category. Sujata Patel; Richard Jenkins; Sharon Elaine Preves; Kogila Moodley; Heribert Adam; Zimitri Erasmus; Margo Anderson; Stephen E. Fienberg; Nandini Sundar. **Curr. Sociol.** 48:3 7:2000 pp.1-126. *Collection of 7 articles*.

2437 Sotsial'naia struktura rossiiskogo obshchestva:itogi vos'mi let reform. *[In Russian]*; (The social stratification of Russia.) N. Tikhonova. **Obshch. Nauki Sovrem.** 3 2000 pp.5-15.

2438 Sotsial'noe iadro natsii (Srednie sloi v sovremennom rossiiskom obshchestve). *[In Russian]*; (The middle strata in modern Russian society.) A. Andreev. **Obshch. Nauki Sovrem.** 3 2000 pp.76-86.

2439 Splendeurs et misères de la vie intellectuelle (I). *[In French]*; [The splendour and misery of intellectual life: Part 1]. Olivier Mongin; Marc-Olivier Padis; Laurence Guellec; Paul Garapon; Thierry Pech; Olivier Abel; Jean-Louis Schlegel; Jacques Julliard; Michel Winock; Esprit [Interviewer]; Daniel Lindenberg; Éric Marty; François George; Vincent Descombes. **Esprit** 262 3-4:2000 pp.7-176. *Collection of 14 articles*.

2440 Stratification, class and health: class relations and health inequalities in high modernity. Graham Scambler; Paul Higgs. **Sociology** 33:2 5:1999 pp.275-296.

2441 Subaltern alternatives on caste, class and ethnicity. Rudolf C. Heredia. **Contr. I. Soc.** 34:1 1-4:2000 pp.37-62.

2442 Tackling inequalities: where are we now and what can be done. David Gordon [Ed.]; Christina Pantazis [Ed.]. Bristol: Policy Press, 1999. 132p. *ISBN: 1861341466*.

2443 Taste formation in pluralistic societies: the role of rhetorics and institutions. Heinz-Dieter Meyer. **Int. Sociol.** 15:1 3:2000 pp.33-56.

E: STRUCTURE SOCIALE

2444 'Too much money off other people's backs': status in late modern societies; *[Summary in French]*. Michèle Ollivier. **Can. J. Soc.** 25:4 Fall:2000 pp.441-470.
2445 Toward a sounder basis for class analysis. Aage B. Sørensen; Erik Olin Wright [Comments by]; John H. Goldthorpe [Comments by]; Dietrich Rueschemeyer [Comments by]; James Mahoney [Comments by]. **A.J.S.** 105:6 5:2000 pp.1523-1591.
2446 Towards a global ruling class: globalization and the transnational capitalist class. William I. Robinson; Jerry Harris. **Sci. Soc.** 64:1 Spring:2000 pp.11-54.
2447 Unfolding social hierarchies. Fernando Vega-Redondo. **J. Econ. Theo.** 90:2 2:2000 pp.177-203.
2448 Ungleichheit, Exklusion und Gerechtigkeit. *[In German]*; (Inequality, exclusion and justice.) *[Summary]*. Volker H. Schmidt. **Soz. Welt.** 51:4 2000 pp.383-400.
2449 Women without class: *chicas, cholas,* trash, and the presence/absence of class identity. Julie Bettie. **Signs** 26:1 Autumn:2000 pp.1-35.
2450 Working-class power, capitalist-class interests, and class compromise. Erik Olin Wright. **A.J.S.** 105:4 1:2000 pp.957-1002.
2451 Die Zitadellengesellschaft: Soziale Exklusion durch Privatisierung und Befestigung urbaner Lebenswelten. *[In German]*; (The fortified society: social exclusion as a result of privatization and fortification of space.) *[Summary]*. Stefan A. Litz. **Berl. J. Soziol.** 10:4 2000 pp.535-554.

Disability
Invalidité

2452 Abuse and disabled people: vulnerability or social indifference? Rosemary Calderbank. **Dis. and Soc.** 15:3 5:2000 pp.521-534.
2453 Challenges that educators meet when teaching children with hearing impairment at resource units in Harare, Zimbabwe. Jane Mutasa. **Dis. and Soc.** 15:6 10:2000 pp.923-942.
2454 Creating enforceable civil rights for disabled students in higher education: an institutional theory perspective. Ozcan Konur. **Dis. and Soc.** 15:7 12:2000 pp.1041-1063.
2455 A critical evaluation of the contradictions for disabled workers arising from the emergence of the flexible labour market in Britain. Debbie Jolly. **Dis. and Soc.** 15:5 8:2000 pp.795-810.
2456 La disabilità smentita: i percorsi nell'arte, nel pensiero e nella natura. *[In Italian]*; [Denied disability: journeys in art, thought and nature]. Luigi Fruidà; Michele Marotta; Luisa Danieli; Maria Caterina Federici; Fabrizio Vescovo; Romolo Guasco; Cristina De Luca; Anna Fusco di Ravello; Nicola Beranzoli; Maurizzio Picciurro; Andreas Maydorm; Laura Lombardi; Sally Reynolds; Monica Oerke; Mary Kealy. **Sociologia [Rome]** XXXIV:1(Supp.) 2000 pp.3-60.
2457 Disability and the labour market: an analysis of British males. Michael P. Kidd; Peter J. Sloane; Ivan Ferko. **J. Health Econ.** 19:6 11:2000 pp.961-981.
2458 Disability and the restructuring of welfare: employment, benefits and the law. Sheila Riddell; Nick Watson; Robert F. Drake; Colin Barnes; Charlotte Pearson; Alastair Wilson; Stephen Baron; Dan Goodley; Caroline Gooding. **Crit. Soc. Pol.** 20:4 (65) 11:2000 pp.411-550. *Collection of 7 articles.*
2459 Disability, dependency and the New Deal for disabled people. Alan Roulstone. **Dis. and Soc.** 15:3 5:2000 pp.427-444.
2460 Disability, human rights and education: cross-cultural perspectives. Felicity Armstrong [Ed.]; Len Barton [Ed.]. Buckingham, Philadelphia PA: Open University Press, 1999. xi, 237p. *ISBN: 0335204589, 0335204570. Includes bibliographical references and index.* (*Series:* Disability, human rights and society).
2461 Disability politics, language planning and inclusive social policy. Mairian Corker. **Dis. and Soc.** 15:3 5:2000 pp.445-462.
2462 Disability studies: the old and the new; *[Summary in French]*. Tanya Titchkosky. **Can. J. Soc.** 25:2 Spring:2000 pp.197-224.

E: SOCIAL STRUCTURE

2463 Disability, the family, and society: listening to mothers. Janet Read. Philadelphia PA: Open University Press, 2000. *ISBN: 0335203116, 0335203108. Includes bibliographical references and index. (Series:* Disability, human rights, and society).

2464 Disabled children, parents and professionals: partnership on whose terms? Pippa Murray. **Dis. and Soc.** 15:4 6:2000 pp.683-698.

2465 Disabled people, health professionals and the social model of disability: can there be a research relationship? Gillian Bricher. **Dis. and Soc.** 15:5 8:2000 pp.781-793.

2466 Disabling employment interviews: warfare to work. Paul S. Duckett. **Dis. and Soc.** 15:7 12:2000 pp.1019-1039.

2467 Disabling environments and the geography of access policies and practices. Rob Imrie. **Dis. and Soc.** 15:1 1:2000 pp.5-24.

2468 Doing disability research: activist lives and the academy. Dan Goodley; Michele Moore. **Dis. and Soc.** 15:6 10:2000 pp.861-882.

2469 An employment project as a route to social inclusion for people with learning difficulties? Vashti Gosling; Lesley Cotterill. **Dis. and Soc.** 15:7 12:2000 pp.1001-1018.

2470 Ethnicity, disability, and chronic illness. Waqar Ihsan-Ullah Ahmad [Ed.]. Buckingham, Philadelphia PA: Open University Press, 2000. 154p. *ISBN: 0335199836, 0335199828. Includes bibliographical references and index. (Series:* Race, health, and social care).

2471 Feminist perspectives on disability. Barbara Fawcett. New York: Pearson Education, 2000. 180p. *ISBN: 058236941X. Includes bibliographical references and index. (Series:* Feminist perspectives).

2472 *Grooming que zi*: marriage exclusion and identity formation among disabled men in contemporary China. Matthew Kohrman. **Am. Ethn.** 26:4 11:1999 pp.890-909.

2473 Grounding hierarchies of acceptance: the social construction of disability in NIMBY conflicts. Robert Wilton. **Urban Geogr.** 21:7 10-11:2000 pp.586-608.

2474 A history of disability. Henri-Jacques Stiker. Ann Arbor MI: University of Michigan Press, 1999. 239p. *ISBN: 0472110632, 047208626X. Translated from the French Corps infirmes et sociétés. Includes bibliographical references. (Series:* Corporealities).

2475 An inclusive future? Disability, social change and opportunities for greater inclusion by 2010. Ian Christie; Gavin Mensah-Coker. London: Demos, 1999. 110p. *ISBN: 1841800007.*

2476 Interviewing non-disabled people about their disability-related attitudes: seeking methodologies. Claire Tregaskis. **Dis. and Soc.** 15:2 3:2000 pp.343-353.

2477 Meanings, models and metaphors. Bill Hughes; John Swain; Sally French; Susan Peters; M. Miles; Bob Sapey; Alison Pedlar; Peggy Hutchinson; Barbara Riddick. **Dis. and Soc.** 15:4 6:2000 pp.555-652. *Collection of 7 articles.*

2478 La minusvalía psíquica: implicaciones éticas. *[In Spanish]*; [Mental disability: ethical implications] *[Summary]*. Eduardo López Azpitarte. **Rev. Fom. Soc.** 55:217 1-3:2000 pp.85-104.

2479 Missed connections: hard of hearing in a hearing world. Barbara Stenross. Philadelphia PA: Temple University Press, 1999. xii, 139p. *ISBN: 1566396816, 1566396824. Includes bibliographical references (p. 123-124) and index.*

2480 Multiculturalism and disability: a critical perspective. Stephen French Gilson; Elizabeth DePoy. **Dis. and Soc.** 15:2 3:2000 pp.207-218.

2481 Museums and the visually impaired: the spatial politics of access. Kevin Hetherington. **Sociol. Rev.** 48:3 8:2000 pp.444-463.

2482 Mystery or typical teen? The social construction of academic engagement and disability. Robin M. Smith. **Dis. and Soc.** 15:6 10:2000 pp.909-922.

2483 Official development assistance to disabled people in Ghana. Robert L. Metts; Nansea Metts. **Dis. and Soc.** 15:3 5:2000 pp.475-488.

2484 Oppression within the counselling room. Donna Reeve. **Dis. and Soc.** 15:4 6:2000 pp.669-682.

2485 Philosophical and ethical problems in mental handicap. Peter Byrne. Basingstoke: Macmillan, 2000. 200p. *ISBN: 0333801164. Includes index.*

E: STRUCTURE SOCIALE

2486 Promoting inclusive play and leisure opportunities for children with disabilities. Blanche Thompson; Helen Taylor; Roy McConkey. **Child C. Pract.** 6:2 4:2000 pp.108-123.

2487 A qualitative study of the perceptions of individuals with disabilities concerning health and rehabilitation professionals. Ross Crisp. **Dis. and Soc.** 15:2 3:2000 pp.355-367.

2488 Refocusing on the parent: what are the social issues of concern for parents of disabled children. Stephen Case. **Dis. and Soc.** 15:2 3:2000 pp.271-292.

2489 The relationship of adaptive and maladaptive behaviour to social outcomes for individuals with developmental disabilities. Deborah Ann White; Richard A. Dodder. **Dis. and Soc.** 15:6 10:2000 pp.897-908.

2490 The researched opinions on research: disabled people and disability research. Rob Kitchen. **Dis. and Soc.** 15:1 1:2000 pp.25-47.

2491 Researching disability projects, or, some problems with the social model in practice. Jill C. Humphrey. **Dis. and Soc.** 15:1 1:2000 pp.63-85.

2492 Restricted access: lesbians on disability. Susan Raffo [Ed.]; Victoria A. Brownworth [Ed.]. Seattle WA: Seal Press, 1999. xxii, 296p. *ISBN: 158005028X*.

2493 'Sense and sensibility': social-spatial experiences of the visually-impaired in Singapore. C.P. Pow. **Sing. J. Trop. Geogr.** 21:2 7:2000 pp.166-182.

2494 Social networks of visually impaired and blind adolescents. Structure and effect on well-being. S. Kef; J.J. Hox; H.T. Habekothé. **Soc. Networks** 22:1 1:2000 pp.73-91.

2495 Trouble in paradise — a disabled person's right to the satisfaction of a self-defined need: some conceptual and practical problems. Peter Handley. **Dis. and Soc.** 15:2 3:2000 pp.313-325.

2496 We have choices: globalisation and welfare user movements. Peter Beresford; Chris Holden. **Dis. and Soc.** 15:7 12:2000 pp.973-989.

2497 What's in a name? The implications of diagnosis for people with learning difficulties and their family carers. Maureen Gillman; Bob Heyman; John Swain. **Dis. and Soc.** 15:3 5:2000 pp.389-410.

2498 Why rights are never enough: rights, intellectual disability and understanding. Damon A. Young; Ruth Quibell. **Dis. and Soc.** 15:5 8:2000 pp.747-764.

2499 Women with intellectual disabilities: finding a place in the world. Rannveig Traustadóttir [Ed.]; Kelley Johnson [Ed.]. Philadelphia PA: Jessica Kingsley Publishers, 2000. 303p. *ISBN: 1853028460. Includes bibliographical references and index.*

2500 Working with the experts: collaborative research with people with an intellectual disability. Marie Knox; Magdalena Mok; Trevor R. Parmenter. **Dis. and Soc.** 15:1 1:2000 pp.49-61.

2501 'You're not a retard, you're just wise': disability, social identity, and family networks. Steven J. Taylor. **J. Contemp. Ethnog.** 29:1 2:2000 pp.58-92.

E.3: **Social change**
Changement social

2502 Africa and the road ahead. Hamdy Abdel-Rahman. **Afr. Q.** 40:1 2000 pp.17-40.

2503 After progress: finding the old way forward. Anthony O'Hear. London: Bloomsbury, 1999. xi, 270p. *ISBN: 0747543860. Includes bibliographical references and index.*

2504 American culture, American tastes: social change and the 20th century. Michael G. Kammen. New York: Knopf, 1999. xxvii, 320p. *ISBN: 0679427406. Includes bibliographical references (p. 263-303) and index.*

2505 Architecture of societies in transition — the case of the Maasai of Kenya. R.W. Rukwaro; K.M. Mukono. **Hab. Int.** 25:1 3:2001 pp.81-98.

2506 Bowling alone: the collapse and revival of American community. Robert D. Putnam. New York: Simon & Schuster, 2000. 541p. *ISBN: 0684832836. Includes bibliographical references (p. [445]-504) and index.*

2507 Brazil in the aftershock of neoliberalism. James N. Green; Ricardo Antunes; Héctor Alimonda; Nise Jinkings; Luis Felipe Miguel; Peggy A. Lovell. **Lat. Am. Pers.** 27:6 11:2000 pp.5-102. *Collection of 5 articles.*

E: SOCIAL STRUCTURE

2508   The challenge of civilizational transition. Ervin Laszlo [Ed.]; Duane Elgin; Peter M. Allen; Robert Artigiani; Sally J. Goerner. **Wor. Futur.** 55:1 2000 pp.1-103. *Collection of 5 articles.*

2509   Chinese society: change, conflict, and resistance. Elizabeth J. Perry [Ed.]; Mark Selden [Ed.]. London, New York: Routledge, 2000. xii, 249p. *ISBN: 0415204909, 0415223342. Includes bibliographical references and index. (Series:* Routledge studies in Asia's transformations).

2510   Cultural trauma: the other face of social change. Piotr Sztompka. **Eur. J. Soc. Theory** 3:4 11:2000 pp.449-466.

2511   Culture change among a Mamanua group of northeastern Mindanao. Marcelino N. Maceda. **Phil. Q. Cult. Soc.** 26:1-2 3-6:1998 pp.14-32.

2512   Development and social change: a global perspective. Philip McMichael. Thousand Oaks CA: Pine Forge Press, 2000. xlii, 364p. *ISBN: 0761986928, 0761986677. Includes bibliographical references (p. 321-344) and index. (Series:* Sociology for a new century).

2513   Dynamics and policy implications of the global reforms at the end of the second millennium: a comparative perspective. Tukumbi Lumumba-Kasongo; Julius O. Ihonvbere; Mark Ginsburg; Don Adams; Thomas Clayton; Martha Mantilla; Judy Sylvester; Yidan Wang; Kent Klitgaard; Amiya Kumar Bagchi; N'Dri Thérèse Assié-Lumumba; Arild Schou. **Int. J. Comp. Soc** XLI:1 2000 pp.1-143. *Collection of 7 articles.*

2514   The dynamics of social change in Latin America. Henry Veltmeyer; James F. Petras. Basingstoke; New York: Macmillan Press; St. Martin's Press, 2000. xi, 210p. *ISBN: 0333749375, 0312222777. Includes bibliographical references (p. 191-205) and index. (Series:* International political economy series).

2515   *Enkurma Sikitoi*: commoditization, drink, and power among the Maasai. Justin Willis. **Int. J. Afr. H. S.** 32:2-3 1999 pp.339-357.

2516   The exemplary society: human improvement, social control, and the dangers of modernity in China. Børge Bakken. Oxford; New York: Clarendon Press; Oxford University Press, 1999. 516p. *ISBN: 0198295235. Includes bibliographical references and index. (Series:* Studies on contemporary China).

2517   Gender, love and education in three generations: the way out and up. Harriet Bjerrum Nielsen; Monica Rudberg. **Eur. J. Wom. Stud.** 7:4 11:2000 pp.423-453.

2518   The idea of a united Europe: political, economic and cultural integration since the fall of the Berlin Wall. M.J. Wintle [Ed.]; Jamal Shahin [Ed.]. Basingstoke: Macmillan, 2000. 176p. *ISBN: 0333914775. Includes index.*

2519   K některým sociálním aspektům a posunům v koncepcích post-industriální a informační společnosti. *[In Czech];* (Comments on some social aspects and advancements in conceptions of the post-industrial and information society.) *[Summary].* Tomáš Kolomazník. **Soc. Čas.** 36:2 2000 pp.221-232.

2520   The last great revolution: turmoil and transformation in Iran. Robin B. Wright. New York: Alfred A. Knopf, 2000. xxiv, 339p. *ISBN: 0375406395. Includes bibliographical references (p. 315-320) and index.*

2521   Living in a more violent world. Mayra Buvinić; Andrew R. Morrison. **Foreign Pol.** 118 Spring:2000 pp.58-73.

2522   McLuhan's world — and ours. David Skinner. **Publ. Inter.** 138 Winter:2000 pp.52-64.

2523   Problems of multilingualism and social change in Asian and African contexts. Florian Coulmas [Ed.]; Joshua A. Fishman [Ed.]; Minglang Zhou; Yuling Pan; Shoji Takano; Vivian de Klerk; Abdul Karim Bangura; Francis X. Karam. **Int. J. S. Lang.** 146 2000 pp.1-136. *Collection of 6 articles.*

2524   Qué talantes, qué cultura y qué fe para la transformación social. *[In Spanish];* [Which attitudes, culture and faith are necessary for social change?] *[Summary].* Josep Miralles Massanés [Comments by]; Joaquín García Roca. **Rev. Fom. Soc.** 55:220 10-12:2000 pp.539-568.

2525   Religion, ethnicity, and social change. Jo Campling [Ed.]; Liz Fawcett. Basingstoke; New York: Macmillan; St. Martin's Press, 2000. xvi, 220p. *ISBN: 0333720474, 0312225679. Includes bibliographical references and index.*

E: STRUCTURE SOCIALE

2526 Riflessioni sociologiche alla fine del secondo millennio. *[In Italian]*; [Sociological reflections at the end of the second millennium]. Franco Ferrarotti. **Sociologia [Rome]** XXXIV:1 2000 pp.9-21.

2527 Scanning the future: 20 eminent thinkers on the world of tomorrow. Yorick Blumenfeld [Ed.]. London: Thames & Hudson, 1999. 304p. *ISBN: 0500280452*. (*Series:* Prospects for tomorrow).

2528 Social change in Melanesia: development and history. Paul Sillitoe. Cambridge, New York: Cambridge University Press, 2000. xx, 264p. *ISBN: 0521778069, 0521771412*.

2529 Social change in provincial Russia: the intelligentsia in a Raion centre. Anne White. **Eur.-Asia Stud.** 52:4 6:2000 pp.677-694.

2530 Social changes in globalised societies and the redefinition of identities: social psychological perspectives. X. Chryssochoou; L. Timotijevic; G.M. Breakwell; A. Triandafyllidou; G. Philogène; K. Deaux. **J. Comm. App. Soc. Psychol.** 10:5 9-10:2000 pp.343-431. *Collection of 6 articles*.

2531 Social theory and social change. Trevor Noble. Basingstoke: Macmillan, 2000. 260p. *ISBN: 033391239X, 0333912381, 0312233280, 0312233299. Includes bibliographical references*.

2532 Society and sociology: Britain in 2025. David Mason; Roger Penn; David McCrone; Richard Kiely; Trevor Noble; Jonathan Bradshaw; Robert Reiner; Sara Delamont; Grace Davie; Steve Harrison; Waqar I.U. Ahmad; Peter Dickens; Peter Golding; Sallie Westwood. **Sociology** 34:1 2:2000 pp.1-202. *Collection of 12 articles*.

2533 A society transformed: Hungary in time-space perspective. Rudolf Andorka [Ed.]; Tamás Kolosi [Ed.]; Richard Rose [Ed.]; György Vukovich [Ed.]. Budapest: Central European University Press, 1999. 203p. *ISBN: 9639116491. Includes bibliographical references*.

2534 Ten years of shame: arguments about blame. Aleksandr Tarasov. **Rus. Pol. Law** 38:3 5-6:2000 pp.49-68.

2535 Tenevizatsiia rossiiskovo obshchestva: prichiny i posledstviia. *[In Russian]*; (Shadowing of Russia's society: reasons and effects.) *[Summary]*. R.V. Ryvkina. **Sot. Issle.** 12 2000 pp.3-13.

2536 Trauma kulturowa. Druga strona zmiany społecznej. *[In Polish]*; (Cultural trauma: the other side of social transformation.) *[Summary]*. Piotr Sztompka. **Prz. Soc.** XLIX:1 2000 pp.9-30.

2537 Two generations: life stories and social change in Malaysia. Merete Lie. **J. Gender St.** 9:1 3:2000 pp.27-44.

2538 «Um» i «serdtse» moego sovremennika. *[In Russian]*; [The hearts and minds of my contemporaries. Part 2]. A. Razumov. **Svobod. Mysl'** 6 2000 pp.46-65.

2539 Ursachen und Theoreien regionaler Entwicklungskrisen - Das Beispiel der Asienkrise. *[In German]*; [Causes and theories of regional development crises: the example of the Asian crisis]. Renate Schubert. Berlin: Duncker & Humblot, 2000. 239p.

2540 Vzgliad iz XXI veka. *[In Russian]*; [The outlook for the 21st century]. E. Arab-Ogly. **Svobod. Mysl'** 12 2000 pp.60-70.

2541 World system history: the social science of long-term change. Robert Allen Denemark [Ed.]; et al. New York: Routledge, 2000. 345p. *ISBN: 0415232767, 0415232775. Includes bibliographical references and index*.

2542 The world we have lost: further explored. Peter Laslett. London: Routledge, 2000. 376p. *ISBN: 0415228336*.

Globalization
Mondialisation

2543 À quoi sert l'identité? *[In French]*; (What use is identity?) Georges Labica. **Hom. Soc.** 135 1-3:2000 pp.71-86.

E: SOCIAL STRUCTURE

2544 The anthropology of the state in the age of globalization: close encounters of the deceptive kind. Michel-Rolph Trouillot; Chris Hann [Comments by]; László Kűrti [Comments by]. **Curr. Anthr.** 42:1 2:2001 pp.125-138.
2545 China's Big Mac attack. James L. Watson. **Foreign Aff.** 79:3 5-6:2000 pp.120-135.
2546 The chronopolitan ideal: time, belonging and globalization. Saulo B. Cwerner. **Time Soc.** 9:2-3 6-9:2000 pp.331-354.
2547 Competing cultures: Canada and the World Trade Organization — the lessons from *Sports Illustrated*. Myra J. Tawfik. **Can. Yb. Int. Law** XXXVI 1998 pp.279-302.
2548 Cultura, ciudadanía y desarrollo en tiempos de globalización. *[In Spanish]*; [Culture, citizenship and development in times of globalization] *[Summary]*. Martín Hopenhayn. **Rev. Cien. Soc.** 5 6:1998 pp.30-50.
2549 Culture change in India: identity and globalization. Yogendra Singh. Jaipur: Rawat Publications, 2000. 260p. *Includes bibliographical references and index*.
2550 Ethnicity and globalization: from migrant worker to transnational citizen. Stephen Castles. London: Sage Publications, 2000. 228p. *ISBN: 0761956123, 0761956115*.
2551 Global capitalism: what's race got to do with it? Karen Brodkin. **Am. Ethn.** 27:2 5:2000 pp.237-256.
2552 Global culture/individual identity: searching for home in the cultural supermarket. Gordon Mathews. New York: Routledge, 2000. 232p. *ISBN: 0415206154. Includes bibliographical references and index*.
2553 Globalisation, the nation-state and global society. James Fulcher. **Sociol. Rev.** 48:4 11:2000 pp.522-543.
2554 Globalisierung. *[In German]*; (Globalization.) Richard Münch; Franz-Xaver Kaufmann; Joachim Wiemeyer; Rotraud Wielandt; Karl Gabriel; Hans J. Münk; Martin Maier; Hermann Schalück; Klaus Müller; Heinz-Gerhard Justenhoven. **Jahr. Christ. Sozialwiss.** 41 2000 pp.14-196. *Collection of 10 articles*.
2555 Globalisierung als Herrschaft. Eine Auseinandersetzung mit dem makrosoziologischen Neoinstitutionalismus von Meyer et al. *[In German]*; (Globalization as domination. A critical comment on John W. Meyer's macro-sociological institutional theory.) *[Summary]*. Monika Schäfer. **Soz. Welt.** 51:3 2000 pp.355-375.
2556 Globalisierung, Raum und Gesellschaft: Elemente einer modernen Soziologie des Raumes. *[In German]*; (Globalization, space and society. Elements of a modern sociology of space.) *[Summary]*; *[Summary in French]*. Peter Noller. **Berl. J. Soziol.** 10:1 2000 pp.21-48.
2557 La globalización como cambio cultural: más allá del capitalismo y del nacionalismo. *[In Spanish]*; (Globalisation as a cultural change: beyond capitalism and nationalism.) *[Summary]*. Jaime Loring Miró. **Rev. Fom. Soc.** 55:218 4-6:2000 pp.247-269.
2558 Globalización e historiografía en el mediterráneo y América Latina. *[In Spanish]*; [Globalization and historiography in the Mediterranean and Latin America]. Juan Manuel Santana Pérez. **Cuad. Am.** 79:1 1-2:2000 pp.199-213.
2559 La globalización subterránea. *[In Spanish]*; [Underground globalization]. Edit Antal; Remedios Gómez Amau; Argentino Mendoza; Aurora Tovar; Jesús Tamayo; Laís Abramo. **Acta Sociol. [Mexico]** 24 9-12:1998 pp.11-110. *Collection of 5 articles*.
2560 Globalización y regionalización. Respuestas regionales a los problemas no económicos. *[In Spanish]*; [Globalization and regionalization: regional answers to non-economic problems]. Antonio Remiro Brotons. **Rev. Mexicana Cien. Pol.** XLIV:176 5-8:1999 pp.119-136.
2561 Globalization. Günseli Berik; Stephanie Seguino; Elizabeth Fussell; Nahid Aslanbeigui; Gale Summerfield; Ushma D. Upadhyay; Marilyn Carr; Martha Alter Chen; Jane Tate. **Fem. Econ.** 6:3 11:2000 pp.1-142. *Collection of 6 articles*.
2562 Globalization: a critical introduction. Jan Aart Scholte. Basingstoke: Macmillan, 2000. xix, 361p. *ISBN: 0312236328, 0333660218, 031223631X, 0333660226. Includes bibliographical references and index*.
2563 Globalization and strategy. Fredric Jameson. **New Left R.** 4 7-8:2000 pp.49-68.
2564 Globalization and the erosion of class compromise in contemporary Australia. Rob Lambert. **Polit. Soc.** 28:1 3:2000 pp.93-118.

E: STRUCTURE SOCIALE

2565 Globalization and the nation-state: an appraisal of the discussion. Pertti Alasuutari. **Acta Sociol.** 43:3 2000 pp.259-270.
2566 Globalization, cultural symbols, and group consciousness: culture as an adaptive complex system. Richard Jenner. **Wor. Futur.** 56:1 2000 pp.21-39.
2567 Globalization revisited. Johann P. Arnason; Claus Offe; David Roberts; Sigrid Meuschel; John A. Hall; Barnard Turner. **Thes. Elev.** 63 11:2000 pp.1-88. *Collection of 6 articles.*
2568 Globalizations are plural. Göran Therborn; Jens Bartelson; Paul Bairoch; Aníbal Quijano; John W. Meyer; Immanuel Wallerstein; Henry Wai-chung Yeung; Gary Hamilton; Robert Feenstra; Wongi Choe; Chung Ku Kim; Eun Mie Lim; Asa Cristina Laurell; Banu Helvacioglu; Daniel Mato; Mamadou Diawara; Saskia Sassen; David Held. **Int. Sociol.** 15:2 6:2000 pp.149-408. *Collection of 15 articles.*
2569 Globalization's cultural consequences. Robert Holton. **Ann. Am. Poli.** 570 7:2000 pp.140-152.
2570 Globalizatsiia: protsess i osmyslenie. *[In Russian]*; (Globalization: the process and its conceptualization. Part 1.) A. Utkin. **Svobod. Mysl'** 11 2000 pp.28-38.
2571 Globalizing cities. L. Kong [Ed.]; E. Clark; A. Lund; P. Breathnach; B. Warf; A. Löfgren. **Soc. Sci. Q.** 31:4 11:2000 pp.465-511. *Collection of 5 articles.*
2572 A globalizing world? Culture, economics, politics. David Held [Ed.]. London: Routledge, 2000. 188p. *ISBN: 0415222931.* (*Series:* An introduction to the social sciences: understanding social change).
2573 McGuggenisation? National identity and globalisation in the Basque Country. Donald McNeill. **Pol. Geogr.** 19:4 5:2000 pp.473-494.
2574 The meanings of work in contemporary Palau: policy implications of globalization in the Pacific. Karen L. Nero; Fermina Brel Murray; Michael L. Burton. **Cont. Pac.** 12:2 Fall:2000 pp.319-348.
2575 The natural and cultural invariants of the representation of time in face of globalization. Hervé Barreau. **Time Soc.** 9:2-3 6-9:2000 pp.303-318.
2576 Otázky globalizácie alebo nové pohl'ady na spoločnost' a mládež? *[In Slovak]*; [Issues of globalisation: new views on society and youth?] Peter Ondrejkovič. **Sociologia [Brat.]** 32:1 2000 pp.31-42.
2577 Predatory globalization: a critique. Richard Falk. Malden MA. Polity Press, 1999. x, 217p. *ISBN: 074560935X, 0745609368. Includes bibliographical references (p. [185]-213) and index.*
2578 The process of globalisation and class transformation in the West. Sophia N. Antonopoulou. **Demo. & Nat.** 6:1 3:2000 pp.37-54.
2579 Prospects for globalization. Yong-Hak Kim. **Kor. Foc.** 8:1 1-2:2000 pp.84-98.
2580 Public domain and the new world order in knowledge. John Frow. **Soc. Sem.** 10:2 8:2000 pp.173-186.
2581 www.timeandglobalization.com/narrative. Paul Andre Harris. **Time Soc.** 9:2-3 6-9:2000 pp.319-330.

F: POPULATION. FAMILY. GENDER. ETHNIC GROUPS
POPULATION. FAMILLE. SEXE. GROUPE ETHNIQUE

F.1: Age groups
Groupes d'âges

2582 African American grandparents raising grandchildren: a national profile and health characteristics. Esme Fuller-Thomson; Meredith Minkler. **Health Soc. Work** 25:2 5:2000 pp.109-118.
2583 Age, depression, and attrition in the National Survey of Families and Households. John Mirowsky; John R. Reynolds. **Sociol. Meth.** 28:4 5:2000 pp.476-504.
2584 Age vitality across eleven nations. Howard Giles; Kim Noels; Hiroshi Ota; Sik Hung Ng; Cindy Gallois; Ellen B. Ryan; Angie Williams; Tae-seop Lim; LilnaBeth Somera; Hongyin Tao; Itesh Sachdev. **J. Multiling.** 21:4 2000 pp.308-323.
2585 Attitudes of the student youth and middle aged persons towards the elderly. Visweswara Rao; B. Devi Prasad; Ch. Avataramu. **Indian J. Soc. W.** 61:1 1:2000 pp.42-53.
2586 Bridging the generation gap. Young-soon Kim; Myung-hee Han; Jung Ok Lee [Tr.]. **Inter-Asia Cult. St.** 1:3 12:2000 pp.503-512.
2587 Le choc des générations. *[In French]*; [The generation schock]. Bernard Préel. Paris: La Découverte, 2000. 262p. *ISBN: 2707129496*.
2588 Communication media use in the grandparent-grandchild relationship. Jake Harwood. **J. Comm.** 50:4 Autumn:2000 pp.56-78.
2589 Degrees of connection: a critique of Rawls's theory of mutual disinterest. Frances Woolley. **Fem. Econ.** 6:2 7:2000 pp.1-21.
2590 Intergenerational solidarity networks of instrumental and cultural transfers within migrant families in Turkey. Sibel Kalaycioglu; Helga Rittersberger-Tiliç. **Age. Soc.** 20:5 9:2000 pp.523-542.
2591 Intergenerationeller sozialer Abstieg in Schweizer Akademikerfamilien: Eine Fallanalyse. *[In German]*; (Intergenerational downward mobility in Swiss academic families: a case study.) *[Summary]*; *[Summary in French]*. Martin Schmeiser. **Schweiz. Z. Soziologie** 26:3 12:2000 pp.637-662.
2592 Młodzież i dorośli: rodzice i nauczyciele. Wybrane problemy kulturowych relacji międzygenaracyjnych. *[In Polish]*; (Youth and adults: parents and teachers. Selected issues of cultural relations between generations.) *[Summary]*. Barbara Fatyga. **Prz. Soc.** XLVIII:2 1999 pp.55-76.
2593 Parental background and lifestyle differentiation in Eastern Europe: social, political, and cultural intergenerational transmission in five former socialist societies. Gerbert Kraaykamp; Paul Nieuwbeerta. **Soc. Sci. R.** 29:1 3:2000 pp.92-122.
2594 Rapports de générations: transferts intrafamiliaux et dynamique macrosociale. *[In French]*; (Relations between generations. Intrafamily transfer and macrosocial dynamics.) *[Summary]*. Claudine Attias-Donfut. **Rev. Fr. Soc.** 41:4 10-12:2000 pp.643-684.
2595 A time to join, a time to quit: the influence of life cycle transitions on voluntary association membership. Thomas Rotolo. **Soc. Forc.** 78:3 3:2000 pp.1133-1162.

Children
Enfants

2596 After the death of childhood: growing up in the age of electronic media. David Buckingham. Malden MA: Polity Press, 2000. 245p. *ISBN: 0745619339. Includes bibliographical references and index.*
2597 The body, childhood and society. Alan Prout [Ed.]. Basingstoke: Macmillan, 2000. 224p. *ISBN: 0312221444, 033365949X, 0333659481. Includes index.*

F: POPULATION. FAMILLE. SEXE. GROUPE ETHNIQUE

2598 Child development. Laura E. Berk. Boston MA: Allyn & Bacon, 2000. *ISBN: 0205286348. Includes bibliographical references and index.*
2599 Child development. John W. Santrock. Boston MA: McGraw-Hill, 1998. xxvii, 692p. *ISBN: 0071155465. Includes bibliographical references (p. 621-664) and indexes.*
2600 Childhood in a changing society at the end of the second millenium. Rivka Bar-Yosef. **Megamot** XL:3 8:2000 pp.365-381.
2601 Childhood studies: a reader in perspectives of childhood. Jean Mills [Ed.]; Richard W. Mills [Ed.]. London, New York: Routledge, 2000. 224p. *ISBN: 0415214149, 0415214157. Includes bibliographical references and index.*
2602 Children and childhood at the start of the new millennium. John Coleman; John Tomlinson; Vivienne Little; Susan Tomlinson; Emily Bower; Helen S. Heussler; Leon Polnay; Manuel Katz; Robbie Gilligan; Michael Freeman; Peter K. Smith; Alan Prout; Roger Smith. **Child. Soc.** 14:4 9:2000 pp.230-325. *Collection of 8 articles.*
2603 Children and theories of social justice. Hilde Bojer. **Fem. Econ.** 6:2 7:2000 pp.23-39.
2604 'Children, fooles, and mad-men': children's relationship to citizenship in Britain from Thomas Hobbes to Bernard Crick. Tom Cockburn. **Sch. Field** X:3-4 Autumn-Winter:1999 pp.65-83.
2605 Children's participation: control and self-realisation in British late modernity. Alan Prout. **Child. Soc.** 14:4 9:2000 pp.304-315.
2606 Deti v sovremennom obshchestve. *[In Russian]*; [Children in contemporary society] *[Summary]*. E.B. Breeva. Moscow: Editorial URSS, 1999. 211p. *ISBN: 5901006917. Includes bibliographical references (p. [199]-206).*
2607 Educating sensibilities: the image of 'the lesson' in children's talk about punishment. Marion Smith; Richard Sparks; Evi Girling. **Pun. & Soc.** 2:4 10:2000 pp.395-415.
2608 From crib to campus. Mike Crang; Mary Thomas; Stuart C. Aitken; Elizabeth A. Gagen; Sarah L. Holloway; Gill Valentine; Nick Bingham; Melissa S. Hyams. **Envir. Plan. A.** 32:4 4:2000 pp.577-654. *Collection of 5 articles.*
2609 Kinetic tactile-kinesthetic bodies: ontogenetical foundations of apprenticeship learning. Maxine Sheets-Johnstone. **Human St.** 23:4 10:2000 pp.343-370.
2610 Studying children in context: theories, methods, and ethics. M. Elizabeth Graue; Daniel J. Walsh; Deborah Ceglowski; et al. Thousand Oaks CA, London: Sage Publications, 1998. xviii, 270p. *ISBN: 0803972563, 0803972571. Includes bibliographical references (p. 250-257) and index.*

Youth
Jeunesse

2611 Adolescence, affect and health. Donna Spruijt-Metz. Hove: Psychology Press, 1999. xvii, 221p. *ISBN: 0863775187. Includes bibliographical references and index. European Association for Research on Adolescence.* (*Series:* Studies in adolescent development).
2612 Adolescent alcohol abstainers: traditional patterns in new groups. Willy Pedersen; Arne Kolstad. **Acta Sociol.** 43:3 2000 pp.219-234.
2613 Adolescent siblings in stepfamilies: family functioning and adolescent adjustment. E. Mavis Hetherington; Sandra H. Henderson; David Reis; Edward R. Anderson; James H. Bray. Chicago IL: University of Chicago Press, 1999. vi, 222p. *Includes bibliographical references.* (*Series:* Monographs of the Society for Research in Child Development).
2614 The China Youth Corps in Taiwan. Thomas A. Brindley. New York: Peter Lang, 1999. xi, 155p. *ISBN: 0820442968. Includes bibliographical references (p. 133-145) and index.* (*Series:* American University studies. XIV, Education - 46).
2615 Cognitive and moral development and academic achievement in adolescence. Richard M. Lerner [Intro.]; Jasna Jovanovic [Ed.]. New York, London: Garland Publishing, 1999. xii, 364p. *ISBN: 0815332912. Includes bibliographical references.* (*Series:* Adolescence: development, diversity, and context - 2).

F: POPULATION. FAMILY. GENDER. ETHNIC GROUPS

2616 Comunicación e identidades juveniles. *[In Spanish]*; [Communication and identities of youth]. Delia Crovi Druetta. **Rev. Mexicana Cien. Pol.** XLIV:176 5-8:1999 pp.101-118.

2617 Confucian rappers and rockers? Singaporean youth in the nineties. Alfred L. Oehlers. **Int. Asien.** 30:1-2 5:1999 pp.97-108.

2618 La construction de l'identité: de l'enfance à l'âge adulte. *[In French]*; [The construction of identity, from childhood to adulthood]. Colette Sabatier; Martine Kaluszynski; Gérard Neyrand; Claude Dubar; Serge Lesourd; Serge Tisseron; Claire Calogirou; Marc Touché; Gérard Mauger; Laurence Ould Ferhat; Olivier Galland; Sylvie Wieviorka; Isabelle Amrouni; Jean-François Montes; Françis Bailleau; Jacques Pain; Hervé Hamon; Louis Chauvel. **Inf. Soc.** 84 2000 pp.4-163. *Collection of 17 articles.*

2619 The enemy has a face: the Seeds of Peace experience. John Wallach; Michael Wallach. Washington DC: United States Institute of Peace Press, 2000. xvii, 119p. *ISBN: 1878379976, 1878379968.*

2620 Esélyek és orientációk. Fiatalok az ezredfordulón. *[In Hungarian]*; [Prospects and orientations: youth at the turn of the century]. Ferenc Gaszó; László Laki. Budapest: Okker Kiadó, 1999. 180p. *ISBN: 9637315837. Includes bibliographical references (p. 179-180).*

2621 Experience and knowledge of young people regarding illicit drug use, 1969-99. J. Denham Wright; Laurence Pearl. **Addiction** 95:8 8:2000 pp.1225-1235.

2622 Exploring children and young people's narratives of identity. G. Valentine. **Geoforum** 31:2 5:2000 pp.257-268.

2623 Feminism and youth culture. Angela McRobbie. Basingstoke: Macmillan, 2000. 256p. *ISBN: 0333770323, 0333770315.*

2624 Generation status, social capital, and the routes out of high school. Michael J. White; Jennifer E. Glick. **Sociol. For.** 15:4 12:2000 pp.671-691.

2625 Getting a life: the emergence of the life story in adolescence. Tilmann Habermas; Susan Bluck. **Psychol. B.** 126:5 9:2000 pp.748-769.

2626 Jeunes: l'âge des indépendances. *[In French]*; [Youth: the age of independence]. Olivier Galland; Daniel Courgeau; Catherine Villeneuve-Gokalp; Véronique Simonnet; Valérie Ulrich; Brigitte Dormont; Sandrine Dufour-Kippelen; Florence Audier; Dominique Meurs; Sophie Ponthieux; Marc-Antoine Estrade; Nathalie Missègue. **Écon. Stat.** 337-338 2000 pp.13-178. *Collection of 8 articles.*

2627 La jeunesse dans quatre pays d'Europe. *[In French]*; (Youth in four European countries.) *[Summary]*. John Bynner; Alessandro Cavalli; Hugh Cunningham; Olivier Galland; Walter R. Heinz. **Rev. de l'OFCE** 72 1:2000 pp.185-228.

2628 Percepção de atitudes parentais pelo filho adolescente: uma abordagem psicanalítica da adolescência. *[In Portuguese]*; [An adolescent son's perception of parental attitudes: a psychoanalytic approach to adolescence] *[Summary]*. Cirilo Magagnin. **Aletheia** 10 1999 pp.33-50.

2629 Percepção de atitudes parentais pelo filho adolescente: uma abordagem sistêmica da adolescência. *[In Portuguese]*; [An adolescent son's perception of parental attitudes: a systemic approach to adolescence] *[Summary]*. Cirilo Magagnin. **Aletheia** 9 1999 pp.51-62.

2630 Porozhdenie reform: britogolovye, oni zhe skinkhedy. Novaia fashistskaia molodezhaia subkul'tura v Rossii. *[In Russian]*; [The results of reform: the shaven-headed are still 'skinheads'. The new fascist youth subculture in Russia]. A. Tarasov. **Svobod. Mysl'** 5 2000 pp.39-56.

2631 Ports of entry and obstacles: teenagers' access to volunteer activities. Richard A. Sundeen; Sally A. Raskoff. **Non. Manag. Leader.** 11:2 Winter:2000 pp.179-198.

2632 The relationship between adolescent nonmarital childbearing and educational expectations: a cohort and period comparison. Ann M. Beutel. **Sociol. Q.** 41:2 Spring:2000 pp.297-314.

2633 The relationship between family factors and adolescent substance use in rural, suburban, and urban settings. Scott D. Scheer; Lynne M. Borden; Joseph F. Donnermeyer. **J. Child Fam. Stud.** 9:1 3:2000 pp.105-116.

2634 Social protest and self-enhancement: a conditional relationship. Howard B. Kaplan; Xiaoru Liu. **Sociol. For.** 15:4 12:2000 pp.595-616.

F: POPULATION. FAMILLE. SEXE. GROUPE ETHNIQUE

2635 The sociology of adolescence and youth in the 1990s: a critical commentary. Frank F. Furstenberg. **J. Marriage Fam.** 62:4 11:2000 pp.896-910.

2636 Staying out of trouble: community resources and problem behavior among high-risk adolescents. Lori Kowaleski-Jones. **J. Marriage Fam.** 62:2 5:2000 pp.449-464.

2637 Surviving post-communism: young people in the former Soviet Union. S.C. Clark; A. Adibekian; Kenneth Roberts. Northampton MA: Edward Elgar Publishing, 2000. 242p. *ISBN: 1840641037. Includes bibliographical references and index. (Series:* Studies of communism in transition).

2638 Sustainable human development: youth empowerment for the new millennium. Peggy A. David. **J. Third World Spect.** 7:1 Spring:2000 pp.1-15.

2639 System wartości rodzinnych młodzieży końca XX wieku (na przykładzie województwa poznańskiego). *[In Polish]*; (The family values of young people at the end of the 20th century (the example of Poznań province).) Walentyna Ignatczyk. **Stud. Demogr.** 1(135) 1999 pp.91-112.

2640 Teen expectations for significant life events. Baruch Fischhoff; Andrew M. Parker; Wändi Bruine De Bruin; Julie Downs; Claire Palmgren; Robyn Dawes; Charles F. Manski. **Publ. Opin. Q.** 64:2 Summer:2000 pp.189-205.

2641 Teenage dreams: feminism, psychoanalysis, and adolescence. Janet Sayers. **Signs** 25:3 Spring:2000 pp.817-839.

2642 Teenage family life, life chances, lifestyles and health: a comparison of two contemporary cohorts. Margaret Ely; Patrick West; Helen Sweeting; Martin Richards. **Int. J. Law Policy Fam.** 14:1 4:2000 pp.1-30.

2643 Telling tales in school: youth culture and conflict narratives. Calvin Morrill; Christine Yalda; Madelaine Adelman; Michael Musheno; Cindy Bejarano. **Law Soc. Rev.** 34:3 2000 pp.521-566.

2644 Using food as a metaphor for care: middle-school kids talk about family, school, and class relationships. Elaine Bell Kaplan. **J. Contemp. Ethnog.** 29:4 8:2000 pp.474-509.

2645 Van *Yes* en dingen die voorbijgaan: tienermeisjes, interpretatieve repertoires en identiteitsconstructie. *[In Dutch]*; (*Yes* and the things that pass by: teenage girls, interpretive repertoires and identity construction.) *[Summary]*. Ellen Hijmans. **Sociol. Gids** XLVII:2 3-4:2000 pp.95-111.

2646 Winners and losers: transformation processes and their consequences for adolescents. Ines Steinke. **Soc. Sci. Info.** 39:1 3:2000 pp.131-154.

2647 Young people in Britain at the beginning of a new century. John Coleman. **Child. Soc.** 14:4 9:2000 pp.230-242.

2648 Youth and coping in twelve countries: surveys of 18-20 year-old young people. Janice Gibson-Cline [Ed.]. London: Routledge, 2000. 240p. *ISBN: 0415217156.*

2649 Youth in a changing Karelia: a comparative study of everyday life, future orientations and political culture of youth in north-west Russia and eastern Finland. Vesa Puuronen [Ed.]; et al. Aldershot: Ashgate, 2000. 266p. *ISBN: 075462028X.*

2650 Youth lifestyles in a changing world. Steven Miles. Philadelphia PA: Open University Press, 2000. 177p. *ISBN: 0335200982, 0335200990. Includes bibliographical references and index.*

Older persons
Personnes âgées

2651 Ageing in an autobiographical context. Riitta-Liisa Heikkinen. **Age. Soc.** 20:4 7:2000 pp.467-484.

2652 Aging, gender and widowhood: perspectives from rural West Bengal. Sarah Lamb. **Contr. I. Soc.** 33:3 9-12:1999 pp.541-570.

2653 Agricultores idosos de Trás-os-Montes: exclusão e reconhecimento. *[In Portuguese]*; (Elderly farmers in Trás-os-Montes: exclusion and recognition.) *[Summary]; [Summary in French]*. António Fragata; José Portela. **Anál. Soc.** XXXV:156 Autumn:2000 pp.721-738.

F: POPULATION. FAMILY. GENDER. ETHNIC GROUPS

2654 The Berlin ageing study: ageing from 70 to 100. Karl Ulrich Mayer [Ed.]; Paul B. Baltes [Ed.]. Cambridge, New York: Cambridge University Press, 1999. xii, 552p. *ISBN: 0521621348. Includes bibliographical references and index.*

2655 Beyond church attendance: religiosity and mental health among rural older adults. Jim Mitchell; Dave Weatherly. **J. Cr-Cult. Gerontol.** 15:1 3:2000 pp.37-54.

2656 A concepção sobre a família na geriatria e na gerontologia Brasileiras: ecos dos dilemas da multidisciplinaridade. *[In Portuguese]*; (The concept of family in Brazilian geriatrics and gerontology: echoes from multidisciplinary dilemma.) Simoni Lahud Guedes. **Rev. Bras. Ciên. Soc.** 15:43 6:2000 pp.69-82.

2657 Des vieillards aux seniors: l'émergence de la société multigénérationnelle. *[In French]*; (From the elderly to seniors: the emergence of multigenerational society.) *[Summary]*. Michel Loriaux. **Recher. Sociolog.** XXXI:1 2000 pp.159-172.

2658 Difference and the negotiation of 'old age'. Rachel Pain; Graham Mowl; Carol Talbot. **Envir. Plan. D.** 18:3 6:2000 pp.377-394.

2659 The effects of environmental context and personal resources on depressive symptomatology in older age: a test of the Lawton model. C.P.M. Knipscheer; M.I. Broese Van Groenou; G.J.F. Leene; A.T.F. Beekman; D.J.H. Deeg. **Age. Soc.** 20:2 3:2000 pp.183-202.

2660 Faith and health self-management of rural older adults. Thomas A. Arcury; Sara A. Quandt; Juliana McDonald; Ronny A. Bell. **J. Cr-Cult. Gerontol.** 15:1 3:2000 pp.55-74.

2661 Gossip in sheltered housing: its cultural importance and social implications. John Percival. **Age. Soc.** 20:3 5:2000 pp.303-325.

2662 Indian elderly: some views of populace. S. Irudaya Rajan; U.S. Mishra; P.S. Sarma. **Indian J. Soc. W.** 60:4 10:1999 pp.487-507.

2663 An introduction to three studies of rural elderly people: effects of religion and culture on health. Wil Gesler; Thomas A. Arcury; Harold G. Koenig. **J. Cr-Cult. Gerontol.** 15:1 3:2000 pp.1-12.

2664 Lifestyles of belief: narrative and culture in a retirement community. Simon Biggs; Miriam Bernard; Paul Kingston; Hilary Nettleton. **Age. Soc.** 20:6 11:2000 pp.649-672.

2665 The mirror has two faces. Elizabeth W. Markson; Carol A. Taylor. **Age. Soc.** 20:2 3:2000 pp.137-160.

2666 Modeling life satisfaction among the aged: a comparison of Chinese and Americans. Philip Silverman; Laura Hecht; J. Daniel McMillin. **J. Cr-Cult. Gerontol.** 15:4 2000 pp.289-305.

2667 Negotiating lifestyle options in later life. Angie Williams; Virpi Ylänne-McEwen; Justine Coupland; Jake Harwood; Mei-chen Lin; Melanie Morgan; Mary Lee Hummert; Jacqui Guendouzi; Kevin Wright; Kristen Harrison; Renée A. Botta. **J. Comm.** 50:3 Summer:2000 pp.9-159. *Collection of 8 articles.*

2668 Nonagenarians: a qualitative exploration of individual differences in wellbeing. Pernilla K. Hillerås; Penelope Pollitt; Jo Medway; Kjerstin Ericsson. **Age. Soc.** 20:6 11:2000 pp.673-698.

2669 Nursing home entry in Germany and the United States. Christine L. Himes; Gert G. Wagner; Douglas A. Wolf; Hakan Aykan; Deborah D. Dougherty. **J. Cr-Cult. Gerontol.** 15:2 2000 pp.99-118.

2670 Perceptions and consequences of ageism: views of older people. Victor Minichiello; Jan Browne; Hal Kendig. **Age. Soc.** 20:3 5:2000 pp.253-278.

2671 Political disempowerment among older people in Hong Kong. Ping-kwong Kam. **J. Cr-Cult. Gerontol.** 15:4 2000 pp.307-329.

2672 Politics, power and old age. John A. Vincent. Buckingham: Open University Press, 1999. viii, 164p. *ISBN: 0335201660, 0335201652. Includes bibliographical references (p. [147]-158) and index.* (*Series:* Rethinking ageing).

2673 Religion, spirituality and older people. Kenneth Howse. London: Centre for Policy on Ageing, 1999. 126p. *ISBN: 090413993X.* (*Series:* CPA reports - 25).

F: POPULATION. FAMILLE. SEXE. GROUPE ETHNIQUE

2674 Social and democratic participation in residential settings for older people: realities and aspirations. Stephen Abbott; Malcolm Fisk; Louise Forward. **Age. Soc.** 20:3 5:2000 pp.327-340.
2675 Sociological studies on the aged in Vietnam. Truyen Duc Nguyen; Huong Thi Nguyen; Phuong Le; Tam Quach; Thièn Chi Duong. **Viet. Soc. Sci.** 2:76 2000 pp.90-114.
2676 Sooner rather than later? Younger and middle-aged adults preparing for retirement. Michael Anderson; Yaojun Li; Frank Bechhofer; David McCrone; Robert Stewart. **Age. Soc.** 20:4 7:2000 pp.445-466.
2677 La tercera edad en México: imágenes y perspectivas. *[In Spanish]*; [The Third Age in Mexico: images and perspectives]. Héctor Luis Zarauz; José Arellano S.; Margarita Santoyo R.; Marco Antonio Sánchez Saldaña; Juan Bello Domínguez; Mariana del Rocío Aguilar Bobadilla; Tania Brito Castrejón. **Acta Sociol. [Mexico]** 30 9-12:2000 pp.11-144. *Collection of 5 articles.*
2678 Understanding old age: critical and global perspectives. Gail Wilson. London: Sage publications, 2000. ix, 194p. *ISBN: 0761960112, 0761960120. Includes bibliographical references (p. [171]-186) and index.*
2679 Viellir: l'avancée en âge. *[In French]*; [Ageing: advancing in age]. Pierre Sansot; Jean Mantovani; Monique Membrado; Xavier Gaullier; Marcel Drulhe; Nathalie Des Gayets; Marie-Eve Joël; Pierre-Alain Greciano; Anne-Marie Guillemard; Claudine Attias-Donfut; Nicole Lapierre; Bernard Ennuyer; Isabelle Mallon; Jean-Philippe Virot Durandal; Bernadette Puijalon. **Inf. Soc.** 88 2000 pp.4-121. *Collection of 13 articles.*
2680 Vietnamese-Australian grandparenthood: the changing roles and psychological well-being. James Vo-Thanh-Xuan; Pranee Liamputtong Rice. **J. Cr-Cult. Gerontol.** 15:4 2000 pp.265-288.

F.2: **Demography**
Démographie

2681 Age period cohort characteristic models. Robert M. O'Brien. **Soc. Sci. R.** 29:1 3:2000 pp.123 139.
2682 Die Beziehungen zwischen den Generationen in Frankreich. *[In German]*; [Intergenerational relations in France]. Xavier Gaullier. **Dokumente** 56:2 4:2000 pp.129-139.
2683 Census and social reality. A.M. Shah; M. Vijayanunni; M.K. Premi; Satish Deshpande. **Sociol. Bul.** 48:1-2 3-9:1999 pp.235-262. *Collection of 4 articles.*
2684 Česká republika a země Evropské unie (demografické podobnosti a rozdíly). *[In Czech]*; (The Czech Republic and countries of the European Union (demographic similarities and differences).) Vladimíra Dvořáková; Helena Horská; Ladislav Rabušic; Jitka Rychtaříková; Felix Koschin. **Demografie** 42:4 2000 pp.277-298.
2685 Chelovecheskii potentsial pog ugrozoi. *[In Russian]*; [Human potential under threat]. Iu. Granin. **Svobod. Mysl'** 9 2000 pp.74-84.
2686 Demografický vývoj na Slovensku v roku 1998. *[In Czech]*; (Demographic development in Slovakia in 1998.) *[Summary]*. Michal Tirpák; Viera Pilinská. **Demografie** 42:1 2000 pp.1-18.
2687 The demographic status of and perspectives for the Russian Federation. Piotr Eberhardt. **Geogr. Pol.** 73:1 Spring:2000 pp.63-76.
2688 Demographics of the gay and lesbian population in the United States: evidence from available systematic data sources. Dan Black; Gary Gates; Seth Sanders; Lowell Taylor. **Demography** 37:2 5:2000 pp.139-154.
2689 Die demographische Struktur Polens im Transformationsprozeß. Entwicklung und räumliche Gliederung. *[In German]*; [Poland's demographic structure in the process of transformation]. Olaf Kühne. **Osteuropa** 50:8 8:2000 pp.872-884.

F: POPULATION. FAMILY. GENDER. ETHNIC GROUPS

2690 Demography: measuring and modeling population processes. Samuel H. Preston; Michel Guillot; Patrick Heuveline. Malden MA: Blackwell Publishers, 2000. 291p. *ISBN: 1557864519, 1557862141. Includes bibliographical references and index.*

2691 The demography of industrializing cities. Patrice Bourdelais; William Robert Lee; Peter Marschalck; Michel Oris; Anders Brändström; Jan Sundin; Lars-Göran Tedebrand; Arantza Pareja Alonso; Cezary Kuklo; Mariann Villa. **Hist. Fam.** 5:4 2000 pp.363-450. *Collection of 5 articles.*

2692 Educational assortative mating across marriage markets: non-Hispanic Whites in the United States. Susan K. Lewis; Valerie K. Oppenheimer. **Demography** 37:1 2:2000 pp.29-40.

2693 The effects of migration on the population distribution in Hong Kong. Paul S.F. Yip; Joseph Lee. **Asian J. Pub. Admin.** 22:1 6:2000 pp.90-104.

2694 The encyclopedia of global population and demographics. Immanuel Ness; James Ciment. Chicago IL, London: Fitzroy Dearborn, 1999. vii, 967p. *ISBN: 1579581803.*

2695 L'évolution démographique des Balkans depuis la fin de la décennie 1980. *[In French];* (Demographic change in the Balkans since the end of the 1980s.) *[Summary]; [Summary in Spanish].* J.P. Sardon. **Population** 55:4-5 7-10:2000 pp.765-786.

2696 L'évolution démographique récente en France. *[In French];* (Recent demographic change in France.) *[Summary]; [Summary in Spanish].* F. Prioux. **Population** 55:3 5-6:2000 pp.441-476.

2697 Les évolutions démographiques des territoires entre 1975 et 1999. *[In French];* (Changes in the population of the French regions between 1975 and 1999.) *[Summary]; [Summary in Spanish].* C. Rieu. **Population** 55:3 5-6:2000 pp.477-502.

2698 Évolutions récentes de la démographie des pays développés. *[In French];* (Recent changes in the demographic situation of the developed countries.) *[Summary]; [Summary in Spanish].* J.P. Sardon. **Population** 55:4-5 7-10:2000 pp.729-764.

2699 The fifth cell: correlation bias in U.S. census adjustment. Kenneth W. Wachter; David A. Freedman. **Eval. Rev.** 24:2 4:2000 pp.191-211.

2700 Forecast accuracy and efficiency: an evaluation of *ex ante* substate long-term forecasts. David G. Lenze. **Int. Reg. Sci. R.** 23:2 4:2000 pp.201-226.

2701 Genetic diversity and population structure among thirteen endogamous populations of Purnia, Bihar. B.N. Pandey; T.S. Vasulu; P.K.L. Das; P.K. Panka. **Mankind Q.** XL:4 Summer:2000 pp.355-380.

2702 Graying Japan, swaying the policymaker. Hideyuki Morito. **Int. J. Comp. L. L. I. R.** 16:1 Spring:2000 pp.25-38.

2703 The impact of postmarital residence on fertility, early childhood mortality, and child health in southern Ethiopia. Gebre-Egziabher Kiros; David I. Kertzer. **J. Comp. Fam. Stud.** XXXI:4 Autumn:2000 pp.503-518.

2704 The importance of international demographic research for the United States. N. Sastry. **Pop. Res. Pol. R.** 19:3 6:2000 pp.199-232.

2705 Irish demography in a comparative context: European transition theory vs. a post-colonial understanding. Timothy J. White. **Irish J. Soc.** 9 1999 pp.60-76.

2706 The law of increasing returns. Ronald Bailey. **Nat. Inter.** 59 Spring:2000 pp.113-150.

2707 Life in an older America. Lawrence K. Grossman [Ed.]; Mia R. Oberlink [Ed.]; Robert N. Butler [Ed.]. New York: Century, 1999. vi, 287p. *ISBN: 0870784242. Includes bibliographical references (p. 239-271) and index.*

2708 Marianne au foyer. Révolution politique et transition démographique en France et aux États-Unis. *[In French];* (Marianne at home. Political revolution and demographic transition in France and the United States.) *[Summary]; [Summary in Spanish].* R. Binion. **Population** 55:1 1-2:2000 pp.81-104.

2709 Monitoring demographic and socioeconomic characteristics of intercensal populations: a British local authority perspective. Nigel Walford; Ann Hockey. **Plan. Pract. Res.** 15:1-2 2-5:2000 pp.51-64.

F: POPULATION. FAMILLE. SEXE. GROUPE ETHNIQUE

2710 One quarter of humanity: Malthusian mythology and Chinese realities, 1700-2000. James Z. Lee; Wang Feng. Cambridge MA, London: Harvard University Press, 1999. xii, 248p. *ISBN: 0674639081. Includes bibliographical references (p. [159]-239) and index.*
2711 An optimum world population. David Willey. **Med. Conf. Surv.** 16:1 1-3:2000 pp.72-93.
2712 Population ageing: challenges for policies and programmes in developed and developing countries. Robert Cliquet [Ed.]; Mohammed Nizamuddin [Ed.]. New York: United Nations Population Fund, Population and Family Study Centre, 1999. 288p.
2713 Population ageing in developed and developing regions: implications for health policy. Peter Lloyd-Sherlock. **Soc. Sci. Med.** 51:6 9:2000 pp.887-896.
2714 Population crises and population cycles. Claire Russell; W.M.S. Russell. **Med. Conf. Surv.** 16:4 10-12:2000 pp.383-410.
2715 Population, food, and knowledge. D. Gale Johnson. **Am. Econ. Rev.** 90:1 3:2000 pp.1-14.
2716 Recensements et géographie. *[In French]*; [Censuses and geography]. Yves Guermond; Denise Pumain; Jean-Philippe Damais; Roger Brunet; Alexandre Kych; Michel Bussi; Catherine Rhein; Véronique Mondou; Isabelle Thomas; Sarah Curtis; Lena Sanders; Pierre Riquet; John Mollenkopf; Benoît Antheaume; Hervé Théry; Philippe Waniez; Philippe Cadène. **Espace Géogr.** 29:1 2000 pp.1-63. *Collection of 15 articles.*
2717 The relationships of population and forest trends. A.S. Mather; C.L. Needle. **Geogr. J.** 166:1 3:2000 pp.2-13.
2718 La reprise démographique rurale en Wallonie et en Europe du Nord-Ouest. *[In French]*; (Rural population renewal in Walloonia and North-Western Europe.) Laurence Thomsin. **Espace Pop. Soc.** 1 2000 pp.83-100.
2719 Russie: l'horreur démographique. *[In French]*; [Demographic horror in Russia]. Jean-Claude Chesnais. **Polit. Int.** 89 Autumn:2000 pp.211-240.
2720 Srovnáni demografické situace České republiky s vybranými zeměmi Evropské unie. *[In Czech]*; (A comparison of thedemographic situation of the Czech Republic with that of selected countries of the European Union.) *[Summary]*. Aneta Dvořáková. **Demografie** 42:4 2000 pp.253-265.
2721 The state of population management in Bihar: problems and prospects. J.P. Singh. **Man India** 80:1-2 1-6:2000 pp.141-155.
2722 Understanding the sex ratio in India: a simulation approach. Paula Griffiths; Zoë Matthews; Andrew Hinde. **Demography** 37:4 11:2000 pp.477-488.
2723 The US decennial census: political questions, scientific answers. Kenneth Prewitt. **Pop. Dev. Rev.** 26:1 3:2000 pp.1-16.
2724 Vývoj obyvatelstva České Republiky v roce 1999 (z výsledků zpracování Českého statistického úřadu). *[In Czech]*; (Population development in the Czech Republic in 1999 (with results processed by the Czech Statistical Office).) *[Summary]*. Milan Kučera; Miroslav Šimek. **Demografie** 42:3 2000 pp.169-182.
2725 Women, poverty and demographic change. Brígida García [Ed.]. Oxford: Oxford University Press, 2000. xii, 311p. *ISBN: 0198294867. Includes bibliographical references and index. (Series:* International studies in demography).

F.3: **Demographic trends and population policy**
Tendances démographiques et politique démographique

Family planning
Planning familial

2726 The 1998 Canadian contraception study. William A. Fisher; Richard Boroditsky; Martha L. Bridges. **Canad. J. Human Sex.** 8:3 1999 pp.161-216.
2727 Adolescent girls with illegally induced abortion in Dar es Salaam: the discrepancy between sexual behaviour and lack of access to contraception. Vibeke Rasch; Margrethe

F: POPULATION. FAMILY. GENDER. ETHNIC GROUPS

Silberschmidt; Yasinta Mchumvu; Vumilia Mmary. **Reprod. Health Mat.** 8:15 5:2000 pp.52-62.

2728 Are births underreported in rural China? Manipulation of statistical records in response to China's population policies. M. Giovanna Merli; Adrian E. Raftery. **Demography** 37:1 2:2000 pp.109-126.

2729 Birth planning and sterilization in China. Susan E. Short; Ma Linmao; Yu Wentao. **Pop. Stud.** 54:3 11:2000 pp.279-292.

2730 Competitive framing processes in the abortion debate: polarization-vilification, frame saving, and frame debunking. Dawn McCaffrey; Jennifer Keys. **Sociol. Q.** 41:1 Winter:2000 pp.41-62.

2731 Contraception across cultures: technologies, choices, constraints. Elisa Janine Sobo [Ed.]; Mary Thompson [Ed.]; Andrew Russell [Ed.]. Oxford: Berg Publishers, 2000. 224p. *ISBN: 1859733867, 1859733816. Includes index.*

2732 The contraceptive revolution in Israel: changing family planning practices among ethnoimmigrant groups. Esther I. Wilder. **Soc. Sci. R.** 29:1 3:2000 pp.70-91.

2733 Correlates of female sterilization regret in the southern states of India. Mala Ramanathan; U.S. Mishra. **J. Biosoc. Sc.** 32:4 10:2000 pp.547-558.

2734 Creation ethics: the moral status of early fetuses and the ethics of abortion. Elizabeth Harman. **Philos. Pub.** 28:4 Fall:1999 pp.310-324.

2735 Demographic implications of reproductive technologies. E.H. Stephen. **Pop. Res. Pol. R.** 19:4 8:2000 pp.301-316.

2736 Determinants of contraceptive use and method choice in Turkey. Ismet Koc. **J. Biosoc. Sc.** 32:3 7:2000 pp.329-342.

2737 Disability, space and sexuality: access to family planning services. Paul Anderson; Rob Kitchin. **Soc. Sci. Med.** 51:8 10:2000 pp.1163-1174.

2738 The effect of pregnancy intention on child development. Theodore J. Joyce; Robert Kaestner; Sanders Korenman. **Demography** 37:1 2:2000 pp.83-94.

2739 Effects of child gender preference on contraceptive use in rural Bangladesh. Akiko Nosaka. **J. Comp. Fam. Stud.** XXXI:4 Autumn:2000 pp.485-502.

2740 Family planning programs, socioeconomic characteristics, and contraceptive use in Malawi. B. Cohen. **World Dev.** 28:5 5:2000 pp.843-860.

2741 The fertility impact of temporary migration in China: a detachment hypothesis. Xiushi Yang. **Eur. J. Pop.** 16:2 6:2000 pp.163-184.

2742 Genetic technology and family conflict. Deborah B. Gentry. **Med. Q.** 18:1 Fall:2000 pp.5-18.

2743 Husbands' versus wives' fertility goals and use of contraception: the influence of gender context in five Asian countries. Karen Oppenheim Mason; Herbert L. Smith. **Demography** 37:3 8:2000 pp.299-312.

2744 Induced abortion ratio in modern Sweden falls with age, but rises again before menopause. Birgitta S. Tullberg; Virpi Lummaa. **Evol. Hum. Behav.** 22:1 1:2001 pp.1-10.

2745 Informed policy making for the prevention of unwanted pregnancy. Carol Chetkovich; Jane Mauldon; Claire Brindis; Sylvia Guendelman. **Eval. Rev.** 23:5 10:1999 pp.527-552.

2746 Is low income a constraint to contraceptive use among the Pakistani poor? Sohail Agha. **J. Biosoc. Sc.** 32:2 4:2000 pp.161-175.

2747 Local and foreign models of reproduction in Nyanza province, Kenya. Susan Cotts Watkins. **Pop. Dev. Rev.** 26:4 12:2000 pp.725-760.

2748 Mass media exposure and its impact on family planning in Bangladesh. M. Mazharul Islam; A.H.M. Saidul Hasan. **J. Biosoc. Sc.** 32:4 10:2000 pp.513-526.

2749 Population education and family planning. India Health Foundation; P.N. Sinha. New Delhi: AuthorsPress, 2000. vi, 260p. *ISBN: 8172730160. Includes bibliographical references (p. [255]-257) and index. India Health Foundation.*

2750 Postabortion care: lessons from operations research. Dale Huntington [Ed.]; Nancy J. Piet-Pelon [Ed.]. New York: Population Council, 1999. xv, 218p. *ISBN: 0878341005. Includes bibliographical references.*

F: POPULATION. FAMILLE. SEXE. GROUPE ETHNIQUE

2751 Racial differences in Norplant use in the United States. Jennifer Malat. **Soc. Sci. Med.** 50:9 5:2000 pp.1297-1308.
2752 Relatos de la esterilización: entre el acomodo y la resistencia. *[In Spanish]*; [Reports on sterilization: between compromise and resistance] *[Summary]*. Lourdes Lugo-Ortiz. **Rev. Cien. Soc.** 6 1:1999 pp.208-226.
2753 Religiosity and contraceptive method choice: the Jewish population of Israel. Barbara S. Okun. **Eur. J. Pop.** 16:2 6:2000 pp.109-132.
2754 Reproductive and sexual rights. Sofia Gruskin; Nafis Sadik; Rosalind Petchesky; Tomris Türmen; Carmel Shalev; Alice M. Miller; Bonnie Shepard; Barbara Klugman; Marlene Gerber Fried; Judit Sandor; Bartholomew Dean; Eliana Elías Valdeavellano; Michelle McKinley; Rebekah Saul; International Coordinating Committee. **Health Hum. Rights** 4:2 2000 pp.1-234. *Collection of 12 articles.*
2755 Reproductive genetics, gender and the body: 'Please doctor, may I have a normal baby?' Elizabeth Ettorre. **Sociology** 34:3 8:2000 pp.402-420.
2756 Šetření rodiny a reprodukce — mezinárodní komparace. *[In Czech]*; (Family and reproduction survey - international comparison.) *[Summary]*. Eva Čákiová. **Demografie** 42:3 2000 pp.208-218.
2757 Sharing genetic origins information in third party assisted conception: a case for Victorian family values? Eric Blyth. **Child. Soc.** 14:1 2:2000 pp.11-22.
2758 Social impacts of technological diffusion: prenatal diagnosis and induced abortion in Brazil. Hillegonda Maria Dutilh Novaes. **Soc. Sci. Med.** 50:1 1:2000 pp.41-52.
2759 Social networks, ideation, and contraceptive behavior in Bangladesh: a longitudinal analysis. D. Lawrence Kincaid. **Soc. Sci. Med.** 50:2 1:2000 pp.215-231.
2760 Socioeconomic and cultural determinants of abortion among Jewish women in Israel. Esther I. Wilder. **Eur. J. Pop.** 16:2 6:2000 pp.133-162.
2761 Spousal communication and contraceptive use among the Yoruba of Nigeria. B.J. Feyisetan. **Pop. Res. Pol. R.** 19:1 2:2000 pp.29-46.
2762 Transforming family planning programmes: a framework for advancing the reproductive rights agenda. Jodi L. Jacobson. **Reprod. Health Mat.** 8:15 5:2000 pp.21-32.
2763 Unmet need for family planning in developing countries and implications for population policy. John B. Casterline; Steven W. Sinding. **Pop. Dev. Rev.** 26:4 12.2000 pp.691-724.
2764 Welfare generosity, pregnancies and abortions among unmarried AFDC recipients. L.M. Argys; S.L. Averett; D.I. Rees. **J. Pop. Ec.** 13:4 2000 pp.569-594.
2765 What husbands in northern India know about reproductive health: correlates of knowledge about pregnancy and maternal and sexual health. Shelah S. Bloom; Amy Ong Tsui; Marya Plotkin; Sarah Bassett. **J. Biosoc. Sc.** 32:2 4:2000 pp.237-251.

Fertility
Fécondité

2766 Analysis of birth intervals in a non-contracepting Indian population: an evolutionary ecological approach. Dilip C. Nath; Donna L. Leonetti; Matthew S. Steele. **J. Biosoc. Sc.** 32:3 7:2000 pp.343-354.
2767 Are there crisis-led fertility declines? Evidence from central Cameroon. P.M. Eloundou-Enyegue; C.S. Stokes; G.T. Cornwell. **Pop. Res. Pol. R.** 19:1 2:2000 pp.47-72.
2768 Childbearing following marital dissolution in Britain; *[Summary in French]*. Julie Jefferies; Ann Berrington; Ian Diamond. **Eur. J. Pop.** 16:3 9:2000 pp.193-210.
2769 Coitus, the proximate determinant of conception: inter-country variance in Sub-Saharan Africa. Mark Simon Brown. **J. Biosoc. Sc.** 32:2 4:2000 pp.145-160.
2770 Conditioning factors for fertility decline in Bengal: history, language identity, and openness to innovations. Alaka Malwade Basu; Sajeda Amin. **Pop. Dev. Rev.** 26:4 12:2000 pp.761-794.
2771 Couples' views about planning fertility in the Philippines. Lindy Williams; Teresa Sobieszczyk; Aurora Perez. **Rural Sociol.** 65:3 9:2000 pp.484-514.

F: POPULATION. FAMILY. GENDER. ETHNIC GROUPS

2772 Cyberspace time and infertility: thoughts on social time and the environment. Heather Menzies. **Time Soc.** 9:1 3:2000 pp.75-89.
2773 Demographic and health status risk factors in childbearing among Indian women. Evidence from hospital data for the later stages of fertility decline. Kirsty McNay. **J. Biosoc. Sc.** 32:2 4:2000 pp.191-206.
2774 Demographic, socio-economic, and regional fertility differentials in Pakistan. Abdul Hakim. **Pak. Dev. R.** 38:4(II) Winter:1999 pp.643-660.
2775 Did the economic crisis cause the fertility decline in Russia: evidence from the 1994 microcensus; *[Summary in French]*. Tatiana L. Kharkova; Evgueny M. Andreev. **Eur. J. Pop.** 16:3 9:2000 pp.211-233.
2776 Diverging fertility among U.S. women who delay childbearing past age 30. Steven P. Martin. **Demography** 37:4 11:2000 pp.523-533.
2777 Un exemple de réduction de la fécondité sous contraintes: la région du delta du fleuve Rouge au Viêt Nam. *[In French]*; (An example of fertility reduction within limits: the region of the Red River Delta in Vietnam.) C. Scornet. **Population** 55:2 3-4:2000 pp.265-300.
2778 Factors influencing choice of delivery sites in Rakai district of Uganda. B. Amooti-Kaguna; F. Nuwaha. **Soc. Sci. Med.** 50:2 1:2000 pp.203-213.
2779 La fécondité Chinoise à l'aube du XXIe siècle: constats et incertitudes. *[In French]*; (Chinese fertility on the eve of the 21st century: fact and uncertainty.) I. Attané. **Population** 55:2 3-4:2000 pp.233-264.
2780 Fertility and mortality differentials among selected population groups of north-western and eastern India. A.K. Kapoor; Gautam K. Kshatriya. **J. Biosoc. Sc.** 32:2 4:2000 pp.253-264.
2781 Fertility and the male life-cycle in the era of fertility decline. Caroline H. Bledsoe [Ed.]; Susana Lerner [Ed.]; Jane I. Guyer [Ed.]. Oxford, New York: Oxford University Press, 2000. x, 376p. *ISBN: 0198294441. Includes bibliographical references and index. (Series: International studies in demography).*
2782 Fertility decline as a coordination problem. H.P. Kohler. **J. Dev. Econ.** 63:2 12:2000 pp.231-264.
2783 Fertility, mortality and gender bias among tribal population: an Indian perspective. Arup Maharatna. **Soc. Sci. Med.** 50:10 5:2000 pp.1333-1351.
2784 Fertility of Mexican immigrant women in the U.S.: a closer look. Marion Carter. **Soc. Sci. Q.** 81:4 12:2000 pp.1073-1086.
2785 Formuła Bongaartsa-Feeneya — zastosowania dla Polski. *[In Polish]*; (Bongaarts-Feeney's formula — an application for Poland.) *[Summary]*. Ewa Frątczak; Aneta Ptak-Chmielewska. **Stud. Demogr.** 2(136) 1999 pp.43-61.
2786 Gender equity in theories of fertility transition; *[Summary in French]*. Peter McDonald. **Pop. Dev. Rev.** 26:3 9:2000 pp.427-440.
2787 The impact of education, income, and mortality on fertility in Jamaica. S. Handa. **World Dev.** 28:1 1:2000 pp.173-186.
2788 The limits to low fertility: a biosocial approach. Caroline Foster. **Pop. Dev. Rev.** 26:2 6:2000 pp.209-234.
2789 Living with infertility: experiences from urban slum populations in Bangladesh. Nahar Papreen; Anjali Sharma; Keith Sabin; Lutfa Begum; S. Khaled Ahsan; Abdulla H. Baqui. **Reprod. Health Mat.** 8:15 5:2000 pp.33-44.
2790 Pastoralists, agropastoralists and migrants: interactions between fertility and mobility in northern Burkina Faso. Kate Hampshire; Sara Randall. **Pop. Stud.** 54:3 11:2000 pp.247-262.
2791 Płodność pozamałżeńska w Polsce. *[In Polish]*; (Extra-marital fertility in Poland.) *[Summary]*. Piotr Szukalski. **Stud. Demogr.** 2(136) 1999 pp.109-124.
2792 Politics and fertility: a new approach to population policy analysis. L. Lush; J. Cleland; K. Lee; G. Walt. **Pop. Res. Pol. R.** 19:1 2:2000 pp.1-28.
2793 Population and resources: an exploration of reproductive and environmental externalities. Partha Dasgupta. **Pop. Dev. Rev.** 26:4 12:2000 pp.643-690.

F: POPULATION. FAMILLE. SEXE. GROUPE ETHNIQUE

2794 Predictive intervals for age-specific fertility; *[Summary in French]*. Nico Keilman; Dinh Quang Pham. **Eur. J. Pop.** 16:1 3:2000 pp.41-66.
2795 Protracted national conflict and fertility change: Palestinians and Israelis in the twentieth century; *[Summary in French]*. Philippe Fargues. **Pop. Dev. Rev.** 26:3 9:2000 pp.441-482.
2796 The recent rise in Palestinian fertility: permanent or transient? Marwan Khawaja. **Pop. Stud.** 54:3 11:2000 pp.331-346.
2797 Recent trends in Tanzanian fertility. Andrew Hinde; Akim J. Mturi. **Pop. Stud.** 54:2 7:2000 pp.177-192.
2798 Rekonstrukcja dzietności małżeńskiej kobiet w późniejszym wieku na podstawie ankiety retrospektywnej. *[In Polish]*; (Reconstruction of completed marital fertility of women in post-reproductive age based on a retrospective survey.) Jan Paradysz. **Stud. Demogr.** 1(135) 1999 pp.13-34.
2799 Relative cohort size: source of a unifying theory of global fertility transition? Diane J. Macunovich. **Pop. Dev. Rev.** 26:2 6:2000 pp.235-261.
2800 Seasonal variation of births in rural West Bengal: magnitude, direction and correlates. Uma Chatterjee; Rajib Acharya. **J. Biosoc. Sc.** 32:4 10:2000 pp.443-458.
2801 Secular trend and intrapopulational variation in age at menopause in Spanish women. C. Varea; C. Bernis; P. Montero; S. Arias; A. Barroso; B. González. **J. Biosoc. Sc.** 32:3 7:2000 pp.383-394.
2802 Shrinking kin networks in Italy due to sustained low fertility; *[Summary in French]*. Cecilia Tomassini; Douglas A. Wolf. **Eur. J. Pop.** 16:4 12:2000 pp.353-372.
2803 Subsequent fertility among teen mothers: longitudinal analyses of recent national data. Jennifer Manlove; Carrie Mariner; Angela Romano Papillo. **J. Marriage Fam.** 62:2 5:2000 pp.430-448.
2804 Teenage pregnancy — unravelling the issues. Ann McGuigan. **Child C. Pract.** 6:2 4:2000 pp.182-205.
2805 Zmiana wzorca płodności w projekcji demograficznej dla Polski. *[In Polish]*; (Changes in the fertility pattern in a population projection for Poland.) *[Summary]*. Grażyna Marciniak. **Stud. Demogr.** 2(136) 1999 pp.89-108.

Morbidity
Morbidité

2806 AIDS into the 21st century: some critical considerations. Elizabeth Pisani. **Reprod. Health Mat.** 8:15 5:2000 pp.63-76.
2807 Death and deprivation: an exploratory analysis of deaths in the health and lifestyle survey. Kelvyn Jones; Myles I. Gould; Craig Duncan. **Soc. Sci. Med.** 50:7-8 4:2000 pp.1059-1080.
2808 A multilevel analysis of income inequality and cardiovascular disease risk factors. Ana V. Diez-Roux; Bruce G. Link; Mary E. Northridge. **Soc. Sci. Med.** 50:5 3:2000 pp.673-687.
2809 On the 'physiological dope' problematic in housing and illness research: towards a critical realism of home and health. C. Allen. **Hous. Th. Soc.** 17:2 2000 pp.49-67.
2810 The potential demographic impact of HIV/AIDS in the Pacific. Dennis A. Ahlburg; Heidi J. Larson; Tim Brown. **Pac. Stud.** 21:4 12:1998 pp.67-81.
2811 The racial crossover in comorbidity, disability, and mortality. Nan E. Johnson. **Demography** 37:3 8:2000 pp.267-283.
2812 Racial differences in birth health risk: a quantitative genetic approach. Edwin J.C.G. van den Oord; David C. Rowe. **Demography** 37:3 8:2000 pp.285-298.
2813 Social inequalities in cancer survival. Øystein Kravdal. **Pop. Stud.** 54:1 3:2000 pp.1-18.
2814 Zdravi nejen do roku 2000 (Česká republika a mezinárodní srovnáni). *[In Czech]*; [Health up to and beyond 2000 (Comparison of Czech Republic and international data)]. Alena Petráková; Marcela Gregůrková; Zdeňka Vandasová; Zdeňka Skodová; Marek Malý; Růžena Kubínová; Zuzana Kamberská; Radka Kočová; Ladislav Csémy; Dagmar Dzúrová; Eva Dragomirecká; Jitka Rychtaříková; Jan Bruthans; Marcela Ambrožová.

F: POPULATION. FAMILY. GENDER. ETHNIC GROUPS

Demografie 42:1 2000 pp.19-55. *Papers presented at the XXIXth conference of the Czech Demographic Society.*

Mortality
Mortalité

2815 Active life expectancy estimates for the U.S. elderly population: a multidimensional continuous-mixture model of functional change applied to completed cohorts, 1982-1996. Kenneth G. Manton; Kenneth C. Land. **Demography** 37:3 8:2000 pp.253-266.

2816 Alcohol regulation and auto fatalities. Douglas J. Young; Thomas W. Likens. **Int. R. Law Econ.** 20:1 3:2000 pp.107-126.

2817 Analysis of cervical cancer mortality and incidence data from England and Wales: evidence of a beneficial effect of screening. Peter D. Sasieni; Joanna Adams. **J. Roy. Stat. Soc. A.** 163:2 2000 pp.191-210.

2818 Bayesian analysis of multivariate mortality data with large families. M.H. Chen; D.K. Dey; D. Sinha. **J. R. Stat. Soc.** 49:1 2000 pp.129-144.

2819 Beverage-specific alcohol consumption and cirrhosis mortality in a group of English-speaking beer-drinking countries. William C. Kerr; Kaye Middleton Fillmore; Paul Marvy; Paul J. Gruenewald [Comments by]; John A. Hermos [Comments by]; Jürgen Rehm; Gerhard Gmel; Minghao Her [Comments by]; Ole-Jørgen Skog [Comments by]. **Addiction** 95:3 3:2000 pp.339-358.

2820 Changing patterns of death and dying. Clive Seale. **Soc. Sci. Med.** 51:6 9:2000 pp.917-930.

2821 Correlates of child mortality in Pakistan: a hazards model analysis. Jannifer Bennett. **Pak. Dev. R.** 38:1 Spring:1999 pp.85-118.

2822 Determinants of infant and child mortality in the West Bank and Gaza Strip. Jon Pedersen. **J. Biosoc. Sc.** 32:4 10:2000 pp.527-546.

2823 The effects of water supply and sanitation on childhood mortality in urban Eritrea. Gebremariam Woldemicael. **J. Biosoc. Sc.** 32:2 4:2000 pp.207-227.

2824 Les effets sur la mortalité de quelques maux contemporains: sida, hépatite, alcool et tabac. *[In French]*; (The mortality effects of some modern health problems: AIDS, hepatitis, alcohol and tobacco consumption.) *[Summary]*; *[Summary in Spanish]*. A. Nizard. **Population** 55:3 5-6:2000 pp.503-566.

2825 Environmental factors, situation of women and child mortality in southwestern Nigeria. Iyun B. Folasade. **Soc. Sci. Med.** 51:10 11:2000 pp.1473-1490.

2826 Fatal train accidents on Britain's mainline railways. A.W. Evans. **J. Roy. Stat. Soc. A.** 163:1 2000 pp.99-119.

2827 Household vulnerability to food crisis and mortality in the drought-prone areas of northern Ethiopia. Markos Ezra; Gebre-Egziabher Kiros. **J. Biosoc. Sc.** 32:3 7:2000 pp.395-410.

2828 Indices and sociodemographic determinants of childhood mortality in rural upper Egypt. Khaled M. Yassin. **Soc. Sci. Med.** 51:2 7:2000 pp.185-198.

2829 An information statistical approach to the modifiable areal unit problem in incidence rate maps. Tomoki Nakaya. **Envir. Plan. A.** 32:1 1:2000 pp.91-110.

2830 Living and dying in the USA: behavioral, health, and social differentials of adult mortality. Richard G. Rogers; Charles B. Nam; Robert A. Hummer. San Diego CA: Academic Press, 2000. xx, 354p. *ISBN: 0125931301. Includes bibliographical references (p. 323-342) and indexes.*

2831 Monitoring suicide mortality: a Bayesian approach; *[Summary in French]*. Peter Congdon. **Eur. J. Pop.** 16:3 9:2000 pp.251-284.

2832 La mortalité maternelle en milieu rural au Sénégal. *[In French]*; (Maternal mortality in rural Senegal.) *[Summary]*; *[Summary in Spanish]*. G. Pison; B. Kodio; E. Guyavarch; J.F. Etard. **Population** 55:6 11-12:2000 pp.1003-1020.

2833 The mortality crisis in transitional economies. Renato Paniccià [Ed.]; Giovanni Andrea Cornia [Ed.]. New York: Oxford University Press, 2000. 456p. *ISBN: 0198297416.*

F: POPULATION. FAMILLE. SEXE. GROUPE ETHNIQUE

Includes bibliographical references and index. *(Series:* UNU/WIDER studies in development economics).

2834 Mortality differentials among women: the Israel longitudinal mortality study. Orly Manor; Zvi Eisenbach; Avi Israeli; Yechiel Friedlander. **Soc. Sci. Med.** 51:8 10:2000 pp.1175-1188.

2835 Natężenie zgonów według wieku jako czynnik przyrostu trwania życia ludności dolnego Śląska w latach 1980-1998. *[In Polish]*; (The contribution of age-specific mortality to the rise of life expectancy at birth in Lower Silesia in the years 1980-1998.) *[Summary].* Ireneusz Kuropka. **Stud. Demogr.** 2(136) 1999 pp.3-16.

2836 Perceiving mortality decline. Mark R. Montgomery. **Pop. Dev. Rev.** 26:4 12:2000 pp.795-820.

2837 Prognoza umieralności w Polsce do 2050 r. *[In Polish]*; (Mortality forecast in Poland until 2050.) *[Summary].* Longina Rutkowska. **Stud. Demogr.** 2(136) 1999 pp.17-42.

2838 Searching for socioeconomic risk factors in perinatal mortality in Kuwait: a case control study. Nasra M. Shah; Makhdoom A. Shah; Abdul Aziz Khalaf; Mustafa Mohammad Mustafa; Ali Al Sayed. **Soc. Sci. Med.** 51:4 8:2000 pp.539-550.

2839 Sibling mortality correlation in Kenya. Lawrence Ikamari. **J. Biosoc. Sc.** 32:2 4:2000 pp.265-278.

2840 Social class differences in mortality using the national statistics socio-economic classification — too little, too soon: a reply to Chandola. D. Rose; D.J. Pevalin; T. Chandola [Comments by]. **Soc. Sci. Med.** 51:7 10:2000 pp.1121-1134.

2841 Socioeconomic status and infant mortality in Australia: a national study of small urban areas, 1985-89. Gavin Turrell; Kerrie Mengersen. **Soc. Sci. Med.** 50:9 5:2000 pp.1209-1226.

2842 Thank God it's Friday: the weekly cycle of mortality in Israel. J. Anson; O. Anson. **Pop. Res. Pol. R.** 19:2 4:2000 pp.143-154.

2843 Urban-rural mortality differentials: controlling for material deprivation. Martyn Senior; Huw Williams; Gary Higgs. **Soc. Sci. Med.** 51:2 7:2000 pp.289-306.

2844 Widening inequality in mortality between 160 regions of 15 European countries in the early 1990s. Mary Shaw; Scott Orford; Nicola Brimblecombe; Daniel Dorling. **Soc. Sci. Med.** 50:7-8 4:2000 pp.1047-1058.

F.4: Marriage and family
Mariage et famille

Divorce
Divorce

2845 The association between health-related behaviours and the risk of divorce in the USA. Haishan Fu; Noreen Goldman. **J. Biosoc. Sc.** 32:1 1:2000 pp.63-88.

2846 Child support and the postdivorce economic well-being of mothers, fathers, and children. Judi Bartfeld. **Demography** 37:2 5:2000 pp.203-214.

2847 Children, feelings and divorce: finding the best outcome. Heather Smith. London: Free Association, 1999. xiv, 178p. *ISBN: 1853434345. Includes bibliographical references (p. [172]-174) and index.*

2848 The consequences of divorce for adults and children. Paul R. Amato. **J. Marriage Fam.** 62:4 11:2000 pp.1269-1287.

2849 Divorce: a psychosocial study. Shelley Day Sclater. Aldershot: Ashgate, 1999. 248p. *ISBN: 1840149000. Includes bibliographical references.*

2850 Divorce adjustment and mediation: theoretically grounded process research. Andrew J. Bickerdike; Lyn Littlefield. **Med. Q.** 18:2 Winter:2000 pp.181-201.

2851 Divorce in Ethiopia: the impact of early marriage and childlessness. Dana Tilson; Ulla Larsen. **J. Biosoc. Sc.** 32:3 7:2000 pp.355-372.

F: POPULATION. FAMILY. GENDER. ETHNIC GROUPS

2852 Heterogamie en echtscheiding gebrek aan overeenkomst in voorkeuren of gebrek aan sociale steun? *[In Dutch]*; (Heterogamy and divorce: lack of similarity in preferences or lack of social support?) *[Summary]*. Jacques P.G. Janssen; Paul M. de Graaf. **Mens Maat.** 75:4 12:2000 pp.298-319.

2853 Parental divorce and outcomes for children: evidence and interpretation. Máire Ni Bhrolcháin; Roma Chappell; Ian Diamond; Catherine Jameson. **Eur. Sociol. R.** 16:1 3:2000 pp.67-92.

2854 The party of the last part: ethical and process implications for children in divorce mediation. Bruce Menin. **Med. Q.** 17:3 Spring:2000 pp.281-294.

2855 Predictors of divorce adjustment: stressors, resources, and definitions. Hongyu Wang; Paul R. Amato. **J. Marriage Fam.** 62:3 8:2000 pp.655-668.

2856 The psychosocial well-being of Black and White mothers following marital dissolution. Mary W. McKelvey; Patrick C. McKenry. **Psychol. Wom. Quart.** 24:1 3:2000 pp.4-14.

2857 Rozwód w opinii społecznej w latach 1990. *[In Polish]*; (Social opinion on divorce in the 1990s.) Paweł Rydzewski. **Stud. Demogr.** 1(135) 1999 pp.73-90.

2858 Separation and divorce: effect on family structures and life conditions. Alessandra De Rose. **Labour [Italy]** 14:1 3:2000 pp.145-160.

2859 Working with children and parents through separation and divorce: the changing lives of children. Emilia Dowling; Gill Gorell Barnes. Basingstoke: Macmillan, 1999. 192p. *ISBN: 0333719522. Includes bibliographical references.*

Domestic violence
Violence dans la famille

2860 Assessing assault self-reports by batterer program participants and their partners. D. Alex Heckert; Edward W. Gondolf. **J. Fam. Viol.** 15:2 6:2000 pp.181-198.

2861 Attachment, emotional regulation, and the function of marital violence: differences between secure, preoccupied, and dismissing violent and nonviolent husbands. Julia C. Babcock; Neil S. Jacobson; John M. Gottman; Timothy P. Yerington. **J. Fam. Viol.** 15:4 12:2000 pp.391-409.

2862 Attributions of negative partner behavior by men who physically abuse their partners. Santina Tonizzo; Kevin Howells; Andrew Day; Daniel Reidpath; Irene Froyland. **J. Fam. Viol.** 15:2 6:2000 pp.155-168.

2863 Battered women and their animal companions: symbolic interaction between human and nonhuman animals. Clifton P. Flynn. **Soc. and. Anim.** 8:2 2000 pp.99-128.

2864 Can restorative justice reduce battering? Some preliminary considerations. Lois Presser; Emily Gaarder. **Soc. Just.** 27:1 Spring:2000 pp.175-195.

2865 Changing violent men. R. Emerson Dobash; et al. Thousand Oaks CA: Sage Publications, 1999. ix, 210p. *ISBN: 0761905340, 0761905359. Includes bibliographical references.* (*Series:* Sage series on violence against women).

2866 Conjugal violence in Korean American families: a residue of the cultural tradition. Jae Yop Kim; Kyu-taik Sung. **J. Fam. Viol.** 15:4 12:2000 pp.331-345.

2867 A descriptive analysis of same-sex relationship violence for a diverse sample. Susan C. Turell. **J. Fam. Viol.** 15:3 9:2000 pp.281-293.

2868 The domestic violence arrest decision: examining demographic, attitudinal, and situational variables. Amanda L. Robinson; Meghan S. Chandek. **Crime Delin.** 46:1 1:2000 pp.18-37.

2869 Domestic violence: guidelines for research-informed practice. Ernest N. Jouriles [Ed.]; John P. Vincent [Ed.]. Philadelphia PA: Jessica Kingsley Publishers, 2000. 208p. *ISBN: 1853028541. Includes bibliographical references and index.*

2870 Domestic violence in the South Asian immigrant community. Helen E. Sheehan; Rafael Art. Javier; Theresa Thanjan; Shamita Das Dasgupta; Habibeh Rahim; Bandana Purkayastha; Margaret Abraham; Ruksana Ayyub; Munira Merchant. **J. Soc. Distr. Home.** 9:3 7:2000 pp.167-259. *Collection of 7 articles.*

F: POPULATION. FAMILLE. SEXE. GROUPE ETHNIQUE

2871 The effects of domestic violence on children's adjustment at school. Samia Dawud-Noursi; Michael Lamb; Kathleen Sternberg. **Megamot** XL:1 11:1999 pp.72-102.
2872 Effects of parental substance abuse on current levels of domestic violence: a possible elaboration of intergenerational transmission processes. Keneth Corvo; Elizabeth H. Carpenter. **J. Fam. Viol.** 15:2 6:2000 pp.123-136.
2873 How domestic violence came to be viewed as a public issue and policy object. Kathya Araujo; Virginia Guzmán; Amalia Mauro. **CEPAL R.** 70 4:2000 pp.137-150.
2874 Incidence and correlates of posttraumatic stress disorder in Australian victims of domestic violence. Peter Mertin; Philip B. Mohr. **J. Fam. Viol.** 15:4 12:2000 pp.411-422.
2875 The incidence of wife abuse and battering and some sociodemographic correlates as revealed by two national surveys in Palestinian society. Muhammad M. Haj-Yahia. **J. Fam. Viol.** 15:4 12:2000 pp.347-374.
2876 The intergenerational transmission of spouse abuse: a meta-analysis. Sandra M. Stith; Karen H. Rosen; Kimberly A. Middleton; Amy L. Busch; Kirsten Lundeberg; Russell P. Carlton. **J. Marriage Fam.** 62:3 8:2000 pp.640-654.
2877 Inter-rater reliability of the report form for aggressive episodes. Stål Bjørkly. **J. Fam. Viol.** 15:3 9:2000 pp.269-279.
2878 It hurts to be a girl: growing up poor, White, and female. Julia Hall. **Gender Soc.** 14:5 10:2000 pp.630-643.
2879 Leaving an abusive dating relationship: an investment model comparison of women who stay versus women who leave. Dana M. Truman-Schram; Arnie Cann; Lawrence Calhoun; Lori Vanwallendael. **J. Soc. Clin. Psychol.** 19:2 Summer:2000 pp.161-183.
2880 The lived body experience of domestic violence survivors: an interrogation of female identity. Jennifer K. Wesely; Maria T. Allison; Ingrid E. Schneider. **Wom. St. Inter. For.** 23:2 3-4:2000 pp.211-222.
2881 Lone motherhood: the impact on living standards of leaving a violent relationship. Paula Wilcox. **Soc. Pol. Admin.** 34:2 6:2000 pp.176-190.
2882 The multi-agency approach to domestic violence: new opportunities, old challenges. Gill Hague [Ed.]; Ellen Malos [Ed.]; Nicola Harwin [Ed.]. London: Whiting & Birch, 1999. xiv, 292p. *ISBN: 1861770022, 1861770030. Includes bibliographical references (p. 271-285) and index.*
2883 The normative protection of women from violence. Richard B. Felson. **Sociol. For.** 15:1 3:2000 pp.91-116.
2884 Parenting by men who abuse women: issues and dilemmas. Einat Peled. **Br. J. Soc. W.** 30:1 2:2000 pp.25-36.
2885 Patterns of violence against engaged Arab women from Israel and some psychological implications. Muhammad M. Haj-Yahia. **Psychol. Wom. Quart.** 24:3 9:2000 pp.209-219.
2886 Predictive models of domestic violence and fear of intimate partners among migrant and seasonal farm worker women. Nikki R. Van Hightower; Joe Gorton; Casey Lee DeMoss. **J. Fam. Viol.** 15:2 6:2000 pp.137-154.
2887 Predictors of physical spousal/intimate violence in Chinese American families. Alice G. Yick. **J. Fam. Viol.** 15:3 9:2000 pp.249-267.
2888 Predictors of underreporting of male violence by batterer program participants and their partners. D. Alex Heckert; Edward W. Gondolf. **J. Fam. Viol.** 15:4 12:2000 pp.423-443.
2889 The process of leaving an abusive relationship: the role of risk assessments and decision-certainty. Andrea J. Martin; Kathy R. Berenson; Sascha Griffing; Robert E. Sage; Lorraine Madry; Lewis E. Bingham; Beny J. Primm. **J. Fam. Viol.** 15:2 6:2000 pp.109-122.
2890 The process of recovery and rebuilding among abused women in the conservative evangelical subculture. Norman Giesbrecht; Irene Sevcik. **J. Fam. Viol.** 15:3 9:2000 pp.229-248.
2891 Research on domestic violence in the 1990s: making distinctions. Michael P. Johnson; Kathleen J. Ferraro. **J. Marriage Fam.** 62:4 11:2000 pp.948-963.
2892 Threat vigilance in child witnesses of domestic violence: a pilot study utilizing the ambiguous situations paradigm. Joseph J. Coyne; Paula M. Barrett; Amanda L. Duffy. **J. Child Fam. Stud.** 9:3 9:2000 pp.377-388.

F: POPULATION. FAMILY. GENDER. ETHNIC GROUPS

2893 Les troubles extériorisés et intériorisés des enfants témoins de violence conjugale et leurs variables associées: une recension des écrits. *[In French]*; (Internalized and externalized disorders in children witnesses to conjugal violence and their associated variables: a literature review.) *[Summary]*; *[Summary in Spanish]*. Isabelle Émond; Laurier Fortin; Égide Royer; Pierre Potvin. **San. Ment. Qué** XXV:1 Spring:2000 pp.258-287.

2894 Verbal aggression among male alcoholic patients and their wives in the year before and two years after alcoholism treatment. Timothy J. O'Farrell; Christopher M. Murphy; Tara M. Neavins; Valerie Van Hutton. **J. Fam. Viol.** 15:4 12:2000 pp.295-310.

2895 Violence conjugale pendant la grossesse: recension des écrits. *[In French]*; (Conjugal violence during pregnancy: a literature review.) *[Summary]*. Louise Séguin; Michel Pimont; Maryse Rinfret-Raynor; Solange Cantin. **San. Ment. Qué** XXV:1 Spring:2000 pp.288-312.

Family relations
Liens de famille

2896 Adolescents and their families: structure, function, and parent-youth relationships. Richard M. Lerner [Intro.]; Domini R. Castellino [Ed.]. New York: Garland Publishing, 1999. xiii, 375p. *ISBN: 0815332939*. *Includes bibliographical references.* (*Series:* Adolescence: development, diversity, and context - 4).

2897 Adolescents' plans for family formation: is parental socialization important? Marjorie E. Starrels; Kristen E. Holm. **J. Marriage Fam.** 62:2 5:2000 pp.416-429.

2898 African American children: socialization and development in families. Shirley A. Hill. Thousand Oaks CA: Sage Publications, 1999. xxiii, 192p. *ISBN: 0761904336, 0761904344*. *Includes bibliographical references (p. 173-184) and index.* (*Series:* Understanding families - 14).

2899 An analysis of kin-provided child care in the context of intrafamily exchanges: linking components of family support for parents raising young children. Peter D. Brandon. **Am. J. Econ. S.** 59:2 4:2000 pp.191-216.

2900 The Beavers systems model of family functioning. Robert Beavers; Robert B. Hampson. **J. Fam. Ther.** 22:2 5:2000 pp.128-143.

2901 Beyond kinship and households: godparents and orphans. Claude Morin; Gísli Ágúst Gunnlaugsson; Loftur Guttormsson; Tom Ericsson; Ana Maria Lugão Rios; Sylvie Perrier; Alain Bideau; Guy Brunet; Fabrice Foroni; Claudine Attias-Donfut; Nicole Lapierre; Solveig Fagerlund. **Hist. Fam.** 5:3 2000 pp.255-357. *Collection of 8 articles.*

2902 Born and bred: idioms of kinship and new reproductive technologies in England. Jeanette Edwards. Oxford: Oxford University Press, 2000. xiv, 264p. *ISBN: 0198233949*. *Includes bibliographical references (p. [249]-257) and index.* (*Series:* Oxford studies in social and cultural anthropology).

2903 The changing family and child development. Claudio Violato [Ed.]; Elizabeth Oddone-Paolucci [Ed.]; Mark Genuis [Ed.]. Aldershot: Ashgate, 2000. xxiv, 301p. *ISBN: 075461025X*. *Papers presented at the First International Congress on The Changing Family and Child Development held at the University of Calgary, July 1997. Includes bibliographical references.*

2904 Child quantity versus 'quality': a general dilemma in Israeli terms. Ilana Brosch; Yochanan Peres. **Megamot** XL:2 3:2000 pp.185-198.

2905 Circumplex model of marital and family systems. David H. Olson. **J. Fam. Ther.** 22:2 5:2000 pp.144-167.

2906 Las conductas de ocio de la familia puertorriqueña. *[In Spanish]*; [Leisure and the Puerto Rican family] *[Summary]*. Nelson Meléndez Brau. **Rev. Cien. Soc.** 6 1:1999 pp.227-243.

2907 A conscious and inclusive family studies. Katherine R. Allen. **J. Marriage Fam.** 62:1 2:2000 pp.4-17.

2908 Cross-cultural mediation: a critical view of the dynamics of culture in family disputes. Sonia Nourin Shah-Kazemi. **Int. J. Law Policy Fam.** 14:3 12:2000 pp.302-325.

F: POPULATION. FAMILLE. SEXE. GROUPE ETHNIQUE

2909 Culture and co-residence: an exploration of variation in home-returning among Canadian young adults. Barbara A. Mitchell; Andrew V. Wister; Ellen M. Gee. **Can. R. Soc. A.** 37:2 5:2000 pp.197-222.

2910 Daughters' dilemmas: grief resolution in girls whose widowed fathers remarry early. Gordon Riches; Pam Dawson. **J. Fam. Ther.** 22:4 11:2000 pp.360-374.

2911 The divorce of marriage and parenthood. Steven Nock; John Byng-Hall [Comments by]. **J. Fam. Ther.** 22:3 8:2000 pp.245-272.

2912 Early separation and sibling incest: a test of the revised Westermarck theory. Irene Bevc; Irwin Silverman. **Evol. Hum. Behav.** 21:3 5:2000 pp.151-162.

2913 East-Indian college students' perceptions of family strengths. Nilufer P. Medora; Jeffry H. Larson; Parul B. Dave. **J. Comp. Fam. Stud.** XXXI:4 Autumn:2000 pp.407-426.

2914 Economic restructuring and changing prevalence of female-headed families in America. Diane K. McLaughlin; Erica L. Gardner; Daniel T. Lichter. **Rural Sociol.** 64:3 9:1999 pp.394-416.

2915 Emergent and reconfigured forms of family life. Lora Bex Lempert; Marjorie L. De Vault; Gillian A. Dunne; Susan E. Dalton; Denise D. Bielby; Jane D. Bock; Vivienne Elizabeth; Catherine Kohler Riessman; Susan J. Ferguson; Christine E. Edwards; Christine L. Williams; Sharon Sassler. **Gender Soc.** 14:1 2:2000 pp.6-209. *Collection of 9 articles.*

2916 Emotional and social adjustment of adolescents who show role-reversal in the family. Yisraela Herer; Ofra Mayseless. **Megamot** XL:3 8:2000 pp.413-441.

2917 Ethnicity and gender in non-traditional family forms: studies of families pushing normative boundaries. R. Robin Miller; Sandra Lee Browning; Linda Bell; David Bell; Jessie M. Tzeng; Myra J. Hird; Kimberly Abshoff; Judy Singleton; Barbara H. Vinick; Susan Lanspery; Katherine Brown Rosier; Scott L. Feld. **J. Comp. Fam. Stud.** XXXI:3 Summer:2000 pp.301-394. *Collection of 8 articles.*

2918 Exploring twins: towards a social analysis of twinship. Elizabeth Stewart. Basingstoke: Macmillan, 2000. 240p. *ISBN: 0333803612. Includes index.*

2919 Families in the middle and later years: a review and critique of research in the 1990s. Katherine R. Allen; Rosemary Blieszner; Karen A. Roberto. **J. Marriage Fam.** 62:4 11:2000 pp.911-926.

2920 Family assessment measure (FAM) and process model of family functioning. Harvey Skinner; Paul Steinbauer; Gill Sitarenios. **J. Fam. Ther.** 22:2 5:2000 pp.190-210.

2921 Family of origin environment and coping with situations which vary by level of stress intensity. Stephanie Lewis Harter; Robert J. Vanecek. **J. Soc. Clin. Psychol.** 19:4 2000 pp.463-479.

2922 Family policy and public attitudes in Germany and Israel. Noah Lewin-Epstein; Haya Stier; Michael Braun; Bettina Langfeldt. **Eur. Sociol. R.** 16:4 12:2000 pp.385-402.

2923 Family structure and children's success: a comparison of widowed and divorced single-mother families. Timothy J. Biblarz; Greg Gottainer. **J. Marriage Fam.** 62:2 5:2000 pp.533-548.

2924 Family structure and youths' outcomes: which correlations are causal? Gary Painter; David I. Levine. **J. Hum. Res.** 35:3 Summer:2000 pp.524-549.

2925 Handbook of marriage and the family. Marvin B. Sussman [Ed.]; Suzanne K. Steinmetz [Ed.]; Gary W. Peterson [Ed.]. New York, London: Plenum Press, 1999. xvii, 822p. *ISBN: 0306457547. Includes bibliographical references and index.*

2926 House division: divided yet continued and united — a study of house division institutions in China. Guoqing Ma. **Soc. Sci. China** XXI:3 Autumn:2000 pp.22-34.

2927 Intergenerational exchanges in Vietnam: family size, sex composition, and the location of children. John Knodel; Jed Friedman; Truong Si Anh; Bui The Cuong. **Pop. Stud.** 54:1 3:2000 pp.89-104.

2928 Interparental conflict and child adjustment: testing the mediational role of appraisals in the cognitive-contextual framework. John H. Grych; Frank D. Fincham; Ernest N. Jouriles; Renee McDonald. **Child. Devel.** 71:6 11-12:2000 pp.1648-1661.

2929 Leaving home in Britain and Spain. Clare Holdsworth. **Eur. Sociol. R.** 16:2 6:2000 pp.201-222.

F: POPULATION. FAMILY. GENDER. ETHNIC GROUPS

2930 Le lien de germanité à l'âge adulte: une approche par l'étude des fréquentations. *[In French]*; (Sibling ties in adulthood. Based on frequency-of-meetings approach.) *[Summary]*. Emmanuelle Crenner; Jean-Hugues Déchaux; Nicolas Herpin. **Rev. Fr. Soc.** 41:2 4-6:2000 pp.211-240.

2931 Marital conflict and children's emotions: the development of an anger organization. Jennifer M. Jenkins. **J. Marriage Fam.** 62:3 8:2000 pp.723-736.

2932 Moral tales of the child and the adult: narratives of contemporary family lives under changing circumstances. Jane Ribbens McCarthy; Rosalind Edwards; Val Gillies. **Sociology** 34:4 11:2000 pp.785-816.

2933 Moving into adulthood: family residential mobility and first-union transitions. Scott M. Myers. **Soc. Sci. Q.** 81:3 9:2000 pp.782-797.

2934 The nature of support from adult *sansei* (third generation) children to older *nisei* (second generation) parents in Japanese Canadian families. Karen M. Kobayashi. **J. Cr-Cult. Gerontol.** 15:3 2000 pp.185-206.

2935 Neighborhood attributes as determinants of children's outcomes: how robust are the relationships? Donna Ginther; Robert Haveman; Barbara Wolfe. **J. Hum. Res.** 35:4 Fall:2000 pp.603-642.

2936 Parent-adolescent language use and relationships among immigrant families with East Asian, Filipino, and Latin American backgrounds. Vivian Tseng; Andrew J. Fuligni. **J. Marriage Fam.** 62:2 5:2000 pp.465-476.

2937 Pathways to problems — an exploratory study of how problems evolve vs dissolve in families. Rudi Dallos; Louise Hamilton-Brown. **J. Fam. Ther.** 22:4 11:2000 pp.375-393.

2938 Perspectives on American kinship in the later 1990s. Colleen L. Johnson. **J. Marriage Fam.** 62:3 8:2000 pp.623-639.

2939 Polygyny, gender relations, and reproduction in Ghana. Victor Agadjanian; Alex Chika Ezeh. **J. Comp. Fam. Stud.** XXXI:4 Autumn:2000 pp.427-442.

2940 Power in Turkish migrant families. Erica Huls. **Disc. Soc.** 11:3 7:2000 pp.345-372.

2941 Privacy in the family: its hierarchical and asymmetric nature. Ying-keung Chan. **J. Comp. Fam. Stud.** XXXI:1 Winter:2000 pp.1-18.

2942 Public and media perception of bereaved families in Israel: a national survey. Victor Florian; Asa Kasher; Ruth Malkinson. **Megamot** XL:2 3:2000 pp.280-297.

2943 Refracted knowledge: viewing families through the prism of social science. Alexis J. Walker. **J. Marriage Fam.** 62:3 8:2000 pp.595-608.

2944 Regional differences in household composition and family formation patterns in Vietnam. Danièle Bélanger. **J. Comp. Fam. Stud.** XXXI:2 Spring:2000 pp.171-190.

2945 Relations et dépendances familiales: regards croisés sur les étudiants Français et Italiens. *[In French]*; [Family relations and dependence: a glance at French and Italian students] *[Summary]*. Marco Oberti. **Rev. de l'OFCE** 73 4:2000 pp.259-276.

2946 Resilience concepts and findings: implications for family therapy. Michael Rutter; Gill Gorell Barnes [Comments by]; Gerrilýn Smith [Comments by]. **J. Fam. Ther.** 21:2 5:1999 pp.119-160.

2947 The role of family support in interparental conflict and adolescent academic achievement. Donald G. Unger; Laurie Ellis McLeod; Margaret B. Brown; Patricia A. Tressell. **J. Child Fam. Stud.** 9:2 6:2000 pp.191-202.

2948 Socioeconomic reach and heterogeneity in the extended family: contours and consequences. Joshua R. Goldstein; John Robert Warren. **Soc. Sci. R.** 29:3 9:2000 pp.382-404.

2949 Stepfamily as dyads — direct and indirect relationships. Irene Levin; Jan Trost. **J. Comp. Fam. Stud.** XXXI:2 Spring:2000 pp.137-154.

2950 'The normal American family' as an interpretive structure of family life among grown children of Korean and Vietnamese immigrants. Karen Pyke. **J. Marriage Fam.** 62:1 2:2000 pp.240-255.

2951 Wanted and unwanted sexual experiences and family dysfunction during adolescence. Nancy D. Kellogg; Sandra Burge; Elizabeth R. Taylor. **J. Fam. Viol.** 15:1 3:2000 pp.55-68.

F: POPULATION. FAMILLE. SEXE. GROUPE ETHNIQUE

2952 We are family: sibling relationships in placement and beyond. Audrey Mullender [Ed.]. London: British Agencies for Adoption and Fostering, 1999. 340p. *ISBN: 1873868790.*
2953 Work/family border theory: a new theory of work/family balance. Sue Campbell Clark. **Human Relat.** 53:6 6:2000 pp.747-770.
2954 Young people's participation within the family: parents' accounts. Smiljka Tomanović-Mihajlović. **Int. J. Child. Rig.** 8:2 2000 pp.151-167.

Marriage and cohabitation
Mariage et concubinage

2955 Age at marriage in rural Bangladesh: determinants, trends and patterns. K.N.S. Yadava; M.Z. Hossain. **Asian Prof.** 28:4 8:2000 pp.319-338.
2956 Attributions in marriage: state or trait? A growth curve analysis. Benjamin R. Karney; Thomas N. Bradbury. **J. Pers. Soc. Psychol.** 78:2 2:2000 pp.295-309.
2957 Changes in housework after retirement: a panel analysis. Maximiliane E. Szinovacz. **J. Marriage Fam.** 62:1 2:2000 pp.78-92.
2958 Cohabitation in Great Britain: not for long, but here to stay. John Ermisch; Marco Francesconi. **J. Roy. Stat. Soc. A.** 163:2 2000 pp.153-172.
2959 Decade review: observing marital interaction. John M. Gottman; Clifford I. Notarius. **J. Marriage Fam.** 62:4 11:2000 pp.927-947.
2960 Depression and power in marriage. Michael Byrne; Alan Carr. **J. Fam. Ther.** 22:4 11:2000 pp.408-427.
2961 Dynamics of marriage change in Chinese rural society in transition: a study of a northern Chinese village. Weiguo Zhang. **Pop. Stud.** 54:1 3:2000 pp.57-70.
2962 L'effet du type d'union sur la stabilité des familles dites «intactes». *[In French]*; [The impact of type of marriage on the stability of so-called 'intact' families] *[Summary]*. Céline Le Bourdais; Ghyslaine Neill; Nicole Marcil-Gratton. **Rech. Sociogr.** XLI:1 1-4:2000 pp.53-74.
2963 L'évolution de la nuptialité des adolescentes au Cameroun et ses déterminants. *[In French]*; (Adolescent nuptiality in Cameroon: change and its determinants.) *[Summary]*; *[Summary in Spanish]*. B. Kuate-Defo. **Population** 55:6 11-12:2000 pp.941-974.
2964 Families formed outside of marriage. Judith A. Seltzer. **J. Marriage Fam.** 62:4 11:2000 pp.1247-1268.
2965 Family stress during the Czech transformation. Joseph Hraba; Frederick O. Lorenz; Zdeňka Pechačová. **J. Marriage Fam.** 62:2 5:2000 pp.520-532.
2966 Fire and ice in marital communication: hostile and distancing behaviors as predictors of marital distress. Linda J. Roberts. **J. Marriage Fam.** 62:3 8:2000 pp.693-707.
2967 La flexibilité du marché matrimonial. *[In French]*; (Flexibility in the marriage market.) *[Summary]*; *[Summary in Spanish]*. M. Ní Bhrolcháin. **Population** 55:6 11-12:2000 pp.899-940.
2968 Hard living, perceived entitlement to a great marriage, and marital dissolution. Laura Sanchez; Constance T. Gager. **J. Marriage Fam.** 62:3 8:2000 pp.708-722.
2969 Have changes in gender relations affected marital quality? Stacy J. Rogers; Paul R. Amato. **Soc. Forc.** 79:2 12:2000 pp.731-753.
2970 How does personality matter in marriage? An examination of trait anxiety, interpersonal negativity, and marital satisfaction. John P. Caughlin; Ted L. Huston; Renate M. Houts. **J. Pers. Soc. Psychol.** 78:2 2:2000 pp.326-336.
2971 Husbands' views on family planning and labor force participation of wives in Metro Cebu, the Philippines. Socorro A. Gultiano. **Phil. Q. Cult. Soc.** 27:3-4 9-12:1999 pp.133-160.
2972 Just how do I love thee? Marital relations in urban China. Ellen Efron Pimentel. **J. Marriage Fam.** 62:1 2:2000 pp.32-47.
2973 Leaving your wife and your brothers: when polyandrous marriages fall apart. Kimber A. Haddix. **Evol. Hum. Behav.** 22:1 1:2001 pp.47-60.

F: POPULATION. FAMILY. GENDER. ETHNIC GROUPS

2974 Marriage or cohabitation: a competing risks analysis of first-partnership formation among the 1958 British birth cohort. Ann Berrington; Ian Diamond. **J. Roy. Stat. Soc. A.** 163:2 2000 pp.127-152.

2975 Nonstandard work schedules and marital instability. Harriet B. Presser. **J. Marriage Fam.** 62:1 2:2000 pp.93-110.

2976 (Nuptiality patterns and differentials in Jordan in the past two decades.); *[Text in Arabic]*. Issa Al Masarweh. **Dirasat Hum. Soc. Sc.** 26:Supp. 12:1999 pp.731-748.

2977 Psikhologicheskie problemy supruzheskikh otnoshenii. *[In Russian]*; (Psychological issues in marital relations.) *[Summary]*. T.V. Andreeva. **Vest. San.-Peter. Univ.** 3(20) 9:1999 pp.81-93.

2978 Religion, race, and the debate over *Mut'a* in Dar es Salaam. Richa Nagar. **Fem. Stud.** 26:3 Fall:2000 pp.661-690.

2979 Research on the nature and determinants of marital satifaction: a decade in review. Thomas N. Bradbury; Frank D. Fincham; Steven R.H. Beach. **J. Marriage Fam.** 62:4 11:2000 pp.964-980.

2980 Romancing the honeymoon: consummating marriage in modern society. Kris Bulcroft; Linda E. Smeins; Richard Bulcroft. Thousand Oaks CA: Sage Publications, 1999. xviii, 229p. *ISBN: 076190803X, 0761908048. Includes bibliographical references (p. 211-218) and index. (Series:* Understanding families - 16).

2981 Sexual infidelity among married and cohabiting Americans. Judith Treas; Deirdre Giesen. **J. Marriage Fam.** 62:1 2:2000 pp.48-60.

2982 Shotgun weddings and the meaning of marriage in Russia: an event history analysis. Kimberly D. Cartwright. **Hist. Fam.** 5:1 2000 pp.1-22.

2983 The social ecology of marriage and other intimate unions. Ted L. Huston. **J. Marriage Fam.** 62:2 5:2000 pp.298-321.

2984 Son preference, sex ratios, and marriage patterns. Lena Edlund. **J. Polit. Ec.** 107:6(1) 12:1999 pp.1275-1304.

2985 Structural flaws in the bridge from basic research on marriage to interventions for couples. Scott M. Stanley; Thomas N. Bradbury; Howard J. Markman; John Gottman [Comments by]; Sybil Carrère [Comments by]; Catherine Swanson [Comments by]; James A. Coan [Comments by]. **J. Marriage Fam.** 62:1 2:2000 pp.256-273.

2986 A theory of marital sexual life. Chien Liu. **J. Marriage Fam.** 62:2 5:2000 pp.363-374.

2987 Time-out and writing in distressed couples: an experimental trial into the effects of a short treatment. Alfred Lange; Charlotte van der Wall; Paul Emmelkamp. **J. Fam. Ther.** 22:4 11:2000 pp.394-407.

2988 Trends in cohabitation and implications for children's family contexts in the United States. Larry Bumpass; Hsien-hen Lu. **Pop. Stud.** 54:1 3:2000 pp.29-42.

2989 Union transitions among cohabitors: the significance of relationship assessments and expectations. Susan L. Brown. **J. Marriage Fam.** 62:3 8:2000 pp.833-846.

2990 La vie plurielle. Les régimes d'union dans le nouveau cadre législatif: pour tout savoir sur leurs avantages et leurs inconvénients. *[In French]*; [Conjugal life. Types of union in the new legislative arena: information for all on the advantages and disadvantages]. Jean-Pierre Thiollet. Boulogne-Billancourt: Axiome, 1999. 128p. *ISBN: 2844620361. Includes bibliographical references (p. 117-118) and index.*

2991 What do low-income single mothers say about marriage? Kathryn Edin. **Soc. Prob.** 47:1 2:2000 pp.112-133.

2992 Which Indonesian women marry youngest, and why? Gavin W. Jones. **J. SE. As. Stud.** 32:1 2:2001 pp.67-78.

One-parent families
Famille monoparentale

2993 Age and partnership as public symbols: stigma and non-marital motherhood in an Irish context. Abbey Hyde. **Eur. J. Wom. Stud.** 7:1 2:2000 pp.71-90.

F: POPULATION. FAMILLE. SEXE. GROUPE ETHNIQUE

2994 Children in one-parent families: survival as an indicator of the role of the parents. Frans van Poppel. **J. Fam. Hist.** 25:3 7:2000 pp.269-290.
2995 Deciphering community and race effects on adolescent premarital childbearing. Scott J. South; Eric P. Baumer. **Soc. Forc.** 78:4 6:2000 pp.1379-1408.
2996 The dynamics of single mothers' living arrangements. R.A. London. **Pop. Res. Pol. R.** 19:1 2:2000 pp.73-96.
2997 Lone mothers and policy discourse in New Zealand. Stephen Uttley. **J. Soc. Pol.** 29:3 7:2000 pp.441-458.
2998 Premarital childbearing in urban Cameroon: paternal recognition, child care and financial support. Anne-Emmanuèle Calvès. **J. Comp. Fam. Stud.** XXXI:4 Autumn:2000 pp.443-462.
2999 Social policies and the pathways to inequalities in health: a comparative analysis of lone mothers in Britain and Sweden. Margaret Whitehead; Bo Burström; Finn Diderichsen. **Soc. Sci. Med.** 50:2 1:2000 pp.255-270.
3000 A theory of out-of-wedlock childbearing. Robert J. Willis. **J. Polit. Ec.** 107:6(2) 12:1999 pp.33-64.
3001 Welfare, marital prospects, and nonmarital childbearing. Mark R. Rosenzweig. **J. Polit. Ec.** 107:6(2) 12:1999 pp.3-32.

Parenthood
Paternité-maternité

3002 Agreement between mothers and other female adults on infants' communicative behaviours. Gordon Elias; Denis Meadows. **Fst. Lang.** 20(2):59 6:2000 pp.125-140.
3003 L'alimentation dans la prime enfance diffusion et réception des normes de puériculture. *[In French]*; (Feeding in young childhood. Diffusion and reception of paediatric standards.) *[Summary]; [Summary in German]; [Summary in Spanish]*. Séverine Gojard. **Rev. Fr. Soc.** 41:3 7-9:2000 pp.475-512.
3004 Attachment to transitional objects: role of maternal personality and mother-toddler interaction. Alison J. Steier; Elyse Brauch Lehman. **Am. J. Orthopsy.** 70:3 7:2000 pp.340-350.
3005 Baby entertainer, bumbling assistant and line manager: discourses of fatherhood in parentcraft texts. Jane Sunderland. **Disc. Soc.** 11:2 4:2000 pp.249-274.
3006 Bullies and delinquents: personal characteristics and parental styles. A.C. Baldry; D.P. Farrington. **J. Comm. App. Soc. Psychol.** 10:1 1-2:2000 pp.17-32.
3007 'But I *am* a good mom': the social construction of motherhood through health-care conversations. Rebecca W. Tardy. **J. Contemp. Ethnog.** 29:4 8:2000 pp.433-473.
3008 The changing culture of fatherhood in comic-strip families: a six-decade analysis. Ralph LaRossa; Charles Jaret; Malati Gadgil; G. Robert Wynn. **J. Marriage Fam.** 62:2 5:2000 pp.375-387.
3009 Childrearing practices in the Philippines and Japan. Leslie E. Bauzon; Aurora F. Bauzon. **Phil. Stud.** 48:3 2000 pp.287-314.
3010 Children and the family, yesterday and today. Vū Thi Chín. **Viet. Stud.** 3(133) 1999 pp.74-86.
3011 Comparisons of parenting attitudes among five ethnic groups in the United States. Saigeetha Jambunathan; Diane C. Burts; Sarah Pierce. **J. Comp. Fam. Stud.** XXXI:4 Autumn:2000 pp.395-406.
3012 Conservative Protestant child discipline: the case of parental yelling. John P. Bartkowski; W. Bradford Wilcox. **Soc. Forc.** 79:1 9:2000 pp.265-290.
3013 Constructions and reconstructions: Latino parents' values for children. Emily Arcia; María E. Reyes-Blanes; Elia Vazquez-Montilla. **J. Child Fam. Stud.** 9:3 9:2000 pp.333-350.
3014 Contemporary research on parenting: the case for nature and nurture. W. Andrew Collins; Eleanor E. Maccoby; Laurence Steinberg; E. Mavis Hetherington; Marc H. Bornstein. **Am. Psychol.** 55:2 2:2000 pp.218-232.

F: POPULATION. FAMILY. GENDER. ETHNIC GROUPS

3015 Dependency and self-criticism among first-time mothers: the roles of global and specific support. Beatriz Priel; Avi Besser. **J. Soc. Clin. Psychol.** 19:4 2000 pp.437-450.

3016 Development of children of female commercial sex workers in Vijayawada. Hannah Anandraj. **Indian J. Soc. W.** 60:4 10:1999 pp.552-565.

3017 Emotional availability: conceptualization and research findings. Zeynep Biringen. **Am. J. Orthopsy.** 70:1 1:2000 pp.104-114.

3018 Evolution and proximate expression of human paternal investment. David C. Geary. **Psychol. B.** 126:1 1:2000 pp.55-77.

3019 Factors related to successful outcomes among preschool children born to low-income adolescent mothers. Tom Luster; Laura Bates; Hiram Fitzgerald; Marcia Vandenbelt; Judith Peck Key. **J. Marriage Fam.** 62:1 2:2000 pp.133-146.

3020 Families with young children: a review of research in the 1990s. David H. Demo; Martha J. Cox. **J. Marriage Fam.** 62:4 11:2000 pp.876-895.

3021 Fragile self-esteem in children and its associations with perceived patterns of parent-child communication. Michael H. Kernis; Anita C. Brown; Gene H. Brody. **J. Personal.** 68:2 4:2000 pp.225-252.

3022 The fruits of their labors: a longitudinal exploration of parent personality and adjustment in their adult children. Marjorie Solomon. **J. Personal.** 68:2 4:2000 pp.281-308.

3023 Gender preference and anxiety of pregnant women. S.S. Yadav; V.S. Badari. **Indian J. Soc. W.** 60:4 10:1999 pp.538-551.

3024 Impact of racial identity on African American child-rearing beliefs. Anita Jones Thomas. **J. Black Psychol.** 26:3 8:2000 pp.317-329.

3025 The influence of parenthood on work effort of married men and women. Gayle Kaufman; Peter Uhlenberg. **Soc. Forc.** 78:3 3:2000 pp.931-948.

3026 Intergenerational influences on the entry into parenthood: mothers' preferences for family and nonfamily behavior. Jennifer S. Barber. **Soc. Forc.** 79:1 9:2000 pp.319-348.

3027 Low-income mothers' views on breastfeeding. Nurit Guttman; Deena R. Zimmerman. **Soc. Sci. Med.** 50:10 5:2000 pp.1457-1473.

3028 Maternal experience and the boundaries of Christian sexual ethics. Cristina L.H. Traina. **Signs** 25:2 Winter:2000 pp.369-406.

3029 Maternal versus nonmaternal care and seven domains of children's development. Osnat Erel; Yael Oberman; Nurit Yirmiya. **Psychol. B.** 126:5 9:2000 pp.727-747.

3030 Milk bottle, messenger, monitor, spy: children's experiences of contact. Brynna Kroll. **Child C. Pract.** 6:3 7:2000 pp.215-228.

3031 Moderating effects of mothers' attribution on the relationships between their affect and parenting behaviors and children's aggressive behaviors. Emiko Katsurada; Alan I. Sugawara. **J. Child Fam. Stud.** 9:1 3:2000 pp.39-50.

3032 Momentum in child compliance and opposition. Paul S. Strand; Robert G. Wahler; Melissa Herring. **J. Child Fam. Stud.** 9:3 9:2000 pp.363-375.

3033 Mothering the self: mothers, daughters, subjects. Stephanie Lawler. London: Routledge, 2000. 229p. *ISBN: 0415170842, 0415170834.*

3034 Mothers' personality and its interaction with child temperament as predictors of parenting behavior. Lee Anna Clark; Grazyna Kochanska; Rebecca Ready. **J. Pers. Soc. Psychol.** 79:2 8:2000 pp.274-285.

3035 Noguchi Shika: the eternal mother of modern Japan. Kweku Ampiah. **Jpn. Forum** 12:1 2000 pp.77-86.

3036 The outcome of parenting: what do we really know? Judith Rich Harris. **J. Personal.** 68:3 6:2000 pp.625-638.

3037 Parental illness. John S. Rolland; Barbara Dale; Jenny Altschuler; Riva Miller; Derval Murray; Jo Aldridge; Saul Becker; Anne McFadyen. **J. Fam. Ther.** 21:3 8:1999 pp.242-336. *Collection of 5 articles.*

3038 Parental investment, self-control, and sex differences in the expression of ADHD. Joan C. Stevenson; Don C. Williams. **Hum. Nature** 11:4 2000 pp.405-422.

3039 Parental leave and child health. Christopher J. Ruhm. **J. Health Econ.** 19:6 11:2000 pp.931-960.

F: POPULATION. FAMILLE. SEXE. GROUPE ETHNIQUE

3040 Parenthood, gender and sickness absence. Arne Mastekaasa. **Soc. Sci. Med.** 50:12 6:2000 pp.1827-1842.

3041 Parents' affect, adolescent cognitive representations, and adolescent social development. Blair Paley; Rand D. Conger; Gordon T. Harold. **J. Marriage Fam.** 62:3 8:2000 pp.761-776.

3042 Perceived fairness and compliance with child support obligations. I-Fen Lin. **J. Marriage Fam.** 62:2 5:2000 pp.388-398.

3043 Perceived paternal and maternal acceptance and rural African American and European American youths' psychological adjustment. Robert A. Veneziano. **J. Marriage Fam.** 62:1 2:2000 pp.123-132.

3044 'Poppa' psychology: the role of fathers in children's mental well-being. Vicky Phares. Westport CT: Praeger, 1999. xv, 150p. *ISBN: 0275963675. Includes bibliographical references (p. [113]-143) and index.*

3045 Refracted selves? A study of changes in self-identity in the transition to motherhood. Lucy Bailey. **Sociology** 33:2 5:1999 pp.335-352.

3046 Reinventing fatherhood in Japan and Canada. Susanne Steinberg; Laurence Kruckman; Stephanie Steinberg. **Soc. Sci. Med.** 50:9 5:2000 pp.1257-1272.

3047 The relationship between parenting style and children's adjustment: the parents' perspective. Dagmar Kaufmann; Ellis Gesten; Raymond C. Santa Lucia; Octavio Salcedo; Gianna Rendina-Gobioff; Ray Gadd. **J. Child Fam. Stud.** 9:2 6:2000 pp.231-245.

3048 (Relationship of coping strategies to parental practices, gender, grade, and emotional state of 7th, 8th and 9th grade students.); *[Text in Arabic].* N. Dawod; K. Yahya. **Dirasat Ed.** 26:2 9:1999 pp.514-528.

3049 Relationships among paternal involvement and young children's perceived self-competence and behavioral problems. Rex E. Culp; Stephanie Schadle; Linda Robinson; Anne M. Culp. **J. Child Fam. Stud.** 9:1 3:2000 pp.27-38.

3050 Responsive parenting and child socialization: integrating two contexts of family life. Paul S. Strand. **J. Child Fam. Stud.** 9:3 9:2000 pp.269-281.

3051 Scholarship on fatherhood in the 1990s and beyond. William Marsiglio; Paul Amato; Randal D. Day; Michael E. Lamb. **J. Marriage Fam.** 62:4 11:2000 pp.1173-1191.

3052 Sibling comparison of differential parental treatment in adolescence: gender, self-esteem, and emotionality as mediators of the parenting-adjustment association. Mark E. Feinberg; Jenae M. Neiderhiser; Sam Simmens; David Reiss; E. Mavis Hetherington. **Child. Devel.** 71:6 11-12:2000 pp.1611-1628.

3053 Step in or stay out? Parents' roles in adolescent siblings' relationships. Susan M. McHale; Kimberly A. Updegraff; Corinna J. Tucker; Ann C. Crouter. **J. Marriage Fam.** 62:3 8:2000 pp.746-760.

3054 'Swapping' families: serial parenting and economic support for children. Wendy D. Manning; Pamela J. Smock. **J. Marriage Fam.** 62:1 2:2000 pp.111-122.

3055 Thinking ahead: complexity of expectations and the transition to parenthood. S. Mark Pancer; Michael Pratt; Bruce Hunsberger; Margo Gallant. **J. Personal.** 68:2 4:2000 pp.253-280.

3056 Timing of parental separation and attachment to parents in adolescence: results of a prospective study from birth to age 16. Lianne Woodward; David M. Fergusson; Jay Belsky. **J. Marriage Fam.** 62:1 2:2000 pp.162-174.

3057 A useful extension of Bourdieu's conceptual framework? Emotional capital as a way of understanding mothers' involvement in their children's education? Diane Reay. **Sociol. Rev.** 48:4 11:2000 pp.568-585.

F.5: **Gender and gender relations**
Sexe et relations des sexes

3058 African-American women: an ecological perspective. Norma J. Burgess [Ed.]; Eurnestine Brown [Ed.]. New York: Garland Publishing, 1999. 196p. *ISBN: 0815315910. Includes*

F: POPULATION. FAMILY. GENDER. ETHNIC GROUPS

bibliographical references and index. (*Series:* Michigan State University series on children, youth, and families - 6).

3059 Beyond the usual: the modification of gender in a British dating ads column. Carol Marley. **Text** 20:3 2000 pp.271-306.

3060 Changing femininity, changing concepts of citizenship in public and private spheres. Madeleine Arnot; Helena Araújo; Kiki Deliyanni; Gabrielle Ivinson. **Eur. J. Wom. Stud.** 7:2 5:2000 pp.149-168.

3061 Critical regionalities: gender and sexual diversity in South East and East Asia. Mark Johnson; Peter Jackson; Gilbert Herdt; Antonia Chao; Ronald Baytan; Megan Sinnott; Saskia E. Wieringa; Mark McLelland. **Cult. Health. Sex.** 2:4 10-12:2000 pp.361-472. *Collection of 7 articles.*

3062 The epistemology of the gendered organization. Dana M. Britton. **Gender Soc.** 14:3 6:2000 pp.418-434.

3063 Experiments in knowing: gender and method in the social sciences. Ann Oakley. Cambridge: Polity Press, 2000. viii, 402p. *ISBN: 0745622569, 0745622577. Includes bibliographical references (p. 343-384) and index.*

3064 Frauen zwischen Tradition und Moderne. Zum traditionellen Geschlechterverhältnis in der modernen Gesellschaft: Korea. *[In German]*; (Women between tradition and modernity. Traditional gender relations in a modern society: Korea.) Duk-yung Kim; Eun-ju Kim Lee. **Soz. Welt.** 51:1 2000 pp.87-110.

3065 Gender and citizenship in transition. Barbara Hobson [Ed.]. Basingstoke: Macmillan, 1999. 336p. *ISBN: 0333753690. Includes index.*

3066 Gender and environment. Susan Buckingham-Hatfield. New York: Routledge, 2000. 144p. *ISBN: 0415168198, 0415168201. Includes bibliographical references.*

3067 Gender and ethnicity. Haleh Afshar; Mary Maynard; Peter Chua; Kum-Kum Bhavnani; John Foran; Priya A. Kurian; Sallie Westwood; Annelies Moors; Philomena Essed; Myfanwy Franks. **Ethn. Racial** 23:5 9:2000 pp.805-929. *Collection of 8 articles.*

3068 Gender and global restructuring: sightings, sites and resistances. Marianne H. Marchand [Ed.]; Anne Sisson Runyan [Ed.]. London: Routledge, 2000. xix, 260p. *ISBN: 0415221749, 0415221757. Includes bibliographical references (p. [231]-254) and index. (Series:* Routledge/RIPE studies in global political economy).

3069 Gender and local economic development. Irene Bruegel; Rose Gilroy; Christine Booth; Fiona Forsyth; Suzanne Speak; Clive Collis; Anne Green; Tony Mallier; Anna Webb; Massimiliano Di Luca; Jeff Turner; Margaret Grieco; Nana Apt; Len Holmes. **Local. Ec.** 15:1 5:2000 pp.2-73. *Collection of 8 articles.*

3070 Gender and nationalism. Deniz Kandiyoti; Glenda Sluga; Sylvia Walby; Tricia Cusack; Wendy Bracewell; Michel Huysseune; Cynthia Cockburn. **Nat. Nat.** 6:4 10:2000 pp.491-629. *Collection of 7 articles.*

3071 Gender and society: the Herbert Spencer lectures. Colin Blakemore [Ed.]; Susan D. Iversen [Ed.]. Oxford, New York: Oxford University Press, 2000. 205p. *ISBN: 0198297920. Includes bibliographical references and index.*

3072 Gender, nationality and cultural representations of Ireland: an Irish woman's place? Lorna Stevens; Stephen Brown; Pauline MacLaran. **Eur. J. Wom. Stud.** 7:4 11:2000 pp.405-421.

3073 Geographies of new femininities. Nina Laurie; et al. Harlow: Pearson Education, 1999. 225p. *ISBN: 0582320240.*

3074 Human rights and gender politics in the Asia-Pacific. Anne-Marie Hilsdon [Ed.]; et al. London: Routledge, 2000. 256p. *ISBN: 0415191734.*

3075 Itinerarios vitales: educación, trabajo y fecundidad de las mujeres. *[In Spanish]*; [Important stages: education, work and fertility in women]. Marga Marí-Klose; Anna Nos Colom. Madrid: Centro de Investigaciones Sociológicas, 1999. 123p. *ISBN: 8474762901. Includes bibliographical references.*

3076 Khasi women and matriliny: transformations in gender relations. Tiplut Nongbri. **Gen. Tech. Dev.** 4:3 9-12:2000 pp.359-395.

3077 Neither separate nor equal: women, race, and class in the South. Barbara E. Smith [Ed.]. Philadelphia PA: Temple University Press, 1999. ix, 286p. *ISBN: 1566396794,*

F: POPULATION. FAMILLE. SEXE. GROUPE ETHNIQUE

1566396808. Includes bibliographical references and index. (Series: Women in the political economy).

3078 Networking women: a history of ideas, issues and developments in women's studies in Britain. Sue Jackson. **Wom. St. Inter. For.** 23:1 1-2:2000 pp.1-12.

3079 Perspectives on Africa. Aili Mari Tripp; Amy Kaler; Chikwenye Ogunyemi; Wanjira Muthoni; Susan Arndt [Interviewer]. **Signs** 25:3 Spring:2000 pp.649-726. *Collection of 3 articles.*

3080 The politics of social justice: women's struggle for equality and one man's lament. Judy Fudge. **Acadiensis** XXIX:2 Spring:2000 pp.170-187.

3081 Reconceptualizing gender in postsocialist transformation. Elizabeth C. Rudd. **Gender Soc.** 14:4 8:2000 pp.517-539.

3082 Sexual politics: an introduction. Richard Dunphy. Edinburgh: Edinburgh University Press, 2000. 240p. *ISBN: 0748612475.*

3083 Sitting on the fence: biology, feminism and gender-bending environments. Lynda Birke. **Wom. St. Inter. For.** 23:5 9-10:2000 pp.587-599.

3084 Sotsiokul'turnie determinanty razvitiia gendernoi teorii v Rossii i na Zapade. *[In Russian]*; [Socio-cultural patterns of the development of gender theory in Russia and Western countries]. O. Voronina. **Obshch. Nauki Sovrem.** 4 2000 pp.9-20.

3085 Stigmatized spaces: gender and mobility under crisis in south Sulawesi, Indonesia. Rachel M. Silvey. **Gend. Place Cult.** 7:2 6:2000 pp.143-162.

3086 The trouble with modernity: gender and the remaking of social theory. Susan Thistle. **Sociol. Theory** 18:2 7:2000 pp.275-288.

3087 Using gender to undo gender: a feminist degendering movement. Judith Lorber. **Fem. Theo.** 1:1 4:2000 pp.79-96.

3088 White women: critical perspectives on race and gender. Madi Gilkes [Ed.]; Ann Kaloski-Naylor [Ed.]; Heloise Brown [Ed.]. York: Raw Nerve Books, 1999. 264p. *ISBN: 0953658503. Includes bibliographical references and index.*

3089 Women and power: fighting patriarchy and poverty. Janet Townsend. London: Zed Books, 1999. 200p. *ISBN: 1856498034, 1856498042. Includes bibliographical references.*

3090 Women, culture, development: a new paradigm for development studies? Peter Chua; Kum-Kum Bhavnani; John Foran. **Ethn. Racial** 23:5 9:2000 pp.820-841.

3091 Women in contemporary France. Abigail Gregory [Ed.]; Ursula Tidd [Ed.]. Oxford: Berg Publishers, 2000. 227p. *ISBN: 1859733581, 1859733530. Includes index.*

3092 Zur Codierung des Körpers: Geschlecht, Gesellschaft und Kultur. *[In German]*; [On the coding of the body: gender, society and culture]. Herbert Willems; York Kautt. **Social. Int.** 37:2 1999 pp.131-156.

Feminism
Féminisme

3093 The abject space: its gifts and complaints. Christine Bousfield. **J. Gender St.** 9:3 11:2000 pp.329-346.

3094 Age, gender and slavery in and out of the Persian harem: a different story. Haleh Afshar. **Ethn. Racial** 23:5 9:2000 pp.905-916.

3095 Assessing women's feminist identity development: studies of convergent, discriminant, and structural validity. Ann R. Fischer; David M. Tokar; Marija M. Mergl; Glenn E. Good; Melanie S. Hill; Sasha A. Blum. **Psychol. Wom. Quart.** 24:1 3:2000 pp.15-29.

3096 Baudrillard's challenge: a feminist reading. Victoria Grace. London: Routledge, 2000. vii, 212p. *ISBN: 0415180759, 0415180767. Includes bibliographical references and index.*

3097 Beyond armchair feminism. Debra E. Meyerson; Deborah M. Kolb; Gill Coleman; Ann Rippin; Robin J. Ely; Jeff Hearn; Joan Acker. **Organization** 7:4 11:2000 pp.553-632. *Collection of 5 articles.*

F: POPULATION. FAMILY. GENDER. ETHNIC GROUPS

3098   The Black feminist reader. T. Denean Sharpley-Whiting [Ed.]; Joy James [Ed.]. Malden MA: Blackwell Publishers, 2000. 302p. *ISBN: 0631210067, 0631210075. Includes bibliographical references and index.*
3099   Black feminist thought: knowledge, consciousness, and the politics of empowerment. Patricia Hill Collins. New York: Routledge, 2000. xvi, 335p. *ISBN: 0415924839, 0415924847. Includes bibliographical references and index. (Series:* Perspectives on gender).
3100   Building on the strengths of the socialist feminist tradition. Sue Ferguson. **Crit. Sociol.** 25:1 1999 pp.1-15.
3101   The Cambridge companion to feminism in philosophy. Miranda Fricker [Ed.]; Jennifer Hornsby [Ed.]. Cambridge, New York: Cambridge University Press, 2000. xiii, 280p. *ISBN: 0521624517. Includes bibliographical references (p. 264-275) and index. (Series:* Cambridge companions to philosophy).
3102   Discursive desire: Catherine Belsey's feminism. Marysa Demoor; Jürgen Pieters. **Feminist R.** 66 Autumn:2000 pp.25-45.
3103   The dynamics of governmental structure and the advancement of women: a comparison of Sri Lanka and Malaysia. Barbara Morris. **J. As. Afr. S.** XXXIV:4 11:1999 pp.403-426.
3104   Empowerment without antagonism: a case for reformulation of women's empowerment approach. S.L. Sharma. **Sociol. Bul.** 49:1 3:2000 pp.19-39.
3105   Engendering transition in Russia: an interview. Valerie Sperling; Nanette Funk [Interviewer]. **New Polit.** VIII:1 Summer:2000 pp.122-132.
3106   Equality with a difference: gender and citizenship in transition Palestine. Rema Hammami; Penny Johnson. **Soc. Polit.** 6:3 Fall:1999 pp.314-343.
3107   Feminism and autobiography: texts, theories, methods. Tess Cosslett [Ed.]; Penny Summerfield [Ed.]; Celia Lury [Ed.]. London: Routledge, 2000. 265p. *ISBN: 0415232023, 0415232015. Includes index. (Series:* Transformations).
3108   Feminism and Chinese philosophy. Karyn Lai; Eva Kit Wah Man; Sandra A. Wawrytko; Chenyang Li; Linyu Gu; Julia Po-Wah Laitao. **J. Ch. Philos.** 27:2 6:2000 pp.127-215. *Collection of 7 articles.*
3109   Feminism and the biological body. Lynda Birke. Edinburgh: Edinburgh University Press, 1999. 192p. *ISBN: 0748610510, 0748610529. (Series:* Gender, science and technology).
3110   Feminism and the body. Londa Schiebinger [Ed.]. Oxford: Oxford University Press, 2000. ix, 500p. *ISBN: 0198731914. Includes bibliographical references and index. (Series:* Oxford readings in feminism).
3111   Feminism and the family: politics and society in the UK and USA. Jennifer Somerville. Basingstoke: Macmillan, 2000. 279p. *ISBN: 0333517024, 0333517016. Includes bibliographical references.*
3112   Feminism and the politics of resistance. Rajeswari Sunder Rajan; U. Kalpagam; Srimati Basu; Kalyani Dutta; V. Padma; Nira Gupta-Cassale; Brinda Bose; Maitrayee Chaudhuri; Ritu Menon; Sandra Ponzanesi. **Ind. J. Gend. Stud.** 7:2 7-12:2000 pp.153-318. *Collection of 10 articles.*
3113   Feminism, femininity, and popular culture. Joanne Hollows. New York: Manchester University Press, 1999. 229p. *ISBN: 0719043948, 0719043956. Includes bibliographical references and index.*
3114   Feminism, the state and social policy. Nickie Charles; Jo Campling. Houndmills; New York: Macmillan; St. Martin's Press, 2000. viii, 245p. *ISBN: 0333655559, 0333655567, 0312226756. Includes bibliographical references (p. [218]-238) and index.*
3115   Feminisms at a millennium. Judith A. Howard [Ed.]; Carolyn Allen [Ed.]; Catharine R. Stimpson; Mary Romero; Elizabeth Grosz; Cynthia Enloe; Paola Bono; Federica Giardini; Drucilla Cornell; Sandra Harding; Laura Brace; Julia O'Connell Davidson; Kathy Rudy; Sue-Ellen Case; Rosi Braidotti; Liana Borghi; Ilaria Sborgi; Małgorzata Fuszara; Mrinalini Sinha; Uma Narayan; Therese Saliba; Oyeronke Oyewumi; Tani Barlow; Patricia Fernández-Kelly; Edna Acosta-Belén; Christine E. Bose; Dorothy Q. Thomas; Hilary Rose; Henrietta L. Moore; Beth E. Richie; Michelle Fine; Lois Weis; Dorothy E. Smith; Ruth-Ellen Boetcher Joeres; Catherine Belsey; Elaine Marks; Sydney Janet Kaplan; Londa

F: POPULATION. FAMILLE. SEXE. GROUPE ETHNIQUE

Schiebinger; Julie A. Nelson; Barrie Thorne; Judith Stacey; Irene Dölling; Sabine Hark; Barbara Charlesworth Gelpi; Jean F. O'Barr; Noliwe M. Rooks; Barbara Ransby; Karen Brodkin; France Winddance Twine; Barbara Laslett; Johanna Brenner; Tina Chanter; Traise Yamamoto; Devon A. Mihesuah; Anne Fausto-Sterling; Judith Kegan Gardiner; Thomas J. Gerschick; Nancy Fugate Woods; David L. Eng; Susan McClary; Ellie M. Hisama; Tamara L. Underiner; Dale M. Bauer; Priscilla Wald. **Signs** 25:4 Summer:2000 pp.1007-1303. *Collection of 54 articles*.

3116 Feminist imagination: genealogies in feminist theory. Vikki Bell. London: Sage Publications, 1999. viii, 168p. *ISBN: 0803979703, 0803979711. Includes bibliographical references and index. (Series:* Theory, culture & society).

3117 Feminist interpretations and challenges. Terry Threadgold. **Soc. Sem.** 10:1 4:2000 pp.109-123.

3118 Feminist participatory action research: methodological and ethical issues. Bev Gatenby; Maria Humphries. **Wom. St. Inter. For.** 23:1 1-2:2000 pp.89-106.

3119 Feminist perspectives on ethics. Elisabeth J. Porter. London, New York: Longman, 1999. xiii, 215p. *ISBN: 0582356350. Includes bibliographical references (p. 189-211) and index. (Series:* Feminist perspectives).

3120 Feminist theory and literary practice. Deborah L. Madsen. London: Pluto Press, 2000. 253p. *ISBN: 0745316018, 0745316026*.

3121 Feminist views of the social sciences. Christine Williams [Ed.]; Ravina Aggarwal; Judith D. Auerbach; Maxine Baca Zinn; Dana M. Britton; Lynn S. Chancer; Kelley Hays-Gilpin; Pierrette Hondagneu-Sotelo; Gretchen Ritter; Nicole Mellow; Lynn A. Staeheli; Patricia M. Martin; S. Craig Watkins; Rana A. Emerson; Amy S. Wharton; Judith Worell. **Ann. Am. Poli.** 571 9:2000 pp.14-196. *Collection of 12 articles*.

3122 Framing Nawal El Saadawi: Arab feminism in a transnational world. Amal Amireh. **Signs** 26:1 Autumn:2000 pp.215-249.

3123 The future of differences: truth and method in feminist theory. Susan J. Hekman. Malden MA: Polity Press, 1999. vi, 173p. *ISBN: 0745623786. Includes bibliographical references (p. [158]-168) and index*.

3124 Gender and agency: reconfiguring the subject in feminist and social theory. Lois McNay. Cambridge, Malden MA: Polity Press, 2000. vii, 190p. *ISBN: 0745613497, 0745613489. Includes bibliographical references and index*.

3125 Gendered appetites: feminisms, Dorothy Allison, and the body. Christina Jarvis. **Wom. Stud.** 29:6 2000 pp.763-792.

3126 Generating power: gender, ethnicity and empowerment in India's Narmada valley. Priya A. Kurian. **Ethn. Racial** 23:5 9:2000 pp.842-856.

3127 Hat die Emanzipation ausgedient? *[In German]*; [Has emancipation had its day?] *[Summary]*. Christine Bergmann; Gabriele Bruns; Hildegard M. Nickel; Ursula Hornung; Angela McRobbie; Christina von Braun; Sigrid Meier; Annette Ohme-Reinicke. **Gewerk. Monat.** 51:12 12:2000 pp.665-727. *Collection of 8 articles*.

3128 Identity in transit: nomads, cyborgs and women. Irene Gedalof. **Eur. J. Wom. Stud.** 7:3 8:2000 pp.337-354.

3129 Is feminist philosophy philosophy? Emanuela Bianchi [Ed.]. Evanston IL: Northwestern University Press, 1999. xxvii, 266p. *ISBN: 0810115948, 0810115956. Includes bibliographical references. (Series:* Northwestern University studies in phenomenology and existential philosophy).

3130 'Is it simple to be a feminist in philosophy?' Althusser and feminist theoretical practice. Hasana Sharp. **Rethink. Marx.** 12:2 Summer:2000 pp.18-34.

3131 Is the body essential for ecofeminism? Terri Field. **Org. Environ.** 13:1 3:2000 pp.39-60.

3132 Katoliccy moderniści wobec problemu emancypacji kobiet. *[In Polish]*; (Roman Catholic modernists and emancipation of women.) *[Summary]*. Tomasz Woźniak. **Stud. Socj.** 3(158) 2000 pp.93-110.

3133 Language and liberation: feminism, philosophy, and language. Kelly Oliver [Ed.]; Christina Hendricks [Ed.]. Albany NY: State University of New York Press, 1999. vii,

F: POPULATION. FAMILY. GENDER. ETHNIC GROUPS

402p. *ISBN: 0791440516, 0791440524. Includes bibliographical references and index.* (*Series:* SUNY series in contemporary continental philosophy).

3134 Lesbians' contribution to the autonomous women's movement in (West-)Germany, exemplified by a state capital city. Agnes Senganata Münst. **Wom. St. Inter. For.** 23:5 9-10:2000 pp.601-612.

3135 Life in theory: three feminist thinkers on transition(s). Kathy Davis; Helma Lutz. **Eur. J. Wom. Stud.** 7:3 8:2000 pp.367-378.

3136 Martha Nussbaum's feminist internationalism. Hilary Charlesworth. **Ethics** 111:1 10:2000 pp.64-78.

3137 Merely cultural. Judith Butler. **New Left R.** 227 1-2:1998 pp.33-44.

3138 *Mujhe jawab do!* (Answer me!): Women's grass-roots activism and social spaces in Chitrakoot (India). Richa Nagar. **Gend. Place Cult.** 7:4 12:2000 pp.341-362.

3139 Mutant enunciations: feminist practices and the anoedipal. Estelle Barrett. **Soc. Sem.** 10:3 12:2000 pp.253-263.

3140 Obstacles and opportunities to women's empowerment under neoliberal reform. Cathy A. Rakowski. **J. Dev. Soc.** XVI:1 2000 pp.115-138.

3141 Overloaded: popular culture and the future of feminism. Imelda Whelehan. London: Women's Press, 2000. x, 202p. *ISBN: 0704346176. Includes bibliographical references and index.*

3142 Philosophy matters: a review of recent work in feminist philosophy. Linda Martín Alcoff. **Signs** 25:3 Spring:2000 pp.841-882.

3143 'Point of departure': feminist locations and the politics of travel in India. Ravina Aggarwal. **Fem. Stud.** 26:3 Fall:2000 pp.535-562.

3144 Political theory and feminist social criticism. Brooke A. Ackerly. Cambridge: Cambridge University Press, 2000. xii, 234p. *ISBN: 0521659841, 0521650194. Includes bibliographical references (p. 204-229) and index.* (*Series:* Contemporary political theory).

3145 The politics of the goddess: feminist spirituality and the essentialism debate. Kathryn Rountree. **Soc. Anal. [Adelaide]** 43(2) 1:2000 pp.138-165.

3146 Protesting like a girl: embodiment, dissent and feminist agency. Wendy Parkins. **Fem. Theo.** 1:1 4:2000 pp.59-78.

3147 Questionable claims: colonialism redux, feminist style. Delia D. Aguilar. **Race Class** 41:3 1-3:2000 pp.1-12.

3148 Reading 'India's bandit queen': a trans/national feminist perspective on the discrepancies of representation. Leela Fernandes. **Signs** 25:1 Autumn:1999 pp.123-152.

3149 Second-wave feminism and the politics of relationships. Mary Holmes. **Wom. St. Inter. For.** 23:2 3-4:2000 pp.235-246.

3150 Sotsial'noe vosproizvodstvo kak problema feministskoi teorii. *[In Russian]*; (Social reproduction as a problem of feminist theory.) T.Iu. Zhurzhenko. **Obshch. Nauki Sovrem.** 4 2000 pp.27-40.

3151 El sujeto en el feminismo. *[In Spanish]*; [The subject in feminism] *[Summary]*. Claudia de Lima Costa. **Rev. Mexicana Cien. Pol.** XLIII:174 10-12:1998 pp.83-114.

3152 Taking stands: a feminist perspective on 'other' women's activism in forestry communities of northern Vancouver Island. Maureen G. Reed. **Gend. Place Cult.** 7:4 12:2000 pp.363-388.

3153 Thinking feminism with and against Bourdieu. Terry Lovell. **Fem. Theo.** 1:1 4:2000 pp.11-32.

3154 Transnational feminist networks: collective action in an era of globalization. Valentine M. Moghadam. **Int. Sociol.** 15:1 3:2000 pp.57-86.

3155 Una apuesta por el feminismo global. *[In Spanish]*; [Betting on global feminism]. María José Guerra Palmero. **Leviatán** 80 Summer:2000 pp.101-116.

3156 U.S. feminism - grrrl style! Youth (sub)cultures and the technologics of the third wave. Ednie Kaeh Garrison. **Fem. Stud.** 26:1 Spring:2000 pp.141-170.

3157 Visionary politics? Feminist interventions in the culture of images. Eva Cherniavsky. **Fem. Stud.** 26:1 Spring:2000 pp.171-186.

F: POPULATION. FAMILLE. SEXE. GROUPE ETHNIQUE

3158 Whose body matters? Feminist sociology and the corporeal turn in sociology and feminism. Anne Witz. **Bod. Soc.** 6:2 6:2000 pp.1-24.

3159 Wild science: reading feminism, medicine, and the media. Janine Marchessault [Ed.]; Kim Sawchuk [Ed.]. New York: Routledge, 2000. 259p. *ISBN: 0415204305. Includes bibliographical references and index. (Series:* Writing corporealities).

3160 Women and human development: the capabilities approach. Martha Craven Nussbaum. Oxford, New York: Cambridge University Press, 2000. xxi, 312p. *ISBN: 0521660866. Includes bibliographical references and indexes.*

3161 Women and the women's movement in Britain, 1914-1999. Martin Pugh. Basingstoke: Macmillan, 2000. 400p. *ISBN: 0333732669, 0333732650. Includes index.*

3162 The women's movement in India today - new agendas and old problems. U. Kalpagam. **Fem. Stud.** 26:3 Fall:2000 pp.645-660.

3163 Zum Profil weiblicher 'Ulama' in Iran: Neue Rollenmodelle für 'islamische Feministinnen'? *[In German]*; [On the profile of female *Ulama* in Iran: new role models for 'Islamic feminists'?] Roswitha Badry. **Welt Islams** 40:1 March:2000 pp.7-40.

Gender differentiation
Différenciation sexuelle

3164 Accommodating purdah to the workplace: gender relations in the office sector in Pakistan. Jasmin Mirza. **Pak. Dev. R.** 38:2 Summer:1999 pp.187-206.

3165 Action research for gender equity. Britt-Marie Berge; Hildur Ve. Philadelphia PA: Open University Press, 1999. 157p. *ISBN: 0335200230. Includes bibliographical references and index. (Series:* Feminist educational thinking).

3166 Assimilation, choice, or constraint? Testing theories of gender differences in the careers of lawyers. Kathleen E. Hull; Robert L. Nelson. **Soc. Forc.** 79:1 9:2000 pp.229-264.

3167 Biological limits of gender construction. J. Richard Udry. **Am. Sociol. R.** 65:3 6:2000 pp.443-457.

3168 Changing status of women in Korean society. Young-hee Shim. **Kor. Foc.** 8:2 3-4:2000 pp.70-92.

3169 Children and family policy. Nancy Folbre; Susan Himmelweit; Anita Nyberg; Eileen Trzcinski; Cristina Carrasco; Arantxa Rodríguez; Carmen Sirianni; Cynthia Negrey; Barbara R. Bergmann; Jo Murphy-Lawless; Iulie Aslaksen; Charlotte Koren; Marianne Stokstad; Diane Perrons; Susan Donath; Deborah Levison. **Fem. Econ.** 6:1 3:2000 pp.1-134. *Collection of 11 articles.*

3170 Chinese husbands' participation in household labor. Zai Zai Lu; Marcia L. Bellas; David J. Maume. **J. Comp. Fam. Stud.** XXXI:2 Spring:2000 pp.191-216.

3171 Country gender profile: South Africa. Sally Baden; Shireen Hasim; Sheila Meintjes. Brighton: University of Sussex Press, 1998. 125p. *ISBN: 1858642361. Institute of Development Studies. Swedish International Development Centre. (Series:* BRIDGE Report - 45).

3172 Crossing the borders of whiteness? White Muslim women who wear the *hijab* in Britain today. Myfanwy Franks. **Ethn. Racial** 23:5 9:2000 pp.917-929.

3173 Los desafíos del desarrollo humano desde una perspectiva de género. *[In Spanish]*; [The challenges of human development with regard to gender]. María Eugenia Piola. **Rev. Parag. Sociol.** 36:106 9-12:1999 pp.145-162.

3174 Development for women: methods and priorities. Sarath Amarasinghe. **Sri Lanka J. Soc. Sci.** 21:1-2 6-12:1998 pp.105-134.

3175 'Dim dross': marginalised women both inside and outside the academy. Diane Reay. **Wom. St. Inter. For.** 23:1 1-2:2000 pp.13-22.

3176 Domestic knowledge, inequalities and differences. Xavier Rambla. **Eur. J. Wom. Stud.** 7:2 5:2000 pp.189-208.

F: POPULATION. FAMILY. GENDER. ETHNIC GROUPS

3177 Education, employment, and gender inequality amongst couples: a comparative analysis of Britain and Germany. Malcolm Brynin; Jürgen Schupp. **Eur. Sociol. R.** 16:4 12:2000 pp.349-366.

3178 Emancipatiewaarden en de levensloop van jong-volwassen vrouwen: een panelanalyse van wederzijdse invloeden. *[In Dutch]*; [Emancipation values in the life course of young adult women: a panel analysis of mutual influences]. Miranda Jansen; Matthijs Kalmijn. **Sociol. Gids** XLVII:4 7-8:2000 pp.293-314.

3179 The environment of gender and science: status and perspectives of women and men in physical geography. Sheryl Luzzadder-Beach; Allison M. MacFarlane. **Prof. Geogr.** 52:3 8:2000 pp.407-424.

3180 Equality and cumulative disadvantage. Dana M. Britton; Christine L. Williams; Myra Marx Ferree; Bandana Purkayastha; Erik Olin Wright [Comments by]; Janeen Baxter [Comments by]. **Gender Soc.** 14:6 12:2000 pp.809-821.

3181 Gender differences in coping: a comparison of trait and momentary assessments. Laura S. Porter; Christine A. Marco; Joseph E. Schwartz; John M. Neale; Saul Shiffman; Arthur A. Stone. **J. Soc. Clin. Psychol.** 19:4 2000 pp.480-498.

3182 Gender differences in moral orientation: a meta-analysis. Sara Jaffee; Janet Shibley Hyde. **Psychol. B.** 126:5 9:2000 pp.703-726.

3183 The 'gender gap' in final examination results at Oxford University. Jane Mellanby; Maryanne Martin; John O'Doherty. **Br. J. Psy.** 91:3 8:2000 pp.377-390.

3184 Gender in oblivion: women in the Democratic People's Republic of Korea (North Korea). Sonya Ryang. **J. As. Afr. S.** XXXV:3 2000 pp.323-349.

3185 Gender inequalities in health. Ellen Annandale [Ed.]; Kate Hunt [Ed.]. Buckingham, Philadelphia PA: Open University Press, 1999. 214p. *ISBN: 0335203655, 0335203647. Includes bibliographical references and index.*

3186 Gender relations and witches among the indigenous communities of Jharkhand, India. Samar Bosu Mullick. **Gen. Tech. Dev.** 4:3 9-12:2000 pp.333-358.

3187 Ireland: a man's world? Pat O'Connor. **Econ. Soc. R.** 31:4 1:2000 pp.81-102.

3188 Is anyone doing the housework? Trends in the gender division of household labor. Suzanne M. Bianchi; Melissa A. Milkie; Liana C. Sayer; John P. Robinson. **Soc. Forc.** 79:1 9:2000 pp.191-228.

3189 Maintaining masculinity: men who do 'women's work'. Ben Lupton. **Br. J. Manag.** 11:Special 9:2000 pp.33-48.

3190 Market success or female autonomy? Income, ideology, and empowerment among microentrepreneurs in the Dominican Republic. Sherri Grasmuck; Rosario Espinal. **Gender Soc.** 14:2 4:2000 pp.231-255.

3191 Migrant Filipina domestic workers and the international division of reproductive labor. Rhacel Salazar Parreñas. **Gender Soc.** 14:4 8:2000 pp.560-580.

3192 Moć — volja za moć i moć za žene. *[In Croatian]*; (Power — the will for power and power for women.) *[Summary]*. Jasenka Kodrnja. **Pol. Misao** 37:3 2000 pp.86-101.

3193 A mulher e o poder local em Moçambique. *[In Portuguese]*; [Women and local power in Mozambique]. Helena Zefanias. **Stud. Afr.** 11 3:2000 pp.84-95.

3194 Opyt kross-natsional'nogo analiza gendernogo uklada. *[In Russian]*; (A cross-national analysis of gender arrangements.) B. Pfau-Effinger. **Sot. Issle.** 11 2000 pp.24-35.

3195 Predicting the impact of policy: gender-auditing as a means of assessing the probable impact of policy initiatives on women (Ireland). Mary Donnelly; Olivia Smith; Siobhán Mullally. Liverpool: University of Liverpool, 1999. 121p. *ISBN: 0952214849. Includes bibliographical references. Feminist Legal Research Unit.*

3196 Predicting the impact of policy: gender-auditing as a means of assessing the probable impact of policy initiatives on women (Portugal). João Casqueira Cardoso. Liverpool: University of Liverpool, 1999. 63p. *ISBN: 0952214857. Includes bibliographical references. Feminist Legal Research Unit.*

3197 Predicting the impact of policy: gender-auditing as a means of assessing the probable impact of policy initiatives on women (Sweden). Minna Gillberg. Liverpool: University of

F: POPULATION. FAMILLE. SEXE. GROUPE ETHNIQUE

Liverpool, 1999. 55p. *ISBN: 0952214873. Includes bibliographical references. Feminist Legal Research Unit.*

3198 Predicting the impact of policy: gender-auditing as a means of assessing the probable impact of policy initiatives on women (UK). Fiona Beveridge; Kylie Stephen; Sue Nott. Liverpool: University of Liverpool, 1999. 120p. *ISBN: 0952214881. Includes bibliographical references. Feminist Legal Research Unit.*

3199 Quelques conséquences de la différence «psychanalytique» des sexes. *[In French]*; [Consequences of the 'psychoanalytical' difference between the sexes]. Michel Tort. **Temps Mod.** 55:609 6-8:2000 pp.176-215.

3200 The rush hour: the character of leisure time and gender equity. Michael Bittman; Judy Wajcman. **Soc. Forc.** 79:1 9:2000 pp.165-189.

3201 Sex differences in aggression between heterosexual partners: a meta-analytic review. John Archer; Irene Hanson Frieze [Comments by]; K. Daniel O'Leary [Comments by]; Jacquelyn W. White [Comments by]; Paige Hall Smith [Comments by]; Mary P. Koss [Comments by]; A.J. Figueredo [Comments by]. **Psychol. B.** 126:5 9:2000 pp.651-702.

3202 Son preference and sex composition of children: evidence from India. Shelley Clark. **Demography** 37:1 2:2000 pp.95-108.

3203 Status of women in India: an interstate comparison. Tara Kanitkar; Malika Mistry. **Indian J. Soc. W.** 61:3 7:2000 pp.366-383.

3204 Subordinación de las mujeres e identidad femenina. Diferencias y conexiones. *[In Spanish]*; [Subordination of women and female identity: differences and connections] *[Summary]*. Estela Serret. **Rev. Mexicana Cien. Pol.** XLIII:174 10-12:1998 pp.145-158.

3205 Sur la différence des sexes, et celle des féminismes. *[In French]*; [On the difference between the sexes, and between feminisms]. Liliane Kandel. **Temps Mod.** 55:609 6-8:2000 pp.283-306.

3206 Über Frauen und Frauenarbeit. *[In German]*; [Women and women's work]. Gisela Steineckert; Susanne Bauermann; Ursula Schröter; Sabine Kebir; Elke Kasten-Heitmann; Marlies Mrotzek; MASCH-Kollektiv; Ayse Düzkan; Gisela Blomberg [Interviewer]; Die Hängematten e.V.; Petra Lehmann [Interviewer]. **Marx. Blät** 38:2 2:2000 pp.15-51. *Collection of 9 articles.*

3207 Women and Islam in Bangladesh: beyond subjection and tyranny. Taj ul-Islam Hashmı. Basingstoke: Macmillan, 1999. 288p. *ISBN: 0333749596. Includes bibliographical references and index.*

3208 Women in Swaziland. Zakhe Hlanze; Lolo Mkhabela. Harare; Mbabane: Southern African Research and Documentation Centre; Women and Law in Southern Africa Research Trust, 1998. iv, 64p. *ISBN: 07974175836. Includes bibliographical references (p. 57-58). (Series: Beyond inequalities).*

3209 Women in Zambia. Southern African Research and Documentation Centre; Women in Development Southern Africa Awareness Programme; Zambia Association for Research and Development; Mercy Siame; et al. Lusaka; Harare: Zambia Association for Research and Development; Southern African Research and Documentation Centre, 1998. iv, 102p. *ISBN: 0797417605. Includes bibliographical references (p. 91-96). (Series: Beyond inequalities).*

3210 Women's power and anthropometric status in Zimbabwe. Michelle J. Hindin. **Soc. Sci. Med.** 51:10 11:2000 pp.1517-1528.

Gender roles
Rôles de sexe

3211 Absent and problematic men: demographic accounts of male reproductive roles. Margaret E. Greene; Ann E. Biddlecom. **Pop. Dev. Rev.** 26:1 3:2000 pp.81-116.

3212 The adolescent femininity ideology scale: development and validation of a new measure for girls. Deborah L. Tolman; Michelle V. Porche. **Psychol. Wom. Quart.** 24:4 12:2000 pp.365-376.

F: POPULATION. FAMILY. GENDER. ETHNIC GROUPS

3213 Adolescents' sex-typed friendship experiences: does having a sister versus a brother matter? Kimberly A. Updegraff; Susan M. McHale; Ann C. Crouter. **Child. Devel.** 71:6 11-12:2000 pp.1597-1610.

3214 Assimilation and masquerade: self-constructions of Indo-Dutch women. Pamela Pattynama. **Eur. J. Wom. Stud.** 7:3 8:2000 pp.281-300.

3215 Attitude toward women's societal roles moderates the effect of gender cues on target individuation. Tracie L. Stewart; Patricia M. Vassar; Diana T. Sanchez; Susannah E. David. **J. Pers. Soc. Psychol.** 79:1 7:2000 pp.143-157.

3216 Barbie girls versus sea monsters: children constructing gender. Michael A. Messner. **Gender Soc.** 14:6 12:2000 pp.765-784.

3217 British nonelite road running and masculinity: a case of 'running repairs'? Stuart L. Smith. **Men. Masc.** 3:2 10:2000 pp.187-208.

3218 Bruce Lee's fictional models of masculinity. Jachinson W. Chan. **Men. Masc.** 2:4 4:2000 pp.371-387.

3219 Caring and gender. Francesca M. Cancian; Stacey J. Oliker. Thousand Oaks CA: Pine Forge Press, 2000. xvi, 183p. *ISBN: 0803990960. Includes bibliographical references (p. 161-177) and index. (Series:* The gender lens).

3220 Changing gender relations and policy. Linda Hantrais [Ed.]. Loughborough: Loughborough University, 1999. iv, 39p. *ISBN: 1898564116. Includes bibliographical references. European Research Centre. (Series:* Cross-national research papers. Fifth series, Socio-demographic change, social and economic policies in the European Union - 4).

3221 Conceptualizing and measuring gender ideology as an identity. Amy Kroska. **Gender Soc.** 14:3 6:2000 pp.368-394.

3222 Constructing Chinese masculinity for the modern world: with particular reference to Lao She's *The Two Mas.* Kam Louie. **China Quart.** 164 12:2000 pp.1062-1078.

3223 The cook, the cooker and the gendering of the kitchen. Elizabeth B. Silva. **Sociol. Rev.** 48:4 11:2000 pp.612-628.

3224 Da madri a figlie. Le trasformazioni del ruolo delle donne. *[In Italian]*; [From mothers to daughters: the transformation in the role of women]. Piera Rella; Roberto Cavarra. **Critica Sociol.** 135 Autumn:2000 pp.82-92.

3225 Desire and the literary machine: capitalism, male sexuality, and Stratemeyer series books for boys. Kent Baxter. **Men. Masc.** 3:2 10:2000 pp.168-186.

3226 Do women or men have the less healthy jobs? An analysis of gender differences in sickness absence. Arne Mastekaasa; Harald Dale-Olsen. **Eur. Sociol. R.** 16:3 9:2000 pp.267-286.

3227 Exiles from power: marginality and the female self in postcommunist and postcolonial spaces. Maria-Sabina Draga-Alexandru. **Eur. J. Wom. Stud.** 7:3 8:2000 pp.355-366.

3228 Fetal attractions: the limit of cyborg theory. Marilyn Maness Mehaffy. **Wom. Stud.** 29:2 2000 pp.177-194.

3229 Filial or rebellious daughters? *Dagongmei* in the Pearl River Delta region, south China in the 1990s. Yuen-fong Woon. **Asian Pacif. Migrat. J.** 9:2 2000 pp.137-170.

3230 Gender at a distance: identity, performance and contemporary travel writing. Debbie Lisle. **Int. Fem. J. Pol.** 1:1 1999 pp.66-88.

3231 Gender relations and housing: a cross-community analysis. Girija Shrestha. **Gen. Tech. Dev.** 4:1 1-4:2000 pp.61-86.

3232 Geschlechtliche Normierung von Studienfächern und Karrieren im Wandel. *[In German]*; [Gender normalization of subjects of study and changing careers] *[Summary]*. Ilse Costas; Bettina Roß; Stefan Suchi. **Hist. Soc. R.** 25:2 2000 pp.23-53.

3233 Gli studi sulla mascolinità. Scoperte e problemi di un campo di ricerca. *[In Italian]*; (The challenge of masculinity: problems and suggestions from a new field of research.) *[Summary]*. Simonetta Piccone Stella. **Rass. It. Soc.** XLI:1 1-3:2000 pp.81-107.

3234 I'd rather be rude than ruled: gender, place and communal politics among South Asian communities in Dar es Salaam. Richa Nagar. **Wom. St. Inter. For.** 23:5 9-10:2000 pp.571-585.

F: POPULATION. FAMILLE. SEXE. GROUPE ETHNIQUE

3235 Imagined masculinities: male identity and culture in the modern Middle East. Emma Sinclair-Webb [Ed.]; Mai Ghoussoub [Ed.]. London: Saqi, 2000. 294p. *ISBN: 0863560423, 0863560970. Includes bibliographical references and index.*

3236 Incorporating masculine domination: theoretical and ethnographic elaborations. Allon Uhlmann. **Soc. Anal. [Adelaide]** 44:1 4:2000 pp.142-161.

3237 Influences on gender-role attitudes during the transition to adulthood. Pi-Ling Fan; Margaret Mooney Marini. **Soc. Sci. R.** 29:2 6:2000 pp.258-283.

3238 Institutions, relations and outcomes: a framework and case studies for gender-aware planning. Naila Kabeer [Ed.]; Ramya Subrahmanian [Ed.]. London: Zed Books, 2000, 1999. xi, 410p. *ISBN: 1856498964, 1856498956. Includes bibliographical references and index.*

3239 Intrafamiliar congruence in gender-role ideology: husband-wife versus parents-offspring. Liat Kulik. **J. Comp. Fam. Stud.** XXXI:1 Winter:2000 pp.91-106.

3240 Literature of the U.S. men's movements. Kenneth Clatterbaugh. **Signs** 25:3 Spring:2000 pp.883-904.

3241 Managing marginalised masculinities: men and probation. Sally Holland; Jonathan B. Scourfield. **J. Gender St.** 9:2 7:2000 pp.199-211.

3242 Masculinity and nationalism: gender and sexuality in the making of nations. Joane Nagel. **Ethn. Racial** 21:2 3:1998 pp.242-269.

3243 Masculinity, femininity, and servitude: domestic workers in Calcutta in the late twentieth century. Raka Ray. **Fem. Stud.** 26:3 Fall:2000 pp.691-718.

3244 Materializing Thailand. Penny Van Esterik. Oxford: Berg Publishers, 2000. 274p. *ISBN: 1859733069.*

3245 Men and women on the move: dramas of the road. Jessica Enevold. **Euro. Journ. Cult. Stud.** 3:3 9:2000 pp.403-420.

3246 Men, management and multiple masculinities in organisations. L. McDowell. **Geoforum** 32:2 5:2000 pp.181-198.

3247 Modernity and veiled women. Ibrahim Kaya. **Eur. J. Soc. Theory** 3:2 5:2000 pp.195-214.

3248 The more things change: *The Rules* and late eighteenth-century conduct books for women. Barbara Darby. **Wom. Stud.** 29:3 2000 pp.333-355.

3249 Mothering, work, and gender in Urban Asante ideology and practice. Gracia Clark. **Am. Anthrop.** 101:4 12:1999 pp.717-729.

3250 "Mujeres excéntricas": identidades nacionales, de clase y de género en las narrativas autobiográficas de las Puertorriqueñas. *[In Spanish]*; ['Eccentric women': national, class and gender identities in the autobiographical narratives of Puerto Rican women] *[Summary]*. Aileen Schmidt. **Rev. Cien. Soc.** 5 6:1998 pp.208-241.

3251 Nation and gender — historical perspective. Mohini Anjum. **Sociol. Bul.** 49:1 3:2000 pp.111-141.

3252 'New lads'? Masculinities and the 'new sport' participant. Belinda Wheaton. **Men. Masc.** 2:4 4:2000 pp.434-456.

3253 'Oh no! I'm a NERD!' Hegemonic masculinity on an online forum. Lori Kendall. **Gender Soc.** 14:2 4:2000 pp.256-274.

3254 Osobost' arkhetipov zhenskogo/devich'ego yspekha v russkoi skazke. *[In Russian]*; (The archetypes of women's and girls' success in Russian stories.) V.N. Liusin. **Obshch. Nauki Sovrem.** 4 2000 pp.88-102.

3255 Les parcours de vie des femmes: travail, familles et représentations publiques. *[In French]*; [The paths of women's lives: work, family and public representation]. Anne Guillou [Ed.]; Simone Pennec [Ed.]. Paris: L'Harmattan, 1999. 238p. *ISBN: 273848431X. Includes bibliographical references.*

3256 Personal collections: women's clothing use and identity. Alison Guy; Maura Banim. **J. Gender St.** 9:3 11:2000 pp.313-327.

3257 Philippine commonwealth and cult of masculinity. Alfred W. McCoy. **Phil. Stud.** 48:3 2000 pp.315-346.

3258 The politics of breastfeeding: assessing risk, dividing labor. Jules Law. **Signs** 25:2 Winter:2000 pp.407-450.

F: POPULATION. FAMILY. GENDER. ETHNIC GROUPS

3259 Racial warriors and weekend warriors: the construction of masculinity in mythopoetic and White supremacist discourse. Abby L. Ferber. **Men. Masc.** 3:1 7:2000 pp.30-56.

3260 Real men or real teachers? Contradictions in the lives of men elementary teachers. Paul Sargent. **Men. Masc.** 2:4 4:2000 pp.410-433.

3261 Reflections on gender issues in Africa. Patricia McFadden [Ed.]; Keshia Nicole Abraham; et al. Harare: Southern African Regional Institute for Policy Studies, 1999. 111p. *ISBN: 1779050844. Includes bibliographical references and indexes. (Series:* Gender).

3262 Seduction, simulacra and the feminine: spectacles and images in Muriel Spark's *The Public Image*. Fotini Apostolou. **J. Gender St.** 9:3 11:2000 pp.281-298.

3263 Shifting boundaries of self and other: Moroccan migrant women in Italy. Ruba Salih. **Eur. J. Wom. Stud.** 7:3 8:2000 pp.321-336.

3264 Signs of masculinism in an 'uneasy' place: advertising for 'Big Brothers'. Jeff Hopkins. **Gend. Place Cult.** 7:1 3:2000 pp.31-55.

3265 South Asian women in East London: the impact of education. Kalwant Bhopal. **Eur. J. Wom. Stud.** 7:1 2:2000 pp.35-52.

3266 To veil or not to veil? A case study of identity negotiation among Muslim women in Austin, Texas. Jen'nan Ghazal Read; John P. Bartowski. **Gender Soc.** 14:3 6:2000 pp.395-417.

3267 Trabalho doméstico e poder familiar: práticas, normas e ideais. *[In Portuguese]*; (Domestic work and power in the family: practices, norms and ideals.) *[Summary]*. Gabrielle Poeschl. **Anál. Soc.** XXXV:156 Autumn:2000 pp.695-720.

3268 Tradition and change in domestic roles and food preparation. Debbie Kemmer. **Sociology** 34:2 5:2000 pp.323-346.

3269 Ulstermen and loyalist ladies on parade. Linda Racioppi; Katherine O'Sullivan See. **Int. Fem. J. Pol.** 2:1 2000 pp.1-29.

3270 Unbending gender: why family and work conflict and what to do about it. Joan Williams. Oxford, New York: Oxford University Press, 2000. xii, 338p. *ISBN: 0195094646. Includes bibliographical references (p. [277]-333) and index.*

3271 Uncertain masculinities: youth, ethnicity and class in contemporary Britain. Mike O'Donnell; Sue Sharpe. London: Routledge, 2000. 208p. *ISBN: 0415153476, 0415153468.*

3272 Virtual virility, or, does medicine make the man? Elizabeth Haiken. **Men. Masc.** 2:4 4:2000 pp.388-409.

3273 When no means no: disbelief, disregard, and deviance as discourses of voluntary childlessness. Rosemary Gillespie. **Wom. St. Inter. For.** 23:2 3-4:2000 pp.223-234.

3274 White guy *habitus* in the classroom: challenging the reproduction of privilege. Michael A. Messner. **Men. Masc.** 2:4 4:2000 pp.457-469.

3275 'Women forget that men are the masters': gender antagonism and socio-economic change in Kisii district, Kenya. Margrethe Silberschmidt. Uppsala: Nordiska Africainstitutet, 1999. 186p. *ISBN: 9171064397. Includes bibliographical references (p. [179]-186).*

3276 Women who become men: Albanian sworn virgins. Antonia Young. Oxford, New York: Berg Publishers, 2000. xxvi, 168p. *ISBN: 1859733352, 1859733409. Includes bibliographical references (p. 153-163) and index. (Series:* Dress, body, culture).

3277 Women, work and Islamism: ideology and resistance in Iran. Maryam Poya. London, New York: Zed Books, 1999. xvii, 186p. *ISBN: 1856496813, 1856496821. Includes bibliographical references and index.*

3278 Women working in Oman: individual choice and cultural constraints. Dawn Chatty. **Int. J. M. E. Stud.** 32:2 5:2000 pp.241-254.

3279 Women's autonomy, women's status and fertility-related behavior in Zimbabwe. M.J. Hindin. **Pop. Res. Pol. R.** 19:3 6:2000 pp.255-282.

3280 Women's health in relation with their family and work roles: France in the early 1990s. Myriam Khlat; Catherine Sermet; Annick Le Pape. **Soc. Sci. Med.** 50:12 6:2000 pp.1807-1826.

3281 Zhenshchina-rukovoditel': delovye strategii obraz 'Ia'. *[In Russian]*; (Women managers: business strategies and self-image.) A.E. Chirikova; O.N. Krichevskaia. **Sot. Issle.** 11 2000 pp.45-56.

F: POPULATION. FAMILLE. SEXE. GROUPE ETHNIQUE

Sex discrimination
Discrimination sexuelle

3282 Badgering or bantering? Gender differences in experience of, and reactions to, sexual harassment among U.S. high school students. Jeanne Z. Hand; Laura Sanchez. **Gender Soc.** 14:6 12:2000 pp.718-746.

3283 Beyond prejudice as simple antipathy: hostile and benevolent sexism across cultures. Peter Glick; Susan T. Fiske; Antonio Mladinic; José L. Saiz; Dominic Abrams; Barbara Masser; Bolanle Adetoun; Johnstone E. Osagie; Adebowale Akande; Amos Alao; Annetje Brunner; Tineke M. Willemsen; Kettie Chipeta; Benoit Dardenne; Ap Dijksterhuis; Daniel Wigboldus; Thomas Eckes; Iris Six-Materna; Francisca Expósito; Miguel Moya; Margaret Foddy; Hyun-Jeong Kim; Maria Lameiras; Maria José Sotelo; Angelica Mucchi-Faina; Myrna Romani; Nuray Sakalli; Bola Udegbe; Mariko Yamamoto; Miyoko Ui; Maria Cristina Ferreira; Wilson López López. **J. Pers. Soc. Psychol.** 79:5 11:2000 pp.763-775.

3284 Discriminatory experiences of women police. A comparison of officers serving in England and Wales, Scotland, Northern Ireland and the Republic of Ireland. J. Brown. **Int. J. S. Law** 28:2 6:2000 pp.91-112.

3285 The effect of occupational sex composition on the gender gap in workplace authority. Vered Kraus; Yuval P. Yonay. **Soc. Sci. R.** 29:4 12:2000 pp.583-605.

3286 Entering the political elite in Canada: the case of minority women as parliamentary candidates and MPs. Jerome H. Black. **Can. R. Soc. A.** 37:2 5:2000 pp.143-166.

3287 Experiencing the streets: harassment and perceptions of safety among women. Ross MacMillan; Annette Nierobisz; Sandy Welsh. **J. Res. Crim. Delin.** 37:3 8:2000 pp.306-322.

3288 Hegemonic masculinity and male feminisation: the sexual harassment of men at work. Deborah Lee. **J. Gender St.** 9:2 7:2000 pp.141-155.

3289 A psychoanalytic dialectical model for sexual and other forms of workplace harassment. Stuart W. Twemlow. **J. App. Psy. Stud.** 1:3 7:1999 pp.249-272.

3290 Sexual harassment: analyses and bibliography. V.P. Argos [Comp.]; Tatiana Shohov [Comp.]. Commack NY: Nova Science Publishers, 1999. 180p. *ISBN: 156072711X. Includes bibliographical references and indexes.*

3291 Sexual harassment in university and college compuses in Mumbai. Asha Bajpai. **Indian J. Soc. W.** 60:4 10:1999 pp.606-623.

3292 The social construction of sexual harassment and assault of university students. Fiona Wilson. **J. Gender St.** 9:2 7:2000 pp.171-187.

3293 The subjective experience of sexual harassment: cases of students. Fiona Wilson. **Human Relat.** 53:8 8:2000 pp.1081-1098.

F.6: **Sexual behaviour**
Comportement sexuelle

3294 Adolescent sexual and reproductive health in Canada: a review of national data sources and their limitations. Eleanor Maticka-Tyndale; Michael Barrett; Alexander McKay. **Canad. J. Human Sex.** 9:1 2000 pp.41-66.

3295 Anarchism and sexuality. Martha Ackelsberg; Richard Cleminson; Ulrike Heider; Karen Goaman; Mo Dodson. **Anarch. St.** 8:2 10:2000 pp.99-152. *Collection of 4 articles.*

3296 Attitudes toward people in exclusive dating relationships who initiate condom use. Jennifer Davidson-Harden; William A. Fisher; Paul R. Davidson. **Canad. J. Human Sex.** 9:1 2000 pp.1-14.

3297 Bisexuality and the eroticism of everyday life. Marjorie B. Garber. New York: Routledge, 2000. 606p. *ISBN: 0415926610. Includes bibliographical references (p. [529]-584) and index.*

3298 Classifying sexual behavior. Janice Haaken; Sharon Lamb; Carol Tavris; David Spiegel; Julia A. Ericksen. **Society** 37:4 5-6:2000 pp.7-25. *Collection of 4 articles.*

F: POPULATION. FAMILY. GENDER. ETHNIC GROUPS

3299 Condoms and the making of 'testosterone man': a cultural analysis of the male sex drive in AIDS research on safer heterosex. Nicole Vitellone. **Men. Masc.** 3:2 10:2000 pp.152-167.

3300 Contemporary patterns of adolescent sexuality in urban Botswana. Dominique Meekers; Ghyasuddin Ahmed. **J. Biosoc. Sc.** 32:4 10:2000 pp.467-486.

3301 Desire/disgust: mapping the moral contours of heterosexuality. Philip Hubbard. **Prog. H. Geog.** 24:2 6:2000 pp.191-218.

3302 Feminism and pornography. Drucilla Cornell [Ed.]. New York: Oxford University Press, 2000. 671p. *ISBN: 0198782500. Includes bibliographical references and index. (Series:* Oxford readings in feminism).

3303 French letters and English overcoats: sexual fallacies and fads from ancient Greece to the millennium. Richard Death. London: Robson, 2000. xv, 204p. *ISBN: 1861053231.*

3304 From Westermarck's effect to Fox's law: paradox and principle in the relationship between incest taboos and exogamy. Alex Walter. **Soc. Sci. Info.** 39:3 9:2000 pp.467-488.

3305 The function of the fetish in: the *Rocky Horror Picture Show* and *Priscilla, Queen of the Desert*. Betty Robbins; Roger Myrick. **J. Gender St.** 9:3 11:2000 pp.269-280.

3306 Gender differences in erotic plasticity: the female sex drive as socially flexible and responsive. Roy F. Baumeister; Janet Shibley Hyde [Comments by]; Amanda M. Durik [Comments by]; Barbara L. Andersen [Comments by]; Jill M. Cyranowski [Comments by]; Susan Aarestad [Comments by]; Kathleen R. Catanese [Comments by]; W. Keith Campbell [Comments by]; Dianne M. Tice [Comments by]. **Psychol. B.** 126:3 5:2000 pp.347-389.

3307 Gendered heteronormativity: empirical illustrations in everyday life. Joyce McCarl Nielson; Glenda Walden; Charlotte A. Kunkel. **Sociol. Q.** 41:2 Spring:2000 pp.283-296.

3308 Genetic and environmental influences on sexual orientation and its correlates in an Australian twin sample. J. Michael Bailey; Michael P. Dunne; Nicholas G. Martin. **J. Pers. Soc. Psychol.** 78:3 3:2000 pp.524-536.

3309 Highway cowboys, old hands, and Christian truckers: risk behavior for human immunodeficiency virus infection among long-haul truckers in Florida. Dale Stratford; Tedd V. Ellerbrock; J. Keith Akins; Heather L. Hall. **Soc. Sci. Med.** 50:5 3:2000 pp.737-749.

3310 How do people evaluate social sexual conduct at work? A psycholegal model. Richard L. Wiener; Linda E. Hurt. **J. Appl. Psychol.** 85:1 2:2000 pp.75-85.

3311 Intravaginal practises in Zimbabwe: which women engage in them and why? Janneke van de Wijgert; Michael Mbizvo; Sabada Dube; Magdalene Mwale; Prisca Nyamapfeni; Nancy Padian. **Cult. Health. Sex.** 3:2 4-6:2001 pp.133-148.

3312 Let every child be wanted: how social marketing is revolutionizing contraceptive use around the world. Philip D. Harvey. Westport CT: Auburn House, 1999. x, 251p. *ISBN: 0865692823. Includes bibliographical references and index.*

3313 The love between 'beautiful boys' in Japanese women's comics. Mark J. McLelland. **J. Gender St.** 9:1 3:2000 pp.13-26.

3314 Making sexual history. Jeffrey Weeks. Oxford, Malden MA: Polity Press, 2000. x, 256p. *ISBN: 0745621147, 0745621155. Includes bibliographical references and index. Blackwell Publishers.*

3315 Making up for war: sexuality and citizenship in wartime culture. Page Dougherty Delano. **Fem. Stud.** 26:1 Spring:2000 pp.33-68.

3316 Nebulous margins: sexuality and social constructions of risks in rural areas of Central Mexico. Xóchitl Castañeda; Claire Brindis; Itzá Castañeda Camey. **Cult. Health. Sex.** 3:2 4-6:2001 pp.203-219.

3317 Neither 'saints' nor 'prostitutes': sexual discourse in the Filipina domestic worker community in Hong Kong. Kimberly A. Chang; Julian McAllister Groves. **Wom. St. Inter. For.** 23:1 1-2:2000 pp.73-88.

3318 Non-verbal behavior as courtship signals: the role of control and choice in selecting partners. Karl Grammer; Kirsten Kruck; Astrid Juette; Bernhard Fink. **Evol. Hum. Behav.** 21:6 11:2000 pp.371-390.

F: POPULATION. FAMILLE. SEXE. GROUPE ETHNIQUE

3319 On prostitution, STDs and the law in South Africa: the state as pimp. John M. Luiz; Leon Roets. **J. Contemp. Afr. St.** 18:1 1:2000 pp.21-38.

3320 'On the beach of elsewhere': Angela Carter's moral pornography and the critique of gender archetypes. Gregory J. Rubinson. **Wom. Stud.** 29:6 2000 pp.717-740.

3321 L'orientation sexuelle en Europe: esquisse d'une politique publique antidiscriminatoire. *[In French]*; [Sexual orientation in Europe: an outline of antidiscriminatory public policy]. Daniel Borrillo. **Temps Mod.** 55:609 6-8:2000 pp.263-282.

3322 The politics of sex and other essays: on conservatism, culture, and imagination. Raymond Tallis [Foreword]; Robert Grant. Basingstoke; New York: Macmillan; St. Martin's Press, 2000. 248p. *ISBN: 0333760069, 0312230249. Includes bibliographical references and index.*

3323 Politics/sexuality. Meaghan Morris; Antonia Chao; Audrey Yue; J. Neil C. Garcia; Josephine Chuen-Juei Ho; Naifei Ding. **Inter-Asia Cult. St.** 1:2 8:2000 pp.219-318. *Collection of 6 articles.*

3324 Pornographies. Leslie Green. **J. Polit. Phil.** 8:1 3:2000 pp.27-52.

3325 Prostitution: collectives and the politics of regulation. Jackie West. **Gend. Work & Org.** 7:2 4:2000 pp.106-118.

3326 Prostitution in Malawi and the HIV/AIDS risk. Peter G. Forster. **Nord. J. Afr. St.** 9:1 2000 pp.1-19.

3327 Protecting the rights of sex workers: the Indian experience; *[Summary in French]*; *[Summary in Spanish]*. Geetanjali Misra; Ajay Mahal; Rima Shah. **Health Hum. Rights** 5:1 2000 pp.88-115.

3328 Raging hormones, regulated love: adolescent sexuality and the constitution of the modern individual in the United States and the Netherlands. Amy T. Schalet. **Bod. Soc.** 6:1 3:2000 pp.75-105.

3329 Reconstructing the sexuality of men with learning disabilities: empirical evidence and theoretical interpretations of need. Paul Cambridge; Bryan Mellan. **Dis. and Soc.** 15:2 3:2000 pp.293-311.

3330 Rethinking sexuality. Diane Richardson. London: Sage Publications, 2000. 176p. *ISBN: 0761967095, 0761967087. Includes bibliographical references and index.*

3331 Revisiting 'the myth of the vaginal orgasm': the female orgasm in American sexual thought and second wave feminism. Jane Gerhard. **Fem. Stud.** 26:2 Summer:2000 pp.449-476.

3332 Selling sex in the time of AIDS: the psycho-social context of condom use by sex workers on a Southern African mine. Catherine Campbell. **Soc. Sci. Med.** 50:4 2:2000 pp.479-494.

3333 Sex for sale: prostitution, pornography, and the sex industry. Ronald John Weitzer [Ed.]. New York: Routledge, 2000. vi, 310p. *ISBN: 0415922941, 041592295X. Includes bibliographical references (p. 265-300) and index.*

3334 Sex work in Southeast Asia: the place of desire in a time of AIDS. Lisa Law. London: Routledge, 2000. 160p. *ISBN: 0415218055.*

3335 Sexes et sexualités: bonnes et mauvaises différences. *[In French]*; [Sex and sexuality: good and bad differences]. Evelyne Pisier. **Temps Mod.** 55:609 6-8:2000 pp.156-175.

3336 The sexual behavior of married Mexican immigrant men in North Carolina. Claire I. Viadro; Jo Anne L. Earp. **Soc. Sci. Med.** 50:5 3:2000 pp.723-735.

3337 Sexual behaviour and contraception among unmarried adolescents and young adults in greater Accra and eastern regions of Ghana. William K.A. Agyei; Richard B. Biritwum; A.G. Ashitey; Robert B. Hill. **J. Biosoc. Sc.** 32:4 10:2000 pp.495-512.

3338 Sexual delinquency and exploitation. D.J. West; Roxanne Lieb; Hans Boutellier; Martin Killias; Sarah Alexander; Stan Meuwese; Annemieke Wolthuis; Stefan Bogaerts; Geert Vervaeke; Johan Goethals; Frans Van Dijk; Jaap De Waard. **Eur. J. Crim. Pol. Res.** 8:4 12:2000 pp.399-527. *Collection of 7 articles.*

3339 Sexual identity, identification and difference: a psychoanalytic contribution to discourse theory. Jason Glynos. **Philos. Soc. Crit.** 26:6 11:2000 pp.85-108.

3340 Sexual orientation and gender identity in America's urban schools. Ian K. MacGillivray; Genét Kozik-Rosabal; Glorianne M. Leck; Monica E. Schneider; Robert E. Owens; David

F: POPULATION. FAMILY. GENDER. ETHNIC GROUPS

S. Buckel; Eric Rofes; Margaret D. LeCompte. **Educ. Urban. Soc.** 32:3 5:2000 pp.287-429. *Collection of 8 articles.*

3341 Sexual rhetoric: media perspectives on sexuality, gender, and identity. Susan C. Zavoina [Ed.]; Meta G. Carstarphen [Ed.]. Westport CT: Greenwood Press, 1999. xviii, 304p. *ISBN: 0313307881. Includes bibliographical references and index. (Series:* Contributions to the study of mass media and communications - 57).

3342 Sexuality and perversion a hundred years on: discovering what Freud discovered; *[Summary in French]; [Summary in German]; [Summary in Spanish].* Michael Parsons. **Int. J.Psy.** 81:1 2:2000 pp.37-51.

3343 Sexuality in marriage, dating, and other relationships: a decade review. F. Scott Christopher; Susan Sprecher. **J. Marriage Fam.** 62:4 11:2000 pp.999-1017.

3344 Social motives and cognitive power-sex associations: predictors of aggressive sexual behavior. Eileen L. Zurbriggen. **J. Pers. Soc. Psychol.** 78:3 3:2000 pp.559-581.

3345 Taxometric analyses of sexual orientation and gender identity. Steven W. Gangestad; J. Michael Bailey; Nicholas G. Martin. **J. Pers. Soc. Psychol.** 78:6 6:2000 pp.1109-1121.

3346 'The essence of the hard on': hegemonic masculinity and the cultural construction of 'erectile dysfunction'. Annie Potts. **Men. Masc.** 3:1 7:2000 pp.85-103.

3347 'The worst thing is the screwing' (1): consumption and the management of identity in sex work. Joanna Brewis; Stephen Linstead. **Gend. Work & Org.** 7:2 4:2000 pp.84-97.

3348 Tourism and sex: culture, commerce, and coercion. Stephen Clift [Ed.]; Simon Carter [Ed.]. London, New York: Pinter, 2000. xiii, 297p. *ISBN: 1855675498, 1855676362. Includes bibliographical references and indexes. (Series:* Tourism, leisure, and recreation series).

3349 Towards a dubious liberation: masculinity, sexuality and power in South African lowveld schools, 1953-1999. Isak Niehaus. **J. S. Afr. Stud.** 26:3 9:2000 pp.387-407.

3350 'When a man is with a woman, it feels like electricity': subjectivity, sexuality and contraception among men in Central Mexico. Roberto Castro. **Cult. Health. Sex.** 3:2 4-6:2001 pp.149-165.

3351 Willingness to engage in casual sex: the role of parental qualities and perceived risk of aggression. Michele K. Surbey; Colette D. Conohan. **Hum. Nature** 11:4 2000 pp.367-386.

3352 Women's sexualities: new perspectives on sexual orientation and gender. Linda D. Garnets; Letitia Anne Peplau; Esther D. Rothblum; Paula C. Rodríguez Rust; Evelyn Blackwood; Beverly Greene; Gregory M. Herek; Rosemary C. Veniegas; Terri D. Conley; Janet Shibley Hyde; Sara R. Jaffee; Lisa M. Diamond; Ritch C. Savin-Williams; Suzanna Rose; Sheila James Kuehl. **J. Soc. Issues** 56:2 Summer:2000 pp.181-359. *Collection of 12 articles.*

3353 Working in the fantasy factory: the attention hypothesis and the enacting of masculine power in strip clubs. Elizabeth Anne Wood. **J. Contemp. Ethnog.** 29:1 2:2000 pp.5-31.

Homosexuality
Homosexualité

3354 Accessing homosexuality: truth, evidence and the legal practices for determining refugee status — the case of Ioan Vraciu. Derek McGhee. **Bod. Soc.** 6:1 3:2000 pp.29-50.

3355 Australian gay porn videos: the national identity of despised cultural objects. Alan McKee. **Int. Jour. Cult. Stud.** 2:2 8:1999 pp.178-198.

3356 Cracks in the feminist mirror? Research and reflections on lesbians and gay men working together. Jill C. Humphrey. **Feminist R.** 66 Autumn:2000 pp.95-130.

3357 Delineating differences: sub-communities in the San Francisco gay community. Ben Peacock; Stephen L. Eyre; Sandra Crouse Quinn; Susan Kegeles. **Cult. Health. Sex.** 3:2 4-6:2001 pp.183-201.

3358 Egg seeks sperm. End of story…? Articulating gay parenting in small ads for reproductive partners. Susan Hogben; Justine Coupland. **Disc. Soc.** 11:4 10:2000 pp.459-485.

F: POPULATION. FAMILLE. SEXE. GROUPE ETHNIQUE

3359 «Faces cachées de l'urbain» ou éléments d'une nouvelle centralité? Les lieux de la culture homosexuelle à Berlin. *[In French]*; ('The hidden side of urban life' or elements in a new centrality. Places of homosexual culture in Berlin.) *[Summary]*; *[Summary in German]*. Boris Grésillon. **Espace Géogr.** 29:4 2000 pp.301-314.

3360 Family relationships of lesbians and gay men. Charlotte J. Patterson. **J. Marriage Fam.** 62:4 11:2000 pp.1052-1069.

3361 Feminism, the family, and the politics of the closet: lesbian and gay displacement. Cheshire Calhoun. Oxford: Oxford University Press, 2000. vii, 172p. *ISBN: 0198295596. Includes bibliographical references and index.*

3362 Gay and Greek: the identity paradox of gay fraternities. King-to Yeung; Mindy Stombler. **Soc. Prob.** 47:1 2:2000 pp.134-152.

3363 Gay and lesbian language. Don Kulick. **Ann. R. Anthr.** 29 2000 pp.243-285.

3364 Get used to it! gay and lesbian parents and their children. Myra Hauschild; Patricia Rosier. Christchurch; Hadleigh: Canterbury University Press; BRAD, 1999. 128p. *ISBN: 0908812868.*

3365 Heroes and invaders: gay and lesbian pride parades and the public/private distinction in New Zealand media accounts. Chris Brickell. **Gend. Place Cult.** 7:2 6:2000 pp.163-178.

3366 Homosexuality and Christian faith: questions of conscience for the churches. Walter Wink [Ed.]. Minneapolis MN: Fortress Press, 1999. viii, 133p. *ISBN: 0800631862. Includes bibliographical references (p. 70).*

3367 Intimidade, norma e diferença: a modernidade gay em Lisboa. *[In Portuguese]*; (Intimacy, norms and difference: gay modernity in Lisbon.) Inês Meneses. **Anál. Soc.** XXXIV:153 Spring:2000 pp.933-956.

3368 Inverted appellation and discursive gender insubordination: an Austrian case study in gay male conversation. Matti Bunzl. **Disc. Soc.** 11:2 4:2000 pp.207-236.

3369 Lesbian and gay studies: an introductory interdisciplinary approach. Theo Sandfort [Ed.]. London: Sage Publications, 2000. xi, 236p. *ISBN: 076195418X, 0761954171.*

3370 The lesbian, gay & bisexual youth program (LGBYP): a model for communities seeking to improve quality of life for lesbian, gay and bisexual youth. Robb Travers; Dino Paoletti. **Canad. J. Human Sex.** 8:4 1999 pp.293-303.

3371 Listening to queer maps of the city: gay men's narratives of pleasure and danger in London's East End. Gavin Brown. **Oral Hist.** 29:1 Spring:2001 pp.48-61.

3372 'Macho man': clones and the development of a masculine stereotype. Shaun Cole. **Fash. Theory** 4:2 6:2000 pp.125-140.

3373 Negotiating health care: the experiences of young lesbian and bisexual women. Teresa Scherzer. **Cult. Health. Sex.** 2:1 1-3:2000 pp.87-102.

3374 'No experts—guaranteed!': do-it-yourself sex radicalism and the production of the lesbian sex zine. Brat Attack; Dana Collins. **Signs** 25:1 Autumn:1999 pp.65-90.

3375 Postcards from the edge: decoding Winnipeg's 'one gay city' campaign. Janice Oakley. **Ethnologies** 21:1 1999 pp.177-192.

3376 Queer theory and feminism. Kathy Rudy. **Wom. Stud.** 29:2 2000 pp.195-216.

3377 Die Queer-Debatte. *[In German]*; (The queer debate.) *[Summary]*. Elisabeth Holzleithner. **Fors. Jour. Soz. Beweg.** 13:4 12:2000 pp.14-23.

3378 'Queering' development: exploring the links between same-sex sexualities, gender, and development. Susie Jolly. **Gen. Dev.** 8:1 3:2000 pp.78-88.

3379 La recherche sur les lesbiennes: enjeux théoriques, méthodologiques et politiques. *[In French]*; [Theoretical, methodological and political issues in lesbian research]. Denise Veilleux [Ed.]. Ottawa: Institut canadien de recherches sur les femmes/Canadian Research Institute for the Advancement of Women, 1999. ii, 101p. *ISBN: 0919653812. Includes bibliographical references.*

3380 The relations of power and intimacy motives to genitoerotic role preferences in gay men: a pilot study. Will Damon. **Canad. J. Human Sex.** 9:1 2000 pp.15-29.

3381 Responding to the support needs of HIV positive lesbian, gay and bisexual youth. Robb Travers; Dino Paoletti. **Canad. J. Human Sex.** 8:4 1999 pp.271-292.

F: POPULATION. FAMILY. GENDER. ETHNIC GROUPS

3382 Sexuality: so what's the issue? Maeve Malley; Fiona Tasker; Damian McCann; David Spellman; Layne A. Prest; Robin Russel; Henry D'Souza; Volker Thomas; Robert A. Lewis; Ian Bennun. **J. Fam. Ther.** 21:1 2:1999 pp.3-112. *Collection of 6 articles.*
3383 Sexualizing the sociological: queering and querying the intimate substructure of social life. Joane Nagel. **Sociol. Q.** 41:1 Winter:2000 pp.1-18.
3384 Simple pleasures: lesbian community and *Go Fish*. Lisa Henderson. **Signs** 25:1 Autumn:1999 pp.37-64.
3385 Something to tell you: the road families travel when a child is gay. Gilbert H. Herdt; Bruce Koff. New York, Chichester: Columbia University Press, 2000. 192p. *ISBN: 0231104383.*
3386 Straight with a twist: queer theory and the subject of heterosexuality. Joseph O. Aimone; Catherine A.F. MacGillivray; Calvin Thomas [Ed.]. Urbana IL: University of Illinois Press, 2000. 290p. *ISBN: 0252024958, 0252068130. Includes bibliographical references and index.*
3387 Subkultura homosexuálů v Brně. *[In Czech]*; (Gay subculture in Brno.) *[Summary].* Kateřina Nedbálková. **Soc. Čas.** 36:3 2000 pp.317-332.
3388 'The bars, the bogs, and the bushes': the impact of locale on sexual cultures. Paul Flowers; Claire Marriott; Graham Hart. **Cult. Health. Sex.** 2:1 1-3:2000 pp.69-86.
3389 This is what lesbian looks like: dyke activists take on the 21st century. Kris Kleindienst [Ed.]. Ithaca NY: Firebrand Books, 1999. 278p. *ISBN: 1563411164, 1563411172.*

F.7: **Race and ethnicity**
Race et ethnicité

Ethnicity
Ethnicité

3390 Accommodating ethnic diversity in a modernizing democratic state: theory and practice in the case of Mauritius. Barbara Wake Carroll; Terrance Carroll. **Ethn. Racial** 23:1 1:2000 pp.120-147.
3391 The African American male in American life and thought. Tracy D. Snipe; Jake C. Miller; Jacob U. Gordon; I. Peter Ukpokodu; Garry A. Mendez, Jr.; Quintard Taylor; Lewis Diuguid; Adrienne Rivers; Festus E. Obiakor; Sunday O. Obi; Patrick Grant; John A. Rich; Susan Williams McElroy; Leon T. Andrews, Jr. **Ann. Am. Poli.** 569 5:2000 pp.10-175. *Collection of 10 articles.*
3392 'Ain't I a Filipino (woman)?' An analysis of authorship/authority through the construction of 'Filipina' on the Net. Emily Noelle Ignacio. **Sociol. Q.** 41:4 Fall:2000 pp.551-572.
3393 Ambiguous insiders: an investigation of Arab American invisibility. Nadine Naber. **Ethn. Racial** 23:1 1:2000 pp.37-61.
3394 Asian American ethnic identification by surname. D.S. Lauderdale; B. Kestenbaum. **Pop. Res. Pol. R.** 19:3 6:2000 pp.283-300.
3395 Being African in South Africa: the dynamics of exclusion and inclusion. Gerhard Schutte. **Soc. Ident.** 6:2 6:2000 pp.207-222.
3396 Beyond Black and White: Latinos and social science research on immigration, race, and ethnicity in America. Silvia Pedraza. **Soc. Sci. Hist.** 24:4 Winter:2000 pp.697-726.
3397 The challenges of measuring the ethno-cultural diversity of Britain in the new millennium; *[Summary in French]; [Summary in Spanish].* Peter Aspinall. **Policy Pol.** 28:1 1:2000 pp.109-118.
3398 Competing identities? Race, ethnicity and panethnicity among Dominicans in the United States. Jose Itzigsohn; Carlos Dore-Cabral. **Sociol. For.** 15:2 6:2000 pp.225-247.
3399 Correlates of race, ethnicity and national origin in the United States Virgin Islands. Klaus de Albuquerque; Jerome L. McElroy. **Soc. Econ. S.** 48:3 9:1999 pp.1-42.
3400 Curry goat as a metaphor for the Indian/Jamaican future. Kirk Meighoo. **Soc. Econ. S.** 48:3 9:1999 pp.43-60.

F: POPULATION. FAMILLE. SEXE. GROUPE ETHNIQUE

3401 A Darwinian theory of ethnicity, 'race,' and nationality. Walter L. Wallace. **Int. J. Comp. Soc** XLI:2 2000 pp.147-202.
3402 La desvalorizacion de la identidad, un problema de la situacion de contacto. I parte. *[In Spanish]*; [The devaluation of identity, a problem of contact: Part I] *[Summary]*. Laura Collin Harguindeguy. **Scr. Ethn.** XXI 1999 pp.59-80.
3403 Dominance and difference: rival visions of ethnicity in Nigeria. Obi Igwara. **Ethn. Racial** 24:1 1:2001 pp.86-103.
3404 Ethnic jokes and social function in Hawai'i. Kimie Oshima. **Humor** 13:1 2000 pp.41-58.
3405 Ethnicity and acculturation in a culturally diverse country: identifying ethnic markets. Guilherme D. Pires; P.J. Stanton. **J. Multiling.** 21:1 2000 pp.42-57.
3406 Ethnicity and farm entry behavior. John A. Cross; Douglas Jackson-Smith; Bradford Barham. **Rural Sociol.** 65:3 9:2000 pp.461-483.
3407 O etnicite príslušníkov slovenskej inteligencie v mad'arsku — relácie medzi stupňom etnickej identity a etnoidentifikačnými kategóriami. *[In Slovak]*; (On the ethnicity of members of the Slovak intelligentsia in Hungary - relations between degree of ethnic identity and ethno-identification categories.) Mária Homišinová. **Sociologia [Brat.]** 32:5 2000 pp.471-482.
3408 Etnikai besorolás és statisztika. Elvi alapvetés a gömöri cigányok három évszázados jelenlétének vizsgálatához. *[In Hungarian]*; (Attempting to classify the Gypsies in Gömör and the question of their statistical identity.) Róbert Keményfi. **Regio** 10:1 1999 pp.137-155.
3409 Finno-Ugrians of Russia: vanishing cultural communities? Seppo Lallukka. **Nat. Pap.** 29:1 3:2001 pp.9-39.
3410 The formation of Azerbaijani collective identity in Iran. Brenda Shaffer. **Nat. Pap.** 28:3 9:2000 pp.449-478.
3411 Formation of ethnic and racial identities: narratives by young Asian-American professionals. Pyong Gap Min; Rose Kim. **Ethn. Racial** 23:4 7:2000 pp.735-767.
3412 From Black to African American: a new social representation. Serge Moscovici [Foreword]; Gina Philogène. Westport CT, London: Praeger, 1999. xviii, 237p. *ISBN: 0275962849. Includes bibliographical references (p. [221]-233) and index.*
3413 Les gangs hispaniques dans le quartier de la Mission (San Francisco, Californie). *[In French]*; [Hispanic street gangs in the Mission Bay area (San Francisco, California)]; *[Summary in Spanish]*. Sonia Lehman-Frisch. **Cah. Amer. Lat.** 33 2000 pp.173-200.
3414 Group images and possible selves among adolescents: linking stereotypes to expectations by race and ethnicity. Grace Kao. **Sociol. For.** 15:3 9:2000 pp.407-430.
3415 Handbook of language and ethnic identity. Joshua A. Fishman [Ed.]. New York: Oxford University Press, 1999. xii, 468p. *ISBN: 0195124286. Includes bibliographical references and index.*
3416 In the politics of the rainbow: creoles and civil society in Mauritius. Rosabelle Laville. **J. Contemp. Afr. St.** 18:2 7:2000 pp.277-294.
3417 Intersections among tribalism, ethnicity and gender in the light of African data. Edwin S. Segal. **Sociol. Bul.** 49:1 3:2000 pp.1-17.
3418 Jewish identity and the meaning of community in contemporary Denmark. Andrew Buckser. **Ethn. Racial** 23:4 7:2000 pp.712-734.
3419 Liberal ethnicity: beyond liberal nationalism and minority rights. Eric Kaufmann. **Ethn. Racial** 23:6 11:2000 pp.1086-1119.
3420 The limits of tolerance: nation-state building and what it means for minority groups. Mark Levene. **Patt. Prej.** 34:2 4:2000 pp.19-40.
3421 Między grupą etniczną a narodem. *[In Polish]*; (Between ethnic group and nation.) *[Summary]*. Iwona Kabzińska. **Etn. Polska** XLVII:2 2000 pp.39-62.
3422 Migrant belongings: memory, space and identity. Anne-Marie Fortier. Oxford: Berg Publishers, 2000. 224p. *ISBN: 1859734103, 1859734057. Includes index.*
3423 Minorités. *[In French]*; [Minorities]. André Langlois; Simon Laflamme; Rachid Bagaoui; Denise Helly; Marc Lavallée; Marie McAndrew; Patrick D. Clarke. **Rech. Sociogr.** XLI:2 5-8:2000 pp.211-366. *Collection of 4 articles.*

F: POPULATION. FAMILY. GENDER. ETHNIC GROUPS

3424 Minorities research: a collection of studies by Hungarian authors. Győző Cholnoky [Ed.]. Budapest: Lucidus Kiadó, 1999. 152p. *ISBN: 963859540X.*
3425 Le mouvement de conservation d'une ethnie en voie d'extinction, les Youkaguirs. *[In French]*; (The defense movement in favor of a nearly extinct ethnic group, the Yukagirs.) *[Summary].* Marine Leberre-Semenov. **Cah. Mon. Russe** 41:2-3 4-9:2000 pp.401-429.
3426 The myth of a Finno-Ugrian community in practice. Sirkka Saarinen. **Nat. Pap.** 29:1 3:2001 pp.41-52.
3427 Occupation and ethnicity: constructing identity among professional Romani (Gypsy) musicians in Romania. Margaret H. Beissinger. **Slavic R.** 60:1 Spring:2001 pp.24-49.
3428 Race and ethnicity and the controversy over the US census. Margo Anderson; Stephen E. Fienberg. **Curr. Sociol.** 48:3 7:2000 pp.87-110.
3429 Race and ethnicity in the United States: issues and debates. Stephen Steinberg [Ed.]. Malden MA: Blackwell Publishers, 2000. xvii, 342p. *ISBN: 0631208305. Includes bibliographical references and index.*
3430 Race and nation in post-apartheid South Africa. Kogila Moodley; Heribert Adam. **Curr. Sociol.** 48:3 7:2000 pp.51-69.
3431 Race and place in Birmingham: the civil rights and neighborhood movements. Bobby M. Wilson. Lanham MD: Rowman & Littlefield, 2000. ix, 275p. *ISBN: 0847694828. Includes bibliographical references (p. 229-255) and index.*
3432 'Race' as an interaction order phenomenon: W.E.B. Du Bois's 'double consciousness' thesis revisited. Anne Warfield Rawls. **Sociol. Theory** 18:2 7:2000 pp.241-274.
3433 'Race', ethnicity and adoption. Derek Kirton. Buckingham: Open University Press, 2000. 162p. *ISBN: 0335200036, 0335200028. Includes bibliographical references and index.* (*Series:* Race, health, and social care).
3434 Race, ethnicity and nativity, family structure, socioeconomic status and welfare dependency. Hiromi Ono; Rosina M. Becerra. **Int. Migr. Rev.** 34:3 Fall:2000 pp.739-765.
3435 Racial politics, pedagogy and the crisis of representation in academic multiculturalism. Henry A. Giroux. **Soc. Ident.** 6:4 12:2000 pp.493-510.
3436 Racial situations: class predicaments of whiteness in Detroit. John Hartigan, Jr. Princeton NJ: Princeton University Press, 1999. xii, 354p. *ISBN: 0691028869, 0691028850. Includes bibliographical references and index.*
3437 Racism and democracy reconsidered. Carol C. Gould. **Soc. Ident.** 6:4 12:2000 pp.425-439.
3438 Recognition through pleasure, recognition through violence: gendered coloured subjectivities in South Africa. Zimitri Erasmus. **Curr. Sociol.** 48:3 7:2000 pp.71-85.
3439 The relationships among racial identity, perceived ethnic fit, and organizational involvement for African American students at a predominantly White university. Tabbye M. Chavous. **J. Black Psychol.** 26:1 2:2000 pp.79-100.
3440 Revising and improving the African-American acculturation scale. Elizabeth A. Klonoff; Hope Landrine. **J. Black Psychol.** 26:2 5:2000 pp.235-261.
3441 Scattered belongings: cultural paradoxes of 'race,' nation and gender. Jayne O. Ifekwunigwe. London, New York: Routledge, 1999. xvii, 221p. *ISBN: 0415170958, 0415170966. Includes bibliographical references (p. 197-214) and index.*
3442 Social identity and preferred ethnic/racial labels for Blacks in Canada. Sharon J. Boatswain; Richard N. Lalonde. **J. Black Psychol.** 26:2 5:2000 pp.216-234.
3443 Touristic ethnicity: a brief itinerary. Robert E. Wood. **Ethn. Racial** 21:2 3:1998 pp.218-241.
3444 Tre perspektiver på hviterusserne i Polen. *[In Norwegian]*; (Three perpectives on Belarusians in Poland.) Jørn Holm-Hansen. **Int. Pol.** 58:1 2000 pp.63-80.
3445 Tupi, Guarani, Português, Negro, Mestiço, Mulato, Italiano, Polaco, Brasileiro. Kształtowanie się tożsamości Polonii brazylijskiej na tle przemian tożsamości mieszkańców Brazylii. *[In Polish]*; (*Tupi, Guarani, Português, Negro, Mestiço, Mulato, Italiano, Polaco, Brasileiro.* Formation of Brazilian Poles' national identity against a background of Brazilians' identity changes.) *[Summary].* Władysław T. Miodunka. **Prz. Pol.** XXVI:3(97) 2000 pp.29-52.

F: POPULATION. FAMILLE. SEXE. GROUPE ETHNIQUE

3446 Urban Aboriginal-Australian and Anglo-Australian children: in-group preference, self-concept, and teachers' academic evaluations. A. Pedersen; I. Walker. **J. Comm. App. Soc. Psychol.** 10:3 5-6:2000 pp.183-198.

3447 Uygurs that eat pork: a note on ethnic consciousness in Changde's Uygur-Hui townships. Chih-yu Shih. **Iss. Stud.** 36:3 5-6:2000 pp.180-198.

3448 Varieties of authenticity in contemporary Jewish identity. Stuart Z. Charmé. **Jew. Soc. Stud.** 6:2 Winter:2000 pp.133-155.

3449 Whiteness: feminist philosophical reflections. Kim Q. Hall [Ed.]; Chris J. Cuomo [Ed.]. Lanham MD: Rowman & Littlefield, 1999. viii, 133p. *ISBN: 0847692949, 0847692957. Includes bibliographical references (p. 119-127) and index.*

3450 Who, what, when, where, and why is Polish Jewry? Envisioning, constructing, and possessing Polish Jewry. Scott Ury. **Jew. Soc. Stud.** 6:3 Spring-Summer:2000 pp.205-228.

Interethnic relations
Relations interethniques

3451 L'accès à la transaction immobilière: un des mécanismes du processus de ségrégation résidentielle ethnique. *[In French]*; [Access to real estate transactions: one of the mechanisms allowing residential segregation on grounds of ethnicity] *[Summary]*. Sylvie Paré. **Rech. Sociogr.** XLI:3 9-12:2000 pp.509-528.

3452 Albatros rasismu. *[In Czech]*; (The racist albatross: social science, Jörg Haider, and *Widerstand*.) *[Summary]*. Immanuel Wallerstein. **Soc. Čas.** 36:4 2000 pp.459-474.

3453 Another step in the study of race relations. Luigi Esposito; John W. Murphy. **Sociol. Q.** 41:2 Spring:2000 pp.171-188.

3454 Antiracist activism in Ecuador: Black-Indian community alliances. Adam Halpern; France Winddance Twine. **Race Class** 42:2 10-12:2000 pp.19-31.

3455 Antisemitische Einstellungen in Deutschland zwischen 1994 und 1998. *[In German]*; (Anti-semitic attitudes in Germany between 1994 and 1998.) *[Summary]*. Reinhard Wittenberg. **Kölner Z. Soz. Soz. Psy.** 52:1 3:2000 pp.118-131.

3456 As long as they don't move next door: segregation and racial conflict in American neighborhoods. Stephen Grant Meyer. Lanham MD: Rowman & Littlefield, 2000. x, 344p. *ISBN: 0847697002. Includes bibliographical references and index.*

3457 Black men, racial stereotyping, and violence in the U.S. South and Cuba at the turn of the century. Aline Helg. **Comp. Stud. S.** 42:3 7:2000 pp.576-604.

3458 Bullying and racism among Asian schoolchildren in Britain. Mike Eslea; Kafeela Mukhtar. **Educat. Res.** 42:2 Summer:2000 pp.207-217.

3459 Changing profile of Chinese Americans: some general and preliminary observations. Pao-min Chang. **Asian Prof.** 27:4 8:1999 pp.283-308.

3460 Citizenship, housing and minority ethnic groups: an approach to multiculturalism. A. Bowes; N. Dar; D. Sim. **Hous. Th. Soc.** 17:2 2000 pp.83-95.

3461 Classical and modern racial prejudice: a study of attitudes toward immigrants in Sweden. Nazar Akrami; Bo Ekehammar; Tadesse Araya. **Eur. J. Soc. Psychol.** 30:4 7-8:2000 pp.521-532.

3462 Co-existence in selected mixed Arab-Jewish cities in Israel: by choice or by default? Ghazi Falah; Michael Hoy; Rakhal Sarker. **Urban Stud.** 37:4 4:2000 pp.775-796.

3463 The contemporary structure of Canadian racial supremacism: networks, strategies and new technologies; *[Summary in French]*. Sean P. Hier. **Can. J. Soc.** 25:4 Fall:2000 pp.471-494.

3464 Contents and correlates of Whites' and Blacks' racial attitudes. Margo J. Monteith; C. Vincent Spicer. **J. Exp. S. Psychol.** 36:2 3:2000 pp.125-154.

3465 A cultural explanation of collapse into civil war: escalation of tension in Nigeria. Nancy Spalding. **Cult. Psyc.** 6:1 3:2000 pp.51-87.

3466 Demonizing the other: antisemitism, racism and xenophobia. Robert S. Wistrich [Ed.]. Amsterdam: Harwood Academic Publishers, 1999. 392p. *ISBN: 9057024977. Includes index.*

F: POPULATION. FAMILY. GENDER. ETHNIC GROUPS

3467 The difference between a Surinamese and a Turk: ethnic jokes and the position of ethnic minorities in the Netherlands. Giselinde Kuipers. **Humor** 13:2 2000 pp.141-175.
3468 Dilemmas at the border. Janet Bauer; Vijay Prashad; Leora Auslander; Gerdien Jonker; Asale Angel-Ajani; Alejandro Lugo; Lewis R. Gordon. **Cult. Dyn.** 12:3 11:2000 pp.275-383. *Collection of 6 articles.*
3469 Država i etnička manjina. *[In Croatian]*; (State and ethnic minority.) *[Summary]*. Dušan Janjić. **Pol. Misao** 37:3 2000 pp.102-114.
3470 Education and racism: a cross national inventory of positive effects of education on ethnic tolerance. Shervin Nekuee [Ed.]; Louk Hagendoorn [Ed.]. Aldershot: Ashgate, 1999. xix, 248p. *ISBN: 0754611418. Includes bibliographical references and index.*
3471 The end of tolerance: engaging cultural differences. Marcelo M. Suárez-Orozco; Katherine Pratt Ewing; Unni Wikan; Usha Menon; David L. Chambers; Martha Minow; Austin Sarat; Nomi Maya Stolzenberg; Lawrence G. Sager; Richard A. Shweder; Hazel Rose Markus; Claude M. Steele; Dorothy M. Steele. **Dædalus** 129:4 Fall:2000 pp.1-259. *Collection of 9 articles.*
3472 Ethnic conflict. Michael Banton. **Sociology** 34:3 8:2000 pp.481-498.
3473 Ethnic conflict in India: a case-study of Punjab. Gurharpal Singh. Basingstoke; New York: Macmillan; St. Martin's Press, 2000. xv, 231p. *ISBN: 0312228384. Includes bibliographical references (p. 223-225) and index.*
3474 Ethnic mobilization and the state: the Roma in Eastern Europe. Zoltan Barany. **Ethn. Racial** 21:2 3:1998 pp.308-327.
3475 Ethnic protest in core and periphery states. Susan Olzak. **Ethn. Racial** 21:2 3:1998 pp.187-217.
3476 An examination of the nature and correlates of ethnic harassment experiences in multiple contexts. Kimberly T. Schneider; Robert T. Hitlan; Phanikiran Radhakrishnan. **J. Appl. Psychol.** 85:1 2:2000 pp.3-12.
3477 Examining and responding to conflict between African American and Jewish American students on a college campus. Warren J. Blumenfeld; Lisa D. Robinson. **Med. Q.** 17:3 Spring:2000 pp.231-264.
3478 The experience and consequences of perceived racial discrimination: a study of African-Americans. Clifford L. Broman; Roya Mavaddat; Shu-yao Hsu. **J. Black Psychol.** 26:2 5:2000 pp.165-180.
3479 A glimpse of the Thai in north-west Vietnam. Quoc Su Trinh. **Viet. Stud.** 36:2(136) 2000 pp.8-18.
3480 'Good-enough' isn't so bad: thinking about success and failure in ethnic conflict management. Marc Howard Ross. **Peace Con.** 6:1 2000 pp.27-47.
3481 How segregated are middle-class African Americans? Richard D. Alba; John R. Logan; Brian J. Stults. **Soc. Prob.** 47:4 11:2000 pp.543-558.
3482 If not reconciliation, then what? Samuel L. Myers, Jr. **R. Soc. Econ.** LVIII:3 9:2000 pp.361-380.
3483 Israel's ethnic demon: inside the bottle, on a slow flame. Yariv Tsfati. **Megamot** XL:1 11:1999 pp.5-30.
3484 Koreans in Japan: critical voices from the margin. Sonia Ryang [Ed.]. London, New York: Routledge, 2000. 229p. *ISBN: 041521999X. Includes bibliographical references and index. (Series:* Routledge studies in Asias transformations).
3485 The manipulation of ethnicity: from ethnic cooperation to violence and war in Yugoslavia. Anthony Oberschall. **Ethn. Racial** 23:6 11:2000 pp.982-1001.
3486 The moral surveillance of Aboriginal applicants for public housing in New South Wales. George Morgan. **Aust. Abor. S.** 2 1999 pp.3-14.
3487 The Mordvins: dilemmas of mobilization in a biethnic community. Valerii Iurchenkov. **Nat. Pap.** 29:1 3:2001 pp.85-95.
3488 Multicultural Washington, DC: the changing social and economic landscape of a post-industrial metropolis. Robert D. Manning. **Ethn. Racial** 21:2 3:1998 pp.328-355.
3489 Multiculturalism in practice: Irish, Jewish, Italian and Pakistani migration to Scotland. Suzanne Audrey. Aldershot: Ashgate, 2000. xiv, 256p. *ISBN: 0754615111. Includes*

F: POPULATION. FAMILLE. SEXE. GROUPE ETHNIQUE

bibliographical references and index. (Series: Interdisciplinary research series in ethnic, gender, and class relations).

3490 Multikulturalizmus — veszély vagy esély? *[In Hungarian]*; [Multiculturalism — danger or chance?] Gabriella Kiss. **Valóság** 42:1 1999 pp.30-42.

3491 Multiracialism and meritocracy: Singapore's approach to race and inequality. R. Quinn Moore. **R. Soc. Econ.** LVIII:3 9:2000 pp.339-360.

3492 Nationalism and ethnic conflict: philosophical perspectives. Nenad Miscevic [Ed.]. Chicago IL: Open Court, 2000. vi, 331p. *ISBN: 0812694155. Includes bibliographical references and index.*

3493 Nationalism and rationality. Michael Hechter. **Stud. Comp. Int. Dev.** 35:1 Spring:2000 pp.3-19.

3494 New ethnicities, old racisms? Phil Cohen [Ed.]. London, New York: Zed Books, 1999. 243p. *ISBN: 1856496511. Includes bibliographical references and index.*

3495 Nine lives: ethnic conflict in the Polish-Ukrainian borderlands. Waldemar Lotnik; Julian Preece. London: Serif, 1999. 224p. *ISBN: 1897959400. Includes bibliographical references.*

3496 Obraz „svojho" a „iných" etník v orálnej histórii nemeckého obyvatel'stva Švedlára. *[In Slovak]*; (The picture of 'our' and 'other' ethnic groups in the oral history of the German population at Švedlár.) Zuzana Búriková. **Slov. Národop.** 48:1 2000 pp.24-52.

3497 On not looking German: ethnicity, diaspora and the politics of vision. Ming-Bao Yue. **Euro. Journ. Cult. Stud.** 3:2 5:2000 pp.173-194.

3498 Overrepresentation and underrepresentation of African Americans and Latinos as lawbreakers on television news. Travis L. Dixon; Daniel Linz. **J. Comm.** 50:2 Spring:2000 pp.131-156.

3499 The Palestinian citizens of Israel, the concept of trapped minority and the discourse of transnationalism in anthropology. Dan Rabinowitz. **Ethn. Racial** 24:1 1:2001 pp.64-85.

3500 The paradox of diversity: the construction of a multicultural Canada and 'women of color'. Himani Bannerji. **Wom. St. Inter. For.** 23:5 9-10:2000 pp.537-560.

3501 A place in the sun: re-creating the Australian way of life. Bill Cope; Mary Kalantzis. Pymble, New York: HarperCollins, 2000. 389p. *ISBN: 0732265223. Includes bibliographical references and index.*

3502 The 'post-Holocaust Jew' and the instrumentalization of philosemitism. Thomas Altfelix. **Patt. Prej.** 34:2 4:2000 pp.41-56.

3503 ¡Qué tal raza! *[In Spanish]*; [Considering race]. Aníbal Quijano. **Tareas** 105 5-8:2000 pp.119-129.

3504 Race and racism in theory and practice. Berel Lang [Ed.]. Lanham MD: Rowman & Littlefield, 2000. 266p. *ISBN: 0847696936.*

3505 Race in cyberspace. Beth E. Kolko [Ed.]; Lisa Nakamura [Ed.]; Gilbert B. Rodman [Ed.]. New York: Routledge, 1999. *ISBN: 0415921627. Includes bibliographical references and index.*

3506 Race, media, and the crisis of civil society: from Watts to Rodney King. Ronald N. Jacobs. New York: Cambridge University Press, 2000. 189p. *ISBN: 052162360X. Includes bibliographical references and index. (Series:* Cambridge cultural social studies).

3507 'Race', racism and anti-racism: challenging contemporary classifications. Alana Lentin. **Soc. Ident.** 6:1 3:2000 pp.91-106.

3508 Racism and discourse. Ruth Wodak; Peter Teo; Eduardo Bonilla-Silva; Tyrone A. Forman; Benjamin Bailey. **Disc. Soc.** 11:1 1:2000 pp.5-108. *Collection of 4 articles.*

3509 Racism and young girls' peer-group relations: the experiences of South Asian girls. Paul Connolly. **Sociology** 34:3 8:2000 pp.499-519.

3510 Racism, mimesis and anthropology in Brazil. Fernando Rosa-Ribeiro. **Crit. Anthr.** 20:3 9:2000 pp.221-241.

3511 Racismo y discriminación en la Argentina. *[In Spanish]*; [Racism and discrimination in Argentina]. Víctor Ramos. Buenos Aires: Editorial Catálogos, 1999. 213p. *ISBN: 9508950544. Includes bibliographical references (p. [207]-209).*

F: POPULATION. FAMILY. GENDER. ETHNIC GROUPS

3512 Rasa i etniczność: konstrukcja porządku społecznego w amerykańskim tyglu. *[In Polish]*; (Race and ethnicity: constructing social order in American melting pot.) Jarosław Rokicki. **Prz. Pol.** XXV:4(94) 1999 pp.5-44.

3513 Realism and racism: concepts of race in sociological research. Bob Carter. London: Routledge, 2000. 208p. *ISBN: 0415233739, 0415233720. Includes index.*

3514 Reclaiming a Du Boisian perspective on racial attitudes. Lawrence D. Bobo. **Ann. Am. Poli.** 568 3:2000 pp.186-202.

3515 Reconciling context and contact effects on racial attitudes. Robert M. Stein; Stephanie Shirley Post; Allison L. Rinden. **Pol. Res. Q.** 53:2 6:2000 pp.285-304.

3516 Reconsidering the environmental determinants of racial attitudes. J. Eric Oliver; Tali Mendelberg. **Am. J. Pol. Sc.** 44:3 7:2000 pp.574-589.

3517 Reducing racial prejudice, discrimination, and stereotyping: translating research into programs. Frances E. Aboud; Sheri R. Levy; Vladimir T. Khmelkov; Maureen T. Hallinan; Robert E. Slavin; Robert Cooper; Fred Genesee; Patricia Gándara; Rebecca S. Bigler; Sherryl Browne Graves; Walter G. Stephan; Krystina Finlay; Virginia Fenwick; Anthony R. Pratkanis; Marlene E. Turner. **J. Soc. Issues** 55:4 Winter:1999 pp.621-815. *Collection of 10 articles.*

3518 Reflexiones sobre el significado del holocausto. *[In Spanish]*; [Reflections on the meaning of the Holocaust]. Yahuda Bauer; Michael R. Marrus; Judit Bokser; Gilda Waldman M.; Susana Ralsky Cimet; Blanca Solares; Abraham Sutzkever; Samuel Kassow; Nechama Tec; David Bankier; Sergio DellaPergola; José Gordon; Alan Astro; Gilda Waldman M. **Acta Sociol. [Mexico]** 26-27 5-12:1999 pp.13-261. *Collection of 12 articles.*

3519 Relations interethniques et processus d'identification à Carthagène (Colombie). *[In French]*; [Interethnic relations and identification processes in Cartagena (Colombia)]; *[Summary in Spanish]*. Elisabeth Cunin. **Cah. Amer. Lat.** 33 2000 pp.127-151.

3520 Romalincselések Romániában. *[In Hungarian]*; (Roma lynching in Romania.) István Haller. **Regio** 10:1 1999 pp.178-193.

3521 School racial composition and adolescent racial homophily. Kara Joyner; Grace Kao. **Soc. Sci. Q.** 81:3 9:2000 pp.810-825.

3522 Situating social attitudes toward cultural pluralism: between culture wars and contemporary racism. Dennis J. Downey. **Soc. Prob.** 47:1 2:2000 pp.90-111.

3523 The social construction of racism: the case of second generation Bangladeshis. B. Ahmed; P. Nicolson; C. Spencer. **J. Comm. App. Soc. Psychol.** 10:1 1-2:2000 pp.33-48.

3524 Social control and deviance: a South Asian community in Scotland. Ali Wardak. Aldershot: Ashgate, 2000. xii, 275p. *ISBN: 1840145889. Includes bibliographical references. (Series:* Interdisciplinary research series in ethnic, gender and class relations).

3525 The southern albatross: race and ethnicity in the American South. Philip D. Dillard [Ed.]; Randal L. Hall [Ed.]. Macon GA: Mercer University Press, 1999. 282p. *ISBN: 0865546665. Includes bibliographical references.*

3526 The spirit of Alberta Indian treaties. Richard Price [Ed.]. Edmonton: University of Alberta Press, 1999. *ISBN: 0888643276. Includes bibliographical references.*

3527 Stereotypes in contemporary Anglo-German relations. Rainer Emig [Ed.]. Basingstoke: Macmillan, 2000. 256p. *ISBN: 0333793412. Includes bibliographical references and index. Anglo-German Foundation for the Study of Industrial Society.*

3528 The study of African American problems: W.E.B. Du Bois's agenda, then and now. Tukufu Zuberi; W.E.B. Du Bois; Farah Jasmine Griffin; Patricia Hill Collins; Elijah Anderson; William Julius Wilson; Mary Frances Berry; Michael B. Katz; Gerald D. Jaynes; James E. Bowman; Fatimah L.C. Jackson; Lawrence D. Bobo; Henry Louis Gates, Jr.; Anthony Monteiro; Barbara Dianne Savage; Herman Beavers; Lewis R. Gordon; Lucius T. Outlaw, Jr.; Martin Kilson. **Ann. Am. Poli.** 568 3:2000 pp.9-313. *Collection of 20 articles.*

3529 Theories of race and racism: a reader. Les Back [Ed.]; John Solomos [Ed.]. New York: Routledge, 1999. 646p. *ISBN: 0415156718, 0415156726. Includes bibliographical references and index.*

3530 They ask if we eat frogs: social boundaries, ethnic categorisation, and the Garo people of Bangladesh. Ellen Bal. Delft: Eburon, 2000. 247p. *ISBN: 9051667647.*

F: POPULATION. FAMILLE. SEXE. GROUPE ETHNIQUE

3531 Violence and the crisis of conciliation: Suri, Dizi and the state in south-west Ethiopia; *[Summary in French]*. J. Abbink. **Africa [Edinburgh]** 70:4 2000 pp.527-550.

3532 Die Walser-Bubis-Debatte: Eine Dokumentation. *[In German]*; [The Walser-Bubis debate: documents]. Frank Schirrmacher [Ed.]. Frankfurt am Main: Suhrkamp, 1999. 682p. *ISBN: 3518410733. Includes bibliographical references.*

3533 Where East meets West: the last stand of Finns and Karelians in contemporary Karelia? Antti Laine. **Nat. Pap.** 29:1 3:2001 pp.53-67.

3534 Whiteness in the field. John Hartigan, Jr.; Ira Bashkow; Galen Joseph; Mary Weismantel. **Identities** 7:3 9:2000 pp.269-440. *Collection of 5 articles.*

3535 *Youth associations* und Ethnizität in Nordghana. *[In German]*; (Youth associations and ethnicity in Northern Ghana.) *[Summary]*; *[Summary in French]*. Carola Lentz. **Af. Spec.** 34:3 1999 pp.305-320.

3536 Die Zukunftsperspektiven türkischer Jugendlicher in der Bundesrepublik Deutschland. *[In German]*; [Perspectives on the future of Turkish youths in Germany]. Hüseyin Azizefendioglu. Herbolzheim: Centaurus, 2000. 120p. *ISBN: 3825502317.*

F.8: Migration
Migration

3537 Arguments within geographies of movement: the theoretical potential of migrants' stories. Victoria A. Lawson. **Prog. H. Geog.** 24:2 6:2000 pp.173-190.

3538 Gender and migration in Southern Europe: women on the move. Floya Anthias [Ed.]; Gabriella Lazaridis [Ed.]. Oxford: Berg Publishers, 2000. ix, 263p. *ISBN: 1859732313, 1859732364. Includes bibliographical references and index.* (*Series:* Mediterranea).

3539 Home and away: narratives of migration and estrangement. Sara Ahmed. **Int. Jour. Cult. Stud.** 2:3 12:1999 pp.329-347.

3540 Inside, outside, upside down, backward, forward, round and round: a case for ethnographic studies in migration. Kevin E. McHugh. **Prog. H. Geog.** 24:1 2000 pp.71-89.

3541 Migration, mobility and modernization. David Siddle [Ed.]. Liverpool: Liverpool University Press, 2000. viii, 225p. *ISBN: 0853238839. Includes bibliographical references.* (*Series:* Liverpool studies in European population - 7).

3542 Open borders: the case against immigration controls. Teresa Hayter. London: Pluto Press, 2000. 224p. *ISBN: 0745315429, 074531547X.*

3543 Theoretical and methodological issues in migration research: interdisciplinary, intergenerational and international perspectives. Biko Agozino [Ed.]. Aldershot, Brookfield VT: Ashgate, 2000. 243p. *ISBN: 1840145579.*

3544 Towards a sociology of Asian migration and settlement: focus on Japan. Kenichiro Hirano; Stephen Castles; Patrick Brownlee. **Asian Pacif. Migrat. J.** 9:3 2000 pp.243-254.

3545 Transformations: immigration and immigration research in the United States. Rubén G. Rumbaut; Nancy Foner; Steven J. Gold; Mary C. Waters; George J. Sanchez; Aristide R. Zolberg; Josh DeWind; Herbert J. Gans; Howard Markel; Alexandra Minna Stern; Jennifer S. Hirsch; Steven S. Zahniser; Rafael Alarcón; Jennifer Lee; Jane Junn; Gaspar Rivera-Salgado; Ayumi Takenaka. **Am. Behav. Sc.** 42:9 6-7:1999 pp.1258-1474. *Collection of 15 articles.*

Immigrant adaptation
Adaptation des immigrants

3546 Acculturation and health in Korean Americans. Soo-kyung Lee; Jeffery Sobal; Edward A. Frongillo, Jr. **Soc. Sci. Med.** 51:2 7:2000 pp.159-174.

3547 Acculturation discrepancies and well-being: the moderating role of conformity. Sonia Roccas; Gabriel Horenczyk; Shalom H. Schwartz. **Eur. J. Soc. Psychol.** 30:3 5-6:2000 pp.323-334.

F: POPULATION. FAMILY. GENDER. ETHNIC GROUPS

3548 Acting Brazilian in Japan: ethnic resistance among return migrants. Takeyuki Gaku Tsuda. **Ethnology** XXXIX:1 Winter:2000 pp.55-71.

3549 L'activité des femmes immigrées du Portugal à l'arrivée en France, reflet d'une diversité de stratégies familiales et individuelles. *[In French]*; (Female migration from Portugal and activity on arrival in France: a variety of personal and family strategies.) S. Condon. **Population** 55:2 3-4:2000 pp.301-330.

3550 Assortative mating among married new legal immigrants to the United States: evidence from the new immigrant survey pilot. Guillermina Jasso; Douglas S. Massey; Mark R. Rosenzweig; James P. Smith. **Int. Migr. Rev.** 34:2 Summer:2000 pp.443-459.

3551 Characteristics and migration experience of Africans in Canada with specific reference to Ghanaians in greater Toronto; *[Summary in French]*. Kwadwo Konadu-Agyemang. **Can. Geogr.** 43:4 Winter:1999 pp.400-414.

3552 Clima de actitudes en los inmigrantes respecto de la sociedad chilena. *[In Spanish]*; [Immigrants' attitudes regarding Chilean society]. Orlando Mella; Astrid Stoherel. **Rev. Parag. Sociol.** 36:106 9-12:1999 pp.179-194.

3553 The consumer market of the enclave economy: a study of advertisements in a Chinese daily newspaper in Toronto. Peter S. Li; Yahong Li. **Can. Ethn. Stud.** XXXI:2 1999 pp.43-60.

3554 Cultural identity and adaptation among participants in the Naale 16 project. Uzi Ben-Shalom; Gabriel Horenczyk. **Megamot** XL:2 3:2000 pp.199-217.

3555 Culture and language. Edward P. Lazear. **J. Polit. Ec.** 107:6(2) 12:1999 pp.95-126.

3556 Culture and social adjustment: migrant workers in Korea and local workers in overseas Korean firms. Kiseon Chung; Hyunho Seok. **Asian Pacif. Migrat. J.** 9:3 2000 pp.287-310.

3557 Diasporic subjects and identity negotiations: women in and from Asia. Shirlena Huang; Peggy Teo; Brenda S.A. Yeoh; Pauline Gardiner Barber; Nobue Suzuki; Yu Zhou; Sally Lloyd Evans; Sophia Bowlby; Claire Dwyer; Rebecca Elmhirst; Rachel M. Silvey. **Wom. St. Inter. For.** 23:4 7-8:2000 pp.391-516. *Collection of 9 articles.*

3558 Ethnic return migration from the East and the West: the case of Estonia in the 1990's. Hill Kulu; Tiit Tammaru. **Eur.-Asia Stud.** 52:2 3:2000 pp.349-370.

3559 Ethnicity and labour market performance among recent immigrants from the former Soviet Union to Israel. Yitchak Haberfeld; Moshe Semyonov; Yinon Cohen. **Eur. Sociol. R.** 16:3 9:2000 pp.287-300.

3560 Les flux migratoires: nouveaux profils des immigrés, mutations dans les sociétés d'accueil. *[In French]*; [Migration trends: new immigrant profiles and changes in the host society]. Faouzi Malleh. **R. Tun. Sci. Soc.** 36:118 1999 pp.27-42.

3561 Forced relocation, language use, and ethnic identity of Koreans in Central Asia. In-jin Yoon. **Asian Pacif. Migrat. J.** 9:1 2000 pp.35-64.

3562 La France africaine: Islam, intégration, insécurité. Infos et intox, essai. *[In French]*; [African France: Islam, integration, insecurity. Information and disinformation, an essay]. Jean-Paul Gourévitch. Paris: Pré aux Clercs, 2000. 371p. *ISBN: 2842280660.*

3563 From Latin American immigrant to 'Hispanic' citizen: the role of social capital in seeking U.S. citizenship. Susan González Baker; Marilyn Espitia. **Soc. Sci. Q.** 81:4 12:2000 pp.1053-1063.

3564 Hebrew language proficiency, occupation and attachment to Israel among immigrants from the former Soviet Union in the 1990s. Gila Menachem; Idit Gejst. **Megamot** XL:1 11:1999 pp.131-148.

3565 Hispanics in America in 2000. Jorge Durand; Douglas S. Massey; Fernando Charvet; William Kandel; Grace Kao; Julie A. Phillips; Rubén Hernández-León; Víctor Zúñiga; Susan Welch; Lee Sigelman; Gilda Laura Ochoa; Lisa García Bedolla; Kenneth J. Meier; Robert D. Wrinkle; Melissa R. Michelson; Natasha Hritzuk; David K. Park; R. Michael Alvarez; Tara L. Butterfield; Lina Y. Newton; M.V. Hood, III; Irwin L. Morris; Robert R. Bezdek; David M. Billeaux; Juan Carlos Huerta; Scott Graves; Jongho Lee; Robert W. Brown; R. Todd Jewell; Jeffrey J. Rous; Sean M. Bolks; Diana Evans; J.L. Polinard; Alberto Dávila; Marie T. Mora; Jana L. Jasinski; Marta Tienda; Rebeca Raijman; Deborah

F: POPULATION. FAMILLE. SEXE. GROUPE ETHNIQUE

A. Cobb-Clark; Sherrie A. Kossoudji; Matthew O. Hunt; Larry L. Hunt; Matthew T. Lee; Ramiro Martinez, Jr.; S. Fernando Rodriguez; Jacqueline L. Angel; Ronald J. Angel; Kyriakos S. Markides; Frank D. Bean; C. Gray Swicegood; Ruth Berg; Brian Karl Finch; Jason D. Boardman; Bohdan Kolody; William A. Vega; Douglas Forbes; W. Parker Frisbie; Starling G. Pullum; Samuel Echevarria; Robert A. Hummer; Richard G. Rogers; Sarit H. Amir; Ralph Catalano; Ethel Adrete; Sergio Aguilar-Gaxiola. **Soc. Sci. Q.** 81:1 3:2000 pp.1-487. *Collection of 31 articles.*

3566 The hyphenated American: the hidden injuries of culture. John Papajohn. Westport CT: Greenwood Press, 1999. xvii, 148p. *ISBN: 0313309302. Includes bibliographical references (p. [137]-140) and index. (Series:* Contributions in psychology - 38).

3567 Immigrant acculturation attitudes and host country identification. Drew Nesdale; Anita S. Mak. **J. Comm. App. Soc. Psychol.** 10:6 11-12:2000 pp.483-495.

3568 Immigrants and assimilation. Jan Rath; John Mollenkopf; Robert Kloosterman; Susan S. Fainstein; Malcolm Cross; Kees van Kersbergen; Enzo Mingione; Enrico Pugliese; Hans Vermeulen; Tjino Venema; Ad van Iterson; Herman G. van de Werfhorst; Gerbert Kraaykamp; Nan Dirk de Graaf; Martha Meerman; Marike van IJssel; René van der Vlist. **Neth. J. Soc. Sci.** 36:2 2000 pp.117-229. *Collection of 12 articles.*

3569 Immigrants in Japan. Hiroshi Komai. **Asian Pacif. Migrat. J.** 9:3 2000 pp.311-326.

3570 Immigrants' pathways to business ownership: a comparative ethnic perspective. Marta Tienda; Rebeca Raijman. **Int. Migr. Rev.** 34:3 Fall:2000 pp.682-706.

3571 Immigrants, schooling and social mobility: does culture make a difference? Hans Vermeulen [Ed.]; Joel Perlmann [Ed.]. Basingstoke: Macmillan, 2000. 288p. *ISBN: 0333793439, 0333793420. Includes index.*

3572 Immigration and opportunity: race, ethnicity, and employment in the United States. Frank D. Bean [Ed.]; Stephanie Bell-Rose [Ed.]. New York: Russell Sage Foundation, 1999. x, 425p. *ISBN: 0871541238. Includes bibliographical references and index.*

3573 Immigrazioni e problematiche religiose. *[In Italian]*; [Immigration and religious problems]. Ugo Taucer. **St. Pol. Soc.** II:1 6:2000 pp.51-67.

3574 Les immigrés nigérians à Douala — problèmes et stratégies d'insertion des étrangers en milieu urbain. *[In French]*; (Integrated Nigerian immigrants in Douala — problems and insertation strategies.) *[Summary]*. Blaise-Jacques Nkene. **Verf. Rec. Über.** 33:1 2000 pp.43-59.

3575 Inmigracion espanola en la Argentina. *[In Spanish]*; [Spanish immigrants in Argentina]. Alejandro E. Fernandez. Buenos Aires: Biblos, 1999. 271p. *ISBN: 9507862277.*

3576 L'intégration politique et culturelle des ethnies minoritaires au Nord-Laos: l'exemple des Phou Noï. *[In French]*; [Political and cultural integration of ethnic minorities in North Laos: the example of Phou Noï]. Olivier Evrard. **Péninsule** 37:2 1998 pp.23-42.

3577 Judging not only by color: ethnicity, nativity, and neighborhood attainment. Michael J. White; Sharon Sassler. **Soc. Sci. Q.** 81:4 12:2000 pp.997-1013.

3578 Korean immigrants and the challenge of adjustment. Moon H. Jo. Westport CT: Greenwood Press, 1999. xix, 189p. *ISBN: 0313309183. Includes bibliographical references (p. [179]-185) and index. (Series:* Contributions in sociology - 127).

3579 Los laberintos de la exclusión: relatos de inmigrantes ilegales en Argentina. *[In Spanish]*; [The labyrinths of exclusion: tales of illegal immigrants in Argentina]. Diego Casaravilla. Buenos Aires: Lumen Humanitas, 1999. 191p. *ISBN: 9507249117. Includes bibliographical references (p. 185-[192]).*

3580 The language ability of U.S. immigrants: assimilation and Cohort effects. Geoffrey Carliner. **Int. Migr. Rev.** XXXIV:1 Spring:2000 pp.158-182.

3581 Life satisfaction of Indian immigrants in Canada. Neharika Vohra; John Adair. **Psychol. Devel. Soc.** 12:2 7-12:2000 pp.109-138.

3582 A model of 'reasonable integration': summary of the first report on the integration of immigrants in Italy. Giovanna Zincone. **Int. Migr. Rev.** 34:3 Fall:2000 pp.956-968.

3583 New Chinese migrants in Europe: the case of the Chinese community in Hungary. Pál Nyíri. Aldershot: Ashgate, 1999. 180p. *ISBN: 075461154X. Includes bibliographical references.*

F: POPULATION. FAMILY. GENDER. ETHNIC GROUPS

3584 The new Germany and migration in Europe. Barbara Marshall. Manchester; New York: Manchester University Press; St. Martin's Press, 2000. 186p. *ISBN: 0719043360, 0719043352*. Includes bibliographical references and index. (*Series:* Europe in change).

3585 (New Slovak immigrants in New York: social networks and adjustment.); *[Text in Slovak]*. Anna Zajacová. **Sociologia [Brat.]** 32:3 Spring:2000 pp.257-272.

3586 Newcomers to Canada from former Yugoslavia: settlement issues. Usha George; A. Ka Tat Tsang. **Int. Soc. Work** 43:3 7:2000 pp.381-402.

3587 *Nikkei* Brazilians and local residents: a study of the H housing complex in Toyota City. Kurumi Tsuzuki. **Asian Pacif. Migrat. J.** 9:3 2000 pp.327-342.

3588 Public assistance receipt across immigrant generations. Peter Brandon; Curt Tausky. **Soc. Sci. R.** 29:2 6:2000 pp.208-222.

3589 Rebuilding the ancestral village: Singaporeans in China. Kuah Khun Eng. Aldershot: Ashgate, 2000. xv, 283p. *ISBN: 075461137X*. Includes bibliographical references and index.

3590 Relations between deprivation and immigrant groups in large Canadian cities. David Ley; Heather Smith. **Urban Stud.** 37:1 1:2000 pp.37-62.

3591 Relationship of perceived culture shock, length of stay in the U.S., depression, and self-esteem in elderly Russian-speaking immigrants. Sergei Tsytsarev; Lana Krichmar. **J. Soc. Distr. Home.** 9:1 1:2000 pp.35-50.

3592 Return migration: changing roles of men and women. Despina Sakka; Maria Dikaiou; Grigoris Kiosseoglou. **Int. Migr.** 37:4 1999 pp.741-764.

3593 The role of Ghanaian immigrant associations in Toronto, Canada. Thomas Y. Owusu. **Int. Migr. Rev.** 34:132 Winter:2000 pp.1155-1181.

3594 Selbständigkeit von Immigranten in Deutschland — Ausgrenzung oder Weg der Integration? *[In German]*; (Self-employment of immigrants in Germany: exclusion or a path to integration?) *[Summary]*. Veysel Özcan; Wolfgang Seifert. **Soz. Welt.** 51:3 2000 pp.289-302.

3595 Slavic and Norwegian language and culture in contact: the influence of the Norwegian language and culture on immigrant youth from the former Yugoslavia; *[Summary in Russian]*; *[Summary in Norwegian]*; *[Summary in Croatian]*. Branka Lie. **Migrac. Teme** 16:1-2 2000 pp.47-64.

3596 Soziale und identifikative Assimilation türkischer Jugendlicher. *[In German]*; (Social and identificational assimilation of young Turkish people.) *[Summary]*; *[Summary in French]*. Robert Kecskes. **Berl. J. Soziol.** 10:1 2000 pp.61-78.

3597 A study of Asian immigrants in global city Tokyo. Junko Tajima. **Asian Pacif. Migrat. J.** 9:3 2000 pp.349-364.

3598 «Translations» politiques et culturelles: les proscrits français et l'Angleterre. *[In French]*; (Political and cultural 'translations': French exiles and England.) Sylvie Aprile. **Genèses** 38 3:2000 pp.33-55.

3599 Transnationalism, African immigration, and new migrant spaces in South Africa. Jonathan Crush; David A. McDonald; Sally Peberdy; Christian Rogerson; Stephen C. Lubkemann; Theresa Ulicki; Maxine Reitzes; Sivuyile Bam; Belinda Dodson; Catherine Oelofse; Brij Maharaj; Vadi Moodley. **Can. J. Afr. St.** 34:1 2000 pp.1-160. *Collection of 8 articles.*

3600 Uncertain travelers: conversations with Jewish women immigrants to America. Marjorie Agosin; Mary G. Berg [Ed.]. Hanover NH: University Press of New England, 1999. vii, 214p. *ISBN: 0874519454*. (*Series:* Brandeis series on Jewish women).

3601 The whore and the other: Israeli images of female immigrants from the former USSR. Dafna Lemish. **Gender Soc.** 14:2 4:2000 pp.333-349.

3602 Women, immigration and identities in France. Jane Freedman [Ed.]; Carrie Tarr [Ed.]. Oxford: Berg Publishers, 2000. 256p. *ISBN: 1859734367, 1859734316*. Includes index.

3603 You can go home again: evidence from longitudinal data. Patricia B. Reagan; Randall J. Olsen. **Demography** 37:3 8:2000 pp.339-350.

3604 You can't take it with you? Immigrant assimilation and the portability of human capital. Rachel M. Friedberg. **J. Labor Ec.** 18:2 4:2000 pp.221-251.

F: POPULATION. FAMILLE. SEXE. GROUPE ETHNIQUE

3605 Zuwanderung nach Deutschland: Strukturen, Wirkungen, Perspektiven. *[In German]*; [Emigration to Germany: structures, consequences, perspectives]. Rainer Münz; Wolfgang Seifert; Ralf E. Ulrich. Frankfurt am Main, New York: Campus, 1999. 225p. *ISBN: 3593363747. Includes bibliographical references (p. [206]-224).*

Internal migration
Migration interne

3606 Age selectivity and inter-provincial net migration in Spain. John Stillwell; Arlinda Garcia Coll. **Espace Pop. Soc.** 1 2000 pp.57-70.
3607 Changing places: migration's social and environmental consequences. Catherine Locke; W. Neil Adger; P. Mick Kelly. **Environment** 42:7 9:2000 pp.24-35.
3608 Commuting, migration, and rural-urban population dynamics. Mitch Renkow; Dale Hoover. **J. Reg. Sc.** 40:2 5:2000 pp.261-288.
3609 The crisis and international population movement in Indonesia. Graeme Hugo. **Asian Pacif. Migrat. J.** 9:1 2000 pp.93-130.
3610 Determinants of migration intentions in Hubei province, China: individual versus family migration. Xiushi Yang. **Envir. Plan. A.** 32:5 5:2000 pp.769-788.
3611 Emergency and development: the case of *Imidugudu*, villagization in Rwanda. Dorothea Hilhorst; Mathijs Van Leeuwen. **J. Refug. S.** 13:3 9:2000 pp.264-280.
3612 Emigration urbaine, crise économique et mutations des campagnes en Côte d'Ivoire. *[In French]*; (Urban emigration, economic crisis and transformations of rural areas in Ivory Coast.) Cris Beauchemin. **Espace Pop. Soc.** 3 1999 pp.399-410.
3613 Expectations, gender, and norms in migration decision-making. Gordon F. De Jong. **Pop. Stud.** 54:3 11:2000 pp.307-320.
3614 Impact of religious involvement on migration. Scott Myers. **Soc. Forc.** 79:2 12:2000 pp.755-766.
3615 Internal displacement in Burma. Steven Lanjouw; Graham Mortimer; Vicky Bamforth. **Disasters** 24:3 9:2000 pp.228-239.
3616 Internal migration in today's Japan. Satoshi Nakagawa. **Geogr. Pol.** 73:1 Spring:2000 pp.127-140.
3617 The interstate migration of U.S. immigrants: individual and contextual determinants. Douglas T. Gurak; Mary M. Kritz. **Soc. Forc.** 78:3 3:2000 pp.1017-1040.
3618 Labor migration and allocation of human resources in Taiwan: return and onward cases. Ji-ping Lin; Ching-lung Tsay. **Asian Pacif. Migrat. J.** 9:1 2000 pp.1-34.
3619 Labour migration as a social security mechanism for smallholder households in Sub-Saharan Africa: the case of Cameroon. Gertrud Schrieder; Béatrice Knerr. **Ox. Dev. Stud.** 28:2 6:2000 pp.223-236.
3620 Migration and age: the effect of age on sensitivity to migration stimuli; *[Summary in French]*; *[Summary in German]*. Jim Millington. **Reg. Stud.** 34:6 8:2000 pp.521-534.
3621 Migration and remittances in island microstates: a comparative perspective on the South Pacific and the Caribbean; *[Summary in French]*. John Connell; Dennis Conway. **Int. J. Urban Reg. Res.** 24:1 3:2000 pp.52-78.
3622 Problems and solutions in the measurement of migration intensities: Australia and Britain compared. Philip Rees; Martin Bell; Oliver Duke-Williams; Marcus Blake. **Pop. Stud.** 54:2 7:2000 pp.207-222.
3623 Residence spells and migration: a comparison for men and women. Cecile Détang-Dessendre; Ian Molho. **Urban Stud.** 37:2 2:2000 pp.247-260.
3624 Through the developmentalist's looking glass: conflict-induced displacement and involuntary resettlement in Colombia. Robert Muggah. **J. Refug. S.** 13:2 6:2000 pp.133-164.
3625 Types and patterns of later-life migration. William H. Walters. **Geogr. Ann. B.** 82(B):3 2000 pp.129-148.

F: POPULATION. FAMILY. GENDER. ETHNIC GROUPS

3626 The urban factors and transition of China's rural surplus labor. Zhaohui Hong; Hong Liang. **Asian Prof.** 28:2 4:2000 pp.87-98.

3627 V dvizhenii dobrovol'nom i vynuzhdennom: postsovetskie migratsii v Evrazii. *[In Russian]*; (On the move, voluntarily and involuntarily: migration in Eurasia.) *[Summary]*. S.A. Panarin [Ed.]; N.P Kosmarskaia [Ed.]; Anatolii Rudol'fovich Viatkin [Ed.]. Moscow: Izd-vo Natalis, 1999. 319p. *ISBN: 5806200094. Includes bibliographical references and index.*

3628 'We came for the work': situating employment migration in B.C.'s small resource-based, communities; *[Summary in French]*. Greg Halseth. **Can. Geogr.** 43:4 Winter:1999 pp.363-381.

International migration
Migration internationale

3629 Peopling skilled international migration: Indian doctors in the UK; *[Summary in French]*; *[Summary in Spanish]*. Vaughan Robinson; Malcolm Carey. **Int. Migr.** 38:1 2000 pp.89-108.

3630 Anti-immigrant sentiment and the problem of reproduction/maintenance in Mexican immigration to the United States. Tamar Diana Wilson. **Crit. Anthr.** 20:2 6:2000 pp.191-213.

3631 Aussiedler seit 1989 — Bilanz und Perspektiven. *[In German]*; [Emigrants since 1989 - outcome and perpectives]. Klaus F. Zimmermann. **Jahrb. Wirt. Gesch.** 1 2000 pp.225-237.

3632 *Beyond the Melting Pot* thirty-five years later: on the relevance of a sociological classic for the immigration metropolis of today. Richard Alba; Alejandro Portes; Philip Kasinitz; Nancy Foner; Elijah Anderson; Nathan Glazer. **Int. Migr. Rev.** XXXIV:1 Spring:2000 pp.243-279.

3633 The brain drain. Will the outflow of skilled people kill the African renaissance? David A. McDonald; Jonathan Crush; Robert Mattes; Wayne Richmond; C.M. Rogerson; J.M. Rogerson; Mercy Brown; David Kaplan; Jean-Baptiste Meyer; Eugene K. Campbell; John O. Oucho; John Gay. **Afr. Insight** 30:2 10:2000 pp.5-74. *Collection of 8 articles.*

3634 Citizenship and migration: globalization and the politics of belonging. Stephen Castles; Alastair Davidson. Basingstoke: Macmillan, 2000. 272p. *ISBN: 0333643100, 0333643097. Includes index.*

3635 Dépasser l'exil. Degrés de médiation et stratégies de transfert littéraire chez des exilés de l'Europe de l'Est en France. *[In French]*; (Getting beyond exile. Degrees of mediation and strategies of literary transfer adopted by Eastern Europeans exiled in France.) Ioana Popa. **Genèses** 38 3:2000 pp.5-32.

3636 Diaspora żydowska: refleksje nowszej literatury przedmiotu. *[In Polish]*; (The Jewish diaspora in the latest publications.) Adam Walaszek. **Prz. Pol.** XXV:4(94) 1999 pp.45-72.

3637 The effects of development on migration: theoretical issues and new empirical evidence. M. Vogler; R. Rotte. **J. Pop. Ec.** 13:3 2000 pp.485-508.

3638 *El ghorba*: from original sin to collective lie. Abdelmalek Sayad. **Ethnog.** 1:2 12:2000 pp.147-172.

3639 Eldorado or fortress? Migration in Southern Europe. Russell King [Ed.]; Gabriella Lazaridis [Ed.]; Charalambos Tsardanidis [Ed.]. Basingstoke: Macmillan, 2000. xiv, 351p. *ISBN: 0333747909, 0312226152. Includes bibliographical references and index.*

3640 Ethnocide: a cultural narrative of refugee detention in Hong Kong. Joe Thomas. Aldershot: Ashgate, 2000. xii, 255p. *ISBN: 1840148292. Includes bibliographical references. (Series: Social and political studies from Hong Kong).*

3641 Exodus? Some social and policy implications of return migration from the UK to the Commonwealth Caribbean in the 1990s. Harry Goulbourne. **Policy St.** 20:3 9:1999 pp.157-172.

F: POPULATION. FAMILLE. SEXE. GROUPE ETHNIQUE

3642 Exporting people: the Philippines and contract labor in Palau. Dean Alegado; Gerard Finin. **Cont. Pac.** 12:2 Fall:2000 pp.359-370.
3643 Fact or fable? The consequences of migration for educational achievement and labor market participation. Cluny Macpherson; Richard Bedford; Paul Spoonley. **Cont. Pac.** 12:1 Spring:2000 pp.57-82.
3644 The Filipino 'entertainers' in Japan. Nobuhiko Fuwa. **Phil. Stud.** 47:3 1999 pp.319-350.
3645 Gender and transnational household strategies: Singaporean migration to China; *[Summary in French]*; *[Summary in German]*. Katie D. Willis; Brenda S.A. Yeoh. **Reg. Stud.** 34:3 5:2000 pp.253-264.
3646 Gendering the Irish diaspora: questions of enrichment, hybridization and return. Breda Gray. **Wom. St. Inter. For.** 23:2 3-4:2000 pp.167-186.
3647 German and Jewish migration from the former Soviet Union to Germany: background, trends and implications. Barbara Dietz. **J. Eth. Migr. St.** 26:4 10:2000 pp.635-652.
3648 Global migration, ethnic media and ethnic identity. Shigehiko Shiramizu. **Asian Pacif. Migrat. J.** 9:3 2000 pp.273-286.
3649 Guess who's coming to dinner: migration from Lesotho, Mozambique and Zimbabwe to South Africa. David A. McDonald; Lovemore Zinyama; John Gay; Fion de Vletter; Robert Mattes. **Int. Migr. Rev.** 34:3 Fall:2000 pp.813-841.
3650 The Hindu diaspora: comparative patterns. Steven Vertovec. London: Routledge, 2000. 192p. *ISBN: 0415238935, 0415238927. Includes bibliographical references and index.*
3651 Imagining the future of migration and families in Asia. Maruja M.B. Asis. **Asian Pacif. Migrat. J.** 9:3 2000 pp.255-272.
3652 L'immigrazione albanese in Puglia: saggi interdisciplinari. *[In Italian]*; [Albanian immigration in Puglia: interdisciplinary studies]. Giovanna Da Molin [Ed.]. Bari: Cacucci, 1999. 211p. *Includes bibliographical references.*
3653 Immigrazione, multicultura, intercultura: tematiche dei nostri tempi. *[In Italian]*; [Immigration, multiculturalism, interculturalism: themes of our time]. Maria Immacolata Macioti. **Sociologia [Rome]** XXXIV:1 2000 pp.23-32.
3654 India and experience of Indian diaspora in Africa. Ajay Kumar Dubey. **Afr. Q.** 40:2 2000 pp.69-92.
3655 Indonesian immigrant settlements in Peninsular Malaya. Azizah Kassim. **SOJOURN** 15:1 4:2000 pp.100-122.
3656 Into the margins: migration and exclusion in Southern Europe. Floya Anthias [Ed.]; Gabriella Lazaridis [Ed.]. Aldershot: Ashgate, 1999. xi, 222p. *ISBN: 1840141166. Includes index.*
3657 Issues and challenges of foreign workers in Asia. Raymond K.H. Chan; Moha Asri Abdullah. **Asian Prof.** 27:5 10:1999 pp.441-456.
3658 Japan and labor migration: theoretical and methodological implications of negative cases. David Bartram. **Int. Migr. Rev.** XXXIV:1 Spring:2000 pp.5-32.
3659 Las migraciones en un mundo globalizado. *[In Spanish]*; (Migration in a globalised world.) *[Summary]*. André Linard. **Rev. Fom. Soc.** 55:218 4-6:2000 pp.271-288.
3660 Migration and threat to identity. L. Timotijevic; G.M. Breakwell. **J. Comm. App. Soc. Psychol.** 10:5 9-10:2000 pp.355-372.
3661 Migration of Mexican seasonal farm workers to Canada and development: obstacles to productive investment. Tanya Basok. **Int. Migr. Rev.** XXXIV:1 Spring:2000 pp.79-97.
3662 The motivation to migrate: the ethnic and sociocultural constitution of the Japanese-Brazilian return-migration system. Takeyuki Tsuda. **Econ. Dev. Cult. Change** 48:1 10:1999 pp.1-32.
3663 Nepalese labour migration to Japan: from global warriors to global workers. Keiko Yamanaka. **Ethn. Racial** 23:1 1:2000 pp.62-93.
3664 Les parcours migratoires des réfugiés vers la Suède et l'Europe du Nord. *[In French]*; [Migration flow of refugees towards Sweden and Northern Europe]. Mohamed Kamel Doraï. **R. Et. Palest.** 75:23 Spring:2000 pp.38-52.
3665 Pathways abroad: gender and international migration recruitment choices in northern Thailand. Teresa Sobieszczyk. **Asian Pacif. Migrat. J.** 9:4 2000 pp.391-428.

F: POPULATION. FAMILY. GENDER. ETHNIC GROUPS

3666 Psychosocial wellness of refugees: issues in qualitative and quantitative research. Frederick L. Ahearn, Jr. [Ed.]. New York, Oxford: Berghahn Books, 2000. xvii, 251p. *ISBN: 1571812059, 1571812040. Volume 7. Includes bibliographical references and index.* (*Series:* Studies in forced migration).

3667 Push-and-pull migration and satisficing versus optimizing migratory behavior: a review and Nepalese evidence. Clem Tisdell; Gopal Regmi. **Asian Pacif. Migrat. J.** 9:2 2000 pp.213-230.

3668 Raspad CCCP: etnicheskie migratsii i problema diaspor. *[In Russian]*; (Decomposition of the USSR: ethnic migration and the diaspora problem.) A. Vishnevskii. **Obshch. Nauki Sovrem.** 3 2000 pp.115-130.

3669 Reconstructing an inclusive citizenship for a new millennium: globalization, migration and difference. Yasmeen Abu-Laban. **Int. Politics** 37:4 12:2000 pp.509-526.

3670 Reframing the migration question: an analysis of men, women, and gender in Mexico. Shawn Malia Kanaiaupuni. **Soc. Forc.** 78:4 6:2000 pp.1311-1348.

3671 Regional cooperation on labor issues. Fung-yea Huang. **Asian Pacif. Migrat. J.** 9:2 2000 pp.199-212.

3672 Regulating immigration in a global age: a new policy landscape. Saskia Sassen. **Ann. Am. Poli.** 570 7:2000 pp.65-77.

3673 Relative success of male workers in the host country, Kuwait: does the channel of migration matter? Nasra M. Shah. **Int. Migr. Rev.** XXXIV:1 Spring:2000 pp.59-78.

3674 Repatriation and self-settled refugees in Zambia: bringing solutions to the wrong problems. Oliver Bakewell. **J. Refug. S.** 13:4 12:2000 pp.356-373.

3675 Rights and ratios? Evaluating the relationship between social rights and immigration. Brian K. Gran; Elizabeth J. Clifford. **J. Eth. Migr. St.** 26:3 7:2000 pp.417-448.

3676 The role of the maternal in diasporic cultural reproduction—Australia, Canada and Greece. Georgina Tsolidis. **Soc. Sem.** 11:2 8:2001 pp.193-208.

3677 Stable instability of displaced people in western Georgia: a food-security and gender survey after five years. Jose Luis Vivero Pol. **J. Refug. S.** 12:4 12:1999 pp.349-366.

3678 Strategies for global migration among Pakistani workers in Japan. Yasumasa Igarashi. **Asian Pacif. Migrat. J.** 9:3 2000 pp.375-386.

3679 Sunset lives: British retirement migration to the Mediterranean. Russell King; Allan M. Williams; Tony Warnes. Oxford: Berg Publishers, 2000. 235p. *ISBN: 185973362X, 1859733573. Includes index.*

3680 'They got game' asylum rights and marginality in the diaspora: the World Cup and Iranian exiles. Manuchehr Sanadjian. **Soc. Ident.** 6:2 6:2000 pp.143-164.

3681 Transboundary population movements: refugees, environment and politics. Nesrin Algan; Özlen Künçek. **Turk. Year. Int. Rel.** XXVIII 1998 pp.75-103.

3682 Les transformations de la migration internationale au Mexique: conditions de crise et logiques territoriales dans les années 1990. *[In French]*; [The transformation of international migration in Mexico: crisis conditions and territorial logic in the 1990s]. Laurent Faret. **Cah. Amer. Lat.** 31-32 1999 pp.231-260.

3683 Transnationalization in international migration: implications for the study of citizenship and culture. Thomas Faist. **Ethn. Racial** 23:2 3:2000 pp.189-222.

3684 The turbulence of migration: globalization, deterritorialization, and hybridity. Nikos Papastergiadis. Malden MA: Polity Press, 2000. 246p. *ISBN: 0745614302, 0745614310. Includes bibliographical references and index.*

3685 Új ázsiai migráció Kelet-Európába: a magyarországi kínaiak. *[In Hungarian]*; (New Asian migration to Eastern Europe: the case of Chinese in Hungary.) *[Summary]*. Pál Nyíri. **Regio** 10:3-4 1999 pp.93-104.

3686 The volume and dynamics of international migration. Thomas Faist. Oxford, New York: Oxford University Press, 2000. 380p. *ISBN: 0198293917, 0198297262. Includes bibliographical references and index.*

G: ENVIRONMENT. COMMUNITY. RURAL. URBAN
ENVIRONNEMENT. COMMUNAUTÉ. RURAL. URBAIN

G.1: Environment. Ecology. Geography. Human settlements
Environnement. Écologie. Géographie. Établissements humains

3687 Being constructive: social constructionism and the environment. Kate Burningham; Geoff Cooper. **Sociology** 33:2 5:1999 pp.297-316.
3688 Bioregionalism. Michael Vincent McGinnis [Ed.]. London, New York: Routledge, 1999. xvii, 231p. *ISBN: 0415154448, 0415154456. Includes index.*
3689 Culture, landscape, and the environment: the Linacre lectures, 1997. Kate Flint [Ed.]; Howard Morphy [Ed.]. Oxford, New York: Oxford University Press, 2000. xii, 225p. *ISBN: 0198233787. Includes bibliographical references and index. (Series:* The Linacre lectures).
3690 Drought: a global assessment. Donald A. Wilhite [Ed.]. London: Routledge, 2000. *ISBN: 0415168333, 0415168341, 0415214181. Includes bibliographical references and indexes. (Series:* Routledge hazards and disasters).
3691 Environments and historical change. Paul Slack [Ed.]. Oxford, New York: Oxford University Press, 1999. x, 196p. *ISBN: 0198233884. Includes bibliographical references and index. (Series:* Linacre lectures - 1998).
3692 Från altarring till prästgårdskök. *[In Swedish]*; (From the altar rails to the kitchen of the vicarage: on place, space and gender.) Birgitta Meurling. **Rig** 4 2000 pp.206-219.
3693 Geografía y teoría social: los actores y la construcción del territorio. *[In Spanish]*; [Geography and social theory: the actors and the construction of territory]. Rocío Rosales Ortega. **Acta Sociol.** [Mexico] 25 1-4:1999 pp.81-104.
3694 Geographical perspectives on the public good. Bryan Massam. **Can. Geogr.** 43:4 Winter:1999 pp.346-362.
3695 Loss, healing, and the power of place. Helen M. Cox; Colin A. Holmes. **Human St.** 23:1 1:2000 pp.63-78.
3696 Natuur en gezondheid een verkennend onderzoek naar de relatie tussen volksgezondheid en groen in de leefomgeving. *[In Dutch]*; (Nature and health: an exploratory investigation of the relationship between health and green space in the living environment.) *[Summary]*. Sjerp de Vries; Robert A. Verheij; Peter P. Groenewegen. **Mens Maat.** 75:4 12:2000 pp.320-339.
3697 Privileged narratives and fictions of consent in environmental discourse. Simon Bourke; Tony Meppem. **Loc. Env.** 5:3 8:2000 pp.299-310.
3698 Resource, Arcadia, lifeworld. Nature concepts in environmental sociology. C.S.A. Kris van Koppen. **Sociol. Rur.** 40:3 7:2000 pp.300-318.
3699 Response to disaster: fact versus fiction & its repercussion : the sociology of disaster. Henry W. Fischer. Lanham MD: University Press of America, 1998. 218p. *Includes bibliographical references and index.*
3700 Social science and the absence of nature: uncertainty and the reality of extremes. Reiner Grundmann; Nico Stehr. **Soc. Sci. Info.** 39:1 3:2000 pp.155-180.
3701 Theoretical stances and environmental debates: reconciling the physical and the symbolic. Steve Kroll-Smith; Valerie Gunter; Shirley Laska. **Am. Sociol.** 31:1 Spring:2000 pp.44-61.
3702 Urban hazards and risks; consequences of large eruptions and earthquakes. Jean-Claude Thouret; James K. Mitchell; Avijit Gupta; Rafi Ahmad; Jan J. Nossin; C. Bardinet; E. Bournay; Omkar M. Shrestha; Achyuta Koirala; Jörg Hanisch; Klaus Busch; Martin Kerntke; Stefan Jäger; Franck Lavigne; J.L. Chatelain; B. Tucker; B. Guillier; F. Kaneko; H. Yepes; J. Fernandez; J. Valverde; G. Hoefer; M. Souris; E. Dupérier; T. Yamada; G. Bustamante; C. Villacis; Anne-Catherine Chardon; Pascale Metzger; Robert D'Ercole; Alexis Sierra; Frédéric Leone; Jean-Christophe Gaillard. **Geojournal** 49:2 1999 pp.131-238. *Collection of 11 articles.*

G: ENVIRONMENT. COMMUNITY. RURAL. URBAN

3703 The value of nature's otherness. Simon A. Hailwood. **Environ. Values** 9:3 8:2000 pp.353-372.
3704 World risk society. Ulrich Beck. Malden MA: Polity Press, 1999. viii, 184p. *ISBN: 0745622208, 0745622216. Includes bibliographical references (p. [161]-167) and index.*

Ecology
Écologie

3705 The accommodation of value in environmental decision-making. Ronan Palmer; Paul Anand; James Lenman; Clive L. Spash; Anthony C. Burton; Susan M. Chilton; Martin K. Jones; Arild Vatn; Jonathan Burney; John O'Neill. **Environ. Values** 9:4 11:2000 pp.411-542. *Collection of 8 articles.*
3706 Actitudes y comportamientos hacia el medioambiente en España. *[In Spanish]*; [Attitudes and behaviour towards the environment in Spain]. Cristóbal Gómez Benito; Francisco Javier Noya; Ángel Paniagua Mazorra. Madrid: Centro de Investigaciones Sociológicas, 1999. 150p. *ISBN: 8474762790.*
3707 The ambiguity of 'watershed': the politics of people and conservation in northern Thailand. Pinkaew Laungaramsri. **SOJOURN** 15:1 4:2000 pp.52-75.
3708 The assessment of vulnerability and adaptation to climatic change impacts in Tanzania. Mark J. Mwandosya; Buruhani S. Nyenzi; Mathew L. Luhanga. Dar es Salaam: CEEST, 1998. xx, 235p. *ISBN: 9987612113. Includes bibliographical references. Centre for Energy, Environment, Science and Technology.*
3709 Beaches and dunes of developed coasts. Karl F. Nordstrom. New York: Cambridge University Press, 2000. xiii, 338p. *ISBN: 0521470137. Includes bibliographical references (p. 287-332) and index.*
3710 Beyond birds: biopower and birdwatching in the world of Audubon. Timothy W. Luke. **Cap. Nat. Social.** 11(3):43 9:2000 pp.7-37.
3711 The carbon war: global warming at the end of the oil era. Jeremy Leggett. London, New York: Penguin, 2000. xiii, 341p. *ISBN: 014028494X.*
3712 Classical sociology and the restoration of nature: the relevance of Émile Durkheim and Georg Simmel. Matthias Gross. **Org. Environ.** 13:3 9:2000 pp.277-291.
3713 Conciencia (post-) moderna de la crisis: reflexiones acerca de posibles soluciones a la catástrofe. *[In Spanish]*; [(Post)modern awareness of crisis: reflections on possible solutions to catastophe] *[Summary]*. Harald Holz. **Apuntes** 45 1999 pp.107-120.
3714 Coping with changing environments: social dimensions of endangered ecosystems in the developing world. Helmut Geist [Ed.]; Beate Lohnert [Ed.]. Aldershot: Ashgate, 1999. xxi, 330p. *ISBN: 1840149582. Includes index.*
3715 Demographic covariates of residential recycling efficiency. Julie Owens; Sharyn Dickerson; David L. MacIntosh. **Envir. Behav.** 32:5 9:2000 pp.637-650.
3716 Demographic transition in ecological focus. Edward M. Crenshaw; Matthew Christenson; Doyle Ray Oakey. **Am. Sociol. R.** 65:3 6:2000 pp.371-391.
3717 Discourses of the environment. Éric Darier [Ed.]. Oxford: Blackwell Publishers, 1999. xii, 276p. *ISBN: 0631211233, 0631211225. Includes bibliographical references and index.*
3718 Ecological modernisation around the world: perfectives and critical debates. Arthur P.J. Mol [Ed.]; David Allan Sonnenfeld [Ed.]. London, Portland OR: Frank Cass, 2000. 300p. *ISBN: 071468113X, 0714650641. Includes bibliographical references and index.*
3719 Ecology today: beyond the bounds of science. Mohan K. Wali. **Nat. Resour.** 35:2 4-6:1999 pp.38-50.
3720 Ecosocialism and feminism: deep materialism and the contradictions of capitalism. Alan Dordoy; Mary Mellor. **Cap. Nat. Social.** 11(3):43 9:2000 pp.41-61.
3721 Endless/end-less natures: environmental futures at the Fin de Millennium. Rob Bartram; Sarah Shobrook. **Ann. As. Am. G.** 90:2 6:2000 pp.370-380.

G: ENVIRONNEMENT. COMMUNAUTÉ. RURAL. URBAIN

3722   Environment and global modernity. A. P. J. Mol [Ed.]; Frederick H. Buttel [Ed.]; Gert. Spaargaren [Ed.]. London: Sage Publications, 2000. 256p. *ISBN: 0761967672, 0761967664.*

3723   Environment, education, and society in the Asia-Pacific: local traditions and global discourses. David Yencken [Ed.]; John Fien [Ed.]; Helen Sykes [Ed.]. New York: Routledge, 2000. 341p. *ISBN: 0415205816. Includes bibliographical references and index.*

3724   Environmental education and attitudes: emotions and beliefs are what is needed. Julie Ann Pooley; Moira O'Connor. **Envir. Behav.** 32:5 9:2000 pp.711-723.

3725   The environmental impact of suburbanization. Matthew E. Kahn. **J. Policy An.** 19:4 Fall:2000 pp.569-586.

3726   Environmental values, beliefs, and actions: a situational approach. José A. Corraliza; Jaime Berenguer. **Envir. Behav.** 32:6 11:2000 pp.832-848.

3727   Environnement et mondialisation: de la confusion à la convergence des discours. *[In French]*; [Environment and globalization: from confusion to convergence of the discourse] *[Summary]*. René Blais. **Can. Geogr.** 44:3 Fall:2000 pp.286-297.

3728   Following the flow of Japan's river culture. Paul Waley. **Jpn. Forum** 12:2 2000 pp.199-217.

3729   How green is my valley? Tracking rural and urban environmentalism in the Southern Appalachian ecoregion. Robert Emmet Jones; J. Mark Fly; H. Ken Cordell. **Rural Sociol.** 64:3 9:1999 pp.482-499.

3730   In the name of solidarity: the politics of representation and articulation in support of the Labrador Innu. Jennifer Barron. **Cap. Nat. Social.** 11(3):43 9:2000 pp.87-112.

3731   Income distribution and environmental degradation in the Argentine interior. Larry Sawers. **Lat. Am. Res. R.** 35:2 2000 pp.3-33.

3732   Indigenous people, traditional people, and conservation in the Amazon. Manuela Carneiro da Cunha; Mauro W.B. de Almeida. **Dædalus** 129:2 Spring:2000 pp.315-338.

3733   Intensification, degradation and soil improvement: utilising structuration theory for a differentiated analysis of population and pressure outcomes in highland Tanzania. Samantha Jones. **Sing. J. Trop. Geogr.** 21:2 7:2000 pp.131-148.

3734   Is trust a realistic goal of environmental risk communication? Lillian Trettin; Catherine Musham. **Envir. Behav.** 32:3 5:2000 pp.410-426.

3735   Islands of rainforest: agroforestry, logging and eco-tourism in the Solomon Islands. Edvard Hviding; Tim Bayliss-Smith. Aldershot: Ashgate, 2000. xvii, 390p. *ISBN: 0754612333. Includes bibliographical references and index. University of London, School of Oriental and African Studies. (Series:* SOAS studies in development geography).

3736   Leaving a person behind: history, personhood, and struggles over forest resources in the Sangha Basin of equatorial Africa. Tamara Giles-Vernick. **Int. J. Afr. H. S.** 32:2-3 1999 pp.311-338.

3737   Life and environment in the Mediterranean. L. Trabaud [Ed.]. Southampton: WIT, 1999. 300p. *ISBN: 1853126802.*

3738   Living in the environment: principles, connections and solutions. G. Tyler Miller, Jr. Belmont CA, London: Brooks/Cole, 2000. xxiii, 815p. *ISBN: 053456268X, 0534562698.*

3739   Local forest protection, gender and caste — Dhani Hill, Orissa, India. Madelene Ostwald; Ranjan Baral. **Geogr. Ann. B.** 82(B):3 2000 pp.115-128.

3740   The matter of freedom: ecofeminist lessons for social ecology. John Clark. **Cap. Nat. Social.** 11(3):43 9:2000 pp.62-80.

3741   Modélisation d'une interaction individus, espace et société par les systèmes multi-agents: pâture en forêt virtuelle. *[In French]*; (Using multi-agent systems to model interaction between individuals, space and society: pasture in a virtual forest.) *[Summary]*. Jean-Luc Bonnefoy; François Bousquet; Juliette Rouchier. **Espace Géogr.** 30:1 2001 pp.13-25.

3742   Mujer y cultura ecológica. *[In Spanish]*; [Women and ecological culture]. Elizabeth Maier. **Tareas** 104 1-4:2000 pp.123-144.

3743   A multinational perspective on the relation between Judeo-Christian religious beliefs and attitudes of environmental concern. P. Wesley Schultz; Lynnette Zelezny; Nancy J. Dalrymple. **J. App. Behav. Sc.** 32:4 7:2000 pp.576-591.

G: ENVIRONMENT. COMMUNITY. RURAL. URBAN

3744 Nature, purity, ontology. Piers H.G. Stephens. **Environ. Values** 9:3 8:2000 pp.267-294.
3745 The nearshore as public space: controlling access to the coastal ocean. Michael Craghan; James DeFilippis. **Urban Geogr.** 21:3 4-5:2000 pp.193-204.
3746 Polar bonds: environmental relationships in the polar regions. G. Daniel Steel. **Envir. Behav.** 32:6 11:2000 pp.796-816.
3747 Politicized moral geographies debating biodiversity conservation and ancestral domain in the Philippines. Raymond L. Bryant. **Pol. Geogr.** 19:6 8:2000 pp.673-705.
3748 Postawy wobec środowiska naturalnego i ich korelaty. Z badań nad mieszkańcami gmin. *[In Polish]*; (Attitudes towards natural environment and their correlates. Findings of surveys focussed on rural inhabitants.) *[Summary]*. Ewa Rokicka. **Prz. Soc.** XLIX:1 2000 pp.121-146.
3749 Promoting environmentalism. Lynnette C. Zelezny; P. Wesley Schultz; Stuart Oskamp; Paul Stern; Riley Dunlap; Kent Van Liere; Angela Mertig; Robert Emmet Jones; Poh-Pheng Chua; Christina Aldrich; Susan Clayton; Susan Opotow; Leah Weiss; Stephen Kaplan; Raymond De Young; Renee Bator; Robert Cialdini; Doug McKenzie-Mohr; Robert D. Bullard; Glenn S. Johnson. **J. Soc. Issues** 56:3 Fall:2000 pp.365-578. *Collection of 13 articles.*
3750 Recent representations in popular environmental discourse: individualism, wastefulness and the global economy; *[Summary in French]*. Glenda Wall. **Can. R. Soc. A.** 37:3 8:2000 pp.249-266.
3751 Response to disaster: psychosocial, community, and ecological approaches. Richard Gist [Ed.]; Bernard Lubin [Ed.]. Philadelphia PA: Brunner/Mazel, 1999. xiv, 363p. *ISBN: 0876309988, 0876309996. Includes bibliographical references and index. (Series:* Series in clinical and community psychology).
3752 Revealing the vulnerability of people and places: a case study of Georgetown county, South Carolina. Susan L. Cutter; Jerry T. Mitchell; Michael S. Scott. **Ann. As. Am. G.** 90:4 12:2000 pp.713-737.
3753 The reworking of conservation geographies: nonequilibrium landscapes and nature-society hybrids. Karl S. Zimmerer. **Ann. As. Am. G.** 90:2 6:2000 pp.356-369.
3754 Rights to land and resources in Argentina's Alerces national park. D. Aagesen. **B. Lat. Am. Res.** 19:4 10:2000 pp.547-570.
3755 Sage scrub revolution? Property rights, political fragmentation, and conservation planning in southern California under the federal endangered species act. Thomas D. Feldman; Andrew E.G. Jonas. **Ann. As. Am. G.** 90:2 6:2000 pp.256-292.
3756 Social and ecological resilience: are they related? W. Neil Adger. **Prog. H. Geog.** 24:3 9:2000 pp.347-364.
3757 The spatial association between U.S. immigrant residential concentration and environmental hazards. Lori M. Hunter. **Int. Migr. Rev.** 34:2 Summer:2000 pp.460-488.
3758 The study of environmental beliefs by facet analysis: research in the Canary Islands, Spain. Bernardo Hernández; Ernesto Suárez; Juan Martínez-Torvisco; Stephany Hess. **Envir. Behav.** 32:5 9:2000 pp.612-636.
3759 Symposium: is humanity destined to self-destruct? Gary Bryner; Heiner Benking; Herman E. Daly; Bruna De Marchi; Lorraine Elliott; Joel E. Cohen; David E. Bloom; Gerard Fairtlough; Mario Giampietro; Max Falque; Renato Guimaraes, Jr.; Garrett Hardin; Sheila Jasanoff; Martin W. Lewis; T.N. Khoshoo; Mohamed Kassas; Kai N. Lee; Lennart J. Lundqvist; Giridhari Lal Pandit; Tatu Vanhanen; Carlos Martin-Cantarino; Donald N. Michael; David Pimentel; Marcia Pimentel; Yvonne Rydin; Kristin Shrader-Frechette; Leslie Paul Thiele; S. Holly Stocking; Geoffrey Wandesforde-Smith; Nicholas Watts; Lynton Keith Caldwell. **Polit. Life Sci.** 18:2 9:1999 pp.201-284. *Collection of 29 articles.*
3760 To what extent can direct selling of farm produce offer a more environmentally friendly type of farming? Some evidence from France. A.W. Gilg. **J. Environ. Manag.** 60:3 11:2000 pp.195-214.
3761 Tourism, development, wetland degradation and beach erosion in Antigua, West Indies; *[Summary in French]*. Jeff Baldwin. **Tour. Geog.** 2:2 5:2000 pp.193-218.

G: ENVIRONNEMENT. COMMUNAUTÉ. RURAL. URBAIN

3762 Transboundary environmental problems and cultural theory: the protection of the Rhine and the Great Lakes. Marco Verweij. Basingstoke; New York: Palgrave; St. Martin's Press, 2000. 260p. *ISBN: 0333915631. Includes bibliographical references and index.*

3763 La valorisation du tourisme dans les espaces protégés européens: quelles orientations possibles? *[In French]*; (The enhanced value of tourism in Europe's protected areas: which possible directions?) L. Laurens; B. Cousseau. **Ann. Géogr.** 109:613 5-6:2000 pp.240-258.

3764 Visions of a new earth: religious perspectives on population, consumption, and ecology. Harold G. Coward [Ed.]; Daniel C. Maguire [Ed.]. Albany NY: State University of New York Press, 2000. vii, 234p. *ISBN: 0791444570, 0791444589. Includes bibliographical references and index.*

3765 The whole house book: ecological building design and materials. Pat Borer; Cindy Harris; Graham Preston [Illus.]; Benedicte Foo [Illus.]. Machynlleth: National Centre for Alternative Technology, 1998. 312p. *ISBN: 1898049211. Includes bibliographical references (p. 299-300) and index.*

3766 Why people oppose dams: environment and culture in subsistence economies. Vinod Raina. **Inter-Asia Cult. St.** 1:1 4:2000 pp.145-161.

Human geography
Géographie humaine

3767 Actors, activities, and the geographical scene. Studies on time-geography, mobility, and gender. Kajsa Ellegård; Ben de Pater; Bo Lenntorp; María Ángeles Díaz-Muñoz; María Jesús Salado-García; Concepción Díaz-Castillo; Bertil Vilhelmson; Joos Droogleever Fortuijn; Martin Dijst; Hiroo Kamiya; Masaki Kawase; B. Folasade Iyun; Yoga Rasanayagam; Joan Fairhurst; Moserwa Rosina Phalatse; Alba Caballé; María José Prados Velasco. **Geojournal** 48:3 1999 pp.149-258. *Collection of 14 articles.*

3768 Amazonie: la fin d'une frontière? *[In French]*; [Amazonia: the end of a frontier?] *[Summary]*; *[Summary in Portuguese]*. Martine Droulers; François-Michel Le Tourneau. **Caravelle** 75 2000 pp.109-136.

3769 Atlas of changing South Africa. A.J. Christopher. London: Routledge, 2000. 216p. *ISBN. 0415211786, 0415211778. Includes bibliographical references.*

3770 Development geography. Rupert Hodder. New York: Routledge, 2000. 176p. *ISBN: 0415142105, 0415142113. Includes bibliographical references and index. (Series: Routledge contemporary human geography series).*

3771 Development of settlements and regions. Erik Bylund; Riccardo Petrella; Denise Pumain; Assefa Mehretu; Bruce Wm. Pigozzi; Lawrence M. Sommers; R.G. Ironside. **Geogr. Ann. B.** 82(B):2 2000 pp.57-114. *Collection of 5 articles.*

3772 The 'eager gaze of the tourist' meets 'our grandfathers' guns': producing and contesting the land of enchantment in Gallup, New Mexico. Bruce D'Arcus. **Envir. Plan. D.** 18:6 12:2000 pp.693-714.

3773 L'essentiel de la géographie économique et humaine de la France. *[In French]*; [The foundations of economic and human geography in France]. Paul Busuttil. Paris: Gualino éditeur, 1999. 95p. *ISBN: 2842002229. Includes bibliographical references (p. [92]).*

3774 Human geography today. John Allen [Ed.]; Philip Sarre [Ed.]; Doreen B. Massey [Ed.]. Cambridge; Malden MA: Polity Press; Blackwell Publishers, 1999. xi, 340p. *ISBN: 0745621899, 0745621880. Includes bibliographical references and index.*

3775 Institutional geographies. L. Kong [Ed.]; C. Philo; V.J. Del Casino, Jr.; A.J. Grimes; S.P. Hanna; J.P. Jones, III; G. Davies; J. Holloway; J. Tooke; O. Valins; L. Saugeres. **Soc. Sci. Q.** 31:4 11:2000 pp.513-599. *Collection of 7 articles.*

3776 Insulares Südostasien. *[In German]*; [Island Southeast Asia] *[Summary]*. Lothar Schwarzkopf; Hans-Ulrich Schmincke; Ulrich Scholz; Harald Leisch; Samuel Wälty; Frauke Kraas; Hans Fischer; Stefan Seitz; Klaus-Albrecht Pretzell; Stefan Thiebes. **Geogr. Rund.** 52:4 4:2000 pp.4-63. *Collection of 11 articles.*

G: ENVIRONMENT. COMMUNITY. RURAL. URBAN

3777 Interpreting the Civil Rights movement: place, memory, and conflict. Owen J. Dwyer. **Prof. Geogr.** 52:4 11:2000 pp.660-671.

3778 The Irish diaspora. Andy Bielenberg [Ed.]. Harlow, New York: Longman, 2000. *ISBN: 0582369983, 0582369975. Includes bibliographical references and index.*

3779 Landscape and identity: geographies of nation and class in England. Wendy Joy Darby. Oxford: Berg Publishers, 2000. 224p. *ISBN: 1859734308, 1859734251. Includes bibliographical references.*

3780 Moral progress in human geography: transcending the place of good fortune. David M. Smith. **Prog. H. Geog.** 24:1 2000 pp.1-18.

3781 Place, social relations and the fear of crime: a review. Rachel Pain. **Prog. H. Geog.** 24:3 9:2000 pp.365-388.

3782 Postcolonial geographies: an exploratory essay. James D. Sidaway. **Prog. H. Geog.** 24:4 12:2000 pp.591-612.

3783 Reality, society and geographical/environmental organization: searching for an integrated order. Martin Hample. Prague: Department of Social Geography and Regional Development, Charles University of Prague, 2000. 112p. *ISBN: 8090268625. Includes bibliographical references (p. 105-110) and index.*

3784 Reconsidering the legacy of urban public facility location theory in human geography. Geoffrey DeVerteuil. **Prog. H. Geog.** 24:1 2000 pp.47-70.

3785 Representations and identities in tourism map spaces. Vincent J. Del Casino, Jr.; Stephen P. Hanna. **Prog. H. Geog.** 24:1 2000 pp.23-46.

3786 The social construction of scale. Sallie A. Marston. **Prog. H. Geog.** 24:2 6:2000 pp.219-242.

3787 Spaces of hope. David Harvey. Berkeley CA: University of California Press, 2000. x, 293p. *ISBN: 0520225775, 0520225783. Includes bibliographical references (p. 282-288) and index. (Series:* California studies in critical human geography - 7).

3788 Spaces of performance. Nigel Thrift [Ed.]; Gillian Rose [Ed.]; John-David Dewsbury; Nicky Gregson; Robyn Longhurst; Paul Harrison. **Envir. Plan. D.** 18:4 8:2000 pp.411-517. *Collection of 5 articles.*

3789 Thinking 'postnationally': dialogue across multicultural, indigenous, and settler spaces. Kay Anderson. **Ann. As. Am. G.** 90:2 6:2000 pp.381-391.

3790 Thinking space. Mike Crang [Ed.]; Nigel Thrift [Ed.]. New York: Routledge, 2000. 384p. *Includes bibliographical references and index. (Series:* Critical geographies).

3791 Tourism and migration; *[Summary in French].* Allan M. Williams [Ed.]; C. Michael Hall [Ed.]; Russell King; Tony Warnes; Guy Patterson; Sophie Kyung-Mi Kang; Stephen J. Page; Carmen Aitken; Martin Bell; Gary Ward. **Tour. Geog.** 2:1 2:2000 pp.5-107. *Collection of 5 articles.*

3792 Tourism geography. Stephen Williams. London: Routledge, 1998. x, 212p. *ISBN: 0415142148, 0415142156. Includes bibliographical references (p. 198-206) and index. (Series:* Routledge contemporary human geography series).

3793 Trafficking in Bangladeshi women and girls. Bimal Kanti Paul; Syed Abu Hasnath. **Geogr. Rev.** 90:2 4:2000 pp.268-284.

3794 Using survival analysis to study spatial point patterns in geographical epidemiology. Steven Reader. **Soc. Sci. Med.** 50:7-8 4:2000 pp.985-1000.

3795 Weaving demography into society, economy and culture: progress and prospect in population geography. Philip E. Ogden. **Prog. H. Geog.** 24:4 12:2000 pp.627-640.

Sustainable development
Développement soutenable

3796 Amazonia at the crossroads: the challenge of sustainable development. Anthony L. Hall [Ed.]. London: Institute of Latin American Studies, 2000. vi, 257p. *ISBN: 1900039311. Includes bibliographical references (p. [iii]). Papers presented at Amazonia 2000: Development, Environment and Geopolitics, London, 1998.*

G: ENVIRONNEMENT. COMMUNAUTÉ. RURAL. URBAIN

3797 The challenge of globalization and sustainability. Elisabet Sahtouris; Nitamo Federico Montecucco; Min Jiayin; Ralph H. Abraham; Piero Bassetti; Vadim Zagladin. **Wor. Futur.** 55:2 2000 pp.105-181. *Collection of 6 articles.*

3798 Changing the culture of underdevelopment and unsustainability. Timothy J. Downs. **J. Environ. Plan. Manag.** 43:5 9:2000 pp.601-621.

3799 Ecological-oriented consumption: a pluriactoral approach. Edwin Zaccaï. **Int. Journ. Sust. Dev.** 3:1 2000 pp.26-39.

3800 An ethics-based system approach to indicators of sustainable development. J. Peet; H. Bossel. **Int. Journ. Sust. Dev.** 3:3 2000 pp.221-238.

3801 Global sustainable development in the twenty-first century. A.J. Holland [Ed.]; Keekok Lee [Ed.]; Desmond McNeill [Ed.]. Edinburgh: Edinburgh University Press, 2000. 232p. *ISBN: 185331241X. Includes bibliographical references and index.*

3802 Globalization, localization and sustainable livelihood. Leo de Haan. **Sociol. Rur.** 40:3 7:2000 pp.339-365.

3803 Der instrumentelle Gebrauch der Theorie der nachhaltigen Entwicklung in Lateinamerika. *[In German];* (The instrumental use of the theory of sustained development in Latin America.) *[Summary].* Hugo-Celso F. Mansilla. **Schweiz. Z. Soziologie** 26:2 7:2000 pp.401-423.

3804 Instruments of change: motivating and financing sustainable development. Todor Panaïotov; United Nations Environment Programme. London: Earthscan, 1998. xi, 228p. *ISBN: 185383467X. Includes bibliographical references (p. [203]-222) and index.*

3805 Kerala: the development experience, reflections on sustainability and replicability. Govindan Parayil [Ed.]. London: Zed Books, 2000. x, 274p. *ISBN: 1856497267, 1856497275. Includes bibliographical references and index.*

3806 Market versus non-market values: where to draw the line? Beat Bürgenmeier. **Int. Journ. Sust. Dev.** 3:1 2000 pp.1-15.

3807 Monitoring and evaluating outcomes of community involvement — the LITMUS experience. Florian Sommer. **Loc. Env.** 5:4 11:2000 pp.483-492.

3808 A new space for sustainable development? Regional environmental governance in the North West and West Midlands of England. Aidan While; Stephen Littlewood; David Whitney. **Town Plan. R.** 71:4 10:2000 pp.395-414.

3809 Reforming social policy: changing perspectives on sustainable human development. Jennifer L. Moher [Ed.]; Daniel A. Morales-Gomez [Ed.]; Neclâ Yongaçoğlu Tschirgi [Ed.]. Ottawa: International Development Research Centre, 2000. viii, 160p. *ISBN: 0889368783. Includes bibliographical references.*

3810 Sustainability. T. O'Riordan; R. Preston-Whyte; R. Hamann; M. Manquele; L. Booth; C. Oelofse; Z. Patel. **S. Afr. Geogr. J.** 82:2 2000 pp.1-43. *Collection of 4 articles.*

3811 'Sustainability' in ecological economics, ecology and livelihoods: a review. Christopher S. Sneddon. **Prog. H. Geog.** 24:4 12:2000 pp.521-549.

3812 Sustainability, systems and meaning. Joachim Schütz. **Environ. Values** 9:3 8:2000 pp.373-388.

3813 Sustainable cities revisited III. Ian Roberts; Gururaja Budhya; Solomon Benjamin; John Thompson; Ina T. Porras; Elisabeth Wood; James K. Tumwine; Mark R. Mujwahuzi; Munguti Katui-Katua; Nick Johnstone; Jane Hobson; Ana Hardoy; Ricardo Schusterman; Samson W. Mwangi; David Sanderson; Vincent Ifeanyi Ogu; Jorge Morello; Gustavo D. Buzai; Claudia A. Baxendale; Andrea F. Rodríguez; Silvia Diana Matteucci; R.E. Godagnone; R.R. Casas; Shahab Fazal; Helen Ross; Anuchat Poungsomlee; Sureeporn Punpuing; Krittaya Archavanitkul; Sara Ojeda-Benitez; Carolina Armijo de Vega; Ma. Elizabeth Ramírez-Barreto; Happy Santosa; Asef Bayat; Eric Denis; Eliana Riggio; Theresa Kilbane. **Environ. Urban.** 12:2 10:2000 pp.9-206. *Collection of 15 articles.*

3814 Sustainable community development: integrating environmental, economic and social objectives. Mark Roseland. **Prog. Plan.** 54:2 2000 pp.73-132.

3815 Sustainable development and integrated appraisal in a developing world. Norman Lee [Ed.]; C. H. Kirkpatrick [Ed.]. Northampton MA: Edward Elgar Publishing, 2000. 250p.

G: ENVIRONMENT. COMMUNITY. RURAL. URBAN

ISBN: 1840641622. Papers presented at a conference held at University of Manchester, October 1998.

3816 Sustainable development and social justice: expanding the Rawlsian framework of global justice. Oluf Langhelle. **Environ. Values** 9:3 8:2000 pp.295-323.

3817 Sustainable development in Mozambique. Barry Munslow [Ed.]; Bernardo Ferraz [Ed.]. Trenton NJ; Oxford: Africa World Press; James Currey, 1999. xiv, 242p. *ISBN: 0865437483, 0865437491, 085255821X, 0852558201. Includes bibliographical references and index. MICOA.*

3818 Sustainable development: the challenge of transition. Jurgen Schmandt [Ed.]; C.H. Ward [Ed.]. New York: Cambridge University Press, 2000. 223p. *ISBN: 0521653053. Includes index.*

3819 Sustainable measures: evaluation and reporting of environmental and social performance. Peter James [Ed.]; Martin Bennett [Ed.]; Leon Klinkers [Ed.]. Sheffield: Greenleaf, 1999. 586p. *ISBN: 1874719160. Includes bibliographical references and index.*

3820 Sustainable tourism. Richard W. Butler; Allan M. Williams; Armando Montanari; Jean-Michel Dewailly; Wim G.M. van der Knaap; Myriam Jansen-Verbeke; Anne-Marie d'Hauteserre; Nacima Baron-Yelles. **Tour. Geog.** 1:1 2:1999 pp.7-120. *Collection of 7 articles.*

3821 Tourism and sustainable development: monitoring, planning, managing, decision making, a civic approach. R.W. Butler [Ed.]; Geoffrey Wall [Ed.]; J.G. Nelson [Ed.]. Canada: University of Waterloo Press, 1999. *ISBN: 0921083602. Heritage Resources Centre.* (*Series:* Geography publications series. Heritage Resources Centre joint publication - 52).

3822 Tourism in the Yunnan Great Rivers National Parks System Project: prospects for sustainability. Erlet A. Cater. **Tour. Geog.** 2:4 11:2000 pp.472-489.

3823 The unfinished symphony: an evolutionary perspective on the conception of sustainable development. T. Jackson. **Int. Journ. Sust. Dev.** 3:3 2000 pp.199-220.

G.2: **Local community**
Collectivités locales

3824 Accounting for the uncountable: tenant participation in housing modernisation. Ian Cole; Paul Hickman; Barbara Reid. Coventry: Chartered Institute of Housing, 1999. 76p. *ISBN: 1900396335. Joseph Rowntree Foundation.*

3825 The active community: innovative consultation and participation methods for housing. Frauke Sinclair. London: London Housing Unit, 1999. 84p. *ISBN: 1872527469.*

3826 The British on the Costa del Sol: transnational identities and local communities. Karen O'Reilly. London: Routledge, 2000. 187p. *ISBN: 1841420476, 1841420484. Includes bibliographical references and index.*

3827 Community development: globalization from below. Gary Craig; Marjorie Mayo; Marilyn Taylor; Mick Carpenter; Paul Hoggett; Chris Miller; Crescy Cannan; Helen M. Hintjens; Keith Popple; Mark Redmond; Mae Shaw; Ian Martin; Alan Kay. **Comm. Dev. J.** 35:4 10:2000 pp.323-424. *Collection of 8 articles.*

3828 Community development in democratic South Africa. Scott Bollens. **Comm. Dev. J.** 35:2 4:2000 pp.167-180.

3829 Community engagement with the state: a case study of the Plymouth Hoe citizen's jury. Val Woodward. **Comm. Dev. J.** 35:3 7:2000 pp.233-244.

3830 Community participation in the development of services: a move towards community empowerment? Shelia Watt; Cassie Higgins; Andrew Kendrick. **Comm. Dev. J.** 35:2 4:2000 pp.120-132.

3831 The community planning handbook: how people can shape their cities, towns and villages in any part of the world. Nick Wates. London: Earthscan, 1999. 240p. *ISBN: 1853836540.*

3832 Complex community development projects: collaboration, comprehensive programs, and community coalitions in complex society. Ted K. Bradshaw. **Comm. Dev. J.** 35:2 4:2000 pp.133-145.

G: ENVIRONNEMENT. COMMUNAUTÉ. RURAL. URBAIN

3833   The contingent meaning of neighborhood stability for residents' psychological well-being. Catherine E. Ross; John R. Reynolds; Karlyn J. Geis. **Am. Sociol. R.** 65:4 8:2000 pp.581-597.
3834   Critical alliance: Black and White women working together for social justice. Margaret Ledwith; Paula Asgill. **Comm. Dev. J.** 35:3 7:2000 pp.290-309.
3835   The declining significance of neighborhoods? Marital transitions in community context. Scott J. South; Kyle D. Crowder. **Soc. Forc.** 78:3 3:2000 pp.1067-1099.
3836   Developing communities for the future: community development in Australia. Susan Kenny. Melbourne: Nelson ITP, 1999. xii, 356p. *ISBN: 017010205X. Includes bibliographical references (p. [339]-352) and index.*
3837   Empowering communities through public work, science, and local food systems: revisiting democracy and globalization. William B. Lacy. **Rural Sociol.** 65:1 3:2000 pp.3-26.
3838   (Environment, community, and mathematical approach: toward a collaboration with 'life environmentalism' and 'community co-management approach'.) *[Summary]; [Text in Japanese].* Keiji Hasegawa. **Rir. To Ho.** 15:2 10:2000 pp.249-260.
3839   Experiences from a community nature project in a housing estate in Singapore. Foo Tuan Seik. **Loc. Env.** 5:3 8:2000 pp.285-298.
3840   Helping each other out? Community exchange in deprived neighbourhoods. Colin C. Williams; Jan Windebank. **Comm. Dev. J.** 35:2 4:2000 pp.146-156.
3841   Indicators of citizen participation: lessons from learning teams in rural EZ/EC communities. Janice Morrissey. **Comm. Dev. J.** 35:1 1:2000 pp.59-74.
3842   Individualization strategies among city dwellers in contemporary Africa: balancing the shortcomings of community solidarity and the individualism of the struggle for survival. Alain Marie. **Int. Rev. S. H.** 45:Supp.8 2000 pp.137-157.
3843   Kerklidmaatschap en participatie in vrijwilligerswerk: een kwestie van psychologische dispositie of sociale organisatie? *[In Dutch];* [Church society and participation in voluntary work: a question of psychological disposition or social organizations?] René Bekkers. **Sociol. Gids** XLVII:4 7-8:2000 pp.268-292.
3844   The Ladd report. Everett Carll Ladd. New York: Free Press, 1999. xiii, 210p. *ISBN: 0684837358. Includes bibliographical references (p. 199-206) and index.*
3845   Living together: community life on mixed tenure estates. Ben Jupp; James Sainsbury; Oliver Akers-Douglas. London: Demos, 1999. 103p. *ISBN: 1898309159.*
3846   Marriage and social support in a British-Asian community. R. Goodwin; D. Cramer. **J. Comm. App. Soc. Psychol.** 10:1 1-2:2000 pp.49-62.
3847   Measuring social capital in five communities. Jenny Onyx; Paul Bullen. **J. App. Behav. Sc.** 36:1 3:2000 pp.23-42.
3848   The mediate community: the nature of local and extralocal ties within the metropolis. Avery M. Guest. **Urban Aff. Rev.** 35:5 5:2000 pp.603-627.
3849   Penal communities. R.A. Duff. **Pun. & Soc.** 1:1 7:1999 pp.27-43.
3850   Reconciling process and outcome in evaluating community initiatives. Mike Hughes; Tish Traynor. **Evaluation** 6:1 1:2000 pp.37-49.
3851   Restoring community and place in a global economy. Michael Vincent McGinnis. **Cap. Nat. Social.** 11(1):41 3:2000 pp.93-104.
3852   Rural financial schemes' contribution to community development. N.J. Vermaak. **Comm. Dev. J.** 36:1 1:2001 pp.42-52.
3853   Secular and faith-based organisations as reliable information sources for residents of environmentally stressed neighbourhoods. Michael R. Greenberg; Lynda Osafo. **Loc. Env.** 5:2 5:2000 pp.171-190.
3854   A sense of identity and a sense of place: oral history and preserving the past in the mining community of Broken Hill. Christine Landorf. **Oral Hist.** 28:1 Spring:2000 pp.92-102.
3855   Social capital and community development. Autar S. Dhesi. **Comm. Dev. J.** 35:3 7:2000 pp.199-214.
3856   Social capital construction and the role of the local state. Mildred Warner. **Rural Sociol.** 64:3 9:1999 pp.373-393.

G: ENVIRONMENT. COMMUNITY. RURAL. URBAN

3857 Social capital formation and healthy communities: insights from the Colorado healthy communities initiative. Michael Murray. **Comm. Dev. J.** 35:2 4:2000 pp.99-108.
3858 Social disorganization and parochial control: religious institutions and their communities. Dina R. Rose. **Sociol. For.** 15:2 6:2000 pp.339-358.
3859 Susjedstvo i prijateljstvo povratnika i useljenika u predratnom, ratnom i poslijeratnom socijalnom ambijentu Brodsko-Posavske županije. *[In Croatian]*; [Returnees and immigrants - neighbours and friendship in the pre-war, wartime and post-war social setting of the Brod-Posavina county *[Summary]*; *[Summary in French]*. Dragutin Babić. **Migrac. Teme** 16:1-2 2000 pp.7-28.
3860 Time, temporality and the dynamics of community. Elizabeth Kenyon. **Time Soc.** 9:1 3:2000 pp.21-41.
3861 Top down meets bottom up: neighbourhood management. Marilyn Taylor. York: York Publishing Services, 2000. 62p. *ISBN: 1859350542. Joseph Rowntree Foundation.*
3862 Toward a new balance between governmental and non-governmental community work: the case of Israel. Yossi Korazim-Körösy. **Comm. Dev. J.** 35:3 7:2000 pp.276-289.
3863 Trusting community developers: the influence of the form and origin of community groups on residents' support in Northern Ireland. Andreas Cebulla. **Comm. Dev. J.** 35:2 4:2000 pp.109-119.
3864 The view of our town from the hill: communities on display as local heritage. Bella Dicks. **Int. Jour. Cult. Stud.** 2:3 12:1999 pp.349-368.
3865 The well-connected community: networking to the 'edge of chaos'. Alison Gilchrist. **Comm. Dev. J.** 35:3 7:2000 pp.264-275.

G.3: **Rural and urban relations**
Rapports rurale et urbaine

3866 À propos de l'arrivée de nouvelles populations et de ses conséquences sur les espaces ruraux. *[In French]*; (On the arrival of new populations and its consequences for rural areas.) *[Summary]*. Véronique Roussel. **R. Ec. Reg. Urb.** 1 2000 pp.45-62.
3867 Defining the peri-urban: rural-urban linkages and institutional connections. D.L. Iaquinta; A.W. Drescher. **Land Ref. Land Sett. Coop.** 2 2000 pp.8-27.
3868 Livelihood, linkages and policy paradoxes. Deborah Fahy Bryceson; Leslie Bank; Vali Jamal; Kate Meagher; Barth Chukwuezi; Victor Muzvidziwa; Rachel Slater; Deborah James; Catherine Cross. **J. Contemp. Afr. St.** 19:1 1:2000 pp.5-147. *Collection of 9 articles.*
3869 Un maroc en transition: alternance et continuités. *[In French]*; [Morocco in transition: changeover and continuity]. Mohammed Naciri; Noureddine El Aoufi; Abdellatif Felk; Mohamed Tozy. **Mon. Ar. Mag. Mack.** 164 4-6:1999 pp.3-84. *Collection of 4 articles.*
3870 Rural and urban differences in economic experiences, anxiety and support for the post-communist reforms in the Czech and Slovak republics. Joseph Hraba; Allan L. McCutcheon; Jiří Večerník. **Rural Sociol.** 64:3 9:1999 pp.439-463.
3871 Territoire: contrôler ou développer, le dilemme du pouvoir depuis un siècle. *[In French]*; (Territory: control or development, the dilemma of power for the last century.) *[Summary]*. Mohammed Naciri. **Mon. Ar. Mag. Mack.** 164 4-6:1999 pp.9-35.
3872 Town and country planning in the UK. J. Barry Cullingworth; Vincent Nadin. London, New York: Routledge, 2000. 432p. *ISBN: 0415221692.*

G.3.1: **Rural sociology**
Sociologie rurale

3873 After farming: emotional health trajectories of farm, nonfarm, and displaced farm couples. Frederick O. Lorenz; Glen H. Elder, Jr.; Wan-Ning Bao; K.A.S. Wickrama; Rand D. Conger. **Rural Sociol.** 65:1 3:2000 pp.50-71.

G: ENVIRONNEMENT. COMMUNAUTÉ. RURAL. URBAIN

3874 Alternatives to census-based indicators of social disadvantage in rural communities. Gary Higgs; Sean White. **Prog. Plan.** 53:1 2000 pp.1-76.
3875 Beyond the farm gate: production-consumption networks and agri-food research. Stewart Lockie; Simon Kitto. **Sociol. Rur.** 40:1 1:2000 pp.3-19.
3876 Centralised spatial planning practice and land development realities in rural Tanzania. Fred Lerise. **Hab. Int.** 24:2 6:2000 pp.185-200.
3877 Collaboration among rural nonprofit organizations. Keith Snavely; Martin B. Tracy. **Non. Manag. Leader.** 11:2 Winter:2000 pp.145-166.
3878 The Common Agricultural Policy and the re-invention of the rural in the European Community. John Gray. **Sociol. Rur.** 40:1 1:2000 pp.30-52.
3879 Community worldview and rural systems: a study of five communities in Iowa. Janel M. Curry. **Ann. As. Am. G.** 90:4 12:2000 pp.693-712.
3880 Contingent or structural crisis in British agriculture. Ian Drummond; Hugh Campbell; Geoffrey Lawrence; David Symes. **Sociol. Rur.** 40:1 1:2000 pp.111-127.
3881 The dark side of the force: a case study of restructuring and social capital. Michael D. Schulman; Cynthia Anderson. **Rural Sociol.** 64:3 9:1999 pp.351-372.
3882 Delta sugar: Louisiana's vanishing plantation landscape. John B. Rehder. Baltimore MD: Johns Hopkins University Press, 1999. xiv, 355p. *ISBN: 0801861314. Includes bibliographical references (p. [323]-344) and index. (Series:* Creating the North American landscape).
3883 Diminished access, diverted exclusion: women and land tenure in Sub-Saharan Africa; *[Summary in French].* Leslie Gray; Michael Kevane. **Afr. Stud. R.** 42:2 9:1999 pp.15-39.
3884 Does it cost less to live in rural areas? Evidence from new data on food security and hunger. Mark Nord. **Rural Sociol.** 65:1 3:2000 pp.104-125.
3885 England's village services in the late 1990s: entrepreneurialism, community involvement and the state. Malcolm J. Moseley. **Town Plan. R.** 71:4 10:2000 pp.415-434.
3886 Estate villages revisited: a second, up-dated edition of a study of the Oxfordshire (formerly Berkshire) villages of Ardington and Lockinge. Michael Havinden; Douglas Thornton [Contrib.]; Peter Wood [Contrib.]. Reading: Rural History Centre, University of Reading, 1999. 252p. *ISBN: 0704910519. Includes index.*
3887 Famine, land, and culture in Ireland. Carla King [Ed.]. Dublin: University College Dublin Press, 2000. x, 227p. *ISBN: 1900621479, 1900621487. Includes bibliographical references and index.*
3888 Farming visions: agriculture in French culture. Susan Carol Rogers. **Fre. Pol. Cult. Soc.** 18:1 Spring:2000 pp.50-70.
3889 Four milestones in the social and economic development of Czech agriculture. Věra Majerová. **Czech Soc. Rev.** VIII:2 Fall:2000 pp.157-176.
3890 Innowacyjność kobiet wiejskich. *[In Polish];* (Innovation propensity of rural women.) *[Summary].* Maria Strykowska. **Prz. Soc.** XLIX:1 2000 pp.89-120.
3891 Justice et sociétés rurales. *[In French];* [Justice and rural societies]. Juan Carlos Garavaglia; Bruno Lemesle; Hugues Neveux; Frédérique Langue; Rosa Congost; Jorge Gelman; Raúl Fradkin; Jane Burbank; Claudio Ingerflom [Interviewer]; Mukulika Banerjee; Sanjay Subrahmanyam; Lygia Sigaud. **Rural Stud.** 149-150 1-6:1999 pp.9-228. *Collection of 13 articles.*
3892 Maintaining solidarity: a look back at the Mormon village. Todd Goodsell. **Rural Sociol.** 65:3 9:2000 pp.357-375.
3893 Measuring social capital: the Danish co-operative dairy movement. Gunnar L.H. Svendsen; Gert T. Svendsen. **Sociol. Rur.** 40:1 1:2000 pp.72-86.
3894 Migration, place and class: youth in a rural area. Lynn Jamieson. **Sociol. Rev.** 48:2 5:2000 pp.203-223.
3895 Options for rural poverty reduction in Latin America and the Caribbean. Rubén G. Echeverria. **CEPAL R.** 70 4:2000 pp.151-164.
3896 Perspectives on the peasantries of Europe. Terence J. Byres. **J. Peasant Stud.** 27:2 1:2000 pp.132-168.

G: ENVIRONMENT. COMMUNITY. RURAL. URBAN

3897 Poverty in nonmetropolitan America: impacts of industrial, employment, and family structure variables. Don E. Albrecht; Carol Mulford Albrecht; Stan L. Albrecht. **Rural Sociol.** 65:1 3:2000 pp.87-103.

3898 Predicting community satisfaction among rural residents: an integrative model. Rebecca Filkins; John C. Allen; Sam Cordes. **Rural Sociol.** 65:1 3:2000 pp.72-86.

3899 Registered households and micro-social structure in China: residential patterns in three settlements in Beijing area. Zhongwei Zhao. **J. Fam. Hist.** 26:1 1:2001 pp.39-65.

3900 Rural audit: A health check on rural Britain. Rural Group of Labour MPs [Comp.]. London: 1999. 96p. *ISBN: 0953609405. Cooperative Wholesale Society.*

3901 Rural Black women and depression: a contextual analysis. Anita C. Brown; Gene H. Brody; Zolinda Stoneman. **J. Marriage Fam.** 62:1 2:2000 pp.187-198.

3902 Rural community life and the importance of reciprocal survival strategies. Henk Meert. **Sociol. Rur.** 40:3 7:2000 pp.319-338.

3903 The rural exodus in the context of economic crisis, globalization and reform in Brazil. Stephen G. Perz. **Int. Migr. Rev.** 34:3 Fall:2000 pp.842-881.

3904 Rural life courses in Norway: living within the rural-urban complementarity. Mariann Villa. **Hist. Fam.** 5:4 2000 pp.473-490.

3905 Rural poverty in Latin America. Ramon E. López [Ed.]; Alberto Valdés [Ed.]. Basingstoke: Macmillan, 2000. 343p. *ISBN: 0333792904. Includes bibliographical references and index.*

3906 Rural second homes in Europe: examining housing supply and planning control. Nick Gallent; Mark Tewdwr-Jones. Aldershot, Burlington VT: Ashgate, 2000. x, 166p. *ISBN: 184014582X. Includes bibliographical references (p. 156-166).*

3907 Rural weekly markets and the dynamics of time, space and community in Senegal. Donna Perry. **J. Mod. Afr. S.** 38:3 9:2000 pp.461-486.

3908 Tourism, place identities and social relations in the European rural periphery. Moya Kneafsey. **Eur. Urban Reg. Stud.** 7:1 1:2000 pp.35-50.

3909 Transformations in trade and the constitution of gender and rank in northeast India. Romy Borooah. **Am. Ethn.** 27:2 5:2000 pp.371-399.

3910 What is social capital? A study of interaction in a rural community. Ian Falk; Sue Kilpatrick. **Sociol. Rur.** 40:1 1:2000 pp.87-110.

Rural development
Développement rural

3911 Beyond empowerment: changing power relations in rural Bangladesh. Thomas Costa. Dhaka: CDL, 1999. 188p.

3912 Can rural voices effect rural choices? Contesting deregulation in New Zealand's apple industry. Megan K.L. McKenna. **Sociol. Rur.** 40:3 7:2000 pp.366-383.

3913 Contrasting approaches to the management of common property resources: an institutional analysis of fisheries development strategies in Shetland and the Soloman islands. Kevin Crean. **Aust. Geogr.** 31:3 11:2000 pp.367-382.

3914 'Culture clash' revisited: newcomer and longer-term residents' attitudes toward land use, development, and environmental issues in rural communities in the Rocky Mountain West. Michael D. Smith; Richard S. Krannich. **Rural Sociol.** 65:3 9:2000 pp.396-421.

3915 Customary law and rural development in Vietnam today. Ngo Duc Thinh. **Viet. Soc. Sci.** 1:75 2000 pp.20-38.

3916 Innovation and rural development: some lessons from Britain and Western Europe. Malcolm J. Moseley. **Plan. Pract. Res.** 15:1-2 2-5:2000 pp.95-116.

3917 Občiansky potenciál ako diferencujúci faktor rozvoja sídla. *[In Slovak]*; (Civic potential as the differentiating factor of the development of settlements.) *[Summary]*. Martin Slosiarik. **Sociologia [Brat.]** 32:2 2000 pp.153-179.

3918 The 'other' agrarian transition? Structure, institutions and agency in sustainable rural development. Subir Sinha. **J. Peasant Stud.** 27:2 1:2000 pp.169-204.

G: ENVIRONNEMENT. COMMUNAUTÉ. RURAL. URBAIN

3919 Promotion collective et développement dans la France rurale progressive: l'exemple des Monts du Lyonnais. *[In French]*; (Collective development in rural progressive France: the Monts du Lyonnais' example.) J.P. Houssel. **Ann. Géogr.** 109:611 1-2:2000 pp.21-42.
3920 Regional development in rural Malaysia and the 'tribal question'. Zawawi Ibrahim. **Mod. Asian S.** 34:1 2:2000 pp.99-137.
3921 Rolling back the state and physical development planning: the case of Barbados. Jonathan Pugh; Robert B. Potter. **Sing. J. Trop. Geogr.** 21:2 7:2000 pp.183-199.
3922 State-NGO relations in an era of globalisation: the implications for agricultural development in Africa. Korbla P. Puplampu; Wisdom J. Tettey. **Rev. Afr. Pol. Ec.** 27:84 6:2000 pp.251-272.
3923 Sustainable economic development in rural America. Adam S. Weinberg. **Ann. Am. Poli.** 570 7:2000 pp.173-185.
3924 Sustainable rural livelihoods in Mali. Karen Brock; Ngolo Coulibaly. Brighton: Institute of Development Studies, 1999. x, 162p. *ISBN: 1858642698. Includes bibliographical references (p. 158-162). University of Sussex. (Series:* Research report - 35).
3925 Tourism and development in mountain regions. P. Godde [Ed.]; Martin F. Price [Ed.]; F. M. Zimmerman [Ed.]. Wallingford, New York: CABI Publishing, 1999. 357p. *ISBN: 0851993915. Includes bibliographical references and index.*

G.3.2: **Urban sociology**
   Sociologie urbaine

3926 Les animaux dans la cité: pour une histoire urbaine de la nature. *[In French]*; (Animals in the city: towards an urban history of nature.) Caroline Hodak. **Genèses** 37 12:1999 pp.156-169.
3927 Asia's global cities. Anne Haila; Toshio Kamo; Richard Child Hill; June Woo Kim; Kuniko Fujita; Sirat Morshidi; Kyoung-ho Shin; Michael Timberlake; Bob Jessop; Ngai-ling Sum; Mike Douglass; K.C. Ho; Gavin Shatkin; Lisa B.W. Drummond. **Urban Stud.** 37:12 11:2000 pp.2141-2391. *Collection of 12 articles.*
3928 Australian cities: continuity and change. Clive A. Forster. Melbourne: Oxford University Press, 1999. xvi, 191p. *ISBN: 0195510364. Includes bibliographical references and index. (Series:* Meridian, Australian geographical perspectives).
3929 'Bigness' in context: some regressive tendencies in Rem Koolhaas' urban theory. Jorge Otero-Pailos. **City** 4:3 11:2000 pp.379-389.
3930 Ces risques qui nous menacent: enquête sur les inquiétudes des Helvètes. *[In French]*; (Threatening risks: a study of the anxieties of the Swiss population.) *[Summary]*. Jean Kellerhals; Noelle Languin; Luca Pattaroni. **Schweiz. Z. Soziologie** 26:2 7:2000 pp.297-317.
3931 The city and 'the city': the representation of social reality in a local weekly. Ayelet Kohn. **Megamot** XL:1 11:1999 pp.149-166.
3932 City A-Z. Steve Pile [Ed.]; N.J. Thrift [Ed.]. New York: Routledge, 2000. 319p. *ISBN: 0415207274, 0415207282. Includes bibliographical references and index.*
3933 The city cultures reader. Malcolm Miles [Ed.]; Iain Borden [Ed.]; Tim Hall [Ed.]. New York: Routledge, 2000. 338p. *ISBN: 0415207339, 0415207347.*
3934 The city in Central Europe: culture and society from 1800 to the present. Malcolm Gee [Ed.]; Tim Kirk [Ed.]; Jill Steward [Ed.]. Aldershot, Brookfield VT: Ashgate, 1999. x, 276p. *ISBN: 1859284426. Includes bibliographical references (p. [255]-265) and index.*
3935 City profile: Cape Town. Peter Wilkinson. **Cities** 17:3 6:2000 pp.195-206.
3936 City profile: Maputo. Paul Jenkins. **Cities** 17:3 6:2000 pp.207-218.
3937 City-centre revitalisation: problems of fragmentation and fear in the evening and night-time city. Colin J. Thomas; Rosemary D.F. Bromley. **Urban Stud.** 37:8 7:2000 pp.1403-1430.

G: ENVIRONMENT. COMMUNITY. RURAL. URBAN

3938 Code of the street: decency, violence, and the moral life of the inner city. Elijah Anderson. New York, London: W.W. Norton & Company, 1999. 352p. *ISBN: 0393040232. Includes bibliographical references (p. [333]-342) and index.*

3939 A companion to the city. Gary Bridge [Ed.]; Sophie Watson [Ed.]. Malden MA: Blackwell Publishers, 2000. 640p. *ISBN: 0631210520. Includes bibliographical references and index.*

3940 Cultural production, place and politics on the South Bank of the Thames; *[Summary in French]*. Peter Newman; Ian Smith. **Int. J. Urban Reg. Res.** 24:1 3:2000 pp.9-24.

3941 The English urban landscape. P.J. Waller [Ed.]. Oxford: Oxford University Press, 2000. 352p. *Includes bibliographical references and index.*

3942 From rentiers to rantiers: 'active entrepreneurs', 'structural speculators' and the politics of marketing the city. Kevin G. Ward. **Urban Stud.** 37:7 6:2000 pp.1093-1108.

3943 Hong Kong as a global metropolis. David R. Meyer. Cambridge, New York: Cambridge University Press, 2000. xiii, 272p. *ISBN: 0521643449. Includes bibliographical references (p. 248-269) and index. (Series:* Cambridge studies in historical geography - 30).

3944 Hospitality and violence: contradictions in a southern city. Harvey K. Newman. **Urban Aff. Rev.** 35:4 3:2000 pp.541-558.

3945 Identités urbaines et identités nationales. *[In French]*; [Urban identities and national identities]. Sylvaine Bulle. **R. Et. Palest.** 74:22 Winter:2000 pp.35-47.

3946 Isolement résidentiel et normativité sociale dans les quartiers urbains. Le jeune isolé comme figure de la modernité. *[In French]*; (Residential isolation and social normativity in urban areas: solitary youth as an emblem of modernity.) *[Summary]*. Xavier Leloup. **Recher. Sociolog.** XXXI:1 2000 pp.135-146.

3947 Lima. John B. Leonard. **Cities** 17:6 12:2000 pp.433-446.

3948 Mega-cities... and mega-city regions. Part 2: world. John G. Papaioannou; Calogero Muscarà; José Manuel Gomez Vazquez Aldana; Koichi Tonuma; Liangyong Wu; Edward Leman; William Michelson; Laila El-Hamamsy; Petros Petsimeris; Voula Mega; S.K. Chandhoke; Gerald B. Dix; Margery al- Chalabi; Eiichi Isomura; Lawrence Wai Chung Lai. **Ekistics** 65:388-390 1-6:1998 pp.6-159. *Collection of 15 articles.*

3949 Modernism, postmodernism and the identity of Korean cities. Won Bae Kim; Yong-woong Kim; Seong-kyu Ha; Tae-jin Yi; Myung-rae Cho; Kwi-gon Kim; Kweesoon Kim. **Korea J.** 39:3 Autumn:1999 pp.5-178. *Collection of 6 articles.*

3950 New York City. Fred Siegel. **Publ. Inter.** 139 Spring:2000 pp.88-98.

3951 Notas sobre a população — Lisboa: área metropolitana e cidade. *[In Portuguese]*; (Notes on the population — Lisbon: metropolitan area and city.) Maria João Valente Rosa. **Anál. Soc.** XXXIV:153 Spring:2000 pp.1045-1058.

3952 The paradigmatic city. Jan Nijman. **Ann. As. Am. G.** 90:1 3:2000 pp.135-145.

3953 Pensar la ciudad desde la perspectiva del habitar. *[In Spanish]*; [Thinking about the town from the point of view of living there]. Cruz Elena Espinal Pérez. **Rev. Univ. EAFIT** 117 1-3:2000 pp.29-42.

3954 Polite politics: a sociological analysis of an urban protest in Hong Kong. Kwok-leung Denny Ho. Aldershot: Ashgate, 2000. 388p. *ISBN: 1840143339. Includes bibliographical references. (Series:* Social and political studies from Hong Kong).

3955 The postmodern urban condition. M.J. Dear. Oxford, Malden MA: Blackwell Publishers, 2000. xii, 337p. *ISBN: 0631209875, 0631209883. Includes bibliographical references and index.*

3956 Re-imaging a post-industrial city: the Leeds St. Valentine's fair as a civic spectacle. Tony Harcup. **City** 4:2 7:2000 pp.215-232.

3957 Revisiting fear and place: women's fear of attack and the built environment. H. Koskela; R. Pain. **Geoforum** 31:2 5:2000 pp.269-280.

3958 Revisiting Rio De Janeiro and São Paulo. Brian J. Godfrey. **Geogr. Rev.** 89:1 1:1999 pp.94-121.

3959 Revitalizing the state's urban 'nerve tips'. Benjamin L. Read. **China Quart.** 163 9:2000 pp.806-820.

3960 Services et métropoles: formes urbaines et changement économique. *[In French]*; [Services and metropoles: urban forms and economic change]. Jean Philippe [Ed.]; Pierre-

G: ENVIRONNEMENT. COMMUNAUTÉ. RURAL. URBAIN

Yves Léo [Ed.]; Louis-M. Boulianne [Ed.]. Paris: L'Harmattan, 1998. 300p. *ISBN: 2738482112. Includes bibliographical references (p. 275-288). Réseau européen sur les services et l'espace.*

3961   Squatter settlements: their sustainability, architectural contributions, and socio-economic roles. Cedric Pugh. **Cities** 17:5 10:2000 pp.325-337.

3962   Sydney: the emergence of a world city. John Connell [Ed.]. Melbourne, Oxford: Oxford University Press, 2000. 256p. *ISBN: 0195507487. Includes index.*

3963   'The basic assumptions as regards the nature and requirements of a capital city': identity, modernization and urban form at Mafikeng's margins. Peris Sean Jones. **Int. J. Urban Reg. Res.** 24:1 3:2000 pp.25-51.

3964   Third world cities. D.W. Drakakis-Smith. New York: Routledge, 2000. 190p. *ISBN: 041519881X, 0415198828. Includes bibliographical references and index. (Series: Routledge introductions to development series).*

3965   Town centre management awareness: an aid to developing young people's citizenship. Helen Woolley. **Cities** 17:6 12:2000 pp.453-464.

3966   Understanding land markets in African urban areas: the case of Dar es Salaam, Tanzania. J.M. Lusugga Kironde. **Hab. Int.** 24:2 6:2000 pp.151-166.

3967   Urban community development: an examination of the Perkins model. Timothy Essenburg. **R. Soc. Econ.** LVIII:2 6:2000 pp.197-223.

3968   Urban social movements and housing in Hong Kong: from antagonism to guided participation. Ngai Ming Yip. **Iss. Stud.** 35:6 11-12:1999 pp.144-166.

3969   La ville: savoirs urbains, normes et citoyenneté. *[In French]*; (The town: urban savvy, norms and citizenship.) *[Summary]*. Bernard Francq. **Recher. Sociolog.** XXXI:1 2000 pp.85-96.

3970   Visual image of the city: tourists' versus residents' perception of Simla, a hill station in northern India. Rajinder S. Jutla. **Tour. Geog.** 2:4 11:2000 pp.404-420.

3971   The vitality and viability of town centres. Neil Ravenscroft. **Urban Stud.** 37:13 12:2000 pp.2533-2550.

Housing
Logement

3972   An approach to improved housing delivery in large cities of less developed countries. Alpana Sivam; David Evans; Ross King; David Young. **Hab. Int.** 25:1 3:2001 pp.99-113.

3973   Assessment of the design participation school of thought. Antônio Reis. **J. Arch. Plan. Res.** 17:1 Spring:2000 pp.1-15.

3974   Bastee eviction and housing rights: a case of Dhaka, Bangladesh. Mohammed Mahbubur Rahman. **Hab. Int.** 25:1 3:2001 pp.49-68.

3975   Current housing policy issues in Barbados: with particular reference to vacant subdivisions. Robert B. Potter; Mark R. Watson. **Third World Plan. R.** 21:3 8:1999 pp.237-260.

3976   The housing allowance scheme in Guangzhou. Eddie Chi-Man Hui; Bill Seabrooke. **Hab. Int.** 24:1 3:2000 pp.19-30.

3977   Housing associations: the policy and practice of registered social landlords. Helen Cope. London: Macmillan Education, 1999. 361p. *ISBN: 0333731999. (Series: Macmillan building and surveying).*

3978   Housing Black and minority ethnic people in Sheffield: a research report. Gidley Glen; David Robinson; M.L. Harrison. Sheffield: Centre for Regional Economic and Social Research, 1999. 118p. *ISBN: 0863998308. Includes bibliographical references. Sheffield City Council Housing Department. Housing Corporation.*

3979   Housing vouchers, tenant quality, and apartment values. John D. Benjamin; Peter Chinloy; G. Stacy Sirmans. **J. Real Est. Finan. Econ.** 20:1 1:2000 pp.37-48.

3980   More American than the United States. Housing in urban Canada in the twentieth century. Richard Harris. **J. Urban Hist.** 26:4 5:2000 pp.456-478.

G: ENVIRONMENT. COMMUNITY. RURAL. URBAN

3981 Out of sight, out of mind: the assessment of and provision for Black and minority ethnic housing needs in the South West. A. Jones; D. Mullins. Birmingham: Univiversity of Birmingham, 1998. 56p. *ISBN: 0704485125. Centre for Urban and Regional Studies.* (*Series:* Housing research at CURS - 3).

3982 Owner-occupation, social mix and neighbourhood impacts; *[Summary in French]*; *[Summary in Spanish]*. Rowland Atkinson; Keith Kintrea. **Policy Pol.** 28:1 1:2000 pp.93-108.

3983 Planning, politics and housing in Britain. Andrzej Olechnowicz; Nick Tiratsoo; Junichi Hasegawa; Andrew Homer; Tatsuya Tsubaki; Harriet Jones; Peter Weiler; Mark Clapson. **Contemp. Br. Hist.** 14:1 Spring:2000 pp.3-174. *Collection of 8 articles.*

3984 Preservation through change: renovating modern architecture. M. Vittoria Giuliani; Valeria Bucchignani. **J. Arch. Plan. Res.** 17:1 Spring:2000 pp.34-46.

3985 Rent differentials, housing benefit and management of the public housing stock in the United Kingdom. C.J. Mackay. **Loc. Govt. St.** 26:1 Spring:2000 pp.81-96.

3986 The social consequences of housing. Edward L. Glaeser; Bruce Sacerdote. **J. Hous. Ec.** 9:1-2 3-6:2000 pp.1-23.

3987 Status, quality and the other trade-off: towards a new theory of urban residential location. Hoang Huu Phe; Patrick Wakely. **Urban Stud.** 37:1 1:2000 pp.7-36.

3988 Subsidized housing and neighborhood racial transition: an empirical investigation. Lance Freeman; William Rohe. **Hous. Pol. Deb.** 11:1 2000 pp.67-90.

3989 Urban housing and the role of 'underclass' processes: the case of Ireland; *[Summary in French]*. Brian Nolan; Christopher T. Whelan. **J. Europe. Soc. Pol.** 10:1 2:2000 pp.5-21.

3990 Windfall sites for housing: an underestimated resource. William Walton. **Urban Stud.** 37:2 2:2000 pp.391-410.

Social differentiation and segregation
Différenciation et ségrégation urbaine

3991 Area deprivation in Scotland: a new assessment. Ade Kearns; Kenneth Gibb; Daniel MacKay. **Urban Stud.** 37:9 8:2000 pp.1535-1560.

3992 Armut in der Stadt: Zur Segregation benachteiligter Gruppen in Deutschland. *[In German]*; [Poverty in the city: on the segregation of disadvantaged groups in Germany]. Carsten Keller. Opladen: Westdeutscher Verlag, 1999. 152p. *ISBN: 3531134825. Includes bibliographical references (p. [143]-152).*

3993 Attitudinal differentiation between African-American urbanities and suburbanities. Lee Sigelman; Lars Willnat. **Urban Aff. Rev.** 35:5 5:2000 pp.677-694.

3994 The compact city: just or just compact? A preliminary analysis. Elizabeth Burton. **Urban Stud.** 37:11 10:2000 pp.1969-2006.

3995 The emergence of crack cocaine and the rise in urban crime rates. Jeff Grogger; Michael Willis. **Rev. Econ. St.** LXXXII:4 11:2000 pp.519-529.

3996 An empirical assessment of four perspectives on the declining fortunes of the African-American male. James H. Johnson, Jr.; Walter C. Farrell, Jr.; Jennifer A. Stoloff. **Urban Aff. Rev.** 35:5 5:2000 pp.695-716.

3997 An examination of extreme urban poverty: the effect of metropolitan employment and demographic dynamics. John B. Strait. **Urban Geogr.** 21:6 8-9:2000 pp.514-542.

3998 Gated communities in the USA — a new trend in urban development. Klaus Frantz. **Espace Pop. Soc.** 1 2000 pp.101-114.

3999 Gentrification within Australia's 'problem city': inner Newcastle as a zone of residential transition. M.W. Rofe. **Aust. Geogr. Stud.** 38:1 3:2000 pp.54-70.

4000 Geographic variation in mortgage discrimination: evidence from Los Angeles. Michael Reibel. **Urban Geogr.** 21:1 1-2:2000 pp.45-60.

4001 The ghetto model and ethnic concentration in Australian cities. M.F. Poulsen; R.J. Johnston. **Urban Geogr.** 21:1 1-2:2000 pp.26-44.

G: ENVIRONNEMENT. COMMUNAUTÉ. RURAL. URBAIN

4002 The global ethnopolis: Chinatown, Japantown and Manilatown in American society. Michel S. Laguerre. Basingstoke; New York: Macmillan; St. Martin's Press, 2000. xii, 199p. *ISBN: 0333777891, 0312226128. Includes bibliographical references (p. 167-186) and index.*

4003 The local housing system in Craigavon, N. Ireland: ethno-religious residential segregation, socio-tenurial polarisation and sub-markets. A.S. Adair; J.N. Berry; W.S.J. McGreal; B. Murtagh; C. Paris. **Urban Stud.** 37:7 6:2000 pp.1079-1092.

4004 Measuring gentrification and displacement in Greater London. Rowland Atkinson. **Urban Stud.** 37:1 1:2000 pp.149-166.

4005 Minorities in European cities: the dynamics of social integration and social exclusion at the neighbourhood level. Marco Martiniello [Ed.]; Sophie Body-Gendrot [Ed.]. Basingstoke: Macmillan, 2000. 262p. *ISBN: 0333754182. Includes index.*

4006 Neighborhood poverty and the social isolation of inner-city African American families. Bruce H. Rankin; James M. Quane. **Soc. Forc.** 79:1 9:2000 pp.139-164.

4007 Neighbourhood poverty in Canadian cities; *[Summary in French]*. A. Kazemipur; S.S. Halli. **Can. J. Soc.** 25:3 Summer:2000 pp.369-381.

4008 New Labour's approach to age-old problems: renewing and revitalising poor neighbourhoods — the national strategy for neighbourhood renewal. Nick Oatley. **Local. Ec.** 15:2 7:2000 pp.86-97.

4009 The new poverty in Canada: ethnic groups and ghetto neighbourhoods. Abdolmohammad Kazemipur; Shivalingappa S. Halli. Toronto: Thompson Educational Publishing, 2000. 193p. *ISBN: 1550571086.*

4010 New Urbanism and the city: potential applications and implications for distressed inner-city neighborhoods. Charles C. Bohl; Michael Pyatok [Comments by]; Shelley R. Poticha [Comments by]. **Hous. Pol. Deb.** 11:4 2000 pp.761-820.

4011 Pauvreté et espaces quotidiens à Niamey. *[In French]*; (Poverty and everyday urban space in Niamey.); *[Summary]*. Lourdes Diaz-Olvera; Didier Plat; Pascal Pochet. **Espace Géogr.** 29:4 2000 pp.329-340.

4012 Plural cities in comparative perspective. Ralph D. Grillo. **Ethn. Racial** 23:6 11:2000 pp.957-981.

4013 Race-based neighbourhood projection: a proposed framework for understanding new data on racial integration. Ingrid Gould Ellen. **Urban Stud.** 37:9 8:2000 pp.1513-1534.

4014 The racial context of White mobility: an individual-level assessment of the White flight hypothesis. Kyle Crowder. **Soc. Sci. R.** 29:2 6:2000 pp.223-257.

4015 Racial residential segregation by level of socioeconomic status. Craig St. John; Robert Clymer. **Soc. Sci. Q.** 81:3 9:2000 pp.701-715.

4016 A reappraisal of gentrification: towards a 'geography of gentrification'. Loretta Lees. **Prog. H. Geog.** 24:3 9:2000 pp.389-408.

4017 The reassertion of economics: 1990s gentrification in the Lower East Side; *[Summary in French]*. Neil Smith; James DeFilippis. **Int. J. Urban Reg. Res.** 23:4 1999 pp.638-653.

4018 Social polarisation and socioeconomic segregation in a welfare state: the case of Oslo. Terje Wessel. **Urban Stud.** 37:11 10:2000 pp.1947-1967.

4019 Spatial and socioeconomic analysis of Latin Americans and Whites in the Toronto CMA. Joe T. Darden; Sameh M. Kamel. **J. Dev. Soc.** XVI:2 2000 pp.245-270.

4020 The spatial separation of the poor in Canadian cities. Eric Fong; Kumiko Shibuya. **Demography** 37:4 11:2000 pp.449-459.

4021 La ville éclatée: quartiers et peuplement. *[In French]*; [The broken town: quarters and population]. Jean-Pierre Lévy [Ed.]; Nicole Haumont [Ed.]; Marie-Hélène Bacqué. Paris: L'Harmattan, 1998. 261p. *ISBN: 2738462626. Includes bibliographical references.*

4022 Why voucher and certificate users live in distressed neighborhoods. Rolf Pendall. **Hous. Pol. Deb.** 11:4 2000 pp.881-910.

G: ENVIRONMENT. COMMUNITY. RURAL. URBAN

Urban planning and infrastructure
Aménagement et infrastructure urbaine

4023 L'adaptation des transports en commun à l'évolution urbaine (l'exemple de Rouen). *[In French]*; (Public transportation adaptation to urban development (the case study of Rouen).) Véronique Mondou. **Espace Pop. Soc.** 3 1999 pp.411-424.

4024 The American metropolis at century's end: past and future influences. Robert Fishman. **Hous. Pol. Deb.** 11:1 2000 pp.199-213.

4025 Assessment methodologies for urban infrastructure. Jan Rotmans; Marjolein van Asselt; Pier Vellinga; Christopher Tweed; Phil Jones; Enrique J. Calderón; Corrado Diamantini; Bruno Zanon; Daniel Hellström; Ulf Jeppsson; Erik Kärrman; Jean-Luc Bertrand-Krajewski; Sylvie Barraud; Bernard Chocat; Michiel A. Rijsberman; Frans H.M. van de Ven; Birgitte Hoffmann; Susanne Balslev Nielsen; Morten Elle; Søren Gabriel; Anne Marie Eilersen; Mogens Henze; Peter Steen Mikkelsen; Kine Halvorsen Thorén; Irmeli Harmaajärvi; Anke Valentin; Joachim H. Spangenberg; Rosa Arce; Natalia Gullón; Oddvar G. Lindholm; Terje Nordeide. **Envir. Imp. Assess. Rev.** 20:3 6:2000 pp.265-423. *Collection of 14 articles.*

4026 Bournville: model village to garden suburb. Michael Harrison. Chichester: Phillimore, 1999. xvi, 272p. *ISBN: 1860771173.*

4027 Britain's regional shopping centres: new urban forms? Michelle S. Lowe. **Urban Stud.** 37:2 2:2000 pp.261-274.

4028 Building the 21st century home: the sustainable urban neighbourhood. David Rudlin; Nicholas Falk. Oxford: Architectural Press, 1999. xvi, 271p. *ISBN: 0750625287. Includes index.*

4029 Certainty and discretion in planning control: a case study of office development in Hong Kong. Bo-sin Tang; Lennon H.T. Choy; Joshua K.F. Wat. **Urban Stud.** 37:13 12:2000 pp.2465-2484.

4030 Chinese urban planning at fifty: an assessment of the planning theory literature. Wing-shing Tang. **J. Plan. Lit.** 14:3 2:2000 pp.347-366.

4031 Cities and infrastructure networks. Stephen Graham; Maria Kaika; Erik Swyngedouw; Ricardo Toledo Silva; Jean-Marc Offner. **Int. J. Urban Reg. Res.** 24:1 3:2000 pp.114-200. *Collection of 5 articles.*

4032 Cities working together to improve urban services in developing areas: the Toronto-São Paulo example. W.E. Ted Hewitt. **Stud. Comp. Int. Dev.** 34:1 Spring:1999 pp.27-44.

4033 City center revitalization in Portugal. Lessons from two medium size cities. Carlos J. Lopes Balsas. **Cities** 17:1 2:2000 pp.19-31.

4034 Les «communautés fermées» dans les villes des États-Unis. Aspects géographiques d'une sécession urbaine. *[In French]*; (Gated communities in the cities of the United States: geographical aspects of an urban secession.) *[Summary]*. Renaud Le Goix. **Espace Géogr.** 30:1 2001 pp.81-93.

4035 Community roles in urban regeneration new partnerships on London's South Bank. Tim Brindley. **City** 4:3 11:2000 pp.363-378.

4036 Consensus planning: the relevance of communicative planning theory in Dutch infrastructure development. Johan Woltjer. Aldershot, Burlington VT: Ashgate, 2000. xiii, 308p. *ISBN: 0754614301. Includes bibliographical references (p. 249-283) and index.* (*Series:* Urban and regional planning and development).

4037 Creating sustainable cities. Herbert Girardet. Totnes: Green Books, 1999. 77p. *ISBN: 1870098773. Schumacher Society.* (*Series:* Schumacher Briefings - 2).

4038 The creative city: a toolkit for urban innovators. Charles Landry. London: Comedia, Earthscan, 2000. xviii, 300p. *ISBN: 1853836133. Includes bibliographical references (p. 276-284).*

4039 The dead zone and the architecture of transgression. Gil M. Doron. **City** 4:2 7:2000 pp.247-262.

4040 Eastern promise: education and social renewal in London's Docklands. Tim Butler [Ed.]. London: Lawrence and Wishart, 2000. 254p. *ISBN: 0853158983.*

G: ENVIRONNEMENT. COMMUNAUTÉ. RURAL. URBAIN

4041 Ecological and political modernisation: the challenge for planning. Andrew Blowers. **Town Plan. R.** 71:4 10:2000 pp.371-394.

4042 Éléments de réflexion pour une révision de l'aménagement des villes en Afrique. *[In French]*; (Elements of reflections on the revision of town planning in Africa.) *[Summary]*; *[Summary in French]*. René Joly Assako Assako. **Af. Spec.** 34:3 1999 pp.349-374.

4043 Evaluation of community-based regeneration in Northern Ireland: between social and economic regeneration. Andreas Cebulla; Jim Berry; Stanley McGreal. **Town Plan. R.** 71:2 4:2000 pp.169-190.

4044 Evaluations of a community regeneration project: case studies of Cruddas Park Development Trust, Newcastle upon Tyne. Andrew McCulloch. **J. Soc. Pol.** 29:3 7:2000 pp.397-419.

4045 Formation of hub cities: transportation cost advantage and population agglomeration. Hideo Konishi. **J. Urban Ec.** 48:1 7:2000 pp.1-28.

4046 The geography of a tourist business: hotel distribution and urban development in Xiamen, China. Stéphane Bégin. **Tour. Geog.** 2:4 11:2000 pp.448-471.

4047 Growing greener: putting conservation into local plans and ordinances. Randall Arendt. Washington DC: Island Press, 1999. xxv, 236p. *ISBN: 1559637420. Includes bibliographical references (p. 223-225) and index.*

4048 High-speed rail developments and spatial restructuring. A case study of the capital region in South Korea. Kwang Sik Kim. **Cities** 17:4 8:2000 pp.251-262.

4049 Housing and development objectives in India. Piyush Tiwari. **Hab. Int.** 25:2 6:2001 pp.229-254.

4050 Housing, planning and cadre influence on Chinese urban social space: through the looking glass of social areas of Beijing. Victor F.S. Sit. **Asian Prof.** 28:1 2:2000 pp.1-18.

4051 A hundred years of town planning and the influence of Ebenezer Howard. Max Steuer. **Br. J. Soc.** 51:2 6:2000 pp.377-386.

4052 Inclusive regeneration? Integrating social and economic regeneration in English local authorities. Paul Lawless; David Robinson. **Town Plan. R.** 71:3 7:2000 pp.289-310.

4053 The influence of urban form on travel: an interpretive review. Randall Crane. **J. Plan. Lit.** 15:1 8:2000 pp.3-18.

4054 Innovation in the control of residential design: what lessons for wider practice? Matthew Carmona. **Town Plan. R.** 70:4 10:1999 pp.501-528.

4055 Institutional restructuring in Taiwan's planning paradigm. Tsu-lung Chou. **Third World Plan. R.** 21:3 8:1999 pp.331-346.

4056 Intelligent urban development. Margaret Grieco; Jeff Turner; Len Holmes; Frances C. Hodgson; Chris Carter; Mahizhnan Arun; Mui Teng Yap; Julian Hine; Derek Swan; Judith Scott; David Binnie; John Sharp; Paul Corrigan; Paul Joyce; Perry Morrison; Kerry Hamilton; Linda Jenkins; Mark Stubbs; Mark Lemon; Phil Longhurst; Stephen E. Little; Pascale de Berranger; Mary C.R. Meldrum; David Crowther; K.W. Axhausen; Stephen Denning; Kenneth I. MacDonald. **Urban Stud.** 37:10 9:2000 pp.1719-1892. *Collection of 15 articles.*

4057 Khartoum blues: the 'deplanning' and decline of a capital city. Adil Mustafa Ahmad. **Hab. Int.** 24:3 9:2000 pp.309-326.

4058 Land use and the limits to (regional) governance: some lessons from planning for housing and minerals in England; *[Summary in French]*. Richard Cowell; Jonathan Murdoch. **Int. J. Urban Reg. Res.** 23:4 1999 pp.654-669.

4059 The landscape of towns. Michael Aston; James Bond. Stroud: Sutton, 2000. 259p. *ISBN: 0750924896. Includes bibliographical references (p. 225-244) and index. (Series:* Sutton history handbooks*).*

4060 Leisure, property, and the viability of town centres. Neil Ravenscroft; Jo Reeves; Martha Rowley. **Envir. Plan. A.** 32:8 8:2000 pp.1359-1374.

4061 Leitbilder der räumlichen Stadtentwicklung in der kommunalen Planungspraxis. *[In German]*; (Spatial concepts in municipal planning practice.) *[Summary]*. Klaus Spiekermann. **Arc. Kommunal.** 39:2 2000 pp.289-311.

G: ENVIRONMENT. COMMUNITY. RURAL. URBAN

4062 Levels of activity relating to safer routes to school type projects and green transport plans. Ruth Bradshaw; et al. London: University of Westminster, Transport Studies Group, 1998. 101p.
4063 London: pathways to the future. John Jopling. London: Sustainable London Trust, 2000. 136p. *ISBN: 0953768007.*
4064 Managing change in the new millennium: fine tuning or radical reform? Andrew W. Gilg; Michael P. Kelly. **Town Plan. R.** 71:3 7:2000 pp.269-288.
4065 The materiality of urban discourse: rational planning in the restructuring of the early twentieth-century ghetto. Christopher Mele. **Urban Aff. Rev.** 35:5 5:2000 pp.628-648.
4066 Metropoli in trasformazione. *[In Italian]*; [Cities in transformation]. Hartmut Häußermann; Katja Simons; John Andersen; Lucia Cavola; Serena Vicari. **Rass. It. Soc.** 41:4 2000 pp.477-538. *Collection of 3 articles.*
4067 Metropolitan strategic planning in England: strategies in transition. Kevin Thomas; Peter Roberts. **Town Plan. R.** 71:1 1:2000 pp.25-50.
4068 Mobilité quotidienne des citadins à faibles ressources. Les enseignements de Ouagadougou. *[In French]*; (Daily mobility of underprivileged urban dwellers. Lessons from Ouagadougou.) Lourdes Diaz Olvera; Didier Plat; Pascal Pochet. **R. T-Monde** XL:160 10-12:1999 pp.829-848.
4069 Modernisierung der Regionalplanung. Ein Diskussionsbeitrag zur Steuerung der Siedlungsentwicklung in den Stadtregionen. *[In German]*; (Modernisation of regional planning. A contribution to the discussion about the management of settlement development in city regions.) Jürgen Aring. **Inf. Raum.** 9 1999 pp.645-660.
4070 Neighborhood recovery: reinvestment policy for the new hometown. John Kromer. New Brunswick NJ: Rutgers University Press, 1999. x, 262p. *ISBN: 0813527163, 0813527171. Includes bibliographical references (p. 245-248) and index.*
4071 The new American city faces its regional future: a Cleveland perspective. Kathryn Wertheim Hexter [Ed.]; David Beach [Ed.]; David C. Sweet [Ed.]. Athens OH: Ohio State University Press, 1999. xxi, 230p. *ISBN: 0821412787. Includes bibliographical references and index.*
4072 New approaches to delineating metropolitan and nonmetropolitan settlement: geographers drawing the line. Donald C. Dahmann. **Urban Geogr.** 20:8 11-12:1999 pp.683-694.
4073 New directions in planning theory. Susan S. Fainstein. **Urban Aff. Rev.** 35:4 3:2000 pp.451-478.
4074 New urbanism and the culture of criticism. Emily Talen. **Urban Geogr.** 21:4 5-6:2000 pp.318-341.
4075 Obduracy and urban sociotechnical change. Changing *Plan Hoog Catharijne*. Anique Hommels. **Urban Aff. Rev.** 35:5 5:2000 pp.649-676.
4076 Of railroads and regime shifts. Downtown renewal in Providence, Rhode Island. Mark T. Motte; Laurence A. Weil. **Cities** 17:1 2:2000 pp.7-18.
4077 On the edge: regenerating a Dublin suburb. David Prichard. **City** 4:1 4:2000 pp.65-80.
4078 Our towns and cities. The future: delivering an urban renaissance. Department of the Environment, Transport and the Regions, House of Commons, UK. London: Stationery Office, 2000. 160p. *ISBN: 0101491123. (Series:* Cm.4911).
4079 Placing (post-)socialism: the making and remaking of Nowa Huta, Poland. Alison Stenning. **Eur. Urban Reg. Stud.** 7:2 4:2000 pp.99-118.
4080 Planned abandonment: the neighborhood life-cycle theory and national urban policy. John T. Metzger; Anthony Downs [Comments by]; Kenneth Temkin [Comments by]; George C. Galster [Comments by]. **Hous. Pol. Deb.** 11:1 2000 pp.7-66.
4081 Planning and conservation in historic Chinese cities: the case of Xi'an. Ya Ping Wang. **Town Plan. R.** 71:3 7:2000 pp.311-332.
4082 Planning, governance and spatial strategy in Britain: an institutionalist analysis. Geoff Vigar; et al. Basingstoke: Macmillan, 2000. x, 314p. *ISBN: 0312231253, 0333773160, 0333773179. Includes bibliographical references (p. 290-307) and index. (Series:* Planning, environment, cities).

4083 Planning the evolution of a city: a case study of Abidjan. Ferdinando Semboloni. **Third World Plan. R.** 21:2 5:1999 pp.201-235.
4084 Planning theories and environmental impact assessment. David P. Lawrence. **Envir. Imp. Assess. Rev.** 20:6 12:2000 pp.607-626.
4085 The politics of city-region planning and governance: reconciling the national, regional and urban in the competing voices of institutional restructuring. Mark Tewdwr-Jones; Donald McNeill. **Eur. Urban Reg. Stud.** 7:2 4:2000 pp.119-134.
4086 The problem with community in planning. Emily Talen. **J. Plan. Lit.** 15:2 11:2000 pp.171-183.
4087 Public health and urban planning. Ximena de la Barra; Talia McCray; H. Patricia Hynes; Doug Brugge; Julie Watts; Jody Lally. **Plan. Pract. Res.** 15:1-2 2-5:2000 pp.5-50. *Collection of 3 articles.*
4088 Public-private partnerships for urban land development in Mexico: a victory for hope versus expectation? Gareth A. Jones; Rosaria A. Pisa. **Hab. Int.** 24:1 3:2000 pp.1-18.
4089 Race and planning: the UK experience. Huw Thomas. London: UCL Press, 2000. 192p. *ISBN: 1857283570.*
4090 Reactive, proactive or interactive? Community perceptions of waterfront change in Canadian port cities. Brian Hoyle. **Town Plan. R.** 70:4 10:1999 pp.455-478.
4091 Rebuilding sustainable communities: assessing Glasgow's urban village experiment. Andrew McArthur. **Town Plan. R.** 71:1 1:2000 pp.51-70.
4092 Reconstructed production landscapes in the postmodern city: applied design and creative services in the metropolitan core. Thomas A. Hutton. **Urban Geogr.** 21:4 5-6:2000 pp.285-317.
4093 Reflections on Nigerian urban planning issues. Waheed A. Kadiri [Ed.]. Abeokuta: Desi-Oga Publications, 1998. 173p. *ISBN: 9783129554.*
4094 Regeneration: story of the Dome. Adam Nicolson. London: HarperCollins, 1999. 255p.
4095 Regional wars and chances for the reconstruction of Balkan cities in a global information society: cities and citizens, urbanity and multiculture in the past, present and future of Balkan civilization. Milan Prodanovic. **City** 4:2 7:2000 pp.277-288.
4096 Rethinking sustainable development in the post-apartheid reconstruction of South African cities. Zarina Patel. **Loc. Env.** 5:4 11:2000 pp.383-400.
4097 Rethinking the Urban Development Corporation 'experiment': the case of central Manchester, Leeds and Bristol. Iain Deas; Brian Robson; Michael Bradford. **Prog. Plan.** 54:1 2000 pp.1-72.
4098 Revisiting inner-city strips: a framework for community and economic development. Anastasia Loukaitou-Sideris. **Econ. Devel. Q.** 14:2 5:2000 pp.165-181.
4099 Self-help planning of migrants in Rome and Madrid. Volker Kreibich. **Hab. Int.** 24:2 6:2000 pp.201-212.
4100 Some problems in the co-ordination of planning: managing interdependencies in the planning of Delhi, India. Ashok Kumar. **Spa. & Pol.** 4:2 11:2000 pp.167-185.
4101 South Africa: urban transformation. John James Williams. **Cities** 17:3 6:2000 pp.167-184.
4102 Spatial data infrastructures for cities in developing countries. Lessons from the Bangkok experience. Ian D. Bishop; Francisco J. Escobar; Sadasivam Karuppannan; Ian P. Williamson; Paul M. Yates; Ksemsan Suwarnarat; Haider W. Yaqub. **Cities** 17:2 4:2000 pp.85-96.
4103 Spatial structure of a metropolitan area with an agricultural hinterland. Fumio Takuma; Komei Sasaki. **J. Urban Ec.** 48:2 9:2000 pp.307-320.
4104 Stadtentwicklungsplanung und Nachhaltigkeit — neuer Wein in alten Schläuchen? Bemerkungen über die Perspektiven eines nicht mehr ganz neuen Leitbegriffs in der Planung. *[In German]*; (Urban development planning and sustainability — new wine in old bottles? Remarks on the perspectives of a not really new leading planning concept.) *[Summary].* Karolus Heil. **Inf. Raum.** 1 2000 pp.21-32.
4105 Strategy and partnership in cities and regions: economic development and urban regeneration in Pittsburgh, Birmingham, and Rotterdam. Brian D. Jacobs. Basingstoke;

G: ENVIRONMENT. COMMUNITY. RURAL. URBAN

New York: Macmillan; St. Martin's Press, 1999. 220p. *ISBN: 0333777824, 0312230281. Includes bibliographical references and index.*

4106 Tall buildings and the urban skyline: the effect of visual complexity on preferences. Tom Heath; Sandy G. Smith; Bill Lim. **J. App. Behav. Sc.** 32:4 7:2000 pp.541-556.

4107 Urban and ecological planning in Chicago: science, policy and dissent. Margarita Alario. **J. Environ. Plan. Manag.** 43:4 7:2000 pp.489-504.

4108 Urban development, planning and environment in Asia. Tai-chee Wong; Andrew M. Marton; Sun Sheng Han; Chun Xing He; Roger C.K. Chan; Yao Shimou; Kee-bom Nahm; Huong Ha; P. Agrawal; Belinda Yuen; Lily Kong; Clive Briffett. **Geojournal** 49:3 1999 pp.239-338. *Collection of 10 articles.*

4109 Urban regeneration and sustainable development in Britain. The example of the Liverpool Ropewalks Partnership. Chris Couch; Annekatrin Dennemann. **Cities** 17:2 4:2000 pp.137-148.

4110 Urban renewal and its aftermath. Jon C. Teaford. **Hous. Pol. Deb.** 11:2 2000 pp.443-466.

4111 Urban renewal and the culture of conservatism: changing perceptions of the tower block and implications for contemporary renewal initiatives. Keith Jacobs; Tony Manzi. **Crit. Soc. Pol.** 18:2(55) 5:1998 pp.157-174.

4112 Urban renewal, heritage planning and the remaking of an inner-city suburb: a case study of heritage planning in Auckland, New Zealand. Alan Latham. **Plan. Pract. Res.** 15:4 11:2000 pp.285-298.

4113 Urban waterfront regeneration and local governance in Tallinn. Merje Feldman. **Eur.-Asia Stud.** 52:5 7:2000 pp.829-850.

4114 Verkehrsberuhigung in Stadtzentren. Ihre Auswirkungen auf Politik, Ökonomie, Mobilität, Ökologie und Verkehrssicherheit — unter besonderer Berücksichtigung des Fallbeispiels Lüneburg. *[In German]*; (Traffic reduction in town centres. Impact on policy, economy, mobility, ecology and traffic safety illustrated by the Lüneburg case study.) Peter Pez. **Arc. Kommunal.** 39:1 2000 pp.117-151.

4115 Views from above and below: the Petronas Twin Towers and/in contesting visions of development in contemporary Malaysia. Tim Bunnell. **Sing. J. Trop. Geogr.** 20:1 6:1999 pp.1-23.

4116 Voices from the barrio: oral testimony and informal housing processes. Peter Kellett. **Third World Plan. R.** 22:2 5:2000 pp.189-205.

4117 We can work it out: a community planning approach to neighbourhood regeneration. Peter Duncan; Andrew A. McArthur. London: National Housing Federation, 1999. ix, 73p. *ISBN: 0862974186. Includes bibliographical references (p. 72-73).*

4118 When strangers become neighbours: managing cities of difference. Leonie Sandercock. **Plan. Th. Pract.** 1:1 9:2000 pp.13-30.

Urban space
Espace urbain

4119 21st century living spaces. James D. Wright; Thomas J. DiLorenzo; Daniel J. Monti, Jr.; Michael Greenberg; Leonard I. Ruchelman. **Society** 38:1 11-12:2000 pp.3-38. *Collection of 5 articles.*

4120 Centros e margens: produção e práticas culturais na área metropolitana de Lisboa. *[In Portuguese]*; (Centres and fringes: cultural practices and production in the Lisbon metropolitan area.) Pedro Costa. **Anál. Soc.** XXXIV:153 Spring:2000 pp.957-984.

4121 A cidade Brasileira como espaço cultural. *[In Portuguese]*; (The Brazilian city as a cultural space.) *[Summary]*. Barbara Freitag-Rouanet. **Tempo Soc.** 12:1 5:2000 pp.29-46.

4122 Cities in the telecommunications age: the fracturing of geographies. James O. Wheeler [Ed.]; Yuko Aoyama [Ed.]; Barney Warf [Ed.]. New York: Routledge, 2000. 350p. *ISBN: 0415924413, 0415924421. Includes bibliographical references and index.*

4123 Classification and use of open space in the context of increasing urban capacity. Chris Nicol; Ron Blake. **Plan. Pract. Res.** 15:3 8:2000 pp.193-210.

G: ENVIRONNEMENT. COMMUNAUTÉ. RURAL. URBAIN

4124   Cyberspace and physical space in an urban economy. Hiroyuki Shibusawa. **Pap. Reg. Sci.** 79:3 7:2000 pp.253-270.

4125   La diaspora antillaise au Royaume-Uni et le religieux: appropriation d'un espace symbolique et reformulations des identités urbaines. *[In French]*; (The West Indian diaspora in the United Kingdom and religion: appropriation of a symbolic space and reshaping of urban identities.) *[Summary]*. Christine Chivallon. **Espace Géogr.** 29:4 2000 pp.315-328.

4126   Gender, culture, and architecture in Ahmedabad and Berlin. Krishna Kakad. **Gen. Tech. Dev.** 4:2 5-8:2000 pp.201-224.

4127   Globalizing cities: a new spatial order. Peter Marcuse [Ed.]; Ronald van Kempen [Ed.]. Oxford, Malden MA: Blackwell Publishers, 2000. xviii, 318p. *ISBN: 0631212892, 0631212906. Includes bibliographical references (p. [276]-301) and index. (Series: Studies in urban and social change).*

4128   History repeats itself, but how? City character, urban tradition, and the accomplishment of place. Harvey Molotch; William Freudenburg; Krista E. Paulsen. **Am. Sociol. R.** 65:6 12:2000 pp.791-823.

4129   Living differences: ethnicity and fearless girls in public spaces. Nora Räthzel. **Soc. Ident.** 6:2 6:2000 pp.119-142.

4130   La localisation des fonctions stratégiques: entre attractivité métropolitaine et convivialité résidentielle. *[In French]*; (Strategic functions location: between metropolitan attractivity and residential amenities].) *[Summary]*. Jean Ollivro; Guy Baudelle. **R. Ec. Reg. Urb.** 2 2000 pp.195-214.

4131   Louis Sullivan, architectural modernism, and the creation of democratic space. James R. Abbott. **Am. Sociol.** 31:1 Spring:2000 pp.62-85.

4132   Market places, social spaces in Cuzco, Peru. Linda J. Seligmann. **Int. J. Hum. Res. Man.** 29:1 Spring:2000 pp.1-68.

4133   The place of historic parks and gardens in the English planning system: towards statutory controls? John Pendlebury. **Town Plan. R.** 70:4 10:1999 pp.479-500.

4134   Public space, urban space and electronic space: would the real city please stand up? Mike Crang. **Urban Stud.** 37:2 2:2000 pp.301-318.

4135   Retail and the urban. Michelle Lowe; Neil Wrigley. **Urban Geogr.** 21:7 10-11:2000 pp.640-653.

4136   Social areas in Beijing. Victor F.S. Sit. **Geogr. Ann. B.** 81(B):4 1999 pp.203-221.

4137   Tales of the city: situating urban discourse in place and time. Simon Parker. **City** 4:2 7:2000 pp.233-246.

4138   The Thames Embankment and the disciplining of nature in modernity. Stuart Oliver. **Geogr. J.** 166:3 9:2000 pp.227-238.

4139   'That's the only place where you can hang out': urban young people and the space of the mall. Robert M. Vanderbeck; James H. Johnson, Jr. **Urban Geogr.** 21:1 1-2:2000 pp.5-25.

4140   'The gaze without eyes': video-surveillance and the changing nature of urban space. Hille Koskela. **Prog. H. Geog.** 24:2 6:2000 pp.243-265.

4141   Theming cities, taming places: insights from Singapore. T.C. Chang. **Geogr. Ann. B.** 82(B):1 2000 pp.35-54.

4142   Urban agriculture in Mexico City: functions provided by the use of space for dairy based livelihoods. H. Losada; R. Bennett; R. Soriano; J. Vieyra; J. Cortés. **Cities** 17:6 12:2000 pp.419-432.

4143   Urban morphology and the shaping of the transmissable city. Mike Crang. **City** 4:3 11:2000 pp.303-315.

4144   Urban space and representation. Maria Balshaw [Ed.]; Liam Kennedy [Ed.]. London, Sterling VA: Pluto Press, 2000. viii, 201p. *ISBN: 0745313493. Includes bibliographical references and index.*

4145   Views and visions of land use in the United Kingdom. Margaret Robertson; Rex Walford. **Geogr. J.** 166:3 9:2000 pp.239-254.

4146   Walking the city: an essay on peripatetic practices and politics. David MacAuley. **Cap. Nat. Social.** 11:4(44) 12:2000 pp.3-44.

G: ENVIRONMENT. COMMUNITY. RURAL. URBAN

4147 Women and the city: visibility and voice in urban space. Roberta Woods [Ed.]; Jane Darke [Ed.]; Sue Ledwith [Ed.]. New York: St. Martin's Press, 2000. 222p. *ISBN: 033377485X*. Includes bibliographical references and index.

4148 'You gotta love this city': The Whitlams and inner Sydney. Jessica Carroll; John Connell. **Aust. Geogr.** 31:2 7:2000 pp.141-154.

Urbanization and development
Urbanisation et développement urbain

4149 Aktuelle Aspekte der Urbanisierung in Jabotabek: Räumlicher und sektoraler Wandel in Metro-Jakarta. *[In German]*; [Current aspects of urbanization in Jabotabek: spatial and sectoral change in metropolitan Jakarta]. Günter Spreitzhofer; Martin Heintel. **Int. Asien.** 30:1-2 5:1999 pp.131-152.

4150 Beyond edge cities: job decentralization and urban sprawl. Chengri Ding; Richard D. Bingham. **Urban Aff. Rev.** 35:6 7:2000 pp.837-864.

4151 Beyond optimal city size: an evaluation of alternative urban growth patterns. Roberta Capello; Roberto Camagni. **Urban Stud.** 37:9 8:2000 pp.1479-1496.

4152 The changing face of the rural hinterland of a fast growing town. Case study: Gurgaon and its hinterland. Monis Khan; Shashi Shekhar. **Ind. J. Reg. Sci.** XXXII 2000 pp.106-117.

4153 Compliance with urban development and planning regulations in Ibadan, Nigeria. Ben C. Arimah; Demola Adeagbo. **Hab. Int.** 24:3 9:2000 pp.279-294.

4154 Conceptualizing small towns as urban places: the process of downtown redevelopment in Galena, Illinois. Thomas W. Paradis. **Urban Geogr.** 21:1 1-2:2000 pp.61-82.

4155 Continuity and change in a Middle Eastern city: the social ecology of Irbid City, Jordan. Mohammed Suleiman Shunnaq; William A. Schwab. **Int. J. Hum. Res. Man.** 29:1 Spring:2000 pp.69-98.

4156 Dynamiques foncières et immobilières: explosion urbaine à Cotonou. *[In French]*; (Real estate and land development dynamics: urban expansion in Cotonou, Benin.) *[Summary]*. Jean-Claude Grisoni Niaki. **Cah. Outre-mer** 53:211 7-9:2000 pp.231-252.

4157 Entitlement to patronage: social construction of household claims on slum improvement project, Bangladesh. Shayer Ghafur. **Hab. Int.** 24:3 9:2000 pp.261-278.

4158 Évolutions des organisations urbaines et mobilités quotidiennes: espace de référence et analyse des processus. *[In French]*; [Daily mobility and changes in urban organisation: a reference space and an analysis of processes of change] *[Summary]*. Jean-Marie Halleux. **Espace Géogr.** 30:1 2001 pp.67-80.

4159 Exploring the local: international initiatives, regeneration and participation. Robert A. Beauregard; Jon Pierre; Paul Foley; Steve Martin; Suzanne Fitzpatrick; Annette Hastings; Keith Kintrea. **Policy Pol.** 28:4 10:2000 pp.465-510. *Collection of 3 articles*.

4160 From world cities to gateway cities: extending the boundaries of globalization theory. John Rennie Short; Carrie Breitbach; Steven Buckman; Jamey Essex. **City** 4:3 11:2000 pp.317-340.

4161 Housing-sector performance in global perspective: a cross-city investigation. Ben C. Arimah. **Urban Stud.** 37:13 12:2000 pp.2551-2580.

4162 An institutional analysis of the process of urbanization in China from the bottom up. Gu Shengzu; Li Zhengyou. **Soc. Sci. China** XXI:1 Spring:2000 pp.67-78.

4163 International municipal cooperation: an enabling approach to development for small and intermediate urban centres? W.E. Hewitt. **Third World Plan. R.** 22:3 8:2000 pp.335-360.

4164 Land readjustment and metropolitan growth: an examination of suburban land development and urban sprawl in the Tokyo metropolitan area. André Sorensen. **Prog. Plan.** 53:4 2000 pp.217-330.

4165 Main street development in Dagupan. Norbert Dannhaeuser. **Phil. Stud.** 48:2 2000 pp.143-174.

4166 Monitoring growth in rapidly urbanizing areas using remotely sensed data. Douglas Ward; Stuart R. Phinn; Alan T. Murray. **Prof. Geogr.** 52:3 8:2000 pp.371-385.

G: ENVIRONNEMENT. COMMUNAUTÉ. RURAL. URBAIN

4167 Nachhaltige Kommunikation. Stadtentwicklung als Verständigungsarbeit — Entwicklungslinien, Stärken, Schwächen und Folgerungen. *[In German]*; (Sustainable communication? Urban development as a process of agreement — development trends, strengths, weaknesses and conclusions.) *[Summary]*. Klaus Selle. **Inf. Raum.** 1 2000 pp.9-20.

4168 Post-socialist urban transition in Eastern and Central Europe. Zoltán Kovács; Ulrike Sailer-Fliege; Vic Duke; Mike Ingham; Zoltán Dövényi; Keith Grime; Reinhard Wießner; Herman Kok; Alain Dingsdale; Luděc Sýkora; Tuna Tasan; G.J. Ashworth; J.E. Tunbridge; Andrei Treivish; Izolde Brade; Tatyana Nefedova. **Geojournal** 49:1 1999 pp.1-129. *Collection of 12 articles.*

4169 Poverty reduction and urban governance. Shyam S. Dutta; Mariken Vaa; Solomon Benjamin; Felisa U. Etemadi; Steven Russell; Elizabeth Vidler; Andrés Cabanas Díaz; Emma Grant; Paula Irene del Cid Vargas; Verónica Sajbin Velásquez; Jo Beall; Owen Crankshaw; Susan Parnell; Nick Devas; David Korboe; Paul Jenkins; Carole Rakodi; Rose Gatabaki Kamau; Eduardo Dockemdorff; Alfredo Rodríguez; Lucy Winchester; Philip Amis; Sashi Kumar. **Environ. Urban.** 12:2 4:2000 pp.3-196. *Collection of 13 articles.*

4170 Rapid urbanisation in the Gambia: its implications for land use planning. Paul Caprani. **Third World Plan. R.** 21:2 5:1999 pp.155-175.

4171 Le rôle des acteurs publics et privés dans l'urbanisation des villes de la région de Bizerte. *[In French]*; [The role of public and private actors in the urbanization of towns in the Bizerte region]. Mourad Ben Jalloul. **R. Tun. Sci. Soc.** 36:119 1999 pp.65-90.

4172 Urban development and new towns in the Third World: lessons from the New Bombay experience. Alain R.A. Jacquemin. Aldershot, Brookfield VT: Ashgate, 1999. xvii, 313p. *ISBN: 0754610519. Includes bibliographical references. (Series:* SOAS studies in development geography).

4173 Urban process and change in Africa. Abdou Maliq Simone. Dakar: CODESRIA, 1998. 122p. *Includes bibliographical references (p. 115-122). (Series:* Working paper - 3/97).

4174 Urban regeneration: a handbook. Hugh Sykes [Ed.]; Peter W. Roberts [Ed.]. London: Sage Publications, 2000. xvi, 320p. *ISBN: 0761967168, 0761967176. Includes bibliographical references and index.*

4175 Urbanisation. *[In French]*; [Urbanization]. Philippe Julien; Pascale Bessy-Pietri; Chantal Brutel; Maryse Jegou; Carole Rieu; Anne Rozan; Anne Stenger; Élizabeth Kremp; Patrick Sevestre. **Écon. Stat.** 336 6:2000 pp.3-92. *Collection of 5 articles.*

4176 Urbanisation in the outer city: a case study in Ho Chi Minh City's suburbs. Lisa Drummond. **Malay. J. Trop. Geogr.** 29:1 6:1998 pp.23-38.

4177 'Urbanisation of everybody', institutional imperatives, and social transformation in Pakistan. Mohammad A. Qadeer; Mohammad Afzal [Comments by]. **Pak. Dev. R.** 38:4(II) Winter:1999 pp.1193-1210.

4178 Vietnam's urban edge: the administration of urban development in Hanoi. Michael Leaf. **Third World Plan. R.** 21:3 8:1999 pp.297-316.

H: ECONOMIC LIFE
VIE ÉCONOMIQUE

H.1: Economic sociology
Sociologie économique

4179 Beni & Servizi. *[In Italian]*; [Goods and Services]. Carla Ravaioli. **Crit. Marx.** 2 3-4:2000 pp.55-68.
4180 Beyond homo economicus: new developments in theories of social norms. Elizabeth Anderson. **Philos. Pub.** 29:2 Spring:2000 pp.170-200.
4181 Carl Menger's theory of invisible-hand explanations. Markus Haller. **Soc. Sci. Info.** 39:4 12:2000 pp.529-566.
4182 The changing commercial structure of non-metropolitan urban centres and vacancy rates; *[Summary in French]*. Maurice Yeates; Dan Montgomery. **Can. Geogr.** 43:4 Winter:1999 pp.382-399.
4183 Do individuals try to maximize general satisfaction? Paul Frijters. **J. Econ. Psyc.** 21:3 6:2000 pp.281-304.
4184 Does cultural origin affect saving behavior? Evidence from immigrants. Christopher D. Carroll; Byung-kun Rhee; Changyong Rhee. **Econ. Dev. Cult. Change** 48:1 10:1999 pp.33-50.
4185 Essays on social conflict and reform. Anders Bornefalk. Stockholm: Stockholm School of Economics, 2000. *ISBN: 9172585285. Includes bibliographical references.*
4186 From value to consumption. A social-theoretical perspective on Simmel's *Philosophie des Geldes*. Roberta Sassatelli. **Acta Sociol.** 43:3 2000 pp.207-218.
4187 Honor, status, and aggression in economic exchange. Vern Baxter; A.V. Margavio. **Sociol. Theory** 18:3 11:2000 pp.399-416.
4188 The impact of perceived material wealth and perceiver personality on first impressions. Andrew N. Christopher; Barry R. Schlenker. **J. Econ. Psyc.** 21:1 2:2000 pp.1-19.
4189 In search of research: approaches to socio-economic issues in contemporary Namibia. Direcktoratet for utviklingshjelp; Christian Michelsens Institutt for Videnskap og Andsfrihet; Namibian Economic Policy Research Unit; Multidisciplinary Research Centre, University of Namibia. Windhoek: NEPRU, 1998. viii, 173p. *ISBN: 999163804X. Papers presented at a NORAD-sponsored workshop of the Christian Michelsen Institute (CMI), the Namibian Economic Policy Research Unit (NEPRU), and the Social Science Division (SSD) of the Multidisciplinary Research Centre at the University of Namibia. Includes bibliographical references. (Series:* NEPRU publication - 6).
4190 Institutions meet mind: the way out of an impasse. Salvatore Rizzello; Margherita Turvani. **Constit. Pol. Econ.** 11:2 6:2000 pp.165-180.
4191 An interview with Barbara Bergmann: leading feminist economist. Barbara Bergmann; Lisa F. Saunders [Interviewer]; Mary C. King [Interviewer]. **R. Pol. Econ.** 12:3 7:2000 pp.305-316.
4192 Die Macht Des Geldes — 100 Jahre „Philosophie Des Geldes". *[In German]*; (The power of money — 100 years of 'philosophy of money'.) Christoph Deutschmann; Viviana A. Zelizer; Steffen Sigmund; Neil Fligstein; Helga Krüger; René Levy; Jörg Rössel. **Berl. J. Soziol.** 10:3 2000 pp.301-422. *Collection of 6 articles.*
4193 Markets and money in social theory: what role for economics? Ben Fine; Costas Lapavitsas; Viviana Zelizer [Comments by]. **Econ. Soc.** 29:3 8:2000 pp.357-389.
4194 Methodological altruism as an alternative foundation for individual optimization. Christian Arnsperger. **Ethic. Theory Moral P.** 3:2 6:2000 pp.115-136.
4195 Penser ensemble l'économie et la société. *[In French]*; [Thinking about both society and the economy together]. Jean-Louis Laville; Benoît Levesque. **Esprit** 264 6:2000 pp.207-221.

H: VIE ÉCONOMIQUE

4196 The rational choice generalization of neoclassical economics reconsidered: any theoretical legitimation for economic imperialism? Milan Zafirovski. **Sociol. Theory** 18:3 11:2000 pp.448-471.
4197 Social capital: promise and pitfalls of its role in development. Alejandro Portes; Patricia Landolt. **J. Lat. Am. St.** 32:2 5:2000 pp.529-548.
4198 Tschechische, österreichische und deutsche Kulturstandards in der Wirtschaftskooperation. *[In German]*; [Czech, Austrian and German cultural standards in economic cooperation]. Gerhard Fink; Ivan Nový; Sylvia Schroll-Machl. **J. E. Eur. Man. Stud.** 5:4 2000 pp.361-376.
4199 The uses of authority in economics: shared intellectual frameworks as the foundation of personal persuasion. Morgan Marietta; Mark Perlman. **Am. J. Econ. S.** 59:2 4:2000 pp.151-190.
4200 What constitutes a good society? Bent Greve [Ed.]. Basingstoke: Macmillan, 2000. xiii, 192p. *ISBN: 0333775023, 0312228260. Includes bibliographical references and index.*

H.2: **Economic and production systems**
Systèmes économiques et de production

4201 Autogestion: apprentissages et projets. *[In French]*; [Self-management: training and projects]. Maurice Decaillot. **Pensée** 321 1-3:2000 pp.25-42.
4202 Blade Runner capitalism, the transnational corporation, and commodification: implications for cultural integrity. Marc T. Jones. **Cult. Dyn.** 10:3 11:1998 pp.287-306.
4203 Bringing Putnam to the European regions: on the relevance of social capital for economic growth. Gerald Schneider; Thomas Plümper; Steffen Baumann. **Eur. Urban Reg. Stud.** 7:4 10:2000 pp.307-318.
4204 Cadre capitalism in Hungary and Poland: property accumulation among communist-era elites. Eric Hanley. **E. Eur. Pol. Soc.** 14:1 Winter:2000 pp.143-178.
4205 Capitalism's impending dangers for global humane development. Mahmoud Dhaouadi. **Am. J. Islam. Soc. Sci.** 17:1 Spring:2000 pp.39-64.
4206 Coffee anyone? Recent research on Latin American coffee societies. Steven C. Topik. **Hisp. Am. Hist. Rev.** 80:2 5:2000 pp.225-266.
4207 Confucian pragmatism vs. Brahmanical idealism: understanding the divergent roots of Indian and Chinese economic performance. Rajesh Kumar. **J. As. Bus.** 16:2 2000 pp.49-70.
4208 Consolidating states, restructuring economies, and confronting workers and peasants: the antinomies of Bolivian neoliberalism. Harry Sanabria. **Comp. Stud. S.** 41:3 7:1999 pp.535-562.
4209 Controversies and evidence in the market transition debate. Yang Cao; Victor G. Nee; Xueguang Zhou [Comments by]. **A.J.S.** 105:4 1:2000 pp.1175-1195.
4210 Creating an ecological socialist future. Aaran Gare. **Cap. Nat. Social.** 11(2):42 6:2000 pp.23-40.
4211 Critique de l'économie «apolitique». *[In French]*; (The unsupportable flexibility of being: citizenship and precarity.) Rémy Herrera. **Hom. Soc.** 135 1-3:2000 pp.87-104.
4212 The cultural basis of a regional economy: the Vega Baja del Segura in Spain. Susana Narotzky. **Ethnology** XXXIX:1 Winter:2000 pp.1-14.
4213 Cyber-Marx: cycles and circuits of struggle in high-technology capitalism. Nick Dyer-Witheford. Urbana IL: University of Illinois Press, 1999. x, 344p. *ISBN: 0252024796, 0252067959. Includes bibliographical references (p. [301]-332) and index.*
4214 Du produit marchandise à «l'entreprise marchandise»: une clé possible de lecture de la «pensée unique» contemporaine. *[In French]*; (From merchandise product to merchandise enterprise.) Jean-Claude Delaunay. **Hom. Soc.** 135 1-3:2000 pp.157-173.
4215 An exchange: socialism and the market. Roy Morrison; David McNally. **New Polit.** VII:4 Winter:2000 pp.53-65.

H: ECONOMIC LIFE

4216 Exhausting modernity: grounds for a new economy. Teresa Brennan. New York: Routledge, 2000. 216p. *ISBN: 041523705X, 0415237068.*

4217 El fin de la dialéctica: pobreza sin revolución y capitalismo sin riqueza. *[In Spanish]*; [The end of the dialectic: poverty without revolution and capitalism without wealth]. Raúl Augusto Hernández. **Rev. Parag. Sociol.** 36:106 9-12:1999 pp.35-60.

4218 Flexible families: capitalist development and crisis in rural Peru. Susan Vincent. **J. Comp. Fam. Stud.** XXXI:2 Spring:2000 pp.155-170.

4219 Flexible production, households, and fieldwork: multisited Zapotec weavers in the era of late capitalism. W. Warner Wood. **Ethnology** XXXIX:2 Spring:2000 pp.133-148.

4220 Forms of property rights or class capacities. The example of Tuscan sharecropping. Rebecca J. Emigh. **Eur. J. Soc.** XLI:1 2000 pp.22-52.

4221 Globalization and ideology: the competing images of the contemporary Japanese economic system in the 1990s. Bai Gao. **Int. Sociol.** 15:3 9:2000 pp.435-454.

4222 Globalization, Europeanization and the end of Scandinavian social democracy? Robert Geyer [Ed.]; Jonathon Moses [Ed.]; Christine Ingebritsen [Ed.]. Basingstoke: Macmillan, 1999. 256p. *ISBN: 033372710X. Includes bibliographical references.*

4223 Grands commerçants musulmans au bord de la crise? Ajustement structurel, dévaluation et pétrole au Tchad. *[In French]*; [Muslim merchants on the verge of crisis? Structural adjustment, devaluation and petrol in Chad]. Claude Arditi. **Islam Soc. S. Sah.** 13 12:1999 pp.103-118.

4224 L'homme, l'économe de l'homme. Fatalité de l'économie ou économie existentielle? *[In French]*; (Man, man's treasurer. The fatality of the economy or existential economy?) Philippe Caumartin. **Pensée** 321 1-3:2000 pp.43-54.

4225 Housing, home ownership and social change in Hong Kong. James Z. Lee. Aldershot: Ashgate, 1999. ix, 242p. *ISBN: 1840145625. Includes bibliographical references (p. 225-237) and index. (Series:* Social and political studies from Hong Kong).

4226 In and out of the milking parlour: a cross-national comparison of gender, the dairy industry and the state. Sally Shortall. **Wom. St. Inter. For.** 23:2 3-4:2000 pp.247-258.

4227 Millennial capitalism and the culture of neoliberalism. Jean Comaroff; John L. Comaroff; Irene Stengs; Hylton White; Caitrin Lynch; Jeffrey A. Zimmermann; Fernando Coronil; Michael Storper; Peter Geschiere; Francis Nyamnjoh; Luiz Paulo Lima; Scott Bradwell; Seamus Walsh; Rosalind C. Morris; Robert P. Weller. **Publ. Cult.** 12:2 Spring:2000 pp.291-498. *Collection of 8 articles.*

4228 Miracles with a system: the economic rise of East Asia and the role of sociocultural patterns. Boris Holzer. **Int. Sociol.** 15:3 9:2000 pp.455-478.

4229 The morality of immigrant home ownership: gender, work and Italian-Australian *sistemazione*. Mariastella Pulvirenti. **Aust. Geogr.** 31:2 7:2000 pp.237-250.

4230 Néo-libéralisme ou keynésianiśme rénové: la fausse alternative. *[In French]*; (Keynesianism against neoliberalism: a real alternative?) Denis Collin. **Hom. Soc.** 135 1-3:2000 pp.45-70.

4231 On two 'models' of capitalism. John Rosenthal. **Sci. Soc.** 64:4 Winter:2000-2001 pp.424-459.

4232 The People's Republic of Yoker: a case study of tenant management in Scotland. Suzie Scott. **J. Co-op. St.** 33:1 4:2000 pp.15-38.

4233 Property cycles in a global economy. Alireza Dehesh; Cedric Pugh. **Urban Stud.** 37:13 12:2000 pp.2581-2602.

4234 Le sens des mots dans le débat sur l'après-Fordisme ou le capitalisme fin-de-siècle au-delà des mythes. *[In French]*; (The meaning of terms used in the debate on post-Fordism or end-of-century capitalism, beyond the myths.) *[Summary]*. R. Bellofiore. **Ec. Sociét.** XXXIV:1 1:2000 pp.5-31.

4235 Solidarity-based third sector organizations in the 'proximity services' field: a European francophone perspective. Jean-Louis Laville; Marthe Nyssens. **Voluntas** 11:1 3:2000 pp.67-84.

4236 Structural adjustment and social disarticulation: the case of Argentina. Miguel Teubal. **Sci. Soc.** 64:4 Winter:2000-2001 pp.460-488.

H: VIE ÉCONOMIQUE

4237 Le «tiers secteur»: le retour de la troisième voie. *[In French]*; (The 'tiertiary sector' or the return of the third way.) Daniel Bachet. **Hom. Soc.** 135 1-3:2000 pp.139-156.
4238 Tourism and the development of handicraft production in the Maltese islands; *[Summary in French]*. Marion C. Markwick. **Tour. Geog.** 3:1 2:2001 pp.29-51.
4239 Tres notas sobre *El espíritu del capitalismo* en Weber, para pensar América Latina. *[In Spanish]*; [Three points on Weber's *The Spirit of Capitalism* with relation to Latin America] *[Summary]*. José Gandarilla Salgado. **Est. Latinam.** VI:11 1-6:1999 pp.21-31.
4240 Trust, networks and norms: the creation of social capital in agricultural economies in Ghana. F. Lyon. **World Dev.** 28:4 4:2000 pp.663-682.
4241 Understanding China's transition to capitalism: the contributions of Victor Nee and Andrew Walder. Doug Guthrie. **Sociol. For.** 15:4 12:2000 pp.727-749.
4242 The universal capitalism movement in the United States. Ward Morehouse; Stuart Speiser; Ken Taylor. **R. Soc. Econ.** LVIII:1 3:2000 pp.63-80.
4243 Viejos y nuevos actores: la pluriactividad en las explotaciones familiares de la región Pampeana Argentina. *[In Spanish]*; [Old and new actors: diversification in family operations in the Pampeana region of Argentina]. Clara Craviotti. **Rev. Parag. Sociol.** 36:104 1-4:1999 pp.123-146.

H.3: **Economic conditions and living standards**
Conditions économiques et niveau de vie

4244 Adverse living conditions and political protest after communism. Karl-Dieter Opp. **Soc. Forc.** 79:1 9:2000 pp.29-65.
4245 Ajustement et mobilité économique à Lima. *[In French]*; (Adjustment and economic mobility in Lima.) Javier Herrera. **Prob. Am. Lat.** 38 7-9:2000 pp.71-100.
4246 Assessing the impact of agricultural research on poverty alleviation. Douglas Pachico [Ed.]; Reed Hertford [Ed.]; Alain de Janvry [Ed.]; Elisabeth Sadoulet; Shenngen Fan; Peter Hazell; T. Haque; Derek Byerlee; Keijiro Otsuka; Mitch Renkow; Sara J. Scherr; Gordon Rausser; Leo Simon; Holly Ameden; Thomas S. Walker. **Food Pol.** 25:4 8:2000 pp.379-530. *Collection of 9 articles.*
4247 Benefit take-up and the geography of poverty in Scotland; *[Summary in French]*; *[Summary in German]*. Glen Bramley; Sharon Lancaster; David Gordon. **Reg. Stud.** 34:6 8:2000 pp.507-520.
4248 Las causas de la pobreza rural en América Latina y políticas para reducirla, con referencia especial al Paraguay. *[In Spanish]*; [The causes of rural poverty in Latin America and policies to alleviate it, with special reference to Paraguay]. Albert Berry. **Rev. Parag. Sociol.** 36:106 9-12:1999 pp.7-34.
4249 The colour of poverty: a study of the poverty of ethnic and immigrant groups in Canada; *[Summary in French]*; *[Summary in Spanish]*. Abdolmohammad Kazemipur; Shiva S. Halli. **Int. Migr.** 38:1 2000 pp.69-88.
4250 Crisis effects in South Korea. Su-dol Kang; Hee-yeon Cho; Kwang-yeong Shin; Myung Koo Kang; Ok-sang Lim; Bul-dong Park; Seong-nae Kim; Keehyeung Lee; Jin Kyoon Kim; Young-soon Kim; Myung-hee Han; Jung Ok Lee [Tr.]. **Inter-Asia Cult. St.** 1:3 12:2000 pp.393-456. *Collection of 4 articles.*
4251 ¿Cuán eficiente es el mapa de NBIs como instrumento para la focalización del gasto? *[In Spanish]*; [How efficient is the map of Basic Unsatisfied Needs as an instrument for focusing social expenditure?] *[Summary]*. Nelson Shack. **Apuntes** 45 1999 pp.13-36.
4252 Demografía y pobreza. *[In Spanish]*; [Demography and poverty]. Joaquín Leguina. **Leviatán** 80 Summer:2000 pp.31-46.
4253 Development in Sub-Saharan Africa: cultural influences and managers' decision behaviour. J.C. Munene; S.H. Schwartz; P.B. Smith. **Publ. Adm. D.** 20:4 10:2000 pp.339-352.
4254 The effects of foreign aid on women's attainment of their economic and social human rights. Clair Apodaca. **J. Third World St.** XVII:2 Fall:2000 pp.205-222.

H: ECONOMIC LIFE

4255 Equality, participation, transition: essays in honour of Branko Horvat. Milica Uvalić [Ed.]; Vojmir Franičević [Ed.]. Basingstoke: Macmillan, 2000. 209p. *ISBN: 031223225X, 0333776402*. Includes bibliographical references and index.

4256 Finansovyi krizis i sotsial'naia zashchita. *[In Russian]*; (Financial crisis and social defence.) M. Dmitriev. **Obshch. Nauki Sovrem.** 3 2000 pp.16-31.

4257 From austerity to prosperity? Migration and child poverty among mainland and island Puerto Ricans. R.S. Oropesa; Nancy S. Landale. **Demography** 37:3 8:2000 pp.323-338.

4258 From modernization to globalization: perspectives on development and social change. J. Timmons Roberts [Ed.]; Amy Hite [Ed.]. Malden MA: Blackwell Publishers, 1999. *ISBN: 0631210962, 0631210970*. Includes bibliographical references and index. (Series: Blackwell readers in sociology).

4259 Gender, poverty and empowerment. John Andersen; Jørgen Elm Larsen. **Crit. Soc. Pol.** 18:2(55) 5:1998 pp.241-258.

4260 Globalización, economía de mercado y desarrollo humano: desafíos y riesgos para Centro América en los umbrales del siglo XXI. *[In Spanish]*; [Globalization, the market economy and human development: challenges and risks facing Central America at the beginning of the 21st century]. Eugenio Ortega. Guatemala: Instituto Centroamericano de Estudios Políticos (INCEP), 1999. 88p.

4261 Globalization and socio-economic restructuring in Andalusia: challenges and possible alternatives. Francisco Entrena; Jesús Gómez-Mateos; Jean Stephenson [Tr.]. **Eur. Sociol. R.** 16:1 3:2000 pp.93-114.

4262 Hodnotenie spravodlivosti pravidiel distribúcie zdrojov so zretel'om na situačný kontext. *[In Slovak]*; [A situation context evaluation of the justice of resource distribution rules]. Eva Bolfíková. **Sociologia [Brat.]** 32:5 2000 pp.449-470.

4263 Household strategies for survival 1600-2000: fission, faction and cooperation. Laurence Fontaine; Jürgen Schlumbohm; Thomas Sokoll; Jeremy Boulton; Montserrat Carbonell-Esteller; Sabine Ullmann; Dennis A. Frey, Jr.; Alain Marie; Hotze Lont; Danyu Wang. **Int. Rev. S. H.** 45:Supp.8 2000 pp.1-196. *Collection of 9 articles.*

4264 How and why has poverty in China changed? A study based on microdata for 1988 and 1995. Björn Gustafsson; Wei Zhong. **China Quart.** 164 12:2000 pp.983-1006.

4265 How is household vulnerability gendered? Female-headed households in the collectives of Suleimaniyah, Iraqi Kurdistan. Louise Waite. **Disasters** 24:2 6:2000 pp.153-172.

4266 How segregation concentrates poverty. Douglas S. Massey; Mary J. Fischer. **Ethn. Racial** 23:4 7:2000 pp.670-691.

4267 Human development report 1999. United Nations Development Programme. New York, Oxford: Oxford University Press, 1999. xiv, 262p. *ISBN: 0195215621*. Includes bibliographical references (p. 251-252) and index.

4268 Human rights to food, health and education. Siddiqur Rahman Osmani. **J. Hum. Dev.** 1:2 7:2000 pp.273-298.

4269 The hyper-shantytown: neo-liberal violence(s) in the Argentine slum. Javier Auyero. **Ethnog.** 1:1 7:2000 pp.93-116.

4270 Identifying poverty in rural England; *[Summary in French]*; *[Summary in Spanish]*. Michael Noble; Gemma Wright. **Policy Pol.** 28:3 7:2000 pp.293-308.

4271 Inequality, welfare state, and homicide: further support for the institutional anomie theory. Jukka Savolainen. **Criminology** 38:4 11:2000 pp.1021-1042.

4272 International inclusiveness: publicizing Cuba's development of the 'good life'. AnaMaria Goicoechea-Balbona; Enrique Conill-Mendoza. **Int. Soc. Work** 43:4 10:2000 pp.435-452.

4273 Involution and destitution in capitalist Russia. Michael Burawoy; Pavel Krotov; Tatyana Lytkina. **Ethnog.** 1:1 7:2000 pp.43-66.

4274 Is inequality bad for our health? Jeffrey Milyo; Jennifer M. Mellor. **Crit. Rev.** 13:3-4 Summer-Fall:1999 pp.359-372.

4275 Making the economic *habitus*: Algerian workers revisited. Pierre Bourdieu. **Ethnog.** 1:1 7:2000 pp.17-42.

4276 Measuring living standards with proxy variables. Mark R. Montgomery; Michele Gragnolati; Kathleen A. Burke; Edmundo Paredes. **Demography** 37:2 5:2000 pp.155-174.

H: VIE ÉCONOMIQUE

4277 Methoden der Armutsmessung. Einkommens-, Unterversorgungs-, Deprivations- und Sozialhilfekonzept im Vergleich. *[In German]*; (Concepts of poverty measurement: a comparison of four different approaches.) *[Summary]*. Andreas Klocke. **Z. Soziol.** 29:4 8:2000 pp.313-329.

4278 The new economy, globalisation and the impact on African-Americans. Randolph B. Persuad; Clarence Lusane. **Race Class** 42:1 7-9:2000 pp.21-34.

4279 A new model of development for the new millennium. D. Paul Schafer. **Wor. Futur.** 55:4 2000 pp.293-328.

4280 The paradox of Africa's poverty: the role of indigenous knowledge, traditional practices and local institutions - the case of Ethiopia. Tirfe Mammo. Lawrenceville NJ: Red Sea Press, 1999. xv, 268p. *ISBN: 1569020485, 1569020493. Includes bibliographical references (p. 241-257) and index.*

4281 Política económica, distribución del ingreso, y pobreza en Paraguay. *[In Spanish]*; [Economic policy, income distribution and poverty in Paraguay]. Gustavo Indart. **Rev. Parag. Sociol.** 36:106 9-12:1999 pp.61-106.

4282 Poverty and inequality in South Africa: meeting the challenge. Julian May [Ed.]. London: Zed Books, 2000. xiv, 304p. *ISBN: 1856498077, 1856498085. Includes bibliographical references and index.*

4283 Poverty and social exclusion in Britain. David Gordon; et al. York: Joseph Rowntree Foundation, 2000. 101p. *ISBN: 1859350593.*

4284 Poverty, rural financial institution building and gender sensitive demand analysis in the North-West and West Province of Cameroon. Gertrud Schrieder. **Sav. Develop.** XXIV:1 2000 pp.95-110.

4285 Recasting economic inequality. Ashwini Deshpande. **R. Soc. Econ.** LVIII:3 9:2000 pp.381-399.

4286 Recherches sur la pauvreté: état des lieux. Contribution à la définition d'une problématique. *[In French]*; (Research on poverty: a state of affairs. Contribution to the definition of a problematic.) Marguerite Bey. **R. T-Monde** XL:160 10-12:1999 pp.871-900.

4287 Re-framing development for the 21st century. A. Thomas; T. Allen; E.A. Brett; J. Chataway; D. Wield; D. Styan; J. Beall; D. Weinhold; J. Hanlon. **J. Int. Dev.** 12:6 8:2000 pp.769-901. *Collection of 8 articles.*

4288 The riddle of the modern world: of liberty, wealth and equality. Alan MacFarlane. Basingstoke: Macmillan, 2000. 272p. *ISBN: 033379270X. Includes bibliographical references and index.*

4289 Singapore's economic internationalization and its effects on work and family. Audrey Chia. **SOJOURN** 15:1 4:2000 pp.123-138.

4290 Social capital and culture: master keys to development. Bernardo Kliksberg. **CEPAL R.** 69 12:1999 pp.83-102.

4291 Social inequalities, stressors and self reported health status among African American and White women in the Detroit metropolitan area. A. Schulz; B. Israel; D. Williams; E. Parker; A. Becker; S. James. **Soc. Sci. Med.** 51:11 12:2000 pp.1639-1653.

4292 Socioeconomic transformation in Russia: where is the rural elite? Stephen K. Wegren. **Eur.-Asia Stud.** 52:2 3:2000 pp.237-272.

4293 Soziale Gerechtigkeit. *[In German]*; [Social justice]. Birgit Mahnkopf; Peter Lohauß; Norbert Reuter; Hans Georg Zilian; Bernd Ladwig; Urs Müller-Plantenberg; Enrique Leff. **Prokla Zeit. Krit. Soz.** 30:4 12:2000 pp.489-633. *Collection of 7 articles.*

4294 The super-rich: the unjust new world of global capitalism. Stephen Haseler. Basingstoke; New York: Macmillan; St. Martin's Press, 2000. xviii, 208p. *ISBN: 0333764285, 0312230052. Includes bibliographical references and index.*

4295 Usloviia zhizni v Rossii. *[In Russian]*; (Living conditions in Russia.) *[Summary]*. F. Ronge. **Sot. Issle.** 3 2000 pp.59-69.

4296 Valores posmaterialistas entre los menos privilegiados en el Puerto Rico de hoy. *[In Spanish]*; [Post-materialist values among the under-privileged of Puerto Rico today] *[Summary]*. Jorge Benítez Nazario. **Rev. Cien. Soc.** 6 1:1999 pp.165-179.

H: ECONOMIC LIFE

4297 Das vereinte Deutschland — Eine lebenswerte Gesellschaft? Zur Bewertung von Freiheit, Sicherheit und Gerechtigkeit in Ost und West. *[In German]*; (The unified Germany — a society worth living in? The assessment of freedom, security and social justice in East and West.) *[Summary]*. Thomas Bulmahn. **Kölner Z. Soz. Soz. Psy.** 52:3 9:2000 pp.405-427.

4298 Współczesna rzeczywistość, współczesna bieda (wybrane teoretyczne i empiryczne podstawy analizy biedy). *[In Polish]*; (Contemporary reality, contemporary poverty (selected theoretical and empirical foundations of poverty analysis).) *[Summary]*. Jolanta Grotowska Leder. **Prz. Soc.** XLIX:1 2000 pp.31-58.

Income
Revenu

4299 Budgets précaires. *[In French]*; [Precarious budgets]. Jean-Michel Belorgey; Daniel Verger; Chloé Mirau; Hugues Moutouh; Daniel Lenoir; Liane Mozère; Taoufik Souami; Gilles Nezosi; Philippe Steck; Pierre Concialdi; François Aballéa; Jean-Noël Chopart. **Inf. Soc.** 86 2000 pp.4-117. *Collection of 12 articles.*

4300 The concentration of African-American poverty and the dispersal of the working class: an ethnographic study of three inner-city areas; *[Summary in French]*. Martín Sánchez-Jankowski. **Int. J. Urban Reg. Res.** 23:4 1999 pp.619-637.

4301 Economic transformation and income inequality in urban China: evidence from panel data. Xueguang Zhou. **A.J.S.** 105:4 1:2000 pp.1135-1174.

4302 The home as workplace: a study of income-generating activities within the domestic setting. Peter Kellett; A. Graham Tipple. **Environ. Urban.** 12:2 4:2000 pp.203-214.

4303 Income of the urban elderly in postreform China: political capital, human capital, and the state. James M. Raymo; Yu Xie. **Soc. Sci. R.** 29:1 3:2000 pp.1-24.

4304 Income-related inequality in life-years and quality-adjusted life-years. Ulf-G Gerdtham; Magnus Johannesson. **J. Health Econ.** 19:6 11:2000 pp.1007-1026.

4305 An intergenerational model of wages, hours, and earnings. Joseph G. Altonji; Thomas A. Dunn. **J. Hum. Res.** 35:2 Spring:2000 pp.221-258.

4306 Jak vnímáme příjmové nerovnosti a jaké bychom je chtěli mít. *[In Czech]*; (Perceived and desired income inequalities.) *[Summary]*. Blanka Řeháková. **Soc. Čas.** 36:1 2000 pp.23-40.

4307 Minimum wage and justice? Oren M. Levin-Waldman. **R. Soc. Econ.** LVIII:1 3:2000 pp.43-62.

4308 The poverty and heterogeneity among female-headed households revisited: the case of Panama. N. Fuwa. **World Dev.** 28:8 8:2000 pp.1515-1542.

4309 Rural nonagricultural employment and poverty in Ecuador. Peter Lanjouw. **Econ. Dev. Cult. Change** 48:1 10:1999 pp.91-122.

H.4: **Markets and consumption**
Marchés et consommation

4310 Accounting at home. Sue Llewellyn [Ed.]; Stephen P. Walker [Ed.]; Naoko Komori; Christopher Humphrey; Deryl Northcott; Bill Doolin; Jan Pahl; Michael-Burkhard Piorkowsky; Julie Froud; Colin Haslam; Sukhdev Johal; Karel Williams. **Acc. Aud. Accountab. J.** 13:4 2000 pp.418-560. *Collection of 7 articles.*

4311 Capitalism, democracy, and *Ralph's Pretty Good Grocery*. John E. Mueller. Princeton NJ: Princeton University Press, 1999. xi, 335p. *ISBN: 0691001146. Includes bibliographical references (p. 255-315) and index.*

4312 Crossing borders: globalization as myth and charter in American transnational consumer marketing. Kalman Applbaum. **Am. Ethn.** 27:2 5:2000 pp.257-282.

4313 Driving south: the globalization of auto consumption and its social organization of space. Peter Freund; George Martin. **Cap. Nat. Social.** 11:4(44) 12:2000 pp.51-72.

H: VIE ÉCONOMIQUE

4314 Economy/society: markets, meanings, and social structure. Bruce G. Carruthers; Sarah L. Babb. Thousand Oaks CA: Pine Forge Press, 2000. x, 254p. *ISBN: 0761986413. Includes bibliographical references (p. 227-241) and index.* (*Series:* Sociology for a new century).

4315 Geographies of retailing and consumption. Louise Crewe. **Prog. H. Geog.** 24:2 6:2000 pp.275-290.

4316 Grassroots-based organic foods distributors, retailers, and consumer cooperatives in Japan: broadening the organic farming movement. Darrell Gene Moen. **Hito. J. Soc. Stud.** 32:2 12:2000 pp.55-76.

4317 If you build it, will they come? A simulation of financial product holdings among low-to-moderate income households. Jeanne M. Hogarth; Kevin H. O'Donnell. **J. Consum. Pol.** 23:4 12:2000 pp.409-444.

4318 Marketing across cultures. Jean-Claude Usunier. New York: Prentice Hall, 1999. *ISBN: 0130106682. Includes bibliographical references and index.*

4319 Marketing and feminism: current issues and research. Lorna Stevens; Pauline Maclaran; Miriam Catterall. London: Routledge, 2000. 296p. *ISBN: 0415219736, 0415219728.*

4320 On the origin and distinctness of skepticism toward advertising. Carl Obermiller; Eric R. Spangenberg. **Market. Lett.** 11:4 11:2000 pp.311-322.

4321 Le prestataire, le client et le consommateur. Sociologie d'une relation marchande. *[In French]*; (The provider, the customer and the consumer. Sociology of a trade relation.) Sophie Dubuisson-Quellier. **Rev. Fr. Soc.** XL:4 10-12:1999 pp.671-688.

4322 Les professionnels du marché. *[In French]*; [The market professionals]. Franck Cochoy; Sophie Dubuisson-Quellier; Lucien Karpik; Alexandre Mallard; François Eymard-Duvernay; Emmanuelle Marchal; Thomas Debril; Sandrine Barrey; Pascale Trompette; Olivier Boissin. **Sociol. Trav.** 42:3 7-9:2000 pp.359-504. *Collection of 7 articles.*

4323 Why the microbrewery movement? Organizational dynamics of resource partitioning in the U.S. brewing industry. Glenn R. Carroll; Anand Swaminathan. **A.J.S.** 106:3 11:2000 pp.715-762.

Consumerism
Consumérisme

4324 Advertising and consumer citizenship: gender, images and rights. Anne M. Cronin. London: Routledge, 2000. 179p. *ISBN: 0415223245, 0415223237. Includes index.* (*Series:* Transformations).

4325 Consumer culture and the commodification of policing and security. Ian Loader. **Sociology** 33:2 5:1999 pp.373-392.

4326 Consumer rationality and consumer sovereignty. William H. Redmond. **R. Soc. Econ.** LVIII:2 6:2000 pp.177-196.

4327 The consumer revolution in urban China. Deborah S. Davis [Ed.]. Berkeley CA: University of California Press, 2000. xiii, 366p. *ISBN: 0520216393, 0520216407. Includes bibliographical references (p. 323-344) and index.* (*Series:* Studies on China).

4328 The consumer society reader. Martyn J. Lee [Ed.]. Malden MA, Oxford: Blackwell Publishers, 2000. xxvi, 325p. *ISBN: 063120797X, 0631207988. Includes bibliographical references and indexes.*

4329 Consumerism, disorientation and postmodern space: a modest test of an immodest theory. Ian Woodward; Michael Emmison; Philip Smith. **Br. J. Soc.** 51:2 6:2000 pp.339-354.

4330 Consumers against capitalism? Consumer cooperation in Europe, North America, and Japan, 1840-1990. Carl Strikwerda [Ed.]; Ellen Furlough [Ed.]. Lanham MD, Oxford: Rowman & Littlefield, 1999. 377p. *ISBN: 0847686485, 0847686493. Includes bibliographical references and index.*

4331 (Consumer's attitudes towards boycotting the consumption of products in Jordan — a case study of coffee.) *[Summary]*; *[Text in Arabic]*. M. Obaidat; M. Ta'ani. **Dirasat Ad. Sc.** 26:2 7:1999 pp.366-388.

H: ECONOMIC LIFE

4332 Consumption and material culture in contemporary Japan. Michael Ashkenazi; J.R. Clammer. London: Kegan Paul International, 2000. 319p. *ISBN: 0710306180. Includes bibliographical references and index.* (*Series:* Japanese studies).

4333 Consumption caught in the 'cash nexus'. Tim Dant. **Sociology** 34:4 11:2000 pp.655-670.

4334 Consumption in Asia: lifestyle and identities. Beng-Huat Chua [Ed.]. London: Routledge, 2000. 272p. *ISBN: 0415232449, 0415213118.*

4335 Consumption pattern of the floating population in Shanghai. Kangqing Zhang. **Hemispheres** 14 1999 pp.129-142.

4336 Fetishizing fetishism: commodities, goods, and the meaning of consumer culture. David R. Shumway. **Rethink. Marx.** 12:1 Spring:2000 pp.1-15.

4337 From rugs to riches: housework, consumption and modernity in Germany. Jennifer Loehlin. Oxford: Berg Publishers, 1999. 224p. *ISBN: 1859732844.*

4338 Pauvreté et convergence des consommations au Canada. *[In French]*; [Poverty and convergence of consumptions in Canada]. François Gardes; Patrice Gaubert; Simon Langlois. **Can. R. Soc. A.** 37:1 2:2000 pp.1-28.

4339 The pleasure of possessions: affective influences and personality in the evaluation of consumer items. Joseph Ciarrochi; Joseph P. Forgas. **Eur. J. Soc. Psychol.** 30:5 9-10:2000 pp.631-649.

4340 Psychology of the consumer and its development: an introduction. Robert C. Webb. New York: Kluwer Academic Publishers; Plenum Publishers, 1999. xiii, 362p. *ISBN: 0306460734. Includes bibliographical references (p. 329-352) and index.* (*Series:* The Plenum series in adult development and aging).

4341 Seeing through the eyes of the color-deficient shopper: consumer issues for public policy. Carol Kaufman-Scarborough. **J. Consum. Pol.** 23:4 12:2000 pp.461-492.

4342 The soul of the new consumer. Authenticity - what we buy and why in the new economy. David Lewis; Darren Bridger. London, Naperville IL: Nicholas Brealey, 2000. x, 246p. *ISBN: 1857882466. Includes bibliographical references (p. [225]-239) and index.*

4343 (Super-long-term memories of advertising and brands. Part 1: a review of theoretical and empirical studies in memory research.); *[Text in Japanese]*. Shizue Kishi. **J. Tokyo Keizai Uni.** 216 2:2000 pp.117-136.

4344 'When you're trying something on you picture yourself in a place where they are playing this kind of music' — musically sponsored agency in the British clothing retail sector. Tia de Nora; Sophie Belcher. **Sociol. Rev.** 48:1 2:2000 pp.80-101.

4345 The why of consumption: contemporary perspectives on consumer motives, goals and desires. David Glen Mick [Ed.]; Cynthia Huffman [Ed.]; S. Ratneshwar [Ed.]. London: Routledge, 2000. 330p. *ISBN: 0415220955. Includes index.* (*Series:* Routledge interpretive marketing research).

H.5: Finance
Finance

4346 Entscheiden unter Ungewissheit: Bankwirtschaftliche Standortsuche in Mittel- und Osteuropa. *[In German]*; (Decision making under uncertainty: banking locations in Central and Eastern Europe.) *[Summary]*. Herbert Kalthoff. **Z. Soziol.** 29:2 4:2000 pp.103-120.

4347 Geld — Krise — Generation. Soziomonetäre Streifzüge im 20. Jahrhundert. *[In German]*; (Money — crisis — generation. Socio-monetary journeys through the 20th century.) *[Summary]*. Tilman Heisterhagen; Rainer W. Hoffmann; Frank Mußmann; Marc Pleimann; Sibyll-Annett Strecker. **Soz. Welt.** 51:4 2000 pp.463-485.

4348 Die Herstellung von Evidenz. Firmenkredite und Risikoanalyse in Mittel- und Osteuropa. *[In German]*; (The production of evidence. Corporate banking and risk-analysis in Central Europe.) *[Summary]*. Herbert Kalthoff. **Soz. Welt.** 51:4 2000 pp.417-442.

4349 Kapital i rossiiskie bankiry. *[In Russian]*; (Capital and Russian bankers.) *[Summary]*. N.P. Evdokimova-Dinello. **Sot. Issle.** 2 2000 pp.75-86.

H: VIE ÉCONOMIQUE

4350 Monetized time-space: derivatives — money's 'new imaginary'? Michael Pryke; John Allen. **Econ. Soc.** 29:2 5:2000 pp.264-284.
4351 La monnaie des science sociales. *[In French]*; [The currency of the social sciences]. Jean-Yves Grenier; Frédéric Lordon; Stéphane Breton. **Annales** 55:6 11-12:2000 pp.1335-1366. *Collection of 3 articles.*
4352 Religion, ethics and stock trading: the case of an Islamic equities market. Shahnaz Naughton; Tony Naughton. **J. Busin. Ethics** 23:2 1:2000 pp.145-160.
4353 Which pension? Women, risk and pension choice. Kay Peggs. **Sociol. Rev.** 48:3 8:2000 pp.349-364.

I: LABOUR
TRAVAIL

I.1: Sociology of industry and work
Sociologie de l'industrie et du travail

4354 The 'anti-Wapping'? Technological innovation and workplace reorganization at the *Financial Times*. Timothy Marjoribanks. **Media Cult. Soc.** 22:5 9:2000 pp.575-594.

4355 El balance social como herramienta de auditoría organizacional. *[In Spanish]*; [Using social balance as a tool in business auditing]. Mery Gallego. **Rev. Univ. EAFIT** 115 7-9:1999 pp.27-40.

4356 Behavior in organizations: understanding and managing the human side of work. Jerald Greenberg; Robert A. Baron. Upper Saddle River NJ: Prentice Hall, 1999. xxvi, 687p. *ISBN: 0130850268.*

4357 'Collaborative production' and the Irish boom: work organisation, partnership and direct involvement in Irish workplaces. William K. Roche; John F. Geary. **Econ. Soc. R.** 31:4 1:2000 pp.1-36.

4358 Corporate greening as amoralization. Andrew Crane. **Organ. Stud.** 21:4 2000 pp.673-696.

4359 Cultural diversity and ethical behaviour at workplace — an analysis. Neelu Rohmetra. **Ind. J. Ind. Rel.** 35:3 1:2000 pp.301-326.

4360 The development of new paradigm values, thinkers, and business. Dafna Eylon; Robert A. Giacalone; Hazel Henderson; Kazimierz Gozdz; Daniel C. Feldman; Søren Christensen; Ann Westenholz; Judi Neal; Benyamin M. Bergmann Lichtenstein. **Am. Behav. Sc.** 43:8 5:2000 pp.1213-1366. *Collection of 8 articles.*

4361 A dialogue on self and work. Marianne Knuth. **Organization** 7:3 8:2000 pp.477-488.

4362 Diversity at work: paradoxes, possibilities and problems in the Swedish discourse on diversity. Paulina de los Reyes. **Econ. Ind. Dem.** 21:2 5:2000 pp.253-266.

4363 Effect of supervisor-subordinate *guanxi* on supervisory decisions in China: an empirical investigation. Kenneth S. Law; Chi-sum Wong; Duanxu Wang; Lihua Wang. **Int. J. Hum. Res. Man.** 11:4 8:2000 pp.751-765.

4364 Effective public relations. Scott M. Cutlip; Allen H. Center; Glen M. Broom. London: Prentice Hall, 2000. xx, 588p. *ISBN: 0130254452, 0130254452. Includes bibliographical references and index.* (*Series:* Prentice Hall International editions).

4365 ¿El fin del trabajo? Debates desde una mirada moderna, postindustrial y posmoderna. *[In Spanish]*; [The end of work? Discussions from a modernist, postindustrialist and postmodernist viewpoint] *[Summary]*. Bernice E. Tapia González. **Rev. Cien. Soc.** 5 6:1998 pp.51-70.

4366 Embeddedness, social identity and mobility: why firms leave the NASDAQ and join the New York Stock Exchange. Hayagreeva Rao; Gerald F. Davis; Andrew Ward. **Adm. Sci. Qua.** 45:2 6:2000 pp.268-292.

4367 Employee demography, organizational commitment, and turnover intentions in China: do cultural differences matter? Zhen Xiong Chen; Anne Marie Francesco. **Human Relat.** 53:6 6:2000 pp.869-887.

4368 The end of work and the 'marginal mass' thesis. José Nun. **Lat. Am. Pers.** 27:1 1:2000 pp.6-32.

4369 Entrepreneurship and the evolution of angel financial networks. Lloyd Steier; Royston Greenwood. **Organ. Stud.** 21:1 2000 pp.163-192.

4370 European business cultures. Robert Crane [Ed.]. New York: Financial Times, Prentice Hall, 1999. 215p. *ISBN: 0135745594. Includes index.*

4371 Family matters: gender, networks, and entrepreneurial outcomes. Linda A. Renzulli; Howard Aldrich; James Moody. **Soc. Forc.** 79:2 12:2000 pp.523-546.

I: TRAVAIL

4372 Les femmes entrepreneurs en France. *[In French]*; [Women entrepreneurs in France]. Bertrand Duchéneaut; Muriel Orhan. Paris: Seli Arslan, 2000. 384p. *ISBN: 2842760484. Includes bibliographical references (p. [373]-384).*

4373 La filosofía del trabajo solidario en la economía sumergida latinoamericana. *[In Spanish]*; [The philosophy of shared work in the Latin American informal economy]. Antonio Colomer Viadel. **Cuad. Am.** 79:1 1-2:2000 pp.161-171.

4374 Friendships among competitors in the Sydney hotel industry. Paul Ingram; Peter W. Roberts. **A.J.S.** 106:2 9:2000 pp.387-423.

4375 Funky business: talent makes capital dance. Kjell A. Nordström; Jonas Ridderstråle. London: Financial Times Management, 1999. 256p. *ISBN: 0273645919.*

4376 Gender, race, ethnicity, and networks: the factors affecting the status of employees' network members. Gail M. McGuire. **Work Occup.** 27:4 11:2000 pp.500-523.

4377 Gender-related effects of information technology implementation. Sabine Zauchner; C. Korunka; A. Weiss; A. Kafka-Lützow. **Gend. Work & Org.** 7:2 4:2000 pp.119-132.

4378 The globalisation of positional competition? Phillip Brown. **Sociology** 34:4 11:2000 pp.633-654.

4379 Healthy culture and unhealthy culture. Hideo Yamashita. Aldershot: Ashgate, 2000. xi, 211p. *ISBN: 0754614441. Includes bibliographical references (p. 209-211).*

4380 How inter-firm co-operation depends on social embeddedness: a vignette study. Gerrit Rooks; Werner Raub; Robert Selten; Frits Tazelaar. **Acta Sociol.** 43:2 2000 pp.123-138.

4381 Intercorporate ties in Singapore. Xiaowei Zang. **Int. Sociol.** 15:1 3:2000 pp.87-106.

4382 Labouring under an illusion? The labour process of software development in the Australian information industry. Rowena Barrett. **New Tech. Work. Empl.** 16:1 3:2000 pp.18-34.

4383 Learning from academia: the importance of relationships in professional life. Connie J.G. Gersick; Jean M. Bartunek; Jane E. Dutton. **Acad. Manag. J.** 43:6 12:2000 pp.1026-1044.

4384 Learning from cross-functional teamwork. P. Kettley; P. Hirsh. Brighton: Institute for Employment Studies, 2000. 57p. *ISBN: 1851842853.* (*Series:* IES report - 356).

4385 The logic of membership of sectoral business associations. Robert J. Bennett. **R. Soc. Econ.** LVIII:1 3:2000 pp.17-42.

4386 Measuring organizational culture clashes: a two-nation post-hoc analysis of a cultural compatibility index. John Veiga; Michael Lubatkin; Roland Calori; Philippe Very. **Human Relat.** 53:4 4:2000 pp.539-558.

4387 Obscene profits: the entrepreneurs of pornography in the cyber age. Frederick S. Lane, III. New York: Routledge, 2000. xxiii, 305p. *ISBN: 0415920965. Includes bibliographical references and index.*

4388 On the use of the prisoners' dilemma to analyze the relations between employment security, trust, and effort. Michael R. Smith. **R. Soc. Econ.** LVIII:2 6:2000 pp.153-175.

4389 Organizational culture and identity: unity and division at work. Martin Parker. Thousand Oaks CA, London: Sage Publications, 2000. 272p. *ISBN: 076195242X, 0761952438.*

4390 Partners in evaluation: modelling quality in partnership projects. Hazel Kemshall; Liz Ross. **Soc. Pol. Admin.** 34:5 12:2000 pp.551-566.

4391 Pourquoi faire ce qu'on ne veut pas faire? *[In French]*; [Why do what you don't want to do?] Veronica Velo. **R. Econ. Soc.** 58:3 9:2000 pp.131-151.

4392 Power, subjectivity and British industrial and organisational sociology: the relevance of the work of Norbert Elias. Tim Newton. **Sociology** 33:2 5:1999 pp.411-450.

4393 Prior knowledge and the discovery of entrepreneurial opportunities. Scott Shane. **Organiz. Sci.** 11:4 7-8:2000 pp.448-469.

4394 Producing against poverty: female and male micro-entrepreneurs in Lima, Peru. Annelou Ypeij. Amsterdam; London: Amsterdam University Press; Eurospan, 1999. 252p. *ISBN: 9053563776.*

4395 Produzione del consenso ed estrazione della conoscenza tacita. Studio di caso alla Fiat-Hitachi. *[In Italian]*; [Producing consent and extracting tacit knowledge: a case study of Fiat and Hitachi]. Igor Piotto. **Quad. Sociol.** XLIV:22 2000 pp.105-131.

I: LABOUR

4396 Regulation: the social control of business between law and politics. Michael Clarke. Basingstoke; New York: Macmillan; St. Martin's Press, 2000. 249p. *ISBN: 0312231040. Includes bibliographical references and index.*

4397 Research and knowledge at work: perspectives, case-studies and innovative strategies. Carl Rhodes [Ed.]; John Garrick [Ed.]. London, New York: Routledge, 2000. xiv, 285p. *ISBN: 041521338X, 0415213371. Includes bibliographical references and index.*

4398 Researching work and learning. Keith Forrester; Nick Frost; Kevin Ward; D.W. Livingstone; Anne Munro; Lesley Holly; Helen Rainbird; James C. Fisher; Larry G. Martin; Kaori H. Okano; Colin Symes; David Boud; John McIntyre; Nicky Solomon; Mark Tennant; Jianzhong Hong; Madhu Singh; Bernd Owerwien. **Int. R. Educat.** 46:6 11:2000 pp.483-640. *Collection of 9 articles.*

4399 Rethinking public relations: the spin and the substance. Kevin Moloney. London: Routledge, 2000. 196p. *ISBN: 0415217598.*

4400 Rethinking the labor process. Mark L. Wardell [Ed.]; Thomas L. Steiger [Ed.]; Peter Meiksins [Ed.]. Albany NY: State University of New York Press, 1999. ix, 279p. *ISBN: 0791442810, 0791442829. Includes bibliographical references (p. 233-263) and index. (Series: SUNY series, the new inequalities).*

4401 Rule enforcement among peers: a lateral content regime. Emmanuel Lazega. **Organ. Stud.** 21:1 2000 pp.193-214.

4402 Societal effects meet sectoral effects: work organization, competencies and payment systems in the Volvo commercial vehicle division. Terry Wallace. **Int. J. Hum. Res. Man.** 11:4 8:2000 pp.714-735.

4403 Sociologie de l'entreprise. *[In French]*; [Sociology of the firm]. Jean-Michel Morin. Paris: Presses Universitaires de France, 1999. 127p. *ISBN: 2130504094. Includes bibliographical references (p. 125-126) and index.*

4404 Sociologie du travail. *[In French]*; [Sociology of work]. Claude Durand. Toulouse: Octarès Éditions, 2000. 259p. *ISBN: 2906769592.*

4405 Sociology and the future of work: contemporary discourses and debates. Paul Ransome. Aldershot: Ashgate, 1999. x, 287p. *ISBN: 0754611590. Includes bibliographical references.*

4406 Stretching the iron cage: the constitution and implications of routine workplace resistance. Pushkala Prasad; Anshuman Prasad. **Organiz. Sci.** 11:4 7-8:2000 pp.387-403.

4407 Testing a psychological typology of entrepreneurship using business founders. John B. Miner. **J. App. Behav. Sc.** 36:1 3:2000 pp.43-69.

4408 Top management-team diversity and firm performance: examining the role of cognitions. Martin Kilduff; Reinhard Angelmar; Ajay Mehra. **Organiz. Sci.** 11:1 1-2:2000 pp.21-34.

4409 Towards a process model of corporate greening. Monika I. Winn; Linda C. Angell. **Organ. Stud.** 21:6 2000 pp.1119-1148.

4410 Trabajo y ciudadanía: estudios sobre la crisis de la sociedad salarial. *[In Spanish]*; [Work and citizenship: studies on the crisis of the salaried society]. L.E. Alonso Benito. Madrid: Editorial Trotta, 1999. 281p. *ISBN: 8481643025. Includes bibliographical references (p. 257-281). Fundación 1º de Mayo.*

4411 Trasformazioni del lavoro, nuove forme di precarizzazione lavorativa e politiche di welfare: alcune riflessioni preliminari. *[In Italian]*; (Transformations of work and new kinds of employment precariousness: some reflections.) *[Summary]*. Roberto Rizza. **Sociol. Lav.** 78-79 2000 pp.13-27.

4412 Understanding the latent structure of job performance ratings. Steven E. Scullen; Michael K. Mount; Maynard Goff. **J. Appl. Psychol.** 85:6 12:2000 pp.956-970.

4413 Viewpoint: the sociology of organizations and the organization of sociology: some reflections on the making of a division of labour. Martin Parker. **Sociol. Rev.** 48:1 2:2000 pp.124-146.

4414 *Vive la différence*: the gendering of occupational structures in a case study of Irish and French retailing. Anne-Marie McGauran. **Wom. St. Inter. For.** 23:5 9-10:2000 pp.613-627.

I: TRAVAIL

4415 Women enterpreneurs of Eastern UP: challenges and strategies of empowerment. Shailendra Singh; S.C. Saxena. **Ind. J. Ind. Rel.** 36:1 7:2000 pp.67-78.

4416 Workers, customers, and clients: challenges of the service economy for the sociology of work. Holly J. McCammon; Larry J. Griffin; Bonnie H. Erickson; Patricia Albanese; Slobodan Drakulic; Barbara A. Gutek; Bennett Cherry; Anita D. Bhappu; Sherry Schneider; Loren Woolf; Jennifer Lee; William Finlay; James E. Coverdill; Lisa Troyer; Charles W. Mueller; Pavel L. Osinsky. **Work Occup.** 27:3 8:2000 pp.278-427. *Collection of 6 articles.*

Business ethics
Déontologie commerciale

4417 Business challenging business ethics: new instruments for coping with diversity in international business. Henk J.L. Van Luijk; John Rosthorn; Bryan W. Husted; David B. Allen; André Nijhof; Olaf Fisscher; Jan Kees Looise; Laura J. Spence; José Félix Lozano; Reggy Hooghiemstra; Robert Van Es; Tiemo L. Meijlink; Eberhard Schnebel; Gael McDonald; Chris J. Moon; Peter Woolliams; Mari Meel; Maksim Saat; Warren French; Alexander Weis; Peter Koslowski; Rodger Spiller; John Kaler; Alejo José G. Sison; Yves Fassin; Wesley Cragg. **J. Busin. Ethics** 27:1-2 9:2000 pp.3-214. *Collection of 19 articles.*

4418 Compulsory ethics education and the cognitive moral development of salespeople: a quasi-experimental assessment. George Izzo. **J. Busin. Ethics** 28:3 12:2000 pp.223-242.

4419 Do internal due process systems permit adequate political and moral space for ethics voice, praxis, and community? Richard P. Nielsen. **J. Busin. Ethics** 24:1 3:2000 pp.1-28.

4420 Ethical and societal issues in marketing and business. Victoria D. Bush; Beverly T. Venable; Alan J. Bush; Brett A. Boyle; Anna Zarkada-Fraser; Isabelle Maignan; O.C. Ferrell; Morgan P. Miles; Jeffrey G. Covin; Debbie Thorne LeClair; Linda Ferrell; Michael R. Hyman; Catharine M. Curran. **J. Busin. Ethics** 23:3 2:2000 pp.235-337. *Collection of 7 articles.*

4421 Ethics of individuals. Zygmunt Bauman. **Can. J. Soc.** 25:1 Winter:2000 pp.83-96.

4422 Focus on Africa. Gedeon J. Rossouw; Belinda Barkhuysen; Christine Gichure, Peter Kanyandago; Tina Uys; Steve Krummeck; Patricia H. Werhane. **Bus. Eth. Eur. Rev.** 9:4 10:2000 pp.225-275. *Collection of 7 articles.*

4423 Human rights and corporate responsibility. Shelley Wright [Ed.]; Stuart Rees [Ed.]. Pluto Press, 2000. 339p. *ISBN: 1864031190.*

4424 Intrapreneurship as a peaceful and ethical transition strategy toward privatization. Richard P. Nielsen. **J. Busin. Ethics** 25:2 5:2000 pp.157-168.

4425 The power of money: a cross-cultural analysis of business-related beliefs. Swee Hoon Ang. **J. W. Bus.** 35:1 Spring:2000 pp.43-60.

4426 (A study on business ethics in Japan: particular references with group oriented behavior.); *[Text in Japanese].* Keiko Negishi. **J. Tokyo Keizai Uni.** 216 2:2000 pp.79-96.

4427 Studying moral ethos using an adapted Kohlbergian model. Robin S. Snell. **Organ. Stud.** 21:1 2000 pp.267-296.

4428 Teamwork and morality: comparing lean production and sociotechnology. Harry Hummels; Jan De Leede. **J. Busin. Ethics** 26:1 7:2000 pp.75-88.

I.2: Employment and labour market
Emploi et marché du travail

4429 The changing significance of ties: an exploration of the hiring channels in the Russian transitional labor market. Valery Yakubovich; Irina Kozina. **Int. Sociol.** 15:3 9:2000 pp.479-500.

4430 Child workers: the shifting debate. Jeremy Seabrook. **Race Class** 42:2 10-12:2000 pp.80-90.

I: LABOUR

4431 Class, race, and job matching in contemporary urban labor markets. James R. Elliott. **Soc. Sci. Q.** 81:4 12:2000 pp.1036-1052.

4432 The determinants of immigrant self-employment in Australia. Anh T. Le. **Int. Migr. Rev.** XXXIV:1 Spring:2000 pp.183-214.

4433 The dismissal of injured workers and workers' compensation arrangements in Australia. Kevin Purse. **Int. J. Health. Ser.** 30:4 2000 pp.849-872.

4434 The dynamics of the U.S. occupational structure during the 1990s. Edward T. Gullason. **J. Labor Res.** XXI:2 Spring:2000 pp.363-375.

4435 Early work histories of urban youth. Doris R. Entwisle; Karl L. Alexander; Linda Steffel Olson. **Am. Sociol. R.** 65:2 4:2000 pp.279-297.

4436 Een postindustriële klassenstructuur? Het klassenschema van Esping-Andersen toegepast op Nederland, Amsterdam en Rotterdam. *[In Dutch]*; (A post-industrial class-structure? The Esping-Andersen class scheme applied to employment structure in the Netherlands, Amsterdam and Rotterdam.) *[Summary]*. Bram Steijn; Erik Snel; Lambert van der Laan. **Sociol. Gids** XLVII:2 3-4:2000 pp.77-94.

4437 The effect of geographic mobility on male labor-force participants in the United States. Joan R. Rodgers; John L. Rodgers. **J. Labor Res.** XXI:1 Winter:2000 pp.117-132.

4438 Eliminating race differences in school attainment and labor market success. Michael P. Keane; Kenneth I. Wolpin. **J. Labor Ec.** 18:4 10:2000 pp.614-652.

4439 Employability, adaptability and flexibility: changing labour market prospects; *[Summary in French]*; *[Summary in German]*. Ron Martin; Peter Tyler; Christina Beatty; Stephen Fothergill; Rob MacMillan; Nick Bailey; Ivan Turok; Mike Campbell; Graham Haughton; Martin Jones; Jamie Peck; Adam Tickell; Aidan While; Irene Hardill; Sandra MacDonald; John Stillwell; Arlinda García Coll. **Reg. Stud.** 34:7 10:2000 pp.601-711. *Collection of 7 articles.*

4440 English skills, earnings, and the occupational sorting of Mexican Americans working along the U.S.-Mexico border. Marie T. Mora; Alberto Davila. **Int. Migr. Rev.** XXXIV:1 Spring:2000 pp.133-157.

4441 Existe-t-il un modèle européen de structure sociale? *[In French]*; (Is there a common model of social structure in Europe?) *[Summary]*. Louis Chauvel. **Rev. de l'OFCE** 71 10:1999 pp.283-298.

4442 The exploited child. Bernard Schlemmer [Ed.]. London: Zed Books, 2000. 352p. *ISBN: 1856497216, 1856497208. Translated from the French L'enfant exploité. Includes index.*

4443 Filipina migrant workers on the periphery. Kyoko Kikuchi. **US-Jap. Wom. J.** 16 1999 pp.138-158.

4444 Free to be unfree: Mexican guest workers in Canada; *[Summary in French]*. Tanya Basok. **Labour Cap. Soc.** 32:2 11:1999 pp.192-221.

4445 From incorporation to exclusion: the employment experience of Taiwanese urban aborigines. Jou-juo Chu. **China Quart.** 164 12:2000 pp.1025-1043.

4446 From textile mills to taxi ranks: experiences of migration, labour and social changes. Virinder S. Kalra. Aldershot: Ashgate, 2000. x, 230p. *ISBN: 1840148659. Includes bibliographical references (p. 212-229) and index. (Series: Research in migration and ethnic relations).*

4447 Giovani e lavoro nel Mezzogiorno: le carriere del precariato fra stato e mercato. *[In Italian]*; (Young people and work in southern Italy: the careers of the temporary workers.) *[Summary]*. Anna Cortese. **Sociol. Lav.** 78-79 2000 pp.277-324.

4448 I rapporti di collaborazione tra dipendenza e autonomia: una ricerca in Emilia Romagna. *[In Italian]*; [Labour-only sub-contracting between dependence and autonomy: a study in Emilia Romagna] *[Summary]*. Claudia Dall'Agata; Patrizia Grazioli. **Sociol. Lav.** 78-79 2000 pp.109-129.

4449 Illegal child labor in the United States: prevalence and characteristics. Douglas L. Kruse; Douglas Mahony. **Ind. Lab. Rel.** 54:1 10:2000 pp.17-40.

4450 The impact of export processing zone development on employment creation in Kenya. Caleb Mireri. **Sing. J. Trop. Geogr.** 21:2 7:2000 pp.149-165.

4451 It pays to value family: work and family tradeoffs reconsidered. Peter Cappelli; Jill Constantine; Clint Chadwick. **Ind. Relat.** 39:2 4:2000 pp.175-198.

4452 Labor force participation and household work of urban schoolchildren in Mexico: characteristics and consequences. Melissa Binder; David Scrogin. **Econ. Dev. Cult. Change** 48:1 10:1999 pp.123-154.

4453 Labor market marginalization of youth in San Antonio, Texas. Harald Bauder; Bob Sharpe. **Prof. Geogr.** 52:3 8:2000 pp.531-543.

4454 Labour participation of higher education students. Jean-Luc Demeulemeester; Denis Rochat. **Labour [Italy]** 14:3 9:2000 pp.503-522.

4455 Labour standards in the aftermath of structural adjustment programme: the case of India. Sasmita Palo; Nayantara Padhi; Sweta Panigrahi. **Ind. J. Ind. Rel.** 35:3 1:2000 pp.381-398.

4456 Lavoro atipico e politiche del lavoro a livello locale: un'indagine empirica in Emilia Romagna. *[In Italian]*; [Atypical forms of employment and labour politics at a local level: research from Emilia Romagna] *[Summary]*. Diletta D'Imperio; Roberto Rizza. **Sociol. Lav.** 78-79 2000 pp.130-148.

4457 Life role salience: a study of dual-career couples in the Indian context. Ujvala Rajadhyaksha; Deepti Bhatnagar. **Human Relat.** 53:4 4:2000 pp.489-512.

4458 Maquiladoras et développement rural au nord du Yucatan, Mexique. *[In French]*; (Maquiladoras and rural development in Northern Yucatan, Mexico.) Marie France Labrecque. **Labour Cap. Soc.** 32:2 11:1999 pp.132-157.

4459 Market, state and the quality of new self-employment jobs among men in the United States and Western Germany. Patricia A. McManus. **Soc. Forc.** 78:3 3:2000 pp.865-906.

4460 Men N the hood: skill, spatial, and social mismatch among male workers in Los Angeles county. Manuel Pastor, Jr.; Enrico A. Marcelli. **Urban Geogr.** 21:6 8-9:2000 pp.474-496.

4461 La metropoli e gli immigrati. *[In Italian]*; (Metropolis and immigrants.) *[Summary]*. Maurizio Ambrosini. **Sociol. Lav.** 78-79 2000 pp.200-224.

4462 Mexican immigrant women and the new domestic labor. María de la Luz Ibarra. **Human. Org.** 59:4 Winter:2000 pp.452-464.

4463 Migration and the employment and wages of native and immigrant workers. Franklin D. Wilson; Gerald Jaynes. **Work Occup.** 27:2 5:2000 pp.135-167.

4464 Mobilizing social resources: race, ethnic, and gender differences in social capital and persisting wage inequalities. Sandra S. Smith. **Sociol. Q.** 41:4 Fall:2000 pp.509-537.

4465 Occupational age structure and access for older workers. Barry T. Hirsch; David A. Macpherson; Melissa A. Hardy. **Ind. Lab. Rel.** 53:3 4:2000 pp.401-418.

4466 L'offerta di lavoro femminile tra partecipazione e squilibri. Un'analisi su un campione di donne residenti nel comune di Trento. *[In Italian]*; (Female labour supply between participation and imbalances: analysis of a sample of women living in the municipality of Trento.) *[Summary]*. Carlo Borzaga; Elena Contrini. **Ec. Lav.** XXXIII:3-4 7-12:1999 pp.57-73.

4467 Organising around women and labour in China: uneasy shadows, uncomfortable alliances. Jude Howell. **Comm. Post-Comm. Stud.** 33:3 9:2000 pp.355-377.

4468 Organizational ecology and job mobility. Takako Fujiwara-Greve; Henrich R. Greve. **Soc. Forc.** 79:2 12:2000 pp.547-585.

4469 Percepción y tipología del trabajo de los menores: un acercamiento cualitativo al caso de Andalucía. *[In Spanish]*; (Establishing and classifying types of child-labour: a qualitative look at the case of Andalusia.) Rafael Serrano del Rosal. **Rev. Fom. Soc.** 55:219 7-9:2000 pp.391-418.

4470 Poverty and work effort among urban Latino men. Susan M. Hauan; Nancy S. Landale; Kevin T. Leicht. **Work Occup.** 27:2 5:2000 pp.188-222.

4471 Precarizzazione lavorativa, flessibilità e deregolazione: riflessioni introduttive sulla situazione spagnola. *[In Italian]*; [Labour insecurity, flexibility and deregulation: some introductory reflections on the Spanish situation] *[Summary]*. Ernesto Cano. **Sociol. Lav.** 78-79 2000 pp.325-341.

I: LABOUR

4472 Racializing class, classifying race: labour and difference in Britain, the USA and Africa. Peter Alexander [Ed.]; Rick Halpern [Ed.]. Basingstoke; New York: Macmillan; St. Martin's Press, 2000. xi, 250p. *ISBN: 0333730925, 0312229992.* Includes bibliographical references and index. (Series: St. Antony's).

4473 Self-employment, family background, and race. Michael Hout; Harvey S. Rosen. **J. Hum. Res.** 35:4 Fall:2000 pp.670-692.

4474 Self-employment in post-communist Eastern Europe: a refuge from poverty or road to riches? Eric Hanley. **Comm. Post-Comm. Stud.** 33:3 9:2000 pp.379-402.

4475 Sources of work-family conflict: a Sino-U.S. comparison of the effects of work and family demands. Nini Yang; Chao C. Chen; Jaepil Choi; Yimin Zou. **Acad. Manag. J.** 43:1 2:2000 pp.113-123.

4476 The state of working Britain. Paul Gregg [Ed.]; Jonathan Wadsworth [Ed.]. Manchester: Manchester University Press, 1999. xvii, 285p. *ISBN: 0719056462, 0719056470.* Includes bibliographical references and index.

4477 To garden, to market: gendered meanings of work on an African urban periphery. Susanne Freidberg. **Gend. Place Cult.** 8:1 3:2001 pp.5-24.

4478 Travail et emploi des femmes. *[In French];* [Women's work and employment]. Margaret Maruani. Paris: La Découverte, 2000. 124p. *ISBN: 2707131806.* Includes bibliographical references (p. 110-[121]).

4479 Trends in self-employment among White and Black men during the twentieth century. Robert W. Fairlie; Bruce D. Meyer. **J. Hum. Res.** 35:4 Fall:2000 pp.643-669.

4480 Type of work matters: women's labor force participation and the child sex ratio in Turkey. G. Berik; C. Bilginsoy. **World Dev.** 28:5 5:2000 pp.861-878.

4481 Una socialización desalentadora: la iniciación laboral de los jóvenes. *[In Spanish];* [A discouraging socialization: the initiation of youth into work]. Martín J. Moreno; Nora J. Goren. **Rev. Parag. Sociol.** 36:104 1-4:1999 pp.147-162.

4482 Visible wars and invisible girls, shadow industries, and the politics of not-knowing. Carolyn Nordstrom. **Int. Fem. J. Pol.** 1:1 1999 pp.14-33.

4483 The winding road from employee to complainant: situational and psychological determinants of wrongful-termination claims. E. Allan Lind; Jerald Greenberg; Kimberly S. Scott; Thomas D. Welchans. **Adm. Sci. Qua.** 45:3 9:2000 pp.557-590.

4484 Worker perceptions of job insecurity in the mid-1990s: evidence from the survey of economic expectations. Charles F. Manski; John D. Straub. **J. Hum. Res.** 35:3 Summer:2000 pp.447-479.

4485 Workers without traditional employment: an international study of non-standard work. John Mangan. Northampton MA: Edward Elgar Publishing, 2000. 205p. *ISBN: 184064267X.* Includes bibliographical references and index.

4486 The workplace at the millennium. Diane Perrons; Peter Sunley; Ron Martin; Adrian Smith; Andrew Herod; Giles Atkinson; Fernando Machado; Susana Mourato; Alan G. Phipps; Chris Brooks; Sotiris Tsolacos; John Adams; Malcolm Greig; Ronald W. McQuaid; Rob Crouchley; Reza Oskrochi; Ian Hodge; Jessica Dunn; Sarah Monk; Caroline Kiddle. **Envir. Plan. A.** 32:10 10:2000 pp.1719-1888. *Collection of 10 articles.*

Employment discrimination
Discrimination dans l'emploi

4487 Ageism and employment: controversies, ambiguities and younger people's perceptions. Wendy Loretto; Colin Duncan; Phil J. White. **Age. Soc.** 20:3 5:2000 pp.279-302.

4488 Ageism and sexism at work: the middle-aged women of Hong Kong. Kwong-leung Tang. **Gen. Tech. Dev.** 4:2 5-8:2000 pp.225-254.

4489 Are suburban firms more likely to discriminate against African-Americans? Steven Raphael; Michael A. Stoll; Harry J. Holzer. **J. Urban Ec.** 48:3 11:2000 pp.485-508.

4490 Black applicants, Black employees, and urban labor market policy. Harry J. Holzer; Jess Reaser. **J. Urban Ec.** 48:3 11:2000 pp.365-387.

I: TRAVAIL

4491 Challenging race discrimination at work. Karon Monaghan. London: Institute of Employment Rights, 2000. 96p. *Includes bibliographical references.*

4492 The changing face of urban bureaucracy: is there interethnic competition for municipal government jobs? Brinck Kerr; Will Miller; Margaret Reid. **Urban Aff. Rev.** 35:6 7:2000 pp.770-793.

4493 Chronicity of sexual harassment and generalized work-place abuse: effects on drinking outcomes. Kathleen M. Rospenda; Judith A. Richman; Joseph S. Wislar; Joseph A. Flaherty. **Addiction** 95:12 12:2000 pp.1805-1820.

4494 Combatting discrimination at a Japanese university. Cynthia Worthington. **Asian Persp.** [S. Korea] 24:4 2000 pp.131-157.

4495 The cost of discrimination in Latin America. Harry Patrinos. **Stud. Comp. Int. Dev.** 35:2 Summer:2000 pp.3-17.

4496 Discrimination: a guide to the relevant case law on race and sex discrimination and equal pay. Michael Rubenstein. London: Eclipse Group, 2000. 102p. *ISBN: 1870771494.*

4497 Discrimination and affirmative action and public policy. Rhonda M. Williams; William E. Spriggs; Harold A. Black; Robert Cherry; Curtis Haynes, Jr.; Jessica Gordon Nembhard; Sherri Leronda Wallace; Major G. Coleman. **Rev. Bl. Pol. Ec.** 27:1 Summer:1999 pp.9-127. *Collection of 6 articles.*

4498 Earnings differentials among ethnic groups in Canada: a review of the research. Morton Stelcner. **R. Soc. Econ.** LVIII:3 9:2000 pp.295-317.

4499 Employers' estimates of market wages: implications for wage discrimination in the U.S. Marlene Kim. **Fem. Econ.** 6:2 7:2000 pp.97-114.

4500 Ethnic employment penalties in Britain. Richard Berthoud. **J. Eth. Migr. St.** 26:3 7:2000 pp.389-416.

4501 Ethnic penalties in unemployment and occupational attainment: evidence for Britain. F. Carmichael; R. Woods. **Int. R. Applied Ec.** 14:1 1:2000 pp.71-98.

4502 Evolution, green beards, and skin hue wage discrimination. Gregory N. Price. **Wor. Futur.** 55:4 2000 pp.341-355.

4503 Gender and the labour market: econometric evidence of obstacles to achieving gender equality. Danièle Meulders [Ed.]; Siv Gustafsson [Ed.]. Basingstoke: Macmillan, 2000. 320p. *ISBN: 0333804422. Includes index.*

4504 Gender as an impediment to labor market success: why do young women report greater harm? Heather Antecol; Peter Kuhn. **J. Labor Ec.** 18:4 10:2000 pp.702-728.

4505 Incarceration and racial inequality in men's employment. Bruce Western; Becky Pettit. **Ind. Lab. Rel.** 54:1 10:2000 pp.3-16.

4506 'Occupationalized credentialism' in Germany: a gendered allocation mechanism? Heike Solga; Dirk Konietzka. **Schweiz. Z. Soziologie** 26:1 3:2000 pp.111-148.

4507 Offering a job: meritocracy and social networks. Trond Petersen; Ishak Saporta; Marc-David L. Seidel. **A.J.S.** 106:3 11:2000 pp.763-816.

4508 Pregnant workers and sex discrimination: the limits of purposive non-comparative methodology. Paul Lewis. **Int. J. Comp. L. L. I. R.** 16:1 Spring:2000 pp.55-69.

4509 Race, gender and regional labor market inequalities in Brazil. Peggy A. Lovell. **R. Soc. Econ.** LVIII:3 9:2000 pp.277-293.

4510 Race-related differences in promotions and support: underlying effects of human and social capital. Erika Hayes James. **Organiz. Sci.** 11:5 9-10:2000 pp.493-508.

4511 Reflections of African-American women on their careers in urban policing. Their experiences of racial and sexual discrimination. M. Pogrebin; M. Dodge; H. Chatman. **Int. J. S. Law** 28:4 12:2000 pp.311-326.

4512 Sexual orientation discrimination and its challenges for nonprofit managers. Dennis W. Hostetler; Joan E. Pynes. **Non. Manag. Leader.** 11:1 Fall:2000 pp.49-64.

I: LABOUR

Gender issues
Questions de sexe

4513 Analysing change in women's careers: culture, structure and action dimensions. Julia Evetts. **Gend. Work & Org.** 7:1 1:2000 pp.57-67.

4514 Balancing gender in higher education: a study of the experience of senior women in a 'new' UK university. Sue Ledwith; Simonetta Manfredi. **Eur. J. Wom. Stud.** 7:1 2:2000 pp.7-34.

4515 Bridging home and work in the transition to motherhood: a discursive study. Lucy Bailey. **Eur. J. Wom. Stud.** 7:1 2:2000 pp.53-70.

4516 Changing profile of female employment in India — an analysis. U.T. Damayanthi. **Ind. J. Reg. Sci.** XXXI:2 1999 pp.22-37.

4517 Child care and employment turnover. S. Hofferth; N. Collins. **Pop. Res. Pol. R.** 19:4 8:2000 pp.357-395.

4518 Choosing children over career? Changes in the postpartum labor force behavior of professional women. L. Whittington; S. Averett; D. Anderson. **Pop. Res. Pol. R.** 19:4 8:2000 pp.339-355.

4519 Climbing the corporate ladder: do female and male executives follow the same route? Karen S. Lyness; Donna E. Thompson. **J. Appl. Psychol.** 85:1 2:2000 pp.86-101.

4520 Compromising positions: emergent neo-Fordisms and embedded gender contracts. Heidi Gottfried. **Br. J. Soc.** 51:2 6:2000 pp.235-259.

4521 Cultural stereotypes and the gendering of senior management. Nickie Charles; Charlotte Aull Davies. **Sociol. Rev.** 48:4 11:2000 pp.544-567.

4522 Cutting at the wrong edge: gender, part-time work and the Irish retail sector. Roland Tormey. **Irish J. Soc.** 9 1999 pp.77-96.

4523 Determinantes de la participación intermitente de las mujeres en el mercado de trabajo del area metropolitana de Buenos Aires. *[In Spanish]*; [Determinants of female labour market participation in metropolitan Buenos Aires] *[Summary]*. Marcela Cerrutti. **Desar. Econ.** 39:156 1-3:2000 pp.619-638.

4524 The determinants of work efforts of working married women — a case study of the Chittagong metropolitan area, Bangladesh. Mohammad Abdul Hossain; Omar Haider; N. Bashar; Mohammad M. Siddiqui; Mohammad S. Siddiqui. **Asian Prof.** 27:4 8:1999 pp.349-360.

4525 The devaluation of women's work: a comment on Tam. Paula England; Joan M. Hermsen; David A. Cotter; Tony Tam [Comments by]. **A.J.S.** 105:6 5:2000 pp.1741-1760.

4526 The division of domestic labour: twenty years of change? Oriel Sullivan. **Sociology** 34:3 8:2000 pp.437-456.

4527 (Do gender role attitudes affect the aspirations of female high-school students? A quantitative study on determinants of aspirations of female high-school students.) *[Summary]*; *[Text in Japanese]*. Hiroshi Kanbayashi. **Rir. To Ho.** 15:2 10:2000 pp.359-374.

4528 Does the availability of child care influence the employment of mothers? Findings from Western Germany. M. Kreyenfeld; K. Hank. **Pop. Res. Pol. R.** 19:4 8:2000 pp.317-338.

4529 Doing the dirty work? The global politics of domestic labour. Bridget Anderson. New York: Zed Books, 2000. 213p. *ISBN: 1856497607, 1856497615. Includes bibliographical references and index.*

4530 Economic dependence, gender, and the division of labor in the home: a replication and extension. Theodore N. Greenstein. **J. Marriage Fam.** 62:2 5:2000 pp.322-335.

4531 The effects of children on married and lone mothers' employment in the United States and (West) Germany. Sonja Drobnič. **Eur. Sociol. R.** 16:2 6:2000 pp.137-157.

4532 Employment decisions of married women: evidence and explanations. Daniela Del Boca; Marilena Locatelli; Silvia Pasqua. **Labour [Italy]** 14:1 3:2000 pp.35-52.

4533 The evolution of sex segregation regimes. Mariko Lin Chang. **A.J.S.** 105:6 5:2000 pp.1658-1701.

I: TRAVAIL

4534 Extending the 'bright line': feminism, breastfeeding, and the workplace in the United States. Judith Galtry. **Gender Soc.** 14:2 4:2000 pp.295-317.

4535 The extra burden of Moslem wives: clues from Israeli women's labor supply. Shoshana Grossbard-Shechtman; Shoshana Neuman. **Econ. Dev. Cult. Change** 46:3 4:1998 pp.491-518.

4536 Feminising the masculine? Women in non-traditional employment. Margaret Whittock. Aldershot: Ashgate, 2000. x, 246p. *ISBN: 0754610470. Includes bibliographical references.*

4537 Gender and collective bargaining. Linda Dickens; Mia Latta; Anni Weiler; Riitta Martikainen; Myriam Bergamaschi; Jeanne de Bruijn; Inge Bleijenbergh; Birgit Buchinger; Ulrike Gschwandtner; Erika Pircher. **Transfer** 6:2 Summer:2000 pp.187-306. *Collection of 8 articles.*

4538 Gender and the new inequality: explaining the college/non-college wage gap. Leslie McCall. **Am. Sociol. R.** 65:2 4:2000 pp.234-255.

4539 Gender differences in pay. Francine D. Blau; Lawrence M. Kahn. **J. Econ. Pers.** 14:4 Fall:2000 pp.75-99.

4540 Gender discrimination in wages and employment practices in Japan. Mori Masumi. **US-Jap. Wom. J.** 16 1999 pp.103-137.

4541 Gender, family and employment in comparative perspective: the realities and representations of equal opportunities in Britain and France; *[Summary in French].* Rosemary Crompton; Nicky Le Feuvre. **J. Europe. Soc. Pol.** 10:4 11:2000 pp.334-348.

4542 Gender, pay equity and human service work: a New South Wales case study. Natasha Cortis. **Aust. J. Pol. Sci** 35:1 3:2000 pp.49-62.

4543 Gender-based barriers to senior management positions: understanding the scarcity of female CEOs. Judith G. Oakley. **J. Busin. Ethics** 27:4 10:2000 pp.321-334.

4544 Gendered organization and workplace culture in Japanese customer services. Karen Shire. **Soc. Sci. Jap. J.** 3:1 4:2000 pp.37-58.

4545 The gendering of inequalities: women, men and work. Jacqueline Laufer [Ed.]; Margaret Maruani [Ed.]; Jane Jenson [Ed.]. Aldershot: Ashgate, 2000. xv, 319p. *ISBN: 0754612368. Translated from the French Les nouvelles frontières de l'inégalité: Hommes et femmes sur le marchè du travail.*

4546 The globalised woman: reports from a future of inequality. Patrick Camiller [Tr.]; Christa Wichterich. New York: Zed Books, 2000. 180p. *ISBN: 1856497402, 1856497410. Translated from the German Globalisierte Frau. Includes bibliographical references and index.*

4547 Having none of it: women, men and the future of work. Suzanne Franks. London: Granta, 1999. xi, 289p. *ISBN: 1862071640. Includes bibliographical references and index.*

4548 How do children matter? A comparison of gender earnings inequality for young adults in the former East Germany and the former West Germany. Heike Trappe; Rachel A. Rosenfeld. **J. Marriage Fam.** 62:2 5:2000 pp.489-507.

4549 The impact of military presence in local labor markets on the employment of women. Bradford Booth; William W. Falk; David R. Segal; Mady Wechsler Segal. **Gender Soc.** 14:2 4:2000 pp.318-332.

4550 The incompatibility of decentralized bargaining and equal employment opportunity in Australia. Glenda Strachan; John Burgess. **Br. J. Ind. R.** 38:3 9:2000 pp.361-382.

4551 Inside medical marriages: the effect of gender on income. Susan Waldoch Hinze. **Work Occup.** 27:4 11:2000 pp.464-499.

4552 Labour market transformations and changing gender relations. Diane Perrons; Maria-Dolors García-Ramon; Anna Ortiz; Anne Lise Ellingsæter; Wuokko Knocke; Barbara Poggio. **Econ. Ind. Dem.** 21:3 8:2000 pp.283-402. *Collection of 5 articles.*

4553 Labour supply and employment probabilities in Italy: a gender analysis in a regional perspective; *[Summary in Italian].* Tindara Addabbo. **Ec. Lav.** XXXIII:3-4 7-12:1999 pp.189-207.

I: LABOUR

4554 Learning to serve? Employment aspirations and attitudes of young working-class men in an era of labour market restructuring. Linda McDowell. **Gend. Place Cult.** 7:4 12:2000 pp.389-416.

4555 A look backward and forward at American professional women and their families. Rita James Simon [Ed.]. Lanham MD: University Press of America, 2000. 166p. *ISBN: 0761815813, 0761815821.*

4556 Male/female earnings differences in self-employment: the effects of marriage, children, and the household division of labor. Greg Hundley. **Ind. Lab. Rel.** 54:1 10:2000 pp.95-114.

4557 Married women's employment over the life course: attitudes in cross-national perspective. Judith Treas; Eric D. Widmer. **Soc. Forc.** 78:4 6:2000 pp.1409-1436.

4558 Men at work: labour, masculinities, development. Cecile Jackson; Ann Whitehead; Elizabeth Harrison; Javier Pineda; Norma Fuller; Ann Varley; Maribel Blasco; Diane Alméras; Elaine Unterhalter; Penny Vera-Sanso; Sylvia Chant; Ruth Pearson. **Euro. J. Dev. Res.** 12:2 12:2000 pp.1-237. *Collection of 11 articles.*

4559 Opportunities lost? Race, industrial restructuring, and employment among young women heading households. Irene Browne. **Soc. Forc.** 78:3 3:2000 pp.907-930.

4560 'Progress' in Zimbabwe: is 'it' a 'woman?' Christine Sylvester. **Int. Fem. J. Pol.** 1:1 1999 pp.89-118.

4561 Quality and demand of child care and female labour supply in Italy. Maria Concetta Chiuri. **Labour [Italy]** 14:1 3:2000 pp.97-118.

4562 Senior female international managers: why so few? Margaret Linehan. Aldershot, Brookfield VT: Ashgate, 2000. ix, 216p. *ISBN: 0754612007. Includes bibliographical references (p. 200-213) and index.*

4563 The social construction of gendered equal opportunities in UK universities: a case study of women technicians. Jackie Goode; Barbara Bagilhole. **Crit. Soc. Pol.** 18:2(55) 5:1998 pp.175-192.

4564 Strategies to increase the representation of women on the academic staff of the Faculty of Medicine at Monash University. Louise McCall; Merilyn Liddell; Jo O'Neil; Greg Coman. **High. Educ.** 39:2 3:2000 pp.131-150.

4565 Under the Northern Lights: the reflection of gender on the career of women managers in Finnish municipalities. Anna Liisa Westman. Joensuu: Joensuun yliopisto, 2000. 460p. *ISBN: 9517088515.*

4566 Voces de mujeres. La esfera laboral urbana en el marruecos de finales del siglo XX. *[In Spanish]*; [Women's voices: urban labour in Morocco at the end of the 20th century]. Yolanda Aixelà. **Stud. Afr.** 11 3:2000 pp.39-59.

4567 Vrouwen gezocht: de sociaal-economische positie van vrouwen in de culturele sector. *[In Dutch]*; (Wanted: women: the socio-economic position of women in the cultural sector.) *[Summary]*. Ineke van Hamersveld. **Boekmancahier** 12:44 6:2000 pp.131-146.

4568 Weaving work and motherhood. Anita Ilta Garey. Philadelphia PA: Temple University Press, 1999. xi, 239p. *ISBN: 1566396999, 1566397006. Includes bibliographical references (p. 219-230) and index. (Series:* Women in the political economy).

4569 Why not ascription? Organizations' employment of male and female managers. Barbara F. Reskin; Debra Branch McBrier. **Am. Sociol. R.** 65:2 4:2000 pp.210-233.

4570 Women and work in the information age. Celia Stanworth. **Gend. Work & Org.** 7:1 1:2000 pp.20-32.

4571 Women in science, engineering and technology (SET): a report on the Indonesian experience. Wati Hermawati; Achie S. Luhulima. **Gen. Tech. Dev.** 4:1 1-4:2000 pp.87-100.

4572 Women in the construction professions: achieving critical mass. Clara Greed. **Gend. Work & Org.** 7:3 7:2000 pp.181-196.

4573 Women in transition: changes in gender wage differentials in Eastern Europe and the former Soviet Union. Elizabeth Brainerd. **Ind. Lab. Rel.** 54:1 10:2000 pp.138-162.

4574 Women, work, and computerization: charting a course to the future. Ellen Balka [Ed.]; Richard Smith [Ed.]. Boston MA: Kluwer Academic Publishers, 2000. x, 307p. *ISBN:*

I: TRAVAIL

0792378644. Papers presented at the 7th IFIP TC9/WG9.1 International conference on women, work, and computerization, Vancouver 2000. Includes bibliographical references. (Series: IFIP - 44).

4575 Women's employment and its effects on Bengali households of Shillong, India. Mousumee Dutta. **J. Comp. Fam. Stud.** XXXI:2 Spring:2000 pp.217-230.

4576 Women's work in Britain and France: practice, theory, and policy. Abigail Gregory; Jan Windebank. Basingstoke, New York: Macmillan, St. Martin's Press, 2000. xi, 226p. *ISBN: 0333683064, 0312231059. Includes bibliographical references (p. 195-219) and index.*

4577 Work and employment in small businesses: perpetuating and challenging gender traditions. Susan Baines; Jane Wheelock. **Gend. Work & Org.** 7:1 1:2000 pp.45-56.

4578 Work design for flexible work scheduling: barriers and gender implications. Ann M. Brewer. **Gend. Work & Org.** 7:1 1:2000 pp.33-44.

Unemployment
Chômage

4579 Adjustment to job loss in Britain's major cities; *[Summary in French]*; *[Summary in German]*. Nick Bailey; Ivan Turok. **Reg. Stud.** 34:7 10:2000 pp.631-653.

4580 Ammortizzatori sociali, traiettorie biografiche e rischi di precarizzazione. *[In Italian]*; (Social policies, biographical trajectories and risks of precariousness.) *[Summary]*. Antonella Spanò; Paola Clarizia. **Sociol. Lav.** 78-79 2000 pp.149-199.

4581 Confrontation de modèles normatifs dans l'exemple des chômeurs en fin de parcours. *[In French]*; (The terminally unemployed and normative models.) *[Summary]*. Nathalie Burnay. **Recher. Sociolog.** XXXI:1 2000 pp.173-184.

4582 Une décomposition du non-emploi en France. *[In French]*; (A breakdown of non-employment in France.) *[Summary]*. Guy Laroque; Bernard Salanié. **Écon. Stat.** 331 1:2000 pp.47-66.

4583 The effects of level of education on mobility between employment and unemployment in the Netherlands. Maarten H.J. Wolbers. **Eur. Sociol. R.** 16:2 6:2000 pp.185-200.

4584 Gendernye aspekty strategii bezrabotnykh. *[In Russian]*; (Gender aspects of strategies of the unemployed.) I.N. Tartakovskaya. **Sot. Issle.** 11 2000 pp.73-83.

4585 Insertion, le droit à l'identité: l'expérience de l'accompagnement des chômeurs de l'association ALICE. *[In French]*; [Integration and the right to identity: the experience of shadowing unemployed people from the ALICE association]. Pascale Domonique Russo. Paris: C.-L. Meyer, 1999. 85p. *ISBN: 2843770041.*

4586 Jobless men and women: a comparative analysis of job search intensity, attitudes toward unemployment, and related responses. Liat Kulik. **J. Occup. Organ. Psychol.** 73:4 12:2000 pp.487-500.

4587 Labour markets and welfare. Ken Mayhew; Peter Robinson; Richard Blundell; Phil Agulnik; Stephen Bazen; Colin Crouch; Paul Davies; Mark Freedland; Richard Dickens; Paul Gregg; Jonathan Wadsworth; David Webster; Angela Brennan; John Rhodes; Peter Tyler. **Ox. R. Econ. Pol.** 16:1 Spring:2000 pp.1-146. *Collection of 10 articles.*

4588 Predictors and outcomes of networking intensity among unemployed job seekers. Connie R. Wanberg; Ruth Kanfer; Joseph T. Banas. **J. Appl. Psychol.** 85:4 8:2000 pp.491-503.

4589 Reconnecting the long term unemployed to labour market opportunity: the case for a 'local active labour market policy'; *[Summary in French]*; *[Summary in German]*. Mike Campbell. **Reg. Stud.** 34:7 10:2000 pp.655-668.

4590 Récurrence du chômage dans l'insertion des jeunes: des trajectoires hétérogènes. *[In French]*; (Recurring unemployment among young people entering the labour market: heterogeneous trajectories.) *[Summary]*. Stéfan Lollivier. **Écon. Stat.** 334 4:2000 pp.49-63.

4591 Slipping into and out of underemployment: another disadvantage for nonmetropolitan workers? Leif Jensen; Jill L. Findeis; Wan-ling Hsu; Jason P. Schachter. **Rural Sociol.** 64:3 9:1999 pp.417-438.

I: LABOUR

4592 Soziales Kapital und Arbeitslosigkeit. Eine empirische Analyse zu den Schweizer Kantonen. *[In German]*; (Social capital and unemployment. Swiss cantons in a comparative perspective.) *[Summary]*. Markus Freitag. **Z. Soziol.** 29:3 6:2000 pp.186-201.

4593 Sposoby adaptatsii bezrabotnykh v trudnoi zhiznenoi situatsii. *[In Russian]*; [Tactics of the unemployed in adapting to harsh living conditions] *[Summary]*. A.N. Demin; I.P. Popova. **Sot. Issle.** 5 2000 pp.35-46.

4594 A theory of employment, unemployment and sickness; *[Summary in French]*; *[Summary in German]*. Christina Beatty; Stephen Fothergill; Rob MacMillan. **Reg. Stud.** 34:7 10:2000 pp.617-630.

4595 Unemployment determinants for women in Spain. Nieves Lázaro; María Luisa Moltó; Rosario Sánchez. **Labour [Italy]** 14:1 3:2000 pp.53-78.

4596 Unemployment in Southern Europe. Katrina Burgess; Omar G. Encarnación; Seraphim Seferiades; Miguel Glatzer; W. Rand Smith; Mario Bacalhau; Thomas Bruneau; Ugo M. Amoretti; M. Margarida Marques; Martin Baldwin-Edwards; Constantina Safilios Rothschild; Manuel Villaverde Cabral; Neovi M. Karakatsanis; Nancy G. Bermeo. **S. Euro. Soc. Pol.** 4:3 Winter:1999 pp.1-287. *Collection of 12 articles.*

4597 Work incentives and welfare provision: the pathological theory of unemployment. Doris Schroeder. Aldershot, Brookfield VT: Ashgate, 2000. ix, 220p. *ISBN: 0754612074. Includes bibliographical references (p. 197-216) and index. (Series:* Avebury series in philosophy).

4598 Youth unemployment and the NDE self-employment programmes. Abayomi Adebayo. **Nig. J. Econ. Soc. Stud.** 41:1 3:1999 pp.81-104.

I.3: **Personnel management and working conditions**
Administration du personnel et conditions de travail

Human resources
Ressources humaines

4599 *Assessment centers* in België: de resultaten van een onderzoek naar de voorspellende kracht en de billijkheid. *[In Flemish]*; (Assessment centers in Belgium: the results of a study on predictive validity and fairness.) *[Summary]*. Filip Lievens; Etienne Van Keer. **Econ. Soc. Tijd.** 54:1 3:2000 pp.67-88.

4600 Change and development in pluralistic settings: an exploration of HR practices in Chinese township and village enterprises. Irene Hau Siu Chow; Ping Ping Fu. **Int. J. Hum. Res. Man.** 11:4 8:2000 pp.822-836.

4601 Ethical standards for human resource management professionals: a comparative analysis of five major codes. Carolyn Wiley. **J. Busin. Ethics** 25:2 5:2000 pp.93-114.

4602 High-performance workplaces, training, and the distribution of skills. Keith Whitfield. **Ind. Relat.** 39:1 1:2000 pp.1-25.

4603 HR shared services and the realignment of HR. P. Reilly. Brighton: Institute of Employment Studies, 2000. 62p. *ISBN: 1851842985. (Series:* IES Report - 368).

4604 Human resource accounting: advances in concepts, methods, and applications. Eric Flamholtz. Boston MA: Kluwer Academic Publishers, 1999. xviii, 390p. *ISBN: 0792382676. Includes bibliographical references (p. [359]-375) and index.*

4605 Human resource development in Malaysia: a synoptic view. B.N. Ghosh. **S. E. Asian R.** XXIII:1-2 1-12:1998 pp.29-41.

4606 Human resources of Eastern Europe. David Turnock [Ed.]; Doris Schmied; Andrew H. Dawson; Bronislaw Górz; Wlodzimierz Kurek; Hans-Joachim Bürkner; Francis W. Carter; Fiona Simpson; Branislav S. Djurdjev; Liliana Guran; Wilfried Heller; Nicolae Muica; Veselina Urucu; Krzysztof R. Mazurski; Daniela Nancu; Tassilo Herrschel; Craig Young; Sylwia Kaczmarek; Vladimir Drgona; Derek Hall; Erika Nagy; Lesław Czetwertynski-

Sytnik; Edward Kozioł; Vasile Surd; Joseph J. Gallagher; Philip J.J. Tucker. **Geojournal** 50:2-3 2000 pp.75-309. *Collection of 22 articles.*

4607 The impact of development centre participation and the role of individual differences in changing self-assessments. Freyja Halman; Clive Fletcher. **J. Occup. Organ. Psychol.** 73:4 12:2000 pp.423-442.

4608 In search of perfect people: teamwork and team players in the Scottish spirits industry. Patricia Findlay; Alan McKinlay; Abigail Marks; Paul Thompson. **Human Relat.** 53:12 12:2000 pp.1549-1574.

4609 Knowledge in organizations: access to thinking at work. John Sparrow. London, Thousand Oaks CA: Sage Publications, 1998. x, 260p. *ISBN: 0803978294, 0803978286. Includes bibliographical references (p. [229]-250) and index.*

4610 Knowledge management and the role of HR. Chris Harman; Sue Brelade. London: Financial Times, Prentice Hall, 2000. xvii, 106p. *ISBN: 0273644564. Includes bibliographical references (p. 104-106). (Series:* Management briefings).

4611 Managing AIDS in Africa: HRM challenges in Tanzania. Yehuda Baruch; Patricia Claney. **Int. J. Hum. Res. Man.** 11:4 8:2000 pp.789-806.

4612 Paradigms lost and paradigms regained? Recent developments and new directions for HRM/OB in the UK and USA. Philip Morgan. **Int. J. Hum. Res. Man.** 11:4 8:2000 pp.853-866.

4613 Qui calcule trop finit par déraisonner: les experts du marché du travail. *[In French];* (Overcalculating nonsense: labor market experts.) *[Summary].* François Eymard-Duvernay; Emmanuelle Marchal. **Sociol. Trav.** 42:3 7-9:2000 pp.411-432.

4614 Relationships between ability requirements and human errors in job tasks. Louis C. Buffardi; Edwin A. Fleishman; Ray A. Morath; Patrick M. McCarthy. **J. Appl. Psychol.** 85:4 8:2000 pp.551-564.

4615 Selection based on merit versus demography: implications across race and gender lines. Marcus M. Stewart; Debra L. Shapiro. **J. Appl. Psychol.** 85:2 4:2000 pp.219-231.

4616 Sociological paradigms and human resources: an African context. Ken N. Kamoche. Aldershot: Ashgate, 2000. ix, 209p. *ISBN: 1840148551. Includes bibliographical references.*

4617 Team work in Japan: revolution, evolution or no change at all? Anne Sey. **Econ. Ind. Dem.** 21:4 11:2000 pp.475-503.

4618 Teamworking. Frank Mueller [Ed.]; Stephen Procter [Ed.]; David Buchanan [Ed.]; Nicolas Bacon; Paul Blyton; Rick Delbridge; James Lowe; Nick Oliver; David Knights; Darren McCabe; Christine A. Sprigg; Paul R. Jackson; Sharon K. Parker. **Human Relat.** 53:11 11:2000 pp.1387-1544. *Collection of 6 articles.*

Management
Gestion

4619 Applied psychology in human resource management. Wayne F. Cascio. Upper Saddle River NJ: Prentice Hall, 1998. xv, 399p. *ISBN: 0138342288. Includes bibliographical references (p. 333-385) and indexes.*

4620 The arts of leadership. Keith Grint. New York: Oxford University Press, 2000. 440p. *ISBN: 019829445X. Includes bibliographical references and index.*

4621 At the critical moment: conditions and prospects for critical management studies. Valérie Fournier; Chris Grey. **Human Relat.** 53:1 1:2000 pp.7-32.

4622 Becoming a leader in a complex organization. Jean-Louis Denis; Ann Langley; Marc Pineault. **J. Manag. Stu.** 37:8 12:2000 pp.1063-1099.

4623 Boundary management tactics and logics of action: the case of peer-support providers. Samuel B. Bacharach; Peter Bamberger; Valerie McKinney. **Adm. Sci. Qua.** 45:4 12:2000 pp.704-736.

I: LABOUR

4624 Business leadership and culture: national management styles in the global economy. Björn Bjerke. Cheltenham, Northampton MA: Edward Elgar Publishing, 2000. 287p. *ISBN: 1840641711*. Includes bibliographical references.

4625 CEO succession research: methodological bridges over troubled waters. P. Pitcher; S. Chreim; V. Kisfalvi. **Strat. Manage. J.** 21:6 6:2000 pp.625-648.

4626 Consequences of abusive supervision. Bennett J. Tepper. **Acad. Manag. J.** 43:2 4:2000 pp.178-190.

4627 Consequences of the psychological contract for the employment relationship: a large scale survey. Jackie Coyle-Shapiro; Ian Kessler. **J. Manag. Stu.** 37:7 11:2000 pp.903-930.

4628 Critical turns in the evolution of diversity management. Anna Lorbiecki; Gavin Jack. **Br. J. Manag.** 11:Special 9:2000 pp.17-32.

4629 Cultural effects in East Asian strategic decision-making. Bob Phelps; Oui Krabuanrat. **Asia Pac. Bus. Rev.** 6:2 Winter:1999 pp.44-58.

4630 Cultural variation of leadership prototypes across 22 European countries. Felix C. Brodbeck; et al. **J. Occup. Organ. Psychol.** 73:1 3:2000 pp.1-30.

4631 Determinants of managerial performance: a cross-cultural comparison of the perceptions of middle-level managers in four countries. James P. Neelankavil; Anil Mathur; Yong Zhang. **J. Int. Bus. Stud.** 31:1 2000 pp.121-140.

4632 Dynamics and dilemmas of women leading women. Jean Bartunek. **Organiz. Sci.** 11:6 11-12:2000 pp.589-610.

4633 The effect of human resource management practices on firm performance in Russia. Carl F. Fey; Ingmar Björkman; Antonina Pavlovskaya. **Int. J. Hum. Res. Man.** 11:1 2:2000 pp.1-18.

4634 Effect of human resources management (HRM) practices on firm performance in India. Kuldeep Singh. **Ind. J. Ind. Rel.** 36:1 7:2000 pp.1-23.

4635 The effect of organizational context on the motivation of raters to produce lenient appraisals. Denis Morin; Stéphane Renaud. **Int. Rev. Admin. Sci.** 66:4 12:2000 pp.637-654.

4636 The ethnomethodological approach of management: a new perspective on constructivist research. Jean-Michel Plane. **J. Busin. Ethics** 26:3 8:2000 pp.233-244.

4637 *Filogenez liderstva. [In Russian]*; (Phylogenesis of leadership.) *[Summary]*. V.K. Vasilev. **Vest. San.-Peter. Univ.** 1(6) 3:1999 pp.47-57.

4638 Five-factor model of personality and transformational leadership. Timothy A. Judge; Joyce E. Bono. **J. Appl. Psychol.** 85:5 10:2000 pp.751-765.

4639 Frankenstein's manager: leadership's missing links. Bill McAnerney. Dublin: Oak Tree Press, 1999. 304p. *ISBN: 1860761496*.

4640 *Haute couture* and *prêt-à-porter*: the popular press and the diffusion of management practices. Carmelo Mazza; José Luis Alvarez. **Organ. Stud.** 21:3 2000 pp.567-588.

4641 How experience and network ties affect the influence of demographic minorities on corporate boards. James D. Westphal; Laurie P. Milton. **Adm. Sci. Qua.** 45:2 6:2000 pp.366-398.

4642 The human face of corporate governance. Lynn McGregor. Basingstoke: Macmillan Business, 2000. 224p. *ISBN: 0333772059*.

4643 Human resource management: the new agenda. Mick Marchington [Ed.]; Paul Sparrow [Ed.]. London; Washington DC: Financial Times; Pitman Publishing, 1998. xix, 346p. *ISBN: 0273628232. Includes bibliographical references (p. 315-336) and index.*

4644 The impact of cultural value orientations on individual HRM preferences in developing countries: lessons from Kenyan organizations. Stephen M. Nyambegera; Paul Sparrow; Kevin Daniels. **Int. J. Hum. Res. Man.** 11:4 8:2000 pp.639-663.

4645 Leadership into perspective. Jeff Katz [Foreword]; Eoin Banahan; Pierre Casse; Paul Claudel; et al. Paris: Éditions des Écrivains, 1999. 172p. *ISBN: 2844341624*.

4646 Leadership style, organizational culture and performance: empirical evidence from UK companies. Emmanuel Ogbonna; Lloyd C. Harris. **Int. J. Hum. Res. Man.** 11:4 8:2000 pp.766-788.

4647 Leaning on lean: the reception of a management fashion in Germany. Jos Benders; Mark von Bijsterveld. **New Tech. Work. Empl.** 15:1 3:2000 pp.50-64.
4648 Locus of control and managerial effectiveness: a study of private sector managers. S.K. Nair; S. Yuvaraj. **Ind. J. Ind. Rel.** 36:1 7:2000 pp.41-52.
4649 A longitudinal analysis of technical and organizational uncertainty in management theory. Ely Weitz; Yehouda Shenhav. **Organ. Stud.** 21:1 2000 pp.243-266.
4650 The making and remaking of HRM: the practice of managing people in the Eastern Cape Province, South Africa. Geoffrey Wood; Candice Els. **Int. J. Hum. Res. Man.** 11:1 2:2000 pp.112-125.
4651 Management aptitude of entrepreneurs. Daniel J. Knutson. New York, London: Garland Publishing, 2000. xii, 114p. *ISBN: 0815335032. Includes bibliographical references and index.* (*Series:* Garland studies in entrepreneurship).
4652 Management in Western Europe. Peter A. Lawrence; Vincent Edwards. Basingstoke; New York: Macmillan; St. Martin's Press, 1999. 251p. *ISBN: 0333733037, 0312229445. Includes bibliographical references and index.*
4653 Managing human resources: a partnership perspective. Susan E. Jackson; Randall S. Schuler. Cincinnati OH: South Western College Publishing, 1998. xiv, 776p. *ISBN: 032400415X. Includes bibliographical references and index.*
4654 Managing know-who based companies: a multinetworked approach to knowledge and innovation management. Sigvald Harryson. Cheltenham: Edward Elgar Publishing, 2000. xiv, 281p. *ISBN: 1840643145. Includes bibliographical references and index.*
4655 Managing strategy. David Watson. Buckingham, Philadelphia PA: Open University Press, 2000. xix, 156p. *ISBN: 0335203450, 0335203469. Includes bibliographical references and index.* (*Series:* Managing universities and colleges).
4656 Move it or lose it: an examination of the evolving role of the human resource professional in New Zealand. Jacqui Cleland; Karl Pajo; Paul Toulson. **Int. J. Hum. Res. Man.** 11:1 2:2000 pp.143-160.
4657 Las mujeres en cargos de dirección: obstáculos y cultura organizativa en las compañías privadas. *[In Spanish]*; [Women in management positions: obstacles and organizational culture in private companies] *[Summary]*. Gina Zabludovsky. **Rev. Mexicana Cien. Pol.** XLIII:174 10-12:1998 pp.115-144.
4658 New trends in international and multicultural management. Phillipe Hermel; David A. Ralston; Nguyen Van Thang; Nancy K. Napier; Michael E. Whitman; Anthony M. Townsend; Anthony R. Hendrickson; John W. Cadogan; Adamantios Diamantopoulos; Charles Pahud de Mortanges; Sharon Leiba-O'Sullivan; Sanjeev Agarwal; Thomas E. DeCarlo; Shyam B. Vyas; Elizabeth Goad Oliver; Karen S. Cravens; Rajnandini Pillai; Terri A. Scandura; Ethlyn A. Williams; Tomasz Lenartowicz; Kendall Roth; Kevin Y. Au. **J. Int. Bus. Stud.** 30:4 1999 pp.649-812. *Collection of 10 articles.*
4659 Organization and management in an Anglo-French consortium: the case of Transmanche-Link. Graham M. Winch; Naomi Clifton; Carla Millar. **J. Manag. Stu.** 37:5 7:2000 pp.663-686.
4660 Organizational justice and human resource management. Robert Folger; Russell Cropanzano. London: Sage Publications, 1998. xxvi, 278p. *ISBN: 0803956878, 080395686X. Includes bibliographical references (p. 236-263) and indexes.* (*Series:* Foundations for organizational science).
4661 Questioning the notion of feminine leadership: a critical perspective on the gender labelling of leadership. Yvonne Due Billing; Mats Alvesson. **Gend. Work & Org.** 7:3 7:2000 pp.144-157.
4662 Relationship between managers' authority power and perception of their subordinates' behaviour. Shailendra Singh. **Ind. J. Ind. Rel.** 35:3 1:2000 pp.275-300.
4663 Revisiting the dichtomy: managers versus leaders. Thiruvenkatam Ravichandran; Dakoju Nagabrahmam. **Ind. J. Ind. Rel.** 35:4 4:2000 pp.486-506.
4664 Self-management training for improving job performance: a field experiment involving salespeople. Colette A. Frayne; J. Michael Geringer. **J. Appl. Psychol.** 85:3 6:2000 pp.361-372.

I: LABOUR

4665 Small business: critical perspectives on business and management. D.J. Storey [Ed.]. New York: Routledge, 2000. *ISBN: 0415184681. Includes bibliographical references and index.*

4666 Strategic decision making, discourse, and strategy as social practice. John Hendry. **J. Manag. Stu.** 37:7 11:2000 pp.955-977.

4667 A strategic planning process for a small nonprofit organization: a hospice example. Cynthia Massie Mara. **Non. Manag. Leader.** 11:2 Winter:2000 pp.211-224.

4668 Strategic positioning: creating growth, generating profits, and achieving high performance. Paul Temporal. New York: Oxford University Press, 2000. xvii, 241p. *ISBN: 9835600570, 9835600589. Includes index.*

4669 Thinking about management: implications of organizational debates for practice. Ian Palmer; Cynthia Hardy. London: Sage Publications, 2000. 344p. *ISBN: 0761955356, 0761955364. Includes bibliographical references and index.*

4670 To your heart's content: a model of affective diversity in top management teams. Sigal G. Barsade; Andrew J. Ward; Jean D.F. Turner; Jeffrey A. Sonnenfeld. **Adm. Sci. Qua.** 45:4 12:2000 pp.802-836.

4671 Using psychology in management training: the psychological foundations of management skills. David A. Statt. New York: Routledge, 2000. 204p. *ISBN: 0415178630, 0415178649. Includes bibliographical references and index.*

4672 Validation of a multi-dimensional measure of strategy development processes. Andy Bailey; Gerry Johnson; Kevin Daniels. **Br. J. Manag.** 11:2 6:2000 pp.151-162.

4673 Work-family human resource bundles and perceived organizational performance. Jill E. Perry-Smith; Terry C. Blum. **Acad. Manag. J.** 43:6 12:2000 pp.1107-1117.

Working conditions
Conditions de travail

4674 Agricultural 'killing fields': the poisoning of Costa Rican banana workers. Robert Sass. **Int. J. Health. Ser.** 30:3 2000 pp.491-514.

4675 Assertiveness at work: a practical guide to handling awkward situations. Ken Back; Kate Back. London: McGraw-Hill, 1999. xiii, 207p. *ISBN: 0077095332.*

4676 Bad jobs in America: standard and nonstandard employment relations and job quality in the United States. Arne L. Kalleberg; Barbara F. Reskin; Ken Hudson. **Am. Sociol. R.** 65:2 4:2000 pp.256-278.

4677 The brave new world of work. Ulrich Beck. Malden MA: Polity Press, 2000. 202p. *ISBN: 0745623972, 0745623980. Includes bibliographical references and index.*

4678 The changing face of Japanese retail: working in a chain store. Louella Matsunaga. New York: Routledge, 2000. 209p. *ISBN: 0415229758. Includes bibliographical references and index.*

4679 Consequences of satisfaction with pay systems: two field studies. Marcia P. Miceli; Paul W. Mulvey. **Ind. Relat.** 39:1 1:2000 pp.62-87.

4680 Coping, health, and organizations. Philip Dewe [Ed.]; Michael P. Leiter [Ed.]; Tom Cox [Ed.]. London, New York: Taylor & Francis, 1999. xxi, 295p. *ISBN: 074840824X, 0748408231. Includes bibliographical references and index. (Series:* Issues in occupational health).

4681 Creating competitive capacity: labor market institutions and workplace practices in Germany and the United States. Peter Berg [Ed.]. Berlin: Sigma, 2000. 166p.

4682 The dark side of Taiwan's globalization success story. Robert Sass. **Int. J. Health. Ser.** 30:4 2000 pp.699-716.

4683 Deviance in the workplace. James Tucker; A.V. Margavio; Shirley Laska; Elaine Draper; Kitty Calavita; Vladimir Shlapentokh; Peter K. Manning; Paul M. Roman; Terry C. Blum; Gary T. Marx; Bridget M. Hutter; Joyce Rothschild; Terance D. Miethe. **Res. Soc. Work** 8 1999 pp.1-227. *Collection of 10 articles.*

4684 Does attitude toward money moderate the relationship between intrinsic job satisfaction and voluntary turnover? Thomas Li-Ping Tang; Jwa K. Kim; David Shin-Hsiung Tang. **Human Relat.** 53:2 2:2000 pp.213-246.

4685 Employment and distributional effects of restricting working time. R. Marimon; F. Zilibotti. **Eur. Econ. R.** 44:7 6:2000 pp.1291-1326.

4686 Employment and health: psychosocial stress in the workplace. Jennie Grimshaw. London: British Library, 1999. xx, 418p. *ISBN: 0712308474. Includes bibliographical references and indexes.* (*Series:* Social policy).

4687 Enriching Swedish women's work environment: the case of social enterprises in day care. Victor A. Pestoff. **Econ. Ind. Dem.** 21:1 2:2000 pp.39-70.

4688 Entrapped by the 'electronic panopticon'? Worker resistance in the call centre. Peter Bain; Phil Taylor. **New Tech. Work. Empl.** 15:1 3:2000 pp.2-18.

4689 An examination of the mediating role of psychological empowerment on the relations between the job, interpersonal relationships, and work outcomes. Robert C. Liden; Sandy J. Wayne; Raymond T. Sparrowe. **J. Appl. Psychol.** 85:3 6:2000 pp.407-416.

4690 Friends in high places: the effects of social networks on discrimination in salary negotiations. Marc-David L. Seidel; Jeffrey T. Polzer; Katherine J. Stewart. **Adm. Sci. Qua.** 45:1 3:2000 pp.1-24.

4691 Harassment, bullying and violence at work: a practical guide to combating employee abuse. Angela Ishmael; Bunmi Alemoru. London: Industrial Society, 1999. 317p. *ISBN: 1858351049.*

4692 Health effects of job insecurity among employees in the Swiss general population. Gianfranco Domenighetti; Barbara D'Avanzo; Brigitte Bisig. **Int. J. Health. Ser.** 30:3 2000 pp.477-490.

4693 Healthy and productive work: an international perspective. Lawrence R. Murphy [Ed.]; Cary L. Cooper [Ed.]. New York: Taylor & Francis, 2000. 256p. *ISBN: 0748408398. Includes bibliographical references and index.*

4694 Highlights of women workers in the global garment industry. Tran Angie Ngoc. **Viet. Stud.** 2(132) 1999 pp.141-152.

4695 Industrial legislation in 1999. Anna Chapman. **J. Ind. Relat.** 42:1 3:2000 pp.29-40.

4696 Inequality in the social consequences of illness: how well do people with long-term illness fare in the British and Swedish labor markets? Bo Burström; Margaret Whitehead; Christina Lindholm; Finn Diderichsen. **Int. J. Health. Ser.** 30:3 2000 pp.435-451.

4697 The influence of job familiarity and impression management on self-report measure scale scores and response latencies. Nicholas L. Vasilopoulos; Richard R. Reilly; Julia A. Leaman. **J. Appl. Psychol.** 85:1 2:2000 pp.50-63.

4698 Insomnia and its relationship to work and health in a working-age population. Steven J. Linton; Ing-Liss Bryngelsson. **J. Occupat. Rehabil.** 10:2 6:2000 pp.169-184.

4699 Institutional context and stress appraisal: the experience of life insurance agents in Singapore. Gina Lai; Kwok Bun Chan; Yiu Chung Ko; Kam Weng Boey. **J. As. Afr. S.** XXXV:2 2000 pp.209-228.

4700 Interactive effects of absence culture salience and group cohesiveness: a multi-level and cross-level analysis of work absenteeism in the Chinese context. Jia Lin Xie; Gary Johns. **J. Occup. Organ. Psychol.** 73:1 3:2000 pp.31-52.

4701 Is everyone in agreement? An exploration of within-group agreement in employee perceptions of the work environment. Katherine J. Klein; Amy Buhl Conn; D. Brent Smith; Joann Speer Sorra. **J. Appl. Psychol.** pp.3-16.

4702 Job demands, perceptions of effort-reward fairness and innovative work behaviour. Onne Janssen. **J. Occup. Organ. Psychol.** 73:3 9:2000 pp.287-302.

4703 Job insecurity and health. Peggy McDonough. **Int. J. Health. Ser.** 30:3 2000 pp.453-476.

4704 Job satisfaction, comparison earnings, and gender. P.J. Sloane; H. Williams. **Labour [Italy]** 14:3 9:2000 pp.473-501.

4705 Job satisfaction of commercial bank employees in Bangladesh: a comparative study of private and public sectors. Md. Mosharraf Hossain. **Ind. J. Ind. Rel.** 35:3 1:2000 pp.347-361.

I: LABOUR

4706 Job strain, effort-reward imbalance and employee well-being: a large-scale cross-sectional study. Jan de Jonge; Hans Bosma; Richard Peter; Johannes Siegrist. **Soc. Sci. Med.** 50:9 5:2000 pp.1317-1328.

4707 Linking employee satisfaction to business results. Paula S. Topolosky. New York: Garland Publishing, 2000. ix, 103p. *ISBN: 0815334877. Includes bibliographical references (p. 73-87) and index. (Series:* Garland studies on industrial productivity).

4708 Locality and *habitus*: the origins of sickness absence practices. Pekka Virtanen; Risto Nakari; Hanna Ahonen; Jussi Vahtera; Jaana Pentti. **Soc. Sci. Med.** 50:1 1:2000 pp.27-40.

4709 Meaningful work: rethinking professional ethics. Mike W. Martin. New York, Oxford: Oxford University Press, 2000. xiii, 252p. *ISBN: 0195133250. Includes bibliographical references and index. (Series:* Practical and professional ethics).

4710 Measures of five aspects of affective well-being at work. Kevin Daniels. **Human Relat.** 53:2 2:2000 pp.275-294.

4711 The moderating role of hostility in the relationship between enriched jobs and health. Deborah J. Dwyer; Marilyn L. Fox. **Acad. Manag. J.** 43:6 12:2000 pp.1086-1096.

4712 'Monday I've got Friday on my mind': working time in the hospitality industry. Alison Barnes; Diane Fieldes. **J. Ind. Relat.** 42:4 12:2000 pp.535-550.

4713 More tasks, less secure, working harder: three dimensions of labour utilisation. Cameron Allan; Michael O'Donnell; David Peetz. **J. Ind. Relat.** 41:4 12:1999 pp.519-535.

4714 Non-pecuniary advantages versus pecuniary disadvantages; job satisfaction among male and female academics in Scottish universities. Melanie E. Ward; Peter J. Sloane. **Scot. J. Poli. Econ.** 47:3 8:2000 pp.273-303.

4715 Pandora's box: the paradox of flexibility in today's workplace. Lynne Gouliquer. **Curr. Sociol.** 48:1 1:2000 pp.29-40.

4716 Passing the word: toward a model of gossip and power in the workplace. Nancy B. Kurland; Lisa Hope Pelled. **Acad. Man. Rev.** 25:2 4:2000 pp.428-438.

4717 Perceived overqualification and dimensions of job satisfaction: a longitudinal analysis. Gloria Jones Johnson; W. Roy Johnson. **J. Psychol.** 134:5 9:2000 pp.537-555.

4718 Personal control in organizations: a longitudinal investigation with newcomers. Blake E. Ashforth; Alan M. Saks. **Human Relat.** 53:3 3:2000 pp.311-340.

4719 Personality and job satisfaction: the mediating role of job characteristics. Timothy A. Judge; Joyce E. Bono; Edwin A. Locke. **J. Appl. Psychol.** 85:2 4:2000 pp.237-249.

4720 The personality, job satisfaction and turnover intentions of African-American male and female accountants: an examination of the human capital and structural/class theories. H.D. Glover; P.G. Mynatt; R.G. Schroeder. **Crit. Persp. Acc.** 11:2 4:2000 pp.173-192.

4721 Predictors and outcomes of openness to changes in a reorganizing workplace. Connie R. Wanberg; Joseph T. Banas. **J. Appl. Psychol.** 85:1 2:2000 pp.132-142.

4722 Predictors and outcomes of proactivity in the socialization process. Connie R. Wanberg; John D. Kammeyer-Mueller. **J. Appl. Psychol.** 85:3 6:2000 pp.373-385.

4723 Quand les salariés jugent leur salaire. *[In French]*; (What employees think of their wages.) *[Summary]*. Olivier Godechot; Marc Gurgand. **Écon. Stat.** 331 1:2000 pp.3-24.

4724 Reduced-hours employment: the relationship between difficulty of trade-offs and quality of life. Rosalind Chait Barnett; Karen C. Gareis. **Work Occup.** 27:2 5:2000 pp.168-187.

4725 The relationship between job and life satisfaction: evidence from a remote mining community. Roderick D. Iverson; Catherine Maguire. **Human Relat.** 53:6 6:2000 pp.807-840.

4726 Retail change: effects on employees' job demands and home life. Adelina Broadbridge; Vivien Swanson; Christine Taylor. **Int. R. Ret. Dist. Cons. Res.** 10:4 10:2000 pp.417-432.

4727 Risicos in bedrijf: omgaan met gezondheidsrisicos op de werkvloer. *[In Dutch]*; (Risks at work: handling health risks on the shop floor.) *[Summary]*. Peter Mascini. Rotterdam: Erasmus University, 1999. 201p. *ISBN: 9073235979. Includes bibliographical references (p. [167]-172).*

4728 The role of participation in decision-making in the organizational politics-job satisfaction relationship. L.A. Witt; Martha C. Andrews; K. Michele Kacmar. **Human Relat.** 53:3 3:2000 pp.341-358.

4729 Security abeyance: coping with the erosion of job conditions and treatments. Jerry Hallier. **Br. J. Manag.** 11:1 3:2000 pp.71-89.
4730 Sick from work: the body in employment. Paul Bellaby. Aldershot: Ashgate, 1999. ix, 252p. *ISBN: 0754610411. Includes bibliographical references and index.*
4731 Sindrome de burnout: um problema do indivíduo ou do seu contexto de trabalho? *[In Portuguese]*; (Burnout syndrome: an individual problem or a job-related problem?) *[Summary]*. Mary Sandra Carlotto; Maria Dolores Gobbi. **Aletheia** 10 1999 pp.103-114.
4732 Social capital at work: networks and employment at a phone center. Roberto M. Fernandez; Emilio J. Castilla; Paul Moore. **A.J.S.** 105:5 3:2000 pp.1288-1356.
4733 Social context at work: a multilevel analysis of job satisfaction. Amy S. Wharton; Thomas Rotolo; Sharon R. Bird. **Sociol. For.** 15:1 3:2000 pp.65-90.
4734 Strategic stress management: an organizational approach. Valerie J. Sutherland; Cary L. Cooper. Basingstoke: Macmillan, 2000. vi, 263p. *ISBN: 0333774876. Includes bibliographical references and index.*
4735 Stress and coping of Singapore teachers: a quantitative and qualitative analysis. Yiu-chung Ko; Kwok-bun Chan; Gina Lai; Kam-weng Boey. **J. Dev. Soc.** XVI:2 2000 pp.181-200.
4736 A struggle for recognition: work life reform in the domestic services industry. Gabrielle Meagher. **Econ. Ind. Dem.** 21:1 2:2000 pp.9-38.
4737 Surviving layoffs: the effects on organizational commitment and job performance. Leon Grunberg; Richard Anderson-Connolly; Edward S. Greenberg. **Work Occup.** 27:1 2:2000 pp.7-31.
4738 Teleworking benefits and pitfalls as perceived by professionals and managers. Yehuda Baruch. **New Tech. Work. Empl.** 15:1 3:2000 pp.34-49.
4739 Tolkninger af vilkår og situationer i arbejdslivet. *[In Danish]*; [Interpreting situations in working life] *[Summary]*. Steen Scheuer. **Led. Erhv.** 64:2 6:2000 pp.69-82.
4740 Umanizzazione del lavoro: storia e limiti di un paradigma. *[In Italian]*; [Humanization of labour: history and limits of a paradigm]. Fabrizio Pirro. **Quad. Sociol.** XLIII:21 1999 pp.168-187.
4741 Unrewarding work, coworker support, and job satisfaction: a test of the buffering hypothesis. Lori J. Ducharme; Jack K. Martin. **Work Occup.** 27:2 5:2000 pp.223-243.
4742 What determines job quality in nursing homes? Larry W. Hunter. **Ind. Lab. Rel.** 53:3 4:2000 pp.463-481.
4743 Who is stressed and why? Occupational specific stress among staff in an Irish human service organization. Niamh Flanagan; Tom Moriarty; Antoinette Daly. **Economica** 67:265 2:2000 pp.70-90.
4744 Why is this happening? A causal attribution approach to work exhaustion consequences. Jo Ellen Moore. **Acad. Man. Rev.** 25:2 4:2000 pp.335-349.
4745 Work attitudes, work conditions and hours constraints: an explorative, cross-national analysis. Alfonso Sousa-Poza; Fred Henneberger. **Labour [Italy]** 14:3 9:2000 pp.351-372.
4746 Work stress among six professional groups: the Singapore experience. Kwok Bun Chan; Gina Lai; Yiu Chung Ko; Kam Weng Boey. **Soc. Sci. Med.** 50:10 5:2000 pp.1415-1432.
4747 Workaholism and extra-work satisfactions. Ronald J. Burke. **Intern. J. Organiz. Anal.** 7:4 10:1999 pp.352-364.
4748 Working conditions and employee commitment in indigenous private manufacturing firms in Nigeria: managing business organisations for industrial development. Chikwendu Christian Ukaegbu. **J. Mod. Afr. S.** 38:2 6:2000 pp.295-324.
4749 Working time: theory and policy implications. François Contensou; Radu Vranceanu. Cheltenham: Edward Elgar Publishing, 2000. xvii, 232p. *ISBN: 1858989965. Includes bibliographical references and index.*
4750 Workplace accommodation as a social process. Lauren B. Gates. **J. Occupat. Rehabil.** 10:1 3:2000 pp.85-98.
4751 Work-time reduction in France: the role of collective bargaining in implementing the law. Philippe Auvergnon. **Int. J. Comp. L. L. I. R.** 16:3 Autumn:2000 pp.201-216.

I: LABOUR

I.4: Vocational training, occupations and careers
Formation professionnelle, professions et carrières

4752 Age and the quality of work: the case of modern American painters. David W. Galenson; Bruce A. Weinberg. **J. Polit. Ec.** 108:4 8:2000 pp.761-777.
4753 Diskontinuität im Erwerbsverlauf und betrieblicher Kontext. *[In German]*; [Discontinuity in working life and the firm] *[Summary]*. Stefan Bender; Dirk Konietzka; Peter Sopp. **Kölner Z. Soz. Soz. Psy.** 52:3 9:2000 pp.475-499.
4754 Divisions of labour: social groups and occupational allocation. Maria Charles. **Eur. Sociol. R.** 16:1 3:2000 pp.27-42.
4755 Is occupational mobility declining in the United States? Steven Rytina. **Soc. Forc.** 78:4 6:2000 pp.1227-1276.

Career development
Déroulement de carrière

4756 Career concerns and the acquisition of firm-specific skills. Bernard Sinclair-Desgagné; Olivier Cadot. **J. Jap. Int. Ec.** 14:3 9:2000 pp.204-217.
4757 Career frontiers: new conceptions of working lives. Maury Peiperl [Ed.]. New York: Oxford University Press, 2000. xvii, 290p. *ISBN: 0198296916. Includes bibliographical references and index.*
4758 Career jobs, survival jobs, and employee deviance: a social investment model of workplace misconduct. Jessica Huiras; Christopher Uggen; Barbara McMorris. **Sociol. Q.** 41:2 Spring:2000 pp.245-264.
4759 Developing managers: the functional, the symbolic, the sacred and the profane. Ken Kamoche. **Organ. Stud.** 21:4 2000 pp.747-774.
4760 Effects of task performance and contextual performance on systemic rewards. James R. Van Scotter; Stephan J. Motowidlo; Thomas C. Cross. **J. Appl. Psychol.** 85:4 8:2000 pp.526-535.
4761 High hopes: organizational position, employment experiences, and women's and men's promotion aspirations. Naomi Cassirer; Barbara Reskin. **Work Occup.** 27:4 11:2000 pp.438-463.
4762 The influence of further education on occupational mobility in Switzerland. Jiang Hong Li; Markus König; Marlis Buchmann; Stefan Sacchi. **Eur. Sociol. R.** 16:1 3:2000 pp.43-66.
4763 Job assignment and promotion. Irene Valsecchi. **J. Econ. Sur.** 14:1 2:2000 pp.31-52.
4764 Het loon als maatstaf voor de aansluiting tussen baan- en opleidingsniveau. *[In Dutch]*; [Matching educational and job levels] *[Summary]*. P. Van Eijs; J.A.M. Heijke. **Maan. Econ.** 64:3 6:2000 pp.191-206.
4765 Partner en kinderen: belemmerend of bevorderend voor beroepssucces? Beroepsmobiliteit van mannen en vrouwen met verschillende huwelijksen ouderschapscarrières. *[In Dutch]*; [Partner and children: burden or asset for occupational attainment? Occupational mobility of men and women with different marriage and parenthood careers] *[Summary]*. Pearl A. Dykstra; Tineke Fokkema. **Mens Maat.** 75:2 6:2000 pp.110-128.
4766 The professional career of sociologists: a graphical chain model reflecting early influences and associations. Iris Pigeot; Astrid Heinicke; Angelika Caputo; Josef Brüderl. **All. Stat. A.** 84:1 2000 pp.3-22.

Occupations
Professions

4767 Amateurs et professionnels. *[In French]*; [Amateurs and professionals]. Éliane Del Col; Hubert Cukrowicz; Philippe Coulangeon; Sylvain Robert. **Genèses** 36 9:1999 pp.6-91. *Collection of 4 articles.*

4768 Amateurs in public service: volunteering, service-learning, and community service. Charles T. Clotfelter [Ed.]; Eleanor Brown; Helmut K. Anheier; Lester M. Salamon; Emmett D. Carson; Sally A. Raskoff; Richard A. Sundeen; Rodney A. Smolla; John Wilson; Marc Musick; Steven Rathgeb Smith; Robert R. Korstad; James L. Leloudis; Jean Baldwin Grossman; Kathryn Furano; Jeffrey L. Brudney. **Law Cont. Pr.** 62:4 Autumn:1999 pp.1-263. *Collection of 12 articles.*

4769 The British engineer problem: a comparison of careers, employment and skills. Bryn Jones; Peter Scott; Brian Bolton; Alan Bramley; Fred Manske. **Policy St.** 21:1 3:2000 pp.5-24.

4770 The 'bureaucratization' of professional roles: the case of clinical directors in UK hospitals. Martin Kitchener. **Organization** 7:1 2:2000 pp.129-154.

4771 Changes in occupational structure and occupational practice: a challenge to education. Elly de Bruijn; Monique Volman. **Eur. J. Wom. Stud.** 7:4 11:2000 pp.455-474.

4772 Education, profession and culture: some conceptual questions. David Carr. **Br. J. Educ. S.** 48:3 9:2000 pp.248-268.

4773 An empirical evaluation of the interpersonal and organisational correlates of professionalism in internal auditing. Timothy J. Fogarty; Lawrence P. Kalbers. **Acc. Bus. Res.** 30:2 Spring:2000 pp.125-136.

4774 Housing management: the social construction of an occupational role. D. Clapham; B. Franklin; L. Saugères. **Hous. Th. Soc.** 17:2 2000 pp.68-82.

4775 Identidad y profesión en la agricultura familiar. *[In Spanish]*; [Identity and profession on family farms]. Cristóbal Gómez Benito; Juan Jesús González; Roberto Sancho Hazak. Madrid: Centro de Investigaciones Sociológicas, 1999. 134p. *ISBN: 8474762804. Includes bibliographical references (p. 93-94).*

4776 The impact of carpal tunnel syndrome on work status: implications of job characteristics for staying on the job. Julia Faucett; Paul D. Blanc; Edward Yelin. **J. Occupat. Rehabil.** 10:1 3:2000 pp.55-84.

4777 Intergenerationele overdracht van status en sekse-typering van beroepen: de invloed van vader en moeder op hun dochters en zonen. *[In Dutch]*; (How parents' jobs influence children's jobs: interrelating occupational status and sex-typing in the Netherlands.) Sylvia E. Korupp; Karin Sanders; Harry B.G. Ganzeboom. **Mens Maat.** 75:1 3:2000 pp.22-39.

4778 The ministry as an occupational labor market: intentions to leave an employer (church) versus intentions to leave a profession (ministry). Elaine M. McDuff; Charles W. Mueller. **Work Occup.** 27:1 2:2000 pp.89-116.

4779 Le mirage de la compétence. *[In French]*; [The mirage of skills]. Patrick Rozenblatt [Ed.]; Isabelle Auriel; et al. Paris: Éditions Syllepse, 2000. 267p. *ISBN: 2913165184. Includes bibliographical references.*

4780 Une nouvelle carte de la mobilité professionnelle. *[In French]*; (A new professional mobility map.) *[Summary]*. Simone Chapoulie. **Écon. Stat.** 331 1:2000 pp.25-46.

4781 Pochodzenie społeczne i wybór zawodu kowala na Kaszubach i Kociewiu. *[In Polish]*; (Social background and the choice of the profession of blacksmith in the Kashuby and Kotsievie area.) Jerzy Kuniewski. **Lud** 83 1999 pp.89-108.

4782 The professionalisation of financial advice in Britain. Michael Clarke. **Sociol. Rev.** 48:1 2:2000 pp.58-79.

4783 The professionalization of everyone? A comparative study of the development of the professions in the United Kingdom and Germany. Mark Neal; John Morgan. **Eur. Sociol. R.** 16:1 3:2000 pp.9-26.

I: LABOUR

4784 Skilled international migration: the experience of nurses in the UK; *[Summary in French]*; *[Summary in German]*. Irene Hardill; Sandra MacDonald. **Reg. Stud.** 34:7 10:2000 pp.681-692.

4785 Stavovi i mišljenja studenata novinarstva fakulteta političkih znanosti o novinarstvu. *[In Croatian]*; [The attitudes and opinions towards journalism as a profession shown by students of journalism in the faculty of political science] *[Summary]*. Marko Sapunar. **Pol. Misao** 37:3 2000 pp.194-206.

4786 The strategic choice of operator skills in CNC installations. Mark Pagell; Alison E. Barber. **New Tech. Work. Empl.** 15:1 3:2000 pp.65-86.

4787 Transformationen im Journalismus. Entdifferenzierung der Organisationen und Qualifikationen im Formatjournalismus. *[In German]*; (Transformations in journalism. 'De-differentiation' of organizations and qualifications in format journalism.) *[Summary]*. Klaus-Dieter Altmeppen; Patrick Donges; Kerstin Engels. **Publizistik** 45:2 6:2000 pp.200-218.

4788 Unravelling a profession: the case of engineers in a British regional electricity company. C. Carter; D. Crowther. **Crit. Persp. Acc.** 11:1 1:2000 pp.23-49.

4789 Whither welfare professionalism? Peggy Foster; Paul Wilding. **Soc. Pol. Admin.** 34:2 6:2000 pp.143-159.

Training
Formation

4790 Berufliche Qualifizierung für Arbeitslose. Zur Effektivität AFG-finanzierter Weiterbildung im Transformationsprozess. *[In German]*; (Training programs for the unemployed: the efficiency of publicly financed training measures in the German transformation process.) *[Summary]*. Matthias Wingens; Reinhold Sackmann; Michael Grotheer. **Kölner Z. Soz. Soz. Psy.** 52:1 3:2000 pp.60-80.

4791 Core competence and education. Gary Holmes; Nick Hooper. **High. Educ.** 40:3 10:2000 pp.247-258.

4792 Correlates of training: an analysis using both employer and employee characteristics. Harley Frazis; Maury Gittleman; Mary Joyce. **Ind. Lab. Rel.** 53:3 4:2000 pp.443-462.

4793 Développement et individualisation des politiques de formation des adultes. *[In French]*; (The growth and individualisation of adult training policies.) *[Summary]*. Christian Maroy; Bernard Conter. **Recher. Sociolog.** XXXI:1 2000 pp.41-54.

4794 Do male dropouts benefit from obtaining a GED, postsecondary education, and training? John B. Willett; Richard J. Murnane; Kathryn Parker Boudett. **Eval. Rev.** 23:5 10:1999 pp.475-502.

4795 Evaluating public sector sponsored training in East Germany. Bernd Fitzenberger; Hedwig Prey. **Ox. Econ. Pap.** 52:3 7:2000 pp.497-520.

4796 Exploring the relationship between performance management and program impact: a case study of the job training partnership act. Burt S. Barnow. **J. Policy An.** 19:1 Winter:2000 pp.118-141.

4797 Formations en alternance et appariement: rôle de la gouvernance régionale. *[In French]*; (Vocational training on a rotational basis and job matching: the role of regional governance.) *[Summary]*. François Mambi-El-Sendengele. **R. Ec. Reg. Urb.** 2 2000 pp.301-322.

4798 The impact of training on labour mobility: individual and firm-level evidence from Britain. Francis Green; Alan Felstead; Ken Mayhew; Alan Pack. **Br. J. Ind. R.** 38:2 6:2000 pp.261-276.

4799 Les jeunes et les petites entreprises: vers de nouvelles cohérences territoriales. *[In French]*; [Young people and small firms: toward a new territorial understanding]. Stéphane Michun. **R.E.M.** 48:1-2 2000 pp.147-168.

I: TRAVAIL

4800 Predictive validity of personal statements and the role of the five-factor model of personality in relation to medical training. Eamonn Ferguson; Andrea Sanders; Fiona O'Hebir; David James. **J. Occup. Organ. Psychol.** 73:3 9:2000 pp.321-344.
4801 Teaching English grammar in initial teacher training. Robert Jeffcoate. **Educat. Res.** 42:1 Spring:2000 pp.73-84.
4802 Toward an integrative theory of training motivation: a meta-analytic path analysis of 20 years of research. Jason A. Colquitt; Jeffrey A. LePine; Raymond A. Noe. **J. Appl. Psychol.** 85:5 10:2000 pp.678-707.
4803 Training for a smart workforce. Rodney Gerber [Ed.]; Colin Lankshear [Ed.]. London, New York: Routledge, 2000. 248p. *ISBN: 0415195519, 0415195527. Includes bibliographical references and index.*
4804 Training in the new private sector in Russia. Simon Clarke; Tanya Metalina. **Int. J. Hum. Res. Man.** 11:1 2:2000 pp.19-36.
4805 Vocational and technical higher education in the United Kingdom. Michael Connolly; Peter Hodson; Norah Jones. **Administration** 48:1 Spring:2000 pp.18-39.
4806 Vocational schools in Turkey: an administrative and organizational analysis; *[Summary in French]; [Summary in German]; [Summary in Spanish]; [Summary in Russian]*. Hasan Simsek; Ali Yildirim. **Int. R. Educat.** 46:3-4 7:2000 pp.327-342.
4807 What do people need to know about writing in order to write in their jobs? Chris Davies; Maria Birbili. **Br. J. Educ. S.** 48:4 12:2000 pp.429-445.

I.5: **Labour relations**
Relations du travail

4808 'Ain't misbehavin'? Opportunities for resistance under new forms of 'quality' management. David Knights; Darren McCabe. **Sociology** 34:3 8:2000 pp.421-436.
4809 Codetermination in Sweden: myth and reality. Klas Levinson. **Econ. Ind. Dem.** 21:4 11:2000 pp.457-473.
4810 A 'Copernican revolution' in French industrial relations: are the times a' changing? Stephen Jeffcrys. **Br. J. Ind. R.** 38:2 6:2000 pp.241-260.
4811 Cross-border trade with Mexico and the prospect for worker solidarity: the case of Mexico. Steve Babson. **Crit. Sociol.** 26:1-2 2000 pp.13-35.
4812 Employee buyouts and employee involvement: a case study investigation of employee attitudes. Lisa Trewhitt. **Ind. Relat. J.** 31:5 12:2000 pp.437-453.
4813 Employee representation on health and safety and European works councils. David Walters. **Ind. Relat. J.** 31:5 12:2000 pp.416-436.
4814 Employer associations and industrial relations change. Peter Sheldon [Ed.]; Louise Thornthwaite [Ed.]. St. Leonards: Allen & Unwin, 1999. 267p. *ISBN: 1864487488.*
4815 Experiences of tripartite relations in Central and Eastern European countries. Giuseppe Casale. **Int. J. Comp. L. L. I. R.** 16:2 2000 pp.129-142.
4816 Feminism facing industrial relations in Britain. Judy Wajcman. **Br. J. Ind. R.** 38:2 6:2000 pp.183-202.
4817 Gesamtwirtschaftliche Leistungseffekte betrieblicher Arbeitnehmervertretung im internationalen Vergleich. *[In German]*; (The institutionalization of enterprise worker representation and economy-wide performance in comparative perspective.) *[Summary]*. Bernhard Kittel. **Indust. Bezieh.** 7:3 2000 pp.211-229.
4818 Globalisation and labour regulation. Mark Bray; Gregor Murray; Anthony Giles; Nigel Haworth; Stephen Hughes; Nick Wailes; Christian Lévesque; Guylaine Vallée; Frederic C. Deyo; Pierre Verge; Russell Lansbury; Peter Fairbrother; Duncan MacDonald. **J. Ind. Relat.** 42:2 6:2000 pp.167-333. *Collection of 9 articles.*
4819 Globalisation, development and labour strategies: Ireland in context. Ronaldo Munck. **Irish J. Soc.** 9 1999 pp.97-114.
4820 The illusion of union-management cooperation in postcommunist Central Eastern Europe. Carola M. Frege. **E. Eur. Pol. Soc.** 14:3 Fall:2000 pp.636-660.

I: LABOUR

4821 Immigrant organizing and the new labor movement in Los Angeles. Ruth Milkman. **Crit. Sociol.** 26:1-2 2000 pp.59-81.

4822 The impact of representation and other factors on the outcomes of employee-initiated workers' compensation appeals. Douglas Hyatt; Boris Kralj. **Ind. Lab. Rel.** 53:4 7:2000 pp.665-683.

4823 Industrial democracy and institutional environments: a comparison of Germany and Taiwan. Tzu-shian Han; Su-fen Chiu. **Econ. Ind. Dem.** 21:2 5:2000 pp.147-182.

4824 Industrial relations in Japan: trends, challenges and future prospects. Ajay Singh. **Ind. J. Ind. Rel.** 35:3 1:2000 pp.362-380.

4825 Integración económica y relaciones laborales en América Latina: el caso de Centroamérica. *[In Spanish]*; [Economic integration and labour relations in Latin America: the case of Central America] *[Summary]*. Dídimo Castillo. **Est. Latinam.** VI:11 1-6:1999 pp.47-66.

4826 Japanese industrial relations. Taishirō Shirai. Tokyo: Japan Institute of Labour, 2000. iv, 160p. *ISBN: 4538760056. Includes bibliographical references. (Series:* Japanese economy and labor - 5).

4827 Jobs and fairness: the logic and experience of employee ownership. Robert Oakeshott. Norwich: Michael Russell, 2000. 710p. *ISBN: 085955256X. Includes bibliographical references and index.*

4828 La négociation collective en Belgique: crise de l'emploi et modification du référentiel d'échange. *[In French]*; (Collective bargaining in Belgium: unemployment and procedural change.) *[Summary]*. Xavier Leloup; Philippe Barré; Évelyne Léonard; Pierre Walthéry. **Recher. Sociolog.** XXXI:1 2000 pp.55-66.

4829 New collective labor relation mechanisms in the workplace: the collective contract system in mainland China. Ngok Kinglun. **Iss. Stud.** 35:6 11-12:1999 pp.119-143.

4830 New employee relations strategies in Britain: towards individualism or partnership? Nicholas Bacon; John Storey. **Br. J. Ind. R.** 38:3 9:2000 pp.407-428.

4831 Restructuring in the service industries: management reform and workplace relations in the UK service sector. Gavin Poynter. London, New York: Mansell, 2000. xii, 260p. *ISBN: 0720123410. Includes bibliographical references (p. 243-252) and index. (Series:* Employment and work relations in context).

4832 The resurgence of labor as citizenship movement in the new labor relations environment. Paul Johnston. **Crit. Sociol.** 26:1-2 2000 pp.139-160.

4833 Rethinking 'regional industrial relations': space, place and the social relations of work. Bradon Ellem; John Shields. **J. Ind. Relat.** 41:4 12:1999 pp.536-560.

4834 Skilled workers' solidarity: the American experience in comparative perspective. Antoine Joseph. New York, London: Garland Publishing, 2000. xvii, 227p. *ISBN: 0815333366. Includes bibliographical references (p. 203-223) and index. (Series:* States and society - 7).

4835 Social dialogues: an interim report on recent results and prospects. Berndt Keller; Matthias Bansbach. **Ind. Relat. J.** 31:4 10-11:2000 pp.291-307.

4836 Ten years of post-communist Central Eastern Europe: labour's tenuous foothold in the regulation of the employment relationship. Anna Pollert. **Econ. Ind. Dem.** 21:2 5:2000 pp.183-210.

4837 Theorieansätze zur Analyse industrieller Beziehungen. *[In German]*; [Theoretical approaches to the analysis of industrial relations]. Holger Lengfeld; Stefan Liebig; Carsten Wirth; Berndt Keller; Ralf Rogowski. **Indust. Bezieh.** 7:1 2000 pp.10-126. *Collection of 4 articles.*

4838 The transformation of Swedish industrial relations from below. Göran Brulin. **Econ. Ind. Dem.** 21:2 5:2000 pp.237-252.

4839 Worker control: the bases of women's support. Ed Collom. **Econ. Ind. Dem.** 21:2 5:2000 pp.211-236.

I: TRAVAIL

Labour disputes
Conflits du travail

4840 Accounting for strikes: evidence from UK manufacturing in the 1980s. Daphne Nicolitsas. **Labour [Italy]** 14:3 9:2000 pp.417-440.
4841 Centralized collective bargaining and the problem of 'compliance': lessons from the Italian experience. Lucio Baccaro. **Ind. Lab. Rel.** 53:4 7:2000 pp.579-601.
4842 Decentralised collective bargaining in Hungary. László Neumann. **Int. J. Comp. L. L. I. R.** 16:2 2000 pp.113-128.
4843 Hinges in collective action: strategic innovation in the Pittston coal strike. Karen Beckwith. **Mobilization** 5:2 2000 pp.179-199.
4844 How attorney representation and adjudication affect Canadian arbitration and labor relations board decisions. Mark Harcourt. **J. Labor Res.** XXI:1 Winter:2000 pp.149-160.
4845 Industrial dispute tactics in Australian manufacturing. James Ted McDonald. **Ind. Relat.** 39:1 1:2000 pp.115-138.
4846 Lawful industrial action and the employment relationship in Denmark. Ole Hasselbalch. **Int. J. Comp. L. L. I. R.** 16:2 2000 pp.143-153.
4847 No news is good news: the relationship between media attention and strike duration. Francis J. Flynn. **Ind. Relat.** 39:1 1:2000 pp.139-160.
4848 The 'revenge of history': collective memories and labor protests in northeastern China. Ching Kwan Lee. **Ethnog.** 1:2 12:2000 pp.217-238.
4849 South Australian workers' compensation disputes: from conciliation to adjudication and back again. Frances Meredith. **J. Ind. Relat.** 42:3 9:2000 pp.398-416.
4850 STRIKES! Past and present. Margaret Levi; David Olson; Victoria Johnson; Peter Turnbull; Chris McConville; Frances Fox Piven; Richard A. Cloward. **Polit. Soc.** 28:3 9:2000 pp.309-430. *Collection of 5 articles.*
4851 'The parliaments call them thugs': public space, identity and union protest. Janis Bailey; Kurt Iveson. **J. Ind. Relat.** 42:4 12:2000 pp.517-534.

Trade unions
Syndicats

4852 Ageism, early exit, and British trade unions. Colin Duncan; Wendy Loretto; Phil White. **Ind. Relat. J.** 31:3 9:2000 pp.220-234.
4853 Breaking the iron law of oligarchy: union revitalization in the American labor movement. Kim Voss; Rachel Sherman. **A.J.S.** 106:2 9:2000 pp.303-349.
4854 British trade unions facing the future. Peter Fairbrother. **Cap. Class** 71 Summer:2000 pp.47-78.
4855 The changing trade unions in China. Seung Wook Baek. **J. Cont. Asia** 30:1 2000 pp.46-66.
4856 Comparative union responses to mass immigration: evidence from an immigrant city. Guillermo Grenier; Bruce Nissen. **Crit. Sociol.** 26:1-2 2000 pp.82-108.
4857 Diversity, identities and strategies of women trade union activists. Fiona Colgan; Sue Ledwith. **Gend. Work & Org.** 7:4 10:2000 pp.242-257.
4858 Explaining variation in workplace restructuring: the role of local union capabilities. Ann C. Frost. **Ind. Lab. Rel.** 53:4 7:2000 pp.559-578.
4859 Gewerkschaften und Sozialdemokratie. *[In German]*; [Trade unions and social democracy]. Hans O. Hemmer; Hans-Jürgen Arlt; Thomas Meyer; Hans-Joachim Schabedoth; Helmuth Schütte; Hartmut Soell; Klaus Kempter; Jürgen Walter; Bodo Zeuner. **Gewerk. Monat.** 51:1 1:2000 pp.1-46. *Collection of 8 articles.*
4860 Gewerkschaftsreformen in den USA. *[In German]*; (Trade union reform in the United States: a critical assessment of the 'organizing model'.) *[Summary]*. Carola M. Frege. **Indust. Bezieh.** 7:3 2000 pp.260-280.

I: LABOUR

4861 How do people become empowered? A case study of union activists. Michelle Kaminski; Jeffrey S. Kaufman; Robin Graubarth; Thomas G. Robins. **Human Relat.** 53:10 10:2000 pp.1357-1383.

4862 IAPB e sindicato: duas estruturas interligadas. *[In Portuguese]*; (The IAPB and labor unions: two interconnected structures.) Ana Lucia Oliveira. **Rev. Soc. Polit.** 13 1999 pp.141-152.

4863 Identidades sindicais européias em tempos de globalização. *[In Portuguese]*; (European trade union identities in times of globalization.) *[Summary]*. Hermes Augusto Costa. **Tempo Soc.** 12:1 5:2000 pp.165-186.

4864 Labor and the Left in South Africa. Allison Drew; Lucien van der Walt; Peter Alexander; Vladimir Shubin; Phil Eidelberg; Andrew Nash; Lungisile Ntsebeza; Leonard Gentle. **Comp. Stud. S. As. Af. Mid. East** XIX:1 1999 pp.1-102. *Collection of 8 articles.*

4865 A Marxist critique of Black radical theories of trade-union racism. Satnam Virdee. **Sociology** 34:3 8:2000 pp.545-565.

4866 La modernización y la estructura sindical de México. *[In Spanish]*; [Modernization and union structure in Mexico]. Javier Aguilar García. **Acta Sociol. [Mexico]** 25 1-4:1999 pp.9-24.

4867 Neoliberal restructuring and U.S. unions: toward social movement unionism? Ian Robinson. **Crit. Sociol.** 26:1-2 2000 pp.109-138.

4868 The new unionism and the new bargaining agenda: UNISON-employer partnerships on workplace learning in Britain. Anne Munro; Helen Rainbird. **Br. J. Ind. R.** 38:2 6:2000 pp.223-240.

4869 Organizing the next generation: influences on young workers' willingness to join unions in Canada. Graham S. Lowe; Sandra Rastin. **Br. J. Ind. R.** 38:2 6:2000 pp.203-222.

4870 Right-to-work laws: new evidence from the stock market. Steven E. Abraham; Paula B. Voos. **S. Econ. J.** 67:2 10:2000 pp.345-362.

4871 Self-organization and trade union democracy. Jill C. Humphrey. **Sociol. Rev.** 48:2 5:2000 pp.262-282.

4872 Towards a reform agenda? European trade unions in transition. Jeremy Waddington. **Ind. Relat. J.** 31:4 10-11:2000 pp.317-330.

4873 Trade unions at the crossroads. Peter Fairbrother. New York: Mansell, 2000. xv, 365p. *ISBN: 0720122023. Includes bibliographical references (p. 345-359) and index. (Series: Employment and work relations in context).*

4874 The TUC: from the general strike to new unionism. Robert Taylor. New York: St. Martin's Press, 2000. 299p. *ISBN: 0333930657. Includes bibliographical references and index.*

4875 The TUC's organising academy: an assessment. Edmund Heery; Melanie Simms; Rick Delbridge; John Salmon; Dave Simpson. **Ind. Relat. J.** 31:5 12:2000 pp.400-415.

4876 Union governance and democracy — Part I. Bruce E. Kaufman; Clyde W. Summers; Michael J. Goldberg; Michael Lynk; Paul F. Clark; Lois S. Gray; Robert Bruno; Richard W. Hurd. **J. Labor Res.** XXI:1 Winter:2000 pp.1-115. *Collection of 7 articles.*

4877 Union governance and democracy — Part II. Bruce E. Kaufman; George Strauss; Paul Jarley; Jack Fiorito; John T. Delaney; Samuel Estreicher; Ann C. Frost; David Witwer. **J. Labor Res.** XXI:2 Spring:2000 pp.189-303. *Collection of 6 articles.*

4878 Union wage differentials for covered members and nonmembers in Great Britain. Andrew K.G. Hildreth. **J. Labor Res.** XXI:1 Winter:2000 pp.133-148.

4879 Union weakness in Hong Kong: workplace industrial relations and the Federation of Trade Unions. Andy W. Chan; Ed Snape. **Econ. Ind. Dem.** 21:2 5:2000 pp.117-146.

4880 Unionization of faculty salaries: new evidence from the 1990s. James Monks. **J. Labor Res.** XXI:2 Spring:2000 pp.305-314.

4881 Unions and employment growth: panel data evidence. Mark Wooden; Anne Hawke. **Ind. Relat.** 39:1 1:2000 pp.88-107.

4882 Women, power and trade union government in the UK. Geraldine Healy; Gill Kirton. **Br. J. Ind. R.** 38:3 9:2000 pp.343-360.

4883 Women working in a greedy institution: commitment and emotional labour in the union movement. Suzanne Franzway. **Gend. Work & Org.** 7:4 10:2000 pp.258-268.

J: POLITICS. STATE. INTERNATIONAL RELATIONS
POLITIQUE. ÉTAT. RELATIONS INTERNATIONALES

J.1: Political sociology
Sociologie politique

4884 Contemporary political sociology: globalization, politics and power. Kate Nash. Malden MA: Blackwell Publishers, 1999. 309p. *ISBN: 0631206604, 0631206612. Includes bibliographical references and index.*

4885 Un contributo sociologico all'analisi della politica. *[In Italian]*; [A sociological contribution to political analysis]. Fabio de Nardis. **Sociologia [Rome]** XXXIV:1 2000 pp.75-90.

4886 The development of charismatic leaders. Micha Popper. **Polit. Psych.** 21:4 12:2000 pp.729-744.

4887 Discourse theory and political analysis: identities, hegemonies, and social change. David R. Howarth [Ed.]; Aletta J. Norval [Ed.]; Yannis Stavrakakis [Ed.]. New York: Manchester University Press, 2000. 243p. *ISBN: 0719056632, 0719056640. Includes bibliographical references and index.*

4888 Le legs de l'Ecole de Chicago à la théorie de l'action collective. *[In French]*; [The legacy of the Chicago School and the theory of collective action]. David Snow; Daniel Cefai [Interviewer]; Danny Trom [Interviewer]. **Politix** 13:50 2000 pp.151-162.

4889 Macht und Herrschaft: sozialwissenschaftliche Konzeptionen und Theorien. *[In German]*; [Power and dominion: concepts and theories in social science]. Peter Imbusch. Opladen: Leske + Budrich, 1998. 374p. *ISBN: 3810019119.*

4890 Mobilisierung, Staat und Demokratie: Eine Reinterpretation einer modernisierungstheoretischen These. *[In German]*; (Mobilization, state, and democracy: a re-interpretation of a thesis of modernization theory.) Jörg Rössel. **Kölner Z. Soz. Soz. Psy.** 52:4 12:2000 pp.609-635.

4891 Political sociology: a critical introduction. Keith Faulks. New York; Edinburgh: New York University Press; Edinburgh University Press, 1999. 256p. *ISBN: 0814727093, 0814727085, 0748613560. Includes bibliographical references and index.*

4892 Primitive globalization? State and locale in neoliberal global engagement. William Sites. **Sociol. Theory** 18:1 3:2000 pp.121-144.

4893 Processes and mechanisms of democratization. Charles Tilly. **Sociol. Theory** 18:1 3:2000 pp.1-16.

4894 Propos sur le champ politique. *[In French]*; [A word on politics]. Philippe Fritsch [Intro.]; Pierre Bourdieu. Lyon: Presses Universitaires de Lyon, 2000. 110p. *ISBN: 2729706496.*

4895 Psychotherapy and politics. Nick Totton. London: Sage Publications, 2000. 186p. *ISBN: 0761958509, 0761958495. Includes bibliographical references and index. (Series: Perspectives on psychotherapy).*

4896 Readings in contemporary political sociology. Kate Nash [Ed.]. Malden MA: Blackwell Publishers, 1999. 361p. *ISBN: 0631213635, 0631213643. Includes bibliographical references and index.*

4897 Sciences du politique. *[In French]*; [Political science]. Loïc Blondiaux; Philippe Veitl; Mario Grynszpan; Yves Viltard; Véronique Dimier. **Genèses** 37 12:1999 pp.4-92. *Collection of 4 articles.*

4898 Splendeurs et misères de la vie intellectuelle (II). *[In French]*; [The splendour and misery of intellectual life. Part II]. O. Mongin; Monique Canto-Sperber; Goulven Boudic; Pierre Grémion; Jean-Philippe Béja; Pierre Hassner; Marc Lazar; Aleksander Smolar; Nicolas Baverez; Claude Habib; Irène Théry; Véronique Nahoum-Grappe; Sandra Laugier; Vincent Descombes. **Esprit** 265 5:2000 pp.6-174. *Collection of 15 articles.*

4899 Die Wiederentdeckung der Handlungs-potentiale — Problemstellungen politischer Soziologie unter den Bedingungen reflexiver Modernisierung. *[In German]*; [Problems of

J: POLITICS. STATE. INTERNATIONAL RELATIONS

political sociology under conditions of reflexive modernization] *[Summary]*. Ronald Hitzler. **Z. Polit.** 47:2 6:2000 pp.183-200.

J.2: **Political thought**
Pensée politique

4900 Adolph Lowe on freedom, education and socialization. Mathew Forstater. **R. Soc. Econ.** LVIII:2 6:2000 pp.225-239.
4901 Ciudadanía y democracia: la mirada de las ciencias sociales. *[In Spanish]*; [Citizenship and democracy: a view from the social sciences]. Juan Enrique Opazo Marmentini. **Metapolítica** 4:15 7-9:2000 pp.52-79.
4902 Cosmopolitanism and the circle of reason. Pratap Bhanu Mehta. **Polit. Theory** 28:5 10:2000 pp.619-639.
4903 ...*created equal*. Lockes negatives Argument zur Begründung der Menschenrechte. *[In German]*; [...created equal. Locke's negative argument on the foundation of human rights] *[Summary]*. Heinz-Gerd Schmitz. **Arc. Recht. Soz.** 86:1 2000 pp.29-47.
4904 La crítica Marxista del posmodernismo. *[In Spanish]*; [The Marxist critique of postmodernism] *[Summary]*. Carlos Rojas Osorio. **Rev. Cien. Soc.** 5 6:1998 pp.71-95.
4905 Culture, citizenship, and community: a contextual exploration of justice as evenhandedness. Joseph H. Carens. Oxford, New York: Oxford University Press, 2000. ix, 284p. *ISBN: 0198297513, 0198297688. Includes bibliographical references (p. [265]-273) and index.*
4906 Democratic epistemology and accountability. Russell Hardin. **Soc. Philos. Pol.** 17:1 Winter:2000 pp.110-126.
4907 Dimensionen der Demokratiefähigkeit. Politik und rhetorische Rechtstheorie. *[In German]*; [Dimensions of the capabilities of democracy] *[Summary]*. Hans-Rudolf Horn. **Arc. Recht. Soz.** 86:3 2000 pp.400-411.
4908 *Expedit esse deos*. *[In German]*; [*Expedit esse deos*] *[Summary]*. Reinhold Zippelius. **Arc. Recht. Soz.** 86:1 2000 pp.109-121.
4909 Fair play and social obligation: paying my debt to Bert and Ernie. Scott C. Lowe. **Publ. Aff. Q.** 14:1 1:2000 pp.73-85.
4910 Figli della libertà: contro il lamento sulla caduta dei valori. *[In Italian]*; (The sons of liberty: against the fear of the 'absence of values'.) *[Summary]*. Ulrich Beck. **Rass. It. Soc.** XLI:1 1-3:2000 pp.3-27.
4911 From actor to spectator: Hannah Arendt's 'two theories' of political judgment. Majid Yar. **Philos. Soc. Crit.** 26:2 3:2000 pp.1-27.
4912 Idéologie et rhétorique dans l'histoire. Sur la réitération des discours de l'ordre. *[In French]*; (Ideology and historicity: on the reiteration of discourses about order.) Jean De Martelaere. **Hom. Soc.** 135 1-3:2000 pp.105-118.
4913 Imagining membership: the conception of Europe in the political thought of T.G. Masaryk and Václav Havel. Josette Baer. **Stud. East. Eur. Th.** 52:3 9:2000 pp.203-226.
4914 In the shadow of the state: intellectuals and the quest for national identity in twentieth-century Spanish America. Nicola Miller. London, New York: Verso, 1999. 342p. *ISBN: 1859847382, 1859842054. Includes bibliographical references (p. [323]-334) and index.* (*Series:* Critical studies in Latin American and Iberian cultures).
4915 Liberalism and collective investments in repertoires. Arthur L. Stinchcombe. **J. Polit. Phil.** 8:1 3:2000 pp.1-26.
4916 El liberalismo del siglo XX como cultura. *[In Spanish]*; [Liberalism in the 20th century as culture]. Paloma de la Nuez Sánchez-Cascado. **Rev. Fom. Soc.** 54:216 10-12:1999 pp.419-442.
4917 Lie or Utopia? The problem of the subject in two contemporary liberal theories. Maria Chiara Pievatolo. **Arc. Recht. Soz.** 86:1 2000 pp.70-87.
4918 The mosaic moment: an early modernist critique of modernist theories of nationalism. Philip S. Gorski. **A.J.S.** 105:5 3:2000 pp.1428-1468.

J: POLITIQUE. ÉTAT. RELATIONS INTERNATIONALES

4919 Narrating nationalisms: Black Marxism and Jewish communists through the eyes of Harold Cruse. Alan Wald. **Sci. Soc.** 64:4 Winter:2000-2001 pp.400-423.
4920 New threats to freedom. J. Swindal. **Human St.** 23:2 4:2000 pp.179-194.
4921 On the site of distributive justice: reflections on Cohen and Murphy. Thomas W. Pogge. **Philos. Pub.** 29:2 Spring:2000 pp.137-169.
4922 Overcoming false dichotomies: Mill, Marx and the welfare state. Peter Lindsay. **Hist. Polit. Thou.** XXI:4 Winter:2000 pp.657-681.
4923 La «pensée unique» et son double. *[In French]*; (*Pensée unique* and its double.) Jean-Pierre Garnier. **Hom. Soc.** 135 1-3:2000 pp.7-44.
4924 Peoples, cultures, and nations in political philosophy. Paul Gilbert. Edinburgh: Edinburgh University Press, 2000. vii, 223p. *ISBN: 074861091X. Includes bibliographical references and index.*
4925 Post-Marxism: an intellectual history. Stuart Sim. London: Routledge, 2000. 198p. *ISBN: 0415218144. Includes index. (Series:* Routledge studies in social and political thought - 29).
4926 Pour une philosophie émancipatrice. *[In French]*; [For an emancipatory philosophy]. Yvon Quiniou. **Pensée** 321 1-3:2000 pp.135-146.
4927 Quasi-rights: participatory citizenship and negative liberties in democratic Athens. Josiah Ober. **Soc. Philos. Pol.** 17:1 Winter:2000 pp.27-61.
4928 Radical democracy, personal freedom, and the transformative potential of politics. Steven Wall. **Soc. Philos. Pol.** 17:1 Winter:2000 pp.225-254.
4929 Raison laïque: troisième dimension. *[In French]*; (Secular reason: the third dimension.) Pierre Hayat. **Pensée** 321 1-3:2000 pp.91-102.
4930 Reception of nation and national dynamics in the work of Alexander Hirner. Eva Laiferová. **Sociologia [Brat.]** 32:6 Fall:2000 pp.539-554.
4931 Relativity, universality and peaceful coexistence. J.F.C. van Velsen. **Arc. Recht. Soz.** 86:1 2000 pp.88-108.
4932 Revisiting the notion of 'public' in Habermas's theory: towards a theory of politics of public credibility. Agnes S. Ku. **Sociol. Theory** 18:2 7:2000 pp.216-240.
4933 The right to privacy. Richard A. Epstein; Lloyd L. Weinreb; R.G. Frey; Alexander Rosenberg; Richard J. Arneson; H. Tristram Engelhardt, Jr.; Mark Tushnet; Scott D. Gerber; David Friedman; Judith Wagner Decew; A.M. Capron; Tom L. Beauchamp; Frederick Schauer. **Soc. Philos. Pol.** 17:2 Summer:2000 pp.1-309. *Collection of 13 articles.*
4934 Socialisme, démocratie, autogestion. *[In French]*; (Socialism, democracy, self-management.) Jacques Texier. **Pensée** 321 1-3:2000 pp.5-24.
4935 Tribute to Renato Constantino. Peter Limqueco; James Petras; Bruce McFarlane; Johan Saravanamuttu; István Mészáros; Rosalinda P. Ofreneo; Arnold S. Tenorio; Edilberto N. Alegre; Frederic Clairmont; K.S. Jomo; Rajah Rasiah; Leonor M. Briones; Rolando G. Simbulan; Ledivina V. Cariño; Letizia R. Constantino. **J. Cont. Asia** 30:3 2000 pp.291-411. *Collection of 15 articles.*
4936 Trust, social dilemmas and collective memories. Bo Rothstein. **J. Theor. Pol.** 12:4 10:2000 pp.477-501.
4937 Welfare should be the currency of justice. Richard J. Arneson. **Can. J. Phil.** 30:4 12:2000 pp.497-524.
4938 Where and when was democracy invented? John Markoff. **Comp. Stud. S.** 41:4 10:1999 pp.660-690.

J.3: **Political systems**
Systèmes politique

4939 Citizenship 2000. Cindy Patton; Robért L. Caserio; Laurent Dubois; Carol Mason; Heidi Marie Rimke; Michael J. Shapiro. **Cult. St.** 14:1 1:2000 pp.1-98. *Collection of 5 articles.*

J: POLITICS. STATE. INTERNATIONAL RELATIONS

4940 Civil society at the millennium. Marcus Akuhata-Brown; et al. West Hartford CT: Kumarian Press, 1999. xi, 211p. *ISBN: 1565491017. Includes bibliographical references.*

4941 Constructing inequality: city spaces and the architecture of citizenship. Susan Bickford. **Polit. Theory** 28:3 6:2000 pp.355-376.

4942 The Cuban experiment: economic reform, social restructuring, and politics. Haroldo Dilla Alfonso. **Lat. Am. Pers.** 27:1 1:2000 pp.33-44.

4943 The cultural construction of politics in Asia. Hans Antlöv [Ed.]; Tak-wing Ngo [Ed.]. Richmond: Curzon Press, 2000. viii, 263p. *ISBN: 0700706127. Includes bibliographical references (p. 241-259) and index. (Series: Democracy in Asia - 2).*

4944 Daughters of the goddess, daughters of imperialism: African women struggle for culture, power and democracy. Ifi Amadiume. London; New York: Zed Books; St. Martin's Press, 2000. xix, 300p. *ISBN: 1856498050, 1856498069. Includes bibliographical references and index.*

4945 Déclin de l'État-providence et résurgence de l'idée de communauté. *[In French]*; (The decline of the welfare state and the resurgence of the community.) *[Summary].* Gilbert Larochelle. **Recher. Sociolog.** XXX1:2 2000 pp.133-156.

4946 Des buts et des moyens: quel projet autogestionnaire socialiste? *[In French]*; (Aims and means: which project of a self-managed society?) Catherine Samary. **Pensée** 321 1-3:2000 pp.55-70.

4947 Determinants of democracy. Robert J. Barro. **J. Polit. Ec.** 107:6(2) 12:1999 pp.158-183.

4948 The development of civil society in Indonesia and the role of voluntary organizations. M. Habib Chirzin. **Am. J. Islam. Soc. Sci.** 17:1 Spring:2000 pp.21-37.

4949 Dossiê FHC — 1° governo. *[In Portuguese]*; [Dossier on the first government of Fernando Henrique Cardoso]. Alain Touraine; Brasilio Sallum, Jr.; Argelina Cheibub Figueiredo; Fernando Limongi; Ana Luzia Valente; Eduardo Kugelmas; Lourdes Sola; Gilson Schwartz; José de Souza Martins; Sérgio Adorno; Iram Jácome Rodrigues; Amélia Cohn; Maria Helena Oliva Augusto; Olavo Viana Costa; Maria Arminda do Nascimento Arruda; Eunice Ribeiro Durham. **Tempo Soc.** 11:2 10:1999 pp.1-254. *Collection of 12 articles.*

4950 Le droit à... *[In French]*; [The right to...]. Michel Borgetto; Emmanuelle Betton; John Rawls; Amartya Kunar Sen; Sami Castro; Nathalie Martin-Papineau; Pedro Meca; Gilles Jeannot; Patrick Doutreligne; Hélène Strohl; Robert Lafore; Nadia Kesteman; Andrea Caizzi; Jean-Michel Belorgey; Renée David-Aeschlimann; Gwénaële Calvès. **Inf. Soc.** 81 2000 pp.4-127. *Collection of 14 articles.*

4951 Élites e cittadinanza societaria: una teoria relazionale del pluralismo dopomoderno. *[In Italian]*; [Elites and societal citizenship: a relational theory of postmodern pluralism]. Pierpaolo Donati. **Sociologia [Rome]** XXXIV:1 2000 pp.47-58.

4952 'European citizenship', or where neoliberalism meets ethno-culturalism: analysing the European Union's citizenship discourse. Peo Hansen. **Euro. Soc.** 2:2 2000 pp.139-166.

4953 La genèse de l'État moderne: Max Weber revisité. *[In French]*; (The genesis of the modern state: back to Max Weber.) *[Summary].* Patrice Mann. **Rev. Fr. Soc.** 41:2 4-6:2000 pp.331-344.

4954 Government by appearances. Peter Wollen. **New Left R.** 3 5-6:2000 pp.91-106.

4955 Human agency and democratic challenges in Africa. Wisdom J. Tettey. **Afr. Q.** 40:2 2000 pp.13-50.

4956 Interacting with the state. Louise Chappell. **Int. Fem. J. Pol.** 2:2 2000 pp.244-275.

4957 Ist Europa „demokratiefähig"? *[In German]*; (Can Europe be democratized?) *[Summary].* Andreas Heinemann-Grüder. **Berl. J. Soziol.** 10:4 2000 pp.501-516.

4958 Lady liberty's allure: political agency, citizenship and *The Second Sex*. Sharon Krause. **Philos. Soc. Crit.** 26:1 1:2000 pp.1-24.

4959 Language, region and national identity. M.N. Karna. **Sociol. Bul.** 48:1-2 3-9:1999 pp.75-96.

4960 Limites et actualité du concept de société civile. *[In French]*; (Limits and contemporary relevance of the idea of civil society.) Nasser Etemadi. **Hom. Soc.** 136-137 2-3:2000 pp.95-110.

J: POLITIQUE. ÉTAT. RELATIONS INTERNATIONALES

4961 Marx, l'État moderne et la sociologie de l'État. *[In French]*; [Marx, The modern state and the sociology of the state]. Antoine Artous. **Hom. Soc.** 136-137 2-3:2000 pp.111-126.

4962 Les méandres de la laïcité. *[In French]*; (Twists and turns of laicity.) Yuki Shiose; Jacques Zylberberg; Raphaël Ntambue Tshimbulu; Dominique MacNeill; Bérengère Massignon; Lina Molokotos Liederman; Jean-Paul Willaime; Albert Bastenier. **Soc. Compass** 47:3 9:2000 pp.299-409. *Collection of 8 articles.*

4963 Miteinander oder gegeneinander? Zum schwierigen Verhältnis von Rat und Verwaltung. *[In German]*; (Harmony or discord? The difficult relationship between elected council members and administration officers.) Paul von Kodolitsch. **Arc. Kommunal.** 39:2 2000 pp.199-224.

4964 Politische Institutionen im gesellschaftlichen Wandel. Einbürgerung zwischen Erwartungen von Migranten und staatlicher Vorgabe. *[In German]*; (Political institutions in societal change. Naturalization procedures: between immigrant expectations and institutional specifications in present-day Germany.) *[Summary]*. Theresa Wobbe; Roland Otte. **Z. Soziol.** 29:6 12:2000 pp.444-462.

4965 Problems in the study of democratization in Latin America: regime analysis vs cultural studies. Paulo J. Krischke. **Int. Sociol.** 15:1 3:2000 pp.107-126.

4966 Projekt Demokratisches Europa. *[In German]*; (Democratic Europe as a project.) *[Summary]*; *[Summary in French]*. Peter Flora; Klaus Eder; Dieter Rucht; Peter A. Kraus; Willfried Spohn; Michael Mann. **Berl. J. Soziol.** 10:2 2000 pp.151-277. *Collection of 6 articles.*

4967 Reading the small print in global civil society: the inexorable hegemony of the liberal self. Stephen Hopgood. **Millennium** 29:1 2000 pp.1-26.

4968 The reconstitution of power and democracy in the age of capital globalization. Lucio Fernando Oliver Costilla. **Lat. Am. Pers.** 27:1 1:2000 pp.82-104.

4969 La République face à ses communautés. *[In French]*; [The Republic faces its communities]. Hugues Moutouh. **Temps Mod.** 55:608 3-5:2000 pp.117-129.

4970 Sotsiopoliticheskie strategii razvitiia Rossii. *[In Russian]*; (Sociopolitical strategies for Russia's development.) *[Summary]*. V.K. Levashov. **Sot. Issle.** 7 2000 pp.12-25.

4971 The South African Truth Commission. Kenneth Christie. Basingstoke: Macmillan, 2000. 224p. *ISBN: 0333691261. Includes bibliographical references and index.*

4972 Die staatliche Willensbildung in der differenzierten Gesellschaft. *[In German]*; [Democratic government in a pluralistic society] *[Summary]*. Toru Mori. **Arc. Recht. Soz.** 86:2 2000 pp.185-206.

4973 Theories of totalitarianism and modern dictatorships: a tentative approach. Sigrid Meuschel. **Thes. Elev.** 61 5:2000 pp.87-98.

4974 Youth and the creation of civil society in Slovakia. Ladislav Macháček. **Sociologia [Brat.]** 32:3 Spring:2000 pp.241-256.

J.4: **Social control**
Régulation sociale

4975 The African legislature: constitutional functions and political experience. Ali A. Mazrui. **Afr. Q.** 40:2 2000 pp.1-12.

4976 Civil society and social order: demarcating and combining market, state and community. Claus Offe. **Eur. J. Soc.** XLI:1 2000 pp.71-96.

4977 Colombie, la société prise en otage. *[In French]*; [Colombia: a society taken hostage?] Daniel Pécaut. **Esprit** 270 12:2000 pp.138-188.

4978 Community and the state: the relationship between normative and legal controls. Christine Horne. **Eur. Sociol. R.** 16:3 9:2000 pp.225-244.

4979 Costruzione e controllo della devianza in Italia. *[In Italian]*; [Construction and control of deviance in Italy]. Anna Rita Calabrò; Sandro Segre; Luigi Berzano; Renzo Gallini. **Quad. Sociol.** XLIV:22 2000 pp.7-79. *Collection of 3 articles.*

4980　Crime, protest and police in modern British society: essays in memory of David J.V. Jones. David Howell [Ed.]; Kenneth O. Morgan [Ed.]. Cardiff: University of Wales Press, 1999. x, 248p. *ISBN: 0708315550. Includes bibliographical references (p. [238]-240).*

4981　Cultural life and cultural control in rural China: where is the Party? Stig Thøgersen. **China J.** 44 7:2000 pp.129-156.

4982　Doing research on crime and justice. Roy D. King [Ed.]; Emma Wincup [Ed.]. New York: Oxford University Press, 2000. xxi, 441p. *ISBN: 0198765401. Includes bibliographical references and index.*

4983　¿Dónde se juega la justicia en nuestro entorno en los próximos diez años? *[In Spanish]*; (What part will justice play in our environment in the next few years?) *[Summary].* Luis de Sebastián. **Rev. Fom. Soc.** 55:220 10-12:2000 pp.509-520.

4984　Gun control. Hugh LaFollette. **Ethics** 110:2 1:2000 pp.263-281.

4985　Labor markets, delinquency and social control theory: an empirical assessment of the mediating process. Tim Wadsworth. **Soc. Forc.** 78:3 3:2000 pp.1041-1066.

4986　The maximum surveillance society: the rise of CCTV. Clive Norris; Gary Armstrong. Oxford, New York: Berg Publishers, 1999. viii, 248p. *ISBN: 1859732216, 1859732267. Includes bibliographical references (p. 231-243) and index.*

4987　Post-panopticism. Roy Boyne. **Econ. Soc.** 29:2 5:2000 pp.285-307.

4988　Privacy in the face of new technologies of surveillance. Mark Tunick. **Publ. Aff. Q.** 14:3 7:2000 pp.259-277.

4989　Regulation, crime, and freedom. John Braithwaite. Aldershot; Burlington VT: Ashgate; Dartmouth Publishing, 2000. xix, 360p. *ISBN: 0754620050. Includes bibliographical references and index.* (*Series:* Collected essays in law).

4990　Righting wrongs on Anuta. Richard Feinberg. **Pac. Stud.** 21:3 9:1998 pp.29-49.

4991　The social control of cities? A comparative perspective. Sophie Body-Gendrot. Oxford: Blackwell Publishers, 2000. xi, 286p. *ISBN: 0631205217, 0631205209. Includes bibliographical references and index.* (*Series:* Studies in urban and social change).

4992　Les tendances contemporaines de la répression disciplinaire. *[In French]*; [Current trends of disciplinary repression]. Joëlle Pralus-Dupuy. **Rev. Sci. Crim. D. P.** 3 7-9:2000 pp.545-558.

4993　La théorie de la «vitre cassée» en France. Incivilités et désordres en public. *[In French]*; (The 'broken window' theory in France. Public incivilities and disorders.) *[Summary].* Sebastian Roché. **R. Fr. Sci. Pol.** 50:3 6:2000 pp.387-412.

4994　Working wrongly and seeking the straight: remedial remedies on Enewetak Atoll. Laurence Marshall Carucci. **Pac. Stud.** 21:3 9:1998 pp.1-27.

4995　'You'll never walk alone': CCTV surveillance, order and neo-liberal rule in Liverpool city centre. Roy Coleman; Joe Sim. **Br. J. Soc.** 51:4 12:2000 pp.623-640.

4996　Young people and community safety: inclusion, risk, tolerance and disorder. Lynda Measor; Peter Squires. Aldershot: Ashgate, 2000. ix, 277p. *ISBN: 0754611310. Includes bibliographical references and index.*

Criminal justice
Justice pénale

4997　Building violence: how America's rush to incarcerate creates more violence. John P. May [Ed.]; Khalid R. Pitts [Ed.]. Thousand Oaks CA: Sage Publications, 2000. xviii, 188p. *ISBN: 0761914595, 0761914609. Includes bibliographical references and index.*

4998　Cannabis law and the young adult user: reflections on South Australia's Cannabis Expiation Notice System. A. Sutton. **Int. J. S. Law** 28:2 6:2000 pp.147-162.

4999　Caring to death: health care professionals and capital punishment. Cary Federman; Dave Holmes. **Pun. & Soc.** 2:4 10:2000 pp.441-451.

5000　Charting a new course for juvenile justice: listening to outsiders. Thomas F. Geraghty; Steven A. Drizin. **J. Crim. Law Criminol.** 90:1 Fall:1999 pp.363-389.

J: POLITIQUE. ÉTAT. RELATIONS INTERNATIONALES

5001 Confess and be hanged: Scottish crime and punishment through the ages. Sheila Livingstone. Edinburgh: Birlinn, 2000. viii, 226p. *ISBN: 1841580023*.

5002 Corrections in Canada. Colin H. Goff. Cincinnati OH: Anderson Publishing, 1999. xi, 213p. *ISBN: 0870843222. Includes bibliographical references and index.*

5003 Countries in transition: effects of political, social and economic change on crime and criminal justice — sanctions and their implementation. Hans-Jörg Albrecht. **Eur. J. Crime Crim. Law Crim. Just.** 7:4 1999 pp.448-480.

5004 Crime and punishment in America. Elliott Currie. New York: Henry Holt, 1998. vi, 230p. *ISBN: 0805060162. Includes bibliographical references (p. [195]-220) and index.*

5005 Crime control as industry: towards gulags, Western style. Nils Christie. Oslo; London, New York: Scandinavian University Press; Routledge, 2000. 244p. *ISBN: 0415234875. Translated from the Norwegian. Includes bibliographical references and index.*

5006 Criminal justice 2000: strategies for a new century. Michael Cavadino; Iain Crow; James Dignan. Winchester: Waterside Press, 1999. 224p. *ISBN: 1872870775. Includes bibliographical references and index. (Series:* Criminal policy).

5007 Criminal justice policies in Commonwealth Africa: trends and prospects. Simon Coldham. **J. Afr. Law** 44:2 2000 pp.218-238.

5008 The culture of high crime societies: some preconditions of recent 'law and order' policies. David Garland. **Br. J. Crimin.** 40:3 Summer:2000 pp.347-375.

5009 Dangerous offenders: punishment and social order. John Pratt [Ed.]; Mark Brown [Ed.]. London: Routledge, 2000. ix, 197p. *ISBN: 0415200482, 0415200474. Includes bibliographical references and index.*

5010 Desperately seeking safety: witnesses' experiences of intimidation, protection and relocation. Nicholas R. Fyfe; Heather McKay. **Br. J. Crimin.** 40:4 Autumn:2000 pp.675-691.

5011 Docile bodies? Chemical restraints and the female inmate. Kathleen Auerhahn; Elizabeth Dermody Leonard. **J. Crim. Law Criminol.** 90:2 Winter:2000 pp.599-634.

5012 Doing her own time? Women's responses to prison in the context of the old and the new penology. Candace Kruttschnitt; Rosemary Gartner; Amy Miller. **Criminology** 38:3 8:2000 pp.681-717.

5013 Doing time: an introduction to the sociology of imprisonment. Roger Matthews. New York; Basingstoke: St. Martin's Press; Macmillan, 1999. xi, 288p. *ISBN: 0333752309, 0333752317, 0312222394. Includes bibliographical references (p. 262-284) and index.*

5014 Emerging criminal justice: three pillars for a proactive justice system. Paul H. Hahn. Thousand Oaks CA: Sage Publications, 1998. xiv, 218p. *ISBN: 0761912827, 0761912835. Includes bibliographical references (p. 175-208) and index.*

5015 Emotive and ostentatious punishment: its decline and resurgence in modern society. John Pratt. **Pun. & Soc.** 2:4 10:2000 pp.417-439.

5016 Enfermements. *[In French]*; [Confinement]. Frédéric Gros; Thierry Pech; Charles Amourous; Pierre Landreville; Pierre Victor Tournier; Véronique Lagandré; Philippe Combessie; Julien Damon; Jean-Pierre Martin; Paul Court; Didier Haas; Hervé Levilain; Vincent Caradec. **Inf. Soc.** 82 2000 pp.4-117. *Collection of 12 articles.*

5017 Ethnicity and sentencing outcomes in U.S. federal courts: who is punished more harshly? Darrell Steffensmeier; Stephen Demuth. **Am. Sociol. R.** 65:5 10:2000 pp.705-729.

5018 From social justice to criminal justice: poverty and the administration of criminal law. John Kleinig [Ed.]; William C. Heffernan [Ed.]. New York: Oxford University Press, 2000. 304p. *ISBN: 0195129857. Includes indexes. (Series:* Practical and professional ethics series).

5019 'Healthy prisons': a contradiction in terms? Catrin Smith. **Can. R. Soc. A.** 37:3 8:2000 pp.339-353.

5020 *Justice de proximité* — the growth of 'houses of justice' and victim/offender mediation in France: a very unFrench legal response? Adam Crawford. **Soc. Leg. Stud.** 9:1 3:2000 pp.29-54.

5021 Language and the administration of justice: the international framework. Kristin Henrard. **Int. J. Min. Gr. Rights** 7:2 2000 pp.75-108.

J: POLITICS. STATE. INTERNATIONAL RELATIONS

5022 Managed health care in prisons as cruel and unusual punishment. Ira P. Robbins. **J. Crim. Law Criminol.** 90:1 Fall:1999 pp.195-237.
5023 The mentor/monitor debate in criminal justice: 'what works' for offenders. Monica Barry. **Br. J. Soc. W.** 30:5 10:2000 pp.575-595.
5024 Penal policy making: elitist, populist or participatory? Gerry Johnstone. **Pun. & Soc.** 2:2 4:2000 pp.161-180.
5025 La place du droit pénal dans la société contemporaine. *[In French]*; [The place of penal law in contemporary society]. Mireille Delmas-Marty; Michel van de Kerchove; Bernard Bouloc; Alain Cœuret; Elisabeth Fortis; Alain Prothais; Jacques Francillon; Jean-François Renucci; Stefano Manacorda; Michel Massé; Régis de Gouttes; Christine Lazerges; Hubert Delesalle; Denis Salas; Marie Elisabeth Cartier. **Rev. Sci. Crim. D. P.** 1 1-3:2000 pp.1-192. *Collection of 13 articles.*
5026 Prisons that empower: neo-liberal governance in Canadian women's prisons. Kelly Hannah-Moffat. **Br. J. Crimin.** 40:3 Summer:2000 pp.510-531.
5027 Psychiatric aspects of justification, excuse, and mitigation: the jurisprudence of mental abnormality in Anglo-American criminal law. Alec Buchanan. Philadelphia PA, London: Jessica Kingsley Publishers, 1999. 160p. *ISBN: 1853027979. Includes bibliographical references and index. (Series:* Forensic focus - 17).
5028 Psychology and criminal justice: international review of theory and practice. Iván Münnich [Ed.]; Márton Szegedi [Ed.]; János Boros [Ed.]. Berlin, New York: Walter de Gruyter, 1998. xxii, 460p. *ISBN: 3110163292. Papers presented at the 5th Conference of the European Association of Psychology and Law, Budapest, 1995. Includes bibliographical references and index. (Series:* Publications of the European Association of Psychology and Law).
5029 Punishing repeat offenders more severely. C.Y. Cyrus Chu; Sheng-cheng Hu; Ting-yuan Huang. **Int. R. Law Econ.** 20:1 3:2000 pp.127-140.
5030 Punishment and the question of ownership: groupwork in the criminal justice system. Liz Dixon. **Groupwork** 12:1 2000 pp.6-25.
5031 Racial disparity in arrest rates as an explanation of racial disparity in commitment to Pennsylvania's prisons. Roy L. Austin; Mark D. Allen. **J. Res. Crim. Delin.** 37:2 5:2000 pp.200-220.
5032 Restoring respect for justice: a symposium. Roger Graef [Foreword]; Martin Wright. Winchester: Waterside Press, 1999. 224p. *ISBN: 1872870783. Includes bibliographical references (p. 210-216) and index.*
5033 Social integration and mental well-being among jail inmates. Christine H. Lindquist. **Sociol. For.** 15:3 9:2000 pp.431-455.
5034 The story of justice: retribution, mercy, and the role of emotions in the capital sentencing process. Mary Sigler. **Law Philos.** 19:3 5:2000 pp.339-368.
5035 Tackling offending on bail. Anthea Hucklesby; Emma Marshall. **Howard J. Crim. Just.** 39:2 5:2000 pp.150-170.
5036 Theorizing sanctioning in a criminalized juvenile court. Daniel P. Mears; Samuel H. Field. **Criminology** 38:4 11:2000 pp.983-1019.
5037 Too much time: women in prison. Jane Evelyn Atwood. London: Phaidon, 2000. 192p. *ISBN: 0714839736.*
5038 Transparent adjudication and social science research in constitutional criminal procedure. Tracey L. Meares; Bernard E. Harcourt. **J. Crim. Law Criminol.** 90:3 Spring:2000 pp.733-798.
5039 Trial and sentencing: judicial independence, training and appointment of judges, structure of criminal procedure, sentencing patterns, the role of the defense in the countries in transition. Károly Bárd. **Eur. J. Crime Crim. Law Crim. Just.** 7:4 1999 pp.433-447.
5040 Two cheers for vindictiveness. Jeffrie G. Murphy. **Pun. & Soc.** 2:2 4:2000 pp.131-144.
5041 Understanding miscarriages of justice: law, the media, and the inevitability of crisis. Richard Nobles; David Schiff. Oxford, New York: Oxford University Press, 2000. xvi, 279p. *ISBN: 0198298935. Includes bibliographical references (p. [263]-273) and index.*

J: POLITIQUE. ÉTAT. RELATIONS INTERNATIONALES

5042 Voluntary after-care and the probation service: a case of diminishing responsibility. Mike Maguire; Peter Raynor; Maurice Vanstone; Jocelyn Kynch. **Howard J. Crim. Just.** 39:3 8:2000 pp.234-248.

5043 Why not hang them all: the virtues of inefficient punishment. David Friedman. **J. Polit. Ec.** 107:6(2) 12:1999 pp.259-269.

Criminology
Criminologie

5044 Adolescent victimization and income deficits in adulthood: rethinking the costs of criminal violence from a life-course perspective. Ross MacMillan. **Criminology** 38:2 5:2000 pp.553-588.

5045 Alcohol abuse and crime: a fixed-effects regression analysis. David M. Fergusson; L. John Horwood. **Addiction** 95:10 10:2000 pp.1525-1536.

5046 American delinquency: its meaning and construction. LaMar Taylor Empey; Mark C. Stafford; Carter H. Hay. Belmont CA: Wadsworth, 1999. xxvii, 428p. *ISBN: 0534507077. Includes bibliographical references and index.*

5047 As contradições da 'sociedade punitiva': o caso britânico. *[In Portuguese]*; (The contradictions of the 'punitive society': the British case.) David Garland. **Rev. Soc. Polit.** 13 1999 pp.59-80.

5048 Big brother and his science kit: DNA databases for 21st century crime control? Paul E. Tracy; Vincent Morgan. **J. Crim. Law Criminol.** 90:2 Winter:2000 pp.635-690.

5049 Buurten en geweldscriminaliteit: een multilevel-analyse. *[In Dutch]*; (Neighbourhoods and violent crime: a multilevel analysis.) *[Summary]*. Karin Wittebrood. **Mens Maat.** 75:2 6:2000 pp.92-109.

5050 The causes and costs of crime and a controversial cure. David T. Lykken. **J. Personal.** 68:3 6:2000 pp.559-606.

5051 Childhood and adolescent predictors of physical assault: a prospective longitudinal study. Lianne J. Woodward; David M. Fergusson. **Criminology** 38:1 2:2000 pp.233-262.

5052 Class, gender, and arrest: an intergenerational analysis of workplace power and control. Christopher Uggen. **Criminology** 38:3 8:2000 pp.835-862.

5053 Concentrated poverty, race, and homicide. Matthew R. Lee. **Sociol. Q.** 41:2 Spring:2000 pp.189-206.

5054 'Condemn a little more, understand a little less': the political context and rights implications of the domestic and European rulings in the Venables-Thompson case. Deena Haydon; Phil Scraton. **J. Law Soc.** 27:3 9:2000 pp.416-448.

5055 Corruption à São Paulo: affaire de droit commun ou problème politique? *[In French]*; (Corruption in São Paulo. An issue for common law or a political problem?) *[Summary]*. Jair Pinheiro. **Pensée** 324 10-12:2000 pp.39-50.

5056 Crime and Punishment (Scotland) Act 1997: a survey of psychiatrists' views concerning the Scottish 'hybrid order'. Rajan Darjee; John Crichton; Lindsay Thomson. **J. For. Psy.** 11:3 12:2000 pp.608-620.

5057 Crime as a social cost of poverty and inequality: a review focusing on developing countries. F. Bourguignon. **Desar. Soc.** 44 9:1999 pp.61-99.

5058 Crime, gender, and society in India: insights from homicide data. Jean Drèze; Reetika Khera. **Pop. Dev. Rev.** 26:2 6:2000 pp.335-363.

5059 Crime in context: a critical criminology of market societies. Ian Taylor. Oxford: Polity, 1999. 300p. *ISBN: 0745606660, 0745606679. Includes index.*

5060 Crime: manifestations, patterns and trends of crime 'traditional' versus 'new' crime; juvenile crime; fear of crime. Jerzy Jasinski. **Eur. J. Crime Crim. Law Crim. Just.** 7:4 1999 pp.374-386.

5061 Crime, risk and insecurity: law and order in everyday life and political discourse. Tim Hope [Ed.]; Richard Sparks [Ed.]. London: Routledge, 2000. 275p. *ISBN: 0415243440, 0415243432. Includes bibliographical references.*

J: POLITICS, STATE, INTERNATIONAL RELATIONS

5062 Crime, violence and minority youths. Becky L. Tatum. Aldershot: Ashgate, 2000. xiii, 116p. *ISBN: 1840149620. Includes bibliographical references and index. (Series:* Interdisciplinary research series in ethnic, gender, and class relations).

5063 Crime-fighting and urban renewal. Eli Lehrer. **Publ. Inter.** 141 Fall:2000 pp.91-103.

5064 Crimes and markets: essays in anti-criminology. Vincenzo Ruggiero. New York: Oxford University Press, 2000. 208p. *ISBN: 0198268386. Includes bibliographical references and index. (Series:* Clarendon studies in criminology).

5065 Crimes et cultures. *[In French]*; [Crime and culture]. Jean-Michel Bessette [Ed.]. Paris: L'Harmattan, 1999. 310p. *ISBN: 2738485197. Papers presented at the 32nd Congress of the Association française de criminologie, Besançon, December 1998. Includes bibliographical references (p. [293]-310) and index.*

5066 Criminal behavior: a psychosocial approach. Curt R. Bartol. Upper Saddle River NJ: Prentice Hall, 1999. xi, 492p. *ISBN: 0137876491. Includes bibliographical references (p. 425-480) and indexes.*

5067 Culture as a determinant of crime: an alternative perspective. Ronald Burns. **Envir. Behav.** 32:3 5:2000 pp.347-360.

5068 Délinquance juvénile, droit des mineurs et violences collectives. *[In French]*; [Juvenile delinquency, children's rights and collective violence]. Alain Bruel; Dominique Youf; Thierry Pech; Hugues Lagrange; Marc-Olivier Padis. **Esprit** 268 10:2000 pp.75-173. *Collection of 5 articles.*

5069 Developmental timing of onsets of disruptive behaviors and later delinquency of inner-city youth. Patrick H. Tolan; Deborah Gorman-Smith; Rolf Loeber. **J. Child Fam. Stud.** 9:2 6:2000 pp.203-220.

5070 Different measures of vulnerability in their relation to different dimensions of fear of crime. Martin Killias; Christian Clerici. **Br. J. Crimin.** 40:3 Summer:2000 pp.437-450.

5071 Do disadvantaged neighborhoods cause well-adjusted children to become adolescent delinquents? A study of male juvenile serious offending, individual risk and protective factors, and neighborhood context. Per-Olof H. Wikström; Rolf Loeber. **Criminology** 38:4 11:2000 pp.1109-1142.

5072 Educationally disaffected young offenders: youth court and agency responses to truancy and school exclusion. Caroline Ball; Jo Connolly. **Br. J. Crimin.** 40:4 Autumn:2000 pp.594-616.

5073 The empirical status of Gottfredson and Hirschi's general theory of crime: a meta-analysis. Travis C. Pratt; Francis T. Cullen. **Criminology** 38:3 8:2000 pp.931-964.

5074 An empirical, theoretical, and historical overview of organized crime. Don Liddick. Lewiston NY, Lampeter: Edwin Mellen Press, 1999. xiii, 264p. *ISBN: 077348583X, 0773479651. Includes bibliographical references and index. (Series:* Criminology studies - 6).

5075 Ein empirischer Vergleich zwischen der Theorie geplanten Verhaltens von Icek Ajzen und der Allgemeinen Theorie der Kriminalität von Michael R. Gottfredson und Travis Hirschi. *[In German]*; (An empirical comparison of the theory of planned behavior of Icek Ajzen and the general theory of crime of Michael R. Gottfredson and Travis Hirschi.) *[Summary]*. Christian Seipel. **Z. Soziol.** 29:5 10:2000 pp.397-410.

5076 Études sur la criminalité féminine, approche bibliographique. *[In French]*; [Studies on female criminality: a bibliographic approach]. Abdallah Maaouia. **R. Tun. Sci. Soc.** 36:118 1999 pp.95-120.

5077 An examination of gender, ethnicity, class and delinquency; *[Summary in French]*. M. Reza Nakhaie; Robert A. Silverman; Teresa C. LaGrange. **Can. J. Soc.** 25:1 Winter:2000 pp.35-59.

5078 Explanations for apparent late onset criminality in a high-risk sample of children followed up in adult life. James Elander; Michael Rutter; Emily Simonoff; Andrew Pickles. **Br. J. Crimin.** 40:3 Summer:2000 pp.497-509.

5079 Factors influencing gun carrying among young urban males over the adolescent-young adult life course. Alan J. Lizotte; Marvin D. Krohn; James C. Howell; Kimberly Tobin; Gregory J. Howard. **Criminology** 38:3 8:2000 pp.811-834.

J: POLITIQUE. ÉTAT. RELATIONS INTERNATIONALES

5080 Fear of crime among British holidaymakers. R.I. Mawby; P. Brunt; Z. Hambly. **Br. J. Crimin.** 40:3 Summer:2000 pp.468-479.

5081 Fear of crime among Korean Americans in Chicago communities. Min Sik Lee; Jeffery T. Ulmer. **Criminology** 38:4 11:2000 pp.1173-1206.

5082 'Fear of crime', vulnerability and poverty: evidence from the British crime survey. Christina Pantazis. **Br. J. Crimin.** 40:3 Summer:2000 pp.414-436.

5083 Forgiveness and fundamentalism: reconsidering the relationship between correctional attitudes and religion. Brandon K. Applegate; Francis T. Cullen; Bonnie S. Fisher; Thomas Vander Ven. **Criminology** 38:3 8:2000 pp.719-753.

5084 From the lab to the police station: a successful application of eyewitness research. Gary L. Wells; Roy S. Malpass; R.C.L. Lindsay; Ronald P. Fisher; John W. Turtle; Solomon M. Fulero. **Am. Psychol.** 55:6 6:2000 pp.581-598.

5085 Furthering the integration of routine activity and social disorganization theories: small units of analysis and the study of street robbery as a diffusion process. William R. Smith; Sharon Glave Frazee; Elizabeth L. Davison. **Criminology** 38:2 5:2000 pp.489-524.

5086 Gender and crime among felony offenders: assessing the generality of social control and differential association theories. Leanne Fiftal Alarid; Velmer S. Burton, Jr.; Francis T. Cullen. **J. Res. Crim. Delin.** 37:2 5:2000 pp.171-199.

5087 Gender, structural disadvantage, and urban crime: do macrosocial variables also explain female offending rates? Darrell Steffensmeier; Dana Haynie. **Criminology** 38:2 5:2000 pp.403-438.

5088 Going equipped: criminology, situational crime prevention and the resourceful offender. Paul Ekblom; Nick Tilley. **Br. J. Crimin.** 40:3 Summer:2000 pp.376-398.

5089 Greek adolescents in custody: psychological morbidity, family characteristics and minority groups. Miltos Livaditis; Maria Fotiadou; Filitsa Kouloubardou; Maria Samakouri; Grigoris Tripsianis; Florika Gizari. **J. For. Psy.** 11:3 12:2000 pp.597-607.

5090 Juvenile involvement in occupational delinquency. John Paul Wright; Francis T. Cullen. **Criminology** 38:3 8:2000 pp.863-896.

5091 Khaos i kriminal. *[In Russian]*; (Chaos and crime.) B. Erasov. **Svobod. Mysl'** 9 2000 pp.13-29.

5092 Les «mafias» de l'est un phénomène hétérogène et inédit. *[In French]*; (The Eastern 'mafias'. A heterogenous and surprising phenomenon.) Bruno Drweski. **Pensée** 324 10-12:2000 pp.27-38.

5093 The meaning of age differences in the fear of crime: combining quantitative and qualitative approaches. Marian Tulloch. **Br. J. Crimin.** 40:3 Summer:2000 pp.451-467.

5094 Mobsters are human too: behavioural science and organized crime investigation. Petrus C. Van Duyne. **Cr. Law Soc. Chan.** 34:4 12:2000 pp.369-390.

5095 On the association among self-control, crime, and analogous behaviors. Raymond Paternoster; Robert Brame. **Criminology** 38:3 8:2000 pp.971-982.

5096 Onset age, persistence, and offending versatility: comparisons across gender. Paul Mazerolle; Robert Brame; Ray Paternoster; Alex Piquero; Charles Dean. **Criminology** 38:4 11:2000 pp.1143-1172.

5097 Pathways to violent crimes by children in South Africa and the UK. Wandile Walter Zwane. Norwich: University of East Anglia Press, 2000. ii, 52p. *ISBN: 1857840739. Includes bibliographical references (p. 47-51).* (*Series:* Social work monographs - 177).

5098 Paulo Egídio e a sociologia criminal em São Paulo. *[In Portuguese]*; (Paulo Egídio and criminal sociology in São Paulo.) *[Summary]*. Fernando Salla; Marcos César Alvarez. **Tempo Soc.** 12:1 5:2000 pp.101-122.

5099 Perceived sanction threats, gender, and crime: a test and elaboration of power-control theory. Brenda Sims Blackwell. **Criminology** 38:2 5:2000 pp.439-488.

5100 Psychological profile of pedophiles and child molesters. John B. Murray. **J. Psychol.** 134:2 3:2000 pp.211-224.

5101 Psychology and crime: myths and reality. Peter B. Ainsworth. New York: Longman, 2000. *ISBN: 0582414245. Includes bibliographical references and index.* (*Series:* Longman criminology series).

5102 Race, crime, and public housing in Atlanta: testing a conditional effect hypothesis. Thomas L. McNulty; Steven R. Holloway. **Soc. Forc.** 79:2 12:2000 pp.707-729.

5103 Race, crime, and the American dream. Stephen A. Cernkovich; Peggy C. Giordano; Jennifer L. Rudolph. **J. Res. Crim. Delin.** 37:2 5:2000 pp.131-170.

5104 Race, gender, and class in criminology: the intersections. Dragan Milovanovic [Ed.]; Martin D. Schwartz [Ed.]. New York: Garland Publishing, 1999. xv, 311p. *ISBN: 0815337264. Includes bibliographical references and index. (Series:* Garland reference library of social science).

5105 Resistance and adaptation to criminal identity: using secondary analysis to evaluate classic studies of crime and deviance. Nigel G. Fielding; Jane L. Fielding. **Sociology** 34:4 11:2000 pp.671-690.

5106 Rethinking social reactions to crime: personal and altruistic fear in family households. Mark Warr; Christopher G. Ellison. **A.J.S.** 106:3 11:2000 pp.551-578.

5107 Secure foundations: key issues in crime prevention, crime reduction and community safety. Scott Ballintyne; Ken Pease; Vic McLaren. London: IPPR, 2000. 312p. *ISBN: 186030088X.*

5108 Self-control and resistance to school; *[Summary in French].* M. Reza Nakhaie; Robert A. Silverman; Teresa C. LaGrange. **Can. R. Soc. A.** 37:4 11:2000 pp.443-460.

5109 Self-reported gang involvement and officially recorded delinquency. G. David Curry. **Criminology** 38:4 11:2000 pp.1253-1274.

5110 Social changes and rising crime rates: the case of Central and Eastern Europe. Miklós Lévay. **Eur. J. Crime Crim. Law Crim. Just.** 8:1 2000 pp.35-50.

5111 The social psychology of crime: groups, teams, and networks. David Canter; Laurence J. Alison. Aldershot, Brookfield VT: Ashgate, 1999. *ISBN: 1840144351, 1840144971. (Series:* Offender Profiling - 111).

5112 Stalkers and their victims. Paul E. Mullen; Rosemary Purcell; Michele Pathé. Cambridge, New York: Cambridge University Press, 2000. x, 310p. *ISBN: 0521669502.*

5113 The structural context of homicide: accounting for racial differences in process. Lauren J. Krivo; Ruth D. Peterson. **Am. Sociol. R.** 65:4 8:2000 pp.547-559.

5114 Subcultural diversity and the fear of crime and gangs. Jodi Lane; James W. Meeker. **Crime Delin.** 46:4 10:2000 pp.497-521.

5115 The validity of juvenile arrestees' drug use reporting: a gender comparison. Julia Yun Soo Kim; Michael Fendrich; Joseph S. Wislar. **J. Res. Crim. Delin.** 37:4 11:2000 pp.419-437.

5116 Victims' needs and support for victims in Prague. R.I. Mawby; E. Koubova; I. Brabcova. **Int. J. S. Law** 28:2 6:2000 pp.129-146.

5117 Vllast' i prestuplenie v politicheskoi kriminologii Dostoyevskogo. *[In Russian];* (Authority and crime in Dostoyevsky's political criminology.) V.A. Bachinin. **Polis [Moscow]** 5(58) 2000 pp.155-166.

5118 Voices from the barrio: Chicano/a gangs, families, and communities. Marjorie S. Zatz; Edwardo L. Portillos. **Criminology** 38:2 5:2000 pp.369-402.

5119 Why is there more crime in cities? Edward L. Glaeser; Bruce Sacerdote. **J. Polit. Ec.** 107:6(2) 12:1999 pp.225-258.

5120 Why men commit crimes (and why they desist). Satoshi Kanazawa; Mary C. Still. **Sociol. Theory** 18:3 11:2000 pp.434-447.

5121 Work as a turning point in the life course of criminals: a duration model of age, employment, and recidivism. Christopher Uggen. **Am. Sociol. R.** 65:4 8:2000 pp.529-546.

Police
Police

5122 Age and race deference reversals: extending Turk on police-citizen conflict. Lonn Lanza-Kaduce; Richard G. Greenleaf. **J. Res. Crim. Delin.** 37:2 5:2000 pp.221-236.

J: POLITIQUE. ÉTAT. RELATIONS INTERNATIONALES

5123 Archives policières: les répertoires de procès-verbaux des commissariats parisiens. *[In French]*; (Police archives; the minute-books of Paris police stations.) *[Summary]*. Jean-Claude Farcy. **Rech. Cont.** 5 1998-1999 pp.5-44.

5124 Catching offenders in the act: an empirical study of police effectiveness in handling 'immediate response' residential burglary. T. Coupe; M. Griffiths. **Int. J. S. Law** 28:2 6:2000 pp.163-176.

5125 Civilian oversight of police: a test of capture theory. Tim Prenzler. **Br. J. Crimin.** 40:4 Autumn:2000 pp.659-674.

5126 Core issues in policing. Barry Loveday [Ed.]; Stephen P. Savage [Ed.]; Frank Leishman [Ed.]. London: Longman, 2000. xvii, 326p. *ISBN: 058236986X. Includes bibliographical references and index.*

5127 The crowned harp: policing Northern Ireland. Graham Ellison; Jim Smyth. Sterling Va: Pluto Press, 2000. 218p. *ISBN: 0745313981. Includes bibliographical references and index. (Series:* Contemporary Irish studies).

5128 Cultural influences on Taiwanese police management and patrol practices: an exploratory investigation of Ouchi's theory Z. L.F. Alarid; H.M. Wang. **Int. J. S. Law** 28:2 6:2000 pp.113-128.

5129 Examining police/Black relations: what's in a story? Nadia Joanne Britton. **Ethn. Racial** 23:4 7:2000 pp.692-711.

5130 The fabrication of social order: a critical theory of police power. Mark Neocleous. Sterling VA: Pluto Press, 2000. xv, 160p. *ISBN: 0745314899. Includes bibliographical references (p. 119-156) and index.*

5131 Gender and policing: comparative perspectives. Jennifer Brown; Frances Heidensohn. Basingstoke: Macmillan, 2000. 203p. *ISBN: 0333730615, 0333730607. Includes index.*

5132 Interviewing child witnesses within memorandum guidelines. A survey of police officers in England and Wales. Michelle Aldridge; Joanne Wood. **Child. Soc.** 14:3 6:2000 pp.168-181.

5133 Patterns of provocation: police and public disorder. Richard Bessel [Ed.]; Clive Emsley [Ed.]; European Centre for the Study of Policing. New York: Berghahn Books, 2000. 153p. *ISBN: 1571812288, 157181227X. Includes bibliographical references and index.*

5134 Police. Amadeu Recasens. **Eur. J. Crime Crim. Law Crim. Just.** 7:4 1999 pp.397-411.

5135 Police complaints and the complainants' experience. Ian Waters; Katie Brown. **Br. J. Crimin.** 40:4 Autumn:2000 pp.617-638.

5136 Police, probation, and protecting the public. Mike Nash. London: Blackstone Press, 1999. x, 228p. *ISBN: 1854317350. Includes bibliographical references and index.*

5137 Police station diversion schemes: role and efficacy in central London. David James. **J. For. Psy.** 11:3 12:2000 pp.532-555.

5138 Police violence occasioning citizen complaint: an empirical analysis of time-space dynamics. Tim Phillips; Philip Smith. **Br. J. Crimin.** 40:3 Summer:2000 pp.480-496.

5139 Policing and human rights. James Sheptycki; Christopher E. Stone; Heather H. Ward; Thomas E. Perez; Boris Pustintsev; Istvan Szikinger; Monica L. Macovei; Jorge Da Silva; Jerry Sanders. **Poli. Soc.** 10:1 2000 pp.1-141. *Collection of 8 articles.*

5140 Policing Britain: risk, security and governance. Les Johnston. Harlow: Longman, 1999. 240p. *ISBN: 0582298865.*

5141 Polizeialltag und Habitus: Eine sozialökologische Fallstudie. *[In German]*; (Police routine and *habitus*: a social-ecological study.) Jörg Hüttermann. **Soz. Welt.** 51:1 2000 pp.7-24.

5142 Race and policing: a study of police custody. Nadia Joanne Britton. **Br. J. Crimin.** 40:4 Autumn:2000 pp.639-658.

5143 Relation between police image and police visibility. Satu Salmi; Marinus J.M. Voeten; Esko Keskinen. **J. Comm. App. Soc. Psychol.** 10:6 11-12:2000 pp.433-447.

5144 Risk, fear, harm: immigrant women's perceptions of the 'policing solution' to woman abuse. Sandra Wachholz; Baukje Miedema. **Cr. Law Soc. Chan.** 34:3 10:2000 pp.301-317.

J: POLITICS. STATE. INTERNATIONAL RELATIONS

5145 Rounding up the usual suspects? Developments in contemporary law enforcement intelligence. Peter Gill. Aldershot: Ashgate, 2000. xv, 290p. *ISBN: 184014923X. Includes bibliographical references and index.*

5146 Social police and the mechanisms of prevention: Patrick Colquhoun and the condition of poverty. Mark Neocleous. **Br. J. Crimin.** 40:4 Autumn:2000 pp.710-726.

5147 The Stephen Lawrence murder and the Macpherson Inquiry and Report. Liz Stanley; Simon Holdaway; Kusminder Chahal; Nira Yuval-Davis; John Solomos; Nigel Fielding; Larry Ray; David Smith; Liz Wastell; Floya Anthias; Martin Innes; Louis Kushnick; P.A.J. Waddington. **Sociol. Res. Online** 4:1 3:1999 p. *Collection of 11 articles.*

5148 Transforming police organizations from within: police dissident groupings in South Africa. Monique Marks. **Br. J. Crimin.** 40:4 Autumn:2000 pp.557-573.

J.5: Law
Loi

5149 Censure theory and intuitions about punishment. Thaddeus Metz. **Law Philos.** 19:4 7:2000 pp.491-512.

5150 The collapse of the harm principle. Bernard E. Harcourt. **J. Crim. Law Criminol.** 90:1 Fall:1999 pp.109-194.

5151 Dealing with insolvency and indebted individuals in respect to law and morality. Bo Carlsson; David Hoff. **Soc. Leg. Stud.** 9:2 6:2000 pp.293-318.

5152 „Die wahre Verantwortung eines Missetäters kann nicht mit Bestimmtheit festgestellt werden". Vor gut vierzig Jahren erschienen: Albert Camus' Betrachtungen zur Todesstrafe. *[In German]*; ["The true responsibility for a crime can not be conclusively determined". Albert Camus' thoughts on the death penalty] *[Summary]*. Josef Pechtl. **Arc. Recht. Soz.** 86:2 2000 pp.251-262.

5153 'Dirty words' and the offense principle. David W. Shoemaker. **Law Philos.** 19:5 9:2000 pp.545-584.

5154 Do the 'haves' still come out ahead? Herbert M. Kritzer [Ed.]; Susan S. Silbey [Ed.]; Joel B. Grossman; Stewart Macaulay; Donald R. Songer; Reginald S. Sheehan; Susan Brodie Haire; Kathryn Hendley; Peter Murrell; Randi Ryterman; Catherine Albiston; Beth Harris; Lauren B. Edelman; Mark C. Suchman; Karyl A. Kinsey; Loretta J. Stalans; Patricia Ewick; Donald J. Farole, Jr.; Yoav Dotan; Kenneth G. Dau-Schmidt; Charles R. Epp; Richard Lempert; Marc Galanter. **Law Soc. Rev.** 33:4 1999 pp.803-1123. *Collection of 14 articles.*

5155 Does judge gender matter? Decision making in state supreme courts. Donald R. Songer; Kelley A. Crews-Meyer. **Soc. Sci. Q.** 81:3 9:2000 pp.750-762.

5156 Les données juridiques de l'identité culturelle. *[In French]*; [Legal data on cultural identity]. Jean-Marie Pontier. **R. Droit Pub.** 5 9-10:2000 pp.1271-1290.

5157 The effects of peer review and evidence quality on judge evaluations of psychological science: are judges effective gatekeepers? Margaret Bull Kovera; Bradley D. McAuliff. **J. Appl. Psychol.** 85:4 8:2000 pp.574-586.

5158 Émile Durkheim: law in a moral domain. Roger Cotterell. Stanford CA: Stanford University Press, 1999. xii, 276p. *ISBN: 0804738084, 0804738238. (Series:* Jurists - profiles in legal theory).

5159 The empowered self: law and society in the age of individualism. Thomas M. Franck. New York: Oxford University Press, 1999. xiii, 312p. *ISBN: 0198298412. Includes bibliographical references and index.*

5160 Empty votes in jury deliberations. Kim Taylor-Thompson. **Harv. Law Rev.** 113:6 4:2000 pp.1261-1320.

5161 The end of human rights: critical legal thought at the turn of the century. Costas Douzinas. Oxford: Hart Publishing, 2000. ix, 410p. *ISBN: 1901362914, 1841130001. Includes bibliographical references and index.*

J: POLITIQUE. ÉTAT. RELATIONS INTERNATIONALES

5162 The enigma of free speech: Speakers' Corner, the geography of governance and a crisis of rationality. John Michael Roberts. **Soc. Leg. Stud.** 9:2 6:2000 pp.271-292.

5163 Faith in law: essays in legal theory. Sionaidh Douglas-Scott [Ed.]; Victor Tadros [Ed.]; Peter Oliver [Ed.]. Oxford, Portland OR: Hart Publishing, 2000. 153p. *ISBN: 1901362957.*

5164 Family law in Bulgaria: legal norms and social norms. Velina Todorova. **Int. J. Law Policy Fam.** 14:2 8:2000 pp.148-181.

5165 La fonction subversive du droit comparé. *[In French]*; [The subversive function of comparative law] *[Summary]*. Horatia Muir-Watt. **Rev. Int. Droit C.** 52:3 7-9:2000 pp.503-528.

5166 From critical to socio-legal studies: three dialectics in search of a subject. Alan Norrie. **Soc. Leg. Stud.** 9:1 3:2000 pp.85-114.

5167 The future of tradition: customary law, common law, and legal pluralism. Leon Shaskolsky Sheleff. London, Portland OR: Frank Cass, 2000. viii, 512p. *ISBN: 0714649538, 0714680125. Includes bibliographical references (p. [487]-497) and index.*

5168 Grupos, lealtades y prácticas: el caso de la justicia penal Argentina. *[In Portuguese]*; (Groups, loyalties and practices: the case of the Argentine penal justice system.) Maria José S. Oliveira. **Rev. Soc. Polit.** 13 1999 pp.81-104.

5169 'Heard it through the grapevine': Chinese walls and former client confidentiality in law firms. Harry McVea. **Camb. Law J.** 59:2 7:2000 pp.370-389.

5170 I don't think it's an answer to the question: silencing Aboriginal witnesses in court. Diana Eades. **Lang. Soc.** 29:2 6:2000 pp.161-196.

5171 Institutional racism: judicial conduct and a new theory of racial discrimination. Ian F. Haney López. **Yale Law J.** 109:8 6:2000 pp.1717-1884.

5172 Judicial rhetoric, meaning-making, and the institutionalization of hate crime law. Scott Phillips; Ryken Grattet. **Law Soc. Rev.** 34:3 2000 pp.567-606.

5173 The jurisprudence of laws: form and substance. Robert S. Summers. Aldershot, Brookfield VT: Ashgate, 2000. xii, 309p. *ISBN: 0754620247. Includes bibliographical references (p. [311]) and index. (Series:* Collected essays in law).

5174 Justice in the age of sentencing guidelines. David Dolinko. **Ethics** 110:3 4:2000 pp.563-585.

5175 Justifying justice: therapeutic law and the victimization defense strategy. James L. Nolan, Jr.; Saundra Davis Westervelt. **Sociol. For.** 15:4 12:2000 pp.617-646.

5176 Law, pornography and crime: the Danish experience. Berl Kutchinsky; Annika Snare [Ed.]. Oslo: Pax Forlag, 1999. 391p. *ISBN: 8253018282. Includes bibliographical references (p. [349]-374). The Scandinavian Research Council for Criminology. (Series:* Scandinavian studies in criminology - volume 16).

5177 Legal interpretation, morality, and semantic fetishism. Amir Horowitz. **Am. Phil. Q.** 37:4 10:2000 pp.335-357.

5178 Legal traditions of the world: sustainable diversity in law. H. Patrick Glenn. New York: Oxford University Press, 2000. 370p. *ISBN: 0198765754. Includes bibliographical references and index.*

5179 Legal validity as doxastic obligation: from definition to normativity. Giovanni Sartor. **Law Philos.** 19:5 9:2000 pp.585-625.

5180 Moral and legal argumentation as a practice. Sebastián Urbina; Agnes Heller; Riccardo Guastini; Aleksander Peczenik; José Antonio Marina. **Ethic. Theory Moral P.** 3:3 9:2000 pp.231-325. *Collection of 5 articles.*

5181 The moral world of the law. Peter R. Coss [Ed.]. Cambridge, New York: Cambridge University Press, 2000. xi, 262p. *ISBN: 0521640598. Includes bibliographical references and index. (Series:* Past and present publications).

5182 My body and other stories: anorexia nervosa and the legal politics of embodiment. Kirsty Keywood. **Soc. Leg. Stud.** 9:4 12:2000 pp.495-514.

5183 The myth of legality and public evaluation of the Supreme Court. John M. Scheb, II; William Lyons. **Soc. Sci. Q.** 81:4 12:2000 pp.928-940.

5184 Negotiating negotiation: the collaborative production of resolution in small claims mediation hearings. Angela Cora Garcia. **Disc. Soc.** 11:3 7:2000 pp.315-344.

J: POLITICS. STATE. INTERNATIONAL RELATIONS

5185 A non-essentialist version of legal pluralism. Brian Z. Tamanaha. **J. Law Soc.** 27:2 6:2000 pp.296-321.
5186 Paths to justice: what people do and think about going to law. Hazel Genn. Oxford: Hart Publishing, 1999. 288p. *ISBN: 1841130397.*
5187 Postcolonial law in the global economy: the case of Hong Kong. W.M. Sin; Y.W. Chu. **Int. J. S. Law** 28:4 12:2000 pp.291-310.
5188 Postmodern liberalism and the expressive function of law. N. Scott Arnold. **Soc. Philos. Pol.** 17:1 Winter:2000 pp.87-109.
5189 Post-war Japan and the law: mapping discourses of legalization and modernization. Seigo Hirowatari. **Soc. Sci. Jap. J.** 3:2 10:2000 pp.155-169.
5190 Private law and social inequality in the industrial age: comparing legal cultures in Britain, France, Germany and the United States. Willibald Steinmetz [Ed.]. Oxford: Oxford University Press, 2000. xii, 565p. *ISBN: 0199202362. Includes bibliographical references and index.* (*Series:* Studies of the German Historical Institute London).
5191 Prosecuting and defending rape: perspectives from the bar. Jennifer Temkin. **J. Law Soc.** 27:2 6:2000 pp.219-248.
5192 Psicologia jurídica. *[In Portuguese];* [Legal psychology]. Fernando de Jesus Souza; Betina Tabajaski; Miriam Gaiger; Rosane Borges Rodrigues; Paola Giacomini Fachini; Ana Celina Garcia Albornoz; Suzana Santa Maria Rodrigues; Magaly Andriotti Fernandes; Dirce Maria de Lemos Minella; Sonia Liane Reichert Rovinski; Maria do Céu Scribel da Silva; Tânia Maria Vanoni Polanczyk; Claudia Anaf; Ivone Patrício; Gislene Magalhães; Raquel Policelli; Renata Ferreira; Valéria Camargo; Margarida Calligaris Mamede; Sidney Shine; Gecelda A. Nunes da Silva; Ana Lúcia S. Duarte; Clair Ana Mariuza; Deborah Pierini Cidade; Jorge Trindade. **Aletheia** 7 1998 pp.5-140. *Collection of 16 articles.*
5193 Psychology and the legal system. Lawrence S. Wrightsman; Michael T. Nietzel; William H. Fortune. Pacific Grove CA: Brooks/Cole, 1998. xvii, 573p. *ISBN: 0534340857. Includes bibliographical references (p. 505-542) and indexes.*
5194 Psychology, law, and eyewitness testimony. Peter B. Ainsworth. Chichester: John Wiley & Sons, 1998. xii, 194p. *ISBN: 0471969311, 0471982385. Includes bibliographical references and index.* (*Series:* Wiley series in psychology of crime, policing, and law).
5195 Punishment: self-protection and desert. Joseph Carcasole. **Publ. Aff. Q.** 14:3 7:2000 pp.225-244.
5196 Queer readings of Europe: gender identity, sexual orientation and the (im)potency of rights politics at the European Court of Justice. Nico J. Beger. **Soc. Leg. Stud.** 9:2 6:2000 pp.249-270.
5197 Rawlssche Gerechtigkeitstheorie und die Rationierung medizinischer Leistungen — kann ein theoretisches Konzept in der Praxis angewandt werden? *[In German];* [Rawlsian theory of justice and the rationing of medical care] *[Summary].* Konrad Obermann. **Arc. Recht. Soz.** 86:3 2000 pp.412-422.
5198 Readings in the philosophy of law. Jules L. Coleman [Ed.]. New York: Garland Publishing, 1999. 680p. *ISBN: 0815337183. Includes bibliographical references.*
5199 Reflections on the methodological issues of the sociology of law. Reza Banakar. **J. Law Soc.** 27:2 6:2000 pp.273-295.
5200 Reproductive rights, advocacy and changing the law. Marta Lamas; Sharon Bissell; Bishakha Datta; Geetanjali Misra; Ruth Fletcher; Aida Seif El Dawla; Shereen Usdin; Nicola Christofides; Lebo Malepe; Aadielah Maker; Alessandra Casanova Guedes; Wilza Vieira Villela; Maria José de Oliveira Araújo; Prathibha Varkey; Padma Priya Balakrishna; Jasmine Helan Prasad; Sulochana Abraham; Abraham Joseph; Susan Pick; Martha Givaudan; Jeremy Brown; Sanjani Jane Varkey; Sharon Fonn; Mpefe Ketlhapile; Susannah H. Mayhew; Kirti Iyengar; Sharad D. Iyengar; Violet Naanyu Yebei; Chewe Luo; Anna Forbes; Lori Heise. **Reprod. Health Mat.** 8:16 11:2000 pp.10-159. *Collection of 15 articles.*
5201 Rhetorik und Demokratie. *[In German];* [Rhetoric and democracy] *[Summary].* Waldemar Schreckenberger. **Arc. Recht. Soz.** 86:3 2000 pp.367-399.

J: POLITIQUE. ÉTAT. RELATIONS INTERNATIONALES

5202 Scratching the surface of collaborative and associative governance: identifying the diversity of social action in institutional capacity building. Nicholas A. Phelps; Mark Tewdwr-Jones. **Envir. Plan. A.** 32:1 1:2000 pp.111-130.
5203 Selecting solicitors in Scotland: gender issues. Gerda Siann; Fiona Raitt; Murray Rowan. **J. Gender St.** 9:2 7:2000 pp.213-226.
5204 Sociologie du droit. *[In French]*; [Sociology of law]. Évelyne Serverin. Paris: La Découverte, 2000. 118p. *ISBN: 2707129739. Includes bibliographical references (p. 105-116).*
5205 Some experimental influences of lawyers' complicated questions on eyewitness confidence and accuracy. Mark R. Kebbell; David C. Giles. **J. Psychol.** 134:2 3:2000 pp.129-139.
5206 Sotsiologiia prava v sisteme obshchestvovedeniia. *[In Russian]*; (Sociology of law within the system of the social sciences.) V.V. Lapaeva. **Gos. Pravo** 4 4:2000 pp.81-90.
5207 The sovereign state v. Foucault: law and disciplinary power. Carole Smith. **Sociol. Rev.** 48:2 5:2000 pp.283-306.
5208 Toleranz als nicht-relatives Rechtsausübungsprinzip. Eine „diskursive" Annäherung. *[In German]*; [Tolerance as a non-relative legal practice principle] *[Summary]*. Massimo La Torre. **Arc. Recht. Soz.** 86:3 2000 pp.351-366.
5209 O trabalho do psicólogo no juizado da infância e da juventude de Porto Alegre/RS. *[In Portuguese]*; [The work of the psychologist in the Child and Juvenile Court in Porto Alegre, RS] *[Summary]*. Betina Tabajaski; Miriam Gaiger; Rosane Borges Rodrigues. **Aletheia** 7 1998 pp.9-18.
5210 Die Völkerrechtsphilosophie, Versuch einer Grundlegung in den Hauptzügen. *Pro scientia ethica iuris inter gentes. [In German]*; [The philosophy of international law] *[Summary]*. Panos Terz. **Arc. Recht. Soz.** 86:2 2000 pp.168-184.
5211 Weber's misunderstanding of traditional Chinese law. Robert M. Marsh. **A.J.S.** 106:2 9:2000 pp.281-302.

J.6: **Public administration**
Administration publique

5212 Citizens versus the new public manager: the problem of mutual empowerment. B. Guy Peters; Jon Pierre. **Admin. Soc.** 32:1 3:2000 pp.9-28.
5213 Does civil society speak for the people? Evidence from a survey of Scottish teachers. Lindsay Paterson. **Sociol. Rev.** 48:1 2:2000 pp.102-123.
5214 The ethnic dimension to bureaucratic encounters in postcommunist Europe: perceptions and experience. Åse B. Grødeland; William L. Miller; Tatyana Y. Koshechkina. **Nat. Nat.** 6:1 1:2000 pp.43-66.
5215 (Handicapped human resources: a study on the central civil service agencies in Riyadh city.); *[Text in Arabic]*. Moaddi Al Methheb; Salem Al Qahtani. **Dirasat Ad. Sc.** 27:1 1:2000 pp.120-138.
5216 Managerial strategies of domination. Power in soft bureaucracies. David Courpasson. **Organ. Stud.** 21:1 2000 pp.141-162.
5217 Managing through contracts: the employment effects of compulsory competitive tendering in Australian local government. Janet Walsh; Janine O'Flynn. **Ind. Relat. J.** 31:5 12:2000 pp.454-469.
5218 Opinion publique et politique en Belgique: une crise de légitimité? *[In French]*; (Public opinion and Belgian politics — a crisis in legitimacy?) *[Summary]*. André-Paul Frognier; Benoît Rihoux. **Recher. Sociolog.** XXXI:1 2000 pp.147-158.
5219 Parteienstaat am Ende? *[In German]*; [The end of the party state?] Heribert Prantl; Ulrich von Alemann; Klaus von Beyme; Richard Stöss; Oskar Niedermayer; Everhard Holtmann; Franz Walter. **Gewerk. Monat.** 51:2 2:2000 pp.65-119. *Collection of 7 articles.*
5220 Reforma administrativa e relações trabalhistas no setor público: dilemas e perspectivas. *[In Portuguese]*; (Administrative reform and labour relations in the public sector: dilemmas and perspectives.) Zairo B. Cheibub. **Rev. Bras. Ciên. Soc.** 15:43 6:2000 pp.115-146.

J: POLITICS. STATE. INTERNATIONAL RELATIONS

5221 Shades of green in local authority policy-making: a regional case study. Kate Muir; Martin Phillips; Mick Healey. **Area** 32:4 12:2000 pp.369-382.

5222 State-society relations in the making of Canadian immigration policy during the Mulroney era. John W.P. Veugelers. **Can. R. Soc. A.** 37:1 2:2000 pp.95-110.

5223 Structural adjustment, budget structure, and women's share of employment in Nigeria's federal civil service. P. Kassey Garba. **Nig. J. Econ. Soc. Stud.** 41:1 3:1999 pp.125-158.

5224 Surviving the routinization of evaluation: the administrative use of evaluations in Danish municipalities. Peter Dahler-Larsen. **Admin. Soc.** 32:1 3:2000 pp.70-92.

5225 When institutions fail: can viable social policies then be formulated? Ralph Scott. **Mankind Q.** XL:4 Summer:2000 pp.435-472.

J.7: **Political parties, pressure groups and political movements**
Partis politiques, groupes de pression et mouvements politiques

5226 Challenging the colonial contract: the Zapatistas' insurgent imagination. Patricia Huntington. **Rethink. Marx.** 12:3 Fall:2000 pp.58-80.

5227 The class embeddedness of corporate political action: leadership in defense of the NAFTA. Michael C. Dreiling. **Soc. Prob.** 47:1 2:2000 pp.21-48.

5228 Comunità virtuali, comunità reali e azione collettiva. *[In Italian]*; (Real communities, virtual communities, and collective action.) *[Summary]*. Mario Diani. **Rass. It. Soc.** XLI:1 1-3:2000 pp.29-51.

5229 From 'dangerous classes' to 'quiet rebels': politics of the urban subaltern in the global South. Asef Bayat. **Int. Sociol.** 15:3 9:2000 pp.533-558.

5230 In the net: an Internet guide for activists. James Walch. London: Zed Books, 1999. xii, 188p. *ISBN: 1856497585, 1856497593. Includes bibliographical references (p. [176]-181) and index.*

5231 Information and common knowledge in collective action. Arieh Gavious; Shlomo Mizrahi. **Econ. Polit.** 12:3 11:2000 pp.297-319.

5232 Jumping borders with pleasure: Chicano cultural resistance to neo-liberalism. Barbara Jenkins; Rob Aitken. **Stud. Pol. Ec.** 63 Autumn:2000 pp.87-110.

5233 Pedagogical guerrillas, armed democrats, and revolutionary counterpublics: examining paradox in the Zapatista uprising in Chiapas Mexico. Josée Johnston. **Theory Soc.** 29:4 8:2000 pp.463-505.

5234 Political parties, interest groups, and political campaigns. Ronald J. Hrebenar; Robert C. Benedict; Matthew J. Burbank. Boulder CO: Westview Press, 1999. 322p. *ISBN: 0813380073, 0813380081. Includes bibliographical references.*

5235 Political processes and local newspaper coverage of protest events: from selection bias to triadic interactions. Pamela E. Oliver; Gregory M. Maney. **A.J.S.** 106:2 9:2000 pp.463-505.

5236 Protest and decision-making in a society of blame. Giancarlo Corsi. **Demo. & Nat.** 6:3 11:2000 pp.361-374.

5237 Protest, tree ordination, and the changing context of political ritual. Nicola Tannenbaum. **Ethnology** XXXIX:2 Spring:2000 pp.109-128.

5238 Right-wing extremism in contemporary France: a 'silent counterrevolution'? John W.P. Veugelers. **Sociol. Q.** 41:1 Winter:2000 pp.19-40.

5239 The sense and non-sense of revolt. Julia Kristeva; Jeanine Herman [Tr.]. New York: Columbia University Press, 2000. 243p. *ISBN: 0231109962. Translated from the French Sens et non-sens de la révolte. Includes bibliographical references and index. (Series: European perspectives. The powers and limits of psychoanalysis).*

5240 Spaces of contention. Charles Tilly. **Mobilization** 5:2 2000 pp.135-159.

5241 Translating contention: culture, history, and the circulation of collective action. Sean Scalmer. **Alternatives** 25:4 10-12:2000 pp.491-514.

5242 Transnational mobilization and civil rights in Northern Ireland. Gregory M. Maney. **Soc. Prob.** 47:2 5:2000 pp.153-179.

J: POLITIQUE. ÉTAT. RELATIONS INTERNATIONALES

5243   Was tun gegen rechts. *[In German]*; [What can be done against the Right?] Richard Stöss; Margarete Jäger; Siegfried Jäger; Micha Brumlik; Dietmar Sturzbecher; Detlef Landua; Hajo Funke. **Gewerk. Monat.** 51:11 11:2000 pp.601-646. *Collection of 5 articles.*

Social movements
Mouvements sociaux

5244   Advances in environmental justice: research, theory, and methodology. Dorceta E. Taylor [Ed.]; David N. Pellow; Andrew Szasz; Michael Meuser; David R. Simon; Eugene S. Uyeki; Lani J. Holland; Edna Molina; Mangala Subramaniam; Francis O. Adeola. **Am. Behav. Sc.** 43:4 1:2000 pp.501-728. *Collection of 8 articles.*

5245   Are Latin American peasant movements still a force for change? Some new paradigms revisited. James Petras; Henry Veltmeyer. **J. Peasant Stud.** 28:2 1:2001 pp.83-118.

5246   Articulating the world: social movements, the self-transcendence of society and the question of culture. Martin Fuchs. **Thes. Elev.** 61 5:2000 pp.65-86.

5247   Australian gay activists: from movement to community. Graham Willett. **Rad. Hist. R.** 76 Winter:2000 pp.169-187.

5248   Complexity, cultural pluralism and democracy: collective action in the public space. Alberto Melucci; Leonardo Avritzer. **Soc. Sci. Info.** 39:4 12:2000 pp.507-528.

5249   (Cross-national analysis of social movements: effectiveness of the concept of political opportunity structure.); *[Text in Japanese]*. Tsutomu Watanabe. **Rir. To Ho.** 15:1 6:2000 pp.135-148.

5250   Democratisation and the decline of social movements: the effects of regime change on collective action in Eastern Europe, Southern Europe and Latin America. Christopher J. Pickvance. **Sociology** 33:2 5:1999 pp.353-372.

5251   Disappearing social movements: clandestinity in the New Left protest cycle in the U.S., Japan, Germany and Italy. Gilda Zwerman; Patricia G. Steinhoff; Donatella della Porta. **Mobilization** 5:1 2000 pp.83-100.

5252   Embodying ecological citizenship: rethinking the politics of grassroots globalization in the United States. Herbert Reid; Betsy Taylor. **Alternatives** 25:4 10-12:2000 pp.439-466.

5253   Engendering social movements: cultural images and movement dynamics. Rachel L. Einwohner; Jocelyn A. Hollander; Toska Olson. **Gender Soc.** 14:5 10:2000 pp.679-699.

5254   Environmental discourse and practice: a reader. John R. Short [Ed.]; Lisa M. Benton [Ed.]. Malden MA: Blackwell Publishers, 2000. xvi, 272p. *ISBN: 0631216375, 0631216367. Includes bibliographical references and index.*

5255   Explaining environmentalism: in search of a new social movement. Philip W. Sutton. Aldershot: Ashgate, 2000. x, 238p. *ISBN: 0754613127.*

5256   Global change, local angst: class and the American Patriot Movement. Carolyn Gallaher. **Envir. Plan. D.** 18:6 12:2000 pp.667-691.

5257   Global social movements. Shirin Rai [Ed.]; Robin Cohen [Ed.]. London: Athlone Press, 2000. 256p. *ISBN: 0485006154, 0485004194.*

5258   Ideas, ideologies, and social movements: the United States experience since 1800. Stuart W. Bruchey [Ed.]; Peter A. Coclanis [Ed.]. Columbia SC: University of South Carolina Press, 1999. xviii, 231p. *ISBN: 1570033137. Includes bibliographical references (p. 187-222) and index.*

5259   Identidad cultural, procesos étnico-nacionales y movimientos sociales en América Latina. *[In Spanish]*; (Cultural identity, ethnic-national processes and social movements in Latin America.) Concepción Rodríguez. **Cuad. Nues. Am.** XIII:25 1-6:2000 pp.52-75.

5260   Is the South African women's movement an easy rider? Interdependencies, foci, and strategies of social movements in the Third World; *[Summary in German]*. Miriam Abu Sharkh. **Sociologus** 49:2 1999 pp.207-246.

5261   The Landless Rural Workers Movement (MST) in Brazil. Wilder Robles. **J. Peasant Stud.** 28:2 1:2001 pp.146-161.

J: POLITICS. STATE. INTERNATIONAL RELATIONS

5262 The liminal effects of social movements: Red Guards and the transformation of identity. Guobin Yang. **Sociol. For.** 15:3 9:2000 pp.379-406.

5263 The making of a 'bad' public: ethnonational mobilization in post-communist Bulgaria. Peter Stamatov. **Theory Soc.** 29:4 8:2000 pp.549-572.

5264 The making of the White March: the mass media as a mobilizing alternative to movement organizations. Stefaan Walgrave; Jan Manssens. **Mobilization** 5:2 2000 pp.217-239.

5265 Mouvements sociaux, enjeux institutionnels et démocratisation. *[In French]*; [Social movements, institutional issues and democratization]. Pierre Hamel; Louis Maheu; Jean-Guy Vaillancourt; Rachel Laforest; Marc Lemire; Jean-Marc Fontan; Juan-Luis Klein; Serge Denis; Réjean Pelletier; Daniel Guérin. **Pol. et Soc.** 19:1 2000 pp.3-161. *Collection of 6 articles.*

5266 Movement socialization in art workshops: a case from Pinochet's Chile. Jacqueline Adams. **Sociol. Q.** 41:4 Fall:2000 pp.615-638.

5267 El movimiento estudiantil: actualidad y retrospectiva. *[In Spanish]*; [The student movement: past and present] *[Summary]*. José Luis Hoyo Arana. **Rev. Mexicana Cien. Pol.** XLIV:177-178 9-4:1999-2000 pp.255-276.

5268 Los movimientos estudiantiles de 1968 y 1999: contextos históricos y reflexiones críticas. *[In Spanish]*; [Student movements in 1968 and 1999: historical contexts and criticisms] *[Summary]*. Gilda Waldman. **Rev. Mexicana Cien. Pol.** XLIV:177-178 9-4:1999-2000 pp.277-294.

5269 New social and political movements of dalits: a study of Meerut district. Sudha Pai. **Contr. I. Soc.** 34:2 5-8:2000 pp.189-220.

5270 New social movements and the 'centri sociali' in Milan. Vincenzo Ruggiero. **Sociol. Rev.** 48:2 5:2000 pp.167-185.

5271 The outcomes of homeless mobilization: the influence of organization, disruption, political mediation, and framing. Daniel M. Cress; David A. Snow. **A.J.S.** 105:4 1:2000 pp.1063-1104.

5272 Percepción de las relaciones sociales globales y formulación de alternativas para los movimientos sociales. *[In Spanish]*; (The perception of global social relations and the formulation of alternatives for social movements.) Francois Houtart. **Cuad. Nues. Am.** XIII:25 1-6:2000 pp.32-51.

5273 Policing, collective action and social movement theory: the case of the Northern Ireland civil rights campaign. Graham Ellison; Greg Martin. **Br. J. Soc.** 51:4 12:2000 pp.681-700.

5274 The popular movement dimensions of contemporary militant Islamism: socio-spatial determinants in the Cairo urban setting. Salwa Ismail. **Comp. Stud. S.** 42:2 4:2000 pp.363-393.

5275 Protesta senza movimenti? *[In Italian]*; [Protest without movements?] Mario Diani; Donatella della Porta; Marco Giugni; Massimiliano Andretta; Nicholas Dines. **Quad. Sociol.** XLIII:21 1999 pp.3-111. *Collection of 5 articles.*

5276 Radical social movement organizations: a theoretical model. Kathleen J. Fitzgerald; Diane M. Rodgers. **Sociol. Q.** 41:4 Fall:2000 pp.573-592.

5277 Return of the repressed: the fall and rise of emotions in social movement theory. Jeff Goodwin; James M. Jasper; Francesca Polletta. **Mobilization** 5:1 2000 pp.65-82.

5278 Social movements in advanced capitalism: the political economy and cultural construction of social activism. Steven M. Buechler. New York: Oxford University Press, 2000. xiii, 240p. *ISBN: 0195126033, 0195126041. Includes bibliographical references (p. 215-232) and index.*

5279 Thailand's assembly of the poor: background, drama, reaction. Chris Baker. **S.E. Asia Res.** 8:1 3:2000 pp.5-29.

5280 Transnational diffusion and the African American reinvention of Gandhian repertoire. Sean Chabot. **Mobilization** 5:2 2000 pp.201-216.

J: POLITIQUE. ÉTAT. RELATIONS INTERNATIONALES

J.8: Political behaviour and elections
Comportement politique et élections

5281 Academics in politics. Aleksandr V. Iurevich. **Rus. Pol. Law** 38:3 5-6:2000 pp.24-48.
5282 Corruption, libéralisation, démocratisation. *[In French]*; [Corruption, liberalization, democratization]. Jean Cartier-Bresson; Béatrice Hibou; Mohamed Tozy; Fatiha Talahite; Jean-François Médard; Johann Graf Lambsdorff; Michael Johnston; Iréne Hors; Jean-Marc Guillelmet. **R. T-Monde** XLI:161 1-3:2000 pp.9-214. *Collection of 8 articles.*
5283 Do politics perceptions relate to political behaviors? Tests of an implicit assumption and expanded model. Matthew Valle; Pamela L. Perrewe. **Human Relat.** 53:3 3:2000 pp.359-386.
5284 Elites in post-communist Russia: a changing of the guard? Sharon Werning Rivera. **Eur.-Asia Stud.** 52:3 5:2000 pp.413-432.
5285 Les formes du sentiment de responsabilité dans les mentalités contemporaines: une étude empirique. *[In French]*; (The different forms of the sense of responsibility in contemporary mentality: an empirical study.) *[Summary]*. Jean Kellerhals; Noëlle Languin; Gilbert Ritschard; Massimo Sardi. **Rev. Fr. Soc.** 41:2 4-6:2000 pp.307-330.
5286 Homeownership and politics: testing the political incorporation thesis; *[Summary in French]*. Norine Verberg. **Can. J. Soc.** 25:2 Spring:2000 pp.169-196.
5287 Market, state, or don't know? Education, economic ideology, and voting in contemporary Russia. Theodore Gerber. **Soc. Forc.** 79:2 12:2000 pp.477-521.
5288 On-line interaction and why candidates avoid it. Jennifer Stromer-Galley. **J. Comm.** 50:4 Autumn:2000 pp.111-132.
5289 The opinion poll as a cultural form. Justin Lewis. **Int. Jour. Cult. Stud.** 2:2 8:1999 pp.199-221.
5290 Opiniones y actitudes de los españoles ante el proces de integración europea. *[In Spanish]*; [Public opinion and attitudes towards European integration in Spain]. Inmaculada Szmolka. Madrid: Centro de Investigaciones Sociológicas, 1999. 159p. *ISBN: 8474762774. Includes bibliographical references (p. 133-135).*
5291 (Political communication patterns in Saudi families: limitations and results.) *[Summary]*; *[Text in Arabic]*. Sa'ud Otaibi. **Dirasat Hum. Soc. Sc.** 27:1 2:2000 pp.13-29.
5292 Political participation and ethnic minorities: Chinese overseas in Malaysia, Indonesia, and the United States. Amy L. Freedman. New York: Routledge, 2000. xvi, 231p. *ISBN: 0415924456. Includes bibliographical references (p. [209]-222) and index.*
5293 Politicheskii smekh: latentnye funktsii v sovremennoi Rossii. *[In Russian]*; [Political humour]. V. Razuvaev. **Svobod. Mysl'** 8 2000 pp.27-38.
5294 Politische Kultur in den Zeiten der Konfliktenttarnung: Zur postkommunistischen Modernisierung kollektiver Erinnerungspraktiken. *[In German]*; (Political culture in times of the unveiling of conflict: on postcommunist modernization of collective commemorative practices.) *[Summary]*. Andreas Langenohl. **Berl. J. Soziol.** 10:4 2000 pp.517-534.
5295 Reluctant Europeans: Britain and European integration, 1945-1998. D.A. Gowland; Arthur Turner. New York: Addison Wesley Longman, 1999. 391p. *ISBN: 0582369576, 0582369568. Includes bibliographical references and index.*
5296 Social dominance orientation, anti-egalitarianism and the political psychology of gender: an extension and cross-cultural replication. Jim Sidanius; Shana Levin; James Liu; Felicia Pratto. **Eur. J. Soc. Psychol.** 30:1 1-2:2000 pp.41-67.
5297 Studies of political elites in Russia: issues and alternatives. Vladimir Gel'man; Inessa Tarusina. **Comm. Post-Comm. Stud.** 33:3 9:2000 pp.311-329.
5298 Le terrorisme intellectuel de 1945 à nos jours. *[In French]*; [Intellectual terrorism from 1945 to today]. Jean Sévillia. Paris: Perrin, 2000. 263p. *ISBN: 2262013438. Includes bibliographical references (p. [259]-262).*
5299 When is the personal political? The President's penis and other stories. Mary Holmes. **Sociology** 34:2 5:2000 pp.305-322.

J: POLITICS. STATE. INTERNATIONAL RELATIONS

Elections
Élections

5300   Crosscutting social circles and political choice: effects of personal network composition on voting behavior in the Netherlands. Paul Nieuwbeerta; Henk Flap. **Soc. Networks** 22:4 10:2000 pp.313-335.
5301   Les dons dans le jeu électoral au Cameroun. *[In French]*; (Gifts in Cameroonian election campaigns.) Antoine Socpa. **Cah. Ét. Afr.** XL(1):157 2000 pp.91-108.
5302   The effects of class mobility on class voting in post-war Western industrialized countries. Paul Nieuwbeerta; Nan Dirk de Graaf; Wout Ultee. **Eur. Sociol. R.** 16:4 12:2000 pp.327-348.
5303   Em busca da racionalidade perdida: alguns determinantes do voto no Distrito Federal. *[In Portuguese]*; (Searching for the lost rationality: some determinants of the popular vote in the Federal District.) Gláucio Ary Dillon Soares. **Rev. Bras. Ciên. Soc.** 15:43 6:2000 pp.5-24.
5304   Ethnic group leaders and the mobilization of voter turnout: evidence from five Montreal communities. Miriam Lapp. **Can. Ethn. Stud.** XXXI:2 1999 pp.17-42.
5305   Is there a duty to vote? Loren E. Lomasky; Geoffrey Brennan. **Soc. Philos. Pol.** 17:1 Winter:2000 pp.62-86.
5306   Kruising van sociale kringen en politieke keuze: de invloed van de sociale samenstelling van persoonlijke netwerken op stemgedrag. *[In Dutch]*; (Cross-cutting social circles and political choice the effects of social composition of personal networks on voting behaviour.) Paul Nieuwbeerta; Henk Flap. **Mens Maat.** 75:1 3:2000 pp.40-61.
5307   Panelové šetření — metoda a výsledky výzkumu *The People's Choice*. *[In Czech]*; (Panel analysis — method and results of 'The People's Choice' research project.) *[Summary]*. Hynek Jeřábek. **Soc. Čas.** 36:2 2000 pp.201-220.

J.9:   **International relations**
Relations internationales

5308   America's world identity: the politics of exclusion. Neil Renwick. Basingstoke: Macmillan, 2000. xii, 261p. *ISBN: 0333774604, 0312223226. Includes bibliographical references (p. 229-250) and indexes.*
5309   Confucianism and human rights: rhetoric and reality. Ivy Y.Y. Lau; Richard Cullen. **Int. Asien.** 30:1-2 5:1999 pp.75-96.
5310   Constructing a new orthodoxy? Wendt's 'social theory of international politics' and the constructivist challenge. Friedrich Kratochwil. **Millennium** 29:1 2000 pp.73-104.
5311   Crimes against humanity: Hannah Arendt and the Nuremberg debates. Robert Fine. **Eur. J. Soc. Theory** 3:3 8:2000 pp.293-311.
5312   Criminology and genocide. George S. Yacoubian, Jr.; David O. Friedrichs; L. Edward Day; Margaret Vandiver; John M. Steiner; Frank M. Afflitto; Michael H. Hoffman. **Cr. Law Soc. Chan.** 34:1 7:2000 pp.7-110. *Collection of 6 articles.*
5313   Crossing borders - confronting history: intercultural adjustment in a post-Cold War world. Jerry L. Johnson. Lanham MD: University Press of America, 2000. xi, 230p. *ISBN: 0761815368. Includes bibliographical references (p. [219]-226) and index.*
5314   Cultures of insecurity: states, communities, and the production of danger. Jutta Weldes [Ed.]; George Marcus [Foreword]; et al. Minneapolis MN, London: University of Minnesota Press, 1999. xix, 432p. *ISBN: 081663307X, 0816633088. Includes bibliographical references (p. 363-412) and index.* (*Series:* Borderlines - 14).
5315   The dialogue of civilisations and international public spheres. Marc Lynch. **Millennium** 29:2 2000 pp.307-330.
5316   Ethics, economics and international relations: transparent sovereignty in the commonwealth of life. Peter G. Brown. Edinburgh: Edinburgh University Press, 2000. xii,

J: POLITIQUE. ÉTAT. RELATIONS INTERNATIONALES

180p. *ISBN: 0748608923. Includes bibliographical references. (Series:* Edinburgh studies in world ethics).

5317 Gender in international relations. Diana Thorburn; V. Spike Peterson; Azar Nafisi; Samantha Ravich; Shirin Tahir-Kheli; Alison Jamieson; Madeleine K. Albright; Roberta Cohen; Jill Benderly; Mahnaz Afkhami. **SAIS R.** XX:2 Summer-Fall:2000 pp.1-92. *Collection of 8 articles.*

5318 Gender justice and reconciliation. Susan McKay. **Wom. St. Inter. For.** 23:5 9-10:2000 pp.561-570.

5319 The graceful and generous liberal gesture: making racism invisible in American international relations. Robert Vitalis. **Millennium** 29:2 2000 pp.331-356.

5320 Human rights violations in East and Central Africa and the issue of cultural relativity. Santosh Saha. **Scand. J. Dev. Alt. A. Stud.** 18:2-3 6-9:1999 pp.79-94.

5321 L'humanitaire appartient-il à tout le monde? *[In French]*; (Is humanitarian action everybody's affair? Reflections on an overworked concept.) *[Summary].* Jean-Luc Blondel. **Int. R. Red Cross** 82:838 6:2000 pp.327-338.

5322 International justice. A.J. Coates [Ed.]. Aldershot, Burlington VT: Ashgate, 2000. viii, 302p. *ISBN: 1840149450. Includes bibliographical references. Association for Legal and Social Philosophy. (Series:* Avebury series in philosophy).

5323 An intimate history of killing: face-to-face killing in twentieth-century warfare. Joanna Bourke. London: Granta, 2000. viii, 564p. *ISBN: 186207321X. Includes index.*

5324 Kriegsdienstverweigerung in der Bundesrepublik Deutschland. *[In German]*; (Conscientious objection in Germany.) *[Summary].* Margarete Haberhauer; Helmut Maneval. **Jahrb. N. St.** 220:2 3:2000 pp.129-146.

5325 El Mediterráneo y América Latina. *[In Spanish]*; [The Mediterranean and Latin America]. Marcos Aguinis; Leopoldo Zea; José Luis Rubio Cordón; Juan Hung Hui; Tullo Vigevani. **Cuad. Am.** 79:1 1-2:2000 pp.61-160. *Collection of 5 articles.*

5326 Mezhdunarodnaia zashchita sotsial'nykh prav zhenshchin (Printsip universal'nosti i kul'turnogo raznoobraziia). *[In Russian]*; (International protection of women's social rights.) S. Polenina. **Obshch. Nauki Sovrem.** 3 2000 pp.172-182.

5327 Les «pacifistes» et la guerre sans la guerre. *[In French]*; (The 'pacifists' and war without war.) Ariane Lantz. **Hom. Soc.** 135 1-3:2000 pp.119-138.

5328 Pan-Africanism: exploring the contradictions. Politics, identity and development in Africa and the African diaspora. William Ackah. Aldershot: Ashgate, 1999. xvii, 123p. *ISBN: 1840143754. Includes bibliographical references and index. (Series:* Interdisciplinary research series in ethnic, gender and class relations).

5329 Pour une analyse critique du discours dans l'étude des relations internationales. Exemple d'application à des éditoriaux américains sur la guerre en Tchétchénie. *[In French]*; [In favour of a critical discourse analysis of international relations, with the example of American editorials on the war in Chechnya] *[Summary].* Elisabeth Le. **Ét. Int.** XXXI:3 9:2000 pp.489-516.

5330 Réflexions et convictions sur l'humanitaire d'aujourd'hui et de demain. *[In French]*; (Considerations and convictions with regard to humanitarian action today and tomorrow.) *[Summary].* Cornelio Sommaruga. **Int. R. Red Cross** 82:838 6:2000 pp.295-310.

5331 Scarred minds: the psychological impact of war on Sri Lankan Tamils. Daya Somasundaram. New Delhi, Thousand Oaks CA: Sage Publications, 1998. 352p. *ISBN: 0761992677. Includes bibliographical references and index.*

5332 Sociology after Bosnia and Kosovo: recovering justice. Keith Doubt. Lanham MD: Rowman & Littlefield, 2000. 183p. *ISBN: 0847693775, 0847693767.*

5333 Speak clearly into the chandelier: cultural politics between Britain and Russia. John C.Q Roberts. Richmond: Curzon Press, 2000. 316p. *ISBN: 0700712968.*

5334 The state and identity construction in international relations. Sarah Owen Vandersluis [Ed.]. Basingstoke: Macmillan, 2000. 264p. *ISBN: 033373291X, 0333732901. Includes bibliographical references and index.*

J: POLITICS. STATE. INTERNATIONAL RELATIONS

5335 Tourisme et relations internationales. *[In French]*; [Tourism and international relations]. G. Chabaud; A. Rauch; V. Patin; L. Tissot; R. Mazuy; V. Claeys; J. van Praet; G. Cazes. **Relat. Int.** 102 Summer:2000 pp.141-245. *Collection of 7 articles.*

5336 What's the use of international relations? Michael Nicholson. **Rev. Int. Stud.** 26:2 4:2000 pp.183-198.

5337 Why do they do it like this? An analysis of the factors influencing mediation behavior in international conflicts. Jacob Bercovitch; Allison Houston. **Confl. Resolut.** 44:2 4:2000 pp.170-202.

Military sociology
Sociologie militaire

5338 Army retirement rites: formal and informal. Nissan Rubin; Drora Peer. **Megamot** XL:1 11:1999 pp.103-130.

5339 Brothers and others in arms: managing gay identity in combat units of the Israeli army. Danny Kaplan; Eyal Ben-Ari. **J. Contemp. Ethnog.** 29:4 8:2000 pp.396-432.

5340 Civil-military relations in the Kosovo crisis: an emerging hegemony? Michael Pugh. **Secur. Dial.** 31:2 6:2000 pp.229-242.

5341 Civil-military relations in the transition to democracy: the case of Mozambique. Joao Bernado Honwana. **Afr. Devel.** XXIV:3-4 1999 pp.135-176.

5342 Conscription in Scandinavia during the last quarter century: developments and arguments. Henning Sørensen. **Arm. Forces Soc.** 26:2 Winter:2000 pp.313-334.

5343 Culture at all points, including militarism. Félix Díaz Martínez. **Cult. Psyc.** 6:3 9:2000 pp.333-352.

5344 Duty, honor, country: the social identity of West Point cadets. Volker C. Franke. **Arm. Forces Soc.** 26:2 Winter:2000 pp.175-202.

5345 Effects of work-related absences on families: evidence from the Gulf War. Joshua D. Angrist; John H. Johnson, IV. **Ind. Lab. Rel.** 54:1 10:2000 pp.41-58.

5346 Female participation in war: bio-cultural interactions. Azar Gat. **J. Strat. Stud.** 23:4 12:2000 pp.21-31.

5347 The first wave: gender integration and military culture. Regina F. Titunik. **Arm. Forces Soc.** 26:2 Winter:2000 pp.229-258.

5348 The great illusion: women in the military. Martin van Creveld; Christopher Coker [Comments by]; Jean Bethke Elshtain [Comments by]. **Millennium** 29:2 2000 pp.429-460.

5349 Healing the social wounds of war. Murray Last. **Med. Conf. Surv.** 16:4 10-12:2000 pp.370-382.

5350 'How can she claim equal rights when she doesn't have to do as many push-ups as I do?' the framing of men's opposition to women's equality in the military. Carol Cohn. **Men. Masc.** 3:2 10:2000 pp.131-151.

5351 The imprint of the Intifada: response of kibbutz-born soldiers to military service in the West Bank and Gaza. Yechezkel Dar; Shaul Kimhi; Nurit Stadler; Alek D. Epstein. **Arm. Forces Soc.** 26:2 Winter:2000 pp.285-312.

5352 It could be you! Military conscription and selection bias in rural Honduras. Samuel Cameron; Grail Dorling; Andy Thorpe. **R. Eur. Lat.am. Caribe** 68 4:2000 pp.47-63.

5353 Less than we can be: men, women and the modern military. Martin van Creveld. **J. Strat. Stud.** 23:4 12:2000 pp.1-20.

5354 Measuring the cohesion of military communities. Peggy McClure; Walter Broughton. **Arm. Forces Soc.** 26:3 Spring:2000 pp.473-488.

5355 Morality and contemporary warfare. James Turner Johnson. New Haven CT: Yale University Press, 1999. ix, 259p. *ISBN: 0300078374. Includes bibliographical references (p. [249]-255) and index.*

5356 Politics and the military: back to the future? Tolstoy and post-communist Russian military politics. John P. Moran. **J. Slav. Mil. Stud.** 12:4 12:1999 pp.54-77.

J: POLITIQUE. ÉTAT. RELATIONS INTERNATIONALES

5357 Racial equity, the United States Army, operations research, and social science. Andrew G. Loerch; Carl M. Harris; Edward Rattner. **Socio. Econ.** 34:2 6:2000 pp.73-84.

5358 Saving the males: the sociological implications of the Virginia Military Institute and the Citadel. Michael Kimmel. **Gender Soc.** 14:4 8:2000 pp.494-516.

5359 Senior officer training: applying Zhukov's command heritage to military training and reform in today's world. Makhmut A. Gareev; Robert R. Love [Tr.]. **J. Slav. Mil. Stud.** 12:4 12:1999 pp.78-113.

5360 The use and evolution of stories as a mode of problem representation: Soviet and French military officers face the loss of empire. Tanya Charlick-Paley; Donald A. Sylvan. **Polit. Psych.** 21:4 12:2000 pp.697-728.

5361 Violence, coercion, and rights in the Americas. Anthony W. Pereira; Diane E. Davis; Jorge Zaverucha; Deena I. Abu-Lughod; Susan D. Burgerman; Eduardo González-Cueva. **Lat. Am. Pers.** 27:3 5:2000 pp.3-102. *Collection of 5 articles.*

5362 Women and the military. Caroline Kennedy-Pipe. **J. Strat. Stud.** 23:4 12:2000 pp.32-50.

K: SOCIAL PROBLEMS. SOCIAL WELFARE. SOCIAL WORK
PROBLÈMES SOCIAUX. BIEN-ÊTRE SOCIAL. TRAVAIL SOCIAL

K.1: Social problems
Problèmes sociaux

5363 AIDS: issues in the global pandemic. Quarraisha Abdool Karim; Mary Crewe; Chris Desmond; Karen Michael; Jeff Gow; Charlotte Faty Ndiaye; John Rwomushana; Tamar Rénaud; Jeremy Hess; Mário Scheffer; Richard Delate; Gina Buijs; Jenny Hadingham; Greg Mills; Alan Thorold; Susan K. Glover; Beverly L. Peters; Naudé Malan; Gareth Elliot; Laura Hastings; Nkosazana Dlamini-Zuma [Speech by]; Thabo Mbeki [Speech by]; F.W. de Klerk [Speech by]; Moeletsi Mbeki. **S. Afr. J. Int. Affairs** 7:2 Winter:2000 pp.1-223. *Collection of 20 articles.*

5364 Alcohol sales to underage adolescents: an unobtrusive observational field study and evaluation of a police intervention. Paul Willner; Kenneth Hart; John Binmore; Margaret Cavendish; Elizabeth Dunphy. **Addiction** 95:9 9:2000 pp.1373-1388.

5365 Criminalità ed occupazione: lo stato dell'arte. *[In Italian]*; [Crime and employment] *[Summary]*. Donato Masciandaro. **Riv. Int. Sci. Soc.** CVII:1 1-3:1999 pp.85-117.

5366 Dark heart: the shocking truth about hidden Britain. Nick Davies. London: Vintage, 1998. ix, 304p. *ISBN: 0099583011.*

5367 Explaining the drug-crime link: theoretical, policy and research issues. Toby Seddon. **J. Soc. Pol.** 29:1 1:2000 pp.95-107.

5368 Fiesta as tradition, fiesta as change: ritual, alcohol and violence in a Mexican community. Ramona L. Pérez. **Addiction** 95:3 3:2000 pp.365-374.

5369 First person accounts and sociological explanations of delinquency. James J. Teevan; Heather B. Dryburgh. **Can. R. Soc. A.** 37:1 2:2000 pp.77-94.

5370 Juvenile delinquency in Israel and its treatment: background, policy and future trends. Meir Hovav. **Soc. Sec.** 6 2:2000 pp.206-230.

5371 Pedophilia and the culture wars. G.E. Zuriff. **Publ. Inter.** 138 Winter:2000 pp.29-39.

5372 The weight of the world: social suffering in contemporary society. Pierre Bourdieu; et al; Priscilla Parkhurst Ferguson [Tr.]. Cambridge: Polity Press, 1999. x, 646p. *ISBN: 0745615929, 0745615937. Translated from the French La misère du monde. Includes bibliographical references and index.*

5373 Young people and prostitution: an end to the beginning? Patrick Ayre; David Barrett. **Child. Soc.** 14:1 2:2000 pp.48-59.

Addiction
Dépendance

5374 Capture-recapture estimates of drug misuse in urban and non-urban settings in the north east of Scotland. Gordon Hay. **Addiction** 95:12 12:2000 pp.1795-1804.

5375 The characteristics of 'new users' of cocaine and heroin unknown to treatment agencies: results from the Swiss hidden population study. Daniel Kuebler; Dominique Hausser; Jean-Pierre Gervasoni. **Addiction** 95:10 10:2000 pp.1561-1571.

5376 Coming clean: overcoming addiction without treatment. Stanton Peele [Foreword]; Robert Granfield; William Cloud. New York, London: New York University Press, 1999. xxi, 296p. *ISBN: 0814715818, 0814715826. Includes bibliographical references (p. [251]-287) and index.*

5377 Contemporary issues and future directions for research into pathological gambling. Mark Dickerson; Ellen Baron. **Addiction** 95:8 8:2000 pp.1145-1159.

5378 Death by heroin: recovery by hope. Mary Kenny. Dublin: New Island, 1999. 240p. *ISBN: 1902602110.*

K: PROBLÈMES SOCIAUX. BIEN-ÊTRE SOCIAL. TRAVAIL SOCIAL

5379 Disciplining addictions: the bio-politics of methadone and heroin in the United States. Philippe Bourgois. **Cult. Medic. Psych.** 24:2 6:2000 pp.165-196.
5380 Diversion of prescribed drugs by drug users in treatment: analysis of the UK market and new data from London. Jane Fountain; John Strang; Michael Gossop; Michael Farrell; Paul Griffiths. **Addiction** 95:3 3:2000 pp.393-406.
5381 Does cannabis use encourage other forms of illicit drug use? David M. Fergusson; L. John Horwood. **Addiction** 95:4 4:2000 pp.505-520.
5382 Drug abuse and partner violence among women in methadone treatment. Nabila El Bassel; Louisa Gilbert; Robert Schilling; Takeshi Wada. **J. Fam. Viol.** 15:3 9:2000 pp.209-228.
5383 Drug injectors and prison mandatory drug testing. Rhidian Hughes. **Howard J. Crim. Just.** 39:1 2:2000 pp.1-13.
5384 The effectiveness of the Minnesota model approach in the treatment of adolescent drug abusers. Ken C. Winters; Randy D. Stinchfield; Elizabeth Opland; Christine Weller; William W. Latimer. **Addiction** 95:4 4:2000 pp.601-612.
5385 Effects of increasing income on polydrug use: a comparison of heroin, cocaine, and alcohol abusers. Nancy M. Petry. **Br. J. Addict.** 95:5 5:2000 pp.705-717.
5386 Emergent trends in illicit drug-use behaviors. Merrill Singer [Ed.]; Robert G. Carlson; Russel S. Falck; Harvey A. Siegal; Philippe Bourgois; Julie Bruneau; J. Bryan Page; Maria José Míguez-Burbano; Joy Ann Juvalis; Margaret Weeks; Jean J. Schensul; Cristina Huebner; Marvin Snow; Pablo Feliciano; Lorie Broomhall; Teri A. Strenski; Patricia A. Marshall; Jessica K. Gacki; Clifton W. Sanchez; Claire E. Sterk; Kirk W. Elifson. **Med. Anthrop.** 18:4 2000 pp.299-455. *Collection of 8 articles.*
5387 Gambling problems in substance abusers are associated with increased sexual risk behaviors. Nancy M. Petry. **Addiction** 95:7 7:2000 pp.1089-1100.
5388 Gender differences in alcohol consumption and adverse drinking consequences: cross-cultural patterns. Richard W. Wilsnack; Nancy D. Vogeltanz; Sharon C. Wilsnack; T. Robert Harris. **Addiction** 95:2 2:2000 pp.251-266.
5389 A genetic analysis of smoking behavior in family members of older adult males. Li Shu-Chuan Cheng; Gary E. Swan; Dorit Carmelli. **Addiction** 95:3 3:2000 pp.427-436.
5390 Genetic and environmental influences on alcohol use: DF analysis of NLSY kinship data. Maury A. Buster; Joseph Lee Rodgers. **J. Biosoc. Sc.** 32:2 4:2000 pp.177-189.
5391 'I already stopped': abstinence prior to treatment. David B. Rosengren; Lois Downey; Dennis M. Donovan. **Addiction** 9:51 1:2000 pp.65-76.
5392 Illicit drug use, unemployment, and occupational attainment. Ziggy MacDonald; Stephen Pudney. **J. Health Econ.** 19:6 11:2000 pp.1089-1115.
5393 A latent class analysis of antisocial personality disorder symptom data from a multi-centre family study of alcoholism. K.K. Bucholz; V.M. Hesselbrock; A.C. Heath; J.R. Kramer; M.A. Schuckit. **Addiction** 95:4 4:2000 pp.553-568.
5394 A longitudinal study of cannabis use and mental health from adolescence to early adulthood. Rob McGee; Sheila Williams; Richie Poulton; Terrie Moffitt. **Addiction** 95:4 4:2000 pp.491-504.
5395 A longitudinal study of male buprenorphine addicts attending an addiction clinic in India. Debasish Basu; Surendra K. Mattoo; Anil Malhotra; Nitin Gupta; Rama Malhotra. **Addiction** 95:9 9:2000 pp.1363-1372.
5396 Maternal addiction, child maladjustment, and socio-demographic risks: implications for parenting behaviors. Nancy E. Suchman; Suniya S. Luthar. **Addiction** 95:9 9:2000 pp.1417-1428.
5397 Motivating illegal drug use recovery: evidence for a culturally congruent intervention. Douglas Longshore; Cheryl Grills. **J. Black Psychol.** 26:3 8:2000 pp.288-301.
5398 Natural and treatment-assisted recovery from gambling problems: a comparison of resolved and active gamblers. David C. Hodgins; Nady el- Guebaly. **Br. J. Addict.** 95:5 5:2000 pp.777-789.
5399 Natural recovery from alcohol and drug problems: methodological review of the research with suggestions for future directions. Linda C. Sobell; Tomothy P. Ellingstad; Mark B. Sobell. **Br. J. Addict.** 95:5 5:2000 pp.749-764.

K: SOCIAL PROBLEMS. SOCIAL WELFARE. SOCIAL WORK

5400 'One day at a time' and other slogans for everyday life: the ethical practices of Alcoholics Anonymous. Mariana Valverde; Kimberley White-Mair. **Sociology** 33:2 5:1999 pp.393-410.

5401 One year follow-up of opiate injectors treated with oral methadone in a GP-centred programme. Sharon J. Hutchinson; Avril Taylor; Laurence Gruer; Catherine Barr; Carl Mills; Lawrence Elliott; David J. Goldberg; Robert Scott; Gail Gilchrist. **Addiction** 95:7 7:2000 pp.1055-1068.

5402 Opium in 20th-century Britain: pharmacists, regulation and the people. Stuart Anderson; Virginia Berridge. **Addiction** 9:51 1:2000 pp.23-36.

5403 Prevalence of alcohol use and the association between onset of use and alcohol-related problems in a general population sample in Germany. Ludwig Kraus; Kim Bloomfield; Rita Augustin; Anneke Reese. **Addiction** 95:9 9:2000 pp.1389-1401.

5404 The process of relapse in severely dependent male problem drinkers. Steve Allsop; Bill Saunders; Mike Phillips. **Addiction** 9:51 1:2000 pp.95-106.

5405 Psychiatric symptoms and deviance in early adolescence predict heavy alcohol use 3 years later. Kirsti Kumpulainen. **Addiction** 95:12 12:2000 pp.1847-1857.

5406 Research perspectives on alcohol craving. Cherry Lowman; Walter A. Hunt; Raye Z. Litten; D. Colin Drummond; Ting-Kai Li; Herman H. Samson; George F. Koob; John Littleton; Terry E. Robinson; Kent C. Berridge; Anthony A. Grace; Stephen T. Tiffany; Cynthia A. Conklin; Raymond Niaura; Harriet de Wit; Saul Shiffman; Brian L. Carter; Edward G. Singleton; Michael A. Sayette; Christopher S. Martin; William G. Shadel; Raymond F. Anton; Roger E. Meyer; Peter M. Monti; Damaris J. Rohsenow; Kent E. Hutchison; David B. Abrams. **Addiction** 95:2(Supp.) 8:2000 pp.45-255. *Collection of 19 articles.*

5407 Smoking reduction: efficacy and implementation. John R. Hughes; Peter Anderson; Michael Kunze; Chris T. Bolliger; David Sweanor; Robert West. **Addiction** 95:1(Supp.) 1:2000 pp.3-34. *Collection of 6 articles.*

5408 Studies on natural recovery from alcohol dependence: sample selection bias by media solicitation? H.J. Rumpf; G. Bischof; U. Hapke; C. Meyer; U. John. **Br. J. Addict.** 95:5 5:2000 pp.765-775.

5409 Substance abuse prevention. Sandra S. Chipungu; John Hermann; Soledad Sambrano; Mary Nistler; Elizabeth Sale; J. Fred Springer; Faye Z. Belgrave; Deborah Ridley Brome; Carl Hampton; Kathleen Burlew; DeKimberlen Neely; Candace Johnson; Tonya Hucks; Bruce Purnell; Jacqueline Butler; Marilyn Lovett; Randi Burlew; Tiffany G. Townsend; Harolyn M.E. Belcher; Paula J. Lockhart; Susan Perkins-Parks; Margaret McNally; Harriet Curtis-Boles; Valata Jenkins-Monroe; Michelle Deaneen Owens; Karen Allen; Tinaz Vevaina. **J. Black Psychol.** 26:4 11:2000 pp.360-486. *Collection of 7 articles.*

5410 Substance dependence, family history of alcohol dependence, and neuropsychological functioning in adolescence. Susan F. Tapert; Sandra A. Brown. **Addiction** 95:7 7:2000 pp.1043-1054.

5411 'The lizard in the green bottle': 'aging out' of problem drinking among Navajo men. Gilbert Quintero. **Soc. Sci. Med.** 51:7 10:2000 pp.1031-1046.

5412 Understanding problem gamblers: a practitioners guide to effective intervention. Paul Bellringer. London: Free Association, 1999. 220p. *ISBN: 1853434620, 1853434639.*

5413 What works? A review of evaluated alcohol misuse interventions among Aboriginal Australians. Dennis Gray; Sherry Saggers; Brooke Sputore; Deirdre Bourbon. **Addiction** 9:51 1:2000 pp.11-22.

Homelessness
Sans-abri

5414 Changing attitudes toward the homeless: the effects of prosocial communication with the homeless. John E. Hocking; Samuel G. Lawrence. **J. Soc. Distr. Home.** 9:2 4:2000 pp.91-110.

5415 Ex-servicemen on the road: travel and homelessness. Paul Higate. **Sociol. Rev.** 48:3 8:2000 pp.331-348.
5416 Family homelessness: more than simply a lack of housing. Karleen Jackson. New York, London: Garland Publishing, 2000. xx, 158p. *ISBN: 0815335814. Includes bibliographical references (p. 145-153) and index. (Series:* Garland studies on children of poverty).
5417 The hidden and emerging spaces of rural homelessness. Paul Cloke; Paul Milbourne; Rebekah C. Widdowfield. **Envir. Plan. A.** 32:1 1:2000 pp.77-90.
5418 Homelessness and rurality: 'out-of-place' in purified space? Paul Cloke; Paul Milbourne; Rebekah Widdowfield. **Envir. Plan. D.** 18:6 12:2000 pp.715-736.
5419 Imaging homelessness and homeless people: visions and strategies within the movement(s). Rob Rosenthal. **J. Soc. Distr. Home.** 9:2 4:2000 pp.111-126.
5420 Itinérance et santé mentale. *[In French]*; [Homelessness and mental health]. Danielle Laberge; Daphné Morin; Shirley Roy; Marielle Rozier; Michel Parazelli; Véronique Lussier; Mario Poirier; Diane Aubin; Joyce Tryssenaar; Shannon Wilkinson; Cathy Bailey; Michel Simard; Marie-France Thibaudeau; Jean Fortier; Hélène Denoncourt; Marcel Desilets; Marie-Carmen Plante; Johanne Lapante; Micheline Choquet; Hugues Poirier; Jean-Pierre Bonin; Alain Lesage; Daniel Reinharz. **San. Ment. Qué** XXV:2 Autumn:2000 pp.9-215. *Collection of 9 articles.*
5421 Linking practice and science in the substance abuse treatment of homeless persons. Joseph E. Schumacher; Jesse B. Milby; Molly Engle; James M. Raczynski; Max Michael. **J. App. Behav. Sc.** 36:3 9:2000 pp.297-313.
5422 Meeting homeless people's needs: service development and practice for the older excluded. A.M. Warnes; Maureen Crane. London: King's Fund Publishing, 2000. xii, 198p. *ISBN: 1857172531.*
5423 La misère dans la rue. *[In French]*; [Destitution in the street]. Jean-Claude Girardin. **Temps Mod.** 55:609 6-8:2000 pp.363-382.
5424 Of nomads and vagrants: single homelessness and narratives of home as place. Jon May. **Envir. Plan. D.** 18:6 12:2000 pp.737-759.
5425 'Please ask me how I am': experiences of family homelessness in the context of single mothers' lives. Thomas H. Styron; Ronnie Janoff-Bulman; Larry Davidson. **J. Soc. Distr. Home.** 9:2 4:2000 pp.143-165.
5426 Response to homelessness in Tempe, Arizona: public opinion and government policy. Sarah J. Brinegar. **Urban Geogr.** 21:6 8-9:2000 pp.497-513.
5427 Still running: children on the streets in the UK. Safe on the Streets Research Team. London: Children's Society, 1999. 196p. *ISBN: 1899783318.*
5428 Street children in Africa: a Nairobi case study. Aylward Shorter; Edwin Onyancha. Nairobi: Paulines Publications, 1999. 120p. *Includes bibliographical references.*
5429 Sub city: young people, homelessness and crime. Julia Wardhaugh. Aldershot: Ashgate, 1999. 170p. *ISBN: 1859725104.*
5430 Surviving on the streets of Java: homeless children's narratives of violence. Laine Berman. **Disc. Soc.** 11:2 4:2000 pp.149-174.
5431 Young homeless people. Suzanne Fitzpatrick. New York; Basingstoke: St. Martin's Press; Macmillan, 2000. ix, 172p. *ISBN: 0333773349, 0312226179. Includes bibliographical references and index.*

Suicide
Suicide

5432 Effects of societal integration, period, region, and culture of suicide on male age-specific suicide rates: 20 developed countries, 1955-1989. Phillips Cutright; Robert M. Fernquist. **Soc. Sci. R.** 29:1 3:2000 pp.148-172.
5433 Joint heavy use of alcohol, cigarettes and coffee, and the risk of suicide. Antti Tanskanen; Jaakko Tuomilehto; Heimo Vinamäki; Erkki Vartiainen; Johannes Lehtonen; Pekka Puska. **Addiction** 95:11 11:2000 pp.1699-1718.

5434 A last defence: the negotiation of blame within suicide notes. L. McClelland; S. Reicher; N. Booth. **J. Comm. App. Soc. Psychol.** 10:3 5-6:2000 pp.225-240.
5435 Media impacts on suicide: a quantitative review of 293 findings. Steven Stack. **Soc. Sci. Q.** 81:4 12:2000 pp.957-971.
5436 Status integration and suicide: occupational, marital, or both? Jack Gibbs. **Soc. Forc.** 79:2 12:2000 pp.363-384.

Violence
Violence

5437 Aggressive behavior as a function of identity type among individuals and groups. Malca Aleck; Yoel Yinon. **Megamot** XL:3 8:2000 pp.382-412.
5438 Becoming 'real men': adolescent masculinity challenges and sexual violence. James W. Messerschmidt. **Men. Masc.** 2:3 1:2000 pp.286-307.
5439 Candies in hell: women's experiences of violence in Nicaragua. Mary Ellsberg; Rodolfo Peña; Andrés Herrera; Jerker Liljestrand; Anna Winkvist. **Soc. Sci. Med.** 51:11 12:2000 pp.1595-1610.
5440 Community cohesion and violent predatory victimization: a theoretical extension and cross-national test of opportunity theory. Matthew R. Lee. **Soc. Forc.** 79:2 12:2000 pp.683-706.
5441 Comparing the context of immigrant homicides in Miami: Haitians, Jamaicans and Mariels. Ramiro Martinez, Jr.; Matthew T. Lee. **Int. Migr. Rev.** 34:3 Fall:2000 pp.794-812.
5442 Conducting ethical research on sensitive topics: lessons from gender-based violence research in Southern Africa. Rachel Jewkes; Charlotte Watts; Naeema Abrahams; Loveday Penn-Kekana; Claudia García Moreno. **Reprod. Health Mat.** 8:15 5:2000 pp.93-103.
5443 Confronting gender-based violence with international instruments: is a solution to the pandemic within reach? Jennifer L. Ulrich. **Ind. J. Glob. Legal Stud.** 7:2 Spring:2000 pp.629-654.
5444 Courtship violence among college students: a comparison of verbally and physically abusive couples. Nancy J. Shook; Deborah A. Gerrity; Joan Jurich; Allen E. Segrist. **J. Fam. Viol.** 15:1 3:2000 pp.1-22.
5445 Estudios de criminalidad y violencia. *[In Spanish]*; [Studies on criminality and violence]. François Bourguignon; Alfredo Sarmiento Gómez; Manuel Fernando Castro; Jorge Arabia Wartenberg; Andrés Eduardo Celis; Hugo Aristizábal; Juan Carlos Palou. **Rev. Plan. Desar.** XXX:3 7-9:1999 pp.7-172. *Collection of 5 articles.*
5446 Exploring how Chinese define violence against women: a focus group study in Hong Kong. Catherine So-Kum Tang; Day Wong; Fanny M.C. Cheung; Antoinette Lee. **Wom. St. Inter. For.** 23:2 3-4:2000 pp.197-210.
5447 Exposure to community violence: defining the problem and understanding the consequences. Stacy Overstreet. **J. Child Fam. Stud.** 9:1 3:2000 pp.7-26.
5448 Football violence. E.R. Muller; U. Rosenthal; B. Krop; A.G.W. Ruitenberg; Eric Dunning; Julian V. Roberts; Cynthia J. Benjamin; Antonio Roversi; Carlo Balestri; Stéfan De Vreese. **Eur. J. Crim. Pol. Res.** 8:2 6:2000 pp.125-223. *Collection of 5 articles.*
5449 Forced sexual intercourse among intimates. Ida M. Johnson; Robert T. Sigler. **J. Fam. Viol.** 15:1 3:2000 pp.95-108.
5450 Gangs: an international approach. Sean Grennan; et al. Upper Saddle River NJ: Prentice Hall, 2000. 479p. *ISBN: 0133248569. Includes bibliographical references and index.*
5451 Gender, violence and the social order. Jayne Mooney. Basingstoke: Macmillan, 2000. 224p. *ISBN: 0333734807, 033391886X. Includes bibliographical references and index.*
5452 Gewaltkriminalität junger Deutscher und Ausländer. Brisante Befunde, die irritieren: Eine Erwiderung auf Ulrich Mueller. *[In German]*; (Violent crimes committed by native and foreign juveniles in Germany. Empirical results that confuse: a rejoinder to Ulrich Müller.)

K: PROBLÈMES SOCIAUX. BIEN-ÊTRE SOCIAL. TRAVAIL SOCIAL

[Summary]. Dirk Enzmann; Peter Wetzels. **Kölner Z. Soz. Soz. Psy.** 52:1 3:2000 pp.142-156.

5453 Homicidas em Portugal. *[In Portuguese]*; [Homicide in Portugal]. Fernando Almeida. Maia: Instituto Superior da Maia, 1999. 549p. *ISBN: 9729048045. Includes bibliographical references (p. 527-549).*

5454 How the West was one: explaining the similarities in race-specific homicide rates in the West and South. Karen F. Parker; Matthew V. Pruitt. **Soc. Forc.** 78:4 6:2000 pp.1483-1508.

5455 Increasing returns and the evolution of violent crime: the case of Colombia. Alejandro Gaviria. **J. Dev. Econ.** 61:1 2:2000 pp.1-26.

5456 Juvenile-perpetrated sex crimes: patterns of offending and predictors of violence. John A. Hunter; Robert R. Hazelwood; David Slesinger. **J. Fam. Viol.** 15:1 3:2000 pp.81-94.

5457 Male victims of sexual assault. Gillian C. Mezey [Ed.]; Michael B. King [Ed.]. Oxford: Oxford University Press, 2000. xiii, 161p. *ISBN: 0192629328. Includes bibliographical references and index. (Series:* Oxford medical publications).

5458 'Marrying my rapist?!' The cultural trauma among Chinese rape survivors. Tsun-yin Luo. **Gender Soc.** 14:4 8:2000 pp.581-597.

5459 Militarization and gender violence in south Sudan. Jok Madut Jok. **J. As. Afr. S.** XXXIV:4 11:1999 pp.427-442.

5460 Motivation and psychosis in schizophrenic men who sexually assault women. Alan Smith. **J. For. Psy.** 11:1 4:2000 pp.62-73.

5461 Le point de vue des enfants sur la construction des liens sociaux: l'exemple de la violence entre élèves. *[In French]*; (Construction of social ties from the children's point of view: the example of violence among pupils.) *[Summary].* Cléopâtre Montandon; Loraine Dominicé. **Schweiz. Z. Soziologie** 26:2 7:2000 pp.319-344.

5462 Rape and rape avoidance in ethno-national conflicts: sexual violence in liminalized states. Robert M. Hayden. **Am. Anthrop.** 102:1 3:2000 pp.27-41.

5463 Responding to gender violence in Albania: a partnership effort. Mary P. Van Hook; Edlira Haxhiymeri; Eglantina Gjermeni. **Int. Soc. Work** 43:3 7:2000 pp.351-364.

5464 Salokha: a response to communal riots, a social disaster. Helen Joseph. **Indian J. Soc. W.** 61:4 10:2000 pp.664-674.

5465 School violence. Stuart Henry; J. Scott Staples; Ralph Cintron; Douglas E. Thompkins; Peter J. Venturelli; Wayne N. Welsh; Lissa J. Yogan; Ronald C. Kramer; A. Troy Adams; Hal Pepinsky; Susan L. Caulfield; Jane Nicholson; Edward L. Cohn; William G. Hinkle. **Ann. Am. Poli.** 567 1:2000 pp.16-208. *Collection of 13 articles.*

5466 Societies of fear: the legacy of civil war, violence and terror in Latin America. Kees Koonings [Ed.]; Dirk Kruijt [Ed.]. London: Zed Books, 1999. xii, 335p. *ISBN: 1856497666, 1856497674. Includes bibliographical references (p. [301]-327) and index.*

5467 States of conflict: gender, violence, and resistance. Susie M. Jacobs [Ed.]; Ruth Jacobson [Ed.]; Jennifer Marchbank [Ed.]. London; New York: Zed Books, 2000. ix, 246p. *ISBN: 1856496554, 1856496562. Includes bibliographical references and index.*

5468 The systemic conditions leading to violent human behavior. Kenneth G. Roy. **J. App. Behav. Sc.** 36:4 12:2000 pp.389-406.

5469 Violence against women: a threat to Nigerian society. D.O. Akintunde. **Orita** XXXI:1-2 6-12:1999 pp.122-133.

5470 Violence and sexual coercion in high school students' dating relationships. Susan M. Jackson; Fiona Cram; Fred W. Seymour. **J. Fam. Viol.** 15:1 3:2000 pp.23-36.

5471 Violence as a public health issue; *[Summary in French]*; *[Summary in Spanish]*. Jane Keithley; Fred Robinson. **Policy Pol.** 28:1 1:2000 pp.67-77.

5472 La violence des jeunes aux États-Unis. *[In French]*; [Juvenile violence in the U.S.A.]. Patrick Carr. **Projet** 263 9:2000 pp.24-34.

5473 Violent incidents on a medium secure unit: the target of assault and the management of incidents. Gisli Gudjonsson; Sophia Rabe-Hesketh; Claire Wilson. **J. For. Psy.** 11:1 4:2000 pp.105-118.

K: SOCIAL PROBLEMS. SOCIAL WELFARE. SOCIAL WORK

5474 Women, violence and strategies for action: feminist research, policy and practice. Jill Radford [Ed.]; Melissa Friedberg [Ed.]; Lynne Harne [Ed.]. Buckingham, Philadelphia PA: Open University Press, 2000. x, 193p. *ISBN: 0335203701, 0335203698. Includes bibliographical references and index.*

K.2: Social welfare
Bien-être social

5475 Aide et action sociale: qui paye? *[In French]*; [Aid and social action: who's paying?] Philippe Ligneau; Marie Ruault; Pierre Grelley; Louis Souchal; Jean-Pierre Worms; Christine Chognot; Francine Fenet; Johan Priou; Arnaud Vinsonneau; Xavier Bureau; Marie-Ève Joël; Bernard Friot; Nathalie Des Gayets; Marc Loriol. **Inf. Soc.** 87 2000 pp.4-107. *Collection of 11 articles.*
5476 The conduct of philanthropy: the William Sutton Trust, 1900-2000. Patricia L. Garside. New Brunswick NJ: Athlone Press, 1999. 295p. *ISBN: 048511531X. Includes bibliographical references and index.*
5477 Emotional life and the politics of welfare. Paul Hoggett. Basingstoke: Macmillan, 2000. 248p. *ISBN: 0333760719. Includes bibliographical references.*
5478 For-profit and nonprofit human services: a comparative analysis. Hillel Schmid. **Soc. Sec.** 6 2:2000 pp.161-179.
5479 Husbands caring for wives with dementia: a longitudinal study of continuity and change. Betty J. Kramer. **Health Soc. Work** 25:2 5:2000 pp.97-107.
5480 Increasing access and providing social services to improve drug abuse treatment for women with children. Jeanne C. Marsh; Thomas A. D'Aunno; Brenda D. Smith. **Addiction** 95:8 8:2000 pp.1237-1247.
5481 The newer deal: social work and religion in partnership. Ram A. Cnaan; Stephanie C. Boddie; Robert J. Wineburg. New York: Columbia University Press, 1999. xiii, 368p. *ISBN: 0231116241, 023111625X. Includes bibliographical references (p. [315]-346) and indexes.*
5482 Personal social services in Israel: main issues and dilemmas. Joseph Katan. **Soc. Sec.** 6 2:2000 pp.137-160.
5483 Race, gender, social welfare: encounters in a post-colonial society. Gail Lewis. Cambridge: Polity Press, 2000. xiv, 233p. *ISBN: 0745622844, 0745622852. Includes bibliographical references and index.*
5484 Rhetorics of welfare: uncertainty, choice and voluntary associations. Kevin M. Brown. Basingstoke: Macmillan, 2000. 288p. *ISBN: 0333803590. Includes index.*
5485 Risk, trust and welfare. Peter Taylor-Gooby [Ed.]. Basingstoke: Macmillan, 2000. xv, 240p. *ISBN: 0333764900, 0333764935. Includes index.*
5486 The role of the economic sector in the provision of care to trusting clients. Erna Gelles. **Non. Manag. Leader.** 10:3 Spring:2000 pp.233-250.
5487 The stratification of social entitlements in China. Zhiyue Bo. **Asian Prof.** 27:3 6:1999 pp.189-204.
5488 Stress factors and mental health of carers with relatives suffering from schizophrenia in Hong Kong: implications for culturally sensitive practices. Daniel F.K. Wong. **Br. J. Soc. W.** 30:3 6:2000 pp.365-382.
5489 Welfare after communism. Janos Kornai. London: Social Market Foundation, Centre for Post-Collective Studies, 1999. 45p. *ISBN: 1874097380.*
5490 What kind of people are we? 'Race', anti-racism and social welfare research. Margaret Boushel. **Br. J. Soc. W.** 30:1 2:2000 pp.71-90.
5491 Which way for voluntary housing associations in Ireland? Padraic Kenna. **Administration** 48:3 Autumn:2000 pp.21-41.

K: PROBLÈMES SOCIAUX. BIEN-ÊTRE SOCIAL. TRAVAIL SOCIAL

Care of the aged
Aide aux personnes âgées

5492 Acting up: role ambiguity and the legal recognition of carers. Brenda Gillies. **Age. Soc.** 20:4 7:2000 pp.429-444.
5493 The ageing and development report: poverty, independence and the world's older people. Judith Randel [Ed.]; Tony German [Ed.]; Deborah Ewing [Ed.]. London: Earthscan, 1999. xvi, 200p. *ISBN: 1853836486. Includes bibliographical references.*
5494 Ageing in Portugal: regional iniquities in health and health care. Paula Santana. **Soc. Sci. Med.** 50:7-8 4:2000 pp.1025-1036.
5495 Bridging the divide: elders and the assessment process. Sally Richards. **Br. J. Soc. W.** 30:1 2:2000 pp.37-50.
5496 Broadening our vision of housing and community care for older people: innovative examples from Finland, Sweden and England. Judith Phillips [Ed.]; et al. Oxford: Anchor Trust, 1999. 85p. *ISBN: 0906178347.*
5497 Caring for older people: an assessment of community care in the 1990s. Linda Bauld; et al. Aldershot: Ashgate, 2000. xx, 408p. *ISBN: 0754612805. Includes bibliographical references and index. Personal Social Services Research Unit, University of Kent at Canterbury.*
5498 Caring for the elderly in Japan and the US: practices and policies. Susan Orpett Long [Ed.]. New York: Routledge, 2000. 358p. *ISBN: 0415223520. Includes bibliographical references.*
5499 Coming up for care: assessing the post-hospital needs of older patients. Judith Healy; et al. London: Policy Studies Institute, 1999. x, 146p. *ISBN: 0853747679. (Series: PSI report - 866).*
5500 (A comparative study of the welfare services for the aged in Tochigi and Gunma prefectures.); *[Text in Japanese].* Kunio Sue. **J. Tokyo Keizai Uni.** 217 3:2000 pp.33-59.
5501 Continuing to pay: the consequences for family caregivers of an older person's admission to a care home. Fay Wright. **Soc. Pol. Admin.** 34:2 6:2000 pp.191-205.
5502 Dementia in focus: research, care and policy into the 21st century. Centre on Policy on Ageing. London: Centre for Policy on Ageing, 1998. v, 90p. *ISBN: 1901097307. (Series: CPA reports - 24).*
5503 Expectations and attitudes affecting patterns of informal care in farming families in Northern Ireland. Deirdre Heenan. **Age. Soc.** 20:2 3:2000 pp.203-216.
5504 The future of long-term care in Israel. Rachelle Kaye. **Soc. Sec.** 6 2:2000 pp.98-123.
5505 Gender and elder care: social change and the role of the caregiver in Japan. Susan Orpett Long; Phyllis Braudy Harris. **Soc. Sci. Jap. J.** 3:1 4:2000 pp.21-36.
5506 Germany's long-term-care insurance: putting a social insurance model into practice. Max Geraedts; Geoffrey V. Heller; Charlene A. Harrington. **Milbank Q.** 78:3 2000 pp.375-401.
5507 Gesundheitsausgaben, Alter und medizinischer Fortschritt. *[In German];* (Ageing, medical progress and health care expenditures.) *[Summary].* Friedrich Breyer; Volker Ulrich. **Jahrb. N. St.** 220:1 1:2000 pp.1-17.
5508 Health care professionals' support for older carers. Susan Pickard; Sandra Shaw; Caroline Glendinning. **Age. Soc.** 20:6 11:2000 pp.725-744.
5509 Homelike housing for elderly people — materialized ideology. E. Lundgren. **Hous. Th. Soc.** 17:3 2000 pp.109-120.
5510 How important is parenthood? Childlessness and support in old age in England. G. Clare Wenger; Anne Scott; Nerys Patterson. **Age. Soc.** 20:2 3:2000 pp.161-182.
5511 How likely is community care to be an option? Anthea Tinker. **Administration** 48:3 Autumn:2000 pp.62-74.
5512 The impact of modernisation and social policy on family care for older people in Japan. Makoto Kono. **J. Soc. Pol.** 29:2 4:2000 pp.181-203.
5513 Integration of services for the elderly: a proposed model. Jochanan Stessman; Robert Hamerman-Rozenberg; Yoram Maaravi; Aaron Cohen. **Soc. Sec.** 6 2:2000 pp.124-136.

K: SOCIAL PROBLEMS. SOCIAL WELFARE. SOCIAL WORK

5514 Is the health of older persons in OECD countries improving fast enough to compensate for population ageing? S. Jacobzone; Emmanuelle Cambois; Jean-Marie Robine. **OECD Ec. Stud.** 30(1) 2000 pp.149-190.

5515 Long-term care restructuring in rural Ontario: retrieving community service user and provider narratives. Denise Cloutier-Fisher; Alun E. Joseph. **Soc. Sci. Med.** 50:7-8 4:2000 pp.1037-1046.

5516 Meeting the mental health needs of older women: taking social inequality into account. Alisoun Milne; Jennie Williams. **Age. Soc.** 20:6 11:2000 pp.699-724.

5517 Place attachment and social support at continuing care retirement communities. Shiho Sugihara; Gary W. Evans. **Envir. Behav.** 32:3 5:2000 pp.400-409.

5518 Poor health and retirement income: the Canadian case. Lynn McDonald; Peter Donahue. **Age. Soc.** 20:5 9:2000 pp.493-522.

5519 Population aging and the need for long term care: a comparison of the United States and the people's Republic of China. Pamela Arnsberger; Patrick Fox; Xiulan Zhang; Shixun Gui. **J. Cr-Cult. Gerontol.** 15:3 2000 pp.207-228.

5520 Potential and active family caregivers: changing networks and the 'sandwich generation'. Brenda C. Spillman; Liliana E. Pezzin. **Milbank Q.** 78:3 2000 pp.347-374.

5521 Preparation for future care needs: styles of preparation used by older Eastern German, United States, and Canadian women. Silvia Sörensen; Martin Pinquart. **J. Cr-Cult. Gerontol.** 15:4 2000 pp.349-381.

5522 Private residential care for older persons: local impacts of care in the community reforms in England and Wales. Gavin J. Andrews; David R. Phillips. **Soc. Pol. Admin.** 34:2 6:2000 pp.206-222.

5523 The provision of assured support for older people. M Sturge. Manchester Statistical Society, 1999. 20p. *ISBN: 0853361517.*

5524 Regulatory factors of medical care expenditures for older people in Japan — analysis based on secondary medical care areas in Hokkaido. Yoshinori Fujiwara; Tanji Hoshi; Shouji Shinkai; Toru Kita. **Health Pol.** 53:1 8:2000 pp.39-60.

5525 Relying on informal care in the new century? Informal care for elderly people in England to 2031. Linda Pickard; Raphael Wittenberg; Adelina Comas-Herrera; Bleddyn Davies; Robin Darton. **Age. Soc.** 20:6 11:2000 pp.745-772.

5526 (Requesting the operation of the Japanese care insurance system for the elderly: case study on the care insurance system for the elderly in a suburban city of Tokyo.); *[Text in Japanese].* Seiichi Yoda. **J. Tokyo Keizai Uni.** 217 3:2000 pp.125-134.

5527 Researching social care for minority ethnic older people: implications of some Scottish research. A.M. Bowes; N.S. Dar. **Br. J. Soc. W.** 30:3 6:2000 pp.305-322.

5528 The residency decision of elderly Indonesians: a nested logit analysis. Lisa Cameron. **Demography** 37:1 2:2000 pp.17-28.

5529 The role of culture in designing environments for people with dementia: a study of Russian Jewish immigrants. Kristen Day; Uriel Cohen. **Envir. Behav.** 32:3 5:2000 pp.361-399.

5530 The role of family care-givers for an older person resident in a care home. Fay Wright. **Br. J. Soc. W.** 30:5 10:2000 pp.649-661.

5531 The roles of friends and neighbours in providing support for older people. Andrew Nocon; Maggie Pearson. **Age. Soc.** 20:3 5:2000 pp.341-367.

5532 Social support exchange and quality of life among the Korean elderly. Hye-kyung Kim; Mitsuru Hisata; Ichiro Kai; Sung-kook Lee. **J. Cr-Cult. Gerontol.** 15:4 2000 pp.331-347.

5533 Social support in later life: a study of three areas. Judith Phillips; Miriam Bernard; Chris Phillipson; Jim Ogg. **Br. J. Soc. W.** 30:6 12:2000 pp.837-853.

5534 Socialising disease: medical categories and inclusion of the aged. Joanna Latimer. **Sociol. Rev.** 48:3 8:2000 pp.383-407.

5535 SSI eligibility and participation among elderly naturalized citizens and noncitizens. Jennifer Van Hook. **Soc. Sci. R.** 29:1 3:2000 pp.51-69.

5536 Thinking about the production and consumption of long-term care in Britain: does gender still matter? Clare Ungerson. **J. Soc. Pol.** 29:4 10:2000 pp.623-643.

K: PROBLÈMES SOCIAUX. BIEN-ÊTRE SOCIAL. TRAVAIL SOCIAL

Child welfare
Bien-être des enfants

5537 L'accueil des jeunes enfants: concentration des équipements et inégalités d'accès aux services. *[In French]*; (Young child welfare. Facilities concentration and differences in access to family care services.) Olivier David. **Espace Pop. Soc.** 3 1999 pp.483-498.

5538 Adoption. Douglas B. Henderson; Michael F. McGinn; René Hoksbergen; Jan ter Laak; Amanda L. Baden; Robbie J. Steward; Mary Jo Carr; Daniel A. Sass; Diana E. Post. **J. Soc. Distr. Home.** 9:4 10:2000 pp.261-372. *Collection of 7 articles.*

5539 Ambition for change: partnership, children and work. Ann Jamieson; Sue Owen. London: National Children's Bureau, 2000. viii, 104p. *ISBN: 1900990520.*

5540 Assessing the local need for family and child care services: a small area utilization analysis. Andrew Percy; Roy Carr-Hill; Paul Dixon; James Q. Jamison. **Child Wel.** LXXIX:5 9-10:2000 pp.535-554.

5541 Caretakers, child care practices, and growth failure in highland Ecuador. James P. Stansbury; William R. Leonard; Kathleen M. DeWalt. **Med. Anthr. Q.** 14:2 6:2000 pp.224-241.

5542 Child care with gloves on: protecting children and young people in residential care. Jan Horwath. **Br. J. Soc. W.** 30:2 4:2000 pp.179-191.

5543 Child maltreatment: differences in perceptions between parents in low income and middle income neighbourhoods. Ron Shor. **Br. J. Soc. W.** 30:2 4:2000 pp.165-178.

5544 Child sexual assault: feminist perspectives. Joy Trotter [Ed.]; Pat Cox [Ed.]; Sheila Kershaw [Ed.]; Liz Kelly [Foreword]. Basingstoke: Palgrave, 2000. 209p. *ISBN: 0333771532. Includes bibliographical references and index.*

5545 Child sexual exploitation/child prostitution: how can the views of the young people involved inform multi-agency practice towards a more effective means of working in partnership with them? Jane M. Dodsworth. Norwich: School of Social Work, University of East Anglia, 2000. ii, 54p. *ISBN: 1857840720. Includes bibliographical references (p. 49-54). (Series:* Social work monographs - no. 178).

5546 Childhood in question: children, parents and the state. Stephen Hussey [Ed.]; Anthony J. Fletcher [Ed.]. Manchester: Manchester University Press, 1999. 177p. *ISBN: 0719053935, 0719053943. Includes bibliographical references and index.*

5547 Children and social exclusion: towards an understanding and practice that is more inclusive. Keith J. White [Ed.]. London: National Council of Voluntary Child Care Organisations, 1999. 126p. *ISBN: 1870575075.*

5548 Children and the state: whose problem? Jane Tunstill [Ed.]. London: Cassell, 1999. ix, 181p. *ISBN: 0304705217, 0304705209. Includes bibliographical references and index.*

5549 Children and young people with a hidden disability: an examination of the social work role. Judith Cavet. **Br. J. Soc. W.** 30:5 10:2000 pp.619-634.

5550 Children's adjustment over time in foster care: cross-informant agreement, stability and placement disruption. Colette McAuley; Karen Trew. **Br. J. Soc. W.** 30:1 2:2000 pp.91-108.

5551 Children's welfare exposure and subsequent development. Phillip Levine; David J. Zimmerman. Cambridge MA: National Bureau of Economic Research, 2000. 26p. *(Series:* NBER working paper - 7522).

5552 Concept mapping the needs of foster parents. Jason Brown; Peter Calder. **Child Wel.** LXXIX:6 11-12:2000 pp.729-746.

5553 Contested identities: the adoption of American Indian children and the liberal state. M.M. Slaughter. **Soc. Leg. Stud.** 9:2 6:2000 pp.227-248.

5554 Dangerous care: working to protect children. Renuka Jeyarajah Dent [Ed.]. London: Bridge Child Care Development Service, 1998. ix, 102p. *ISBN: 0951608886. Includes bibliographical references.*

5555 Data-based organizational change: the use of administrative data to improve child welfare programs and policy. Diana J. English; Carol C. Brandford; Laura Coghlan. **Child Wel.** LXXIX:5 9-10:2000 pp.499-516.

K: SOCIAL PROBLEMS. SOCIAL WELFARE. SOCIAL WORK

5556 Decision making by senior social workers at point of first referral. Trevor Spratt. **Br. J. Soc. W.** 30:5 10:2000 pp.597-618.
5557 Discovering what children think: connections between research and practice. Nigel Thomas; Clair O'Kane. **Br. J. Soc. W.** 30:6 12:2000 pp.819-836.
5558 Disparition de mineurs: approche comparée du phénomène des disparitions de mineurs et des incriminations relatives aux abus sexuels sur enfants. *[In French]*; [The disappearance of minors: a comparative approach to the phenomenon of missing children and accusations related to sexual abuse of children]. Emmanuel-Roger France. Ramonville Saint-Agne: Erès, 1999. 120p. *ISBN: 2865867382. Includes bibliographical references and index.*
5559 'Don't shake the baby': towards a prevention strategy. Julie Shepherd; Alice Simpson. **Br. J. Soc. W.** 30:6 12:2000 pp.721-735.
5560 The draft for child protection and the public attitudes towards the policy for children in Bulgaria. Velina Todorova. **Int. J. Child. Rig.** 8:2 2000 pp.169-184.
5561 The effectiveness of CASAs in achieving positive outcomes for children. Pat Litzelfelner. **Child Wel.** LXXIX:2 3-4:2000 pp.179-196.
5562 Effects of age and delay on the amount of information provided by alleged sex abuse victims in investigative interviews. Michael E. Lamb; Kathleen J. Sternberg; Phillip W. Esplin. **Child. Devel.** 71:6 11-12:2000 pp.1586-1596.
5563 Ethnoracial awareness in intercountry adoption: US experiences. Carol Carstens; María Juliá. **Int. Soc. Work** 43:1 1:2000 pp.61-74.
5564 Excluding children: autonomy, friendship and the experience of the care system. Tess Ridge; Jane Millar. **Soc. Pol. Admin.** 34:2 6:2000 pp.160-175.
5565 Expensive children in poor families: out-of-pocket expenditures for the care of disabled and chronically ill children in welfare families. Anna Lukemeyer; Marcia K. Meyers; Timothy Smeeding. **J. Marriage Fam.** 62:2 5:2000 pp.399-415.
5566 Fathers and family centres: engaging fathers in preventive services. Deborah Ghate; Catherine Shaw; Neal Hazel. York: York Publishing Services, 2000. 56p. *ISBN: 1902633490. Joseph Rowntree Foundation.*
5567 Father's fair share: helping poor men manage child support and fatherhood. Earl Johnson; Fred C. Doolittle; Ann Levine. New York: Russell Sage Foundation, 1999. xiv, 241p. *ISBN: 0871544113. Includes bibliographical references and index.*
5568 From foster care to fostering care: the need for community. Martha Bauman Power; Brenda Krause Eheart. **Sociol. Q.** 41:1 Winter:2000 pp.85-102.
5569 Future challenges and opportunities in child welfare. Brenda G. McGowan; Elaine M. Walsh; Susan Kelly; Betty J. Blythe; Jane Waldfogel; James K. Whittaker; John R. Seita; Elizabeth M. Tracy; Barbara A. Pine; Anthony N. Maluccio. **Child Wel.** LXXIX:1 1-2:2000 pp.3-122. *Collection of 7 articles.*
5570 Going missing from residential and foster care: linking biographies and contexts. Nina Biehal; Jim Wade. **Br. J. Soc. W.** 30:2 4:2000 pp.211-225.
5571 Hacia un nuevo sistema de políticas públicas: situación de la infancia en la provincia de Buenos Aires. *[In Spanish]*; [Towards a new public policy system: the case of children in the province of Buenos Aires]. Gerardo Codina. Buenos Aires: Fundación Acción para la Comunidad, 1999. 123p. *ISBN: 9879717112.*
5572 Helping parents, protecting children: ideas from Germany. Karen Baistow; Gerti Wilford. **Child. Soc.** 14:5 11:2000 pp.343-354.
5573 The heterogeneity of children and their experiences in kinship care. Laurel K. Leslie; John Landsverk; Mark B. Horton; William Ganger; Rae R. Newton. **Child Wel.** LXXIX:3 5-6:2000 pp.315-334.
5574 Home-Start and the delivery of family support. Nick Frost; Liz Johnson; Mike Stein; Lorraine Wallis. **Child. Soc.** 14:5 11:2000 pp.328-342.
5575 The immunisation status of poor children: an analysis of parental altruism and child well-being. John J. Hisnanick; Dale A. Coddington. **R. Soc. Econ.** LVIII:1 3:2000 pp.81-107.
5576 Implementing the right to community integration for children with disabilities in Russia: a human rights framework for international action; *[Summary in French]*; [Summary in

K: PROBLÈMES SOCIAUX. BIEN-ÊTRE SOCIAL. TRAVAIL SOCIAL

Spanish]. Eric Rosenthal; Elizabeth Bauer; Mary F. Hayden; Andrea Holley. **Health Hum. Rights** 4:1 1999 pp.82-113.

5577 Intercountry, transracial adoption and ethnic identity: a Korean example. Nam Soon Huh; William J. Reid. **Int. Soc. Work** 43:1 1:2000 pp.75-88.

5578 Linking child maltreatment retrospectively to birth and home visit records: an initial examination. David A. Murphey; Moshe Braner. **Child Wel.** LXXIX:6 11-12:2000 pp.711-728.

5579 Listening to children. Martine F. Delfos. **Child C. Pract.** 6:3 7:2000 pp.229-239.

5580 Loving smack or lawful assault? A contradiction in human rights and law. Christina M. Lyon. London: Institute for Public Policy Research, 2000. viii, 113p. *ISBN: 1860301193. Includes bibliographical references.*

5581 Making child care 'affordable' in the United States. Barbara R. Bergmann. **Soc. Polit.** 6:2 Summer:1999 pp.245-262.

5582 Mapping child maltreatment: looking at neighborhoods in a suburban county. Joy Swanson Ernst. **Child Wel.** LXXIX:5 9-10:2000 pp.555-572.

5583 Mediators and moderators in the evaluation of programs for children: current practice and agenda for improvement. Anthony Petrosino. **Eval. Rev.** 24:1 2:2000 pp.47-72.

5584 Men in the nursery: gender and caring work. Claire Cameron; Peter Moss; Charlie Owen. London: Paul Chapman, 1999. 224p. *ISBN: 185396431X, 1853963887.*

5585 Most vulnerable of all: the treatment of unaccompanied refugee children in the UK. Simon Russell. London: Amnesty International United Kingdom, 1999. 119p. *ISBN: 1873328354. Includes bibliographical references (p. [111]-115) and index.*

5586 Picking up the pieces: local government reorganisation and voluntary sector children's services. Gary Craig; Malcolm Hill; Jill Manthorpe; Kay Tisdall; Bernadette Monaghan; Suzanne Wheelaghan. **Child. Soc.** 14:2 4:2000 pp.85-97.

5587 Placement stability for children in out-of-home care: a longitudinal analysis. Daniel Webster; Richard P. Barth; Barbara Needell. **Child Wel.** LXXIX:5 9-10:2000 pp.614-632.

5588 Policy and practice in childcare and nursery education. Helen Penn. **J. Soc. Pol.** 29:1 1:2000 pp.37-54.

5589 The rediscovery of child neglect. Jonathan Scourfield. **Sociol. Rev.** 48:3 8:2000 pp.365-382.

5590 The role of friends, in-laws, and other kin in father-perpetrated child physical abuse. Carol Coohey. **Child Wel.** LXXIX:4 7-8:2000 pp.373-404.

5591 Sponsored day care in a changing world. June Statham; Jean Dillon; Peter Moss. **Child. Soc.** 14:1 2:2000 pp.23-36.

5592 Street children's drawings: windows into their life circumstances and aspirations. Margaret A. DiCarlo; Judith L. Gibbons; Donald C. Kaminsky; James D. Wright; Deborah A. Stiles. **Int. Soc. Work** 43:1 1:2000 pp.107-128.

5593 Suffer the little children: the inside story of Ireland's industrial schools. Mary Raftery; Eoin O'Sullivan. Dublin: New Island, 1999. 424p. *ISBN: 1874597839. Includes bibliographical references and index.*

5594 Training parents reported for or at risk for child abuse and neglect to identify and treat their children's illnesses. Kathryn M. Bigelow; John R. Lutzker. **J. Fam. Viol.** 15:4 12:2000 pp.311-330.

5595 Trust and betrayal in the treatment of child abuse. Virginia Goldner [Foreword]; Laurie K. MacKinnon. New York: Guilford Press, 1998. xii, 260p. *ISBN: 1572302984. Includes bibliographical references (p. 249-254) and index.*

5596 Understanding reentry to out-of-home care for reunified infants. Laura Frame; Jill Duerr Berrick; Melissa Lim Brodowski. **Child Wel.** LXXIX:4 7-8:2000 pp.339-372.

5597 Using administrative data to assess child safety in out-of-home care. Philip C. Garnier; John Poertner. **Child Wel.** LXXIX:5 9-10:2000 pp.597-613.

5598 The welfare of Europe's children: are EU member states converging? J. Micklewright; Kitty Stewart. Bristol: Policy Press, 2000. vii, 158p. *ISBN: 1861342268. Includes bibliographical references and index.*

K: SOCIAL PROBLEMS. SOCIAL WELFARE. SOCIAL WORK

5599 'Who's crying for whom?' Setting up an under five's counselling service in a social services family centre. Julie Long. **J. Soc. Work. Practice** 14:1 5:2000 pp.51-61.
5600 Women, power and policy: comparative studies of childcare. Jen Marchbank. New York: Routledge, 2000. xvi, 197p. *ISBN: 0415239052, 0415239044. Includes bibliographical references and index.*
5601 Young children's rights. Priscilla Alderson. London: Jessica Kingsley Publishers, 2000. 176p. *ISBN: 1853028800. Includes bibliographical references and index.*

Disability support
Invalidité support

5602 Adults only: disability, social policy and the life course. Mark Priestley. **J. Soc. Pol.** 29:3 7:2000 pp.421-439.
5603 Disability as a phenomenon: a discourse of social and biological understanding. Marianne Hedlund. **Dis. and Soc.** 15:5 8:2000 pp.765-780.
5604 The dynamics of being disabled. Tania Burchardt. **J. Soc. Pol.** 29:4 10:2000 pp.645-668.
5605 A global perspective on social security programmes for disabled people. John Dixon; Mark Hyde. **Dis. and Soc.** 15:5 8:2000 pp.709-730.
5606 The needed and the needy: the policy legacies of benefits for disabled war veterans in Israel. John Gal; Michal Bar. **J. Soc. Pol.** 29:4 10:2000 pp.577-598.
5607 Quality of life and quality of service relationships: experiences of people with disabilities. Ruth Marquis; Robert Jackson. **Dis. and Soc.** 15:3 5:2000 pp.411-426.
5608 Respite care for disabled children: micro and macro reflections. Alison Cocks. **Dis. and Soc.** 15:3 5:2000 pp.507-520.

Welfare state
État-providence

5609 Access to services as a civil and social rights issue: the role of welfare professionals in regulating access to and commissioning services for disabled and older people under New Labour. Kirstein Rummery; Caroline Glendinning. **Soc. Pol. Admin.** 34:5 12:2000 pp.529-550.
5610 AFDC benefits and nonmarital births to young women. Saul D. Hoffman; E. Michael Foster. **J. Hum. Res.** 35:2 Spring:2000 pp.376-391.
5611 Après les HLM. *[In French]*; [After low-cost housing blocks]. Eric Le Lann; Philippe Pivion. Paris: L'Harmattan, 2000. 111p. *ISBN: 2738490212. Includes bibliographical references (p. 109-110).*
5612 Assisted housing and the educational attainment of children. Sandra Newman; Joseph Harkness. **J. Hous. Ec.** 9:1-2 3-6:2000 pp.40-63.
5613 Care work: gender, class, and the welfare state. Madonna Harrington Meyer [Ed.]. New York, London: Routledge, 2000. 348p. *ISBN: 041592541X, 0415925428. Includes index.*
5614 Caring capitalism: a new middle class base for the welfare state. Ronald M. Glassman. Basingstoke: Macmillan, 2000. 296p. *ISBN: 0333773845. Includes index.*
5615 Citizenship in the new welfare market: the purposes of housing advice services. Jo Dean; Robina Goodlad; Ann Rosengard. **J. Soc. Pol.** 29:2 4:2000 pp.229-245.
5616 The concept of social care and the analysis of contemporary welfare states. Mary Daly; Jane Lewis. **Br. J. Soc.** 51:2 6:2000 pp.281-298.
5617 Crime and banishment: nuisance and exclusion in social housing. Elizabeth Burney. Winchester: Waterside Press, 1999. 159p. *ISBN: 1872870791.*
5618 Deniable degradation: the finger-imaging of welfare recipients. Harry Murray. **Sociol. For.** 15:1 3:2000 pp.39-63.
5619 (The development of welfare state theories in Japan and characteristics of these theories.); *[Text in Japanese]*. Hideo Okamoto. **J. Tokyo Keizai Uni.** 217 3:2000 pp.135-166.

K: PROBLÈMES SOCIAUX. BIEN-ÊTRE SOCIAL. TRAVAIL SOCIAL

5620 Ending welfare as we know it (again): welfare state retrenchment. Yvonne Zylan; Sarah Soule. **Soc. Forc.** 79:2 12:2000 pp.623-652.

5621 Ethnic minority housing needs and diversity in an area of low housing demand. Stuart Cameron. **Envir. Plan. A.** 32:8 8:2000 pp.1427-1444.

5622 Europe in a comparative global context. Jens Alber; Guy Standing; Ana M. Guillén; Manos Matsaganis; Bob Deacon; Sven E.O. Hort; Stein Kuhnle; Stephen J. Kay. **J. Europe. Soc. Pol.** 10:2 5:2000 pp.99-203. *Collection of 5 articles.*

5623 European welfare futures: towards a theory of retrenchment. Giuliano Bonoli; Peter Taylor-Gooby; Vic George. Cambridge: Polity Press, 2000. ix, 190p. *ISBN: 0745618103, 0745618111. Includes bibliographical references and index.*

5624 Evaluation of the New Deal for lone parents: early lessons from the phase one prototype - synthesis report. Jon Hales; et al. Leeds: Corporate Document Services, 2000. viii, 100p. *ISBN: 1841231878. Includes bibliographical references. Institute for Employment Research. National Centre for Social Research. Centre for Analysis of Social Policy. (Series:* Department of Social Security research report - 108).

5625 Family change, employment transitions, and the welfare state: household income dynamics in the United States and Germany. Thomas A. DiPrete; Patricia A. McManus. **Am. Sociol. R.** 65:3 6:2000 pp.343-370.

5626 A fresh look at the Japanese welfare state. Ito Peng. **Soc. Pol. Admin.** 34:1 3:2000 pp.87-114.

5627 The Gautreaux legacy: what might mixed-income and dispersal strategies mean for the poorest public housing tenants? Susan J. Popkin; Larry F. Buron; Diane K. Levy; Mary K. Cunningham. **Hous. Pol. Deb.** 11:4 2000 pp.911-942.

5628 The gender division of welfare: the impact of the British and German welfare states. Mary E. Daly. Cambridge, New York: Cambridge University Press, 2000. x, 273p. *ISBN: 0521626218, 0521623316. Includes bibliographical references (p. 255-267) and index.*

5629 Gestión y externalización de programas sociales: caso del Fondo de Inversión Social del Paraguay. *[In Spanish];* [Management and externalization of social programmes: the case of Paraguay's Social Investment Fund]. Leonel Tapia. **Rev. Parag. Sociol.** 36:106 9-12:1999 pp.163-178.

5630 Hope and despair at the front line: observations on integrity and change in the human services. Martyn Jones. **Int. Soc. Work** 43:3 7:2000 pp.365-380.

5631 Housing is not enough: the story of St Pancras Housing Association. Malcolm J. Holmes. London: St. Pancras Housing Association, 1999. 119p. *ISBN: 0950294713. Includes bibliographical references and index.*

5632 Immigration and welfare: challenging the borders of the welfare state. Andrew Geddes [Ed.]; Michael Bommes [Ed.]. London: Routledge, 2000. 291p. *ISBN: 0415223725. Includes bibliographical references and index. (Series:* Routledge/EUI studies in the political economy of welfare - 1).

5633 The impact of welfare reform. Ariel Kalil; LaDonna A. Pavetti; Rukmalie Jayakody; Dawn Stauffer; Nathaniel J. Anderson; Richard M. Tolman; Jody Raphael; Julia R. Henly; Sandra Lyons; Rebekah Levine Coley; Ann M. Kuta; P. Lindsay Chase-Lansdale; Ellen K. Scott; Andrew S. London; Kathryn Edin; Sandra L. Hofferth; Julia Smith; Vonnie C. McLoyd; Jonathan Finkelstein; Sandra K. Danziger; Diana Romero; Wendy Chavkin; Paul H. Wise; Diana M. Zuckerman. **J. Soc. Issues** 56:4 Winter:2000 pp.579-820. *Collection of 13 articles.*

5634 Inheritance of welfare recipiency: an intergenerational study of social assistance recipiency in postwar Sweden. Sten-Åke Stenberg. **J. Marriage Fam.** 62:1 2:2000 pp.228-239.

5635 Local authority social services: an introduction. Michael J. Hill [Ed.]. Oxford: Blackwell Publishers, 2000. xv, 224p. *ISBN: 0631209476, 0631209468. Includes bibliographical references and index.*

5636 Lone female headship and welfare policy in Canada. Martin D. Dooley; Stéphane Gascon; Pierre Lefebvre; Philip Merrigan. **J. Hum. Res.** 35:3 Summer:2000 pp.587-602.

5637 Managing to survive: asylum seekers, refugees and access to social housing. Roger Zetter; Martyn Pearl. Bristol: Policy Press, 1999. 93p. *ISBN: 1861341717.*

K: SOCIAL PROBLEMS. SOCIAL WELFARE. SOCIAL WORK

5638   Migration regimes, intra-state conflicts, and the politics of exclusion and inclusion: migrant workers in the Israeli welfare state. Zeev Rosenhek. **Soc. Prob.** 47:1 2:2000 pp.49-67.

5639   Modernising social services: promoting independence, improving protection, raising standards. Department of Health, House of Commons, UK. London: Stationery Office, 1998. 130p. *ISBN: 010141692X.*

5640   National welfare states, European integration and globalization: a perspective for the next century. Stephan Leibfried. **Soc. Pol. Admin.** 34:1 3:2000 pp.44-63.

5641   Les nouvelles politiques sociales: une comparaison internationale. *[In French]*; (New social policies. An international comparison.) Jean-Michel Bonvin; Nathalie Burnay; François-Xavier Merrien; Christian Maroy; Monica Threlfall; Maurizio Ferrera; François Bafoil; Vassil Kirov; Bernard Francq; Thomas Lemaigre; Gilbert Larochelle. **Recher. Sociolog.** XXX1:2 2000 pp.1-156. *Collection of 9 articles.*

5642   La política social. *[In Spanish]*; [Social policy] *[Summary].* Carlos M. Vilas; Fernando Reimers; Bernardo Kliksberg; María Ester Mancebo; Myriam Cardozo Brum; Luiz Antonio Maciel de Paula; Enrique Contreras Suárez. **Acta Sociol.** [Mexico] 28-29 1-8:2000 pp.15-191. *Collection of 7 articles.*

5643   Popular paradigms and welfare values. Hartley Dean. **Crit. Soc. Pol.** 18:2(55) 5:1998 pp.131-156.

5644   Post-Fordism, the welfare state and the personal social services: a comparison of Australia and Britain. John Harris; Catherine McDonald. **Br. J. Soc. W.** 30:1 2:2000 pp.51-70.

5645   Public sector housing law. David Hughes; Stuart Lowe. London: Butterworths, 2000. liv, 482p. *ISBN: 0406983011. Includes bibliographical references and index.*

5646   Social exclusion and housing: context and challenges. Isobel Anderson [Ed.]; Duncan Sim [Ed.]. Coventry: Chartered Institute of Housing, 2000. 256p. *ISBN: 1900396394. (Series: Housing policy and practice).*

5647   Social policy. John Baldock [Ed.]; et al. Oxford: Oxford University Press, 1999. xxx, 594p. *ISBN: 0198781741, 0198781733. Includes bibliographical references and index.*

5648   Sociální dávky a jejich příjemci: na „sociální trampolíně", nebo ve slepé uličce? *[In Czech]*; (Welfare benefits recipients: on a 'social springboard' or at the dead end?) *[Summary].* Tomáš Sirovátka. **Soc. Čas.** 36:2 2000 pp.181-200.

5649   Sociální nájemní bydlení v ČR ve světle komparativního srovnání. *[In Czech]*; (Social housing in the Czech Republic in a comparative context.) *[Summary].* Martin Lux. **Soc. Čas.** 36:2 2000 pp.157-180.

5650   States of welfare: a conceptual challenge. John Veit-Wilson. **Soc. Pol. Admin.** 34:1 3:2000 pp.1-25.

5651   The Swedish welfare state and the emergence of female welfare state occupations. Lars Evertsson. **Gend. Work & Org.** 7:4 10:2000 pp.230-241.

5652   Three pillars of welfare state theory: T.H. Marshall, Karl Polanyi and Alva Myrdal in defence of the national welfare state. John Holmwood. **Eur. J. Soc. Theory** 3:1 2:2000 pp.23-50.

5653   Time and poverty in Western welfare states: united Germany in perspective. Lutz Leisering; Stephan Leibfried; et al; John Veit-Wilson [Tr.]. Cambridge: Cambridge University Press, 1999. xvi, 379p. *ISBN: 0521590132. Translated from the German Zeit der Armut. Includes bibliographical references and index.*

5654   The twilight of liberal welfare reform. Lawrence M. Mead. **Publ. Inter.** 139 Spring:2000 pp.22-34.

5655   User-initiated extensions as housing supply: a study of government-built housing estates in Malaysia. A. Graham Tipple; A. Salim. **Third World Plan. R.** 21:2 5:1999 pp.119-154.

5656   Vouchers versus production revisited. Mark Shroder; Arthur Reiger. **J. Hous. Res.** 11:1 2000 pp.91-107.

5657   Welfare, exclusion and political agency. Janet Batsleer [Ed.]; Beth Humphries [Ed.]. London, New York: Routledge, 2000. xii, 253p. *ISBN: 0415195136, 0415195144. Includes bibliographical references and index. (Series:* The state of welfare).

K: PROBLÈMES SOCIAUX. BIEN-ÊTRE SOCIAL. TRAVAIL SOCIAL

5658 Welfare reform, substance use, and mental health. Rukmalie Jayakody; Sheldon Danziger; Harold Pollack. **J. Health Polit. Pol. Law** 25:4 8:2000 pp.623-651.

5659 The welfare state: a general theory. Paul Spicker. London: Sage Publications, 2000. vii, 193p. *ISBN: 0761967044, 0761967052.*

5660 The welfare state: a reader. Christopher Pierson [Ed.]; Francis G. Castles [Ed.]. Cambridge: Polity Press, 2000. xii, 403p. *ISBN: 0745622526, 0745622534. Includes bibliographical references and index.*

5661 When children pay: US welfare reform and its implications for UK policy. Rosemary J. Link; Anthony A. Bibus; Karen Lyons. London: Child Poverty Action Group, 2000. 169p. *ISBN: 1901698157.*

5662 The working class and the welfare state support for economic redistribution, tolerance for nonconformity, and the conditionality of solidarity with the unemployed. Dick Houtman. **Neth. J. Soc. Sci.** 36:1 2000 pp.37-55.

K.3: **Social work**
Travail social

5663 8008: the measure of a competent child care social worker? Barry Cooper. **J. Soc. Work. Practice** 14:2 11:2000 pp.113-124.

5664 The addicted offender: developments in policy and practice. Judith Rumgay. New York: St. Martin's Press, 2000. 261p. *ISBN: 033375445X. Includes bibliographical references and index.*

5665 'Anti-oppressive practice': emancipation or appropriation? Anne Wilson; Peter Beresford. **Br. J. Soc. W.** 30:5 10:2000 pp.553-574.

5666 Applying a community needs profiling approach to tackling service user poverty. Roger Green. **Br. J. Soc. W.** 30:3 6:2000 pp.287-304.

5667 The assessment relationship: interactions between social workers and parents in child protection assessments. Sally Holland. **Br. J. Soc. W.** 30:2 4:2000 pp.149-164.

5668 Attachment theory and systemic practice: research update. Jane Akister. **J. Fam. Ther.** 20:4 11:1998 pp.353-366.

5669 Attitudes of low-income parents toward seeking help with parenting: implications for practice. JoDee Keller; Katherine McDade. **Child Wel.** LXXIX:3 5-6:2000 pp.285-314.

5670 Casework: a psychosocial therapy. Mary E Woods; Florence Hollis. Boston MA: McGraw-Hill, 2000. xxviii, 667p. *ISBN: 0072901799. Includes bibliographical references (p. 613-652) and index.*

5671 Children's and adolescents' views on family therapy. Lisa Strickland-Clark; David Campbell; Rudi Dallos. **J. Fam. Ther.** 22:3 8:2000 pp.324-341.

5672 Consultancy to groupwork programmes for adult male sex offenders: some reflections on knowledge and processes. Malcolm Cowburn. **Br. J. Soc. W.** 30:5 10:2000 pp.635-648.

5673 Contemporary perspectives in the evaluation of practice. Mansoor A.F. Kazi. **Br. J. Soc. W.** 30:6 12:2000 pp.755-768.

5674 Counselling skills in social work practice. Janet Seden. Buckingham, Philadelphia PA: Open University Press, 1999. x, 166p. *ISBN: 0335199690, 0335199682. Includes bibliographical references (p. [154]-161) and index.*

5675 The Darlington family assessment system: clinical guidelines for practitioners. Ian Wilkinson. **J. Fam. Ther.** 22:2 5:2000 pp.211-224.

5676 Developing reflective practice: making sense of social work in a world of change. Helen Martyn [Ed.]. Bristol: Policy Press, 2000. xxii, 224p. *ISBN: 1861342381.*

5677 Dialectics in social work. Nai Ming Tsang. **Int. Soc. Work** 43:4 10:2000 pp.421-434.

5678 Dilemmas in international and cross-cultural social work education. Géza Nagy; Diane Falk. **Int. Soc. Work** 43:1 1:2000 pp.49-60.

5679 Ethical practice and the abuse of power in social responsibility: leave no stone unturned. Helen Payne [Ed.]; Brian Littlechild [Ed.]. London: Jessica Kingsley Publishers, 1999. 240p. *ISBN: 185302743X.*

K: SOCIAL PROBLEMS. SOCIAL WELFARE. SOCIAL WORK

5680 Evidence-based practice in family therapy and systemic consultation. I. Alan Carr. **J. Fam. Ther.** 22:1 2:2000 pp.29-60.

5681 Evidence-based practice in family therapy and systemic consultation. II: Adult-focused problems. Alan Carr. **J. Fam. Ther.** 22:3 8:2000 pp.273-295.

5682 Exploring the use of family therapy with adults with a learning disability. Beverley Fidell. **J. Fam. Ther.** 22:3 8:2000 pp.308-323.

5683 From war hero to cripple: an interview study on psychosocial intervention and social reconstruction in Nicaragua. Nora Sveaass; Marcia Castillo. **J. Man. Gov.** 6:2 2000 pp.113-134.

5684 Globalisation: an opportunity for dialogue between South African and Asian social work educators. Sandra J. Drower. **Indian J. Soc. W.** 61:1 1:2000 pp.12-31.

5685 Informal care in farming families in Northern Ireland: some considerations for social work. Deirdre Heenan. **Br. J. Soc. W.** 30:6 12:2000 pp.855-866.

5686 Internationalising social work education. David Cox. **Indian J. Soc. W.** 61:2 4:2000 pp.157-173.

5687 Islamic theology and prayer: relevance for social work practice. Alean Al-Krenawi; John R. Graham. **Int. Soc. Work** 43:3 7:2000 pp.289-304.

5688 Launching of an international census of social work, social development and social services education. Ralph Garber. **Indian J. Soc. W.** 61:2 4:2000 pp.174-188.

5689 Learning from personal experience: reflexions on social work practice with mothers in child and family care. Johanna Sheppard. **J. Soc. Work. Practice** 14:1 5:2000 pp.37-50.

5690 Medical social workers in Hong Kong hospitals: expectation, authority structure and role ambiguity. Chack-kie Wong; Becky Chan; Victor Tam. **Int. Soc. Work** 43:4 10:2000 pp.495-524.

5691 The mixed-based nature of self-help groups in Finland. Marianne Nylund. **Groupwork** 12:2 2000 pp.64-85.

5692 On the link between academia and the practice of social work. Mili Mass. **J. Theory Soc. Behav.** 30:1 3:2000 pp.99-125.

5693 A preventive services program model for preserving and supporting families over time. Peg McCartt Hess; Brenda G. McGowan; Michael Botsko. **Child Wel.** LXXIX:3 5-6:2000 pp.227-268.

5694 Professional social work in India: some issues and strategies. Manohar Pawar. **Indian J. Soc. W.** 60:4 10:1999 pp.566-586.

5695 Remote, northern communities: implications for social work practice. Glen G. Schmidt. **Int. Soc. Work** 43:3 7:2000 pp.337-350.

5696 Reshaping child care practice. Robert Holman; Roy Parker; William Utting. London: National Institute for Social Work, 1999. vi, 77p. *ISBN: 1899942327. Includes bibliographical references.*

5697 Self and social work: towards an integrated model of learning. Gillian Ruch. **J. Soc. Work. Practice** 14:2 11:2000 pp.99-112.

5698 Sexualities in health and social care: a textbook. Tamsin Wilton. Philadelphia PA: Open University Press, 2000. 220p. *ISBN: 0335200273, 0335200265. Includes bibliographical references and index.*

5699 The skilled helper: a problem-management approach to helping. Gerard Egan. Pacific Grove CA: Brooks/Cole, 1998. xvii, 377p. *ISBN: 053434948X. Includes bibliographical references (p. 345-363) and index.*

5700 Social development content in the courses of Australian social work schools. Manohar Pawar. **Int. Soc. Work** 43:3 7:2000 pp.277-288.

5701 Social development in Sub-Saharan Africa: lessons for social work practice in South Africa. Ndangwa Noyoo. **Int. Soc. Work** 43:4 10:2000 pp.453-466.

5702 Social work and social problems: working towards social inclusion and social change. Gerald G. Smale; Graham Tuson; Daphne Statham. Basingstoke: Macmillan, 2000. 256p. *ISBN: 0333625641. Includes index.*

K: PROBLÈMES SOCIAUX. BIEN-ÊTRE SOCIAL. TRAVAIL SOCIAL

5703 Social work education in a changing socio-political and economic dispensation: perspectives from South Africa. Dovhani Mamphiswana; Ndangwa Noyoo. **Int. Soc. Work** 43:1 1:2000 pp.21-32.

5704 Social work education in India. Katherine A. Kendall; David Cox; Ralph Garber; P.D. Kulkarni; Manohar Pawar; Shankar Pathak; Murli Desai; K.P. Jayasankar; Anjali Monteiro; P.K. Visvesvaran; Gracy Fernandes; Madhuri Dass; Asha J. Rane; Anjali Dave. **Indian J. Soc. W.** 61:2 4:2000 pp.189-284. *Collection of 7 articles.*

5705 Social work in higher education: demise or development. K.H. Lyons. Aldershot: Ashgate, 1999. xv, 259p. *ISBN: 0754610071. Includes index.*

5706 Social work law in Scotland. Richard H. Mays; Vikki L. Smith; Veronica M. Strachan. Edinburgh: Sweet & Maxwell, 1999. xli, 401p. *ISBN: 0414012232. Includes bibliographical references and index.*

5707 Social work practice: a generalist approach. Louise C. Johnson. Boston MA: Allyn & Bacon, 1998. xviii, 461p. *ISBN: 0205270557. Includes bibliographical references and indexes.*

5708 Social work practice: an introduction. Veronica Coulshed; Joan Orme. London: Macmillan, 1998. xi, 256p. *ISBN: 0333727304. Includes bibliographical references and index. (Series:* Practical social work).

5709 Social work research. Steve Trevillion; Karen Lyons; Nigel Parton; Michael Sheppard; Steve Newstead; Antonietta Di Caccavo; Kate Ryan; Peter Beresford; Judith Phillips; Eric Blyth; Mark Drakeford. **Br. J. Soc. W.** 30:4 8:2000 pp.425-526. *Collection of 8 articles.*

5710 Stress: the perceptions of social work lecturers in Britain. Stewart Collins; Beth Parry-Jones. **Br. J. Soc. W.** 30:6 12:2000 pp.769-794.

5711 Stumbling towards oblivion or discovering new horizons? Observations on the relationship between social work education and practice. Michael Preston-Shoot. **J. Soc. Work. Practice** 14:2 11:2000 pp.87-98.

5712 Supervision of fear in social work. A re-evaluation of reassurance. Martin Smith. **J. Soc. Work. Practice** 14:1 5:2000 pp.17-26.

5713 Tackling institutional racism: anti-racist policies and social work education and training. Laura Penketh. Bristol: Policy Press, 2000. v, 153p. *ISBN: 1861341814. Includes bibliographical references.*

5714 Taking supervision forward: enquiries and trends in counselling and psychotherapy. Barbara Lawton [Ed.]; Colin Feltham [Ed.]. London: Sage Publications, 2000. x, 219p. *ISBN: 0761960090, 0761960104. Includes bibliographical references and index.*

5715 Teamwork in multiprofessional care. Malcolm Payne. London: Macmillan, 2000. 268p. *ISBN: 0333729773. Includes bibliographical references and index.*

5716 Travail social: l'individu, le groupe, le collectif. *[In French]*; [Social work: individual, group and collective]. Blaise Ollivier; Jean-François Garnier; Julien Damon; Brigitte Bouquet; Margot Breton; Philippe Cholet; Maria Maïlat; Christine Farache-Jamet; Luc Diservi; Marie-Rose Le Dain; Cristina De Robertis; Paul Fustier; Pierre Le Quéau; Michel Peroni. **Inf. Soc.** 83 2000 pp.4-140. *Collection of 12 articles.*

5717 Treatment expectations and treatment experience of Chinese families towards family therapy: appraisal of a common belief. Joyce L.C. Ma. **J. Fam. Ther.** 22:3 8:2000 pp.296-307.

5718 Understanding community care: a guide for social workers. Ann McDonald. Basingstoke: Macmillan, 1999. xiii, 265p. *ISBN: 0333675924. Includes bibliographical references (p. 245-259) and index.*

5719 Understanding social work: preparing for practice. Neil Thompson. London: Macmillan, 2000. 190p. *ISBN: 033371749X.*

5720 Who volunteers? Fiona Wardell; Joyce Lishman; Lawrence J. Whalley. **Br. J. Soc. W.** 30:2 4:2000 pp.227-264.

5721 Working therapeutically with children and families. Delia McGuinness; Joanne Carney; Polly Finn; Imelda McGeehan; George Crawford; Bobby Moore; Jim Wilson; Larry Martel; Eamon McMahon; Artie O'Neill; Elizabeth Cormack. **Child C. Pract.** 6:4 10:2000 pp.306-381. *Collection of 7 articles.*

K: SOCIAL PROBLEMS. SOCIAL WELFARE. SOCIAL WORK

5722 Working with creative creatures: towards a Christian paradigm for social work theory, with some practical implications. Graham Bowpitt. **Br. J. Soc. W.** 30:3 6:2000 pp.349-364.
5723 World-wide beginnings of social work education. Katherine A. Kendall. **Indian J. Soc. W.** 61:2 4:2000 pp.141-156.

K.4: Health care
Soins médicaux

5724 Beyond health: essays on control, resistance and renewal. Nicholas J. Fox. London: Free Association, 1999. 224p. *ISBN: 185343468X, 1853434698.*
5725 The corporate practice of medicine: competition and innovation in health care. James C. Robinson. Berkeley CA: University of California Press, 1999. xii, 261p. *ISBN: 0520220757, 0520220765. Includes bibliographical references (p. 237-254) and index.* (*Series:* California/Milbank series on health and the public - 1).
5726 The cultural revolution in health care. Ronald W. Dworkin. **Publ. Inter.** 139 Spring:2000 pp.35-49.
5727 Culture, health, and illness. Cecil Helman. Oxford, Boston MA: Butterworth-Heinemann, 2000. 328p. *ISBN: 0750647868. Includes bibliographical references and index.*
5728 The demography of health and health care. Louis G. Pol; Richard K. Thomas. New York: Plenum Press, 2000. 382p. *ISBN: 0306463369. Includes bibliographical references and index.* (*Series:* The Plenum series on demographic methods and population analysis).
5729 Egészségügyünk jövője. *[In Hungarian]*; (The future of our health care.) Péter Mihályi. **Mag. Tud.** 44:12 1999 pp.1457-1471.
5730 The ethics of genetic research on intelligence. Michael J. Reiss. **Bioethics** 14:1 1:2000 pp.1-15.
5731 Handbook of social studies in health and medicine. Gary L. Albrecht [Ed.]; Ray Fitzpatrick [Ed.]; Susan C. Scrimshaw [Ed.]. London, Thousand Oaks CA: Sage Publications, 2000. xxvii, 545p. *ISBN: 0761956174. Includes bibliographical references and index.*
5732 Health care. Sara L. Beckman; Michael L. Katz; James C. Robinson; Linda Bergthold; Suzanne Olson Koebler; Sara J. Singer; Alain C. Enthoven; Gary J. Young; David M. Gaba; Daniel P. Gitterman. **Calif. Manag. R.** 43:1 Fall:2000 pp.9-120. *Collection of 7 articles.*
5733 Health, medicine, and society: key theories, future agendas. Simon J. Williams [Ed.]; Jonathan Gabe [Ed.]; Michael Calnan [Ed.]. New York: Routledge, 2000. 336p. *ISBN: 0415221358, 0415221366. Includes bibliographical references and index.*
5734 The rise and fall of modern medicine. James Le Fanu. London: Little, Brown & Co, 1999. xxi, 490p. *ISBN: 0316648361.*
5735 Some fundamental questions concerning healthcare from a process-based systems perspective. Elisabeth Dostal; György G. Járos; Barry Baker. **J. Soc. Evol. Sys.** 21:2 1998 pp.193-211.

Community care
Soins en dehors du milieu hospitalier

5736 Community care: exploring the priorities of clients, mental health professionals and community providers. Frank van Hoof; Jaap van Weeghel; Hans Kroon. **Int. J. Soc. Psyc.** 46:3 Autumn:2000 pp.208-219.
5737 Comprehensive community-based interventions for youth with severe emotional disorders: multisystemic therapy and the wraparound process. Barbara J. Burns; Sonja K. Schoenwald; John D. Burchard; Leyla Faw; Alberto B. Santos. **J. Child Fam. Stud.** 9:3 9:2000 pp.283-314.
5738 Defining the outcomes of community care: the perspectives of older people with dementia and their carers. Claire Bamford; Errollyn Bruce. **Age. Soc.** 20:5 9:2000 pp.543-570.

K: PROBLÈMES SOCIAUX. BIEN-ÊTRE SOCIAL. TRAVAIL SOCIAL

5739 The essentials of community care: a guide for practitioners. Peter Sharkey. Basingstoke: Macmillan, 2000. 192p. *ISBN: 033377289X.*

5740 Moral dilemmas and the management of private residential homes: the impact of care in the community reforms in the UK. Gavin J. Andrews; David R. Phillips. **Age. Soc.** 20:5 9:2000 pp.599-622.

5741 The NIMBY phenomenon: community residents' concerns about housing for deinstitutionalized people. Myra Piat. **Health Soc. Work** 25:2 5:2000 pp.127-138.

5742 A therapeutic community approach to care in the community: dialogue and dwelling. Sarah Tucker [Ed.]. London: Jessica Kingsley Publishers, 2000. 240p. *ISBN: 1853027510. Includes index.*

Health care services
Services de santé

5743 Access to elective care: what should really be done about waiting lists. Anthony John Harrison; Bill New. London: King's Fund Publishing, 2000. 131p. *ISBN: 185717299X. Includes bibliographical references.*

5744 Benefit-cost analysis of residential and outpatient addiction treatment in the state of Washington. Michael T. French; Helena J. Salomé; Antoinette Krupski; James R. McKay; Dennis M. Donovan; A. Thomas McLellan; Jack Durell. **Eval. Rev.** 24:6 12:2000 pp.609-634.

5745 Care and support for people living with HIV/AIDS in northern Thailand: findings from an in-depth qualitative study. Anchalee Singhanetra-Renard; Chilaluck Chongsatitmun; Peter Aggleton. **Cult. Health. Sex.** 3:2 4-6:2001 pp.167-182.

5746 Challenges to effective maternal health care delivery: the case of traditional and certified nurse midwives in Zimbabwe. Chishamiso T. Rowley. **J. As. Afr. S.** XXXV:2 2000 pp.251-264.

5747 Changing the culture of a hospital: from hierarchy to networked community. Paul Bate. **Publ. Admin.** 78:3 2000 pp.485-512.

5748 Chronic illicit drug use, health services utilization and the cost of medical care. Michael T. French; Kerry Anne McGeary; Dale D. Chitwood; Clyde B. McCoy. **Soc. Sci. Med.** 50:12 6:2000 pp.1703-1714.

5749 Community accountability among hospitals affiliated with health care systems. Jeffrey A. Alexander; Bryan J. Weiner; Melissa Succi. **Milbank Q.** 78:2 2000 pp.157-184.

5750 Contested decisions: priority setting in the NHS. Christopher Ham; Shirley McIver. London: King's Fund Publishing, 2000. 85p. *ISBN: 1857174186. Includes bibliographical references. (Series:* Policy dilemmas).

5751 A cue for change: global comparisons in health care. Oliver Morgan. London: Social Market Foundation, 1999. xii, 332p. *ISBN: 1874097445. Includes bibliographical references (p. 256-279). (Series:* Paper - 41).

5752 Decision making in health care: theory, psychology, and applications. Gretchen Chapman [Ed.]; Frank Sonnenberg [Ed.]. Cambridge: Cambridge University Press, 2000. xiii, 438p. *ISBN: 0521641594. Includes bibliographical references and index.*

5753 Defining quality of care. S.M. Campbell; M.O. Roland; S.A. Buetow. **Soc. Sci. Med.** 51:11 12:2000 pp.1611-1625.

5754 The demand for private health care in the UK. Carol Propper. **J. Health Econ.** 19:6 11:2000 pp.855-876.

5755 Des rituels et des hommes: la gestion de la qualité en milieu hospitalier au Québec. *[In French]*; [Resistance of quality management controls through administrative 'rituals' in Quebec public hospitals] *[Summary].* D. Lozeau. **Can. Publ. Ad.** 42:4 Winter:1999 pp.542-565.

5756 Determinants of health outcomes in industrialised countries: a pooled, cross-country, time-series analysis. Zeynep Or. **OECD Ec. Stud.** 30(1) 2000 pp.53-78.

K: SOCIAL PROBLEMS. SOCIAL WELFARE. SOCIAL WORK

5757 Determinants of use of maternal-child health services in rural Ghana. Isaac Addai. **J. Biosoc. Sc.** 32:1 1:2000 pp.1-16.

5758 Developing primary care in London: from 1990 to PGCs. Dominique Florin. London: King's Fund Publishing, 1999. 65p. *ISBN: 185717240X. Includes bibliographical references. King Edward's Hospital Fund for London. (Series:* Kings Fund primary care series).

5759 Economic reform, poverty and equity in access to health care: case studies in Viet Nam. Malcolm Segall. Brighton: Institute of Development Studies, 1999. xii, 60p. *ISBN: 1858642531. Includes bibliographical references (p. 59-60). (Series:* Research report / Institute of Development Studies - 34).

5760 Efficiency and administrative costs in primary care. Antonio Giuffrida; Hugh Gravelle; Matthew Sutton. **J. Health Econ.** 19:6 11:2000 pp.983-1006.

5761 Elementary economic evaluation in health care. Tom Jefferson; Vittorio Demicheli; Miranda Mugford. London: B.M.J. Publishing Group, 2000. 132p.

5762 Elephant problems and fixes that fail: the story of a search for new approaches to inter-agency working. John Victor Harries; et al. London: King's Fund Publishing, 1999. 51p. *ISBN: 1857172329. (Series:* Whole systems thinking working paper).

5763 Equity in the delivery of health care in Europe and the US. E. van Doorslaer; A. Wagstaff; H. van der Burg; T. Christiansen; D. De Graeve; I. Duchesne; U.G. Gerdtham; M. Gerfin; J. Geurts; L. Gross; U. Häkkinen; J. John; J. Klavus; R.E. Leu; B. Nolan; O. O'Donnell; C. Propper; F. Puffer; M. Schellhorn; G. Sundberg; O. Winkelhake. **J. Health Econ.** 19:5 9:2000 pp.553-583.

5764 Examining the HIV/AIDS case management process. Roslyn H. Chernesky; Beth Grube. **Health Soc. Work** 25:4 11:2000 pp.243-253.

5765 Factors associated with non-urgent utilization of accident and emergency services: a case-control study in Hong Kong. Albert Lee; Fei-lung Lau; Clarke B. Hazlett; Chak-wah Kam; Patrick Wong; Tai-wai Wong; Susan Chow. **Soc. Sci. Med.** 51:7 10:2000 pp.1075-1086.

5766 Financiële verantwoordelijkheid en betaalbaarheid van de gezondheidszorg. *[In Flemish]*; (Affordable health care and financial responsibility.) Diana De Graeve; Marc Jegers. **Econ. Soc. Tijd.** 54:2 6:2000 pp.139-164.

5767 The framing of teenage health care: organizations, culture, and control. Laura Nader; Roberto J. González. **Cult. Medic. Psych.** 24:2 6:2000 pp.231-258.

5768 Gender differences in children's nutrition and access to health care in Pakistan. Gautam Hazarika. **J. Dev. Stud.** 37:1 10:2000 pp.73-92.

5769 Gesundheitsleistungen für Kinder in Deutschland, Österreich, Großbritannien und Dänemark. *[In German]*; (Health services for children in Germany, Austria, Great Britain, and Denmark.) Claus Wendt. **Soz. Welt.** 51:1 2000 pp.45-66.

5770 The global challenge of health care rationing. Angela Coulter [Ed.]; Christopher Ham [Ed.]. Philadelphia PA: Open University Press, 2000. xii, 267p. *ISBN: 0335204643. Includes bibliographical references and index. (Series:* State of health).

5771 The governance and management of effective community health partnerships: a typology for research, policy, and practice. Shannon M. Mitchell; Stephen M. Shortell. **Milbank Q.** 78:2 2000 pp.241-290.

5772 GPs and purchasing in the NHS: the internal market and beyond. Bernard Dowling. Aldershot, Brookfield VT: Ashgate, 2000. xiv, 262p. *ISBN: 0754611574. Includes bibliographical references (p. 235-259) and index.*

5773 Health crisis in Russia and Eastern Europe. Johannes Siegrist; I.V. McKeehan; William C. Cockerham; Hannele Palosuo; Martin Bobak; Hynek Pikhart; Richard Rose; Clyde Hertzman; Michael Marmot; Maria S. Kopp; Árpád Skrabski; Sándor Szedmák; Per Carlson; Inna Nazarova; Tony Barnett; Alan Whiteside; Lev Khodakevich; Yuri Kruglov; Valentyna Steshenko; Ilkka Henrik Mäkinen. **Soc. Sci. Med.** 51:9 11:2000 pp.1283-1435. *Collection of 10 articles.*

5774 Health insurance, race, and emergency room utilization. Peter Jackson. **Rev. Bl. Pol. Ec.** 27:2 1999 pp.63-81.

K: PROBLÈMES SOCIAUX. BIEN-ÊTRE SOCIAL. TRAVAIL SOCIAL

5775 Healthy relationships: a survey of London health authorities' and trusts' support to the voluntary sector. Ian Mocroft; Cathy Pharoah; Debbie Romney-Alexander. West Malling: Charities Aid Foundation, 1999. 55p. *ISBN: 1859341101.*

5776 Hospitals sponsored by the Roman Catholic Church: separate, equal, and distinct? Kenneth R. White. **Milbank Q.** 78:2 2000 pp.213-240.

5777 How do countries regulate the health sector? Evidence from Tanzania and Zimbabwe. Lilani Kumaranayake; Sally Lake; Phare Mujinja; Charles Hongoro; Rose Mpembeni. **Health Pol. Plan.** 15:4 12:2000 pp.357-367.

5778 Improving services for older people: what are the issues for primary care groups. Emilie Roberts. London: King's Fund Publishing, 2000. 73p. *ISBN: 1857174216.*

5779 In pursuit of an improving National Health Service. Alain C. Enthoven. London: Nuffield Trust, 1999. ix, 126p. *ISBN: 1902089375. Includes bibliographical references (p. 117-126). (Series:* Rock Carling Fellowship).

5780 Innovative approaches to co-operation in health care and social services. Gabriele Ullrich. **J. Co-op. St.** 33:1 4:2000 pp.53-71.

5781 Learning from the NHS internal market. Julian Le Grand [Ed.]; Nicholas Mays [Ed.]; Jo-Ann Mulligan [Ed.]. London: King's Fund Publishing, 1998. xi, 196p. *ISBN: 1857172159. Includes bibliographical references (p. [167]-196).*

5782 Lessons in control: prenatal education in the hospital. Elizabeth M. Armstrong. **Soc. Prob.** 47:4 11:2000 pp.583-605.

5783 Living values in the NHS: stories from the 50th year. Rebecca Malby; Stephen Pattison. London: King's Fund Publishing, 1999. 40p. *ISBN: 1857174038. Includes bibliographical references.*

5784 Managing quality: strategic issues in health care management. Huw T.O. Davies [Ed.]; et al. Aldershot, Brookfield VT: Ashgate, 1999. xiii, 233p. *ISBN: 0754610047. Includes bibliographical references and index.*

5785 The many meanings of deinsuring a health service: the case of in vitro fertilization in Ontario. M. Giacomini; J. Hurley; G. Stoddart. **Soc. Sci. Med.** 50:10 5:2000 pp.1485-1500.

5786 Measuring adverse selection in managed health care. R.G. Frank; J. Glazer; T.G. McGuire. **J. Health Econ.** 19:6 11:2000 pp.829-854.

5787 Measuring appropriate use of acute beds: a systematic review of methods and results. Marian S. McDonagh; David H. Smith; Maria Goddard. **Health Pol.** 53:3 10:2000 pp.157-184.

5788 Medicaid policy, physician behavior, and health care for the low-income population. Laurence C. Baker; Anne Beeson Royalty. **J. Hum. Res.** 35:3 Summer:2000 pp.480-502.

5789 Medicare's DRG-weights in a European environment: the Spanish experience. Francesc Cots; David Elvira; Xavier Castells; Eulalia Dalmau. **Health Pol.** 51:1 2:2000 pp.31-47.

5790 Methodological considerations on the assessment of the implementation of quality management systems. Willem H. van Harten; Ton F. Casparie; Olaf A.M. Fisscher. **Health Pol.** 54:3 12:2000 pp.187-200.

5791 Migration and mainstreaming: matching health services to immigrants' needs in Australia. Margaret Kelaher; Lenore Manderson. **Health Pol.** 54:1 11:2000 pp.1-11.

5792 (Mothers, children and health in Ma'an district: a social study.); *[Text in Arabic].* Ayed Wraikat. **Dirasat Hum. Soc. Sc.** 26:Supp. 12:1999 pp.790-811.

5793 Nationale Krankenversicherungssyteme Europas im Systemwettbewerb. *[In German]*; (National health care systems exposed to institutional competition.) *[Summary].* Frank Daumann. **Jahrb. N. St.** 220:5 9:2000 pp.527-540.

5794 Negotiating quality: total quality management and the complexities of transforming professional organizations. Joan E. Manley. **Sociol. For.** 15:3 9:2000 pp.457-484.

5795 The NHS. Anthony John Harrison; Jennifer Dixon. London: King's Fund Publishing, 2000. xi, 341p. *ISBN: 1857172191. Includes bibliographical references.*

5796 NHS direct: learning from the London experience. Katherine Pearce; Rebecca Rosen. London: King's Fund Publishing, 1999. 71p. *ISBN: 1857174100.*

K: SOCIAL PROBLEMS. SOCIAL WELFARE. SOCIAL WORK

5797   The NHS in Scotland: the legacy of the past and the prospect of the future. Chris Nottingham [Ed.]. Aldershot: Ashgate, 2000. 194p. *ISBN: 0754612767.*
5798   Observing organisations: anxiety, defence and culture in health care. R. D. Hinshelwood [Ed.]; Wilhelm Skogstad [Ed.]. London: Routledge, 2000. 175p. *ISBN: 0415196299, 0415196302.*
5799   Organizational learning in a hospital. Raanan Lipshitz; Micha Popper. **J. App. Behav. Sc.** 36:3 9:2000 pp.345-361.
5800   Perceptions and interactions of vulnerable groups with the government health services. B.V. Babu; G.P. Chhotray; R.K. Hazra; K. Satyanarayana. **Indian J. Soc. W.** 61:1 1:2000 pp.54-65.
5801   Pharmacy-based needle exchange (PBNX) schemes in south east England: a survey of service providers. Janie Sheridan; Selina Lovell; Paul Turnbull; James Parsons; Gerry Stimson; John Strang. **Addiction** 95:10 10:2000 pp.1551-1560.
5802   Physical access to primary health care in Andean Bolivia. Baker Perry; Wil Gesler. **Soc. Sci. Med.** 50:9 5:2000 pp.1177-1188.
5803   Pressures in UK healthcare: challenges for the NHS. Carl Emmerson; Christine Frayne; Alissa Goodman. London: Institute for Fiscal Studies, 2000. 63p. (*Series:* IFS commentary - 81).
5804   Primary care, income inequality, and self-rated health in the United States: a mixed-level analysis. Leiyu Shi; Barbara Starfield. **Int. J. Health. Ser.** 30:3 2000 pp.541-555.
5805   Protecting and promoting the right to health in Latin America: selected experiences from the field; *[Summary in French]; [Summary in Spanish].* Alicia Ely Yamin. **Health Hum. Rights** 5:1 2000 pp.116-148.
5806   La qualité des soins en France. *[In French];* [Quality of care in France]. Jean-Pierre Davant [Foreword]; Jean de Kervasdoué. Paris: Éditions de l'Atelier; Éditions ouvrières; Mutualités françaises, 2000. 180p. *ISBN: 2708235125. Includes bibliographical references (p. 175-178).*
5807   The quality imperative: measurement and management of quality in healthcare. John R. Kimberly [Ed.]; Etienne Minvielle [Ed.]. River Edge NJ: Imperial College Press, 2000. 214p. *ISBN: 1860941737. Includes index.*
5808   Recherche sur les services de santé et évaluation en santé au travail. *[In French];* Health service research and evaluation in occupational health. Jean-François Caillard [Ed.]; Peter Westerholm [Ed.]. Toulouse: Octares éditions, 1999. 352p. *ISBN: 290676955X. Conference papers. Text in English and French. Includes bibliographical references. Institut de médecine du travail de Haute-Normandie. Groupe d'études en santé au travail et ergonomie.*
5809   The recognition of access to health care as a human right in South Africa: is it enough? *[Summary in French]; [Summary in Spanish].* Charles Ngwena. **Health Hum. Rights** 5:1 2000 pp.26-44.
5810   Reforming gendered health care: an assessment of change. Mary K. Zimmerman; Shirley A. Hill. **Int. J. Health. Ser.** 30:4 2000 pp.771-796.
5811   A review of data on the health sector of the United States. Ida Hellander. **Int. J. Health. Ser.** 30:3 2000 pp.641-653.
5812   La riorganizzazione dei sistemi sanitari in Europa: finanza, marketing e produzione in sanità. *[In Italian];* [The reorganization of health systems in Europe: finance, marketing and production in health]. Carla Cattaneo [Ed.]. Milan: Giuffrè, 1999. xii, 153p. *ISBN: 8814080119. Università degli studi di Pavia, Dipartimento di ricerche aziendali.*
5813   The role of 'African chemists' in the health care system of the Eastern Cape province of South Africa. Michelle Cocks; Anthony Dold. **Soc. Sci. Med.** 51:10 11:2000 pp.1505-1516.
5814   La santé, l'expert et le patient. *[In French];* [Health, the expert and the patient]. Marie-Eve Joël; Agnès Granier; Anne-Marie Tockert; Marie-France Fortin; Hervé Tanguy; Gérard de Pouvourville; Thérèse Lebrun; Jean-Claude Sailly; Claude Evin; Jean-Luc Préel. **Projet** 263 9:2000 pp.35-98. *Collection of 7 articles.*

K: PROBLÈMES SOCIAUX. BIEN-ÊTRE SOCIAL. TRAVAIL SOCIAL

5815 Service quality in public and private hospitals in urban Bangladesh: a comparative study. Syed Saad Andaleeb. **Health Pol.** 53:1 8:2000 pp.25-38.

5816 Should St. Merciful Hospital become CorpHealth, Inc.? Ownership and quality in U.S. health care organizations. Renee A. Irvin. **Non. Manag. Leader.** 11:1 Fall:2000 pp.3-20.

5817 Les soins palliatifs en France: un mouvement paradoxal de médicalisation du mourir contemporain. *[In French]*; [Palliative care in France: a contradictory movement toward the medicalization of dying today]. Pierre Moulin. **Cah. Int. Soc.** CVIII 1-6:2000 pp.125-160.

5818 State-of-the-art methodologies in alcohol-related health services. Harold I. Perl; Michael L. Dennis; Robert B. Huebner; A. Thomas McLellan; Robert G. Orwin; Lee A. Kaskutas; Laura A. Schmidt; Constance Weisner; Thomas K. Greenfield; Frances K. Del Boca; Jane A. Noll; Aurelio José Figueredo; Patrick E. McKnight; Katherine M. McKnight; Souraya Sidani; Donald Hedeker; Robin J. Mermelstein; Bruce D. Rapkin; Kimberly A. DuMont; David B. Wilson; Dennis McCarty. **Addiction** 95:3(Supp.) 11:2000 pp.275-447. *Collection of 10 articles.*

5819 Les systèmes de santé: analyse et évaluation comparée dans les grands pays industriels. *[In French]*; [Health care systems: a comparative analysis and evaluation of industrial countries]. Denis-Clair Lambert. Paris: Seuil, 2000. 529p. *ISBN: 2020396203. Includes bibliographical references (p. 505-[506]).*

5820 'The times, are they a-changing?' As the world enters a new millennium are we as paediatricians keeping up with the changing needs of children? Helen S. Heussler; Leon Polnay; Manuel Katz. **Child. Soc.** 14:4 9:2000 pp.254-266.

5821 Traditional medicine, professional monopoly and structural interest: a Korean case. Hyo-Je Cho. **Soc. Sci. Med.** 50:1 1:2000 pp.123-136.

5822 Transforming primary care: personal medical services in the new NHS. Stephen Gillam [Ed.]; Richard Lewis [Ed.]. London: King's Fund Publishing, 1999. viii, 110p. *ISBN: 1857172906.*

5823 Turkish migrant women encountering health care in Stockholm: a qualitative study of somatization and illness meaning. Sofie Bäärnhielm; Solvig Ekblad. **Cult. Medic. Psych.** 24:4 12:2000 pp.431-452.

5824 Visions of primary care. Tom Coffey [Ed.]; et al. London: King's Fund Publishing, 1999. 70p. *ISBN: 1857174089. New Health Network.*

Medical personnel
Personnel médical

5825 Attachment theory and residential treatment: a study of staff-client relationships. Tally Moses. **Am. J. Orthopsy.** 70:4 10:2000 pp.474-490.

5826 Cadaveric donotransplantation: nurses' attitudes, knowledge and behaviour. Magi Sque; Sheila Payne; Ioannis Vlachonikolis. **Soc. Sci. Med.** 50:4 2:2000 pp.541-552.

5827 Career preferences and the work-family balance in medicine: gender differences among medical specialists. Phil J.M. Heiligers; L. Hingstman. **Soc. Sci. Med.** 50:9 5:2000 pp.1235-1246.

5828 Doctor-patient communication about drugs: the evidence for shared decision making. Fiona A. Stevenson; Christine A. Barry; Nicky Britten; Nick Barber; Colin P. Bradley. **Soc. Sci. Med.** 50:6 1:2000 pp.829-840.

5829 The doctor-patient relationship: a survey of attitudes and practices of doctors in Singapore. David Chan; Lee Gan Goh. **Bioethics** 14:1 1:2000 pp.58-76.

5830 The effect of patient race and socio-economic status on physicians' perceptions of patients. Michelle van Ryn; Jane Burke. **Soc. Sci. Med.** 50:6 1:2000 pp.813-828.

5831 Examining relationships between physicians and their patients: a psychoanalytic model. Annette Yonke; Jorge Schneider. **J. App. Psy. Stud.** 2:4 10:2000 pp.347-364.

5832 Gender, race, pay and promotion in the British nursing profession: estimation of a generalized ordered probit model. S. Pudney; M. Shields. **J. Appl. Econ.** 15:4 7-8:2000 pp.367-399.
5833 The influences of drug companies' advertising programs on physicians. Dilek Güldal; Semih Şemin. **Int. J. Health. Ser.** 30:3 2000 pp.585-595.
5834 The management implications of women's employment disadvantage in a female-dominated profession: a study of NHS nursing. Nikala Lane. **J. Manag. Stu.** 37:5 7:2000 pp.705-732.
5835 Managing patient trust in managed care. Huw T.O. Davies; Thomas G. Rundall. **Milbank Q.** 78:4 2000 pp.609-624.
5836 Neutralizing differences: producing neutral doctors for (almost) neutral patients. Brenda L. Beagan. **Soc. Sci. Med.** 51:8 10:2000 pp.1253-1266.
5837 Not just bodies: strategies for desexualizing the physical examination of patients. Patti A. Giuffre; Christine L. Williams. **Gender Soc.** 14:3 6:2000 pp.457-482.
5838 The physicians' role in transition. E. Riska; E. Gjerberg; L. Kjølsrød; B.B. Arnetz; J. Firth-Cozens; M.S. Gerrity; V. Löyttyniemi; E. Falkum; R. Førde; E.O. Rosvold; A. Hjartåker; E. Bjertness; E. Lund; O.G. Aasland; Ø. Ekeberg; T. Schweder; M. Ali; M. Emch; F. Tofail; A.H. Baqui; V.C. Li; W. Shaoxian; W. Kunyi; Z. Wentao; O. Buchthal; G.C. Wong; M.A. Burris; J.C. Umeh; O. Amali; E.U. Umeh; R. Kaestner; T. Joyce; A. Racine; A.C. Gielen; K.A. McDonnell; A.W. Wu; P. O'Campo; R. Faden. **Soc. Sci. Med.** 52:2 1:2001 pp.179-322. *Collection of 9 articles.*
5839 Postmodern nursing. Sarah Glazer. **Publ. Inter.** 140 Summer:2000 pp.3-16.
5840 Professional commitment among US physician executives in managed care. Timothy J. Hoff. **Soc. Sci. Med.** 50:10 5:2000 pp.1433-1444.
5841 Professionals: back to the future? Louise Fitzgerald; Ewan Ferlie. **Human Relat.** 53:5 5:2000 pp.713-739.
5842 Saúde e doença na perspectiva dos profissionais de saúde no hospital. *[In Portuguese]*; [Health and illness from the perspective of two hospital health professionals] *[Summary]*. Jane Biscaia Hartmann. **Aletheia** 9 1999 pp.39-50.
5843 Social perspectives on pregnancy and childbirth for nurses and the caring professions. Julie Kent. Buckingham, Philadelphia PA: Open University Press, 1999. 250p. *ISBN: 0335199119, 0335199127. Includes bibliographical references and index. (Series:* Social science for nurses and the caring professions).
5844 Variations in geographical distribution of foreign and domestically trained physicians in the United States: 'safety nets' or 'surplus exacerbation'? Stephen S. Mick; Shoou-Yih D. Lee; Walter P. Wodchis. **Soc. Sci. Med.** 50:2 1:2000 pp.185-202.
5845 The wineglass model: tracking the locational histories of health professionals. Leonard D. Baer; Wilbert M. Gesler; Thomas R. Konrad. **Soc. Sci. Med.** 50:3 2:2000 pp.317-330.
5846 Workforce diversity: implications for the effectiveness of health care delivery teams. Janice L. Dreachslin; Portia L. Hunt; Elaine Sprainer. **Soc. Sci. Med.** 50:10 5:2000 pp.1403-1414.

Medical sociology
Sociologie médicale

5847 Anorexia nervosa and respecting a refusal of life-prolonging therapy: a limited justification. Heather Draper. **Bioethics** 14:2 4:2000 pp.120-133.
5848 An argument for limited human cloning. David B. Hershenov. **Publ. Aff. Q.** 14:3 7:2000 pp.245-258.
5849 Autonomy, interdependence, and assisted suicide: respecting boundaries/crossing lines. Anne Donchin. **Bioethics** 14:3 7:2000 pp.187-204.
5850 Un avis controversé sur l'euthanasie. *[In French]*; [A controversial recommendation on euthanasia]. Jacques Ricot. **Esprit** 269 11:2000 pp.98-118.

K: PROBLÈMES SOCIAUX. BIEN-ÊTRE SOCIAL. TRAVAIL SOCIAL

5851   The beginning of personhood: a Thomistic biological analysis. Jason T. Eberl. **Bioethics** 14:2 4:2000 pp.134-157.
5852   A betegek jogai. *[In Hungarian]*; [Patients' rights]. Mária Polecsák [Ed.]. Budapest: Vince Kiadó, 1999. 332p. *ISBN: 9639192368*.
5853   Biomedizinische Humanexperimente mit Einwilligungsunfähigen. *[In German]*; [Biomedical human experiments with persons unable to give their consent] *[Summary]*. Wiltrud Christine Radau; Bernhard Losch. **Arc. Recht. Soz.** 86:3 2000 pp.423-444.
5854   Clinical ethics. Laurence B. McCullough; Kathleen E. Powderly; Virginia A. Sharpe; Yanguang Wang; Patricia Illingworth; Christopher Tollefsen; Tuija Takala; Matti Häyry; Rosamond Rhodes. **J. Medic. Philos.** 25:1 2:2000 pp.5-120. *Collection of 9 articles*.
5855   Conscientious objection in medicine. Mark R. Wicclair. **Bioethics** 14:3 7:2000 pp.205-227.
5856   Coping and physical health during caregiving: the roles of positive and negative affect. Douglas W. Billings; Susan Folkman; Michael Acree; Judith Tedlie Moskowitz. **J. Pers. Soc. Psychol.** 79:1 7:2000 pp.131-142.
5857   A darker ribbon: breast cancer, women, and their doctors in the twentieth century. Ellen Leopold. Boston MA: Beacon Press, 1999. xi, 334p. *ISBN: 0807065129. Includes bibliographical references (p. 285-327) and index*.
5858   Decision-making at the end of life: the termination of life-prolonging treatment, euthanasia (mercy-killing), and assisted suicide in Canada and South Africa. B. Sneiderman; D. McQuoid-Mason. **Comp. Int. Law J. S. Afr.** XXXIII:2 7:2000 pp.193-209.
5859   Deviant insiders: medical acupuncturists in New Zealand. Kevin Dew. **Soc. Sci. Med.** 50:12 6:2000 pp.1785-1796.
5860   Embedded altruism: blood collection regimes and the European Union's donor population. Kieran Healy. **A.J.S.** 105:6 5:2000 pp.1633-1657.
5861   Embodying bioethics: recent feminist advances. Anne Donchin [Ed.]; Laura Martha Purdy [Ed.]. Lanham MD, Oxford: Rowman & Littlefield, 1999. ix, 286p. *ISBN: 0847689255, 0847689247. Papers presented at the Feminist Approaches to Bioethics conference, San Franciso, 1996. Includes bibliographical references and index. International Network on Feminist Approaches to Bioethics. (Series:* New feminist perspectives).
5862   End-of-life decisions of physicians in the city of Hasselt (Flanders, Belgium). Freddy Mortier; Luc Deliens; Johan Bilsen; Marc Cosyns; Koen Ingels; Robert Vander Stichele. **Bioethics** 14:3 7:2000 pp.254-267.
5863   The ethics of human cloning. Leon Kass; James Q. Wilson. Washington DC: AEI Press, 1998. xxi, 101p. *ISBN: 0844740500. Includes bibliographical references*.
5864   Genetic technologies and achieving health for populations. Patricia A. Baird. **Int. J. Health. Ser.** 30:2 2000 pp.407-424.
5865   Guidance and justification in particularistic ethics. Ulrik Kihlbom. **Bioethics** 14:4 10:2000 pp.287-309.
5866   How to have theory in an epidemic: cultural chronicles of AIDS. Paula A. Treichler. Durham NC, London: Duke University Press, 1999. 477p. *ISBN: 0822323184, 0822322862. Includes bibliographical references and index*.
5867   Incorporating psycho-social considerations into health valuation: an experimental study. Richard Cookson. **J. Health Econ.** 19:3 5:2000 pp.369-401.
5868   Infanticide and abortion infanticide and the liberal view on abortion. Robert F. Card; Mary Anne Warren [Comments by]. **Bioethics** 14:4 10:2000 pp.340-359.
5869   Informed consent, exploitation and whether it is possible to conduct human subjects research without either one. Dave Wendler. **Bioethics** 14:4 10:2000 pp.310-339.
5870   International research ethics. Udo Schüklenk; Richard Ashcroft. **Bioethics** 14:2 4:2000 pp.158-172.
5871   Is a market in human organs necessarily exploitative? Mark J. Cherry. **Publ. Aff. Q.** 14:4 10:2000 pp.337-360.
5872   'Just testing': race, sex, and the media in New York's 'baby AIDS' debate. Karen M. Booth. **Gender Soc.** 14:5 10:2000 pp.644-661.

5873 Latinas, amniocentesis and the discourse of choice. C.H. Browner; H. Mabel Preloran. **Cult. Medic. Psych.** 24:3 9:2000 pp.353-375.

5874 Lay constructions of HIV and complementary therapy use. Dorothy Pawluch; Roy Cain; James Gillett. **Soc. Sci. Med.** 51:2 7:2000 pp.251-264.

5875 The limits and lies of human genetic research: dangers for social policy. Jonathan Michael Kaplan. New York: Routledge, 2000. xi, 224p. *ISBN: 0415926378, 0415926386. Includes bibliographical references (p. [206]-216) and index.*

5876 The limits of principle: deciding who lives and what dies. Tom Koch. Westport CT, London: Praeger, 1998. x, 176p. *ISBN: 0275964078. Includes bibliographical references (p. [159]-168) and index.*

5877 Living and dying well. Lewis F. Petrinovich. Cambridge MA: MIT Press, 1998. xi, 362p. *ISBN: 026266142X. Includes bibliographical references (p. 329-347) and index.*

5878 Messiahs, pariahs, and donors: the development of social representations of organ transplants. Gail Moloney; Iain Walker. **J. Theory Soc. Behav.** 30:2 6:2000 pp.203-227.

5879 Negotiating natural death in intensive care. Jane Elizabeth Seymour. **Soc. Sci. Med.** 51:8 10:2000 pp.1241-1252.

5880 The new genetics: a social science and humanities research agenda. Nora Machado; Tom R. Burns. **Can. J. Soc.** 25:4 Fall:2000 pp.495-506.

5881 Owning genetic information and gene enhancement techniques: why privacy and property rights may undermine social control of the human genome. Adam D. Moore. **Bioethics** 14:2 4:2000 pp.97-119.

5882 Palliative care vs. euthanasia. The German position: the German medical council's principles for medical care of the terminally ill. Stephan W. Sahm. **J. Medic. Philos.** 25:2 4:2000 pp.195-219.

5883 Patients, families, and organ donation: who should decide? Thomas May; Mark P. Aulisio; Michael A. DeVita. **Milbank Q.** 78:2 2000 pp.323-336.

5884 A philosophical and critical analysis of the European Convention of Bioethics. Gilbert Hottois. **J. Medic. Philos.** 25:2 4:2000 pp.133-146.

5885 The politics of AIDS surveillance. Michelle Cochrane. **Prof. Geogr.** 52:2 5:2000 pp.205-217.

5886 Reefer madness: legal & moral issues surrounding the medical prescription of marijuana. R. Eric Barnes. **Bioethics** 14:1 1:2000 pp.16-41.

5887 'Requested death': a new social movement. Fran McInerney. **Soc. Sci. Med.** 50:1 1:2000 pp.137-154.

5888 A right to life for the unborn? The current debate on abortion in Germany and Norbert Hoerster's legal-philosophical justification for the right to life. Alfred Simon. **J. Medic. Philos.** 25:2 4:2000 pp.220-239.

5889 Sanctity of life and death with dignity. Amos Shapira; Albin Eser; David Heyd; Daniel Sinclair; Shimon M. Glick; Daniel Callahan; Leon Sheleff; Ron L.P. Berghmans; Carmel Shalev; Gerhard Robbers; Norman L. Cantor; George C. Thomas; Louis Waller; Hans-Georg Koch. **Isr. Y.book. Hum. Rig.** 29 1999 pp.1-252. *Collection of 14 articles.*

5890 The social meanings of death from HIV/AIDS: an African interpretative view. Charles Nzioka. **Cult. Health. Sex.** 2:1 1-3:2000 pp.1-14.

5891 Sociobehavioural sciences on AIDS: new challenges. Jean-Paul Moatti; Yves Souteyrand; Nathalie Bajos; Jacques Marquet; Laetitia Atlani; Michel Caraël; Jean-Baptiste Brunet; Timothy Frasca; Nikolai Chaika; François Delor; Michel Hubert; M.A. Schiltz; Th.G.M. Sandfort; Janine Pierret; Margaret A. Chesney; Michel Morin; Lorraine Sherr; Rolf Rosenbrock; Francoise Dubois-Arber; Martin Moers; Patrice Pinell; Doris Schaeffer; Michel Setbon; Sarah Aldrich; Chris Eccleston; Iris Yeung; S.H. Kong; Janet Lee; Warren R. Stanton; Kevin P. Balanda; Amaya M. Gillespie; John B. Lowe; Peter D. Baade; Mohammadreza Hojat; Joseph S. Gonnella; James B. Erdmann; Susan L. Rattner; J. Jon Veloski; Karen Glaser; Gang Xu; Bernard Ineichen; Marjan van den Akker; Frank Buntinx; Job F.M. Metsemakers; J. André Knottnerus. **Soc. Sci. Med.** 50:11 6:2000 pp.1519-1694. *Collection of 14 articles.*

K: PROBLÈMES SOCIAUX. BIEN-ÊTRE SOCIAL. TRAVAIL SOCIAL

5892 Sociological perspectives on the new genetics. Jonathan Gabe [Ed.]; Peter Conrad [Ed.]. Oxford: Blackwell Publishers, 1999. 219p. *ISBN: 0631215999. Includes bibliographical references and index.* (*Series:* Sociology of health and illness monograph).
5893 Terminal illness and coping with loneliness. Ami Rokach. **J. Psychol.** 134:3 5:2000 pp.283-296.
5894 'The last resort would be to go to the GP'. Understanding the perceptions and use of general practitioner services among people with HIV/AIDS. Roland Petchey; Bill Farnsworth; Jacky Williams. **Soc. Sci. Med.** 50:2 1:2000 pp.233-245.
5895 A time to die: the place for physician assistance. Charles F. McKhann. New Haven CT, London: Yale University Press, 1999. xi, 268p. *ISBN: 0300076312. Includes bibliographical references (p. 241-260) and index.*
5896 Towards a 'good' death: end-of-life narratives constructed in an intensive care unit. Nancy Johnson; Deborah Cook; Mita Giacomini; Dennis Willms. **Cult. Medic. Psych.** 24:3 9:2000 pp.275-295.
5897 Uncertain lifetime, life protection, and the value of life saving. Isaac Ehrlich. **J. Health Econ.** 19:3 5:2000 pp.341-367.
5898 Understanding the dynamics of illness and help-seeking: event-structure analysis and a Cambodian-American narrative of 'spirit invasion'. E.S. Uehara. **Soc. Sci. Med.** 52:4 2:2001 pp.519-536.

Mental health
Santé mentale

5899 Are special hospitals needed? Jeremy Coid; Nadji Kahtan. **J. For. Psy.** 11:1 4:2000 pp.17-35.
5900 Attitudes towards mental health in an urban Pakistani community in the United Kingdom. Rashda Tabassum; Ann Macaskill; Iftikhar Ahmad. **Int. J. Soc. Psyc.** 46:3 Autumn:2000 pp.170-181.
5901 Behavioral health care dot-com and beyond: computer-mediated communications in mental health and substance abuse treatment. Simon H. Budman. **Am. Psychol.** 55:11 11:2000 pp.1290-1300.
5902 Behavioral medicine and women: a comprehensive handbook. Elaine A. Blechman [Ed.]; Kelly D. Brownell [Ed.]. New York, London: Guilford Press, 1998. xxxiii, 876p. *ISBN: 1572302186. Includes bibliographical references and index.*
5903 Bilan de la mise en œuvre et des effets des programmes régionaux d'organisation des services (PROS) comme stratégies d'implantation de la réforme des services de santé mentale au Québec. *[In French]*; [Effects of regional programmes of service organization as strategies for the implementation of mental health care reform in Québec: an assessment] *[Summary]*; *[Summary in Spanish]*. Marie-Josée Fleury; Jean-Louis Denis. **San. Ment. Qué** XXV:1 Spring:2000 pp.217-240.
5904 The community care movement in mental health services: implications for social work practice. Kam-shing Yip. **Int. Soc. Work** 43:1 1:2000 pp.33-48.
5905 Comprehensive integrated primary mental health care for South Africa. Pipedream or possibility? Inge Petersen. **Soc. Sci. Med.** 51:3 8:2000 pp.321-334.
5906 Concordance between parent reports of children's mental health services and service records: the services assessment for children and adolescents (SACA). Kimberly Hoagwood; Sarah Horwitz; Arlene Stiffman; John Weisz; Donna Bean; Donald Rae; Wilson Compton; Linda Cottler; Leonard Bickman; Philip Leaf. **J. Child Fam. Stud.** 9:3 9:2000 pp.315-331.
5907 Cultural sensitivity training in mental health: treatment of Orthodox Jewish psychiatric inpatients. Elizabeth Sublette; Brian Trappler. **Int. J. Soc. Psyc.** 46:2 Summer:2000 pp.122-134.
5908 Culturally sensitive social work practice with Arab clients in mental health settings. Alean Al-Krenawi; John R. Graham. **Health Soc. Work** 25:1 2:2000 pp.9-22.

5909 Direct and indirect costs of schizophrenia in community psychiatric services in Italy: the GISIES study. Rosanna Tarricone; S. Gerzeli; R. Montanelli; Lucilla Frattura; Mauro Percudani; Giorgio Racagni. **Health Pol.** 51:1 2:2000 pp.1-18.

5910 Disaster and mental health: responses of mental health professionals. R. Srinivasa Murthy. **Indian J. Soc. W.** 61:4 10:2000 pp.675-692.

5911 Disaster mental health: a current perspective. Srilatha Juvva; P. Rajendran. **Indian J. Soc. W.** 61:4 10:2000 pp.527-541.

5912 Early intervention programs for children with autism: conceptual frameworks for implementation. Heather Whiteford Erba. **Am. J. Orthopsy.** 70:1 1:2000 pp.82-94.

5913 Effectiveness of specialized treatment programs for veterans with serious and persistent mental illness: a three-year follow-up. Frederic C. Blow; Esther Ullman; Kristen Lawton Barry; C. Raymond Bingham; Laurel A. Copeland; Richard McCormick; William Van Stone. **Am. J. Orthopsy.** 70:3 7:2000 pp.389-400.

5914 Ethnicity, marginalisation and mental illness in Hawaii. Tom Olsen; Robert L. Anders. **Dis. and Soc.** 15:3 5:2000 pp.463-474.

5915 Evaluating the role of gender inequalities and rights violations in women's mental health; *[Summary in French]*; *[Summary in Spanish]*. Leyla Gülçür. **Health Hum. Rights** 5:1 2000 pp.46-66.

5916 Families as partners in care: perspectives from AMEND. Nirmala Srinivasan. **Indian J. Soc. W.** 61:3 7:2000 pp.351-365.

5917 Gender violence, trauma, and its impact on women's mental health. Jasjit Purewal; Indira Ganesh. **Indian J. Soc. W.** 61:4 10:2000 pp.542-557.

5918 An investigation of treatment integrity and outcomes in wraparound services. Douglas A. Della Toffalo. **J. Child Fam. Stud.** 9:3 9:2000 pp.351-361.

5919 Leaving the asylum: a psychodynamic observation study of a move from a long stay psychiatric ward to the community. Anne M. Goodwin. **Int. J. Soc. Psyc.** 46:1 Spring:2000 pp.21-33.

5920 Madness and democracy: the modern psychiatric universe. Marcel Gauchet; Gladys Swain. Princeton NJ, Chichester: Princeton University Press, 1999. xxvi, 323p. *ISBN: 0691033722. Translated from the French Pratique de l'esprit humain. Includes bibliographical references (p. [283]-315) and index. (Series:* New French thought).

5921 Memória e trauma numa unidade psiquiátrica. *[In Portuguese]*; (Memory and trauma in a psychiatric unit.) Luís Quintais. **Anál. Soc.** XXXIV:151-152 Winter:2000 pp.673-686.

5922 Mental health care in Italy: organisational structure, routine clinical activity and costs of a community psychiatric service in Lombardy region. Giovanni Fattore; Mauro Percudani; Carla Pugnoli; Agostino Contini; Jennifer Beecham. **Int. J. Soc. Psyc.** 46:4 Winter:2000 pp.250-265.

5923 Mental health care in Marathwada earthquake disaster — 2: short-term outreach counselling. N.R. Pande; S.S. Phadke; M.S. Dalal; P.J. Gadkari; U.S. Nagapurkar; M.M. Agashe. **Indian J. Soc. W.** 61:4 10:2000 pp.640-651.

5924 Multiple imaginings of institutional identity: a case study of a large psychiatric research hospital. Julia D. Harrison. **J. App. Behav. Sc.** 36:4 12:2000 pp.425-455.

5925 Parent perspectives on family involvement in therapeutic foster care. Pauline Jivanjee. **J. Child Fam. Stud.** 8:4 12:1999 pp.451-462.

5926 People with autism: the effectiveness of the TEACCH programme. Lesley Lanning. Norwich: University of East Anglia, 2000. 45p. *ISBN: 1857840755. (Series:* Social work monographs - 181).

5927 Progress or neglect? Reviewing the impact of care in the community for the severely mentally ill. Patrick Sullivan. **Crit. Soc. Pol.** 18:2(55) 5:1998 pp.193-213.

5928 Racism and mental health. David Rollock; Edmund W. Gordon; James E. Dobbins; Judith H. Skillings; David Wellman; Anderson J. Franklin; Nancy Boyd-Franklin; Shelly P. Harrell; Sumie Okazaki; Charles R. Ridley; David W. Chih; Ronald J. Olivera; Jeffrey M. Ring; Heather Whiteford Erba; Maria V. Hammond; Susan H. Landry; Paul R. Swank; Karen E. Smith; Zeynep Biringen; Ariana Shahinfar; Nathan A. Fox; Lewis A. Leavitt;

K: PROBLÈMES SOCIAUX. BIEN-ÊTRE SOCIAL. TRAVAIL SOCIAL

Eric D. Johnson; Mary Elizabeth Collins. **Am. J. Orthopsy.** 70:1 1:2000 pp.5-72. *Collection of 8 articles.*

5929 The relative irrelevance of human rights for the care and protection of the mentally ill. Anthony P. Butcher. **Aust. J. Pol. Sci** 35:1 3:2000 pp.85-97.

5930 Rights and psychiatric patients in East Asia. Ian Neary. **Jpn. Forum** 12:2 2000 pp.157-168.

5931 Risk sharing and the supply of mental health services. Meredith B. Rosenthal. **J. Health Econ.** 19:6 11:2000 pp.1047-1065.

5932 Rites of purification: the aftermath of the Ashworth Hospital inquiry of 1992. Joel Richman; David Mercer. **J. For. Psy.** 11:3 12:2000 pp.621-653.

5933 The role of schools in outcomes for youth: implications for children's mental health services research. Elizabeth M.Z. Farmer; Thomas W. Farmer. **J. Child Fam. Stud.** 8:4 12:1999 pp.377-396.

5934 Services for mentally disordered offenders in community psychiatry teams. Phillip Vaughan; Nick Pullen; Maria Kelly. **J. For. Psy.** 11:3 12:2000 pp.571-586.

5935 Social contingencies in mental health: a seven-year follow-up study of teenage mothers. R. Jay Turner; Ann M. Sorenson; J. Blake Turner. **J. Marriage Fam.** 62:3 8:2000 pp.777-791.

5936 The strengths and limitations of case record reviews in examining family preservation outcome formulation and treatment planning. Marlys Staudt. **J. Child Fam. Stud.** 8:4 12:1999 pp.409-424.

5937 The struggle for mental health in South Africa: psychologists, apartheid and the story of Durban OASSSA. Grahame Hayes. **J. Comm. App. Soc. Psychol.** 10:4 7-8:2000 pp.327-342.

5938 Therapy and learning difficulties: advocacy, participation, and partnership. John Swain [Ed.]; Sally French [Ed.]. Boston MA: Butterworth-Heinemann, 1999. 345p. *ISBN: 0750639628. Includes bibliographical references and index.*

5939 Treating dementia: the complementing team approach of occupational therapy and psychology. Jeremy Keough; Ruth A. Huebner. **J. Psychol.** 134:4 7:2000 pp.375-391.

5940 Will managed care change our way of being? Philip Cushman; Peter Gilford. **Am. Psychol.** 55:9 9:2000 pp.985-996.

5941 Young people's perceptions of mental health. Clare Armstrong; Malcolm Hill; Jenny Secker. **Child. Soc.** 14:1 2:2000 pp.60-74.

Public health
Santé publique

5942 Les acteurs de la santé publique et les réformes. *[In French]*; [Public health officials and reforms]. Alain Letourmy; Jean-Claude Moisdon; Michel Setbon; Laure Amar; Étienne Minvielle; Michel Arliaud; Magali Robelet; Bernard Kahane; Renaud Crespin; Pierre Lascoumes; Sébastien Dalgalarrondo. **Sociol. Trav.** 42:1 1-3:2000 pp.13-184. *Collection of 8 articles.*

5943 Adapting the Thai 100% condom programme: developing a culturally appropriate model for the Dominican Republic. Deanna Kerrigan; Luis Moreno; Santo Rosario; Michael Sweat. **Cult. Health. Sex.** 3:2 4-6:2001 pp.221-240.

5944 The AIDS crisis and the modern self: biographical self-construction in the awareness of finitude. Sebastian Rinken. Boston MA: Kluwer Academic Publishers, 2000. 242p. *ISBN: 079236371X. Includes bibliographical references and index. (Series:* International library of ethics, law, and the new medicine - 3).

5945 AIDS in Europe: new challenges for the social sciences. Jean-Paul Moatti. New York: Routledge, 2000. 268p. *ISBN: 1857285077, 1857285085. Includes bibliographical references and index. (Series:* Social aspects of AIDS).

5946 AIDStimes: representing AIDS in an age of anxiety. John Lynch. **Time Soc.** 9:2-3 6-9:2000 pp.247-268.

5947 Black infant health: where to in the 21st century? Geoffrey Warner. **Rev. Bl. Pol. Ec.** 26:4 Spring:1999 pp.29-54.

5948 The BSE inquiry: the inquiry into BSE and variant CJD in the United Kingdom. Nicholas Phillips. London: Stationery Office, 2000. 16p. *ISBN: 0105569860.* (*Series:* HC 1999-2000. 887).

5949 Child immunization in Madhya Pradesh. Rakesh Munshi; Sang-Hyop Lee. Bombay, Honolulu HI: International Institute for Population Sciences, 2000. 20p. *Includes bibliographical references (p. 25).* (*Series:* National family health survey subject reports - no. 15).

5950 Circumstances of post-neonatal deaths in Ceara, northeast Brazil: mothers' health care-seeking behaviors during their infants' fatal illness. A.C. Terra de Souza; K.E. Peterson; F.M.O. Andrade; J. Gardner; A. Ascherio. **Soc. Sci. Med.** 51:11 12:2000 pp.1675-1693.

5951 Community, responsibility and culpability: HIV risk-management amongst Scottish gay men. Paul Flowers; Barbara Duncan; Jamie Frankis. **J. Comm. App. Soc. Psychol.** 10:4 7-8:2000 pp.285-300.

5952 The deafening silence of AIDS. Edwin Cameron. **Health Hum. Rights** 5:1 2000 pp.7-25.

5953 Developing the professionals: groupwork for health promotion. Ellen E. Reverand; Louis B. Levy. **Groupwork** 12:1 2000 pp.42-57.

5954 Diffusion of ideas about personal hygiene and contamination in poor countries: evidence from Guatemala. N. Goldman; A.R. Pebley; M. Beckett. **Soc. Sci. Med.** 52:1 1:2001 pp.53-70.

5955 Early results from a school alcohol harm minimization study: the school health and alcohol harm reduction project. Nyanda McBride; Richard Midford; Fiona Farringdon; Mike Phillips. **Addiction** 95:7 7:2000 pp.1021-1042.

5956 The effect of tobacco advertising bans on tobacco consumption. Henry Saffer; Frank Chaloupka. **J. Health Econ.** 19:6 11:2000 pp.1117-1137.

5957 The endangered self: managing the social risks of HIV. Gill Green; Elisa Janine Sobo. London: UCL Press, 2000. 248p. *ISBN: 1857289099, 1857289102. Includes bibliographical references.*

5958 Evaluating effectiveness of syringe exchange programmes: current issues and future prospects. F.I. Bastos; S.A. Strathdee. **Soc. Sci. Med.** 51:12 12:2000 pp.1771-1782.

5959 Evaluating WIC. Douglas J. Besharov; Peter Germanis. **Eval. Rev.** 24:2 4:2000 pp.123-190.

5960 From 'reducing' to 'coping with' uncertainty: reconceptualizing the central challenge in breast self-exams. Austin S. Babrow; Kimberly N. Kline. **Soc. Sci. Med.** 51:12 12:2000 pp.1805-1816.

5961 Health outcomes of elementary school students in New Brunswick: the education perspective. Xin Ma. **Eval. Rev.** 24:5 10:2000 pp.435-456.

5962 Health seeking behavior: Q-structures of rural and urban women in India with sexually transmitted diseases and reproductive tract infections. Suprabha Sue Tripathi. **Prof. Geogr.** 52:2 5:2000 pp.218-232.

5963 Healthy neighbourhoods. Natasha Gowman. London: King's Fund Publishing, 1999. 67p. *ISBN: 1857172507.* (*Series:* Public health).

5964 HIV risk and prevention in emergency-affected populations: a review. Adrian J. Khaw; Peter Salama; Brent Burkholder; Timothy J. Dondero. **Disasters** 24:3 9:2000 pp.181-197.

5965 The impact of public testing for human immunodeficiency virus. Michael A. Boozer; Thomas J. Philipson. **J. Hum. Res.** 35:3 Summer:2000 pp.419-446.

5966 'In but free' — an HIV/AIDS intervention in an African prison. Oscar Simooya; Nawa Sanjobo. **Cult. Health. Sex.** 3:2 4-6:2001 pp.241-251.

5967 Injury prevention and control. Dinesh Mohan [Ed.]; Geetam Tiwari [Ed.]. New York: Taylor & Francis, 2000. 160p. *ISBN: 0748409599. Includes bibliographical references and index.*

5968 Maladies émergentes et reviviscentes. *[In French]*; (Emerging and re-emerging diseases.) André Prost; Jeanne-Marie Amat-Roze; Emmanuel Éliot; Pascal Handschumacher; Jean-Marc Duplantier; Suzanne Chanteau; Jean-Pierre Hervouët; Dominique Laffly; Lætitia

K: PROBLÈMES SOCIAUX. BIEN-ÊTRE SOCIAL. TRAVAIL SOCIAL

Cardon; Frédéric Paris; France Meslé; Vladimir Shkolnikov; Valérie Josset; Véronique Merle; Pierre Czernichow; Antoine Bailly; Laurence Husson; Seng Suth Wantha; Peter Godwin; Mean Chhi Vun. **Espace Pop. Soc.** 2 2000 pp.159-308. *Collection of 12 articles.*

5969 Malnutrition in Asia. John Mason; Joseph Hunt; David Parker; Urban Jonsson; Kraisid Tontisirin; Stuart Gillespie; Venkatesh Mannar; Nancy Mock; Lawrence Haddad; Patrice Engle; Howarth Bouis; Susan Horton. **Asian Dev. R.** 17:1-2 1999 pp.1-273. *Collection of 8 articles.*

5970 Managing and treating risk and uncertainty for health: a case study of diabetes among First Nation's people in Ontario, Canada. J. Sunday; J. Eyles. **Soc. Sci. Med.** 52:4 2:2001 pp.635-650.

5971 'Managing' the poor: neoliberalism, Medicaid, HMOs and the triumph of consumerism among the poor. Jeff Maskovsky. **Med. Anthrop.** 19:2 2000 pp.121-146.

5972 Mandatory public health programs: to what standards should they be held? S. Jody Heymann; Randall L. Sell. **Health Hum. Rights** 4:1 1999 pp.193-203.

5973 Multiculturalismo, democracia y género: nuevos caminos y categorías para pensar un estudio de caso en salud pública. *[In Spanish]*; [Multiculturalism, democracy and gender: new ways and categories for thinking about a public health case study]. Paula Vásquez. **Rev. Latin. Estud. Avanz.** 10 1-4:2000 pp.137-156.

5974 A nation in pain: why the HIV/AIDS epidemic is out of control in Zimbabwe. Amson Sibanda. **Int. J. Health. Ser.** 30:4 2000 pp.717-738.

5975 Participatory diagramming as a means to improve communication about sex in rural Zimbabwe: a pilot study. Mike Kesby. **Soc. Sci. Med.** 50:12 6:2000 pp.1723-1742.

5976 Patient education literature and help seeking behaviour: perspectives from an evaluation in the United Kingdom. Timothy Milewa; Michael Calnan; Stephen Almond; Alethea Hunter. **Soc. Sci. Med.** 51:3 8:2000 pp.463-476.

5977 Planning and change: a Cambodian public health case study. Peter S. Hill. **Soc. Sci. Med.** 51:12 12:2000 pp.1711-1722.

5978 Power through choices: the development of a sexuality education curriculum for youths in out-of-home care. Marla G. Becker; Richard P. Barth. **Child Wel.** LXXIX:3 5-6:2000 pp.269-284.

5979 Researching health needs: a community-based approach. Judy Payne. Thousand Oaks CA, London: Sage Publications, 1999. 192p. *ISBN: 076196083X, 0761960848.*

5980 La santé en Afrique: anciens et nouveaux défis. *[In French]*; [Health in Africa: old and new challenges]. Marc-Eric Gruénais; Roland Pourtier; André Prost; Jeanne-Marie Amat-Roze; Dominique Baudon; Jean Jannin; Pierre Cattand; Jacques Prod'hon; Michel Boussinesq; Jean-Marc Hougard; Gérard Salem; Emmanuelle Cadot; Florence Fourmet; Nathalie Lydié; Laurent Vidal; Philippe Msellati; Didier Fassin; Annabel Desgrées du Loû; Patrice Vimard; Jean-Pierre Olivier de Sardan; Adamou Moumouni; Aboubacar Souley; Bernard Maire; Francis Delpeuch; Wim Van Lerberghe; Vincent de Brouwere; Joseph Brunet-Jailly; Alain Le Vigouroux; Raphaël Okalla; Jeanne Maritoux; Carinne Bruneton; Philippe Bouscharain; Alain Letourmy; Carolyne W. Njue; Marie Badaka; Yannick Jaffré; Fatoumata Dicko; Madeleine Yila-Boumpoto; Joseph Tonda. **Afr. Cont.** 195 7-9:2000 pp.3-282. *Collection of 23 articles.*

5981 Sexually transmitted diseases in Morocco: gender influences on prevention and health care seeking behavior. Lisa E. Manhart; Abdessamad Dialmy; Caroline A. Ryan; Jaouad Mahjour. **Soc. Sci. Med.** 50:10 5:2000 pp.1369-1383.

5982 Sida et action publique. *[In French]*; [AIDS and public activity]. Philippe Urfalino [Ed.]; Monika Steffen; Olivier Borraz; Patricia Loncle-Moriceau; Michel Setbon; Nicolas Dodier; Janine Barbot; Sébastien Dalgalarrondo. **Rev. Fr. Soc.** 41:1 1-3:2000 pp.3-158. *Collection of 5 articles.*

5983 Smallpox and the impact of vaccination among the Parsees of Bombay. Jayant Banthia; Tim Dyson. **Indian Ec. Soc. His. R.** XXXVII:1 1-3:2000 pp.27-52.

5984 The social construction of immunity: HIV risk perception and prevention among lesbians and bisexual women. Diane Richardson. **Cult. Health. Sex.** 2:1 1-3:2000 pp.33-50.

K: SOCIAL PROBLEMS. SOCIAL WELFARE. SOCIAL WORK

5985 Taking part in adolescent sexual health promotion in Peru: community participation from a social psychological perspective. Marcelo Ramella; Rosa Bravo de la Cruz. **J. Comm. App. Soc. Psychol.** 10:4 7-8:2000 pp.271-284.
5986 Two pathways to prevention. Robert M. Kaplan. **Am. Psychol.** 55:4 4:2000 pp.382-396.
5987 When is HIV infection prevented and when is it merely delayed? Steven D. Pinkerton; Harrell W. Chesson; David R. Holtgrave; William Kassler; Peter M. Layde. **Eval. Rev.** 24:3 6:2000 pp.251-271.
5988 Working together for health and human rights. Victor W. Sidel. **Med. Conf. Surv.** 16:4 10-12:2000 pp.355-369.

AUTHOR INDEX
INDEX DES AUTEURS

Aagesen, D. 3754
Aarestad, S. 3306
Aasland, O. 5838
Aballéa, F. 4299
Abbès, M. 1822
Abbey, B. 2197
Abbink, J. 3531
Abbinnett, R. 1609
Abbott, A. 440
Abbott, J. 4131
Abbott, S. 2674
ABC Research Group 595
Abdel-Rahman, H. 2502
Abdullah, M. 3657
Abel, O. 161, 1172, 2439
Abercrombie, N. 100, 2305
Aberle-Grasse, M. 2213
Abma, T. 517
Aboud, F. 3517
Abraham, I. 1589
Abraham, K. 3261
Abraham, M. 2870
Abraham, R. 715, 3797
Abraham, S. 4870, 5200
Abrahams, N. 5442
Abramo, L. 2559
Abrams, D. 3283, 5406
Abshoff, K. 2917
Acharya, R. 2800
Ackah, W. 5328
Ackelsberg, M. 3295
Acker, J. 3097
Ackerly, B. 3144
Acosta-Belén, E. 3115
Acree, M. 5856
Adair, A. 4003
Adair, J. 3581
Adam, B. 32
Adam, H. 2436, 3430
Adama, H. 2126
Adams, A. 2194, 5465
Adams, C. 1296, 1523
Adams, D. 1135, 2513
Adams, J. 2104, 2225, 2817, 4486, 5266
Adams, R. 758

Addabbo, T. 4553
Addai, I. 5757
Addison, J. 681
Adeagbo, D. 4153
Adebayo, A. 4598
Adejunmobi, M. 1913
Adelman, M. 2643
Adeola, F. 5244
Adesanmi, P. 1942
Adetoun, B. 3283
Adger, W. 3607, 3756
Adibekian, A. 2637
Adigüzel, M. 2227
Adkins-Covert, T. 1742
Adorno, S. 4949
Adorno, T. 274, 307, 354
Adrete, E. 3565
Affleck, G. 722
Afflitto, F. 5312
Afkhami, M. 5317
Afshar, H. 3067, 3094
Afzal, M. 4177
Agadjanian, V. 2939
Agarwal, S. 4658
Agashe, M. 5923
Aggarwal, R. 3121, 3143
Aggleton, P. 5745
Agha, S. 2746
Agocha, V. 709
Agosin, M. 3600
Agostino, P. D' 846
Agozino, B. 3543
Agrawal, P. 4108
Aguilar, D. 3147
Aguilar-Gaxiola, S. 3565
Aguinis, M. 5325
Agulnik, P. 4587
Agyei, W. 3337
Ahearn, Jr., F. 3666
Ahlburg, D. 2810
Ahmad, A. 4057
Ahmad, I. 5900
Ahmad, R. 3702
Ahmad, W. 2470, 2532
Ahmed, A. 1534

AUTHOR INDEX

Ahmed, B. 3523
Ahmed, G. 3300
Ahmed, S. 3539
Ahmetova, Š. 1527
Ahonen, H. 4708
Ahsan, S. 2789
Ahuja, M. 1660
Aiken, L. 587
Aimone, J. 3386
Ainsworth, P. 5101, 5194
Aitken, C. 3791
Aitken, R. 5232
Aitken, S. 2608
Aixelà, Y. 4566
Ajzner, J. 363
Akande, A. 3283
Åkerlind, G. 2257
Akers-Douglas, O. 3845
Akhtar, N. 624
Akhtar, S. 814, 1947
Akiba, K. 118
Akins, J. 3309
Akintunde, D. 5469
Akister, J. 5668
Akker, M. van den 5891
Akkok, F. 2153
Akrami, N. 3461
Aksoy, A. 1775, 1777
Akudinobi, J. 1880
Akuhata-Brown, M. 4940
Alao, A. 3283
Alapuro, R. 2088
Alarcón, R. 3545
Alarid, L. 5086, 5128
Alario, M. 4107
Alasuutari, P. 1763, 2565
Alba, R. 3481, 3632
Albada, K. 1752
Albanese, P. 4416
Albarracín, D. 549
Albee, G. 775
Alber, J. 5622
Albert, C. 2043
Albiston, C. 5154
Albrecht, C. 3897
Albrecht, D. 3897
Albrecht, G. 5731
Albrecht, H. 5003
Albrecht, S. 3897
Albright, M. 5317
Albuquerque, K. de 3399
Alcoff, L. 3142
Alden, D. 1710
Alden, L. 569
Alderman, H. 2022

Alderson, P. 2157, 5601
Aldísardóttir, L. 1671
Aldrich, C. 3749
Aldrich, H. 4371
Aldrich, S. 5891
Aldridge, A. 1435
Aldridge, J. 3037
Aldridge, M. 521, 5132
Aleck, M. 5437
Alegado, D. 3642
Alegre, E. 4935
Alemann, U. von 5219
Alemoru, B. 4691
Alexander, H. 2177
Alexander, J. 329, 405, 996, 5749
Alexander, K. 4435
Alexander, P. 4472, 4864
Alexander, S. 3338
Alfonso, H. 4942
Algan, N. 3681
Ali, M. 5838
Alimonda, H. 2507
Alison, L. 5111
Allan, C. 4713
Allan, S. 1741
Allana, M. 1533
Allcock, S. 92
Allemann-Ghionda, C. 2117
Allen, C. 2809, 3115
Allen, D. 4417
Allen, J. 3774, 3898, 4350
Allen, K. 2907, 2919, 5409
Allen, M. 833, 1908, 5031
Allen, N. 1118
Allen, P. 2508
Allen, T. 4287
Allison, M. 2880
Allred, K. 1018
Allsop, S. 5404
Almeida, F. 5453
Almeida, M. de 3732
Alméras, D. 4558
Almond, S. 5976
Alonso, A. 2691
Alonso Benito, L. 4410
Alper, J. 1620
Altfelix, T. 3502
Altmeppen, K. 4787
Altonji, J. 4305
Altschuler, J. 3037
Alvarez, J. 4640
Alvarez, M. 5098
Alvarez, R. 3565
Alvesson, M. 416, 432, 1104, 1127, 4661
Amadiume, I. 4944

INDEX DES AUTEURS

Amali, O. 5838
Amar, L. 5942
Amarasinghe, S. 3174
Amato, P. 2848, 2855, 2969, 3051
Amat-Roze, J. 5968, 5980
Amatucci, A. 2196
Amau, R. 2559
Ambrose, M. 1106
Ambrosini, M. 4461
Ambrožová, M. 2814
Ameden, H. 4246
Amin, S. 520, 2770
Amir, S. 3565
Amireh, A. 3122
Amis, P. 4169
Amooti-Kaguna, B. 2778
Amoretti, U. 4596
Amourous, C. 5016
Ampiah, K. 3035
Amrouni, I. 2618
Amstutz, D. 1991
Anaf, C. 5192
Anand, N. 1100
Anand, P. 3705
Anandraj, H. 3016
Anaya, M. 2294
Andaleeb, S. 5815
Anders, R. 5914
Andersen, B. 3306
Andersen, J. 4066, 4259
Andersen, N. 371
Andersen, S. 914
Anderson, B. 4529
Anderson, C. 3881
Anderson, D. 4518
Anderson, E. 2613, 3528, 3632, 3938, 4180
Anderson, I. 5646
Anderson, J. 616
Anderson, K. 3789
Anderson, M. 2436, 2676, 3428
Anderson, N. 5633
Anderson, P. 2737, 5407
Anderson, S. 5402
Anderson, T. 2201
Anderson, W. 1552
Anderson-Connolly, R. 4737
Anderson-Gough, F. 1127
Ando, A. 2210
Andorka, R. 2533
Andrade, F. 5950
Andreas, S. 890
Andreev, A. 2438
Andreev, E. 2775
Andreeva, T. 2977
Andretta, M. 5275

Andrews, B. 812
Andrews, C. 1351
Andrews, G. 5522, 5740
Andrews, Jr., L. 3391
Andrews, M. 4728
Andrews, P. 649
Andrews, R. 96
Andriotti Fernandes, M. 5192
Ang, S. 4425
Angel, J. 3565
Angel, R. 3565
Angel-Ajani, A. 3468
Angell, L. 4409
Angelmar, R. 4408
Angrist, J. 5345
Angus, I. 333
Anh, T. 2927
Anheier, H. 4768
Anjum, M. 3251
Annandale, E. 3185
Annas, J. 2370
Anselin, L. 39
Anson, J. 1544, 2842
Anson, O. 1544, 2842
Antal, E. 2559
Antecol, H. 4504
Antheaume, B. 2716
Anthias, F. 3538, 3656, 5147
Antlöv, H. 4943
Anton, R. 5406
Antonio, W. D' 56
Antonopoulou, S. 2578
Antunes, A. 459
Antunes, R. 2507
Anwar, S. 1089
Anyi, W. 1894
Aoufi, N. El 3869
Aoyama, Y. 4122
Apel, K. 2355
Apfelbaum, E. 870
Apodaca, C. 4254
Aponiuk, N. 2188
Apostolou, F. 3262
Appadurai, A. 52
Appelbaum, R. 39
Applbaum, K. 4312
Applegate, B. 5083
Apprey, M. 814
Aprile, S. 3598
Apt, N. 3069
Arab-Ogly, E. 2540
Araki, K. 463
Araújo, H. 3060
Araujo, K. 2873
Araujo, L. 1128

Author Index

Araya, T. 3461
Arayıcı, A. 2025
Arcand, B. 1607
Arce, R. 4025
Archavanitkul, K. 3813
Archer, J. 3201
Archwamety, T. 2119
Arcia, E. 3013
Arcury, T. 2660, 2663
Arcus, B. D' 3772
Arditi, C. 4223
Arellano S., J. 2677
Arendt, H. 410
Arendt, R. 4047
Arent, R. 944
Aretxaga, B. 2340
Argos, V. 3290
Argys, L. 2764
Arias, S. 2801
Arigoni, A. 481
Arimah, B. 4153, 4161
Aring, J. 4069
Aristizábal, H. 5445
Arkin, R. 725
Arliaud, M. 5942
Arlt, H. 4859
Armeli, S. 722
Arminen, I. 1120
Armitage, C. 941
Arms, J. D' 2361
Armstrong, C. 5941
Armstrong, E. 5782
Armstrong, F. 2460
Armstrong, G. 4986
Arnason, J. 1159, 1263, 2567
Arndt, J. 872, 1081
Arndt, S. 3079
Arneson, P. 904
Arneson, R. 4933, 4937
Arnett, R. 904
Arnetz, B. 5838
Arnold, N. 5188
Arnot, M. 3060
Arnsberger, P. 5519
Arnsperger, C. 4194
Arnstine, B. 2181
Arnstine, D. 2181
Aron, A. 902
Aron, E. 902
Aronowitz, S. 112
Aronson, E. 875
Aroutiunian, I. 9
Artigiani, R. 2508
Artous, A. 4961
Arun, M. 4056

Asaad, D. 2177
Ascherio, A. 5950
Asgill, P. 3834
Ashcroft, R. 5870
Ashforth, B. 4718
Ashitey, A. 3337
Ashiwa, Y. 1467
Ashkenazi, M. 4332
Ashworth, G. 4168
Asis, M. 3651
Aska, K. 2125
Askonas, P. 2433
Aslaksen, I. 3169
Aslanbeigui, N. 2561
Aslanov, C. 1789
ASLIB 79, 80
Aslin, R. 659
Aspinall, P. 3397
Assako, R. 4042
Asselt, M. van 4025
Assié-Lumumba, N. 2513
Assier-Andrieu, L. 2313
Aston, M. 4059
Astro, A. 3518
Ateljevic, I. 1314
Atkinson, D. 1823
Atkinson, G. 4486
Atkinson, R. 565, 3982, 4004
Atkinson, S. 1772
Atlani, L. 5891
Attack, B. 3374
Attané, I. 2779
Attias-Donfut, C. 2594, 2679, 2901
Atwood, J. 5037
Au, K. 4658
Aubé, J. 776
Aubin, D. 5420
Audier, F. 2626
Audini, B. 765
Audrey, S. 3489
Auerbach, J. 3121
Auerhahn, K. 5011
Augustin, R. 5403
Augusto, M. 4949
Aulisio, M. 5883
Aung, S. 1506
Aunno, T. D' 5480
Auriel, I. 4779
Ausch, R. 112
Auslander, L. 3468
Austen, R. 1913
Austin, R. 5031
Auvergnon, P. 4751
Auyero, J. 4269
Avanzo, B. D' 4692

Avataramu, C. 2585
Averett, S. 2764, 4518
Ávila, P. 1610
Aviram, A. 2177
Avis, J. 2279
Avritzer, L. 5248
Avruch, K. 1018
Axhausen, K. 4056
Axsom, D. 688
Axtell, C. 1144
Ayduk, O. 933
Aykan, H. 2669
Ayodele, E. 2015
Ayoub, M. 1525
Ayre, P. 5373
Ayukawa, J. 50
Ayyub, R. 2870
Azenabor, G. 199
Azevedo, M. 1865
Azim, F. 1165
Azizefendioglu, H. 3536
Baade, P. 5891
Bäärnhielm, S. 5823
Babadzan, A. 992
Babb, S. 4314
Babbie, E. 429
Babcock, J. 2861
Babić, D. 3859
Babrow, A. 5960
Babson, S. 4811
Babu, B. 5800
Bacalhau, M. 4596
Baccaro, L. 4841
Bacharach, S. 4623
Bachet, D. 4237
Bachinin, V. 5117
Back, K. 4675
Back, L. 3529
Backus, M. 1227
Bacon, N. 4618, 4830
Bacqué, M. 4021
Badaka, M. 5980
Badari, V. 3023
Badcock, C. 560
Baden, A. 5538
Baden, S. 3171
Badry, R. 3163
Baecker, D. 380
Baek, S. 4855
Baena Paz, G. 2292
Baer, J. 4913
Baer, L. 5845
Baer, M. 1530
Baez, B. 2011
Bafoil, F. 5641

Bagaoui, R. 3423
Bagchi, A. 2513
Bagilhole, B. 4563
Bagozzi, R. 1076
Bahrick, L. 551
Baigrie, B. 288
Baik, E. 2145
Bailey, A. 4672
Bailey, B. 1815, 2188, 3508
Bailey, C. 5420
Bailey, J. 69, 3308, 3345, 4851
Bailey, L. 3045, 4515
Bailey, N. 4439, 4579
Bailey, R. 2706
Bailleau, F. 2618
Bailly, A. 5968
Bain, B. 1789
Bain, J. 1605
Bain, P. 4688
Baine, D. 2186
Baines, S. 4577
Baird, P. 5864
Bairoch, P. 2568
Baistow, K. 5572
Bajos, N. 5891
Bajpai, A. 3291
Bak, P. 827
Baker, B. 5735
Baker, C. 430, 5279
Baker, D. 207, 775
Baker, L. 5788
Bakewell, O. 3674
Bakken, B. 2516
Bal, E. 3530
Balakrishna, P. 5200
Balanda, K. 5891
Balci, A. 2153
Balding, D. 446
Baldock, J. 5647
Baldry, A. 3006
Baldry, C. 1147
Baldwin, J. 3761
Baldwin, S. 13
Baldwin-Edwards, M. 4596
Balestri, C. 5448
Balka, E. 4574
Ball, C. 5072
Ball, K. 1137
Ballara, A. 164
Ballintyne, S. 5107
Balshaw, M. 4144
Balter, L. 546
Baltes, P. 2654
Bam, S. 3599
Bamberger, P. 4623

AUTHOR INDEX

Bamford, C. 5738
Bamforth, V. 3615
Banahan, E. 4645
Banaji, M. 826, 863
Banakar, R. 5199
Banas, J. 4588, 4721
Banerjea, K. 1978
Banerjea, P. 1978
Banerjee, M. 3891
Banerjee, S. 1769
Bangura, A. 2523
Banham, G. 1249
Banim, M. 3256
Bank, L. 3868
Bankier, D. 3518
Banks, A. 655
Bankston, III, C. 2077
Banner, M. 1063
Bannerji, H. 3500
Bansbach, M. 4835
Banthia, J. 5983
Banton, M. 3472
Bao, W. 3873
Baqui, A. 2789, 5838
Bar, M. 5606
Baral, R. 3739
Barany, Z. 3474
Barbalet, J. 314
Barbarito, M. 567
Barber, A. 4786
Barber, J. 3026
Barber, N. 5828
Barber, P. 3557
Barbot, J. 5982
Bárd, K. 5039
Bardinet, C. 3702
Bardram, J. 1040
Bareja-Starzyńska, A. 1470
Barenbaum, N. 870
Bargach, J. 1976
Bargh, J. 591
Barham, B. 3406
Baringer, D. 1647
Barker, J. 1033
Barkhuizen, G. 1813
Barkhuysen, B. 4422
Barlow, D. 731
Barlow, T. 3115
Barlucchi, M. 108
Barnatt, C. 1100
Barnes, A. 4712
Barnes, B. 407
Barnes, C. 2458
Barnes, G. 2859, 2946
Barnes, L. 1419

Barnes, R. 5886
Barnett, C. 1220
Barnett, L. 1908
Barnett, R. 2222, 4724
Barnett, T. 5773
Barngetuny, M. 2078
Barnow, B. 4796
Baron, E. 5377
Baron, R. 884, 4356
Baron, S. 2458
Baron-Yelles, N. 3820
Barou, J. 2313
Barr, C. 5401
Barr, R. 767
Barra, X. de la 4087
Barraud, S. 4025
Barré, P. 4828
Barreau, H. 2575
Barrère, A. 2014
Barrett, D. 5373
Barrett, E. 3139
Barrett, M. 622, 3294
Barrett, P. 2892
Barrett, R. 4382
Barrey, S. 4322
Barro, R. 4947
Barron, J. 3730
Barroso, A. 2801
Barrow, R. 261
Barry, B. 1105
Barry, C. 5828
Barry, K. 5913
Barry, M. 5023
Barsade, S. 4670
Barshack, L. 2327
Bartel, C. 1037
Bartels, E. 1532
Bartelson, J. 2568
Bartfeld, J. 2846
Barth, R. 5587, 5978
Barthold, L. 293
Bartkowski, J. 3012
Bartol, C. 5066
Barton, D. 2006
Barton, L. 2460
Bartowski, J. 3266
Bartram, D. 3658
Bartram, R. 3721
Bartunek, J. 4383, 4632
Baruch, Y. 4611, 4738
Bar-Yosef, R. 2600
Bash, H. 387
Bashar, N. 4524
Bashkirova, E. 2372
Bashkow, I. 3534

INDEX DES AUTEURS

Basinger, D. 1440
Basok, T. 3661, 4444
Bassel, N. El 5382
Bassett, S. 2765
Bassetti, P. 3797
Bastenier, A. 1535, 4962
Bastos, F. 5958
Basturkmen, H. 1648
Basu, A. 2770
Basu, D. 5395
Basu, J. 942
Basu, S. 3112
Batagelj, V. 493
Bate, P. 43, 5747
Bates, D. 256, 1591
Bates, L. 3019
Bates, R. 2
Batie, B. de la 1949
Bator, R. 3749
Batsh, M. 2075
Batsleer, J. 5657
Battah, A. 2183
Battu, H. 2267
Bauchspies, W. 1566
Baudelle, G. 4130
Bauder, H. 4453
Baudon, D. 5980
Bauer, D. 20, 3115
Bauer, E. 5576
Bauer, J. 3468
Bauer, M. 530
Bauer, T. 1131
Bauer, Y. 3518
Bauermann, S. 3206
Bauld, L. 5497
Bauman, Z. 17, 28, 291, 1256, 4421
Baumann, M. 1464
Baumann, S. 4203
Baumeister, R. 657, 717, 718, 873, 3306
Baumer, E. 2995
Bausinger, H. 1003
Bautista, M. 25
Bauzon, A. 3009
Bauzon, L. 3009
Bavelas, J. 919, 945
Baverez, N. 4898
Baxendale, C. 3813
Baxter, J. 3180
Baxter, K. 3225
Baxter, V. 4187
Bayat, A. 3813, 5229
Bayertz, K. 1569
Bayliss-Smith, T. 3735
Bayma, T. 996
Bayraktaroglu, A. 1835

Baytan, R. 3061
Baz, T. 1898
Bazemore, G. 1442
Bazen, S. 4587
Bazin, A. 1004
Bazin, L. 801
Beach, D. 4071
Beach, S. 2979
Beach, W. 1810
Beagan, B. 5836
Beall, J. 4169, 4287
Bean, D. 5906
Bean, F. 3565, 3572
Beaton, J. 2263
Beatty, C. 4439, 4594
Beauchamp, T. 4933
Beauchemin, C. 3612
Beauregard, K. 657
Beauregard, R. 4159
Beavers, H. 3528
Beavers, R. 2900
Becerra, R. 3434
Bechhofer, F. 488, 2676
Beck, D. 1991
Beck, J. 1000
Beck, R. 1437
Beck, U. 32, 3704, 4677, 4910
Becker, A. 4291
Becker, D. 820
Becker, M. 5978
Becker, N. 446
Becker, R. 2048
Becker, S. 3037
Becker, W. 2216
Beckett, M. 5954
Beckford, J. 56
Beckman, S. 5732
Beckwith, J. 1620
Beckwith, K. 4843
Bedford, R. 3643
Bedolla, L. 3565
Beech, N. 1104
Beecham, J. 5922
Beed, C. 356
Beekman, A. 2659
Beer, J. 698
Beger, R. 5196
Bégin, S. 4046
Begum, L. 2789
Behrman, J. 2022
Behuniak, J. 1420
Beijaard, D. 2215
Beilharz, P. 1281
Beiner, G. 986
Beissinger, M. 3427

AUTHOR INDEX

Beitz, C. 2361
Béja, J. 4898
Bejarano, C. 2643
Bekerian, D. 812
Bekker, S. 964
Bekkers, R. 3843
Bélanger, D. 2944
Belar, C. 775
Belardinelli, D. 1502
Belasco, W. 1286
Belcher, H. 5409
Belcher, S. 4344
Belfield, C. 2267
Belgrave, F. 681, 5409
Belin, T. 2020
Belingard, L. 641
Bell, D. 1664, 2917
Bell, J. 418
Bell, Jr., C. 1125
Bell, L. 2917
Bell, M. 20, 3622, 3791
Bell, R. 2660
Bell, V. 990, 3116
Bellaby, P. 4730
Bellas, M. 3170
Bellofiore, R. 4234
Bellringer, P. 5412
Bell-Rose, S. 3572
Belorgey, J. 4299, 4950
Belsey, C. 3115
Belsky, J. 3056
Belton, T. 1711
Ben-Ari, E. 5339
Benbow, S. 1371
Bender, S. 4753
Bendera, S. 2041
Benderly, J. 5317
Benders, J. 4647
Benedict, R. 5234
Benet-Martínez, V. 643, 710
Benin, S. 145
Benjamin, C. 5448
Benjamin, J. 3979
Benjamin, Jr., L. 775
Benjamin, S. 3813, 4169
Benking, H. 3759
Bennert, K. 2217
Bennett, D. 518
Bennett, J. 2821
Bennett, M. 553, 3819
Bennett, R. 4142, 4385
Bennun, I. 3382
Bensimon-Choukroun, G. 1789
Benthall, J. 1258
Benton, L. 5254

Benveniste, L. 2112
Benyahia, S. 1822
Ben-Ze'ev, A. 696
Benzimra, Y. 767
Beranzoli, N. 2456
Bercovitch, J. 5337
Berenguer, J. 3726
Berenson, K. 2889
Beresford, P. 2496, 5665, 5709
Berg, M. 3600
Berg, P. 4681
Berg, R. 3565
Bergamaschi, M. 4537
Bergami, M. 1076
Berge, B. 3165
Berger, C. 574, 1647
Berger, F. 545
Berger, V. 1009
Bergerson, A. 2134
Berghmans, R. 5889
Bergmann, B. 3169, 4191, 5581
Bergmann, C. 3127
Bergmann Lichtenstein, B. 4360
Bergthold, L. 5732
Beriain, J. 403
Berik, G. 2561, 4480
Berk, L. 2598
Berk, M. 914
Berk, R. 434
Berkel, H. van 2053
Berman, L. 5430
Bermeo, N. 4596
Bernard, M. 2664, 5533
Bernard, R. 956
Bernardi, B. de León de 761
Bernardo, A. 2006
Bernecker, W. 165
Bernis, C. 2801
Bernt, J. 1696
Berntson, G. 591
Beroggi, G. 1015
Berranger, P. de 4056
Berrick, J. 5596
Berridge, K. 5406
Berridge, V. 5402
Berrington, A. 2768, 2974
Berry, A. 4248
Berry, J. 4003, 4043
Berry, M. 3528
Berscheid, E. 591
Berthelot, J. 66, 1610
Bertho, S. 1206
Berthoud, R. 4500
Bertram, V. 1945
Bertrand, M. 801

INDEX DES AUTEURS

Bertrand-Krajewski, J. 4025
Bertrando, P. 1275
Berzano, L. 4979
Besharov, D. 419, 5959
Bessel, R. 5133
Besser, A. 3015
Bessette, J. 5065
Bessin, M. 1298
Bessy-Pietri, P. 4175
Best, B. 368
Best, J. 614
Bettie, J. 2449
Betto, F. 1478
Betton, E. 4950
Beutel, A. 2632
Bevc, I. 2912
Beveridge, F. 3198
Bevir, M. 138
Bey, F. 68
Bey, M. 4286
Beyer, P. 56
Beyme, K. von 5219
Bezdek, R. 3565
Bhappu, A. 4416
Bhargava, R. 567
Bhatia, S. 2346
Bhatnagar, D. 4457
Bhavnani, K. 3067, 3090
Bhopal, K. 3265
Bhrolcháin, M. 2853, 2967
Biaggi, E. de 58
Biaggio, M. 570
Biale, D. 145
Bianchi, E. 3129
Bianchi, S. 3188
Biblarz, T. 2923
Bibus, A. 5661
Bickerdike, A. 2850
Bickerton, D. 571
Bickford, S. 4941
Bickman, L. 5906
Biddlecom, A. 3211
Bideau, A. 2901
Bidou-Zachariasen, C. 2374
Biehal, N. 5570
Bielby, D. 2915
Bielenberg, A. 3778
Biesta, G. 2117
Bigelow, K. 5594
Biggs, S. 2664
Bigler, R. 3517
Bijsterveld, M. von 4647
Bikkeinin, N. 1938
Bilginsoy, C. 4480
Billeaux, D. 3565

Billig, M. 632
Billing, Y. 4661
Billings, D. 5856
Bilsen, J. 5862
Bin, Z. 1738
Binas, S. 1331
Binder, M. 4452
Bingham, C. 5913
Bingham, L. 2889
Bingham, N. 2608
Bingham, R. 4150
Binion, R. 2708
Binmore, J. 5364
Binnie, D. 4056
Biott, C. 2099
Bippus, A. 921
Birbili, M. 4807
Birch, D. 1240
Birckmayer, J. 443
Bird, J. 2273
Bird, S. 4733
Biringen, Z. 3017, 5928
Biritwum, R. 3337
Birke, L. 3083, 3109
Birman, P. 1514
Birnbaum, G. 721
Biscaia Hartmann, J. 5842
Bischof, G. 5408
Bishop, I. 4102
Bishop, J. 1048
Bishop, P. 1699
Bisig, B. 4692
Bissell, S. 5200
Bittman, M. 3200
Bittner, S. 2117
Bjerke, B. 4624
Bjertness, E. 5838
Bjork, R. 666
Bjorklund, D. 544
Bjørkly, S. 2877
Björkman, I. 4633
Black, D. 334, 819, 2688
Black, H. 4497
Black, J. 3286
Black, M. 2154
Blackburn, J. 2221
Blackledge, A. 2050
Blackler, F. 1115
Blackman, L. 340
Blackwell, B. 5099
Blackwood, E. 3352
Blair, H. 1891
Blair, J. 496
Blais, R. 3727
Blake, C. 1249

AUTHOR INDEX

Blake, M. 3622
Blake, R. 4123
Blakemore, C. 3071
Blalock, C. 654
Blanc, P. 4776
Blancarte, R. 1431
Blanco, F. 259
Blangero, J. 789
Blanton, H. 843
Blas Arroyo, J. 1839
Blasco, M. 4558
Blasco, P. y 1503
Blaser, C. 1809
Blau, F. 4539
Blaut, J. 152
Blechman, E. 5902
Bledsoe, C. 2781
Bleijenbergh, I. 4537
Blejwas, S. 2009
Blieszner, R. 2919
Bligh, D. 947
Blizek, W. 2181
Blokland, T. 2332
Blom, T. 402
Blomberg, G. 3206
Blomberg, J. 816
Blommaert, J. 1792
Blondel, J. 5321
Blondiaux, L. 4897
Bloom, D. 3759
Bloom, S. 2765
Bloom, W. 1401
Bloomfield, K. 5403
Blöss, T. 2057
Blow, F. 5913
Blowers, A. 4041
Bluck, S. 2625
Blue, I. 2432
Blühdorn, I. 372
Blum, P. 156
Blum, S. 3095
Blum, T. 4673, 4683
Blumenfeld, W. 3477
Blumenfeld, Y. 2527
Blundell, R. 2287, 4587
Blyth, E. 2757, 5709
Blythe, B. 5569
Blyton, P. 4618
Bo, Z. 5487
Boardman, J. 3565
Boatswain, S. 3442
Bobak, M. 5773
Bobo, L. 3514, 3528
Boca, D. Del 4532
Boca, F. Del 5818

Bochonko, H. 2188
Bock, J. 2915
Bock, P. 710
Boddie, S. 5481
Boddy, K. 1907
Bodor, P. 1816
Body-Gendrot, S. 4005, 4991
Boertzel, H. 1010
Boey, K. 4699, 4735, 4746
Bogaerts, S. 3338
Bogard, W. 2322
Bogart, L. 844
Bøgeberg, S. 1348
Bohl, C. 4010
Boidin, G. 1822
Boily, M. 1045
Boissin, O. 4322
Boitet, C. 1822
Bojer, H. 2603
Bokser, J. 3518
Boles, L. 1801
Bolfíková, E. 4262
Bolin, G. 1889
Bolks, S. 3565
Bollas, C. 695
Bollens, S. 3828
Bolliger, C. 5407
Bolmont-Couval, A. 2178
Bolton, B. 4769
Bommes, M. 5632
Bond, J. 4059
Bond, M. 710
Bond, S. 2278
Bondi, L. 2377
Bonilla-Silva, E. 3508
Bonin, J. 5420
Bonnefoy, J. 3741
Bonné-Tamir, B. 1620
Bono, J. 4638, 4719
Bono, P. 3115
Bonoli, G. 5623
Bonvin, J. 5641
Booth, A. 2207
Booth, B. 4549
Booth, C. 3069
Booth, K. 5872
Booth, L. 3810
Booth, N. 5434
Boozer, M. 5965
Boqing, Z. 1895
Borch-Jacobsen, M. 779
Borden, I. 3933
Borden, L. 2633
Bordone, R. 1018
Borer, P. 3765

Borges Rodrigues, R. 5192, 5209
Borgetto, M. 4950
Borghi, L. 3115
Borgoño, M. 1197
Bornat, J. 74
Bornefalk, A. 4185
Bornstein, M. 3014
Boroditsky, L. 642
Boroditsky, R. 2726
Boron, A. 1194, 1221
Borooah, R. 3909
Boros, J. 5028
Borraz, O. 5982
Borrillo, D. 3321
Boruch, R. 426
Borzaga, C. 4466
Bosch, B. 1813
Boschi, S. 758
Bose, B. 3112
Bose, C. 3115
Bosma, H. 4706
Bossel, H. 3800
Bosson, J. 720
Botsko, M. 5693
Botta, R. 2667
Botz-Bornstein, T. 212
Boud, D. 4398
Boudic, G. 4898
Bouis, H. 5969
Boulianne, L. 3960
Bouloc, B. 5025
Boulton, J. 4263
Bouquet, B. 5716
Bourbon, D. 5413
Bourdais, C. Le 2962
Bourdelais, P. 2691
Bourdieu, P. 18, 68, 130, 4275, 4894, 5372
Bourdon, J. 1725
Bourges, H. 1637
Bourgois, P. 5379, 5386
Bourguignon, F. 5057, 5445
Bourke, J. 5323
Bourke, S. 3697
Bournay, E. 3702
Bouscharain, P. 5980
Bousfield, C. 3093
Boushel, M. 5490
Bousquet, F. 3741
Boussinesq, M. 5980
Boutellier, H. 3338
Bouts, J. 510
Bouysse-Cassagne, T. 1433
Boven, L. Van 905
Bower, E. 2187, 2602
Bower, J. 1100

Bower, S. 815
Bowes, A. 3460, 5527
Bowker, G. 70
Bowlby, S. 3557
Bowling, D. 1007
Bowman, J. 1620, 3528
Bowman, P. 808
Bowpitt, G. 5722
Bowring, F. 311
Boychuk, G. 2254
Boyd, M. 609
Boyd-Franklin, N. 5928
Boyer, D. 989
Boyer, M. 1023
Boyer, P. 561
Boykin, A. 2174
Boyle, B. 2241, 4420
Boyle, T. 2241
Boyne, R. 4987
Braa, K. 1040
Brabcova, I. 5116
Brace, L. 3115
Bracewell, W. 3070
Bracke, P. 811
Bradbury, T. 2956, 2979, 2985
Brade, I. 4168
Bradford, M. 4097
Bradley, C. 5828
Bradley, K. 922
Bradley, S. 1010
Bradshaw, J. 2532
Bradshaw, R. 4062
Bradshaw, T. 3832
Bradwell, S. 4227
Braidotti, R. 3115
Brainerd, E. 4573
Braithwaite, J. 4989
Brakel, M. 584
Brame, R. 5095, 5096
Bramley, A. 4769
Bramley, G. 4247
Branco Vicente, L. 740
Brandell, M. 2213
Brandford, C. 5555
Brandon, P. 2899, 3588
Brandstätter, E. 831
Brändström, A. 2691
Brandt, C. 1096
Braner, M. 5578
Brannen, M. 1134
Branskii, V. 1602
Brashers, D. 1059
Brauman, R. 161
Braun, C. von 3127
Braun, M. 2922

AUTHOR INDEX

Bravo de la Cruz, R. 5985
Bray, J. 2613
Bray, M. 4818
Breakwell, G. 2530, 3660
Breathnach, P. 2571
Breen, R. 2108
Breeva, E. 2606
Brehm, S. 883
Breitbach, C. 4160
Brelade, S. 4610
Brennan, A. 4587
Brennan, G. 5305
Brennan, J. 2275
Brennan, K. 918
Brennan, T. 4216
Brenner, I. 814
Brenner, J. 3115
Brentlinger, J. 1444
Breslau, D. 29
Breton, D. Le 1347
Breton, M. 5716
Breton, S. 4351
Brett, E. 4287
Breuer, S. 1411
Breuvart, J. 225
Breward, C. 1254
Brewer, A. 4578
Brewer, J. 1513
Brewin, C. 812
Brewis, J. 3347
Breyer, F. 5507
Brezzo, L. 2205
Bricher, G. 2465
Brick, J. 525
Brickell, C. 3365
Bridge, G. 382, 3939
Bridger, D. 4342
Bridges, M. 2726
Brient, E. 1251
Brier, S. 1628
Briffett, C. 4108
Brighouse, H. 2155
Brimblecombe, N. 2844
Brindis, C. 2745, 3316
Brindley, T. 2614, 4035
Brinegar, S. 5426
Bringle, R. 2213
Brink, R. van den 1060
Briones, L. 4935
Bristow, M. 859
Brito Castrejón, T. 2677
Britt, T. 972
Britten, N. 5828
Britton, D. 3062, 3121, 3180
Britton, N. 5129, 5142

Broadbridge, A. 4726
Broberg, J. 816
Brock, K. 3924
Brockliss, L. 2264
Brock-Utne, B. 2167
Brodbeck, F. 1046, 4630
Brodkin, K. 2551, 3115
Brodowski, M. 5596
Brody, G. 3021, 3901
Brody, R. 1731
Broman, C. 3478
Brome, D. 5409
Bromet, E. 758
Bromley, R. 3937
Bronner, S. 2052
Brooker, W. 1242
Brookman, F. 529
Brooks, C. 4486
Brooks, K. 1744
Brooks, P. 636
Brooksbank Jones, A. 1169
Brooks-Gunn, J. 577
Broom, G. 4364
Broomhall, L. 5386
Brosch, I. 2904
Brose, H. 1200
Brosius, H. 1783
Brotons, A. 2560
Brottman, M. 1882
Broughton, C. 789
Broughton, W. 5354
Brouwere, V. de 5980
Brown, A. 2181, 3021, 3901
Brown, E. 3058, 4768
Brown, G. 644, 3371
Brown, H. 3088
Brown, J. 3284, 5131, 5200, 5552
Brown, K. 5135, 5484
Brown, M. 2241, 2769, 2947, 3633, 5009
Brown, P. 838, 4378, 5316
Brown, R. 881, 1051, 2061, 3565
Brown Rosier, K. 2917
Brown, S. 2989, 3072, 5410
Brown, T. 2810
Browne, I. 4559
Browne, J. 2670
Brownell, K. 5902
Browner, C. 5873
Browning, G. 2331
Brownlee, P. 3544
Brownworth, V. 2492
Brozović, D. 1825
Bruce, E. 5738
Bruce, S. 1377, 1452
Bruchey, S. 5258

INDEX DES AUTEURS

Bruckner, K. 736
Brüderl, J. 4766
Brudney, J. 4768
Bruegel, I. 3069
Bruel, A. 5068
Brugge, D. 4087
Bruijn, E. de 4771
Bruijn, J. de 4537
Bruin, W. De 2640
Brulin, G. 4838
Brumfitt, S. 1653
Brumlik, M. 5243
Bruneau, J. 5386
Bruneau, T. 4596
Brunet, A. 767
Brunet, G. 2901
Brunet, J. 5891
Brunet, R. 2716
Brunet-Jailly, J. 5980
Bruneton, C. 5980
Bruniaux, C. 2270
Brunner, A. 3283
Bruno, R. 4876
Bruno-Jofré, R. 2188
Bruns, G. 3127
Brunt, P. 5080
Brustlein, V. 1433
Brutel, C. 4175
Bruthans, J. 2814
Bruzzi, S. 1740
Bryant, C. 900
Bryant, J. 127
Bryant, R. 3747
Bryner, G. 3759
Bryngelsson, I. 4698
Brynin, M. 3177
Bucchignani, V. 3984
Buchanan, A. 2361, 5027
Buchanan, D. 1119, 4618
Buchanan, M. 193
Buchinger, B. 4537
Buchmann, C. 2035
Buchmann, M. 4762
Bucholz, K. 5393
Buchthal, O. 5838
Buckel, D. 3340
Buckingham, D. 1716, 2596
Buckingham-Hatfield, S. 3066
Buckland, S. 468
Buckley, C. 520
Buckley, S. 1756
Buckman, S. 4160
Buckser, A. 3418
Budhya, G. 3813
Budianta, M. 1195

Budman, S. 5901
Buechler, S. 5278
Buenen, L. 1875
Buetow, S. 5753
Buffardi, L. 4614
Bugental, D. 2301
Buijs, G. 5363
Bulcaen, C. 1792
Bulcroft, K. 922, 2980
Bulcroft, R. 922, 2980
Bull Kovera, M. 5157
Bullard, R. 3749
Bulle, S. 3945
Bullen, P. 3847
Bullock, B. 1940
Bulmahn, T. 4297
Bulmer, M. 520
Bumpass, L. 2988
Bunčák, J. 983
Bunge, M. 287, 288
Bunnell, T. 4115
Buntinx, F. 5891
Bunzl, M. 3368
Burawoy, M. 4273
Burbank, J. 3891
Burbank, M. 5234
Burchard, J. 5737
Burchardt, T. 5604
Bureau, M. 2145
Bureau, X. 5475
Burford, G. 1050
Burg, H. van der 5763
Burge, E. 2172
Burge, S. 2951
Bürgenmeier, B. 3806
Burgerman, S. 5361
Burgess, J. 4550
Burgess, K. 4596
Burgess, N. 3058
Burgh, H. de 1720
Burgoon, J. 574
Burgoyne, J. 1128
Búriková, Z. 3496
Burke, J. 1588, 5830
Burke, K. 4276
Burke, R. 4747
Burkholder, B. 5964
Bürkner, H. 4606
Burleson, B. 1647
Burlew, K. 5409
Burlew, R. 5409
Burnay, N. 4581, 5641
Burney, E. 5617
Burney, J. 3705
Burnham, J. 12

AUTHOR INDEX

Burningham, K. 3687
Burns, B. 5737
Burns, J. 1882
Burns, R. 424, 567, 5067
Burns, T. 12, 765, 5880
Buron, L. 5627
Burridge, K. 1258
Burris, C. 880
Burris, M. 5838
Burrow, J. 214
Burström, B. 2999, 4696
Burt, E. 1673
Burton, A. 188, 3705
Burton, D. 438
Burton, E. 3994
Burton, Jr., V. 5086
Burton, M. 2574
Burtonwood, N. 2143
Burts, D. 3011
Busch, A. 2876
Busch, K. 3702
Bush, A. 4420
Bush, V. 4420
Bushnell, D. 800
Buss, A. 1486
Bussi, M. 2716
Bussing, R. 2020
Bustamante, G. 3702
Buster, M. 5390
Busuttil, P. 3773
Butcher, A. 5929
Butler, B. 1660
Butler, J. 3137, 5409
Butler, R. 639, 2707, 3820, 3821
Butler, T. 4040
Buttel, F. 3722
Butterfield, R. 774
Butterfield, T. 3565
Butts, C. 308
Buvinić, M. 2521
Buxton, W. 65
Buzai, G. 3813
Byerlee, D. 4246
Bylund, E. 3771
Byng-Hall, J. 2911
Bynner, J. 2627
Byres, T. 3896
Byrne, M. 2960
Byrne, P. 2485
Caballé, A. 3767
Cable, D. 1100
Cabral, M. 4596
Caccavo, A. Di 5709
Cacioppo, J. 591
Cacouault-Bitaud, M. 2091

Cadène, P. 2716
Cadogan, J. 4658
Cadot, E. 5980
Cadot, O. 4756
Caglar, A. 1985
Caillard, J. 5808
Cain, R. 5874
Caistor, N. 1756
Caizzi, A. 4950
Čákiová, E. 2756
Calabrò, A. 4979
Calavita, K. 4683
Caldas, S. 2077
Calder, A. 611
Calder, P. 5552
Calderbank, R. 2452
Calderón, E. 4025
Caldwell, L. 3759
Calhoun, C. 2373, 3361
Calhoun, L. 686, 2879
Callahan, D. 5889
Callender, C. 1605
Calligaris Mamede, M. 5192
Callinicos, A. 26
Calnan, M. 5733, 5976
Calogirou, C. 2618
Calori, R. 662, 4386
Calvanese, P. 2154
Calvès, A. 2998
Calvès, G. 4950
Calvet, L. 1989
Calvin, W. 571
Calvo, T. 1433
Camagni, R. 4151
Camargo, V. 5192
Camblin, Jr., L. 2286
Cambois, E. 5514
Cambridge, P. 3329
Cameron, C. 5584
Cameron, D. 1641
Cameron, E. 5952
Cameron, L. 5528
Cameron, S. 5352, 5621
Camoun, A. 1822
Campbell, C. 2138, 3332
Campbell, D. 1145, 5671
Campbell, E. 3633
Campbell, H. 3880
Campbell, J. 726
Campbell, M. 4439, 4589
Campbell, N. 1174
Campbell, S. 1936, 5753
Campbell, W. 896, 3306
Campillo, R. 403, 1677
Campling, J. 2525, 3114

INDEX DES AUTEURS

Cancian, F. 3219
Cann, A. 686, 2879
Cannan, C. 3827
Cannon-Bowers, J. 1056
Cano, E. 4471
Cansino, C. 1199
Canter, D. 5111
Cantin, S. 2895
Cantoni, V. 634
Cantor, N. 5889
Canto-Sperber, M. 4898
Cao, Y. 4209
Capdevila, N. 295
Cape, J. 794
Capello, R. 4151
Caplan, L. 520
Cappai, G. 1231
Cappelli, P. 4451
Caprani, P. 4170
Capron, A. 4933
Caputo, A. 4766
Caputo, N. 145
Caradec, V. 5016
Caraël, M. 5891
Carbonell-Esteller, M. 4263
Carcasole, J. 5195
Card, R. 5868
Cardiel, H. 2294
Cardon, L. 5968
Cardoso, J. 3196
Cardozo Brum, M. 5642
Carens, J. 4905
Carey, M. 3629
Carey, S. 216
Cariño, L. 4935
Carl, B. 2151
Carle, A. 709
Carley, K. 1146, 1660
Carliner, G. 3580
Carlotto, M. 4731
Carlson, P. 5773
Carlson, R. 5386
Carlsson, B. 5151
Carlsson, J. 816
Carlton, R. 2876
Carmelli, D. 5389
Carmichael, F. 4501
Carmona, M. 4054
Carney, J. 5721
Carney, M. 722
Carpenter, D. 2
Carpenter, E. 2872
Carpenter, M. 3827
Carpentier, C. 2212
Carr, A. 2960, 5680, 5681

Carr, D. 4772
Carr, M. 2561, 5538
Carr, P. 5472
Carrasco, C. 3169
Carrasco, P. 2047
Carrasquillo, A. 2232
Carrère, S. 2985
Carr-Hill, R. 5540
Carrithers, M. 1424
Carroll, B. 3390
Carroll, C. 4184
Carroll, G. 4323
Carroll, J. 56, 4148
Carroll, N. 1850
Carroll, T. 3390
Carroll, W. 2263
Carruthers, B. 4314
Carruthers, S. 1732
Carson, E. 4768
Carstarphen, M. 3341
Carstens, C. 5563
Carstensen, L. 682
Carswell, J. 1118
Carter, B. 3513, 5406
Carter, C. 4056, 4788
Carter, F. 4606
Carter, M. 2784
Carter, S. 3348
Cartier, M. 5025
Cartier-Bresson, J. 5282
Cartwright, K. 2982
Cartwright, N. 2235
Caruana, L. 1579
Carucci, L. 4994
Carugati, F. 1077
Carvalho, J. de 961
Casale, G. 4815
Casanova, A. 1478
Casanova Guedes, A. 5200
Casaravilla, D. 3579
Casas, R. 3813
Casassus, C. 67
Cascio, W. 4619
Case, S. 2488, 3115
Caserio, R. 4939
Casino, Jr., V. Del 3775, 3785
Casparie, T. 5790
Caspi, A. 709
Casse, P. 4645
Cassirer, N. 4761
Casswell, S. 1349
Castañeda Camey, I. 3316
Castañeda, X. 3316
Castaños Lomnitz, H. 2251
Castellino, D. 2896

AUTHOR INDEX

Castells, M. 32
Castells, X. 5789
Casterline, J. 2763
Castilla, E. 445, 4732
Castillo, D. 4825
Castillo, M. 5683
Castles, F. 5660
Castles, S. 2550, 3544, 3634
Castoriadis, C. 296
Castro, M. 5445
Castro, R. 3350
Castro, S. 4950
Caswill, C. 13
Catalano, R. 3565
Catanese, K. 3306
Catani, A. 1158
Catanzaro, S. 675
Cater, E. 3822
Catmur, W. 1731
Cattand, P. 5980
Cattaneo, C. 5812
Cattell, N. 547
Catterall, M. 4319
Cattonar, B. 2082
Caughlin, J. 2970
Caulfield, S. 5465
Caumartin, P. 4224
Cavadino, M. 5006
Cavalli, A. 2627
Cavallo, D. 155
Cavarra, R. 3224
Cavendish, J. 1479
Cavendish, M. 5364
Cavet, J. 5549
Cavola, L. 4066
Cazés, D. 2242
Cazes, G. 5335
Cebulla, A. 3863, 4043
Ceci, S. 575
Cecil, J. 426
Cefai, D. 4888
Ceglowski, D. 435, 2610
Celis, A. 5445
Center, A. 4364
Centre on Policy on Ageing 5502
Cerbone, D. 236
Čeredničenko, G. 2238
Cerisier, A. 1323
Cernkovich, S. 5103
Cerrutti, M. 4523
Cervone, D. 561
Cœuret, A. 5025
Cha, J. 54
Chabaud, G. 5335
Chabot, S. 5280

Chace, W. 996
Chadha, K. 1733
Chadwick, C. 4451
Chadwick, K. 1475
Chahal, K. 5147
Chaika, N. 5891
Chalabi, M. al- 3948
Chaloupka, F. 5956
Chamberlayne, P. 74
Chambers, D. 1761, 3471
Chambers, Jr., J. 541
Chambert-Loir, H. 172
Champagne, M. 1055
Champion, F. 1418
Champion, L. 738
Champy, F. 1849, 1857, 1944
Chan, A. 1141, 1660, 4879
Chan, B. 5690
Chan, C. 54
Chan, D. 5829
Chan, J. 3218
Chan, K. 4699, 4735, 4746
Chan, M. 2133
Chan, R. 3657, 4108
Chan, S. 1483, 2103
Chan, Y. 2941
Chancer, L. 3121
Chandek, M. 2868
Chandhoke, S. 3948
Chandler, M. 1161
Chandola, T. 2840
Chang, E. 751
Chang, K. 3317
Chang, M. 4533
Chang, P. 1481, 3459
Chang, T. 4141
Chanson, C. 767
Chant, S. 4558
Chanteau, S. 5968
Chanter, T. 3115
Chao, A. 3061, 3323
Chapman, A. 4695
Chapman, G. 5752
Chapoulie, J. 339
Chapoulie, S. 4780
Chappell, L. 4956
Chappell, R. 2853
Charbonneau, J. 767, 2047
Chardon, A. 3702
Charles, M. 4754
Charles, N. 3114, 4521
Charles, R. 1789
Charlesworth, H. 3136
Charlesworth, S. 2422
Charlick-Paley, T. 5360

Charmé, S. 3448
Charnsangavej, T. 2061
Charvet, F. 3565
Chase-Dunn, C. 2
Chase-Lansdale, P. 5633
Chase-Vaughn, G. 681
Chashab, T. 1470
Chassin, L. 709
Chasteen, J. 1981
Chataway, J. 4287
Chatelain, J. 3702
Chatman, H. 4511
Chatterjee, U. 2800
Chatterton, P. 2252
Chatty, D. 43, 3278
Chaudhuri, M. 3112
Chauvel, L. 2618, 4441
Chaves, M. 1443
Chavez, M. 1654
Chavkin, W. 5633
Chavous, T. 3439
Checkland, P. 376
Cheibub, Z. 5220
Chelli, N. 1464
Chen, C. 4475
Chen, G. 627
Chen, J. 2258
Chen, M. 2561, 2818
Chen, R. 1625
Chen, X. 266
Chen, Z. 607, 4367
Cheng, C. 266
Cheng, L. 5389
Cheng, Y. 2133
Chernesky, R. 5764
Cherniavsky, E. 3157
Cherry, B. 4416
Cherry, F. 870
Cherry, M. 5871
Cherry, R. 4497
Cherry, V. 681
Cheshire, J. 1789
Chesnais, J. 2719
Chesneaux, J. 1200
Chesney, M. 5891
Chesson, H. 5987
Chetkovich, C. 2745
Cheung, C. 1666
Cheung, F. 5446
Chew, P. 1811
Chhotray, G. 5800
Chia, A. 4289
Chiang, S. 1930
Chibout, K. 1822
Chicchi, F. 412

Chih, D. 5928
Chiland, C. 803
Childs, P. 1178
Chilton, S. 3705
Chín, V. 3010
Chinloy, P. 3979
Chipeta, K. 3283
Chipungu, S. 5409
Chirikova, A. 3281
Chirzin, M. 4948
Chitwood, D. 5748
Chiu, C. 643, 864
Chiu, I. 768
Chiu, M. 911
Chiu, S. 4823
Chiuri, M. 4561
Chivallon, C. 4125
Cho, H. 1195, 4250, 5821
Cho Han, H. 1195
Cho, M. 3949
Chocat, B. 4025
Choe, W. 2568
Choe, Y. 1787
Chognot, C. 5475
Choi, I. 676
Choi, J. 4475
Choi, W. 1666
Cholet, P. 5716
Cholnoky, G. 3424
Chong, W. 1885
Chongsatitmun, C. 5745
Choo, C. 1116
Chopart, J. 4299
Choquet, M. 5420
Chou, T. 4055
Chovil, N. 945
Chow, I. 4600
Chow, S. 5765
Choy, L. 4029
Chreim, S. 4625
Chrétien, J. 161
Christensen, A. 932
Christensen, S. 4360
Christenson, M. 3716
Christian, B. 1965
Christian Michelsens Institutt for Videnskap og Andsfrihet 4189
Christiansen, C. 489
Christiansen, T. 5763
Christie, H. 2377
Christie, I. 2475
Christie, K. 4971
Christie, N. 5005
Christofides, N. 5200
Christopher, A. 3769, 4188

AUTHOR INDEX

Christopher, F. 3343
Chrosniak, L. 787
Chryssides, G. 1416
Chryssochoou, X. 2530
Chu, C. 5029
Chu, J. 1365, 4445
Chu, Y. 5187
Chua, B. 4334
Chua, P. 3067, 3090, 3749
Chukwuezi, B. 3868
Chung, K. 3556
Chung, M. 870
Church, A. 678, 710
Chwe, M. 1038
Cialdini, R. 3749
Ciarrochi, J. 4339
Cid Vargas, P. del 4169
Ciment, J. 2694
Cimet, S. 3518
Cinnirella, M. 834
Cintron, R. 5465
Cioffi, F. 268
Císař, O. 328
Cistone, P. 2104
Civic, D. 532
Claeys, V. 5335
Clairmont, F. 4935
Clam, J. 371
Clammer, J. 4332
Clampitt-Dunlap, S. 1819
Claney, P. 4611
Clapham, D. 4774
Clapson, M. 3983
Clarizia, P. 4580
Clark, E. 2571
Clark, G. 3249
Clark, J. 2225, 3740
Clark, L. 591, 3034
Clark, P. 4876
Clark, S. 1578, 2637, 2953, 3202
Clark, T. 1266
Clark, V. 1516
Clarke, A. 1603
Clarke, D. 2226
Clarke, I. 952
Clarke, M. 4396, 4782
Clarke, P. 12, 203, 982, 3423
Clarke, S. 4804
Clatterbaugh, K. 3240
Claudel, P. 4645
Claus-Bachmann, M. 1331
Clawson, R. 1747
Claydon, T. 1119
Claypool, H. 1063
Clayton, M. 349

Clayton, S. 3749
Clayton, T. 2513
Clegg, S. 1148, 2056
Cleland, J. 2792, 4656
Clement, R. 867
Cleminson, R. 3295
Clerici, C. 5070
Cleveland, H. 653
Clifford, E. 3675
Clifford, J. 1258
Clift, S. 3348
Clifton, N. 4659
Cliquet, R. 2712
Cloke, P. 5417, 5418
Clotfelter, C. 4768
Cloud, W. 5376
Clough, P. 1621
Cloutier-Fisher, D. 5515
Cloward, R. 4850
Clyman, D. 1012
Clymer, R. 4015
Cnaan, R. 5481
Coan, J. 2985
Coates, A. 5322
Coates, K. 198
Coates, L. 919
Coates, R. 224
Coats, S. 1063
Cobb, S. 1018
Cobb-Clark, D. 3565
Cochoy, F. 4322
Cochran, L. 2024, 2080
Cochrane, M. 5885
Cock, C. De 1957
Cockburn, C. 3070
Cockburn, T. 2604
Cockerham, W. 5773
Cocking, D. 909
Cocks, A. 5608
Cocks, M. 5813
Cocks, P. 12
Coclanis, P. 5258
Coddington, D. 5575
Codina, G. 5571
Cody, A. 1583
Coe, C. 1668
Coen, S. 1937
Coffey, A. 2189
Coffey, T. 5824
Coghlan, L. 5555
Cohen, A. 5513
Cohen, B. 2740
Cohen, C. 2266
Cohen, J. 235, 525, 3759
Cohen, L. 437

Cohen, P. 3494
Cohen, R. 5257, 5317
Cohen, S. 525
Cohen, U. 5529
Cohen, Y. 3559
Cohen-Émerique, M. 2047
Cohn, A. 4949
Cohn, C. 5350
Cohn, E. 5465
Cohn-Sherbok, D. 1547
Coid, J. 5899
Coker, C. 5348
Cokley, K. 2045
Col, É. Del 4767
Coldham, S. 5007
Cole, I. 3824
Cole, J. 1427
Cole, S. 3372
Coleman, G. 3097
Coleman, J. 2602, 2647, 5198
Coleman, M. 4497
Coleman, R. 4995
Colenso, M. 1114
Coley, R. 5633
Colgan, F. 4857
Coll, A. 3606
Coller, X. 51
Collin, D. 4230
Collins, A. 2028
Collins, D. 3374
Collins, H. 1619
Collins, M. 5928
Collins, N. 935, 4517
Collins, P. 3099, 3528
Collins, R. 5, 288, 2430
Collins, S. 5710
Collins, W. 591, 3014
Collinson, D. 230
Collis, C. 3069
Collom, E. 4839
Colman, A. 604
Colquitt, J. 4802
Colwell, J. 540, 576
Coman, G. 4564
Comaroff, J. 4227
Comas-Herrera, A. 5525
Combessie, P. 5016
Comer, L. 781
Compton, W. 5906
Concialdi, P. 4299
Condominas, G. 1468
Condon, S. 3549
Congdon, P. 2831
Conger, R. 900, 3041, 3873
Congost, R. 3891

Conill-Mendoza, E. 4272
Conklin, C. 5406
Conley, D. 2071
Conley, T. 3352
Conlon, D. 1017, 1019
Conn, A. 4701
Connell, J. 3621, 3962, 4148
Connelly, P. 2240
Conner, M. 648, 941
Connolly, J. 5072
Connolly, M. 4805
Connolly, P. 3509
Conohan, C. 3351
Conrad, F. 509
Conrad, K. 1227
Conrad, P. 1260, 5892
Constantine, J. 4451
Constantino, L. 4935
Contensou, F. 4749
Conter, B. 4793
Contini, A. 5922
Contreras Suárez, E. 5642
Contrini, E. 4466
Contu, A. 1115
Conway, D. 3621
Coohey, C. 5590
Cook, D. 5896
Cook, M. 2034
Cooke, T. 2005
Cookson, R. 5867
Cooley, V. 2104
Cooper, B. 463, 5663
Cooper, C. 4693, 4734
Cooper, D. 1548
Cooper, G. 3687
Cooper, J. 652
Cooper, M. 709, 710
Cooper, R. 3517
Cope, B. 3501
Cope, H. 3977
Copeland, B. 1593
Copeland, L. 5913
Coppock, V. 762
Coq, G. 2114
Corcuff, P. 16
Cordell, H. 3729
Cordero Valdavida, M. 450
Cordes, S. 3898
Cordón, J. 5325
Cordray, D. 426
Corker, M. 2461
Cormack, E. 5721
Cormack, M. 1736
Cornelissen, S. 964
Cornelius, S. 1667

AUTHOR INDEX

Cornell, D. 3115, 3302
Cornia, G. 2833
Corning, A. 824
Corning, P. 2329
Cornish, I. 629
Cornwell, G. 2767
Coronado, V. 525
Coronil, F. 4227
Corraliza, J. 3726
Corrigan, P. 4056
Corsi, G. 5236
Corsini, R. 556
Cortés, J. 4142
Cortese, A. 4447
Cortina, J. 787
Cortis, N. 4542
Corvo, K. 2872
Coss, P. 5181
Cosslett, T. 3107
Costa, A. da 1610
Costa Gomes, P. Da 58
Costa, H. 4863
Costa, Jr., P. 709
Costa, O. 4949
Costa, P. 4120
Costa, T. 3911
Costa-Lascoux, J. 2122
Costas, I. 3232
Costilla, L. 4968
Cosyns, M. 5862
Cots, F. 5789
Cotter, D. 4525
Cotterell, R. 5158
Cotterill, L. 2469
Cottler, L. 5906
Cottret, B. 1478
Cotts Watkins, S. 2747
Couch, C. 4109
Coudassot-Ramirez, S. 1899
Couffignal, G. 58
Coulangeon, P. 1977, 4767
Couldry, N. 1743
Coulibaly, N. 3924
Coulmas, F. 2523
Coulshed, V. 5708
Coulter, A. 5770
Coulter, C. 2306
Counelis, J. 1999
Coupe, T. 5124
Couper, M. 537
Coupland, J. 2667, 3358
Courgeau, D. 2626
Cournoyer, D. 756
Courpasson, D. 5216
Court, P. 5016

Cousseau, B. 3763
Coutinho, M. 2026
Couturier, J. 168
Coverdill, J. 4416
Covin, J. 4420
Coward, H. 3764
Cowburn, M. 5672
Cowell, R. 4058
Cowie, H. 2218
Cowmeadow, P. 800
Cox, D. 736, 5686, 5704
Cox, H. 3695
Cox, M. 3020
Cox, P. 5544
Cox, T. 4680
Coy, P. 1010
Coyle-Shapiro, J. 4627
Coyne, J. 2892
Crabbe, J. 591
Craft, W. 630
Cragg, W. 4417
Craghan, M. 3745
Craig, G. 3827, 5586
Craig, R. 1808
Craig, W. 257, 1571
Cram, F. 5470
Cramer, D. 421, 475, 3846
Crandall, C. 972
Crane, A. 4358
Crane, M. 5422
Crane, R. 4053, 4370
Crang, M. 2608, 3790, 4134, 4143
Crankshaw, O. 4169
Crant, J. 1105
Crary, A. 262
Craven, D. 1801
Cravens, K. 4658
Craviotti, C. 4243
Crawford, A. 5020
Crawford, C. 2017
Crawford, E. 225
Crawford, G. 1327, 5721
Crawford, J. 1785
Crawford, T. 1882
Crean, K. 3913
Creese, H. 1772
Crenner, E. 2930
Crenshaw, E. 3716
Crespin, R. 5942
Cress, D. 5271
Cresswell, R. 135
Creveld, M. van 5348, 5353
Crewe, L. 4315
Crewe, M. 5363
Crews-Meyer, K. 5155

Criblez, B. 2117
Crichton, J. 5056
Crisp, R. 1041, 2487
Crocker, J. 843
Crocombe, J. 555
Croissant, J. 1566
Crompton, R. 2427, 4541
Cronin, A. 4324
Crook, D. 2130
Cropanzano, R. 1106, 4660
Cross, C. 3868
Cross, J. 3406
Cross, M. 3568
Cross, R. 1091
Cross, T. 4760
Crouch, C. 4587
Crouch, M. 1300
Crouchley, R. 4486
Crouter, A. 3053, 3213
Crow, I. 5006
Crowder, K. 3835, 4014
Crowley, D. 1274
Crowther, D. 4056, 4788
Crowther, J. 2010
Crump, N. 1115
Crush, J. 3599, 3633
Cruz, B. 2211
Cruz, J. 2294
Csemicskó, I. 1816
Csémy, L. 2814
Cua, A. 273
Cucó i Giner, J. 931
Cuddon, J. 99
Cui, M. 900
Cukrowicz, H. 4767
Cullen, F. 5073, 5083, 5086, 5090
Cullen, R. 5309
Cullingworth, J. 3872
Culp, A. 3049
Culp, R. 3049
Cunha, M. da 3732
Cunin, E. 3519
Cunningham, H. 2627
Cunningham, M. 5627
Cunningham-Burley, S. 1595
Cuomo, C. 3449
Cuong, B. 2927
Curran, C. 4420
Curran, J. 1702
Currie, E. 5004
Currie, J. 2068
Curry, G. 5109
Curry, J. 3879
Curtis, S. 504, 2716
Curtis-Boles, H. 5409

Cusack, T. 3070
Cushing, J. 1599
Cushman, P. 5940
Custen, G. 1882
Cutler, J. 1909
Cutlip, S. 4364
Cutright, P. 5432
Cutrona, C. 838, 1010
Cutter, S. 3752
Cuypers, S. 2303
Cwerner, S. 1316, 2546
Cyranowski, J. 3306
Czarnocka, J. 796
Czernichow, P. 5968
Czetwertynski-Sytnik, L. 4606
Dabinett, G. 1685
Dąbrowska, A. 2009
Dąbrowska, E. 636
Dachler, M. 607
Dahab, E. 1914
Dahan, Y. 2177
Dahler-Larsen, P. 5224
Dahlgren, P. 1773
Dahlin, M. 635
Dahmann, D. 4072
Dain, M. Le 5716
Dalal, M. 5923
Dale, A. 447
Dale, B. 3037
Dale-Olsen, H. 3226
Dalgalarrondo, S. 5942, 5982
Dall'Agata, C. 4448
Dallaire, C. 979
Dallos, R. 2937, 5671
Dalmau, E. 5789
Dalrymple, N. 3743
Dalton, S. 2915
Daly, A. 4743
Daly, H. 3759
Daly, J. 360
Daly, M. 5616, 5628
Damais, J. 2716
Damayanthi, U. 4516
Damerow, P. 1161
Damon, J. 2313, 5016, 5716
Damon, W. 3380
Danaher, G. 294
Đang, P. 545
Danieli, L. 2456
Daniels, K. 4644, 4672, 4710
Dannhaeuser, N. 4165
Dant, T. 4333
Danziger, K. 870
Danziger, S. 808, 5633, 5658
Dar, N. 3460, 5527

AUTHOR INDEX

Dar, Y. 5351
Darbon, S. 1350
Darby, B. 3248
Darby, W. 3779
Darcovich, N. 2006
Darden, J. 4019
Dardenne, B. 3283
Darier, É. 3717
Darjee, R. 5056
Darke, J. 4147
Darley, A. 1779
Darling, J. 2117
Darton, R. 5525
Das, P. 2701
Das, V. 1002
Dasgupta, N. 826
Dasgupta, P. 2793
Dasgupta, S. Das 2870
Dass, M. 5704
Datta, B. 5200
Daumann, F. 5793
Dauphin, V. 2328
Dau-Schmidt, K. 5154
Davant, J. 5806
Davaz-Mardin, A. 104
Dave, A. 5704
Dave, P. 2913
Davenport, S. 1927
David, O. 5537
David, P. 2638
David, R. 2213
David, S. 3215
David-Aeschlimann, R. 4950
Davidson, A. 3634
Davidson, J. 3115
Davidson, L. 5425
Davidson, P. 3296
Davidson, R. 591, 739
Davidson, S. 1309
Davidson-Harden, J. 3296
Davie, G. 1434, 1450, 2532
Davies, B. 430, 5525
Davies, C. 1194, 4521, 4807
Davies, D. 786
Davies, G. 812, 2106, 3775
Davies, H. 1716, 5784, 5835
Davies, N. 5366
Davies, P. 4587
Davila, A. 3565, 4440
Davis, D. 4327, 5361
Davis, G. 4366
Davis, K. 3135
Davis, M. 716, 2401
Davison, E. 5085
Dawes, R. 2640

Dawla, A. El 5200
Dawod, N. 3048
Dawoud, N. 2065
Dawson, A. 4606
Dawson, P. 2910
Dawud-Noursi, S. 2871
Day, A. 2862
Day, K. 5529
Day, L. 5312
Day, R. 3051
Dayan, D. 1409
Daymon, C. 1701
Deacon, B. 5622
Deakins, S. 772
Dean, A. 1166
Dean, B. 2754
Dean, C. 5096
Dean, H. 5643
Dean, J. 5615
Dear, M. 3955
Dearden, L. 2287
Deas, I. 4097
Death, R. 3303
Deaux, K. 2530
Debril, T. 4322
Decaillot, M. 4201
DeCarlo, T. 4658
Decew, J. 4933
Déchaux, J. 2930
Dechesne, M. 1081
Dederichs, A. 2428
Dee, J. 2258
Deeg, D. 2659
Deem, R. 2305
Deetz, S. 416
DeFilippis, J. 3745, 4017
DeGrandpre, R. 594
Dehesh, A. 4233
Delamont, S. 2189, 2532
Delaney, J. 4877
Delano, P. 3315
Delate, R. 5363
Delaunay, J. 4214
Delbridge, R. 4618, 4875
Delesalle, H. 5025
Delfos, M. 5579
Deliège, R. 1398
Deliens, L. 5862
Deliyanni, K. 3060
Della Toffalo, D. 5918
DellaPergola, S. 3518
Delmas-Marty, M. 5025
Delor, F. 5891
Delpeuch, F. 5980
Demailly, L. 67

INDEX DES AUTEURS

Demerath, III, N. 1459
Demeulemeester, J. 4454
Demicheli, V. 5761
Demick, J. 574
Demin, A. 4593
Demir, C. 2153
Demo, D. 3020
Demoor, M. 3102
DeMoss, C. Lee 2886
Demuth, S. 5017
Denemark, R. 2541
Denis, C. 979
Denis, E. 3813
Denis, J. 4622, 5903
Denis, S. 5265
Dennemann, A. 4109
Denning, S. 4056
Dennis, M. 5818
Denoncourt, H. 5420
DeNora, T. 1982
Densley, L. 833
Dent, R. 5554
Department of Health, House of Commons, UK 5639
Department of the Environment, Transport and the Regions, House of Commons, UK 4078
DePoy, E. 2480
Der, G. 757
Derisley, J. 813
Derksen, L. 498
Derlon, B. 992
Derné, S. 1897
Desai, M. 5704
Desai, S. 2007
DeSanctis, G. 1054, 1660
Descola, P. 381
Descombes, V. 268, 2439, 4898
Deshpande, A. 4285
Deshpande, S. 2683
Desilets, M. 5420
Desmond, C. 5363
Desrosières, A. 2382
Détang-Dessendre, C. 3623
Dettmar, E. 142
Deuchar, M. 610
Deutschmann, C. 4192
Devas, N. 4169
DeVerteuil, G. 3784
Devine, T. 1510
DeVita, M. 5883
Devlieger, P. 1898
Devos, T. 1057
Dew, K. 5859
Dewailly, J. 3820

DeWalt, K. 5541
Dewe, P. 4680
DeWind, J. 3545
Dewitte, S. 665
Dewsbury, J. 3788
Dey, D. 2818
Deyo, F. 4818
Dhaouadi, M. 4205
Dhesi, A. 1998, 3855
Diab, T. 2081, 2173, 2246
Diakite, C. 520
Diakité, D. 2121
Diallo, A. 1822
Dialmy, A. 5981
Diamantini, C. 4025
Diamantopoulos, A. 4658
Diamond, I. 520, 2768, 2853, 2974
Diamond, L. 3352
Diani, M. 5228, 5275
Diawara, M. 2568
Díaz, A. 995, 4169
Díaz Martínez, F. 5343
Díaz Narbona, I. 1925
Diaz Olvera, L. 4068
Díaz Soler, A. 1333
Díaz-Castillo, C. 3767
Díaz-Muñoz, M. 3767
Diaz-Olvera, L. 4011
Diaz-Perez, M. 797
DiCarlo, M. 5592
Dichy, J. 1822
Dickens, L. 4537
Dickens, P. 390, 2532
Dickens, R. 4587
Dickerson, M. 5377
Dickerson, P. 828
Dickerson, S. 3715
Dickey, S. 2421
Dicko, F. 5980
Dicks, B. 3864
Dickter, D. 663
Diderichsen, F. 2999, 4696
Die Hängematten e.V. 3206
Diehl, G. 1331
Diekmann, A. 90
Diene, I. 1822
Diessel, H. 636
Diethrich, G. 1319
Dietz, B. 3647
Dietz, T. 1297
Diez-Roux, A. 2808
DiGirolamo, G. 591
Dignan, J. 5006
DiIulio, Jr., J. 1515
Dijk, F. Van 3338

AUTHOR INDEX

Dijk, L. Van 402
Dijksterhuis, A. 3283
Dijkstra, A. 2239
Dijst, M. 3767
Dikaiou, M. 3592
Dill, E. 2174
Dillard, J. 1647
Dillard, P. 3525
Dilley, F. 1487
Dillon, J. 5591
Dillon, M. 340
DiLorenzo, T. 4119
Dimier, V. 4897
Dindo, R. 1893
Dines, N. 5275
Ding, C. 4150
Ding, N. 3323
Dingsdale, A. 4168
Dintenfass, M. 192
Dionne, E. 1515
DiPrete, T. 5625
Direcktoratet for utviklingshjelp 4189
Diservi, L. 5716
Dishion, T. 709
Dittes, J. 56
Diuguid, L. 3391
Dix, G. 3948
Dixon, J. 839, 5605, 5795
Dixon, L. 5030
Dixon, P. 5540
Dixon, T. 3498
Djupe, P. 1439
Djurdjev, B. 4606
Dlamini-Zuma, N. 5363
Dmitriev, M. 4256
Doan, J. 1227
Doan, K. 2352
Doba, G. 369
Dobash, R. 2865
Dobbelaere, K. 56
Dobbins, J. 5928
Dobesz, U. 2009
Dockemdorff, E. 4169
Dodd, N. 1273
Dodder, R. 2489
Dodge, M. 4511
Dodier, N. 5982
Dodson, B. 3599
Dodson, M. 3295
Dodsworth, J. 5545
Doel, M. 1053
Doeuff, M. Le 1613
Doherty, T. 1882
Doja, A. 965
Dolan, S. 591

Dold, A. 5813
Dolderman, D. 946
Dolev, Y. 222
Dolinko, D. 5174
Dolinski, D. 580
Dolitsky, M. 1789
Dollenmayer, J. 996
Dölling, I. 3115
Domb, R. 1935
Domenighetti, G. 4692
Domingues, J. 324, 391
Domínguez, J. 2677
Dominicé, L. 5461
Dominy, M. 1258
Donahue, P. 5518
Donald, S. 1767
Donath, S. 3169
Donati, P. 4951
Donchin, A. 5849, 5861
Dondero, T. 5964
Donges, P. 4787
Donnelly, C. 2135
Donnelly, J. 2237
Donnelly, M. 3195
Donnermeyer, J. 2633
Donovan, D. 5391, 5744
Donovan, J. 707
Dooley, C. 2188
Dooley, M. 5636
Doolin, K. 4310
Doolittle, F. 5567
Doorslaer, E. van 5763
Doraï, M. 3664
Dorantes, C. 312
Doray, B. 801
Dordoy, A. 3720
Dore-Cabral, C. 3398
Dorling, D. 2844
Dorling, G. 5352
Dormont, B. 2626
Doron, G. 4039
Dostal, E. 5735
Dotan, Y. 5154
Doubt, K. 5332
Dougherty, D. 1865, 2669
Douglass, M. 3927
Douglas-Scott, S. 5163
Doumato, E. 1520
Doumbia, A. 2121
Doutreligne, P. 4950
Douvan, I. 1624
Douville, O. 801
Douzinas, C. 5161
Dövényi, Z. 4168
Dovidio, J. 835, 861

INDEX DES AUTEURS

Dowd, T. 1982
Dowling, B. 5772
Dowling, E. 2859
Downey, D. 3522
Downey, G. 933
Downey, L. 5391
Downing, J. 637
Downs, A. 4080
Downs, J. 2640
Downs, T. 3798
Doyle, M. 1119
Draga-Alexandru, M. 3227
Dragomirecká, E. 2814
Draguns, J. 710
Drakakis-Smith, D. 3964
Drake, R. 2458
Drakeford, M. 5709
Drakulic, S. 4416
Draper, E. 4683
Draper, H. 5847
Drasgow, F. 2335
Drazen, C. 1898
Dreachslin, J. 5846
Dreiling, M. 5227
Drescher, A. 3867
Dreu, C. de 1021, 1022, 1084
Drew, A. 4864
Drèze, J. 5058
Drgona, V. 4606
Drinot, P. 143
Drizin, S. 5000
Drobizheva, L. 9
Drobnič, S. 4531
Drolet, A. 1027
Droulers, M. 58, 3768
Drower, S. 5684
Druetta, D. 2616
Druine, N. 2006
Drulhe, M. 2679
Drummond, D. 5406
Drummond, I. 3880
Drummond, L. 3927, 4176
Drummond, P. 705
Drury, J. 829, 1005, 1042
Drweski, B. 5092
Dryburgh, H. 5369
Drysdale, J. 1053
Du Bois, W. 3528
Du, G. 1894
Duarte, A. 5192
Dubanoski, J. 710
Dubar, C. 2618
Dube, S. 3311
Dubet, F. 2014
Dubey, A. 3654

Dubois, J. 1478
Dubois, L. 4939
Dubois-Arber, F. 5891
Dubuisson-Quellier, S. 4321, 4322
Ducatel, K. 1645
Ducharme, L. 4741
Duchêne, J. 2363
Duchéneaut, B. 4372
Duchesne, I. 5763
Duchnowski, A. 2154
Duckett, P. 2466
Dudgeon, P. 102
Duff, R. 3849
Duffy, A. 2892
Duffy, M. 1064
Dufour, L. 1549
Dufour-Kippelen, S. 2626
Dugan, E. 2028
Duhaldeborde, Y. 633
Duhurt, Q. 1899
Duke, V. 4168
Dukepoo, F. 1620
Duke-Williams, O. 3622
Dumestre, G. 2121
DuMont, K. 5818
Dunbar, M. 757
Duncan, B. 5951
Duncan, C. 500, 2807, 4487, 4852
Duncan, L. 2013
Duncan, P. 4117
Dundes, A. 1258
Dunford, F. 426
Dunford, R. 1127
Dunlap, R. 3749
Dunmore, E. 804
Dunn, J. 4486
Dunn, T. 4305
Dunne, G. 2915
Dunne, M. 3308
Dunning, D. 657, 851, 905
Dunning, E. 5448
Dunphy, E. 5364
Dunphy, R. 3082
Duong, T. Chi 2675
Dupérier, E. 3702
Duplain, M. 1035
Duplantier, J. 5968
Durand, C. 4404
Durand, J. 3565
Durandal, J. 2679
Durell, J. 5744
Durham, E. 4949
Durik, A. 3306
Durnin, J. 2001
Durrheim, K. 839

AUTHOR INDEX

Durrill, W. 2321
Durston, J. 2345
Duru-Bellat, M. 2014, 2115, 2116
Dusci, L. 625
Dushay, R. 772
Dushnik, L. 2084
Dutta, B. 486
Dutta, K. 3112
Dutta, M. 4575
Dutta, S. 4169
Dutton, J. 4383
Duvignaud, J. 58
Duyne, P. Van 5094
Düzkan, A. 3206
Dvořáková, A. 2720
Dvořáková, V. 2684
Dweck, C. 704
Dworkin, R. 5726
Dwyer, C. 3557
Dwyer, D. 917, 4711
Dwyer, O. 3777
Dyck, D. 1025
Dyer-Witheford, N. 4213
Dykstra, P. 4765
Dyson, A. 2066
Dyson, T. 5983
Dzúrová, D. 2814
Eades, D. 5170
Eagleton, M. 669
Eagleton, T. 1225
Earp, J. 3336
Easterby-Smith, M. 1128
Easterman, M. 1756
Easthope, A. 1181
Eaton, L. 711
Eaton, R. 184
Ebbs, G. 297
Eberhardt, C. 1072
Eberhardt, P. 2687
Eberl, J. 5851
Eberle, T. 119
Ebsworth, M. 1819
Ebsworth, T. 1819
Eby, L. 1135
Eccleston, C. 5891
Echevarría, R. 1308
Echevarria, S. 3565
Echeverria, R. 3895
Eckes, T. 3283
Edelman, L. 5154
Eder, K. 4966
Edin, K. 2991, 5633
Edlund, L. 2984
Edström, B. 1230
Edwards, B. 2213

Edwards, C. 2915
Edwards, J. 2902
Edwards, R. 2191, 2932
Edwards, V. 4652
Eemeren, F. Van 1650
Eerola, M. 446
Egan, G. 5699
Eggli, C. 2350
Egholk, K. 2230
Eheart, B. 5568
Ehrlich, I. 5897
Eiche, K. 2213
Eickelman, D. 1263
Eidelberg, P. 4864
Eidson, J. 162
Eiji, O. 977
Eijk, C. van der 423
Eijs, P. Van 4764
Eilders, C. 1730
Eilersen, A. 4025
Einwohner, R. 5253
Eisenbach, Z. 2834
Eisenmann, T. 1100
Eisenstadt, S. 1162, 1263, 1394
Ekblad, S. 5823
Ekblom, P. 5088
Ekeberg, Ø. 5838
Ekehammar, B. 3461
Ekström, M. 1717
Elander, J. 5078
Elder, Jr., G. 900, 3873
Elen, J. 2193
Elford, R. 1410
Elgin, D. 2508
Eliaeson, S. 365
Elias, G. 3002
Elias, R. 2213
Elifson, K. 5386
Éliot, E. 5968
Elizabeth, V. 2915
Ell, K. 766
Elle, M. 4025
Ellegård, K. 3767
Ellem, B. 4833
Ellen, I. 4013
Ellerbrock, T. 3309
Ellinger, B. 1834
Ellingsæter, A. 4552
Ellingstad, T. 5399
Elliot, G. 5363
Elliott, A. 896
Elliott, J. 4431
Elliott, L. 3759, 5401
Elliott, M. 451
Elliott, S. 800

Ellis, B. 920
Ellis, D. 2392
Ellis, G. 1756
Ellis, J. 1765, 1766
Ellis McLeod, L. 2947
Ellison, C. 1074, 5106
Ellison, G. 5127, 5273
Ellsberg, M. 5439
Ellwood, D. 1900
Elmhirst, R. 3557
Eloundou-Enyegue, P. 2767
Els, C. 4650
Elsbach, K. 462
Elshtain, J. 5348
Elson, S. 650
Elster, J. 723
Elston, D. 468
Elvira, D. 5789
Elwood, S. 528
Ely, M. 2642
Ely, R. 3097
Emadi, H. 1536
Emch, M. 5838
Emerson, R. 3121
Emig, R. 3527
Emigh, R. 4220
Emmelkamp, P. 2987
Emmerson, C. 5803
Emmison, M. 1870, 4329
Emmitt, H. 1936
Émond, I. 2893
Empey, L. 5046
Emsley, C. 5133
Encarnación, O. 4596
Enders, D. 1310
Endo, T. 369
Enevold, J. 3245
Enfield, N. 1237
Eng, D. 3115
Eng, K. 3589
Engel, D. 145
Engelhardt, Jr., H. 4933
Engels, K. 4787
Engeström, Y. 1115
England, P. 4525
Engle, M. 5421
Engle, P. 5969
English, D. 5555
Englund, H. 1482
Enloe, C. 3115
Ennuyer, B. 2679
Enriquez, E. 801, 2317
Ensari, N. 837
Enthoven, A. 5732, 5779
Entrena, F. 4261

Entwisle, D. 4435
Entwistle, J. 1325
Enzmann, D. 5452
Epley, N. 851
Epp, C. 5154
Epstein, A. 5351
Epstein, R. 4933
Erasmus, Z. 2436, 3438
Erasov, B. 5091
Erba, H. 5912, 5928
Ercole, R. D' 3702
Erdmann, J. 5891
Erel, O. 3029
Ericksen, J. 522, 3298
Erickson, B. 4416
Erickson, K. 2393
Ericsson, K. 2668
Ericsson, T. 2901
Erikson, R. 2014
Erlich, V. 2057
Erman, T. 1517
Ermisch, J. 2958
Ernest, P. 225
Ernst, D. 847
Ernst, J. 5582
Erskine, R. 747
Ertl, H. 2124
Es, R. Van 4417
Escobar, A. 520
Escobar, F. 4102
Eser, A. 5889
Eshel, I. 463
Eslea, M. 3458
Espinal Pérez, C. 3953
Espinal, R. 3190
Esping-Andersen, G. 32
Espitia, M. 3563
Esplin, P. 5562
Esposito, L. 3453
Esprit 2439
Essed, P. 2118, 3067
Essenburg, T. 3967
Essex, J. 4160
Esterik, P. Van 3244
Estrade, M. 2626
Estreicher, S. 4877
Etard, J. 2832
Etemadi, F. 4169
Etemadi, N. 4960
Ettorre, E. 43, 2755
Etzioni, A. 1442, 2330
Europa Publications Limited 85, 87
European Centre for the Study of Policing 5133
Eva, F. 1000

AUTHOR INDEX

Evans, A. 2826
Evans, D. 3565, 3972
Evans, G. 5517
Evans, J. 631
Evans, N. 2128
Evans, S. 3557
Evans, W. 2034
Evdokimova-Dinello, N. 4349
Everett, E. 758
Evertsson, L. 5651
Every, E. Van 1108
Evetts, J. 4513
Evin, C. 5814
Evlampiev, I. 241
Evrard, O. 3576
Ewen, R. 699
Ewick, P. 5154
Ewing, D. 5493
Exline, J. 717
Expósito, F. 3283
Eyles, J. 5970
Eylon, D. 4360
Eymard-Duvernay, F. 4322, 4613
Eyre, S. 3357
Eysenck, M. 615
Ezeh, A. 2939
Ezra, M. 2827
Ezzati-Rice, T. 525
Fabrigar, L. 713
Faden, R. 5838
Fagerlund, S. 2901
Fah, G. 1540
Fahy Bryceson, D. 3868
Fainstein, S. 3568, 4073
Fairbrother, P. 4818, 4854, 4873
Fairhurst, J. 3767
Fairlie, R. 4479
Fairtlough, G. 3759
Faist, T. 3683, 3686
Falah, G. 3462
Falck, R. 5386
Falit-Baiamonte, A. 461
Falk, D. 5678
Falk, I. 3910
Falk, N. 4028
Falk, P. 1287
Falk, R. 2577
Falk, W. 4549
Falkner, K. 503
Falkum, E. 5838
Falla, R. 59
Falque, M. 3759
Falzon, L. 1043
Fan, P. 3237
Fan, S. 4246

Fanu, J. Le 5734
Farache-Jamet, C. 5716
Fararo, T. 308
Farcy, J. 5123
Faret, L. 3682
Fargues, P. 2795
Farmer, E. 2024, 2146, 5933
Farmer, T. 5933
Farnham, S. 732
Farnsworth, B. 5894
Farole, Jr., D. 5154
Farrell, Jr., W. 3996
Farrell, M. 5380
Farrenkopf, J. 1201
Farringdon, F. 5955
Farrington, D. 426, 3006
Fassin, D. 5980
Fassin, Y. 4417
Fattore, G. 5922
Fatyga, B. 2592
Faubion, J. 1258
Faucett, J. 4776
Faulks, K. 4891
Faure, S. 1858
Fausto-Sterling, A. 3115
Faw, L. 5737
Fawcett, B. 2471
Fawcett, L. 2525
Fay, B. 268
Fayer, J. 1819
Fazal, S. 3813
Feather, H. 1289
Feather, J. 1646
Featherstone, M. 32
Fedderke, J. 2163
Feder, L. 426
Federici, M. 2456
Federman, C. 4999
Feeney, B. 935
Feenstra, R. 2568
Feghali, L. 1822
Fei, L. 1895
Fein, S. 883
Feinberg, M. 3052
Feinberg, R. 4990
Feintuck, M. 1734
Fejfar, M. 709
Feld, S. 2917
Feldman, D. 4360
Feldman, M. 809, 1130, 4113
Feldman, R. 162, 885
Feldman, S. 124
Feldman, T. 3755
Feliciano, P. 5386
Felk, A. 3869

INDEX DES AUTEURS

Felson, R. 2883
Felstead, A. 4798
Feltham, C. 5714
Fendrich, M. 5115
Fenet, F. 5475
Feng, W. 2710
Fengtong, G. 1894
Fennell, J. 114
Fennema, M. 423
Fenton, N. 1269
Fenwick, V. 3517
Fenyvesi, A. 1816
Ferber, A. 3259
Ferguson, A. 1991
Ferguson, D. 1742
Ferguson, E. 694, 741, 1143, 4800
Ferguson, M. 591
Ferguson, S. 2915, 3100
Fergusson, D. 2074, 3056, 5045, 5051, 5381
Fergusson, R. 97
Ferhat, L. 2618
Ferko, I. 2457
Ferlie, E. 5841
Fernandes, G. 5704
Fernandes, L. 3148
Fernandez, A. 3575
Fernandez, J. 3702
Fernandez, R. 4732
Fernández-Kelly, P. 3115
Fernquist, R. 5432
Ferraro, K. 2891
Ferrarotti, F. 2526
Ferraz, B. 3817
Ferree, M. 3180
Ferreira, M. 3283
Ferreira, P. 2358
Ferreira, R. 5192
Ferreira de Oliveira, J. 2147
Ferrell, L. 4420
Ferrell, O. 4420
Ferrer, J. 2294
Ferrera, M. 2320, 5641
Ferry, J. 1694
Feteris, E. 1650
Feuerverger, A. 480
Feuvre, N. Le 4541
Fey, C. 4633
Feyerherm, W. 426
Feyisetan, B. 2761
Fiander, M. 765
Fichman, L. 776
Fidell, B. 5682
Fidler, D. 1308
Fidyk, S. 225
Field, L. 971

Field, S. 5036
Field, T. 3131
Fieldes, D. 4712
Fieldhouse, E. 447
Fielding, J. 499, 5105
Fielding, N. 5105, 5147
Fields, W. 1161
Fien, J. 3723
Fienberg, S. 2436, 3428
Figueiredo, A. 4949
Figueredo, A. 3201, 5818
Filipović, R. 1793
Filkins, R. 3898
Fillmore, K. 2819
Filson, D. 49
Finan, B. 1694
Finch, B. 3565
Fincham, F. 2928, 2979
Fincham, R. 1138
Finckenauer, J. 426
Findeis, J. 4591
Findlay, P. 4608
Findor, A. 984
Fine, B. 4193
Fine, G. 462
Fine, M. 3115
Fine, R. 5311
Finegan, J. 1112
Fineman, S. 1109
Finer, C. 43
Finin, G. 3642
Fink, B. 3318
Fink, G. 4198
Finke, R. 1500
Finke, S. 117
Finkel, A. 149
Finkelstein, J. 5633
Finlay, K. 1075, 3517
Finlay, L. 1053
Finlay, W. 878, 4416
Finlayson, J. 367
Finlayson, R. 1813
Finn, P. 5721
Fiore Ohama, M. 1801
Fiorito, J. 4877
Firminger, K. 792
Firth-Cozens, J. 5838
Fischer, A. 689, 3095
Fischer, H. 3699, 3776
Fischer, L. 1882
Fischer, M. 4266
Fischer-Kerli, D. 501
Fischhoff, B. 2640
Fish, J. 603
Fishbach, A. 760

AUTHOR INDEX

Fisher, A. 1867
Fisher, B. 5083
Fisher, G. 756
Fisher, J. 4398
Fisher, R. 503, 2185, 5084
Fisher, W. 2726, 3296
Fishman, J. 1817, 2523, 3415
Fishman, R. 4024
Fisk, M. 2674
Fiske, E. 2166
Fiske, S. 822, 3283
Fisscher, O. 4417, 5790
Fitzenberger, B. 4795
Fitzgerald, H. 3019
Fitzgerald, K. 5276
Fitzgerald, L. 5841
Fitzpatrick, R. 5731
Fitzpatrick, S. 4159, 5431
Flaherty, J. 4493
Flamholtz, E. 4604
Flanagan, N. 4743
Flap, H. 5300, 5306
Flathman, R. 304
Fleischacker, S. 2354
Fleishman, E. 4614
Fletcher, A. 5546
Fletcher, C. 1147, 4607
Fletcher, R. 5200
Fleury, M. 5903
Flier, H. van der 2288
Fligstein, N. 4192
Flint, K. 3689
Flood, C. 217
Flora, P. 4966
Florian, V. 685, 2942
Florin, A. 545
Florin, D. 5758
Flowers, D. 1991
Flowers, P. 3388, 5951
Fly, J. 3729
Flynn, C. 2863
Flynn, F. 4847
Flynn, M. 225
Flyvbjerg, B. 243
Foddy, M. 3283
Fogarty, T. 4773
Fokkema, T. 4765
Folasade, I. 2825
Folbre, N. 3169
Foley, G. 2049
Foley, P. 4159
Folger, R. 4660
Folkman, S. 5856
Follari, R. 1158
Foner, N. 3545, 3632

Fong, E. 903, 4020
Fonn, S. 5200
Fontaine, L. 4263
Fontan, J. 5265
Foos, C. 2213
Foran, J. 3067, 3090
Forbes, A. 5200
Forbes, D. 3565
Ford, G. 757
Ford, R. 1013
Førde, R. 5838
Forgas, J. 850, 4339
Forges, J. 1906
Forman, T. 3508
Formenti, S. 766
Fornäs, J. 1215
Forness, S. 2020
Foroni, F. 2901
Forrester, K. 4398
Forstater, M. 4900
Forster, C. 3928
Förster, J. 657
Forster, P. 3326
Forsyth, F. 3069
Fortgang, R. 1018
Fortier, A. 3422
Fortier, J. 5420
Fortin, C. 767
Fortin, L. 2893
Fortin, M. 767, 5814
Fortis, E. 5025
Fortuijn, J. 3767
Fortune, W. 5193
Forward, L. 2674
Foster, C. 2788
Foster, E. 5610
Foster, P. 454, 4789
Fothergill, S. 4439, 4594
Fotiadou, M. 5089
Fouché, P. 1323
Fountain, J. 5380
Fourmet, F. 5980
Fournier, V. 4621
Fowler, B. 1962
Fox, M. 4711
Fox, N. 5724, 5928
Fox, P. 5519
Fradkin, R. 3891
Fragata, A. 2653
Fraley, R. 670, 918
Frame, L. 5596
France, E. 5558
Francesco, A. 4367
Francesconi, M. 2958
Francillon, J. 5025

INDEX DES AUTEURS

Francis, D. 1800
Francis, H. 2190
Franck, T. 5159
Francmanis, J. 1973
Francq, B. 3969, 5641
Franičević, V. 4255
Frank, F. 2005
Frank, K. 1541
Frank, R. 5786
Franke, V. 5344
Frankel, E. 1442
Frankel, M. 525
Frankis, J. 5951
Franklin, A. 5928
Franklin, B. 4774
Franks, M. 3067, 3172
Franks, S. 4547
Frantz, K. 3998
Franzen, A. 1670
Franzmann, M. 1463
Franzway, S. 4883
Frasca, T. 5891
Fraser, G. 2136
Frątczak, E. 2785
Frattura, L. 5909
Frau-Meigs, D. 1662
Frayne, C. 4664, 5803
Frazee, S. 5085
Frazer, E. 1751
Frazis, H. 4792
Freedland, M. 4587
Freedman, A. 5292
Freedman, D. 2699
Freedman, J. 3602
Freeman, L. 3988
Freeman, M. 2602
Freeman, S. 2020
Frege, C. 4820, 4860
Freidberg, S. 4477
Freitag, M. 4592
Freitag-Rouanet, B. 4121
French, M. 5744, 5748
French, S. 2477, 5938
French, W. 1125, 4417
Frerichs, P. 2413
Freudenburg, W. 4128
Freund, P. 4313
Freundschuh, S. 613
Frey, Jr., D. 4263
Frey, R. 4933
Fricker, M. 3101
Fridlund, A. 589
Fried, M. 2754
Friedberg, M. 5474
Friedberg, R. 3604

Friedlander, Y. 2834
Friedman, D. 4933, 5043
Friedman, H. 709
Friedman, I. 2096
Friedman, J. 2927
Friedman, R. 660
Friedrichs, D. 5312
Friese, H. 1280
Frieze, I. 3201
Frijters, P. 4183
Friot, B. 5475
Frisbie, W. 3565
Frisina, W. 266
Fritsch, P. 4894
Fritz, C. 666
Fritz, H. 709
Froese, K. 204
Frognier, A. 5218
Frongillo, Jr., E. 3546
Frost, A. 4858, 4877
Frost, N. 4398, 5574
Froud, J. 4310
Frow, J. 1228, 2580
Froyland, I. 2862
Fruidà, L. 2456
Fu, H. 2845
Fu, P. 4600
Fuchs, M. 1208, 5246
Fuchs, S. 5
Fudge, J. 3080
Fuente, E. de la 30
Fuente, J. de la 2294
Fujigaki, Y. 1604
Fujita, F. 687
Fujita, H. 50
Fujita, K. 3927
Fujiwara, Y. 5524
Fujiwara-Greve, T. 4468
Fulcher, J. 2553
Fulero, S. 5084
Fuligni, A. 2936
Fullagar, S. 1176
Fuller, N. 4558
Fuller, S. 75, 288, 1577, 1592
Fuller-Thomson, E. 2582
Funder, D. 711
Fung, W. 473
Funk, N. 3105
Funk, W. 697
Funke, H. 5243
Furano, K. 4768
Furlough, E. 4330
Furman, U. 1531
Furnham, A. 763
Furstenberg, F. 2635

AUTHOR INDEX

Fusco di Ravello, A. 2456
Fussell, E. 2561
Fustier, P. 5716
Fuszara, M. 3115
Fuwa, N. 3644, 4308
Fyfe, N. 5010
Gaarder, E. 2864
Gaba, D. 5732
Gabe, J. 5733, 5892
Gaßner, K. 1040
Gabriel, K. 2554
Gabriel, S. 4025
Gaby, S. 1135
Gacki, J. 5386
Gadd, R. 3047
Gadgil, M. 3008
Gadkari, P. 5923
Gaertner, L. 858
Gagen, E. 2608
Gager, C. 2968
Gaiger, J. 1876
Gaiger, M. 5192, 5209
Gaillard, J. 3702
Gaine, C. 2042
Gaita, R. 209
Gajdukowa, K. 1008
Gajendran, M. 1122
Gal, J. 5606
Galambos, N. 758
Galanter, M. 5154
Galasiński, D. 2217
Galbraith, M. 1499
Galembert, C. de 2313
Galenson, D. 4752
Galinsky, A. 620, 652
Gallagher, J. 4606
Gallaher, C. 5256
Galland, O. 2618, 2626, 2627
Gallant, M. 3055
Gallego, M. 4355
Gallent, N. 3906
Gallini, R. 4979
Gallois, C. 2584
Gallupe, B. 1036
Galster, G. 4080
Galston, W. 2361
Galtry, J. 4534
Games, R. 2213
Gándara, P. 3517
Gane, M. 357
Ganesh, I. 5917
Ganger, W. 5573
Gangestad, S. 3345
Ganguli, H. 788
Gans, C. 1188

Gans, H. 3545
Ganzeboom, H. 4777
Gao, B. 4221
Garapon, P. 2439
Garavaglia, J. 3891
Garba, P. 5223
Garbarini, J. 2313
Garber, M. 3297
Garber, R. 5688, 5704
Garcia, A. 5184
Garcia Albornoz, A. 5192
García, B. 2725
García Coll, A. 4439
García, E. 996
García, J. 3323, 4866
Garcia, R. 1388
García Roca, J. 2524
Garcia, S. 2284
García-Carpintero, M. 1828
García-Ramon, M. 4552
Gardes, F. 4338
Gardiner, J. 103, 3115
Gardner, E. 2914
Gardner, H. 996, 1018
Gardner, J. 5950
Gardner, R. 1757, 2024, 2069
Gardner-Chloros, P. 1789
Gare, A. 1553, 4210
Gareev, M. 5359
Gareis, K. 4724
Garey, A. 4568
Garland, D. 5008, 5047
Garner, J. 670
Garner, R. 1507
Garnets, L. 3352
Garnham, N. 1706
Garnier, J. 4923, 5716
Garnier, P. 728, 5597
Garrick, J. 4397
Garrison, E. 3156
Garside, P. 5476
Gartman, D. 340
Gärtner, C. 1448
Gartner, R. 5012
Garud, R. 1660
Garver, E. 1650
Garzón, F. 617
Gascon, S. 5636
Gaskell, G. 530, 535
Gasparini, G. 1200, 1298
Gasperoni, G. 1203
Gaszó, F. 2620
Gaszyńska-Magiera, M. 2009
Gat, A. 5346
Gatenby, B. 3118

Gates, G. 2688
Gates, Jr., H. 3528
Gates, L. 4750
Gatrell, A. 483
Gaubert, P. 4338
Gauchet, M. 578, 5920
Gaudet, S. 767
Gaullier, X. 2679, 2682
Gavious, A. 5231
Gaviria, A. 5455
Gavis, B. 1066
Gavroglu, K. 1623
Gay, J. 3633, 3649
Gayathri, S. 1122
Gayets, N. Des 2679, 5475
Geaney, J. 266
Geary, D. 3018
Geary, J. 4357
Gedalof, I. 3128
Geddes, A. 5632
Gee, E. 2909
Gee, M. 3934
Geertz, A. 1396, 1445
Geest, S. Van Der 1258
Geis, K. 3833
Geist, H. 3714
Gejst, I. 3564
Gelfand, A. 489
Gelles, E. 5486
Gelman, J. 3891
Gelman, R. 666
Gel'man, V. 5297
Gelpi, B. 3115
Gemser, G. 1100
Gene Moen, D. 4316
Genesee, F. 3517
Genn, H. 5186
Gentle, L. 4864
Gentry, D. 2742
Genuis, M. 2903
Geoffroy-Bernard, F. 1323
George, F. 2439
George, J. 684
George, R. 2042
George, U. 3586
George, V. 5623
Gephart, W. 1855
Geraedts, M. 5506
Geraghty, T. 5000
Geras, N. 1248
Gerber, R. 4803
Gerber, S. 4933
Gerber, T. 5287
Gerdes, Jr., J. 1066
Gerdtham, U. 4304, 5763

Gerfin, M. 5763
Gerhard, J. 3331
Geringer, J. 4664
German, T. 5493
Germanis, P. 419, 5959
Gerrard, M. 709
Gerrity, D. 5444
Gerrity, M. 5838
Gerschheimer, G. 132
Gerschick, T. 3115
Gersick, C. 4383
Gert, J. 131
Gervasoni, J. 5375
Gerzeli, S. 5909
Gerzina, M. 705
Geschiere, P. 4227
Gesler, W. 504, 1399, 2663, 5802, 5845
Gessner, T. 787
Gesten, E. 3047
Gestwa, K. 183
Geurts, J. 5763
Geyer, R. 4222
Ghafur, S. 4157
Ghate, D. 5566
Gherardi, S. 1115
Ghosh, B. 4605
Ghosh, S. 489
Ghoussoub, M. 3235
Giacalone, R. 4360
Giacomini Fachini, P. 5192
Giacomini, M. 5785, 5896
Giampietro, M. 3759
Giardini, F. 3115
Gibb, H. 1543
Gibb, K. 3991
Gibbons, F. 709
Gibbons, J. 5592
Gibbons, M. 13
Gibbs, J. 5436
Gibson, D. 1651
Gibson, M. 1223, 1235
Gibson-Cline, J. 2648
Gichure, C. 4422
Gidley Glen 3978
Giebels, E. 1022
Gielen, A. 5838
Giesbrecht, N. 2890
Giesen, D. 2981
Gigerenzer, G. 595
Gijsberts, M. 2389
Gilbert, D. 688
Gilbert, G. 499
Gilbert, L. 5382
Gilbert, P. 4924
Gilbert-Walsh, J. 205

AUTHOR INDEX

Gilchrist, A. 3865
Gilchrist, G. 5401
Giles, A. 4818
Giles, D. 5205
Giles, H. 2584
Giles, J. 1236
Giles, P. 1243
Giles-Vernick, T. 3736
Gilford, P. 5940
Gilg, A. 3760, 4064
Gilkes, M. 3088
Gill, A. 2023
Gill, P. 5145
Gillam, S. 5822
Gillberg, M. 3197
Gillen, J. 2224
Gilles, R. 1060
Gillespie, A. 5891
Gillespie, Jr., G. 20
Gillespie, R. 3273
Gillespie, S. 5969
Gillett, J. 5874
Gilliam, Jr., F. 1750
Gillies, B. 5492
Gillies, V. 2932
Gilligan, R. 2602
Gillman, M. 2497
Gillmore, M. 532
Gilman, S. 1189
Gilovich, T. 889
Gilroy, R. 3069
Gils, G. van 510
Gilson, S. 2480
Gingras, Y. 1610
Ginsburg, M. 2513
Ginther, D. 2935
Gioia, D. 1127
Giordano, C. 680
Giordano, P. 5103
Girardet, H. 4037
Girardi, G. 1493
Girardin, J. 5423
Giribone, J. 1182
Girling, E. 2607
Girod de l'Ain, B. 2149
Giroux, H. 1196, 1226, 3435
Gist, R. 3751
Gittell, M. 2266
Gittell, R. 2266
Gitterman, D. 5732
Gittleman, M. 4792
Giuffre, P. 5837
Giuffrida, A. 5760
Giugni, M. 5275
Giuliani, M. 3984

Givaudan, M. 5200
Gizari, F. 5089
Gjerberg, E. 5838
Gjermeni, E. 5463
Glaeser, E. 3986, 5119
Gläser, J. 1590
Glaser, K. 5891
Glass, R. 2181
Glassman, R. 5614
Glassner, B. 1173
Glatzer, M. 4596
Glauser, B. 1798
Glazer, J. 5786
Glazer, N. 1171, 3632
Glazer, S. 5839
Glebbeek, A. 11
Gleitman, H. 589
Glendinning, C. 5508, 5609
Glenn, E. 2386
Glenn, H. 5178
Glick, J. 2624
Glick, P. 3283
Glick, S. 5889
Glock, C. 56
Glover, D. 2235
Glover, H. 4720
Glover, K. 1829
Glover, S. 5363
Glynn, M. 1100
Glynn, P. 1442
Glynos, J. 3339
Gmel, G. 2819
Goaman, K. 3295
Gobbi, M. 4731
Gobet, F. 658
Gobo, G. 526
Godagnone, R. 3813
Goddard, A. 1814
Goddard, M. 5787
Gödde, C. 354
Godde, P. 3925
Godechot, O. 4723
Godelier, M. 14, 381
Godfrey, B. 3958
Godlovitch, S. 301
Godwin, P. 5968
Godwin, S. 2402
Goebl, H. 1798
Goerner, S. 2508
Goethals, J. 3338
Goff, C. 5002
Goff, M. 4412
Goh, L. 5829
Goh, R. 1920
Goicoechea-Balbona, A. 4272

INDEX DES AUTEURS

Goix, R. Le 4034
Gojard, S. 3003
Gojawiczyńska, B. 2009
Göker, E. 1517
Golato, A. 1839
Gold, S. 3545
Goldberg, D. 5401
Goldberg, M. 4876
Goldblatt, D. 1587
Golding, P. 2532
Goldman, N. 2845, 5954
Goldner, V. 5595
Goldring, E. 2024, 2051
Goldstein, H. 479
Goldstein, J. 2948
Goldthorpe, J. 2445
Goldzweig, G. 621
Göle, N. 1263
Gomberoff, L. de 743
Gomberoff, M. 743
Gómez Benito, C. 3706, 4775
Gomez, P. 1098
Gómez, R. 2294
Gomez, S. 2006
Gómez-Mateos, J. 4261
Gomm, R. 454
Gondolf, E. 2860, 2888
Gonnella, J. 5891
Gonon, P. 2117
Gonzales, C. 925
González, B. 2801, 4365
González Baker, S. 3563
González, J. 4775
González, M. 2176
González, O. 2298
González, R. 5767
González-Cueva, E. 5361
Good, G. 3095
Good, J. 12, 870
Goodchild, M. 39
Goode, J. 4563
Gooding, C. 2458
Goodlad, R. 5615
Goodley, D. 2458, 2468
Goodman, A. 2287, 5803
Goodsell, T. 3892
Goodwin, A. 5919
Goodwin, C. 1859
Goodwin, G. 1056
Goodwin, J. 1650, 5277
Goodwin, R. 3846
Goor, H. van 460
Gordon, D. 2442, 4247, 4283
Gordon, E. 1010, 5928
Gordon, G. 2249

Gordon, J. 3391, 3518
Gordon, L. 3468, 3528
Gordon, P. 145
Gordon, R. 2379
Gordon, T. 2073
Goren, N. 4481
Görke, A. 1715
Gorman, T. 2425
Gorman-Smith, D. 5069
Gorski, P. 4918
Gorton, J. 2886
Górz, B. 4606
Gosling, V. 2469
Gossop, M. 5380
Gotay, C. 1801
Gotman, A. 2313
Gottainer, G. 2923
Gottfredson, L. 2017
Gottfried, H. 4520
Göttlich, U. 1244
Gottman, J. 2861, 2959, 2985
Gough, G. 2235
Goulbourne, H. 3641
Gould, C. 3437
Gould IV, W. 1308
Gould, M. 2807
Goulet, D. 1221
Gouliquer, L. 4715
Gourévitch, J. 3562
Gouttes, R. de 5025
Governatori, L. 481
Gow, J. 5363
Gowans, C. 255
Gowland, D. 5295
Gowman, N. 5963
Gozdz, K. 4360
Graaf, N. de 1494, 3568, 5302
Graaf, P. de 2852
Grabowski, M. 1660
Grace, A. 5406
Grace, G. 2095
Grace, V. 3096
Graef, R. 5032
Graeve, B. De 1697
Graeve, D. De 5763, 5766
Graf von Krockow, C. 1199
Gragnolati, M. 4276
Graham, A. 202
Graham, C. 1227
Graham, J. 5687, 5908
Graham, N. 1644
Graham, R. 2188
Graham, S. 4031
Graille, C. 992
Gralton, E. 555

AUTHOR INDEX

Grammer, K. 3318
Gran, B. 3675
Grandy, D. 1388
Granfield, R. 5376
Granier, A. 5814
Granin, I. 2685
Granit, E. 1656
Grant, D. 1101, 1104, 1127
Grant, E. 2432, 4169
Grant, P. 3391
Grant, R. 3322
Grasmuck, S. 3190
Grattet, R. 5172
Graubarth, R. 4861
Graue, M. 2610
Gravelle, H. 5760
Graves, S. 3517, 3565
Gray, B. 3646
Gray, D. 5413
Gray, F. 681
Gray, J. 3878
Gray, L. 3883, 4876
Graziano, W. 708
Grazioli, P. 4448
Grazioli, R. 807
Greciano, P. 2679
Greed, C. 4572
Greely, H. 1620
Green, A. 752, 3069
Green, F. 4798
Green, G. 5957
Green, J. 2507
Green, L. 3324
Green, M. 650
Green, R. 2151, 5666
Greenberg, D. 1087
Greenberg, E. 4737
Greenberg, J. 872, 1081, 4356, 4483
Greenberg, M. 3853, 4119
Greene, B. 3352
Greene, J. 1647
Greene, M. 3211
Greene, S. 71
Greenfield, P. 605
Greenfield, T. 5818
Greenleaf, R. 5122
Greenstein, T. 4530
Greenwald, A. 732, 826
Greenwald, M. 1696
Greenwood, J. 870
Greenwood, M. 996
Greenwood, R. 4369
Greer, G. 1918
Gregg, P. 4476, 4587
Gregory, A. 3091, 4576

Gregory, R. 628
Gregson, N. 3788
Gregůrková, M. 2814
Greig, A. 417
Greig, M. 4486
Greiner, G. 596
Greitemeyer, T. 1046
Grelley, P. 5475
Grémion, C. 2424
Grémion, P. 4898
Grenier, G. 4856
Grenier, J. 4351
Grennan, S. 5450
Grésillon, B. 3359
Greve, B. 4200
Greve, H. 4468
Grey, C. 1127, 4621
Grieco, M. 3069, 4056
Grief, A. 2
Grier, S. 854
Griffin, D. 936, 946
Griffin, F. 3528
Griffin, L. 176, 4416
Griffin, R. 1848
Griffing, S. 2889
Griffiths, M. 5124
Griffiths, P. 2722, 5380
Grillo, R. 4012
Grills, C. 5397
Grim, P. 1374, 1638
Grime, K. 4168
Grimes, A. 3775
Grimshaw, J. 4686
Grint, K. 4620
Groarke, V. 1936
Grødeland, Å. 5214
Groenewegen, P. 3696
Groenou, M. Van 2659
Groff, R. 140
Grogger, J. 3995
Gronski, R. 2213
Groot, J. De 1555
Gros, F. 5016
Groshev, I. 1759
Gross, D. 15
Gross, I. 1934
Gross, J. 1986
Gross, L. 5763
Gross, M. 2378, 3712
Gross, S. 1789
Grossbard-Shechtman, S. 4535
Grossin, W. 1298
Grossman, J. 4768, 5154
Grossman, L. 2707
Grosz, E. 3115

Grotheer, M. 4790
Groves, J. 3317
Groves, R. 512
Grow, L. 1959
Grube, B. 5764
Gruénais, M. 5980
Gruenewald, P. 2819
Gruenwald, O. 1388
Gruer, L. 5401
Grumley, J. 1265
Grunberg, L. 4737
Grundmann, R. 1730, 3700
Grundy, E. 1284
Gruskin, S. 2754
Grusky, S. 2213
Grych, J. 2928
Grynszpan, M. 4897
Gschwandtner, U. 4537
Gu, L. 3108
Guagnano, G. 1297
Guanping, W. 1895
Guasco, R. 2456
Guastini, R. 5180
Gudjonsson, G. 5473
Guebaly, N. el- 5398
Guedes, S. 2656
Guellec, L. 2439
Guendelman, S. 2745
Guendouzi, J. 2667
Guérin, D. 5265
Guermond, Y. 2716
Guerra Palmero, M. 3155
Guerriero, S. 1384
Guest, A. 3848
Gui, S. 5519
Guidicelli, C. 1433
Guillelmet, J. 5282
Guillemard, A. 2679
Guillén, A. 5622
Guillier, B. 3702
Guillo, D. 396
Guillot, M. 2690
Guillou, A. 3255
Guimaraes, Jr., R. 3759
Guimond, S. 1052
Gülçür, L. 5915
Güldal, D. 5833
Gullason, E. 4434
Gullón, N. 4025
Gully, S. 627
Gultiano, S. 2971
Gumport, P. 2243
Gunnarsson, B. 1103
Gunnlaugsson, G. 2901
Gunter, B. 425

Gunter, P. 225
Gunter, V. 3701
Gupta, A. 1811, 3702
Gupta, D. 1002
Gupta, N. 5395
Gupta-Cassale, N. 3112
Gurak, D. 3617
Guran, L. 4606
Gurevitch, Z. 378
Gurgand, M. 4723
Gur-Ze'ev, I. 2177
Gusfield, J. 1354
Gustafsson, B. 4264
Gustafsson, K. 2029
Gustafsson, S. 4503
Gutek, B. 4416
Guthrie, D. 4241
Gutiérrez, G. 1158
Guttman, N. 3027
Guttormsson, L. 2901
Guy, A. 3256
Guyavarch, E. 2832
Guyer, J. 2781
Guyer, P. 113
Guzmán, V. 2873
Ha, H. 4108
Ha, S. 3949
Haaken, J. 3298
Haan, L. de 3802
Haaramo, J. 842
Haas, D. 5016
Habaili, H. 1822
Habekothé, H. 2494
Haberfeld, Y. 3559
Haberhauer, M. 5324
Habermas, T. 2625
Habib, C. 4898
Habu, T. 2271
Hackney, S. 996
Haddad, L. 5969
Haddad, Y. 2093
Haddix, K. 2973
Haddon, L. 1687
Hadidi, F. al 2245
Hadingham, J. 5363
Haeri, N. 1802
Hage, G. 1195
Hagen, R. 371
Hagendoorn, L. 3470
Haggis, J. 1219
Hague, G. 2882
Hahlbohm-Helmus, E. 1464
Hahn, P. 5014
Hahn, S. 1853
Haïdara, M. 2121

AUTHOR INDEX

Haider, O. 4524
Haiken, E. 3272
Haila, A. 3927
Hailwood, S. 3703
Haire, S. 5154
Hajji, J. Al 2236
Haj-Yahia, M. 2875, 2885
Hakel, M. 661
Hakim, A. 2774
Hakim, C. 436, 1304
Häkkinen, U. 5763
Halberstadt, J. 683
Halci, A. 2331
Hale, A. 1227
Hales, J. 5624
Hales, S. 133
Haley, J. 1442
Hall, A. 3796
Hall, C. 726, 3791
Hall, D. 4606
Hall, H. 3309
Hall, J. 2567, 2878
Hall, K. 2090, 3449
Hall, P. 53, 480
Hall, R. 3525
Hall, T. 2, 3933
Hallam, M. 573
Hallam, S. 2190
Haller, I. 3520
Haller, M. 4181
Halleux, J. 4158
Hallgarten, J. 2220
Halli, S. 4007, 4009, 4249
Hallier, J. 4729
Hallinan, M. 2000, 3517
Halman, F. 4607
Halpern, A. 3454
Halpern, R. 4472
Halseth, G. 3628
Ham, C. 5750, 5770
Hamada, W. 710
Hamamsy, L. El- 3948
Hamann, R. 3810
Hamberger, J. 866
Hambly, Z. 5080
Hamdi, N. 2184
Hamel, J. 381
Hamel, P. 5265
Hamerman-Rozenberg, R. 5513
Hamersveld, I. van 4567
Hamid al-Junaid, S. 1089
Hamilton, A. 1772
Hamilton, C. 263
Hamilton, D. 907, 1086
Hamilton, G. 2568

Hamilton, K. 4056
Hamilton, M. 2006
Hamilton-Brown, L. 2937
Hammami, R. 3106
Hammer, D. 232
Hammer, E. 125
Hammersley, M. 454
Hammerstein, P. 561
Hammond, J. 1346
Hammond, M. 5928
Hammond, P. 1385, 1731
Hammons, S. 56
Hamon, H. 2618
Hample, M. 3783
Hamplová, D. 1511
Hampshire, K. 2790
Hampson, R. 2900
Hampton, C. 5409
Hamzé, H. 1822
Han, K. 54
Han, M. 2586, 4250
Han, S. 4108
Han, T. 4823
Hanasaki, K. 1195
Hand, J. 3282
Handa, S. 2787
Handley, P. 2495
Handley, S. 631
Handschumacher, P. 5968
Haney López, I. 5171
Hanisch, J. 3702
Hank, K. 4528
Hanley, E. 4204, 4474
Hanlon, J. 4287
Hann, C. 2544
Hanna, G. 2179
Hanna, S. 3775, 3785
Hannah-Moffat, K. 5026
Hannay, A. 244
Hanner, J. 1059
Hannover, B. 825
Hans, G. 2248
Hansen, K. 2270
Hansen, P. 4952
Hanson, D. 1093
Hantrais, L. 3220
Hapke, U. 5408
Haque, T. 4246
Hara, J. 2434
Haralambos, M. 33
Harbans Lal, B. 1376
Harcourt, B. 5038, 5150
Harcourt, M. 4844
Harcup, T. 3956
Hardill, I. 4439, 4784

Hardin, G. 3759
Hardin, R. 4906
Harding, R. 2139
Harding, S. 1568, 3115
Hardoy, A. 3813
Hardt, M. 1229
Hardy, C. 1127, 1148, 4669
Hardy, M. 4465
Harguindeguy, L. 3402
Hark, S. 3115
Harkin, M. 1620
Harkness, J. 5612
Harm, D. 567
Harmaajärvi, I. 4025
Harman, C. 4610
Harman, E. 2734
Harne, L. 5474
Harned, M. 777
Harold, G. 3041
Harpham, T. 2432
Harrell, S. 5928
Harreveld, F. van 890
Harries, J. 5762
Harrington, A. 126, 310
Harrington, C. 5506
Harrington, E. 1144
Harris, A. 2165
Harris, B. 5154
Harris, C. 3765, 5357
Harris, J. 2446, 3036, 5644
Harris, K. 531
Harris, L. 4646
Harris, P. 1083, 2581, 5505
Harris, R. 3980
Harris, S. 389
Harris, T. 5388
Harris, Z. 353
Harris-Hendriks, J. 819
Harrison, A. 1980, 5743, 5795
Harrison, E. 4558
Harrison, J. 2098, 5924
Harrison, K. 2667
Harrison, M. 1053, 3978, 4026
Harrison, P. 3788
Harrison, S. 2532
Harrow, K. 1913
Harry, D. 1620
Harryson, S. 4654
Hart, G. 3388
Hart, K. 5364
Hart, W. 1386
Harten, W. van 5790
Harter, S. 2921
Harthorn, B. 39
Hartigan, Jr., J. 3436, 3534

Hartke, R. 1869
Hartley, J. 1223, 1756
Hartman, M. 2391
Hartmann, K. 1425
Hartway, J. 532
Harvey, D. 2348, 3787
Harvey, J. 795, 924, 2138, 2142
Harvey, P. 3312
Harvey, R. 972
Harvie, D. 2018
Harwin, N. 2882
Harwood, J. 1768, 2588, 2667
Hasan, A. 2748
Hasegawa, J. 3983
Hasegawa, K. 3838
Haseler, S. 4294
Hashmi, T. 3207
Hasim, S. 3171
Haslam, C. 4310
Haslam, N. 847
Haslam, S. 857, 894
Hasnath, S. 3793
Hassard, J. 1090
Hassebrauck, M. 865
Hasselbalch, O. 4846
Hasselbladh, H. 1139
Hassine, O. 1572
Hassner, P. 4898
Hastings, A. 4159
Hastings, L. 5363
Hatch, J. 1863
Hatcher, E. 1345
Hatef, M. 2072
Hattiangadi, J. 288
Hau, K. 862
Hauan, S. 4470
Haughey, M. 2201
Haughton, G. 4439
Hauke, C. 1255
Haumont, N. 4021
Hauschild, M. 3364
Hausen, C. zur 1783
Hausser, D. 5375
Häußermann, H. 4066
Hautecoeur, J. 2006
Hauteserre, A. d' 3820
Haveman, R. 2935
Haviland-Jones, J. 690
Havinden, M. 3886
Havlík, R. 77
Hawke, A. 4881
Haworth, N. 4818
Hawthorne, E. 1960
Haxhiymeri, E. 5463
Hay, C. 5046

AUTHOR INDEX

Hay, D. 2194
Hay, G. 5374
Hayat, P. 4929
Hayden, M. 5576
Hayden, R. 5462
Haydn, T. 2170
Haydon, D. 5054
Hayes, G. 5937
Hayes, S. 737
Haynes, Jr., C. 4497
Haynes, S. 798
Haynie, D. 5087
Häyry, M. 5854
Hays-Gilpin, K. 3121
Hayter, T. 3542
Haythornthwaite, C. 1681
Hazarika, G. 5768
Hazel, N. 5566
Hazell, P. 4246
Hazelwood, R. 5456
Hazez, S. Ben 1822
Hazlett, C. 5765
Hazra, R. 5800
He, C. 4108
Healey, J. 495
Healey, M. 5221
Healy, D. 1933
Healy, G. 4882
Healy, J. 5499
Healy, K. 5860
Healy, P. 1198
Hearn, J. 3097
Heath, A. 5393
Heath, T. 4106
Hecht, L. 2666
Hechter, M. 3493
Heckert, D. 2860, 2888
Heckhausen, J. 561, 704
Hedeen, T. 1010
Hedeker, D. 5818
Hedlund, M. 5603
Hedström, P. 392
Heenan, D. 5503, 5685
Heery, E. 4875
Heffernan, W. 5018
Heffner, T. 1056
Heflin, C. 808
Heideking, J. 1263
Heidensohn, F. 5131
Heider, U. 3295
Heijden, P. van der 510
Heijke, J. 4764
Heikkinen, R. 2651
Heil, K. 4104
Heiligers, P. 5827

Heilman, S. 1545
Heimer, T. 2244
Heinemann-Grüder, A. 4957
Heinicke, A. 4766
Heintel, M. 4149
Heintz, B. 1581
Heinz, W. 2627
Heise, L. 5200
Heisig, J. 265
Heisterhagen, T. 4347
Hekman, S. 3123
Held, D. 2568, 2572
Helg, A. 3457
Helgeson, V. 709
Hellander, I. 5811
Heller, A. 1276, 5180
Heller, G. 5506
Heller, W. 4606
Hellström, D. 4025
Hellström, T. 2260
Helly, D. 3423
Helm, B. 226
Helman, C. 5727
Helsloot, N. 298
Helvacioglu, B. 2568
Hemmer, H. 4859
Henderson, D. 5538
Henderson, G. 2344
Henderson, H. 4360
Henderson, L. 3384
Henderson, S. 2613
Hendley, B. 225
Hendley, K. 5154
Hendricks, C. 3133
Hendrickson, A. 4658
Hendry, J. 1102, 4666
Hendy, D. 1745
Henkemans, A. 1650
Henker, B. 781
Henkin, A. 2258
Henley, D. 2188
Henly, J. 5633
Henneberg, S. 1969
Henneberger, F. 4745
Hennion, A. 1982
Henochsberg, M. 1896
Henrard, K. 5021
Henry, E. 1972
Henry, S. 5465
Henwood, F. 2039
Henze, M. 4025
Her, M. 2819
Heracleous, L. 1102
Herbst, J. 709
Herdt, G. 3061, 3385

Heredia, R. 2441
Herek, G. 3352
Herer, Y. 2916
Herlinghaus, H. 1158
Herman, A. 1693
Hermann, J. 5409
Heřmanová, S. 2411
Hermawati, W. 4571
Hermel, P. 4658
Hermes, J. 1191, 1921
Hermos, J. 2819
Hermsen, J. 4525
Hermsen, S. 861
Hernández, B. 3758
Hernández, R. 4217
Hernández-León, R. 3565
Herod, A. 4486
Herpin, N. 2930
Herreiner, D. 463
Herrera, A. 5439
Herrera, J. 4245
Herrera, R. 4211
Herring, M. 3032
Herrmann, W. 1645
Herrschel, T. 4606
Herschmann, M. 1735
Hersen, M. 570
Hershenov, D. 5848
Hershock, P. 1466
Hertel, G. 1061
Hertford, R. 4246
Hertzman, C. 5773
Hervouët, J. 5968
Hess, J. 5363
Hess, L. 679
Hess, P. 5693
Hess, S. 3758
Hesse, F. 664
Hesselbrock, V. 5393
Hessling, R. 838
Hester, S. 1800
Hetherington, E. 2613, 3014, 3052
Hetherington, K. 1340, 2481
Heuchert, J. 710
Heurtaux, J. 24
Heussler, H. 2602, 5820
Heuveline, P. 2690
Hewitt, W. 4032, 4163
Hewlett, N. 217
Hewstone, M. 865, 866, 1041
Hexter, K. 4071
Heyd, D. 5889
Heyman, B. 2497
Heyman, R. 902
Heymann, S. 5972

Hibou, B. 5282
Hickford, C. 938
Hickman, P. 3824
Hicks, C. 1682
Hier, S. 3463
Hiernaux, J. 1383
Higate, P. 5415
Higgins, C. 1660, 3830
Higgins, E. 638, 657, 1071
Higgins, G. 1513
Higgs, G. 2843, 3874
Higgs, P. 2440
Hightower, N. Van 2886
Hijmans, E. 2645
Hildreth, A. 4878
Hilhorst, D. 3611
Hill, A. 1703
Hill, M. 3095, 5586, 5635, 5941
Hill, P. 1381, 2138, 5977
Hill, R. 3337, 3927
Hill, S. 100, 1308, 2898, 5810
Hillage, J. 2016
Hillerås, P. 2668
Hilsdon, A. 3074
Himes, C. 2669
Himmelfarb, G. 1192
Himmelweit, S. 3169
Hinck, S. 2213
Hinde, A. 2722, 2797
Hindin, M. 3210, 3279
Hindle, P. 94
Hine, J. 4056
Hingstman, L. 5827
Hinkle, W. 5465
Hinshelwood, R. 5798
Hinskens, F. 1798
Hintjens, H. 3827
Hinze, S. 4551
Hirano, K. 3544
Hird, M. 2917
Hirose, Y. 1830
Hirowatari, S. 5189
Hirsch, B. 4465
Hirsch, J. 3545
Hirsch, P. 1100
Hirsh, P. 4384
Hirst, W. 830
Hisama, E. 3115
Hisata, M. 5532
Hisnanick, J. 5575
Hitchcock, P. 1880
Hite, A. 4258
Hitlan, R. 3476
Hitzler, R. 119, 4899
Hjartåker, A. 5838

AUTHOR INDEX

Hlanze, Z. 3208
Ho, D. Ngoc 545
Ho, J. 3323
Ho, K. 3927, 3954
Ho, S. 898
Hoad, N. 1258
Hoag, A. 1660
Hoaglin, D. 525
Hoagwood, K. 5906
Hoàng, C. 545
Hoare, R. 1820
Hobart, M. 1707
Hobson, B. 3065
Hobson, J. 3813
Hochschild, M. 1415
Hockey, A. 2709
Hocking, J. 5414
Hodak, C. 3926
Hodder, R. 1186, 3770
Hodge, I. 4486
Hodgins, D. 5398
Hodgson, F. 4056
Hodson, P. 4805
Hoefer, C. 1586, 1605
Hoefer, G. 3702
Hoefer, R. 411
Hoewyk, J. Van 519
Hoff, D. 5151
Hoff, T. 5840
Hofferth, S. 4517, 5633
Hoffman, D. 1007
Hoffman, M. 5312
Hoffman, S. 5610
Hoffmann, B. 4025
Hoffmann, R. 4347
Hogan, P. 2164
Hogarth, J. 4317
Hogben, S. 3358
Hogetsu, M. 50
Hogg, M. 1034, 1044
Hoggart, R. 1223
Hoggett, P. 3827, 5477
Hohl, J. 2047
Hohmann, H. 1650
Hojat, M. 5891
Hoksbergen, R. 5538
Holborn, M. 33
Holdaway, S. 5147
Holden, C. 2218, 2496
Holden, D. 2402
Holden, P. 1951
Holdstock, J. 774
Holdstock, T. 592
Holdsworth, C. 447, 2929
Holland, A. 3801

Holland, C. 2005
Holland, L. 5244
Holland, S. 3241, 5667
Hollander, J. 5253
Holley, A. 5576
Holliday, R. 444, 1090
Hollinger, R. 1584
Hollis, F. 5670
Holloway, J. 3775
Holloway, S. 2325, 2608, 5102
Hollows, J. 3113
Hollway, W. 516
Holly, L. 4398
Holm, K. 2897
Holman, D. 1144
Holman, R. 5696
Holmes, C. 3695
Holmes, D. 4999
Holmes, G. 4791
Holmes, J. 76, 908, 936, 939, 946
Holmes, L. 3069, 4056
Holmes, M. 1277, 3149, 5299, 5631
Holm-Hansen, J. 3444
Holmwood, J. 5652
Holt, R. 1305
Holtgrave, D. 5987
Holtmann, E. 5219
Holton, G. 1271
Holton, R. 2569
Holtug, N. 1620
Holz, H. 3713
Holzer, B. 4228
Holzer, H. 4489, 4490
Holzer, J. 1004
Holzleithner, E. 3377
Homer, A. 3983
Homišinová, M. 3407
Hommels, A. 4075
Honan, E. 430
Hondagneu-Sotelo, P. 3121
Hong, J. 4398
Hong, S. 191, 663
Hong, Y. 247, 643, 864
Hong, Z. 3626
Hongoro, C. 5777
Honwana, J. 5341
Hood, III, M. 3565
Hood, Jr., R. 56, 1381
Hoof, F. van 5736
Hooghiemstra, R. 4417
Hook, J. Van 5535
Hook, M. Van 5463
Hooper, N. 4791
Hoover, D. 3608
Hope, T. 5061

INDEX DES AUTEURS

Hopenhayn, M. 2548
Hopgood, S. 4967
Hopkins, J. 800, 3264
Hoppe, H. 1040
Hoppe, M. 532
Hoppers, W. 2144
Hopton, J. 762
Horcasitas, I. 457
Horenczyk, G. 3547, 3554
Horn, H. 4907
Horn, J. 698
Horne, C. 4978
Horne, J. 1368
Hornsby, J. 3101
Hornung, U. 3127
Horowitz, A. 5177
Hors, I. 5282
Horská, H. 2684
Horstmeier, S. 964
Hort, S. 5622
Hortaçsu, N. 1058
Horton, J. 268
Horton, M. 5573
Horton, S. 5969
Horváth, F. 2269
Horwath, J. 5542
Horwitz, S. 5906
Horwood, L. 5045, 5381
Hosali, P. 1805
Hoshi, A. 2256
Hoshi, T. 5524
Hossain, M. 2955, 4524, 4705
Hostetler, D. 4512
Hottois, G. 5884
Hougard, J. 5980
Hourmant, L. 1464
Houseal, M. 567
Houssel, J. 3919
Houston, A. 5337
Houston, D. 2352
Hout, M. 4473
Houtart, F. 5272
Houtlosser, P. 1650
Houtman, D. 5662
Houts, R. 2970
Hovav, M. 5370
Hovey, J. 805
Howard, C. 1844
Howard, G. 5079
Howard, J. 3115
Howarth, D. 4887
Howarth, K. 179
Howden, P. 20
Howell, D. 4980
Howell, J. 4467, 5079

Howell, W. 814
Howells, K. 2862
Howitt, D. 421, 475
Howley, K. 1756
Howsam, L. 1557
Howse, K. 2673
Hox, J. 510, 2494
Hoxby, C. 2027
Hoy, M. 3462
Hoyer, W. 1710
Hoyle, B. 4090
Hoyle, R. 709
Hoyo Arana, J. 5267
Hoz, R. 2054
Hraba, J. 2965, 3870
Hrebenar, R. 5234
Hritzuk, N. 3565
Hrvatin, S. 1731
Hsia, Y. 1620
Hsu, H. 211
Hsu, S. 3478
Hsu, W. 4591
Hu, S. 5029
Hu, Y. 473
Hua, J. 1895
Hua, Z. 1839
Huang, F. 3671
Huang, S. 1811, 3557
Huang, T. 5029
Huang, Y. 266
Hubbard, B. 910, 937
Hubbard, P. 3301
Hubert, M. 5891
Hucklesby, A. 5035
Hucks, T. 5409
Hudders, M. 1819
Hudson, K. 4676
Hudson, P. 163
Huebner, C. 5386
Huebner, R. 5818, 5939
Huerta, J. 3565
Huffman, C. 4345
Huffman, D. 1495
Hughes, A. 86
Hughes, B. 2477
Hughes, D. 5645
Hughes, J. 5407
Hughes, M. 3850
Hughes, R. 5383
Hughes, S. 4818
Hugo, G. 3609
Huh, N. 5577
Huh, W. 247
Hui, E. 3976
Hui, J. 5325

AUTHOR INDEX

Huiras, J. 4758
Hull, K. 3166
Hulland, J. 1660
Hulme, C. 644
Huls, E. 2940
Humfrey, C. 2274
Hummels, H. 4428
Hummer, R. 2830, 3565
Hummert, M. 2667
Hummon, N. 1085
Humphrey, C. 4310
Humphrey, J. 2491, 3356, 4871
Humphreys, K. 2086
Humphries, B. 5657
Humphries, M. 583, 3118
Hundley, G. 4556
Hundt, G. 43
Hunkin, N. 774
Hunsberger, B. 3055
Hunt, A. 2356
Hunt, J. 5969
Hunt, K. 757, 3185
Hunt, L. 1429, 3565
Hunt, M. 1429, 1580, 3565
Hunt, P. 5846
Hunt, S. 1474
Hunt, W. 5406
Hunter, A. 5976
Hunter, I. 208
Hunter, J. 1460, 5456
Hunter, L. 3757, 4742
Huntington, D. 2750
Huntington, P. 5226
Hurd, R. 4876
Hurley, J. 5785
Hursh, D. 2182
Hurt, L. 3310
Hurtz, G. 707
Husain, F. 1532
Hussain, M. 1532
Hussain, S. 1165
Hussey, S. 5546
Husson, L. 5968
Husted, B. 4417
Huston, T. 2970, 2983
Hutchby, I. 901
Hutchinson, P. 2477
Hutchinson, S. 5401
Hutchison, K. 5406
Hutnyk, J. 1978
Hutter, B. 4683
Hüttermann, J. 2376, 5141
Hutton, J. 453
Hutton, T. 4092
Hutton, V. Van 2894

Huxham, C. 1032
Huyssen, A. 994
Huysseune, M. 3070
Hviding, E. 3735
Hwang, K. 321
Hyams, M. 2608
Hyatt, D. 4822
Hyde, A. 2993
Hyde, J. 3182, 3306, 3352
Hyde, M. 5605
Hyland, P. 2207
Hyman, M. 4420
Hynes, H. 4087
Hysong, S. 567
Iacono, W. 2304
Iacovetta, F. 178
Ianni, O. 1199
Iaquinta, D. 3867
Ibarra, H. 2294
Ibrahim, Z. 1756, 3920
Ifekwunigwe, J. 3441
Igarashi, Y. 3678
Iggers, G. 158
Ignacio, E. 3392
Ignatczyk, W. 2639
Igwara, O. 3403
Ihonvbere, J. 2513
IJssel, M. van 3568
Ikamari, L. 2839
Ikei, M. 1308
Illingworth, P. 5854
Illouz, E. 1361
Imada, T. 2434
Imbusch, P. 4889
Imperio, D. D' 4456
Imrie, R. 2467
Indart, G. 4281
India Health Foundation 2749
Ineichen, B. 5891
Ingebritsen, C. 4222
Ingels, K. 5862
Ingerflom, C. 3891
Ingham, M. 4168
Inglis, D. 1277
Ingram, P. 4374
Inkster, I. 1663
Innes, M. 5147
Innes-Ker, A. 683
Inoue, N. 1393
Inozemtsev, V. 2412
Insko, C. 858
Institut sotsiologii 23
International Coordinating Committee 2754
Introvigne, M. 1457
Ironside, R. 3771

INDEX DES AUTEURS

Irvin, R. 5816
Irvine, L. 548
Isaac, C. 774
Isajiw, W. 903
Ishmael, A. 4691
Islam, M. 2748
Ismail, S. 5274
Isomura, E. 3948
Israel, B. 4291
Israel, M. 636
Israeli, A. 2834
Issakainen, J. 907
Iterson, A. van 3568
Ito, K. 369
Itzigsohn, J. 3398
Iurchenkov, V. 3487
Iurevich, A. 5281
Ivanitskii, V. 1954
Ivantyšyn, R. 1764
Iversen, S. 3071
Iverson, R. 4725
Iveson, K. 4851
Ivinson, G. 3060
Iwamoto, T. 2256
Iyengar, K. 5200
Iyengar, S. 606, 1750, 5200
Iyun, B. 3767
Izzo, G. 4418
Jaarsma, S. 1258
Jack, D. 672
Jack, G. 4628
Jackson, B. 1104
Jackson, C. 4558
Jackson, D. 591, 735
Jackson, F. 1620, 3528
Jackson, K. 5416
Jackson, L. 880
Jackson, M. 376
Jackson, N. 2247
Jackson, P. 1744, 3061, 4618, 5774
Jackson, R. 5607
Jackson, S. 3078, 4653, 5470
Jackson, T. 3823
Jackson-Smith, D. 3406
Jacob, M. 2260
Jacobs, B. 4105
Jacobs, J. 1551
Jacobs, K. 4111
Jacobs, L. 539
Jacobs, R. 2001, 3506
Jacobs, S. 1650, 5467
Jacobson, D. 2361
Jacobson, J. 2762
Jacobson, N. 932, 1559, 2861
Jacobson, R. 5467

Jacobzone, S. 5514
Jacquemin, A. 4172
Jadwin, L. 1897
Jaffal, M. 1518
Jaffee, S. 3182, 3352
Jaffré, Y. 5980
Jäger, M. 5243
Jäger, S. 3702, 5243
Jagers, R. 583
Jain, R. 533
Jalloul, M. 4171
Jamal, V. 3868
Jambunathan, S. 3011
James, A. 555
James, D. 3868, 4800, 5137
James, E. 4510
James, I. 2429
James, J. 3098
James, P. 3819
James, S. 4291
Jameson, C. 2853
Jameson, F. 1229, 2563
Jamieson, A. 5317, 5539
Jamieson, L. 3894
Jamison, J. 5540
Ja'nini, N. 2316
Janjić, D. 3469
Jannin, J. 5980
Janoff-Bulman, R. 5425
Jansen, M. 3178
Jansen-Verbeke, M. 3820
Janssen, J. 2852
Janssen, O. 4702
Janssens, M. 2110
Janvry, A. de 4246
Japp, K. 2309
Jaret, C. 3008
Jarley, P. 4877
Jarman, N. 1343
Jarnagin, S. 20
Járos, G. 286, 5735
Jarvenpaa, S. 1660
Jarvie, I. 288
Järvinen, M. 508
Jarvis, C. 3125
Jarvis, P. 93
Jasanoff, S. 3759
Jasinskaja-Lahti, I. 842
Jasinski, J. 3565, 5060
Jasper, J. 5277
Jasso, G. 3550
Jauréguiberry, F. 1298
Javier, R. 2870
Jay, M. 337, 1307
Jayakody, R. 5633, 5658

AUTHOR INDEX

Jayaprakash, Y. 1756
Jayasankar, K. 5704
Jaynes, G. 3528, 4463
Jeannot, G. 4950
Jeffcoate, R. 4801
Jefferies, J. 2768
Jefferson, T. 516, 5761
Jeffery, L. 938
Jefferys, S. 4810
Jeffries, V. 1403
Jegede, O. 2103
Jegers, M. 5766
Jegou, M. 4175
Jelonkiewicz, M. 2009
Jenkins, B. 5232
Jenkins, J. 2931
Jenkins, L. 4056
Jenkins, P. 3936, 4169
Jenkins, R. 2436
Jenkins, T. 1620
Jenkins-Monroe, V. 5409
Jenner, R. 2566
Jennings, Z. 2040
Jensen, L. 4591
Jenson, J. 4545
Jepperson, R. 306
Jeppsson, U. 4025
Jeřábek, H. 5307
Jerrentrup, A. 1331
Jerusel, J. 1705
Jervis, J. 1279
Jessop, B. 3927
Jesus Souza, F. de 5192
Jetten, J. 1044
Jewell, R. 3565
Jewers, C. 1332
Jewkes, R. 5442
Jiayin, M. 3797
Jin, P. 710
Jin, Y. 323
Jing, X. 1895
Jingmei, N. 1895
Jinkings, N. 2507
Jinyue, W. 1895
Jiqun, T. 1895
Jisa, H. 1789
Jivanjee, P. 5925
Jo, M. 3578
Jodoin, M. 2047
Joël, M. 2679, 5475, 5814
Joeres, R. 3115
Johal, S. 4310
Johannesson, M. 4304
Johansson, T. 1272
John, J. 5763

John, O. 710
John, U. 5408
Johnes, M. 962
Johns, A. 1557
Johns, G. 4700
Johnson, A. 81, 2056
Johnson, C. 636, 877, 1013, 2938, 5409
Johnson, D. 2715
Johnson, E. 5567, 5928
Johnson, G. 3749, 4672, 4717
Johnson, H. 756
Johnson, I. 5449
Johnson, IV, J. 5345
Johnson, J. 835, 1941, 5313, 5355
Johnson, Jr., J. 3996, 4139
Johnson, K. 916, 1729, 2499
Johnson, L. 5574, 5707
Johnson, M. 2235, 2891, 3061
Johnson, N. 2811, 5896
Johnson, P. 3106
Johnson, T. 919
Johnson, V. 4850
Johnson, W. 4717
Johnston, J. 5233
Johnston, L. 859, 5140
Johnston, M. 5282
Johnston, P. 4832
Johnston, R. 84, 4001
Johnstone, G. 5024
Johnstone, N. 3813
Joiner, Jr., T. 876
Joiner, R. 1083
Jok, J. 5459
Jokelainen, M. 483
Jokisch, R. 403
Jolin, A. 426
Jolly, D. 2455
Jolly, S. 3378
Jomo, K. 4935
Jonas, A. 3755
Jones, A. 197, 1937, 2156, 3981
Jones, B. 1098, 2188, 4769
Jones, D. 1127
Jones, G. 2992, 4088
Jones, H. 91, 3983
Jones, III, J. 3775
Jones, K. 500, 1563, 2807
Jones, M. 1840, 3705, 4202, 4439, 5630
Jones, N. 4805
Jones, P. 3963, 4025
Jones, R. 95, 330, 1811, 3729, 3749
Jones, S. 3733
Jones, T. 8
Jong, G. De 3613
Jongbloed, B. 2259

Jonge, J. de 4706
Jonker, G. 3468
Jonsson, J. 2014, 2108
Jonsson, U. 5969
Jopling, J. 4063
Jordán, J. 1819
Jordan, P. 78
Jordan, S. 1901
Joseph, A. 4834, 5200, 5515
Joseph, G. 3534
Joseph, H. 5464
Joseph, J. 285, 383, 1811
Josephs, I. 585
Joshi, S. 513
Josset, V. 5968
Jost, J. 852
Jouriles, E. 2869, 2928
Jovanovic, J. 2615
Jowell, R. 520
Joyce, A. 782
Joyce, M. 4792
Joyce, P. 4056
Joyce, T. 2738, 5838
Joyner, K. 3521
Judd, C. 88, 832
Judge, T. 4638, 4719
Juette, A. 3318
Juliá, M. 5563
Julien, P. 4175
Julliard, J. 2439
Jun, H. 1895
Junn, J. 3545
Jupp, B. 3845
Jurich, J. 5444
Justenhoven, H. 2554
Jutla, R. 3970
Juvalis, J. 5386
Juvva, S. 5911
Kabeer, N. 3238
Kabzińska, I. 3421
Kacmar, K. 4728
Kaczmarek, S. 4606
Kadiri, W. 4093
Kadt, E. de 1813
Kadt, R. de 2163
Kaestner, R. 2738, 5838
Kafka, T. 1004
Kafka-Lützow, A. 4377
Kahana, N. 949
Kahane, B. 5942
Kahn, L. 4539
Kahn, M. 3725
Kahne, J. 2218
Kahtan, N. 5899
Kai, I. 5532

Kaika, M. 4031
Kain, R. 91
Kainan, A. 2054
Kaitatzi-Whitlock, S. 1730
Kakad, K. 4126
Kalakanis, L. 573
Kalantzis, M. 3501
Kalaycioglu, S. 2590
Kalbach, M. 954
Kalbach, W. 954
Kalbers, L. 4773
Kaler, A. 3079
Kaler, J. 4417
Kalil, A. 5633
Kalin, N. 591
Kalleberg, A. 4676
Kallen, J. 1798
Kallinikos, J. 1139
Kalmijn, M. 3178
Kalof, L. 1297
Kaloski-Naylor, A. 3088
Kalpagam, U. 3112, 3162
Kalra, V. 1978, 4446
Kalthoff, H. 4346, 4348
Kaluszynski, M. 2618
Kalvenes, J. 1066
Kam, C. 5765
Kam, P. 2671
Kamarás, I. 1384
Kamau, R. 4169
Kamberská, Z. 2814
Kamel, G. 1822
Kamel, S. 4019
Kaminski, M. 4861
Kaminsky, D. 5592
Kamiya, H. 3767
Kammen, M. 2504
Kammeyer-Mueller, J. 4722
Kamo, T. 3927
Kamoche, K. 4616, 4759
Kamolnick, P. 343
Kamps, D. 2028
Kamwangamalu, N. 1813
Kanaiaupuni, S. 3670
Kanazawa, S. 5120
Kanbayashi, H. 4527
Kandel, L. 3205
Kandel, W. 3565
Kandiyoti, D. 3070
Kane, K. 1227
Kané, S. 2121
Kaneko, F. 3702
Kanfer, R. 4588
Kang, M. 4250
Kang, S. 3791, 4250

AUTHOR INDEX

Kanitkar, T. 3203
Kanouté, M. 2121
Kanovský, M. 27
Kant, I. 113
Kanyandago, P. 4422
Kao, G. 3414, 3521, 3565
Kapcia, A. 1167
Kaplan, D. 3633, 5339
Kaplan, E. 2644
Kaplan, H. 2634
Kaplan, J. 5875
Kaplan, M. 2295
Kaplan, R. 5986
Kaplan, S. 3115, 3749
Kaplan, T. 819
Kapoor, A. 1123, 2780
Karachalios, A. 1623
Karakatsanis, N. 4596
Karam, F. 2523
Karides, M. 2200
Karim, Q. 5363
Karna, M. 4959
Karney, B. 2956
Karpik, L. 4322
Karreman, D. 1104, 1127
Kärrman, E. 4025
Karuppannan, S. 4102
Karvalics, L. 1675
Karylowski, J. 869
Käser, L. 1258
Kasher, A. 2942
Kashima, Y. 868
Kasinitz, P. 3632
Kaskutas, L. 5818
Kaspersen, L. 41
Kass, A. 950
Kass, L. 950, 5863
Kassas, M. 3759
Kassim, A. 3655
Kassin, S. 883
Kassler, W. 5987
Kassow, S. 3518
Kasten-Heitmann, E. 3206
Katan, J. 5482
Katičić, R. 1794
Katigbak, M. 710
Katrňák, T. 926
Katsiyannis, A. 2119
Katsurada, E. 3031
Katui-Katua, M. 3813
Katz, J. 692, 4645
Katz, M. 2602, 3528, 5732, 5820
Kaufman, B. 4876, 4877
Kaufman, G. 3025
Kaufman, J. 1013, 2021, 4861

Kaufmann, D. 213, 3047
Kaufmann, E. 3419
Kaufmann, F. 2554
Kaufmann, J. 1283
Kaufman-Scarborough, C. 4341
Kaur, R. 1978
Kautt, Y. 3092
Kavanagh, J. 1822
Kaviraj, S. 1263
Kavoori, A. 1733
Kawakami, C. 574
Kawakami, K. 861
Kawase, M. 3767
Kawka, Z. 2140
Kay, A. 3827
Kay, S. 5622
Kaya, I. 3247
Kaye, H. 2416
Kaye, R. 5504
Kazemipur, A. 4007, 4009, 4249
Kazi, M. 5673
Kazumi, Y. 1948
Kealy, M. 2456
Kealy, W. 2299
Keane, J. 611
Keane, M. 615, 1360, 4438
Kearns, A. 3991
Kearns, D. 2142
Kebbell, M. 5205
Kebede, M. 1204
Kebir, S. 3206
Kecskes, R. 3596
Kee, Y. 2145
Keeble, R. 1731
Keenan, W. 37
Keenoy, T. 1101, 1104, 1127
Keer, E. Van 4599
Keeter, S. 512
Kef, S. 2494
Kegeles, S. 3357
Kehl, D. 1967
Keijser, A. 1885
Keilman, N. 2794
Keith, B. 38
Keithley, J. 5471
Kekäle, J. 2283
Kekes, J. 1387
Kelaher, M. 5791
Kelasev, V. 439
Keller, B. 4835, 4837
Keller, C. 3992
Keller, H. 561
Keller, J. 5669
Keller, R. 1190
Keller, S. 913

Kellerhals, J. 3930, 5285
Kellett, P. 4116, 4302
Kelley, P. 1716
Kellogg, N. 2951
Kelly, A. 2180
kelly, L. 5544
Kelly, M. 4064, 5934
Kelly, P. 3607
Kelly, R. 2203
Kelly, S. 5569
Kember, D. 2008, 2195
Kember, S. 1234
Kemeny, M. 781
Keményfi, R. 3408
Kemmer, D. 3268
Kempen, R. van 4127
Kempter, K. 4859
Kemshall, H. 43, 4390
Ken, C. 1895
Kendall, K. 5704, 5723
Kendall, L. 1339, 3253
Kendall, P. 754
Kendig, H. 2670
Kendrick, A. 3830
Kenna, P. 5491
Kennedy, B. 1664
Kennedy, L. 4144
Kennedy, R. 744
Kennedy, S. 285
Kennedy-Pipe, C. 5362
Kennet-Cohen, T. 2052
Kennett, J. 909
Kenny, M. 181, 5378
Kenny, S. 3836
Kent, J. 5843
Kenworthy, J. 2019
Kenyon, E. 3860
Keough, J. 5939
Keough, K. 2061
Kerchove, M. van de 5025
Keren, M. 1916
Kerlinger, F. 422
Kernis, M. 3021
Kerntke, M. 3702
Kerr, A. 1595
Kerr, B. 4492
Kerr, D. 2171
Kerr, N. 1061
Kerr, W. 2819
Kerrigan, D. 5943
Kers, C. 559
Kersbergen, K. van 3568
Kershaw, S. 5544
Kershnar, S. 2359
Kershner, R. 2229

Kertzer, D. 2703
Kervasdoué, J. de 5806
Kesby, M. 427, 5975
Keskinen, E. 5143
Kessler, I. 4627
Kessler, T. 1067
Kesteman, N. 4950
Kestenbaum, B. 3394
Ketlhapile, M. 5200
Kettley, P. 4384
Kevane, M. 3883
Key, J. 3019
Keys, J. 2730
Keywood, K. 5182
Khalaf, A. 2838
Khalfa, J. 218
Khan, M. 4152
Khan, Z. 1532
Kharkova, T. 2775
Khaw, A. 5964
Khawaja, M. 2796
Khera, R. 5058
Khlat, M. 3280
Khmelkov, V. 3517
Khodakevich, L. 5773
Khoshoo, T. 3759
Khubchandani, L. 1805
Kidd, J. 1620
Kidd, K. 1620
Kidd, M. 2457
Kiddle, C. 4486
Kieffer, A. 2115, 2116
Kiely, R. 2532
Kihlbom, U. 5865
Kiklewicz, A. 2009
Kikuchi, E. 219
Kikuchi, K. 4443
Kilb, N. 1638
Kilbane, T. 3813
Kilcullen, R. 627
Kilduff, M. 1127, 4408
Killias, M. 3338, 5070
Kilpatrick, S. 3910
Kilson, M. 3528
Kim, C. 2568
Kim, D. 3064
Kim, H. 54, 2141, 3283, 5532
Kim, J. 44, 247, 342, 2866, 3927, 4250, 4684, 5115
Kim, K. 5, 54, 1787, 3949, 4048
Kim Lee, E. 3064
Kim, M. 4499
Kim, R. 3411
Kim, S. 1262, 4250
Kim, W. 3949

Kim, Y. 2579, 2586, 3949, 4250
Kimball, K. 2104
Kimberly, J. 5807
Kimhi, S. 5351
Kimmel, M. 5358
Kincaid, D. 2759
Kincaid, H. 116
Kincanon, E. 5
Kinchin, I. 2194
King, A. 406, 969, 2300
King, C. 1887, 3887
King, M. 4191, 5457
King, N. 2344
King, R. 3639, 3679, 3791, 3972, 4982
King, S. 767
Kinglun, N. 4829
Kingston, P. 2664
Kinsey, K. 5154
Kintrea, K. 3982, 4159
Kiosseoglou, G. 3592
Kirk, N. 988
Kirk, T. 3934
Kirkpatrick, C. 3815
Kironde, J. 3966
Kiros, G. 2703, 2827
Kirov, V. 5641
Kirsch, I. 675
Kirsch, S. 1597
Kirton, D. 3433
Kirton, G. 4882
Kisfalvi, V. 1153, 4625
Kishi, S. 4343
Kisriev, E. 1529
Kiss, G. 3490
Kita, T. 5524
Kitchen, R. 2490
Kitchener, M. 4770
Kitchin, R. 613, 2737
Kittel, B. 4817
Kitto, S. 3875
Kitzinger, C. 455
Kiyonari, T. 656
Kjølsrød, L. 5838
Klausmann, H. 1798
Klavus, J. 5763
Kleiman, N. 2266
Klein, G. 1556
Klein, J. 5265
Klein, K. 4701
Klein, T. 501
Kleindienst, K. 3389
Kleinig, J. 5018
Kleinsorge, S. 584
Klemke, E. 1584
Klerk, F. de 5363

Klerk, V. de 1813, 1841, 2523
Klicker, R. 724
Kliksberg, B. 4290, 5642
Kline, A. 1584
Kline, K. 5960
Klinkers, L. 3819
Klitgaard, K. 2513
Klobucký, R. 144
Klocke, A. 4277
Klonoff, E. 3440
Kloosterman, R. 414, 3568
Klotman, P. 1909
Klugman, B. 2754
Knaap, W. van der 3820
Kneafsey, M. 3908
Kneebone, I. 804
Knerr, B. 3619
Knez, I. 559
Knežević-Hočevar, D. 987
Knight, N. 332
Knights, D. 4618, 4808
Knippenberg, D. van 1111
Knipscheer, C. 2659
Knobel, M. 430
Knöbl, W. 1253
Knocke, W. 4552
Knodel, J. 2927
Knott, K. 1384
Knottnerus, J. 1074, 5891
Knox, M. 2500
Knudsen, S. 2202
Knuth, M. 4361
Knutson, D. 4651
Ko, Y. 4699, 4735, 4746
Kobayashi, J. 420
Kobayashi, K. 2934
Koc, I. 2736
Koch, H. 5889
Koch, T. 1039, 5876
Kochanska, G. 3034
Kočová, R. 2814
Kodio, B. 2832
Kodolitsch, P. von 4963
Kodrnja, J. 3192
Kody, Z. 1822
Koebler, S. 5732
Koenig, H. 2663
Koenis, S. 1175
Koestner, R. 776
Koff, B. 3385
Kohler, H. 2782
Köhler, S. 1302
Kohli, M. 953
Kohn, A. 3931
Kohring, M. 1715

Kohrman, M. 2472
Kohut, A. 512
Koirala, A. 3702
Kok, H. 4168
Kokalis, T. 1638
Kolb, D. 1018, 3097
Koliba, C. 2213
Kolin, P. 1241
Kolko, B. 3505
Kolody, B. 3565
Kolomazník, T. 2519
Kolosi, T. 2533
Kolossov, V. 1000
Kolstad, A. 2612
Koltsova, E. 1731
Komai, H. 3569
Komori, N. 4310
Kompridis, N. 139
Komter, A. 929
Konadu-Agyemang, K. 3551
Konarzewski, K. 869
Kondo, H. 2434
Kong, C. 862
Kong, L. 2571, 3775, 4108
Kong, S. 5891
Konieczny, M. 1443
Konietzka, D. 4506, 4753
König, M. 4762
Konishi, H. 4045
Kono, M. 5512
Konotey-Ahulu, F. 1620
Konrad, T. 5845
Konstantinovskij, D. 2123
Kontra, M. 1816
Konur, O. 2454
Koob, G. 5406
Koole, S. 1084
Koomen, W. 840, 855
Koonings, K. 5466
Kopp, M. 5773
Koppen, C. van 3698
Koppett, L. 1308
Korazim-Körösy, Y. 3862
Korboe, D. 4169
Korcz, K. 107
Koren, C. 3169
Korenman, S. 434, 2738
Kornai, J. 5489
Korstad, R. 4768
Korunka, C. 4377
Korupp, S. 4777
Koschin, F. 2684
Koshar, R. 1329
Koshechkina, T. 5214
Koskela, H. 3957, 4140

Koslowski, P. 4417
Kosmarskaia, N. 3627
Kosnick, K. 1698, 1777
Kosonen, K. 1000
Koss, M. 3201
Kosso, P. 1574
Kossoudji, S. 3565
Kostelecký, T. 2407
Kostiuk, K. 1505
Kota, J. 77
Kotthoff, H. 1839
Kotzé, E. 1813
Koubova, E. 5116
Kouloubardou, F. 5089
Kovács, Z. 4168
Koven, M. 1912
Kowaleski-Jones, L. 2636
Kowalikowa, J. 2009
Kowzan, T. 1862
Kozik-Rosabal, G. 3340
Kozina, I. 4429
Kozioł, E. 4606
Kozlarek, O. 393
Kraas, F. 3776
Kraaykamp, G. 2593, 3568
Krabbe, E. 1650
Krabuanrat, O. 4629
Kragh, H. 1623
Kralj, B. 4822
Kramer, B. 5479
Kramer, D. 668
Kramer, J. 5393
Kramer, R. 5465
Krannich, R. 3914
Kratochwil, F. 5310
Kraus, L. 5403
Kraus, P. 1826, 4966
Kraus, V. 3285
Krause, S. 4958
Kraut, R. 1660
Kravdal, Ø. 2813
Kraye, J. 237
Kreibich, V. 4099
Kreitzman, L. 1282
Krejčí, J. 1185
Kremer, M. 120
Kremp, É. 4175
Krenawi, A. Al- 5687, 5908
Krenske, L. 1974
Kretsedemas, P. 1639
Kreyenfeld, M. 4528
Krichevskaia, O. 3281
Krichmar, L. 3591
Kriel, M. 1813
Krindač, A. 1436

AUTHOR INDEX

Krischke, P. 4965
Kristel, O. 650
Kristeva, J. 5239
Kritz, M. 3617
Kritzer, H. 5154
Krivo, L. 5113
Krohn, M. 5079
Kroll, B. 3030
Kroll-Smith, S. 3701
Kromer, J. 4070
Kroon, H. 5736
Krop, B. 5448
Kroska, A. 3221
Krotov, P. 4273
Kruck, K. 3318
Kruckman, L. 3046
Krueger, J. 867
Krueger, R. 507, 709, 712
Krüger, H. 4192
Kruglov, Y. 5773
Kruijt, D. 5466
Krull, J. 709
Krummeck, S. 4422
Krupski, A. 5744
Kruse, D. 4449
Krutous, V. 1421
Kruttschnitt, C. 5012
Krylova, A. 710
Krystal, M. 1170
Kshatriya, G. 2780
Ku, A. 4932
Kuate-Defo, B. 2963
Kubey, R. 1690
Kubínová, R. 2814
Kučera, M. 2724
Kudomi, Y. 2101
Kuebler, D. 5375
Kuechler, M. 520
Kuehl, S. 3352
Kugelmas, E. 4949
Kuhlman, D. 709
Kuhn, P. 593, 4504
Kühne, O. 2689
Kühnen, U. 825
Kuhnle, S. 5622
Kuipers, G. 3467
Kukkonen, T. 271, 272
Kukla, A. 1615
Kuklo, C. 2691
Kukushkina, E. 1
Kulick, D. 3363
Kulik, L. 3239, 4586
Kulkarni, P. 5704
Kulu, H. 3558
Kumar, A. 4100

Kumar, R. 2351, 2394, 4207
Kumar, S. 4169
Kumaranayake, L. 5777
Kumpulainen, K. 5405
Künçek, Ö. 3681
Küng-Shankleman, L. 1718
Kuniewski, J. 4781
Kunkel, C. 3307
Kunyi, W. 5838
Kunze, M. 5407
Kupczyk, M. 2009
Kurasawa, F. 338
Kurek, W. 4606
Kurian, P. 3067, 3126
Kurland, N. 4716
Kuropka, I. 2835
Kűrti, L. 2544
Kurz, T. 1331
Kushner, S. 428
Kushnick, L. 5147
Kuta, A. 5633
Kutash, K. 2154
Kutchinsky, B. 5176
Kverndokk, K. 976
Kwan-Terry, A. 1811
Kwok, B. 1477
Kwon, C. 2009
Kwon, P. 691
Kwon, S. 1021
Kwon, Y. 54
Kych, A. 2716
Kydd, A. 927
Kynch, J. 5042
Laak, J. 5538
Laan, L. van der 4436
Laban, Y. Abu- 3669
Laberge, D. 5420
Labib, T. 1528
Labica, G. 2543
Labrecque, M. 4458
Lacassin, F. 1323
Lacey, K. 1756
Lacey, N. 1739
Lachance, L. 767
Lachapelle, J. 1216
Lacouture, M. 2152
Lacy, M. 496
Lacy, W. 3837
Ladd, E. 3844
Ladd, H. 2166
Laden, A. 129
Ladwig, D. 4293
Laermans, R. 1866
LaFarge, L. 784
Laffly, D. 5968

Laflamme, S. 3423
LaFollette, H. 4984
Lafore, R. 4950
Laforest, R. 5265
Lafuze, J. 750
Lagandré, V. 5016
Lago, A. Dal 335
Lagopoulos, A. 1803
Lagrange, H. 5068
LaGrange, T. 5077, 5108
Laguerre, M. 4002
Lai, G. 4699, 4735, 4746
Lai, K. 3108
Lai, L. 3948
Laiferová, E. 4930
Laine, A. 3533
Laitao, J. 3108
Laitin, D. 1845
Lake, S. 5777
Laki, L. 2620
Lalande, G. 767
Lalli, P. 1649
Lalljee, M. 830
Lallukka, S. 3409
Lally, J. 4087
Lalonde, R. 3442
Lam, A. 1149
Lam, C. 806
Lam, S. 550, 582
Lamas, M. 5200
Lamb, M. 2871, 3051, 5562
Lamb, S. 2652, 3298
Lambert, D. 5819
Lambert, R. 2564
Lambsdorff, J. 5282
Lameiras, M. 3283
Lammers, K. 173
Lamont, M. 2021
Lampel, J. 1100
Lamprecht, M. 2324
Lan, D. 1895
Lancaster, S. 4247
Land, K. 471, 2815
Landale, N. 4257, 4470
Landolt, P. 4197
Landorf, C. 3854
Landreville, P. 5016
Landrine, H. 3440
Landry, C. 4038
Landry, L. 315
Landry, S. 5928
Landsverk, J. 5573
Landua, D. 5243
Lane, III, F. 4387
Lane, J. 377, 5114

Lane, N. 5834
Lang, B. 3504
Lang, D. 2289
Lange, A. 2987
Lange, P. Van 928
Langenohl, A. 5294
Langer, E. 574
Langfeldt, B. 2922
Langhelle, O. 3816
Langley, A. 4622
Langlois, A. 3423
Langlois, J. 573
Langlois, S. 1607, 4338
Langman, J. 1816
Langue, F. 3891
Languin, N. 3930, 5285
Lanjouw, P. 4309
Lanjouw, S. 3615
Lankshear, C. 4803
Lann, E. Le 5611
Lanning, L. 5926
Lansbury, R. 4818
Lanspery, S. 2917
Lanstyák, I. 1816
Lant, T. 1100
Lantz, A. 5327
Lantz, P. 1200
Lanuza, G. 1417, 1449
Lanz, R. 1158
Lanza-Kaduce, L. 5122
Lapaeva, V. 5206
Lapante, J. 5420
Lapavitsas, C. 4193
Laperrousaz, E. 1478
Lapierre, N. 2679, 2901
Lapp, M. 5304
Lappin, J. 630
Lara, P. de 358
Larochelle, G. 4945, 5641
Laroque, G. 4582
LaRossa, R. 3008
Laroussi, F. 1931
Larsen, J. 4259
Larsen, N. 1158
Larsen, U. 2851
Larson, A. 573
Larson, D. 1381
Larson, H. 2810
Larson, J. 2913
Larsson, S. 907
Lascoumes, P. 5942
Laska, S. 3701, 4683
Laslett, B. 2384, 3115
Laslett, P. 2542
Lassman, P. 268

AUTHOR INDEX

Last, M. 5349
Laszlo, E. 2508
László, R. 993
LaTendresse, D. 1078
Latham, A. 4112
Latham, K. 1318
Latimer, J. 5534
Latimer, W. 5384
Latour, B. 32, 1596
Latta, M. 4537
Lau, F. 5765
Lau, I. 5309
Lauderdale, D. 3394
Laufer, J. 4545
Laugier, S. 4898
Laungaramsri, P. 3707
Laurell, A. 2568
Laurens, H. 161
Laurens, L. 3763
Laurie, N. 3073
Lavalette, M. 2390
Lavallée, M. 3423
Lavaud, J. 2294
Lavelle, J. 758
Lavigne, F. 3702
Laville, J. 4195, 4235
Laville, R. 3416
Lavin, D. 2266
Lavy, V. 2022
Law, D. 1413
Law, J. 1115, 1598, 3258
Law, K. 4363
Law, L. 3334
Law, S. 1708
Lawler, E. 1047
Lawler, J. 2335
Lawler, S. 3033
Lawless, P. 4052
Lawrence, C. 741
Lawrence, D. 4084
Lawrence, G. 3880
Lawrence, P. 4652
Lawrence, S. 5414
Lawrence, W. 1082
Lawson, S. 992, 1789
Lawson, V. 3537
Lawton, B. 5714
Lay-Chenchabi, K. 1949
Layde, P. 5987
Lazar, A. 816
Lazar, J. 2311
Lazar, M. 4898
Lazaridis, G. 3538, 3639, 3656
Lázaro, N. 4595
Lazear, E. 3555

Lazega, E. 1068, 1151, 4401
Lazerges, C. 5025
Le, A. 4432
Le, E. 5329
Le Grand, J. 5781
Lê, K. 545
Le, P. 2675
Leaf, M. 4178
Leaf, P. 5906
Leaman, J. 4697
Leary, M. 697
Leavitt, L. 5928
Leberre-Semenov, M. 3425
Lebrun, J. 801
Lebrun, M. 2047
Lebrun, T. 5814
Leck, G. 3340
Lecker, T. 949
LeClair, D. 4420
LeCompte, M. 3340
Leder, J. 4298
Ledwith, M. 3834
Ledwith, S. 4147, 4514, 4857
Lee, A. 5446, 5765
Lee Browning, S. 2917
Lee, C. 4848
Lee, D. 394, 3288
Lee, H. 422
Lee, J. 54, 2693, 2710, 3545, 3565, 4225, 4416, 5891
Lee, K. 1118, 1222, 2145, 2792, 3759, 3801, 4250
Lee, M. 3565, 4328, 5053, 5081, 5440, 5441
Lee, N. 3815
Lee, S. 54, 247, 3546, 5532, 5844, 5949
Lee, W. 2691
Leede, J. De 4428
Leedham, B. 766
Leene, G. 2659
Leerssen, J. 160
Lees, L. 4016
Lee-Treweek, G. 48
Leeuwen, M. Van 3611
Lefebvre, M. 2047
Lefebvre, P. 5636
Lefebvre, Y. 767
Leff, E. 4293
Leff, M. 1650
Legendre, B. 1323
Leggett, J. 3711
Legros, E. 1383
Leguina, J. 4252
Lehman, E. 3004
Lehman-Frisch, S. 3413
Lehmann, P. 3206

Index des auteurs

Lehmann-Rommel, R. 2117
Lehman-Wilzig, S. 1689
Lehrer, E. 5063
Lehtonen, J. 5433
Lehtonen, M. 1796
Leiba-O'Sullivan, S. 4658
Leibfried, S. 5640, 5653
Leicht, K. 4470
Leidner, D. 1660
Leigh, D. 2023
Leildé, A. 964
Leisch, H. 3776
Leisering, L. 5653
Leishman, F. 5126
Leisse, U. 1067
Leite Lopes, J. 1315
Leite, M. 1514
Leite Nahra, C. 791
Leiter, B. 264
Leiter, M. 4680
Leloudis, J. 4768
Leloup, X. 3946, 4828
Lemaigre, T. 5641
Leman, E. 3948
Lemasson, J. 2278
Lemesle, B. 3891
Lemieux, V. 1035
Lemire, F. 2047
Lemire, M. 5265
Lemish, D. 3601
Lemon, M. 4056
Lemonnier, P. 381
Lemos, C. De 1161
Lemos Minella, D. de 5192
Lempert, L. 2915
Lempert, R. 5154
Lemyre, L. 767
Lenartowicz, T. 4658
Leng, K. 340
Lengfeld, H. 4837
Lenman, J. 3705
Lennon, J. 1946
Lenntorp, B. 3767
Lenoir, D. 4299
Lenoir-Achdjian, A. 1990
Lens, W. 665
Lentin, A. 3507
Lentz, C. 3535
Lenze, D. 2700
Lenzen, D. 2218
Leo, J. Di 1233
Léo, P. 3960
Leonard, E. 4828, 5011
Leonard, J. 3947
Leonard, W. 5541

Leone, F. 3702
Leonetti, D. 2766
Leopold, E. 5857
Leoussi, A. 1164, 1679
LePine, J. 4802
Lepper, M. 606
Lepperhoff, N. 458
Lerat, P. 1822
Lerberghe, W. Van 5980
Lerise, F. 3876
Lerner, J. 598, 650
Lerner, R. 598, 679, 2615, 2896
Lerner, S. 2781
Lesage, A. 5420
Leslie, E. 299
Leslie, L. 5573
Lesourd, S. 2618
Letonturier, É. 67
Letourmy, A. 5942, 5980
Létourneau, J. 147
Leu, R. 5763
Leudar, D. 818, 1748
Leuenberger, C. 746
Levashov, V. 4970
Levasseur, A. 1882
Lévay, M. 5110
Levene, M. 3420
Leventhal, T. 577
Levering, B. 1997
Leverton, T. 800
Levesque, B. 4195
Lévesque, C. 4818
Levi, M. 2, 4850
Levilain, H. 5016
Levin, D. 1129
Levin, I. 1157, 2949
Levin, S. 5296
Levine, A. 5567
Levine, D. 373, 2924
Levine, J. 146, 440
Levine, P. 5551
Levine, R. 2223
Levinson, K. 4809
Levin-Waldman, O. 4307
Levison, D. 3169
Levy, C. 68
Levy, D. 2318, 5627
Levy, G. 2177
Lévy, J. 4021
Levy, Jr., M. 65
Levy, L. 5953
Levy, N. 206
Levy, R. 4192
Levy, S. 3517
Lew, J. 1489

AUTHOR INDEX

Lew, R. 2310
Lewandowski, J. 401
Lewin-Epstein, N. 2922
Lewiński, P. 2009
Lewis, A. 1086
Lewis, D. 1373, 4342
Lewis, G. 5483
Lewis, J. 43, 1669, 5289, 5616
Lewis, M. 690, 3759
Lewis, P. 1756, 2319, 4508
Lewis, R. 3382, 5822
Lewis, S. 2692
Lewkowicz, D. 552
Ley, D. 3590
Leydesdorff, L. 359, 1604
Li, C. 3108
Li, J. 4762
Li, P. 3553
Li, T. 5406
Li, V. 5838
Li, W. 1894
Li, Y. 2676, 3553
Liang, H. 3626
Liao, C. 1811
Licha, I. 1566
Lichtblau, K. 408
Lichter, D. 2914
Lickel, B. 1086
Lickliter, R. 551
Liddell, M. 4564
Liddick, D. 5074
Liden, R. 4689
Lie, B. 3595
Lie, M. 2537
Lieb, R. 3338
Liebig, S. 2396, 4837
Liebkind, K. 842
Liebman, C. 1024
Liechtenhan, F. 151
Liégeois, J. 2067
Liere, K. Van 3749
Lievens, F. 4599
Light, A. 2253
Light, D. 1328
Lightfoot, C. 1161
Lightfoot, J. 2044
Lightly, N. 1474
Ligneau, P. 5475
Likens, T. 2816
Lilja, J. 907
Liljestrand, J. 5439
Lim, B. 4106
Lim, E. 2568
Lim, H. 54
Lim, O. 4250

Lim, T. 2584
Lima Costa, C. de 1915, 3151
Lima, L. 4227
Limongi, F. 4949
Limqueco, P. 4935
Lin, A. 1811
Lin, I. 3042
Lin, J. 3618
Lin, M. 2667
Linard, A. 3659
Lind, E. 4483
Linde, C. 162
Lindell, M. 1096
Linden, M. van der 176
Lindenberg, D. 2439
Lindholm, C. 4696
Lindholm, O. 4025
Lindquist, C. 5033
Lindsay, P. 4922
Lindsay, R. 5084
Lindzey, G. 726
Linehan, M. 4562
Lines, P. 2192
Link, B. 772, 2808
Link, R. 5661
Linkogle, S. 48
Linmao, M. 2729
Linstead, S. 3347
Linton, S. 4698
Linz, D. 3498
Lippard, L. 1342
Lipshitz, R. 1095, 5799
Lishman, J. 5720
Lisle, D. 3230
Lissenburgh, S. 2139
Lissitz, R. 511
Litten, R. 5406
Little, D. 154
Little, R. 451
Little, S. 4056
Little, V. 2187, 2602
Littlechild, B. 5679
Littlefield, L. 2850
Littlejohn, S. 1655
Littleton, J. 5406
Littlewood, S. 3808
Litz, S. 2451
Litzelfelner, P. 5561
Liu, C. 2986
Liu, H. 434
Liu, J. 833, 5296
Liu, S. 1423
Liu, X. 456, 2634
Liusin, V. 3254
Livaditis, M. 5089

Livingstone, D. 4398
Livingstone, S. 5001
Lizotte, A. 5079
Llewellyn, S. 4310
Lloyd, D. 1227
Lloyd-Sherlock, P. 2713
Llull, L. 2294
Llywelyn, D. 998
Loader, I. 4325
Lober, K. 476
Locatelli, M. 4532
Lochery, N. 57
Lock, A. 1161
Lock, M. 1620
Locke, C. 3607
Locke, E. 4719
Locke, L. 2282
Lockhart, P. 5409
Lockie, S. 3875
Loeber, R. 5069, 5071
Loehlin, J. 4337
Loerch, A. 5357
Loewenstein, G. 905
Loewenstein, J. 1018
Löfgren, A. 2571
Loft, J. 525
Logan, J. 3481
Lohan, M. 1562, 1659
Lohauß, P. 4293
Lohnert, B. 3714
Lollivier, S. 4590
Lom, P. 352
Lomasky, L. 5305
Lombardi, L. 2456
Loncle-Moriceau, P. 5982
London, A. 5633
London, R. 2996
Long, J. 2188, 5599
Long, S. 5498, 5505
Longhurst, P. 4056
Longhurst, R. 3788
Longshore, D. 5397
Lonkila, M. 2088
Lont, H. 4263
Looise, J. 4417
Lopes Balsas, C. 4033
López Azpitarte, E. 2478
López, K. de 636
López López, W. 3283
López, M. 2298
López, R. 3905
Lopi, B. 1760
Lorber, J. 3087
Lorbiecki, A. 4628
Lordon, F. 4351

Lorenz, F. 2965, 3873
Lores, A. 329
Loretto, W. 4487, 4852
Loriaux, M. 2657
Loring Miró, J. 2557
Loriol, M. 5475
Losada, H. 4142
Losch, B. 5853
Losch, H. 1797
Loscocco, K. 1290
Lotnik, W. 3495
Lotz, A. 449
Loû, A. du 5980
Loughlin, J. 1566
Louie, K. 3222
Louis, M. 1091
Loukaitou-Sideris, A. 4098
Loukas, A. 709
Love, K. 2208
Love, N. 859
Loveday, B. 5126
Loveless, T. 2079
Lovell, P. 2507, 4509
Lovell, S. 5801
Lovell, T. 3153
Lovett, M. 5409
Low, E. 2387
Low, H. 463
Lowe, G. 4869
Lowe, J. 4618, 5891
Lowe, M. 4027, 4135
Lowe, S. 4909, 5645
Lowman, C. 5406
Löwy, M. 1478
Lowyck, J. 2193
Löytönen, M. 483
Löyttyniemi, V. 5838
Lozano, J. 4417
Lozeau, D. 5755
Lu, H. 2988
Lu, Z. 3170
Lubatkin, M. 662, 4386
Lubek, I. 870
Lubin, B. 3751
Lubkemann, S. 3599
Luca, C. De 2456
Luca, M. Di 3069
Lucas, R. 687
Luchtenberg, S. 1757
Luciano, A. 2037
Lugão Rios, A. 2901
Lugg, D. 567
Lughod, D. Abu- 5361
Lugo, A. 3468
Lugo-Ortiz, L. 2752

AUTHOR INDEX

Luhanga, M. 3708
Luhmann, N. 403
Luhrmann, T. 1258
Luhulima, A. 4571
Luijk, H. Van 4417
Luiz, J. 2163, 3319
Luke, T. 3710
Lukemeyer, A. 5565
Lukens, E. 772
Lukes, S. 268
Lumby, C. 1714
Lummaa, V. 2744
Lumumba-Kasongo, T. 2513
Lund, A. 2571
Lund, E. 5838
Lund, H. 2247
Lundby, K. 1409
Lundeberg, K. 2876
Lundgren, E. 5509
Lundqvist, L. 3759
Lunt, I. 2109
Luo, C. 5200
Luo, T. 5458
Lupfer, M. 1438, 2352
Lupton, B. 3189
Lupton, D. 714
Lury, C. 3107
Lusane, C. 4278
Lush, L. 2792
Lussier, V. 5420
Luster, T. 3019
Lüter, A. 1730
Luthar, S. 5396
Lutz, H. 3135
Lutzker, J. 5594
Lux, M. 5649
Luz Ibarra, M. de la 4462
Luzzadder-Beach, S. 3179
Lydié, N. 5980
Lykken, D. 2304, 5050
Lynch, A. 1321
Lynch, C. 4227
Lynch, J. 5946
Lynch, M. 268, 309, 725, 5315
Lyness, K. 4519
Lynk, M. 4876
Lyon, C. 5580
Lyon, D. 19, 1405
Lyon, F. 4240
Lyons, E. 878
Lyons, K. 5661, 5705, 5709
Lyons, S. 5633
Lyons, W. 5183
Lyra, M. 1161
Lysa, H. 1207

Lytkina, T. 4273
M., G. 3518
Ma, E. 1758
Ma, G. 2926
Ma, J. 5717
Ma, X. 5961
Maaouia, A. 5076
Maaravi, Y. 5513
Maasilta, P. 483
McAleer, J. 1955
McAndrew, M. 2047, 3423
McAnerney, B. 4639
McArthur, A. 4091, 4117
Macaskill, A. 5900
Macaulay, S. 5154
McAuley, C. 5550
MacAuley, D. 4146
McAuliff, B. 5157
McBride, N. 5955
McBrier, D. 4569
McC. Adams, R. 996
McCabe, D. 4618, 4808
McCabe, J. 1991
McCaffrey, D. 2730
McCall, L. 4538, 4564
McCalman, J. 1094
McCammon, H. 4416
McCann, D. 3382
McCarthy, A. 1737
McCarthy, D. 2361
McCarthy, J. 2932
McCarthy, P. 4614
McCarty, D. 5818
McCarty, J. 524
McCauley, M. 503
McClary, S. 3115
McClelland, L. 5434
McClintock, M. 591
McClure, J. 833
McClure, P. 5354
Maccoby, E. 3014
McCombs, B. 2017
McConkey, R. 2486
McConville, C. 4850
McCormack, C. 469, 470
McCormick, R. 5913
McCoy, A. 3257
McCoy, C. 5748
McCrae, R. 709, 710
McCray, T. 4087
McCrone, D. 2532, 2676
McCullagh, C. 148
McCullagh, M. 563
McCulloch, A. 4044
McCullough, L. 5854

McCullough, M. 1381
McCutcheon, A. 3870
McCutcheon, R. 1445
McDade, K. 5669
McDonagh, M. 5787
McDonald, A. 5718
MacDonald, B. 361
McDonald, B. 1293
McDonald, C. 5644
MacDonald, D. 719, 991, 4818
McDonald, D. 3599, 3633, 3649
MacDonald, G. 908, 2318
McDonald, G. 4417
McDonald, J. 2660, 4845
MacDonald, K. 4056
McDonald, L. 5518
McDonald, P. 2786
McDonald, R. 2928
McDonald, S. 1115
MacDonald, S. 4439, 4784
MacDonald, Z. 5392
McDonnell, K. 5838
MacDonogh, S. 1952
McDonough, P. 4703
MacDougall, D. 1911
McDowell, L. 3246, 4554
McDuff, E. 4778
Maceda, M. 2511
McElroy, J. 3399
McElroy, S. 3391
Macer, D. 1620
McEwan, P. 2112
McFadden, P. 3261
McFadyen, A. 3037
MacFarlane, A. 3179, 4288
McFarlane, B. 4935
McFarlane, W. 772
McGauran, A. 4414
McGeary, K. 5748
McGee, R. 5394
McGeehan, I. 5721
McGhee, D. 826, 3354
McGill, A. 854
MacGillivray, C. 3386
MacGillivray, I. 3340
McGinn, M. 5538
McGinnis, M. 3688, 3851
McGivney, V. 2031
McGowan, B. 5569, 5693
McGreal, S. 4043
McGreal, W. 4003
McGregor, L. 4642
McGue, M. 2304
McGuigan, A. 2804
McGuigan, J. 1261

McGuinness, D. 5721
McGuiran, J. 955
McGuire, G. 4376
McGuire, T. 5786
Macháček, L. 62, 4974
Machado, F. 4486
Machado, N. 5880
McHale, S. 3053, 3213
Mchitarjan, I. 2117
Machlin, S. 525
Machuca Becerra, R. 159
McHugh, K. 3540
Mchumvu, Y. 2727
Maciel de Paula, L. 5642
McInerney, F. 5887
MacIntosh, D. 3715
McIntyre, J. 4398
McIntyre, L. 22
Macioti, M. 3653
McIver, S. 5750
McKay, A. 2160, 3294
Mackay, C. 3985
MacKay, D. 3991
McKay, H. 5010
McKay, I. 170
McKay, J. 1726, 1974, 5744
McKay, S. 5318
McKee, A. 3355
McKeehan, I. 5773
McKelvey, M. 2856
McKenna, C. 902
McKenna, E. 1092
McKenna, M. 3912
McKenry, P. 2856
McKenzie-Mohr, D. 3749
McKhann, C. 5895
Mackie, D. 882, 1057
McKie, L. 1133
McKimmie, B. 1034
McKinlay, A. 4608
McKinley, M. 2754
McKinney, V. 4623
MacKinnon, L. 5595
MacKinnon, R. 748
McKittrick, K. 1917
McKnight, K. 5818
McKnight, P. 5818
Maclagan, M. 1847
Maclaran, P. 3072, 4319
McLaren, V. 5107
McLaughlin, D. 2914
McLaughlin, T. 489
McLellan, A. 5744, 5818
McLelland, M. 3061, 3313
McLennan, G. 34

AUTHOR INDEX

McLoughlin, L. 1722
McLoyd, V. 5633
McMahon, E. 5721
McManus, B. 1010
McManus, P. 4459, 5625
MacMartin, C. 870
McMichael, P. 2512
McMillan, J. 2276
MacMillan, R. 3287, 4439, 4594, 5044
McMillin, J. 2666
McMorris, B. 4758
McMullen, K. 1936
McNally, D. 4215
McNally, M. 5409
McNay, K. 2773
McNay, L. 3124
McNeill, D. 636, 2573, 3801, 4085
MacNeill, D. 4962
McNulty, T. 5102
McOuat, G. 1558
Macovei, M. 5139
McPherran, M. 270
Macpherson, C. 3643
Macpherson, D. 4465
McQuaid, R. 4486
McQueen, R. 1036
McQuillan, B. 756
McQuoid-Mason, D. 5858
McRobbie, A. 2623, 3127
Macron, E. 161
Macrory, G. 2087
Macunovich, D. 2799
McVea, H. 5169
McWilliam, R. 171
Madajczyk, P. 1004
Madison, D. 579
Madry, L. 2889
Madsen, D. 3120
Madsen, F. 1384
Mäenpää, P. 1287
Magagnin, C. 2628, 2629
Magalhães, G. 5192
Magaš, D. 1000
Magnusson, J. 2188
Magsino, R. 2188
Maguire, C. 4725
Maguire, D. 3764
Maguire, J. 1330
Maguire, M. 5042
Magyar, B. 1675
Mahal, A. 3327
Maharaj, B. 3599
Maharatna, A. 2783
Maher, M. 519
Maheu, L. 5265

Mahjour, J. 5981
Mahnkopf, B. 4293
Mahoney, J. 180, 497, 2445
Mahony, D. 586, 4449
Mahroof, M. 190
Mahroum, S. 2262
Maier, E. 3742
Maier, M. 1715, 2554
Maignan, I. 4420
Maïlat, M. 5716
Maire, B. 5980
Majerová, V. 3889
Mak, A. 3567
Maker, A. 5200
Mäkinen, I. 5773
Malamuth, N. 920
Malan, N. 5363
Malat, J. 2751
Malby, R. 5783
Malepe, L. 5200
Malhotra, A. 5395
Malhotra, R. 5395
Malkinson, R. 2942
Mallard, A. 4322
Malleh, F. 3560
Malley, M. 3382
Mallier, T. 3069
Mallikarachchi, D. 1471
Mallon, I. 2679
Maloney, W. 2203
Malos, E. 2882
Malos, S. 2055
Malpass, R. 5084
Maltais, D. 767
Maluccio, A. 5569
Malý, M. 2814
Mamadouh, V. 1000
Mambi-El-Sendengele, F. 4797
Mammo, T. 4280
Mamphiswana, D. 5703
Man, E. 3108
Man, G. 1882
Manacorda, S. 5025
Mancebo, M. 5642
Mandalios, J. 1160
Mander, M. 1712
Manderson, L. 5791
Manesse, D. 2006
Maneval, H. 5324
Maney, G. 5235, 5242
Manfredi, S. 4514
Mangan, I. 1356, 4485
Mangez, É. 2082
Manghi, S. 1573
Mangini, M. 673

INDEX DES AUTEURS

Manhart, L. 5981
Maniglier, P. 348
Manion, L. 437
Manlapaz, E. 1943
Manley, J. 5794
Manlove, J. 2803
Mann, M. 4966
Mann, P. 4953
Mannar, V. 5969
Manning, E. 2
Manning, P. 4683
Manning, R. 3488
Manning, W. 3054
Manor, J. 2397
Manor, O. 1053, 2834
Manquele, M. 3810
Manser, M. 97
Mansilla, H. 3803
Manske, F. 4769
Manski, C. 2640, 4484
Manssens, J. 5264
Manstead, A. 1044
Manthorpe, J. 5586
Mantilla, M. 2513
Manton, K. 2815
Mantovani, J. 2679
Manusov, V. 1824
Manzenreiter, W. 1353
Manzi, T. 4111
Maoz, I. 1014, 1026
Mara, C. 4667
Marcelli, E. 4460
Marchal, E. 4322, 4613
Marchand, M. 3068
Marchant, P. 2090
Marchbank, J. 5467, 5600
Marchessault, J. 3159
Marchi, B. De 3759
Marchi, N. De 1859
Marchington, M. 4643
Marcil-Gratton, N. 2962
Marciniak, G. 2805
Marco, C. 3181
Marcus, G. 5314
Marcuse, P. 4127
Mareš, P. 2385
Margavio, A. 4187, 4683
Marginson, S. 2277
Margolin, J. 683
Marie, A. 3842, 4263
Marietta, M. 4199
Marí-Klose, M. 3075
Marí-Klose, P. 115
Marimon, R. 4685
Marina, J. 5180

Mariner, C. 2803
Marini, M. 3237
Maritoux, J. 5980
Mariuza, C. 5192
Marjoribanks, T. 4354
Mark, V. 1986
Markel, H. 3545
Markham, I. 1410
Markides, K. 3565
Markman, H. 2985
Markoff, J. 4938
Markov, B. 241
Marks, A. 4608
Marks, C. 1882
Marks, E. 3115
Marks, J. 340, 1620
Marks, M. 1065, 5148
Markson, E. 2665
Markus, H. 3471
Markwick, M. 4238
Marley, C. 3059
Marmot, M. 5773
Marotta, M. 2456
Marotta, V. 397
Maroy, C. 4793, 5641
Marques, M. 4596
Marquet, J. 5891
Marquis, R. 5607
Marr, D. 975
Marriott, C. 3388
Marrus, M. 3518
Marschalck, P. 2691
Marsella, A. 710
Marsh, H. 862
Marsh, J. 5480
Marsh, R. 5211
Marshak, R. 1104
Marshall, B. 3584
Marshall, E. 5035
Marshall, L. 1647
Marshall, P. 5386
Marshall, R. 748
Marsiglio, W. 3051
Marston, S. 3786
Martel, C. 767
Martel, L. 5721
Martelaere, J. De 4912
Martens, L. 1322
Martikainen, R. 4537
Martin, A. 2889
Martin, C. 5406
Martin, D. 528
Martin, G. 542, 4313, 5273
Martin, I. 2010, 3827
Martin, J. 543, 1937, 4741, 5016

AUTHOR INDEX

Martin, L. 4398
Martin, M. 3183, 4709
Martin, N. 3308, 3345
Martin, O. 1610, 1617
Martin, P. 3121
Martin, R. 727, 1357, 4439, 4486
Martin, S. 2776, 4159
Martin, T. 710
Martín-Barbero, J. 1194, 1199
Martín-Barrero, J. 2298
Martin-Cantarino, C. 3759
Martinec, R. 1842
Martinez, Jr., R. 3565, 5441
Martinez, M. 1610
Martinez, P. 755
Martínez, R. 2294
Martínez-San Miguel, Y. 1224
Martínez-Torvisco, J. 3758
Martiniello, M. 4005
Martin-Iverson, M. 625
Martin-Papineau, N. 4950
Martocchio, J. 2335
Marton, A. 4108
Martuccelli, D. 2014
Marty, É. 2439
Martyn, H. 5676
Martyniuk, W. 2009
Maruani, M. 4478, 4545
Marullo, S. 2213
Marvy, P. 2819
Marx, G. 65, 4683
Masarweh, I. Al 2976
MASCH-Kollektiv 3206
Masciandaro, D. 5365
Mascini, P. 4727
Maskovsky, J. 5971
Mason, C. 4939
Mason, D. 2532
Mason, J. 5969
Mason, K. 2743
Mass, M. 5692
Massam, B. 3694
Mâsse, B. 1045
Massé, M. 5025
Masser, B. 3283
Massey, D. 536, 3550, 3565, 3774, 4266
Massignon, B. 4962
Massumi, B. 292
Mastekaasa, A. 3040, 3226
Masters, III, H. 709
Mastor, K. 710
Masumi, M. 4540
Matejů, M. 1205
Mateos, A. 978
Máté-Tóth, A. 2297

Mather, A. 2717
Mathews, G. 2552
Mathiassen, L. 1113
Mathieu, J. 1056, 1065
Mathur, A. 4631
Maticka-Tyndale, E. 3294
Mato, D. 2568
Matsaganis, M. 5622
Matsui, A. 464
Matsuki, K. 162
Matsumoto, Y. 50
Matsunaga, L. 4678
Mattes, R. 3633, 3649
Matteucci, S. 3813
Matthews, G. 741
Matthews, P. 1313
Matthews, R. 5013
Matthews, S. 1964
Matthews, Z. 2722
Mattis, J. 1372
Mattoo, S. 5395
Matuchniak-Krasuska, A. 1852
Mauger, G. 2618
Mauldon, J. 2745
Maume, D. 3170
Maurice, T. 161
Mauro, A. 2873
Mauss, A. 56
Mauws, M. 1104, 1856
Mavaddat, R. 3478
Mawby, R. 5080, 5116
Mawdsley, R. 2024
Mawhinney, M. 362
May, C. 1674
May, J. 4282, 4997, 5424
May, T. 5883
Maydorm, A. 2456
Mayer, A. 1612
Mayer, K. 431, 2654
Mayes, A. 774
Mayes, G. 137
Mayfield, A. 755
Mayhew, K. 4587, 4798
Mayhew, S. 5200
Maynard, M. 3067
Mayo, M. 3827
Mayr, U. 682
Mays, N. 5781
Mays, R. 5706
Mayseless, O. 2916
Mazaud, J. 1323
Mazerolle, P. 5096
Mazlish, B. 2314
Mazrui, A. 4975
Mazurski, K. 4606

Mazuy, R. 5335
Mazza, C. 4640
Mazzoldi, B. 2298
Mbeki, M. 5363
Mbeki, T. 5363
Mbizvo, M. 3311
Mboya, M. 2041
Mead, L. 5654
Meadows, D. 3002
Meagher, G. 4736
Meagher, K. 3868
Meaney, M. 767
Meares, P. 792
Meares, R. 785
Meares, T. 5038
Mearns, J. 675
Mears, D. 5036
Measor, L. 4996
Meca, P. 4950
Médard, J. 5282
Medora, N. 2913
Medvec, V. 889
Medvene, L. 915
Medway, J. 2668
Meeker, J. 5114
Meekers, D. 3300
Meeks, L. 2024, 2062
Meeks, W. 2024, 2062
Meel, M. 4417
Meerman, M. 3568
Meert, H. 3902
Mega, V. 3948
Mehaffy, M. 3228
Mehra, A. 4408
Mehretu, A. 3771
Mehta, P. 4902
Meier, K. 3565
Meier, S. 3127
Meighoo, K. 3400
Meijl, T. van 992, 1259
Meijlink, T. 4417
Meiksins, P. 4400
Meintjes, S. 3171
Meints, K. 636
Mejor, M. 1470
Meldrum, M. 4056
Mele, C. 4065
Meléndez Brau, N. 2906
Meléndez, H. 1221
Mella, O. 3552
Mellan, B. 3329
Mellanby, J. 3183
Mellers, B. 591
Melleuish, G. 1163
Mellman, L. 748

Mellor, J. 4274
Mellor, M. 3720
Mellow, N. 3121
Melton, J. 1378
Melucci, A. 5248
Membrado, M. 2679
Menachem, G. 3564
Mendelberg, T. 3516
Mendes Catani, A. 2147
Mendez, Jr., G. 3391
Mendoza, A. 2559
Mendoza-Denton, R. 933
Mendras, H. 355, 2357
Meneses, I. 3367
Menestrel, S. Le 1367
Mengersen, K. 2841
Menin, B. 2854
Menkel-Meadow, C. 1018
Mennecke, B. 1704
Menon, R. 2022, 3112
Menon, T. 864
Menon, U. 671, 3471
Mensah-Coker, G. 2475
Menzies, H. 2772
Meppem, T. 3697
Mercer, D. 5932
Merchant, M. 2870
Meredith, F. 4849
Mergl, M. 3095
Merle, P. 2014, 2111
Merle, V. 5968
Merli, M. 2728
Mermelstein, R. 5818
Mero, N. 1117
Merriam, S. 2145
Merrien, F. 5641
Merrigan, P. 5636
Merritt, M. 733
Merson, M. 2100
Mertig, A. 3749
Mertin, P. 2874
Meslé, F. 5968
Messaoudi, L. 1822
Messé, L. 1061
Messerschmidt, J. 5438
Messner, M. 3216, 3274
Mészáros, I. 4935
Metalina, T. 4804
Methheb, M. Al 5215
Metsemakers, J. 5891
Metts, N. 2483
Metts, R. 2483
Metz, T. 5149
Metzger, J. 4080
Metzger, P. 3702

AUTHOR INDEX

Meulders, D. 4503
Meulemann, H. 1375
Meuret, D. 2014
Meurling, B. 817, 3692
Meurs, D. 2626
Meuschel, S. 2567, 4973
Meuser, M. 5244
Meuwese, S. 3338
Meyer, B. 4479
Meyer, C. 5408
Meyer, D. 3943
Meyer, H. 2443
Meyer, I. 1822
Meyer, J. 306, 1642, 1647, 2568, 3633
Meyer, M. 5613
Meyer, R. 5406
Meyer, S. 3456
Meyer, T. 4859
Meyerowitz, B. 766
Meyers, J. 688
Meyers, M. 5565
Meyers, R. 1059
Meyerson, D. 3097
Mezey, G. 5457
Mezias, J. 1100
Mezias, S. 1100
Mezvinsky, N. 1546
Miagkov, A. 527
Miceli, M. 4679
Michael, D. 3759
Michael, K. 5363
Michael, M. 5421
Michela, J. 680
Michelson, M. 3565
Michelson, W. 3948
Michie, P. 625
Michon, J. 1323
Michun, S. 4799
Mick, D. 4345
Mick, S. 5844
Micklewright, J. 5598
Middleton, K. 2876
Middleton, S. 1093
Middleton, T. 1236
Middleton, W. 1083
Midford, R. 5955
Miedema, B. 5144
Miedema, S. 2117
Miell, D. 841
Miethe, T. 4683
Miguel, L. 2507
Míguez-Burbano, M. 5386
Mihályi, P. 5729
Mihesuah, D. 3115
Mikkelsen, P. 4025

Miklowitz, P. 251
Mikulecky, D. 1606
Mikulincer, M. 685, 721
Milbourne, P. 5417, 5418
Milby, J. 5421
Miles, M. 2477, 3933, 4420
Miles, S. 2650
Miles, W. 951
Milewa, T. 5976
Milkie, M. 3188
Milkman, R. 4821
Millar, C. 4659
Millar, J. 5564
Miller, A. 2754, 5012
Miller, C. 512, 1437, 3827
Miller, D. 843, 1395
Miller, J. 178, 709, 1770, 3391
Miller, Jr., G. 3738
Miller, N. 837, 856, 925, 4914
Miller, P. 600
Miller, R. 2917, 3037
Miller, T. 1357
Miller, W. 223, 4492, 5214
Millington, J. 3620
Mills, C. 5401
Mills, D. 845
Mills, G. 5363
Mills, J. 2601
Mills, M. 490
Mills, R. 2601
Millward, L. 655
Milne, A. 5516
Milovanovic, D. 5104
Milton, L. 999, 4641
Milyo, J. 4274
Mimroth, P. 2394
Min, P. 3411
Minato, K. 1956
Minca, C. 1362
Miner, J. 4407
Mingione, E. 3568
Minichiello, V. 2670
Minicz, W. 2009
Mininberg, E. 2104
Minkler, M. 2582
Minow, M. 3471
Minvielle, É. 5807, 5942
Miodunka, W. 2009, 3445
Miotto Wright, M. 2213
Miralles Massanés, J. 2524
Mirau, C. 4299
Mireri, C. 4450
Mirowsky, J. 2583
Mirza, H. 2161
Mirza, J. 3164

Index des auteurs

Miscevic, N. 3492
Mischel, W. 933
Mishra, U. 2662, 2733
Misra, G. 3327, 5200
Misra, J. 2200
Missègue, N. 2626
Mistry, M. 771, 3203
Mitchel, L. 2104
Mitchell, B. 2909
Mitchell, J. 2655, 3702, 3752
Mitchell, L. 897
Mitchell, S. 5771
Mitchinson, W. 178
Mitterauer, M. 195
Mizrahi, S. 5231
Mkhabela, L. 3208
Mladinic, A. 3283
Mmary, V. 2727
Moatti, J. 5891, 5945
Moberg, D. 56
Mock, N. 5969
Mocroft, I. 5775
Modak, M. 2313
Modood, T. 1535
Moers, M. 5891
Moffitt, T. 709, 5394
Moghadam, V. 3154
Moghaddam, F. 888
Mohan, D. 5967
Mohan, J. 2403
Mohay, T. 1414
Moher, J. 3809
Mohr, P. 2874
Moilanen, P. 568
Moisdon, J. 5942
Mok, M. 2500
Mol, A. 3718, 3722
Moldoveanu, M. 574
Molho, I. 3623
Molin, G. Da 3652
Molina, E. 5244
Molina y Vedia, S. 350
Moliterno, G. 1180
Moll, J. 861
Mollenkopf, J. 2716, 3568
Möller, H. 1473
Mollison, D. 446
Mollon, P. 812
Molloy, M. 1886
Molokotos Liederman, L. 4962
Moloney, G. 5878
Moloney, K. 4399
Molotch, H. 4128
Moltó, M. 4595
Monacelli, N. 1077

Monaghan, B. 5586
Monaghan, K. 4491
Mondada, L. 1561
Mondou, V. 2716, 4023
Monga, Y. 1177
Monge, P. 1660
Mongin, O. 161, 2439, 4898
Monk, S. 4486
Monks, J. 4880
Montague, L. 624
Montanari, A. 3820
Montandon, C. 5461
Montanelli, R. 5909
Montecucco, N. 3797
Monteiro, A. 3528, 5704
Monteith, M. 3464
Montejano, B. 2294
Montenegro, A. 186
Montero, P. 2801
Montes, J. 2618
Montgomery, D. 4182
Montgomery, K. 1099
Montgomery, M. 2836, 4276
Montgomery, R. 1492
Monthoux, P. de 1868
Monti, Jr., D. 4119
Monti, P. 5406
Montoya, J. 2176
Moodley, K. 2436, 3430
Moodley, V. 3599
Moody, J. 4371
Moody, M. 2021
Moon, C. 4417
Moon, H. 1017
Moon, Y. 574
Mooney, G. 2390
Mooney, J. 5451
Moore, A. 5881
Moore, B. 5721
Moore, H. 3115
Moore, J. 4744
Moore, M. 225, 2468
Moore, P. 4732
Moore, R. 1905, 3491
Moores, S. 1728
Moors, A. 3067
Mora, M. 3565, 4440
Moral, F. 978
Morales, A. 1819
Morales-Gomez, D. 3809
Moran, J. 1217, 5356
Morath, R. 4614
Morehouse, W. 4242
Moreland, J. 257
Morello, J. 3813

AUTHOR INDEX

Moreno, C. 5442
Moreno, J. 2294
Moreno, L. 5943
Moreno, M. 4481
Morera, E. 1250
Moretti, F. 1919
Morgan, A. 2134
Morgan, B. 220
Morgan, D. 242
Morgan, E. 1936
Morgan, G. 3486
Morgan, J. 4783
Morgan, K. 4980
Morgan, M. 2667
Morgan, N. 1317
Morgan, O. 5751
Morgan, P. 4612
Morgan, V. 2136, 5048
Mori, T. 4972
Moriarty, S. 756
Moriarty, T. 4743
Morin, C. 2901
Morin, D. 4635, 5420
Morin, J. 4403
Morin, M. 5891
Morito, H. 2702
Morley, D. 1252
Morphy, H. 3689
Morrill, C. 2643
Morris, A. 2384
Morris, B. 3103
Morris, I. 3565
Morris, M. 539, 643, 864, 1027, 3323
Morris, P. 666
Morris, R. 4227
Morrison, A. 2521
Morrison, D. 532, 845
Morrison, K. 437
Morrison, P. 2038, 4056
Morrison, R. 4215
Morrissey, J. 3841
Morse, H. 710
Morshidi, S. 3927
Mortanges, C. de 4658
Mortier, F. 5862
Mortimer, G. 3615
Morton, J. 812
Moscovici, S. 3412
Moseley, M. 3885, 3916
Moses, J. 4222
Moses, T. 5825
Mosini, V. 1623
Moskowitz, G. 620, 657, 848
Moskowitz, J. 5856
Moss, P. 5584, 5591

Motes, M. 869
Motowidlo, S. 4760
Motta, R. 1431
Motte, M. 4076
Mou, B. 1458
Moulin, P. 5817
Moumouni, A. 5980
Mounkoro, P. 520
Mount, M. 4412
Moura Castro, C. de 1996
Mourato, S. 4486
Moursund, J. 747
Moutouh, H. 4299, 4969
Mouzelis, N. 399
Mowbray, C. 792
Mowl, G. 2658
Moya, M. 895, 3283
Mozère, L. 4299
Mozersky, J. 1627
Mpembeni, R. 5777
Mrotzek, M. 3206
M'Roué, H. 280
Mrvar, A. 493
Msellati, P. 5980
Mtimde, L. 1756
Mturi, A. 2797
Mu, D. 1894
Mučalo, M. 1749
Mucchi-Faina, A. 3283
Mucha, J. 1193, 2009
Mueller, C. 4416, 4778
Mueller, F. 1080, 4618
Mueller, J. 4311
Mueller, U. 90
Mugford, M. 5761
Muggah, R. 3624
Muggleton, D. 1335
Mühlenbrock, M. 1040
Muica, N. 4606
Muir, K. 5221
Muir, L. 2127
Muir-Watt, H. 5165
Mujinja, P. 5777
Mujwahuzi, M. 3813
Mukerji, S. 567
Mukherjee, A. 1710
Mukherjee, S. 2044
Mukhtar, K. 3458
Mukono, K. 2505
Mulder, N. 1961
Mulholland, P. 1484
Mullally, S. 3195
Mullen, B. 877
Mullen, C. 2299
Mullen, P. 5112

Mullender, A. 2952
Muller, E. 5448
Müller, F. 801
Müller, K. 2554
Müller-Böling, D. 2296
Müller-Plantenberg, U. 4293
Müller-Schneider, T. 441
Mullick, S. 3186
Mulligan, J. 5781
Mullins, D. 3981
Multidisciplinary Research Centre, University of Namibia 4189
Mulvey, P. 4679
Mummendey, A. 1067
Münch, R. 2554
Munck, R. 1169, 1194, 4819
Mundt, H. 1074
Munene, J. 4253
Munier, F. 1565
Münk, H. 2554
Münnich, I. 5028
Munoz, P. 2363
Munro, A. 4398, 4868
Munro, I. 2337
Munshi, R. 5949
Munslow, B. 3817
Münst, A. 3134
Munz, P. 288
Münz, R. 3605
Murao, M. 763
Muraven, M. 657, 718
Murdin, L. 778
Murdoch, J. 4058
Murdock, G. 1773
Murnane, R. 633, 4794
Murphey, D. 5578
Murphy, C. 2894
Murphy, F. 769
Murphy, J. 3453, 5040
Murphy, L. 4693
Murphy-Lawless, J. 3169
Murray, A. 4166
Murray, D. 3037
Murray, F. 2574
Murray, G. 4818
Murray, H. 5618
Murray, J. 5100
Murray, M. 3857
Murray, P. 2464
Murray, S. 936, 946
Murrell, P. 5154
Murry, V. 838
Murtagh, B. 4003
Murthy, R. 5910
Musau, P. 1723

Muscarà, C. 3948
Musham, C. 3734
Musheno, M. 2643
Musick, M. 4768
Musselin, C. 2014
Mußmann, F. 4347
Mussweiler, T. 871
Mustafa, M. 2838
Mutasa, J. 2453
Muthoni, W. 3079
Mutti, A. 1267, 1431
Muzvidziwa, V. 3868
Mwale, M. 3311
Mwandosya, M. 3708
Mwangi, S. 3813
Mwenifumbo, L. 2089
Myburgh, C. 710
Myers, Jr., S. 3482
Myers, K. 2076
Myers, S. 2933, 3614
Myers-Scotton, C. 1789
Mynatt, P. 4720
Myrick, R. 3305
Na, E. 54
Naber, N. 3393
Nachmias, O. 721
Naciri, M. 3869, 3871
Nader, L. 5767
Nadin, V. 3872
Nadine, C. 1239
Natarrate, J. 403
Naffati, H. 1822
Nafisi, A. 5317
Nagabrahmam, D. 4663
Nagapurkar, U. 5923
Nagar, R. 2978, 3138, 3234
Nagel, J. 3242, 3383
Nagy, E. 4606
Nagy, G. 5678
Nagy, N. 538
Nagy-Zekmi, S. 2294
Nahm, K. 4108
Nahoum-Grappe, V. 4898
Nail, P. 2318
Naimy, N. 1932
Nair, S. 4648
Nakabayashi, N. 1476
Nakagawa, S. 3616
Nakamura, L. 3505
Nakano, L. 734
Nakari, R. 4708
Nakaya, T. 2829
Nakhaie, M. 5077, 5108
Nam, C. 2830

AUTHOR INDEX

Namibian Economic Policy Research Unit 4189
Nance, J. 686
Nancu, D. 4606
Nanopoulos, K. 1565
Napier, N. 4658
Naples, N. 20
Narayan, U. 3115
Nardis, F. de 4885
Narotzky, S. 4212
Nascimento, A. Do 2047
Nascimento Arruda, M. do 4949
Nash, A. 4864
Nash, C. 1232
Nash, K. 4884, 4896
Nash, M. 5136
Nasr, S. 1537
Nass, C. 574
Nasson, B. 957
Nasur, H. 2105
Nath, D. 2766
Nathan, L. 1656
Nathan, P. 591, 775
Nauck, B. 90
Naughton, S. 4352
Naughton, T. 4352
Navarro, V. 1923
Naved, R. 520
Naylor, P. 2218
Nazario, J. 4296
Nazarova, I. 5773
Ndiaye, C. 5363
Neal, C. 786
Neal, J. 4360
Neal, M. 4783
Neale, J. 3181
Neary, I. 5930
Neavins, T. 2894
Nedbálková, K. 3387
Nee, C. 2266
Nee, V. 4209
Need, A. 1494
Needell, B. 5587
Needle, C. 2717
Neelankavil, J. 4631
Neely, D. 5409
Nefedova, T. 4168
Negash, G. 1880
Negishi, K. 4426
Negra, D. 1227
Negrey, C. 3169
Negrin, L. 1214
Neiderhiser, J. 3052
Neill, G. 2962
Neitz, M. 56

Nekuee, S. 3470
Nekvapil, J. 1748, 1816
Nelson, J. 3115, 3821
Nelson, K. 1161
Nelson, R. 3166
Nembhard, J. 4497
Nemes, K. 1890
Neocleous, M. 5130, 5146
Nero, K. 2574
Nesbitt, N. 1988
Nesdale, D. 3567
Ness, I. 2694
Nesselroade, J. 682
Nesti, A. 1384
Nettleton, H. 2664
Neuman, S. 4535
Neumann, F. 1331
Neumann, L. 4842
Neumann, R. 703
Neusner, J. 1380
Neveux, H. 3891
New, B. 5743
Newby, M. 520
Newell, S. 1155
Newman, H. 3944
Newman, M. 2061
Newman, P. 3940
Newman, S. 5612
Newstead, S. 5709
Newton, L. 3565
Newton, R. 5573
Newton, T. 4392
Newton-Smith, W. 1560
Neyrand, G. 2618
Nezosi, G. 4299
Ng, S. 836, 2584
Ngangura, M. 1880
Ngo, T. 4943
Ngoc, T. 4694
Nguyen, Đ. Minh 545
Nguyen, H. 545
Nguyen, H. Thi 545, 2675
Nguyen, K. 545
Nguyen, P. Ngoc 545
Nguyen, T. Duc 2675
Nguyen, T. Xuan 545
Ngwena, C. 5809
Niaki, J. 4156
Niaura, R. 5406
Nichols, L. 65
Nicholson, I. 870
Nicholson, J. 5465
Nicholson, M. 5336
Nickel, H. 3127
Nicol, C. 4123

Nicolini, D. 1115
Nicolitsas, D. 4840
Nicolson, A. 4094
Nicolson, N. 716
Nicolson, P. 3523
Niedenthal, P. 683
Niedermayer, O. 5219
Niehaus, I. 3349
Nielsen, H. 1910, 2517
Nielsen, J. 1519
Nielsen, P. 1113
Nielsen, R. 4419, 4424
Nielsen, S. 4025
Nielson, J. 3307
Nierobisz, A. 3287
Nietzel, M. 5193
Nieuwbeerta, P. 2389, 2593, 5300, 5302, 5306
Nigg, J. 790
Nightingale, J. 742
Nijhof, A. 4417
Nijman, J. 3952
Nikitina, A. 167
Nilan, P. 1772
Nimmo-Smith, I. 611
Nind, M. 783
Ning, W. 1268
Niranjana, T. 1195
Nisbet, J. 2117
Nisbett, R. 676
Nishizaka, A. 369
Nissen, B. 780, 4856
Nistler, M. 5409
Nivison, D. 1420
Nizamuddin, M. 2712
Nizard, A. 2824
Njue, C. 5980
Nkene, B. 3574
Noaks, L. 529
Noam, E. 1753
Noble, M. 4270
Noble, T. 2531, 2532
Nobles, R. 5041
Nock, S. 2911
Nocks, L. 1576
Nocon, A. 5531
Noe, R. 4802
Noels, K. 2584
Nohrstedt, S. 1730
Nolan, B. 3989, 5763
Nolan, Jr., J. 5175
Noll, J. 5818
Noller, P. 2556
Nongbri, T. 3076
Nonoyama, H. 50
Nora, T. de 4344

Nord, M. 3884
Nordeide, T. 4025
Nordstrom, C. 4482
Nordström, K. 3709, 4375
Norkus, Z. 364
Norman, C. 902
Norman, P. 941
Norrie, A. 5166
Norris, C. 1614, 4986
North, K. 996
Northcott, D. 4310
Northridge, M. 2808
Norton, B. 2003
Norton, J. 1605
Norval, A. 4887
Norwich, B. 2109
Nos Colom, A. 3075
Nosaka, A. 2739
Nossin, J. 3702
Notarius, C. 2959
Nott, S. 3198
Nottingham, C. 5797
Nouailhat, R. 2169
Noujaim, A. 1822
Nouweland, A. van den 486
Novaes, H. 2758
Nový, I. 4198
Nowicka, E. 960
Noya, F. 3706
Noyoo, N. 5701, 5703
Ntambue Tshimbulu, R. 4962
Ntsebeza, L. 4864
Nuez Sánchez-Cascado, P. de la 4916
Numrich, P. 1469
Nun, J. 4368
Nunes da Silva, G. 5192
Nussbaum, J. 1647
Nussbaum, M. 3160
Nutini, H. 1498
Nuwaha, F. 2778
Nuyen, A. 1382
Nyamapfeni, P. 3311
Nyambegera, S. 4644
Nyamnjoh, F. 4227
Nyberg, A. 3169
Nye, M. 1623
Nye, R. 599
Nyenzi, B. 3708
Nyíri, P. 3583, 3685
Nylund, M. 5691
Nyssens, M. 4235
Nzioka, C. 5890
Oakeshott, R. 4827
Oakey, D. 3716
Oakley, A. 426, 3063

AUTHOR INDEX

Oakley, J. 3375, 4543
Oatley, N. 4008
Obadia, L. 1464
Obaidat, M. 4331
O'Barr, J. 3115
Obelkevich, J. 174
Ober, J. 4927
Oberlink, M. 2707
Oberman, Y. 3029
Obermann, K. 5197
Obermiller, C. 4320
Oberschall, A. 3485
Oberti, M. 2945
Obi, S. 3391
Obiakor, F. 3391
O'Brien, L. 1010
O'Brien, M. 1532
O'Brien, R. 2681
O'Brien, W. 798
O'Campo, P. 5838
Ochera, J. 812
Ochoa, G. 3565
O'Connor, B. 307
O'Connor, E. 1104
O'Connor, M. 1936, 2131, 3724
O'Connor, P. 3187
Oddone-Paolucci, E. 2903
Oden, H. 1154
O'Doherty, J. 3183
O'Donnell, K. 4317
O'Donnell, M. 3271, 4713
O'Donnell, O. 5763
O'Donnell, P. 1795
Oehlers, A. 2617
Oelkers, J. 2117
Oelofse, C. 3599, 3810
Oerke, M. 2456
Oestermeier, U. 664
Oettingen, G. 657
Oettinger, G. 2070
O'Farrell, T. 2894
Offe, C. 2567, 4976
Offner, J. 4031
O'Flynn, J. 5217
Ofreneo, R. 4935
Ogbonna, E. 4646
Ogden, J. 43
Ogden, P. 3795
Ogden, T. 785
Ogg, J. 5533
Ogien, A. 119
Ogu, V. 3813
Ogunyemi, C. 3079
O'Hear, A. 234, 2503
O'Hebir, F. 4800

Ohlemacher, T. 1705
Ohme-Reinicke, A. 3127
Ohnuma, R. 239
Oishi, S. 588
Ojeda, V. 797
Ojeda-Benitez, S. 3813
Ojo-Ade, F. 1939
Okalla, R. 5980
Okamoto, H. 5619
O'Kane, C. 5557
Okano, K. 4398
Okasha, S. 1629, 1630
Okazaki, S. 5928
Okun, B. 2753
O'Laughlin, B. 2388
Olayyan, K. 2032
Oldberg, I. 963
O'Leary, K. 3201
Olechnowicz, A. 3983
Oleson, K. 725
Oliker, S. 3219
Oliveira, A. 4862
Oliveira Araújo, M. de 5200
Oliveira, B. 2154
Oliveira, M. 5168
Oliven, R. 1363
Oliver, A. 1099
Oliver, E. 4658
Oliver, J. 3516
Oliver, K. 3133
Oliver, N. 4618
Oliver, P. 5163, 5235
Oliver, S. 4138
Olivera, R. 5928
Oliver-Lumerman, A. 2094
Oller, Jr., J. 1787
Ollivier, B. 5716
Ollivier, M. 2444
Ollivro, J. 4130
Olsen, R. 3603
Olsen, T. 5914
Olson, D. 1508, 2905, 4850
Olson, L. 4435
Olson, T. 5253
Olssen, M. 252
Olzak, S. 3475
O'Mahen, H. 872
Omar, R. 479
Omarzu, J. 924
O'Meara, J. 109
Omoniyi, T. 1811, 2218
O'Muircheartaigh, C. 535
Omulecka, A. 2009
Öncü, A. 1777
Ondrejkovič, P. 2364, 2576

INDEX DES AUTEURS

O'Neil, J. 4564
O'Neil, T. 722
O'Neill, A. 5721
O'Neill, B. 1724
O'Neill, G. 1300
O'Neill, J. 3705
O'Neill, P. 446
Ono, H. 3434
Onyancha, E. 5428
Onyx, J. 3847
Oord, E. van den 653, 2812
Opazo Marmentini, J. 4901
Opheim, M. 2121
Opland, E. 5384
Opotow, S. 3749
Opp, K. 4244
Oppenheimer, V. 2692
Or, Z. 5756
Orcajo, Á. 1158
O'Reilly, K. 3826
Oren, C. 2052
Orford, S. 2844
Orhan, M. 4372
O'Riordan, T. 3810
Oris, M. 2691
Orkin, M. 520
Orlando, A. 697
Orme, J. 13, 5708
Oro, A. 1431
Oro, G. D' 110
Oropesa, R. 4257
Ortega, E. 4260
Ortega, R. 3693
Ortiz, A. 4552
Ortiz, R. 1199, 1263
Orwin, R. 5818
Oryol, V. 710
Osafo, L. 3853
Osagie, J. 3283
Osawa, M. 369
Osbaldiston, R. 1073
Osborne, K. 2188, 2204
Osborne, R. 750, 2213
Osgood, R. 2213
Oshima, K. 3404
Osinsky, P. 4416
Oskamp, S. 886, 3749
Oskrochi, R. 4486
Osleeb, J. 461
Osmani, S. 4268
Osorio, C. 4904
Osorio, J. 6
Østerberg, D. 371
Ostwald, M. 3739
O'Sullivan, E. 5593

Osuri, G. 1769
Oswald, D. 2026
Oswick, C. 1101, 1104, 1127
Ota, H. 2584
Otaibi, S. 5291
Otero-Pailos, J. 3929
Otsuka, K. 4246
Otte, R. 1389, 4964
Otten, S. 848
Ottosen, R. 1730
Oucho, J. 3633
Ouellette, F. 767
Ouellette, S. 1488
Oushakine, S. 340
Outlaw, Jr., L. 3528
Over, D. 631
Overskeid, G. 667
Overstreet, S. 5447
Owaidat, A. 2032
Owen, C. 5584
Owen, S. 5539
Owens, D. 136
Owens, J. 3715
Owens, M. 5409
Owens, R. 3340
Owerwien, B. 4398
Owram, D. 178
Owusu, T. 3593
Øyen, E. 2397
Oyeneyin, A. 2015
Oyewumi, O. 3115
Oyserman, D. 792
Özcan, V. 3594
Özdemir, A. 1541
Özkırımlı, U. 1762
Pacherie, E. 618
Pachico, D. 4246
Pack, A. 4798
Padhi, N. 4455
Padian, N. 3311
Padis, M. 2439, 5068
Padma, V. 3112
Pagano, I. 1801
Page, J. 5386
Pagé, M. 2047
Page, S. 3791
Pagell, M. 4786
Pahl, J. 4310
Pai, S. 5269
Paik, H. 413
Pain, J. 2618
Pain, R. 2658, 3781, 3957
Painter, G. 2924
Pajo, K. 4656
Paley, B. 3041

AUTHOR INDEX

Palinkas, L. 567
Palmer, B. 178
Palmer, I. 1127, 4669
Palmer, R. 3705
Palmeri, T. 654
Palmgren, C. 2640
Palo, S. 4455
Palosuo, H. 5773
Palou, J. 5445
Pamanta, D. 2121
Pan, Y. 2523
Pan, Z. 1365
Panaïotov, T. 3804
Panarin, S. 3627
Pancer, S. 3055
Pande, N. 5923
Pandey, B. 2701
Pandey, J. 2231
Pandit, G. 3759
Paniagua Mazorra, Á. 3706
Paniccià, R. 2833
Panigrahi, S. 4455
Panka, P. 2701
Pannekoek, F. 196
Pant, S. 1708, 2046
Pantazis, C. 2442, 5082
Paoletti, D. 3370, 3381
Papa, M. 1708
Papaioannou, J. 3948
Papajohn, J. 3566
Papakosta-Harvey, V. 815
Papastergiadis, N. 3684
Pape, A. Le 3280
Pape, M. Le 161
Paperman, P. 674
Papillo, A. 2803
Papreen, N. 2789
Paradis, T. 4154
Paradysz, J. 2798
Parayil, G. 3805
Parazelli, M. 5420
Parchment, S. 254
Paré, S. 3451
Paredes, E. 4276
Pargament, K. 1381
Parijs, P. Van 1806
Parikh, S. 2
Paris, C. 4003
Paris, F. 5968
Parisi, F. 2308
Park, B. 832, 1623, 4250
Park, C. 187
Park, D. 612, 3565
Park, J. 247, 863, 1408, 1512
Park, M. 1702

Park, S. 2145
Parker, A. 2640
Parker, B. 583
Parker Boudett, K. 4794
Parker, C. 153
Parker, D. 5969
Parker, E. 4291
Parker, K. 5454
Parker, M. 4389, 4413
Parker, R. 5696
Parker, S. 4137, 4618
Parker, W. 710
Parkin, A. 626
Parkins, W. 3146
Parkovnick, S. 870
Parmenter, T. 2500
Parnell, S. 4169
Parr, J. 2002
Parreñas, R. 3191
Parry-Jones, B. 5710
Parsons, J. 5801
Parsons, M. 770, 3342
Parsons, T. 65, 400
Parton, N. 5709
Pasieka, M. 2009
Pasqua, S. 4532
Passey, A. 1156
Pastor, Jr., M. 4460
Pasupathi, M. 682
Patel, S. 2436
Patel, V. 764
Patel, Z. 3810, 4096
Pater, B. de 3767
Paternoster, R. 5095, 5096
Paterson, L. 488, 5213
Pathak, S. 5704
Pathé, M. 5112
Patil, R. 2394
Patin, V. 5335
Patočka, J. 215
Paton, R. 1094
Patrício, I. 5192
Patrinos, H. 4495
Pattaroni, L. 3930
Patterson, C. 3360
Patterson, F. 1143
Patterson, G. 3791
Patterson, L. 1814
Patterson, N. 5510
Pattison, S. 5783
Patton, C. 4939
Patton, K. 697
Pattynama, P. 3214
Paul, B. 3793
Paulhus, D. 569

Paulsen, K. 4128
Paunonen, S. 735
Pauwels, B. 795
Pavetti, L. 5633
Pavitt, C. 1633
Pavlovskaya, A. 4633
Pawar, M. 5694, 5700, 5704
Pawlik, K. 566
Pawluch, D. 5874
Pawson, R. 55
Payne, G. 2431
Payne, H. 5679
Payne, J. 576, 5979
Payne, M. 5715
Payne, S. 46, 5826
Peacock, A. 225
Peacock, B. 3357
Peacock, M. 1570
Peacocke, C. 231, 289
Peake, P. 933
Pear, J. 542
Pearce, B. 1030
Pearce, K. 1640, 5796
Pearce, N. 2220
Pearce, W. 1640
Pearl, L. 2621
Pearl, M. 5637
Pearson, C. 2458
Pearson, M. 5531
Pearson, R. 4558
Pease, K. 5107
Peberdy, S. 3599
Pebley, A. 5954
Pécaut, D. 4977
Pech, T. 2439, 5016, 5068
Pechačová, Z. 2965
Pechtl, J. 5152
Peck, J. 4439
Peczenik, A. 5180
Pedersen, A. 3446
Pedersen, I. 1798
Pedersen, J. 2822
Pedersen, W. 925, 2612
Pedlar, A. 2477
Pedraza, S. 2, 3396
Pedroso de Lima, A. 2398
Peele, S. 5376
Peer, D. 5338
Peerenboom, R. 248
Peet, J. 3800
Peeters, D. 459
Peetz, D. 4713
Peggs, K. 4353
Peiperl, M. 4757
Peiser, W. 1776

Peled, E. 2884
Pelled, L. 1142, 4716
Pellegrini, A. 544
Pellegrini, T. 1194
Pelletier, R. 5265
Pellow, D. 5244
Pels, D. 384
Pels, P. 1258
Pels, T. 1532
Peltz, M. 1937
Peña, R. 5439
Pendall, R. 4022
Pendlebury, J. 4133
Peng, I. 5626
Peng, S. 1895
Penketh, L. 5713
Penn, H. 5588
Penn, R. 2532
Pennebaker, J. 720
Pennec, S. 3255
Pennell, J. 1050
Penn-Kekana, L. 5442
Pentti, J. 4708
Pepinsky, H. 5465
Peplau, L. 3352
Percival, J. 2661
Percudani, M. 5909, 5922
Percy, A. 5540
Percy-Smith, J. 2423
Perea, A. 2294
Pereira, A. 5361
Peres, Y. 2904
Perez, A. 2771
Pérez Campos, G. 1245
Pérez, G. 2250
Pérez, R. 5368
Perez, T. 5139
Perham, N. 631
Peri, A. 567
Perkins, D. 574, 750
Perkins-Parks, S. 5409
Perl, H. 5818
Perl, P. 1481, 1508
Perlman, M. 4199
Perlmann, J. 3571
Perlmutter, D. 729
Peroni, M. 5716
Perret, D. 611
Perrewe, P. 5283
Perrier, S. 2901
Perron, C. 1004
Perrons, D. 3169, 4486, 4552
Perroton, J. 2014
Perrucci, R. 2418
Perry, B. 505, 5802

AUTHOR INDEX

Perry, D. 3907
Perry, E. 2509
Perry-Smith, J. 4673
Persell, C. 2017
Persuad, R. 4278
Perszyk, K. 1412
Péruch, P. 641
Perugini, M. 648
Perz, S. 3903
Pescosolido, B. 2334
Pessin, A. 221
Pestoff, V. 4687
Petchesky, R. 2754
Petchey, R. 5894
Peter, G. 20
Peter, J. 1776
Peter, R. 1453, 4706
Peters, B. 5212, 5363
Peters, M. 1875
Peters, S. 2477
Petersen, I. 5905
Petersen, T. 4507
Peterson, D. 775
Peterson, G. 2925
Peterson, K. 5950
Peterson, R. 1100, 5113
Peterson, V. 5317
Petráková, A. 2814
Petras, J. 2514, 4935, 5245
Petrella, R. 3771
Petrinovich, L. 5877
Petrosino, A. 426, 5583
Petry, N. 5385, 5387
Petsimeris, P. 3948
Pettit, B. 4505
Pettit, P. 268
Petty, S. 1880, 1881
Pevalin, D. 2840
Pez, P. 4114
Pezzin, L. 5520
Pfau-Effinger, B. 3194
Phadke, S. 5923
Phalatse, M. 3767
Pham, D. 2794
Phares, V. 3044
Pharoah, C. 5775
Phe, H. 3987
Phelps, B. 4629
Phelps, N. 5202
Philippe, J. 3960
Philipson, T. 5965
Phillips, D. 1532, 2124, 5522, 5740
Phillips, J. 3565, 5496, 5533, 5709
Phillips, M. 5221, 5404, 5955
Phillips, N. 1127, 5948

Phillips, S. 233, 1742, 5172
Phillips, T. 5138
Phillipson, C. 5533
Philo, C. 3775
Philogène, G. 2530, 3412
Phinn, S. 4166
Phipps, A. 4486
Physick, R. 1305
Piat, M. 5741
Picart, C. 278
Picciurro, M. 2456
Pick, D. 1963
Pick, S. 5200
Pickard, L. 5525
Pickard, S. 5508
Pickering, D. 97
Pickles, A. 5078
Pickvance, C. 5250
Pieler, M. 1754
Pierce, J. 1928
Pierce, M. 1399
Pierce, S. 3011
Pierini Cidade, D. 5192
Pierre, J. 4159, 5212
Pierret, J. 5891
Pierson, C. 5660
Pierucci, A. 1431
Pieters, J. 175, 3102
Piet-Pelon, N. 2750
Pievatolo, M. 4917
Pigeot, I. 4766
Pigg, K. 2213
Pigozzi, B. 3771
Pikhart, H. 5773
Pilar López, O. del 123
Pilardi, J. 283
Pile, S. 3932
Pilgrim, D. 1270
Pilinská, V. 2686
Pilkington, C. 874
Pillai, R. 4658
Pillemer, K. 948
Pillon, P. 992
Pimentel, D. 3759
Pimentel, E. 2972
Pimentel, M. 3759
Pimont, M. 2895
Pina Cabral, J. De 331
Pina-Cabral, J. de 2398
Pine, B. 5569
Pineault, M. 4622
Pineda, J. 4558
Pinell, P. 5891
Pinheiro, J. 5055
Pinkerton, S. 5987

Pinquart, M. 5521
Piola, M. 3173
Piorkowsky, M. 4310
Piotto, I. 4395
Piquero, A. 5096
Pircher, E. 4537
Pires, G. 3405
Pirro, F. 4740
Pisa, R. 4088
Pisani, E. 2806
Piscová, M. 983
Pisier, E. 3335
Pison, G. 2832
Pitcher, P. 4625
Pithers, R. 1992
Pitluk, M. 1658
Pitts, K. 4997
Piven, F. 4850
Pivion, P. 5611
Pizarro, D. 706
Plaks, J. 1071
Planalp, S. 899, 1647
Plane, J. 4636
Plant, K. 230
Plante, M. 5420
Plat, D. 4011, 4068
Platero, S. 1397
Platow, M. 845
Pleasants, N. 268, 303
Pléh, C. 1816
Pleimann, M. 4347
Pligt, J. van der 890
Plomin, R. 591
Plotkin, M. 2765
Plümper, T. 4203
Pochet, P. 4011, 4068
Poehlmann, K. 725
Poel, I. van der 1206
Poel, M. Van Der 1650
Poertner, J. 5597
Poeschl, G. 3267
Pogge, T. 4921
Poggio, B. 4552
Pogoniailo, A. 241
Pogrebin, M. 4511
Pointon, P. 2229
Poirier, H. 5420
Poirier, M. 5420
Pol, J. 3677
Pol, L. 5728
Polecsák, M. 5852
Polenina, S. 5326
Policar, A. 2395
Policelli, R. 5192
Polinard, J. 3565

Polioudakis, E. 2426
Polkinghorne, D. 1161
Pollack, D. 1461
Pollack, H. 5658
Pollert, A. 4836
Polletta, F. 5277
Polley, M. 1305
Pollitt, P. 2668
Polnay, L. 2602, 5820
Polster, C. 2261
Polzer, J. 999, 4690
Pomerantz, E. 588
Poncela, A. 2294
Ponthieux, S. 2626
Pontier, J. 5156
Pontille, D. 1610
Ponzanesi, S. 3112
Poole, S. 1958
Pooley, J. 3724
Popa, I. 3635
Popkin, S. 5627
Popova, I. 4593
Poppel, F. van 2994
Popper, M. 4886, 5799
Popple, K. 3827
Porche, M. 3212
Porhiel, S. 1822
Porras, I. 3813
Porritt, J. 1601
Porta, D. della 5251, 5275
Portela, J. 2653
Porter, D. 1305
Porter, E. 3119
Porter, J. 43
Porter, L. 3181
Portes, A. 347, 3632, 4197
Portillos, E. 5118
Portin, P. 2104
Posner, M. 591
Post, D. 5538
Post, S. 3515
Postlethwaite, K. 2092
Poston, L. 1526
Poticha, S. 4010
Potter, G. 269, 341
Potter, J. 1821
Potter, P. 716
Potter, R. 3921, 3975
Potts, A. 3346
Potucek, J. 2028
Potvin, M. 2047
Potvin, P. 2893
Poulat, É. 1478
Poulin, R. 1045
Pouliot, G. 767

AUTHOR INDEX

Poulsen, M. 4001
Poulton, R. 5394
Pound, R. 1344
Poungsomlee, A. 3813
Pourciau, B. 1585
Pourtier, R. 5980
Pousada, A. 1819
Pouvourville, G. de 5814
Pow, C. 2493
Powderly, K. 5854
Powell, S. 783
Power, M. 738, 5568
Power, S. 2130
Powers, T. 343
Poya, M. 3277
Poynter, G. 4831
Pozdnev, M. 241
Praet, J. van 5335
Pralus-Dupuy, J. 4992
Prandi, R. 1431
Prantl, H. 5219
Prasad, A. 4406
Prasad, B. 2585
Prasad, J. 5200
Prasad, P. 4406
Prashad, V. 3468
Pratkanis, A. 3517
Pratt Ewing, K. 3471
Pratt, G. 60
Pratt, J. 5009, 5015
Pratt, M. 3055
Pratt, T. 5073
Pratto, F. 879, 5296
Preda, A. 2315
Preece, J. 1680, 3495
Preece, T. 644
Préel, B. 2587
Préel, J. 5814
Preisendörfer, P. 1299
Preloran, H. 5873
Premi, M. 2683
Prenzler, T. 5125
Presser, H. 2975
Presser, L. 2864
Presser, S. 512
Prest, L. 3382
Preston, S. 2690
Preston-Shoot, M. 5711
Preston-Whyte, R. 3810
Pretzell, K. 3776
Preves, S. 2436
Prewitt, K. 996, 2723
Prey, H. 4795
Price, G. 4502
Price, J. 773

Price, M. 3925
Price, R. 3526
Prichard, D. 4077
Priel, B. 3015
Priest, R. 1258
Priestley, J. 225
Priestley, M. 5602
Primm, B. 2889
Pringle, D. 1000
Priou, J. 5475
Prioux, F. 2696
Pritchard, A. 1317
Pritchard, D. 1404
Probst, T. 2335
Probyn, E. 1303, 1358
Procter, S. 1080, 4618
Prodanovic, M. 4095
Prod'hon, J. 5980
Proietti, P. 1388
Propper, C. 5754, 5763
Prost, A. 5968, 5980
Prothais, A. 5025
Prout, A. 2597, 2602, 2605
Provencher, D. 1940
Pruitt, M. 5454
Pryke, M. 4350
Ptak-Chmielewska, A. 2785
Puddifoot, J. 2323
Pudney, S. 5392, 5832
Puffer, F. 5763
Pugh, C. 3961, 4233
Pugh, J. 3921
Pugh, M. 3161, 5340
Pugliese, E. 3568
Pugnoli, C. 5922
Puhan, B. 2186
Puhan, G. 2186
Puhan, S. 2186
Puijalon, B. 2679
Pullen, N. 5934
Pullum, S. 3565
Pulvirenti, M. 4229
Pumain, D. 2716, 3771
Punch, K. 415
Punpuing, S. 3813
Puplampu, K. 3922
Purcell, R. 1053, 5112
Purdy, J. 2353
Purdy, L. 5861
Purewal, J. 5917
Purkayastha, B. 2870, 3180
Purnell, D. 5409
Purse, K. 4433
Puska, P. 5433
Pustintsev, B. 5139

INDEX DES AUTEURS

Putnam, R. 2506
Puuronen, V. 2649
Puyol González, Á. 2414
Pyatok, M. 4010
Pyke, K. 2950
Pynes, J. 4512
Pyszczynski, T. 872
Qadeer, M. 4177
Qahtani, S. Al 5215
Qiang, M. 1894
Quach, T. 545, 2675
Quandt, S. 2660
Quane, J. 4006
Quanzhong, S. 1895
Quay, S. 610
Qudah, M. Al 1334
Quéau, P. Le 5716
Queffélec, A. 1822
Quibell, R. 2498
Quijano, A. 2568, 3503
Quiniou, Y. 4926
Quinlan, K. 2257
Quinn, E. 1370
Quinn, S. 3357
Quintais, L. 5921
Quintal de Freitas, M. 893
Quintanilla, M. 2291
Quintero, G. 5411
Rabe-Hesketh, S. 5473
Rabinowitz, D. 3499
Rabušic, L. 477, 2684
Racagni, G. 5909
Racine, A. 5838
Racine-Issa, O. 1709
Racioppi, L. 3269
Raczynski, J. 5421
Radau, W. 5853
Radford, J. 5474
Radhakrishnan, P. 3476
Radke-Yarrow, M. 755
Radovanović, M. 1816
Radtke, H. 870
Rae, D. 5906
Raffo, S. 2492
Raftery, A. 2728
Raftery, M. 5593
Raghuram, S. 1660
Ragon, P. 1433
Ragouet, P. 1610
Rahim, H. 2870
Rahman, M. 3974
Rai, S. 5257
Raijman, R. 3565, 3570
Raina, V. 1195, 3766
Rainbird, H. 4398, 4868

Rainis, M. 1326
Rainnie, A. 1891
Raitt, F. 5203
Rajadhyaksha, U. 4457
Rajan, R. 3112
Rajan, S. 2662
Rajaspera, R. 1822
Rajendran, P. 5911
Rakodi, C. 4169
Rakowski, C. 3140
Raley, R. 531
Ralston, D. 4658
Ram, H. 980
Ram, U. 985, 2177
Ramal, R. 1428
Ramanathan, M. 2733
Ramanathan, S. 2394
Rambla, X. 3176
Ramella, M. 5985
Ramírez, A. 2294
Ramírez-Barreto, M. 3813
Ramos, F. 1247
Ramos, J. 1298
Ramos, V. 3511
Ram-Prasad, C. 245, 246
Ramsay, H. 1867
Ramsey, J. 1623
Randall, R. 1143
Randall, S. 2790
Randel, J. 5493
Rane, A. 5704
Rankin, B. 4006
Ransby, B. 3115
Ransom, M. 491
Ransome, P. 4405
Rao, H. 4366
Rao, V. 2585
Rao, Y. 2394
Raphael, J. 5633
Raphael, S. 4489
Rapkin, B. 5818
Rapport, N. 320
Rasanayagam, Y. 3767
Rasch, V. 2727
Rasiah, R. 4935
Raskoff, S. 2631, 4768
Rastin, S. 4869
Ratcliffe, S. 98
Rath, J. 414, 3568
Räthzel, N. 4129
Ratner, C. 677, 1238
Ratneshwar, S. 4345
Rattner, E. 5357
Rattner, S. 5891
Raub, W. 923, 4380

AUTHOR INDEX

Rauch, A. 5335
Rauschenbach, B. 1004
Rausser, G. 4246
Ravaioli, C. 4179
Ravenhill, W. 91
Ravenscroft, N. 3971, 4060
Ravi, S. 1926
Ravich, S. 5317
Ravichandran, T. 4663
Rawlins, W. 2102
Rawls, A. 3432
Rawls, J. 4950
Ray, L. 404, 5147
Ray, R. 942, 3243
Ray, S. 1213
Raymo, J. 4303
Raynor, P. 5042
Raz, A. 1320
Razumov, A. 2538
Razuvaev, V. 5293
Read, B. 3959
Read, J. 2463, 3266
Read, R. 262
Read, S. 815
Reader, K. 86
Reader, S. 2368, 3794
Ready, R. 3034
Reagan, P. 3603
Reaser, J. 4490
Reay, D. 2161, 3057, 3175
Recasens, A. 5134
Rechtman, R. 801
Reckwitz, A. 597
Redclift, M. 64
Reddy, T. 1122
Redmond, M. 3827
Redmond, W. 4326
Reeber, M. 2313
Reed, H. 2287
Reed, M. 3152
Reeder, G. 896
Rees, D. 2764
Rees, E. 1991
Rees, M. Van 1650
Rees, P. 3622
Rees, S. 4423
Reese, A. 5403
Rees-Miller, J. 930
Reeve, C. 661
Reeve, D. 2484
Reeve, T. 1480
Reeves, J. 4060
Regalado, S. 1308
Regev, M. 1001
Regina, W. 1006

Regmi, G. 3667
Regnerus, M. 1408
Reguillo, R. 1199
Řeháková, B. 4306
Rehder, J. 3882
Rehm, J. 2819
Reibel, M. 4000
Reich, J. 716
Reichelt, G. 2417
Reicher, S. 829, 5434
Reichert Rovinski, S. 5192
Reid, B. 3824
Reid, H. 5252
Reid, I. 2054
Reid, M. 4492
Reid, S. 836, 1274
Reid, W. 5577
Reidpath, D. 2862
Reiger, A. 5656
Reilly, B. 2234
Reilly, P. 4603
Reilly, R. 4697
Reimers, F. 5642
Reimers, S. 1270
Reiner, R. 2532
Reinharz, D. 5420
Reis, A. 3973
Reis, D. 2613
Reis, E. 2397
Reis, H. 88, 591
Reisberg, D. 589
Reis-Bergan, M. 709
Reiss, D. 3052
Reiss, M. 5730
Reiss, S. 574
Reitzes, M. 3599
Rella, P. 3224
Remington, N. 713
Rémond, R. 1432
Renaud, S. 4635
Rénaud, T. 5363
Rendić-Miočević, I. 967
Rendina-Gobioff, G. 3047
Renjie, Z. 1895
Renkow, M. 3608, 4246
Renner, K. 2089
Rentfrow, P. 2061
Renucci, J. 5025
Renwick, N. 5308
Renzulli, L. 4371
Rescher, N. 121
Reskin, B. 4569, 4676, 4761
Resnik, D. 1620
Restivo, S. 1566
Reuter, N. 4293

Revel, J. 974
Reverand, E. 5953
Revill, G. 1979
Revista de Fomento Social 1485
Reyes, A. 1987
Reyes, C. 2294
Reyes, P. de los 4362
Reyes-Blanes, M. 3013
Reynolds, A. 494
Reynolds, J. 2583, 3833
Reynolds, K. 894
Reynolds, S. 813, 2456
Rhee, B. 4184
Rhee, C. 4184
Rhein, C. 2716
Rhein, S. 1331
Rhodes, C. 1140, 4397
Rhodes, G. 938
Rhodes, J. 4587
Rhodes, P. 1138
Rhodes, R. 5854
Riall, L. 1209
Rice, P. 2680
Ricœur, P. 161
Rich, J. 3391
Richards, G. 12
Richards, M. 2642
Richards, S. 5495
Richardson, D. 3330, 5984
Richardson, T. 2011
Riche, M. 996
Richert, A. 756
Riches, G. 2910
Richie, B. 3115
Richman, J. 4493, 5932
Richmond, W. 3633
Ricot, J. 5850
Riddell, S. 2458
Ridderstråle, J. 4375
Riddick, B. 2477
Ridge, M. 702
Ridge, T. 5564
Ridgeway, C. 2393
Ridgley, M. 1039
Riding, R. 2236
Ridley, C. 5928
Riegert, K. 1730
Riessman, C. 2915
Rieu, C. 2697, 4175
Riggio, E. 3813
Rigney, A. 160
Rihoux, B. 5218
Rijsberman, M. 4025
Riley, R. 1324
Rimke, H. 4939

Rincones-Gomez, R. 2104
Rind, M. 300
Rinden, A. 3515
Rindfuss, R. 531
Rinfret-Raynor, M. 2895
Ring, J. 5928
Rink, D. 2312
Rinken, S. 5944
Rip, A. 13
Rippin, A. 3097
Riquet, P. 2716
Riska, E. 5838
Riskind, J. 787
Rispens, S. 460
Ritchhart, R. 574
Ritschard, G. 5285
Ritter, G. 3121
Rittersberger-Tiliç, H. 2590
Ritzer, G. 89, 316, 395
Rivera, S. 5284
Rivera-Salgado, G. 3545
Rivero, J. 1994
Rivers, A. 3391
Rivière, C. 1686
Rizza, R. 4411, 4456
Rizzello, S. 4190
Rizzo, J. 1117
Robbers, G. 5889
Robbins, B. 2383, 3305
Robbins, D. 1212
Robbins, I. 5022
Robbins, P. 507
Robbins, T. 56
Robbins, V. 2154
Robelet, M. 5942
Robert, C. 2313, 2335
Robert, R. 1924
Robert, S. 4767
Robertis, C. De 5716
Roberto, K. 2919
Roberts, B. 520
Roberts, D. 1264, 2567
Roberts, E. 5778
Roberts, I. 3813
Roberts, J. 2172, 2175, 4258, 5162, 5333, 5448
Roberts, Jr., J. 492
Roberts, K. 1660, 2637
Roberts, L. 2966
Roberts, M. 385
Roberts, P. 2006, 4067, 4174, 4374
Robertson, M. 4145
Robichaud, S. 767, 1035
Robine, J. 5514
Robins, K. 1775, 1777

AUTHOR INDEX

Robins, T. 4861
Robinson, A. 2868
Robinson, D. 3978, 4052
Robinson, E. 2268
Robinson, F. 5471
Robinson, I. 4867
Robinson, J. 3188, 5725, 5732
Robinson, L. 1408, 3049, 3477
Robinson, P. 1730, 4587
Robinson, T. 5406
Robinson, V. 3629
Robinson, W. 2446
Robles, W. 5261
Robson, B. 4097
Robson, E. 2066
Robson, G. 1341
Robson, K. 1127
Roccas, S. 3547
Roccor, B. 1331
Rochat, D. 4454
Roché, S. 4993
Roche, W. 4357
Rochford, Jr., E. 1384
Rocío Aguilar Bobadilla, M. del 2677
Rode, C. 561
Rodgers, D. 5276
Rodgers, J. 653, 4437, 5390
Rodman, G. 3505
Rodrigues, I. 4949
Rodrigues, S. 5192
Rodrigues, V. 2394
Rodríguez, A. 3169, 3813, 4169
Rodríguez Araujo, O. 2293
Rodríguez, C. 5259
Rodriguez, E. 1488
Rodriguez, M. 933
Rodriguez, S. 3565
Rodríguez-Bailón, R. 895
Rodriguez-Campos, L. 2104
Roets, L. 3319
Rofe, M. 3999
Rofes, E. 3340
Roger, A. 968
Rogers, A. 2113
Rogers, E. 1708
Rogers, K. 660
Rogers, R. 2830, 3565
Rogers, S. 2969, 3888
Rogerson, C. 3599, 3633
Rogerson, J. 3633
Rogowski, R. 4837
Rohe, W. 3988
Rohmetra, N. 4359
Rohsenow, D. 5406
Rojek, C. 7, 1291, 2326

Rokach, A. 5893
Rokicka, E. 3748
Rokicki, J. 2009, 3512
Roland, M. 5753
Rolland, J. 3037
Rollock, D. 5928
Roloff, M. 916
Rolston, B. 1364
Roman, A. 1822
Roman, P. 4683
Romani, M. 3283
Romanov, A. 1836
Romanovskii, N. 166
Romero, D. 5633
Romero, M. 3115
Rommeluère, É. 1464
Romney-Alexander, D. 5775
Rondelli, E. 1735
Ronen, R. 1832
Roney, C. 730
Ronge, F. 4295
Ronsaville, D. 755
Rookes, P. 646
Rooks, G. 4380
Rooks, N. 3115
Roose, S. 748
Roots, J. 1827
Ropé, F. 2014
Rorty, R. 248
Rosa, M. 3951
Rosa-Ribeiro, F. 3510
Rosario Atuesta, M. Del 2176
Rosario, S. 5943
Rosario-Braid, F. 1683
Rosati, C. 2361
Roschelle, A. 2213
Roscigno, V. 2036
Rose, A. De 2858
Rose, D. 2047, 2840, 3858
Rose, G. 3788
Rose, H. 1620, 3115
Rose, J. 810
Rose, P. 5, 72
Rose, R. 2333, 2533, 5773
Rose, S. 3352
Roseland, M. 3814
Rosen, H. 4473
Rosen, K. 2876
Rosen, R. 5796
Rosen, S. 1894
Rosenberg, A. 1600, 4933
Rosenberg, M. 452
Rosenblatt, Z. 2085
Rosenbrock, R. 5891
Rosenfeld, R. 4548

Rosengard, A. 5615
Rosengren, D. 5391
Rosengren, K. 1635
Rosenhek, Z. 5638
Rosental, C. 1610
Rosenthal, E. 5576
Rosenthal, J. 2, 4231
Rosenthal, M. 5931
Rosenthal, R. 5419
Rosenthal, U. 5448
Rosentraub, M. 1308
Rosenzweig, M. 566, 3001, 3550
Rosier, P. 3364
Rosnet, E. 567
Rospenda, K. 4493
Ross, A. 2218
Roß, B. 3232
Ross, C. 3833
Ross, E. 2182
Ross, H. 3813
Ross, J. 789, 802
Ross, K. 996, 2273
Ross, L. 4390
Ross, M. 562, 1011, 3480
Ross, W. 1019
Rössel, J. 4192, 4890
Rossi, A. 481
Rossini Favretti, R. 1582
Rossiter, A. 799
Rössler, P. 1783
Rossouw, G. 4422
Rosthorn, J. 4417
Rosvold, E. 5838
Roth, K. 1295, 4658
Rothblum, E. 3352
Rothenbacher, F. 101
Rothermund, K. 827
Rothschild, C. 4596
Rothschild, J. 4683
Rothschild, L. 847
Rothstein, B. 4936
Rotmans, J. 4025
Rotolo, T. 2410, 2595, 4733
Rott, H. 141
Rotte, R. 3637
Rouch, J. 1888
Rouchier, J. 3741
Roulston, K. 523
Roulstone, A. 2459
Rouner, L. 701
Rountree, K. 3145
Rountree, P. 471
Rous, J. 3565
Rousseau, J. 2405
Roussel, V. 3866

Routh, D. 775
Routledge 83
Roversi, A. 5448
Rowan, J. 1053
Rowan, M. 5203
Rowe, D. 653, 2812
Rowland, D. 611
Rowley, C. 5746
Rowley, M. 4060
Rowley, S. 2060
Roy, K. 5468
Roy, S. 5420
Royalty, A. 5788
Royer, É. 2893
Rozan, A. 4175
Rozenblatt, P. 4779
Rozier, M. 5420
Rozik, E. 1872
Rozin, P. 561
Rozin, V. 374
Rozmovits, L. 2419
Roznowski, M. 663
Ruault, M. 5475
Ruback, R. 2231
Rubenstein, A. 573
Rubenstein, E. 1871
Rubenstein, M. 4496
Rubin, B. 2334
Rubin, N. 5338
Rubin, P. 2406
Rubinson, G. 3320
Rubio, C. 2399
Ruch, G. 5697
Ruchelman, L. 4119
Rucht, D. 4966
Rudberg, M. 2517
Rudd, E. 3081
Rudge, D. 1584
Rudlin, D. 4028
Rudolph, J. 5103
Rudy, K. 3115, 3376
Ruef, M. 1107
Rueschemeyer, D. 2445
Ruggiero, V. 5064, 5270
Ruhm, C. 3039
Ruhrmann, G. 1715
Ruitenberg, A. 5448
Rukavishnikov, A. 710
Rukwaro, R. 2505
Rumbaut, R. 3545
Rumgay, J. 5664
Rummery, K. 5609
Rumpf, H. 5408
Runciman, W. 319
Rundall, T. 5835

AUTHOR INDEX

Runyan, A. 3068
Rupke, N. 1557
Rural Group of Labour MPs 3900
Rusbult, C. 928
Russel, R. 3382
Russell, A. 2731
Russell, C. 2714
Russell, D. 709, 838
Russell, J. 1135
Russell, S. 4169, 5585
Russell, W. 2714
Russin, A. 861
Russo, P. 1306, 4585
Rust, P. 3352
Ruthrof, H. 1804
Rutkowska, L. 2837
Rutland, A. 834
Rutter, M. 2946, 5078
Ruvio, A. 2085
Rwomushana, J. 5363
Ryan, C. 844, 5981
Ryan, E. 2584
Ryan, K. 5709
Ryan, S. 1692
Ryang, S. 3184, 3484
Rychtaříková, J. 2684, 2814
Ryckeboer, H. 1798
Ryder, A. 569
Rydin, Y. 3759
Rydzewski, P. 2857
Ryn, M. van 5830
Ryterman, R. 5154
Rytina, S. 4755
Ryvkina, R. 2535
Saarinen, S. 3426
Saat, M. 4417
Saavedra, R. 1037
Sabatier, C. 2618
Sabel, C. 483
Sabin, K. 2789
Sacchi, S. 4762
Sacerdote, B. 3986, 5119
Sachdev, I. 1789, 2584
Sachdeva, U. 567
Sachs, A. 1010
Sachs, C. 20
Sackmann, R. 4790
Sacks, P. 2214
Sadik, N. 2754
Sadlak, J. 2265
Sadoulet, E. 4246
Saeed, M. Al 2137
Safe on the Streets Research Team 5427
Saffer, H. 5956
Sagal, M. 567

Sage, L. 1918
Sage, R. 2889
Sager, L. 3471
Saggers, S. 5413
Sagiv, L. 892
Sagy, S. 2033
Saha, S. 5320
Sahm, S. 5882
Sahtouris, E. 3797
Sailer-Fliege, U. 4168
Sailly, J. 5814
Sainsbury, J. 3845
St. John, C. 4015
Saiz, J. 3283
Sajenczuk, M. 2009
Sakalli, N. 3283
Sakamoto, K. 369
Sakka, D. 3592
Saks, A. 4718
Salado-García, M. 3767
Salama, P. 5964
Salamon, L. 4768
Salanié, B. 4582
Salas, D. 5025
Salas, E. 1056
Salau, M. 2015
Salcedo, O. 3047
Sale, E. 5409
Salem, G. 5980
Salgado, J. 4239
Saliba, T. 3115
Salih, R. 3263
Salim, A. 5655
Salk, J. 1134
Salla, F. 5098
Sallum, Jr., B. 4949
Salmi, S. 5143
Salmon, J. 4875
Salomé, H. 5744
Salomon, A. 657
Salomon, J. 1608
Saltaris, C. 776
Salter, B. 2280
Salvemini, B. 973
Salzano, F. 1620
Salzer, M. 891
Samakouri, M. 5089
Samarneh, M. 2093
Samarrai, S. Al- 2234
Samary, C. 4946
Sambrano, S. 5409
Samelson, F. 870
Sampaio Martins de Barros, C. 791
Samson, H. 5406
Samuelson, L. 463

INDEX DES AUTEURS

Sanabria, H. 2339, 4208
Sanadjian, M. 3680
Sanasarian, E. 1441
Sanbar, E. 68
Sanchez, C. 5386
Sanchez, D. 3215
Sanchez, G. 3545
Sanchez, L. 2968, 3282
Sánchez, R. 4595
Sánchez Saldaña, M. 2677
Sánchez-Jankowski, M. 4300
Sancho Hazak, R. 4775
Sandahl, T. 1040
Sandell, R. 816
Sandercock, L. 4118
Sanders, A. 4800
Sanders, J. 5139
Sanders, K. 4777
Sanders, L. 2716
Sanders, S. 2688
Sanderson, D. 3813
Sandford, J. 1179
Sandfort, T. 3369, 5891
Sándor, A. 1812
Sandor, J. 2754
Sándor, K. 1816
Sandqvist, T. 128
Sandri, G. 1582
Sandy, J. 709
Sanjack, M. 800
Sanjobo, N. 5966
Sansone, E. 463
Sansot, P. 2679
Santa Ana, J. 1929
Santa Lucia, R. 3047
Santamarina, C. 1626
Santana, P. 5494
Santana Pérez, J. 2558
Santas, A. 2011
Santiso, J. 1298
Santoro, M. 1982
Santos, A. 5737
Santos, L. 1359
Santosa, H. 3813
Santoyo R., M. 2677
Santrock, J. 2599
Sanusi, A. 1808
Sapey, B. 2477
Saporta, I. 4507
Sapunar, M. 4785
Sarat, A. 3471
Saravanamuttu, J. 4935
Sarbin, T. 1161
Sardan, J. de 5980
Sardi, M. 5285

Sardoč, M. 2218
Sardon, J. 2695, 2698
Sargent, P. 3260
Sarhimaa, A. 1798
Sari, H. 1077
Sarker, R. 3462
Sarma, P. 2662
Sarmiento Gómez, A. 5445
Sarre, P. 3774
Sartor, G. 5179
Sartori, G. 1333
Sasaki, K. 4103
Sasieni, P. 2817
Sass, D. 5538
Sass, R. 4674, 4682
Sassatelli, R. 4186
Sassen, S. 32, 2568, 3672
Sassler, S. 2915, 3577
Sastry, N. 2704
Satô, T. 1218
Satofuka, F. 1663
Satou, T. 369
Satyanarayana, K. 5800
Saucier, G. 860
Saucier, J. 767
Sa'ud, R. 2183
Saugères, L. 3775, 4774
Saukko, P. 506
Saul, R. 2754
Saumade, F. 1350
Saunders, B. 5404
Saunders, L. 4191
Savage, B. 3528
Savage, S. 5126
Savage-Rumbaugh, E. 1161
Savarese, R. 1730
Savin-Williams, R. 3352
Savitsky, K. 889
Savolainen, J. 4271
Sawchuk, K. 3159
Sawdon, C. 1053
Sawers, L. 3731
Sawin, L. 663
Saxena, S. 4415
Saxon, J. 588
Sayad, A. 3638
Sayed, A. Al 2838
Sayer, L. 3188
Sayer, R. 21
Sayers, J. 2641
Sayette, M. 5406
Sborgi, I. 3115
Scalmer, S. 5241
Scambler, G. 2440
Scandura, T. 4658

387

AUTHOR INDEX

Scanff, C. Le 567
Scanlon, T. 302
Scarlata, C. 567
Scazzieri, R. 1582
Schabedoth, H. 4859
Schachter, J. 4591
Schadle, S. 3049
Schaeffer, D. 5891
Schafer, D. 4279
Schäfer, M. 2555
Schäffer, B. 1338
Schalet, A. 3328
Schaller, M. 877
Schalück, H. 2554
Schamess, A. 2213
Schatzki, T. 268, 284
Schaubroeck, J. 550
Schauer, F. 4933
Scheb, II, J. 5183
Schech, S. 1219
Scheer, S. 2633
Scheff, T. 388, 745
Scheffer, M. 5363
Scheibman, J. 1839
Schellenberg, J. 1451
Schellhorn, M. 5763
Schenk, J. 2302
Schensul, J. 5386
Schérer, R. 2313
Scherer-Warren, I. 322
Scherr, S. 4246
Scherzer, T. 3373
Scheuer, J. 1833
Scheuer, S. 4739
Schiappa, E. 1650
Schie, E. van 1111
Schiebinger, L. 3110, 3115
Schiemann, J. 366
Schiff, D. 5041
Schijf, H. 423
Schilbrack, K. 250
Schilling, R. 5382
Schiltz, M. 5891
Schimank, U. 2404
Schimel, J. 872, 1081
Schippers, M. 1352
Schirato, T. 294
Schirrmacher, F. 3532
Schlee, G. 1020
Schlegel, J. 2439
Schlemmer, B. 4442
Schlenker, B. 4188
Schlie, U. 189
Schluchter, W. 345
Schlumbohm, J. 4263

Schmandt, J. 3818
Schmeiser, M. 2591
Schmid, H. 5478
Schmidt, A. 3250
Schmidt, G. 5695
Schmidt, H. 2053, 2343
Schmidt, L. 5818
Schmidt, N. 876
Schmidt, V. 2448
Schmied, D. 4606
Schmincke, H. 3776
Schminke, M. 1106
Schmitz, H. 4903
Schnebel, E. 4417
Schneider, B. 1104
Schneider, G. 4203
Schneider, I. 2880
Schneider, J. 2117, 2244, 5831
Schneider, K. 3476
Schneider, M. 3340
Schneider, S. 4416
Schneider, W. 1652
Schober, M. 509
Schoenwald, S. 5737
Schoeny, M. 1028
Schofer, B. 1575
Scholnick, E. 600
Scholte, J. 2562
Scholz, U. 3776
Schooler, C. 520
Schotten, P. 1388
Schou, A. 2513
Schreckenberger, W. 5201
Schrieder, G. 3619, 4284
Schrimshaw, E. 581
Schrock, D. 2402
Schrøder, K. 1727
Schröder, S. 540
Schröder, T. 274
Schroeder, D. 4597
Schroeder, R. 4720
Schroll-Machl, S. 4198
Schröter, U. 3206
Schubert, J. 816
Schubert, R. 2539
Schuckit, M. 5393
Schudson, M. 996
Schüklenk, U. 1620, 5870
Schuler, R. 4653
Schuller, T. 63
Schulman, M. 3881
Schultz, P. 886, 3743, 3749
Schulz, A. 4291
Schumacher, J. 5421
Schupp, J. 3177

Schüssler Fiorenza, F. 266
Schusterman, R. 3813
Schutte, G. 3395
Schütte, H. 4859
Schütz, J. 3812
Schwab, W. 4155
Schwaber, P. 1937
Schwalbe, M. 2402
Schwartz, B. 996
Schwartz, G. 4949
Schwartz, J. 3181
Schwartz, L. 590
Schwartz, M. 277, 5104
Schwartz, S. 892, 3547, 4253
Schwarz, H. 1213
Schwarz, N. 612, 823
Schwarzkopf, L. 3776
Schweber, S. 1623
Schweder, T. 5838
Schweers, Jr., C. 1819
Schwinn, T. 2409
Sclater, S. 2849
Sconce, J. 1780
Scornet, C. 2777
Scott, A. 1168, 1892, 5510
Scott, D. 1472, 2012
Scott, E. 5633
Scott, J. 2360, 4056
Scott, K. 1048, 4483
Scott, M. 3752
Scott, P. 2132, 4769
Scott, R. 5225, 5401
Scott, S. 4232
Scott, W. 1132
Scotter, J. Van 4760
Scourfield, J. 3241, 5589
Scraton, P. 5054
Scraton, S. 1292
Scribel da Silva, M. 5192
Scrimshaw, S. 5731
Scrogin, D. 4452
Scruton, R. 2342
Scullen, S. 4412
Seabrook, J. 4430
Seabrooke, B. 3976
Seale, C. 2820
Sealey, A. 1788
Sebastián, L. de 4983
Secker, J. 5941
Seddon, T. 5367
Seden, J. 5674
Sedgley, N. 2266
Sedikides, C. 896
See, K. 3269
Seeman, B. 1388

Seeseman, R. 1542
Seferiades, S. 4596
Segal, D. 4549
Segal, E. 3417
Segal, M. 4549
Segall, M. 5759
Segerstråle, U. 1567
Segre, S. 409, 4979
Segrist, A. 5444
Séguin, L. 2895
Seguino, S. 2561
Seidel, M. 4507, 4690
Seifert, W. 3594, 3605
Seigworth, G. 1211
Seik, F. 3839
Seipel, C. 5075
Seita, J. 5569
Seiter, E. 1774
Seitz, S. 3776
Seiyama, K. 2434
Seki, K. 1184
Selden, M. 2509
Seleznev, A. 1539
Seligmann, L. 4132
Selim, M. 801
Sell, J. 1074
Sell, R. 5972
Selle, K. 4167
Sellnow, T. 1097
Selten, R. 4380
Selten-Eisenhardt, M. 2228
Selting, M. 1790
Seltzer, J. 2964
Semán, P. 1431
Semboloni, F. 4083
Semetsky, I. 1799
Semin, G. 853
Şemin, S. 5833
Sémolué, J. 1904
Semyonov, M. 3559
Sen, A. 111, 134, 4950
Senecah, S. 1010
Senior, M. 2843
Seok, H. 3556
Serkei, C. 1721
Sermet, C. 3280
Serow, R. 2285
Serrano del Rosal, R. 4469
Serret, E. 3204
Serverin, É. 5204
Setbon, M. 5891, 5942, 5982
Settersten, R. 572
Sevcik, I. 2890
Sève, M. de 1607
Sevestre, P. 4175

AUTHOR INDEX

Sévillia, J. 5298
Sey, A. 4617
Seymour, F. 5470
Seymour, J. 5879
Seymour, P. 2013
Seynaeve, K. 2110
Shack, N. 4251
Shadel, W. 5406
Shaffer, B. 3410
Shaffer, D. 554
Shah, A. 2683
Shah, M. 2838
Shah, N. 2838, 3673
Shah, R. 3327
Shah, S. 2030
Shah, T. 2275
Shahak, I. 1546
Shahin, J. 2518
Shahinfar, A. 5928
Shah-Kazemi, S. 2908
Shaked, A. 463
Shalev, C. 2754, 5889
Shalom, U. Ben- 3554
Shameem, N. 1818
Shamsie, J. 1100
Shandler, J. 1786
Shane, S. 4393
Shank, B. 1873
Shankland, D. 1524
Shanks, D. 476
Shaoxian, W. 5838
Shaoyang, L. 1894
Shapira, A. 5889
Shapiro, D. 1018, 4615
Shapiro, J. 1258
Shapiro, M. 4939
Sharkey, P. 5739
Sharkh, M. 5260
Sharma, A. 1978, 2789
Sharma, D. 1566
Sharma, S. 1978, 3104
Sharp, H. 3130
Sharp, J. 4056
Sharpe, B. 4453
Sharpe, S. 3271
Sharpe, V. 5854
Sharpley-Whiting, T. 3098
Shatkin, G. 3927
Shaughnessy, M. 2218
Shaver, P. 670
Shaw, C. 5566
Shaw, J. 210, 1064
Shaw, K. 2137
Shaw, M. 2010, 2844, 3827
Shaw, S. 5508

She, H. 2198
Sheared, V. 1991
Sheehan, H. 2870
Sheehan, R. 5154
Sheeran, P. 941
Sheets-Johnstone, M. 2609
Shefner-Rogers, C. 1708
Shekhar, S. 4152
Sheldon, K. 1073
Sheldon, M. 709
Sheldon, P. 4814
Sheleff, L. 5167, 5889
Shen, J. 2104
Shen, Q. 1657
Shengzu, G. 4162
Shenhav, Y. 4649
Shepard, B. 2754
Shepherd, J. 5559
Sheppard, J. 5689
Sheppard, M. 5709
Shepperson, A. 1880
Sheptycki, J. 5139
Sheridan, J. 591, 5801
Sherman, L. 426
Sherman, N. 201
Sherman, R. 4853
Sherman, S. 1086
Sherr, L. 5891
Shevrin, H. 584
Shi, L. 5804
Shibang, Z. 1894
Shibusawa, H. 4124
Shibuya, K. 4020
Shields, J. 4833
Shields, M. 5832
Shiffman, S. 3181, 5406
Shih, C. 3447
Shim, Y. 54, 3168
Shimou, Y. 4108
Shin, K. 3927, 4250
Shine, S. 5192
Shiner, J. 1121
Shiner, R. 700
Shinkai, S. 5524
Shiose, Y. 4962
Shirai, T. 4826
Shiramizu, S. 3648
Shire, K. 4544
Shkolnikov, V. 5968
Shlapentokh, V. 4683
Shobrook, S. 3721
Shoemaker, D. 276, 5153
Shohov, T. 3290
Sholomov, L. 465
Shonholtz, R. 1010

INDEX DES AUTEURS

Shook, N. 5444
Shor, R. 5543
Short, J. 4160, 5254
Short, Jr., J. 426
Short, S. 2729
Shortall, S. 4226
Shortell, S. 5771
Shorter, A. 5428
Shotter, J. 1145, 1161
Shove, E. 13
Showalter, E. 1918
Shrader-Frechette, K. 3759
Shraim, R. 2032
Shrestha, G. 3231
Shrestha, O. 3702
Shroder, M. 5656
Shrum, L. 524
Shubin, V. 4864
Shumaker, J. 1936
Shumway, D. 4336
Shunnaq, M. 4155
Shute, V. 663
Shweder, R. 3471
Shye, S. 621
Siame, M. 3209
Siann, G. 5203
Sibanda, A. 5974
Sibeon, R. 313
Sicot, B. 1922
Sicre, C. 981
Sidani, S. 5818
Sidanius, J. 879, 5296
Sidaway, J. 3782
Siddiqui, M. 4524
Siddle, D. 3541
Sidel, V. 5988
Siefert, K. 808
Siegal, H. 5386
Siegel, F. 3950
Siegel, K. 581
Siegler, R. 607
Siegrist, J. 4706, 5773
Sierra, A. 3702
Sigaud, L. 3891
Sigelman, L. 3565, 3993
Sigler, M. 5034
Sigler, R. 5449
Sigmund, S. 4192
Silbermann, A. 912
Silberschmidt, M. 2727, 3275
Silbey, S. 5154
Sillince, J. 1029
Sillitoe, P. 2528
Silva, E. 3223
Silva, J. Da 5139

Silva, R. 4031
Silver, H. 42
Silverblatt, A. 1694
Silverlock, M. 2199
Silverman, I. 2912
Silverman, P. 2666
Silverman, R. 5077, 5108
Silverman, S. 2282
Silvey, R. 3085, 3557
Sim, D. 3460, 5646
Sim, J. 4995
Sim, S. 4925
Simard, A. 767
Simard, M. 5420
Simbulan, R. 4935
Šimek, M. 2724
Simmens, S. 3052
Simmons, P. 13
Simmons, T. 1971
Simms, M. 4875
Simões, A. 1623
Simon, A. 5888
Simon, D. 5244
Simon, L. 4246
Simon, R. 4555
Simon, S. 1816
Simone, A. 4173
Simonnet, V. 2626
Simonoff, E. 5078
Simons, J. 665, 1864
Simons, K. 4066
Simont, J. 281
Simooya, O. 5966
Simpson, A. 5559
Simpson, C. 922
Simpson, D. 4875
Simpson, F. 4606
Simsek, H. 4806
Sin, W. 5187
Sinclair, D. 5889
Sinclair, F. 3825
Sinclair, P. 20
Sinclair-Desgagné, B. 4756
Sinclair-Webb, E. 3235
Sinding, S. 2763
Singer, E. 519
Singer, M. 5386
Singer, S. 5732
Singh, A. 4824
Singh Bawa, U. 1447
Singh, G. 3473
Singh, J. 2721
Singh, K. 4634
Singh, M. 4398
Singh, R. 789, 898

AUTHOR INDEX

Singh, S. 4415, 4662
Singh, Y. 2549
Singhal, A. 1708
Singhal, D. 1465
Singhanetra-Renard, A. 5745
Singleton, E. 5406
Singleton, J. 2917
Singleton, V. 1598
Sinha, C. 636, 1161
Sinha, D. 2818
Sinha, M. 3115
Sinha, P. 2749
Sinha, S. 3918
Sinnott, M. 3061
Sirianni, C. 3169
Sirmans, G. 3979
Sirotnik, K. 2104
Sirovátka, T. 5648
Sison, A. 4417
Sit, V. 4050, 4136
Sitarenios, G. 2920
Sites, W. 4892
Sivam, A. 3972
Six-Materna, I. 3283
Skaggs Sheldon, M. 1073
Skalska, A. 2009
Skattum, I. 2121
Škiljan, D. 1816
Skillings, J. 5928
Skillnäs, N. 484
Skinner, D. 2522
Skinner, H. 2920
Skocpol, T. 2
Skodová, Z. 2814
Skog, O. 2819
Skogstad, W. 5798
Skoldberg, K. 432
Skorupski, J. 227
Skovsholm, K. 1838
Skrabski, Á. 5773
Skuce, D. 1822
Skurnik, I. 620
Slabbert, S. 1813
Slack, P. 3691
Slade, P. 796
Sladen, D. 540
Slater, R. 3868
Slaton, D. 2206
Slaughter, M. 5553
Slavich, S. 915
Slavin, R. 3517
Slesinger, D. 5456
Slevin, J. 1676
Slikker, M. 486
Slisli, F. 1781

Sloan, P. 1564
Sloan Wilson, D. 601
Sloane, P. 2267, 2457, 4704, 4714
Sloper, P. 2044
Slosiarik, M. 3917
Sluga, G. 3070
Smale, G. 5702
Smart, B. 89, 379
Smeeding, T. 5565
Smeins, L. 2980
Smelser, N. 996
Smeyers, P. 1997
Smith, A. 1305, 4486, 5460
Smith, B. 3077, 5480
Smith, C. 1016, 1512, 5019, 5207
Smith, D. 61, 84, 305, 1730, 2367, 3115, 3780, 4701, 5147, 5787
Smith, E. 882, 1057, 1063
Smith, G. 504, 2946
Smith, H. 2743, 2847, 3590
Smith, I. 3940
Smith, J. 3550, 5633
Smith, K. 874, 5928
Smith Kipp, R. 1258
Smith, M. 1010, 2607, 3914, 4388, 5712
Smith, N. 4017
Smith, O. 3195
Smith, P. 326, 1870, 2602, 3201, 4253, 4329, 5138
Smith, R. 5, 12, 2482, 2602, 4574
Smith, S. 161, 1984, 3217, 4106, 4464, 4768
Smith, V. 5706
Smith, W. 4596, 5085
Smock, P. 3054
Smolar, A. 4898
Smolińska, I. 1504
Smolla, R. 4768
Smoot, M. 573
Smrekar, C. 2024, 2051
Smyth, J. 5127
Smyth, S. 1497
Snape, E. 4879
Snare, A. 5176
Snavely, K. 3877
Sneddon, C. 3811
Sneiderman, B. 5858
Snel, E. 4436
Snell, R. 4427
Snipe, T. 3391
Snodgrass, M. 584
Snoeck Henkemans, A. 940
Snow, D. 4888, 5271
Snow, M. 5386
Snow, N. 906
Snyder, C. 793

Snyder, V. de 797
So, Y. 1462
Soares, G. 5303
Sobal, J. 3546
Sobell, L. 5399
Sobell, M. 5399
Sober, E. 601
Sobieszczyk, T. 2771, 3665
Sobo, E. 2731, 5957
Socher, A. 145
Socpa, A. 5301
Soden, R. 1992
Soell, H. 4859
Soini, T. 647
Sokoll, T. 4263
Sola, L. 4949
Solares, B. 122, 3518
Solga, H. 4506
Solomon, D. 1647
Solomon, M. 3022
Solomon, N. 4398
Solomos, J. 3529, 5147
Solov'eva, N. 1968
Somasundaram, D. 5331
Somera, L. 2584
Somerville, J. 3111
Sommaruga, C. 5330
Sommer, F. 3807
Sommers, L. 3771
Soneira, A. 1509
Song, Y. 247
Songer, D. 5154, 5155
Songgu, C. 177
Sonn, T. 1380
Sonnemans, J. 515
Sonnenberg, F. 5752
Sonnenfeld, D. 3718
Sonnenfeld, J. 4670
Sonuga-Barke, E. 771
Sood, S. 1708
Sopóci, J. 2435
Sopp, P. 4753
Sordo, F. Del 1983
Sorensen, A. 2445, 4164
Sørensen, H. 5342
Sörensen, S. 5521
Sorenson, A. 5935
Soriano, R. 4142
Sorkin, D. 145
Sorra, J. 4701
Sorrentino, R. 730
Sotelo, M. 3283
Soteriou, M. 645
Souami, T. 4299
Souchal, L. 5475

Soukup, C. 1634
Soule, S. 5620
Souley, A. 5980
Soulié, C. 2058
Soumerai, S. 489
Souris, M. 3702
Sousa-Poza, A. 4745
Souteyrand, Y. 5891
South, S. 2995, 3835
Southern African Research and Documentation Centre 3209
Southgate, V. 636
Souza, A. de 5950
Souza, H. D' 3382
Souza, J. 1183
Souza Martins, J. de 4949
Spaargaren, G. 3722
Spain, J. 711
Spalding, N. 3465
Spangenberg, E. 4320
Spangenberg, J. 4025
Spanò, A. 4580
Sparks, R. 2607, 5061
Sparrow, J. 4609
Sparrow, P. 4643, 4644
Sparrowe, R. 4689
Sparti, D. 934
Spash, C. 3705
Speak, S. 3069
Spear, J. 5
Spears, R. 853, 1044
Special Task Group for 1998 Front-Line 1894
Speer, A. 1854
Speer, S. 1821
Speiser, S. 4242
Spelke, E. 619
Spellman, D. 3382
Spence, L. 4417
Spencer, A. 1388
Spencer, C. 3523
Spencer, S. 1965
Sperling, V. 3105
Speziale, F. 1521
Spicer, C. 3464
Spicker, P. 5659
Spiegel, D. 3298
Spiekermann, K. 4061
Spielmann, C. 2313
Spiller, R. 4417
Spillman, B. 5520
Spindler, J. 2099
Spinelli, M. 1756
Spinello, R. 1665
Spirduso, W. 2282
Spitze, G. 1290

AUTHOR INDEX

Spitzform, M. 558
Spohn, W. 4966
Spoonley, P. 3643
Sprainer, E. 5846
Spratt, T. 5556
Sprecher, S. 3343
Spreitzhofer, G. 4149
Sprigg, C. 4618
Spriggs, W. 4497
Springer, J. 5409
Spruijt-Metz, D. 2611
Spuler, M. 1464
Sputore, B. 5413
Squarcini, F. 1384
Sque, M. 5826
Squires, P. 4996
Srinivasan, N. 5916
Stabb, S. 736
Stacey, J. 3115
Stack, S. 5435
Stadler, N. 5351
Staeheli, L. 3121
Stafford, M. 5046
Stalans, L. 5154
Stam, H. 870
Stamatov, P. 5263
Stamm, H. 2324
Standen, P. 749
Standing, G. 5622
Stanek, E. 756
Stange, M. 1970
Stanley, B. 749
Stanley, L. 5147
Stanley, S. 2985
Stansbury, J. 5541
Stanton, P. 3405
Stanton, W. 5891
Stanworth, C. 4570
Stapel, D. 840, 855
Stapleford, J. 1388
Staples, D. 1660
Staples, J. 5465
Star, S. 70
Starfield, B. 5804
Stargardt, N. 157
Stark, E. 1064
Starkey, K. 1100
Starrels, M. 2897
Stastny, P. 772
Statham, D. 5702
Statham, J. 5591
Statt, D. 4671
Staudt, M. 5936
Stauffer, D. 5633
Stavrakakis, Y. 4887

Stebbins, R. 1285, 1301
Steck, P. 4299
Steedman, H. 2270
Steel, D. 518
Steel, G. 567, 3746
Steele, C. 3471
Steele, D. 3471
Steele, K. 1227, 1936
Steele, M. 2766
Steensland, B. 1408
Steffen, M. 5982
Steffen, S. 522
Steffensmeier, D. 5017, 5087
Stefik, M. 1678
Steger, J. 2286
Stegmaier, W. 241
Stehr, N. 1636, 3700
Steier, A. 3004
Steier, L. 4369
Steiger, T. 2223, 4400
Steijn, B. 4436
Stein, J. 2344
Stein, M. 821, 5574
Stein, P. 482
Stein, R. 3515
Steinbauer, P. 2920
Steinberg, L. 3014
Steinberg, S. 3046, 3429
Steineckert, G. 3206
Steinel, W. 1084
Steiner, J. 5312
Steiner, P. 67
Steinfield, C. 1660
Steinhoff, P. 5251
Steinke, I. 2646
Steinmetz, S. 2925
Steinmetz, W. 5190
Stelcner, M. 4498
Stella, S. 3233
Stello, C. 1921
Stenberg, S. 5634
Stenger, A. 4175
Stengs, I. 4227
Stenning, A. 4079
Stenross, B. 2479
Stephan, W. 1075, 3517
Stephen, E. 2735
Stephen, K. 3198
Stephens, C. 1844
Stephens, P. 3744
Sterk, C. 5386
Stern, A. 3545
Stern, D. 282
Stern, P. 1297, 3749
Sternberg, K. 2871, 5562

Sternberg, R. 574, 2168
Steshenko, V. 5773
Stessman, J. 5513
Stetz, M. 1882
Steuer, M. 4051
Stevens, A. 773
Stevens, K. 2206
Stevens, L. 3072, 4319
Stevenson, F. 5828
Stevenson, J. 2104, 3038
Stevenson, N. 1713, 1744
Stevenson, W. 1087
Steward, J. 3934
Steward, R. 5538
Stewart, A. 2433
Stewart, D. 996
Stewart, E. 2918
Stewart, K. 4690, 5598
Stewart, M. 4615
Stewart, R. 2676
Stewart, T. 3215
Stichele, R. 5862
Stichweh, R. 371
Stiemerling, O. 1040
Stier, H. 2922
Stiffman, A. 5906
Stiker, H. 2474
Stiles, D. 5592
Still, A. 12
Still, J. 1950
Still, M. 5120
Stillwell, J. 3606, 4439
Stimpson, C. 3115
Stimson, G. 5801
Stinchcombe, A. 4915
Stinchfield, R. 5384
Stirk, P. 325
Stith, S. 2876
Stivers, R. 1622
Stockden, E. 2188
Stockford, C. 756
Stocking, S. 3759
Stoddart, G. 5785
Stofferahn, C. 20
Stoherel, A. 3552
Stoker, J. 782
Stokes, C. 2767
Stokstad, M. 3169
Stoll, M. 4489
Stoller, T. 1756
Stoloff, J. 3996
Stolzenberg, N. 3471
Stombler, M. 3362
Stone, A. 3181
Stone, C. 5139

Stone, J. 652, 774
Stone, M. 237
Stoneman, Z. 3901
Stora, B. 161
Storey, D. 4665
Storey, J. 4830
Storper, M. 4227
Storry, M. 1178
Stöss, R. 5219, 5243
Stott, C. 1005, 1042
Strachan, G. 4550
Strachan, V. 5706
Strack, F. 657, 703, 871
Strait, J. 3997
Strand, P. 3032, 3050
Strang, J. 5380, 5801
Strasser, H. 2428
Stratford, D. 3309
Strathdee, S. 5958
Strati, A. 1124
Straub, J. 4484
Strauss, G. 4877
Strayer, F. 1161
Strayer, W. 2253
Streckeisen, U. 1631
Strecker, S. 4347
Street, S. 1884
Strenski, T. 5386
Stretch, D. 753
Stricker, G. 775
Strickland-Clark, L. 5671
Strikwerda, C. 4330
Strinati, D. 1337
Stroebe, W. 887
Strohl, H. 4950
Stromer-Galley, J. 5288
Strosahl, K. 737
Strykowska, M. 3890
Stuart, S. 591
Stubbs, M. 1030, 1152, 4056
Stuhlmacher, A. 1055
Stults, B. 3481
Stumpf, H. 710
Sturge, M. 5523
Sturzbecher, D. 5243
Styan, D. 4287
Styron, T. 5425
Su, Z. 2104
Suar, D. 2362
Suárez, E. 3758
Suárez-Íñiguez, E. 229
Suárez-Orozco, M. 3471
Subedi, J. 789
Subedi, S. 789
Sublette, E. 5907

AUTHOR INDEX

Subrahmanian, R. 3238
Subrahmanyam, S. 3891
Subramaniam, M. 5244
Succi, M. 5749
Suchi, S. 3232
Suchman, L. 1115
Suchman, M. 5154
Suchman, N. 5396
Sue, K. 5500
Suedfeld, P. 567
Sugarman, J. 543
Sugawara, A. 3031
Sugihara, S. 5517
Suitor, J. 948
Sukumane, J. 2107
Sułkowski, B. 1953
Sullivan, O. 4526
Sullivan, P. 567, 5927
Sum, N. 3927
Summerfield, G. 2561
Summerfield, P. 3107
Summers, C. 4876
Summers, R. 5173
Sun, G. 1195
Sundar, N. 2381, 2436
Sunday, J. 5970
Sundberg, G. 5763
Sundeen, R. 2631, 4768
Sunderland, J. 3005
Sundin, J. 2691
Sung, K. 2866
Sunley, P. 4486
Surbey, M. 3351
Surd, V. 4606
Surour, N. Al 2233
Susak, Z. 2086
Sussman, M. 2925
Sut, C. 1755
Sutherland, J. 1049
Sutherland, V. 4734
Sutton, A. 2098, 4998
Sutton, M. 5760
Sutton, P. 5255
Sutzkever, A. 3518
Suwarnarat, K. 4102
Suyoufie, F. 1966
Suzuki, N. 3557
Suzuki, Y. 370
Sveaass, N. 5683
Svendsen, G. 3893
Swaan, A. de 2397
Swain, G. 5920
Swain, J. 2225, 2477, 2497, 5938
Swaminathan, A. 4323
Swan, D. 4056

Swan, G. 5389
Swan, J. 1155
Swank, P. 5928
Swann, Jr., W. 720, 999
Swanson, C. 2985
Swanson, V. 4726
Swatos, Jr., W. 56
Sweanor, D. 5407
Sweat, M. 5943
Swedberg, R. 392
Sweet, D. 4071
Sweeting, H. 2642
Świątkiewicz, W. 1202
Swicegood, C. 3565
Swindal, J. 4920
Swingley, D. 659
Swiss, T. 1693
Swyers, J. 1381
Swyngedouw, E. 4031
Sykes, H. 3723, 4174
Sýkora, L. 4168
Sylvan, D. 5360
Sylvester, C. 4560
Sylvester, J. 2513
Symes, C. 4398
Symes, D. 3880
Symon, G. 1672
Symons, G. 2047
Synodinos, N. 534
Szasz, A. 5244
Szedmák, S. 5773
Szegedi, M. 5028
Szikinger, I. 5139
Szinovacz, M. 2957
Szmolka, I. 5290
Sztompka, P. 943, 2510, 2536
Szukalski, P. 2791
Ta'ani, M. 4331
Tabajaski, B. 5192, 5209
Tabani, M. 992
Tabassum, R. 5900
Tacchi, J. 1756
Tacke, V. 386
Tadros, V. 5163
Taeldeman, J. 1798
Tafti, A. 1638
Tahbub, M. 2173
Tahir-Kheli, S. 5317
Tai, E. 410
Taifi, M. 1822
Tait, R. 625
Tajima, J. 3597
Takala, T. 5854
Takano, S. 2523
Takenaka, A. 3545

Takho-Godi, E. 249
Takuma, F. 4103
Talahite, F. 5282
Talbert-Johnson, C. 2024, 2069
Talbot, C. 2658
Talen, E. 4074, 4086
Tall, S. Al 2032
Tallichet, S. 20
Tallis, R. 3322
Tam, T. 4525
Tam, V. 5690
Tamanaha, B. 5185
Tamayo, J. 2559
Tambiah, S. 1263
Tamburrini, C. 1369
Tamis-LeMonda, C. 546
Tammaru, T. 3558
Tanaka, M. 567
Tanaka, Y. 467
Tang, B. 4029
Tang, C. 5446
Tang, D. 4684
Tang, K. 4488
Tang, T. 4684
Tang, W. 4030
Tangney, J. 693
Tanguy, H. 5814
Tanguy, L. 2014
Tanida, S. 656
Tannenbaum, N. 5237
Tannsjo, T. 1369
Tanskanen, A. 5433
Tao, H. 2584
Taormina, R. 1131
Tapert, S. 5410
Tapia, L. 5629
Taplin, M. 2103
Tapper, T. 2280
Tarasov, A. 2534, 2630
Tardy, R. 3007
Tarì, M. 1454
Taris, T. 487
Tarohmaru, H. 40
Tarr, C. 3602
Tarricone, R. 5909
Tartakovskaya, I. 4584
Tarusina, I. 5297
Tasan, T. 4168
Tasker, F. 3382
Tassinary, L. 708
Tatacharya, N. 233
Tate, J. 2561
Tateiwa, S. 369
Tatsuki, D. 1807
Tatum, B. 5062

Taucer, U. 3573
Tausig, M. 789
Tausky, C. 3588
Tavares, A. 2188
Tavris, C. 3298
Tawfik, M. 2547
Taylor, A. 5401
Taylor, B. 5252
Taylor, C. 657, 2665, 4726
Taylor, D. 5244
Taylor, E. 2951
Taylor, H. 2486
Taylor, I. 5059
Taylor, J. 417, 1108, 1673, 2304
Taylor, K. 4242
Taylor, L. 1911, 2688
Taylor, M. 3827, 3861
Taylor, P. 20, 4688
Taylor, Q. 3391
Taylor, R. 849, 4874
Taylor, S. 2501
Taylor-Gooby, P. 5485, 5623
Taylor-Thompson, K. 5160
Tazelaar, F. 4380
Tchoungui, G. 1843
Teaford, J. 4110
Teal, C. 915
Tec, N. 3518
Tedebrand, L. 2691
Tedeschi, E. 1975
Tedman, G. 351
Teekens, H. 2259
Teevan, J. 5369
Teichler, U. 2265
Telecsan, B. 2206
Tellez, F. 2298
Temkin, J. 5191
Temkin, K. 4080
Tempest, S. 1100
Temporal, P. 4668
Tenenbaum, A. 2177
Tennant, M. 4398
Tennen, H. 722
Tenorio, A. 4935
Teo, P. 3508, 3557
Tepper, B. 4626
Terrio, S. 958
Terry, D. 807, 1034
Terz, P. 5210
Testart, A. 2336
Tester, K. 3
Tetlock, P. 650
Tettey, W. 3922, 4955
Teubal, M. 4236
Teulier-Bourgine, R. 1040

AUTHOR INDEX

Tewdwr-Jones, M. 3906, 4085, 5202
Tewissen, F. 1040
Texier, J. 4934
Thabet, A. 753
Thang, N. Van 4658
Thanjan, T. 2870
Théberge, R. 2188
Thélot, C. 2064
Therborn, G. 32, 2568
Thernstrom, A. 2017
Théry, H. 2716
Théry, I. 4898
Thévenot, L. 2382
Thibaudeau, M. 5420
Thiebes, S. 3776
Thiele, L. 3759
Thijs, G. 2288
Thinh, N. 3915
Thiollet, J. 2990
Third, H. 43
Thistle, S. 3086
Thøgersen, S. 4981
Thomas, A. 3024, 4287
Thomas, C. 3386, 3937
Thomas, D. 2068, 3115
Thomas, G. 2268, 5889
Thomas, H. 635, 4089
Thomas, I. 2716
Thomas, J. 1310, 1388, 3640
Thomas, K. 4067
Thomas, M. 2608
Thomas, N. 5557
Thomas, P. 818
Thomas, R. 5728
Thomas, V. 3382
Thompkins, D. 5465
Thompson, B. 2486
Thompson, D. 4519
Thompson, E. 852
Thompson, J. 2266, 3813
Thompson, L. 1018
Thompson, M. 832, 2731
Thompson, N. 5719
Thompson, P. 194, 4608
Thompson, S. 479, 541, 1227, 1851, 2402
Thompson, T. 169
Thompson, V. 631
Thomsin, L. 2718
Thomson, I. 267
Thomson, L. 5056
Thorburn, D. 5317
Thorén, K. 4025
Thorne, B. 3115
Thornthwaite, L. 4814
Thornton, D. 3886

Thorold, A. 5363
Thorpe, A. 5352
Thorpe, J. 525
Thouret, J. 3702
Threadgold, T. 3117
Threlfall, M. 5641
Thrift, N. 3788, 3790, 3932
Thrupp, M. 2158
Thussu, D. 1730, 1731
Thye, S. 433, 1047, 2341
Tian, C. 1456
Tice, D. 657, 3306
Tickell, A. 4439
Tidd, U. 3091
Tienda, M. 3565, 3570
Tietze, N. 2313
Tiffany, S. 5406
Tijs, S. 486
Tikhonova, N. 2437
Tilanduca, L. 1496
Tiller, G. 228
Tilley, J. 2349
Tilley, N. 5088
Tillman, B. 2024, 2080
Tillotson, S. 178
Tilly, C. 2384, 4893, 5240
Tilman, R. 1848
Tilson, D. 2851
Timberlake, M. 3927
Timimi, I. 1822
Timmerman, C. 1532
Timotijevic, L. 2530, 3660
Tinker, A. 5511
Tipple, A. 4302, 5655
Tiratsoo, N. 3983
Tirimanna, V. 1455
Tirpák, M. 2686
Tiryakian, E. 375
Tisdall, K. 5586
Tisdell, C. 3667
Tisseron, S. 2618
Tissot, L. 5335
Titchkosky, T. 2462
Tittle, C. 2410
Titunik, R. 5347
Tiwari, G. 5967
Tiwari, P. 4049
Tobias, S. 2266
Tobin, K. 5079
Tobin, R. 708
Tockert, A. 5814
Todd, P. 561, 595
Todorov, A. 502, 830
Todorova, V. 5164, 5560
Tofail, F. 5838

Tokar, D. 3095
Tolan, P. 5069
Tollefsen, C. 5854
Tolman, D. 3212
Tolman, R. 5633
Toma, E. 2059
Tomanović-Mihajlović, S. 2954
Tomaselli, K. 1880
Tomasello, M. 623, 636
Tomassini, C. 2802
Tomasson, R. 2017
Tominaga, K. 65
Tomka, M. 1407
Tomlinson, J. 2187, 2602
Tomlinson, S. 2187, 2602
Tonda, J. 5980
Tonizzo, S. 2862
Tonkinson, R. 992
Tonkiss, F. 1156
Tontisirin, K. 5969
Tonuma, K. 3948
Tooke, J. 3775
Toolan, M. 1877
Tooley, J. 2150
Tooley, M. 258, 260, 290
Toomela, A. 1210
Topham, J. 1557
Topik, S. 4206
Topolosky, P. 4707
Topper, C. 1146
Toran, J. 772
Tormey, R. 4522
Torrance, M. 2268
Torre, C. de la 2063
Torre, M. La 5208
Torre, R. De La 1199
Torres Nafarrate, J. 279
Torres, Y. 1400
Torretti, R. 1605
Torrivellec, X. Le 966
Torry, R. 1882
Tort, M. 3199
Torti, M. 1982
Tosh, J. 182
Toshchenko, Z. 36
Tosi, H. 1117
Totton, N. 4895
Touché, M. 2618
Toulson, P. 4656
Touraine, A. 2380, 4949
Tourneau, F. Le 3768
Tournier, P. 5016
Tovar, A. 2559
Townsend, A. 4658
Townsend, J. 3089

Townsend, T. 5409
Tozy, M. 3869, 5282
Trabaud, L. 3737
Tracy, E. 5569
Tracy, M. 3877
Tracy, P. 5048
Traina, C. 3028
Trampuž, M. 1731
Tran, M. Thi 545
Tran, T. 545
Traoré, S. 2121
Trappe, H. 4548
Trappler, B. 5907
Traustadóttir, R. 2499
Trautmann, R. 747
Travers, R. 3370, 3381
Trawalter, S. 835
Trayhurn, D. 2056
Traynor, T. 3850
Treas, J. 2981, 4557
Treasure, J. 769
Tregaskis, C. 2476
Treichler, P. 5866
Treivish, A. 4168
Trenkel, V. 468
Tressell, P. 2947
Trettin, L. 3734
Trevillion, S. 5709
Trevisan, M. 503
Trew, K. 5550
Trewhitt, L. 4812
Triandafyllidou, A. 2530
Trice, R. 1747
Trindade, J. 5192
Trinh, Q. 3479
Tripathi, N. 1123
Tripathi, S. 1123, 5962
Tripp, A. 3079
Tripp, T. 1012
Tripsianis, G. 5089
Trivisano, C. 478
Trobst, K. 709
Tröhler, D. 2117
Trom, D. 4888
Trompette, P. 4322
Troop, N. 769
Trope, Y. 760
Trost, J. 2949
Trotter, J. 5544
Trotzer, J. 759
Trouillot, M. 2544
Trow, M. 2129
Troyer, L. 4416
Trudgill, P. 1837
Truman-Schram, D. 2879

AUTHOR INDEX

Trumbore, P. 1023
Tryssenaar, J. 5420
Trzcinski, E. 3169
Tsai, C. 2209
Tsang, A. 3586
Tsang, H. 768
Tsang, J. 972
Tsang, N. 5677
Tsang, W. 1784
Tsardanidis, C. 3639
Tsay, A. 440
Tsay, C. 3618
Tschirgi, N. 3809
Tse, J. 1811
Tseng, V. 2936
Tsfati, Y. 3483
Tsolacos, S. 4486
Tsolidis, G. 3676
Tsubaki, T. 3983
Tsuda, T. 3548, 3662
Tsui, A. 2765
Tsuji, R. 1079
Tsunskii, I. 1874
Tsuzuki, K. 3587
Tsytsarev, S. 3591
Tuazon, R. 1683
Tubbs, N. 253
Tucker, B. 3702
Tucker, C. 3053
Tucker, J. 1522, 4683
Tucker, P. 4606
Tucker, S. 5742
Tuffin, K. 1844
Tullberg, B. 2744
Tulloch, J. 1294
Tulloch, M. 5093
Tulving, E. 640
Tumwine, J. 3813
Tunbridge, J. 4168
Tung, Y. 662
Tunick, M. 4988
Tunstill, J. 5548
Tuomilehto, J. 5433
Turčan, L. 4
Turell, S. 2867
Türmen, T. 2754
Turnbull, P. 4850, 5801
Turner, A. 5295
Turner, B. 7, 100, 317, 400, 2567
Turner, G. 1756, 1771
Turner, H. 800
Turner, J. 5, 398, 894, 3069, 4056, 4670, 5935
Turner, M. 3517
Turner, P. 398
Turner, R. 479, 5935

Turner, S. 318
Turnock, D. 4606
Turnock, R. 1719
Turok, I. 4439, 4579
Turpin, J. 2213
Turpin-Petrosino, C. 426
Turrell, G. 2841
Turtle, J. 5084
Turvani, M. 4190
Tushnet, M. 4933
Tuson, G. 5702
Tweed, C. 4025
Tweg, S. 1882
Twemlow, S. 3289
Twine, F. 3115
Tyack, D. 996
Tyler, J. 633
Tyler, P. 4439, 4587
Tyrell, H. 1406
Tzeng, J. 2917
Tzur, V. 2094
Uberoi, P. 1002
Udegbe, B. 3283
Udry, J. 3167
Uehara, E. 5898
Uggen, C. 4758, 5052, 5121
Uhlenberg, P. 3025
Uhles, A. 1086
Uhlmann, A. 3236
Ui, M. 3283
Ukadike, N. 1880
Ukaegbu, C. 4748
Ukpokodu, I. 3391
Ulicki, T. 3599
Ullman, E. 5913
Ullmann, S. 4263
Ullrich, G. 5780
Ulmer, J. 5081
Ulmer, R. 1097
Ulrich, J. 5443
Ulrich, R. 3605
Ulrich, V. 2626, 5507
Ultee, W. 1494, 5302
Umeh, E. 5838
Umeh, J. 5838
Umeki, D. 1991
Underiner, T. 3115
UNESCO 105
Unger, D. 2947
Ungerson, C. 5536
United Nations Development Programme 4267
United Nations Environment Programme 3804
Unsworth, K. 1144
Unterhalter, E. 4558

Upadhyay, U. 2561
Updegraff, K. 3053, 3213
Upton, G. 2273
Urada, D. 856
Urbina, S. 5180
Urfalino, P. 5982
Urrego, I. 2176
Urry, J. 32
Ursell, G. 1778
Urucu, V. 4606
Ury, S. 3450
Usdin, S. 5200
Ushadevi, M. 2272
Usher, R. 2191
Uslaner, E. 2371
Usunier, J. 4318
Utkin, A. 2570
Utting, W. 5696
Uttley, S. 2997
Uvalić, M. 4255
Uyeki, E. 5244
Uys, T. 4422
Vaa, M. 4169
Vahtera, J. 4708
Vaillancourt, J. 5265
Valacich, J. 1704
Valadez, D. 532
Valaskivi, K. 1695
Valdeavellano, E. 2754
Valdés, A. 3905
Valente, A. 4949
Valentin, A. 4025
Valentine, E. 651
Valentine, G. 2325, 2608, 2622
Valentini, B. 1323
Valins, O. 3775
Valladares, L. 58
Valle, M. 5283
Vallée, D. 1302
Vallée, G. 4818
Vallet, L. 2064
Valliant, R. 525
Vallicella, W. 1391
Valsecchi, I. 4763
Valsiner, J. 514
Valverde, J. 3702
Valverde, M. 178, 5400
Vamplew, W. 1305
Văn, K. Thi 545
Van Stone, W. 5913
Vanclay, F. 20
Vandasová, Z. 2814
Vandenbelt, M. 3019
Vandendorpe, F. 1383
Vanderbeck, R. 4139

Vandersluis, S. 5334
Vandiver, M. 5312
Vanecek, R. 2921
Vangen, S. 1032
Vanhanen, T. 3759
Vanman, E. 708
Vanoni Polanczyk, T. 5192
Vanstone, M. 5042
Vanwallendael, L. 2879
Varea, C. 2801
Vargas, A. 1308
Varkey, P. 5200
Varkey, S. 5200
Varley, A. 4558
Varshavskii, A. 1618
Vartiainen, E. 5433
Vasilev, V. 4637
Vasilopoulos, N. 4697
Vásquez, P. 5973
Vassar, P. 3215
Vasulu, T. 2701
Vatn, A. 3705
Vaughan, P. 5934
Vaughan, R. 748
Vaughan, S. 748
Vaughn, D. 2154
Vault, M. De 2915
Vazquez Aldana, J. 3948
Vazquez-Montilla, E. 3013
Ve, H. 3165
Večernik, J. 3870
Veenstra, R. 2239
Vega, C. de 3813
Vega, W. 3565
Vega-Redondo, F. 2447
Veiga, J. 662, 4386
Veilleux, D. 3379
Veitch, S. 2366
Veitl, P. 4897
Veit-Wilson, J. 5650
Veken, J. Van der 225
Velasco, M. 3767
Velásquez, V. 4169
Vélez, J. 1819
Vellinga, P. 4025
Velo, V. 4391
Veloski, J. 5891
Velsen, J. van 4931
Veltmeyer, H. 2514, 5245
Ven, F. van de 4025
Ven, T. Vander 5083
Venable, B. 4420
Vender, J. 844
Venema, T. 3568
Veneziano, R. 3043

AUTHOR INDEX

Veniegas, R. 3352
Venter, P. 1667
Venturelli, P. 5465
Vera-Sanso, P. 4558
Verberg, N. 5286
Vere Brody, J. De 1903
Verette, J. 928
Verge, P. 4818
Verger, D. 4299
Verheij, R. 3696
Verhoeven, M. 1993
Véricourt, V. de 1433
Verkuyten, M. 2097
Verma, M. 2231
Vermaak, N. 3852
Vermeulen, H. 3568, 3571
Verstegen, I. 564
Vertovec, S. 3650
Vervaeke, G. 3338
Verweij, M. 3762
Verwiebe, R. 2396
Very, P. 662, 4386
Vescovo, F. 2456
Veugelers, J. 5222, 5238
Vevaina, T. 5409
Viadel, A. 4373
Viadro, C. 3336
Vianna, H. 1981
Viatkin, A. 3627
Vibert, S. 1246
Vicari, S. 4066
Vician, C. 1054
Victor, T. 426
Vidal, C. 161
Vidal, D. 58
Vidal, H. 1194
Vidal, J. 2291
Vidal, L. 58, 5980
Vidler, E. 4169
Vieira Villela, W. 5200
Vieyra, J. 4142
Vigar, G. 4082
Vigevani, T. 5325
Vignoles, A. 2270
Vigouroux, A. Le 5980
Viherä, M. 1643
Vijayanunni, M. 2683
Vilas, C. 5642
Vilhelmson, B. 3767
Villa, M. 2691, 3904
Villacis, C. 3702
Villaran, S. 1756
Villeneuve-Gokalp, C. 2626
Vilnat, A. 1822
Viltard, Y. 4897

Vimard, P. 5980
Vinamäki, H. 5433
Vincent, J. 2672, 2869
Vincent, R. 1730
Vincent, S. 4218
Vinick, B. 2917
Vinsonneau, A. 5475
Vintges, K. 410
Violato, C. 2903
Virdee, S. 4865
Virkkunen, J. 1000
Virtanen, P. 4708
Vishnevskii, A. 3668
Visser, P. 713
Visvesvaran, P. 5704
Vitalis, R. 5319
Vitellone, N. 3299
Vlachonikolis, I. 5826
Vletter, F. de 3649
Vliert, E. Van de 1022
Vlist, R. van der 3568
Vobruba, G. 2375
Vodopianova, E. 1594
Voeten, M. 5143
Vogel, J. 520
Vogeltanz, N. 5388
Vogler, M. 3637
Vohra, N. 3581
Vohs, K. 876
Volk, S. 970
Volkan, V. 814
Volman, M. 4771
Voos, P. 4870
Voronina, O. 35, 3084
Voropaev, I. 241
Vos, H. de 11
Voss, G. 1100
Voss, K. 4853
Voss, Z. 1100
Vostanis, P. 753
Vo-Thanh-Xuan, J. 2680
Vouga, F. 1478
Vranceanu, R. 4749
Vreese, S. De 5448
Vries, N. de 890
Vries, S. de 3696
Vries, Y. de 2215
Vugt, M. Van 2307
Vukovich, G. 2533
Vulliamy, G. 2162
Vun, M. 5968
Vyas, S. 4658
Vyzhletsov, P. 241
Waard, J. De 3338
Waardenburg, J. 1422

INDEX DES AUTEURS

Wachholz, S. 5144
Wachter, K. 2699
Wächter, M. 1623
Wacjman, G. 1902
Wacquant, L. 18
Wada, T. 5382
Waddington, I. 1355
Waddington, J. 4872
Waddington, P. 5147
Wade, J. 5570
Wadsworth, J. 4476, 4587
Wadsworth, T. 4985
Waenke, M. 865
Wagg, S. 1305
Wagner, G. 2669
Wagner, K. 2270
Wagner, P. 1280
Wagner-Pacifici, R. 1031
Wagstaff, A. 5763
Wahl, A. 47
Wahler, R. 3032
Wailes, N. 4818
Waite, L. 4265
Wajcman, J. 3200, 4816
Wakelam, A. 2137
Wakely, P. 3987
Walaszek, A. 3636
Walby, S. 3070
Walch, J. 5230
Wald, A. 4919
Wald, P. 3115
Walden, G. 3307
Waldfogel, J. 5569
Waldman, G. 5268
Waldman M., G. 3518
Waldron, V. 574
Waley, P. 3728
Walford, N. 2709
Walford, R. 4145
Walgrave, S. 5264
Wali, M. 3719
Walia, S. 1278
Walker, A. 2943
Walker, G. 13
Walker, I. 3446, 5878
Walker, S. 4310
Walker, T. 4246
Walkington, H. 2218
Wall, C. van der 2987
Wall, G. 3750, 3821
Wall, S. 4928
Wall, T. 1144
Wallace, C. 463
Wallace, J. 2213
Wallace, P. 1684

Wallace, R. 56
Wallace, S. 4497
Wallace, T. 4402
Wallace, W. 3401
Wallach, J. 2619
Wallach, M. 2619
Waller, L. 5889
Waller, N. 918
Waller, P. 3941
Wallerstein, I. 32, 336, 2568, 3452
Walley, E. 1152
Wallis, L. 774, 5574
Wallis, R. 2213
Walmsley, D. 1661
Walsh, D. 2610
Walsh, E. 5569
Walsh, J. 5217
Walsh, S. 4227
Walston, J. 511
Walt, G. 2792
Walt, L. van der 4864
Walter, A. 3304
Walter, F. 5219
Walter, J. 4859
Waltermann, J. 1753
Walters, D. 4813
Walters, W. 3625
Walthéry, P. 4828
Walton, J. 1312
Walton, W. 3990
Wälty, S. 3776
Wan, C. 727
Wanberg, C. 4588, 4721, 4722
Wandesforde-Smith, G. 3759
Wang, D. 4263, 4363
Wang, H. 2855, 5128
Wang, L. 4363
Wang, N. 1366
Wang, X. 561
Wang, Y. 1426, 2513, 4081, 5854
Waniez, P. 1433, 2716
Wantha, S. 5968
Wappner, S. 442
Warburg, M. 1446
Ward, A. 4366, 4670
Ward, C. 3818
Ward, D. 1053, 4166
Ward, G. 1379, 3791
Ward, H. 5139
Ward, K. 1430, 2213, 3942, 4398
Ward, M. 4714
Wardak, A. 3524
Warde, A. 1322, 2305
Wardell, F. 5720
Wardell, M. 4400

AUTHOR INDEX

Wardhaugh, J. 5429
Ware, R. 1529
Warf, B. 2571, 4122
Warfield, W. 1028
Warhurst, A. 73
Warner, G. 5947
Warner, M. 3856
Warnes, A. 5422
Warnes, T. 3679, 3791
Warnick, B. 1824
Warnock, M. 238
Warr, M. 5106
Warr, P. 637
Warren, C. 1257, 2024, 2062
Warren, J. 2948
Warren, M. 5868
Wartenberg, J. 5445
Wasburn, P. 1742
Wasch, H. 675
Washburn, S. 504
Wastell, L. 5147
Wat, J. 4029
Watanabe, T. 5249
Waters, I. 5135
Waters, M. 3545
Waterson, J. 43
Waterson, P. 1144
Wates, N. 3831
Watkins, S. 1632, 3121
Watson, D. 727, 910, 937, 4655
Watson, J. 1703, 2545
Watson, M. 3975
Watson, N. 1133, 2458
Watson, R. 119
Watson, S. 3939
Watson, T. 13, 1110
Watt, S. 3830
Watts, C. 5442
Watts, J. 4087
Watts, N. 3759
Wawrytko, S. 3108
Wax, M. 602
Wayne, S. 4689
Weatherly, D. 2655
Webb, A. 3069
Webb, J. 294
Webb, R. 2162, 4340
Webb, V. 1813
Webber, S. 2156
Weber, K. 2269
Webster, D. 4587, 5587
Webster, F. 2331
Webster, J. 1645
Wee, C. 1195
Weeghel, J. van 5736

Weeks, J. 8, 3314
Weeks, K. 1229, 2352
Weeks, M. 1438, 5386
Weesie, J. 923
Wegenke, G. 2104
Wegner, P. 1879
Wegren, S. 4292
Wei, L. 1839
Weil, L. 4076
Weiler, A. 4537
Weiler, P. 3983
Weimann, G. 1700
Weiming, T. 1263
Weinberg, A. 3923
Weinberg, B. 4752
Weiner, B. 5749
Weingard, R. 1605
Weingart, L. 1021
Weingast, B. 2
Weinhold, D. 4287
Weinreb, L. 4933
Weinrich, H. 1298
Weis, A. 4417
Weis, L. 3115
Weismantel, M. 3534
Weisner, C. 5818
Weiss, A. 4377
Weiss, C. 443
Weiss, K. 567, 1620
Weiss, L. 3749
Weiss, R. 1150
Weissmahr, B. 1491
Weisz, J. 5906
Weitz, E. 4649
Weitzer, R. 3333
Weizsäcker, R. von 2159
Welch, S. 3565
Welchans, T. 4483
Welcomer, S. 1127
Weldes, J. 5314
Weller, C. 5384
Weller, R. 4227
Wellman, D. 5928
Wells, G. 5084
Wells, N. 608
Welsh, S. 3287
Welsh, W. 5465
Wen, J. 1894
Wendler, D. 5869
Wendt, C. 5769
Wenger, E. 1115
Wenger, G. 5510
Wenger, N. 434
Wengraf, T. 74
Wenjin, H. 1894

Wentao, Y. 2729
Wentao, Z. 5838
Wentura, D. 827
Werfhorst, H. van de 3568
Werhane, P. 4422
Wernick, A. 1390
Werth, P. 1392
Wertsch, J. 162
Wertz, D. 1620
Wesely, J. 2880
Wessel, T. 4018
Wessels, B. 1688
West, D. 3338
West, J. 3325
West, P. 2642
West, R. 5407
Westenholz, A. 4360
Westerholm, P. 5808
Westermark, G. 1490
Western, B. 4505
Western, J. 2276
Westervelt, S. 5175
Westheimer, J. 2218
Westman, A. 4565
Westphal, J. 4641
Westwood, S. 2532, 3067
Wetherell, M. 841
Wetzels, P. 5452
Whalley, L. 5720
Wharton, A. 3121, 4733
Whatley, A. 2299
Wheatley, T. 688
Wheaton, B. 3252
Wheelaghan, S. 5586
Wheeler, B. 1704
Wheeler, H. 1611
Wheeler, J. 4122
Wheelock, J. 4577
Whelan, C. 3989
Whelehan, I. 3141
While, A. 3808, 4439
White, A. 2529
White, D. 2489
White, G. 162, 1161
White, H. 4227
White, J. 574, 3201
White, K. 1632, 5547, 5776
White, M. 2624, 3577
White, P. 45, 4487, 4852
White, S. 3874
White, T. 2705
Whitehead, A. 4558
Whitehead, J. 2092
Whitehead, M. 2999, 4696
White-Mair, K. 5400

Whiteman, J. 627
Whiteside, A. 5773
Whitfield, K. 4602
Whitfield, S. 1187
Whitman, M. 4658
Whitmeyer, J. 1070
Whitney, D. 3808
Whittaker, J. 2019, 5569
Whittington, L. 4518
Whittock, M. 4536
Whitty, G. 2120, 2130
Whitworth, B. 1036
Wicclair, M. 5855
Wichterich, C. 4546
Wickens, T. 666
Wicki, M. 2269
Wickrama, K. 3873
Widdowfield, R. 5417, 5418
Widiger, T. 591
Widmer, E. 4557
Wieczorkowska, G. 1086
Wielandt, R. 2554
Wield, D. 4287
Wiemeyer, J. 2554
Wiener, R. 3310
Wieringa, S. 3061
Wierzbicka, E. 2009
Wiese, D. 910, 937
Wiesenfeld, B. 1660
Wießner, R. 4168
Wieten, J. 1773
Wieviorka, M. 67
Wieviorka, S. 2618
Wigboldus, D. 853, 3283
Wiggins, J. 709
Wijgert, J. van de 3311
Wijnberg, N. 1100, 1861
Wikan, U. 3471
Wikström, P. 5071
Wiktorowicz, Q. 1538
Wilcox, P. 2881
Wilcox, W. 1408, 3012
Wildemeersch, D. 2006
Wilder, E. 2732, 2760
Wilding, P. 4789
Wildschut, T. 928
Wiley, C. 4601
Wilford, G. 5572
Wilhite, D. 3690
Wilkesmann, U. 1088
Wilkins, C. 2218
Wilkinson, I. 5675
Wilkinson, P. 3935
Wilkinson, R. 230
Wilkinson, S. 455, 5420

Willaime, J. 4962
Willems, H. 3092
Willemsen, T. 3283
Willer, D. 466, 1062
Willer, R. 466
Willett, G. 5247
Willett, J. 633, 4794
Willey, D. 2711
Williamon, A. 651
Williams, A. 349, 2584, 2667, 3679, 3791, 3820
Williams, B. 1550
Williams, C. 1995, 2915, 3121, 3180, 3840, 5837
Williams, D. 808, 3038, 4291
Williams, E. 4658
Williams, H. 2843, 4704
Williams, J. 3270, 4101, 5516, 5894
Williams, K. 1666, 4310
Williams, L. 2771
Williams, M. 474, 1846
Williams, N. 787
Williams, R. 12, 31, 742, 1554, 4497
Williams, S. 3792, 5394, 5733
Williams, W. 575
Williams-Blangero, S. 789
Williamson, B. 2004
Williamson, I. 4102
Williamson, P. 453
Willigenburg, T. Van 2365
Willis, J. 2515
Willis, K. 3645
Willis, M. 3995
Willis, R. 3000
Willmott, H. 327, 1090, 1115
Willmott, R. 1136
Willms, D. 5896
Willnat, L. 3993
Willner, P. 5364
Wills, C. 1227
Wills, T. 709
Willson, J. 646
Wilsnack, R. 5388
Wilsnack, S. 5388
Wilson, A. 93, 562, 857, 2458, 5665
Wilson, B. 3431
Wilson, C. 5473
Wilson, D. 1137, 5818
Wilson, E. 340, 1311
Wilson, F. 3292, 3293, 4463
Wilson Farmer, B. 2024, 2146
Wilson, G. 2678
Wilson, J. 4768, 5721, 5863
Wilson, K. 737
Wilson, S. 1647

Wilson, T. 688, 3630
Wilson, W. 3528
Wilton, R. 2473
Wilton, T. 5698
Winbinger, B. 2119
Winch, G. 4659
Winchester, I. 225
Winchester, L. 4169
Wincup, E. 529, 4982
Winddance Twine, F. 3454
Windebank, J. 3840, 4576
Windrich, E. 1756
Wineburg, R. 5481
Winfield, B. 1309
Wingens, M. 4790
Winglee, M. 525
Wink, W. 3366
Winkelhake, O. 5763
Winkvist, A. 5439
Winn, M. 4409
Winock, M. 2439
Winship, J. 1782
Winston, A. 870
Winters, K. 5384
Wintle, M. 2518
Wirth, A. 865
Wirth, C. 4837
Wise, C. 2098
Wise, J. 1288
Wise, P. 5633
Wislar, J. 4493, 5115
Wister, A. 2909
Wistrich, R. 3466
Wit, H. de 5406
Witkin, R. 1878
Witt, L. 4728
Witt, P. De 2219
Wittberg, P. 1500
Wittebrood, K. 5049
Wittenberg, R. 3455, 5525
Wittrock, B. 1263
Witwer, D. 4877
Witz, A. 3158
Wobbe, T. 4964
Wodak, R. 959, 3508
Wodchis, W. 5844
Woddis, D. 721
Wódz, J. 997
Wódz, K. 997
Woelke, J. 1715
Wokler, R. 1248
Wolbers, M. 4583
Woldemicael, G. 2823
Wolf, D. 2669, 2802
Wolfe, B. 2935

INDEX DES AUTEURS

Wolff, J. 1860
Wolf-Wendel, L. 2213
Wolkomir, M. 2402
Wollen, P. 1883, 4954
Wolpin, K. 4438
Wolthuis, A. 3338
Woltjer, J. 4036
Women in Development Southern Africa Awareness Programme 3209
Wong, A. 2195
Wong, B. 346
Wong, C. 4363, 5690
Wong, D. 5446, 5488
Wong, G. 5838
Wong, O. 2408
Wong, P. 5765
Wong, S. 1929
Wong, T. 4108, 5765
Woo, S. 767
Wood, A. 113
Wood, E. 3353, 3813
Wood, G. 4650
Wood, J. 521, 567, 680, 904, 5132
Wood, P. 3886
Wood, R. 3443
Wood, W. 4219
Woodberry, R. 1408
Wooden, M. 4881
Woodhouse, H. 225
Woods, J. 106
Woods, M. 5670
Woods, N. 3115
Woods, R. 4147, 4501
Woodward, D. 2273
Woodward, I. 4329
Woodward, L. 2074, 3056, 5051
Woodward, V. 3829
Wooffitt, R. 901
Woolcock, M. 44
Woolf, L. 4416
Woolgar, S. 13
Woolley, F. 2589
Woolley, H. 3965
Woolliams, P. 4417
Woon, Y. 3229
Worell, J. 3121
Worms, F. 2369
Worms, J. 5475
Worthington, C. 4494
Wortley, A. 2098
Woźniak, T. 3132
Wraikat, A. 5792
Wright, B. 1033
Wright, D. 535
Wright, E. 2384, 2445, 2450, 3180

Wright, F. 5501, 5530
Wright, G. 4270
Wright, J. 2621, 4119, 5090, 5592
Wright, K. 2667
Wright, M. 5032
Wright, R. 525, 2520
Wright, S. 1730, 1978, 4423
Wrightsman, L. 5193
Wrigley, N. 4135
Wrinkle, R. 3565
Wu, A. 5838
Wu, L. 440, 3948
Wulf, V. 1040
Wulfhorst, J. 20
Wyatt, G. 781
Wyer, Jr., R. 549
Wyllie, A. 1349
Wynn, G. 3008
Wysong, E. 2418
Xiao, H. 2347
Xiaodong, W. 1895
Xie, J. 550, 4700
Xie, W. 200
Xie, Y. 4303
Xin, K. 1142
Xin, Z. 1894
Xu, G. 5891
Yabo, Z. 1895
Yacoubian, Jr., G. 5312
Yadav, S. 3023
Yadava, K. 2955
Yaeger, A. 709
Yahya, K. 557, 3048
Yaish, M. 2420
Yakubovich, V. 4429
Yalda, C. 2643
Yalin, W. 2338
Yamada, S. 534
Yamada, T. 3702
Yamagishi, T. 656
Yamaguchi, K. 485, 1069
Yamamoto, M. 3283
Yamamoto, T. 3115
Yamanaka, K. 3663
Yamashita, H. 4379
Yamin, A. 5805
Yan, A. 1091
Yan, M. 806
Yan, Z. 1894
Yang, C. 1691
Yang, G. 5262
Yang, M. 479
Yang, N. 4475
Yang, X. 2020, 2741, 3610
Yang, Z. 1895

AUTHOR INDEX

Yangeng, S. 1895
Yanow, D. 1115
Yap, M. 4056
Yaqub, H. 4102
Yar, M. 4911
Yassin, K. 2828
Yasuda, T. 448
Yates, P. 4102
Yeates, M. 4182
Yebei, V. 5200
Yee, J. 54
Yehoshua, N. Ben- 2084
Yelin, E. 4776
Yencken, D. 3723
Yeoh, B. 3557, 3645
Yepes, H. 3702
Yerington, T. 2861
Yeung, H. 2568
Yeung, I. 5891
Yeung, K. 3362
Yeung, L. 1831
Yi, D. 185
Yi, R. 1894
Yi, T. 3949
Yi, W. 1336
Yi, Z. 1895
Yick, A. 2887
Yila-Boumpoto, M. 5980
Yildirim, A. 4806
Yiming, L. 1894
Yimou, Z. 1895
Yin, Z. 609
Ying, X. 1894
Yinon, Y. 5437
Yip, K. 5904
Yip, N. 3968
Yip, P. 2693
Yirigian, B. 756
Yirmiya, N. 3029
Ylänne-McEwen, V. 2667
Ylijoki, O. 2255
Yoda, S. 5526
Yogan, L. 5465
Yogev, A. 2290
Yonah, Y. 2177
Yonay, Y. 3285
Yongzhi, W. 1894
Yonke, A. 5831
Yoon, I. 3561
Yoon, J. 1047
Yoon, Y. 54
Yost, J. 725
Youf, D. 5068
Young, A. 611, 3276
Young, C. 4606

Young, D. 2498, 2816, 3972
Young, G. 5732
Young, J. 2188, 2400
Young, R. De 3749
Yousef, D. 1126
Yovetich, N. 928
Ypeij, A. 4394
Yu, A. 1789
Yu, W. 525
Yuan, Q. 1839
Yúdice, G. 1158
Yue, A. 3323
Yue, M. 3497
Yuen, B. 4108
Yumul, A. 1762
Yuval-Davis, N. 5147
Yuvaraj, S. 4648
Yzerbyt, V. 895
Zaaiman, H. 2288
Zabludovsky, G. 4657
Zaccaï, E. 3799
Zaccaro, S. 1065
Zafirovski, M. 10, 4196
Zagladin, V. 3797
Zagury-Orly, R. 235
Zahn, M. 426
Zahniser, S. 3545
Zaidman, N. 1384
Zajacová, A. 3585
Zalabardo, J. 275
Zaman, N. 1165
Zambia Association for Research and Development 3209
Zang, X. 4381
Zanna, M. 908
Zanon, B. 4025
Zanten, A. van 2014
Zaraté, P. 1040
Zarauz, M. 2677
Zarkada-Fraser, A. 4420
Zarzycka, G. 2009
Zatz, M. 5118
Zauchner, S. 4377
Zautra, A. 716
Zaverucha, J. 5361
Zavoina, S. 3341
Zayani, M. 344
Zea, C. 2176
Zea, L. 240, 2294, 5325
Zefanias, H. 3193
Zelezny, L. 3743, 3749
Zelizer, V. 4192, 4193
Zeng, L. 472
Zenteno, R. 536
Zéphir, F. 2083

Zerai, A. 1566
Zetter, R. 5637
Zeuner, B. 4859
Zhang, J. 1349
Zhang, K. 4335
Zhang, L. 2168
Zhang, Q. 1402
Zhang, W. 2961
Zhang, X. 5519
Zhang, Y. 4631
Zhao, Z. 3899
Zhengyou, L. 4162
Zhong, W. 4264
Zhongqiang, J. 1895
Zhongshun, H. 1895
Zhou, M. 2523
Zhou, X. 4209, 4301
Zhou, Y. 3557
Zhurun, L. 1746
Zhurzhenko, T. 3150
Zi, Y. 1895
Zilian, H. 4293
Zilibotti, F. 4685
Zilsel, E. 1616
Zima, B. 2020
Zimmer, O. 150
Zimmer, R. 2059
Zimmerer, K. 3753
Zimmerman, D. 3027, 5551
Zimmerman, F. 3925
Zimmerman, M. 5810
Zimmermann, J. 4227
Zimmermann, K. 3631
Zincone, G. 3582
Zinn, M. 3121
Zinnbauer, B. 1381
Zinyama, L. 3649
Zippelius, R. 4908
Zipperstein, S. 145
Zobov, R. 439
Zoccatelli, P. 1501
Zogaib Achcar, E. 2281
Zokaei, S. 1532
Zolberg, A. 3545
Zou, Y. 4475
Zuberi, T. 3528
Zuckerman, D. 5633
Zuckerman, M. 709
Zúñiga, V. 3565
Zupnik, Y. 1791
Żurawska, J. 2009
Zurbriggen, E. 3344
Zuriff, G. 5371
Zvobgo, R. 2148
Zwane, W. 5097

Zwart, F. de 2415
Zwerman, G. 5251
Zylan, Y. 5620
Zylberberg, J. 4962
Zylberstein, J. 1323

PLACENAME INDEX
INDEX DES ENDROITS

Afghanistan 1536
Africa 71, 199, 520, 592, 1177, 1204, 1409, 1507, 1566, 1620, 1723, 1756, 1880, 1881, 1925, 1942, 1976, 2041, 2125, 2144, 2259, 2321, 2502, 2513, 2523, 2712, 2767, 2792, 3079, 3112, 3193, 3261, 3378, 3417, 3531, 3633, 3637, 3654, 3674, 3708, 3736, 3842, 3868, 3922, 3966, 4042, 4173, 4227, 4422, 4472, 4477, 4566, 4611, 4616, 4644, 4944, 4955, 4975, 5007, 5181, 5328, 5349, 5952, 5966, 5980
  see also: Central Africa, East Africa, Francophone Africa, North Africa, Southern Africa, Sub-Saharan Africa, West Africa
Alabama 3431
Alaska 5416
Albania 965, 1756, 3276, 3652, 5463
Alberta 979, 3526
Algeria 18, 1781, 1931, 1976, 2792, 3638, 4275
Amazon 58, 2405, 2754, 3732, 3768, 3796
Amazonas 3768
Americas 710, 3402, 3512, 4227
  see also: Central America, Latin America, North America, South America
Andes 1433, 3754, 5802
Andhra Pradesh 2733, 3016, 4558
Angola 1756, 3674
Antarctica 567
Antigua and Barbuda 3761
Arctic Region 3746
Argentina 1509, 1658, 2205, 3511, 3575, 3579, 3731, 3754, 3891, 4236, 4243, 4269, 4523, 5168, 5571
Arizona 5426
Asia 65, 177, 230, 520, 975, 1195, 1207, 1219, 1455, 1464, 1483, 1506, 1733, 1929, 1930, 1956, 2008, 2539, 2561, 2568, 2712, 2714, 2743, 2763, 2771, 2792, 2955, 3074, 3323, 3544, 3556, 3557, 3559, 3569, 3587, 3597, 3626, 3637, 3648, 3651, 3657, 3678, 3702, 3723, 3839, 3852, 3927, 4002, 4050, 4108, 4227, 4334, 4629, 4631, 4935, 4943, 5335, 5363, 5684, 5969
  see also: Central Asia, East Asia, South Asia, Southeast Asia
Asia Pacific Region 3665
Australia 20, 206, 470, 518, 523, 710, 1016, 1093, 1195, 1220, 1756, 1757, 1767, 1771, 1974, 2208, 2276, 2277, 2401, 2465, 2564, 2670, 2680, 2841, 2862, 2874, 3115, 3200, 3236, 3299, 3308, 3323, 3355, 3405, 3446, 3482, 3486, 3501, 3567, 3622, 3676, 3697, 3702, 3724, 3789, 3791, 3827, 3836, 3847, 3854, 3880, 3927, 3928, 3999, 4001, 4056, 4118, 4148, 4166, 4229, 4382, 4398, 4420, 4432, 4433, 4550, 4564, 4695, 4712, 4725, 4814, 4845, 4849, 4851, 4875, 4881, 4883, 4956, 5125, 5170, 5217, 5247, 5413, 5484, 5644, 5700, 5791, 5878, 5889, 5955
  see also: New South Wales, Queensland, South Australia, Tasmania
Austria 593, 959, 1179, 3452, 4198, 4393, 5769
Azerbaijan 3410
Baden-Württemberg 1302
Bahia 58
Bali 1257, 1362, 1707, 3776
Baltic States 1452
Bangladesh 2739, 2748, 2759, 2770, 2789, 2792, 2955, 3207, 3530, 3793, 3852, 3911, 3974, 4157, 4524, 4705, 5815
Barbados 3921, 3975
Bavaria 3468
Belarus 2009, 3444
Belgium 811, 2082, 2363, 2718, 3820, 3902, 4235, 4454, 4599, 4793, 4828, 4962, 5218, 5264, 5766, 5862
Benin 4156
Berlin 1985, 3359, 4066, 5197
Bihar 2046, 2701, 2721
Bolivia 1433, 4208, 5802
Bosnia and Herzegovina 1756, 4095, 5332, 5462
Botswana 2148, 3300, 3633, 4955

PLACENAME INDEX

Brazil 58, 186, 322, 603, 791, 893, 961, 1183, 1315, 1359, 1363, 1384, 1431, 1433, 1514, 1735, 1915, 1981, 1996, 2147, 2507, 2628, 2629, 2758, 2901, 3445, 3510, 3768, 3891, 3903, 3958, 4032, 4121, 4509, 4949, 5055, 5192, 5200, 5209, 5220, 5245, 5261, 5303, 5361, 5363, 5842, 5950
  see also: Amazonas, Bahia, Maranhão, Rio de Janeiro, Rio Grande do Sul, São Paulo
British Columbia 3628, 3694, 4092
Bulgaria 1295, 4486, 5164, 5214, 5263, 5560
Burkina Faso 2790, 4068, 4477
Burma 3615
C.I.S. 36
California 1427, 1699, 2473, 2996, 3216, 3413, 3434, 3755, 3955, 4000, 4098, 4128, 4460, 4462, 4821, 5114, 5573, 5732, 5767, 5965
Cambodia 5363, 5977
Cameroon 1177, 1540, 1843, 2126, 2767, 2963, 2998, 3574, 3619, 4284, 5301, 5968
Canada 60, 147, 149, 168, 170, 196, 198, 767, 954, 956, 979, 982, 1036, 1039, 1301, 1480, 1563, 1914, 2047, 2089, 2145, 2188, 2204, 2254, 2263, 2272, 2278, 2547, 2712, 2726, 2909, 2917, 2934, 3046, 3152, 3264, 3286, 3287, 3294, 3423, 3442, 3463, 3500, 3553, 3581, 3586, 3590, 3593, 3631, 3661, 3676, 3727, 3749, 3750, 3762, 3771, 3809, 3980, 4007, 4009, 4020, 4032, 4090, 4163, 4249, 4338, 4398, 4444, 4498, 4844, 4869, 4876, 4956, 5002, 5010, 5026, 5108, 5144, 5222, 5265, 5286, 5304, 5386, 5518, 5521, 5636, 5695, 5741, 5836, 5858, 5903, 5970
  see also: Alberta, British Columbia, Manitoba, New Brunswick, Ontario, Quebec
Caribbean 1960, 2211, 2548, 3621, 3641, 3650, 3761, 3895, 4125
Catalonia 1795, 1823
Central Africa 5320, 5964
Central America 971, 4260, 4825
Central Asia 1373, 1470, 3561
Central Eastern Europe 3647, 4820
Central Europe 4, 1004, 1816, 2228, 3421, 3934, 4168, 4346, 4348, 4815, 4836, 5110
Chad 4223
Channel Islands 1797, 1840
Chechnya 1731, 5329
Chile 1433, 2873, 3552, 3809, 4558, 5266

China 65, 185, 200, 211, 248, 266, 273, 321, 332, 582, 710, 1185, 1186, 1268, 1336, 1360, 1365, 1382, 1402, 1423, 1426, 1456, 1467, 1473, 1738, 1746, 1758, 1767, 1839, 1861, 1885, 1894, 1895, 2104, 2145, 2168, 2338, 2472, 2509, 2516, 2523, 2545, 2614, 2666, 2710, 2714, 2728, 2729, 2741, 2779, 2926, 2961, 2972, 2984, 3061, 3108, 3170, 3222, 3378, 3447, 3459, 3557, 3589, 3610, 3626, 3640, 3645, 3685, 3702, 3822, 3899, 3959, 3976, 4030, 4046, 4050, 4081, 4108, 4136, 4162, 4207, 4241, 4252, 4264, 4301, 4303, 4327, 4335, 4363, 4367, 4445, 4467, 4600, 4631, 4700, 4829, 4848, 4855, 4981, 5211, 5262, 5309, 5487, 5519, 5854
Colombia 2112, 2176, 3519, 3624, 4116, 4977, 5245, 5386, 5445, 5455
Colorado 3857
Comoros 1534
Connecticut 5386
Costa Rica 4558, 4674
Côte d'Ivoire 3612, 4083, 5968
Croatia 967, 987, 1000, 1794, 1825, 3859
Cuba 1167, 3457, 4272, 4942
Czech Republic 77, 477, 1004, 1205, 1511, 1816, 2407, 2684, 2720, 2724, 2814, 2965, 3387, 3870, 3889, 4168, 4198, 4966, 5116, 5214, 5307, 5648, 5649
Czechoslovakia 477, 1748
  see also: Slovakia
Delhi 3972, 4100
Denmark 173, 1446, 1798, 1833, 2202, 2230, 2571, 3418, 3893, 4066, 4259, 4846, 5176, 5769
Dominica 1815
Dominican Republic 2232, 3190, 5943
East Africa 1534, 3654, 3702, 3813, 5320
East Asia 172, 1263, 1465, 3061, 3927, 4228, 4629, 5309
East Timor 3776
Eastern Europe 520, 965, 993, 1000, 1193, 1274, 1375, 1516, 1594, 1675, 1816, 2228, 2389, 2536, 2593, 2833, 3421, 3474, 3635, 3685, 4168, 4185, 4346, 4474, 4486, 4573, 4606, 4815, 4836, 5110, 5250, 5284, 5773
Ecuador 2063, 3454, 3537, 4309, 5541
Egypt 1504, 1523, 1966, 2828, 5274
El Salvador 5361
England 153, 988, 1181, 1254, 1322, 1341, 1550, 1798, 1941, 2090, 2109, 2130, 2131, 2161, 2241, 2252, 2422, 2542, 2621, 2831, 2902, 3246, 3271, 3284,

INDEX DES ENDROITS

3509, 3680, 3779, 3807, 3808, 3824,
3845, 3885, 3886, 3940-3942, 3956, 3978,
3994, 4026, 4035, 4044, 4054, 4058,
4063, 4067, 4078, 4097, 4105, 4117, 4133,
4232, 4270, 4354, 4386, 4865, 4995,
5132, 5137, 5162, 5240, 5417, 5429,
5510, 5522, 5546, 5591, 5631, 5637,
5645, 5758, 5775, 5796, 5801, 5934
Eritrea 2823
Estonia 1000, 1836, 3558, 4113
Ethiopia 1204, 2703, 2827, 2851, 3531, 4280
Europe 64, 85, 152, 214, 834, 953, 959, 969,
976, 983, 1230, 1324, 1331, 1356, 1432,
1434, 1464, 1516, 1532, 1645, 1773,
1775, 1777, 1826, 1861, 2009, 2067, 2117,
2218, 2264, 2270, 2324, 2423, 2518,
2530, 2554, 2698, 2705, 2712, 2714,
2718, 2756, 2844, 3069, 3115, 3220, 3321,
3338, 3378, 3424, 3468, 3518, 3541,
3542, 3566, 3571, 3584, 3664, 3762,
3763, 3791, 3820, 3878, 3896, 3906,
3908, 4005, 4025, 4077, 4079, 4085,
4200, 4203, 4227, 4252, 4330, 4370,
4402, 4439, 4441, 4537, 4589, 4618,
4630, 4751, 4771, 4813, 4828, 4835,
4863, 4872, 4913, 4952, 4957, 4966,
5003, 5039, 5054, 5060, 5064, 5134,
5181, 5196, 5290, 5295, 5335, 5340,
5496, 5598, 5622, 5623, 5632, 5641,
5789, 5812, 5860, 5882, 5884, 5888,
5889, 5945, 5982
see also: Baltic States, Central Eastern
Europe, Central Europe, Eastern Europe,
Scandinavia, Southeast Europe, Southern
Europe, Western Europe
Fiji 1818
Finland 483, 1000, 1798, 2088, 2255, 2283,
2649, 2651, 4025, 4565, 4708, 5143,
5433, 5691
Florida 3309, 4074, 5441
France 58, 66, 86, 161, 212, 217, 281, 283,
357, 358, 377, 801, 958, 974, 981, 1172,
1182, 1190, 1206, 1239, 1246, 1283, 1323,
1326, 1350, 1351, 1464, 1475, 1613,
1798, 1820, 1849, 1857, 1862, 1892,
1904, 1924, 1940, 1949, 1958, 1977,
1986, 2058, 2091, 2115-2117, 2149, 2152,
2169, 2178, 2270, 2313, 2382, 2391,
2404, 2424, 2439, 2587, 2679, 2682,
2696, 2697, 2708, 2901, 2945, 2990,
3091, 3177, 3280, 3468, 3471, 3549,
3562, 3598, 3602, 3635, 3638, 3760,
3773, 3820, 3888, 3891, 3919, 4023,
4235, 4287, 4299, 4322, 4372, 4386,
4414, 4420, 4478, 4541, 4576, 4582,
4585, 4659, 4723, 4767, 4779, 4780,
4810, 4898, 4954, 4962, 4966, 4992,
4993, 5016, 5020, 5190, 5238-5240, 5298,
5360, 5475, 5537, 5611, 5716, 5806, 5814,
5817, 5850, 5968, 5982
Francophone Africa 1913, 5980
Gambia 4170
Georgia 3677, 3715
Georgia (U.S.A.) 3944, 5102, 5386
Germany 157, 162, 165, 173, 189, 208, 234,
343, 441, 976, 989, 1003, 1004, 1008,
1103, 1134, 1179, 1190, 1244, 1299, 1302,
1328, 1329, 1331, 1425, 1461, 1486,
1569, 1581, 1698, 1715, 1754, 1757,
1777, 1783, 1798, 1839, 2117, 2124, 2149,
2159, 2178, 2217, 2244, 2270, 2296,
2343, 2376, 2378, 2391, 2404, 2413,
2554, 2567, 2654, 2669, 2922, 3127,
3206, 3232, 3455, 3471, 3497, 3527,
3532, 3536, 3584, 3592, 3594, 3596,
3605, 3631, 3637, 3647, 3992, 4061,
4069, 4114, 4126, 4129, 4198, 4231, 4277,
4293, 4297, 4310, 4347, 4409, 4459,
4506, 4647, 4681, 4753, 4783, 4787,
4790, 4823, 4859, 4860, 4907, 4963,
4964, 4966, 5190, 5201, 5219, 5243,
5251, 5312, 5324, 5403, 5452, 5506,
5507, 5572, 5625, 5628, 5653, 5769,
5793, 5853, 5882, 5888
see also: Bavaria, Berlin
Germany (East) 1425, 1705, 2396, 3081,
3455, 4244, 4548, 4790, 4795, 5521
Germany (West) 1264, 3134, 3455, 4337,
4528, 4531, 4548
Ghana 2483, 2939, 3337, 3535, 3809, 3852,
3853, 4240, 5200, 5757
Greece 3592, 3676, 4596, 4927, 5089, 5622
Guadeloupe 2679, 2901
Guatemala 1170, 2345, 5361, 5954
Guyana 2040
Hawaii 1346, 1801, 3404, 5914
Holland
see: Netherlands
Honduras 5352, 5592
Hong Kong 550, 582, 862, 1131, 1318, 1758,
1811, 2103, 2133, 2408, 2671, 2693, 2941,
3317, 3640, 3702, 3954, 3968, 4029,
4225, 4228, 4488, 4879, 5187, 5446,
5690, 5717, 5765
Hungary 993, 1328, 1407, 1414, 1816, 1890,
2134, 2297, 2378, 2533, 2620, 2754,
3407, 3408, 3583, 3685, 4168, 4204,
4842, 4966, 5729, 5852
Iceland 2901
Idaho 4870

PLACENAME INDEX

Illinois 1469, 3570, 3833, 3877, 4107, 4131, 4154, 5386, 5480
India 132, 184, 210, 239, 245, 246, 764, 788, 1002, 1122, 1123, 1263, 1319, 1376, 1384, 1399, 1424, 1566, 1589, 1708, 1729, 1756, 1805, 1897, 1972, 1998, 2186, 2231, 2248, 2335, 2381, 2394, 2415, 2421, 2441, 2549, 2561, 2585, 2683, 2701, 2722, 2733, 2743, 2749, 2765, 2766, 2773, 2780, 2783, 2913, 2984, 3023, 3067, 3076, 3112, 3126, 3138, 3143, 3148, 3162, 3186, 3202, 3203, 3291, 3327, 3473, 3654, 3766, 3813, 3855, 3891, 3909, 3970, 3972, 4049, 4100, 4126, 4152, 4172, 4207, 4285, 4302, 4359, 4415, 4455, 4457, 4516, 4575, 4634, 4648, 4662, 4959, 5058, 5200, 5269, 5395, 5462, 5464, 5694, 5704, 5910, 5911, 5916, 5917, 5923, 5949, 5962, 5968, 5983
  see also: Andhra Pradesh, Bihar, Delhi, Karnataka, Kerala, Madhya Pradesh, Maharashtra, Orissa, Punjab, Rajasthan, Tamil Nadu, Uttar Pradesh, West Bengal
Indian Ocean 3654
Indonesia 1707, 1772, 2992, 3609, 3702, 3776, 3813, 4108, 4149, 4571, 4948, 5292, 5528, 5968
  see also: Bali, East Timor, Java, Sulawesi
Iowa 3879
Iran 980, 1185, 1441, 2520, 3067, 3094, 3163, 3277, 3410, 5315
Iraq 1731, 2072, 4265
Ireland 986, 1227, 1364, 1724, 1736, 1798, 1936, 1941, 1946, 1952, 2090, 2571, 2705, 2993, 3072, 3187, 3195, 3284, 3566, 3646, 3778, 3827, 3887, 3989, 4077, 4357, 4414, 4522, 4819, 5491, 5511, 5593, 5680
Israel 57, 161, 976, 985, 1001, 1008, 1014, 1026, 1544-1546, 1620, 1656, 1791, 1817, 1834, 1916, 1935, 2033, 2052, 2054, 2084, 2085, 2094, 2177, 2290, 2420, 2619, 2732, 2753, 2760, 2795, 2834, 2842, 2885, 2904, 2922, 2942, 3420, 3462, 3483, 3499, 3547, 3554, 3559, 3564, 3601, 3862, 3931, 4535, 5154, 5338, 5339, 5351, 5370, 5482, 5504, 5513, 5606, 5638, 5889
  see also: Israeli Occupied Territories
Israeli Occupied Territories 5351
Italy 538, 564, 934, 973, 1000, 1180, 1203, 1209, 1267, 1275, 1502, 1521, 1755, 1978, 2009, 2037, 2117, 2196, 2802, 2858, 2945, 3115, 3224, 3468, 3573, 3582, 3652, 3984, 4025, 4066, 4099, 4220, 4395, 4411, 4447, 4448, 4456, 4461, 4466, 4532, 4537, 4553, 4561, 4580, 4596, 4841, 4885, 4979, 5208, 5251, 5270, 5275, 5909, 5922
Ivory Coast
  see: Côte d'Ivoire
Jamaica 2787, 3400
Japan 50, 65, 162, 485, 534, 734, 763, 977, 1134, 1195, 1218, 1230, 1320, 1353, 1368, 1393, 1442, 1663, 1695, 1948, 2101, 2145, 2210, 2256, 2434, 2523, 2679, 2702, 2829, 2917, 3009, 3035, 3046, 3061, 3313, 3484, 3544, 3545, 3548, 3569, 3616, 3644, 3658, 3662, 3663, 3671, 3678, 3728, 3767, 4124, 4164, 4221, 4310, 4316, 4330, 4332, 4379, 4395, 4398, 4426, 4443, 4494, 4540, 4544, 4617, 4618, 4678, 4824, 4826, 4962, 5128, 5189, 5251, 5498, 5500, 5512, 5524, 5526, 5619, 5626, 5930
Java 3776, 5430
Jordan 944, 1077, 1334, 1538, 2032, 2065, 2075, 2081, 2093, 2105, 2173, 2184, 2233, 2245, 2246, 2316, 2976, 3048, 4155, 4331, 5792
Karnataka 2733
Kenya 1476, 1632, 1723, 2035, 2078, 2505, 2747, 2839, 3275, 3654, 4450, 4616, 4644, 5428, 5890
Kerala 2662, 2733, 3805
Korea 54, 177, 187, 191, 247, 676, 1195, 1262, 1489, 2009, 2579, 3064, 3168, 3484, 3546, 3556, 3561, 3949, 5532, 5577, 5821, 5930
  see also: North Korea, South Korea
Kosovo 1516, 1730, 1731, 4287, 5332, 5340
Kurdistan 4265
Kuwait 2236, 2838, 3673
Kyrgyzstan 2153
Laos 1468, 3576
Latin America 59, 159, 240, 761, 1158, 1169, 1194, 1197, 1199, 1221, 1397, 1431, 1433, 1493, 1994, 2294, 2298, 2339, 2507, 2513, 2514, 2548, 2558, 2568, 2608, 2712, 2886, 3754, 3813, 3895, 3905, 4163, 4197, 4206, 4239, 4248, 4252, 4290, 4368, 4373, 4398, 4481, 4495, 4914, 4942, 4965, 4968, 5245, 5259, 5325, 5361, 5445, 5466, 5622, 5629, 5642, 5805
Latvia 1836
Lebanon 1932
Lesotho 3633, 3649
Louisiana 1367, 3882, 4870

INDEX DES ENDROITS

Madagascar 5968
Madhya Pradesh 5949
Maharashtra 1729, 4172
Maine 2619
Malawi 1482, 2740, 3326, 5363
Malaysia 710, 952, 1772, 2145, 2537, 2743,
    3103, 3655, 3776, 3920, 4115, 4605, 5292,
    5655
Mali 1913, 2121, 3924
Malta 4238
Manitoba 3375
Maranhão 186
Marshall Islands 4994
Martinique 951
Maryland 4074, 4435
Mauritius 3390, 3416
Mediterranean Region 2558, 3679, 3737, 5325
Melanesia 2528
Mexico 240, 536, 797, 970, 1142, 1400, 1433,
    1498, 1899, 1922, 2242, 2250, 2251,
    2281, 2292, 2293, 2295, 2335, 2559,
    2561, 2677, 3089, 3316, 3350, 3468,
    3545, 3565, 3630, 3670, 3682, 3813,
    3891, 3955, 4088, 4142, 4219, 4440,
    4444, 4452, 4458, 4558, 4811, 4866, 5118,
    5200, 5226, 5233, 5245, 5267, 5268, 5368
Michigan 3436, 4291
Middle East 169, 1531, 1538, 1802, 2137,
    2619, 3106, 3115, 3122, 3235, 3278, 4352,
    5335
Minnesota 712
Mississippi 3877
Moldova 1816
Mongolia 1470
Morocco 161, 1976, 3263, 3471, 3869, 3871,
    5981
Mozambique 2388, 3193, 3649, 3817, 3936,
    4482, 5341
Myanmar
    see: Burma
Namibia 2107, 2379, 4189, 5363
Nebraska 2119, 3898
Nepal 513, 789, 2973, 3231, 3663, 3667, 3702
Netherlands 11, 414, 1015, 1081, 1494, 1532,
    1721, 1875, 1997, 2117, 2940, 3178, 3328,
    3467, 3696, 3767, 3843, 4036, 4075,
    4105, 4436, 4537, 4583, 4702, 4706,
    4727, 4764, 4777, 5200, 5300, 5306,
    5736, 5790, 5827
Nevada 1261, 3955
New Brunswick 168, 5961
New Jersey 3745, 3853
New Mexico 3772
New South Wales 3486, 3697, 3962, 4374,
    4542, 5170

New York 461, 581, 1488, 2571, 3927, 3950,
    4366, 5425, 5764, 5872, 5907
New Zealand 76, 1036, 1349, 1442, 1818,
    1844, 1847, 1886, 2158, 2166, 2997,
    3292, 3365, 3643, 3791, 3800, 3880,
    3912, 4112, 4656, 5051, 5470, 5859
Nicaragua 971, 5361, 5683
Niger 1888, 4011
Nigeria 1474, 1939, 2015, 2429, 2761, 2825,
    3403, 3465, 3574, 3868, 4093, 4153,
    4598, 4748, 4955, 5223, 5343, 5469
North Africa 1949, 1976, 2429, 2714
North America 1384, 1795, 4881, 5145, 5227
North Carolina 3336
North Korea 3184
Northern Ireland 1343, 1484, 1513, 2135,
    2136, 2306, 2340, 2737, 3269, 3284,
    3493, 3863, 4003, 4043, 5127, 5242,
    5273, 5503, 5540, 5685
Norway 1348, 2517, 2612, 2813, 2877, 3226,
    3471, 3771, 3816, 3904, 4018
Ohio 4071, 5386
Oman 3278
Ontario 1912, 3551, 3553, 3661, 4019, 4182,
    4486, 5515, 5785, 5874
Orissa 3471, 3739, 5800
Pacific Region 992, 1818, 2574, 2810, 3074,
    3544, 3556, 3569, 3587, 3597, 3621,
    3642, 3643, 3648, 3651, 3678, 3723
    see also: Melanesia, Polynesia
Pakistan 1537, 2022, 2743, 2746, 2774, 2792,
    2821, 3164, 3460, 3557, 4177, 4446, 5768
Palau 2574, 3642
Palestinian Authority 1008, 1014, 2177, 2795,
    2796, 2822, 3067, 3106, 3420, 5351
Panama 3742, 4308
Papua New Guinea 1490, 3776
Paraguay 995, 2205, 4248, 4281, 5629
Pennsylvania 3514, 3528, 3938, 5031, 5918
Peru 143, 2399, 2754, 3545, 3947, 4132,
    4218, 4245, 4394, 4558, 5361, 5985
Philippines 25, 710, 1417, 1449, 1496, 1683,
    1959, 1961, 2511, 2743, 2771, 2792, 2971,
    3009, 3061, 3191, 3257, 3323, 3702,
    3747, 3776, 4165, 4631, 4935
Poland 960, 997, 1004, 1193, 1202, 1499,
    1852, 1906, 1934, 2009, 2140, 2217,
    2335, 2639, 2689, 2785, 2791, 2805,
    2835, 2837, 3420, 3444, 3450, 3495,
    3748, 3890, 4079, 4168, 4204, 4298,
    4781, 4966
Polynesia 2405, 4990
Portugal 58, 1865, 2653, 3196, 3267, 3367,
    3549, 3951, 4033, 4120, 4596, 5453,
    5494, 5921

PLACENAME INDEX

Puerto Rico 1221, 1224, 1819, 2232, 2752, 2906, 3250, 4257, 4296
Punjab 3473
Quebec 767, 956, 1035, 1795, 1990, 2047, 3423, 5265, 5386, 5755, 5903
Queensland 4166, 5125
Rajasthan 5200
Rhode Island 1815, 4076
Rio de Janeiro 3958
Rio Grande do Sul 791, 2628, 5192, 5209
Romania 1328, 1816, 3227, 3427, 3520
Russia 23, 35, 151, 162, 224, 249, 527, 710, 963, 1185, 1246, 1505, 1798, 2117, 2156, 2238, 2333, 2378, 2437, 2438, 2535, 2775, 2833, 2982, 3084, 3194, 3254, 3281, 3409, 3426, 3487, 3533, 3627, 3668, 3891, 4185, 4256, 4273, 4349, 4584, 4633, 4804, 5287, 5294, 5356, 5576, 5773, 5968
Russian Federation 1, 9, 36, 166, 966, 1000, 1373, 1392, 1421, 1436, 1527, 1529, 1618, 2088, 2372, 2529, 2534, 2538, 2606, 2630, 2637, 2649, 2685, 2687, 2719, 3105, 3425, 4168, 4292, 4295, 4429, 4573, 4593, 4970, 5092, 5154, 5281, 5284, 5293, 5297, 5333, 5359
see also: Chechnya
Rwanda 161, 3611, 5312
São Paulo 3958, 4031, 4121, 5098, 5192
Saudi Arabia 1520, 5215, 5291
Scandinavia 47, 173, 1452, 4222, 5342
Scotland 834, 1510, 1798, 2010, 2249, 2642, 3284, 3489, 3524, 3830, 3894, 3913, 3982, 3991, 4091, 4159, 4232, 4247, 4608, 4714, 5001, 5056, 5203, 5213, 5374, 5527, 5546, 5706, 5797, 5951
Senegal 2832, 3907
Serbia 967, 991, 4095, 5332
Siberia 1527, 1539, 3425
Singapore 1811, 1951, 2145, 2270, 2493, 2617, 3491, 3645, 3839, 4108, 4141, 4228, 4289, 4381, 4699, 4735, 4746, 5829
Slovakia 4, 62, 144, 983, 1764, 1812, 1816, 2364, 2411, 2686, 3585, 3870, 4930, 4974, 5214
Slovenia 987
Solomon Islands 3735, 3913, 4990
South Africa 13, 710, 839, 957, 964, 1008, 1507, 1756, 1813, 1838, 1841, 1942, 2163, 2212, 2288, 2321, 2523, 3171, 3319, 3349, 3395, 3430, 3438, 3471, 3510, 3599, 3633, 3649, 3654, 3769, 3810, 3828, 3852, 3935, 3963, 4096, 4101, 4282, 4313, 4422, 4558, 4650, 4864, 4971, 4975, 5097, 5148, 5200,
5260, 5363, 5442, 5684, 5701, 5703, 5809, 5813, 5858, 5905, 5937
South America 1170, 3624, 3702, 5250, 5363, 5950
see also: Amazon, Andes
South Asia 2870, 3557, 5622, 5969
South Australia 4849, 4998
South Carolina 3752
South China Sea 3776
South Korea 1222, 2141, 2145, 2586, 2984, 3949, 4048, 4228, 4250
Southeast Asia 1926, 2568, 3061, 3334, 3671, 3776, 4108, 4352, 5292, 5622, 5969
Southeast Europe 1731, 2695, 4095
Southern Africa 1760, 2379, 2754, 5442, 5964
Southern Europe 2320, 2530, 3538, 3639, 3656, 4596, 5250
Spain 161, 710, 978, 1000, 1485, 1503, 1626, 1795, 1823, 1839, 1865, 1869, 2043, 2414, 2573, 2801, 2929, 3075, 3115, 3176, 3575, 3606, 3706, 3726, 3758, 3767, 3826, 3891, 4099, 4212, 4261, 4439, 4469, 4471, 4595, 4596, 4775, 4983, 5290, 5622, 5789
see also: Catalonia
Spratly Islands 3776
Sri Lanka 1471, 3103, 3493, 3767, 5331
Sub-Saharan Africa 592, 2167, 2259, 2769, 2806, 3619, 3883, 4011, 4068, 4253, 4558, 5701, 5968, 5980
Sudan 1542, 4057, 5459
Sulawesi 3085
Swaziland 3208
Sweden 559, 816, 907, 1103, 2029, 2108, 2571, 2744, 2901, 2999, 3165, 3197, 3461, 3664, 3692, 3767, 3771, 4304, 4687, 4696, 4698, 4809, 4966, 5151, 5603, 5634, 5651, 5823
Switzerland 150, 1179, 1809, 2269, 2324, 2591, 3812, 3930, 4592, 4692, 4762, 5070, 5375, 5461
Syria 1522
Taiwan 1691, 1811, 1930, 2209, 2258, 2561, 2614, 3061, 3323, 3618, 3702, 4055, 4228, 4445, 4682, 4823, 5128, 5363, 5458, 5930
Tamil Nadu 2662, 2733
Tanzania 1709, 2041, 2113, 2234, 2727, 2797, 2978, 3234, 3708, 3733, 3876, 3966, 4611, 5777
Tasmania 2406
Texas 411, 3266, 4453
Thailand 1207, 2426, 2743, 2792, 3061, 3244, 3665, 3707, 3813, 4102, 5237, 5279, 5363, 5745

416

INDEX DES ENDROITS

Tibet 1464, 1699, 2973
Transcaucasia 3677
Tunisia 2792, 4171
Turkey 104, 1058, 1185, 1517, 1522, 1524, 1530, 1541, 1698, 1762, 1775, 1777, 2025, 2153, 2227, 2590, 2736, 3247, 4480, 4806, 5833
Turkmenistan 2153
U.S.A. 2, 14, 20, 38, 42, 44, 49, 53, 72, 152, 155, 162, 339, 389, 400, 419, 449, 455, 498, 507, 520, 522, 528, 531, 536, 541, 548, 550, 583, 603, 608, 633, 643, 676, 681, 724, 751, 756, 766, 781, 792, 802, 805, 838, 844, 846, 849, 852, 870, 876, 921, 976, 996, 1009, 1010, 1013, 1023, 1024, 1031, 1036, 1066, 1081, 1131, 1151, 1171, 1173, 1174, 1177, 1187, 1206, 1226, 1227, 1233, 1263, 1290, 1304, 1309, 1310, 1319, 1321, 1331, 1337, 1339, 1352, 1370, 1372, 1375, 1384, 1385, 1405, 1408, 1429, 1442, 1443, 1472, 1479, 1495, 1512, 1515, 1549, 1554, 1597, 1620, 1633, 1640, 1696, 1700, 1718, 1737, 1742, 1747, 1750, 1752, 1753, 1756, 1770, 1774, 1785, 1786, 1793, 1801, 1810, 1815, 1819, 1824, 1839, 1873, 1882, 1894, 1895, 1898, 1899, 1903, 1907-1909, 1927, 1929, 1932, 1967, 1974, 1976, 1987, 1991, 2009, 2011, 2021, 2023, 2024, 2026, 2028, 2036, 2045, 2051, 2060, 2062, 2068, 2069, 2077, 2079, 2080, 2083, 2104, 2129, 2138, 2142, 2145, 2146, 2151, 2174, 2179, 2181, 2182, 2192, 2200, 2206, 2211, 2213, 2214, 2226, 2243, 2260, 2266, 2270, 2296, 2328, 2335, 2341, 2346, 2347, 2353, 2356, 2361, 2371, 2378, 2383, 2386, 2405, 2410, 2418, 2425, 2449, 2451, 2454, 2479, 2482, 2489, 2492, 2504, 2506, 2513, 2522, 2530, 2551, 2559, 2571, 2579, 2582, 2608-2610, 2624, 2631, 2640, 2643, 2666, 2667, 2669, 2688, 2692, 2699, 2704, 2707, 2708, 2712, 2751, 2754, 2776, 2784, 2811, 2812, 2815, 2830, 2845, 2861, 2866, 2867, 2869, 2870, 2878, 2887, 2888, 2890, 2894, 2896, 2898, 2900, 2905, 2914, 2917, 2920, 2924, 2938, 2948, 2950, 2980, 2981, 2988, 2995, 2996, 3004, 3011-3013, 3024, 3026, 3027, 3058, 3077, 3099, 3111, 3115, 3120, 3121, 3167, 3179, 3180, 3182, 3188, 3201, 3216, 3218, 3219, 3225, 3240, 3245, 3250, 3253, 3264, 3270, 3282, 3290, 3292, 3328, 3331, 3338, 3340, 3352, 3357, 3361, 3362, 3386, 3389, 3391-3394, 3396, 3398, 3406, 3411, 3412, 3414, 3428, 3429, 3432-3435, 3437, 3439, 3449, 3456, 3457, 3459, 3468, 3471, 3478, 3481, 3488, 3498, 3506, 3515-3517, 3521, 3522, 3525, 3526, 3528, 3545, 3546, 3550, 3555, 3557, 3563, 3565, 3566, 3570-3572, 3577, 3578, 3580, 3585, 3591, 3600, 3603, 3614, 3617, 3625, 3630-3632, 3715, 3716, 3725, 3729, 3749, 3757, 3762, 3775, 3777, 3827, 3844, 3853, 3873, 3881, 3884, 3892, 3897, 3914, 3923, 3967, 3973, 3980, 3993, 3996, 3998, 4002, 4006, 4013, 4015, 4017, 4024, 4031, 4034, 4047, 4070, 4072, 4098, 4105, 4119, 4122, 4131, 4139, 4144, 4219, 4226, 4231, 4242, 4257, 4278, 4291, 4300, 4312, 4314, 4326, 4330, 4398, 4420, 4431, 4434, 4437-4440, 4449, 4453, 4459, 4464, 4470, 4472, 4473, 4479, 4484, 4489, 4490, 4492, 4493, 4497, 4499, 4505, 4512, 4531, 4534, 4539, 4549, 4555, 4568, 4588, 4591, 4612, 4618, 4619, 4631, 4651, 4676, 4681, 4707, 4717, 4720, 4752, 4755, 4760, 4768, 4832, 4834, 4839, 4843, 4847, 4853, 4856, 4860, 4867, 4875, 4876, 4888, 4919, 4933, 4935, 4978, 4997, 4999, 5000, 5004, 5008, 5010-5012, 5014, 5017, 5018, 5022, 5027, 5033, 5038, 5046, 5050, 5052, 5062, 5066, 5067, 5069, 5073, 5074, 5079, 5081, 5083, 5085, 5087, 5090, 5095, 5099, 5103, 5108, 5109, 5113, 5115, 5128, 5150, 5154, 5155, 5157, 5160, 5171, 5172, 5175, 5183, 5190, 5193, 5232, 5234, 5244, 5251-5254, 5256, 5258, 5280, 5288, 5292, 5308, 5315, 5319, 5340, 5344, 5345, 5347, 5350, 5358, 5371, 5379, 5382, 5386, 5396, 5397, 5409, 5421, 5435, 5436, 5441, 5450, 5454, 5465, 5471, 5472, 5479, 5481, 5498, 5519-5521, 5535, 5552, 5553, 5555, 5563, 5567, 5569, 5573, 5575, 5577, 5578, 5581, 5582, 5587, 5594, 5597, 5613, 5618, 5620, 5625, 5633, 5636, 5654, 5656, 5658, 5661, 5669, 5693, 5725, 5726, 5732, 5748, 5782, 5788, 5794, 5804, 5810, 5811, 5816, 5818, 5835, 5839, 5840, 5844, 5872, 5873, 5883, 5885, 5889, 5898, 5904, 5913, 5924, 5928, 5931, 5947, 5959-5961, 5971, 5978
see also: Alabama, Alaska, Arizona, California, Colorado, Connecticut, Florida, Georgia (U.S.A.), Hawaii, Idaho,

PLACENAME INDEX

Illinois, Iowa, Louisiana, Maine, Maryland, Michigan, Minnesota, Mississippi, Nebraska, Nevada, New Jersey, New Mexico, New York, North Carolina, Ohio, Pennsylvania, Rhode Island, South Carolina, Texas, Vermont, Virginia, Washington, Wisconsin
U.S.S.R. 23, 166, 1000, 1221, 2123, 2333, 2637, 3547, 3559, 3564, 3601, 4185, 4349, 5335, 5360
see also: Azerbaijan, Belarus, Estonia, Georgia, Kyrgyzstan, Latvia, Moldova, Russia, Turkmenistan, Ukraine
Uganda 2778, 3654, 4975
Ukraine 3495, 4573, 5214
United Arab Emirates 1126
United Kingdom 41, 43, 75, 78-80, 91, 95, 102, 103, 171, 174, 182, 327, 437, 576, 742, 763, 765, 955, 998, 1005, 1053, 1103, 1110, 1119, 1147, 1156, 1178, 1227, 1233, 1269, 1270, 1304, 1305, 1312, 1327, 1331, 1337, 1340, 1384, 1419, 1450, 1474, 1532, 1535, 1548, 1558, 1673, 1685, 1687, 1688, 1718, 1719, 1726, 1731, 1734, 1736, 1744, 1745, 1751, 1756, 1761, 1766, 1767, 1770, 1782, 1821, 1839, 1882, 1884, 1891, 1918, 1955, 1968, 1973, 1974, 1980, 2002, 2016, 2019, 2030, 2031, 2042, 2050, 2056, 2066, 2076, 2095, 2098, 2099, 2132, 2139, 2143, 2150, 2161, 2170, 2179, 2180, 2187, 2207, 2218, 2220, 2225, 2237, 2247, 2262, 2267, 2270, 2273, 2274, 2283, 2287, 2305, 2326, 2356, 2377, 2378, 2387, 2390, 2404, 2419, 2442, 2454, 2455, 2457, 2458, 2463, 2466-2470, 2475, 2496, 2532, 2602, 2604, 2605, 2607, 2623, 2647, 2673, 2674, 2676, 2709, 2757, 2768, 2807, 2826, 2840, 2865, 2870, 2929, 2958, 2999, 3057, 3059, 3067, 3069, 3078, 3102, 3111, 3127, 3141, 3161, 3172, 3177, 3183, 3189, 3198, 3217, 3241, 3265, 3284, 3288, 3292, 3354, 3356, 3358, 3371, 3386, 3397, 3422, 3433, 3458, 3460, 3509, 3523, 3527, 3539, 3557, 3598, 3620, 3622, 3629, 3641, 3650, 3660, 3679, 3703, 3744, 3765, 3775, 3778, 3781, 3791, 3825-3827, 3829, 3846, 3861, 3872, 3880, 3886, 3900, 3916, 3937, 3965, 3977, 3981, 3983, 3985, 4027, 4028, 4040, 4041, 4051, 4056, 4059, 4062, 4063, 4082, 4089, 4094, 4109, 4123, 4125, 4129, 4138, 4145, 4159, 4283, 4344, 4392, 4398, 4402, 4439, 4472, 4476, 4486, 4487, 4491, 4496, 4500, 4501, 4521, 4541, 4554, 4563, 4576, 4579, 4587, 4589, 4594, 4612, 4618, 4628, 4646, 4655, 4659, 4696, 4704, 4769, 4774, 4782-4784, 4788, 4798, 4800, 4812, 4816, 4830, 4831, 4840, 4852, 4857, 4865, 4868, 4871, 4873-4875, 4878, 4882, 4962, 4966, 4980, 4986, 4996, 5006, 5008, 5010, 5015, 5019, 5023, 5027, 5032, 5035, 5041, 5042, 5047, 5054, 5082, 5097, 5107, 5108, 5124, 5126, 5135, 5136, 5140, 5142, 5145-5147, 5186, 5190, 5221, 5255, 5295, 5333, 5364, 5366, 5367, 5380, 5392, 5402, 5418, 5422, 5424, 5431, 5471, 5474, 5476, 5483, 5485, 5497, 5499, 5502, 5530, 5533, 5536, 5539, 5544-5549, 5551, 5556, 5557, 5559, 5566, 5574, 5580, 5584, 5585, 5588, 5591, 5599, 5602, 5604, 5609, 5617, 5624, 5628, 5635, 5639, 5644, 5646, 5647, 5657, 5661, 5663, 5665, 5666, 5672-5675, 5679, 5696, 5697, 5702, 5705, 5709-5711, 5713, 5718, 5738-5740, 5743, 5747, 5750, 5753, 5754, 5760, 5762, 5769, 5772, 5778, 5779, 5781, 5784, 5795, 5803, 5820, 5822, 5824, 5832, 5834, 5841, 5900, 5904, 5927, 5932, 5938, 5946, 5948, 5963, 5976
see also: Channel Islands, England, Northern Ireland, Scotland, Wales
Uruguay 5642
Uttar Pradesh 4415
Venezuela 5973
Vermont 5578
Vietnam 545, 975, 1933, 1987, 2675, 2680, 2777, 2927, 2944, 3010, 3479, 3607, 3640, 3702, 3915, 4108, 4176, 4178, 4694, 5759
Virgin Islands (U.S.A.) 3399
Virginia 4667
Wales 962, 998, 1756, 2106, 2831, 2843, 3284, 4521, 5132, 5645
Washington 5744
West Africa 3852
West Bengal 2652, 2770, 2800, 3243
Western Europe 101, 1000, 1375, 1519, 2357, 2794, 3916, 4226, 4652
Wisconsin 3406
Yugoslavia 1000, 1730, 1749, 3485, 3493, 3586, 3595, 3660, 4946, 5343
see also: Bosnia and Herzegovina, Croatia, Kosovo, Serbia, Slovenia
Zambia 2148, 2792, 3209, 3674, 4558, 5966

INDEX DES ENDROITS

Zimbabwe 427, 1409, 2148, 2453, 2792, 3210, 3279, 3311, 3649, 4560, 5363, 5442, 5746, 5777, 5974, 5975

SUBJECT INDEX
INDEX DES MATIÈRES EN ANGLAIS

Ability 663, 2084, 2253, 3049
Ability grouping 2014
Abolition of slavery 951
Abolitionism 2, 4984
Aborigines 1769, 3446, 3482, 3486, 3827, 4056, 4445, 5170, 5413
Abortion 1650, 2696, 2724, 2727, 2730, 2734, 2744, 2745, 2750, 2754, 2758, 2760, 2764, 2769, 3337, 4939, 5200, 5851, 5868, 5873, 5888
Abraham, Karl 593
Absenteeism 4698, 4700, 4708, 5345
Absolutism 241
Academic achievement 479, 700, 862, 1626, 1992, 2005, 2008, 2014, 2017, 2020, 2024, 2027, 2032-2034, 2036, 2037, 2041, 2043, 2045, 2047, 2059-2061, 2063, 2068, 2070-2072, 2074, 2075, 2077, 2090, 2097, 2108, 2158, 2162, 2239, 2245, 2253, 2266, 2267, 2482, 2615, 2632, 2642, 2947, 3019, 3177, 3414, 3446, 3643, 4432, 4435, 4438, 4764, 4794, 4800, 5612, 5704
Academic discipline 5, 11, 38, 44, 53, 67, 167, 170, 183, 195, 339, 1491, 1556, 2207, 2216, 2255, 3115, 3232, 3545, 3788, 4413, 5206
Academic freedom 13, 225, 2280, 2295
Academic profession 1, 13, 28, 43, 47, 50, 53, 66, 67, 309, 438, 996, 1217, 1422, 1594, 1618, 2014, 2018, 2091, 2118, 2242, 2281, 2282, 2591, 3179, 3545, 3780, 4383, 4564, 4714, 4766, 5281, 5710
Academic success 2027, 2070, 2090, 2158, 2163, 2276, 2924, 3057, 3183, 4564, 4800
Access to culture 2481
Access to education 93, 2005, 2010, 2015, 2016, 2018, 2019, 2022, 2024, 2025, 2030, 2031, 2035, 2036, 2038, 2039, 2042, 2049, 2052, 2057, 2062, 2064, 2066, 2069, 2092, 2109, 2112, 2114, 2123, 2136, 2145, 2147, 2266, 2273, 2460, 2513, 2548, 2677
Access to employment 4755
Access to health care 2727, 3185, 3327, 4087, 5019, 5575, 5731, 5743, 5751, 5759, 5763, 5766, 5768, 5769, 5774, 5780, 5788, 5792, 5805, 5809, 5811, 5814, 5891, 5915
Access to information 79, 80, 104, 2757, 4320, 4933, 5869
Accidents 2816, 2826, 2844, 5967
Accountability 411, 1029, 1030, 1742, 2097, 4310, 4621, 4906, 5139, 5749, 5854
see also: Transparency
Accountants 2072, 4310, 4720
Accounting 2072, 2097, 4310, 4604, 5789
see also: Business accounting, National accounting, Social accounting
Accounting methods 4310
Accounting research 4310
Acculturation 569, 805, 806, 1246, 1320, 2511, 2552, 2887, 2915, 3405, 3440, 3546, 3547, 3595, 5529, 5908
see also: Immigrant acculturation
Achievement 892, 3391
Achievement motivation
see: Academic achievement
Action research 427, 3118
Action theory 363, 371, 373
Activism 71, 1025, 1479, 1532, 2468, 3061, 3112, 3115, 3138, 3152, 3389, 3454, 3507, 3749, 3772, 3863, 4861, 4868, 4883, 4956, 4960, 5228, 5230, 5251, 5270, 5274, 5278
Activists 1939, 3078, 3134, 3777, 4935, 5171, 5230, 5247, 5254, 5278, 5885
Activity analysis 1210
Actors 310, 323, 854, 1882, 2082, 2375, 2677, 3223, 3693, 3799, 4171, 4837
Acupuncture 5859
Adaptation to change 3708
Addiction 625, 723, 897, 1684, 2874, 2894, 4747, 5374, 5376-5379, 5381, 5382, 5384, 5385, 5387, 5389, 5391, 5395, 5396, 5398, 5399, 5402-5408, 5412, 5413, 5421, 5664, 5744, 5818, 5901
see also: Drug addiction

SUBJECT INDEX

Addicts 723, 5374, 5376, 5395, 5396, 5406
　see also: Drug addicts
Administration 2040, 2137, 2138, 2247, 2286, 2296, 3832, 4178, 4655, 4780, 5224, 5555, 5755, 5758
　see also: Education administration, Health administration, Public administration, School administration, Social administration
Administration of justice 426, 4982, 5000, 5006, 5013, 5014, 5021, 5022, 5025, 5026, 5028, 5043, 5101, 5136, 5149, 5175, 5181, 5186, 5193, 5195, 5370
Administrative control 3869, 3871, 4406
Administrative organization 5758
Administrative reform 4635, 4963, 5220
Administrative science 1037, 1087, 4623, 4641, 4670, 4690
Adolescence 554, 598, 679, 700, 2517, 2596, 2611, 2615, 2618, 2625, 2632, 2635, 2641, 2648, 2896, 2951, 3052, 3056, 3225, 4139, 5384, 5394, 5405, 5410
Adolescents 77, 545, 576, 577, 598, 633, 776, 849, 2074, 2482, 2494, 2602, 2611-2613, 2615, 2616, 2619, 2621, 2623, 2624, 2628, 2629, 2631, 2633, 2636, 2638, 2640, 2642, 2644-2647, 2667, 2727, 2803, 2804, 2853, 2896, 2897, 2916, 2936, 2947, 2954, 2963, 2995, 3041, 3053, 3212, 3213, 3271, 3294, 3300, 3328, 3337, 3352, 3414, 3521, 3554, 4435, 4996, 5036, 5044, 5046, 5052, 5062, 5079, 5089, 5095, 5192, 5200, 5364, 5373, 5429, 5447, 5671, 5680, 5721, 5767, 5906, 5935, 5941, 5978, 5985
Adopted children 2952, 3433
Adornments 3315
Adorno, Theodor W. 213, 1227, 1853, 1988
Adult education 93, 1991, 2005, 2006, 2010, 2016, 2031, 2040, 2049, 2113, 2127, 2145, 2272
Adulthood 2600, 2618, 2930, 3026, 5394
Adults 623, 637, 661, 670, 738, 900, 918, 1544, 1716, 2002, 2592, 2676, 2834, 2909, 3022, 3237, 3352, 4548, 4793, 5054, 5675
Advertising 1227, 1317, 1710, 1738, 1754, 1757, 1759, 1772, 1782, 2094, 2419, 2667, 3059, 3092, 3228, 3264, 3553, 4319, 4320, 4324, 4341, 4343, 5833, 5946, 5956
Aesthetics 2, 7, 30, 117, 241, 278, 300, 320, 340, 351, 573, 938, 1124, 1189, 1279, 1310, 1311, 1323, 1331, 1338, 1573, 1602, 1848, 1850, 1851, 1853, 1854, 1864, 1868, 1876, 1878, 1988, 2477, 2504, 3698, 4344, 4911
Aeta 3776
Affectivity 739, 850, 937
Affiliation 2667, 3344
　see also: Political affiliation, Religious affiliation
Affirmative action 2017, 2055, 2061, 2415, 3517
African National Congress 3349
African organizations 4611
African studies 71, 1482, 1976, 2121, 3326
African-Americans 53, 541, 583, 681, 814, 826, 838, 849, 852, 1321, 1372, 1427, 1429, 1442, 1479, 1620, 1750, 1909, 1991, 2036, 2045, 2060, 2174, 2266, 2530, 2582, 2655, 2751, 2856, 2898, 2917, 2991, 3024, 3043, 3058, 3098, 3115, 3352, 3391, 3412, 3431, 3432, 3439, 3440, 3442, 3456, 3457, 3477, 3478, 3481, 3488, 3498, 3506, 3514, 3521, 3528, 3572, 3632, 3938, 3993, 3996, 4000, 4006, 4015, 4278, 4291, 4300, 4473, 4489, 4497, 4505, 4511, 4919, 5050, 5103, 5280, 5397, 5409, 5563, 5928, 5947
Africans 199, 592, 1204, 1476, 1620, 1813, 2167, 2379, 2429, 2502, 3457, 3468, 3528, 3551, 3562, 3593, 3649, 3736, 4500, 5244, 5328
Afrikaaners 1813
Afro-Brazilian 1431
Age 441, 559, 624, 2231, 2431, 2669, 2744, 2785, 2791, 2805, 2992, 5012, 5096, 5120, 5392, 5838
　see also: Old age
Age at marriage 2691, 2724, 2797, 2825, 2851, 2955, 2961, 2963, 2976, 2992
Age difference 682, 4752, 5093
Age discrimination 2665, 2670, 2702, 4487, 4488, 4852
Age distribution 2089, 2712, 2967
Age groups 534, 1768, 2587, 2597, 2616, 2618, 2620, 2648, 2681, 2724, 2827, 2835, 2852, 2893, 3606, 3620, 3625, 4362, 4581, 4752, 4852, 5432, 5610
Aged 162, 1284, 1687, 2584, 2585, 2651, 2653-2655, 2657, 2659-2664, 2666-2675, 2677-2679, 2682, 2707, 2712, 2811, 2815, 2829, 3219, 3591, 3619, 4303, 4487, 4558, 4852, 5016, 5070, 5493, 5495-5501, 5504, 5506, 5508, 5509, 5511, 5514, 5516-5519, 5521, 5522, 5524-5526, 5528-5535, 5609, 5644, 5738, 5778
　see also: Care of the aged

INDEX DES MATIÈRES EN ANGLAIS

Ageing 612, 716, 1647, 2532, 2583, 2584, 2588, 2590, 2651, 2652, 2654, 2659, 2664-2668, 2670, 2672-2674, 2676, 2678-2680, 2707, 2801, 3272, 4558, 4581, 5479, 5492-5494, 5498, 5502, 5503, 5507, 5508, 5510, 5516, 5518-5520, 5525, 5531, 5532, 5602, 5738, 5740
Agency 162, 306, 308, 313, 320, 345, 358, 391, 407, 677, 709, 793, 1087, 1090, 1437, 1535, 1651, 2361, 3124, 3146, 3147, 3373, 3847, 3918, 4344, 4392, 4515, 4837, 4958, 5438, 5462, 5495, 5849
Aggression 576, 672, 727, 872, 925, 1807, 2876, 2877, 2894, 2931, 3031, 3038, 3201, 3344, 3351, 3531, 4187, 4626, 5192, 5437, 5444, 5456
Agrarian movements 5245
Agrarian reform 3918, 4248, 4949, 5245, 5363
Agrarian society 3889
Agricultural areas 3813
Agricultural development 3889, 3922
Agricultural economics 3889
Agricultural finance 3852
Agricultural history 2715, 3882, 3889
Agricultural industry 3760
Agricultural intensification 3733
Agricultural investment 3922
Agricultural labour 513
Agricultural policy 3760, 3878, 3880, 4142
Agricultural production 3731, 3760, 3875, 3889, 4206, 4240, 4243, 4674, 5948
Agricultural productivity 3890
Agricultural products 4331
Agricultural research 4246
Agricultural sector 3880
Agricultural systems 3879, 4775
Agricultural workers 1359, 2886, 3889, 4558, 4674, 4775
Agriculture 20, 2511, 3708, 3731, 3735, 3873, 3883, 3888, 3889, 3902, 3912, 4142, 4208, 4212, 4674
see also: Agricultural systems, Sharecropping
Aid 767, 2167, 4287, 5349, 5475, 5977
see also: Development aid, Financial aid, Foreign aid, Health aid
Aid institutions 5330
AIDS 489, 581, 781, 1883, 2754, 2797, 2806, 2810, 2824, 3299, 3316, 3326, 3332, 3334, 3349, 3370, 4611, 5363, 5745, 5764, 5773, 5854, 5866, 5872, 5885, 5890, 5891, 5893, 5894, 5944-5946, 5952, 5957, 5965, 5966, 5968, 5974, 5980, 5982
Air force 4614, 4760
Air traffic 4729

Airlines 3927
Airports 3948
Alcohol 908, 1349, 2515, 2612, 2816, 2819, 2824, 4493, 4994, 5045, 5364, 5368, 5385, 5388, 5390, 5392, 5399, 5400, 5403-5406, 5409, 5411, 5413, 5433, 5444, 5818, 5955, 5968
Alcoholism 709, 722, 1349, 2719, 2874, 2894, 4493, 4683, 5045, 5376, 5386, 5388, 5393, 5399, 5400, 5403-5406, 5408, 5410, 5413, 5681, 5767, 5838, 5955
Alexander, Jeffrey 341
Algebra 5029
Algorithms 440, 446, 1043, 1056, 2301, 4755, 5390
Alienation 388, 785, 1677, 1933, 2018, 2634, 5016, 5372
Alliances 1032, 2289
Allison, Dorothy 3125
Allocation of power 2321
Allport, Floyd 870
Allport, Gordon 870
Alternative medicine 5839, 5859, 5900
Althusser, Louis 3130
Altman, Robert 1907
Altruism 61, 601, 649, 915, 931, 949, 1073, 1532, 1684, 2332, 3843, 4194, 4768, 5106, 5575, 5826, 5860
Alzheimer's disease 5529
Ambedkar, Bhimrao Ramji 2394
Ambition 2646, 4582
American Civil War 1263
American studies 1243
Americanization 1895, 2569, 5308
Americans 826, 864, 1187, 1929, 3043, 3098, 3218, 3393, 4463
Amerindians 982, 1620, 1991, 2399, 2751, 3402, 5563
see also: North Amerindians
Analytical philosophy 114, 137, 258, 290, 1231
Anarchism 3295
Anarchists 3295
Anatomy 3109
Ancestry 952, 3589
Ancient history 151
Anglicanism 1409
Animal domestication 2342
Animal experimentation 2342
Animal husbandry 2342, 4142
Animal products 1293, 2342
Animal rights 1296, 1297, 2342, 5258
Animals 386, 561, 1293, 2863, 3926, 4637
see also: Animal rights, Domestic animals
Anonymity 1066, 1862, 3468

423

SUBJECT INDEX

Anorexia nervosa 506, 769, 791, 817, 2667, 5182, 5847
Anthropocentrism 3743
Anthropological analysis 331, 2683, 3540
Anthropological methodology 526, 3143, 3545
see also: Participant observation
Anthropological research 135, 3545
Anthropological theory 14, 109, 381, 449, 929, 1395, 2544
Anthropology 16, 25, 27, 54, 348, 603, 605, 801, 1197, 1802, 3121, 3363, 3499, 3693, 3758, 5338, 5727
see also: Applied anthropology, Cultural anthropology, Historical anthropology, Industrial anthropology, Linguistic anthropology, Medical anthropology, Philosophical anthropology, Physical anthropology, Political anthropology, Rural anthropology, Social anthropology, Sociological anthropology, Urban anthropology, Visual anthropology
Anthropology of law 5170
Anthropology of religion 1433, 1455, 1464, 1483, 1506, 1509
Anthropology of sport 1357
Anthropology of the body 1189
Anthropology of work 59, 2574
Anthropometry 3210
Anti-colonialism 5226
Anti-communism 1262
Anti-imperialism 4935
Anti-nuclear movements 5275
Anti-Semitism 145, 235, 410, 1963, 3455, 3466, 3502, 3518, 3532
Anti-social behaviour 749, 754, 849, 2154, 2235, 3031, 5030, 5051, 5069, 5078, 5393, 5538, 5617
Anxiety 593, 637, 685, 721, 731, 740, 757, 780, 787, 797, 802, 810, 821, 933, 935, 1006, 1173, 1347, 1927, 2646, 2970, 3023, 3870, 3930, 4710, 4724, 5080, 5681, 5710, 5831
Apartheid 2321, 3510, 3769, 4864, 5260, 5703, 5937
see also: Post-apartheid society
APEC 2145
Apostasy 1392, 1494
Appadurai, Arjun 1409
Appeals
see: Court of appeal
Apples 3912
Applied anthropology 5924
Applied general equilibrium models 4045

Applied psychology 546, 550, 556, 627, 661, 663, 798, 814, 886, 891, 1065, 1118, 2335, 4412, 4588, 4614, 4638, 4675, 4701, 4717, 4760, 4802, 5157, 5752
Applied research 90, 443
Applied sociology 67
Apprenticeship 4590
Aptitude 4651
Aptitude tests 2214
Arab-Israeli conflict 1014, 1026, 1791, 2619, 2795, 3664
Arabic language 1802, 1822, 1914, 1932, 1966, 2126
Arabs 280, 753, 1932, 2619, 2885, 3115, 3393, 3462, 5908
Arbitration 1019, 2554, 4844
Archaeology 123, 3121
Architects 1849, 1857, 3973, 4131
Architecture 1849, 1857, 1859, 3854, 3941, 3945, 3962, 3973, 3984, 4026, 4028, 4039, 4094, 4126, 4131, 4941
see also: Urban architecture
Archives 32, 172, 183, 1884, 5123
Arciniegas, Germán 159
Arendt, Hannah 232, 293, 1251, 4911, 5311
Argyris, C. 1095
Aristocracy 2439, 3891, 4954
Aristotle 201, 286, 1555, 1650
Armed conflict 3859, 5318, 5327, 5343, 5346, 5353, 5362, 5445
Armed forces 4549, 5339, 5342, 5344, 5346, 5347, 5352-5354, 5356, 5357, 5359, 5361, 5362
Armenians 1990
Armies 1813, 5338, 5339, 5352, 5359
Arnason, Johann P. 1253
Arnauld, Antoine 106
Arranged marriage 3265
Arrest 2868, 5031, 5052, 5137
Art 202, 241, 579, 1207, 1266, 1279, 1298, 1311, 1342, 1345, 1848, 1850-1855, 1859, 1867-1869, 1873, 1876, 1878, 1890, 1895, 1911, 1937, 1971, 1977, 3139, 4121
see also: Contemporary art, History of art, Performing arts, Philosophy of art, Sociology of art, Visual arts, Works of art
Art galleries 2573
Art market 4219, 4752
Art theory 1848, 1866, 1869
Artifacts 2315
Artificial intelligence 481, 1234, 1576
Artisans 971, 1616, 4263
Artistic tradition 1861
Artists 1852, 1861, 1863, 1868, 1901, 1904, 3115, 4767

INDEX DES MATIÈRES EN ANGLAIS

Arts 1260, 1724, 1739, 1866, 1880, 1963, 3827, 4144, 4954, 5232
Ashkenazi 3483
Asian and Pacific languages 1805
Asian studies 1483, 1506, 2992
Asian-Americans 1987, 2751, 2866, 2950, 3394, 3459, 3578, 5081, 5577, 5898
Asians 676, 710, 771, 1929, 2008, 2917, 2936, 3115, 3218, 3234, 3265, 3323, 3509, 3521, 3524, 3559, 3570, 3673, 3846, 5928
Aspirations 2317, 2425, 2649, 4527, 4781, 5592
Assistance 5895
Associations 408, 2088, 3362, 4385, 4767, 4940, 4950, 4960, 5491
Astrology 1416
Astronomy 1555
Asylum 1177, 2313, 3354, 3680
  see also: Right of asylum
Atheism 1373, 1428, 1451
Athletes 1305, 1344, 1354, 3217, 4767
Atlases 91, 3769
Attention 670, 1717
Attitude formation 520, 676, 851
Attitude scale 890, 3749
Attitudes 117, 142, 228, 485, 524, 527, 549, 574, 582, 648, 676, 696, 714, 763, 791, 823, 825-827, 835, 842, 845, 851, 852, 859-861, 863, 865, 876, 884, 885, 890, 891, 898, 916, 941, 978, 983, 1004, 1034, 1052, 1063, 1111, 1119, 1126, 1135, 1285, 1297, 1437, 1511, 1531, 1710, 1747, 1750, 1774, 1789, 1820, 1821, 1993, 2009, 2086, 2106, 2186, 2235, 2245, 2313, 2357, 2389, 2396-2398, 2417, 2425, 2452, 2473, 2474, 2476, 2487, 2523, 2524, 2538, 2585, 2601, 2619, 2628, 2629, 2636, 2640, 2643, 2652, 2726, 2770, 2778, 2868, 2917, 2922, 2991, 3011, 3046, 3178, 3215, 3221, 3237, 3239, 3274, 3283, 3295, 3296, 3455, 3464, 3470, 3522, 3545, 3547, 3552, 3565, 3601, 3610, 3633, 3674, 3724, 3729, 3734, 3743, 3748, 3749, 3853, 3914, 3930, 3993, 4320, 4360, 4370, 4487, 4527, 4581, 4658, 4670, 4716, 4744, 4747, 4748, 4785, 4793, 4837, 4839, 4914, 5012, 5056, 5083, 5154, 5244, 5290, 5298, 5328, 5407, 5409, 5414, 5419, 5446, 5503, 5560, 5643, 5669, 5829, 5838, 5878, 5891, 5919, 5941
  see also: Management attitudes, Political attitudes, Racial attitudes
Attitudes to work 4356, 4702, 4704, 4745

Audience 425, 449, 1191, 1712, 1716, 1717, 1727, 1733, 1763, 1774, 1776, 1852, 1889, 1897
Auditing 3195-3198, 4355, 4773, 5023
Augustine [Saint] 232, 293
Authoritarian regimes 1467, 5266
Authoritarianism 860, 1674, 4250, 5250, 5303
Authority 203, 1597, 2338, 2515, 3285, 3392, 4199, 4325, 4558, 4662, 4978, 4993, 5052, 5117, 5850, 5883
  see also: Political authority, Religious authorities
Authors 281, 1158, 1187, 1419, 1557, 1913, 1914, 1920, 1932, 1937-1939, 1941, 1943, 1962, 1966, 2282, 2314, 3098, 3122, 3518
Autobiography 181, 283, 1882, 1888, 1938, 1950, 2625, 2651, 2679, 3107, 3250, 4558
Automobile industry 1129, 4617, 4618, 4811
Automobiles 1129, 2816, 4146, 4313
Autonomy 203, 978, 2143, 2147, 2242, 2293, 2347, 3070, 3279, 5267, 5889
Averroes 272
Aznar, José María 1839
Bacon, Francis 1611
Baha'i 1446
Bakhtin, Mikhail 162, 224, 378
Balance of power 1030, 3210, 4354
Bangladeshis 3523, 4500
Bank operations 4705
Bankers 4349
Banking 2507, 3246, 4346, 4348, 4349
Bankruptcy
  see: Personal insolvency
Banks 1091, 1103, 4349, 4541, 4662, 4862
  see also: Commercial banks, World Bank
Bantu 1813, 1822
Baptism 1490, 2901
Bargaining 944, 999, 1006, 1010, 1012, 1015, 1017, 1018, 1021, 1022, 1024, 1040, 1049, 1055, 1084, 1345, 1704, 1829, 2079, 2908, 3472, 4690, 4751, 4837, 4868, 5184
  see also: Collective bargaining, Wage negotiations
Barker, Clive 1920
Barnes, Barry 1610
Bartlett, Frederic C. 868
Baseball 1308
Basic education 1991, 2144
Basic needs 361, 2495, 3827, 3840, 4251, 4299, 5422, 5701, 5979
  see also: Housing needs
Basic rights 2349, 2495, 2754, 4299, 4423, 4433, 4933, 4950, 5188, 5852, 5879, 5929, 5930, 5972

425

SUBJECT INDEX

Basques 1865
Baudrillard, Jean 357, 1227, 3096
Bauman, Zygmunt 305, 335, 1281
Bayesian method 446, 451, 468, 2818, 2831
Beauvoir, Simone de 283
Beck, Ulrich 1609
Bedouin 2054
Beef 5948
Beef market 5948
Beef production 5948
Beggars 5428
Behaviour in groups 2566
Behavioural disorders 545, 591, 756, 2892, 3032, 3050, 5405, 5468, 5901, 5906, 5918
Behavioural sciences 42, 365, 422, 442, 549, 564, 572, 591, 609, 648, 699, 703, 737, 798, 870, 1089, 1125, 2877, 5094, 5799, 5891
Behaviourism 591, 594, 599, 667, 699, 822, 855, 1299
Beliefs 8, 107, 136, 138, 141, 228, 230, 298, 352, 549, 580, 639, 650, 657, 694, 847, 857, 860, 880, 1052, 1300, 1374, 1375, 1383, 1421, 1490, 1606, 1846, 2035, 2198, 2209, 2360, 2655, 3145, 3406, 3724, 3726, 3758, 4221, 4408, 4421, 4425, 5128, 5529, 5962
  see also: Folk beliefs, Medical beliefs, Religious beliefs
Bell, Daniel 2540
Belsey, Catherine 3102
Ben-Gurion, David 1916
Benefit plans 4293
Bengali 4575
Benigni, Roberto 1896
Benjamin, Walter 213, 299
Bentham, Jeremy 4987
Bereavement 716, 724, 815, 819, 948, 2910, 2942, 5721
Berlin, Isaiah 2143
Bhaskar, Roy 140
Bias 109, 460, 507, 512, 806, 832, 837, 881, 1005, 2250, 5235
Bible 145, 169, 1375, 3743
Bibliographies 36, 72, 101, 1667, 3290, 4686, 5076
Biculturalism 956
Bidding 1073
Bilateral relations 2559
Bilingual education 1785, 2050
Bilingualism 610, 1785, 1789, 1809, 1811, 1819, 1836, 2461, 3595
Biodiversity 225, 2711, 3705, 3712, 3737, 3747, 3759, 3798

Bioethics 1039, 1620, 5025, 5730, 5848, 5854, 5861, 5865, 5868, 5880, 5882, 5884, 5888
Biographies 36, 41, 72, 74, 103, 178, 240, 316, 376, 412, 501, 508, 1735, 1853, 1863, 1882, 1893, 1914, 1916, 1934, 1939, 1952, 1960, 1964, 2479, 3094, 4580, 5420, 5944
Biological weapons 5988
Biologists 27, 1578
Biology 236, 396, 598, 1606, 2902, 3083, 3109, 5388, 5406, 5851
  see also: Human biology
Biomedicine 1620, 5817, 5853, 5859, 5962, 5980
Bion, Wilfred R. 225
Biopolitics 5379
Biotechnology 1099, 1563, 1610, 4246, 5864
Birds 3710, 4767
Birth 551, 796, 800, 807, 2632, 2728, 2757, 2758, 2771, 2776, 2791, 2803, 2812, 2832, 2839, 2962, 2971, 2998, 3000, 3046, 5578, 5610, 5782, 5843
Birth control 2706, 2708, 2710, 2729, 2731, 2732, 2740, 2743, 2749, 2750, 2760, 2779, 3079, 3312
Birth intervals 2766
Birth order 653, 698
Birth rate 2686, 2689, 2705, 2706, 2714, 2719, 2728, 2777, 2779, 2784, 2785, 2795, 2798, 2800, 2805
Birth spacing 2822
Bisexuality 786, 3297, 3340, 3352, 3357, 3373, 3381, 5984
Black market 4373
Black politics 3506
Blacks 53, 579, 710, 835, 1367, 1474, 1479, 1813, 1903, 1917, 2017, 2034, 2060, 2080, 2110, 2161, 2856, 3115, 3412, 3440, 3442, 3454, 3464, 3468, 3478, 3519, 3834, 3835, 3901, 3978, 3981, 3993, 4000, 4015, 4278, 4438, 4489, 4490, 4492, 4497, 4559, 4865, 5031, 5053, 5129, 5142, 5148, 5328, 5454, 5947
Blacksmiths 4781
Blasphemy 1867
Blindness 2481, 2493, 2494
  see also: Colour blindness
Blood 5860
Bloor, David 1610
Blue collar workers 4618
Blumenberg, Hans 1251
Body techniques 3272
Boer War 957
Bogdanov, Aleksandr 1553
Boland, Eavan 1936

INDEX DES MATIÈRES EN ANGLAIS

Bonding 1499
Bonds 3115, 4350
Book industry 1557
Books 1323, 1557, 1924
Border regions 987, 1798, 3468, 3768
Borders 173, 987, 1772, 2544, 2953, 3135, 3542, 3630, 3639, 3672, 4440, 4811, 4966
  see also: Border regions
Boredom 4710
Bouglé, Célestin 2395
Bourdieu, Pierre 341, 377, 401, 406, 1212, 1409, 3153, 3509
Bourgeoisie 4273
Bowen, M. 1006
Boycott 4331
Boys 2878, 3216, 3264
Brahmanism 2394, 4207
Brain 571, 591, 628, 630, 739, 5406
Brain drain 1806, 3629, 3633
Brands 1439, 4343
Brandt, Richard 2361
Braverman, Harry 4400
Breast-feeding 3003, 3027, 3258, 4534, 5969
Brecht, Bertholt 1756
Breweries 4323
Brides 2885
British Empire 188
Britons 763
Broadcasting 1683, 1697, 1698, 1718, 1721, 1724, 1725, 1728, 1730, 1732, 1736, 1745, 1749, 1750, 1753, 1756, 1765, 1766, 1770, 1772, 1773, 1775, 1777, 1778, 1783, 4787
  see also: Political broadcasting
Broadcasts 1770
Broszat, Martin 162
Buber, Martin 265
Bubis, Ignatz 3532
Buddhism 212, 239, 247, 286, 952, 1462, 1464-1473, 1699, 3654
Buddhists 1462, 1465, 1471
Budget control 4975
Budgets 42, 5223
  see also: Household budgets
Building materials 3765, 4049
Buildings 1849, 1857, 2233, 3692, 4028, 4065, 4106, 4168
Bullying 2235, 2602, 2885, 3006, 3289, 3458, 4691
Bureaucracy 1149, 3062, 4421, 4492, 4646, 4806, 4871, 4954, 4968, 4973, 5214, 5216, 5222, 5652, 5871
Burial 5890
Business 414, 1092, 1123, 1200, 1308, 1980, 2266, 2362, 2391, 2568, 3553, 3570, 3818, 3863, 3942, 4175, 4207, 4223, 4355, 4360, 4371, 4372, 4375, 4379, 4396, 4624, 4630, 4658, 4791, 5475
  see also: Business economics, Business studies
Business accounting 4773
Business communications 4654, 4675
Business community 4385
Business cycles 4213, 4233
Business economics 4370, 4425
Business ethics 411, 4352, 4358, 4360, 4417-4420, 4422, 4423, 4425, 4426, 4428, 4601, 4636, 4642, 4709
Business management 416, 1101, 4355, 4364, 4645, 4651, 4653, 4654, 4665, 4666, 4668, 4707, 4748
Business partnership 1134, 3166, 3813, 4088, 4357, 4390, 4830
Business practices 4425, 4636
Business services 4385
Business strategies 4420, 4672, 4786, 4791
Business studies 225
Butler, Judith 3788
Cajun 1367
Caldwell, Lynton Keith 3759
Calendars 1544, 2575
Camps 3640
Camus, Albert 5152
Canadians 147, 956, 2917, 4090
Cancer 766, 2813, 2817, 3759, 5838, 5857, 5891, 5893, 5960, 5986
Candidates 5307
Cannabis 1313, 4998, 5381, 5386, 5394, 5886
Cantons 4592
Capital 291, 3057, 3661, 4349, 4432, 4444, 4458, 4793, 5154
  see also: Human capital, Venture capital
Capital accumulation 4204
Capital cities 3940, 3947, 3949, 3963, 4048, 4057, 4066, 4099, 4113, 4136
Capital flow 4935
Capital market 4175, 4352
  see also: International capital market
Capital punishment 4999, 5001, 5043, 5152, 5155
Capitalism 3, 336, 344, 360, 362, 373, 379, 1172, 1214, 1778, 1920, 2018, 2445, 2446, 2450, 2461, 2507, 2540, 2544, 2551, 2557, 2558, 2567, 2578, 3225, 3503, 3720, 3753, 3771, 3786, 3797, 4202, 4204, 4205, 4208, 4210, 4213-4219, 4226, 4227, 4231, 4234, 4239, 4241, 4242, 4273, 4287, 4294, 4311, 4330, 4336, 4373, 4715, 4850, 4904, 4912, 4920, 4923, 4935, 4942, 4968, 5092, 5272, 5278,

SUBJECT INDEX

5343, 5644, 5652
see also: History of capitalism
Capitalist development 2534, 2540
Capitalist economy 1277
Cardoso, Fernando Henrique 4949
Care of the aged 2585, 2654, 2661, 2662, 2669, 2678, 2679, 2712, 2917, 4235, 5016, 5422, 5479, 5482, 5486, 5492, 5493, 5496-5506, 5508, 5509, 5511-5513, 5517, 5520-5527, 5529, 5531-5534, 5685, 5740, 5778
Career development 440, 2091, 2103, 3166, 3232, 4360, 4383, 4398, 4519, 4544, 4565, 4599, 4757, 4758, 4760-4762, 4766, 4780, 4781, 5663
Caring 749, 1050, 2927, 3037, 3108, 3169, 3219, 3740, 4486, 4687, 5479, 5486, 5488, 5501, 5503, 5520, 5525, 5527, 5543, 5613, 5660, 5707, 5708, 5715, 5719, 5739, 5753, 5764, 5843, 5856, 5916
Carnivals 1345, 3956
Carroll, Lewis 1928
Carter, Angela 3320
Cartoons 586, 1257, 1320
Carver, Raymond 1907
Case studies 2, 51, 454, 461, 555, 610, 750, 762, 780, 833, 890, 1010, 1016, 1091, 1140, 1152, 1153, 1338, 1471, 1673, 1702, 1705, 1708, 1984, 2139, 2158, 2218, 2249, 2255, 2299, 2338, 2473, 2649, 2838, 3037, 3068, 3238, 3390, 3473, 3674, 3752, 3760, 3762, 3807, 3827, 3886, 3921, 4023, 4035, 4044, 4083, 4117, 4147, 4152, 4160, 4176, 4200, 4246, 4348, 4358, 4379, 4393, 4397, 4409, 4462, 4472, 4486, 4568, 4616, 4618, 4645, 4653, 4707, 4713, 4849, 5012, 5125, 5133, 5221, 5670, 5707, 5719, 5751, 5759, 5891, 5924, 5932, 5970, 5973, 5975, 5977
Caste 1376, 1424, 2046, 2381, 2394, 2395, 2415, 2441, 2683, 2701, 2766, 2783, 2984, 3739, 4285, 5269
Castoriadis, Cornelius 2317
Castro, Fidel 1167
Catalan language 1795, 1865
Catholic Church 1475, 1478, 1500, 1502, 1514, 3468, 5776
Catholicism 1431, 1460, 1475, 1478, 1482, 1491, 1493, 1496, 1498, 1502, 1509, 1510, 1513, 1514, 2357, 3919
Catholics 1343, 1475, 1479, 1484, 1499, 1510, 1513, 2439, 3132
Causal analysis 45, 107, 193, 290, 618, 620, 751

Causal explanation 193, 356
Causal inference 497, 618
Causality 108, 109, 193, 259, 290, 356, 370, 391, 497, 618, 620, 653, 664, 854, 908, 1152, 1606, 1624, 1633, 2319, 4197, 4744, 5058, 5075, 5954
Cause 45, 137, 193, 290
Cavell, Stanley 934
Celibacy 2976
Cells 5851
Censorship 1243, 1309, 1427, 2358, 3324, 5298
Censuses 447, 451, 513, 2381, 2436, 2683, 2697, 2699, 2709, 2716, 2723, 2775, 2976, 3394, 3397, 3428, 3555, 3874, 4014, 4019, 4184, 5688
see also: Population censuses
Central-local government relations 4076
Centralization 1106, 1146, 3876, 4806, 4954, 5216
Centre-periphery relations 3776, 4011, 4606
Ceremonies 986, 2851, 5338
Channels of communication 1640, 2479
Chaos theory 292, 2323, 5091
Character 241, 673, 684, 702, 706, 717, 726, 728, 733, 921, 1007, 1332, 1862, 1893, 1937, 4637, 5040
see also: National character
Charismatic leaders 4886
Charity 996, 1156, 2313, 3844, 4192, 4768, 5476, 5481, 5719, 5723, 5776, 5860
Checkland, Peter 376
Chekhov, Anton 249
Chemical weapons 5988
Chemicals 3083
Chemistry 1623
Chemists 1623, 5801, 5813
Cherry, Don 979
Chicano 5232
Chiefdom 2405
Chiefs 4994
Child abuse 521, 3298, 5100, 5192, 5371, 5544, 5546, 5549, 5554, 5558, 5562, 5569, 5578, 5579, 5582, 5589, 5590, 5594, 5595, 5597, 5680
Child adoption 698, 2915, 3433, 5192, 5209, 5538, 5553, 5563, 5569, 5577, 5597
Child care 521, 531, 2020, 2486, 2488, 2582, 2846, 2899, 2998, 3003, 3029, 3054, 3169, 3170, 3264, 4235, 4514, 4517, 4528, 4561, 4687, 5192, 5373, 5486, 5490, 5538-5543, 5546-5548, 5550, 5551, 5554, 5556, 5558, 5559, 5561, 5564, 5568, 5569, 5571, 5573, 5576, 5581,

INDEX DES MATIÈRES EN ANGLAIS

5584-5586, 5588, 5591, 5596, 5599, 5600, 5616, 5624, 5663, 5689, 5696, 5721, 5969
Child costs 2998, 4517, 4528
Child development 77, 544, 545, 551, 577, 607, 622, 623, 636, 660, 695, 743, 756, 792, 2301, 2453, 2596, 2598, 2599, 2601, 2606, 2608, 2646, 2685, 2738, 2893, 2898, 2903, 2921, 2928, 2935, 2946, 2988, 3004, 3009, 3013, 3016, 3027, 3029, 3046, 3047, 3049, 3050, 4469, 4777, 5050, 5097, 5447, 5550, 5551, 5571, 5589, 5591, 5633, 5912, 5969
Child fostering 2020, 2952, 3169, 5550, 5552, 5560, 5568-5570, 5587, 5597, 5721, 5925
Child health 545, 753, 754, 783, 2007, 2022, 2703, 2738, 2823, 3039, 5200, 5575, 5757, 5873, 5947, 5949, 5954, 5969
Child labour 2035, 4430, 4442, 4449, 4452, 4455, 4469, 4482, 5366, 5686
Child mortality 2703, 2780, 2821-2823, 2825, 2828, 2839, 2994
Child protection 1050, 5371, 5373, 5542, 5547, 5556, 5558-5560, 5569, 5572-5574, 5576, 5582, 5583, 5585, 5587-5589, 5596, 5597, 5633, 5667
Child psychology 417, 544-547, 554, 588, 598, 607, 619, 635, 654, 660, 743, 753, 754, 782, 819, 2599, 2607, 2610, 2847, 2892, 2893, 2903, 2946, 3004, 3014, 3029, 3032, 3034, 3044, 5097, 5579, 5918
Child rearing 698, 2360, 2582, 2598, 2599, 2608, 2786, 2854, 2899, 2964, 2988, 2994, 2998, 3000, 3001, 3007, 3009, 3011, 3027, 3036, 4518, 5543, 5551, 5589
Child rearing practices 3009
Child welfare 531, 545, 546, 783, 2154, 2488, 2582, 2599, 2610, 2644, 2859, 2867, 2903, 2922, 2928, 2952, 3010, 3030, 3264, 4191, 4442, 4452, 5366, 5396, 5482, 5537, 5539, 5540, 5543, 5546-5548, 5551, 5554, 5555, 5557, 5559, 5560, 5566, 5567, 5569, 5570, 5572-5574, 5576, 5577, 5579, 5582, 5587, 5588, 5590, 5594-5599, 5601, 5661, 5676, 5689, 5693, 5696, 5769, 5949
Childhood 157, 554, 700, 756, 933, 1494, 1913, 2325, 2597, 2599-2602, 2605, 2607, 2610, 2618, 2635, 2780, 2912, 2916, 2922, 2932, 2951, 3004, 3041, 3056, 5051, 5209, 5461, 5557
Children 157, 225, 417, 419, 545, 577, 583, 586, 607, 608, 610, 622-624, 635, 636, 654, 754-756, 771, 782, 783, 1077, 1460, 1711, 1716, 1788, 1789, 1811, 2013, 2026, 2047, 2154, 2174, 2187, 2225, 2272, 2325, 2464, 2596-2598, 2600-2608, 2610, 2622, 2739, 2757, 2846-2848, 2851, 2853, 2854, 2859, 2871, 2884, 2899, 2904, 2923, 2927, 2931, 2934, 2935, 2946, 2950, 2975, 2988, 2994, 3001, 3003, 3004, 3010, 3012, 3014, 3016, 3017, 3019-3022, 3026, 3030-3032, 3034, 3039, 3040, 3042, 3047, 3048, 3050, 3054, 3055, 3169, 3216, 3239, 3260, 3338, 3446, 3651, 3901, 4257, 4430, 4442, 4452, 4469, 4531, 4548, 4765, 4900, 5078, 5132, 5409, 5427, 5428, 5430, 5447, 5461, 5528, 5544, 5546-5550, 5553, 5556-5559, 5561, 5562, 5564, 5565, 5571, 5572, 5579, 5580, 5583, 5586-5588, 5592-5594, 5596, 5598, 5601, 5608, 5612, 5661, 5671, 5675, 5680, 5696, 5721, 5757, 5768, 5769, 5792, 5820, 5838, 5906, 5912, 5918, 5925, 5933, 5936, 5949, 5959
  see also: Adopted children, Disabled children, Gifted children, Infants, Migrants' children
Children in care 5593
Children's rights 417, 2019, 2596, 2602-2604, 3813, 4482, 5068, 5192, 5209, 5560, 5576, 5580, 5585, 5601
Chinese 806, 864, 952, 1186, 1811, 2568, 2941, 3218, 3497, 3553, 3557, 3583, 3685, 4381, 4500, 5292, 5304, 5446, 5458
Chinese languages 1789, 1811, 1831, 1839, 2523
Choice of products 606
Chomsky, Noam 571
Christian Churches 1478, 1480, 1482, 3366
  see also: Anglicanism, Catholic Church, Coptic Church, Hutterites, Lutheranism, Orthodox Church, Russian Orthodox Church
Christian democratic parties 5219
Christian orders
  see: Dominicans, Jesuits
Christian theology 266, 1388
Christianity 145, 169, 247, 1159, 1251, 1258, 1389, 1405, 1407, 1410, 1419, 1432, 1434, 1457, 1460, 1462, 1474, 1476-1478, 1482, 1483, 1485, 1489-1494, 1496, 1497, 1501, 1502, 1504-1506, 1509, 1515, 1551, 1948, 2169, 2394, 2554, 3028, 3366, 3573, 3743, 3967, 4535, 4962, 5722
  see also: Catholicism, Pentecostalism
Christianization 1476, 1492
Christians 249, 505, 1462, 1515, 4125, 5083
  see also: Orthodox Christians
Chronology 1277, 5887

SUBJECT INDEX

Chuang-tse 1426
Chuang-tzu 200, 1473
Chuilleanáin, Eiléan Ni 1936
Church and state 1432, 1475, 1486, 2532, 3471, 4962
Church history 1475, 1478, 2169
Church membership 1415, 3614
Churches 1035, 1375, 1378, 1415, 1429, 1436, 1460, 1474, 1479, 1485, 1490, 1494, 1496, 1508, 1511, 2655, 2890, 3692, 3843, 3967, 5481
Churchill, Winston Spencer 3759
Cinema 1318, 1332, 1337, 1365, 1879-1885, 1888, 1893-1896, 1898-1901, 1904, 1905, 1907, 1911, 1912, 1983, 2665, 3157, 3323
Cities 471, 969, 1164, 1168, 1530, 1892, 1941, 2252, 2264, 2571, 2573, 2677, 2691, 2821, 3206, 3462, 3590, 3632, 3702, 3776, 3813, 3831, 3839, 3926-3929, 3931-3937, 3939, 3941-3943, 3946, 3948-3953, 3956, 3958, 3959, 3962, 3964, 3966, 3970-3972, 3987, 3992, 3994, 3995, 3999, 4001, 4005, 4007, 4010, 4012, 4029, 4031-4034, 4037, 4038, 4042, 4045, 4053, 4059, 4066, 4069, 4073, 4076-4078, 4081-4083, 4086, 4095, 4097, 4098, 4100, 4102, 4105, 4110, 4112, 4115, 4118, 4119, 4121, 4122, 4127, 4128, 4134, 4137, 4140, 4141, 4143, 4144, 4147, 4149, 4151, 4159-4161, 4168, 4169, 4171, 4173, 4233, 4436, 4439, 4492, 4579, 4941, 4991, 4995, 5049, 5085, 5087, 5119, 5215, 5426, 5526
see also: Capital cities, Inner city, Megacities
Citizen participation 61, 1608, 2218, 2631, 3824, 3825, 3844, 3927, 3965, 4255, 4768, 5107, 5257
Citizens 953, 1662, 1742, 2220, 2387, 2604, 3734, 3799, 3814, 4927, 5122, 5138, 5218, 5305, 5535
Citizenship 58, 322, 954, 1184, 1519, 1643, 1688, 1756, 1764, 1921, 1979, 2063, 2170, 2171, 2181, 2188, 2199, 2218, 2220, 2386, 2387, 2419, 2532, 2567, 2604, 2674, 3060, 3065, 3106, 3146, 3315, 3423, 3460, 3471, 3499, 3528, 3563, 3605, 3630, 3634, 3669, 3683, 3827, 3829, 3965, 3969, 4211, 4420, 4445, 4754, 4832, 4893, 4901, 4905, 4906, 4923, 4927, 4932, 4939, 4941, 4951, 4952, 4955, 4958, 4961, 4964, 5159, 5192, 5305, 5484, 5608, 5609, 5615
City size 3929, 3948, 4033

Civic education 2122, 2170, 2171, 2181, 2188, 2203, 2604
Civil defence 3702
Civil law 2642, 2908, 5156, 5190, 5633
Civil liberties 4935, 5153
Civil proceedings 4822
Civil rights 349, 1531, 2454, 2492, 2498, 3115, 3389, 3391, 3431, 3669, 3749, 3777, 4950, 5002, 5048, 5136, 5139, 5159, 5242, 5258, 5273, 5280, 5320, 5357, 5609
see also: Right to education, Right to work
Civil servants 5223
Civil service 3290, 5215, 5223
Civil society 54, 58, 243, 405, 904, 1442, 1479, 1517, 1643, 1675, 1756, 1764, 2088, 2134, 2181, 2203, 2371, 2387, 2506, 3403, 3416, 3423, 3468, 3506, 3683, 3694, 3702, 3802, 3810, 3828, 3917, 3927, 4095, 4119, 4169, 4192, 4215, 4272, 4467, 4768, 4890, 4901, 4916, 4932, 4940, 4948, 4950, 4955, 4960, 4967, 4974, 4976, 4978, 5015, 5125, 5139, 5200, 5213, 5241, 5285, 5294, 5330
Civil war 162, 3465, 5466
Civil-military relations 957, 2502, 5340, 5341, 5352, 5360
Civilians 1009, 5125
Civilization 956, 973, 988, 1003, 1159, 1160, 1162, 1163, 1167, 1171, 1175, 1178-1180, 1185, 1201, 1225, 1226, 1276, 1277, 1280, 1360, 1865, 2508, 2558, 3797, 3887, 3934, 4094, 5315, 5372
see also: Eastern civilization, Modern civilization, Western civilization
Civilization crisis 3713
Clans 2405
Class 339, 441, 854, 1181, 1227, 1310, 1315, 1339, 1341, 1356, 1431, 1517, 1724, 1761, 1859, 1908, 2014, 2018, 2042, 2048, 2063, 2108, 2223, 2295, 2324, 2326, 2347, 2374, 2377-2379, 2381, 2382, 2387-2392, 2401, 2403, 2412, 2413, 2418, 2421, 2422, 2427, 2428, 2430, 2431, 2434, 2436-2438, 2440-2443, 2445, 2449, 2450, 2529, 2532, 2564, 2578, 2608, 2644, 2774, 2840, 2907, 3003, 3057, 3077, 3153, 3175, 3217, 3222, 3271, 3389, 3436, 3486, 3779, 3891, 3909, 3930, 4004, 4204, 4220, 4266, 4304, 4338, 4398, 4431, 4472, 4526, 4708, 4720, 4947, 4968, 5012, 5052, 5077, 5104, 5108, 5227, 5238, 5244, 5245, 5256, 5299, 5302, 5303, 5543, 5662
see also: Aristocracy, Bourgeoisie, Lower class, Lower middle class, Middle class,

INDEX DES MATIÈRES EN ANGLAIS

Ruling class, Underclass, Upper class, Working class
Class behaviour 2065
Class consciousness 2418
Class culture 1305
Class formation 2446
Class relations 1305, 2377, 2426
Class structure 2390, 2445, 2578, 2870, 3528, 4436
Class struggle 2416, 4213
Classification 70, 104, 286, 591, 861, 869, 880, 894, 1408, 2363, 2382, 3408, 4123, 4265, 4436, 4472, 4953, 5650
Classrooms 2027, 2102, 2229, 2231, 2608
Classwork 2027
Clergy 1443, 1481, 3692, 4778
Clientelism 4965, 5282
Climate 1096, 2800, 3708, 4879
  see also: Climate change, Weather
Climate change 1601, 2717, 3708
Clinical psychology 545, 554, 565, 591, 603, 604, 680, 736, 738, 739, 741-745, 747-749, 751-757, 761, 764-766, 769-771, 773-777, 779, 781, 784, 787, 788, 792, 794, 796, 798, 800, 801, 803, 804, 807, 809, 810, 812, 813, 815, 816, 887, 1947, 2874, 2877, 2921, 3015, 3181, 3382, 5377, 5406, 5420, 5435, 5538, 5670, 5710, 5737, 5910, 5911, 5913, 5917, 5920, 5922, 5928
Cliques 1043, 3927
Cloning 1576, 3372, 5848, 5863, 5865
Clothes 1316, 2399, 3067, 3256, 4344
Clothing industry 4694
Clubs 2614
Cluster analysis 735, 4557
Co-operation 463, 911, 1019, 1027, 1068, 2289, 3480, 3517, 3840, 3850, 3919
Co-operatives 3867, 3893, 5780
  see also: Consumer co-operatives, Housing co-operatives
Coal mines 4725
Coal mining 20, 4192
Coastal areas 1312, 3606, 3709, 3820
Coastal fishing 3913
Coasts 3709
  see also: Coastal areas
Cocaine 3995, 5375, 5385, 5386
Coffee 4206, 4331, 5433
Cognatic descent 2930
Cognition 110, 210, 233, 245, 246, 300, 324, 503, 547, 549, 559, 565, 571, 574, 587, 589, 591, 606-608, 611-617, 619-621, 623, 624, 626, 627, 629, 632, 635, 636, 640-644, 646, 648-650, 652, 654, 655, 658, 659, 661, 663, 664, 666-668, 670, 671, 676, 680, 685, 687, 688, 691, 703, 705, 721, 727, 731-733, 737, 741, 758, 760, 787, 790, 804, 807, 808, 823, 825, 831, 840, 845, 846, 851, 861, 863-865, 868, 871, 873, 877, 905, 907, 915, 918, 919, 924, 941, 972, 1031, 1041, 1056, 1063, 1071, 1075, 1076, 1084, 1095, 1126, 1147, 1161, 1166, 1229, 1237, 1261, 1573, 1582, 1590, 1647, 1863, 1992, 2052, 2168, 2193, 2197, 2236, 2309, 2359, 2362, 2892, 2946, 3041, 3344, 4190, 4339, 4391, 4408, 5406
  see also: Social cognition
Cognitive development 553, 598, 600, 612, 619, 626, 633, 740, 2615, 2625, 3182, 4418, 5592
Cognitive dissonance 652, 1075
Cohabitation 902, 2915, 2933, 2958, 2959, 2964, 2974, 2979, 2981, 2988, 2989, 2996
Cohen, Gerald 4921
Cohort analysis 772, 2287, 2651, 2681, 2696, 4548
Cohorts 2632, 2799, 2802, 2974, 3580
Cold War 165, 1597
Collaboration 73, 1681, 2110, 2213, 3877, 4100, 4357, 4374, 4625, 5691, 5746
Collective action 323, 597, 829, 1038, 1068, 2378, 2450, 3154, 3834, 3838, 3855, 4365, 4385, 4843, 4888, 4942, 5228, 5231, 5241, 5248, 5250, 5265, 5266, 5273, 5275, 5276, 5280, 5716, 5942, 5982
Collective bargaining 2079, 4537, 4550, 4751, 4815, 4824, 4828, 4829, 4841, 4842, 4850, 4855, 4870, 4876, 4880
Collective behaviour 391, 1095, 2082, 4888, 5218, 5278
Collective consciousness 1490
Collective memory 147, 161, 162, 181, 223, 247, 951, 958, 974, 976, 982, 985, 986, 993-995, 1004, 1434, 1758, 1951, 2177, 2205, 3468, 4848, 4936
Collective property 974
Collective representation 268
Collectivism 2335, 4658, 5245
Collectivization 3889
Collingwood, R.G. 110
Colonial government 58, 4042, 4897
Colonial history 58, 164, 184, 188, 961, 1165, 1183, 1224, 1913, 1931, 2388, 2415, 2747, 3257, 3654, 3730, 3891, 4935, 4939, 5325, 5921, 5983
Colonialism 957, 1165, 1769, 1926, 1950, 1951, 2148, 2321, 2568, 3214, 3503,

Subject Index

3782, 4206, 4477, 4935, 4939, 5226, 5325
see also: Neocolonialism
Colonies 1165, 1495, 1819
Colonization 58, 977, 1165, 1362, 2167, 3771, 3789, 4893
Colour 1883, 3534
Colour blindness 3471
Colquhoun, Patrick 5146
Coltrane, John 1988
Comedy 244, 1896, 5293
Comics 3008, 3313
Commerce 58, 1977, 3348, 3909, 4179, 4182, 4223, 4238, 4344
Commercial banks 3975, 4705
Commercial workers 944, 4418
Commodification 1873, 2477, 2515, 3705, 3721, 4202, 4238, 4325, 5232
Commodities 303, 342, 4193, 4336
Common Agricultural Policy 3878
Common good 5659
Common law 5055, 5167
Commonwealth 3257, 5007
Communalism 583, 2174, 3473, 4119
Communes 2697
Communication 67, 111, 117, 194, 205, 310, 359, 371, 384, 394, 403, 511, 521, 527, 590, 607, 655, 693, 782-784, 830, 832, 836, 845, 853, 867, 899, 901, 907, 940, 947, 1009, 1016, 1021, 1022, 1038, 1065, 1066, 1088, 1101, 1105, 1108, 1116, 1119, 1120, 1158, 1161, 1199, 1200, 1215, 1268, 1298, 1384, 1393, 1607, 1611, 1626, 1633-1635, 1637-1640, 1642, 1644, 1647, 1649-1653, 1655, 1656, 1658, 1660, 1668, 1669, 1683, 1689, 1690, 1700, 1702-1704, 1715, 1717, 1739, 1743, 1747, 1749, 1753-1756, 1768, 1771, 1776, 1784, 1787, 1799, 1803, 1808, 1827, 1831, 1833, 1835, 1842, 1846, 1853, 1924, 1997, 2001, 2097, 2102, 2392, 2479, 2571, 2588, 2616, 2667, 2771, 2772, 2905, 2920, 2936, 2943, 2966, 2987, 3002, 3021, 3038, 3368, 3508, 3734, 3825, 3849, 3965, 4036, 4167, 4203, 4417, 4666, 4716, 4807, 5205, 5241, 5414, 5557, 5579, 5682, 5828, 5831, 5846, 5901, 5960
see also: Business communications, Channels of communication, Intercultural communication, Interethnic communication, Interpersonal communication, Mass communication, Non-verbal communication, Oral communication, Political communication, Scientific communication, Verbal communication, Visual communication
Communication industry 1754
Communication networks 1632
Communication research 901, 1088, 1161, 1635, 1783
Communication sciences 1635
Communication systems 1108
Communications technology 537, 1015, 1036, 1242, 1634, 1636, 1641, 1643, 1657, 1659, 1660, 1663-1666, 1668, 1670, 1672-1675, 1677, 1679-1681, 1683-1685, 1687, 1689, 1690, 1704, 1732, 2526, 2532, 2571, 4056, 5228, 5901
Communion 709, 1437, 5262
Communism 1167, 1263, 1328, 1360, 1392, 2310, 2333, 3635, 4244, 4349, 4925, 4946, 5489
Communist parties 1910, 4942
Communists 1392, 4204, 4919
Communitarianism 382, 405, 1548, 3419, 3849, 4134, 4232, 4958
Community 12, 39, 162, 205, 408, 538, 577, 724, 767, 838, 893, 904, 995, 1009, 1010, 1107, 1170, 1188, 1242, 1246, 1427, 1430, 1479, 1495, 1503, 1532, 1548, 1550, 1565, 1656, 1661, 1662, 1668, 1669, 1691, 1756, 2066, 2088, 2161, 2239, 2252, 2307, 2330, 2332, 2345, 2451, 2505, 2506, 2543, 2636, 2661, 2664, 2754, 2870, 2995, 3152, 3234, 3323, 3325, 3357, 3384, 3418, 3423, 3426, 3437, 3472, 3487, 3539, 3614, 3628, 3646, 3688, 3697, 3740, 3757, 3833, 3835, 3837, 3839, 3842, 3846-3848, 3851, 3858, 3860, 3864, 3865, 3879, 3898, 3907, 3909, 3967, 3983, 3998, 4008, 4043, 4056, 4074, 4086, 4090, 4159, 4182, 4197, 4419, 4646, 4725, 4966, 4969, 4976, 4978, 4994, 4996, 5014, 5107, 5118, 5129, 5139, 5143, 5212, 5314, 5354, 5363, 5397, 5440, 5447, 5464, 5546, 5568, 5741, 5742, 5800, 5951, 5979
see also: Business community, Ethnic communities, International community, Local communities, Religious communities, Rural communities, Scientific communities, Urban communities
Community care 758, 792, 2458, 2470, 2489, 2497, 2712, 3751, 5137, 5363, 5397, 5400, 5421, 5422, 5490, 5492, 5496, 5497, 5501, 5511, 5533, 5693, 5718, 5736-5742, 5749, 5771, 5787, 5800, 5900,

INDEX DES MATIÈRES EN ANGLAIS

5904, 5909, 5913, 5919, 5922, 5927, 5934, 5940, 5982
Community development 904, 1026, 1685, 2221, 2345, 3431, 3628, 3730, 3805, 3814, 3825, 3827-3832, 3834, 3836, 3838-3841, 3850, 3852, 3854, 3855, 3857, 3861-3863, 3865, 3907, 3911, 3967, 4044, 4052, 4070, 4071, 4117, 4258, 4299, 5107, 5716, 5969
Community integration 1442, 1488, 5576
Community law 3321, 4950, 5025, 5200
Community life 2371, 3845, 3902
Community organization 3431, 3827, 3836, 3858, 3861
Community participation 20, 2127, 2213, 2371, 2529, 3553, 3807, 3810, 3813, 3824, 3825, 3836, 3841, 3844, 3845, 3847, 3856, 3861, 3885, 4066, 4096, 4119, 4169, 4486, 4940, 5288, 5716, 5985
Community power 2338, 3836, 3852
Community satisfaction 3898
Community services 3836, 4768, 5422, 5515, 5527, 5609, 5666, 5934
Commuting 3608, 3969, 4130, 4143
Comparative analysis 74, 154, 243, 323, 409, 471, 497, 520, 562, 1184, 1195, 1246, 1280, 1308, 1452, 1773, 1831, 1992, 1993, 2088, 2104, 2116, 2145, 2157, 2171, 2249, 2254, 2268, 2355, 2396, 2397, 2627, 2632, 2642, 2669, 2684, 2705, 2720, 2756, 2808, 2917, 2923, 2999, 3002, 3011, 3103, 3177, 3226, 3284, 3328, 3446, 3493, 3568, 3622, 3702, 3853, 3980, 3996, 4097, 4226, 4265, 4459, 4521, 4548, 4601, 4625, 4637, 4681, 4705, 4783, 4834, 4860, 4945, 5012, 5053, 5148, 5190, 5297, 5398, 5432, 5448, 5449, 5478, 5641, 5644, 5649, 5751, 5763, 5769, 5815, 5819
Comparative economics 4255, 5486
Comparative law 5165, 5178
Comparative politics 2, 2123, 2238, 3338, 4823, 5218
Comparative religion 1380, 1396, 1400, 1422, 1423, 1445, 1472
Compensation 4433, 4499, 4600, 4822, 4849, 4990, 5514
see also: Damage compensation
Competition 831, 1021, 1358, 1685, 1733, 2166, 2571, 2940, 3018, 3285, 4045, 4132, 4374, 4375, 4378, 4501, 4681, 4817, 5217, 5725, 5793
see also: International competition
Competitive advantage 4504

Competitiveness 2141, 3771, 4374, 4420, 4656, 4713
Complex organization 4622
Complex societies 3832, 5248
Compulsory education 4418
Computer programmes 4667
Computer science 2270, 4574
Computerization 1040, 4179, 4406
Computers 37, 92, 458, 576, 634, 1036, 1339, 1634, 1660, 1664, 1667, 1669, 1676, 1678, 1681, 1688, 1692, 1693, 1779, 2056, 2172, 2197, 2201, 2210, 2223, 2314, 2554, 2581, 2667, 4387, 5228, 5230, 5288, 5901
Concentration camps 5005
Conceptualization 231, 261, 369, 642, 1095, 1161, 2194, 2570, 2656, 3081, 3727, 4096, 4154
Conciliation 3891, 4849
Conditioning 3273
Confidentiality 5169
Conflict 161, 173, 398, 920, 1005, 1009, 1011, 1013, 1016, 1017, 1020, 1026, 1028, 1029, 1064, 1163, 1364, 1427, 1452, 1485, 1529, 1811, 2250, 2473, 2587, 2643, 2742, 2892, 2900, 2969, 3472, 3477, 3485, 3508, 3531, 3615, 3624, 3677, 3749, 3772, 3777, 3816, 3901, 4493, 4837, 5122, 5127, 5294, 5323, 5331, 5332, 5355, 5444, 5466, 5467, 5606, 5686, 5831
see also: Cultural conflicts, Interethnic conflict, International conflicts, Interpersonal conflicts, Linguistic conflict, Marital conflict, Political conflicts, Racial conflict, Religious conflicts, Role conflicts
Conflict resolution 161, 517, 932, 1004, 1006, 1007, 1010, 1011, 1014-1016, 1019, 1024-1028, 1030, 1031, 2366, 3430, 3472, 3480, 3493, 3891, 4849, 5141, 5184, 5186, 5318, 5337, 5687
see also: Third-party intervention
Conflict theory 399, 1011, 1020, 1025, 1028, 2850, 4217, 4378
Conformism 299, 1164, 2318
Confucianism 211, 266, 273, 321, 1171, 1263, 1402, 1423, 1473, 2617, 3108, 4207, 4981, 5309
Confucius 211, 3108
Congestion 2264
Congregations 1443
Consanguineous marriage 2822
Consanguinity 2949
Conscientious objection 5324, 5855
Consciousness 69, 104, 245, 247, 353, 358, 558, 574, 584, 602, 618, 640, 752, 1246,

433

SUBJECT INDEX

1472, 2300, 2566, 3099, 3115, 3432, 3727, 5944
Conscription 5342, 5352, 5361
Consensus 420, 1010, 1059, 4036
see also: Group consensus
Conservation 3707, 3710, 3721, 3732, 3737, 3747, 3753, 3755, 3970, 3984, 4025, 4047, 4081, 4107, 4123, 4168
see also: Energy conservation, Nature conservation, Resource conservation
Conservatism 141, 860, 1207, 1971, 2140, 3012, 3322, 3365, 4111, 5286
Conservative parties 3983
Conservatives 2730
Constitution 3471, 4962, 5038, 5192, 5809
Constitutional law 4933, 5889
Constitutional reform 2513
Constitutionalism 4957
Construction activity 4028, 4049
Construction industry 1565, 4420, 4572
Constructivism 358, 517, 643, 1563, 1615, 2209, 2219, 3700, 3744, 4636, 5310
Consumer behaviour 1322, 2545, 3823, 4320, 4322, 4324, 4326-4328, 4331, 4333, 4335, 4339, 4340, 4342, 4343, 4345
Consumer co-operatives 4316, 4330
Consumer credit 4317, 4341
Consumer goods 4334, 4339
Consumer information 4322, 4341
Consumer policy 4317, 4341
Consumer preferences 1254, 4339
Consumer protection 5732
Consumer society 4328, 4329, 4333, 4342
Consumerism 1207, 1254, 1300, 1688, 1772, 2243, 2674, 3225, 3909, 4227, 4312, 4319, 4322, 4324, 4325, 4328, 4329, 4331-4333, 4336, 4340, 4342, 4345, 5971
Consumers 519, 1268, 1710, 2650, 3059, 3799, 4284, 4315, 4319, 4321, 4326-4328, 4330, 4332, 4334, 4340, 4342, 4345, 4420, 5732
Consumption 342, 379, 395, 994, 1314, 1318, 1337, 1349, 1731, 1920, 2399, 2419, 2504, 2657, 2711, 3333, 3347, 3720, 3725, 3764, 3786, 3799, 3875, 4135, 4186, 4193, 4206, 4276, 4313, 4315, 4322, 4325, 4327, 4328, 4331-4335, 4337, 4340, 4342, 4345, 4410, 5956
see also: Cultural consumption, Food consumption, Household consumption, Mass consumption
Consumption patterns 3799, 4335
Containment 784
Contemporary art 1860, 1866, 1880
Contemporary literature 1930

Content analysis 1749, 3008
Contextual analysis 539, 1647, 1833, 1874
Continuing education 93, 2004, 2010, 2016, 2031, 2049, 2145
Contraception 890, 2726, 2729, 2731, 2732, 2736, 2739, 2740, 2743, 2746, 2751, 2754, 2759, 2763, 2766, 2769-2771, 2774, 2779, 2797, 2804, 3079, 3279, 3296, 3299, 3312, 3332, 3337, 3350, 5200, 5851, 5943, 5945
Contraceptive methods 2753, 2761, 5200
Contracts 13, 2288, 4220, 4380, 4465, 4520, 4552, 4627, 4829, 4846, 5217
see also: Labour contract, Marriage contracts, Social contract
Conurbation 4067
Convergence 1697, 1798, 2034, 2518, 2560, 4221, 4818, 5622
Cooking 3223
Cooperation 656, 927, 1021, 1040, 1151, 1638, 2088, 2307, 2345, 3834, 3838, 4032, 4100, 4163, 4322, 4356, 4497, 4820, 5220, 5780
Copt 1478
Coptic Church 1504
Corporate crime 5244
Corporate culture 1134, 1157, 4370, 4379, 4381, 4386, 4389, 4413, 4420, 4544, 4624, 4644, 4658, 4769, 4798, 5252
Corporate finance 4175
Corporate governance 4417, 4641, 4642
see also: Business management
Corporate planning 4035
Corporatism 4467, 4642, 4820
Correlation 452, 609, 890, 2821, 2831, 2839, 2924, 3476, 4792
Correspondence 162, 593
Correspondence education 2145
Corruption 931, 2535, 3827, 4204, 4427, 4683, 4877, 5055, 5091, 5094, 5219, 5267, 5282
see also: Political corruption
Cosmetics 1189, 1214, 1559, 3272, 3315
Cosmology 259, 271, 1391, 3695, 3823
Cosmopolitanism 1424, 2348, 2546, 4902, 5311
Cost analysis 3979, 5655, 5789, 5909
Cost function 5760
Cost of education 2293
Cost of living 3884
Cost-benefit analysis 532, 2120, 5744
Cost-effectiveness 3895, 5486, 5656
Costs 3784, 3832, 4068, 4497, 4767, 5401, 5565, 5581, 5748, 5754, 5760, 5931

see also: Child costs, Labour costs, Social costs
Council of Europe 5884
Counselling 724, 759, 767, 778, 785, 786, 806, 815, 2484, 2733, 2869, 3370, 3381, 5175, 5595, 5599, 5671, 5674, 5682, 5699, 5714, 5717, 5923
Counsellors 759, 5699
Counterrevolution 5238
Counties 3620, 3886
Countries
see: Eastern countries
Countryside 3915, 5418
Court of appeal 5154
Courts 1010, 3891, 5017, 5054, 5056, 5072, 5132, 5137, 5139, 5154, 5157, 5170, 5172, 5184, 5191, 5205, 5209
see also: Juvenile courts, Military courts, Supreme Court
Courtship 950, 3318, 5444, 5449, 5470
Covariance 482
Cows 5948
Craft 1591, 4219, 4238
Craft workers 1616
Creativity 324, 374, 621, 634, 660, 672, 770, 1182, 1253, 1345, 1863, 2439, 2581, 3812, 4092, 4361, 5262
Credit 4175, 4240, 4317, 4348
see also: Consumer credit, Microfinance, Money and credit, Rural credit
Creole languages 1801
Creoles 1367, 3416
Crime 33, 161, 426, 471, 1442, 1921, 1991, 2119, 2400, 2535, 3036, 3121, 3287, 3338, 3498, 3781, 3849, 3986, 3995, 4007, 4013, 4390, 4949, 4979, 4980, 4982, 4984, 4989, 4992, 4995, 5000, 5001, 5003, 5006-5008, 5010, 5014, 5025, 5028, 5029, 5035, 5036, 5041, 5045, 5048, 5050, 5053, 5054, 5057-5062, 5064, 5066-5068, 5070, 5072, 5075, 5078, 5080-5082, 5085-5088, 5090, 5091, 5093-5095, 5099-5103, 5106, 5108-5116, 5119-5121, 5123, 5125, 5144-5146, 5172, 5176, 5194, 5282, 5312, 5365, 5367, 5370, 5392, 5401, 5428, 5429, 5438, 5440, 5441, 5450, 5451, 5453, 5455, 5456, 5467, 5471, 5544, 5558, 5617, 5899
see also: Corporate crime, International crime, Organized crime, Victims of crime, War crimes
Crime prevention 2203, 2532, 3036, 4390, 4986, 4989, 4997, 5008, 5014, 5024, 5059, 5063, 5088, 5107, 5112, 5124, 5140, 5143, 5448, 5472, 5474

Crimes against humanity 1388, 5311, 5312, 5462
Criminal jurisdiction 4982, 5001, 5004, 5005, 5014, 5018, 5028, 5032, 5083, 5101
Criminal justice 426, 1442, 2532, 2864, 4949, 4979, 4982, 4997-5010, 5013-5020, 5022-5026, 5028-5032, 5035-5038, 5041, 5043, 5059, 5064, 5068, 5098, 5101, 5116, 5119, 5126, 5129, 5132, 5135, 5145, 5150, 5174, 5175, 5193, 5195, 5205, 5364, 5370
Criminal law 311, 4998, 5000, 5005, 5007, 5009, 5018, 5025, 5027, 5028, 5034, 5036, 5038, 5041, 5054, 5056, 5098, 5150, 5166, 5175, 5176, 5192, 5858
see also: International criminal law
Criminal sentencing 5016, 5034, 5039, 5040, 5054
Criminal sociology 5013, 5051, 5064, 5096, 5098, 5102, 5106, 5110, 5120
Criminality 5015, 5027, 5045, 5047, 5052, 5059, 5061, 5064, 5066, 5067, 5076, 5078, 5082, 5088, 5091, 5092, 5099, 5103, 5105, 5113, 5117, 5119, 5121, 5365, 5445, 5634
Criminology 426, 529, 2400, 2532, 2868, 3121, 3241, 4271, 4979, 4980, 4982, 5005, 5008, 5009, 5011, 5025, 5028, 5036, 5038, 5044, 5047-5049, 5051, 5055, 5057, 5059, 5062, 5064-5067, 5069-5071, 5073, 5074, 5076, 5077, 5080-5082, 5084-5088, 5092-5094, 5096, 5097, 5101, 5103, 5104, 5109-5113, 5117-5121, 5138, 5176, 5193, 5194, 5312, 5441, 5445, 5446, 5453, 5456, 5465, 5468, 5472
Crisis management 724, 1018, 1097, 1146, 3713, 5141
Critical path analysis 1126
Critical theory 213, 253, 274, 285, 303, 307, 315, 317, 325, 337, 354, 365, 366, 369, 398, 1221, 1233, 1265, 1278, 1296, 1314, 1566, 1713, 1792, 1848, 1878, 3102, 3144, 3453, 4911, 5166, 5704
Criticism 7, 52, 257, 303, 307, 333, 592, 1102, 1187, 1229, 1247, 1408, 1702, 1909, 1981, 1988, 3098, 3102, 3121, 3144, 3687, 4918, 5165, 5201, 5452
see also: Literary criticism
Croats 967, 1793, 1794, 3859
Crops 3708
see also: Fruit crops
Cross-cultural analysis 65, 164, 338, 550, 633, 650, 763, 870, 1131, 1330, 1464, 1757, 1767, 1791, 1796, 1824, 1885, 2128, 2145, 2265, 2354, 2460, 2584, 2663, 2666, 2908, 2945, 3060, 3231, 3283,

Subject Index

3284, 3419, 3503, 4012, 4198, 4318, 4359, 4425, 4630, 4631, 4658, 5065, 5069, 5296, 5388, 5521, 5891

Cross-national analysis 520, 1134, 1230, 1725, 1736, 2104, 2116, 2179, 2357, 2367, 2405, 2530, 2602, 2627, 2669, 2679, 2704, 2756, 2820, 3039, 3194, 3338, 3470, 3759, 3913, 3961, 4039, 4135, 4252, 4253, 4386, 4430, 4441, 4475, 4557, 4624, 4745, 4764, 4768, 4772, 4860, 4945, 5272, 5284, 5435, 5445, 5450, 5498, 5519, 5605, 5636, 5641, 5717, 5751, 5756, 5769, 5786, 5787, 5858, 5956

Cross-sectional analysis 2595, 4484, 4679

Crowding-out effect 3979

Crowds 829, 1005, 1042, 5133

Cruse, Harold 4919

Cuban Revolution 1167

Cult of the dead 1433

Cults 1228, 1417, 3257

Cultural adaptation 1320, 1777, 3306, 3598, 5008

Cultural anthropology 989, 1161, 1227, 1319, 1331, 1658, 1940, 1958, 1986, 2544, 3323

Cultural areas 1395

Cultural assimilation 3411, 3423, 3427, 3548, 3555, 3562, 3566, 3578, 3580, 3596, 4012

Cultural authenticity 4238

Cultural behaviour 3530, 3548, 5898

Cultural capital 1227, 2402, 2593, 2612, 3996, 4349, 4353, 5154

Cultural change 139, 994, 1136, 1161, 1169, 1182, 1190, 1202, 1205, 1216, 1264, 1268, 1321, 1336, 1554, 1658, 1777, 1841, 2399, 2505, 2511, 2515, 2520, 2532, 2536, 2549, 2557, 2566, 2569, 2675, 2733, 2870, 3586, 3662, 3776, 4177, 4379, 4535, 4866, 4944

Cultural conflicts 3522, 5065, 5294

Cultural consumption 1203

Cultural contact 1384, 2009, 2271, 2569, 3776, 4205, 4386, 5313, 5335

Cultural development 57, 1219, 1797, 1855, 3940

Cultural differences 9, 134, 550, 676, 710, 806, 965, 1072, 1160, 1171, 1177, 1208, 1209, 1230, 1238, 1240, 1831, 2113, 2118, 2232, 2357, 2569, 2731, 3011, 3266, 3328, 3417, 3471, 3548, 4198, 4212, 4312, 4318, 4367, 4417, 4475, 4629, 4630, 5320, 5908

Cultural differentiation 520, 1796, 4184, 4658

Cultural diffusion 1308, 1540, 2401

Cultural diversity 996, 1001, 1010, 1240, 1548, 1806, 1826, 2354, 2909, 2934, 3423, 3500, 3522, 4227, 4359, 4362, 5021, 5326, 5529

Cultural dynamics 868, 1395, 1566, 1682, 2908

Cultural ecology 3531

Cultural environment 4990

Cultural evolutionism 3401

Cultural factors 35, 342, 409, 603, 797, 875, 888, 899, 1134, 1139, 1219, 1232, 1314, 1386, 1442, 1641, 1693, 1770, 1798, 1831, 1979, 2523, 2704, 2731, 2732, 2908, 3084, 3201, 4386, 4457, 4618, 5170, 5268, 5432, 5459, 5866, 5946

Cultural heritage 280, 965, 974, 996, 1172, 1227, 1367, 1845, 1960, 1973, 3406, 3443, 3477, 3589, 3854, 4081, 4133, 5529, 5577

see also: Preservation of cultural heritage

Cultural history 171, 177, 188, 214, 1161, 1178, 1187, 1189, 1210, 1351, 1397, 1557, 1612, 1616, 1797, 1873, 1919, 1943, 1961, 3371, 3426, 3445, 3798, 3934, 5333

Cultural identification 1796

Cultural identity 541, 966, 992, 997, 1184, 1192, 1198, 1202, 1205, 1207, 1230, 1242, 1318, 1331, 1668, 1758, 1880, 1899, 1936, 1949, 2047, 2178, 2394, 2549, 2575, 3355, 3392, 3406, 3422, 3441, 3554, 3589, 3595, 3676, 4141, 4205, 4924, 5156, 5259, 5328, 5409

Cultural imperialism 248, 1733, 1931, 2545

Cultural industry 1100, 1194, 1856

Cultural influence 1770, 1942, 2569, 2630, 2760, 2917, 2944, 3531, 5128

Cultural integration 1321, 1532, 1809, 1813, 1949, 2047, 2419, 2518, 3559, 3562, 3576, 3598, 3826, 5313

Cultural interaction 4207

Cultural life 86, 331, 1175, 1476, 1527, 1889, 2534, 4981

Cultural materialism 1233

Cultural minorities 1755, 3479

Cultural nationalism 1188

Cultural norms 888, 1508, 2021, 2134, 2349, 2821, 2929

Cultural patterns 1395, 2917

Cultural policy 992, 1171, 1175, 1220, 1223, 1235, 1241, 1336, 1360, 1892, 2025, 3322

Cultural practices 952, 1353, 1527, 1804, 3009, 3266, 3315, 3471, 3750, 4120, 4280, 4955

Cultural property 1100, 1172, 1778

Cultural relations 1072, 1231, 1244, 2592, 3479, 3527, 3684, 4198, 5333

see also: International cultural relations

Cultural reproduction 1873, 3676
Cultural Revolution 185, 1264, 2567
Cultural specificity 1240, 3888, 4426, 4624, 5908
Cultural studies 7, 14, 159, 184, 292, 343, 369, 444, 590, 764, 817, 1001, 1018, 1109, 1158, 1166, 1174, 1176, 1178-1180, 1183, 1192-1196, 1199, 1211-1213, 1215-1228, 1231-1236, 1239-1242, 1244, 1245, 1252, 1261, 1272, 1276, 1278, 1288, 1305, 1311, 1314, 1316, 1318, 1321, 1329, 1336, 1337, 1339, 1358, 1360, 1361, 1364, 1365, 1409, 1566, 1609, 1614, 1668, 1669, 1688, 1693, 1695, 1698, 1707, 1726, 1729, 1738, 1740, 1741, 1744, 1746, 1756, 1758, 1771, 1772, 1775, 1777, 1799, 1859, 1862, 1864, 1874, 1880, 1894, 1895, 1920, 1933, 1940, 1955, 1958, 1986, 2211, 2214, 2252, 2298, 2327, 2349, 2504, 2524, 2547, 2565, 2607, 2992, 3072, 3155, 3157, 3225, 3245, 3250, 3311, 3316, 3350, 3355, 3357, 3409, 3415, 3435, 3443, 3465, 3490, 3494, 3569, 3571, 3676, 3683, 3730, 3756, 3766, 3887, 4192, 4202, 4290, 4398, 4477, 4772, 4965, 5259, 5289, 5333, 5343, 5745, 5943, 5966
Cultural systems 2566, 3417
Cultural tradition 561, 1170, 1175, 1267, 1343, 1364, 1367, 2575, 2866
Cultural values 996, 1176, 1203, 1609, 1864, 2505, 2566, 3009, 3660, 4253, 4359, 4823, 5397
Culturalism 597, 3507
Culture 7, 12, 33, 53, 122, 148, 164, 204, 268, 308, 326, 338, 343, 441, 569, 605, 643, 671, 677, 678, 681, 710, 822, 864, 955, 976, 981, 985, 992, 996, 1001, 1100, 1103, 1161, 1162, 1166-1170, 1175, 1177-1180, 1183, 1188, 1193, 1194, 1196, 1197, 1203, 1206-1208, 1211, 1212, 1218-1220, 1223, 1225, 1233, 1236, 1241, 1243, 1244, 1249, 1250, 1253, 1256, 1261, 1266, 1280, 1281, 1288, 1291, 1294, 1313, 1326, 1329, 1335, 1353, 1368, 1566, 1607, 1663, 1664, 1700-1702, 1709, 1713, 1724, 1735, 1743, 1756, 1764, 1811, 1813, 1824, 1837, 1851, 1855, 1856, 1888, 1890, 1892, 1898, 1907, 1908, 1911, 1947, 1959, 2009, 2113, 2252, 2255, 2298, 2328, 2394, 2477, 2502, 2522, 2526, 2543, 2547, 2549, 2552, 2557, 2563, 2663, 2909, 2953, 3067, 3090, 3092, 3115, 3157, 3216, 3253, 3273, 3278, 3306, 3315, 3322, 3388, 3400, 3427, 3440, 3465, 3507, 3540, 3591, 3646, 3683, 3689, 3712, 3756, 3789, 3848, 3933, 4017, 4121, 4126, 4138, 4202, 4212, 4227, 4336, 4359, 4381, 4417, 4567, 4916, 4943, 4994, 5065, 5067, 5232, 5246, 5253, 5277, 5347, 5356, 5363, 5386, 5458, 5529, 5907
see also: Access to culture, Class culture, Corporate culture, Cultural differences, Cultural diversity, Dominant culture, Indigenous culture, Local culture, Mass culture, Material culture, Minority culture, Musical culture, National culture, Political culture, Popular culture, Sociology of culture, Subculture, Theory of culture, Traditional culture, Youth culture
Culture and personality 3427
Curie, Marie 1882
Currencies 4192, 4347
Current research 76
Curriculum 38, 1951, 1995, 2011, 2103, 2110, 2145, 2153, 2167, 2169-2171, 2177, 2180, 2186-2188, 2194, 2199, 2204, 2210, 2212, 2220, 2233, 2248, 2257, 2279, 2296, 2602, 5678, 5704
Curriculum development 2179, 2180
Custine Astolphe De 151
Customary law 2308, 3915, 5167, 5178
Customer service 1127, 4416, 4544
Customers 944, 1697, 3347, 4321, 4416, 5825
see also: Customer service
Customs 992, 1174, 1291, 1322, 1325, 1835, 2429, 2504, 2992, 3303, 3468, 3954
see also: Marriage customs, Sex customs
Cybernetics 1275
Cyclical analysis 2111
Czechs 1004, 1816
Dairy industry 3893, 4142, 4226
Dalit 2394, 5269
Damage compensation 3752
Dams 3728, 3766
Dance 1170, 1232, 1858, 1981, 3391
see also: Traditional dances
Dancers 1346, 1858
Darwin, Charles 571
Darwinism 214, 390, 561, 898, 1558, 1583, 2426
Data analysis 413, 421, 424, 429, 430, 432, 433, 440, 446-448, 450, 452-454, 456, 458, 464-466, 472-481, 483, 485-487, 489, 493, 495, 496, 499, 501, 504, 505, 514, 520, 525, 526, 529-531, 585, 621, 828, 930, 1005, 1033, 1045, 1085, 1847, 2006, 2043, 2053, 2059, 2213, 2396, 2681, 2688, 2692, 2817, 2855, 3025,

SUBJECT INDEX

3178, 3633, 4465, 4613, 4742, 4747, 4752, 4858, 5031, 5093, 5156, 5555, 5592, 5773, 5818, 5825
Data collection 43, 424, 429, 432, 447, 455, 501, 504-513, 515, 516, 518-520, 522, 524-527, 529-536, 538, 585, 1137, 2006, 2053, 2213, 2276, 2476, 2683, 3213, 3381, 3397, 3428, 4270, 4276, 4277, 4737, 4747, 5555, 5582, 5662, 5891
Data processing 2201
Data protection 2716
Databases 92, 166, 450, 481
Dating 3059, 3343, 5444, 5470
Daughters 2910, 2927, 3023, 3033, 3093, 3202, 3229
Davidson, Donald 114, 1231, 1846
Day care centres 4687, 5591
Deafness 1827, 2453, 2479
Death 327, 685, 724, 740, 809, 948, 1081, 1347, 1383, 1398, 1719, 1735, 1883, 1886, 1937, 2807, 2816, 2820, 2826, 2827, 2831, 2842, 2942, 5323, 5327, 5380, 5434, 5817, 5850, 5862, 5877, 5879, 5887, 5889, 5890, 5895, 5896
Death rate 2689, 2819, 2837
Debt 2336, 4351, 5151
  see also: Debt relief, External debt
Debt relief 4287
Deceit 949, 2986
Decentralization 2120, 2258, 3410, 3771, 4150, 4152, 4550, 4797, 4836, 5629
Decision 638, 1299, 4844, 5752
  see also: Employment decision
Decision making 129, 364, 370, 386, 561, 638, 674, 706, 833, 947, 1012, 1015, 1017, 1023, 1028, 1034, 1049, 1054, 1055, 1059, 1070, 1087, 1097, 1116, 1139, 1153, 1608, 1831, 1856, 2038, 2155, 2241, 2256, 2258, 2309, 2595, 2731, 2760, 2762, 2860, 2897, 3190, 3210, 3267, 3279, 3613, 3614, 3667, 3670, 3702, 3705, 3716, 3749, 3806, 3814, 3821, 3917, 3973, 4029, 4253, 4326, 4346, 4353, 4356, 4357, 4360, 4417, 4418, 4629, 4666, 4670, 4698, 4728, 4786, 4809, 4841, 4877, 4931, 5155, 5183, 5236, 5307, 5528, 5704, 5752, 5828, 5847, 5858, 5862, 5869, 5889, 5925, 5987
  see also: Group decision making
Decision models 638
Decision theory 115, 364, 366, 464, 515, 606, 638, 1049, 1050, 1085, 4391, 5752
Decoding 1799
Decolonization 951, 1880, 3945, 4935

Deconstruction 14, 124, 267, 328, 1556, 1621, 3117, 4621
Deduction 1629, 1824
Defence policy 5356, 5359
Deforestation 2717
Degler, Carl 1431
Deindustrialization 3997, 4066
Deities 1431
Deleuze, Gilles 218, 3788
Delinquency 2304, 2618, 3006, 4979, 4985, 4993, 5069, 5072, 5085, 5090, 5095, 5109, 5114, 5115, 5120
  see also: Juvenile delinquency
Demand 2043, 3909, 4791
Demand analysis 4284
Demilitarization 5361
Democracy 170, 173, 243, 955, 981, 1023, 1039, 1164, 1200, 1568, 1595, 1608, 1669, 1679, 1713, 1742, 1756, 2114, 2117, 2181, 2182, 2205, 2218, 2242, 2317, 2395, 2414, 2439, 3199, 3205, 3335, 3390, 3416, 3437, 3469, 3697, 3759, 3771, 3827, 3829, 3837, 3969, 4131, 4227, 4242, 4244, 4311, 4596, 4768, 4838, 4871, 4876, 4877, 4882, 4885, 4898, 4901, 4905-4907, 4913, 4927, 4928, 4933, 4934, 4938, 4943, 4944, 4947, 4951, 4957, 4966, 4968, 4969, 4972, 4975, 5139, 5180, 5201, 5218, 5226, 5233, 5248, 5250, 5261, 5284, 5303, 5352, 5361, 5363, 5973
  see also: Democratic consolidation, Democratic theory, Industrial democracy, Liberal democracy, Social democracy
Democratic consolidation 4938
Democratic theory 3437, 4906, 4907, 4928, 4947
Democratization 52, 1568, 2025, 2111, 2115, 2388, 2513, 3828, 3869, 4055, 4095, 4227, 4281, 4368, 4823, 4836, 4864, 4890, 4893, 4955, 4957, 4965, 4966, 4974, 4976, 5189, 5233, 5250, 5258, 5261, 5282, 5288, 5301
Demographic change 2542, 2574, 2657, 2679, 2684, 2686, 2689-2691, 2695-2698, 2705, 2708, 2710, 2712, 2720, 2724, 2725, 2767, 2781, 2792, 2796, 2797, 2799, 2810, 2835, 2837, 2994, 3397, 3716, 3795, 4252, 5780
Demographic indicators 90, 5968
Demographic research 90, 2687, 2704, 2752, 2792, 2820, 2828, 2868, 2976, 3047, 3607
Demography 90, 451, 536, 1142, 1443, 1508, 1819, 2267, 2626, 2639, 2682, 2684, 2686, 2688-2692, 2694, 2703, 2705, 2706,

INDEX DES MATIÈRES EN ANGLAIS

2709, 2710, 2713, 2714, 2716-2725, 2735, 2740, 2743, 2773, 2774, 2780, 2783, 2785, 2788, 2791, 2795, 2796, 2798, 2799, 2805, 2810-2812, 2814, 2815, 2819-2821, 2824, 2828, 2833, 2835-2837, 2846, 2857, 2904, 2942, 3211, 3423, 3518, 3528, 3603, 3615, 3639, 3715, 3725, 3758, 3764, 3778, 3795, 3951, 4024, 4252, 4276, 4367, 4408, 4615, 4641, 4697, 5626, 5720, 5728, 5757
see also: Ethnic demography
Demonology 1249
Demonstrations 1610, 4843, 5264
Deontology 1420, 1942
Dependence relationships 897, 2679, 5410
Dependency rehabilitation 5382, 5395, 5412, 5421, 5818
Depression 741, 751, 755, 757, 764, 766, 776, 779, 781, 787, 800, 804, 807, 808, 811, 876, 897, 1670, 2583, 2659, 2874, 2885, 2960, 3015, 3055, 3591, 3901, 4710, 5192, 5405, 5433, 5434, 5710, 5838, 5935
Deprivation 819, 824, 2385, 2432, 2807, 2831, 3590, 3874, 3991, 4277, 4283
Deregulation 28, 2564, 3912, 4471, 4836, 4877
Derrida, Jacques 12, 1609, 1621
Descartes, René 221
Descent
see: Cognatic descent, Matrilineal descent
Desegregation 2110
Desert 5195
Design 436, 488, 2197, 3765, 4028
see also: Experiment design, Test design, Urban design
Determinants 2408, 2822, 5757
Determinism 136, 332, 341, 1412, 1636
Deterrence 3849, 5007, 5029
Devaluation 847, 4223
Developed countries 1177, 2712, 3770, 5348, 5870
Developing countries 92, 1177, 1195, 1620, 1702, 2078, 2112, 2113, 2144, 2186, 2432, 2483, 2513, 2712, 2747, 2750, 2763, 2767, 2770, 2771, 2793, 2820, 2836, 2963, 3067, 3085, 3090, 3103, 3148, 3160, 3211, 3238, 3378, 3610, 3637, 3702, 3714, 3759, 3770, 3802, 3804, 3815, 3961, 3964, 3972, 4102, 4116, 4161, 4163, 4169, 4172, 4205, 4258, 4267, 4276, 4280, 4287, 4430, 4571, 4644, 5057, 5229, 5260, 5282, 5363, 5445, 5655, 5684, 5768, 5802, 5813, 5870, 5980
see also: Less developed countries

Development
see: Economic development, Rural development, Socio-economic development, Socioeconomic development, Sustainable development, Urban development
Development aid 5768
Development economics 2782, 2873, 3770, 3805, 3895, 4156, 4279, 5455
Development models 3771, 3811, 4205, 4279
Development planning 3921, 4061, 4067, 4096, 4104, 4116, 4117, 4167, 4177
Development policy 1267, 1923, 3160, 3378, 3796, 3801, 3815, 3817, 3828, 3868, 3915, 3927, 4236, 4254, 4267, 4279, 4287, 5701
Development potential 2685
Development programmes 2286, 3378, 3611, 5493, 5629
Development projects 2483, 2512, 3813, 3822, 3827, 3832, 3841, 5973
Development research 553
Development sciences 572
Development strategies 1221, 2286, 2483, 3104, 3174, 3822, 3832, 4252, 4290
Development studies 92, 2432, 2539, 3770, 3964, 4236, 4268, 4819, 5768
Development theory 585, 1221, 2528, 2539, 2774, 3160, 3770, 3771, 3803, 4177, 4279, 4287
Developmental psychology 544, 547, 572, 575, 682, 731, 755, 1161
Deviance 709, 2358, 2634, 3377, 3524, 4530, 4683, 5011, 5405
Devils 1438
Devolution 2529
Dewey, John 2117
Diabetes 5970
Dialectics 140, 218, 360, 362, 1210, 1650, 5166, 5677
Dialectology 1798
Dialects 1793, 1798, 1801, 1840, 2523
Dialogue 31, 523, 901, 940, 1014, 1462, 1561, 1632, 1640, 1648, 1808, 1824, 1877, 4835
see also: Intercultural dialogue
Diamonds 3067
Diana [Princess of Wales] 1719, 1751
Diary 722
Diaspora 1263, 1836, 1880, 1978, 1985, 1990, 3445, 3497, 3557, 3636, 3646, 3650, 3654, 3668, 3676, 3680, 3778, 4118, 4125, 5328
Dictatorship 2567, 4095, 4973, 5266
Dictionaries 81, 82, 84, 93, 96-98, 100, 103, 556, 1703

SUBJECT INDEX

Diet 419, 941, 1293, 1297, 3546, 5494, 5959, 5961
Dietrich, Marlene 1882
Difference 45, 368, 735, 1279, 2289, 2907, 2915, 3301, 3367, 3386, 3403, 3786, 3834, 4118, 4615
Digital technology 1661, 1667, 1669, 1779, 2596
Dilthey, Wilhelm 126
Diplomacy 5333
Directories 79, 80, 85, 87, 105
Disability 502, 555, 557, 716, 1898, 2019, 2044, 2431, 2452-2478, 2480-2484, 2487-2492, 2494-2496, 2498-2501, 2737, 2755, 2811, 2815, 3013, 3035, 3037, 3329, 4362, 4776, 5514, 5518, 5549, 5565, 5602-5604, 5606-5608, 5916
Disability benefit 5605
Disabled children 783, 2019, 2026, 2154, 2453, 2463, 2486, 2488, 5547, 5576
Disabled persons 2454, 2456, 2458, 2460, 2462, 2466-2471, 2474-2476, 2478, 2480, 2481, 2485, 2487, 2489-2492, 2495, 2496, 2499, 2500, 4750, 5482, 5520, 5565, 5602, 5605, 5609
Disabled rehabilitation 5604
Disabled workers 2455, 2468, 2489, 5215
Disaster relief 3699, 3751, 3813, 5321, 5330
Disasters 767, 1146, 3615, 3690, 3699, 3751, 4265, 5464, 5910, 5911, 5923, 5964
see also: Natural disasters
Discourse 47, 117, 119, 126, 149, 233, 243, 261, 271, 367, 511, 593, 664, 916, 940, 1059, 1102-1104, 1108, 1127, 1139, 1165, 1208, 1313, 1345, 1361, 1428, 1531, 1561, 1567, 1642, 1648, 1650, 1668, 1685, 1727, 1748, 1752, 1772, 1789, 1790, 1792, 1808, 1830, 1832, 1833, 1839, 1844, 1852, 1960, 2208, 2354, 2402, 2468, 2496, 2579, 2588, 2643, 2730, 2940, 3005, 3037, 3061, 3062, 3102, 3117, 3258, 3259, 3266, 3272, 3273, 3317, 3339, 3354, 3365, 3497, 3499, 3500, 3508, 3697, 3700, 3717, 3723, 3727, 3788, 4016, 4065, 4137, 4138, 4265, 4361, 4362, 4515, 4618, 4666, 4912, 4918, 4952, 4966, 5061, 5162, 5165, 5184, 5254, 5299, 5315, 5589, 5603
Discourse analysis 197, 333, 369, 405, 506, 523, 568, 828, 870, 940, 959, 1101-1104, 1120, 1127, 1137, 1227, 1263, 1311, 1365, 1558, 1650, 1722, 1730, 1739, 1748, 1762, 1771, 1784, 1789-1792, 1800, 1801, 1807, 1808, 1810, 1821, 1822, 1824, 1830, 1831, 1833, 1839, 1844, 1856, 1872, 1877, 1957, 2327, 2355, 2607, 3045, 3139, 3184, 3299, 3346, 3358, 3772, 3864, 4065, 4250, 4666, 4887, 5170, 5289, 5329, 5418
Discrimination 349, 822, 858, 894, 1044, 1067, 1308, 1760, 2017, 2057, 2076, 2273, 2452, 2458, 2477, 2484, 2754, 3274, 3286, 3321, 3375, 3451, 3470, 3511, 3657, 3992, 3996, 4285, 4427, 4494, 4495, 4497, 4510, 4628, 5188, 5214, 5243, 5443, 5800, 5872, 5928, 5988
see also: Age discrimination, Employment discrimination, Racial discrimination, Religious discrimination, Sex discrimination, Wage discrimination
Discussion groups 4726
Diseases 386, 446, 453, 483, 484, 1620, 2719, 2762, 2808, 2844, 3309, 3332, 3334, 3794, 4611, 5363, 5534, 5735, 5773, 5838, 5857, 5866, 5891, 5942, 5944-5946, 5948, 5952, 5957, 5958, 5964, 5968, 5972, 5980, 5983, 5986
see also: AIDS, Alzheimer's disease, Anorexia nervosa, Heart disease, Hepatitis, Malaria, Mental illness, Occupational diseases, Sexually transmitted diseases, Smallpox, Trypanosomiasis
Dismissals 4483, 4508, 4737
Dissent 1431, 5275
Dissidents 5148
Distribution 460, 491, 492, 1892, 2818, 4162
Distribution economics 4262
Distributive justice 2603, 4262, 4660, 4921, 4937
Districts 3359, 4149
Divergence 1798, 2776
Diversification 6, 1010, 2363, 3401, 3919, 4234, 4243
Divination 1433
Divinities 1374
Division of labour 513, 1495, 2035, 2406, 2554, 2571, 2915, 3170, 3221, 3236, 3258, 3270, 3693, 4092, 4132, 4389, 4400, 4477, 4486, 4521, 4526, 4530, 4556, 4575, 4577, 4754
see also: International division of labour
Divorce 2696, 2724, 2768, 2845-2859, 2911, 2923, 2924, 2962, 2968, 2975, 3022, 3054, 3056
Dizi 3531
DNA 473, 498, 1620, 5048, 5848
Doctor-patient relationship 694, 740, 778, 897, 5828-5831, 5835, 5837, 5838, 5849, 5858, 5862, 5889, 5908

INDEX DES MATIÈRES EN ANGLAIS

Doctors 249, 794, 2532, 3629, 4770, 5675, 5726, 5753, 5760, 5765, 5772, 5788, 5824, 5827, 5830, 5833, 5835-5838, 5840, 5841, 5853, 5857, 5862, 5878, 5882, 5895, 5982
Documentation 1884
Documents 104, 178, 1040, 3532
Dogma 58, 141
Dogmatism 1552
Domestic animals 2863
Domestic policy 2704
Domestic violence 2860-2876, 2878-2889, 2891-2893, 2895, 2991, 5144, 5382, 5439, 5444, 5451, 5459, 5463, 5469, 5594
Domestic workers 60, 3191, 3243, 3317, 4462, 4736
Dominant culture 2530
Domination 245, 291, 799, 852, 1060, 2340, 2421, 3115, 3187, 3236, 3457, 3881, 4953, 4968, 5016, 5170, 5216, 5438
Dominicans 3398
Downsizing 4411, 4434, 4647, 4737
Downward mobility 2591
Dowry 3265
Drama 171, 249, 1170, 1331, 1695, 1874, 1877, 1964, 2458
Drawing 5592
Dreams 212, 602, 961, 1426, 2641
Dress 1321, 1325, 1335, 3067, 3372
Drinkers 500, 722, 5388, 5404, 5406, 5955
Dropouts 4794, 5578
Drought 2827, 3690
Drug abuse 709, 1307, 1334, 2618, 2621, 4683, 4998, 5115, 5367, 5369, 5374, 5375, 5378, 5380, 5382-5386, 5395-5397, 5399, 5401, 5406, 5409, 5465, 5480, 5664, 5748, 5767, 5801, 5818, 5891
Drug addiction 5367, 5375, 5376, 5379, 5386, 5406, 5664, 5801
Drug addicts 5375, 5376, 5378, 5401, 5801
Drug policy 2559, 5367, 5383
Drug trafficking 2559
Drug use 5115, 5392, 5409, 5664, 5958, 5966
Drugs 1307, 1313, 1344, 1355, 2521, 2621, 3995, 4493, 5011, 5031, 5050, 5079, 5115, 5126, 5374, 5380, 5381, 5383, 5384, 5386, 5394, 5395, 5399, 5402, 5406, 5409, 5480, 5828, 5833, 5862, 5886, 5891, 5958
see also: Cannabis, Cocaine, Drug policy, Drug trafficking, Drug use, Heroin, Opiates
Du Bois, W.E.B. 3432, 3514
Dualism 239, 1136, 2388, 5182
Duda-Gracz, Jerzy 1852

Dumézil, Georges 1395
Dummett, Michael 222
Dumont, Louis 2395
Durkheim, Émile 223, 330, 375, 801, 1245, 5158
Dutch 1798
Duty 1245, 2346, 3471
Dynamic models 445, 466, 1085, 2967
Dynamics 643, 1265, 3971
Dyslexia 2477
Early modern history 237, 1160, 4263
Earman, J. 1586
Earnings 633, 2267, 2948, 2991, 4305, 4306, 4437, 4451, 4454, 4463, 4464, 4539, 4548, 4549, 4551, 4556, 4573, 4704, 4745, 4804, 4878, 5636, 5832
Earthquakes 3702, 5923
East-West relations 134, 989, 1186, 1230, 1268, 2518
Eastern bloc 1274
Eastern civilization 259, 5128
Eastern countries 4631
Eating disorders 506, 744, 777, 791, 817, 2667, 5182, 5847
Eckhart, Meister 220
Ecological analysis 3712
Ecological movements 5252, 5272
Ecologism 3729, 3742, 3768, 3797, 4210
Ecology 22, 225, 558, 561, 1099, 1107, 1237, 1401, 1576, 2766, 2983, 3058, 3131, 3688, 3695, 3700, 3706, 3707, 3709, 3717-3720, 3725, 3730, 3732, 3737, 3740, 3742, 3747, 3751, 3753, 3758, 3759, 3761, 3762, 3766, 3774, 3797, 3798, 3811, 3816, 3820, 3925, 3949, 4114, 4132, 4155, 4293, 4346, 5252, 5911, 5958
see also: Cultural ecology, Human ecology, Social ecology
Econometric models 4264, 4752, 5956
Econometrics 4503, 5832
Economic activity 2653, 2679, 3626, 3761, 4050, 4240, 4372, 4767, 5287
Economic analysis 1861, 2568, 3662, 4220, 4845, 5057
see also: Long-term analysis, Short-term analysis
Economic behaviour 3842, 4180, 4183, 4184, 4190, 4239, 4263, 4275, 4391, 4426
Economic change 177, 975, 1673, 2504, 2507, 2519, 2541, 2563, 2565, 2579, 2837, 2914, 2965, 3488, 3776, 3810, 3916, 3997, 4066, 4218, 4223, 4241, 4255, 4301, 4429, 4434, 4474, 4715, 4726, 4818, 4866, 5187, 5767, 5773

SUBJECT INDEX

Economic conditions 54, 64, 963, 1067, 2514, 2526, 2637, 2707, 2749, 2914, 3077, 3202, 3206, 3261, 3275, 3277, 3551, 3617, 3633, 3682, 3773, 3776, 3805, 3827, 3870, 3924, 3943, 4009, 4016, 4017, 4071, 4088, 4185, 4189, 4195, 4207, 4245, 4256, 4274, 4275, 4278, 4280, 4282, 4299, 4308, 4314, 4334, 4387, 4545, 4576, 4618, 4845, 4947, 5103, 5202, 5268, 5417, 5493, 5567, 5598, 5626, 5628, 5980
Economic cooperation 4198
Economic crisis 1207, 2561, 2579, 2767, 2775, 3612, 3903, 3927, 4011, 4218, 4221, 4250
Economic decline 4066, 4273
Economic dependence 2945, 3625
Economic development 92, 1219, 1685, 2046, 2266, 2420, 2512, 2523, 2528, 2558, 2749, 2961, 3103, 3160, 3615, 3633, 3637, 3642, 3662, 3718, 3722, 3770, 3771, 3776, 3796, 3802, 3814, 3815, 3914, 3923, 3925, 3935, 3940, 3948, 3960, 3971, 4029, 4043, 4077, 4079, 4085, 4092, 4097, 4098, 4109, 4161, 4169, 4197, 4218, 4228, 4233, 4236, 4250, 4253, 4254, 4258, 4267, 4272, 4279, 4286, 4290, 4292, 4296, 4309, 4313, 4450, 4452, 4535, 4600, 4606, 4819, 4866, 5282, 5445, 5519, 5622, 5768
Economic dynamics 4132
Economic efficiency 4061, 4621
Economic elites 3942, 4160, 5227
Economic equality 4242
Economic forecasts 2527
Economic geography 1314, 1892, 3770, 3773, 3927, 4135, 4175, 4247, 4486
Economic growth 2266, 2434, 2561, 2574, 3661, 3815, 3817, 3893, 3986, 4046, 4177, 4203, 4228, 4261, 4264, 4278, 4287, 4289, 4357, 4407, 4558, 4824, 4935, 5626, 5642
see also: Growth theory
Economic hardship 4606
Economic history 1323, 2424, 2512, 2568, 4206, 4214, 4228, 4242, 4272, 4330
Economic incentives 4180
Economic indicators 5756
see also: Signalling
Economic inequality 2371, 2384, 2521, 4274, 4285, 4497, 5057
Economic instability 4299
Economic integration 2518, 4258, 4439, 4825, 4968
Economic justice 3705, 4242

Economic law 2196, 5025
Economic life 1298, 4322
Economic methodology 515, 1140, 1377, 2723, 2943, 3063
Economic models 10, 3923, 4305, 4427, 4791
Economic networks 4369, 4380, 4381, 5227, 5237
Economic performance 1153, 3996, 4207, 4249, 4374, 4592, 4602, 4633
Economic policy 64, 2496, 2561, 2571, 2707, 3615, 3804, 3817, 4052, 4063, 4185, 4189, 4206, 4236, 4248, 4281, 4587, 4817, 5605
see also: Industrial policy
Economic psychology 905, 4183, 4190, 4684
Economic reform 24, 2396, 2507, 2509, 2513, 2833, 3140, 3869, 3870, 3903, 3976, 4136, 4221, 4236, 4245, 4281, 4303, 4829, 4855, 4872, 4942, 5759
Economic relations 4104, 4322, 4380, 5536
see also: International economic relations
Economic research 54, 414, 436, 4744
Economic resources 1443
Economic rights 4268, 5809
Economic sociology 67, 336, 408, 1324, 2526, 3164, 3169, 3907, 4179, 4180, 4182, 4190, 4191, 4194, 4195, 4224, 4235, 4237, 4241, 4263, 4285, 4323, 4326, 4374, 4380, 4403, 4405, 4423, 5365
Economic stability 4949
Economic status 2748, 3996, 4530, 5519
Economic strategies 5445
Economic structure 4942, 5821
Economic surveys 4484
Economic systems 336, 1200, 2320, 3766, 3823, 3869, 4195, 4208, 4215, 4221, 4223, 4224, 4231, 4236, 4946
Economic theory 381, 1098, 1377, 1570, 2447, 2706, 3000, 3705, 3927, 4181, 4196, 4211, 4230, 4351, 4405, 4739
Economic thought 3797, 4179, 4194, 4216, 4336, 4916
Economics 6, 10, 1410, 1859, 2216, 2243, 3115, 4199, 4224, 4311, 4314, 5186, 5316
Economics of education 2167
Economics of sport 1357
Economies of scale 3893, 4151
Economism 373
Economists 375, 1859, 4191, 4255
Ecosystems 3705, 3714, 3721, 3728, 3731, 3754, 3755, 3761
Ecstasy 1347
Education 33, 252, 418, 437, 441, 448, 454, 459, 543, 545, 574, 587, 633, 647, 980, 984, 996, 1018, 1196, 1203, 1331, 1519,

INDEX DES MATIÈRES EN ANGLAIS

1536, 1592, 1644, 1648, 1675, 1692, 1708, 1776, 1819, 1875, 1992, 1993, 1995, 1997-2003, 2005, 2006, 2011, 2012, 2015-2017, 2022, 2024, 2027, 2028, 2031-2033, 2039, 2041, 2042, 2045, 2046, 2048, 2050-2054, 2060, 2065-2068, 2071, 2073, 2074, 2076, 2078-2081, 2083-2087, 2090, 2092, 2094-2096, 2099, 2100, 2102-2108, 2112, 2115, 2117, 2119, 2122, 2125-2127, 2130, 2131, 2135-2137, 2141-2144, 2148, 2150-2152, 2154, 2156, 2160-2162, 2165-2168, 2172, 2175-2177, 2180, 2181, 2185, 2187-2189, 2191-2193, 2196, 2197, 2200-2203, 2206, 2211, 2214, 2217, 2218, 2220, 2221, 2224, 2229, 2230, 2232, 2233, 2237, 2247, 2254, 2258, 2259, 2265, 2270, 2279, 2324, 2361, 2378, 2383, 2391, 2414, 2430, 2434, 2453, 2454, 2464, 2482, 2517, 2602, 2607, 2632, 2636, 2677, 2736, 2749, 2786, 2787, 2803, 2822, 2825, 2871, 2974, 3016, 3019, 3026, 3057, 3067, 3075, 3112, 3115, 3177, 3203, 3237, 3265, 3282, 3414, 3435, 3509, 3517, 3571, 3582, 3604, 3643, 3653, 3671, 3715, 3723, 3724, 3854, 3965, 4040, 4077, 4176, 4268, 4301, 4367, 4393, 4398, 4435, 4441, 4453, 4481, 4506, 4523, 4538, 4586, 4598, 4605, 4762, 4771, 4772, 4779, 4807, 4869, 4900, 4915, 4947, 5072, 5139, 5225, 5266, 5269, 5287, 5335, 5465, 5538, 5569, 5583, 5591, 5593, 5612, 5634, 5642, 5663, 5678, 5684, 5686, 5688, 5694, 5697, 5703, 5704, 5709, 5711, 5713, 5723, 5969, 5976
see also: Access to education, Adult education, Basic education, Bilingual education, Civic education, Compulsory education, Continuing education, Correspondence education, Economics of education, Health education, Higher education, History of education, Mass education, Minority education, Multicultural education, Pedagogy, Political education, Post-secondary education, Primary education, Private education, Public education, Religious education, Returns to education, Secondary education, Special education, Technical education, Tertiary education, Theory of education, Vocational education, Women's education, Workers' education
Education administration 2093, 2095, 2159, 2263, 4806

Education policy 1991, 1992, 1994-1996, 2012, 2014, 2017, 2019, 2024, 2026, 2027, 2044, 2055, 2079, 2095, 2098, 2107, 2109, 2121, 2124, 2129-2133, 2136, 2138, 2144-2148, 2150, 2151, 2153, 2155, 2156, 2162-2164, 2166, 2167, 2169-2171, 2177, 2204, 2210, 2213, 2225, 2228, 2246, 2248, 2258, 2265, 2266, 2269, 2280, 2290, 2292, 2297, 3206, 3470, 3869, 4438, 4768, 4791, 4793, 4949, 4962, 5588, 5641, 5642
Education reform 68, 1224, 2024, 2069, 2079, 2103, 2117, 2122, 2133, 2137, 2138, 2140, 2145, 2146, 2148, 2154, 2156, 2158, 2164, 2210, 2238, 2292, 2513, 3869, 4598, 5225, 5642, 5703
Education systems 50, 93, 437, 1223, 1715, 1991, 1994, 1996, 2010, 2011, 2014, 2016, 2017, 2021, 2024, 2047, 2049, 2054, 2058, 2059, 2063-2065, 2068, 2076, 2077, 2081, 2084, 2085, 2093, 2094, 2108, 2109, 2111-2116, 2120, 2122-2124, 2126, 2128-2131, 2133, 2135-2138, 2140, 2142, 2144-2148, 2150, 2151, 2153, 2155, 2158, 2159, 2161, 2163-2165, 2167, 2169, 2171, 2173, 2176, 2177, 2180, 2181, 2184, 2192, 2204, 2218-2220, 2226, 2230, 2236, 2238, 2245-2247, 2256, 2259, 2260, 2265, 2266, 2275, 2277, 2283-2285, 2296, 2316, 2378, 2460, 3491, 3521, 3869, 4598, 4640, 4805, 4806, 4949, 5678
Educational crisis 2251
Educational development 2007, 2145, 2257
Educational expenditure 2460
Educational institutions 2014, 2048, 2253, 2291, 3290, 5678
Educational needs 2020, 2486
Educational objectives 2139
Educational opportunities 2030, 5358
Educational philosophy 225, 2004, 2082, 2117, 2145, 2177, 2181, 2193, 2226, 4900
Educational psychology 637, 647, 2028, 2168, 2197, 2206, 4671
Educational research 418, 437, 1992, 1999, 2089, 2182, 2924
Educational sociology 50, 77, 1991, 2000, 2002, 2003, 2014, 2030, 2054, 2064, 2071, 2090, 2097, 2108, 2110, 2158, 2164, 2192, 2202, 2225, 2240, 2284, 2532, 3176, 4772
Educational technology 2172, 2175, 2201
Effects 1308, 4347
see also: Environmental effects, Group effects, Psychological effects

443

SUBJECT INDEX

Egalitarianism 657, 2414, 2439, 2708, 2972, 3237, 4201, 5225, 5262, 5296
Egídio, Paulo 5098
Ego 679, 780
Egocentrism 905, 2938
Elections 1427, 1772, 2507, 2671, 3483, 4947, 5301, 5305, 5306, 5363
Elections to the lower chamber 5219
Electoral behaviour 1439, 2671, 5300, 5306
Electoral campaigning 5234, 5288
Electoral platforms 5307
Electorate 5303
Electricity 4788
Electronics 4134
Elias, Norbert 393, 4392, 5015
Eligibility 5535, 5788
Elites 1608, 2223, 2321, 2391, 2397, 2398, 2401, 3803, 4204, 4292, 4897, 4898, 4951, 4965, 5060, 5284, 5335
  see also: Economic elites, Political elites
Elitism 1369, 2290, 2391, 5024
Ellis, Ruth 1882
Emancipation 295, 1960, 2310, 3178, 3206, 3453, 3457
  see also: Women's emancipation
Emigrants 3631, 3638
Emigration 18, 1536, 2705, 3541, 3542, 3575, 3584, 3598, 3603, 3605, 3612, 3631, 3633, 3639, 3652, 3659, 3668, 3679, 3684, 3686, 3778, 3791
Emotions 226, 314, 388, 559, 565, 591, 596, 611, 650, 670, 671, 674, 676, 677, 682-690, 692, 696, 703-706, 708, 711, 713, 715, 718, 720, 723, 726-729, 731, 736, 739, 742, 777, 821, 823, 838, 850, 856, 863, 873, 892, 899, 907, 913, 920, 921, 933, 935, 943, 948, 955, 1013, 1047, 1057, 1075, 1109, 1112, 1210, 1334, 1359, 1573, 1647, 1666, 1844, 1927, 1967, 2733, 2809, 2847, 2850, 2916, 2931, 2977, 3017, 3030, 3034, 3048, 3052, 3057, 3282, 3318, 3724, 3827, 3873, 4106, 4140, 4345, 4697, 5015, 5034, 5040, 5277, 5303, 5434, 5447, 5477, 5680, 5856, 5925, 5939
  see also: Depression, Love
Empathy 583, 747, 831, 905-907, 1075, 1551
Empire
  see: French Empire
Empires 188, 1195, 2553, 3510, 5360
  see also: British Empire, Ottoman Empire
Empirical research 55, 75, 339, 482, 540, 668, 711, 775, 1293, 1574, 2190, 3996, 4020, 4116, 4197, 4409, 4985, 5074, 5285, 5324, 5383, 5709

Empirical tests 477, 2214, 4298, 5073, 5075
Empiricism 75, 133, 141, 292, 304, 369, 1181, 1581, 1611, 2209
Employees 768, 1111, 1135, 1144, 1764, 1977, 2362, 3226, 3325, 3767, 4367, 4376, 4388, 4391, 4397, 4400, 4403, 4406, 4419, 4422, 4483, 4618, 4658, 4684, 4689, 4692, 4700, 4701, 4703, 4705-4707, 4712, 4718, 4722, 4723, 4728, 4729, 4732, 4745, 4746, 4748, 4760, 4779, 4803, 4808, 4809, 4812, 4822, 4827, 4830, 4831, 4844, 4846, 4861, 4862, 4866, 4876, 4880, 5607, 5794
Employers 1147, 3553, 4422, 4449, 4499, 4596, 4712, 4798, 4814, 4815, 4840, 4846, 4850, 4868
Employers' organizations 4814
Employment 314, 414, 550, 768, 772, 1304, 1644, 2040, 2078, 2085, 2094, 2128, 2413, 2424, 2456, 2458, 2466, 2469, 2507, 2561, 2567, 2571, 2626, 2627, 2657, 2677, 2700, 2760, 2878, 3019, 3025, 3069, 3081, 3177, 3187, 3206, 3226, 3255, 3268, 3270, 3536, 3572, 3585, 3586, 3623, 3628, 3643, 3662, 3897, 4049, 4077, 4235, 4257, 4309, 4361, 4372, 4378, 4382, 4402, 4404, 4405, 4411, 4430, 4431, 4436, 4439, 4442-4445, 4453, 4455, 4457, 4459, 4463, 4472-4474, 4476, 4478, 4479, 4483, 4485, 4491, 4492, 4497, 4503, 4515, 4536, 4540, 4541, 4546, 4547, 4550, 4553-4555, 4557, 4568, 4571, 4576, 4577, 4583, 4594, 4596, 4597, 4600, 4614, 4627, 4644, 4647, 4664, 4673, 4676, 4685, 4686, 4688, 4694, 4724, 4732, 4738, 4740, 4753, 4755, 4758, 4760, 4761, 4763, 4769, 4777, 4786, 4793, 4814, 4827, 4828, 4835, 4836, 4842, 4866, 4872, 4881, 4915, 4949, 4983, 5121, 5217, 5265, 5365, 5567, 5624, 5625, 5633, 5642, 5654
  see also: Access to employment, Downsizing, Full-time employment, Illegal employment, Part-time employment, Rural employment, Temporary employment, Urban employment, Women's employment, Youth employment
Employment creation 4447, 4450
Employment decision 4532, 4561
Employment discrimination 2455, 2466, 4487-4489, 4491, 4496, 4498, 4500, 4507, 4509, 4690, 4691, 5203
Employment level 4505, 4881

INDEX DES MATIÈRES EN ANGLAIS

Employment opportunities 2037, 2475, 2532, 2561, 2691, 3608, 4447, 4465, 4523, 4615, 4742, 4761
Employment policy 1891, 2455, 2459, 2554, 2702, 4267, 4438, 4447, 4476, 4489, 4490, 4507, 4516, 4552, 4589, 4598, 4696, 4795, 4797, 4799, 4810, 4824, 4835, 4837, 4872, 5624, 5641
Employment stability 4738
Employment theory 4588, 4597
Empowerment 104, 891, 1006, 2279, 2310, 2335, 2458, 2483, 2638, 3067, 3094, 3099, 3104, 3126, 3140, 3145, 3176, 3192, 3403, 3453, 3480, 3830, 3837, 3841, 3911, 4259, 4316, 4632, 4689, 4808, 4861, 4942, 4945, 5159, 5184, 5212, 5782
Encyclopaedias 83, 86, 1178-1180, 2694, 3528
Endogamy 2701, 2984
Energy 1623, 2508, 4637
   see also: Non-renewable energy, Nuclear energy
Energy conservation 1605, 1623
Energy crisis 3713
Engineering 1554, 3765, 4571
Engineers 4769, 4788
English language 82, 97, 930, 1671, 1757, 1785, 1789, 1790, 1793, 1795, 1801, 1805, 1806, 1813, 1819, 1830, 1831, 1834, 1847, 1914, 1943, 1997, 2081, 2107, 2149, 2173, 3580, 4440, 4807, 5170
Enlightenment thought 123, 242, 247, 248, 256, 315, 372, 1158, 1248, 1578, 1970
Enterprises 49, 371, 1103, 1122, 1127, 1142, 1323, 2263, 2362, 3166, 3791, 3797, 3869, 4214, 4243, 4279, 4309, 4318, 4357, 4358, 4366, 4375, 4380, 4381, 4401, 4403, 4407, 4408, 4422, 4423, 4569, 4634, 4669, 4763, 4773, 4798, 4809, 4812, 4819, 4842, 4881, 4946, 5227, 5267, 5475, 5478, 5725
   see also: Family firms, Foreign enterprises, Multinational enterprises, Private enterprises, Small and medium sized enterprises
Entertainment 1187, 1318, 1320, 1708, 1731, 1753, 1756, 1765, 1772, 1882, 1977, 2486, 2618, 3353, 3391, 3644, 4060, 4787, 4954
Entrepreneurs 582, 3190, 4372, 4387, 4407, 4415
Entrepreneurship 414, 582, 1151, 2571, 3069, 3791, 3885, 3927, 3942, 4209, 4239, 4273, 4311, 4369, 4371, 4372, 4393, 4394, 4407, 4415, 4651, 4665

Environment 225, 483, 558, 575, 641, 769, 2304, 2559, 2659, 2812, 2825, 3014, 3066, 3083, 3090, 3126, 3167, 3308, 3687, 3691, 3696, 3697, 3701, 3703, 3705, 3706, 3717, 3720-3728, 3731, 3734, 3737, 3742, 3746, 3750, 3753, 3758, 3761, 3762, 3765, 3766, 3803, 3815, 4108, 4114, 4146, 4246, 4313, 4358, 4420, 5067, 5244, 5337, 5517, 5529
   see also: Cultural environment, Environment and politics, Environmentalism, Family environment, Human environment, Physical environment, Rural environment, Social environment, Urban environment, Work environment
Environment and politics 3681, 3718, 3759, 5221, 5255
Environmental degradation 2717, 3681, 3700, 3702, 3704, 3712-3714, 3717, 3722, 3731, 3733, 3757, 3759, 3761, 3811, 3813, 3814, 3853, 4216, 4246, 5686, 5700
Environmental economics 2793, 3757, 3799, 3811, 3823
Environmental effects 73, 559, 1567, 1601, 3718, 3760, 3783
Environmental impact studies 3708, 3709, 3767, 3815, 3819, 4025, 4084, 4108
Environmental law 3810, 5244
Environmental management 73, 3707, 3709, 3712, 3760, 3817, 3819, 3838, 4064, 4107, 4114, 4409, 5254
Environmental movements 3729, 3749, 3827, 5244, 5255, 5275
Environmental planning 3810
Environmental policy 64, 2513, 3688, 3705, 3706, 3711, 3718, 3738, 3755, 3759, 3796, 3800, 3803, 3804, 3806, 3808, 3810, 3818, 3819, 4063, 4107, 4246, 4358, 4486
Environmental protection 73, 1010, 1093, 1152, 1601, 2513, 3706, 3711, 3717, 3723, 3724, 3728, 3732, 3739, 3744, 3749, 3754, 3762, 3763, 3765, 3796, 3797, 3803, 3804, 3806, 3810, 3819, 3820, 3914, 4025, 4058, 4062, 4081, 5254, 5255, 5330
Environmental psychology 442, 641, 839, 3749, 4106, 5529
Environmental sociology 3687, 3698, 3700, 3706, 3712, 3730, 3783, 4086
Environmentalism 1093, 1152, 1297, 3705, 3710, 3717, 3729, 3732, 3742, 3743, 3749, 3759, 3797, 3818, 3838, 4062, 4084, 5252, 5254, 5255
Epic literature 1920, 1934

SUBJECT INDEX

Epic poetry 241
Epidemiology 709, 791, 3794, 5891, 5958, 5965, 5968, 5980
Epistemology 8, 12, 20, 29, 30, 52, 107-110, 112-114, 118-120, 123, 125, 127-129, 131-133, 135-137, 140, 161, 254, 260, 261, 289, 300, 301, 309, 356, 363, 385, 409, 427, 494, 1216, 1234, 1396, 1400, 1404, 1422, 1428, 1445, 1552, 1568, 1570, 1573, 1582, 1592, 1606, 1610, 1628-1630, 1863, 1999, 2209, 2216, 2222, 2224, 2226, 2436, 2609, 2809, 3062, 3094, 3528, 3750, 4413, 4621, 4906, 5310
Equal opportunities 349, 2019, 2030, 2076, 2078, 2123, 2273, 2414, 3127, 4272, 4486, 4496, 4512, 4537, 4541, 4550, 4563, 4695, 5197, 5348
Equal pay 4496, 4552
Equality 349, 389, 852, 2030, 2039, 2114, 2314, 2354, 2380, 2384, 2395, 2405, 2414, 2442, 2458, 2484, 3080, 3106, 3121, 3206, 3335, 3713, 3780, 3787, 4200, 4255, 4262, 4282, 4288, 4400, 4441, 4514, 4538, 4550, 4563, 4572, 4903, 4989, 5021, 5171, 5350, 5357
see also: Economic equality, Sex equality, Social equality
Equilibrium 2447, 2782, 4124, 4351, 5455
see also: Market equilibrium, Social equilibrium
Equilibrium models 467
Equity 461, 915, 1290, 3097, 3335, 3694, 3757, 3784, 4096, 4290, 4486, 5445
Equivalence 5763
Ergonomics 4776
Eroticism 3061, 3297, 3353
Error 27, 233, 498, 525, 624, 631, 666
Estates 3886
Estimation 433, 453, 480, 482, 525, 2722, 2794, 4306, 4317, 5390
Ethics 16, 43, 46, 117, 131, 192, 201, 205, 206, 209, 216, 221, 227, 228, 232, 238, 243, 254, 255, 264, 268, 270, 274, 277, 288, 293, 302, 321, 328, 333, 340, 346, 362, 367, 378, 382, 417, 434, 444, 528, 539, 673, 733, 799, 909, 934, 1259, 1358, 1369, 1382, 1388, 1402, 1403, 1410, 1420, 1440, 1486, 1526, 1607, 1620, 1665, 1714, 1767, 1850, 2001, 2084, 2160, 2181, 2342, 2344, 2348-2350, 2354, 2355, 2362, 2365-2368, 2370, 2478, 2485, 2503, 2554, 2610, 2683, 2716, 2734, 2854, 3028, 3118, 3119, 3136, 3142, 3471, 3705, 3764, 3780, 3798-3801, 3919, 4293, 4307, 4359, 4417, 4421, 4422, 4424, 4427, 4497, 4658, 4684, 4772, 4917, 4984, 4988, 5161, 5169, 5174, 5180, 5181, 5208, 5316, 5327, 5330, 5355, 5371, 5400, 5442, 5679, 5704, 5730, 5770, 5817, 5850, 5853, 5854, 5861, 5863, 5865, 5868, 5869, 5871, 5875, 5876, 5883, 5884, 5886
see also: Bioethics, Business ethics, Medical ethics, Professional ethics, Protestant ethic, Work ethic
Ethnic assimilation 2024, 2051, 3409, 3425, 3440, 3487, 3533, 3548
Ethnic cleansing 1730, 3070, 3420, 3485, 4966
Ethnic communities 2047, 3407, 3419, 3531, 3593
Ethnic consciousness 3447, 5263
Ethnic demography 2811, 2812
Ethnic groups 9, 581, 956, 1263, 1373, 1527, 1620, 1777, 1786, 1801, 2063, 2211, 2392, 2436, 2511, 2811, 2812, 2887, 2992, 3011, 3013, 3263, 3323, 3394, 3397, 3399, 3405, 3408, 3409, 3413-3415, 3419, 3421, 3424, 3425, 3428, 3429, 3436, 3440, 3442, 3447, 3450, 3451, 3454, 3456, 3459, 3460, 3475, 3482, 3483, 3487, 3492, 3496, 3501, 3504, 3511, 3512, 3519, 3520, 3525, 3530, 3533, 3545, 3552, 3558, 3567, 3568, 3577, 3583, 3640, 3647, 3685, 3730, 4001, 4009, 4118, 4129, 4249, 4445, 4460, 4479, 4492, 4495, 4498, 4500, 4575, 4776, 4966, 5102, 5226, 5386, 5436, 5441, 5563, 5621, 5791, 5832, 5900
Ethnic minorities 771, 1319, 1532, 1620, 1698, 1721, 1736, 1748, 1777, 1786, 1985, 1986, 2017, 2024, 2026, 2042, 2050, 2051, 2062, 2067, 2069, 2077, 2080, 2089, 2143, 2188, 2376, 2470, 2523, 2866, 2934, 3397, 3407, 3409, 3413, 3414, 3419, 3423-3426, 3428, 3433, 3447, 3458, 3460, 3467-3469, 3474, 3479, 3484, 3507, 3515, 3533, 3563, 3576, 3577, 3631, 3656, 3668, 3978, 3981, 3988, 4009, 4497, 4500, 4507, 5017, 5081, 5089, 5147, 5214, 5292, 5304, 5527, 5621, 5713
Ethnic pluralism 225, 3501, 3642
Ethnic policy 3395, 3474
Ethnicity 33, 681, 903, 952, 954, 964-967, 983, 985, 991, 997, 1000, 1011, 1171, 1195, 1315, 1373, 1392, 1397, 1431, 1452, 1513, 1529, 1551, 1769, 1775, 1777, 1786, 1801, 1811, 1813, 1815, 1823, 1834, 1912, 1978, 2003, 2011, 2014, 2068, 2077,

2083, 2143, 2290, 2359, 2376, 2392, 2431, 2436, 2441, 2470, 2525, 2530, 2532, 2550, 2552, 2608, 2612, 2751, 2760, 2770, 2834, 2841, 2842, 2917, 2950, 3024, 3043, 3061, 3067, 3073, 3076, 3115, 3126, 3222, 3242, 3259, 3263, 3271, 3317, 3323, 3383, 3390, 3392-3419, 3421, 3422, 3426-3429, 3432-3444, 3447-3450, 3461, 3467, 3471, 3472, 3474, 3475, 3478, 3483-3485, 3487, 3488, 3492, 3494, 3497, 3500, 3503, 3507, 3509, 3512, 3517, 3519, 3525, 3529, 3530, 3533-3535, 3537, 3544, 3545, 3548, 3556-3559, 3561, 3567, 3569, 3570, 3572, 3577, 3580, 3587, 3597, 3632, 3647, 3648, 3651, 3654, 3662, 3663, 3668, 3674, 3678, 3963, 3978, 4002, 4003, 4012, 4019, 4020, 4089, 4129, 4227, 4266, 4362, 4376, 4432, 4453, 4464, 4470, 4498, 4501, 4599, 4606, 5017, 5077, 5108, 5139, 5214, 5259, 5263, 5328, 5473, 5490, 5577, 5757, 5836, 5873, 5914, 5973

Ethnocentrism 603, 837, 852, 1198, 1221
Ethnogeography 4001
Ethnographers 1888
Ethnographic research 31, 526, 1791, 2661, 3252, 3260, 3540, 5379
Ethnography 8, 9, 20, 31, 355, 430, 462, 526, 536, 989, 1042, 1110, 1115, 1237, 1581, 1658, 1682, 1800, 1865, 1909, 2511, 2544, 2574, 2878, 3236, 3309, 3367, 3368, 3453, 3781, 4219, 4300, 4406, 5386
Ethnolinguistics 1823, 1834, 2584
Ethnological research 817
Ethnologists 18
Ethnology 338, 801, 1002, 1170, 1509, 1870, 2902, 3530, 3635, 4212, 5314
Ethnomethodology 119, 312, 1561, 1870, 4636
Ethnomusicology 1319, 1331, 1972, 1986
Ethnophilosophy 1166
Ethnopolitics 966
Ethnopsychology 967
Ethnosociology 9
Ethology 596, 649, 656, 2744, 2912, 2973, 4143
Ethos 216, 2135, 5180
Etiology 712, 723, 745, 755, 756, 2304, 4776
Etiquette 2373
Etymology 2313
EU enlargement 4913, 4966
EU membership 4913
European Convention on Human Rights 5054
European Court of Justice 4508, 5196
European integration 983, 1205, 1826, 2178, 2530, 3468, 4222, 4913, 4966, 5290, 5295, 5598, 5640
see also: Euroscepticism
European policy 3878, 4541, 4966, 5295, 5640
European Union 64, 969, 1000, 2423, 2518, 2530, 2684, 2720, 3069, 3220, 3321, 3468, 3878, 3890, 4203, 4439, 4541, 4589, 4783, 4813, 4835, 4837, 4872, 4952, 4957, 4966, 5025, 5290, 5295, 5598, 5622, 5623, 5793
see also: Common Agricultural Policy, EU enlargement
Europeans 152, 1004, 3559, 3566
Euroscepticism 5295
Euthanasia 5847, 5850, 5858, 5877, 5882, 5887, 5889
Evaluation 30, 111, 416, 419, 420, 428, 443, 454, 503, 518, 539, 774, 826, 843, 874, 877, 894, 1012, 1041, 1119, 2132, 2142, 2145, 2195, 2244, 2247, 2275, 2699, 3617, 3815, 3819, 3850, 4044, 4049, 4390, 4459, 4599, 4607, 4613, 4779, 4795, 5186, 5224, 5413, 5561, 5583, 5673, 5704, 5761, 5783, 5808, 5867, 5959
see also: Programme evaluation, Project evaluation
Evangelicalism 1503
Evangelism 1431, 1433, 1442, 1485, 1498, 2890
Evangelization 1493
Everyday life 30, 469, 711, 722, 802, 1211, 1278, 1282, 1283, 1287, 1288, 1291, 1292, 1294, 1295, 1303, 1304, 1316, 1359, 1371, 1728, 1978, 1984, 2157, 2352, 2456, 2606, 2649, 2677, 2679, 2830, 3091, 3255, 3256, 3297, 3387, 3484, 3767, 3845, 4011, 4115, 4295, 5428, 5891, 5894
Evidence 137, 179, 963, 1389, 1629, 4984, 5084, 5132, 5194, 5205, 5680
Evil 293, 326, 1388, 1389, 1451, 1487, 5928
Evolution 49, 390, 420, 463, 571, 573, 596, 601, 649, 773, 1121, 1558, 1578, 1583, 1636, 1638, 2329, 2508, 2744, 2973, 3018, 3797, 4502
see also: Darwinism, Human development, Human evolution, Natural selection
Evolutionary psychology 560, 561, 773, 3304, 3823, 5120
Evolutionism 185
see also: Cultural evolutionism
Examinations 457, 2032, 2256, 3183, 5837

SUBJECT INDEX

Exchange 303, 398, 466, 1062, 1163, 1648, 2341, 3353, 3902, 3907, 4187, 4193, 4351, 4380
  see also: Social exchange
Exchange theory 1062, 2341
Executive power 4949, 5732
Executives 582, 2391, 4370, 4408, 4519, 4543, 4624, 4625, 4645, 4657, 4671
Exhibitions 1851
Exile 814, 1699, 1922, 3227, 3598, 3635, 3638, 3664, 3680
  see also: Political exile
Existentialism 145, 212, 311, 3129
Exogamy 3304
Exoticism 1926
Expansionism 1004, 5319
Expectation 308, 657, 675, 853, 1285, 1622, 1725, 2640, 2677, 2775, 3055, 3613, 3622, 4246, 4484, 4582, 4723, 4964, 5154, 5503, 5919
  see also: Income expectations
Expeditions 567
Expenditure 3814, 5401
  see also: Food expenditure, Health expenditure, Public expenditure
Experiment design 5561
Experimental economics 3063
Experimental methods 45, 426, 584, 1161
Experimental psychology 606, 627, 631, 655, 658, 666, 720, 739, 760, 825, 870
Experimentation 870, 2344, 2581
  see also: Animal experimentation
Experiments 45, 426, 433, 453, 462, 476, 515, 584, 643, 650, 656, 705, 716, 853, 865, 908, 1034, 1438, 1704, 4418, 5407
Experts 309, 348, 1294, 1565, 4346, 4613
Explanation 137, 154, 830, 1570, 1629, 1630, 1633
  see also: Causal explanation
Exploitation 1308, 1620, 1903, 1950, 2384, 3115, 3338, 4201, 4442, 4935, 5869, 5871
  see also: Resource exploitation
Exploration 58, 2179, 3143, 5325, 5335
Exports 1359, 2561, 4206, 4450, 4458, 4658
Extended family 771, 2899, 2932, 2944, 2948, 2949, 3010
External debt 2502, 4287, 5363
Externalities 949, 3806, 4427, 5455
Extreme Right 2630, 3452, 5238, 5243
Extremism 1546, 5238
Extremists 5243
Facial expressions 611, 683, 945
Factor analysis 629, 719, 727, 774, 1299, 3749, 3847, 4262
Factor choice 1299

Factories 4430, 4617
Failure 4580
  see also: School failure
Fair
  see: Fun fairs
Faith 1388, 1403, 1545, 1547, 2524, 2660, 2890
Fame 1217, 1228, 1318, 2383
Family 402, 501, 545, 577, 769, 772, 900, 1050, 1170, 1227, 1267, 1275, 1290, 1495, 1695, 1927, 1936, 1991, 2034, 2036, 2043, 2066, 2070, 2071, 2074, 2372, 2425, 2456, 2463, 2489, 2497, 2501, 2542, 2583, 2590, 2591, 2600, 2602, 2608, 2626, 2635, 2636, 2639, 2644, 2647, 2656, 2662, 2683, 2685, 2725, 2756, 2784, 2786, 2803, 2848, 2849, 2855, 2858, 2866, 2871, 2876, 2891, 2897, 2900, 2901, 2904-2907, 2913, 2916, 2918-2921, 2923, 2925, 2929, 2931, 2932, 2934-2936, 2938, 2941-2943, 2946, 2947, 2950, 2952-2954, 2957, 2959, 2962, 2964-2966, 2968, 2972, 2975, 2977, 2979, 2981-2983, 2985, 2986, 2989, 3008, 3010, 3019, 3020, 3026, 3030, 3032, 3041-3043, 3050, 3051, 3053, 3054, 3056, 3081, 3111, 3115, 3121, 3187, 3191, 3224, 3270, 3280, 3308, 3343, 3360, 3361, 3486, 3582, 3610, 3651, 3835, 3883, 3901, 4006, 4183, 4212, 4243, 4257, 4263, 4289, 4310, 4371, 4451, 4457, 4466, 4473, 4514, 4515, 4530, 4541, 4548, 4555, 4568, 4673, 4725, 4781, 4950, 5106, 5291, 5345, 5389, 5393, 5396, 5416, 5425, 5488, 5510, 5512, 5520, 5530, 5546, 5549, 5554, 5556, 5565, 5573, 5574, 5625, 5633, 5634, 5667, 5668, 5675, 5676, 5689, 5721, 5737, 5822, 5827, 5883, 5896, 5916, 5925, 5935, 5936
  see also: Extended family, Nuclear family, One-parent families, Sociology of the family
Family allowances 4299, 5610, 5624
Family disintegration 2917
Family environment 2947
Family farms 4218, 4775, 5685
Family firms 4218
Family history 2767, 2901, 3899, 4116, 5410
Family income 2036, 4299
Family law 2854, 2860, 2862, 2872, 2886, 2889, 2990, 5164, 5192, 5548
Family life 792, 1284, 1371, 1690, 1809, 2574, 2633, 2898, 2903, 2915, 2921, 2925, 2950, 3050, 3255, 3328, 4557, 5633, 5693

INDEX DES MATIÈRES EN ANGLAIS

Family planning 2721, 2728, 2729, 2731, 2732, 2735-2737, 2739-2741, 2745-2750, 2752, 2759-2764, 2769, 2771, 2792, 2799, 2800, 2804, 2939, 2971, 3337
Family policy 2922, 2997, 3169, 3220, 3312, 5164
Family reconstitution 5569
Family relations 402, 755, 1532, 1752, 1761, 2047, 2369, 2424, 2463, 2585, 2590, 2607, 2613, 2618, 2628, 2629, 2633, 2635, 2677, 2680, 2742, 2848, 2859, 2861, 2863, 2866, 2867, 2869, 2871, 2874, 2875, 2887, 2888, 2891, 2892, 2894, 2896, 2898-2900, 2903, 2908-2910, 2912, 2913, 2916-2921, 2925, 2927, 2933, 2935, 2937, 2939-2942, 2944-2949, 2951, 2952, 2954, 2959, 2960, 2964, 2969, 2977, 2979, 3013, 3020, 3032, 3033, 3037, 3047, 3050, 3051, 3053, 3219, 3220, 3229, 3239, 3267, 3343, 3360, 3382, 3385, 3524, 3645, 4218, 4555, 5118, 5192, 5345, 5382, 5492, 5505, 5510, 5525, 5528, 5530, 5537, 5541, 5552, 5566, 5569, 5577, 5594, 5668, 5671, 5681, 5687, 5693, 5916
Family size 653, 2032, 2741, 2756, 2818, 2904, 2927, 2948
Family structure 50, 771, 1752, 1761, 2035, 2472, 2635, 2642, 2703, 2712, 2742, 2848, 2853, 2858, 2891, 2896, 2899, 2903, 2910, 2913, 2914, 2917, 2919, 2923, 2924, 2926, 2927, 2929, 2933, 2937, 2938, 2941, 2943-2945, 2949, 2951, 2955, 2959, 2964, 2979, 2988, 2989, 2994, 2996, 3020, 3026, 3051, 3115, 3169, 3236, 3343, 3360, 3382, 3434, 3897, 4192, 5528, 5538, 5540, 5552, 5590
Family therapy 402, 1270, 1275, 2613, 2900, 2905, 2910, 2911, 2920, 2937, 2946, 2960, 2987, 3037, 3382, 5566, 5595, 5599, 5668, 5671, 5675, 5680-5682, 5717, 5721
Famine 1923, 2714, 2747, 2827, 3887
Fanaticism 1081
Farmers 2653, 3406, 3873, 3878, 5685
Farming 20, 3873, 3878, 3888, 3889, 4226
Farming methods 20, 3760
Farms 3406, 3599, 3760, 3839
    see also: Family farms, Small farms
Fascism 2630
Fashion 1254, 1274, 1316, 1325, 1335, 3256, 3315, 3372
Fasting 1504
Fatalism 2771, 3989
Fatherhood 2608, 2998, 3005, 3008, 3025, 3046, 3051, 5567

Fathers 1991, 2628, 2629, 2846, 2847, 2884, 3008, 3021, 3025, 3036, 3042, 3044, 3049, 3054, 3239, 5566, 5567
Fauset, Jessie Redmon 1227
Fear 591, 685, 752, 858, 1173, 2860, 2886, 3287, 3293, 3403, 3781, 3937, 3957, 5010, 5059-5061, 5070, 5080-5082, 5093, 5101, 5106, 5114, 5465, 5466, 5712
Federal states 1529, 5155
Federalism 4072, 4949
Federation 3493
Feeding 3003
Feelings 469, 686, 690, 696, 703, 713, 1666, 1947, 3038
Female labour 4414, 4455, 4466, 4467, 4522, 4529, 4532, 4534, 4542, 4549, 4553, 4561
Female sterilization 2729, 2733, 5200
Females 938, 1767, 1970, 2878, 3232, 3306, 3835, 4394, 4527, 5076, 5087, 5099, 5961
Femininity 278, 669, 732, 1239, 1782, 1860, 1886, 1926, 1936, 1940, 1946, 1974, 2608, 2645, 2917, 3060, 3073, 3113, 3115, 3117, 3204, 3212, 3230, 3243, 3248, 3256, 3273, 3305, 3313, 3320, 3383, 3742, 4259
Feminism 47, 117, 188, 204, 340, 369, 570, 669, 955, 1191, 1195, 1269, 1296, 1317, 1549, 1562, 1613, 1659, 1782, 1882, 1915, 1917, 1921, 1936, 1945, 2007, 2039, 2095, 2189, 2340, 2471, 2537, 2586, 2623, 2641, 2730, 2978, 3028, 3061, 3065, 3070, 3072, 3073, 3079, 3080, 3082, 3083, 3086, 3087, 3090, 3093-3102, 3105, 3107-3136, 3138, 3139, 3141-3159, 3161-3163, 3165, 3169, 3172, 3173, 3176, 3178, 3180, 3201, 3204, 3205, 3221, 3230, 3240, 3243, 3251, 3258, 3266, 3277, 3302, 3307, 3315, 3320, 3323, 3331, 3346, 3356, 3361, 3376, 3379, 3383, 3449, 3471, 3500, 3528, 3720, 3740, 4191, 4319, 4405, 4529, 4534, 4536, 4560, 4632, 4661, 4816, 4857, 4883, 4944, 4956, 5200, 5258, 5260, 5299, 5317, 5348, 5446, 5474, 5810, 5849, 5861
Feminist theory 20, 449, 570, 600, 674, 1195, 1234, 1269, 1296, 1449, 1882, 1913, 1915, 2347, 2471, 2589, 2623, 2917, 2978, 3079, 3086, 3087, 3095-3097, 3099-3101, 3107-3113, 3115-3121, 3123-3125, 3129-3131, 3135, 3137-3139, 3141-3144, 3146-3148, 3150-3153, 3155, 3158, 3159, 3162, 3169, 3205, 3228, 3243, 3261, 3282, 3288, 3299, 3302, 3324, 3339, 3377, 3449, 4191, 4839, 4958, 5299, 5474, 5544, 5861

SUBJECT INDEX

Fertility 2532, 2686, 2695, 2696, 2703, 2719, 2724-2726, 2728, 2729, 2736-2738, 2740, 2741, 2743, 2745, 2753, 2756, 2765-2769, 2771, 2773-2777, 2779-2788, 2790, 2791, 2794-2799, 2801, 2803-2805, 2902, 2927, 2971, 3000, 3075, 3203, 3279, 3337, 3716, 3795, 5528, 5610
  see also: Soil fertility
Fertility decline 2698, 2712, 2770, 2773, 2775, 2781, 2782, 2785, 2788, 2797, 2802
Fertility increase 2796
Fertility rate 2698, 2702, 2721, 2735, 2743, 2775, 2784, 2788, 2793, 2795, 2799, 2802, 2805, 2822
Festivals 1340, 1345, 1348, 1912
  see also: Religious festivals
Fetishes 303, 3305
Fetishism 913, 4336
Feudalism 185, 967
Fiction 1191, 1918, 1961, 1966, 1968, 5435
Field work 9, 76, 538, 716, 1110, 1130, 1353, 1581
Filipinos 60, 1943, 2936, 3191, 3317, 3392, 3642, 3644, 4443, 4935
Film industry 1100, 1699, 1891, 1894, 1895, 2677
Film makers 1880
Films 1332, 1365, 1699, 1879-1890, 1892-1911, 1978, 1983, 2665, 2677, 3157, 3305, 3355, 3384, 3391
Finance 1323, 2137, 2259, 2271, 2571, 2713, 2909, 3804, 4317, 4348, 4350
  see also: Agricultural finance, International finance, Local finance, Public finance
Financial aid 3042
Financial control 4310
Financial crisis 2579, 3085, 3609, 4055, 4250, 4256, 4347, 4935, 5622
Financial economics 4256
Financial incentives 2092, 3814, 4438
Financial information 4782
Financial institutions 2561, 4284, 4317
Financial management 4310, 4773
Financial needs 5636
Financial planning 2676, 4310
Financial resources 3877, 4369
Financial risks 4348, 4350, 4353
Financial services 4284, 4782, 4831
Financial systems 3927
Finno-Ugrians 3409, 3426, 3487, 3533
Fire 4098
Firearms 5192
Firm theory 4407, 4753
Fiscal law 2196

Fishery policy 3913
Fishing
  see: Coastal fishing
Flexible hours of work 2917, 4486, 4712, 4715
Floods 767
Flora 1313
Flusser, Vilém 4121
Fodor, Jerry 231
Foetus 5873
Folk beliefs 763, 1414, 1468, 3009
Folk culture 1310, 2354, 3956
Folk music 1973
Folk songs 1972, 1973, 1987
Folk tales 27
Folk traditions 1973
Folklore 801, 817, 981, 1310, 1343, 1912
Folkloristics 817
Folklorists 1367
Folklorization 801
Food 1286, 1300, 1303, 2399, 2622, 2644, 2715, 3837, 4268, 5948
Food consumption 1322
Food expenditure 2715
Food habits 1300, 1303, 1322
Food industry 1286, 2545
Food policy 5969
Food preparation 3268
  see also: Cooking
Food production 1286, 3875
Food security 2706, 3677, 3884
Food supply 2706
Football 969, 1305, 1306, 1315, 1341, 3680, 5448
Forced migration 814, 3561, 3627, 3666
Fordism 4520
  see also: Post-Fordism
Forecasting techniques 4486
Forecasts 456, 500, 688, 722, 1112, 2038, 2700, 2805, 2825, 2837, 3270, 3801, 4276, 4721, 4796
  see also: Economic forecasts, Population forecasts
Foreign affairs 3391, 5363
Foreign aid 2704, 4254
Foreign direct investment 2446, 2571, 4363
Foreign enterprises 4633
Foreign languages 1654, 1793, 2083, 2149, 2227, 2228
Foreign markets 4363
Foreign policy 1023, 3654, 5316, 5317, 5336
Foreign relations 1230, 3527, 5308
Foreign students 2274
Foreign workers 2574, 3572, 3587, 3594, 3597, 3642, 3657, 4363, 4463, 4529, 4856

Foreigners 960, 2313, 2376, 3467, 3496, 3605, 5335, 5452
Forensic psychiatry 5027, 5192, 5194, 5562, 5934
Forensic science 473, 498, 521, 555, 1031, 5084, 5193
Forest management 3705
Forest resources 3739
Forestry 20, 3152, 3735
Forests 2717, 3736, 3739, 3754, 5237
  see also: Rain forest
Formalization 563, 1106
Fortifications 2451
Foucault, Michel 241, 243, 252, 277, 294, 340, 373, 374, 410, 1141, 1220, 1864, 2337, 3717, 4030, 4954, 4987, 5016, 5207
Fraassen, B.C. van 1630
Franco, Francisco 161
Fraternities 3362
Fraud 510, 4422, 4683, 5618
Free riding 929
Free trade 4811
Freedom 136, 220, 232, 245, 246, 343, 1141, 1164, 1412, 1569, 1867, 1987, 2303, 2317, 2361, 3740, 4288, 4297, 4497, 4898, 4900, 4903, 4910, 4911, 4915, 4920, 4926-4928, 4933, 4989, 5016, 5262, 5652, 5871
  see also: Academic freedom, Civil liberties
Freedom of information 4933, 5298
Freedom of religion 1470, 1867, 3471
Freedom of speech 1679, 5162, 5298
Freedom of the press 1723, 1734
Freedom of thought 2295
Freemasonry 1453
Frege, Gottlob 120
Freire, Paulo 2221
French Empire 5360
French language 168, 956, 979, 1182, 1789, 1795, 1798, 1822, 1914, 1931, 1942, 2082, 2126, 3423, 5239
French Revolution 2439
Frequency 631
Freud, Sigmund 12, 579, 593, 599, 602, 632, 1621, 3342
Freyre, Gilberto 58, 1183, 1431
Friedlander, Saul 162
Friendship 896, 903, 909, 915, 937, 939, 942, 1945, 2102, 2313, 2370, 3213, 3352, 3859, 4374, 4690, 5564
Fruit crops 3912
Full-time employment 2281
Fun fairs 3956
Functional analysis 371, 3404, 4837

Functionalism 267, 329, 398, 563, 1350, 1633, 4181, 4217, 4612, 4759
  see also: Structural functionalism
Fund management 5629
Fund-raising 2282
Funerals 1751
Funerary rites
  see: Burial, Funerals
Funkenstein, Amos 145
Future societies 2540
Futures 4352
Futurology 1603, 2532
Gadamer, Hans-Georg 126
Galileo Galilei 1555
Gallery
  see: Art galleries
Gambling 709, 1287, 5377, 5387, 5398, 5412
Game
  see: Two-person games
Game theory 366, 420, 463, 467, 486, 1079, 1638, 2308, 4388, 5154, 5231
Games 576, 656, 927, 949, 979, 2447
Games of strategy 2308
Gangeśa 233
Gangs 1370, 3413, 5046, 5079, 5109, 5114, 5118, 5450, 5465, 5472
Gaos, José 240
Gardens 1928, 4133
Garo 3530
GATT 4935
Gellner, Ernest 968, 4288
Gender 5, 33, 35, 47, 104, 427, 460, 559, 570, 574, 576, 583, 681, 689, 722, 732, 734, 736, 776, 793, 803, 808, 811, 858, 948, 970, 972, 1227, 1239, 1290, 1303, 1317, 1321, 1339, 1352, 1356, 1369, 1433, 1522, 1532, 1533, 1551, 1562, 1572, 1613, 1654, 1684, 1695, 1759, 1761, 1802, 1814, 1822, 1839, 1847, 1860, 1915, 1917, 1918, 1928-1930, 1933, 1936, 1940, 1945, 1946, 1954, 1982, 2023, 2039, 2041, 2042, 2055, 2056, 2061, 2071, 2073, 2089, 2198, 2202, 2231, 2304, 2340, 2347, 2377, 2413, 2431, 2436, 2449, 2457, 2492, 2499, 2517, 2551, 2561, 2589, 2595, 2602, 2608, 2622, 2623, 2626, 2642, 2647, 2652, 2665, 2666, 2722, 2724, 2725, 2739, 2743, 2755, 2783, 2786, 2834, 2842, 2845, 2870, 2876, 2880, 2888, 2893, 2894, 2907, 2909, 2917, 2921, 2940, 2968, 2969, 2975, 3013, 3018, 3023, 3040, 3045, 3052, 3057, 3059, 3061-3063, 3066-3068, 3070-3074, 3076, 3079-3088, 3090-3094, 3096, 3097, 3099, 3104-3108,

Subject Index

3112, 3115, 3116, 3120, 3121, 3123-3127, 3130, 3135, 3137, 3138, 3142, 3152, 3153, 3158, 3159, 3161-3163, 3165-3167, 3169, 3171, 3173, 3175, 3179-3181, 3184-3188, 3190, 3192, 3194-3198, 3200, 3202-3204, 3207-3209, 3212-3219, 3221-3224, 3230, 3232-3235, 3238, 3242, 3244-3247, 3249, 3251, 3253, 3256, 3259, 3262, 3264, 3266, 3268, 3269, 3276, 3281-3283, 3285, 3288, 3302, 3305, 3307, 3308, 3315, 3320, 3323, 3324, 3327, 3330, 3340, 3341, 3345, 3352, 3356, 3363, 3368, 3376-3378, 3384, 3389, 3392, 3417, 3438, 3441, 3486, 3518, 3528, 3537, 3538, 3559, 3599, 3600, 3613, 3645, 3646, 3665, 3692, 3739, 3742, 3786, 3788, 3909, 3957, 4126, 4129, 4147, 4226, 4229, 4250, 4259, 4265, 4284, 4305, 4308, 4315, 4319, 4362, 4367, 4371, 4376, 4377, 4394, 4398, 4414-4416, 4440, 4443, 4464, 4467, 4477, 4478, 4480, 4499, 4503, 4504, 4507, 4513, 4514, 4519-4522, 4525, 4526, 4530, 4533, 4537-4542, 4544, 4545, 4547, 4548, 4552-4554, 4556, 4558, 4560, 4563, 4565, 4569, 4576, 4577, 4584, 4586, 4615, 4628, 4704, 4714, 4754, 4771, 4816, 4857, 4882, 4883, 4944, 4956, 4958, 5033, 5037, 5052, 5058, 5077, 5086, 5087, 5093, 5096, 5099, 5104, 5115, 5118, 5131, 5155, 5196, 5203, 5223, 5253, 5296, 5299, 5317, 5318, 5347, 5348, 5350, 5363, 5392, 5415, 5438, 5443, 5451, 5459, 5463, 5467, 5473, 5483, 5505, 5516, 5518, 5521, 5536, 5584, 5600, 5613, 5616, 5628, 5651, 5652, 5672, 5685, 5768, 5810, 5832, 5836, 5915, 5917, 5961, 5973, 5981
Gender differentiation 20, 557, 583, 689, 708, 776, 914, 1290, 1321, 1544, 1760, 1814, 2025, 2041, 2072, 2076, 2198, 2472, 2561, 2608, 2658, 2743, 2754, 2888, 2894, 2915, 2976, 3005, 3038, 3048, 3064, 3065, 3069, 3070, 3074, 3079, 3087, 3088, 3115, 3131, 3158, 3165-3171, 3176, 3179, 3181-3183, 3187-3189, 3192, 3194-3198, 3200, 3201, 3203, 3206, 3208, 3209, 3216, 3217, 3222, 3226, 3231, 3243, 3244, 3261, 3281, 3306, 3307, 3372, 3592, 3623, 3665, 3677, 3749, 4371, 4377, 4383, 4415, 4477, 4480, 4506, 4519, 4520, 4526, 4533, 4534, 4536, 4537, 4539, 4540, 4543-4546, 4549, 4551, 4557, 4562, 4570, 4571, 4578, 4584, 4586, 4599, 4661, 4720, 4761,

4765, 4777, 4839, 4944, 5096, 5115, 5131, 5160, 5346, 5350, 5353, 5388, 5403, 5505, 5628, 5827, 5838, 5891
Gender relations 1110, 1317, 1352, 1782, 1928, 1930, 1974, 2377, 2708, 2939, 2969, 3060, 3066, 3070, 3076, 3079, 3081, 3097, 3112, 3165, 3170, 3176, 3184, 3186, 3208, 3209, 3220, 3225, 3231, 3234, 3236, 3238, 3240, 3241, 3244, 3252, 3275, 3277, 3283, 3292, 3320, 3330, 3356, 3670, 4126, 4416, 4544, 4552, 4558, 5058, 5317, 5318, 5350, 5442, 5908, 5962, 5975
Gender roles 485, 574, 1290, 1744, 1814, 1910, 1921, 1928, 1930, 1946, 1974, 2330, 2523, 2608, 2786, 2879, 2887, 2915, 2957, 2972, 3040, 3114, 3125, 3132, 3164, 3165, 3170, 3171, 3177, 3181, 3189, 3193, 3194, 3200, 3208, 3209, 3219-3221, 3223, 3228, 3232, 3233, 3235-3241, 3243-3245, 3248-3251, 3257, 3261, 3264, 3267, 3268, 3273-3275, 3281, 3307, 3339, 3358, 3372, 3592, 4324, 4400, 4416, 4521, 4526, 4527, 4544, 4545, 4554, 4558, 4567, 4584, 5131, 5200, 5203, 5350, 5388, 5505, 5584
see also: Men's role, Women's role
Genealogy 1099, 1141, 2426, 5180
General systems theory 1270
General theories 258, 409, 1210, 5108
Generalization 225, 455, 471, 474, 837, 1711
Generation differences 2587, 2592, 4218, 4305, 4755, 5941
Generations 339, 771, 2089, 2360, 2401, 2517, 2532, 2537, 2546, 2589, 2590, 2592, 2594, 2618, 2657, 2735, 2876, 2926, 2943, 3026, 3523, 3543, 3568, 3588, 5302, 5403, 5520, 5602
Genes 591, 712, 1620, 5730, 5864
Genet, Jean 1940
Genetic engineering 1563, 1601, 2742, 5892
Genetic psychology 560
Genetics 596, 625, 712, 769, 773, 1567, 1576, 1595, 1825, 2304, 2701, 2742, 2755, 2757, 2812, 3014, 3308, 4933, 5390, 5730, 5848, 5854, 5863-5865, 5875, 5877, 5880, 5881, 5892
see also: Cloning, DNA, Genetic engineering, Human genetics
Genital mutilation 3471
Genocide 192, 1388, 1896, 1902, 1906, 1990, 3070, 3518, 3611, 3640, 5312, 5462
Geographic distribution 3877
Geographic location 528, 2633, 2748, 3767, 3820, 4046, 4249, 4291, 4833, 5844

INDEX DES MATIÈRES EN ANGLAIS

Geographic mobility 2790, 3613, 3634, 3767, 4521
Geographical information systems 3813, 3820, 4102, 4166, 5582, 5802, 5838, 5968
Geography 91, 461, 500, 504, 528, 1328, 1399, 1597, 1661, 2348, 2367, 2716, 3073, 3121, 3179, 3553, 3688, 3693-3695, 3702, 3727, 3741, 3761, 3774, 3775, 3779, 3790, 3793, 3794, 3811, 3913, 3939, 3969, 3999, 4034, 4152, 4158, 4166, 4315, 4346, 4437, 5162, 5802, 5885, 5962
see also: Economic geography, Historical geography, Human geography, Linguistic geography, Political geography, Population geography, Rural geography, Urban geography
Geometry 1555
Geopolitics 1199, 2687, 3782, 3796, 4228
Geriatrics 2656, 5513
German language 959, 1757, 1798, 1809, 1813, 1839, 2149
German unification 165, 2124, 2567, 2922, 3455, 3532, 4066, 4297, 4795
Germans 1004, 1179, 1816, 3496, 3552, 3647, 5977
Gerontology 2656, 2666, 2668, 2671, 2678, 2680, 5521, 5532-5534
Gestalt psychology 564
Gestures 945, 1839, 1842
Ghetto 3518, 4001, 4009
Gibran, Gibran Khalil 1932
Gibson, William 1920
Giddens, Anthony 41, 75, 2300
Gide, André 1950, 2439
Gift 239, 931, 1839, 4194, 5860
Gifted children 660
Gilligan, Carol 3182
Girls 681, 1928, 2041, 2074, 2449, 2608, 2623, 2632, 2645, 2667, 2727, 2878, 3115, 3156, 3212, 3216, 3254, 3352, 3509, 3793, 4129, 4482, 4527
Global warming 3711
see also: Greenhouse effect
Globalization 52, 134, 159, 379, 393, 397, 931, 953, 977, 1158, 1184, 1199, 1218, 1220, 1221, 1240, 1257, 1265, 1268, 1308, 1363, 1393, 1397, 1409, 1427, 1637, 1645, 1671, 1713, 1729, 1755, 1756, 1777, 1804, 1806, 1895, 1994, 2009, 2191, 2252, 2261, 2263, 2271, 2278, 2294, 2355, 2364, 2386, 2399, 2446, 2461, 2496, 2507, 2519, 2521, 2532, 2543-2549, 2551-2581, 3068, 3070, 3073, 3154, 3155, 3355, 3634, 3659, 3663, 3669, 3672, 3684, 3688, 3693,
3697, 3722, 3727, 3760, 3776, 3791, 3797, 3802, 3827, 3837, 3851, 3903, 3912, 3922, 3923, 3927, 3936, 3943, 3952, 3956, 4119, 4127, 4160, 4192, 4198, 4202, 4221, 4222, 4227, 4234, 4250, 4252, 4258, 4260, 4261, 4278, 4293, 4312, 4313, 4378, 4410, 4430, 4434, 4486, 4546, 4624, 4674, 4682, 4713, 4818, 4819, 4850, 4863, 4884, 4892, 4902, 4910, 4923, 4935, 4967, 4968, 4976, 5187, 5229, 5236, 5241, 5252, 5256, 5259, 5265, 5272, 5313, 5315, 5325, 5335, 5363, 5622, 5640, 5684, 5686
Glossaries 99
Gnosticism 1501
God-parenthood 2901
Goddesses 3145
Godelier, Maurice 381
Gods 221, 254, 293, 1374, 1375, 1389-1391, 1404, 1406, 1412, 1413, 1428, 1438, 1451, 1477, 1487, 1506
Goethe, Johann Wolfgang von 1161
Goffman, Erving 5016
Goldhagen, Daniel J. 410
Gonne, Maud 1227
González, Felipe 1839
Gorz, André 311
Governability 1994, 4949
Governance 1308, 1608, 2134, 2151, 2532, 3759, 3808, 3814, 3922, 3942, 3947, 4041, 4058, 4066, 4085, 4113, 4163, 4169, 4178, 4427, 4608, 4876, 4877, 5140, 5162, 5202, 5216, 5282, 5749, 5771
Government 971, 1169, 1220, 1550, 1742, 2162, 2343, 2379, 2406, 3391, 4030, 4058, 4072, 4596, 4715, 4796, 4828, 4859, 4892, 4907, 4936, 4949, 4966, 4972, 5139, 5154, 5212, 5222, 5292
see also: Colonial government, Local government, Regional government, Subnational government, Urban government
Government departments 42
Government grant 2287
Government information 3633
Government policy 386, 1442, 1891, 2098, 2403, 2442, 2513, 2657, 2707, 2792, 3114, 3312, 3542, 3602, 3640, 3702, 3814, 3817, 3827, 4054, 4078, 4133, 4248, 4354, 4486, 4491, 4497, 4907, 5002, 5243, 5416, 5426, 5497, 5548, 5567, 5600, 5624, 5635, 5664, 5788, 5882
Government programmes 42, 2748, 4251, 5629, 5969
Government relations 3526

SUBJECT INDEX

Grabbe, Lester 169
Graduates 1996, 2253, 2267, 2268, 2274, 3382, 4766, 4769, 5844
Grahn, Judy 1969
Grammar 1518, 1798, 1822, 2087, 2227, 4801
Gramsci, Antonio 1250
Grandparents 771, 2582, 2588, 2667, 2680
Greeks 3566, 3592, 5089, 5304
Greenhouse effect 3711
Gregory, Augusta 1227
Group analysis 881, 947, 1041, 1066, 1079, 1081, 3357, 4701
Group attraction 1047
Group behaviour 842, 848, 1020, 1034, 1037, 1041, 1042, 1044, 1046, 1048, 1054, 1057, 1073, 1082, 1096, 1331, 2028, 3667, 4366, 4384, 4426, 5450
Group cohesiveness 1047, 1072, 4700, 5450
Group consciousness 1096
Group consensus 1096, 4701
Group decision making 1036, 1039, 1049, 1050, 1066, 1070, 1098, 1704, 4316, 4384, 4670
Group dynamics 655, 759, 829, 832, 844, 848, 852, 856, 858, 894, 999, 1011, 1029, 1033, 1037, 1040, 1043, 1046, 1051, 1053, 1057, 1058, 1060, 1061, 1063-1067, 1071, 1074-1077, 1079, 1080, 1083, 1084, 1086, 1095, 1130, 1143, 1639, 1684, 3517, 4366, 4384, 4607, 4632, 5437, 5672, 5831
Group effects 1053
Group functioning 1080, 4701
Group identity 837, 956, 972, 973, 988, 990, 999, 1036, 1044, 1058, 1082, 1252, 2552, 3362, 3386, 3410, 3421, 3545, 3554, 4366, 4472, 4924, 5159, 5328, 5437
Group influence 1059, 4090
Group integration 4608
Group interaction 911, 1036, 1059, 1072, 1080
Group membership 856, 857, 864, 865, 972, 973, 987, 990, 1032, 1037, 1044, 1063, 1086, 3418, 3857, 3863, 4316, 4385, 4512
Group participation 1072, 2371
Group performance 1056, 1072, 1096, 4670
Group solidarity 1047
Group task 1704
Group theory 947, 1029, 1037, 1061, 1074, 1076, 1081
Growth models 3771, 4166
Growth theory 2793
Guerrillas 4864, 5233, 5445
Guilt 3568, 5149, 5152, 5195, 5434
Gulf War 5345
Gypsies 1748, 2067, 3408, 3427, 3474, 3520

Habermas, Jürgen 117, 126, 243, 359, 369, 2567, 4932
Habitats 3755
Habits 1288
see also: Food habits
Haider, Jörg 3452
Hair 3272
Hall, Stuart 1196, 2326
Hamburger, Sidney 1550
Hampâté Bâ, Amadou 1913
Handbooks 89, 90, 102, 179, 438, 530, 566, 1617, 1694, 2274, 2282, 3831
Handicrafts 4238
Hanson, Pauline 1195, 3323
Happiness 229, 591, 683, 687, 688, 690, 3183
Hare Krishna 1384
Harris, Marvin 1431
Harvey, William 1591
Hasidism 1545, 3450
Hatred 3227, 5172
Havel, Vaclav 4913
Hayek, Friedrich A. von 4181
Hazardous waste 461, 1601, 3757
Headhunters 4416
Heads of state 1731, 4949, 4954, 5299
Healers 1520, 5813
Healing 1442, 1520, 2660, 2663, 5349, 5821, 5839, 5859, 5874
Health 504, 541, 709, 780, 789, 887, 941, 1297, 1355, 2007, 2044, 2324, 2424, 2440, 2536, 2582, 2583, 2611, 2660, 2663, 2664, 2666, 2685, 2807-2809, 2811, 2812, 2814, 2815, 2824, 2830, 2833, 2845, 2999, 3159, 3226, 3311, 3316, 3325-3327, 3350, 3357, 3546, 3565, 3696, 4268, 4274, 4291, 4379, 4611, 4674, 4680, 4692, 4695, 4703, 4727, 4730, 4731, 5375, 5376, 5407, 5408, 5411, 5464, 5494, 5514, 5518, 5609, 5633, 5658, 5724, 5727, 5732, 5733, 5735, 5745, 5752, 5753, 5773, 5792, 5795, 5796, 5798, 5803, 5805, 5809, 5814, 5842, 5856, 5867, 5892, 5915, 5942, 5943, 5946, 5952, 5961, 5962, 5966, 5970, 5979, 5980, 5985, 5987
see also: Child health, Men's health, Mental health, Public health, Sexual health, Women's health
Health administration 5726, 5732, 5747, 5750, 5751, 5758, 5761, 5762, 5770, 5772, 5775, 5779, 5784, 5785, 5790, 5797, 5798, 5804, 5807, 5812, 5814, 5840, 5841, 5980
Health aid 5977

Health care 43, 371, 419, 525, 764-766, 789, 800, 887, 2456, 2602, 2750, 2780, 2814, 2817, 2821, 2838, 3007, 3039, 3185, 3311, 3327, 3373, 3382, 4032, 4087, 4304, 4711, 4949, 4999, 5022, 5197, 5392, 5420, 5421, 5479, 5494, 5497-5499, 5502, 5504, 5505, 5507, 5508, 5513, 5521, 5525, 5526, 5530, 5541, 5583, 5614, 5651, 5690, 5698, 5725, 5727-5729, 5731-5733, 5735-5738, 5742, 5745-5747, 5749-5754, 5757, 5760-5767, 5770-5772, 5776-5781, 5784-5787, 5789, 5790, 5793-5798, 5802-5814, 5816-5821, 5825, 5826, 5833, 5835, 5837, 5840, 5841, 5845, 5846, 5852, 5864, 5869, 5873, 5874, 5877, 5879, 5891, 5896, 5897, 5901, 5903, 5905, 5906, 5910, 5911, 5913-5916, 5918, 5922, 5923, 5926, 5927, 5929, 5931, 5937, 5939, 5942, 5947, 5949, 5950, 5952, 5959, 5963, 5972, 5976, 5980-5982, 5986 *see also:* Long-term care, Medical care, Primary health care, Private health care
Health centres 5824
Health economics 3039, 4304, 5507, 5728, 5732, 5740, 5750, 5754, 5756, 5760, 5761, 5770, 5772, 5777, 5785-5787, 5795, 5803, 5811, 5812, 5814, 5821, 5897, 5931, 5942, 5980
Health education 419, 2611, 3300, 3337, 5409, 5782, 5814, 5941, 5946, 5953, 5955, 5959, 5973, 5975, 5980, 5982, 5986
Health expenditure 5524, 5744, 5756, 5761, 5781, 5785, 5787
Health insurance 525, 5506, 5726, 5732, 5774, 5786, 5811, 5838, 5897, 5971
Health management 5022, 5732, 5740, 5747, 5750, 5760, 5761, 5764, 5770, 5772, 5775, 5779, 5784-5786, 5790, 5794-5796, 5798, 5807, 5812, 5814, 5824, 5826, 5840, 5841, 5931, 5980
Health planning 5523, 5724, 5758, 5770, 5777, 5807
Health policy 2712, 2713, 3300, 4274, 4949, 5200, 5506, 5524, 5658, 5726, 5729, 5732, 5743, 5744, 5750, 5754, 5758, 5759, 5770, 5771, 5777, 5779, 5783, 5787, 5790, 5791, 5797, 5802, 5803, 5807, 5810, 5814, 5815, 5819, 5822, 5824, 5841, 5903, 5927, 5942, 5947, 5968, 5972-5974, 5980, 5982, 5986
Health services 502, 525, 753, 797, 1923, 2470, 2679, 2751, 3381, 4032, 4087, 4304, 4433, 4439, 4682, 4784, 4831, 5019, 5197, 5200, 5407, 5420, 5497, 5499, 5522, 5561, 5609, 5726, 5731, 5732, 5735, 5738, 5739, 5741, 5747-5751, 5753, 5754, 5757, 5758, 5760-5763, 5765, 5769-5772, 5774-5777, 5779-5781, 5783-5786, 5790, 5791, 5794-5801, 5803-5812, 5814, 5816, 5818, 5819, 5821, 5822, 5824, 5825, 5834, 5835, 5838, 5840, 5841, 5843, 5846, 5852, 5860, 5894, 5896, 5903, 5905, 5909-5911, 5913, 5918, 5922, 5923, 5926, 5931, 5933, 5938, 5940, 5942, 5963, 5964, 5968, 5971, 5974, 5976, 5980
Hearing 818, 1653
Heart disease 5968
Hebrew 1552, 1817, 1834, 1935, 3564
Hegel, Georg Wilhelm Friedrich 12, 117, 219, 235, 251
Hegemony 328, 331, 368, 383, 1221, 1222, 1314, 1727, 1976, 2326, 2339, 2461, 2563, 3070, 3367, 3788, 4115, 4887, 5340
Heidegger, Martin 202, 236, 267, 1199, 1413
Heinich, Nathalie 1866
Heller, Agnes 1265
Hepatitis 2824, 5968
Hermeneutics 119, 122, 124, 126, 161, 266, 338, 376, 401, 1198, 1215, 1413, 1489, 1874, 2001, 5940
Heroes 961, 1332, 1735, 1887, 3218, 5683
Heroin 5374, 5375, 5378, 5379, 5385, 5386, 5395, 5401
Herzen, Alexander 224
Heterogamy 2852
Heterosexuality 596, 1821, 2608, 3199, 3201, 3218, 3299, 3301, 3307, 3321, 3345, 3352, 3365, 3383, 3386, 5837
Heuristics 63, 138, 595, 656, 863, 2179, 3705
Hierarchy 879, 1038, 1039, 1074, 1100, 1217, 1835, 2301, 2303, 2341, 2395, 2406, 2434, 2441, 2447, 2536, 3180, 3231, 4391, 4657, 4733, 4737, 4761, 5168, 5267
High technology 4213, 4690
Higher education 1, 44, 53, 78, 996, 1196, 1617, 1692, 1996, 2008, 2018, 2030, 2033, 2043, 2048, 2052, 2055-2057, 2072, 2108, 2128, 2129, 2132, 2134, 2139, 2145, 2147, 2159, 2190, 2195, 2196, 2202, 2210, 2213, 2242, 2243, 2247, 2249, 2253, 2254, 2256, 2257, 2259, 2262-2266, 2270-2280, 2283, 2285, 2287, 2289, 2292, 2294, 2297, 2299, 2383, 2454, 2624, 3232, 3292, 3477, 4040, 4454, 4514, 4564, 4655, 4762, 4791, 4794, 4805, 5705
Hindi 1818
Hinduism 245, 246, 1376, 1398, 1399, 2346, 2394

Subject Index

Hindus 771, 1398, 1424, 2394, 3650
Hirner, Alexander 4, 144, 2302, 2411, 4930
Hispanic-Americans 3396, 3563, 4440, 5171
Hispanics 2017, 2036, 2692, 2936, 3336, 3396, 3398, 3413, 3498, 3515, 3521, 3565, 3570, 3996, 4000, 4019, 4453, 4470, 4492, 5244, 5873
Historians 94, 123, 143, 145, 148, 151-153, 159-162, 174, 187, 192, 4935, 4980
Historic monuments 996, 4081
Historic sites 1342
Historical analysis 2, 26, 144, 145, 148, 161, 165-167, 171, 174, 178, 180, 220, 409, 802, 982, 988, 1280, 1308, 1353, 1811, 1819, 1976, 2009, 2207, 2568, 3098, 3496, 3528, 3631, 4206, 4220, 4837, 4959, 4966, 5218
Historical anthropology 195
Historical geography 91, 94, 3958
Historicism 167, 169, 175, 365, 1390, 5246
Historiography 34, 53, 54, 57, 123, 143-170, 172-176, 178-180, 182-198, 241, 958, 980, 986, 996, 1004, 1251, 1612, 1882, 1900, 1916, 1936, 1964, 2204, 2205, 2212, 2312, 2321, 2558, 3314, 3525, 4935
History 12, 15, 103, 110, 143, 146, 148, 150, 153-158, 160, 162-164, 167, 168, 170, 173, 175, 181, 184, 190-194, 196-198, 218, 235, 240, 241, 296, 319, 324, 343, 353, 362, 387, 593, 799, 870, 974, 975, 981, 984, 996, 1163, 1167, 1174, 1201, 1204, 1207, 1251, 1329, 1356, 1405, 1408, 1490, 1510, 1516, 1520, 1553, 1554, 1650, 1772, 1855, 1882, 1884, 1896, 1900, 1902, 1906, 1916, 1936, 1955, 1960, 1963, 1965, 1969, 1990, 2009, 2148, 2170, 2178, 2207, 2212, 2312, 2429, 2512, 2528, 2558, 3072, 3161, 3184, 3303, 3314, 3391, 3401, 3431, 3484, 3511, 3518, 3575, 3691, 3736, 3778, 3826, 3887, 3934, 3943, 3962, 4026, 4059, 4212, 4330, 4874, 4912, 4973, 5001, 5002, 5074, 5325, 5332, 5476, 5734, 5854
see also: Agricultural history, Ancient history, Church history, Colonial history, Cultural history, Early modern history, Economic history, Family history, Industrial history, Labour history, Language history, Life history, Medieval history, Military history, Modern history, Oral history, Philosophy of history, Political history, Post-war history, Pre-Columbian history, Religious history, Rural history, Social history, Urban history

History of art 1853, 1854, 1863, 3342, 4752
History of capitalism 4365
History of education 775, 2091, 2148, 2163, 2204, 2226
History of ideas 106, 205, 208, 214, 217, 223, 232, 234, 237, 241, 242, 247, 251, 256, 262, 263, 265, 268, 271, 274, 288, 294, 296, 299, 315, 318, 361, 365, 377, 761, 775, 1248, 1250, 1271, 1478, 1588, 1591, 1854, 1876, 2540, 2604, 3078, 4239, 4894, 5098
History of law 3891, 5025, 5181, 5211, 5324
History of medicine 484, 779, 5734, 5857
History of music 1979, 1981, 1982
History of philosophy 113, 120, 212, 214, 217, 224, 241, 242, 247, 254, 256, 262, 264, 267, 270-272, 278, 282, 357, 1591, 1611
History of political ideas 274, 307, 325, 2387, 4909, 4911, 4922, 4925, 4927
History of religion 266, 1400, 1434
History of science 288, 1553, 1555, 1557, 1558, 1564, 1585, 1588, 1591, 1592, 1598, 1599, 1605, 1611, 1612, 1616, 1623-1625, 1630, 2226, 3719, 4030
History of sociology 1, 4, 5, 15, 23, 26, 36, 38, 40, 50, 58, 65, 144, 316, 318, 330, 339, 343, 354, 355, 365, 396, 408, 2411, 2435
History of technology 154, 1554, 1588, 1597, 1598, 1621, 1674, 1851
History of the social sciences 4, 71, 144, 304, 564, 4897
History of travels 151, 5335
HIV 427, 581, 781, 1883, 2726, 2754, 2806, 2810, 3037, 3309, 3311, 3316, 3326, 3327, 3329, 3332, 3370, 3380, 3381, 4611, 5200, 5363, 5386, 5387, 5745, 5764, 5773, 5838, 5854, 5856, 5872, 5874, 5885, 5890, 5891, 5894, 5942, 5944, 5945, 5951, 5952, 5957, 5958, 5964-5966, 5968, 5974, 5975, 5980-5982, 5984, 5987
Højrup, Thomas 2230
Holidays 1312, 2330, 3679, 4751, 5080
Holism 287, 376, 378, 676, 1401, 1579, 1839, 2508, 3514
Holocaust 145, 162, 165, 192, 410, 669, 814, 976, 985, 1388, 1547, 1896, 1902, 1906, 3502, 3518, 3532, 5312
Holy war 1380
Home 2626, 2809, 3539, 5424, 5742
Home economics 1283
Home ownership 2377, 3845, 3980, 3986, 4225, 4229, 5286, 5491
Homeless people 5414, 5416, 5419-5422, 5425, 5431

INDEX DES MATIÈRES EN ANGLAIS

Homelessness 2334, 5271, 5414-5421, 5423-5431, 5558, 5592
Homer 241
Homicide 819, 4271, 5053, 5058, 5113, 5192, 5453, 5454
 see also: Murder
Homo oeconomicus 4916
Homophobia 1821, 3061, 3260, 3307, 3375, 3382, 5698, 5872
Homosexuality 786, 1227, 1488, 1691, 1811, 1882, 1950, 2688, 2867, 2990, 3061, 3082, 3137, 3199, 3218, 3264, 3308, 3313, 3314, 3321, 3323, 3324, 3340, 3345, 3352, 3354-3372, 3375-3383, 3385-3389, 4512, 5196, 5247, 5339, 5698, 5951
Honesty 568, 4697
Honour and shame 388, 1358, 3115, 3891, 4187, 4581, 4990, 5141
Hooliganism 1341
Hormones 3083
Horse-racing 1305
Horvat, Branko 4255
Hosain, Rokeya Sakhawat 3112
Hospices 4667
Hospital management 4622, 5747, 5749, 5776, 5787, 5794
Hospital staff 5842
Hospital treatment 5788
Hospitality 2313, 3944
Hospitalization 489, 5838
Hospitals 757, 1040, 1078, 1857, 2773, 4568, 4770, 5016, 5690, 5726, 5743, 5747, 5749, 5755, 5765, 5782, 5789, 5790, 5796, 5799, 5834, 5879, 5899, 5942
 see also: Mental hospitals
Host countries 3567
Hostility 1009, 2966, 2987, 4711
Hotel industry 4046, 4374
Hours of work 3025, 4305, 4551, 4708, 4712, 4724, 4745, 4747, 4749
 see also: Flexible hours of work
House 1283, 1284, 1288, 2421, 3620, 3695, 3786, 3953, 4310
Household budgets 3190, 4263, 4310
Household consumption 4308, 4338
Household economics 2035, 2676, 2858, 3054, 3190, 3619, 3924, 4184, 4263, 4273, 4310, 4317, 4338, 4486, 4556
Household expenditure 4276, 4342, 4561
Household income 2234, 2808, 2858, 3190, 4263, 4299, 4338, 4595, 5655
Households 513, 811, 1283, 1284, 2311, 2313, 2363, 2407, 2421, 2583, 2600, 2683, 2901, 2926, 2930, 2944, 2949, 2965, 3169, 3188, 3223, 3231, 3268, 3645, 3715, 3899, 3924, 4022, 4056, 4068, 4157, 4219, 4263, 4265, 4302, 4310, 4315, 4338, 4452, 4475, 4530, 4559, 4575, 5363, 5514, 5625, 5800
Housewives 3280
Housework 1290, 2272, 2957, 3121, 3170, 3188, 3221, 3267, 3307, 4337, 4452, 4462, 4529
Housing 608, 1283, 2313, 2407, 2424, 2626, 2661, 2683, 2716, 2809, 3231, 3460, 3582, 3587, 3620, 3655, 3765, 3845, 3949, 3961, 3966, 3972-3975, 3977, 3980, 3981, 3984-3987, 3990, 3992, 3994, 4003, 4010, 4011, 4014, 4020, 4049, 4058, 4083, 4091, 4110, 4111, 4113, 4116, 4126, 4136, 4161, 4225, 4229, 4302, 4774, 4950, 5063, 5417, 5476, 5491, 5494, 5496, 5509, 5511, 5523, 5611, 5612, 5615, 5621, 5631, 5637, 5645, 5646, 5655, 5656, 5741
 see also: Rural housing, Social housing, Urban housing
Housing co-operatives 4117, 4232
Housing conditions 3974, 3984
Housing construction 3765, 3983, 4049, 5656
Housing market 2407, 3620, 3906, 3980, 3983, 3987, 4003, 4225, 5621, 5627, 5649, 5655, 5656
Housing needs 3824, 3825, 3978, 3981, 5422
Housing policy 3460, 3825, 3906, 3954, 3961, 3968, 3972, 3975-3978, 3980-3983, 3985, 3988-3990, 4010, 4022, 4024, 4080, 4110, 4232, 5416, 5509, 5611, 5627, 5631, 5637, 5646, 5655, 5656
Housing prices 2407, 3620, 5656
Howard, Ebenezer 4051
Human behaviour 293, 327, 422, 442, 542, 561, 565, 567, 573, 588, 589, 591, 594, 596, 597, 599, 601, 605, 606, 613, 615, 617, 618, 627, 634, 643, 648-650, 657, 667, 668, 680, 682, 692, 705, 709, 711, 717, 720, 723, 727, 735, 737, 749, 760, 791, 833, 838, 846, 851, 859, 870, 876, 887, 907, 912, 914, 928, 941, 943, 1031, 1064, 1073, 1112, 1126, 1282, 1301, 1302, 1652, 1784, 1789, 1842, 2028, 2236, 2304, 2324, 2350, 2532, 2744, 2763, 2788, 2845, 2862, 2879, 2889, 2973, 3014, 3026, 3167, 3181, 3282, 3298, 3318, 3406, 3667, 3695, 3726, 3783, 3843, 4345, 4419, 4422, 4659, 4990, 5075, 5095, 5112, 5135, 5321, 5387, 5460, 5677, 5860, 5874, 5939, 5950
Human biology 3167
Human body 199, 236, 239, 573, 669, 777, 791, 1189, 1214, 1232, 1277, 1325, 1347,

SUBJECT INDEX

1358, 1368, 1497, 1559, 1861, 1970, 2597, 2651, 2755, 2809, 2880, 3045, 3092, 3108-3110, 3125, 3128, 3131, 3146, 3158, 3272, 3311, 3331, 3346, 4730, 4954, 5182, 5589, 5837, 5876
see also: Anthropology of the body, Organs
Human capital 63, 1122, 1998, 2059, 2070, 2457, 2605, 2904, 3177, 3604, 3617, 3621, 3798, 3817, 4209, 4257, 4265, 4267, 4303, 4375, 4458, 4470, 4510, 4598, 4604, 4605, 4609, 4634, 4643, 4648, 4720, 4756, 4790, 4799, 5633, 5773
Human development 572, 575, 591, 726, 1161, 1994, 3160, 3173, 3809, 4260, 5675
Human ecology 2508, 3689, 3691, 3710, 3716, 3719, 3738, 3752, 3756, 3759, 3764, 3779, 3783, 3800, 3820
Human environment 567, 2717, 2801, 3607, 3689, 3757, 3758, 4077, 5252
Human evolution 560, 1161, 1630, 2406, 2426, 2508, 3401, 3716, 3797
Human genetics 591, 1564, 1595, 1620, 2701, 3528, 5875
Human geography 84, 452, 507, 1232, 1657, 1661, 1917, 2367, 2403, 2658, 3073, 3301, 3537, 3540, 3691, 3756, 3767, 3769-3771, 3773-3775, 3778-3790, 3792, 3795, 3811, 3820, 3882, 3948, 3955, 4016, 4072, 4122, 4127, 4135, 4136, 4140, 4148, 4238, 4315, 4606, 5418, 5424
Human nature 390, 1073, 1188, 2350, 3038, 3351, 3749, 5468
Human physiology 3109
Human race 3759
Human relations 680, 747, 870, 914, 921, 928, 934, 1016, 2369, 2667, 3126, 3352, 3550, 3775, 4363, 4608, 5439, 5461
Human resources 707, 1110, 1157, 2022, 2085, 2133, 2274, 2685, 3618, 3877, 4322, 4356, 4403, 4412, 4473, 4599-4606, 4610, 4613, 4616, 4618, 4619, 4621, 4633-4635, 4642, 4643, 4648, 4650, 4653, 4656, 4660, 4673, 4679, 4743, 4768, 5215, 5217
Human rights 248, 349, 1466, 1482, 1650, 1713, 1731, 1781, 1995, 2019, 2030, 2344, 2361, 2460, 2498, 2554, 2754, 3074, 3115, 3327, 3375, 3469, 3542, 3582, 3615, 3624, 3651, 3754, 4254, 4268, 4287, 4299, 4360, 4417, 4423, 4482, 4682, 4903, 4949, 4971, 5021, 5025, 5139, 5159, 5161, 5200, 5244, 5309, 5312, 5320, 5322, 5326, 5361, 5601, 5605, 5700, 5805, 5809, 5853, 5884, 5887, 5889, 5915, 5929, 5930, 5952, 5972, 5988
see also: European Convention on Human Rights, International human rights
Human rights movements 5805
Human settlements 2505, 2511, 3655, 3771, 3774, 3813, 4102
Humanism 29, 237, 241, 348, 374, 599, 1164, 1275, 1331, 1578, 1612, 3528, 4929, 5343, 5839
Humanitarian intervention 1730, 2704, 4287, 5319, 5321, 5330, 5362
Humanities 28, 1224
Humanity 209, 229, 241, 403, 1199, 1390, 1466, 1731, 3703, 3744, 3759, 4637
Humour 244, 586, 686, 729, 921, 1181, 1642, 1710, 1784, 1839, 1887, 1967, 3404, 3467, 5293
see also: Jokes
Hunger 817, 3884
Husbandry
see: Animal husbandry
Husbands 2765, 2965, 2971, 3170, 3188, 4530, 5479
Hutcheson, Francis 12
Hutchins, Robert 225
Hutterites 1495
Hygiene 3775, 4727, 4730, 5902, 5954
Hypnosis 1963
Hypothesis 624, 1034, 1129, 1389, 1438, 1606, 2523, 2850, 4486
Idealism 125, 139, 232, 1243, 2667, 3701, 4207, 4361, 4420, 4785
Identification 60, 872, 1897, 2301, 2436, 2543, 3394, 3407, 5194, 5618
see also: Cultural identification
Identity 53, 57, 110, 118, 162, 240, 276, 282, 350, 362, 374, 379, 548, 569, 673, 684, 734, 770, 828, 834, 839, 894, 926, 951, 952, 955, 963-965, 971, 979, 982, 988-990, 999, 1000, 1002, 1004, 1066, 1077, 1090, 1100, 1120, 1159, 1163, 1167, 1176, 1181, 1185, 1188, 1195, 1197, 1208, 1209, 1214, 1234, 1252, 1261, 1269, 1272, 1288, 1300, 1303, 1328, 1331, 1384, 1392, 1397, 1409, 1424, 1447, 1474, 1488, 1512, 1513, 1519, 1532, 1548, 1549, 1609, 1662, 1684, 1685, 1744, 1758, 1772, 1789, 1811, 1813, 1815, 1816, 1834, 1862, 1881, 1931, 1935, 1960, 1974, 2002, 2003, 2060, 2191, 2218, 2255, 2314, 2325, 2346, 2361, 2381, 2394, 2415, 2436, 2449, 2480, 2497, 2529, 2530, 2543, 2548, 2549, 2552, 2600, 2616, 2618, 2622, 2645, 2646,

458

INDEX DES MATIÈRES EN ANGLAIS

2757, 2880, 2890, 3045, 3061, 3070,
3072, 3092, 3095, 3096, 3123-3125, 3128,
3151, 3157, 3189, 3204, 3218, 3221,
3222, 3230, 3235, 3243, 3245, 3246,
3252, 3253, 3256, 3257, 3260, 3263,
3265, 3266, 3269, 3273, 3295, 3299,
3301, 3323, 3330, 3339-3341, 3345, 3347,
3353, 3354, 3358, 3361, 3374, 3377,
3382, 3392, 3393, 3398, 3402, 3403,
3406, 3408, 3415, 3418, 3423, 3425,
3429, 3430, 3432, 3438, 3439, 3441-3443,
3448, 3450, 3471, 3497, 3519, 3528,
3537, 3539, 3540, 3547, 3552, 3567,
3601, 3646, 3660, 3736, 3779, 3785,
3812, 3864, 3908, 3910, 3949, 3993,
4065, 4148, 4334, 4389, 4472, 4515,
4560, 4585, 4775, 4851, 4857, 4863,
4887, 4939, 4952, 4966, 4969, 4979,
4994, 5046, 5159, 5166, 5196, 5256,
5262, 5272, 5308, 5338, 5339, 5409,
5437, 5529, 5553, 5704, 5776, 5890, 5919
see also: Cultural identity, Group identity,
Identity formation, Identity politics,
National identity, Professional identity,
Regional identity, Social identity
Identity formation 734, 954, 965, 967, 983,
987, 1020, 1161, 1300, 1409, 1990, 2047,
2436, 2501, 2530, 2608, 2618, 2878,
3059, 3227, 3362, 3382, 3410, 3411, 3441,
3445, 4125, 5293, 5334, 5430
Identity politics 397, 966, 992, 1535, 1761,
2326, 2340, 3480, 5156, 5328
Ideology 23, 34, 47, 149, 189, 295, 351, 929,
967, 968, 977, 1028, 1151, 1167, 1209,
1214, 1346, 1353, 1376, 1421, 1449,
1464, 1577, 1612, 1644, 1727, 1761,
1762, 1792, 1802, 1920, 1931, 1935,
1960, 1990, 2113, 2140, 2217, 2339, 2502,
2534, 2540, 2551, 2730, 2975, 3085,
3130, 3132, 3212, 3221, 3239, 3249,
3272, 3508, 3697, 3719, 3851, 3892,
4214, 4221, 4674, 4850, 4866, 4898,
4908, 4912, 4926, 4935, 4962, 4973,
4981, 5154, 5238, 5251, 5258, 5270,
5287, 5289, 5319, 5335, 5509, 5512,
5603, 5817, 5960
see also: Political ideology
Igbo 3868
Illegal employment 4449
Illegal immigrants 3579, 5200
Illegal immigration 3630
Illegitimacy 2791
Illiteracy 1996
Illness 581, 694, 781, 887, 2044, 2470, 2655,
2660, 2809, 3037, 3040, 4692, 4696,

4703, 4708, 5502, 5507, 5518, 5534,
5594, 5727, 5813, 5842, 5847, 5850,
5856, 5866, 5891, 5893, 5898, 5928,
5950, 5960, 5970, 5980
Images 530, 630, 657, 1103, 1168, 1710,
1732, 1737, 1752, 1859, 1900, 1909,
2665, 2677, 3157, 3262, 3372, 3374,
3497, 4166, 4324, 5253, 5924
Imagination 12, 784, 994, 1110, 1711, 1975,
2047, 2664, 3322, 4900
IMF 2561, 4250
Immigrant acculturation 3567
Immigrant adaptation 2029, 2047, 2691, 3459,
3461, 3489, 3546, 3549-3551, 3554, 3556,
3557, 3560, 3561, 3564, 3568, 3569,
3572, 3574, 3578, 3579, 3581, 3585-3587,
3589, 3593-3595, 3597, 3599, 3603, 3605,
3641, 3656, 3678, 3757, 4001
Immigrant assimilation 2033, 2530, 3398,
3471, 3545, 3555, 3563, 3564, 3568,
3573-3578, 3581, 3585, 3588, 3593, 3604,
3653, 3674, 4445, 4964, 5791
Immigrants 414, 766, 805, 806, 954, 1319,
1384, 1427, 1521, 1698, 1737, 1777,
2029, 2033, 2038, 2083, 2232, 2313,
2376, 2612, 2624, 2680, 2732, 2784,
2870, 2936, 2950, 3336, 3413, 3434,
3461, 3511, 3523, 3536, 3538, 3545-3547,
3549, 3550, 3552-3554, 3558-3560, 3562-
3565, 3567, 3570-3575, 3577, 3578, 3580-
3583, 3585, 3588, 3590, 3591, 3593,
3594, 3596, 3599-3605, 3609, 3631, 3633,
3639, 3644, 3647, 3652, 3653, 3655,
3656, 3669, 3675, 3684, 3791, 3826,
3846, 3859, 4009, 4184, 4229, 4249,
4432, 4461-4463, 4473, 4821, 4856, 5081,
5089, 5144, 5292, 5441, 5529, 5632, 5791
see also: Illegal immigrants
Immigration 414, 805, 954, 1834, 1949, 2420,
2532, 2559, 2691, 2784, 2922, 3394,
3398, 3459, 3497, 3541, 3542, 3544,
3545, 3556, 3558, 3564, 3565, 3567,
3569, 3573, 3574, 3578, 3579, 3587,
3591, 3593, 3597, 3599, 3601, 3602,
3604, 3617, 3630, 3632, 3633, 3647,
3648, 3651-3653, 3655, 3672, 3675, 3678,
3682-3684, 3686, 3778, 4002, 4184, 4252,
4479, 4552, 4596, 4821, 4856, 4939,
4952, 4983, 5275, 5632
see also: Illegal immigration
Immigration law 3542, 3550, 3582, 3633
Immigration policy 954, 2693, 2870, 3468,
3542, 3545, 3555, 3584, 3586, 3602,
3605, 3630, 3649, 3658, 3662, 3669,
3673, 4939, 4964, 5222, 5632

459

SUBJECT INDEX

Immunity 5984
Immunization 5575, 5949
Imperfect information 4763
Imperialism 134, 188, 710, 1165, 1392, 1819, 3782, 4196, 4935, 4944
 see also: Cultural imperialism
Imports 1323, 1894, 4142
Impoverishment 4277
In-group 842, 843, 1044, 1058, 1063, 1083, 3446
In-service training 5713
Inbreeding 2426, 3304
Incest 2912, 3304
Income 441, 2410, 2457, 2590, 2700, 2787, 3042, 3715, 3835, 4011, 4014, 4020, 4277, 4295, 4301, 4303-4305, 4307, 4309, 4441, 4524, 4539, 4551, 4571, 4587, 5044, 5475, 5518, 5625, 5642
 see also: Family income, Household income, Income elasticity, Low income, Minimum income, Per capita income
Income distribution 2430, 2830, 3249, 3731, 3805, 4201, 4242, 4281, 4294, 4306, 4921, 5628
Income elasticity 5385
Income expectations 5891
Income inequality 2808, 2840, 3528, 3582, 4018, 4251, 4264, 4266, 4301, 4304, 4306, 4308, 4368, 4431, 4486, 4525, 4542, 5642, 5804
Income redistribution 2406, 4209, 4299, 5662
Income tax 2458
Incomes policy 4542
Indebtedness 2336
Independence 995, 2317, 2318, 2502, 2626, 2667, 2878, 2996, 3024, 3229, 3776, 3891, 4218, 4275, 5511, 5639
Independence movements 951
Indians 567, 3400, 3454, 3581, 3629, 4500, 5002
Indicators 3800, 4486, 5433
 see also: Demographic indicators, Economic indicators, Social indicators
Indigenous culture 3402, 4280, 4981, 5746
Indigenous populations 58, 198, 982, 1431, 1493, 1620, 1723, 1769, 1785, 1840, 2379, 2505, 2515, 2568, 3186, 3468, 3482, 3486, 3519, 3526, 3688, 3732, 3736, 3768, 3772, 3789, 3913, 3920, 4280, 4373, 4495, 5167, 5170, 5259, 5553, 5695, 5970
Indigenous rights 1620, 1769, 3526, 3771
Individual and society 2214, 4904

Individual behaviour 500, 780, 1034, 1046, 1299, 1708, 2351, 2612, 2845, 2850, 3279, 3749, 4186, 4351, 4722, 5902
Individual performance 651, 665, 725, 843, 1012, 2072, 4631, 4664
Individual rights 1620
Individualism 28, 284, 287, 382, 578, 583, 801, 870, 1238, 1247, 1275, 1486, 2174, 2317, 2335, 3328, 3465, 3750, 3771, 3842, 3946, 4194, 4392, 4427, 4658, 4793, 4830, 4910, 4939, 5159, 5849
Individuality 17, 2214
Individuals 103, 178, 181, 203, 219, 228, 241, 268, 277, 287, 306, 320, 323, 406, 428, 471, 577, 582, 594, 652, 691, 696, 715, 718, 726, 730, 763, 845, 867, 869, 896, 911, 1007, 1046, 1048, 1067, 1112, 1115, 1144, 1147, 1152, 1292, 1301, 1304, 1635, 2021, 2082, 2303, 2304, 2311, 2318, 2357, 2378, 2552, 2935, 2983, 3055, 3183, 3610, 3969, 4006, 4183, 4188, 4190, 4421, 4753, 4933, 5016, 5151, 5437, 5716
 see also: Individual performance
Indo-European languages 1793, 1794, 1818, 1825
 see also: Sanskrit
Indonesians 3655
Induction 162, 474, 476, 1824, 2099
Industrial anthropology 801
Industrial areas 3206, 4848
Industrial democracy 4823, 4838, 4839, 4877
Industrial development 1756, 4162, 4323, 4458, 4748
Industrial economics 4559
Industrial history 2691, 3854, 4402
Industrial management 73, 4651, 4668, 4727
Industrial organization 154, 4838, 4879
Industrial policy 3309, 3927, 4103, 4404, 4935
Industrial pollution 73
Industrial psychology 1092, 1118, 1138, 1143, 2335, 4607, 4619, 4638, 4671, 4675, 4802
Industrial revolution 2691
Industrial sector 2139, 4847
Industrial society 2420, 5238, 5630
Industrial sociology 1138, 4323, 4389, 4392, 4400, 4403-4405, 4811
Industrial workers 4618
Industrialization 1200, 2420, 2434, 2537, 2691, 3919, 3949, 4007, 4055, 4108, 4152, 4179, 4287, 4296
Industrialized countries 1620, 2113, 4618, 5819
Industry 73, 1168, 2243, 2914, 3333, 3693, 3704, 3773, 3897, 4200, 4402, 4608,

460

INDEX DES MATIÈRES EN ANGLAIS

4824, 4826, 4840
see also: Agricultural industry, Automobile industry, Book industry, Clothing industry, Communication industry, Construction industry, Cultural industry, Dairy industry, Film industry, Food industry, Hotel industry, Location of industry, Manufacturing, Oil industry, Pharmaceutical industry, Service industry
Inequality 427, 454, 2014, 2025, 2030, 2064, 2115, 2116, 2123, 2141, 2336, 2384, 2386, 2402, 2409, 2424, 2428, 2440, 2442, 2448, 2532, 2813, 2844, 2999, 3286, 3307, 3475, 3671, 3771, 3996, 4169, 4216, 4227, 4269, 4282, 4309, 4460, 4464, 4491, 4495, 4587, 4628, 4696, 4793, 4941, 4949, 4950, 5057, 5154, 5244, 5445, 5465, 5756, 5811, 5988
see also: Economic inequality, Social inequality
Infancy 2641
Infant mortality 419, 2698, 2738, 2783, 2787, 2822, 2839, 2841, 3039, 5959
Infanticide 2710, 5868
Infants 551, 659, 2609, 2828, 2895, 3002, 3020, 3027, 3034, 3622, 5872, 5947, 5950
Infertility 2735, 2772, 2789, 5200
Inflation 4347, 4949
Inflation rate 4347
Informal groups 2127
Informal sector 3190, 4099, 4116, 4373, 4429, 4596, 5380, 5492
Information 451, 481, 613, 639, 853, 867, 1015, 1055, 1088, 1116, 1200, 1261, 1554, 1565, 1634, 1646, 1648, 1656, 1658, 1687, 1704, 1717, 1731, 1749, 2337, 2554, 2829, 3724, 3734, 4056, 4179, 4353, 4610, 4654, 4987, 5231, 5854, 5969, 5976
see also: Access to information, Consumer information, Government information, Imperfect information, Legal information, Social information
Information acquisition 1587
Information dissemination 43, 923, 1200, 1732, 2748, 4933, 5169, 5407, 5965
Information economics 472, 5965
Information exchange 1084, 1113, 2580, 4395, 5954
Information processing 552, 580, 623, 625, 642, 655, 658, 662, 663, 666, 823, 827, 865, 920, 1084, 5579
Information sciences 39, 4574
Information services 37, 78-80, 1646, 5669

Information society 37, 379, 1199, 1636, 1643-1646, 1657, 1658, 1674-1676, 1678, 1683, 1685, 2006, 2210, 2309, 2412, 2477, 2519, 2532, 2548, 4570
Information sources 78-80, 92, 101, 102, 447, 3853, 3874, 4686
Information systems 376, 1040, 1113
Information technology 37, 1200, 1302, 1554, 1634, 1636, 1643-1645, 1659-1665, 1667, 1671-1678, 1680, 1688, 1689, 1692, 1713, 1774, 1779, 2006, 2039, 2056, 2172, 2175, 2176, 2197, 2201, 2210, 2223, 2270, 2325, 2337, 2519, 2526, 2532, 2571, 2578, 2608, 3156, 3253, 3505, 3797, 4056, 4095, 4102, 4213, 4346, 4377, 4382, 4434, 4574, 5228, 5230
see also: Virtual reality
Information theory 1587
Inhabitants 3860, 5741
Inheritance 3112, 3619
Initiation 4481
Injuries 1347, 3201, 5967
Injustice 799, 4935
Inner city 3937, 3938, 3966, 3995, 4009, 4010, 4016, 4091, 4092, 4098, 4112, 4148, 4300, 4489, 4490, 5069, 5386
Innovation 1100, 1144, 1155, 1393, 1673, 2258, 2299, 2770, 3223, 3885, 3890, 3916, 3919, 4038, 4054, 4122, 4287, 4375, 4393, 4397, 4402, 4417, 4654, 4702, 4808, 5496, 5725
Innovation diffusion 484
Input-output models 1059
Insects 5968
Institutional change 1993, 2242, 2292, 2679, 4055, 4085, 4354, 4885, 5629
Institutional reform 2513, 2961, 5282, 5904
Institutionalism 1137, 1566, 2555, 3705, 4877, 4957, 4964, 5171, 5782, 5899
Institutionalization 1130, 1139, 1556, 2134, 4197, 4739, 4817, 5172, 5192, 5473, 5479, 5515, 5899
Institutions 68, 162, 802, 1028, 1120, 1133, 1149, 1155, 1156, 1162, 1190, 1464, 1568, 1608, 1619, 1626, 1826, 2113, 2125, 2289, 2291, 2317, 2345, 2361, 2443, 2679, 3238, 3734, 3775, 3855, 3867, 3918, 3922, 4097, 4178, 4181, 4190, 4280, 4301, 4310, 4380, 4699, 4790, 4791, 4793, 4817, 4845, 4881, 4936, 4946, 4961, 4966, 4971, 4978, 4992, 4993, 5020, 5147, 5202, 5213, 5220, 5225, 5265, 5287, 5358, 5593, 5638, 5641, 5793, 5942
see also: Aid institutions, Educational

SUBJECT INDEX

institutions, Financial institutions, Institutional change, Institutional reform, Political institutions, Religious institutions
Insurance 5526
see also: Health insurance, Life insurance, Unemployment insurance
Insurance companies 4699, 4831
Insurgency 1262, 5226
Integration theory 1494
Intellectual development 661
Intellectual property 2261, 2580, 5870
Intellectual work 4199
Intellectuals 217, 224, 240, 281, 288, 299, 1158, 1187, 1268, 1336, 1363, 1411, 1553, 1608, 1707, 1924, 2294, 2298, 2383, 2412, 2439, 2534, 2554, 3222, 4897, 4898, 4914, 4935, 5281, 5298
Intelligence 621, 639, 653, 660, 661, 663, 715, 898, 1237, 2017, 2052, 2359, 2410, 2904, 3446, 5730
see also: Artificial intelligence
Intelligence services 5145
Intelligence tests 1787
Intelligentsia 2412, 2439, 2529, 2534, 3407, 4914
Interactionism 312, 389
Intercultural communication 1186, 1231, 1894, 1895, 4318, 4370, 5170, 5313
Intercultural dialogue 173, 4386
Intercultural influences 1770, 3653
Interdependence 939, 1022, 2070, 3759, 3771, 4618
Interdisciplinary relations 3, 10, 16, 39, 603, 605, 1628, 2656, 3774, 3788, 4891, 4895, 5206, 5939, 5953
Interdisciplinary research 61, 77, 186, 596, 1155, 2570, 3545, 4310, 4895, 4896, 5329
Interest 4352, 4467
Interest groups 2249, 3768, 4100, 4966, 5234
Interethnic communication 3508
Interethnic conflict 1011, 1731, 1816, 3070, 3128, 3269, 3403, 3420, 3444, 3465, 3466, 3469, 3472, 3473, 3475, 3480, 3485, 3492, 3493, 3495, 3520, 3524, 3531, 3536, 5081, 5462, 5700
Interethnic marriages 1812, 5538
Interethnic relations 9, 57, 903, 1187, 1427, 1550, 1698, 1777, 1797, 1812, 1813, 1816, 2011, 2014, 2063, 2188, 2232, 2867, 2870, 3067, 3390, 3395, 3404, 3411, 3429, 3439, 3451, 3458, 3461, 3470, 3473, 3476, 3479, 3480, 3484, 3486-3490, 3492, 3501, 3507, 3508, 3515-3517, 3519, 3520, 3524, 3525, 3527, 3530, 3533, 3535, 3536, 3545, 3561, 3562, 3566, 3575, 3576, 3578, 3600, 3627, 3859, 4005, 4952, 5331, 5441, 5713
Intergenerational relations 771, 1532, 1647, 1768, 2584-2589, 2591, 2593, 2594, 2672, 2682, 2872, 2917, 2927, 2934, 3237, 4755, 5536, 5634
Intergroup relations 72, 866, 879, 881, 894, 1005, 1041, 1042, 1051, 1052, 1058, 1075, 2110, 2240, 2619, 3464, 3515, 3517, 4285, 5343, 5687
Intermarriage 2917
Internal migration 2944, 3229, 3541, 3557, 3607, 3610, 3614-3616, 3620, 3622, 3627, 3725, 3894, 4439
International capital market 4234, 4486
International community 1344, 4268, 5336
International competition 2512, 4055, 4546
International conferences 3944, 5200
International conflicts 1730, 1731, 5323, 5337
International cooperation 2572, 2577, 3672, 5684, 5973
International crime 3713, 5094
International criminal law 5312
International crisis 1023, 1731, 2539, 3713
International cultural relations 1421, 1942
International division of labour 3191, 4546
International economic policy 5316
International economic relations 2562, 2572, 3068, 3952, 4258, 4260, 5282
International economics 3797
International finance 2446
International human rights 1730, 2354, 3681, 5322, 5326, 5576, 5805
International humanitarian law 5025, 5312
International integration 2507
International jurisdiction 5311, 5322
International law 2554, 3136, 4287, 5025, 5027, 5210, 5311, 5322
see also: International humanitarian law
International life 2570
International migration 805, 2530, 2689, 3541, 3543, 3551, 3568, 3575, 3598, 3629, 3634, 3635, 3637, 3641, 3644, 3648, 3650, 3652-3654, 3658, 3659, 3661, 3664, 3665, 3668, 3673, 3678, 3681, 3683, 3684, 3686, 3791, 4252, 5325, 5678
International monetary system 2446
International organizations 87, 2292, 3803, 4279
International politics 68, 2572, 3681, 4935, 5310
International protection of minorities 5340
International relations 346, 1004, 1213, 2205, 2541, 2550, 2552, 2562, 2570-2572, 2577, 3762, 5025, 5257, 5308, 5314-5317, 5319,

462

INDEX DES MATIÈRES EN ANGLAIS

5325, 5329, 5330, 5333-5335, 5363
  see also: East-West relations
International relations theory 4818, 5315, 5317, 5319, 5336
International security 1995, 5314, 5325
International society 336, 393, 1919, 2191, 2521, 2546, 2550, 2555, 2557, 2570, 2572, 2576, 3659, 3669, 5317
International status 5308
International system 336, 1995, 2541, 2562, 2568, 3672
International trade 2547, 2580, 3791, 3927, 4206, 4294, 5282
  see also: Exports, Imports
International travels 3348
Internationalism 3136, 4002
Internationalization 1235, 1911, 2269, 2278, 2550, 3634, 4234, 4289, 4494, 4818, 5678, 5686
Internet 537, 1234, 1242, 1634, 1637, 1641, 1656, 1665-1668, 1670, 1671, 1674, 1676-1682, 1684, 1687, 1689-1693, 1713, 1756, 1822, 1920, 2129, 2197, 2201, 2223, 2325, 2581, 2667, 3253, 3392, 3463, 3505, 3797, 4056, 5230, 5241, 5288
Interpersonal attraction 573, 898, 938
Interpersonal communication 574, 899, 901, 904, 930, 932, 945, 947, 1632, 1635, 1639, 1641, 1670, 1680, 1686, 1833, 2761, 2943, 2966, 2987, 3021, 3053, 4675, 5671, 5682, 5901, 5975
Interpersonal conflicts 822, 908, 916, 3006
Interpersonal influence 4620
Interpersonal relations 573, 574, 581, 591, 596, 697, 708, 709, 747, 822, 840, 853, 855, 874, 876, 898-900, 902-904, 906, 908, 910, 912-922, 924-928, 931-937, 939, 942, 943, 946, 950, 1004, 1021, 1027, 1036, 1051, 1057, 1061, 1064, 1071, 1078, 1084, 1110, 1119, 1142, 1651, 1660, 1677, 1681, 1810, 1945, 2363, 2667, 2862, 2867, 2879, 2889, 2891, 2918, 2956, 2958, 2959, 2966, 2970, 2989, 2990, 3310, 3343, 3347, 3352, 3411, 3746, 3892, 4240, 4367, 4374, 4383, 4675, 4689, 5012, 5434, 5461, 5468, 5568, 5607, 5668, 5753, 5849, 5954
Interventionism 7
Interviewers 509, 4776
Interviews 20, 62, 186, 424, 469, 470, 503, 506, 508-511, 516, 518-521, 523, 527, 528, 532, 828, 1050, 1191, 1353, 1752, 1833, 2240, 2283, 2298, 2466, 2476, 2490, 2500, 2530, 2626, 2747, 2763, 2778, 3033, 3102, 3260, 3288, 3310,

3381, 3600, 3649, 3660, 3696, 4361, 4406, 4558, 4623, 4735, 5012, 5118, 5132, 5389, 5420, 5562, 5675, 5823, 5842, 5891, 5924
Interwar years 2117
Intifada 5351
Intimacy 69, 785, 916, 926, 935, 2313, 2983, 3344, 3380, 3383, 5919
Intragroup relations 856, 2127, 3446
Inventions 965, 992, 4938
Inventory
  see: Resource inventory
Investment 3661, 4088, 4175, 5575, 5629
  see also: Agricultural investment, Foreign direct investment, Public investment
Investment returns
  see: Rent
Investors 4369
Iranians 1427, 3680
Irrationality 206
Islam 190, 980, 1089, 1126, 1263, 1380, 1389, 1422, 1517, 1519-1521, 1523-1534, 1537-1543, 1781, 1802, 1962, 2054, 2126, 2153, 2520, 2978, 3067, 3115, 3163, 3172, 3207, 3247, 3263, 3266, 3393, 3447, 3562, 3573, 3596, 4205, 4223, 4535, 4948, 4962, 5274, 5315, 5687
  see also: Koran, Sufism
Islam and politics 1524, 3277, 5274
Islamic countries 4352
Islamic law 1380, 1522, 3468, 4352
Islamization 190, 1530, 1540, 4352
Islands 982, 1811, 3621, 3776, 3913
Italian language 1789
Italians 567, 1180, 3422, 3566, 4229, 5304
Itinerants 1340, 5420
Jains 1424
James, William 12, 1472
Jameson, Fredric 1229
Japanese 567, 763, 1353, 2271, 2934, 3313, 3548
Japanese language 1830
Jazz 1878, 1977, 1978, 1988, 4767
Jealousy 821
Jesuits 59
Jews 145, 282, 669, 1001, 1014, 1026, 1187, 1442, 1544-1546, 1548-1550, 1786, 1791, 1902, 1912, 1916, 1935, 2177, 2419, 2551, 2619, 2753, 2760, 2842, 3418, 3448, 3450, 3455, 3462, 3477, 3483, 3502, 3518, 3532, 3566, 3600, 3636, 3647, 4919, 5304, 5529, 5907
Job analysis 550, 4614
Job change 4468
Job description 4689

SUBJECT INDEX

Job enrichment 4760
Job loss 4439, 4484, 4579, 4594, 4737
Job performance 707, 2084, 2096, 4412
Job requirements 550, 4726
Job satisfaction 715, 1111, 1118, 1131, 2093, 2267, 4618, 4662, 4677, 4679, 4680, 4684, 4689, 4697, 4699, 4704-4707, 4709-4711, 4714, 4717, 4719, 4720, 4722-4726, 4728, 4733, 4734, 4736, 4741-4744, 4746, 4758, 4827, 5283
Job search 4429, 4466, 4580, 4586, 4588, 4593
Job security 2085, 4388, 4411, 4471, 4484, 4692, 4703, 4714, 4729
Job seekers 4504, 4582, 4588
Job sharing 4685
Johnson, William 1462
Joint consultation 3825
Joint ventures 1134
Jokes 1839, 3404, 3467
Jones, David 4980
Journalism 455, 1218, 1671, 1696, 1709, 1712, 1714, 1717, 1720, 1726, 1730, 1731, 1738, 1741, 1744, 1746, 1751, 1754, 1760, 1763, 1771, 2250, 3141, 3931, 4785, 4787, 5041, 5235
Journalists 989, 996, 1351, 1714, 1720, 4935
Joy 831, 863
Joyce, James 1937, 1941
Judaism 145, 169, 213, 235, 282, 1171, 1380, 1389, 1460, 1546-1549, 1551, 1817, 1896, 1912, 2177, 2842, 3518, 3743, 4535
see also: Hasidism, Hebrew
Judgement 117, 120, 232, 300, 302, 498, 584, 631, 639, 706, 711, 833, 854, 855, 859, 867, 871, 890, 1049, 1437, 1856, 2352, 4613, 4911, 5850
see also: Social judgement
Judges 3891, 5155, 5157, 5170-5172
Judicial process 5006, 5025, 5068, 5154, 5171, 5204, 5205
Judiciary 4983, 5183
Judiciary power 3891, 5017, 5155
Jung, Carl 593, 1255, 2566
Jünger, Ernst 1199
Juries 5160
Jurisdiction 4497, 5068
see also: Criminal jurisdiction, International jurisdiction
Jurisprudence 2361, 4422, 4992, 5027, 5038, 5158, 5163, 5173, 5177, 5183, 5198, 5206, 5211
Jury system 5157
Justice 124, 161, 186, 209, 270, 360, 674, 1008, 1019, 1442, 2352, 2361, 2439, 2448, 2589, 2603, 3042, 3780, 3787, 3816, 3891, 4293, 4306, 4483, 4599, 4626, 4660, 4702, 4723, 4905, 4909, 4937, 4958, 4971, 4983, 4990, 5010, 5019, 5020, 5032, 5034, 5072, 5110, 5125, 5135, 5147, 5154, 5161, 5174, 5180, 5192, 5197, 5244, 5318, 5332
see also: Administration of justice, Criminal justice, Distributive justice, Economic justice, Social justice
Juvenile courts 5036, 5068, 5192, 5209, 5583
Juvenile delinquency 545, 2532, 2618, 4979, 4996, 5000, 5025, 5036, 5045, 5046, 5062, 5068, 5071, 5077, 5078, 5097, 5115, 5369, 5370, 5429, 5450, 5452, 5465, 5472, 5546
Kabyle 18, 3638, 4275
Kachin 2405
Kahlo, Frida 970
Kant, Immanuel 117, 121, 225, 242, 274, 279, 300, 343, 385, 1586
Kazakh 1527, 1539
Keynesianism 4230
Khasi 3076
Khatemi, Mohammed 5315
Kibbutzim 5351
Kidnapping 3471
Kierkegaard, Søren Aabye 244
King, Rodney 3506
King, Stephen 1927
Kingdoms 172
Kinship 1267, 2426, 2582, 2802, 2901, 2902, 2930, 2938, 3646, 3791, 3899, 4212, 4253, 4725, 5168, 5390, 5536, 5573, 5587, 5590, 5962
Kinship systems 3164
see also: Endogamy, Exogamy
Knowledge 6, 8, 12, 13, 29, 37, 46, 110, 113, 118-120, 123, 125, 128, 133, 137, 140, 142, 166, 245, 246, 250, 261, 279, 289, 301, 309, 369, 376, 385, 481, 498, 517, 533, 597, 619, 637, 654, 661, 668, 801, 871, 989, 1018, 1099, 1115, 1116, 1129, 1131, 1149, 1158, 1261, 1271, 1403, 1412, 1553, 1561, 1565, 1566, 1568, 1569, 1573, 1574, 1582, 1587, 1588, 1598, 1600, 1604, 1607, 1613, 1616, 1628, 1629, 1675, 1858, 1984, 2006, 2128, 2139, 2215, 2219, 2222, 2223, 2226, 2243, 2260-2262, 2278, 2295, 2309, 2412, 2508, 2568, 2580, 2621, 2943, 3003, 3099, 3759, 3910, 4246, 4287, 4346, 4375, 4395, 4397, 4398, 4413, 4510, 4609, 4610, 4640, 4654, 4906, 5105, 5201, 5231, 5409, 5663, 5697, 5709, 5711

see also: Knowledge management, Local knowledge, Public knowledge, Sociology of knowledge
Knowledge management 1088, 1645, 1667, 4395
Koran 1089, 1518, 1525, 1542
Kouchner, B. 4287
Kristeva, Julia 4898
Kuhn, Thomas S. 1582
Kuki, Shūz 212
Kupka, František 1863
Labelling 859, 4265, 4472, 5419
Laboratory 433, 1610
Labour 291, 311, 314, 707, 1282, 1290, 1672, 2372, 2399, 2421, 2457, 2507, 3121, 3188, 3268, 3545, 3633, 3909, 4206, 4231, 4263, 4368, 4395, 4411, 4442, 4444, 4446, 4448, 4453, 4456, 4458, 4467, 4478, 4479, 4485, 4524, 4539, 4558, 4560, 4576, 4591, 4616, 4643, 4649, 4677, 4681, 4715, 4740, 4811, 4812, 4819, 4820, 4825, 4826, 4832, 4853, 4859, 4863, 4864, 4873, 4875
see also: Agricultural labour, Child labour, Division of labour, Female labour
Labour contract 5217
Labour costs 4449
Labour demand 4461
Labour disputes 4826, 4840, 4843, 4845, 4846, 4848, 4850, 4851, 4855
Labour economics 633, 2507, 4449, 4484, 4603, 4643, 4681, 4749, 4792
Labour force 2551, 2561, 3180, 3626, 3630, 3633, 3658, 4437, 4454, 4490, 4506, 4518, 4532, 4582, 4600, 4737, 4803, 4823, 4836, 5520, 5845
see also: Blue collar workers
Labour force planning 4603
Labour history 3541, 4740, 4834, 4850, 4859, 4864
Labour law 1308, 2554, 4483, 4534, 4542, 4585, 4587, 4751, 4810, 4815, 4818, 4825, 4846, 4870, 5025
Labour market 633, 1123, 1305, 1892, 2014, 2037, 2043, 2457, 2554, 2602, 2647, 2712, 2914, 2929, 2999, 3188, 3189, 3559, 3565, 3604, 3620, 3623, 3626, 3633, 3658, 3881, 3996, 4322, 4398, 4415, 4429, 4431, 4436, 4439, 4442-4445, 4447, 4451-4453, 4458-4462, 4466, 4468-4470, 4473, 4476, 4479, 4481, 4482, 4485, 4486, 4490, 4498, 4501-4503, 4506, 4509, 4525, 4533, 4538, 4540, 4545, 4546, 4549, 4552, 4554, 4566, 4579, 4583-4585, 4587-4590, 4594-4596, 4598,

4613, 4634, 4677, 4681, 4714, 4742, 4760, 4771, 4778, 4780, 4784, 4793, 4804, 4810, 4815, 4825, 4835, 4837, 4856, 4869, 4985, 5223, 5365, 5392, 5633, 5642, 5651, 5658
see also: Labour market flexibility
Labour market flexibility 4471
Labour market participation 2399, 2624, 2677, 2971, 3127, 3168, 3169, 3224, 3237, 3279, 3549, 3553, 3568, 3582, 3643, 3677, 3996, 4368, 4437, 4438, 4452, 4454, 4466, 4480, 4481, 4487, 4500, 4504, 4505, 4517, 4518, 4522-4524, 4528, 4532, 4553, 4554, 4558, 4561, 4572, 4573, 4582, 4590, 4687, 4694, 4696, 5365, 5626, 5648
Labour market structure 2434, 2455, 3549, 3594, 3677, 4382, 4429, 4434, 4480, 4516, 4547, 4552, 4554, 4582, 4790, 4856, 4985
Labour migration 2559, 3191, 3229, 3396, 3544, 3552, 3556, 3557, 3569, 3587, 3597, 3609, 3618, 3619, 3628, 3644, 3645, 3648, 3651, 3655, 3657-3659, 3661, 3663, 3665, 3671, 3678, 3791, 3868, 4439, 4443-4445, 4458, 4529, 4784
Labour mobility 2790, 3541, 3545, 3627, 3633, 3636, 3639, 4437, 4444, 4468, 4626, 4780, 4798, 4811
Labour movements 2339, 2416, 2507, 2563, 2586, 4433, 4821, 4823, 4832, 4834, 4839, 4841, 4843, 4850, 4851, 4853, 4859, 4863, 4864, 4867, 4869, 4871, 4876, 5265
Labour parties 1891, 2458, 3808, 3827, 4008, 5609
Labour policy 4456, 4471, 4552, 4576, 4587, 4596, 4696, 4749, 4809, 4810, 4815, 4818, 4829, 4837, 4842, 4850, 4851, 4867
Labour productivity 4465, 4763
Labour redundancy 4483
Labour relations 1117, 1122, 1123, 2559, 4250, 4357, 4363, 4400, 4402, 4415, 4420, 4455, 4465, 4537, 4550, 4602, 4623, 4633, 4634, 4648, 4650, 4663, 4677, 4689, 4691, 4695, 4712, 4713, 4725, 4727, 4728, 4742, 4792, 4798, 4803, 4809-4816, 4818-4826, 4828-4838, 4840-4847, 4849-4853, 4855, 4856, 4858, 4867-4869, 4872-4876, 4879, 4882, 4883, 4949, 5217, 5220
Labour shortage 2270, 3633
Labour supply 4466, 4476, 4535, 4547, 4553, 4561
Labour turnover 4517, 4684, 4720

SUBJECT INDEX

Lacan, Jacques 3339
Laclau, Ernesto 368
Ladino 1817
Laissez-faire 3771
Land 998, 2711, 3732, 3883, 3887, 3896, 3966, 4145, 4232, 5363
Land claims 5361
Land economics 4047, 4156, 4164
Land market 3883, 4017, 4103
Land prices 3986
Land reform 3867, 5261
Land settlement 3867, 3924
Land tenure 3768, 3883, 3887, 3975
Land use 3152, 3611, 3696, 3876, 3914, 4035, 4047, 4058, 4059, 4074, 4082, 4088, 4099, 4108, 4145, 4170, 4189, 5363, 5838, 5968
Landmines 5445, 5988
Landowners 3755, 3891
Landscape 1362, 1589, 1936, 3689, 3719, 3728, 3753, 3777, 3779, 3851, 3879, 3882, 3941, 3970, 4059, 4141, 4145
Language 12, 76, 81, 82, 114, 119, 122, 156, 197, 202, 210, 244, 249, 297, 312, 340, 359, 378, 384, 470, 538, 547, 610, 623, 743, 836, 945, 979, 981, 1029, 1040, 1104, 1182, 1237, 1247, 1275, 1428, 1458, 1518, 1561, 1582, 1649, 1682, 1689, 1712, 1722, 1723, 1736, 1739, 1763, 1777, 1784-1786, 1788-1790, 1792-1794, 1797, 1798, 1801, 1802, 1804, 1806, 1807, 1809, 1811-1815, 1818-1820, 1825, 1828, 1830, 1832, 1834-1840, 1842, 1844-1847, 1865, 1872, 1877, 1894, 1935, 1957, 1990, 1991, 1997, 2003, 2025, 2107, 2121, 2188, 2190, 2227, 2523, 2909, 2936, 3005, 3061, 3133, 3139, 3227, 3363, 3409, 3415, 3426, 3432, 3561, 3564, 3580, 3598, 3931, 4137, 4179, 4421, 4801, 4959, 4969, 5021, 5132, 5153, 5177, 5410
see also: Arabic language, Foreign languages, Hindi, Indo-European languages, National language, Official languages, Philology, Polish language, Portuguese language, Sentences, Sign language, Vernacular languages
Language acquisition 547, 610, 622-624, 636, 1161, 1654, 1788, 1805, 2087, 2149, 3564, 3585
Language barrier 3586
Language change 1723, 1804, 1805, 1816, 1818, 1819, 1841, 1847, 3423
Language disorder 622, 1653
see also: Dyslexia

Language history 1797, 1798, 1805, 2227
Language planning 1795, 1816, 1817, 1823, 1840, 1841, 2107, 2461
Language policy 1000, 1785, 1809, 1816, 1817, 1819, 1823, 1838, 1841, 1843, 2107, 2228, 2461, 3555, 5021
Language teaching 1786, 2083, 2105, 2121, 2227, 2228
Lao-tzu 200, 1382
Large enterprises 4424, 4543, 5154
Lau 3913
Laughter 729, 1967, 5293
Law 95, 426, 498, 1308, 1380, 1611, 1650, 1665, 1678, 1838, 1980, 2361, 2366, 2754, 3319, 3354, 3574, 4299, 4496, 4497, 4751, 4876, 4978, 4992, 5024, 5025, 5054, 5144, 5149, 5151, 5153, 5154, 5158-5163, 5165, 5167, 5171-5174, 5176, 5178-5183, 5185, 5189, 5191, 5193, 5194, 5198, 5199, 5206-5208, 5211, 5219, 5443, 5580, 5585, 5814, 5829, 5853, 5884, 5886, 5889
see also: Anthropology of law, Civil law, Common law, Community law, Comparative law, Constitutional law, Criminal law, Customary law, Economic law, Environmental law, Family law, Fiscal law, History of law, Immigration law, International law, Islamic law, Labour law, Litigation, Marital law, Martial law, Natural law, Parliamentary law, Philosophy of law, Public law, Sociology of law, Traditional law
Law and order 2532, 4683, 4991, 4993, 4996, 5048, 5061, 5091
Law enforcement 5006, 5048, 5124, 5128, 5134, 5136, 5139, 5140, 5145, 5154, 5204, 5282
Lawrence, Stephen 5147
Lawyers 1010, 3166, 4844, 5154, 5169, 5170, 5205
see also: Solicitors
Leaders 1065, 1938, 3423, 3877, 4620, 4622, 4637, 4639, 4886, 4898, 5304
see also: Charismatic leaders, Political leaders
Leadership 684, 1010, 1065, 1068, 1093, 1153, 1336, 2118, 2151, 2240, 2257, 2321, 2398, 2405, 3067, 3115, 3163, 3911, 4253, 4417, 4543, 4615, 4620, 4622, 4624, 4630, 4632, 4637-4639, 4642, 4645, 4646, 4658, 4661, 4663, 4886, 5227, 5932
see also: Political leadership
Learning 63, 225, 376, 540, 547, 555, 594, 607, 617, 622, 624, 627, 637, 647, 651,

658, 663, 665, 666, 1018, 1040, 1046, 1095, 1098, 1113, 1115, 1119, 1128-1130, 1149, 1293, 1542, 1587, 1681, 1708, 1984, 1992, 2003, 2004, 2008, 2017, 2047, 2049, 2053, 2075, 2087, 2127, 2128, 2164, 2168, 2172, 2174-2178, 2182, 2190, 2192-2194, 2199, 2202, 2209, 2213, 2219, 2223, 2229, 2244, 2260, 2271, 2272, 2279, 2299, 2368, 2447, 2453, 2575, 2609, 3003, 4360, 4384, 4398, 4609, 4807, 4868, 5231, 5677, 5697, 5704, 5799, 5831, 5912, 5926, 5953
Learning disabilities 574, 783, 815, 878, 2019, 2026, 2028, 2206, 2225, 2468, 2469, 2482, 2485, 2486, 2489, 2497, 2499, 2500, 3329, 5682, 5720, 5926, 5934, 5938
Left 4864, 4919
    see also: New left
Left wing parties 3137
Legal aspects 2716, 3291, 3354, 4876, 4984, 5219, 5886, 5888
Legal culture 5020, 5165, 5190, 5203
Legal information 95
Legal profession 5169, 5203
Legal protection 4933, 5326, 5585
Legal reform 5039, 5041, 5054, 5154, 5187, 5200
Legal science 5154, 5166, 5204, 5211
Legal status 1520, 1522, 3290, 3471, 3585, 5156, 5580, 5585
Legal systems 1010, 1734, 3136, 3891, 4422, 4823, 4999, 5020, 5025, 5038, 5043, 5054, 5139, 5150, 5154, 5157, 5160, 5163-5165, 5167, 5168, 5173, 5183, 5189-5191, 5193, 5198, 5204, 5207, 5211, 5282, 5546
    see also: Legal culture
Legal theory 1566, 4907, 5025, 5149, 5150, 5152, 5158, 5160, 5161, 5163, 5165, 5166, 5173, 5177, 5179-5181, 5185, 5188, 5197-5199, 5201, 5207, 5208, 5210, 5311, 5322
Legends 3186
Legislation 1030, 1734, 1980, 2458, 2702, 3290, 3630, 3745, 3810, 4133, 4396, 4488, 4496, 4695, 5153, 5164, 5173, 5176, 5200, 5204, 5221, 5492, 5560, 5706
    see also: Social legislation
Legislative power 4949
Legislature 4975
    see also: State legislatures
Legitimacy 431, 895, 1013, 2243, 4351, 4640, 4767, 5040, 5213, 5216, 5218, 5282
Leisure 469, 470, 1282, 1285, 1291, 1292, 1301, 1308, 1312, 1320, 1326, 1347,

INDEX DES MATIÈRES EN ANGLAIS

1366, 2248, 2372, 2486, 2618, 2667, 2880, 2906, 3169, 3644, 4060, 4176, 4451, 4685, 4767
    see also: Sociology of leisure
Leisure time 1301, 3200, 4475
Lenoir, Fréderic 1464
Lepsius, M. Rainer 2312
Lesbianism 1488, 2492, 2688, 2915, 3061, 3125, 3134, 3340, 3352, 3356, 3361, 3363, 3364, 3369, 3373-3375, 3379, 3384, 3389, 5984
Less developed countries 2397, 2432, 2638, 2786, 3629, 3637, 4170
Level of education 1494, 2031, 2037, 2041, 2072, 2333, 2756, 2760, 2852, 2948, 3279, 3670, 3671, 3748, 4447, 4583, 4595, 4717, 4755, 5578, 5757, 5838
Lévi Strauss, Claude 348
Levi, Primo 3518
Levinas, Emmanuel 1382
Lévy, Bernard-Henri 281
Lexicology 659
Liberal democracy 248, 1265, 4287, 4958
Liberal parties 5219
Liberalism 170, 227, 320, 352, 382, 1188, 1197, 1361, 2143, 2361, 2734, 3365, 3419, 3471, 3816, 3849, 4224, 4230, 4898, 4915-4917, 4927, 4928, 4967, 5130, 5155, 5180, 5188, 5343, 5553, 5641, 5654
    see also: Neoliberalism
Liberalization 4245, 4713, 4923, 4998, 5250, 5282, 5793
Liberalization policy 2564
Liberals 4897, 4915
Liberation 295, 2310, 3133, 3134, 3172, 3295, 3298, 3349, 4935
Liberation movements 4864
Liberation theology 1478, 1514
Libertarianism 1412, 5238
Libertarians 1412
Libraries 78-80, 85, 104, 1646
Life cycles 704, 1647, 2595, 2627, 2781, 2925, 4080
Life expectancy 2679, 2685, 2695, 2696, 2719, 2724, 2815, 2833, 2835, 2837, 4304, 5494, 5519, 5897
Life history 179, 431, 490, 2020, 3094, 3268, 5438, 5573
Life insurance 4699
Life satisfaction 482, 2004, 2666, 2668, 3581, 3679, 4725
Life stories 178, 194, 283, 376, 431, 490, 734, 2537, 2625, 3495, 4557, 5420, 5838

Subject Index

Life styles 1371, 1645, 2503, 2593, 2615, 2642, 2650, 2664, 2711, 2814, 3462, 3679, 3791, 4119, 4295, 4334, 4410, 4593
Liminality 1912, 5262, 5462
Linear models 500, 4733
Linguistic anthropology 1161, 1949
Linguistic conflict 1795, 1798
Linguistic contact 1182, 1798, 1804, 1812, 1813, 1825, 2523
Linguistic geography 1798, 1820
Linguistic minorities 979, 1723, 1786, 1793, 1795, 1816, 1823, 2050, 2523, 3423
Linguistic pluralism 1825, 2107
Linguistic research 76, 1798
Linguistic theory 1239, 1722, 1989
Linguistics 76, 138, 231, 359, 538, 547, 636, 729, 735, 1722, 1757, 1789, 1790, 1792-1795, 1797, 1802, 1804, 1807, 1813, 1815, 1817, 1818, 1822, 1823, 1829, 1830, 1838-1842, 1845, 1847, 1872, 1877, 2050, 2107, 3415, 4801
  see also: Sociolinguistics
Linguists 1816
Listeners 919, 1982
Literacy 1694, 1991, 2005, 2006, 2013, 2025, 2040, 2046, 2185, 2221, 3203, 4807, 5058
Literary criticism 99, 241, 299, 1158, 1227, 1239, 1351, 1796, 1874, 1934, 1937, 1939, 1940, 1943, 1949, 1953, 1958, 3120, 3386
Literary genres 1332
Literary history 1913, 1919, 1941, 1956, 3098
Literary movements 1932
Literary theory 99, 669, 1789, 1919, 3102
Literary works 200, 1224, 1913, 1932, 1941, 3250
Literature 57, 86, 99, 247, 281, 540, 975, 1158, 1181, 1187, 1207, 1227, 1243, 1279, 1307, 1323, 1789, 1796, 1865, 1877, 1882, 1901, 1913-1919, 1921, 1922, 1924-1940, 1942-1946, 1948, 1949, 1951, 1954-1970, 2047, 2298, 2314, 2439, 2522, 3051, 3079, 3098, 3120, 3122, 3225, 3245, 3262, 3386, 3539, 3635, 4030, 4056, 4144, 5152, 5356, 5976
  see also: Contemporary literature, Epic literature, Literary history, Novels, Oral literature, Poems, Poetry, Prose, Sociology of literature
Litigation 3891, 5039, 5041, 5154, 5184, 5189-5191, 5205
Living arrangements 2996
Living conditions 58, 1536, 1923, 2020, 2032, 2606, 2707, 2709, 2843, 2999, 3173, 3399, 3845, 3882, 3917, 3991, 3992, 4017, 4040, 4087, 4169, 4244, 4247, 4272, 4295, 4299, 4593, 5428, 5511, 5592, 5701
Loans 1822, 4683
Lobbying 3535, 3912, 4966
Local communities 463, 987, 1205, 1384, 1764, 2101, 2568, 2709, 3530, 3705, 3814, 3826, 3830, 3838, 3848, 3853, 3856, 3859, 3861, 3881, 3894, 4097, 4148, 4600, 4768, 4945, 5716, 5749, 5771
Local culture 1363, 3723, 3894, 4287
Local economy 1733, 3069, 4280, 4439, 4579, 4589
Local finance 3852, 4169, 5635
Local government 2388, 2458, 2467, 2709, 3745, 3807, 3813, 3814, 3829, 3830, 3856, 3885, 3935, 3981, 3985, 3990, 4031, 4052, 4058, 4061, 4066, 4091, 4110, 4113, 4169, 4270, 4537, 4565, 4774, 5217, 5221, 5224, 5426, 5542, 5571, 5586, 5591, 5617, 5635
Local knowledge 123, 3688, 4280
Local politics 1550, 2467, 3856, 5269
Local power 3193
Localization 1268, 1755, 2545, 2568, 3355, 3802, 3851, 3864
Location of industry 4315, 4346
Loggers 3735
Logic 106, 113, 120, 128, 260, 286, 297, 380, 1265, 1391, 1610, 1640, 2508, 4385, 5179, 5201
  see also: Mathematical logic
London, Jack 1323
Loneliness 578, 701, 1670, 2311, 5893
Long-term analysis 431, 2541, 2700, 2796, 3232, 3237, 3675
Long-term care 5504, 5506, 5513, 5515, 5519, 5536
Losev, Alexsei 249
Lotnik, Waldemar 3495
Lotteries 1287, 4262
Louis XIV {King} 4954
Love 209, 293, 674, 897, 900, 913, 920, 922, 939, 942, 950, 1933, 2517, 2629, 3030, 3108, 3227, 3328, 3342, 3746
Low income 2746, 2841, 2991, 3019, 3027, 3625, 3757, 3813, 3984, 4010, 4022, 4087, 4116, 4169, 4299, 4302, 4587, 4593, 5475, 5543, 5565, 5567, 5611, 5627, 5649, 5656, 5669, 5788, 5969
Lowe, Adolph 4900
Lower chamber 4975
  see also: Members of the lower chamber
Lower class 2394, 2415, 4774
Lower middle class 3164, 3973

INDEX DES MATIÈRES EN ANGLAIS

Loyalty 1439, 1794, 2986, 4601, 5168
Luhmann, Niklas 350, 359, 371, 372, 393, 394, 402, 403
Lutheranism 1486
MacDonogh, Steve 1952
Machiavellianism 346, 5117
Machinery 634, 1593
Macroanalysis 308, 471
Macroeconomic policy 2561, 4596
Macroeconomics 4949
Macrosociology 1183, 5388
Madia 1777
Madness 5027, 5919, 5920
Mafia 2203, 5092, 5094, 5317
Magic 1622, 1905
Magyars 1816
Mahfouz, Najib 1966
Mail surveys 524, 527
Majority groups 903, 1052, 1067
Malaria 3708, 5980
Malcolm X 1882
Male sterilization 2729
Male-female relationships 910, 922, 924, 932, 1810, 2761, 2977, 2985, 3066, 3124, 3149, 3201, 3288, 4310, 5449
see also: Partners
Malebranche, Nicolas 221
Males 938, 1897, 3115, 3232, 3346, 3835, 3996, 4394, 4437, 4460, 5079
Malinowski, Bronislaw 12
Malnutrition 3759, 5541, 5969
Malthus, Thomas 2706
Malthusianism 2715
Management 47, 49, 416, 459, 684, 1033, 1049, 1080, 1090, 1094, 1097, 1100, 1103, 1104, 1108, 1110, 1117, 1119, 1121, 1144, 1146, 1157, 1323, 1622, 1660, 1701, 1718, 2104, 2133, 2159, 2241, 2243, 2274, 2279, 2335, 3180, 3246, 3281, 3821, 3824, 3861, 4056, 4064, 4232, 4354, 4360, 4363, 4364, 4370, 4400, 4402, 4406, 4422, 4492, 4510, 4521, 4543, 4562, 4604, 4608, 4612, 4619, 4620, 4622-4625, 4627, 4629, 4631, 4634-4637, 4639, 4642, 4646, 4648, 4650, 4652, 4654, 4655, 4657-4659, 4661, 4663, 4665-4667, 4669-4672, 4683, 4697, 4729, 4742, 4744, 4756, 4774, 4786, 4808, 4816, 4820, 4831, 4844, 4963, 5148, 5216, 5486, 5646, 5732, 5771, 5834
see also: Crisis management, Environmental management, Financial management, Forest management, Health management, Hospital management, Industrial management, Management science, Middle management, Personnel management, Product management, Public management, Resource management, Risk management, Sales management, Top management, University management, Urban management, Waste management, Water management
Management attitudes 4618
Management development 4628, 4671, 4759
Management research 4628
Management science 376, 416, 1090, 2335, 4355, 4413, 4610, 4627, 4630, 4636, 4649, 4651, 4652, 4659, 4663, 4666, 4668, 4669, 5224, 5790, 5834
Management techniques 662, 1094, 1111, 4399, 4420, 4621, 4623, 4625, 4633, 4640, 4647, 4650, 4656, 4667, 4671, 4808, 5128
Managers 1013, 1104, 1119, 1147, 1718, 3281, 4421, 4512, 4565, 4569, 4599, 4627, 4629-4631, 4635, 4645, 4648, 4652, 4656, 4657, 4659, 4661-4663, 4738, 4759, 4774, 4786, 4809
Manufacturing 4212, 4278, 4450, 4682, 4748, 4840, 4845, 4854, 4882
Manufacturing techniques 4617
Maoism 4848
Maori 164
Mapping 58, 1798, 3702, 3785, 3813, 4346, 5552
Maps 94, 1000, 2829, 3371, 3768, 3769, 3785
Marginality 331, 1985, 2073, 2423, 3227, 3579, 3771, 4283
Marginalized people 1310, 2385, 2432, 2458, 3175, 3250, 3416, 3474, 3656, 3754, 4039, 4453, 5299, 5800, 5914
Marital conflict 2861, 2865, 2870, 2876, 2881, 2928, 2931, 2937, 2947, 2960, 2965, 2966, 2987, 5681
Marital interaction 2761
Marital law 2917, 2992, 3471
Marital life 2861, 2911
Marital roles 2761, 2980
Marital satisfaction 2913, 2960, 2966, 2968, 2970, 3382
Marital separation 2768, 2855, 2968, 2969, 2973
Marital stability 2966, 2969
Marital status 2768, 2791, 2938, 2982, 5436, 5510
Market 1508, 1873, 2243, 2244, 3272, 3907, 3966, 4124, 4132, 4192, 4193, 4215, 4237, 4314, 4322, 4355, 4363, 4459, 4715, 4976, 5287, 5740, 5777
see also: Art market, Beef market, Black

SUBJECT INDEX

market, Capital market, Foreign markets, Housing market, Labour market, Land market, World market
Market economy 1738, 2686, 3890, 4179, 4195, 4201, 4208, 4209, 4214, 4230, 4231, 4237, 4260, 4322, 4351, 4481, 4923, 5059
Market efficiency 5615
Market entry 4407
Market equilibrium 4124
Market failure 3806, 5522
Market forces 1604, 3140, 4349
Market mechanisms 1754
Market regulation 3820, 4322
Market research 519, 4341
Market socialism 4215, 4241, 4829
Market structure 4003, 4778
Market theory 2967
Marketing 1317, 1323, 1875, 1895, 3312, 3405, 3749, 3927, 3942, 3965, 4141, 4312, 4318, 4319, 4322, 4343, 4420
see also: Advertising
Marketing research 3312, 4324, 4345
Markievicz, Constance 1936
Markovian processes 446, 492
Marriage 910, 915, 936, 937, 946, 950, 1290, 1795, 2363, 2394, 2408, 2472, 2478, 2635, 2692, 2696, 2710, 2791, 2800, 2822, 2848, 2849, 2851, 2852, 2856-2858, 2861, 2891, 2897, 2901, 2905, 2911, 2915, 2917, 2919, 2925, 2926, 2933, 2944, 2949, 2955-2962, 2965, 2967-2970, 2972-2986, 2988-2992, 3000, 3001, 3015, 3020, 3026, 3046, 3051, 3055, 3170, 3203, 3211, 3221, 3237, 3343, 3360, 3471, 3550, 3557, 3623, 3835, 3846, 3873, 3883, 3901, 4432, 4451, 4531, 4551, 4556, 4575, 5345, 5538
see also: Age at marriage, Arranged marriage, Consanguineous marriage, Interethnic marriages, Intermarriage, Remarriage
Marriage contracts 2917, 2978
Marriage customs 2980, 3304
Married persons 2969, 2990, 4457, 4557
Married women 3210, 4524, 4532
Martial law 3323
Martín-Barbero, Jesús 1158
Marx, Karl 67, 360-362, 4922, 4961
Marxism 6, 23, 144, 252, 280, 284, 285, 299, 332, 342, 351, 360-363, 379, 381, 1194, 1218, 1221, 1229, 1233, 1250, 1444, 1478, 1879, 2384, 2406, 2416, 2440, 2445, 3137, 4179, 4201, 4336, 4373,

4570, 4864, 4865, 4904, 4919, 4925, 4934, 4961, 5286
Masai 2505, 2515
Masaryk, Thomas G. 4913
Masculinity 574, 732, 1191, 1339, 1341, 1503, 1562, 1744, 1782, 1910, 1927, 1940, 1946, 1974, 2608, 3070, 3115, 3189, 3217, 3218, 3222, 3225, 3230, 3233, 3235, 3236, 3240-3243, 3246, 3252, 3253, 3257, 3259, 3260, 3264, 3269, 3271, 3272, 3274, 3288, 3299, 3305, 3320, 3346, 3349, 3350, 3353, 3372, 3383, 4521, 4558, 5358, 5415, 5438
Masochism 3121
Mass communication 1635, 1730, 1734, 4481
Mass consumption 340, 3820
Mass culture 1311, 1323, 1363, 1753, 1873, 1975
Mass education 2129
Mass production 340, 1873
Mass society 1323, 1719, 4119, 5248
Mate selection 898, 3318, 3351
Material culture 1177, 1215, 1274, 1737, 1941, 3882, 4065, 4332, 4333
Materialism 185, 252, 280, 477, 1390, 3720, 4188, 4296, 4315, 4336
see also: Cultural materialism
Maternity leave 3039, 4508
Mathematical analysis 453, 1045, 1085
Mathematical economics 2776, 4796, 5390
Mathematical logic 370
Mathematical methods 40, 413, 424, 452, 456, 464-467, 472, 476, 480, 485, 486, 491-493, 496, 635, 1043, 1045, 3838, 4756, 5154
Mathematical models 452, 461, 463-465, 467, 476, 479, 485, 486, 489, 635, 1069, 2108, 2815, 4185, 4527, 4614, 5157, 5987
Mathematics 225, 380, 440, 463, 465, 486, 496, 1581, 1585, 1602, 1605, 1610, 1623, 2015, 2179, 2288, 4124
Matriarchy 3060
Matrilineal descent 3076
Maya 1170
McCarthyism 4897
McLuhan, Marshall 2522
Means of transport 4062
Measurement 63, 419, 428, 433, 477, 494, 496, 498, 525, 711, 719, 1012, 1060, 1571, 1606, 2166, 2289, 2785, 3464, 3800, 3847, 4166, 4277, 4386, 4625, 4635, 4697, 5959
see also: Welfare measurement
Meat
see: Beef

470

INDEX DES MATIÈRES EN ANGLAIS

Mechanization 2715
Media 425, 590, 835, 989, 994, 996, 1024, 1100, 1190, 1200, 1215, 1226, 1227, 1242, 1252, 1269, 1309, 1318, 1320, 1337, 1351, 1368, 1409, 1431, 1622, 1637, 1649, 1660, 1664, 1669, 1671, 1681, 1683, 1687, 1691, 1693-1697, 1699, 1700, 1702-1709, 1711-1717, 1719-1723, 1726-1744, 1746-1749, 1751, 1753, 1754, 1756, 1758, 1760-1763, 1765-1769, 1771, 1773-1776, 1778, 1779, 1781-1783, 1882, 1887, 1920, 1924, 1955, 2250, 2324, 2507, 2522, 2526, 2548, 2554, 2581, 2596, 2645, 2667, 2748, 2942, 2993, 3061, 3112, 3121, 3127, 3141, 3156, 3159, 3228, 3341, 3358, 3365, 3375, 3384, 3391, 3393, 3498, 3506, 3508, 3517, 3601, 3699, 3775, 3931, 4095, 4134, 4296, 4354, 4640, 4847, 5041, 5235, 5264, 5279, 5288, 5289, 5307, 5329, 5398, 5408, 5435, 5704, 5866, 5872, 5960
see also: Multimedia, Press
Media policy 1733, 1734, 1763
Mediation 925, 1006, 1007, 1009, 1010, 1016, 1019, 1024, 1025, 1030, 1215, 1647, 2850, 2854, 2908, 2928, 2947, 3053, 3635, 3891, 4064, 4985, 5020, 5184, 5337, 5361
Medical anthropology 5386, 5541, 5727
Medical beliefs 5734, 5823, 5898, 5954
Medical care 1564, 2470, 2751, 3185, 5197, 5497, 5524, 5534, 5698, 5734, 5743, 5748, 5750, 5759, 5764, 5778, 5781, 5784, 5797, 5806, 5808, 5812, 5819, 5822-5824, 5835, 5859, 5902, 5971
Medical ethics 1564, 2344, 2485, 5826, 5848, 5850, 5851, 5854, 5855, 5861-5863, 5869, 5870, 5875-5877, 5880, 5887, 5889, 5895
Medical occupations 4800, 5734, 5827
Medical personnel 907, 2487, 2497, 4999, 5651, 5690, 5726, 5736, 5762, 5771, 5772, 5825, 5826, 5835, 5840-5842, 5846, 5889, 5896, 5910, 5953, 5980
Medical research 795, 1620, 5406, 5502, 5853, 5869, 5870, 5875, 5880, 5891, 5942
Medical sociology 400, 2440, 2487, 3900, 4696, 4703, 4800, 4999, 5400, 5731, 5733-5735, 5773, 5804, 5811, 5826, 5852, 5856, 5857, 5859, 5861, 5863, 5864, 5867, 5868, 5875, 5877, 5878, 5880, 5892, 5893, 5896, 5897, 5900
Medical treatment 705, 747-749, 765, 766, 772, 813, 816, 2905, 3010, 5375, 5391, 5395, 5398, 5401, 5406, 5407, 5413, 5420, 5480, 5502, 5670, 5680, 5737,
5743, 5744, 5764, 5766, 5806, 5818, 5847, 5874, 5877, 5879, 5882, 5889-5892, 5902, 5906, 5912, 5913, 5918, 5928, 5936, 5952, 5968, 5971, 5982, 5986
Medicine 2477, 3159, 3272, 4551, 4564, 5380, 5507, 5725, 5727, 5731, 5733, 5734, 5752, 5796, 5813, 5817, 5833, 5839, 5848, 5853, 5855, 5885, 5886, 5889, 5892, 5902, 5921, 5980, 5982
see also: Alternative medicine, Biomedicine, History of medicine, Social medicine, Surgery, Traditional medicine
Medieval history 958
Megacities 3702, 3947
Mehta, Deepa 3112
Melanchthon, Philipp 15
Member States 2145, 5290
Members of the lower chamber 3286
Memoirs 1913, 1938, 1964, 3518, 5423
Memorials 957
Memory 161, 162, 181, 232, 501, 503, 579, 625, 629, 632, 640, 644, 654, 658, 670, 774, 785, 812, 975, 976, 986, 993, 994, 1008, 1384, 1433, 1434, 1621, 1735, 1758, 1822, 1896, 1906, 1965, 2174, 2625, 2679, 3094, 3422, 3532, 3638, 3777, 3782, 4183, 4343, 5349, 5579, 5671, 5831, 5921
see also: Collective memory, National memory
Men 403, 722, 811, 1889, 1910, 2031, 2472, 2781, 2862, 3022, 3025, 3080, 3158, 3179, 3187, 3211, 3218, 3233, 3235, 3240, 3252, 3258-3260, 3272, 3274, 3275, 3307, 3308, 3346, 3350, 3391, 3457, 3670, 3673, 3996, 4437, 4459, 4470, 4548, 4554, 4765, 4794, 5155, 5388, 5404, 5411, 5432, 5457, 5460, 5584
Men's health 2472, 2829, 5411
Men's role 1910, 3211, 3267, 5505
Mencius 266, 1423, 3108
Menger, Carl 4181
Menopause 2744, 2801
Mental health 95, 545, 557, 574, 716, 742, 745, 751, 753, 755-758, 762, 764-768, 771, 776, 778, 780, 781, 783, 786, 788, 789, 792, 794, 795, 797, 800, 805, 807-809, 813, 816, 819, 876, 1053, 1898, 2020, 2154, 2478, 2499, 2602, 2647, 2655, 2660, 2664, 2856, 2877, 2885, 2893, 2895, 2906, 3044, 3048, 3226, 3382, 3666, 3696, 4698, 4699, 4731, 4735, 4746, 5016, 5022, 5033, 5137, 5381, 5393, 5394, 5406, 5420, 5434, 5464, 5488, 5516, 5633, 5658, 5665,

Subject Index

5683, 5710, 5720, 5735-5738, 5823, 5825, 5891, 5898-5901, 5903, 5905-5908, 5910-5912, 5915-5918, 5920, 5922, 5923, 5925-5929, 5931, 5935, 5937, 5939-5941, 5944, 5961
Mental hospitals 95, 5016, 5056, 5192, 5420, 5914, 5920, 5924, 5927, 5930, 5932
Mental illness 95, 506, 738, 740, 743, 745, 750, 753, 762-764, 768, 772, 773, 779, 788, 789, 794, 804, 807, 808, 813, 816, 818, 820, 1947, 2334, 2478, 2659, 4950, 5016, 5027, 5056, 5078, 5137, 5192, 5377, 5420, 5479, 5529, 5604, 5736, 5738, 5891, 5904, 5906, 5907, 5909, 5912-5916, 5919, 5920, 5922, 5926-5930, 5934, 5938, 5939, 5941
Mental stress 545, 550, 581, 716, 721, 722, 741, 742, 751, 764, 766, 767, 795, 796, 805, 807, 819, 820, 887, 1347, 2096, 2855, 2874, 2895, 2921, 2965, 3181, 3478, 3751, 3873, 4291, 4377, 4680, 4686, 4692, 4693, 4698, 4699, 4703, 4705, 4706, 4711, 4713, 4724, 4726, 4731, 4734, 4735, 4743, 4746, 4773, 5033, 5349, 5369, 5488, 5710, 5721, 5838, 5921, 5928, 5935
Mentality 2396, 5285
Mentally disabled 2456, 2485, 5927, 5930, 5938
Merchants 4223
MERCOSUR 2507
Mergers 4876
Meritocracy 3491, 4507, 4551, 4615
Merleau-Ponty, Maurice 215, 225, 3146
Messages 1642, 1647, 1710, 1799
Messiah 1478
Metaphor 12, 225, 642, 1473, 1682, 1780, 1872, 1928, 3719, 5890, 5932
Metaphysics 199, 207, 208, 218, 221, 222, 225, 233, 245, 246, 248, 250, 251, 258, 260, 267, 271, 272, 275, 276, 288-290, 303, 1413, 1574, 1586, 1868, 1871, 3142
Methodology 2, 20, 41, 51, 63, 74, 88, 90, 112, 119, 123, 146, 164, 167, 176, 179, 182, 183, 194, 195, 301, 303, 309, 313, 321, 365, 374, 376, 392, 410, 412, 416, 418-420, 422, 424-426, 429, 430, 432, 435, 438, 439, 441, 444, 448, 457, 462, 480, 482, 484, 487, 488, 490, 497, 503, 509, 514-517, 526, 530, 533, 535, 587, 605, 629, 653, 713, 841, 870, 1102, 1104, 1113, 1244, 1396, 1408, 1552, 1570, 1580, 1582, 1631, 1711, 1800, 1870, 2012, 2224, 2476, 2681, 2699, 2700, 2726, 2785, 2985, 3063, 3118, 3121, 3178, 3406, 3775, 3794, 3795, 3830, 3993, 4025, 4030, 4044, 4265, 4266, 4276, 4312, 4604, 4625, 4659, 5073, 5135, 5173, 5199, 5224, 5329, 5399, 5442, 5452, 5688, 5867, 5876, 5959, 5968
see also: Anthropological methodology, Economic methodology, Sociological methodology
Metropolis 3359, 3632, 3943, 3948, 3953
Metropolitan areas 411, 3590, 3621, 3767, 3933, 3960, 3997, 4015, 4022, 4024, 4066, 4067, 4072, 4103, 4150, 4159, 4164, 4300, 4461
Mexicans 536, 805, 2784, 3336, 4462
Mickiewicz, Adam 1934
Microanalysis 308, 431, 471, 799, 5170
Microeconomics 40, 4348
Microfinance 4263
Middle age 1284, 2584, 2585, 2676
Middle Ages 1789
Middle class 2374, 2394, 2419, 2425, 2438, 2917, 3411, 3481, 3997, 4378, 4864, 5614
Middle management 4631
Midwives 5746
Migrant workers 58, 2550, 2886, 3556, 3568, 3597, 3609, 3662, 3665, 4443, 4552, 5638
Migrants 953, 1987, 1990, 2590, 2691, 2790, 2940, 3085, 3263, 3537, 3539, 3540, 3543, 3548, 3549, 3566, 3592, 3614, 3641, 3643, 3649, 3669, 3680, 4099, 4257, 5200, 5823
Migrants' children 2029
Migration 18, 536, 814, 1174, 1263, 1362, 1528, 1532, 2038, 2047, 2232, 2429, 2574, 2590, 2693, 2697, 2701, 2704, 2722, 2741, 3135, 3214, 3229, 3391, 3489, 3537, 3539, 3540, 3543-3545, 3551, 3554, 3556, 3557, 3560, 3561, 3568, 3569, 3574, 3584, 3587, 3595, 3597, 3603, 3606-3610, 3613, 3614, 3616, 3618, 3620, 3622, 3623, 3625, 3627, 3630, 3633, 3637, 3639, 3642, 3643, 3645-3649, 3651, 3656, 3660-3665, 3667, 3668, 3670, 3671, 3673, 3674, 3678, 3679, 3682, 3685, 3686, 3789, 3791, 3795, 3859, 3866, 3997, 4197, 4227, 4257, 4443, 4446, 4463, 4606, 5232, 5791
see also: Forced migration, Internal migration, International migration, Labour migration, Return migration, Rural-urban migration, Seasonal migration, Urban-rural migration
Migration policy 3459, 3584, 3631, 3639, 3641, 3659, 3669, 3672, 3675, 5638
Militancy 1537, 1936, 5256, 5274

INDEX DES MATIÈRES EN ANGLAIS

Militarism 5343
Militarization 3070, 3630, 5361, 5459
Military 3242, 3290, 3945, 4549, 5347, 5348, 5352, 5354, 5355, 5361
Military alliances
  see: NATO
Military and politics 5341
Military courts 5139
Military history 957, 5356, 5359
Military intervention 1730, 1731, 5340
Military personnel 5339, 5345, 5346, 5348, 5352, 5353, 5356, 5359, 5360, 5415
  see also: Soldiers
Military service 3257, 5339, 5342, 5351
Military sociology 5338-5340, 5342, 5344-5346, 5350, 5351, 5353, 5354, 5356, 5359-5362
Military theory 5348, 5355
Mill, John Stuart 45, 4922
Mills 4446
Mind 12, 199, 221, 254, 293, 615, 654, 658, 760, 1423, 3108, 5182
Miners 2339, 4843
Mines
  see: Coal mines
Minimum income 4299
Minimum wages 4307, 4486, 4587
Mining 801, 3820, 3854, 4208, 4864
  see also: Coal mining
Mining development 3827
Minorities 168, 173, 857, 877, 903, 1000, 1059, 1531, 1723, 1806, 1812, 2025, 2042, 2151, 2188, 2273, 2461, 3077, 3286, 3424, 3453, 3471, 3499, 3511, 3515, 3555, 3920, 4005, 4089, 4398, 4472, 4491, 4497, 4606, 4628, 4641, 5139
  see also: Cultural minorities, Ethnic minorities, International protection of minorities, Linguistic minorities, National minorities, Religious minorities
Minority culture 1441, 3427, 3555
Minority education 2017, 2161
Minority groups 1052, 1067, 1184, 1441, 1823, 2017, 3356, 3382, 3387, 3410, 3420, 3423-3425, 3515, 3548, 3568, 3576, 4005, 4249, 4500, 4501, 4628, 5062, 5089, 5304, 5527
Minority protection 1531
Minority rights 1531, 3419, 4628, 5021
Missionaries 1258, 1392, 1397, 1490, 1492
Mixed economy 2458
Modelling 2, 141, 376, 483, 484, 500, 1055, 1605, 1623, 2014, 2048, 2053, 2213, 2690, 2818, 3310, 3620, 3741, 4049, 4670, 4860, 5384

Models 2, 90, 308, 396, 456, 461, 472, 541, 644, 657, 705, 710, 713, 719, 722, 735, 775, 1006, 1036, 1039, 1042, 1574, 2354, 2458, 2477, 2588, 2681, 2747, 2788, 2850, 2900, 2905, 2920, 3025, 3194, 3218, 3289, 3396, 3625, 3744, 3749, 3784, 4073, 4124, 4244, 4581, 4800, 4963, 5117, 5610, 5675, 5677, 5845
  see also: Decision models, Development models, Dynamic models, Econometric models, Economic models, Growth models, Linear models, Mathematical models, Statistical models, Stochastic models
Modern civilization 32, 305, 1256, 1260, 1261, 1272, 1276, 1279, 1281, 1394, 1622, 1963, 2503, 2527
Modern history 2, 143, 165, 177, 182, 186, 189, 1432
Modern society 28, 32, 243, 386, 801, 1164, 1190, 1199, 1254, 1263, 1383, 1447, 1644, 1679, 1690, 1855, 1964, 2140, 2307, 2331, 2410, 2413, 2438, 2556, 2617, 2980, 3168, 3448, 4298, 4967, 4972, 4976, 4980, 5278
Modernism 543, 1158, 1164, 1250, 1258, 1266, 1279, 1523, 1855, 1864, 1941, 1962, 1988, 2558, 3132, 3949, 4131, 4143, 4288, 4904, 4918, 5180
Modernity 19, 58, 86, 125, 214, 243, 253, 277, 291, 315, 324, 327, 335, 338, 367, 372, 397, 926, 973, 1127, 1160, 1162, 1166, 1194, 1197, 1199, 1200, 1215, 1246, 1248, 1249, 1251, 1253, 1254, 1256, 1257, 1260-1263, 1265, 1267, 1272-1274, 1276, 1277, 1280, 1281, 1361, 1366, 1368, 1405, 1431, 1464, 1589, 1595, 1609, 1706, 1728, 1746, 1780, 1860, 1864, 1951, 2309, 2333, 2388, 2400, 2440, 2505, 2516, 2532, 2602, 2605, 3064, 3086, 3247, 3367, 3537, 3722, 3753, 3869, 3946, 4138, 4216, 4217, 4227, 4332, 4337, 4351, 4365, 4885, 4899, 4904, 5180, 5246, 5294, 5309
Modernization 58, 367, 977, 1190, 1204, 1264, 1267, 1336, 1494, 1533, 1675, 1685, 1724, 1729, 2100, 2137, 2163, 2242, 2364, 2505, 2516, 2517, 2537, 2567, 2691, 2733, 3390, 3541, 3716, 3718, 3776, 3803, 3890, 3963, 4033, 4069, 4108, 4155, 4228, 4243, 4258, 4261, 4287, 4373, 4575, 4866, 4890, 4899, 4904, 4963, 4990, 5189, 5245, 5294, 5512, 5622, 5639
  see also: Political modernization

SUBJECT INDEX

Mokken, R.J. 423
Monarchy 955, 4954
Monasteries 1516
Monetary economics 4350
Monetary systems
 see: International monetary system
Monetary theory 4193
Monetary unions 4185
Money 1177, 1287, 1427, 2314, 4186, 4192, 4193, 4347, 4349-4351, 4425, 4684
Money and credit 4348
Monogamy 4994
Monographs 1557
Monolingualism 1789, 2523
Monopolies 5821
Monopoly power 2502
Monotheism 1406
Monte Carlo simulation 446, 483, 491, 492
Montesquieu, Charles Louis 4288
Mood 559, 680, 687, 709, 726, 850
Moore, George Edward 2350
Moral development 46, 2615
Moral hazard 456, 909, 4756
Moral philosophy 131, 201, 205, 208, 211, 216, 224, 225, 227, 229, 238, 241, 255, 264-266, 270, 273, 274, 302, 333, 389, 673, 702, 733, 1259, 1388, 1402, 1420, 1850, 1867, 2350, 2361, 2365-2367, 2370, 2373, 2485, 3119, 4427, 4933, 4937, 5174, 5177, 5180, 5197, 5865, 5876, 5888
Morality 3, 16, 46, 131, 192, 207, 211, 216, 227, 228, 238, 241, 255, 264-266, 270, 276, 300, 367, 583, 638, 650, 673, 674, 706, 717, 899, 906, 909, 929, 934, 1245, 1258, 1259, 1382, 1387, 1388, 1402, 1420, 1427, 1460, 1482, 1505, 1591, 1731, 1850, 1867, 2021, 2160, 2181, 2203, 2213, 2332, 2342, 2343, 2346, 2349, 2351, 2353, 2355, 2356, 2359, 2361, 2362, 2365, 2367-2369, 2373, 2932, 3085, 3301, 3320, 3366, 3534, 3747, 3780, 4229, 4293, 4358, 4417, 4420, 4427, 4428, 4497, 4898, 4916, 4917, 4984, 4990, 5016, 5117, 5149-5151, 5158, 5174, 5177, 5180, 5181, 5197, 5208, 5210, 5316, 5327, 5355, 5371, 5568, 5679, 5730, 5849, 5854, 5855, 5863, 5871, 5876, 5883, 5886
Morals 48, 227, 241, 255, 276, 346, 1564, 1665, 1955, 2001, 2343, 2344, 2356, 2366, 2367, 2485, 2503, 2587, 2734, 3182, 3749, 3930, 4244, 4418, 4636, 5210, 5316, 5865, 5868, 5876, 5940

Morbidity 327, 694, 788, 2046, 2602, 2778, 2810, 2811, 2814, 2817, 5407, 5727, 5765, 5773, 5804, 5809, 5820, 5897, 5964, 5968
Moreno, Rafael 2294
Morgenthau, Hans Joachim 346
Morphology 4046, 4143, 4158
Morrison, Toni 1965
Mortality 327, 478, 685, 1081, 1544, 2686, 2691, 2695, 2696, 2703, 2719, 2722, 2780, 2783, 2787, 2807, 2810, 2811, 2813-2815, 2817-2820, 2824, 2826, 2827, 2829-2835, 2837-2840, 2842-2844, 3202, 3622, 4304, 5756, 5773, 5838, 5897, 5956, 5968, 5983
 see also: Child mortality, Infant mortality
Mortality decline 2799, 2836
Mortgages 4000, 5286
Mother tongue 1786, 1811, 3407, 3595
Motherhood 792, 800, 1969, 2007, 2725, 2738, 2765, 2856, 2895, 2915, 2958, 2993, 3004, 3007, 3015, 3027, 3028, 3035, 3037, 3045, 3169, 3227, 3249, 3273, 3676, 4515, 4568, 5396, 5578, 5746, 5872, 5950
Mothers 695, 755, 771, 792, 796, 849, 2463, 2803, 2822, 2825, 2832, 2846, 2847, 2917, 2991, 2997, 3002, 3007, 3008, 3011, 3015, 3016, 3019, 3021, 3026, 3027, 3029, 3031-3035, 3040, 3045, 3057, 3093, 3228, 3239, 3270, 3280, 3434, 3676, 4531, 4553, 4568, 5200, 5425, 5480, 5589, 5636, 5757, 5792, 5935, 5950, 5969
 see also: Unmarried mothers, Working mothers
Motivation 276, 561, 648, 657, 665, 667, 684, 704, 725, 822, 946, 1021, 1022, 1061, 1066, 1071, 1084, 1157, 1285, 1293, 2059, 2141, 2285, 2368, 2788, 3042, 3183, 3667, 4180, 4391, 4597, 4707, 4709, 4768, 4794, 4802, 4886, 5397, 5406, 5460, 5470
Motorcycles 1851
Mounsi 1949
Mountains 1353, 2152, 3733, 3820, 3925
Mourning 743, 767, 1751, 1937
Multicultural education 2177, 3470
Multiculturalism 206, 322, 393, 395, 643, 806, 954, 996, 1164, 1174, 1226, 1483, 1535, 1592, 1721, 1865, 2212, 2240, 2326, 2380, 2399, 2433, 2436, 2480, 2532, 2550, 2554, 2917, 3155, 3397, 3401, 3405, 3430, 3435, 3444, 3460, 3488-3490, 3494, 3497, 3500, 3501, 3517, 3519, 3522, 3653, 3716, 3789, 4002, 4012,

INDEX DES MATIÈRES EN ANGLAIS

4902, 4905, 4966, 5248, 5317, 5320, 5791, 5973
Multiethnic countries 903, 2436, 2530, 3428, 3430, 3445
Multilingualism 1000, 1838, 1843, 2523
Multimedia 1634, 1658, 1688
Multinational enterprises 2446, 2545, 3645, 3927, 4202, 4289, 4312, 4318, 4360, 4475, 4562, 4633, 4658, 4674, 4818, 5187, 5244
Multivariate analysis 2746, 2748, 2794, 2818, 3210, 3481, 3588, 3673, 4664, 5049, 5138, 5587
Mumford, Lewis 1674
Municipal council 4963
Murder 2719, 3520, 3944, 5058, 5113, 5147, 5323, 5441, 5453, 5454, 5468, 5472, 5858
Murphy, Liam 4921
Museums 996, 1558, 2481
Music 835, 1309, 1310, 1319, 1331, 1338, 1348, 1745, 1856, 1865, 1878, 1971-1975, 1978-1980, 1982-1984, 1986, 1987, 2233, 3115, 3156, 3391, 3427, 4344
  see also: Ethnomusicology, Folk music, History of music, Pop music, Religious music, Rock music, Sociology of music, Traditional music
Musical culture 3427
Musical performances 1979, 1982, 1984
Musicians 651, 1338, 1977, 1982, 1988, 4148, 4767
Musicology 1972, 1982, 1989
Muslims 280, 771, 1392, 1422, 1519, 1521, 1524, 1527-1535, 1537-1540, 1775, 1777, 2029, 2520, 2554, 2612, 2978, 3067, 3115, 3172, 3207, 3266, 3468, 3471, 3557, 3562, 4352
Mutual intercultural respect 1198
Mysticism 256, 1308
Myth 20, 155, 172, 249, 956, 961, 967, 980, 1167, 1576, 1965, 1969, 2317, 2328, 3115, 3186, 3638
Mythology 977, 986, 1227, 1406
NAFTA 4434, 4458, 5227
Names 118, 258
Naming 1822
Nancy, Jean-Luc 205
Narcissism 586, 803, 1699, 2327
Narcotics 1307, 5386, 5828
Narratives 2, 127, 149, 156, 162, 175, 181, 435, 470, 508, 516, 677, 891, 919, 980, 984, 1104, 1127, 1157, 1161, 1176, 1258, 1270, 1275, 1739, 1766, 1824, 1839, 1882, 1920, 1937, 1957, 2581, 2622, 2625, 2643, 2651, 2664, 2878, 2932, 3214, 3250, 3371, 3495, 3496, 3539, 3640, 3697, 3777, 3864, 5034, 5424, 5430, 5495, 5896, 5898, 5946
Natality 2724
Nation 173, 965, 970, 971, 981, 987, 992, 1192, 1589, 1762, 1886, 1951, 2553, 2567, 3067, 3070, 3251, 3421, 3499, 3534, 3779, 4924, 4930, 4959
Nation building 162, 967, 983, 1772, 2153, 2723, 3242, 3430, 3510, 3789, 4914, 4930, 4966
Nation state 306, 1192, 1220, 1246, 1519, 2386, 2446, 2461, 2532, 2565, 2568, 2570, 3420, 3468, 4227, 4892, 4910, 4939, 4953, 4959, 4966
National accounting 4310
National character 960, 4207
National commemoration 58, 974, 996
National consciousness 150, 953, 959, 962, 970, 976, 1262, 1452, 2573, 3421, 4930, 4935
National culture 150, 196, 662, 958, 962, 968, 989, 992, 996, 1103, 1167, 1181, 1182, 1186, 1188, 1291, 1308, 1329, 1480, 1845, 1881, 1885, 2335, 2573, 2576, 3445, 3595, 3888, 4644, 5259, 5308
National development 4115
National identity 58, 147, 150, 159, 168, 187, 247, 669, 834, 953, 954, 958-965, 968-970, 977, 978, 981, 983-985, 987, 991, 995, 997, 998, 1000, 1003, 1167, 1182, 1192, 1193, 1227, 1315, 1499, 1798, 1813, 1816, 1819, 1845, 1881, 1885, 1973, 1981, 2153, 2177, 2204, 2532, 2538, 2573, 3070, 3214, 3250, 3251, 3355, 3400, 3421, 3441, 3445, 3468, 3487, 3532, 3534, 3548, 3557, 3595, 3634, 3635, 3646, 3676, 3789, 3945, 4221, 4227, 4913, 4914, 4924, 4930, 4959, 4962, 4966, 5218, 5295, 5308
National language 1777, 1794, 1798, 1825, 2025, 2121
National memory 150, 161, 957, 958, 974, 980, 1004, 1262
National minorities 1004, 1812, 1845, 3421, 3424
National parks 3754, 3763, 3822
National security 4949, 4993, 5314, 5353, 5363
National stereotypes 3527
Nationalism 187, 240, 966-968, 970, 971, 977, 980, 984, 985, 991, 992, 1000, 1193, 1195, 1227, 1330, 1358, 1359, 1369, 1607, 1731, 1736, 1762, 1794, 1813, 1819, 1845, 1934, 1936, 1951, 1979, 2177,

SUBJECT INDEX

2218, 2306, 2326, 2532, 2557, 2567, 2630, 2795, 3067, 3070, 3112, 3242, 3269, 3383, 3419-3421, 3426, 3473, 3485, 3492, 3493, 3497, 3499, 4918, 4919, 4924, 4935, 4939, 4966, 5159, 5214, 5263, 5295
see also: Cultural nationalism
Nationalist movements 1935, 3425, 5263
Nationality 18, 147, 981, 987, 1003, 1192, 1243, 1881, 2838, 3009, 3072, 3401, 3409, 3426, 3437, 3487, 3533, 3605
NATO 1730, 1731, 5327, 5340
Natural disasters 767, 3695, 3699, 3702, 3752, 3776, 3813, 5911
Natural history 284, 396, 1558, 3775
Natural law 271, 360, 5161
Natural resources 58, 961, 2793, 3628, 3698, 3707, 3722, 3735, 3749, 3754, 3756, 3796, 3810, 3814, 3816, 3818, 4246
Natural sciences 11, 22, 1574, 1624, 2314
Natural selection 463, 898, 1583, 2329, 3401
Naturalism 22, 257, 284, 285, 1558, 2368
Naturalization 3563, 4964, 5535
Nature 22, 135, 199, 204, 221, 225, 257, 271, 284, 292, 362, 575, 608, 1176, 1225, 1563, 1567, 1574, 1591, 1621, 3014, 3131, 3152, 3306, 3696, 3698, 3700, 3703, 3710, 3721, 3744, 3748, 3749, 3753, 3783, 3839, 3851, 3926, 4108, 4138, 4227
Nature conservation 257, 3747, 3822, 5237
Navaho 5411
Navigation 58
Nazism 165, 189, 326, 410, 1004, 1902, 2567, 3502, 3518, 3532, 3631, 4973, 5312
Nee, Victor 4241
Negritude 1942
Neighbourhood associations 3959
Neighbourhoods 471, 577, 838, 849, 2935, 2995, 3577, 3833, 3835, 3840, 3845, 3853, 3858-3861, 3904, 3988, 4002, 4005-4008, 4010, 4013, 4014, 4022, 4028, 4034, 4056, 4070, 4080, 4086, 4091, 4119, 4155, 5049, 5063, 5071, 5102, 5582, 5612, 5742, 5963
Neoclassical economics 4196, 4203, 4211, 4351, 4393
Neocolonialism 1308, 3782, 4935
Neoinstitutionalism 4346, 5641
Neoliberalism 1994, 2018, 2263, 2292, 2507, 2513, 2558, 2563, 2564, 3140, 3537, 3750, 3880, 3912, 4206, 4208, 4211, 4227, 4230, 4250, 4269, 4373, 4817, 4867, 4892, 4910, 4949, 4952, 5232, 5261, 5630, 5971
Network analysis 466, 492, 493, 1043, 1045, 1085, 3927, 4401

Networks 32, 277, 486, 493, 662, 1040, 1045, 1069, 1100, 1115, 1146, 1155, 1594, 1660, 1672, 2088, 2110, 2210, 2213, 2333, 2334, 2337, 2501, 2802, 3078, 3463, 3673, 3847, 3867, 3881, 4031, 4056, 4108, 4240, 4369, 4371, 4376, 4429, 4588, 4641, 4654, 4732, 5242, 5306, 5510, 5747
see also: Economic networks
Neurology 589, 591, 596, 628, 630, 5406, 5410
Neuroses 593, 731, 743
Neutrality 683, 801, 1025, 5184
New Deal 2459, 4097, 5624
New left 4587, 5251
New right 2100
New technology 511, 1234, 1242, 1593, 1595, 1603, 1662, 1672, 1756, 2129, 2272, 2519, 2532, 2559, 2596, 2667, 4031, 4243, 4315, 4377, 4382, 4400, 4647, 4688, 4786, 4933, 4988, 5880
New towns 3983, 4070, 4172
Newcastle, T.M. 370
Newly industrializing countries 3671, 4228
News 1671, 1683, 1691, 1730, 1741, 1742, 1750, 1766, 1771, 3498, 5329
Nietzsche, Friedrich 241, 251, 263, 264, 267, 278, 298, 319
Nihilism 241, 267, 1249
Nishida, Kitaro 265
Nobility 263, 4954
Noguchi, Shika 3035
Nomads 1340, 3128, 3539
Non-governmental organizations 1485, 3089, 3423, 3611, 3624, 3813, 3922, 3927, 4169, 4940, 4948, 4967, 5279, 5716, 5805
Non-profit organizations 61, 411, 931, 1035, 1100, 3877, 4235, 4512, 4667, 4768, 5478, 5484, 5486, 5491, 5775, 5816
Non-renewable energy 3711
Non-verbal communication 1787, 1827
Non-violence 1025
Normal 5891
North Amerindians 198, 1785, 3526
Norwegian language 3595
Nostalgia 814, 974, 3728
Novelists 1958, 1966
Novels 1191, 1243, 1917-1919, 1926, 1927, 1931, 1933, 1936, 1937, 1954, 1958, 1961, 1962, 1965, 1966, 1968, 1970, 3122, 3262, 3528
Nuclear energy 1597, 3734
Nuclear family 1761, 2944, 3010
Nuclear weapons 5988
Nudity 2912
Numbers 619, 4346

INDEX DES MATIÈRES EN ANGLAIS

Numeracy 1991, 2040
Nuptiality 2691, 2695, 2698, 2724, 2769, 2963
Nurses 4439, 4711, 4784, 5508, 5651, 5746, 5799, 5826, 5832, 5834, 5839, 5843, 5846
Nussbaum, Martha C. 5034
Nutrition 419, 2022, 2715, 5541, 5768, 5959, 5961, 5969
O'Brien, Edna 1936
Object 300, 406, 619, 1832
Objectivity 109, 126, 169, 215, 255, 261, 310, 399, 498, 605, 645, 1005, 1571, 1628, 1705, 2365, 5692
Obligation 4909, 4937
see also: Political obligation
Observation 45, 55, 194, 528, 617, 630, 2893, 5084
Obstacles to development 2539
Occitan language 1986
Occultism 1416, 1511
Occupational achievement 4752
Occupational choice 3166, 4438, 4757, 4781
Occupational diseases 4730
Occupational groups 842, 4501
Occupational health 4683, 4686, 4693, 4698, 4711, 4730, 4743, 4813, 5773, 5808
Occupational mobility 2047, 2089, 2532, 3643, 4245, 4438, 4440, 4468, 4755, 4762, 4780, 5281
Occupational promotion 4175, 4757, 4761, 4763, 4780, 5832
Occupational roles 4618
Occupational safety 4433, 4683, 4727, 4730, 4813
Occupational segregation 3285
Occupational sociology 4533
Occupational status 842, 2382, 2434, 4765, 4776
Occupational stratification 4376, 4755
Occupational structure 2532, 4414, 4434, 4771
Occupational therapy 1053, 5420, 5939
Occupations 478, 637, 705, 842, 1285, 1857, 2094, 2096, 2100, 2125, 2382, 2382, 2410, 2425, 2430, 2434, 2444, 3062, 3115, 3166, 3189, 3200, 3226, 3255, 3391, 4064, 4183, 4306, 4404, 4414, 4440, 4441, 4446, 4457, 4472, 4485, 4513, 4514, 4533, 4539, 4542, 4572, 4574, 4657, 4735, 4746, 4754, 4756-4758, 4762, 4764-4767, 4769, 4771, 4772, 4774-4778, 4781, 4783, 4785, 4787-4789, 4883, 5090, 5096, 5436, 5584, 5651, 5692, 5757, 5794, 5827, 5840, 5841, 5845

see also: Academic profession, Legal profession, Medical occupations
OECD 2679, 5514
Offenders 529, 1442, 1991, 3241, 4422, 4505, 4683, 4985, 4997, 5009, 5015, 5016, 5020, 5023, 5029, 5030, 5032, 5034-5036, 5041, 5042, 5047, 5056, 5064, 5065, 5068, 5071, 5078, 5083, 5086-5088, 5095, 5096, 5100, 5105, 5111, 5121, 5124, 5137, 5192, 5194, 5195, 5370, 5452, 5455, 5664, 5672, 5934
Office workers 3164, 4662
Official languages 1838, 1843, 2121, 2523
Oil industry 3711
Old age 612, 2651, 2658, 2668, 2671, 2678, 5016, 5510, 5511, 5515, 5523, 5526, 5536, 5738
Old age insurance 2712
Older workers 4465
Oligarchy 4683, 4853
One-parent families 1687, 2858, 2878, 2881, 2915, 2923, 2991, 2993-2997, 3000, 3001, 3019, 3036, 3069, 4531, 5425, 5567, 5610, 5624, 5633, 5636, 5961
Ontogeny 1161
Ontology 22, 29, 140, 213, 218, 225, 232, 250, 254, 266, 267, 284, 286, 360, 490, 563, 617, 847, 1216, 1270, 1391, 1571, 1628, 1871, 2300, 2609, 2809, 3744, 3750
Opera 1318, 1971
Operations research 371, 5357
Ophthalmology 628
Opiates 5392, 5395, 5401
Opinion 470, 520, 1173, 1925, 2183, 2215, 2357, 2490, 2538, 2991, 3031, 3545, 3633, 4361, 4723, 5201, 5289, 5291, 5298, 5303, 5423, 5941
see also: Political opinions, Public opinion
Optimism 675, 1008, 3739
Options on stocks 4352
Oral communication 1641
Oral history 179, 186, 194, 3371, 3496, 3854
Oral literature 1913
Oral tradition 986, 1433, 1913
Orchestras 1100
Organic produce 4316
Organization 359, 396, 439, 1113, 1141, 1142, 1145, 1148, 1157, 1282, 1316, 1993, 2088, 3097, 4322, 4409, 4412, 4419, 4510, 4569, 4646, 4659, 4732, 4733, 4821, 4837, 4856, 4860, 4871, 5148, 5202, 5265, 5732, 5798, 5903
see also: Administrative organization, Community organization, Complex organization, Industrial organization,

SUBJECT INDEX

Social organization, Sociology of organizations, Work organization
Organization of space 4313
Organization theory 396, 1019, 1032, 1033, 1089-1094, 1098, 1100, 1101, 1104-1111, 1114, 1115, 1117, 1118, 1120-1123, 1125, 1127-1130, 1132, 1133, 1136-1138, 1140-1143, 1145, 1148, 1150, 1154, 1157, 1672, 1701, 1957, 2555, 3097, 3705, 3775, 4346, 4360, 4408, 4409, 4412, 4424, 4427, 4428, 4468, 4607, 4609, 4612, 4617, 4618, 4622, 4627, 4632, 4638, 4648, 4649, 4669, 4672, 4770, 4802, 5216, 5555, 5799, 5932
Organizational analysis 684, 1104, 1108, 1115, 1125, 1127, 1131, 1148, 1150, 1157, 4357, 4366, 4389, 4426, 4510, 4641, 4652, 4659, 4669, 4679, 4747, 4823
Organizational behaviour 1048, 1068, 1092, 1096, 1101, 1105, 1106, 1109, 1115, 1117, 1118, 1124, 1125, 1130, 1138, 1139, 1141-1143, 1145, 1148, 1151, 1385, 1672, 3097, 4323, 4356, 4367, 4381, 4389, 4409, 4412, 4422, 4638, 4658, 4660, 4671, 4802, 4812, 5732
Organizational change 1094, 1104, 1114, 1118, 1119, 1125, 1126, 1130, 1134, 1135, 1152, 1154, 2134, 2243, 2250, 3097, 4362, 4379, 4400, 4408, 4424, 4632, 4721, 4726, 4729, 4759, 4788, 4867, 5148, 5732, 5924, 5932
Organizational culture 1095, 1100, 1105, 1122, 1123, 1132, 4323, 4358, 5924
Organizational effectiveness 1114, 1128, 1132, 1133, 1154, 4618
Organizational goals 1129, 2139, 4667
Organizational research 1104, 1107, 1140, 1148, 4406
Organizational structure 1087, 1094, 1096-1100, 1105-1107, 1114, 1125, 1132, 1133, 1140, 1149, 1153, 1154, 1384, 1385, 1443, 1660, 1718, 2133, 2250, 2251, 3097, 3362, 3813, 4356, 4395, 4424, 4609, 4623, 4632, 4656, 4660, 4680, 4734, 4737, 4773, 4787, 4788, 5154, 5267, 5799
Organizations 49, 306, 386, 1008, 1029, 1033, 1040, 1064, 1068, 1076, 1080, 1088, 1090-1093, 1102-1104, 1109, 1110, 1112, 1114-1116, 1120-1124, 1126, 1127, 1137, 1138, 1144-1146, 1148, 1151-1156, 1200, 1384, 1635, 1660, 1701, 1718, 1957, 2307, 2450, 3062, 3097, 3154, 3246, 3416, 3775, 3803, 3828, 3853, 3863, 4100, 4355, 4386, 4397, 4402, 4422, 4468, 4483, 4622, 4628, 4640, 4644, 4648, 4654, 4657, 4669, 4672, 4673, 4680, 4718, 4728, 4729, 4734, 4767, 4847, 4861, 4876, 4940, 5276, 5279, 5283, 5400, 5478, 5732, 5767, 5794, 5798, 5799, 5854
see also: Employers' organizations, International organizations, Non-governmental organizations, Non-profit organizations, Organizational culture, Professional organizations, Voluntary organizations, Women's organizations, Youth organizations
Organized crime 2203, 5055, 5074, 5092, 5094, 5139, 5317
Organs 5871, 5878, 5883
Orientalism 1165, 1209, 1566, 1699, 1978, 3094, 3497
Orphanages 5576
Orphans 2901
Orthodox Christians 1516
Orthodox Church 1504, 1516, 1545
Ottoman Empire 1522
Out-groups 843, 2376
Output rate 662
Overpopulation 5417
Overseas territories 951
Ownership 3471, 3570, 4827, 4984, 5030, 5816
Pacifism 5327
Paganism 1392, 1421, 1539
Painters 1863
Painting 1852, 1861, 1869, 3139, 4767
Palestinians 985, 1014, 1026, 1077, 1791, 2177, 2619, 3499
Pan-Africanism 5328
Pan-Islamism 1543
Panel surveys 811, 2636, 2803, 3835, 4014, 4881, 5307
Panic 731
Pantomimes 1787
Paradigms 27, 46, 54, 170, 182, 399, 821, 837, 858, 1025, 1150, 1194, 1197, 1431, 1489, 1607, 1625, 1630, 2502, 2508, 3090, 3497, 3749, 3952, 4360, 4612, 5244
Parapsychology 540, 1780
Parent-child relations 545, 695, 755, 819, 1647, 2613, 2626, 2628, 2629, 2667, 2682, 2847, 2853, 2859, 2893, 2895-2897, 2903, 2909, 2917, 2928, 2936, 2947, 2950, 2954, 3004, 3006, 3010, 3012, 3014, 3017, 3021, 3022, 3024, 3026, 3030-3032, 3034, 3037, 3041, 3043, 3044, 3047, 3049, 3052, 3053, 3056, 3057, 3228, 3364, 3385, 4777, 5538, 5539, 5546, 5575, 5578, 5692, 5693, 5848

INDEX DES MATIÈRES EN ANGLAIS

Parental discipline 5580
Parenthood 77, 545, 756, 792, 849, 1761, 1998, 2035, 2488, 2608, 2854, 2884, 2897, 2898, 2901, 2911, 2915, 2916, 2932, 3004, 3005, 3007, 3011, 3013-3015, 3017, 3018, 3024-3026, 3030-3032, 3034, 3036, 3038-3040, 3043-3045, 3047-3051, 3054-3056, 3237, 3249, 3358, 3391, 4765, 5050, 5396, 5510, 5546, 5550, 5552, 5559, 5589, 5594, 5634, 5667, 5669, 5689, 5906
Parents 900, 1494, 2029, 2054, 2065, 2155, 2230, 2236, 2347, 2360, 2425, 2463, 2464, 2488, 2592, 2593, 2603, 2757, 2847, 2859, 2872, 2894, 2896, 2899, 2916, 2929, 2934, 2974, 2994, 2996, 3000, 3001, 3006, 3009, 3012, 3017, 3022, 3024, 3037-3039, 3045, 3351, 3364, 4985, 5052, 5386, 5572, 5577, 5667, 5669, 5689, 5925, 5936
  see also: Step-parents
Parishes 1502
Parliament 3286, 4975, 5213
Parliamentary law 5025
Parsons, Talcott 373, 375, 400
Part-time employment 2281, 2653, 4299, 4456, 4520, 4522, 4676, 4678
Participant observation 1005, 1912
Partners 463, 900, 902, 908, 910, 916, 920, 926, 935, 936, 946, 1134, 2862, 2917, 2956, 2958, 2974, 2977, 2985, 3055, 3336, 4169, 4310, 4457, 4765, 5439, 5449
Party financing 5219
Party members 5219
Passions 314, 897
Past 148, 150, 158, 166, 182, 196, 222, 353, 549, 793, 799, 951, 963, 974, 975, 994, 1008, 1413, 1965, 4800
Pastoralism 2790
Paternalism 5838, 5889
Pathology 738, 739, 750, 2937, 5377, 5968
Patients 747, 748, 752, 761, 784, 794, 803, 809, 810, 813, 816, 5726, 5732, 5753, 5787, 5814, 5815, 5830, 5835-5837, 5852, 5854, 5879, 5882, 5883, 5889, 5893, 5896, 5899, 5904, 5919, 5929, 5930, 5976, 5982
Patriarchy 967, 1277, 1296, 1549, 2880, 3089, 3096, 3138, 3173, 3186, 3187, 3240, 3251, 3262, 3313, 3793, 5058
Patriotism 962, 975, 2614, 5256
Patrizi, Francesco 156
Patronage 2314
Pay 4539, 4676, 4679, 4704, 5217
  see also: Equal pay

Payment systems 4402, 5789, 5931
Payments 927, 5552
Peace 57, 105, 161, 1007, 1008, 1014, 4931, 5465
  see also: Peace agreement
Peace agreement 5273
Peace keeping 5344, 5362
Peace movements 5275
Peace negotiations 5317
Peace research 2619
Peace studies 1995
Peasant movements 3891, 5245, 5261
Peasantry 355, 3891, 4206
Peasants 1476, 2345, 2426, 3888, 3896, 3919, 3920, 4275
Pedagogy 15, 225, 574, 930, 1018, 1196, 1819, 1879, 1902, 2000, 2009, 2011, 2014, 2053, 2081, 2099, 2101, 2103, 2105, 2112, 2121, 2125, 2145, 2164, 2171-2173, 2175-2177, 2180-2182, 2184, 2185, 2188, 2189, 2191-2193, 2200-2202, 2206-2208, 2213, 2215-2217, 2220-2224, 2237, 2247, 2284, 2299, 3115, 3435, 3869
Pedestrian areas 4146
Peer groups 577, 1068, 1639, 1654, 2028, 2059, 2174, 2206, 2218, 2643, 2753, 2897, 3509, 4401, 4608, 5369, 5450, 5933
Peformance
  see: Job performance
Peirce, Charles Sanders 494
Penal codes 311, 5004, 5029, 5192, 5200
Penal policy 426, 4992, 5002, 5004-5008, 5018, 5024, 5026, 5032, 5083, 5114
Penitentiary systems 5192
Pensions 2676, 2679, 2682, 2707, 2712, 4353, 4587, 4676, 5518, 5605, 5622
  see also: Retirement pensions
Pentecostalism 1431, 1474, 1482, 1507
Per capita income 2855, 5621
Perception 233, 327, 551, 573, 589, 611, 615, 620, 630, 634, 639, 643, 646, 654, 658, 714, 827, 849, 855, 859, 865, 866, 876, 884, 885, 891, 905, 918, 928, 942, 1086, 1096, 1105, 1112, 1144, 1177, 1606, 1719, 1819, 1820, 1859, 1871, 1942, 1989, 2008, 2055, 2195, 2218, 2360, 2397, 2473, 2628, 2629, 2670, 2755, 2836, 2913, 3021, 3042, 3287, 3462, 3478, 3496, 3727, 3748, 3930, 3970, 4145, 4351, 4484, 4487, 4631, 4673, 4701, 4702, 4717, 4785, 5283, 5308, 5426, 5542, 5543, 5690, 5830, 5894
  see also: Social perception, Visual perception

Subject Index

Perception of others 219, 552, 657, 840, 844, 851, 867, 878, 894, 937, 983, 1186, 1230, 1525, 1528, 1776, 2205, 2301, 2313, 3562, 3649

Performance 60, 627, 631, 633, 639, 655, 663, 666, 697, 833, 919, 990, 1041, 1046, 1061, 1064-1066, 1071, 1115, 1118, 1143, 1147, 1158, 1232, 1294, 1319, 1344-1346, 1598, 1839, 1868, 1964, 1992, 2022, 2096, 2099, 2166, 2920, 3146, 3153, 3230, 3301, 3368, 3788, 3819, 4161, 4187, 4363, 4408, 4412, 4600, 4602, 4607, 4625, 4634, 4638, 4646, 4668, 4673, 4689, 4760, 4779, 4802, 4954, 5410, 5760

Performers 1346, 1982

Performing arts 2458

Periodicals 56, 1351, 1557, 1662, 1722, 1726, 1744, 2645, 3374, 3636, 3827, 3931

Personal aggression 672, 925, 5437

Personal insolvency 5151

Personal power 4199

Personality 88, 241, 326, 561, 565, 569, 578, 586-589, 606, 673, 675, 678-680, 682, 684, 687, 690, 691, 694, 696-700, 702, 704, 707-714, 716, 719-721, 725-730, 733, 735, 742, 760, 787, 790, 827, 840, 842, 870, 873, 910, 914, 920, 928, 933, 937, 949, 1003, 1007, 1057, 1061, 1147, 1486, 1967, 2304, 2318, 2970, 3004, 3021, 3022, 3034, 3055, 3212, 3351, 4188, 4199, 4339, 4391, 4407, 4588, 4625, 4638, 4719, 4720, 4722, 4800, 5393, 5670, 5899

Personality development 553, 679, 698

Personality disorders 695, 731, 788, 790, 820

Personality measurement 1143, 4607

Personality tests 587

Personality traits 678, 694, 698, 710, 727, 735, 855

Personnel management 3290, 4356, 4403, 4512, 4544, 4601, 4603, 4605, 4610-4612, 4616, 4618, 4619, 4620, 4633, 4635, 4640, 4643, 4644, 4650, 4653, 4656, 4658, 4660, 4670, 4673, 4678, 4679, 4683, 4743, 4779, 4831

Personnel selection 4569

Persuasion 1730, 3749, 4199

Pessimism 675, 691, 725, 1008, 4145

Pesticides 4674

Petrol 4223

Pharmaceutical industry 5811, 5833

Pharmaceuticals 5380, 5801, 5833, 5864, 5980

Phenomenology 161, 215, 218, 224, 225, 228, 232, 236, 250, 310, 312, 599, 645, 746, 1419, 1682, 1725, 1953, 2422, 2609, 3129, 3146, 3695

Philanthropy 61, 996, 3844, 5476

Phillips, D.Z. 1428

Philology 241, 1798, 2009

Philosophers 12, 121, 126, 139, 145, 200, 201, 208, 211, 215, 218-220, 225, 230, 235, 240, 249, 251, 256, 262, 265, 266, 273, 282, 288, 296, 298, 299, 340, 344, 405, 1552, 1555, 2361, 3108, 5180

Philosophical anthropology 209, 1201

Philosophical thought 12, 111, 114, 124-126, 133, 139, 142, 145, 201, 202, 204, 205, 207, 208, 211, 212, 215-218, 222, 224, 225, 230, 234-237, 240, 241, 244, 250, 257, 258, 262-267, 272, 273, 275, 279, 280, 282, 283, 288-290, 293, 295-298, 405, 563, 645, 1158, 1160, 1176, 1280, 1374, 1382, 1386, 1402, 1404, 1413, 1423, 1426, 1456, 1466, 1591, 1596, 1599, 1828, 1854, 1864, 1871, 1876, 2303, 2327, 2538, 3108, 3129, 3953, 4898, 4929, 5849

Philosophy 12, 21, 29, 54, 68, 83, 89, 106-108, 110-113, 118, 120, 121, 128-131, 133, 136, 138-142, 144-146, 151, 152, 156, 158, 160, 161, 193, 199-203, 208-224, 226, 228, 229, 231, 233-242, 244-248, 250-253, 257, 259-266, 268, 269, 272, 273, 275-278, 280-284, 286-289, 291, 292, 294, 296-298, 300, 301, 303-305, 311, 312, 315-318, 332, 333, 335, 340-342, 344, 351, 357, 367, 385, 403, 404, 407, 490, 568, 596, 617, 645, 701, 702, 728, 906, 909, 913, 934, 1028, 1124, 1176, 1188, 1195, 1204, 1206, 1216, 1231, 1239, 1247, 1248, 1250, 1253, 1256, 1259, 1266, 1271, 1276, 1289, 1292, 1379, 1382, 1387, 1388, 1420, 1423, 1426, 1449, 1456, 1458, 1464, 1466, 1473, 1552, 1563, 1569, 1578, 1579, 1583, 1586, 1593, 1596, 1599, 1600, 1602, 1611, 1615, 1638, 1655, 1706, 1828, 1832, 1848, 1853, 1854, 1864, 1868, 1876, 1988, 2298, 2300, 2303, 2319, 2327, 2350, 2362, 2368, 2400, 2503, 2531, 2609, 3101, 3108, 3129, 3130, 3133, 3142, 3449, 3492, 3703, 3790, 3801, 3851, 4192, 4194, 4216, 4350, 4405, 4894, 4904, 4920, 4926, 4937, 5153, 5158, 5179, 5180, 5201, 5673, 5716, 5850, 5865, 5866, 5884, 5888
see also: Analytical philosophy, Dualism,

INDEX DES MATIÈRES EN ANGLAIS

Educational philosophy, History of philosophy, Moral philosophy, Political philosophy, Social philosophy
Philosophy of art 1850
Philosophy of history 152, 153, 156, 160, 193, 1201
Philosophy of language 114, 1846
Philosophy of law 2313, 4917, 4933, 5149, 5152, 5153, 5158, 5161, 5163, 5167, 5173, 5177, 5179, 5181, 5182, 5188, 5192, 5195, 5198, 5208, 5210, 5311
Philosophy of religion 132, 200, 249, 266, 273, 1379, 1382, 1386, 1389, 1391, 1402, 1412, 1413, 1423, 1426, 1428, 1440, 1448, 1451, 1456, 1472, 1473, 1487
Philosophy of science 5, 22, 135, 288, 1271, 1553, 1555, 1560, 1564, 1568, 1571, 1574, 1575, 1577, 1579, 1582-1586, 1592, 1593, 1599-1602, 1605, 1606, 1611, 1612, 1614, 1615, 1623-1625, 1627, 1628, 1630, 1871, 2209, 4360
Phonetics 1847
Phonology 1798, 1847, 1989, 3002
Photography 1346, 1737, 1870, 2188, 3375, 5037
Phylogeny 1161
Physical activity 503, 609, 1326, 1368, 1497, 3546, 4146, 5350, 5961
Physical anthropology 3528
Physical appearance 573, 938, 3272
Physical environment 559, 608, 1602, 3692, 3701, 3748, 3781, 3921, 4087
Physically disabled 2456
Physician-patient relationship 5887
Physicians 5844, 5894
Physics 1555, 1574, 1589, 1599, 1602, 1605, 1619, 1623, 1627
see also: Quantum physics
Physiology 628, 630, 1593, 3110, 5406
see also: Human physiology
Picasso, Pablo 1869
Pidgin languages 1805
Pidginization 2523
Pilgrimages 1399, 1433, 1499
Pinter, Harold 1877
Pipelines 3813
Planning methods 1030, 2676, 3624, 3821, 3831, 3872, 3876, 4029, 4047, 4055, 4057, 4064, 4069, 4073, 4082, 4083, 4086, 4099, 4101, 4104, 4108, 4112, 4118, 4167, 5521, 5758, 5936, 5977
Planning systems 1030, 3921
Planning theory 3814, 4030, 4036, 4041, 4073, 4084, 4118
Plantations 3882

Plato 270, 1650, 2370
Play 782, 1350, 2608
Plots 1015
Pluralism 147, 199, 474, 964, 1002, 1201, 1216, 1455, 1548, 2083, 2181, 2365, 2380, 2443, 3441, 3489, 3490, 3501, 3522, 3789, 4012, 4195, 4494, 4905, 4928, 4951, 4972, 5167, 5185, 5859
see also: Ethnic pluralism, Linguistic pluralism, Religious pluralism
Poems 1934
Poetry 186, 241, 1227, 1239, 1853, 1901, 1922, 1936, 1943, 1945-1947, 1959, 1969, 1989
see also: Epic poetry
Poles 960, 997, 1004, 1499, 1934, 3445, 3450
Police 705, 1009, 1844, 2860, 2868, 2888, 3284, 3325, 4683, 4980, 5006, 5010, 5109, 5122, 5123, 5125-5127, 5129-5148, 5243, 5364, 5448, 5765
Police officers 1009, 5135, 5142, 5192
Policing 2532, 2868, 4325, 4422, 4511, 4683, 4986, 4991, 4995, 5014, 5035, 5084, 5109, 5122-5124, 5126, 5128, 5130, 5131, 5133-5136, 5138-5141, 5143-5145, 5147, 5240, 5243, 5273, 5364, 5370, 5448
Policy analysis 891, 2792, 3196-3198, 4044, 4859, 5555, 5565, 5597, 5609, 5810, 5854, 5888, 5942, 5973
Policy implementation 43, 1094, 3810, 4043, 4069, 4108, 4667, 5200, 5638
Policy making 43, 71, 347, 866, 1023, 2702, 2745, 3121, 3319, 3352, 3486, 3649, 3705, 3808, 3830, 4041, 4497, 4587, 4611, 4789, 4858, 5024, 5212, 5221, 5225, 5317, 5471, 5604, 5627, 5641, 5647, 5814
Policy research 64, 426
Policy studies 426, 4673
Polish language 2009
Political action 1070, 4104, 4899, 4950, 5230, 5231, 5292
Political activity 155, 328, 1517, 4914, 4966, 5227, 5228, 5275, 5281, 5292
Political affiliation 5307
Political anthropology 4943
Political attitudes 512, 1730, 2372, 4596
Political authority 5237
Political behaviour 1439, 2324, 2343, 4887, 4895, 5214, 5283, 5291, 5300, 5301, 5363
Political broadcasting 1772
Political change 161, 177, 1000, 1169, 1673, 2507, 2520, 2523, 2541, 2563, 2565, 3660, 3776, 3828, 3869, 3890, 4854, 4859, 4866, 4885, 5341, 5773
Political cleavages 2389, 5238

SUBJECT INDEX

Political commitments 3635
Political communication 1639, 1730, 5061, 5235, 5291, 5293, 5360
Political conditions 4, 54, 161, 991, 1169, 1199, 1798, 2306, 2520, 3106, 3206, 3551, 3565, 3626, 3827, 3968, 4050, 5255, 5268, 5279, 5361, 5980
Political conflicts 1791, 3776, 5127, 5212, 5240, 5318
Political control 42, 2340, 3457
Political cooperation 3776
Political corruption 5219, 5282
Political crises 1781, 5218, 5219
Political culture 1004, 1159, 1169, 1226, 1679, 2439, 2649, 4203, 4898, 4939, 4955, 4966, 5293, 5294, 5301
Political development 57, 2795, 4392, 4885, 4970
Political economy 379, 1950, 2551, 3730, 3896, 3918, 4073, 4074, 4193, 4210, 4211, 4214, 4224, 4231, 4752, 4854, 4922, 5146, 5278, 5363
Political education 2170, 2181
Political elites 24, 3286, 3942, 4066, 4292, 4640, 4897, 5284, 5297
Political exile 3598
Political forces 1979, 4898, 5227
  see also: Pressure groups
Political geography 1000, 3747
Political history 58, 143, 149, 151, 155, 159, 161, 177, 256, 1000, 1004, 1169, 1263, 1515, 1798, 1813, 1819, 2293, 2379, 2439, 3452, 3528, 3532, 3533, 3759, 3869, 4228, 4272, 4596, 4859, 4935, 4938, 4954, 5268
  see also: Recent political history
Political ideas 1199, 1879
  see also: History of political ideas
Political ideology 187, 232, 968, 1221, 1263, 1351, 2280, 4925, 5258, 5285, 5309
Political influences 348, 1976, 2671, 5307
Political instability 3677
Political institutions 4885, 4938, 4956, 4964, 4968, 5218, 5282
Political integration 1826, 2518, 3576, 4966
Political leaders 326, 2266, 4935, 5284, 5288
Political leadership 1731, 2579, 4886, 4955, 5295
Political life 1298, 1889, 4895, 5299
Political majority 5248
Political mobilization 994, 3814, 4974, 5242
Political modernization 4041
Political movements 1010, 1453, 2573, 3162, 3391, 4558, 4960, 5226, 5233, 5234, 5241, 5242, 5247, 5258, 5265, 5266,
5269, 5270, 5275, 5276, 5280
  see also: Anti-nuclear movements
Political obligation 4909, 5305
Political opinions 2593, 3809, 4898, 5286, 5298
Political opposition 189, 4850, 4898, 5226, 5240, 5275, 5284, 5320
Political order 28, 2140
Political participation 71, 955, 1517, 1535, 1939, 2317, 2386, 2461, 2513, 2671, 2674, 3103, 3391, 3545, 3829, 3830, 3863, 3959, 4879, 4914, 4927, 4940, 4956, 4958, 4960, 4974, 5024, 5228, 5257, 5281, 5286, 5292, 5305, 5642
  see also: Activism
Political parties 3070, 4293, 4596, 5219, 5234, 5265, 5269
  see also: Christian democratic parties, Communist parties, Conservative parties, Labour parties, Left wing parties, Liberal parties, Right-wing parties, Social democratic parties, Socialist parties
Political philosophy 129, 278, 281, 295, 307, 337, 366, 1194, 1251, 1466, 2117, 2369, 4230, 4894, 4898, 4900-4903, 4906, 4909, 4911, 4913, 4915-4917, 4920, 4921, 4923, 4924, 4926, 4928, 4929, 4931, 4933, 4934, 4937, 4938, 4969, 4972, 4973, 5188, 5207, 5305, 5311, 5327
Political power 2671, 4884, 4889, 4942, 4944, 4953, 4968, 5207, 5269
Political protest 4244, 4966, 4980, 5235, 5237, 5240, 5247, 5251, 5253, 5275
Political psychology 3527, 4886, 4895, 5239, 5296, 5328, 5360
Political reform 24, 1746, 2147, 2509, 2567, 3140, 3869, 4301, 4971, 5003, 5039, 5092, 5094, 5219, 5341
Political refugees 1987, 3640, 3664
Political regimes 1023, 1746, 2389, 3869, 4250, 4965, 4973, 5250, 5282, 5352
  see also: Authoritarian regimes
Political representation 2723, 4961, 5265, 5271, 5299
Political science 2281, 3121, 3900, 4885, 4891, 4892, 4894, 4896, 4897, 4935, 5146
Political science research 4891, 5297
Political scientists 4897
Political socialization 1827, 2181, 2614, 2671, 3206, 3869, 4956
Political society 1245
Political sociology 16, 307, 325, 335, 368, 400, 1360, 1364, 2312, 4884, 4885, 4887-4891, 4894-4899, 4901, 4915, 4921, 4932, 4936, 4943, 4951, 4953, 4961, 4974,

5227, 5233, 5235, 5238, 5277, 5281,
5289, 5297, 5300, 5302, 5307, 5466
Political structure 3418, 4966, 4973, 5249
Political systems 1195, 1200, 2389, 2502,
2507, 2559, 3323, 4201, 4938, 4956,
4966, 4970, 5207, 5219, 5282, 5325
Political theory 307, 325, 352, 368, 393, 1039,
1194, 1221, 1250, 1265, 2546, 3144, 4889,
4890, 4897, 4901, 4902, 4907, 4918,
4922, 4924, 4925, 4932, 4936, 4941,
4953, 4972, 5055, 5201, 5336, 5886
Political thought 224, 278, 335, 1199, 3144,
4210, 4884, 4888, 4894, 4898, 4899,
4902, 4905-4907, 4909, 4911, 4913, 4915,
4916, 4925, 4927, 4928, 4932, 4941,
4960, 5188, 5207
Political unrest 4977, 5466
Political violence 186, 1000, 1262, 1546,
1707, 1781, 2340, 5233, 5466
Politicians 348, 1550, 1553, 1725, 3323, 5222,
5281, 5301, 5363
Politicization 3149, 3365, 4974
Politics 6, 25, 47, 253, 268, 346, 799, 971,
1110, 1207, 1234, 1275, 1356, 1517, 1553,
1742, 1838, 1839, 1882, 1921, 1933,
1978, 2361, 2502, 2672, 3078, 3080,
3258, 3356, 3391, 3497, 3508, 3574,
3707, 3755, 3942, 3945, 4303, 4311, 4596,
4877, 4897, 4908, 5196, 5213, 5218,
5271, 5333
Pollet, Jean-Daniel 1901
Polls 5289
see also: Public opinion polls
Pollution 1010, 3722, 3757, 3823, 4114, 4156
see also: Industrial pollution, Transfrontier pollution
Polyandry 2973
Polyarchy 4965
Polygyny 2406, 2939
Polysemy 1246, 1822
Polytheism 1406
Ponge, Francis 1901
Poor 608, 1747, 2375, 2397, 2746, 2878,
3667, 3992, 4020, 4246, 4263, 4299,
4300, 5082, 5279, 5366, 5565, 5653, 5971
Pop music 1745, 1975, 1982, 1985
Popular culture 86, 104, 763, 835, 962, 976,
981, 1174, 1187, 1207, 1222, 1226, 1242,
1257, 1268, 1274, 1278, 1289, 1294,
1306, 1308-1312, 1319, 1320, 1325, 1328,
1333, 1336-1339, 1343, 1352, 1359-1361,
1363, 1365, 1370, 1371, 1668, 1724,
1728, 1738, 1740, 1745, 1746, 1753,
1758, 1761, 1770, 1771, 1780, 1859,
1879, 1882, 1889, 1899, 1903, 1907,
1908, 1921, 1974, 1976, 1985, 2504,
2522, 2617, 2618, 2630, 3113, 3141, 3157,
3216, 3305, 3355, 3919, 4332
Popular music 1309, 1331, 1338, 1351, 1364,
1370, 1971, 1981, 1982, 1986, 4148
Popular religion 1378, 1414, 1431
Population 447, 467, 473, 500, 963, 2532,
2683, 2687, 2689, 2690, 2693, 2694,
2700, 2701, 2705, 2709, 2714-2716, 2720,
2725, 2749, 2770, 2779, 2788, 2799,
2802, 2813, 2815, 2832, 2836, 2904,
2963, 2967, 3459, 3518, 3764, 3898,
3951, 4021, 4045, 4252, 5049, 5728
see also: Indigenous populations, Rural population, Urban population, World population
Population ageing 2654, 2656, 2657, 2669,
2677, 2679, 2693, 2702, 2707, 2712,
2713, 2802, 2805, 2934, 3951, 5498,
5512, 5514, 5519
Population censuses 3791
Population composition 2702
Population decline 2698, 2719, 2767, 4611
Population density 2686, 2714, 2736
Population distribution 2690, 2694, 2697,
2699, 2723, 3616
Population dynamics 468, 2706, 2713, 2717,
2718, 2779, 3606, 3607, 4439, 5507
Population economics 1099, 2764, 3637
Population forecasts 2687, 2794
Population geography 1252, 2752, 3606, 3795
Population growth 2638, 2686, 2693, 2697,
2706, 2710, 2711, 2714, 2715, 2721, 2747,
2752, 2774, 2792, 2793, 3608, 3713,
3818, 4083, 4170, 4606, 5780
Population increase 2796, 3972
Population movements 2790, 3609, 3636,
3639, 3650, 3674, 3681, 3684, 3686,
3791, 3866, 3903, 4004
Population policy 2712, 2721, 2728, 2752,
2763, 2770, 2792
Population pressure 3733
Population statistics 2690, 2694, 2712, 2805,
2835, 3773
Populism 4897, 5024
Pork 3447
Pornography 1243, 1684, 3121, 3147, 3302,
3320, 3323, 3324, 3333, 3338, 3355,
4387, 5176
Ports 4090
Portuguese language 1865
Positivism 112, 126, 127, 304, 568, 1150,
2558, 4621, 5182
Post-apartheid society 957, 964, 1507, 1880,
1942, 2436, 3171, 3395, 3430, 3438,

SUBJECT INDEX

3471, 3599, 3769, 4096, 4101, 4282, 4971, 5703
Post-Cold War 1004, 1174, 3552, 4168, 4898, 5313
Post-colonial societies 184, 951, 995, 1158, 1224, 1268, 1962, 2388, 2415, 3148, 3227, 3642, 5328
Post-communist societies 24, 477, 992, 993, 1000, 1328, 1470, 1505, 1511, 1746, 1816, 2088, 2156, 2217, 2228, 2333, 2407, 2437, 2438, 2533-2536, 2538, 2593, 2606, 2637, 2649, 2689, 2695, 2837, 3081, 3105, 3227, 3455, 3469, 3627, 4079, 4168, 4209, 4227, 4273, 4349, 4429, 4474, 4486, 4606, 4790, 4820, 4836, 4898, 4925, 4974, 5003, 5039, 5060, 5116, 5134, 5214, 5263, 5281, 5284, 5294, 5297, 5356, 5489
Post-Fordism 397, 2100, 2532, 4234, 5644
Post-industrial society 2412, 2519, 2540, 3396, 3956, 4227, 4298, 4365, 4436, 4459, 5630
Post-materialism 477, 4296, 5238, 5270
Post-secondary education 2145
Post-Soviet studies 1000, 1470, 3564, 3627
Post-structural analysis 340, 410, 1214
Post-structuralism 197, 292, 328, 340, 344, 346, 1214, 3117, 3346, 4065
Post-war history 101, 149, 165, 173, 355, 1004, 1274, 1305, 1442, 1612, 1956, 2117, 2305, 2374, 2434, 3638, 3658, 3983, 4079, 5189, 5295, 5302, 5324, 5432
Postcolonial societies 1195, 1213, 1227, 1589, 1880, 3417, 3445, 3641, 3782, 4975, 5007, 5187
Postcolonialism 1165, 1213, 1913, 2148, 2705, 3072, 3230, 3392, 3782, 3869, 3871, 5483
Postmodernism 14, 19, 30, 67, 109, 124, 127, 135, 158, 175, 184, 196, 261, 292, 305, 315, 335, 363, 369, 374, 382, 385, 393, 395, 543, 605, 922, 1141, 1150, 1158, 1194, 1221, 1222, 1225, 1229, 1247, 1250, 1252, 1255, 1258, 1259, 1261, 1266, 1268-1271, 1273, 1275, 1276, 1278, 1281, 1300, 1335, 1362, 1388, 1405, 1449, 1505, 1590, 1610, 1661, 1669, 1832, 1920, 1930, 1968, 2012, 2189, 2326, 2334, 2540, 2558, 3117, 3125, 3339, 3377, 3540, 3782, 3949, 3955, 4084, 4213, 4227, 4329, 4365, 4560, 4904, 4951, 4976, 5219, 5839
Poverty 808, 1493, 1536, 1747, 1923, 1994, 2046, 2266, 2385, 2397, 2432, 2532, 2561, 2577, 2585, 2638, 2712, 2713,
2725, 2789, 2843, 2881, 3035, 3089, 3323, 3416, 3694, 3776, 3814, 3833, 3840, 3961, 3992, 4006-4009, 4021, 4157, 4189, 4191, 4216, 4217, 4227, 4246, 4247, 4249, 4251, 4252, 4257, 4259, 4263-4266, 4268-4270, 4277, 4280-4284, 4286, 4290, 4296, 4298-4300, 4307-4309, 4353, 4373, 4394, 4430, 4453, 4470, 4474, 4495, 4587, 4593, 4606, 4950, 4991, 5018, 5050, 5053, 5057, 5063, 5082, 5146, 5279, 5366, 5416, 5419, 5423, 5425, 5428, 5431, 5465, 5475, 5493, 5565, 5567, 5575, 5592, 5593, 5611, 5618, 5633, 5642, 5643, 5650, 5653, 5654, 5666, 5686, 5700, 5759, 5968
see also: Poverty alleviation, Rural poverty, Urban poverty
Poverty alleviation 59, 1994, 2532, 3813, 3827, 3895, 3967, 3974, 4008, 4169, 4246, 4248, 4263, 4264, 4281, 4286, 4287, 4299, 4309, 4587, 4949, 5063, 5330, 5423, 5660, 5666, 5694, 5701, 5768
Power 37, 243, 319, 340, 374, 410, 476, 895, 912, 930, 982, 1013, 1029, 1060, 1069, 1070, 1151, 1196, 1197, 1200, 1220, 1235, 1253, 1427, 1499, 1532, 1562, 1576, 1685, 1743, 1792, 1897, 2006, 2050, 2221, 2314, 2322, 2336, 2337, 2339-2341, 2421, 2430, 2450, 2515, 2672, 2940, 2960, 3060, 3067, 3089, 3096, 3115, 3121, 3126, 3149, 3172, 3187, 3192, 3306, 3344, 3349, 3353, 3380, 3435, 3775, 3869, 3881, 3945, 4140, 4259, 4301, 4392, 4482, 4625, 4662, 4828, 4854, 4882, 4889, 4953, 4954, 4968, 5052, 5125, 5216, 5430, 5608, 5679, 5704, 5920
see also: Political power, Power relations
Power relations 444, 449, 528, 1151, 1823, 2250, 2337, 3193, 3267, 3410, 3911
Practice 43, 60, 183, 301, 308, 376, 651, 775, 1010, 1115, 1253, 1565, 1610, 1878, 2004, 2082, 2189, 2218, 2413, 2428, 3153, 3274, 4287, 5246, 5254, 5557, 5673, 5676, 5677, 5709, 5714, 5829, 5940
Pragmatics 266, 1789, 1807, 1808, 1829, 1830, 1833, 1839, 1872, 1877
Pragmatism 248, 1472, 1650, 1957, 3827, 4084, 4207, 5854
Prayer 1428, 5687
Pre-Columbian history 2677
Pre-industrial society 2542
Preferences 1038, 1733, 2256, 2739, 2967, 2984, 3026, 3345, 3705, 4013, 4106, 4130, 4284, 4305, 5154, 5529

INDEX DES MATIÈRES EN ANGLAIS

Pregnancy 551, 767, 800, 2074, 2638, 2734, 2738, 2740, 2743, 2745, 2763-2765, 2769, 2773, 2778, 2804, 2832, 2895, 2982, 2993, 3023, 3045, 3046, 3228, 3300, 3337, 3788, 4508, 5782, 5843, 5873, 5978
Prejudice 350, 657, 674, 822, 847, 857, 1052, 1075, 1748, 1781, 1821, 2417, 2452, 2464, 2477, 2484, 2497, 3283, 3319, 3455, 3461, 3518, 3562, 5928
  see also: Racial prejudice
Preservation of cultural heritage 3744, 3820, 3984, 4081, 4133, 5237
Press 455, 996, 1000, 1637, 1683, 1696, 1709, 1712, 1714, 1720, 1728, 1730, 1741, 1742, 1751, 1760, 1924, 2679, 3156, 3391, 3506, 3553, 5235, 5264, 5329, 5361
Pressure groups 2870, 3912, 5234, 5257
Prestige 2434, 2444
Preston, Ronald H. 1410
Prevention 791, 1010, 2817, 4731, 5146, 5409, 5467, 5554, 5566, 5814, 5950, 5964, 5967, 5968, 5981, 5983, 5986, 5987
Price policy 3868
Price regulation 5649
Prices
  see: Housing prices, Land prices, Water prices
Pricing 4767
Pride 862, 1358, 2667
Primary education 1996, 2106, 2211, 2217, 2229, 2230, 2232, 3260, 5588
Primary health care 5751, 5758, 5759, 5762, 5778, 5822, 5824, 5905, 5953
Primary schools 2212, 2218, 2231, 2234
Primates 619, 1161
Primatology 2406
Primitive society 1964
Principal-agent theory 4416
Prisoner rehabilitation 5030, 5032
Prisoners 1991, 4997, 4999, 5002, 5011-5013, 5022, 5026, 5033, 5037, 5042, 5068, 5100, 5192, 5664
  see also: Prisoner rehabilitation
Prisoners' dilemma 1073, 1638, 4388
Prisons 311, 426, 3391, 4979, 5005, 5011-5013, 5015, 5016, 5019, 5021, 5022, 5026, 5031, 5035, 5037, 5042, 5043, 5068, 5089, 5098, 5105, 5383, 5966
Privacy 69, 1361, 2941, 4988
  see also: Right of privacy
Privacy protection 4933
Private education 2029, 2141, 2251
Private enterprises 2514, 4657, 4748, 5591
Private health care 5754, 5776
Private property 3471, 3755, 4113

Private schools 1998, 2077, 2126
Private sector 371, 1119, 1122, 1123, 3862, 4054, 4537, 4648, 4705, 4804, 4881, 4949, 5478, 5522, 5754, 5777, 5815
Private sphere 110, 371, 1371, 1659, 1662, 1751, 1938, 2313, 2451, 2941, 3060, 3365, 3946, 4171, 4933, 4984, 4988, 5299, 5982
Privatization 28, 2120, 2150, 2292, 2407, 2451, 3813, 4041, 4079, 4204, 4211, 4424, 4788, 5287, 5478, 5725
Probability 473, 494, 525, 631, 833, 923, 2595, 2640, 2764, 2768, 2989, 4518, 5508
Probation system 3241, 5002, 5016, 5030, 5042, 5136, 5370, 5672
Problem solving 595, 705, 911, 947, 1604, 2053, 2061, 2179, 2850, 4074, 4395, 5699
Processions 3269
Procreation 2912
Product management 4322
Product safety 5200
Production 303, 379, 381, 1200, 1314, 2551, 3090, 3875, 4124, 4219, 4246, 4302, 4394, 4428, 4647, 5287, 5656
  see also: Agricultural production, Beef production, Mass production
Production factors 4833
Production specialization 2406
Production systems 308, 1892, 2627, 3893, 4243, 4818, 4838, 4934
Productivity 2457, 3896, 3910, 4246, 4253, 4262, 4309, 4693, 4764, 5969
  see also: Agricultural productivity, Labour productivity, Productivity growth
Productivity growth 4668
Profane 1471
Professional ethics 43, 48, 539, 2218, 2366, 4709, 4772, 5192, 5679, 5690
Professional identity 11, 4563, 4775, 5924
Professional organizations 4782
Professional workers 799, 802, 1285, 1305, 1977, 2082, 3175, 4383, 4457, 4518, 4555, 4601, 4738, 4770, 4779, 4782, 4788, 4789, 4793, 4876, 5709, 5845, 5925, 5953
Professionalism 1354, 3411, 4767, 4773, 4954
Professionalization 11, 1217, 4322, 4649, 4767, 4770, 4771, 4782, 4783, 5677
Professors 1631, 2089, 2444, 4935
Profit 1015, 1894, 3797, 3823, 4668, 5816, 5871
Profit rate 4234
Programme evaluation 411, 2281, 5958, 5960
Programming 1749
Prohibition 3325

SUBJECT INDEX

Project evaluation 3807, 3813, 3839, 4075, 5977
Propaganda 1360, 1546, 1781
Property 258, 2571, 2926, 3940, 3990, 4060, 4097, 4109, 4204, 4220, 4226, 4233, 4474
 see also: Cultural property, Intellectual property, Private property, Real estate
Property rights 3755, 3891, 4220, 5881
Prophecy 1401
Prophets 1525
Prose 1968
Prosody 1810
Prosperity 2523
Prostitution 171, 1370, 1950, 3016, 3147, 3319, 3323, 3325-3327, 3332-3334, 3347, 3348, 3601, 4979, 5366, 5373, 5545, 5686, 5943
Protectionist measures 5010
Protest movements 3777, 3827, 3954, 4039, 4848, 5235, 5236, 5265, 5266, 5274, 5275
Protestant ethic 314, 370
Protestantism 208, 1431, 1481, 1498, 1510, 1513, 2357, 4239
Protestants 1343, 1484, 1495, 1512, 1513, 2439, 3012
Provinces 2254, 2529, 3606, 5571
Psychiatrists 5056, 5683
Psychiatry 555, 604, 615, 699, 754, 758, 762, 768, 772, 773, 775, 779, 788, 799, 801, 1053, 2877, 2946, 5016, 5056, 5089, 5137, 5387, 5405, 5420, 5460, 5473, 5899, 5907, 5909, 5913, 5920, 5921, 5930, 5932
 see also: Forensic psychiatry, Social psychiatry
Psychoanalysis 12, 218, 340, 388, 558, 579, 584-586, 593, 599, 604, 632, 695, 699, 743, 744, 747, 748, 752, 761, 770, 779, 780, 782, 784, 801-803, 809, 810, 814, 816, 821, 897, 942, 1006, 1255, 1816, 1869, 1897, 1937, 1947, 2327, 2328, 2340, 2628, 2641, 2848, 3199, 3289, 3304, 3305, 3339, 3342, 5239, 5538, 5599, 5831, 5940
Psychodrama 740
Psycholinguistics 547, 622, 1653
Psychological anthropology 875
Psychological effects 755, 767, 883, 2893, 2895, 3471, 4324, 4347, 4626, 5838
Psychological factors 548, 550, 797, 875, 883, 1189, 1963, 3751, 5089, 5752
Psychologist
 see: Social psychologists
Psychologists 564, 592, 599, 604, 802, 868, 4731, 5084, 5192, 5209, 5412

Psychology 12, 25, 181, 199, 203, 215, 231, 289, 319, 326, 340, 388, 421, 422, 475, 503, 540, 541, 543, 544, 549-554, 556, 558-560, 562-567, 569, 570, 574, 575, 577-580, 582-592, 594, 596, 598, 600-602, 604-606, 608, 609, 613-617, 619-621, 625-629, 632, 635, 638, 640, 644, 646, 648-652, 654, 655, 658, 661, 663, 665-667, 670-672, 676, 678-682, 687, 689, 690, 693, 696, 699, 702, 707-710, 712, 713, 715, 717-721, 723, 725, 726, 729-733, 735-739, 741, 746, 750, 751, 755, 757, 759-762, 775, 777, 778, 782, 786, 787, 790, 794-796, 804, 806-810, 812, 813, 815, 818, 824, 829, 834, 838, 840, 845, 846, 849-851, 871-873, 879, 880, 883-885, 887, 892, 902, 905, 907, 914, 918-921, 928, 933, 936-939, 941, 943, 994, 1013, 1048, 1056, 1065, 1071, 1076, 1082, 1092, 1096, 1105, 1106, 1118, 1143, 1144, 1210, 1238, 1255, 1272, 1372, 1381, 1454, 1460, 1464, 1472, 1559, 1621, 1622, 1666, 1672, 1684, 1700, 1821, 1869, 1887, 1905, 1937, 1963, 1967, 2002, 2013, 2028, 2045, 2052, 2060, 2168, 2174, 2224, 2301, 2323, 2335, 2611, 2625, 2641, 2659, 2680, 2849, 2856, 2861, 2888, 2918, 2956, 2970, 2977, 2979, 3010, 3012, 3018, 3021, 3024, 3029, 3043, 3044, 3095, 3121, 3182, 3183, 3201, 3212, 3226, 3235, 3271, 3295, 3308, 3310, 3342, 3344, 3382, 3412, 3439, 3476, 3478, 3566, 3695, 3699, 3744, 3790, 4188, 4340, 4343, 4360, 4391, 4393, 4407, 4412, 4519, 4586, 4607, 4614, 4615, 4619, 4627, 4638, 4675, 4689, 4697, 4701, 4710, 4719, 4721, 4802, 4895, 5028, 5066, 5100, 5101, 5105, 5157, 5159, 5175, 5192-5194, 5331, 5377, 5397, 5409, 5410, 5434, 5453, 5457, 5516, 5687, 5752, 5773, 5798, 5856, 5893, 5901, 5902, 5936, 5939, 5957
 see also: Applied psychology, Child psychology, Clinical psychology, Developmental psychology, Economic psychology, Educational psychology, Environmental psychology, Evolutionary psychology, Experimental psychology, Genetic psychology, Gestalt psychology, Industrial psychology, Political psychology, Social psychology
Psychometrics 421, 475, 768, 3029
Psychopathology 589, 591, 632, 709, 739, 750, 757, 765, 787, 790

Psychophysiology 628
Psychoses 740, 758, 5460, 5681
Psychosociology 693, 767, 5066, 5867, 5891
Psychotherapy 402, 591, 695, 737, 740, 746
  748, 752, 778, 780, 782, 784-786, 793, 794,
  803, 804, 812, 813, 816, 819, 820, 1442, 1464,
  4895, 5192, 5349, 5406, 5420, 5595, 5599,
  5670, 5682, 5683, 5714, 5907, 5938, 5940
Public administration 1857, 2254, 4635, 4961,
  4993, 5212, 5638
Public choice 465, 3705, 3759, 4916
Public economics 5620
Public education 2147, 2199, 2242, 2251,
  2281, 2293, 2295
Public expenditure 4251, 4790, 5620, 5630
  see also: Government grant
Public finance 2196, 2259, 5475, 5514
Public goods 3694
Public health 43, 709, 1349, 2602, 2719, 2726,
  2762, 2817, 2823, 2830, 3115, 3300, 3311,
  3326, 3327, 3757, 3827, 3961, 4087,
  4274, 5386, 5397, 5445, 5471, 5525,
  5658, 5731, 5744, 5745, 5754, 5759,
  5781, 5788, 5789, 5791, 5801, 5813-5815,
  5819, 5820, 5824, 5864, 5867, 5885,
  5942, 5943, 5948, 5949, 5952, 5953,
  5956, 5958, 5960, 5962-5964, 5966-5974,
  5977, 5979-5982, 5986, 5988
Public infrastructure 3868, 3986, 4025, 4031,
  4036, 4051, 4066, 4093, 4102, 4108,
  4169, 4768
Public interest 1734, 3759
Public investment 5969
Public knowledge 427
Public law 5025, 5156
Public management 4635, 5747
Public opinion 455, 502, 519, 524, 534, 535,
  537, 963, 978, 1004, 1327, 1658, 1705,
  1719, 1731, 1747, 1752, 1781, 2311, 2396,
  2401, 2857, 2922, 3352, 3522, 3527,
  3706, 3734, 3983, 4090, 4094, 4145,
  4847, 5083, 5135, 5143, 5186, 5186,
  5200, 5213, 5214, 5218, 5219, 5255,
  5289, 5290, 5329, 5426, 5783, 5891
Public opinion polls 512
Public opinion research 509, 512, 520, 524,
  535
Public ownership 3927
Public policy 426, 633, 1857, 2026, 2602,
  2605, 2679, 3046, 3121, 3321, 3324,
  3352, 3423, 3528, 3694, 3749, 3752,
  3809, 4101, 4261, 4341, 4517, 4518,
  4528, 4796, 4830, 4949, 4984, 4988,
  5471, 5571
Public relations 4364, 4399

Public sector 371, 1119, 1122, 1123, 3862,
  4161, 4163, 4705, 4768, 4795, 4854,
  4857, 4871, 4949, 5212, 5220, 5223,
  5645, 5691, 5754, 5755
Public servants 5214, 5220
Public services 1745, 1778, 1849, 2873, 3784,
  3885, 3960, 4032, 4159, 4169, 4768,
  4818, 4832, 4950
Public spaces 1320, 1348, 1371, 1767, 2403,
  2451, 2580, 2679, 3234, 3255, 3365,
  3387, 3745, 3788, 3792, 3925, 4034,
  4039, 4118, 4123, 4126, 4129, 4132-4134,
  4140, 4146, 4851, 5248, 5361
Public sphere 44, 106, 110, 196, 371, 955,
  1190, 1196, 1199, 1659, 1751, 1782, 1826,
  1889, 1938, 2434, 2439, 3060, 3134,
  3365, 3946, 4171, 4851, 4932, 4933,
  4966, 5162, 5263, 5279, 5299, 5982
Public transport 1299, 2716, 3994, 4023,
  4068, 5093
Public works 1849
Public-private partnership 2139, 3813, 4035,
  4088, 4105, 4995, 5969
Publishing 1323, 1557, 1726, 1754, 1952,
  1955, 2269, 3112
Punishment 161, 1993, 2607, 3012, 3849,
  4990, 4992, 4999, 5001, 5004, 5005,
  5007, 5009, 5015-5017, 5022, 5029, 5030,
  5034, 5040, 5043, 5047, 5149, 5174,
  5192, 5195, 5465, 5580
  see also: Capital punishment
Pupils 435, 479, 2014, 2044, 2047, 2058,
  2065, 2097, 2102, 2163, 2198, 2218,
  2229, 2235, 2608, 2621, 2644, 3274,
  3458, 3517, 4062, 5470, 5955
Purchasing power 4193
Putnam, Robert D. 4203
Qualifications 2064, 2249, 4429, 4441, 4583,
  4717, 4757, 4769
Qualitative analysis 20, 427, 430, 431, 435,
  449, 455, 457, 462, 469, 470, 504, 514,
  517, 520, 528, 529, 585, 651, 1488, 1727,
  2194, 2530, 2646, 3164, 3666, 3852,
  4486, 4726, 4759, 4837, 5563, 5816,
  5838, 5842, 5925
Quality control 1604, 1783, 2244, 5784, 5794,
  5807, 5815
Quality of life 1923, 2480, 2680, 2711, 2814,
  3370, 3581, 3793, 3857, 3904, 3991,
  4123, 4247, 4296, 4297, 4693, 4724,
  4740, 5372, 5531, 5532, 5607, 5738,
  5838, 5889
Quality of service 1998, 2014, 2733, 3885,
  4159, 4390, 5743, 5755, 5806, 5838, 5942
Quality of work 4702, 4740

SUBJECT INDEX

Quality standards 2214, 2253, 2260, 2275, 5743
Quantitative analysis 63, 163, 457, 462, 490, 507, 514, 520, 585, 651, 1488, 1791, 3666, 3784, 4527, 5075, 5563
Quantum physics 1602, 1614, 1623
Questionnaires 460, 509, 520, 527, 532, 629, 711, 712, 742, 763, 768, 800, 833, 1798, 1820, 2157, 2183, 2530, 2775, 2913, 3292, 3739, 3749, 4119, 4618, 4698, 5221, 5403, 5691, 5710, 5792, 5829, 5891
Quine, W.V.O 1231
Race 33, 603, 669, 808, 814, 861, 964, 972, 1078, 1195, 1227, 1297, 1339, 1427, 1433, 1443, 1474, 1620, 1750, 1761, 1815, 1880, 1917, 1965, 1978, 2011, 2017, 2042, 2055, 2061, 2068, 2077, 2151, 2161, 2232, 2359, 2436, 2551, 2602, 2631, 2647, 2699, 2751, 2811, 2812, 2978, 2995, 3024, 3058, 3088, 3121, 3214, 3222, 3242, 3259, 3383, 3389, 3393, 3396, 3398, 3399, 3401, 3411, 3414, 3428-3430, 3432-3439, 3442, 3443, 3449, 3454, 3457, 3463, 3464, 3472, 3474, 3475, 3481, 3484, 3486, 3488, 3503-3506, 3510-3513, 3516, 3517, 3519, 3525, 3528, 3529, 3534, 3545, 3632, 3938, 4012-4014, 4020, 4089, 4291, 4376, 4416, 4431, 4435, 4464, 4472, 4473, 4479, 4496, 4497, 4502, 4505, 4507, 4510, 4559, 4615, 4628, 4733, 4865, 4939, 5017, 5031, 5053, 5081, 5102-5104, 5139, 5142, 5148, 5280, 5357, 5409, 5454, 5465, 5483, 5490, 5563, 5577, 5672, 5774, 5830, 5832, 5836, 5846, 5914
Race relations 835, 1075, 1431, 1442, 1926, 1949, 2011, 2060, 2240, 2530, 3077, 3088, 3099, 3395, 3412, 3429, 3431, 3436, 3439, 3441, 3444, 3449, 3452-3454, 3456, 3462, 3463, 3466, 3472, 3476, 3477, 3482, 3489, 3494, 3503-3507, 3509, 3511, 3512, 3515-3517, 3521, 3524-3526, 3529, 3534, 3599, 3641, 3769, 3950, 3988, 4002, 4013, 4015, 4089, 4472, 4491, 4865, 4919, 4971, 5050, 5142, 5147, 5713
Racial attitudes 1308, 3412, 3461, 3508, 3514-3516
Racial conflict 1009, 3172, 3456, 3522
Racial differentiation 2017, 2034, 2380, 4000, 4438, 5113, 5774
Racial discrimination 2060, 2232, 2266, 3451, 3466, 3478, 3483, 3497, 3505, 3507, 3517, 3521, 3529, 3599, 3654, 3981, 4000, 4015, 4416, 4491, 4501, 4502, 4511, 4690, 5031, 5129, 5142, 5160, 5171, 5490

Racial inequality 1431, 2036, 2062, 2212, 3454, 3482, 3491, 3514, 3528, 4505, 4509
Racial prejudice 844, 1431, 3461, 3463, 3467, 3468, 3476, 3494, 3504, 3508, 3514, 3515, 3517, 3528, 3529, 5703
Racial segregation 1429, 2068, 3451, 3481, 3988, 4019, 4266
Racial stereotypes 1308, 3517
Racism 1620, 1748, 1917, 2011, 2063, 2163, 2630, 3172, 3433, 3437, 3449, 3452, 3456, 3458, 3461, 3463, 3464, 3466-3468, 3470, 3476, 3494, 3502-3504, 3507-3511, 3513, 3516-3518, 3522, 3523, 3529, 3534, 3542, 4919, 5147, 5171, 5243, 5319, 5713, 5872, 5928
Radicalism 155, 1311, 1394, 1553, 2117, 3374, 4316, 4928, 5276
Radicals 4865
Radio 1709, 1724, 1745, 1749, 1755, 1756, 1780, 2748
Railway transport 2826, 4048, 4076
Rain forest 3735, 3768, 3796
Rape 3070, 3112, 3298, 3534, 5191, 5449, 5457-5459, 5462, 5546
Rational behaviour 364, 923, 3493
Rational choice 2, 10, 40, 115, 129, 323, 364, 366, 458, 1069, 1299, 1377, 2048, 4013, 4180, 4194, 4196, 4326, 4739, 4837, 4936, 5075
Rationalism 113, 212, 224, 256, 382, 1391, 1622, 2355, 3493, 4084, 4929, 5117
Rationality 40, 106, 107, 116, 117, 121, 122, 129, 131, 133, 242, 261, 268, 272, 279, 314, 315, 324, 366, 370, 371, 465, 561, 602, 1020, 1127, 1197, 1198, 1247, 1271, 1277, 1280, 1570, 1630, 2311, 2351, 2575, 4030, 4065, 4180, 4275, 4326, 4388, 4428, 4739, 4778, 4920, 5162, 5303
Rationalization 1139, 1860, 2548
Rationing 5197, 5750, 5770
Rawls, John 2361, 2448, 2589, 4293
Readers 78
Reading 1140, 1637, 1921, 2028, 2040
Real estate 3451, 4080, 4156, 5649
see also: Real estate market
Real estate market 2571, 3927
Realism 21, 55, 140, 207, 222, 258, 275, 285, 330, 341, 346, 360, 383, 391, 1136, 1235, 1270, 1428, 1570, 1578, 1596, 1610, 1752, 2319, 2809, 3687, 3700, 3701, 3775, 4361, 5310
Reason 106, 107, 111-113, 121, 122, 126, 130, 131, 134, 136, 139, 141, 206, 226, 244, 268, 271, 360, 667, 1127, 1271, 1591, 2362, 2366, 3744, 4902, 4920

INDEX DES MATIÈRES EN ANGLAIS

Reasoning 30, 111, 129, 137, 583, 619, 664, 706, 823, 940, 1389, 1808, 1824, 2179, 2208, 2351, 2625, 3182, 5179
Rebellions 986, 5239
Recent political history 1723
Recession 4007, 4828
Recidivism 4997, 5121
Reciprocity 656, 1016, 1632, 2308, 2987, 3800, 3847, 4351, 4931, 5508
Recording 1982
Recreation 1291, 1312, 2906, 3792, 3925, 4139
Recruitment 1446, 2092, 2256, 2274, 2631, 3286, 3665, 3673, 4429, 4439, 4489, 4490, 4569, 4603, 4613, 4615, 4732, 4784, 4875, 5352, 5845
Recycling 3715
Reference works 36, 81-83, 85-87, 90, 91, 93, 95-103, 105, 566, 1617, 1703, 2067
Reflexivity 18, 32, 183, 309, 359, 384, 386, 389, 401, 507, 1141, 1562, 1595, 2645, 2809, 4344, 4360, 5246, 5709
Reform 419, 2132, 2294, 3325, 4818, 4848, 4876, 5139, 5212, 5361, 5622, 5810, 5903, 5959
    see also: Administrative reform, Agrarian reform, Constitutional reform, Economic reform, Education reform, Land reform, Legal reform, Political reform, Religious reform, Social reform
Refugees 814, 1536, 2218, 2530, 3354, 3586, 3611, 3624, 3660, 3664, 3666, 3674, 3677, 3680, 3681, 5585, 5637
    see also: Political refugees
Regime transition 746, 1942, 2533, 2534, 4292, 4971, 5003, 5341
Regional analysis 2697
Regional cooperation 3671
Regional development 1892, 2539, 3069, 3682, 3768, 3771, 3792, 3820, 3836, 3920, 3948, 4069, 4085, 4097, 4105, 4261, 4509, 4606, 4995, 5445
Regional disparities 2234, 2560, 2774, 3069, 3620, 3895, 3981
Regional economics 3927, 3997, 4058, 4069, 4833, 4935
Regional government 4797, 4963
Regional identity 963, 969, 1202, 1363, 1820
Regional integration 2205, 2507, 2560, 3776
Regional organizations
    see: African organizations
Regional planning 1324, 3755, 3808, 3872, 3900, 3908, 4071, 4079, 4082, 4084, 4085, 4203, 5903
Regional politics 5221

Regional security 3776
Regional trade 4811
Regional variation 1209, 2701, 2844, 2944, 3773, 4281, 4587, 5454, 5494, 5537, 5968
Regionalism 969, 997, 1000, 1202, 1209, 2009, 2553, 2560, 2573, 3423, 4067, 4969, 5202, 5328, 5363
Regionalization 2560, 2576, 3808
Regions 966, 1429, 2649, 2700, 2835, 2962, 3061, 3688, 3772, 4203, 4212, 4439, 4441, 4594, 4959, 5303, 5432, 5445, 5757
    see also: Regional politics
Regression analysis 485, 489, 662, 1112, 1129, 1443, 1512, 2612, 2666, 2746, 2800, 2816, 2841, 3029, 3182, 3201, 3592, 3929, 4453, 4523, 4721, 4741, 4795, 5045, 5408, 5507, 5918
Regulation 220, 1133, 1190, 1756, 2100, 2280, 2356, 2580, 2741, 2816, 3325, 3672, 3673, 3734, 3814, 3880, 3922, 4153, 4235, 4352, 4396, 4587, 4617, 4683, 4751, 4782, 4818, 4976, 4989, 5125, 5402, 5407, 5524, 5777, 5870, 5880, 5881, 5884, 5888, 5942
    see also: Market regulation, Price regulation, Wage regulation
Regulatory policy 4396
Reincarnation 1398
Relativism 135, 206, 241, 261, 268, 309, 405, 543, 1158, 1198, 1231, 1270, 1455, 1575, 1610, 1627, 2349, 4186, 4931, 5320
Reliability 433, 455, 501
Religion 33, 56, 145, 169, 208, 221, 223, 230, 235, 237, 245, 246, 254, 270, 701, 880, 1171, 1199, 1372, 1373, 1375, 1378, 1379, 1381, 1385, 1386, 1388, 1392, 1393, 1395-1400, 1403, 1405, 1406, 1408, 1409, 1415, 1418, 1422, 1425, 1430, 1433-1435, 1437, 1439, 1441, 1444, 1445, 1448, 1450-1455, 1457, 1459-1461, 1463, 1465, 1466, 1469, 1470, 1474, 1478, 1481, 1483, 1485, 1486, 1490, 1493-1502, 1504-1509, 1511, 1513-1515, 1519, 1523, 1524, 1528, 1530, 1533, 1535, 1541, 1543, 1548, 1549, 1551, 1948, 1990, 2136, 2298, 2372, 2394, 2429, 2524, 2525, 2532, 2663, 2673, 2852, 2890, 2963, 2974, 2978, 3012, 3024, 3112, 3266, 3382, 3448, 3557, 3565, 3573, 3614, 3775, 3858, 3945, 4003, 4908, 4929, 4947, 5400, 5481, 5722, 5757, 5862, 5893, 5907
    see also: Anthropology of religion, Comparative religion, History of religion, Monotheism, Philosophy of religion, Popular religion, Religious texts,

SUBJECT INDEX

Sociology of religion, Traditional religion, World religions
Religion and politics 1394, 1410, 1431, 1470, 1475, 1515, 1537, 1550, 3528, 4962
see also: Islam and politics
Religiosity 880, 1372, 1375, 1383, 1433, 1437, 1438, 1461, 1469, 1481, 1500, 1509, 1512, 1544, 2239, 2655, 2732, 2753, 2982, 3448, 3614, 5238
Religious affiliation 1429, 5083
Religious authorities 2330
Religious behaviour 1452, 1461
Religious beliefs 145, 247, 295, 701, 1263, 1376, 1380, 1388, 1389, 1398, 1404, 1407, 1412, 1414, 1416, 1417, 1421, 1424, 1428, 1431, 1434-1436, 1438, 1441, 1447, 1451, 1454, 1457, 1463, 1469, 1470, 1476-1478, 1481, 1487-1491, 1500, 1501, 1503, 1504, 1508, 1511, 1515, 1523, 1526, 1527, 1538-1541, 1544, 1545, 1550, 2313, 2532, 2631, 2731, 2753, 2756, 3447, 3743, 3764
Religious change 1199, 1384, 1415, 1418, 1425, 1431, 1433, 1448, 1474, 1486, 1489, 1509, 1516, 4477
Religious communities 1409, 1430, 1447, 1478, 1484, 1498, 1499, 1506, 1509, 1512, 1516, 1521, 1532, 1536, 1540, 1550, 1912, 3468, 3879, 4125
Religious conflicts 145, 1484-1486, 1510, 1513, 1529, 1537
Religious conversion 1397, 1446, 1489, 1492, 1493, 1496, 1526
Religious discrimination 3172, 4962
Religious doctrines 132, 1498, 2870
Religious education 225, 1396, 1400, 1419, 1422, 1445, 1542, 2126, 2169, 4962
Religious experiences 1307, 1373, 1388, 1459
Religious festivals 1534
Religious forces 1407, 1414, 1491
Religious fundamentalism 1394, 1411, 1505, 1523, 1541, 1543, 1546, 2520, 5083
Religious groups 1394, 1408, 1417, 1427, 1431, 1433, 1446, 1478, 1496, 1503, 1517, 1521, 2554, 3573, 3843, 3853, 3892, 3919
Religious history 145, 1405, 1432-1434, 1478, 1514, 1516, 1525, 1542
Religious ideas 1379
Religious influences 1438, 1480, 1512, 2753
Religious institutions 1385, 1479, 3858
Religious leaders 326
Religious life 998, 1407, 1433, 1520, 2673
Religious minorities 1441, 1519, 1532, 1536, 2143, 3397
Religious missions 1433, 1492
Religious movements 56, 1384, 1394, 1397, 1401, 1418, 1425, 1430, 1448, 1450, 1457, 1463, 1485, 1495, 1500, 1501, 1509, 1538, 1541, 1543, 3650, 5272, 5274
Religious music 1975, 1983
Religious orders 1521
Religious participation 1429, 1461, 1467, 1529, 3844, 4962
Religious pluralism 1377, 1424, 1425, 1440, 1448, 1525, 1547, 2532, 4962
Religious practice 1001, 1263, 1376, 1429, 1431, 1435, 1436, 1467, 1504, 1507, 1511, 1515, 1518, 1527, 1539, 1544, 1545, 2842, 3202, 3468, 4535
Religious protest 1444
Religious reform 145, 1433
Religious revival 1467, 1470
Religious studies 56, 169, 1386, 1396, 1400, 1418, 1419, 1422, 1445, 1462, 1472, 2297
Religious symbolism 1418
Religious syncretism 1539
Religious teachings 3108
Religious texts 200, 233, 266, 1382, 1402, 1426, 1458, 1473, 1478, 1518, 1534, 1552
Religious thought 145, 211, 233, 266, 272, 293, 1374, 1379, 1381, 1386, 1388, 1402, 1404, 1419, 1435, 1442, 1444, 1449, 1451, 1457, 1458, 1477, 1478, 1501, 1867
Religious traditions 1408, 1442, 1444, 1456, 1504
Remarriage 2910, 2924
Renaissance 237, 1436, 1859
Renewable resources 3810
Rent 3845, 3985, 4486, 5491, 5612, 5649
Rent-seeking 4204
Representations of the body 1861, 3228, 3788
Repression 632, 994, 3147, 3204, 3349, 4269, 4992, 5251, 5320
Reproductive technology 2735, 2902, 5785, 5851, 5863
Republicanism 1970, 2439, 4969
Research 49, 52, 54, 57, 71, 74, 76, 105, 168, 173, 195, 416, 430, 435-437, 454, 457, 517, 533, 538, 996, 1450, 1569, 1590, 1604, 1618, 1647, 1659, 1763, 1850, 1997, 1999, 2018, 2095, 2162, 2215, 2265, 2279, 2282, 2291, 2362, 2468, 2490, 2491, 2500, 2601, 2716, 2905, 2907, 2985, 3014, 3118, 3121, 3175, 3513, 3543, 3758, 3780, 4098, 4246, 4397, 4398, 4510, 5076, 5452, 5490, 5495, 5709, 5808, 5818, 5933
see also: Accounting research, Action research, Agricultural research,

INDEX DES MATIÈRES EN ANGLAIS

Anthropological research, Applied research, Communication research, Current research, Demographic research, Development research, Economic research, Educational research, Empirical research, Ethnographic research, Ethnological research, Interdisciplinary research, Linguistic research, Management research, Market research, Marketing research, Medical research, Operations research, Organizational research, Peace research, Policy research, Political science research, Public opinion research, Scientific research, Social research, Social science research, Sociological research
Research and development 42, 1604
Research financing 43, 1618, 4805
Research foundations 42, 2448
Research methods 20, 31, 88, 119, 163, 179, 180, 183, 411-418, 420-427, 429, 431, 432, 434, 436-438, 440, 442, 443, 450, 454, 456, 458, 472, 474, 475, 482, 487, 488, 490, 495, 497, 502, 505-508, 510, 514-516, 518, 520, 522, 526, 529, 531, 536, 537, 539, 591, 595, 603, 653, 713, 748, 841, 1293, 1445, 1590, 2012, 2282, 2465, 2610, 3666, 4625, 4982, 5073, 5367, 5557, 5709, 5720, 5818, 5898, 5979
see also: Field work
Research policy 2269
Research priorities 415, 442
Research programmes 1618
Research projects 43, 60, 1620, 2397, 2465
Research strategies 60, 415, 1005, 2344, 4181
Research trends 4, 25, 50, 56, 66, 67, 75, 174, 182, 191, 339, 1218, 3067, 3233, 5673
Research workers 423, 528, 2465
Residence 2901
Resident satisfaction 3824
Residential areas 3481, 3899, 3970, 3987, 4022, 4054, 4098, 4130, 4136, 4153, 4165
Residential care 2674, 2679, 5016, 5479, 5496, 5499, 5501, 5504, 5513, 5522, 5530, 5542, 5569, 5570, 5596, 5607, 5608, 5740, 5741, 5978
Residential mobility 3085, 3622, 3628, 4004, 4014, 4130, 5415
Residential segregation 3383, 3451, 3481, 3994, 4003, 4019, 4020, 4034, 4125
Resistance 982, 1141, 1240, 1363, 1978, 2569, 2915, 3112, 3234, 3548, 4206, 4406, 4688, 4808, 5122, 5229, 5232, 5349, 5467, 5755, 5937
see also: Resistance movements
Resistance movements 2339, 2563

Resistance to change 2509
Resistance to integration 1442
Resource allocation 49, 2018, 3618, 4136, 4251, 4270, 5540, 5785
Resource conservation 1093, 3804, 4047
Resource exploitation 3736
Resource inventory 92
Resource management 459, 3690, 3756, 3810, 3811, 3838, 3913, 4047, 4099, 4768
Resource utilization 3713, 3735, 4246
Responsibility 73, 111, 205, 407, 830, 896, 934, 1097, 1607, 1620, 2058, 2151, 2439, 2534, 2991, 3328, 3749, 3750, 4417, 4422, 4423, 4427, 4907, 4963, 5166, 5285, 5548, 5678, 5679, 5854, 5883, 5889
Retail trade 1144, 1738, 3545, 3937, 4135, 4344, 4414, 4522, 4552, 4559, 4678, 4726
see also: Shopping centres
Retired persons 3625
Retirement 1285, 2664, 2667, 2670, 2676, 2679, 2707, 2957, 3679, 3791, 5338, 5517, 5518
Retirement pensions 4353
Return migration 3558, 3592, 3603, 3618, 3621, 3641, 3662, 3859
Returns to education 2023, 2035, 2037, 2287, 4764
Revenge 263, 5040
Revisionism 1209, 4206
Revolt 2618, 5239
Revolution 1167, 1185, 1585, 1625, 1683, 2205, 2293, 2520, 2558, 2708, 3121, 4213, 4327, 5233, 5239, 5325
see also: Cuban Revolution, Cultural Revolution, French Revolution, Industrial revolution
Rhetoric 12, 15, 106, 156, 346, 870, 1029, 1095, 1642, 1650, 1839, 1988, 2443, 3070, 3341, 4265, 4346, 4907, 4912, 5172, 5201, 5484
Rhodes, Cecil 1882
Ricœur, Paul 161
Rich, Adrienne 669
Right 2361, 5883
see also: Extreme Right, New right
Right of asylum 3680, 5637
Right of privacy 1714, 4933, 4986, 4988
Right to education 2014
Right to work 4870
Right-wing parties 3452, 5243, 5256
Rights 1466, 1484, 2346, 2461, 2495, 2734, 3205, 3335, 3675, 4324, 4915, 4933, 4950, 5161, 5196, 5247, 5271, 5326, 5854
see also: Basic rights, Children's rights, Civil rights, Economic rights, Human

SUBJECT INDEX

rights, Indigenous rights, Individual rights, Minority rights, Property rights, Social rights, Women's rights
Riots 2618, 5133, 5448, 5464
Risk 17, 386, 461, 467, 471, 483, 489, 561, 709, 714, 787, 838, 922, 923, 1349, 1563, 1595, 1609, 1660, 2309, 2320, 2636, 2640, 2773, 2808, 2836, 2838, 2845, 2933, 2962, 2981, 2995, 3067, 3309, 3316, 3326, 3351, 3624, 3700, 3702, 3704, 3734, 3752, 3759, 3930, 3979, 4260, 4353, 4416, 4417, 4552, 4580, 4984, 5009, 5061, 5071, 5080, 5081, 5140, 5383, 5386, 5387, 5407, 5433, 5468, 5485, 5554, 5570, 5578, 5773, 5838, 5867, 5891, 5942, 5948, 5957, 5964, 5970, 5978, 5984, 5987
  see also: Financial risks, Risk sharing
Risk management 43, 1660, 3702, 4346, 4348, 4727, 5951
Risk sharing 5931
Rites of passage 1321
Ritual 245, 246, 952, 953, 976, 1074, 1348, 1433, 1442, 1534, 1964, 2330, 3092, 3418, 4315, 5338, 5368, 5932
Rivalry 2166
Rivers 2777, 3728, 3822
Road traffic 1302
Robotics 1576
Rock music 1309, 1352, 1364
Rogers, Carl 599
Rokkan, Stein 4966
Role 1054, 1532, 2439, 2920, 4773, 5209
Role change 2680, 4770
Role conflicts 5690
Role models 3254, 3264
Role playing 60
Role prescriptions 1105
Role theory 4416
Rom 3520
Roman Empire 1159
Romanticism 1197, 1968
Rorty, Richard 248
Rose, Gillian 253
Rosen, Robert 1606
Rubber 3732
Rule of law 4909, 4955, 4989, 5154, 5181, 5187
Ruling class 2321, 2446
Rural anthropology 3920
Rural areas 1343, 1468, 2186, 2234, 2655, 2660, 2663, 2675, 2712, 2718, 2739, 2800, 2843, 2886, 2939, 2961, 3010, 3043, 3612, 3626, 3767, 3776, 3841, 3866, 3876, 3884, 3886, 3897, 3900, 3901, 3905, 3908, 3915, 3924, 4108, 4292, 4558, 5417, 5757, 5838, 5954, 5962, 5975
Rural communities 20, 797, 1813, 2338, 2653, 3628, 3837, 3852, 3868, 3874, 3885, 3892, 3898, 3899, 3907, 3910, 3911, 3914, 3923, 5200, 5515, 5695
Rural credit 4284
Rural development 3535, 3612, 3813, 3852, 3866, 3867, 3871, 3876, 3895, 3914-3920, 3923-3925, 4240, 4458, 5261, 5968
Rural economics 3852, 3868, 3884, 3897, 3898, 3903, 3915, 3916, 3923, 4248, 4264, 4486
Rural employment 4516
Rural environment 3877, 3925
Rural geography 3879
Rural history 3886
Rural housing 3906
Rural life 1363, 3886-3888, 3895, 3904, 3916
Rural planning 2152, 3876, 3906
Rural policy 3880, 3908, 3915, 4248
Rural population 1476, 2832, 3170, 3608, 3748, 3866, 3905, 3915, 4103, 4218
Rural poverty 2793, 3619, 3776, 3869, 3871, 3884, 3895, 3897, 3902, 3905, 4246, 4248, 4270, 4309, 5279
Rural society 3891, 3916
Rural sociology 20, 788, 1632, 2022, 2152, 2532, 3619, 3729, 3742, 3870, 3872-3875, 3878, 3881, 3884, 3892, 3894, 3897-3899, 3902, 3910, 3912, 3917, 3920, 4270, 4591, 4981, 5374, 5418
Rural unemployment 4591
Rural women 2787, 3138, 3890, 4284
Rural youth 3894
Rural-urban migration 2689, 3551, 3608, 3619, 3626, 3813, 3868, 3894, 3903, 3964, 4162, 4177
Rural-urban relations 2843, 3867-3869, 3871, 5279
Ruskin, John 1928
Russian language 1834
Russian Orthodox Church 1436, 1505
Russians 710, 1836, 2033, 2538, 3591, 5529
Saadawi, Nawal el 3122
Sacred 650, 1381, 1393, 1399, 1459, 1471, 1962
Sacrifice 239
Sadness 683, 690, 863, 948
Safety 1115, 1601, 2826, 2879, 3287, 3745, 3937, 3998, 4325, 4695, 4995, 5082, 5107, 5200, 5443, 5808, 5967
  see also: Occupational safety, Product safety

INDEX DES MATIÈRES EN ANGLAIS

Said, Edward 1165, 1386
Saint-Martin, Louis Claude de 256
Sales 4320, 4420
Sales management 4658
Sales techniques 4418
Samba 1981
Sample surveys 705, 3617, 3853
Samples 460, 525, 534, 2722, 2778, 2839, 2876, 2928, 3476, 3715, 4518, 4778, 5408
Sampling 451, 468, 491, 504, 2595, 3182, 4262
San 2379
Sanctions 5099
Sanitation services 2823, 3813
Sanskrit 132
Santayana, George 228
Saro-Wiwa, Ken 1939
Sartre, Jean Paul 311
Sartre, Jean-Paul 215, 218, 281
Satire 5293
Satisfaction 831, 946, 1285, 2495, 3462, 3973, 4183
    see also: Community satisfaction, Job satisfaction, Life satisfaction, Marital satisfaction, Resident satisfaction
Saussure, Ferdinand de 12
Savanna 5968
Savimbi, Jonas 1756
Savings 2676, 4184, 4326
Scandals 5219
Scarcity 4179
Scepticism 352, 358, 1404, 1552, 5265
Schatzki, Theodore 597
Schizophrenia 555, 758, 763, 765, 788, 5460, 5909, 5916, 5922
Schmitt, Carl 1199
Schön, D.A. 1095
School administration 2133, 2159, 2237, 2241, 4806
School attendance 2014
School discipline 2119
School failure 2020
School leaving 2054
School-community relationship 4486
Schooling 225, 544, 980, 1331, 1809, 1991, 2011, 2017, 2022, 2023, 2034, 2041, 2042, 2047, 2054, 2058, 2064, 2066, 2068, 2074, 2095, 2097, 2109, 2120, 2121, 2124, 2130, 2131, 2133, 2141, 2142, 2152, 2155, 2156, 2159-2161, 2163, 2166, 2177, 2187, 2188, 2192, 2225, 2234, 2532, 2602, 2624, 2813, 2935, 3047, 3057, 3115, 3571, 4962
Schools 435, 459, 577, 862, 1875, 1990, 1993, 1998, 2000, 2014, 2017, 2024, 2029, 2034, 2036, 2038, 2044, 2051, 2059, 2062, 2065-2069, 2073, 2076, 2079, 2086, 2094, 2096, 2101, 2104, 2105, 2108-2111, 2114, 2116, 2121, 2122, 2124, 2125, 2131, 2135, 2138, 2142, 2143, 2146, 2151-2153, 2155, 2157, 2159, 2165, 2166, 2177, 2188, 2204, 2205, 2230, 2237, 2316, 2608, 2622, 2636, 2644, 2871, 2878, 3115, 3274, 3340, 3349, 3458, 3517, 3521, 3554, 4398, 5108, 5225, 5461, 5465, 5593, 5814, 5933, 5955
    see also: Primary schools, Private schools, Secondary schools, State schools
Schopenhauer, Arthur 229
Schudson, Michael 1409
Schutz, Alfred 310
Science 13, 15, 22, 106, 126, 135, 225, 268, 279, 301, 334, 385, 396, 572, 775, 1150, 1234, 1271, 1286, 1401, 1416, 1558, 1560, 1563, 1566-1570, 1572-1574, 1577, 1579, 1580, 1582-1584, 1586, 1589, 1592, 1594, 1596-1598, 1600, 1603, 1605, 1607-1609, 1613-1615, 1618, 1619, 1623, 1626, 1628, 1629, 1631, 1633, 1871, 1996, 2015, 2209, 2237, 2262, 2288, 2309, 2350, 3115, 3719, 3759, 3823, 3837, 4571, 5201, 5839
    see also: Behavioural sciences, Communication sciences, Computer science, Forensic science, History of science, Information sciences, Natural sciences, Philosophy of science
Science policy 1577, 1594, 1618
Scientific and technical progress 1608, 2120
Scientific communication 1619
Scientific communities 1557, 1565, 1594, 1619, 3719
Scientific discoveries 288, 1601, 1619
Scientific progress 434, 1576, 1580, 1594, 1603, 1604, 1613, 2350, 2704
Scientific publications 1557
Scientific research 56, 73, 434, 1566, 1569, 1594, 1601, 1607, 1610, 1613, 1618, 1620, 1631, 2262, 2344, 5853, 5942
Scientific thought 214, 1391, 1555, 1569, 1580, 1589, 1600, 1619, 1627, 1630
Scientists 775, 1572, 1605, 1610, 1612, 1613, 1618, 1620, 1624, 1625, 3179
    see also: Political scientists, Social scientists
Scientology 1378
Scots 5213
Scripts 671
Sea 3745
Seacole, Mary 1960

493

Subject Index

Seasonal fluctuations 2800
Seasonal migration 3791
Seasonal workers 3661
Seasonality 3745
Second homes 3791, 3906
Second language 2003, 2009
Secondary analysis 5105
Secondary education 1257, 1419, 2072, 2082, 2087, 2091, 2092, 2109, 2124, 2130, 2149, 2159, 2178, 2179, 2210, 2237-2239, 2241, 3300, 3759, 4527, 4768, 4806
Secondary schools 2070, 2077, 2085, 2088, 2124, 2130, 2158, 2235, 2236, 2240, 2241, 5470, 5955
Secrecy 5169
Sectarianism 1394, 1484, 1510
Sectoral development 4385
Sects 56, 1498, 1536
Secularism 1386, 1535, 2346, 2439, 3853, 4929, 4962
Secularization 1175, 1228, 1375, 1386, 1508, 1514, 1529, 2025, 4962
Segovia, Tomás 1922
Segregation 491, 2024, 2136, 2403, 2935, 3189, 3456, 3992, 3998, 4003, 4015, 4018, 4020, 4034, 4266, 4533, 5576
  see also: Occupational segregation, Racial segregation, Residential segregation
Self 69, 106, 199, 207, 219, 220, 236, 245, 246, 266, 276, 283, 340, 541, 543, 558, 569, 601, 602, 657, 679, 699, 702, 718, 732, 734, 737, 744, 785, 803, 809, 814, 825, 839, 840, 851, 871, 873, 874, 878, 894, 915, 933, 937, 991, 1063, 1147, 1161, 1214, 1251, 1361, 1426, 1454, 1551, 1937, 1947, 1949, 1960, 1964, 2021, 2303, 2566, 3033, 3045, 3059, 3108, 3115, 3135, 3227, 3256, 3263, 3395, 3418, 4349, 4392, 4967, 5073, 5095, 5159, 5697, 5944
Self-categorization 828, 878, 999, 1042, 1083, 2436, 2530, 3660
Self-concept 219, 562, 569, 639, 681, 862, 867, 871, 872, 874, 880, 896, 1161, 2045, 2487, 2670, 2953, 3021, 3049, 3446
Self-consciousness 20, 219, 541, 563
Self-determination 139, 892, 982, 2093, 2310
Self-employed workers 3594, 4432, 4456, 4459, 4461, 4473, 4474, 4479, 4556, 4598, 4665, 4676, 4780
Self-esteem 576, 681, 693, 720, 725, 732, 843, 849, 852, 876, 881, 908, 933, 936, 972, 1064, 1076, 1156, 1198, 1666, 2885, 3021, 3049, 3052, 3055, 3183, 3591, 4187, 4615, 4719, 4750

Self-evaluation 562, 639, 840, 871, 1143, 2086, 2378, 3281, 4607, 4615, 4703, 4719
Self-government 17, 864, 995, 2258, 2532, 3919, 4618, 5553, 5849
Self-help 548, 4939, 5260, 5376, 5691
Self-interest 382, 1073, 3493, 4181, 5077
Self-management 439, 4201, 4618, 4664, 4934, 4946, 5376
Self-perception 142, 548, 549, 557, 562, 580, 609, 675, 679, 697, 801, 828, 874, 880, 896, 936, 960, 999, 1156, 1186, 1367, 1446, 2625, 2667, 2677, 3049, 3402, 3432, 4775, 5773
Self-reliance 704, 2712, 3642
Self-sufficiency 704
Sellars, Wilfred 1871
Semantics 139, 210, 231, 494, 563, 596, 617, 721, 729, 1638, 1804, 1822, 1828, 1842, 1989, 2250, 5177
Seminars 1024
Semiology 1989
Semiotics 326, 342, 1233, 1237, 1418, 1611, 1767, 1787, 1799, 1803, 1804, 1832, 1842, 1862, 1898, 2208, 3061, 3139, 3676, 4612
Sen, Amartya 1923, 5642
Sensation 551, 552, 1347
Senses 1984, 2493
  see also: Hearing, Sight, Taste
Sentences 563, 617, 825, 5034
Separatism 1000, 3400, 3475, 4494
Sephardim 3483
Serbs 967, 991, 3859
Service industry 1977, 3927, 4092, 4179, 4235, 4237, 4321, 4416, 4459, 4736, 4831
Sex 709, 869, 913, 938, 1018, 1334, 1370, 1613, 2071, 2304, 2669, 2699, 2771, 2835, 2951, 2986, 3115, 3121, 3167, 3199, 3297, 3303, 3314, 3322, 3323, 3330-3333, 3335, 3344, 3347, 3348, 3353, 3374, 4387, 4551, 4733, 4761, 4777, 5470
Sex customs 522, 3303
Sex differentiation 689, 858, 1814, 2266, 3063, 3071, 3133, 3185, 3199, 3205, 3335, 4704
Sex discrimination 20, 1613, 2041, 2076, 2783, 3105, 3171, 3180, 3275, 3284, 3285, 3290, 3352, 4488, 4504, 4508, 4511, 4512, 4540, 4562, 4576, 5358
Sex distribution 2712
Sex education 2160, 2721, 3316, 3329, 3349, 5200, 5975, 5978
Sex equality 1369, 1626, 2786, 2939, 3104, 3136, 3155, 3169, 3174, 3180, 3185,

INDEX DES MATIÈRES EN ANGLAIS

3204, 3205, 3267, 4254, 4526, 4534, 4538, 4541, 4542, 4549, 4552, 4569, 5358
Sex inequality 2561, 2870, 2875, 3076, 3087, 3165, 3177, 3178, 3186, 3200, 3203, 3207-3209, 3275, 3283, 3288, 3292, 4496, 4503, 4509, 4540, 4545, 4546, 4558, 4562, 4573, 4576, 5203, 5348, 5350, 5363, 5832, 5915
Sex roles 776, 3065, 3066, 3071, 3077, 3082, 3124, 3141, 3165, 3212, 3219, 3220, 3238, 3244, 3261, 3276, 3277, 3341, 3380, 5104, 5584, 5613
Sex workers 2561, 3323, 3326, 3327, 3334, 3348, 4387, 4979, 5200, 5366, 5545, 5745, 5943
Sexism 1613, 1760, 1810, 1821, 3141, 3283, 3310, 4488, 4508, 4519, 5872
Sexology 522, 3295, 3314
Sexual abuse 593, 777, 812, 2867, 2875, 2885, 2951, 3298, 3329, 4493, 5100, 5371, 5373, 5430, 5449, 5456, 5457, 5474, 5544-5546, 5558, 5562, 5672
Sexual assault 2340, 2885, 3070, 3292, 3338, 4482, 5438, 5456-5460, 5462, 5463, 5469
Sexual behaviour 522, 897, 1303, 2608, 2688, 2727, 2806, 2912, 2980, 2981, 3085, 3294, 3295, 3297, 3298, 3300, 3302, 3303, 3306, 3310, 3316, 3318-3321, 3329, 3330, 3336-3338, 3342-3344, 3347, 3348, 3351, 3357, 3369, 3377, 3379, 3380, 3388, 5100, 5387, 5767, 5891, 5943, 5945, 5965, 5966, 5974, 5975, 5978, 5984, 5987
Sexual harassment 777, 3282, 3284, 3287-3293, 3310, 4493, 4537, 5347
Sexual health 2160, 2638, 2726, 2754, 2765, 2777, 2789, 3294, 3296, 3331, 5200, 5981, 5985
Sexual intercourse 3311, 3350, 3351, 5449
Sexual permissiveness 3300
Sexual reproduction 2692, 2706, 2726, 2744, 2747, 2754-2757, 2759, 2762, 2766, 2777, 2789, 2798, 2902, 2904, 2917, 2939, 2973, 3083, 3090, 3211, 3228, 3299, 3358, 5200
Sexuality 361, 593, 695, 769, 786, 926, 1258, 1317, 1352, 1358, 1488, 1761, 1821, 1882, 1897, 1929, 1940, 1950, 1969, 2160, 2478, 2608, 2641, 2652, 2708, 2737, 2817, 2880, 2907, 2986, 3018, 3028, 3061, 3085, 3090, 3115, 3121, 3137, 3149, 3199, 3225, 3242, 3248, 3253, 3294, 3295, 3297, 3298, 3301, 3303, 3305-3309, 3311, 3313-3317, 3321, 3323, 3324, 3328-3331, 3333, 3335, 3336, 3339-3343, 3345, 3346, 3349-3352, 3356, 3357, 3360, 3361, 3363, 3368, 3369, 3372, 3374, 3376-3379, 3382, 3383, 3385, 3386, 3389, 4512, 5100, 5196, 5371, 5438, 5459, 5698, 5745, 5837, 5943, 5946, 5966
see also: Bisexuality, Heterosexuality, Homosexuality, Lesbianism, Transsexuality
Sexually transmitted diseases 2765, 2806, 3296, 3309, 3319, 3334, 3336, 5200, 5866, 5891, 5945, 5957, 5962, 5964, 5965, 5978, 5981
Shamanism 1401
Shan 5237
Shanty towns 4269
Shapiro, Francine 5721
Sharecropping 3896, 4220
She, Lao 3222
Shelley, Mary 1970
Shift work 2975
Shopping 4341, 4678
Shopping centres 4182, 4315, 4329
Short-term analysis 2796
Shortage
  see: Labour shortage
Shu-hsien, Liu 1477
Siblings 769, 2070, 2071, 2613, 2839, 2901, 2912, 2930, 2952, 3052, 3053, 3213
Siegfried, André 4897
Sight 628, 1897
Sign language 2461
Signalling 1787
Signs 342, 1161, 1210, 1787, 1799, 1804
Sikhism 1376, 1447
Sikhs 1376, 1447
Simmel, Georg 373, 4186, 4192
Simulation 458, 492, 620, 1085, 1623, 2231, 2693, 2722, 2802, 3741, 4317, 4486
Sin 1460
Singhalese 1471
Sisters 769
Skill differentials 4486
Skilled workers 1806, 2270, 3545, 3629, 3633, 3645, 3791, 4431, 4834, 5674
Skills 651, 660, 661, 715, 729, 1018, 1093, 2017, 2040, 2098, 2186, 2199, 2253, 2262, 2286, 2410, 3580, 3603, 3604, 3671, 4398, 4439, 4440, 4460, 4465, 4571, 4602, 4645, 4664, 4671, 4717, 4756, 4769, 4779, 4784, 4786, 4798, 4804, 4807, 5492, 5552
see also: Skill differentials
Skin colour 3468, 3500, 4502
Skinner, Burrhus Frederic 599
Slave trade 3793

SUBJECT INDEX

Slavery 1620, 2336, 2901, 3067, 3094
  see also: Abolition of slavery
Slaves 263, 2901, 3528, 3793
Slavic languages 1793, 1794, 1825, 3595
Slavic studies 3427
Slavs 1816
Sleep 4698
Slums 58, 2789, 3974, 4157, 4169
Small and medium sized enterprises 1170, 3069, 3545, 3599, 4371, 4372, 4382, 4394, 4407, 4417, 4577, 4665, 4799
Small farms 2653, 3907
Small groups 999
Small towns 2841, 4119
Smallpox 5983
Smart, Ninian 1419
Smith, Adam 12, 4288
Smoking 625, 709, 890, 2738, 2845, 5389, 5407, 5433, 5956, 5968, 5986
Sobhuza, II [King] 12
Sociability 1680, 1686
Social acceptance 1313, 2733
Social accounting 4310
Social action 59, 306, 347, 365, 375, 589, 597, 1053, 1098, 1208, 1479, 1652, 2049, 2315, 2353, 2480, 3463, 3800, 3827, 4196, 4217, 4299, 4899, 4940, 5202, 5230, 5231, 5262, 5264, 5276, 5280, 5475, 5716, 5982
Social adaptation 567, 2318
Social administration 5648
Social anthropology 14, 837, 1020, 1259, 1316, 1949, 3143, 3510, 4759, 5259
Social behaviour 10, 67, 321, 334, 383, 463, 542, 561, 567, 582, 597, 652, 714, 827, 836, 845, 846, 867, 870, 896, 898, 920, 941, 1111, 1294, 1439, 2313, 2318, 2462, 2489, 2692, 2807, 2830, 3002, 3041, 3050, 3241, 3530, 3835, 3843, 4593, 4659, 4753, 4987, 5157, 5389, 5721, 5891
Social capital 61, 63, 1267, 1998, 2333, 2345, 2357, 2506, 2593, 2624, 2909, 3563, 3617, 3661, 3814, 3847, 3855-3857, 3881, 3893, 3910, 3986, 4031, 4197, 4203, 4240, 4265, 4290, 4349, 4371, 4464, 4510, 4592, 4641, 4732, 4936, 5773
Social change 19, 28, 52, 59, 166, 177, 185, 195, 243, 294, 347, 398, 477, 543, 734, 822, 829, 964, 975, 992, 1010, 1025, 1182, 1199, 1205, 1221, 1244, 1260, 1264, 1284, 1298, 1300, 1351, 1461, 1507, 1514, 1517, 1532, 1540, 1590, 1646, 1656, 1673, 1678, 1690, 1708, 1727, 1729, 1744, 1961, 2129, 2151, 2156, 2161, 2182, 2213, 2295, 2314, 2329, 2333, 2360, 2363, 2364, 2372, 2375, 2400, 2402, 2410, 2424, 2437, 2439, 2475, 2503, 2504, 2506, 2508-2510, 2512, 2514, 2516, 2517, 2519, 2521-2534, 2537, 2538, 2541, 2542, 2550, 2553, 2555, 2557, 2562, 2563, 2567, 2576, 2578, 2579, 2587, 2594, 2602, 2606, 2639, 2646, 2647, 2650, 2657, 2679, 2691, 2772, 2791, 2806, 2911, 2914, 2933, 2938, 2955, 2961, 2963, 3008, 3062, 3065, 3073, 3086, 3105, 3106, 3127, 3147, 3168, 3189, 3217, 3223, 3224, 3252, 3268, 3278, 3459, 3488, 3560, 3569, 3584, 3651, 3660, 3722, 3769, 3776, 3786, 3787, 3809, 3810, 3890, 3916, 3999, 4041, 4066, 4075, 4077, 4090, 4101, 4149, 4155, 4158, 4177, 4181, 4223, 4225, 4228, 4241, 4256, 4258, 4269, 4287, 4292, 4297, 4298, 4316, 4334, 4337, 4361, 4429, 4446, 4526, 4575, 4859, 4887, 4928, 4964, 4974, 4976, 4991, 5039, 5091, 5110, 5134, 5144, 5255, 5265, 5357, 5363, 5505, 5539, 5641, 5643, 5691, 5702, 5773, 5892
Social cognition 588, 589, 615, 650, 657, 680, 682, 708, 720, 760, 825, 850, 861, 864, 870, 914, 928, 1057, 1061, 1063, 3517
Social cohesion 1697, 1941, 1990, 2431, 2905, 4978, 5440
Social conditions 155, 322, 353, 400, 477, 811, 870, 956, 973, 1002, 1169, 1172, 1173, 1199, 1222, 1251, 1256, 1260, 1274, 1315, 1333, 1520, 1522, 1533, 1537, 1557, 1728, 1793, 2058, 2078, 2305, 2306, 2320, 2328, 2353, 2364, 2379, 2382, 2418, 2438, 2460, 2463, 2474, 2475, 2491, 2506, 2509, 2514, 2516, 2520-2522, 2524, 2526, 2528, 2532-2535, 2542, 2596, 2617, 2637, 2639, 2648-2650, 2682, 2685, 2707, 2772, 2807, 2825, 2830, 2857, 2896, 2902, 2911, 3058, 3065, 3068, 3071, 3074, 3075, 3077, 3088, 3089, 3091, 3111, 3161, 3171, 3195-3198, 3207, 3235, 3240, 3255, 3261, 3271, 3275, 3276, 3319, 3430, 3431, 3516, 3524, 3538, 3562, 3571, 3579, 3583, 3602, 3638, 3640, 3714, 3773, 3805, 3833, 3882, 3897, 3898, 3955, 4005, 4009, 4040, 4071, 4195, 4258, 4260, 4274, 4275, 4282, 4297, 4314, 4337, 4446, 4555, 4944, 4947, 4977, 4981, 4993, 4996, 4997, 5059, 5065, 5068, 5118, 5164, 5236, 5247, 5307, 5366, 5371, 5466, 5493, 5546, 5573, 5600, 5626, 5641, 5646, 5647, 5653

INDEX DES MATIÈRES EN ANGLAIS

Social conflicts 578, 879, 1031, 1078, 1199, 1484, 1712, 2306, 2509, 2587, 2643, 3496, 3914, 4185, 4400, 4404, 5190, 5206, 5240, 5372, 5445
Social consciousness 1916, 4418
Social construction 20, 109, 340, 358, 386, 387, 409, 671, 677, 968, 982, 1161, 1238, 1273, 1353, 1556, 1598, 1610, 1614, 1615, 1716, 1844, 2073, 2397, 2405, 2415, 2473, 2482, 2497, 2501, 2652, 2656, 2917, 2937, 3007, 3087, 3246, 3328, 3417, 3432, 3453, 3510, 3523, 3698, 3721, 3879, 3904, 4157, 4226, 4774, 4943, 4979, 5046, 5278, 5458, 5885
Social contract 953, 2589, 2603, 2604, 2657, 4420
Social control 393, 409, 1070, 1707, 2321, 2322, 2356, 2364, 2421, 2516, 2741, 2891, 3524, 3775, 3858, 3891, 3945, 4074, 4131, 4187, 4396, 4683, 4718, 4908, 4912, 4933, 4973, 4975, 4977, 4979, 4981, 4985-4988, 4991, 4995, 5005, 5011, 5015, 5037, 5048, 5060, 5085-5087, 5098, 5099, 5103, 5104, 5107-5109, 5114, 5126, 5130, 5131, 5133, 5134, 5143, 5154, 5364, 5369, 5465, 5608, 5767, 5881
Social costs 1442, 3752, 4065, 4251, 5057, 5622
Social democracy 3950, 4018, 4066, 4215, 4222, 4859
Social democratic parties 955, 4293, 4859
Social desirability 1313
Social development 353, 598, 1107, 1301, 1368, 1415, 1542, 1729, 2046, 2364, 2503, 2511, 2519, 2528, 2535, 2609, 2685, 2898, 3016, 3041, 3067, 3174, 3203, 3528, 3615, 3642, 3836, 4040, 4097, 4254, 4267, 4286, 4290, 4392, 4481, 4560, 4571, 4970, 5519, 5629, 5683, 5688, 5694, 5695, 5700, 5701
Social differentiation 1322, 2238, 2393, 2409, 2411, 2418, 2428, 2444, 2813, 2915, 3460, 3896, 4292, 5285
Social disadvantage 797, 2924, 2995, 3874, 4287, 4486, 4774, 5454
Social disorganization 2536, 3858
Social distance 1083, 3164
Social dynamics 387, 1043, 1051, 1469, 2161, 2302, 2313, 2329, 2419, 2514, 2594, 2967, 3509, 3892, 4132, 5265
Social ecology 3720, 3740, 3741, 4468
Social economics 2496, 5057, 5475, 5786
Social environment 9, 649, 660, 827, 1324, 1480, 2995, 3701, 4506, 5447

Social equality 2024, 2380, 2384, 2433, 3127, 3994, 4251, 5643
Social equilibrium 1920, 3404
Social exchange 656, 1047, 1062, 1069, 4146
Social exclusion 576, 1666, 1687, 1991, 2037, 2073, 2119, 2332, 2375, 2385, 2386, 2399, 2400, 2403, 2423, 2432, 2448, 2451, 2456, 2459, 2461, 2469, 2474, 2479, 2548, 2577, 2634, 2653, 2737, 3370, 3381, 3416, 3460, 3537, 3579, 3594, 3605, 3656, 3781, 3802, 3902, 3982, 3989, 4056, 4169, 4247, 4283, 4299, 4368, 4445, 4587, 4590, 4950, 4952, 5016, 5367, 5418, 5420, 5422-5424, 5547, 5564, 5617, 5620, 5638, 5642, 5653, 5657, 5741, 5914, 5951
Social factors 35, 64, 268, 548, 875, 899, 1189, 1309, 1322, 1340, 1385, 1564, 1589, 1693, 1694, 1827, 2155, 3084, 3334, 3704, 3820, 3827, 4122, 4267, 4618, 5064, 5186, 5254, 5386, 5468, 5866, 5944
Social facts 387
Social forces 2402
Social group work 2199, 5030
Social history 1, 18, 149, 155, 157, 159, 166, 171, 174, 176-178, 180, 247, 288, 294, 322, 330, 355, 522, 660, 1226, 1260, 1263, 1305, 1307, 1311, 1312, 1323, 1326, 1432, 1480, 1522, 1557, 1873, 1916, 1946, 1973, 2091, 2264, 2277, 2306, 2356, 2386, 2424, 2426, 2434, 2439, 2504, 2528, 2530, 2542, 2691, 2901, 2915, 2994, 3210, 3232, 3295, 3338, 3371, 3396, 3459, 3882, 3934, 3983, 4192, 4206, 4242, 4263, 4330, 4731, 4767, 4768, 4898, 5042, 5254, 5268, 5298, 5335, 5357, 5546, 5723
Social housing 891, 3486, 3491, 3775, 3824, 3845, 3977, 3979, 3981-3983, 3985, 3988, 3989, 4087, 4111, 4117, 4225, 4232, 4774, 5102, 5491, 5509, 5611, 5612, 5617, 5621, 5627, 5631, 5637, 5645, 5646, 5649, 5655
Social identity 548, 829, 834, 836, 848, 854, 859, 880, 881, 893, 973, 1020, 1034, 1042, 1044, 1057, 1076-1078, 1111, 1232, 1755, 1880, 1965, 2110, 2255, 2358, 2381, 2436, 2491, 2498, 2501, 2600, 3153, 3323, 3395, 3435, 3437, 3442, 3602, 3781, 4366, 4857, 5344
Social indicators 2408, 3294, 3590, 3752, 3874
Social inequality 1, 824, 2048, 2064, 2073, 2115, 2116, 2324, 2378, 2384, 2386, 2396, 2402, 2407, 2409, 2413, 2430, 2431, 2442, 2498, 2602, 2605, 2714, 2838,

SUBJECT INDEX

3488, 4004, 4271, 4274, 4290, 4291, 4293, 4304, 4486, 4983, 5190, 5244, 5445, 5475, 5516, 5603, 5642, 5665
Social influence 836, 845, 1036, 1038, 1494, 1567, 1770, 2756, 2778, 3167, 3178, 4620, 5154, 5306
Social information 3874
Social infrastructure 1817, 4042
Social integration 59, 388, 391, 709, 1026, 1321, 1494, 1532, 1685, 1809, 2033, 2047, 2073, 2136, 2312, 2375, 2403, 2404, 2409, 2429, 2433, 2459, 2469, 2474, 2475, 2483, 2530, 2585, 2618, 2664, 3439, 3444, 3471, 3537, 3554, 3562, 3568, 3577, 3582, 3594, 3602, 3607, 3611, 3635, 3802, 3826, 3833, 3902, 3983, 4001, 4005, 4091, 4287, 4585, 4722, 5033, 5420, 5432, 5436, 5638, 5702, 5741, 5904
Social interaction 13, 20, 366, 406, 463, 540, 545, 573, 703, 828, 850, 875, 911, 917, 927, 935, 944, 945, 1026, 1082, 1098, 1113, 1120, 1208, 1298, 1573, 1632, 1647, 1649, 1655, 1708, 1755, 1788, 1831, 1846, 2135, 2198, 2252, 2308, 2318, 2323, 2329, 2373, 2402, 2482, 2489, 2491, 2493, 2619, 2661, 2782, 2931, 3318, 3432, 3505, 3517, 3565, 3585, 3741, 3798, 3839, 3910, 4389, 4404, 4416, 4701, 4741, 4774, 5170, 5267, 5313, 5337, 5414, 5607, 5954
Social isolation 567, 2423, 2498, 4006, 5016, 5646, 5900
Social judgement 823, 830, 856, 869, 878, 889
Social justice 59, 1010, 1028, 2001, 2050, 2118, 2155, 2361, 2414, 2433, 2448, 2458, 2502, 2603, 3080, 3121, 3136, 3155, 3528, 3694, 3705, 3749, 3805, 3816, 3827, 3834, 3837, 4061, 4255, 4262, 4286, 4291, 4293, 4297, 4306, 4307, 4398, 4587, 4837, 4921, 4937, 4950, 4983, 4994, 5018, 5096, 5190, 5261, 5322, 5440
Social legislation 95
Social life 268, 284, 310, 320, 331, 334, 369, 387, 406, 1174, 1200, 1219, 1238, 1245, 1291, 1292, 1294, 1298, 1304, 1322, 1333, 1340, 1442, 1590, 1686, 1728, 2003, 2217, 2301, 2334, 2337, 2373, 2429, 2504, 2555, 2683, 3383, 3514, 3596, 3785, 3864, 3888, 3949, 3954, 4125, 4262, 4298, 4768, 4977, 5123, 5215, 5308, 5716
Social medicine 2344, 4730, 5724, 5727, 5728, 5731, 5733

Social mobility 448, 2314, 2383, 2420, 2434, 2435, 2517, 2591, 2594, 2926, 3085, 3571, 4245, 4474, 4583, 5268, 5302
Social mobilization 2730, 3766, 3814, 5240, 5263-5265, 5273, 5280, 5969
Social movements 799, 1010, 1087, 2010, 2514, 2522, 2634, 2730, 3070, 3137, 3154, 3162, 3391, 3454, 3766, 3771, 3775, 3827, 3968, 4242, 4398, 4832, 4853, 4867, 4871, 4898, 4949, 4950, 4960, 4965, 4966, 4989, 5183, 5226, 5228, 5229, 5241, 5244, 5246-5260, 5262, 5264-5266, 5269-5273, 5275-5280, 5419, 5887
Social networks 54, 67, 379, 466, 493, 874, 948, 1035, 1038, 1043, 1045, 1060, 1062, 1069, 1074, 1085, 1087, 1146, 1512, 1610, 1632, 1636, 1680, 1681, 1686, 1990, 2314, 2315, 2333, 2334, 2357, 2456, 2494, 2646, 2666, 2667, 2747, 2759, 2782, 2836, 2901, 2948, 3585, 3670, 3843, 3848, 3865, 3875, 3910, 3938, 4004, 4006, 4197, 4374, 4383, 4460, 4507, 4690, 5092, 5111, 5237, 5244, 5282, 5300, 5306, 5517, 5533, 5590, 5709, 5962
Social norms 243, 458, 650, 894, 1034, 1112, 1482, 1993, 2082, 2271, 2308, 2313, 2345, 2353, 2356, 2358, 2363-2365, 2369, 2373, 2375, 2421, 2661, 2755, 2799, 2880, 2920, 2929, 2990, 3199, 3307, 3806, 3847, 3946, 3969, 4180, 4240, 4295, 4457, 4581, 4793, 5122, 5128, 5164, 5335, 5368
Social order 28, 458, 1047, 2140, 2315, 2634, 3512, 3833, 4255, 4933, 4976, 4990, 4995, 5009, 5130, 5151, 5343, 5445, 5451
Social organization 277, 893, 1238, 1324, 1415, 1469, 1481, 1500, 1656, 2302, 2309, 2364, 2395, 2426, 2462, 2917, 3171, 3368, 3518, 3528, 3783, 3858, 4195, 4313, 4373, 4511, 4979, 5016, 5085, 5091, 5231
Social origin 4229, 4781, 5284
Social participation 71, 383, 687, 952, 1755, 1764, 2115, 2353, 2456, 2634, 2674, 2675, 2954, 3599, 3844, 3973, 4006, 4159, 4722, 4768, 4817, 5642
Social perception 607, 831, 850, 889, 895, 1173, 2393, 2755, 4111, 4188
Social philosophy 108, 121, 285, 295, 302, 353, 1553, 2313, 2498, 4898
Social planning 3238, 4131
Social policy 43, 50, 64, 426, 852, 1991, 2385, 2390, 2397, 2423, 2433, 2442, 2458, 2461, 2467, 2496, 2498, 2521, 2532,

INDEX DES MATIÈRES EN ANGLAIS

2539, 2602, 2677, 2688, 2707, 2745, 2763, 2804, 2870, 2873, 2997, 2999, 3091, 3114, 3220, 3261, 3312, 3491, 3809, 3869, 3895, 3981, 3989, 4008, 4044, 4052, 4063, 4111, 4185, 4259, 4274, 4283, 4298, 4299, 4497, 4563, 4580, 4686, 4789, 4835, 4862, 4872, 4945, 4949, 5004, 5017, 5023, 5126, 5146, 5225, 5367, 5371, 5414, 5416, 5463, 5471, 5477, 5482, 5496, 5498, 5504, 5509, 5512, 5513, 5532, 5537, 5541, 5547, 5548, 5569, 5571, 5574, 5588, 5591, 5602-5605, 5613, 5620, 5622-5624, 5627, 5629, 5630, 5633-5635, 5639, 5641-5643, 5647, 5649, 5650, 5654, 5661, 5665, 5666, 5716, 5786, 5927, 5929, 5958

Social problems 43, 50, 572, 574, 709, 717, 1173, 1199, 1349, 1976, 1991, 2104, 2119, 2162, 2332, 2358, 2400, 2404, 2473, 2521, 2524, 2535, 2618, 2636, 2804, 2861, 2865, 2871, 2873-2875, 2881, 2882, 2888, 3319, 3528, 3982, 3996, 4004, 4007, 4139, 4250, 4259, 4270, 4271, 4469, 4493, 4626, 4708, 4908, 4977, 4979, 5036, 5068, 5069, 5071, 5081, 5102, 5109, 5112, 5147, 5364, 5367, 5368, 5372, 5374, 5380-5382, 5384, 5396, 5400, 5403, 5407, 5411, 5414, 5418, 5419, 5421, 5424, 5425, 5427, 5429, 5431, 5435, 5436, 5440, 5445, 5450, 5455, 5464, 5471, 5472, 5534, 5546, 5570, 5596, 5670, 5702

Social protest 1976, 2339, 2567, 2634, 4244, 4980, 5236, 5240, 5257, 5275

Social psychiatry 753, 763, 765, 5736, 5900, 5919, 5922

Social psychologists 870

Social psychology 45, 88, 442, 462, 548, 554, 556, 562, 565, 570, 575, 577, 588, 590, 601, 603, 604, 606, 620, 639, 650, 652, 676, 682, 683, 687-689, 700, 703, 707, 708, 712, 720, 722, 724, 727, 730, 732, 760, 776, 781, 821-841, 843-848, 850-870, 872-896, 898, 907, 908, 911, 914-917, 919, 925, 928, 930, 935, 939, 941, 942, 945, 946, 972, 979, 999, 1021, 1022, 1027, 1034, 1037, 1041, 1044, 1046, 1047, 1052, 1056-1058, 1061, 1063, 1067, 1071, 1076, 1081-1084, 1086, 1124, 1161, 1245, 1272, 1297, 1334, 1339, 1551, 1653, 1684, 1844, 1953, 2061, 2301, 2313, 2318, 2323, 2346, 2352, 2393, 2530, 2632, 2763, 2836, 2849, 2906, 2921, 3006, 3015, 3037, 3181, 3215, 3283, 3304, 3344, 3345, 3464, 3514, 3523, 3527, 3547, 3567, 3660, 3705, 3734, 3743, 3749, 3843, 4339, 4379, 4426, 4586, 4593, 4701, 4731, 4847, 4935, 5047, 5111, 5143, 5239, 5296, 5372, 5437, 5447, 5668, 5721, 5818, 5937, 5957, 5985

Social reform 2156, 2437, 2513, 2535, 2564, 3809, 4256, 4975

Social rehabilitation 5544

Social relations 67, 321, 368, 388, 435, 517, 591, 700, 708, 728, 733, 843, 870, 872, 895, 904, 917, 923, 929, 939, 1051, 1060, 1079, 1244, 1277, 1372, 1568, 1610, 1642, 1677, 1878, 2011, 2313, 2321, 2322, 2332, 2369, 2372, 2384, 2465, 2565, 2609, 2901, 2953, 2993, 3149, 3176, 3241, 3301, 3503, 3747, 3791, 3845, 3865, 3904, 3908, 3956, 4126, 4137, 4212, 4215, 4272, 4321, 4333, 4349, 4376, 4389, 4401, 4833, 4893, 4922, 4939, 5033, 5090, 5272, 5313, 5328, 5536, 5564, 5568, 5607, 5677, 5891

Social representations 982, 1649, 1707, 1761, 2205, 2360, 3148, 3255, 3412, 3741, 5046, 5842, 5878

Social reproduction 383, 1074, 1727, 2300, 3080, 3150, 3786, 4462, 4552

Social research 31, 42, 43, 48, 50, 52, 53, 59, 64, 101, 108, 116, 180, 310, 415, 417, 423, 428, 429, 436, 438, 443, 488, 495, 499, 502, 514, 520, 522, 529, 530, 537, 568, 653, 923, 1139, 1150, 1164, 1354, 1377, 2017, 2211, 2375, 2466, 2681, 2906, 2938, 3298, 3379, 3543, 3545, 4119, 4345, 4979, 5206, 5297, 5436, 5502, 5647, 5687, 5891

Social rights 3675, 4299, 4950, 4952, 5326, 5609, 5615, 5652, 5809, 5814

Social roles 734, 745, 1038, 1861, 1981, 2439, 2508, 2529, 2653, 2677, 2679, 2916, 2953, 3273, 3280, 3315, 3391, 4068, 5776

Social science research 2, 13, 16, 25, 43, 45, 46, 54, 56, 70, 74, 167, 195, 356, 415, 418, 423, 424, 428, 431, 438, 439, 442, 445, 469, 470, 502, 514, 516, 520, 801, 890, 2809, 3182, 3396, 3545, 3666, 3978, 5038, 5880, 5960

Social sciences 2, 5, 6, 10, 13, 15, 21, 22, 24, 25, 27, 32, 38, 39, 41, 48, 56, 70, 74, 89, 100, 101, 112, 116, 174, 190, 268, 269, 301, 304, 309, 333, 334, 356, 369, 385, 396, 415, 418, 423, 429, 436, 439, 445, 447, 450, 457, 488, 495, 499, 507, 530, 533, 572, 801, 870, 912, 1089, 1102, 1216, 1224, 1231, 1244, 1245, 1289, 1366, 1610, 1628, 1870, 2182, 2227, 2281,

SUBJECT INDEX

2284, 2462, 2716, 2907, 3063, 3700, 3774, 3790, 3795, 4181, 4205, 4351, 4889, 4901, 4948, 5075, 5206, 5297, 5310, 5357, 5704
Social scientists 48, 1620
Social security 2458, 2657, 2677, 2712, 2846, 3001, 3169, 3588, 3619, 3985, 4191, 4247, 4293, 4299, 4411, 4439, 4456, 4479, 4580, 4594, 4595, 4862, 5475, 5487, 5504, 5506, 5507, 5535, 5551, 5581, 5603, 5606, 5610, 5617, 5620, 5622-5624, 5634, 5641, 5642, 5645, 5648, 5654, 5660, 5766, 5806
Social security financing 5605
Social services 43, 767, 2463, 2469, 2477, 3630, 4152, 4169, 4585, 5373, 5422, 5478, 5480-5482, 5492, 5500, 5513, 5526, 5537, 5544, 5548, 5549, 5556, 5559, 5569, 5581, 5586, 5591, 5596, 5599, 5613, 5614, 5619, 5623, 5629, 5630, 5635, 5639, 5641, 5644, 5647, 5653, 5663, 5665, 5666, 5674, 5679, 5688, 5693, 5697, 5698, 5702, 5705-5708, 5711, 5712, 5715, 5716, 5718, 5719, 5739, 5780, 5820, 5903, 5904
Social space 334, 1979, 2385, 3138, 3387, 3772, 3788, 4050, 4136, 4329
Social status 710, 1686, 1835, 1861, 2078, 2376, 2378, 2386, 2393, 2408, 2410, 2430, 2444, 2449, 2474, 2545, 2591, 2631, 2677, 2679, 2917, 3013, 3192, 3215, 3407, 3410, 3563, 3996, 4187, 4376, 4567, 4781, 5168, 5296, 5300, 5436
Social stereotypes 832, 5842
Social stratification 33, 65, 285, 308, 879, 1205, 1227, 1376, 1513, 2035, 2063, 2223, 2324, 2374-2377, 2381, 2382, 2384, 2385, 2387-2391, 2393-2395, 2398, 2405, 2410-2412, 2417, 2418, 2420, 2422, 2427, 2430-2438, 2440, 2441, 2444, 2445, 2447, 2449, 2466, 2468, 2476, 2487, 2499, 2524, 2548, 2591, 3076, 3171, 3436, 3443, 3512, 3820, 3992, 3996, 4065, 4187, 4209, 4271, 4294, 4474, 4533, 4921, 4983, 5016, 5077, 5215, 5296, 5423, 5430, 5487, 5625
Social structure 40, 41, 65, 285, 326, 329, 347, 368, 372, 394, 837, 1002, 1062, 1074, 1079, 1087, 1222, 1800, 1878, 1974, 2064, 2300, 2305, 2312, 2319, 2320, 2322, 2326, 2327, 2334, 2338, 2384, 2391-2394, 2398, 2400, 2427, 2430, 2434, 2435, 2437, 2438, 2441, 2445, 2494, 2532, 2535, 2536, 2555, 2564, 2578, 2591, 2597, 2657, 2675, 2701, 2870,
2923, 3087, 3418, 3668, 3899, 3909, 3917, 3927, 4314, 4441, 4746, 4921, 4942, 4977, 5092, 5104, 5245, 5302
Social success 2923, 3254
Social support 767, 771, 793, 935, 948, 1054, 1691, 2299, 2494, 2585, 2712, 2852, 2881, 2890, 2934, 2979, 3015, 3048, 3293, 3370, 3381, 3586, 3619, 3846, 4448, 4741, 5033, 5116, 5244, 5400, 5413, 5463, 5475, 5488, 5492, 5517, 5521, 5525, 5531-5533, 5552, 5566, 5572, 5574, 5590, 5669, 5687, 5693, 5716, 5736, 5742
Social surveys 477, 527, 2683, 3210, 3271, 3588, 4119, 5433, 5449
Social systems 65, 279, 287, 306, 318, 336, 359, 368, 369, 372, 380, 381, 391, 392, 394, 402, 403, 408, 439, 821, 1054, 1121, 1282, 1545, 2140, 2300, 2302, 2305, 2310, 2312, 2320, 2322, 2329, 2384, 2391, 2394, 2395, 2405, 2411, 2420, 2427, 2435, 2436, 2445, 2532, 2758, 2955, 2984, 2990, 3800, 3865, 4050, 4228, 4837, 4970, 5306, 5821
Social theory 6, 10, 14, 21, 26, 32, 34, 35, 41, 53, 68, 75, 89, 108, 121, 158, 214, 217, 243, 253, 268, 269, 275, 277, 285, 287, 294, 296, 307-309, 311, 315-318, 320, 322, 325, 326, 328-330, 332, 334, 335, 337, 340, 341, 343, 345, 348, 351-354, 357, 358, 361-363, 366-368, 371, 372, 375, 377, 378, 381, 383-385, 387, 390, 392, 393, 395, 397, 401, 403-407, 410, 430, 439, 463, 474, 575, 825, 875, 881, 922, 968, 990, 1011, 1031, 1039, 1053, 1074, 1081, 1115, 1130, 1139, 1158, 1166, 1194, 1199, 1210, 1214, 1215, 1221, 1235, 1238, 1245, 1250, 1253, 1263, 1272, 1273, 1276, 1278, 1280, 1281, 1289, 1325, 1351, 1366, 1390, 1403, 1598, 1614, 1647, 1651, 1706, 1792, 1848, 1879, 1921, 2211, 2217, 2300, 2302, 2310, 2317, 2319, 2330, 2331, 2346, 2349, 2384, 2395, 2402, 2413, 2417, 2428, 2433, 2465, 2477, 2528, 2531, 2546, 2568, 2589, 2622, 2742, 3084, 3086, 3100, 3101, 3124, 3130, 3139, 3142, 3144, 3151, 3339, 3368, 3376, 3444, 3453, 3504, 3629, 3693, 3698, 3721, 3788, 3802, 4180, 4181, 4186, 4193, 4196, 4360, 4419, 4837, 4865, 4889, 4893, 4894, 4898, 4911, 4918, 4920-4922, 4925, 4987, 5049, 5074, 5086, 5122, 5130, 5246, 5273, 5309, 5369, 5372, 5603, 5619, 5650, 5652
see also: Post-structural analysis

INDEX DES MATIÈRES EN ANGLAIS

Social unrest 4977, 4993
Social values 160, 1292, 2283, 2313, 2343, 3081, 3589, 3806, 4318, 4642
Social welfare 461, 929, 1121, 1480, 1590, 2307, 2390, 2454, 2455, 2466, 2469, 2489, 2496, 2648, 2764, 2865, 2866, 2870, 2882, 3169, 3528, 3555, 3675, 3775, 4111, 4169, 4231, 4256, 4259, 4283, 4299, 4469, 4563, 4979, 4983, 5023, 5071, 5096, 5126, 5143, 5151, 5366, 5427, 5475-5477, 5482-5484, 5490, 5521, 5530, 5532, 5533, 5545, 5549, 5556, 5559, 5572, 5574, 5581, 5598, 5600, 5601, 5611-5614, 5616, 5619, 5628, 5632, 5633, 5639, 5642-5644, 5647, 5658-5661, 5665, 5672, 5676, 5685, 5691, 5696, 5699, 5700, 5706, 5708, 5711, 5716, 5717, 5739, 5742, 5795, 5796, 5806, 5819, 5927
Social work 764, 1053, 2423, 2456, 2582, 2602, 2859, 2865, 2869, 2884, 2887, 2952, 3586, 4585, 5016, 5023, 5373, 5427, 5464, 5481, 5483, 5488, 5490, 5495, 5527, 5530, 5533, 5540, 5542-5545, 5549, 5550, 5554, 5556, 5557, 5559, 5566, 5569, 5570, 5572, 5574, 5578, 5586, 5589, 5599, 5635, 5647, 5657, 5663-5667, 5669, 5670, 5672-5674, 5676-5679, 5683-5689, 5692-5716, 5719, 5720, 5722, 5723, 5739, 5764, 5904, 5908, 5910, 5911, 5917, 5923
Social workers 2464, 2882, 4789, 5023, 5483, 5488, 5501, 5527, 5530, 5540, 5545, 5549, 5556, 5569, 5572, 5595, 5630, 5663, 5666, 5667, 5672, 5674, 5676, 5685, 5687, 5689, 5690, 5692, 5694, 5695, 5697, 5700, 5701, 5705-5714, 5716, 5718, 5719, 5722
Socialism 284, 1936, 1979, 2416, 2563, 3100, 4210, 4213, 4215, 4222, 4864, 4898, 4922, 4934, 4942, 4946
see also: Market socialism, State socialism
Socialist parties 4293
Socialist societies 1295
Socialist states 23, 1274, 5130
Socialization 359, 573, 677, 1052, 1131, 1512, 1542, 1626, 1788, 2301, 2304, 2316, 2325, 2447, 2631, 2870, 2897, 2898, 2909, 3011, 3026, 3173, 3216, 3271, 3568, 4320, 4427, 4481, 4543, 4608, 4622, 4722, 4900, 5050, 5108, 5266, 5344, 5534, 5538, 5563
see also: Political socialization
Society 6, 7, 17, 279, 284, 301, 329, 394, 397, 403, 405, 406, 408, 439, 441, 763, 1195, 1200, 1333, 1417, 1432, 1461, 1483, 1493, 1495, 1524, 1590, 1609, 1646, 1729, 1756, 1790, 1815, 1837, 1852, 1933, 1961, 2305, 2310, 2322, 2324, 2327, 2328, 2337, 2343, 2392, 2414, 2437, 2438, 2440, 2451, 2463, 2507, 2527, 2556, 2563, 2567, 2600, 2614, 2662, 2942, 2961, 2983, 3071, 3092, 3111, 3262, 3552, 3707, 3712, 3723, 3753, 3783, 3861, 3998, 4196, 4200, 4206, 4256, 4307, 4349, 4351, 4444, 4458, 4469, 4983, 5047, 5058, 5159, 5246, 5294, 5332, 5338
see also: Agrarian society, Civil society, Complex societies, Consumer society, Future societies, Individual and society, Industrial society, Information society, International society, Mass society, Modern society, Political society, Post-communist societies, Post-industrial society, Pre-industrial society, Primitive society, Rural society, Socialist societies, Urban society
Socio-economic development 982, 2514, 2568, 2606, 2740, 2767, 4189, 4195, 4197, 4261, 4279, 4793, 4948
Sociobiology 27, 596, 649, 656, 1567, 2744, 2912, 2973, 2983, 3304, 3318
Socioeconomic development 2833, 3086, 3275, 3624, 3801, 4066, 4203, 4337, 4347, 4495, 4606, 4890
Socioeconomic status 577, 710, 766, 1078, 2013, 2021, 2032, 2047, 2055, 2119, 2276, 2347, 2382, 2407, 2432, 2444, 2612, 2624, 2652, 2709, 2732, 2760, 2828, 2840, 2841, 2843, 2875, 2887, 2948, 3057, 3182, 3278, 3391, 3394, 3399, 3434, 3459, 3516, 3538, 3577, 3603, 3696, 3715, 3835, 3901, 3992, 4015, 4018, 4087, 4152, 4249, 4257, 4264, 4271, 4291, 4292, 4454, 4495, 4567, 5071, 5144, 5382, 5396, 5445, 5475, 5636, 5763, 5773, 5804, 5830, 5844, 5961
Sociography 24
Sociolinguistics 76, 538, 571, 610, 622, 853, 916, 930, 940, 945, 959, 979, 1120, 1689, 1722, 1784, 1788, 1790, 1791, 1793-1796, 1799, 1801-1803, 1805, 1807, 1808, 1810, 1811, 1813-1821, 1825-1827, 1832, 1833, 1835, 1837, 1838, 1843, 1846, 1847, 2121, 2208, 2523, 2936, 2940, 3358, 3363, 5170
Sociological analysis 28, 50, 65, 167, 180, 323, 347, 409, 413, 448, 482, 497, 1020, 1162, 1306, 1354, 1366, 1561, 1595, 1629, 1639, 1652, 1743, 1944, 1962, 2302,

SUBJECT INDEX

2315, 2319, 2330, 2374, 2404, 2427, 2445, 2456, 2526, 2556, 2645, 2683, 3463, 3514, 3565, 3617, 3638, 3848, 3860, 3946, 4298, 4344, 4584, 4930, 4959, 4966, 5046, 5117, 5249, 5264, 5276, 5285
Sociological anthropology 2544
Sociological associations 38, 4766
Sociological methodology 4, 34, 41, 50, 51, 55, 65, 112, 119, 312, 321, 330, 358, 364, 374, 377, 391, 392, 412, 413, 415, 423, 440, 474, 485, 491, 496, 510, 515, 526, 527, 921, 2315, 2411, 2583, 3194, 4930, 5435
Sociological research 1, 4, 5, 9, 20, 47, 50, 51, 54, 55, 62, 65, 66, 69, 75, 77, 81, 119, 166, 180, 321, 339, 347, 356, 412, 414, 416, 419, 423, 433, 440, 441, 444, 449, 450, 454, 456, 463, 466, 472, 474, 497, 511, 523, 710, 836, 1032, 1191, 1327, 1408, 1459, 1563, 2404, 2435, 2436, 2448, 2462, 2465, 2583, 2635, 2675, 2848, 2869, 2891, 2919, 2959, 2964, 2979, 3020, 3051, 3067, 3233, 3343, 3360, 3407, 3424, 3513, 3544, 3748, 4090, 4192, 4891, 4982, 5072, 5073, 5095, 5135, 5206, 5277, 5296, 5557, 5673, 5892, 5959, 5979
Sociological theory 5, 7, 14-16, 21, 23, 26, 27, 29-31, 33, 34, 41, 44, 51, 55, 65-67, 69, 72, 75, 115, 119, 122, 143, 197, 223, 243, 248, 269, 275, 287, 288, 292, 294, 304, 306, 307, 312-314, 316-319, 321, 323, 324, 327, 328, 330, 332, 334-337, 339, 341, 345, 347, 350-352, 354-357, 361, 363, 364, 369-374, 377, 378, 381, 383, 386-390, 394-396, 398-400, 402-404, 406, 408, 474, 563, 567, 745, 759, 875, 943, 1062, 1110, 1120, 1152, 1194, 1196, 1201, 1211, 1212, 1229, 1233, 1251, 1263-1266, 1273, 1350, 1352, 1395, 1403, 1406, 1446, 1449, 1570, 1575, 1581, 1621, 1633, 1640, 1649, 1651, 1693, 1705, 1706, 1715, 1800, 1842, 1858, 1866, 1944, 2117, 2300, 2302, 2312, 2315, 2319, 2322, 2329, 2341, 2384, 2397, 2430, 2435, 2436, 2440, 2448, 2510, 2519, 2531, 2540, 2555, 2568, 2953, 3057, 3086, 3100, 3101, 3142, 3151, 3194, 3514, 3528, 3632, 3701, 3705, 3712, 3946, 4187, 4196, 4239, 4329, 4404, 4616, 4888, 4953, 4987, 5073, 5075, 5095, 5120, 5270, 5276, 5277, 5319, 5332, 5336, 5668, 5709, 5817, 5878
Sociologists 1, 4, 11, 23, 36, 44, 50, 58, 62, 65-68, 72, 75, 144, 288, 316, 330, 341, 343, 347, 373-375, 377, 388, 395, 398, 400, 402, 403, 423, 801, 1212, 1431, 1866, 2302, 2411, 4195, 4241, 4766, 4888, 4898, 4930, 5098, 5225
Sociology 3, 5, 10, 11, 16-18, 23, 25, 26, 28, 31, 32, 36, 38, 40, 41, 44, 51, 55, 58, 62, 66, 67, 72, 77, 81, 100, 130, 166, 269, 288, 318, 319, 329, 330, 334, 338, 343, 348, 354, 359, 371, 385, 392, 395, 396, 398, 401, 404, 407, 450, 801, 912, 1002, 1047, 1107, 1553, 1858, 1870, 1944, 2331, 2393, 2462, 2853, 2918, 2930, 3158, 3513, 3693, 3699, 3704, 3900, 4131, 4314, 4323, 4413, 4507, 4754, 4762, 4783, 4978, 5106, 5166, 5204, 5332, 5485, 5523, 5665, 5817
see also: Applied sociology, Criminal sociology, Economic sociology, Educational sociology, History of sociology, Industrial sociology, Medical sociology, Military sociology, Occupational sociology, Political sociology, Rural sociology, Sociology of education, Sociology of science, Teaching of sociology, Urban sociology
Sociology of art 1852, 1855, 1866
Sociology of culture 1192, 1855, 2443
Sociology of education 2024, 2051, 2062, 2069, 2080, 2104, 2146, 3340
Sociology of knowledge 5, 70, 127, 130, 746, 1115, 1116, 1411, 1556, 1575, 1587, 1595, 1610, 1614, 1617, 1629, 2565, 3176, 4610, 5885
Sociology of law 3284, 4511, 4998, 5025, 5124, 5150, 5151, 5153, 5154, 5158, 5166, 5168, 5172, 5183, 5185, 5187-5189, 5192, 5199, 5204, 5206, 5211
Sociology of leisure 1301, 2906
Sociology of literature 1927, 1953
Sociology of music 1309, 1972, 1982, 1987, 1988
Sociology of organizations 416, 1064, 1090, 1109, 1115, 1132, 1142, 1145, 1385, 4355, 4392, 4403, 4409, 4413, 4622, 4627, 4731
Sociology of religion 56, 400, 1228, 1377, 1381, 1385, 1401, 1403, 1406, 1410, 1411, 1415, 1418, 1425, 1430, 1431, 1433-1435, 1437, 1446, 1448-1450, 1461, 1464, 1475, 1492, 1508, 1521, 3919, 5722
Sociology of science 29, 498, 537, 1556, 1561, 1562, 1575, 1577, 1579, 1584, 1596, 1610, 1614, 1616, 1617, 1619, 5885

INDEX DES MATIÈRES EN ANGLAIS

Sociology of sport 962, 1305, 1306, 1326, 1330, 1341, 1355-1358, 1369, 3217
Sociology of the family 50, 2899, 2903, 2906, 2917, 2948, 2971, 3047
Sociology of theatre 1862
Sociology of work 412, 440, 715, 2953, 3062, 3347, 4289, 4365, 4368, 4373, 4377, 4378, 4382, 4389, 4395, 4398, 4401, 4403-4405, 4411, 4416, 4448, 4456, 4461, 4468, 4469, 4471, 4477, 4488, 4616, 4700, 4702, 4704, 4715, 4718, 4732, 4740, 4745, 4758, 4761, 4771, 4821, 4832, 4856, 4867
Socrates 270
Software 1667, 2179, 4382
Soil degradation 3733
Soil fertility 3813
Soil improvement 3733
Sokal, Alan 135
Soldiers 5606
Solicitors 5203
Solidarity 371, 923, 929, 931, 1151, 1499, 2313, 2332, 2590, 2682, 3155, 3730, 3842, 3892, 4250, 4299, 4834, 4850, 4945, 4970, 5151
see also: Group solidarity
Solzhenitsyn, Aleksandr 4898
Songhay 1888
Songs 1334, 1364, 1972, 1973, 1976, 1978, 1987, 1989, 4990
see also: Folk songs
Sons 2628, 2629, 2927, 2984, 3023, 3202
Soul 220
Sovereignty 2547, 2553, 3672, 4287, 4939, 4957, 5207, 5232, 5256, 5334
Soviet studies 166, 183
see also: Post-Soviet studies
Space 291, 313, 572, 976, 1031, 1195, 1200, 1220, 1292, 1302, 1316, 1317, 1348, 1362, 1365, 1399, 1586, 1928, 1984, 2191, 2325, 2493, 2546, 3093, 3422, 3692, 3741, 3772, 3787, 3790, 3864, 4082, 4127, 4144, 4219, 4489, 4521, 5240, 5418, 5424
see also: Spatial analysis
Space economics 3790
Spaniards 710, 3575
Spanish Civil War 1869
Spanish language 240, 1795, 1819, 1839, 1865, 4914
Spark, Muriel 3262
Spatial analysis 1302, 1657, 2493, 4019, 5838, 5968
Spatial dimension 39, 382, 613, 641, 642, 982, 1298, 1393, 1605, 1661, 1920, 2413, 2421, 2481, 2556, 2658, 3231, 3301, 3540, 3693, 3757, 3775, 3780, 3785, 3786, 3788, 3860, 3876, 3907, 3945, 3969, 3996, 4048, 4065, 4102, 4120, 4124, 4129, 4131, 4134, 4140, 4149, 4168, 4315, 4329, 4346, 4350, 4939, 5845
Spatial distribution 452, 1362, 1657, 3625, 3773, 3879, 4046, 4092
Spatial models 39
Special education 2019, 2026, 2154, 2225
Species 1558, 3755, 3759
Speech 378, 703, 818, 901, 1639, 1642, 1647, 1650, 1653, 1788-1790, 1807, 1808, 1810, 1815, 1827, 1829, 1830, 1840, 1846, 1872, 1877, 2523, 2940, 3002, 5184, 5444
Speech analysis 1652
Spencer-Brown, G. 380
Spielberg, Steven 1882
Spinoza, Benedictus de 254
Spirit possession 5898
Spirits 263, 2819
Spirituality 225, 581, 719, 998, 1249, 1372, 1381, 1384, 1416, 1421, 1424, 1427, 1444, 1446, 1454, 1457, 1477, 1501, 1549, 1551, 1975, 1983, 2106, 2673, 2890, 3145, 3382, 4360, 5409
Sport 962, 1326
see also: Anthropology of sport, Sociology of sport
Sports 951, 979, 1081, 1305, 1306, 1308, 1315, 1327, 1330, 1341, 1344, 1347, 1350, 1353-1358, 1368, 1369, 2321, 2618, 3217, 3252, 4767, 5448
see also: Baseball, Football
Squatters 3961, 3974, 4169, 4302
Staff 411, 1010, 2240, 4662, 5919
see also: Hospital staff
Stakeholder 411, 1097, 1127, 1146, 1308, 2110, 4417, 4420
Stalinism 4973
Standard of living 1177, 2123, 2695, 2833, 3661, 3984, 4163, 4250, 4263, 4272, 4276, 4295, 4299, 4334, 4606, 4947, 5286, 5598
Standardization 1794, 1826, 2214, 2448, 4601, 5763
Stars 1217, 1228, 2618
State 173, 351, 578, 1164, 2137, 2143, 2170, 2230, 2265, 2307, 2336, 2414, 2415, 2544, 2662, 3070, 3085, 3114, 3187, 3323, 3410, 3469, 3474, 3475, 3499, 3531, 3568, 3624, 3829, 3862, 3896, 3921, 3922, 4208, 4226, 4237, 4303, 4459, 4782, 4816, 4818, 4828, 4893, 4907, 4932, 4949, 4953, 4956, 4959, 4961,

SUBJECT INDEX

4966, 4968, 4976, 4978, 5130, 5162, 5287, 5314, 5334, 5445, 5546, 5553, 5626, 5644
see also: Church and state, Heads of state, Nation state, Socialist states, State theory, State-society relations
State and law 5192
State formation 151, 3420, 3475, 4206, 4890
State fragmentation 4892
State intervention 3806, 4235
State legislatures 4133
State of emergency 3611
State schools 2131, 4962
State socialism 746
State structure 5227
State theory 4961
State-society relations 1199, 1467, 2576, 2752, 3106, 3474, 3922, 4169, 4774, 4823, 4832, 4945, 4951, 4969, 4970, 5048, 5148, 5162, 5214, 5222, 5237
Statics 1555
Statistical analysis 101, 163, 453, 473, 478, 479, 481, 524, 1749, 1798, 2523, 2629, 2817, 2829, 2958, 2974, 2996, 3407, 3528, 4766, 5324, 5448, 5965, 5983
Statistical data 92, 478, 481, 512, 520, 2381
Statistical decision 638
Statistical methods 163, 421, 424, 445, 447, 453, 468, 475, 479-481, 491, 494, 495, 499
Statistical models 446, 468, 478, 479, 482, 489, 2116, 4486, 4766
Statistics 101, 116, 421, 433, 434, 451, 468, 475, 478, 480, 494-496, 499, 502, 631, 1059, 1431, 1442, 1610, 2089, 2101, 2234, 2533, 2626, 2688, 2716, 2776, 2794, 2808, 2823, 2829, 2840, 2852, 3408, 4175, 4266, 4582, 4646, 4723, 4780, 4796, 5324, 5389, 5728, 5744
see also: Population statistics
Steel 4079
Steel industry 4618
Step-parents 2613, 2917, 2932, 2949
Stereotypes 20, 574, 657, 822, 824, 826, 832, 834, 835, 843, 846, 853, 854, 857, 859, 861, 863, 865, 866, 877, 880, 881, 891, 895, 1014, 1310, 1339, 1768, 1899, 1909, 1946, 2009, 2061, 2584, 2657, 2665, 2677, 2900, 2950, 3181, 3229, 3245, 3248, 3257, 3281, 3372, 3382, 3404, 3414, 3416, 3457, 3527, 3562, 3649, 3894, 4265, 4472, 4521, 4543, 4661, 5253, 5717, 5837
see also: National stereotypes, Racial stereotypes, Social stereotypes

Sterilization 2726, 2752
see also: Female sterilization, Male sterilization
Stimuli 594, 643, 667, 686
Stochastic models 446
Stochastic processes 1638
Stock exchange 2571, 4352, 4366, 4870
Stock exchange speculation 4352
Stockholders 4420, 4422, 4870
Stocks 4242, 4812
Stores 4027, 4678
Stories 470, 1157, 1810, 1907, 1936, 1943, 2233, 3254, 3537, 5360
see also: Life stories
Story telling 919, 1717, 2643
Strategic planning 920, 1055, 1127, 2268, 3821, 3857, 3945, 4067, 4312, 4409, 4655, 4666-4668, 5271, 5337, 5740, 5977
Stratemeyer, Edward 3225
Strike, Kenneth A. 2218
Strikes 1027, 2251, 4840, 4843, 4845-4847, 4850, 4874
Structural adjustment 2513, 2568, 2767, 3868, 4223, 4236, 4245, 4278, 4455, 4682, 4968
Structural analysis 308, 345, 391, 471, 948, 1069, 1136, 1146, 1632, 2413, 2428, 4014, 4837, 5075, 5277, 5300
Structural change 1011, 2123, 2833, 4221
Structural functionalism 400
Structural unemployment 2519
Structuralism 14, 1068, 1221, 2384, 3117, 3775, 4612, 5245
Student behaviour 2065
Student movements 1264, 2250, 2251, 2293, 2294, 2567, 3295, 5267, 5268
Students 11, 469, 541, 557, 588, 631, 710, 724, 751, 791, 942, 1014, 1024, 1058, 1083, 1203, 1626, 1654, 1993, 2002, 2008, 2009, 2021, 2028, 2033, 2045, 2052, 2055-2057, 2060, 2072, 2075, 2077, 2102, 2104, 2129, 2157, 2168, 2183, 2186, 2190, 2193-2195, 2206, 2223, 2238, 2239, 2245, 2246, 2248, 2253, 2268, 2276, 2277, 2288, 2290, 2444, 2454, 2482, 2523, 2585, 2913, 2945, 3232, 3274, 3282, 3291-3293, 3296, 3362, 3477, 3517, 3860, 4062, 4435, 4454, 4785, 5444, 5470, 5697, 5704, 5844, 5955, 5961
see also: Foreign students, Women students
Study
see: American studies
Subaltern 1978, 3148, 5162, 5229
Subcontracting 4448

Subculture 155, 1331, 1335, 1340, 1352, 1370, 1974, 1986, 2630, 3156, 3387, 4007, 5108, 5429
Subject 406, 744, 2322, 3151
Subjectivity 20, 109, 148, 162, 204, 226, 300, 320, 391, 399, 428, 507, 645, 744, 801, 839, 892, 1137, 1161, 1195, 1232, 1289, 1876, 1917, 3130, 3153, 3293, 3350, 3438, 3537, 3788, 3953, 4392, 4808, 5084, 5166, 5430, 5692
Subnational government 5213
Subsidies 3169, 3590, 3979, 3988, 4587, 4756
Substance abuse 508, 723, 2621, 2633, 2845, 2872, 2951, 3995, 4683, 5381-5385, 5387, 5388, 5391-5394, 5396, 5402, 5407, 5409-5411, 5413, 5421, 5480, 5658, 5818
see also: Dependency rehabilitation
Substance use 5409
Suburban areas 2451, 2633, 3725, 3983, 3993, 4026, 4077, 4112, 4119, 4150, 4164, 4175, 4176, 4489, 4490, 5426, 5526
Subversion 3368, 5165
Succession 2398, 4625
Suffrage 3146
Sufism 1521
Sugar cane 3882
Suicide 793, 2719, 2831, 2844, 4994, 5432-5436, 5773, 5838, 5849, 5858, 5882, 5887, 5889, 5895
Sullivan, Louis 4131
Sunni 1537
Supermarkets 4678
Supernatural 1438
Supervisors 1783, 4363, 5712
Supply 4136, 4380
see also: Food supply, Labour supply, Water supply
Supply and demand 4322
Supreme Court 5034, 5038, 5154, 5155, 5160, 5171, 5183
Surgery 1189, 3272, 5878
Suri 3531
Surname 3394
Surveillance 178, 2709, 4140, 4683, 4954, 4986-4988, 4995, 5016, 5881, 5885
Survey analysis 434, 509, 520, 525, 531, 535, 2768, 4618, 5763, 5788
Survey data 500, 512, 518-520, 524, 525, 531, 535, 2157, 2759, 3633, 5891
Surveys 198, 424, 448, 501, 502, 509, 510, 512, 513, 519, 520, 522, 534-537, 751, 791, 1119, 1327, 1349, 1715, 1783, 1841, 2006, 2145, 2583, 2648, 2692, 2726, 2732, 2834, 2875, 2930, 2942, 3025, 3434, 3455, 3570, 3633, 3748, 3991, 3993, 3996, 4145, 4253, 4276, 4277, 4306, 4499, 4723, 4837, 4985, 5114, 5132, 5213, 5773, 5829, 5872
see also: Economic surveys, Mail surveys, Panel surveys, Sample surveys, Social surveys
Survival strategy 596, 1995, 3574, 3902, 4273, 5229, 5430
Sustainability 1093, 1152, 3697, 3705, 3749, 3759, 3765, 3771, 3796, 3801, 3805, 3808-3811, 3813, 3817, 3819-3822, 3827, 3924, 3961, 4028, 4037, 4061, 4163
Sustainable development 1221, 1565, 2508, 2638, 3126, 3694, 3698, 3702, 3715, 3735, 3756, 3761, 3763, 3766, 3796, 3797, 3799-3805, 3807-3823, 3857, 3918, 3923, 3924, 3949, 4025, 4037, 4041, 4061, 4063, 4082, 4096, 4102, 4104, 4109, 4123, 4166, 4170, 5221
Swahili 1709
Symbolic interaction 2645
Symbolism 331, 342, 380, 955, 982, 1258, 1308, 1343, 1347, 1383, 1418, 1799, 1868, 1928, 3093, 3128, 3367, 3418, 4065, 4115, 4349, 4759
see also: Religious symbolism
Symbols 8, 122, 348, 810, 961, 963, 1000, 1100, 1161, 1238, 1899, 3701, 4192
Syncretism
see: Religious syncretism
Syntax 623, 5170
Systematization 121
Systems analysis 634, 4428
Systems theory 345, 350, 359, 371, 372, 376, 380, 386, 402, 552, 1006, 1115, 1652, 1705, 1999, 2323, 2409, 2411, 2508, 3037, 3705, 4833, 4970, 5236, 5668, 5735
Taboo 650, 1822, 2394, 3304
Tales
see: Folk tales
Tamils 5331
Taoism 200, 1382, 1456, 1458, 1473
Tarde, Gabriel 67
Taste 1745
Tatar 1392
Tax revenue 5620
Taxation 4281, 5475
Taxes 5793
see also: Income tax
Taxonomy 650, 1408, 1999, 2308, 3345
Taylor, Charles 206, 207, 266
Teacher training 2090, 2095, 2098, 2103, 4801, 5642
Teacher-student relationship 2027, 2118, 3292, 3509

SUBJECT INDEX

Teachers 435, 523, 1654, 2014, 2024, 2044, 2079-2086, 2088, 2090, 2091, 2093-2106, 2112, 2118, 2121, 2146, 2173, 2184, 2187, 2189, 2195, 2198, 2200, 2202, 2215, 2218, 2225, 2235, 2237, 2241, 2246, 2316, 2453, 2592, 2602, 3031, 3260, 4494, 4735, 4772, 5213, 5465, 5550, 5642

Teaching 47, 53, 1018, 1224, 1226, 1236, 1592, 1631, 1715, 1858, 1991, 1992, 2009, 2011, 2015, 2027, 2056, 2075, 2079, 2084-2087, 2091, 2092, 2094-2096, 2098, 2099, 2101-2104, 2114, 2116, 2121, 2148, 2164, 2169, 2174, 2176-2178, 2181-2183, 2185, 2187-2189, 2191, 2195, 2196, 2198, 2202, 2204, 2206-2208, 2212, 2215, 2216, 2218-2220, 2225, 2229, 2233, 2237, 2279, 2285, 2288, 2291, 2294, 2453, 2602, 3102, 3115, 4735, 4772, 4801, 5704
see also: Language teaching, Religious teachings

Teaching methods 2098, 2145, 2172, 2173, 2175, 2184, 2200, 2201

Teaching of sociology 38, 44, 2200

Teamwork 463, 655, 1033, 1048, 1056, 1065, 1071, 1072, 1080, 1091, 1135, 1660, 4356, 4384, 4408, 4428, 4607, 4608, 4617, 4618, 4670, 4741, 5715, 5846, 5934

Technical education 2125, 4805, 4806

Technicians 4563, 4769

Technocracy 340, 2219

Technological change 532, 537, 1149, 1172, 1199, 1226, 1333, 1554, 1563, 1576, 1593, 1603, 1621, 1641, 1667, 1689, 1693, 1725, 2139, 2295, 2527, 2565, 2566, 2571, 2579, 2581, 2679, 2772, 3223, 3776, 3820, 4031, 4075, 4122, 4213, 4354, 4382, 4387, 4393, 4397, 4434, 4750, 5372, 5877

Technological forecasting 1603, 2527

Technology 37, 39, 291, 634, 1054, 1113, 1154, 1275, 1286, 1554, 1559, 1562, 1563, 1566, 1568, 1588, 1595, 1598, 1609, 1616, 1621, 1622, 1626, 1656, 1663, 1679, 1690, 1697, 1759, 1822, 1851, 1996, 2039, 2176, 2262, 2266, 2286, 2328, 2508, 2563, 2731, 2758, 3127, 3206, 3223, 3700, 3704, 4030, 4049, 4056, 4179, 4417, 4428, 4570, 4571, 4574, 4649, 4658, 4715, 4738, 4744, 4763, 4786, 5790, 5864, 5879
see also: Biotechnology, Communications technology, Digital technology, Educational technology, High technology, History of technology, Information technology, New technology, Reproductive technology

Technology transfer 2580

Telecommunications 1298, 1302, 1634, 1637, 1641, 1657, 1660, 1661, 1663, 1678, 1686, 1688, 1732, 1780, 2554, 3927, 4095, 4122, 4124, 4167, 4688, 4738

Telematics 1688, 2201

Telephone 518, 532, 1686, 1687, 2588, 4732

Television 449, 1100, 1191, 1223, 1227, 1333, 1334, 1336, 1337, 1359-1361, 1641, 1687, 1690, 1695, 1698, 1701, 1707, 1709-1711, 1716, 1717, 1719, 1725, 1729, 1731, 1732, 1737, 1738, 1740, 1748, 1750, 1752, 1753, 1758, 1764-1768, 1770-1778, 1783, 1882, 1908, 2419, 2507, 2522, 2554, 2667, 2748, 3127, 3498, 3517, 3775

Telework 4738

Temples 1384

Temporal dimension 32, 223, 236, 290, 297, 490, 552, 562, 639, 642, 1298, 1571, 2408, 2651, 2772, 3169, 3188, 3200, 3540, 3767, 3848, 3860, 3907, 4350

Temporary employment 2741, 3229, 3791, 4299, 4447, 4456, 4676

Tenants 3824, 3979, 4220, 4232, 5286, 5491, 5611

Terminology 81, 100, 300, 408, 1822, 2374, 2375, 4960

Territoriality 58, 1000, 1806

Territory 966, 987, 1000, 1288, 1362, 3684, 3693, 3869, 3871, 3953
see also: Overseas territories

Terror 685, 752, 1081, 1781, 3457, 4973, 5466

Tertiary education 102, 2055, 2057, 2128, 2134, 2183, 2190, 2210, 2213, 2222, 2259, 2260, 2263, 2267, 2269, 2273, 2275, 2277, 2278, 2283-2287, 2290, 2291, 2293, 2296, 4794, 5703

Test design 587, 774, 5982

Textbooks 162, 318, 980, 2121, 2205, 2211, 2212, 2217, 3035

Textiles 3881, 4219, 4446

Texts 138, 151, 169, 530, 666, 984, 1353, 1757, 1796, 1832, 1874, 1924, 1944, 2190, 3775

Thai 3479

Thanatology 1383

Theatre 171, 1100, 1862, 1868, 1872, 1874, 1875, 3112, 3391
see also: Sociology of theatre

Theatrical performance 1862

Theft 471, 5067, 5085, 5367, 5369

Theology 3, 15, 145, 220, 221, 239, 267, 272, 1379, 1388, 1390, 1391, 1410, 1413,

INDEX DES MATIÈRES EN ANGLAIS

1452, 1455, 1462, 1477, 1478, 1483, 1487, 1491, 1497, 1506, 1526, 1547, 1564, 3028, 5687, 5722
see also: Christian theology, Liberation theology
Theory of culture 1395
Theory of education 647, 2004, 2011, 2164, 2168, 2170, 2171, 2177, 2181, 2224, 2280
Therapeutic groups 548
Therapeutics 5721
Therapy 705, 737, 742, 746, 747, 749, 767, 770, 772, 782, 794, 799, 813, 2628, 3093, 5175, 5391, 5406, 5412, 5413, 5538, 5668, 5675, 5699, 5721, 5737, 5742, 5839, 5847, 5870, 5874, 5884, 5925, 5928, 5936, 5938
see also: Family therapy, Occupational therapy
Thesauri 82, 97
Theses 457, 2282
Third Reich 173, 189, 3532
Third-party intervention 1731, 5321, 5330, 5361
Thomasius, Christian 208
Threat 173, 895, 2892, 5010
Tilly, Charles 2384
Time 212, 222, 254, 290, 291, 313, 387, 409, 441, 572, 1031, 1055, 1161, 1200, 1282, 1292, 1301, 1365, 1413, 1586, 1627, 1966, 2533, 2546, 2575, 2581, 3820, 3864, 3956, 4137, 4751, 5240, 5604, 5946
Time series 445, 2800, 2819, 3767, 5324, 5636, 5756
Tobacco 2824, 5407, 5956
Tocqueville, Alexis de 4288
Tolerance 350, 352, 1058, 1547, 1995, 2380, 2990, 3420, 3462, 3470, 4422, 4962, 4996, 5208, 5662
Tolstoy, Leo 5356
Top management 4408, 4620
Topology 1605, 3358
Totalitarianism 410, 1253, 2567, 4973
Tourism 1170, 1257, 1314, 1317, 1324, 1328, 1329, 1342, 1346, 1362, 1366, 1367, 1950, 2545, 3143, 3334, 3348, 3375, 3443, 3709, 3735, 3745, 3754, 3761, 3763, 3771, 3772, 3776, 3777, 3785, 3791, 3792, 3820-3822, 3854, 3908, 3914, 3925, 3944, 3970, 4113, 4219, 4238, 5080, 5335
Tourist policy 3820
Tourist trade 1342, 1366, 3792, 4046, 4238, 5335
Town centre 3359, 3937, 3965, 3971, 4081

Towns 2338, 3447, 3831, 3932, 3941, 3945, 3946, 3953, 3964, 3969, 3971, 3992, 4021, 4029, 4051, 4060, 4078, 4122, 4152, 4154, 4161, 4165, 4171, 4233
see also: New towns, Shanty towns, Small towns
Toys 635
Trade 1471, 3909, 4322, 4811, 5871
see also: Free trade, International trade, Regional trade, Retail trade, Slave trade, Tourist trade
Trade policy 5227
Trade relations 3654, 4321
Trade union action 4856
Trade union members 4875, 4878, 4880
Trade union membership 4587, 4854, 4870, 4875
Trade unionism 2507, 4417, 4813, 4854, 4864, 4874, 4875, 4880, 4949, 5220
Trade unions 1891, 2079, 2450, 3127, 4208, 4250, 4354, 4537, 4587, 4596, 4618, 4650, 4679, 4682, 4813, 4815, 4816, 4819-4822, 4824, 4829, 4832, 4835, 4836, 4843, 4847, 4850-4883, 5148, 5243, 5265
Trade-off 3987, 4451, 4475, 4724, 5766
Tradition 134, 892, 965, 975, 992, 1002, 1183, 1257, 1343, 1408, 1533, 1549, 2388, 2516, 2915, 3064, 3221, 3265, 3266, 3268, 3362, 3646, 3723, 3736, 3869, 3949, 4128, 4141, 4201, 4243, 4367, 4577, 4864, 5317, 5529
see also: Cultural tradition, Folk traditions, Oral tradition, Religious traditions
Traditional culture 58, 185, 992, 2575, 2733, 3776, 5320, 5746
Traditional dances 1346
Traditional law 5167, 5211
Traditional medicine 5813, 5821, 5823, 5962, 5980
Traditional music 1973
Traditional religion 1431, 1464
Traditionalism 992, 1222, 1363, 4217
Traffic 1302, 4053, 4114
see also: Air traffic, Road traffic
Training 105, 759, 775, 861, 1007, 1054, 1065, 2031, 2099, 2105, 2125, 2176, 2199, 2218, 2754, 3382, 3671, 4398, 4420, 4600, 4602, 4605, 4664, 4750, 4759, 4768, 4779, 4790, 4792-4800, 4802-4805, 4807, 4861, 4875, 5132, 5139, 5157, 5344, 5641, 5663, 5684, 5694, 5700, 5703, 5709, 5711, 5716, 5912, 5928
see also: In-service training, Teacher training, Vocational training

SUBJECT INDEX

Training methods 4671
Trains 2826
Transfer 846
  see also: Technology transfer
Transfrontier pollution 3762
Transition economies 2593, 2686, 2712, 2833, 2961, 3455, 3870, 4168, 4209, 4241, 4255, 4292, 4429, 4573, 4790, 5003, 5773
Transition from school to work 2626
Translation 132, 1231, 1534, 1557, 1582, 1689, 1822, 1915, 1978, 2227, 2461
Transnationalism 52, 983, 1240, 1263, 1268, 1363, 1467, 1737, 2446, 2545, 2553, 2562, 2571, 3148, 3499, 3540, 3599, 3632, 3645, 3683, 3826, 4032, 4768, 4957, 5241, 5242, 5252, 5313, 5335
Transparency 1608, 3807, 4227, 4955, 4963
Transplants 1039, 5826, 5878, 5883, 5891
Transport 291, 1299, 1302, 3877, 4045, 4051, 4062, 4068, 4083, 4124, 5225, 5335
  see also: Means of transport, Public transport, Railway transport, Urban transport
Transport economics 4045, 4048, 4062
Transport infrastructure 4023
Transport planning 3900
Transport policy 4313
Transsexuality 786, 803
Transvestism 3276
Trauma 742, 764, 767, 779, 785, 795, 796, 812, 814, 815, 819, 820, 1004, 1844, 2510, 2536, 2874, 5349, 5458, 5683, 5721, 5910, 5917, 5921, 5923
Travel 65, 1176, 1329, 1393, 1528, 2826, 3143, 3230, 3245, 3443, 4053, 5313, 5335, 5415
  see also: History of travels, International travels
Treaties 3526
Trees 5237
Tribalism 3417, 5363
Tribes 2379, 2505, 2515, 2783, 3736, 3776, 3920, 5553
Tropical zones 5980
Trucks 5067
Trust 927, 943, 1024, 1079, 1142, 1155, 1156, 1660, 2345, 2353, 2357, 2371, 2991, 3067, 3403, 3734, 3847, 3863, 4240, 4388, 4893, 4936, 4993, 5012, 5169, 5485, 5595, 5835
Truth 106, 120, 140, 146, 202, 209, 213, 224, 256, 261, 277, 296, 297, 455, 494, 568, 579, 926, 1008, 1018, 1110, 1403, 1472, 1578, 1581, 1731, 1878, 3354
Trypanosomiasis 5968

Tsung-hsi, Huang 1423
Turing, Alan 1593
Turks 1985, 2227, 2940, 3536, 3596, 3605, 5823
Turner, Stephen 597
Twins 712, 2918, 3308
Two-person games 949
Typological analysis 1505, 4584
Typology 399, 1459, 1569, 1999, 2111, 2363, 2646, 3192, 3625, 3930, 4407, 4582, 4584, 4623, 4994, 5460, 5771
UN Conventions 3813, 5601
Uncertainty 17, 357, 386, 668, 714, 730, 1098, 1261, 1766, 2222, 2309, 2536, 2640, 2794, 4346, 5236, 5484, 5690, 5945, 5970
Underclass 3656, 3775, 3989
Underdevelopment 3702, 3798, 4205, 4261
Underemployment 20, 4398, 4591
Unemployed 460, 4580-4582, 4585, 4586, 4593, 4790, 5662
Unemployment 510, 1285, 2046, 2577, 2714, 2855, 3568, 3590, 3594, 3840, 3870, 4250, 4269, 4368, 4439, 4463, 4476, 4481, 4501, 4505, 4532, 4579-4590, 4592, 4594-4597, 4696, 4713, 4753, 4790, 4796, 4828, 4848, 4866, 5063, 5222, 5365, 5392, 5700, 5838
  see also: Rural unemployment, Structural unemployment, Youth unemployment
Unemployment duration 4590, 4595, 5648
Unemployment insurance 5648
Unemployment levels 4592, 4685
Uneven development 3927
UNHCR 3611, 3674
UNICEF 5973
Unionism 2079, 3269, 4832, 4852, 4861, 4862, 4867, 4868
United Nations 1923, 2602, 3173, 4267, 5361
  see also: UN Conventions
Universalism 255, 340, 382, 405, 888, 1198, 1208, 1240, 1267, 1269, 2212, 2348, 2349, 2563, 3335, 4923, 4931, 5320
Universities 47, 50, 85, 102, 191, 225, 339, 376, 775, 996, 1155, 1158, 1203, 1217, 1604, 1617, 1631, 1715, 2009, 2018, 2033, 2045, 2052, 2057, 2075, 2089, 2118, 2129, 2139, 2145, 2147, 2183, 2188, 2195, 2196, 2200, 2207, 2213, 2222, 2223, 2226, 2242-2245, 2248, 2249, 2251-2264, 2266-2269, 2274, 2277, 2278, 2280, 2281, 2283-2286, 2290, 2291, 2293-2296, 2298, 2299, 2361, 2383, 2454, 3067, 3078, 3115, 3175, 3183, 3291, 3293, 3296, 3439, 4398, 4494, 4514, 4563, 4564, 4655, 4714, 4733, 4935, 4949, 5267, 5268

INDEX DES MATIÈRES EN ANGLAIS

University campuses 996
University management 2251
Unmarried mothers 2881, 2995, 2998-3001, 4531, 5119
Unmarried persons 2311, 5415
Upper class 5335
Upward mobility 2383
Urban agglomeration 3776, 3813, 3948, 3964, 4119
Urban anthropology 4012
Urban architecture 4038, 4106, 4126
Urban areas 471, 2104, 2151, 2234, 2451, 2789, 2841, 2843, 2889, 2998, 3010, 3300, 3359, 3612, 3696, 3784, 3848, 3933, 3939-3942, 3946, 3948, 3949, 3951, 3953, 3957, 3958, 3960, 3963, 3966, 3971, 3976, 3995, 3999-4001, 4016, 4021, 4025, 4029, 4031, 4042, 4048, 4050, 4057, 4058, 4060, 4065, 4072, 4075, 4077, 4093, 4099, 4101, 4107, 4120, 4128, 4139, 4142, 4149, 4151, 4153, 4157, 4159, 4161, 4163, 4165, 4168, 4174, 4175, 4182, 4233, 4301, 4303, 4492, 4511, 4558, 4566, 5053, 5119, 5271, 5386, 5815, 5962
Urban communities 1205, 1813, 2878, 3359, 3842, 3931, 3939, 3959, 3967, 4039, 4117, 4119, 4148, 4155, 4169
Urban decline 4021
Urban design 3941, 3970, 4026, 4054, 4075
Urban development 2024, 2138, 2571, 3755, 3813, 3868, 3927, 3928, 3935, 3936, 3940, 3941, 3947-3949, 3958, 3961, 3962, 3964, 3972, 3974, 3975, 3983, 3987, 3990, 3994, 3998, 4018, 4023-4025, 4031-4033, 4036, 4040, 4045, 4046, 4051, 4056, 4060, 4061, 4066, 4069, 4071, 4076, 4078, 4080, 4081, 4087, 4088, 4097, 4100, 4103-4105, 4108, 4109, 4113, 4115, 4117, 4120, 4127, 4136-4138, 4141, 4149, 4153, 4155, 4158, 4159, 4162, 4164, 4165, 4167, 4169, 4172-4175, 4178
Urban economics 2571, 3927, 4045, 4070, 4103, 4124, 4162, 4174, 4245, 4264, 4327, 4453, 4490, 5475
Urban employment 4130, 4147, 4461, 4516, 4566
Urban environment 608, 3807, 3813, 3926, 4028, 4037, 4096, 4102, 4106, 4114, 4123, 4145, 4166
Urban geography 1657, 2473, 3745, 3928, 3932, 3948, 3958, 3997, 4000, 4001, 4034, 4072, 4074, 4092, 4122, 4135, 4139, 4154, 4158, 4460, 5426
Urban government 3947, 3959, 4066

Urban growth 3702, 3771, 3928, 3936, 3949, 3958, 4060, 4151, 4156, 4166, 4167, 4175
Urban history 2901, 3371, 3926, 3928, 3935, 3941, 3947, 3950, 3980, 3983, 4026, 4030, 4042, 4057, 4128, 4132, 4137
Urban housing 3948, 3968, 3972, 3974, 3978, 3982, 3989, 4024, 4111, 4169, 5611
Urban life 2377, 2633, 2679, 3359, 3387, 3848, 3928, 3929, 3933, 3934, 3939, 3948, 3949, 3953, 3955, 3993, 3996, 4021, 4027, 4065, 4119, 4132, 4135, 4144, 4147, 4148, 4155, 5429
Urban management 3702, 3942, 3948, 4032, 4064, 4093
Urban movements 3954, 3968, 5270, 5275
Urban planning 1324, 1657, 1829, 2152, 3702, 3872, 3900, 3908, 3928, 3945, 3947, 3948, 3983, 3994, 4010, 4018, 4024-4027, 4029-4031, 4033-4039, 4041-4043, 4047, 4050-4054, 4058, 4059, 4061, 4064-4067, 4071, 4073-4075, 4079-4081, 4083-4091, 4093, 4096, 4098, 4100, 4105-4108, 4110, 4113, 4114, 4117, 4133, 4140, 4141, 4146, 4147, 4153, 4168-4170, 4172, 4178
Urban policy 2138, 3702, 3928, 3942, 3976, 3983, 4035, 4037, 4038, 4044, 4052, 4070, 4078, 4080, 4093, 4097, 4100, 4109, 4114, 4174, 4287, 4991
Urban politics 3927, 3950, 3959, 3968, 4100, 4169, 4941, 5229
Urban population 2797, 3170, 3585, 3948, 4053, 4068, 4156, 4176, 4245, 4470, 4490, 5229
Urban poverty 58, 3842, 3927, 3967, 3989, 3992, 3997, 4006, 4007, 4011, 4087, 4169, 4246, 4470, 4991, 5053
Urban renewal 3807, 3937, 3965, 3975, 3982, 4008, 4028, 4035, 4038-4040, 4043, 4044, 4052, 4056, 4066, 4070, 4071, 4076-4078, 4091, 4094, 4097, 4105, 4109-4113, 4154, 4159, 4174, 4995, 5063
Urban services 4176
Urban society 50, 3842, 3939, 3959, 4027, 4092, 4128
Urban sociology 32, 50, 788, 1168, 1365, 1530, 1991, 2024, 2062, 2069, 2104, 2146, 2532, 2972, 3340, 3413, 3610, 3632, 3725, 3729, 3842, 3860, 3870, 3872, 3926, 3929-3933, 3937, 3938, 3944-3946, 3950-3952, 3954, 3957, 3959-3961, 3963, 3966-3969, 3971, 3972, 3974, 3978, 3982, 3983, 3987, 3991, 3994, 3995, 3998-4000, 4005, 4012, 4013, 4015-4017, 4021, 4029, 4031, 4043, 4051, 4056, 4059, 4073, 4076, 4108, 4111, 4121, 4127,

509

SUBJECT INDEX

4128, 4139, 4143, 4144, 4149, 4151,
4154, 4159-4161, 4165, 4168, 4172, 4173,
4233, 4327, 4431, 4436, 4445, 4892,
5079, 5119, 5270, 5274, 5275, 5279, 5374,
5424, 5900
Urban space 1737, 2716, 3359, 3814, 3927,
3956, 4011, 4023, 4038, 4078, 4089, 4102,
4118, 4120, 4121, 4123, 4125-4128, 4131,
4132, 4134-4137, 4139-4142, 4144, 4146,
4147, 4155, 4156, 4941
Urban sprawl 3867
Urban structure 3948, 4053, 4103
Urban transport 3982, 4037, 4053, 4062,
4074, 4087
Urban women 4147
Urban youth 4435
Urban-rural migration 2718, 3618, 3725,
3866, 3868, 3904, 4168
Urbanism 3929, 3955, 4010, 4023, 4033
Urbanization 1540, 2561, 2718, 2733, 3010,
3486, 3612, 3616, 3702, 3755, 3813,
3867, 3927, 3932, 3947-3949, 3955, 3960,
3962, 3964, 4011, 4142, 4149-4152, 4156,
4158, 4160, 4162-4166, 4168, 4170-4173,
4175-4178, 4197, 5055, 5686
Utilitarianism 276, 346, 373, 375, 2445, 5886
Utility functions 1085, 4124
Utility theory 342, 464, 3705
Utopianism 1622, 1941
Utopias 295, 801, 1229, 3697, 3787, 4210,
4917
Validity 4599, 5179
Valuation 905, 4186, 4716
Value 2, 472, 638, 1246, 1716, 1859, 2018,
2341, 2412, 2639, 3402, 3703, 3705,
3744, 3763, 4186, 4351, 4390
Value orientation 1203
Value systems 524, 1205
Value theory 288, 4186
Values 11, 48, 170, 206, 226, 241, 264, 319,
393, 524, 650, 737, 892, 986, 1012, 1073,
1095, 1112, 1156, 1183, 1247, 1285, 1359,
1369, 1387, 1388, 1406, 1421, 1440,
1642, 2084, 2186, 2218, 2347, 2351-2353,
2357, 2359, 2361, 2362, 2365, 2366,
2372, 2373, 2502, 2587, 2646, 2675,
2920, 2945, 3013, 3178, 3202, 3324,
3486, 3547, 3726, 3818, 3914, 4148,
4229, 4296, 4307, 4417, 4422, 4497,
4644, 4658, 4910, 4962, 5208, 5409,
5529, 5630, 5704, 5783, 5829
   see also: Cultural values
Vampires 1239
Vandalism 5369
Vargas, Fred 1958

Variance 496, 668, 866, 2304
Veblen, Thorstein Bunde 1848
Vedism 1384
Vegetarianism 1296
Veils 3172, 3266
Venture capital 4369
Verbal communication 664, 901, 1805, 2523
Vernacular languages 31
Veterans 5361, 5913
Victim support 2873, 5116
Victims 471, 767, 814, 1719, 2235, 2863,
3289, 3458, 3624, 5020, 5044, 5112, 5116,
5123, 5175, 5321, 5440, 5457, 5458, 5683
   see also: Victim support
Victims of crime 5040, 5061, 5080, 5101,
5106
Victims of rape 5457
Victims of violence 2878, 5192, 5321, 5457,
5470
Victorian Age 171, 5723
Videos 444, 686, 1018, 1711, 1779, 1889,
1909, 2175
Vidyālankāra, Raghunātha 132
Vietnamese 975
Viewers 1327, 1725, 1774, 5448
Villages 1295, 1707, 2152, 2338, 3644, 3739,
3776, 3831, 3855, 3885, 3886, 3890,
3892, 3899, 3916, 3917, 4477, 5279
Violence 801, 835, 872, 908, 1199, 1341,
1887, 1889, 2119, 2321, 2340, 2369, 2521,
2643, 2754, 2860-2863, 2865-2867, 2871,
2872, 2874, 2875, 2877, 2882, 2883,
2886-2890, 2892, 2894, 2951, 2979, 3138,
3201, 3438, 3457, 3468, 3485, 3492,
3520, 3531, 3930, 3938, 3944, 3957,
4269, 4482, 4691, 4977, 4984, 4993,
4997, 5044, 5050, 5058, 5062, 5068,
5069, 5097, 5114, 5133, 5138, 5139, 5251,
5256, 5327, 5331, 5349, 5361, 5368,
5430, 5437-5440, 5442-5452, 5454, 5456,
5461-5473, 5580, 5594, 5838, 5914, 5917,
5934
   see also: Domestic violence, Political
   violence
Violent crime 801, 1750, 2864, 2868, 4997,
5000, 5009, 5044, 5045, 5049-5051, 5070,
5079, 5097, 5102, 5113, 5120, 5440, 5441,
5448, 5453, 5455, 5456, 5471, 5474
Virtual reality 641, 1656, 2772, 3820
Visual anthropology 1346, 1767, 1870
Visual arts 970, 1100, 1866, 1870, 1880, 1900,
3375
Visual communication 1803, 1870
Visual perception 444, 628, 645, 664, 1767,
1827, 2481, 3970

INDEX DES MATIÈRES EN ANGLAIS

Vocabulary 100, 4179
Vocational education 2031, 2145, 4771, 4805, 4806
Vocational guidance 48, 1726
Vocational training 2037, 2626, 4448, 4792, 4797, 4799, 4803, 4804
Volcanoes 3702, 3776
Voluntary organizations 61, 1035, 1156, 1673, 2371, 2595, 2631, 3827, 3856, 4235, 4390, 4768, 4948, 5491, 5574, 5720, 5775
Voluntary work 59, 61, 734, 1035, 1156, 1285, 1512, 2371, 3843, 3844, 3862, 4768, 5484, 5586, 5615, 5719, 5723
Voters 5219, 5300, 5301, 5305
Voting behaviour 472, 1070, 2389, 3483, 4596, 4966, 5160, 5287, 5300, 5303, 5305-5307
Voting intentions 5303
Voting turnout 472, 5304
Vraciu, Ioan 3354
Vygotsky, Lev 162, 1161, 2224
Wage determination 4842
Wage differentials 2023, 4305, 4464, 4495, 4498, 4499, 4502, 4503, 4509, 4525, 4538, 4539, 4547, 4551, 4556, 4573, 4878, 4880, 5891
Wage discrimination 2457, 4499, 4502, 4540, 4573
Wage earners 2679
Wage levels 4459, 4460, 4679, 4723
Wage negotiations 4824, 4842
Wage policy 3868
Wage regulation 4841
Wage structure 4763
Wages 2023, 2561, 2799, 4295, 4305, 4306, 4368, 4402, 4410, 4431, 4437, 4438, 4440, 4449, 4452, 4454, 4455, 4463, 4464, 4471, 4499, 4503, 4525, 4538, 4540, 4573, 4587, 4690, 4714, 4723, 4742, 4795, 4880, 5223
see also: Minimum wages
Walder, Andrew 4241
Walser, Martin 3532
Walzer, Michael 2448
Wampar 3776
War 162, 1195, 1731, 1732, 1906, 2205, 2348, 3315, 3485, 3624, 3631, 3859, 4095, 4482, 5318, 5323, 5327, 5329-5332, 5346, 5349, 5355, 5362, 5467, 5683, 5921, 5988
see also: Civil war, Cold War, Holy war, Warfare
War crimes 1902, 1906, 5311, 5312
Warfare 5323, 5346, 5353, 5355, 5362, 5445
Washington, Booker T. 3528

Waste 1277, 3715, 3750
see also: Hazardous waste
Waste management 1190, 3813, 4025
Water 484, 2711
Water management 3690, 3762, 4025
Water prices 3813
Water quality 2825, 3762
Water resources 3690, 3707, 3798
Water supply 2823, 3702, 3813, 4025
Way of life 1175, 2627, 2667, 3387, 3679, 3904, 5415, 5773
Wealth 1287, 1670, 2445, 2982, 3191, 3667, 3814, 4177, 4188, 4227, 4288, 4294, 4425, 4870, 5154, 5643
Weapons 4984, 5050, 5079
see also: Biological weapons, Chemical weapons, Landmines, Nuclear weapons
Weather 767
Weaving 4568
Weber, Max 314, 318, 343, 364, 365, 370, 373, 408, 409, 801, 1406, 4239, 5211
Weddings 2982
Weil, Eric 225
Welfare 510, 1151, 2307, 2403, 2452, 2458, 2577, 2793, 2997, 3001, 3434, 3588, 3603, 4271, 4308, 4398, 4531, 4587, 4597, 4686, 4789, 4937, 5321, 5482, 5485, 5487, 5489, 5494, 5500, 5526, 5535, 5536, 5565, 5569, 5585, 5609, 5610, 5614, 5618-5620, 5628, 5633, 5634, 5648, 5653, 5657, 5659, 5661, 5711, 5793, 5936, 5982
see also: Social welfare
Welfare economics 4200, 5489
Welfare measurement 4251
Welfare policy 2459, 3862, 4411, 4456, 5477, 5512, 5537, 5546, 5548, 5602, 5615, 5616, 5622, 5623, 5625, 5631-5633, 5636, 5637, 5639-5641, 5647, 5654, 5657, 5660
Welfare reform 1991, 2455, 3976, 4439, 5618, 5633, 5639, 5643, 5654, 5658, 5661
Welfare state 1480, 2320, 2455, 2554, 2567, 2682, 2945, 3065, 3169, 4018, 4192, 4231, 4247, 4259, 4271, 4520, 4596, 4922, 4945, 4987, 5482, 5484, 5506, 5602, 5604, 5606, 5613-5616, 5619, 5620, 5622, 5623, 5625, 5626, 5628, 5631, 5632, 5637, 5638, 5640-5645, 5648, 5650-5654, 5659-5662, 5766, 5814, 5819, 5982
see also: Welfare reform
Well-being 482, 505, 577, 673, 675, 693, 717, 892, 936, 1480, 2351, 2494, 2642, 2668, 2680, 2814, 2846, 2977, 3012, 3018, 3029, 3547, 3666, 3833, 4265, 4618, 4706, 4710, 4931, 5373, 5575, 5838, 5842

Subject Index

Wendt, Alex 5310
Weor, Samael Aun 1501
West Indians 4125, 4500
Western civilization 152, 259, 695, 1246, 1279, 1464, 1679, 3402, 5128
Western countries 35, 191, 1384, 1464, 1486, 2930, 3084, 3117, 3452, 3949, 4631, 5005, 5968
Westernization 1183, 1185, 1699, 1702, 2569
White collar workers 4441, 4618
Whitehead, Alfred North 225
Whites 710, 826, 835, 1195, 1479, 1761, 1767, 2034, 2692, 2856, 2991, 3067, 3088, 3259, 3274, 3436, 3439, 3449, 3464, 3534, 3565, 3570, 3588, 3834, 3835, 3996, 4014, 4019, 4291, 4497, 5053, 5454
Widowhood 2910
Widows 186, 2652, 2923
Wilde, Oscar 1882
Wildlife protection 3710, 3763
Willingness-to-pay 3705
Winch, Peter 268, 303, 304
Winfrey, Oprah 1361
Witchcraft 303, 3186
Witches 3186
Withdrawal 780, 4684
Wittgenstein, Ludwig 225, 262, 268, 282, 303, 304, 1846
Wives 2965, 2971, 3035, 3188, 4530, 5479
Wolof 3907
Women 5, 60, 104, 204, 278, 419, 469, 485, 570, 574, 581, 672, 722, 736, 777, 781, 797, 811, 824, 838, 1177, 1214, 1227, 1232, 1304, 1372, 1443, 1463, 1520, 1522, 1533, 1572, 1613, 1659, 1760, 1767, 1782, 1847, 1886, 1903, 1915, 1918, 1925, 1929, 1936, 1943, 1945, 1954, 1969, 2002, 2015, 2039, 2041, 2078, 2080, 2271, 2272, 2408, 2449, 2492, 2499, 2515, 2523, 2537, 2551, 2561, 2712, 2725, 2752, 2760, 2771, 2773, 2776, 2784, 2798, 2825, 2860, 2864, 2868, 2870, 2875, 2879, 2880, 2882, 2883, 2885, 2886, 2889, 2890, 2915, 2917, 2976, 3002, 3007, 3022, 3023, 3025, 3028, 3033, 3038, 3058, 3064, 3065, 3067, 3068, 3071, 3072, 3074-3078, 3080, 3085, 3088-3091, 3093, 3094, 3098, 3105-3107, 3110, 3112, 3114, 3115, 3118, 3125, 3128, 3135, 3138, 3141, 3143, 3145, 3148, 3149, 3151, 3152, 3154-3156, 3158, 3161-3163, 3169, 3172-3175, 3178-3180, 3184, 3189, 3193, 3195-3198, 3203, 3204, 3207-3209, 3214, 3227, 3245, 3247, 3250, 3252, 3254-3256, 3258, 3261, 3262, 3265, 3269, 3273, 3274, 3276, 3284, 3286, 3287, 3293, 3302, 3306-3308, 3315, 3317, 3318, 3332, 3352, 3374, 3384, 3392, 3500, 3518, 3538, 3549, 3557, 3565, 3582, 3599-3602, 3646, 3670, 3676, 3742, 3793, 3834, 3901, 3957, 4226, 4259, 4265, 4308, 4316, 4353, 4372, 4415, 4478, 4503, 4511, 4536, 4545-4548, 4555, 4558-4560, 4563, 4564, 4566, 4567, 4570-4572, 4574, 4576, 4694, 4765, 4857, 4882, 4883, 4944, 5002, 5011, 5012, 5026, 5070, 5076, 5099, 5112, 5144, 5155, 5223, 5244, 5260, 5318, 5326, 5346, 5348, 5353, 5362, 5363, 5382, 5386, 5388, 5409, 5439, 5443, 5446, 5451, 5467, 5469, 5474, 5480, 5483, 5516, 5521, 5546, 5600, 5628, 5633, 5685, 5823, 5843, 5857, 5915, 5917, 5959
see also: Married women, Rural women, Urban women
Women and politics 3079, 3111, 3116, 3184, 3206, 3277, 4944, 5317
Women students 2299
Women workers 513, 2091, 3040, 3075, 3127, 3229, 3232, 3267, 3270, 3280, 3325, 3557, 3670, 4415, 4443, 4462, 4478, 4480, 4488, 4504, 4508, 4513, 4516, 4517, 4523, 4524, 4536, 4557, 4558, 4565, 4566, 4568, 4570, 4575, 4632, 4694, 4839, 4883, 5131, 5203, 5651, 5838
Women's education 2007, 2023, 2721, 5358
Women's emancipation 3132, 3134
Women's employment 2023, 2914, 2971, 2997, 3022, 3224, 3277, 3538, 4372, 4414, 4416, 4466, 4467, 4478, 4480, 4516, 4520, 4522, 4523, 4525, 4528-4532, 4543, 4549, 4552, 4553, 4559, 4567, 4569, 4573-4575, 4595, 5834
Women's health 2726, 2750, 2751, 2754, 2758, 2765, 2777, 2779, 2792, 2798, 2801, 2817, 2832, 2834, 2999, 3083, 3095, 3115, 3210, 3231, 3280, 3373, 4291, 5200, 5746, 5782, 5838, 5902, 5917, 5947, 5960, 5962, 5980
Women's movements 1463, 1549, 2586, 2730, 2870, 2879, 3079, 3080, 3105, 3106, 3112, 3115, 3122, 3134, 3161, 3162, 4857, 5200, 5258, 5260
Women's organizations 3070, 4467
Women's participation 1925, 3160, 3193
Women's rights 2730, 2754, 2761, 2762, 2883, 3074, 3079, 3089, 3114, 3206, 3215, 3883, 4254, 4944, 5326

INDEX DES MATIÈRES EN ANGLAIS

Women's role 513, 1463, 2091, 2675, 2756, 2939, 3069, 3079, 3103, 3104, 3114, 3127, 3140, 3160, 3162, 3168, 3169, 3171, 3174, 3195, 3215, 3224, 3247, 3248, 3251, 3313, 3471, 4273, 4524, 4535, 5317, 5347, 5459, 5505
Women's status 2449, 2873, 2891, 2955, 3079, 3081, 3087, 3091, 3103, 3104, 3111, 3112, 3131, 3140, 3160, 3168, 3169, 3174, 3184, 3192, 3193, 3196-3198, 3203, 3206, 3215, 3224, 3234, 3247, 3251, 3262, 3277-3279, 3290, 3549, 3767, 3793, 4535, 4537, 4564, 5969
Women's studies 1970, 3078, 3079, 3107, 3115, 3122, 3123, 3234, 3248, 3363, 3376, 3379, 3665
Women's work 3194, 3206, 3281, 3677, 4480, 4525, 4536, 4544, 4560, 5969
Woolf, Virginia 1941
Words 197, 210, 624, 659, 1757, 1822, 2313, 3205
Work at home 1283, 2141, 4302
Work environment 2229, 4383, 4389, 4400, 4687, 4692, 4693, 4701, 4703, 4710, 4718, 4730, 5283, 5584, 5630
Work ethic 1126, 4239, 4365, 4597, 4709
Work experience 4393
Work incentives 4587
Work motivation 4702, 4736
Work organization 397, 1040, 1091, 1117, 2125, 3062, 3568, 4357, 4362, 4365, 4389, 4395, 4398, 4401, 4544, 4618, 4634, 4643, 4647, 4650, 4652, 4838, 4872
Work place 1339, 2086, 3246, 3285, 3289, 3290, 3310, 3356, 3568, 4354, 4357, 4359, 4362, 4383, 4384, 4389, 4397, 4398, 4404, 4406, 4416, 4419, 4422, 4451, 4486, 4488, 4493, 4515, 4534, 4544, 4552, 4578, 4602, 4613, 4617, 4626, 4628, 4639, 4677, 4678, 4681, 4683, 4688, 4691, 4709, 4710, 4716, 4721, 4731, 4740, 4741, 4746, 4750, 4753, 4758, 4792, 4807, 4809, 4820, 4829, 4833, 4838, 4858, 4868, 4877, 4879, 5052, 5090
Work study 4702
Workers 1111, 1927, 3553, 3633, 3663, 3671, 3673, 4263, 4275, 4403, 4416, 4433, 4441, 4444, 4448, 4471, 4485, 4558, 4591, 4599, 4698, 4700, 4702, 4726, 4729, 4739, 4741, 4745, 4803, 4809, 4813, 4815, 4817, 4821, 4822, 4826, 4840, 4849, 4850, 4855, 4858, 4869
see also: Agricultural workers, Commercial workers, Disabled workers, Domestic workers, Foreign workers, Industrial workers, Migrant workers, Office workers, Older workers, Professional workers, Research workers, Seasonal workers, Self-employed workers, Skilled workers, White collar workers, Women workers
Workers' education 4484
Workers' movements 2339, 4834, 4879, 5261
Workers' participation 4812, 4838, 4839
Workers' representation 4819, 4853, 4855, 4863, 4871, 4873
Workers' rights 4360, 4849
Workers' stock ownership 4812, 4827
Working class 1310, 1811, 2005, 2158, 2416, 2422, 2425, 2450, 3218, 3236, 3468, 4004, 4300, 4410, 4472, 4554, 4848, 4864, 4865, 5162, 5595, 5662
Working conditions 1053, 1305, 2100, 2421, 2975, 3075, 3226, 3288, 4206, 4250, 4356, 4377, 4416, 4433, 4446, 4448, 4455, 4471, 4478, 4522, 4578, 4626, 4644, 4676-4678, 4680, 4682, 4683, 4686-4688, 4691, 4692, 4694, 4695, 4699, 4702-4704, 4706, 4708, 4709, 4711, 4712, 4716, 4717, 4721, 4723, 4729, 4733-4736, 4740, 4742, 4743, 4745, 4746, 4748-4750, 4757, 4810, 4839, 5630
Working groups 1111
Working life 1304, 1645, 3255, 4738, 4739, 4757
Working mothers 3169, 3270, 4517, 4528, 4534, 4555, 4557, 4568
Working parents 5624
Working time 3169, 4305, 4475, 4524, 4685, 4712, 4724, 4751, 4810
Works councils 4813
Works of art 1247, 1866, 1869, 1876
Workshops 1014, 5928
World Bank 2292, 2561, 3961, 4161, 4287, 5282
World economy 336, 379, 1131, 2128, 2446, 2554, 2559, 2562, 2567, 2571, 2572, 2578, 3663, 3693, 3750, 3797, 3851, 3927, 3952, 4202, 4205, 4206, 4212, 4233, 4486, 4558, 4825, 4850, 4863, 5187, 5622
World Health Organization 2814, 3827, 5407, 5904, 5911
World market 2571
World order 2580, 3452
World politics 2541, 2553, 2572, 3723
World population 2694, 2711

SUBJECT INDEX

World religions 1378
  see also: Christianity, Hinduism, Islam, Judaism
World Trade Organization 2547, 3827, 4935, 5265
World view 982, 2218, 2477, 2538, 3727, 3879, 4207, 4360, 4962
World War Two 189, 976, 1004, 1218, 1888, 1902, 1976, 3495, 3502, 3518, 4898
Worship 952, 1372, 1424, 2106
Writers 249, 281, 283, 1901, 1918, 1922, 1925, 1936, 1937, 1939, 1945, 1948, 1956, 1959, 2439, 3107, 3120, 3122, 4898, 4935
  see also: Novelists
Writing 17, 99, 151, 178, 198, 200, 415, 1140, 1637, 1711, 1763, 1858, 1907, 1914, 1915, 1919, 1922, 1924, 1925, 1936, 1938, 1944, 1959, 2005, 2040, 2206, 2268, 2314, 2588, 3079, 3112, 3230, 3931, 4807
Xenophobia 1705, 3452, 3455, 3466, 3485, 3502, 3599
Xhosa 1841, 2523
Yeats, William Butler 1227
Yi, Cheng 266
Yoruba 1431, 2761
Youth 77, 155, 900, 921, 978, 1014, 1338, 1494, 1809, 1820, 1875, 1889, 1982, 2047, 2119, 2218, 2248, 2576, 2584, 2585, 2592, 2602, 2614, 2616, 2618, 2620-2623, 2626, 2627, 2634, 2635, 2637, 2639, 2640, 2648-2650, 2870, 2909, 2924, 2929, 2954, 3043, 3156, 3237, 3313, 3323, 3337, 3338, 3370, 3385, 3413, 3535, 3536, 3595, 3596, 3946, 3965, 4139, 4145, 4159, 4344, 4361, 4453, 4481, 4487, 4504, 4548, 4559, 4758, 4799, 4869, 4974, 4996, 5000, 5019, 5050, 5054, 5068, 5069, 5072, 5079, 5090, 5097, 5209, 5361, 5370, 5386, 5409, 5420, 5427, 5429, 5431, 5456, 5465, 5542, 5546, 5570, 5737, 5814, 5933, 5941, 5978
  see also: Rural youth, Urban youth
Youth and politics 2617, 2638, 5243
Youth culture 1319, 1331, 1978, 1985, 1986, 2614, 2617, 2620, 2623, 2630, 2643, 5046, 5472
Youth employment 4435, 4447, 4449, 4454
Youth organizations 2614
Youth policy 4799
Youth unemployment 412, 4505, 4590, 4598, 4797
Yugoslavs 4255
Yukagir 3425

Zen 202, 250, 1464
Zionism 985, 991, 1380, 1546, 2177, 3420, 3450
Zoning 4450

SUBJECT INDEX IN FRENCH
INDEX DES MATIÈRES

Abandon d'études 4794, 5578
Abolition de l'esclavage 951
Abolitionnism 2, 4984
Aborigènes 1769, 3446, 3482, 3486, 3827, 4056, 4445, 5170, 5413
Abraham, Karl 593
Absentéisme 4698, 4700, 4708, 5345
Absolutisme 241
Abus de drogues 709, 1307, 1334, 2618, 2621, 4683, 4998, 5115, 5367, 5369, 5374, 5375, 5378, 5380, 5382-5386, 5395-5397, 5399, 5401, 5406, 5409, 5465, 5480, 5664, 5748, 5767, 5801, 5818, 5891
Abus de substances toxiques 508, 723, 2621, 2633, 2845, 2872, 2951, 3995, 4683, 5381-5385, 5387, 5388, 5391-5394, 5396, 5402, 5407, 5409-5411, 5413, 5421, 5480, 5658, 5818
  voir aussi: Réhabilitation de l'état de dépendance
Abus sexuel 593, 777, 812, 2867, 2875, 2885, 2951, 3298, 3329, 4493, 5100, 5371, 5373, 5430, 5449, 5456, 5457, 5474, 5544-5546, 5558, 5562, 5672
Acceptation sociale 1313, 2733
Accès à la culture 2481
Accès à l'éducation 93, 2005, 2010, 2015, 2016, 2018, 2019, 2022, 2024, 2025, 2030, 2031, 2035, 2036, 2038, 2039, 2042, 2049, 2052, 2057, 2062, 2064, 2066, 2069, 2092, 2109, 2112, 2114, 2123, 2136, 2145, 2147, 2266, 2273, 2460, 2513, 2548, 2677
Accès à l'emploi 4755
Accès à l'information 79, 80, 104, 2757, 4320, 4933, 5869
Accès aux soins médicaux généraux 2727, 3185, 3327, 4087, 5019, 5575, 5731, 5743, 5751, 5759, 5763, 5766, 5768, 5769, 5774, 5780, 5788, 5792, 5805, 5809, 5811, 5814, 5891, 5915
Accidents 2816, 2826, 2844, 5967
Accomplissement 892, 3391
Accord de paix 5273
Accroissement de la productivité 4668

Accroissement de population 2796, 3972
Acculturation 569, 805, 806, 1246, 1320, 2511, 2552, 2887, 2915, 3405, 3440, 3546, 3547, 3595, 5529, 5908
Acculturation des immigrants 3567
Accumulation de capital 4204
Acier 4079
Acquisition de connaissances 63, 225, 376, 540, 547, 555, 594, 607, 617, 622, 624, 627, 637, 647, 651, 658, 663, 665, 666, 1018, 1040, 1046, 1095, 1098, 1113, 1115, 1119, 1128-1130, 1149, 1293, 1542, 1587, 1681, 1708, 1984, 1992, 2003, 2004, 2008, 2017, 2047, 2049, 2053, 2075, 2087, 2127, 2128, 2164, 2168, 2172, 2174-2178, 2182, 2190, 2192-2194, 2199, 2202, 2209, 2213, 2219, 2223, 2229, 2244, 2260, 2271, 2272, 2279, 2299, 2368, 2447, 2453, 2575, 2609, 3003, 4360, 4384, 4398, 4609, 4807, 4868, 5231, 5677, 5697, 5704, 5799, 5831, 5912, 5926, 5953
Acquisition d'information 1587
Acquisition du langage 547, 610, 622-624, 636, 1161, 1654, 1788, 1805, 2087, 2149, 3564, 3585
Acteurs 310, 323, 854, 1882, 2082, 2375, 2677, 3223, 3693, 3799, 4171, 4837
Action collective 323, 597, 829, 1038, 1068, 2378, 2450, 3154, 3834, 3838, 3855, 4365, 4385, 4843, 4888, 4942, 5228, 5231, 5241, 5248, 5250, 5265, 5266, 5273, 5275, 5276, 5280, 5716, 5942, 5982
Action politique 1070, 4104, 4899, 4950, 5230, 5231, 5292
Action sociale 59, 306, 347, 365, 375, 589, 597, 1053, 1098, 1208, 1479, 1652, 2049, 2315, 2353, 2480, 3463, 3800, 3827, 4196, 4217, 4299, 4899, 4940, 5202, 5230, 5231, 5262, 5264, 5276, 5280, 5475, 5716, 5982
Action syndicale 4856
Actionnaires 4420, 4422, 4870
Actionnariat ouvrier 4812, 4827
Actions 4242, 4812

SUBJECT INDEX IN FRENCH

Activisme 71, 1025, 1479, 1532, 2468, 3061, 3112, 3115, 3138, 3152, 3389, 3454, 3507, 3749, 3772, 3863, 4861, 4868, 4883, 4956, 4960, 5228, 5230, 5251, 5270, 5274, 5278
Activistes 1939, 3078, 3134, 3777, 4935, 5171, 5230, 5247, 5254, 5278, 5885
Activité bancaire 2507, 3246, 4346, 4348, 4349
Activité de construction 4028, 4049
Activité économique 2653, 2679, 3626, 3761, 4050, 4240, 4372, 4767, 5287
Activité militante 1537, 1936, 5256, 5274
Activité physique 503, 609, 1326, 1368, 1497, 3546, 4146, 5350, 5961
Activité politique 155, 328, 1517, 4914, 4966, 5227, 5228, 5275, 5281, 5292
Acupuncture 5859
Adaptation au changement 3708
Adaptation culturelle 1320, 1777, 3306, 3598, 5008
Adaptation des immigrants 2029, 2047, 2691, 3459, 3461, 3489, 3546, 3549-3551, 3554, 3556, 3557, 3560, 3561, 3564, 3568, 3569, 3572, 3574, 3578, 3579, 3581, 3585-3587, 3589, 3593-3595, 3597, 3599, 3603, 3605, 3641, 3656, 3678, 3757, 4001
Adaptation sociale 567, 2318
Adhérents au parti 5219
Adhésion à l'Union européenne 4913
Adhésion syndicale 4587, 4854, 4870, 4875
Administration 2040, 2137, 2138, 2247, 2286, 2296, 3832, 4178, 4655, 4780, 5224, 5555, 5755, 5758
Administration coloniale 58, 4042, 4897
Administration de la justice 426, 4982, 5000, 5006, 5013, 5014, 5021, 5022, 5025, 5026, 5028, 5043, 5101, 5136, 5149, 5175, 5181, 5186, 5193, 5195, 5370
Administration de la santé 5726, 5732, 5747, 5750, 5751, 5758, 5761, 5762, 5770, 5772, 5775, 5779, 5784, 5785, 5790, 5797, 5798, 5804, 5807, 5812, 5814, 5840, 5841, 5980
Administration de l'enseignement 2093, 2095, 2159, 2263, 4806
Administration locale 2388, 2458, 2467, 2709, 3745, 3807, 3813, 3814, 3829, 3830, 3856, 3885, 3935, 3981, 3985, 3990, 4031, 4052, 4058, 4061, 4066, 4091, 4110, 4113, 4169, 4270, 4537, 4565, 4774, 5217, 5221, 5224, 5426, 5542, 5571, 5586, 5591, 5617, 5635
Administration publique 1857, 2254, 4635, 4961, 4993, 5212, 5638
Administration régionale 4797, 4963
Administration scolaire 2133, 2159, 2237, 2241, 4806
Administration sociale 5648
Administration territoriale 5213
ADN 473, 498, 1620, 5048, 5848
Adolescence 554, 598, 679, 700, 2517, 2596, 2611, 2615, 2618, 2625, 2632, 2635, 2641, 2648, 2896, 2951, 3052, 3056, 3225, 4139, 5384, 5394, 5405, 5410
Adolescents 77, 545, 576, 577, 598, 633, 776, 849, 2074, 2482, 2494, 2602, 2611-2613, 2615, 2616, 2619, 2621, 2623, 2624, 2628, 2629, 2631, 2633, 2636, 2638, 2640, 2642, 2644-2647, 2667, 2727, 2803, 2804, 2853, 2896, 2897, 2916, 2936, 2947, 2954, 2963, 2995, 3041, 3053, 3212, 3213, 3271, 3294, 3300, 3328, 3337, 3352, 3414, 3521, 3554, 4435, 4996, 5036, 5044, 5046, 5052, 5062, 5079, 5089, 5095, 5192, 5200, 5364, 5373, 5429, 5447, 5671, 5680, 5721, 5767, 5906, 5935, 5941, 5978, 5985
Adoption d'enfant 698, 2915, 3433, 5192, 5209, 5538, 5553, 5563, 5569, 5577, 5597
Adorno, Theodor W. 213, 1227, 1853, 1988
Adultes 623, 637, 661, 670, 738, 900, 918, 1544, 1716, 2002, 2592, 2676, 2834, 2909, 3022, 3237, 3352, 4548, 4793, 5054, 5675
Aéroports 3948
Aeta 3776
Affaires 414, 1092, 1123, 1200, 1308, 1980, 2266, 2362, 2391, 2568, 3553, 3570, 3818, 3863, 3942, 4175, 4207, 4223, 4355, 4360, 4371, 4372, 4375, 4379, 4396, 4624, 4630, 4658, 4791, 5475
  voir aussi: Économie de l'entreprise, Études commerciales
Affaires étrangères 3391, 5363
Affectation des ressources 49, 2018, 3618, 4136, 4251, 4270, 5540, 5785
Affectivité 739, 850, 937
Affiliation 2667, 3344
Affiliation politique 5307
Affiliation religieuse 1429, 5083
Africains 199, 592, 1204, 1476, 1620, 1813, 2167, 2379, 2429, 2502, 3457, 3468, 3528, 3551, 3562, 3593, 3649, 3736, 4500, 5244, 5328
Afrikaans 1813
Afro-américains 53, 541, 583, 681, 814, 826, 838, 849, 852, 1321, 1372, 1427, 1429, 1442, 1479, 1620, 1750, 1909, 1991, 2036, 2045, 2060, 2174, 2266, 2530,

INDEX DES MATIÈRES

2582, 2655, 2751, 2856, 2898, 2917, 2991, 3024, 3043, 3058, 3098, 3115, 3352, 3391, 3412, 3431, 3432, 3439, 3440, 3442, 3456, 3457, 3477, 3478, 3481, 3488, 3498, 3506, 3514, 3521, 3528, 3572, 3632, 3938, 3993, 3996, 4000, 4006, 4015, 4278, 4291, 4300, 4473, 4489, 4497, 4505, 4511, 4919, 5050, 5103, 5280, 5397, 5409, 5563, 5928, 5947
Afro-brésilien 1431
Âgé 162, 1284, 1687, 2584, 2585, 2651, 2653-2655, 2657, 2659-2664, 2666-2675, 2677-2679, 2682, 2707, 2712, 2811, 2815, 2829, 3219, 3591, 3619, 4303, 4487, 4558, 4852, 5016, 5070, 5493, 5495-5501, 5504, 5506, 5508, 5509, 5511, 5514, 5516-5519, 5521, 5522, 5524-5526, 5528-5535, 5609, 5644, 5738, 5778
  voir aussi: Aide aux personnes âgées
Âge 441, 559, 624, 2231, 2431, 2669, 2744, 2785, 2791, 2805, 2992, 5012, 5096, 5120, 5392, 5838
  voir aussi: Vieillesse
Âge adulte 2600, 2618, 2930, 3026, 5394
Âge au mariage 2691, 2724, 2797, 2825, 2851, 2955, 2961, 2963, 2976, 2992
Agence 162, 306, 308, 313, 320, 345, 358, 391, 407, 677, 709, 793, 1087, 1090, 1437, 1535, 1651, 2361, 3124, 3146, 3147, 3373, 3847, 3918, 4344, 4392, 4515, 4837, 4958, 5438, 5462, 5495, 5849
Agglomération urbaine 3776, 3813, 3948, 3964, 4119
Âgisme 2665, 2670, 2702, 4487, 4488, 4852
Agression personnelle 672, 925, 5437
Agression sexuelle 2340, 2885, 3070, 3292, 3338, 4482, 5438, 5456-5460, 5462, 5463, 5469
Agressivité 576, 672, 727, 872, 925, 1807, 2876, 2877, 2894, 2931, 3031, 3038, 3201, 3344, 3351, 3531, 4187, 4626, 5192, 5437, 5444, 5456
Agriculteurs 2653, 3406, 3873, 3878, 5685
Agriculture 20, 2511, 3708, 3731, 3735, 3873, 3883, 3888, 3889, 3902, 3912, 4142, 4208, 4212, 4674
  voir aussi: Métayage, Systèmes agricoles
Agriexploitation 20, 3873, 3878, 3888, 3889, 4226
Agroindustrie 3760
Aide 767, 2167, 4287, 5349, 5475, 5977
Aide à l'étranger 2704, 4254
Aide au développement 5768
Aide aux enfants 521, 531, 2020, 2486, 2488, 2582, 2846, 2899, 2998, 3003, 3029, 3054, 3169, 3170, 3264, 4235, 4514, 4517, 4528, 4561, 4687, 5192, 5373, 5486, 5490, 5538-5543, 5546-5548, 5550, 5551, 5554, 5556, 5558, 5559, 5561, 5564, 5568, 5569, 5571, 5573, 5576, 5581, 5584-5586, 5588, 5591, 5596, 5599, 5600, 5616, 5624, 5663, 5689, 5696, 5721, 5969
Aide aux personnes âgées 2585, 2654, 2661, 2662, 2669, 2678, 2679, 2712, 2917, 4235, 5016, 5422, 5479, 5482, 5486, 5492, 5493, 5496-5506, 5508, 5509, 5511-5513, 5517, 5520-5527, 5529, 5531-5534, 5685, 5740, 5778
Aide aux victimes de crime 2873, 5116
Aide financière 3042
Aide sanitaire 5977
Aires culturelles 1395
Aires métropolitaines 411, 3590, 3621, 3767, 3933, 3960, 3997, 4015, 4022, 4024, 4066, 4067, 4072, 4103, 4150, 4159, 4164, 4300, 4461
Ajustement structurel 2513, 2568, 2767, 3868, 4223, 4236, 4245, 4278, 4455, 4682, 4968
Alcool 908, 1349, 2515, 2612, 2816, 2819, 2824, 4493, 4994, 5045, 5364, 5368, 5385, 5388, 5390, 5392, 5399, 5400, 5403-5406, 5409, 5411, 5413, 5433, 5444, 5818, 5955, 5968
Alcoolisme 709, 722, 1349, 2719, 2874, 2894, 4493, 4683, 5045, 5376, 5386, 5388, 5393, 5399, 5400, 5403-5406, 5408, 5410, 5413, 5681, 5767, 5838, 5955
ALÉNA 4434, 4458, 5227
Alexander, Jeffrey 341
Algèbre 5029
Algorithme 440, 446, 1043, 1056, 2301, 4755, 5390
Aliénation 388, 785, 1677, 1933, 2018, 2634, 5016, 5372
Alimentation 3003
Aliments 1286, 1300, 1303, 2399, 2622, 2644, 2715, 3837, 4268, 5948
Allaitement naturel 3003, 3027, 3258, 4534, 5969
Allègement de la dette 4287
Allemands 1004, 1179, 1816, 3496, 3552, 3647, 5977
Alliances 1032, 2289
Alliances militaires
  voir: OTAN
Allison, Dorothy 3125
Allocations familiales 4299, 5610, 5624
Allport, Floyd 870
Allport, Gordon 870

SUBJECT INDEX IN FRENCH

Alphabétisation 1694, 1991, 2005, 2006, 2013, 2025, 2040, 2046, 2185, 2221, 3203, 4807, 5058
Althusser, Louis 3130
Altman, Robert 1907
Altruisme 61, 601, 649, 915, 931, 949, 1073, 1532, 1684, 2332, 3843, 4194, 4768, 5106, 5575, 5826, 5860
Ambedkar, Bhimrao Ramji 2394
Ambition 2646, 4582
Âme 220
Amélioration du sol 3733
Aménagement de l'espace 4313
Aménagement d'habitation 2996
Aménagement hydraulique 3690, 3762, 4025
Aménagement urbain 1324, 1657, 1829, 2152, 3702, 3872, 3900, 3908, 3928, 3945, 3947, 3948, 3983, 3994, 4010, 4018, 4024-4027, 4029-4031, 4033-4039, 4041-4043, 4047, 4050-4054, 4058, 4059, 4061, 4064-4067, 4071, 4073-4075, 4079-4081, 4083-4091, 4093, 4096, 4098, 4100, 4105-4108, 4110, 4113, 4114, 4117, 4133, 4140, 4141, 4146, 4147, 4153, 4168-4170, 4172, 4178
Américain d'origine asiatique 1987, 2751, 2866, 2950, 3394, 3459, 3578, 5081, 5577, 5898
Américains 826, 864, 1187, 1929, 3043, 3098, 3218, 3393, 4463
Américanisation 1895, 2569, 5308
Amérindiens 982, 1620, 1991, 2399, 2751, 3402, 5563
Amérindiens du Nord 198, 1785, 3526
Amitié 896, 903, 909, 915, 937, 939, 942, 1945, 2102, 2313, 2370, 3213, 3352, 3859, 4374, 4690, 5564
Amour 209, 293, 674, 897, 900, 913, 920, 922, 939, 942, 950, 1933, 2517, 2629, 3030, 3108, 3227, 3328, 3342, 3746
Analphabétisme 1996
Analyse à courte terme 2796
Analyse à longue terme 431, 2541, 2700, 2796, 3232, 3237, 3675
Analyse anthropologique 331, 2683, 3540
Analyse causale 45, 107, 193, 290, 618, 620, 751
Analyse comparative 74, 154, 243, 323, 409, 471, 497, 520, 562, 1184, 1195, 1246, 1280, 1308, 1452, 1773, 1831, 1992, 1993, 2088, 2104, 2116, 2145, 2157, 2171, 2249, 2254, 2268, 2355, 2396, 2397, 2627, 2632, 2642, 2669, 2684, 2705, 2720, 2756, 2808, 2917, 2923, 2999, 3002, 3011, 3103, 3177, 3226, 3284, 3328, 3446, 3493, 3568, 3622, 3702, 3853, 3980, 3996, 4097, 4226, 4265, 4459, 4521, 4548, 4601, 4625, 4637, 4681, 4705, 4783, 4834, 4860, 4945, 5012, 5053, 5148, 5190, 5297, 5398, 5432, 5448, 5449, 5478, 5641, 5644, 5649, 5751, 5763, 5769, 5815, 5819
Analyse conjoncturelle 2111
Analyse contextuelle 539, 1647, 1833, 1874
Analyse coût-avantage 532, 2120, 5744
Analyse d'activité 1210
Analyse de contenu 1749, 3008
Analyse de discours 197, 333, 369, 405, 506, 523, 568, 828, 870, 940, 959, 1101-1104, 1120, 1127, 1137, 1227, 1263, 1311, 1365, 1558, 1650, 1722, 1730, 1739, 1748, 1762, 1771, 1784, 1789-1792, 1800, 1801, 1807, 1808, 1810, 1821, 1822, 1824, 1830, 1831, 1833, 1839, 1844, 1856, 1872, 1877, 1957, 2327, 2355, 2607, 3045, 3139, 3184, 3299, 3346, 3358, 3772, 3864, 4065, 4250, 4666, 4887, 5170, 5289, 5329, 5418
Analyse de données croisées 2595, 4484, 4679
Analyse de groupe 881, 947, 1041, 1066, 1079, 1081, 3357, 4701
Analyse de la demande 4284
Analyse de régression 485, 489, 662, 1112, 1129, 1443, 1512, 2612, 2666, 2746, 2800, 2816, 2841, 3029, 3182, 3201, 3592, 3929, 4453, 4523, 4721, 4741, 4795, 5045, 5408, 5507, 5918
Analyse de réseau 466, 492, 493, 1043, 1045, 1085, 3927, 4401
Analyse de systèmes 634, 4428
Analyse d'enquête 434, 509, 520, 525, 531, 535, 2768, 4618, 5763, 5788
Analyse des coûts 3979, 5655, 5789, 5909
Analyse des données 413, 421, 424, 429, 430, 432, 433, 440, 446-448, 450, 452-454, 456, 458, 464-466, 472-481, 483, 485-487, 489, 493, 495, 496, 499, 501, 504, 505, 514, 520, 525, 526, 529-531, 585, 621, 828, 930, 1005, 1033, 1045, 1085, 1847, 2006, 2043, 2053, 2059, 2213, 2396, 2681, 2688, 2692, 2817, 2855, 3025, 3178, 3633, 4465, 4613, 4742, 4747, 4752, 4858, 5031, 5093, 5156, 5555, 5592, 5773, 5818, 5825
Analyse des politiques gouvernementales 891, 2792, 3196-3198, 4044, 4859, 5555, 5565, 5597, 5609, 5810, 5854, 5888, 5942, 5973
Analyse des tâches 550, 4614
Analyse du chemin critique 1126
Analyse du discours 1652

INDEX DES MATIÈRES

Analyse écologique 3712
Analyse économique 1861, 2568, 3662, 4220, 4845, 5057
  voir aussi: Analyse à courte terme, Analyse à longue terme
Analyse factorielle 629, 719, 727, 774, 1299, 3749, 3847, 4262
Analyse fonctionnelle 371, 3404, 4837
Analyse historique 2, 26, 144, 145, 148, 161, 165-167, 171, 174, 178, 180, 220, 409, 802, 982, 988, 1280, 1308, 1353, 1811, 1819, 1976, 2009, 2207, 2568, 3098, 3496, 3528, 3631, 4206, 4220, 4837, 4959, 4966, 5218
Analyse mathématique 453, 1045, 1085
Analyse multivariée 2746, 2748, 2794, 2818, 3210, 3481, 3588, 3673, 4664, 5049, 5138, 5587
Analyse organisationnelle 684, 1104, 1108, 1115, 1125, 1127, 1131, 1148, 1150, 1157, 4357, 4366, 4389, 4426, 4510, 4641, 4652, 4659, 4669, 4679, 4747, 4823
Analyse par cohorte 772, 2287, 2651, 2681, 2696, 4548
Analyse par grappe 735, 4557
Analyse post-structurale 340, 410, 1214
Analyse qualitative 20, 427, 430, 431, 435, 449, 455, 457, 462, 469, 470, 504, 514, 517, 520, 528, 529, 585, 651, 1488, 1727, 2194, 2530, 2646, 3164, 3666, 3852, 4486, 4726, 4759, 4837, 5563, 5816, 5838, 5842, 5925
Analyse quantitative 63, 163, 457, 462, 490, 507, 514, 520, 585, 651, 1488, 1791, 3666, 3784, 4527, 5075, 5563
Analyse régionale 2697
Analyse secondaire 5105
Analyse sociologique 28, 50, 65, 167, 180, 323, 347, 409, 413, 448, 482, 497, 1020, 1162, 1306, 1354, 1366, 1561, 1595, 1629, 1639, 1652, 1743, 1944, 1962, 2302, 2315, 2319, 2330, 2374, 2404, 2427, 2445, 2456, 2526, 2556, 2645, 2683, 3463, 3514, 3565, 3617, 3638, 3848, 3860, 3946, 4298, 4344, 4584, 4930, 4959, 4966, 5046, 5117, 5249, 5264, 5276, 5285
Analyse spatiale 1302, 1657, 2493, 4019, 5838, 5968
Analyse statistique 101, 163, 453, 473, 478, 479, 481, 524, 1749, 1798, 2523, 2629, 2817, 2829, 2958, 2974, 2996, 3407, 3528, 4766, 5324, 5448, 5965, 5983

Analyse structurale 308, 345, 391, 471, 948, 1069, 1136, 1146, 1632, 2413, 2428, 4014, 4837, 5075, 5277, 5300
Analyse transculturelle 65, 164, 338, 550, 633, 650, 763, 870, 1131, 1330, 1464, 1757, 1767, 1791, 1796, 1824, 1885, 2128, 2145, 2265, 2354, 2460, 2584, 2663, 2666, 2908, 2945, 3060, 3231, 3283, 3284, 3419, 3503, 4012, 4198, 4318, 4359, 4425, 4630, 4631, 4658, 5065, 5069, 5296, 5388, 5521, 5891
Analyse transnationale 520, 1134, 1230, 1725, 1736, 2104, 2116, 2179, 2357, 2367, 2405, 2530, 2602, 2627, 2669, 2679, 2704, 2756, 2820, 3039, 3194, 3338, 3470, 3759, 3913, 3961, 4039, 4135, 4252, 4253, 4386, 4430, 4441, 4475, 4557, 4624, 4745, 4764, 4768, 4772, 4860, 4945, 5272, 5284, 5435, 5445, 5450, 5498, 5519, 5605, 5636, 5641, 5717, 5751, 5756, 5769, 5786, 5787, 5858, 5956
Analyse typologique 1505, 4584
Anarchisme 3295
Anarchistes 3295
Anatomie 3109
Anciens combattants 5361, 5913
Anglicanisme 1409
Angoisse 593, 637, 685, 721, 731, 740, 757, 780, 787, 797, 802, 810, 821, 933, 935, 1006, 1173, 1347, 1927, 2646, 2970, 3023, 3870, 3930, 4710, 4724, 5080, 5681, 5710, 5831
Animaux 386, 561, 1293, 2863, 3926, 4637
  voir aussi: Droits des animaux
Animaux domestiques 2863
Anonymat 1066, 1862, 3468
Anorexie 506, 769, 791, 817, 2667, 5182, 5847
Anthropocentrisme 3743
Anthropologie 16, 25, 27, 54, 348, 603, 605, 801, 1197, 1802, 3121, 3363, 3499, 3693, 3758, 5338, 5727
Anthropologie appliquée 5924
Anthropologie culturelle 989, 1161, 1227, 1319, 1331, 1658, 1940, 1958, 1986, 2544, 3323
Anthropologie du corps 1189
Anthropologie du droit 5170
Anthropologie du sport 1357
Anthropologie du travail 59, 2574
Anthropologie historique 195
Anthropologie industrielle 801
Anthropologie linguistique 1161, 1949
Anthropologie médicale 5386, 5541, 5727
Anthropologie philosophique 209, 1201

SUBJECT INDEX IN FRENCH

Anthropologie physique 3528
Anthropologie politique 4943
Anthropologie psychologique 875
Anthropologie religieuse 1433, 1455, 1464, 1483, 1506, 1509
Anthropologie rurale 3920
Anthropologie sociale 14, 837, 1020, 1259, 1316, 1949, 3143, 3510, 4759, 5259
Anthropologie sociologique 2544
Anthropologie urbaine 4012
Anthropologie visuelle 1346, 1767, 1870
Anthropométrie 3210
Anticipations du revenu 5891
Anticolonialisme 5226
Anticommunisme 1262
Antiimpérialisme 4935
Antillais 4125, 4500
Antisémitisme 145, 235, 410, 1963, 3455, 3466, 3502, 3518, 3532
Apartheid 2321, 3510, 3769, 4864, 5260, 5703, 5937
  voir aussi: Société post-apartheid
APEC 2145
Apostasie 1392, 1494
Appadurai, Arjun 1409
Apparence physique 573, 938, 3272
Appartenance au groupe 856, 857, 864, 865, 972, 973, 987, 990, 1032, 1037, 1044, 1063, 1086, 3418, 3857, 3863, 4316, 4385, 4512
Appartenance ecclésiale 1415, 3614
Appel
  voir: Cours d'appel
Apprentissage 4590
Approvisionnement en eau 2823, 3702, 3813, 4025
Après-guerre 101, 149, 165, 173, 355, 1004, 1274, 1305, 1442, 1612, 1956, 2117, 2305, 2374, 2434, 3638, 3658, 3983, 4079, 5189, 5295, 5302, 5324, 5432
Aptitude 4651
Arabes 280, 753, 1932, 2619, 2885, 3115, 3393, 3462, 5908
Arbitrage 1019, 2554, 4844
Arbres 5237
Archéologie 123, 3121
Architecte 1849, 1857, 3973, 4131
Architecture 1849, 1857, 1859, 3854, 3941, 3945, 3962, 3973, 3984, 4026, 4028, 4039, 4094, 4126, 4131, 4941
Architecture urbaine 4038, 4106, 4126
Archives 32, 172, 183, 1884, 5123
Arciniegas, Germán 159
Arendt, Hannah 232, 293, 1251, 4911, 5311

Argent 1177, 1287, 1427, 2314, 4186, 4192, 4193, 4347, 4349-4351, 4425, 4684
Argyris, C. 1095
Aristocratie 2439, 3891, 4954
Aristotle 201, 286, 1555, 1650
Armée 3242, 3290, 3945, 4549, 5347, 5348, 5352, 5354, 5355, 5361
Armée de l'air 4614, 4760
Armée de terre 1813, 5338, 5339, 5352, 5359
Arméniens 1990
Armes 4984, 5050, 5079
  voir aussi: Mines antipersonnel
Armes á feu 5192
Armes biologiques 5988
Armes chimiques 5988
Armes nucléaires 5988
Arnason, Johann P. 1253
Arnauld, Antoine 106
Arrestation 2868, 5031, 5052, 5137
Art 202, 241, 579, 1207, 1266, 1279, 1298, 1311, 1342, 1345, 1848, 1850-1855, 1859, 1867-1869, 1873, 1876, 1878, 1890, 1895, 1911, 1937, 1971, 1977, 3139, 4121
  voir aussi: Arts du spectacle, Arts visuels, Histoire de l'art, Oeuvres d'art, Philosophie de l'art, Sociologie de l'art
Art contemporain 1860, 1866, 1880
Art culinaire 3223
Art de la guerre 5323, 5346, 5353, 5355, 5362, 5445
Artisanat 4238
Artisans 971, 1616, 4263
Artistes 1852, 1861, 1863, 1868, 1901, 1904, 3115, 4767
Artistes du spectacle 1346, 1982
Artistes peintres 1863
Arts 1260, 1724, 1739, 1866, 1880, 1963, 3827, 4144, 4954, 5232
Arts du spectacle 2458
Arts visuels 970, 1100, 1866, 1870, 1880, 1900, 3375
Ascendance 952, 3589
Ashkenaze 3483
Asiatiques 676, 710, 771, 1929, 2008, 2917, 2936, 3115, 3218, 3234, 3265, 3323, 3509, 3521, 3524, 3559, 3570, 3673, 3846, 5928
Asile 1177, 2313, 3354, 3680
  voir aussi: Droit d'asile
Aspects juridiques 2716, 3291, 3354, 4876, 4984, 5219, 5886, 5888
Aspirations 2317, 2425, 2649, 4527, 4781, 5592
Assimilation culturelle 3411, 3423, 3427, 3548, 3555, 3562, 3566, 3578, 3580, 3596, 4012

INDEX DES MATIÈRES

Assimilation des immigrants 2033, 2530, 3398, 3471, 3545, 3555, 3563, 3564, 3568, 3573-3578, 3581, 3585, 3588, 3593, 3604, 3653, 3674, 4445, 4964, 5791
Assimilation ethnique 2024, 2051, 3409, 3425, 3440, 3487, 3533, 3548
Assistance 5895
Assistance socio-psychologique 724, 759, 767, 778, 785, 786, 806, 815, 2484, 2733, 2869, 3370, 3381, 5175, 5595, 5599, 5671, 5674, 5682, 5699, 5714, 5717, 5923
Association commerciale 1134, 3166, 3813, 4088, 4357, 4390, 4830
Associations 408, 2088, 3362, 4385, 4767, 4940, 4950, 4960, 5491
Associations de quartier 3959
Associations de sociologie 38, 4766
Assurance chômage 5648
Assurance maladie 525, 5506, 5726, 5732, 5774, 5786, 5811, 5838, 5897, 5971
Assurance vie 4699
Assurance vieillesse 2712
Assurances 5526
   voir aussi: Assurance chômage, Assurance maladie, Assurance vie
Astrologie 1416
Astronomie 1555
Ateliers 1014, 5928
Athéisme 1373, 1428, 1451
Athlètes 1305, 1344, 1354, 3217, 4767
Atlas 91, 3769
Attention 670, 1717
Attitude envers le travail 4356, 4702, 4704, 4745
Attitude moraliste envers le travail 1126, 4239, 4365, 4597, 4709
Attitudes 117, 142, 228, 485, 524, 527, 549, 574, 582, 648, 676, 696, 714, 763, 791, 823, 825-827, 835, 842, 845, 851, 852, 859-861, 863, 865, 876, 884, 885, 890, 891, 898, 916, 941, 978, 983, 1004, 1034, 1052, 1063, 1111, 1119, 1126, 1135, 1285, 1297, 1437, 1511, 1531, 1710, 1747, 1750, 1774, 1789, 1820, 1821, 1993, 2009, 2086, 2106, 2186, 2235, 2245, 2313, 2357, 2389, 2396-2398, 2417, 2425, 2452, 2473, 2474, 2476, 2487, 2523, 2524, 2538, 2585, 2601, 2619, 2628, 2629, 2636, 2640, 2643, 2652, 2670, 2726, 2770, 2778, 2868, 2917, 2922, 2991, 3011, 3046, 3178, 3215, 3221, 3237, 3239, 3274, 3283, 3295, 3296, 3455, 3464, 3470, 3522, 3545, 3547, 3552, 3565, 3601, 3610, 3633, 3674, 3724, 3729, 3734, 3743, 3748, 3749, 3853, 3914, 3930, 3993, 4320, 4360, 4370, 4487, 4527, 4581, 4658, 4670, 4716, 4744, 4747, 4748, 4785, 4793, 4837, 4839, 4914, 5012, 5056, 5083, 5154, 5244, 5290, 5298, 5328, 5407, 5409, 5414, 5419, 5446, 5503, 5560, 5643, 5669, 5829, 5838, 5878, 5891, 5919, 5941
Attitudes patronales 4618
Attitudes politiques 512, 1730, 2372, 4596
Attitudes raciales 1308, 3412, 3461, 3508, 3514-3516
Attraction du groupe 1047
Attraction interpersonnelle 573, 898, 938
Attribution du nom 1822
Auditeurs 919, 1982
Audition 818, 1653
Auditions musicales 1979, 1982, 1984
Augustine [Saint] 232, 293
Auteur 281, 1158, 1187, 1419, 1557, 1913, 1914, 1920, 1932, 1937-1939, 1941, 1943, 1962, 1966, 2282, 2314, 3098, 3122, 3518
Authenticité culturelle 4238
Autoassistance 548, 4939, 5260, 5376, 5691
Autobiographies 181, 283, 1882, 1888, 1938, 1950, 2625, 2651, 2679, 3107, 3250, 4558
Autodétermination 139, 892, 982, 2093, 2310
Autodéveloppement 704, 2712, 3642
Autogestion 439, 4201, 4618, 4664, 4934, 4946, 5376
Automobiles 1129, 2816, 4146, 4313
Autonomie 17, 203, 864, 978, 995, 2143, 2147, 2242, 2258, 2293, 2347, 2532, 3070, 3279, 3919, 4618, 5267, 5553, 5849, 5889
Autoritarisme 860, 1674, 4250, 5250, 5303
Autorité 203, 1597, 2338, 2515, 3285, 3392, 4199, 4325, 4558, 4662, 4978, 4993, 5052, 5117, 5850, 5883
Autorité politique 5237
Autorités religieuses 2330
Autosuffisance 704
Avantage compétitif 4504
Averroes 272
Avocat 5203
Avortement 1650, 2696, 2724, 2727, 2730, 2734, 2744, 2745, 2750, 2754, 2758, 2760, 2764, 2769, 3337, 4939, 5200, 5851, 5868, 5873, 5888
Aznar, José María 1839
Bacon, Francis 1611
Bahaï 1446
Baisse de la fécondité 2698, 2712, 2770, 2773, 2775, 2781, 2782, 2785, 2788, 2797, 2802
Baisse de la mortalité 2799, 2836
Bakhtin, Mikhail 162, 224, 378

SUBJECT INDEX IN FRENCH

Bandes 1370, 3413, 5046, 5079, 5109, 5114, 5118, 5450, 5465, 5472
Bandes dessinées 3008, 3313
Bangladeshis 3523, 4500
Banque mondiale 2292, 2561, 3961, 4161, 4287, 5282
Banques 1091, 1103, 4349, 4541, 4662, 4862
Banques commerciales 3975, 4705
Banquiers 4349
Bantou 1813, 1822
Baptisme 1490, 2901
Barker, Clive 1920
Barnes, Barry 1610
Barrages 3728, 3766
Barrière linguistique 3586
Bartlett, Frederic C. 868
Base-ball 1308
Bases de données 92, 166, 450, 481
Basques 1865
Bâtiment 1849, 1857, 2233, 3692, 4028, 4065, 4106, 4168
Baudrillard, Jean 357, 1227, 3096
Bauman, Zygmunt 305, 335, 1281
Beauvoir, Simone de 283
Beaux-parents 2613, 2917, 2932, 2949
Beck, Ulrich 1609
Bédouin 2054
Behaviorisme 591, 594, 599, 667, 699, 822, 855, 1299
Bell, Daniel 2540
Belsey, Catherine 3102
Bengali 4575
Ben-Gurion, David 1916
Benigni, Roberto 1896
Benjamin, Walter 213, 299
Bentham, Jeremy 4987
Berlin, Isaiah 2143
Besoins de logement 3824, 3825, 3978, 3981, 5422
Besoins d'éducation 2020, 2486
Besoins financiers 5636
Besoins fondamentaux 361, 2495, 3827, 3840, 4251, 4299, 5422, 5701, 5979
Bhaskar, Roy 140
Bible 145, 169, 1375, 3743
Bibliographies 36, 72, 101, 1667, 3290, 4686, 5076
Bibliothèques 78-80, 85, 104, 1646
Biculturalisme 956
Bidonville 4269
Bidonvilles 58, 2789, 3974, 4157, 4169
Bien commun 5659
Bien-être 510, 1151, 2307, 2403, 2452, 2458, 2577, 2793, 2997, 3001, 3434, 3588, 3603, 4271, 4308, 4398, 4531, 4587, 4597, 4686, 4789, 4937, 5321, 5482, 5485, 5487, 5489, 5494, 5500, 5526, 5535, 5536, 5565, 5569, 5585, 5609, 5610, 5614, 5618-5620, 5628, 5633, 5634, 5648, 5653, 5657, 5659, 5661, 5711, 5793, 5936, 5982
Bien-être des enfants 531, 545, 546, 783, 2154, 2488, 2582, 2599, 2610, 2644, 2859, 2867, 2903, 2922, 2928, 2952, 3010, 3030, 3264, 4191, 4442, 4452, 5366, 5396, 5482, 5537, 5539, 5540, 5543, 5546-5548, 5551, 5554, 5555, 5557, 5559, 5560, 5566, 5567, 5569, 5570, 5572-5574, 5576, 5577, 5579, 5582, 5587, 5588, 5590, 5594-5599, 5601, 5661, 5676, 5689, 5693, 5696, 5769, 5949
Bien-être (personnel) 482, 505, 577, 673, 675, 693, 717, 892, 936, 1480, 2351, 2494, 2642, 2668, 2680, 2814, 2846, 2977, 3012, 3018, 3029, 3547, 3666, 3833, 4265, 4618, 4706, 4710, 4931, 5373, 5575, 5838, 5842
Bien-être social 461, 929, 1121, 1480, 1590, 2307, 2390, 2454, 2455, 2466, 2469, 2489, 2496, 2648, 2764, 2865, 2866, 2870, 2882, 3169, 3528, 3555, 3675, 3775, 4111, 4169, 4231, 4256, 4259, 4283, 4299, 4469, 4563, 4979, 4983, 5023, 5071, 5096, 5126, 5143, 5151, 5366, 5427, 5475-5477, 5482-5484, 5490, 5521, 5530, 5532, 5533, 5545, 5549, 5556, 5559, 5572, 5574, 5581, 5598, 5600, 5601, 5611-5614, 5616, 5619, 5628, 5632, 5633, 5639, 5642-5644, 5647, 5658-5661, 5665, 5672, 5676, 5685, 5691, 5696, 5699, 5700, 5706, 5708, 5711, 5716, 5717, 5739, 5742, 5795, 5796, 5806, 5819, 5927
Biens culturels 1100, 1172, 1778
Biens de consommation 4334, 4339
Biens publics 3694
Bilinguisme 610, 1785, 1789, 1809, 1811, 1819, 1836, 2461, 3595
Biodiversité 225, 2711, 3705, 3712, 3737, 3747, 3759, 3798
Bioéthique 1039, 1620, 5025, 5730, 5848, 5854, 5861, 5865, 5868, 5880, 5882, 5884, 5888
Biographies 36, 41, 72, 74, 103, 178, 240, 316, 376, 412, 501, 508, 1735, 1853, 1863, 1882, 1893, 1914, 1916, 1934, 1939, 1952, 1960, 1964, 2479, 3094, 4580, 5420, 5944
Biologie 236, 396, 598, 1606, 2902, 3083, 3109, 5388, 5406, 5851
Biologie humaine 3167

INDEX DES MATIÈRES

Biologistes 27, 1578
Biomédicine 1620, 5817, 5853, 5859, 5962, 5980
Bion, Wilfred R. 225
Biopolitique 5379
Biotechnologie 1099, 1563, 1610, 4246, 5864
Bisexualité 786, 3297, 3340, 3352, 3357, 3373, 3381, 5984
Blancs 710, 826, 835, 1195, 1479, 1761, 1767, 2034, 2692, 2856, 2991, 3067, 3088, 3259, 3274, 3436, 3439, 3449, 3464, 3534, 3565, 3570, 3588, 3834, 3835, 3996, 4014, 4019, 4291, 4497, 5053, 5454
Blasphème 1867
Bloc oriental 1274
Bloor, David 1610
Blumenberg, Hans 1251
Bogdanov, Aleksandr 1553
Bohémiens 1748, 2067, 3408, 3427, 3474, 3520
Boland, Eavan 1936
Bonheur 229, 591, 683, 687, 688, 690, 3183
Bouddhisme 212, 239, 247, 286, 952, 1462, 1464-1473, 1699, 3654
Bouddhistes 1462, 1465, 1471
Bouglé, Célestin 2395
Bourdieu, Pierre 341, 377, 401, 406, 1212, 1409, 3153, 3509
Bourgeoisie 4273
Bourse 2571, 4352, 4366, 4870
Bowen, M. 1006
Boycottage 4331
Brahmanisme 2394, 2207
Brandt, Richard 2361
Brasserie 4323
Braverman, Harry 4400
Brecht, Bertholt 1756
Britanniques 763
Broszat, Martin 162
Brutalité 2235, 2602, 2885, 3006, 3289, 3458, 4691
Buber, Martin 265
Bubis, Ignatz 3532
Bûcherons 3735
Budgets 42, 5223
Budgets des ménages 3190, 4263, 4310
Bureaucratie 1149, 3062, 4421, 4492, 4646, 4806, 4871, 4954, 4968, 4973, 5214, 5216, 5222, 5652, 5871
But de l'organisation 1129, 2139, 4667
Butler, Judith 3788
Buveurs 500, 722, 5388, 5404, 5406, 5955
Cadres 582, 2391, 4370, 4408, 4519, 4543, 4624, 4625, 4645, 4657, 4671
Cadres moyens 4631

Cadres supérieurs 4408, 4620
Café 4206, 4331, 5433
Cajun 1367
Caldwell, Lynton Keith 3759
Calendriers 1544, 2575
Camions 5067
Camp 3640
Campagne 3915, 5418
Campagne électorale 5234, 5288
Camps de concentration 5005
Campus universitaire 996
Camus, Albert 5152
Canadien 147, 956, 2917, 4090
Canaux de communication 1640, 2479
Cancer 766, 2813, 2817, 3759, 5838, 5857, 5891, 5893, 5960, 5986
Candidats 5307
Cannabis 1313, 4998, 5381, 5386, 5394, 5886
Canne à sucre 3882
Cantons 4592
Caoutchouc 3732
Capacité 663, 2084, 2253, 3049
Capacités au calcul 1991, 2040
Capital 291, 3057, 3661, 4349, 4432, 4444, 4458, 4793, 5154
Capital culturel 1227, 2402, 2593, 2612, 3996, 4349, 4353, 5154
Capital humain 63, 1122, 1998, 2059, 2070, 2457, 2605, 2904, 3177, 3604, 3617, 3621, 3798, 3817, 4209, 4257, 4265, 4267, 4303, 4375, 4458, 4470, 4510, 4598, 4604, 4605, 4609, 4634, 4643, 4648, 4720, 4756, 4790, 4799, 5633, 5773
Capital risque 4369
Capital social 61, 63, 1267, 1998, 2333, 2345, 2357, 2506, 2593, 2624, 2909, 3563, 3617, 3661, 3814, 3847, 3855-3857, 3881, 3893, 3910, 3986, 4031, 4197, 4203, 4240, 4265, 4290, 4349, 4371, 4464, 4510, 4592, 4641, 4732, 4936, 5773
Capitalisme 3, 336, 344, 360, 362, 373, 379, 1172, 1214, 1778, 1920, 2018, 2445, 2446, 2450, 2461, 2507, 2540, 2544, 2551, 2557, 2558, 2567, 2578, 3225, 3503, 3720, 3753, 3771, 3786, 3797, 4202, 4204, 4205, 4208, 4210, 4213-4219, 4226, 4227, 4231, 4234, 4239, 4241, 4242, 4273, 4287, 4294, 4311, 4330, 4336, 4373, 4715, 4850, 4904, 4912, 4920, 4923, 4935, 4942, 4968, 5092, 5272, 5278, 5343, 5644, 5652
voir aussi: Histoire du capitalisme
Caractère 241, 673, 684, 702, 706, 717, 726, 728, 733, 921, 1007, 1332, 1862, 1893, 1937, 4637, 5040

523

SUBJECT INDEX IN FRENCH

Caractère national 960, 4207
Cardoso, Fernando Henrique 4949
Carnavals 1345, 3956
Carroll, Lewis 1928
Carter, Angela 3320
Cartes géographiques 94, 1000, 2829, 3371, 3768, 3769, 3785
Cartographie 58, 1798, 3702, 3785, 3813, 4346, 5552
Carver, Raymond 1907
Castes 1376, 1424, 2046, 2381, 2394, 2395, 2415, 2441, 2683, 2701, 2766, 2783, 2984, 3739, 4285, 5269
Castoriadis, Cornelius 2317
Castro, Fidel 1167
Catastrophes naturelles 767, 3695, 3699, 3702, 3752, 3776, 3813, 5911
Catégorisation de soi 828, 878, 999, 1042, 1083, 2436, 2530, 3660
Catholicisme 1431, 1460, 1475, 1478, 1482, 1491, 1493, 1496, 1498, 1502, 1509, 1510, 1513, 1514, 2357, 3919
Catholiques 1343, 1475, 1479, 1484, 1499, 1510, 1513, 2439, 3132
Causalité 108, 109, 193, 259, 290, 356, 370, 391, 497, 618, 620, 653, 664, 854, 908, 1152, 1606, 1624, 1633, 2319, 4197, 4744, 5058, 5075, 5954
Cause 45, 137, 193, 290
Cavell, Stanley 934
Cécité 2481, 2493, 2494
Cécité des couleurs 3471
Célibat 2976
Célibataires 2311, 5415
Cellules 5851
Censure 1243, 1309, 1427, 2358, 3324, 5298
Centralisation 1106, 1146, 3876, 4806, 4954, 5216
Centre ville 3359, 3937, 3965, 3971, 4081
Centres commerciaux 4182, 4315, 4329
Cérémonie de mariage 2982
Cérémonies 986, 2851, 5338
Cerveau 571, 591, 628, 630, 739, 5406
Chamanisme 1401
Chances d'éducation 2030, 5358
Chances d'obtenir un emploi 2037, 2475, 2532, 2561, 2691, 3608, 4447, 4465, 4523, 4615, 4742, 4761
Changement culturel 139, 994, 1136, 1161, 1169, 1182, 1190, 1202, 1205, 1216, 1264, 1268, 1321, 1336, 1554, 1658, 1777, 1841, 2399, 2505, 2511, 2515, 2520, 2532, 2536, 2549, 2557, 2566, 2569, 2675, 2733, 2870, 3586, 3662, 3776, 4177, 4379, 4535, 4866, 4944

Changement de climat 1601, 2717, 3708
Changement de rôle 2680, 4770
Changement démographique 2542, 2574, 2657, 2679, 2684, 2686, 2689-2691, 2695-2698, 2705, 2708, 2710, 2712, 2720, 2724, 2725, 2767, 2781, 2792, 2796, 2797, 2799, 2810, 2835, 2837, 2994, 3397, 3716, 3795, 4252, 5780
Changement d'organisation 1094, 1104, 1114, 1118, 1119, 1125, 1126, 1130, 1134, 1135, 1152, 1154, 2134, 2243, 2250, 3097, 4362, 4379, 4400, 4408, 4424, 4632, 4721, 4726, 4729, 4759, 4788, 4867, 5148, 5732, 5924, 5932
Changement économique 177, 975, 1673, 2504, 2507, 2519, 2541, 2563, 2565, 2579, 2837, 2914, 2965, 3488, 3776, 3810, 3916, 3997, 4066, 4218, 4223, 4241, 4255, 4301, 4429, 4434, 4474, 4715, 4726, 4818, 4866, 5187, 5767, 5773
Changement linguistique 1723, 1804, 1805, 1816, 1818, 1819, 1841, 1847, 3423
Changement politique 161, 177, 1000, 1169, 1673, 2507, 2520, 2523, 2541, 2563, 2565, 3660, 3776, 3828, 3869, 3890, 4854, 4859, 4866, 4885, 5341, 5773
Changement religieux 1199, 1384, 1415, 1418, 1425, 1431, 1433, 1448, 1474, 1486, 1489, 1509, 1516, 4477
Changement social 19, 28, 52, 59, 166, 177, 185, 195, 243, 294, 347, 398, 477, 543, 734, 822, 829, 964, 975, 992, 1010, 1025, 1182, 1199, 1205, 1221, 1244, 1260, 1264, 1284, 1298, 1300, 1351, 1461, 1507, 1514, 1517, 1532, 1540, 1590, 1646, 1656, 1673, 1678, 1690, 1708, 1727, 1729, 1744, 1961, 2129, 2151, 2156, 2161, 2182, 2213, 2295, 2314, 2329, 2333, 2360, 2363, 2364, 2372, 2375, 2400, 2402, 2410, 2424, 2437, 2439, 2475, 2503, 2504, 2506, 2508-2510, 2512, 2514, 2516, 2517, 2519, 2521-2534, 2537, 2538, 2541, 2542, 2550, 2553, 2555, 2557, 2562, 2563, 2567, 2576, 2578, 2579, 2587, 2594, 2602, 2606, 2639, 2646, 2647, 2650, 2657, 2679, 2691, 2772, 2791, 2806, 2911, 2914, 2933, 2938, 2955, 2961, 2963, 3008, 3062, 3065, 3073, 3086, 3105, 3106, 3127, 3147, 3168, 3189, 3217, 3223, 3224, 3252, 3268, 3278, 3459, 3488, 3560, 3569, 3584, 3651, 3660, 3722, 3769, 3776, 3786, 3787, 3809, 3810, 3890, 3916, 3999, 4041, 4066, 4075, 4077, 4090, 4101, 4149, 4155, 4158, 4177, 4181,

4223, 4225, 4228, 4241, 4256, 4258,
4269, 4287, 4292, 4297, 4298, 4316,
4334, 4337, 4361, 4429, 4446, 4526,
4575, 4859, 4887, 4928, 4964, 4974,
4976, 4991, 5039, 5091, 5110, 5134, 5144,
5255, 5265, 5357, 5363, 5505, 5539,
5641, 5643, 5691, 5702, 5773, 5892
Changement structurel 1011, 2123, 2833,
4221
Changement technologique 532, 537, 1149,
1172, 1199, 1226, 1333, 1554, 1563, 1576,
1593, 1603, 1621, 1641, 1667, 1689,
1693, 1725, 2139, 2295, 2527, 2565,
2566, 2571, 2579, 2581, 2679, 2772,
3223, 3776, 3820, 4031, 4075, 4122,
4213, 4354, 4382, 4387, 4393, 4397,
4434, 4750, 5372, 5877
Chansons populaires 1972, 1973, 1987
Chants 1334, 1364, 1972, 1973, 1976, 1978,
1987, 1989, 4990
Charbonnages 20, 4192
Charité 996, 1156, 2313, 3844, 4192, 4768,
5476, 5481, 5719, 5723, 5776, 5860
Chasseurs de tête 4416
Châtiment 161, 1993, 2607, 3012, 3849, 4990,
4992, 4999, 5001, 5004, 5005, 5007,
5009, 5015-5017, 5022, 5029, 5030, 5034,
5040, 5043, 5047, 5149, 5174, 5192,
5195, 5465, 5580
voir aussi: Peine de mort
Checkland, Peter 376
Chefs 4994
Chefs d'entreprise 582, 3190, 4372, 4387,
4407, 4415
Chefs d'État 1731, 4949, 4954, 5299
Chekhov, Anton 249
Cherchant revenus d'investissement 4204
Chercheurs 423, 528, 2465
Cherry, Don 979
Chicano 5232
Chimie 1623
Chimistes 1623, 5801, 5813
Chinois 806, 864, 952, 1186, 1811, 2568,
2941, 3218, 3497, 3553, 3557, 3583,
3685, 4381, 4500, 5292, 5304, 5446, 5458
Chirurgie 1189, 3272, 5878
Choix collectif 465, 3705, 3759, 4916
Choix de produits 606
Choix des facteurs 1299
Choix du conjoint 898, 3318, 3351
Choix d'une profession 3166, 4438, 4757,
4781
Choix rationnel 2, 10, 40, 115, 129, 323, 364,
366, 458, 1069, 1299, 1377, 2048, 4013,

4180, 4194, 4196, 4326, 4739, 4837,
4936, 5075
Chômage 510, 1285, 2046, 2577, 2714, 2855,
3568, 3590, 3594, 3840, 3870, 4250,
4269, 4368, 4439, 4463, 4476, 4481,
4501, 4505, 4532, 4579-4590, 4592, 4594-
4597, 4696, 4713, 4753, 4790, 4796,
4828, 4848, 4866, 5063, 5222, 5365,
5392, 5700, 5838
Chômage des jeunes 412, 4505, 4590, 4598,
4797
Chômage partiel 20, 4398, 4591
Chômage rural 4591
Chômage structurel 2519
Chômeurs 460, 4580-4582, 4585, 4586, 4593,
4790, 5662
Chomsky, Noam 571
Chrétiens 249, 505, 1462, 1515, 4125, 5083
Chrétiens orthodoxes 1516
Christianisation 1476, 1492
Christianisme 145, 169, 247, 1159, 1251,
1258, 1389, 1405, 1407, 1410, 1419,
1432, 1434, 1457, 1460, 1462, 1474,
1476-1478, 1482, 1483, 1485, 1489-1494,
1496, 1497, 1501, 1502, 1504-1506, 1509,
1515, 1551, 1948, 2169, 2394, 2554,
3028, 3366, 3573, 3743, 3967, 4535,
4962, 5722
voir aussi: Catholicisme, Pentecôtisme
Chronologie 1277, 5887
Chuang-tse 1426
Chuang-tzu 200, 1473
Chuilleanáin, Eiléan Ni 1936
Churchill, Winston Spencer 3759
Cinéastes 1880
Cinéma 1318, 1332, 1337, 1365, 1879-1885,
1888, 1893-1896, 1898-1901, 1904, 1905,
1907, 1911, 1912, 1983, 2665, 3157, 3323
Circonscriptions administratives 3359, 4149
Circulation 1302, 4053, 4114
Circulation aérienne 4729
Circulation routière 1302
Citoyenneté 58, 322, 954, 1184, 1519, 1643,
1688, 1756, 1764, 1921, 1979, 2063,
2170, 2171, 2181, 2188, 2199, 2218,
2220, 2386, 2387, 2419, 2532, 2567,
2604, 2674, 3060, 3065, 3106, 3146,
3315, 3423, 3460, 3471, 3499, 3528,
3563, 3605, 3630, 3634, 3669, 3683,
3827, 3829, 3965, 3969, 4211, 4420, 4445,
4754, 4832, 4893, 4901, 4905, 4906,
4923, 4927, 4932, 4939, 4941, 4951,
4952, 4955, 4958, 4961, 4964, 5159,
5192, 5305, 5484, 5608, 5609, 5615

SUBJECT INDEX IN FRENCH

Citoyens 953, 1662, 1742, 2220, 2387, 2604, 3734, 3799, 3814, 4927, 5122, 5138, 5218, 5305, 5535
Civil 1009, 5125
Civilisation 956, 973, 988, 1003, 1159, 1160, 1162, 1163, 1167, 1171, 1175, 1178-1180, 1185, 1201, 1225, 1226, 1276, 1277, 1280, 1360, 1865, 2508, 2558, 3797, 3887, 3934, 4094, 5315, 5372
Civilisation contemporaine 32, 305, 1256, 1260, 1261, 1272, 1276, 1279, 1281, 1394, 1622, 1963, 2503, 2527
Civilisation occidentale 152, 259, 695, 1246, 1279, 1464, 1679, 3402, 5128
Civilisation orientale 259, 5128
Clans 2405
Classe 339, 441, 854, 1181, 1227, 1310, 1315, 1339, 1341, 1356, 1431, 1517, 1724, 1761, 1859, 1908, 2014, 2018, 2042, 2048, 2063, 2108, 2223, 2295, 2324, 2326, 2347, 2374, 2377-2379, 2381, 2382, 2387-2392, 2401, 2403, 2412, 2413, 2418, 2421, 2422, 2427, 2428, 2430, 2431, 2434, 2436-2438, 2440-2443, 2445, 2449, 2450, 2529, 2532, 2564, 2578, 2608, 2644, 2774, 2840, 2907, 3003, 3057, 3077, 3153, 3175, 3217, 3222, 3271, 3389, 3436, 3486, 3779, 3891, 3909, 3930, 4004, 4204, 4220, 4266, 4304, 4338, 4398, 4431, 4472, 4526, 4708, 4720, 4947, 4968, 5012, 5052, 5077, 5104, 5108, 5227, 5238, 5244, 5245, 5256, 5299, 5302, 5303, 5543, 5662
voir aussi: Aristocratie, Bourgeoisie, Petite bourgeoisie, Sous-classe
Classe dirigeante 2321, 2446
Classe inférieure 2394, 2415, 4774
Classe moyenne 2374, 2394, 2419, 2425, 2438, 2917, 3411, 3481, 3997, 4378, 4864, 5614
Classe ouvrière 1310, 1811, 2005, 2158, 2416, 2422, 2425, 2450, 3218, 3236, 3468, 4004, 4300, 4410, 4472, 4554, 4848, 4864, 4865, 5162, 5595, 5662
Classe supérieure 5335
Classification 70, 104, 286, 591, 861, 869, 880, 894, 1408, 2363, 2382, 3408, 4123, 4265, 4436, 4472, 4953, 5650
Clergé 1443, 1481, 3692, 4778
Client 944, 1697, 3347, 4321, 4416, 5825
voir aussi: Service clientèle
Clientélisme 4965, 5282
Clignotement des indicateurs économiques 1787

Climat 1096, 2800, 3708, 4879
voir aussi: Changement de climat, Temps
Cliques 1043, 3927
Clivages politiques 2389, 5238
Clonage 1576, 3372, 5848, 5863, 5865
Clubs 2614
Cocaïne 3995, 5375, 5385, 5386
Code déontologique des affaires 411, 4352, 4358, 4360, 4417-4420, 4422, 4423, 4425, 4426, 4428, 4601, 4636, 4642, 4709
Code déontologique médical 1564, 2344, 2485, 5826, 5848, 5850, 5851, 5854, 5855, 5861-5863, 5869, 5870, 5875-5877, 5880, 5887, 5889, 5895
Code pénal 311, 5004, 5029, 5192, 5200
Cognition 110, 210, 233, 245, 246, 300, 324, 503, 547, 549, 559, 565, 571, 574, 587, 589, 591, 606-608, 611-617, 619-621, 623, 624, 626, 627, 629, 632, 635, 636, 640-644, 646, 648-650, 652, 654, 655, 658, 659, 661, 663, 664, 666-668, 670, 671, 676, 680, 685, 687, 688, 691, 703, 705, 721, 727, 731-733, 737, 741, 758, 760, 787, 790, 804, 807, 808, 823, 825, 831, 840, 845, 846, 851, 861, 863-865, 868, 871, 873, 877, 905, 907, 915, 918, 919, 924, 941, 972, 1031, 1041, 1056, 1063, 1071, 1075, 1076, 1084, 1095, 1126, 1147, 1161, 1166, 1229, 1237, 1261, 1573, 1582, 1590, 1647, 1863, 1992, 2052, 2168, 2193, 2197, 2236, 2309, 2359, 2362, 2892, 2946, 3041, 3344, 4190, 4339, 4391, 4408, 5406
Cognition sociale 588, 589, 615, 650, 657, 680, 682, 708, 720, 760, 825, 850, 861, 864, 870, 914, 928, 1057, 1061, 1063, 3517
Cohabitation 902, 2915, 2933, 2958, 2959, 2964, 2974, 2979, 2981, 2988, 2989, 2996
Cohen, Gerald 4921
Cohésion du groupe 1047, 1072, 4700, 5450
Cohésion sociale 1697, 1941, 1990, 2431, 2905, 4978, 5440
Cohortes 2632, 2799, 2802, 2974, 3580
Collaboration 73, 1681, 2110, 2213, 3877, 4100, 4357, 4374, 4625, 5691, 5746
Collecte de fonds 2282
Collectivisation 3889
Collectivisme 2335, 4658, 5245
Collectivité 12, 39, 162, 205, 408, 538, 577, 724, 767, 838, 893, 904, 995, 1009, 1010, 1107, 1170, 1188, 1242, 1246, 1427, 1430, 1479, 1495, 1503, 1532, 1548, 1550, 1565, 1656, 1661, 1662, 1668, 1669, 1691, 1756, 2066, 2088, 2161, 2239,

INDEX DES MATIÈRES

2252, 2307, 2330, 2332, 2345, 2451, 2505, 2506, 2543, 2636, 2661, 2664, 2754, 2870, 2995, 3152, 3234, 3323, 3325, 3357, 3384, 3418, 3423, 3426, 3437, 3472, 3487, 3539, 3614, 3628, 3646, 3688, 3697, 3740, 3757, 3833, 3835, 3837, 3839, 3842, 3846-3848, 3851, 3858, 3860, 3864, 3865, 3879, 3898, 3907, 3909, 3967, 3983, 3998, 4008, 4043, 4056, 4074, 4086, 4090, 4159, 4182, 4197, 4419, 4646, 4725, 4966, 4969, 4976, 4978, 4994, 4996, 5014, 5107, 5118, 5129, 5139, 5143, 5212, 5314, 5354, 5363, 5397, 5440, 5447, 5464, 5546, 5568, 5741, 5742, 5800, 5951, 5979
voir aussi: Communauté internationale, Communauté scientifique, Communautés ethniques, Communautés religieuses, Milieux d'affaires
Collectivités locales 463, 987, 1205, 1384, 1764, 2101, 2568, 2709, 3530, 3705, 3814, 3826, 3830, 3838, 3848, 3853, 3856, 3859, 3861, 3881, 3894, 4097, 4148, 4600, 4768, 4945, 5716, 5749, 5771
Collectivités rurales 20, 797, 1813, 2338, 2653, 3628, 3837, 3852, 3868, 3874, 3885, 3892, 3898, 3899, 3907, 3910, 3911, 3914, 3923, 5200, 5515, 5695
Collectivités urbaines 1205, 1813, 2878, 3359, 3842, 3931, 3939, 3959, 3967, 4039, 4117, 4119, 4148, 4155, 4169
Collingwood, R.G. 110
Colonialisme 957, 1165, 1769, 1926, 1950, 1951, 2148, 2321, 2568, 3214, 3503, 3782, 4206, 4477, 4935, 4939, 5226, 5325
voir aussi: Néocolonialisme
Colonies 1165, 1495, 1819
Colonisation 58, 977, 1165, 1362, 2167, 3771, 3789, 4893
Colonisation rurale 3867, 3924
Colquhoun, Patrick 5146
Cols blancs 4441, 4618
Cols bleus 4618
Coltrane, John 1988
Comédie 244, 1896, 5293
Comités d'entreprise 4813
Commerce 58, 1471, 1977, 3348, 3909, 4179, 4182, 4223, 4238, 4322, 4344, 4811, 5871
voir aussi: Libre échange, Tourisme international
Commerce de détail 1144, 1738, 3545, 3937, 4135, 4344, 4414, 4522, 4552, 4559, 4678, 4726
voir aussi: Centres commerciaux
Commerce des esclaves 3793

Commerce international 2547, 2580, 3791, 3927, 4206, 4294, 5282
voir aussi: Exportations, Importations
Commerce régional 4811
Commodification 1873, 2477, 2515, 3705, 3721, 4202, 4238, 4325, 5232
Commonwealth 3257, 5007
Communalisme 583, 2174, 3473, 4119
Communauté internationale 1344, 4268, 5336
Communauté scientifique 1557, 1565, 1594, 1619, 3719
Communautés ethniques 2047, 3407, 3419, 3531, 3593
Communautés religieuses 1409, 1430, 1447, 1478, 1484, 1498, 1499, 1506, 1509, 1512, 1516, 1521, 1532, 1536, 1540, 1550, 1912, 3468, 3879, 4125
Communes 2697
Communication 67, 111, 117, 194, 205, 310, 359, 371, 384, 394, 403, 511, 521, 527, 590, 607, 655, 693, 782-784, 830, 832, 836, 845, 853, 867, 899, 901, 907, 940, 947, 1009, 1016, 1021, 1022, 1038, 1065, 1066, 1088, 1101, 1105, 1108, 1116, 1119, 1120, 1158, 1161, 1199, 1200, 1215, 1268, 1298, 1384, 1393, 1607, 1611, 1626, 1633-1635, 1637-1640, 1642, 1644, 1647, 1649-1653, 1655, 1656, 1658, 1660, 1668, 1669, 1683, 1689, 1690, 1700, 1702-1704, 1715, 1717, 1739, 1743, 1747, 1749, 1753-1756, 1768, 1771, 1776, 1784, 1787, 1799, 1803, 1808, 1827, 1831, 1833, 1835, 1842, 1846, 1853, 1924, 1997, 2001, 2097, 2102, 2392, 2479, 2571, 2588, 2616, 2667, 2771, 2772, 2905, 2920, 2936, 2943, 2966, 2987, 3002, 3021, 3038, 3368, 3508, 3734, 3825, 3849, 3965, 4036, 4167, 4203, 4417, 4666, 4716, 4807, 5205, 5241, 5414, 5557, 5579, 5682, 5828, 5831, 5846, 5901, 5960
voir aussi: Canaux de communication
Communication confidentielle 5169
Communication dans l'entreprise 4654, 4675
Communication de masse 1635, 1730, 1734, 4481
Communication interculturelle 1186, 1231, 1894, 1895, 4318, 4370, 5170, 5313
Communication interethnique 3508
Communication interpersonnelle 574, 899, 901, 904, 930, 932, 945, 947, 1632, 1635, 1639, 1641, 1670, 1680, 1686, 1833, 2761, 2943, 2966, 2987, 3021, 3053, 4675, 5671, 5682, 5901, 5975
Communication non-verbale 1787, 1827

527

SUBJECT INDEX IN FRENCH

Communication orale 1641
Communication politique 1639, 1730, 5061, 5235, 5291, 5293, 5360
Communication scientifique 1619
Communication verbale 664, 901, 1805, 2523
Communication visuelle 1803, 1870
Communion 709, 1437, 5262
Communisme 1167, 1263, 1328, 1360, 1392, 2310, 2333, 3635, 4244, 4349, 4925, 4946, 5489
Communistes 1392, 4204, 4919
Communitarianisme 382, 405, 1548, 3419, 3849, 4134, 4232, 4958
Compagnies d'assurance 4699, 4831
Compensation 4433, 4499, 4600, 4822, 4849, 4990, 5514
    voir aussi: Dédommagement
Compétences 651, 660, 661, 715, 729, 1018, 1093, 2017, 2040, 2098, 2186, 2199, 2253, 2262, 2286, 2410, 3580, 3603, 3604, 3671, 4398, 4439, 4440, 4460, 4465, 4571, 4602, 4645, 4664, 4671, 4717, 4756, 4769, 4779, 4784, 4786, 4798, 4804, 4807, 5492, 5552
    voir aussi: Différentiel de qualifications
Compétitivité 2141, 3771, 4374, 4420, 4656, 4713
Complots 1015
Comportement antisocial 749, 754, 849, 2154, 2235, 3031, 5030, 5051, 5069, 5078, 5393, 5538, 5617
Comportement collectif 391, 1095, 2082, 4888, 5218, 5278
Comportement culturel 3530, 3548, 5898
Comportement de classe 2065
Comportement de l'étudiant 2065
Comportement de l'organisation 1048, 1068, 1092, 1096, 1101, 1105, 1106, 1109, 1115, 1117, 1118, 1124, 1125, 1130, 1138, 1139, 1141-1143, 1145, 1148, 1151, 1385, 1672, 3097, 4323, 4356, 4367, 4381, 4389, 4409, 4412, 4422, 4638, 4658, 4660, 4671, 4802, 4812, 5732
Comportement des électeurs 472, 1070, 2389, 3483, 4596, 4966, 5160, 5287, 5300, 5303, 5305-5307
Comportement du consommateur 1322, 2545, 3823, 4320, 4322, 4324, 4326-4328, 4331, 4333, 4335, 4339, 4340, 4342, 4343, 4345
Comportement du groupe 842, 848, 1020, 1034, 1037, 1041, 1042, 1044, 1046, 1048, 1054, 1057, 1073, 1082, 1096, 1331, 2028, 3667, 4366, 4384, 4426, 5450
Comportement économique 3842, 4180, 4183, 4184, 4190, 4239, 4263, 4275, 4391, 4426

Comportement électoral 1439, 2671, 5300, 5306
Comportement en groupe 2566
Comportement humain 293, 327, 422, 442, 542, 561, 565, 567, 573, 588, 589, 591, 594, 596, 597, 599, 601, 605, 606, 613, 615, 617, 618, 627, 634, 643, 648-650, 657, 667, 668, 680, 682, 692, 705, 709, 711, 717, 720, 723, 727, 735, 737, 749, 760, 791, 833, 838, 846, 851, 859, 870, 876, 887, 907, 912, 914, 928, 941, 943, 1031, 1064, 1073, 1112, 1126, 1282, 1301, 1302, 1652, 1784, 1789, 1842, 2028, 2236, 2304, 2324, 2350, 2532, 2744, 2763, 2788, 2845, 2862, 2879, 2889, 2973, 3014, 3026, 3167, 3181, 3282, 3298, 3318, 3406, 3667, 3695, 3726, 3783, 3843, 4345, 4419, 4422, 4659, 4990, 5075, 5095, 5112, 5135, 5321, 5387, 5460, 5677, 5860, 5874, 5939, 5950
Comportement individuel 500, 780, 1034, 1046, 1299, 1708, 2351, 2612, 2845, 2850, 3279, 3749, 4186, 4351, 4722, 5902
Comportement politique 1439, 2324, 2343, 4887, 4895, 5214, 5283, 5291, 5300, 5301, 5363
Comportement rationnel 364, 923, 3493
Comportement religieux 1452, 1461
Comportement sexuel 522, 897, 1303, 2608, 2688, 2727, 2806, 2912, 2980, 2981, 3085, 3294, 3295, 3297, 3298, 3300, 3302, 3303, 3306, 3310, 3316, 3318-3321, 3329, 3330, 3336-3338, 3342-3344, 3347, 3348, 3351, 3357, 3369, 3377, 3379, 3380, 3388, 5100, 5387, 5767, 5891, 5943, 5945, 5965, 5966, 5974, 5975, 5978, 5984, 5987
Comportement social 10, 67, 321, 334, 383, 463, 542, 561, 567, 582, 597, 652, 714, 827, 836, 845, 846, 867, 870, 896, 898, 920, 941, 1111, 1294, 1439, 2313, 2318, 2462, 2489, 2692, 2807, 2830, 3002, 3041, 3050, 3241, 3530, 3835, 3843, 4593, 4659, 4753, 4987, 5157, 5389, 5721, 5891
Composition de la population 2702
Comptabilité 2072, 2097, 4310, 4604, 5789
Comptabilité de l'entreprise 4773
Comptabilité nationale 4310
Comptabilité sociale 4310
Comptables 2072, 4310, 4720
Comtés 3620, 3886
Conception 436, 488, 2197, 3765, 4028
    voir aussi: Esthétique urbaine, Plan d'expérience

INDEX DES MATIÈRES

Conception de soi 219, 562, 569, 639, 681, 862, 867, 871, 872, 874, 880, 896, 1161, 2045, 2487, 2670, 2953, 3021, 3049, 3446
Conception de test 587, 774, 5982
Conceptualisation 231, 261, 369, 642, 1095, 1161, 2194, 2570, 2656, 3081, 3727, 4096, 4154
Conciliation 3891, 4849
Concurrence 831, 1021, 1358, 1685, 1733, 2166, 2571, 2940, 3018, 3285, 4045, 4132, 4374, 4375, 4378, 4501, 4681, 4817, 5217, 5725, 5793
Concurrence internationale 2512, 4055, 4546
Condamnation pénale 5016, 5034, 5039, 5040, 5054
Conditionnement 3273
Conditions de logement 3974, 3984
Conditions de travail 1053, 1305, 2100, 2421, 2975, 3075, 3226, 3288, 4206, 4250, 4356, 4377, 4416, 4433, 4446, 4448, 4455, 4471, 4478, 4522, 4578, 4626, 4644, 4676-4678, 4680, 4682, 4683, 4686-4688, 4691, 4692, 4694, 4695, 4699, 4702-4704, 4706, 4708, 4709, 4711, 4712, 4716, 4717, 4721, 4723, 4729, 4733-4736, 4740, 4742, 4743, 4745, 4746, 4748-4750, 4757, 4810, 4839, 5630
Conditions de vie 58, 1536, 1923, 2020, 2032, 2606, 2707, 2709, 2843, 2999, 3173, 3399, 3845, 3882, 3917, 3991, 3992, 4017, 4040, 4087, 4169, 4244, 4247, 4272, 4295, 4299, 4593, 5428, 5511, 5592, 5701
Conditions économiques 54, 64, 963, 1067, 2514, 2526, 2637, 2707, 2749, 2914, 3077, 3202, 3206, 3261, 3275, 3277, 3551, 3617, 3633, 3682, 3773, 3776, 3805, 3827, 3870, 3924, 3943, 4009, 4016, 4017, 4071, 4088, 4185, 4189, 4195, 4207, 4245, 4256, 4274, 4275, 4278, 4280, 4282, 4299, 4308, 4314, 4334, 4387, 4545, 4576, 4618, 4845, 4947, 5103, 5202, 5268, 5417, 5493, 5567, 5598, 5626, 5628, 5980
Conditions politiques 4, 54, 161, 991, 1169, 1199, 1798, 2306, 2520, 3106, 3206, 3551, 3565, 3626, 3827, 3968, 4050, 5255, 5268, 5279, 5361, 5980
Conditions sociales 155, 322, 353, 400, 477, 811, 870, 956, 973, 1002, 1169, 1172, 1173, 1199, 1222, 1251, 1256, 1260, 1274, 1315, 1333, 1520, 1522, 1533, 1537, 1557, 1728, 1793, 2058, 2078, 2305, 2306, 2320, 2328, 2353, 2364, 2379, 2382, 2418, 2438, 2460, 2463, 2474, 2475, 2491, 2506, 2509, 2514, 2516, 2520-2522, 2524, 2526, 2528, 2532-2535, 2542, 2596, 2617, 2637, 2639, 2648-2650, 2682, 2685, 2707, 2772, 2807, 2825, 2830, 2857, 2896, 2902, 2911, 3058, 3065, 3068, 3071, 3074, 3075, 3077, 3088, 3089, 3091, 3111, 3161, 3171, 3195-3198, 3207, 3235, 3240, 3255, 3261, 3271, 3275, 3276, 3319, 3430, 3431, 3516, 3524, 3538, 3562, 3571, 3579, 3583, 3602, 3638, 3640, 3714, 3773, 3805, 3833, 3882, 3897, 3898, 3955, 4005, 4009, 4040, 4071, 4195, 4258, 4260, 4274, 4275, 4282, 4297, 4314, 4337, 4446, 4555, 4944, 4947, 4977, 4981, 4993, 4996, 4997, 5059, 5065, 5068, 5118, 5164, 5236, 5247, 5307, 5366, 5371, 5466, 5493, 5546, 5573, 5600, 5626, 5641, 5646, 5647, 5653
Conférences internationales 3944, 5200
Confiance 927, 943, 1024, 1079, 1142, 1155, 1156, 1660, 2345, 2353, 2357, 2371, 2991, 3067, 3403, 3734, 3847, 3863, 4240, 4388, 4893, 4936, 4993, 5012, 5169, 5485, 5595, 5835
Conflit 161, 173, 398, 920, 1005, 1009, 1011, 1013, 1016, 1017, 1020, 1026, 1028, 1029, 1064, 1163, 1364, 1427, 1452, 1485, 1529, 1811, 2250, 2473, 2587, 2643, 2742, 2892, 2900, 2969, 3472, 3477, 3485, 3508, 3531, 3615, 3624, 3677, 3749, 3772, 3777, 3816, 3901, 4493, 4837, 5122, 5127, 5294, 5323, 5331, 5332, 5355, 5444, 5466, 5467, 5606, 5686, 5831
Conflit conjugal 2861, 2865, 2870, 2876, 2881, 2928, 2931, 2937, 2947, 2960, 2965, 2966, 2987, 5681
Conflit israélo-arabe 1014, 1026, 1791, 2619, 2795, 3664
Conflits armés 3859, 5318, 5327, 5343, 5346, 5353, 5362, 5445
Conflits culturels 3522, 5065, 5294
Conflits de rôles 5690
Conflits du travail 4826, 4840, 4843, 4845, 4846, 4848, 4850, 4851, 4855
Conflits interethniques 1011, 1731, 1816, 3070, 3128, 3269, 3403, 3420, 3444, 3465, 3466, 3469, 3472, 3473, 3475, 3480, 3485, 3492, 3493, 3495, 3520, 3524, 3531, 3536, 5081, 5462, 5700
Conflits internationaux 1730, 1731, 5323, 5337
Conflits interpersonnels 822, 908, 916, 3006
Conflits linguistiques 1795, 1798

SUBJECT INDEX IN FRENCH

Conflits politiques 1791, 3776, 5127, 5212, 5240, 5318
Conflits raciaux 1009, 3172, 3456, 3522
Conflits religieux 145, 1484-1486, 1510, 1513, 1529, 1537
Conflits sociaux 578, 879, 1031, 1078, 1199, 1484, 1712, 2306, 2509, 2587, 2643, 3496, 3914, 4185, 4400, 4404, 5190, 5206, 5240, 5372, 5445
Conformisme 299, 1164, 2318
Confucianisme 211, 266, 273, 321, 1171, 1263, 1402, 1423, 1473, 2617, 3108, 4207, 4981, 5309
Confucius 211, 3108
Congé de maternité 3039, 4508
Congestion 2264
Congrégations 1443
Congrès National Africain 3349
Conjoncture démographique 2790, 3609, 3636, 3639, 3650, 3674, 3681, 3684, 3686, 3791, 3866, 3903, 4004
Connaissance 6, 8, 12, 13, 29, 37, 46, 110, 113, 118-120, 123, 125, 128, 133, 137, 140, 142, 166, 245, 246, 250, 261, 279, 289, 301, 309, 369, 376, 385, 481, 498, 517, 533, 597, 619, 637, 654, 661, 668, 801, 871, 989, 1018, 1099, 1115, 1116, 1129, 1131, 1149, 1158, 1261, 1271, 1403, 1412, 1553, 1561, 1565, 1566, 1568, 1569, 1573, 1574, 1582, 1587, 1588, 1598, 1600, 1604, 1607, 1613, 1616, 1628, 1629, 1675, 1858, 1984, 2006, 2128, 2139, 2215, 2219, 2222, 2223, 2226, 2243, 2260-2262, 2278, 2295, 2309, 2412, 2508, 2568, 2580, 2621, 2943, 3003, 3099, 3759, 3910, 4246, 4287, 4346, 4375, 4395, 4397, 4398, 4413, 4510, 4609, 4610, 4640, 4654, 4906, 5105, 5201, 5281, 5409, 5663, 5697, 5709, 5711
voir aussi: Management de l'information, Sociologie de la connaissance
Connaissance indigène 123, 3688, 4280
Connaissance publique 427
Connaissance sociale 1916, 4418
Consanguinité 2949
Conscience 69, 104, 245, 247, 353, 358, 558, 574, 584, 602, 618, 640, 752, 1246, 1472, 2300, 2566, 3099, 3115, 3432, 3727, 5944
Conscience collective 1490
Conscience de classe 2418
Conscience de groupe 1096
Conscience de soi 20, 219, 541, 563
Conscience ethnique 3447, 5263

Conscience nationale 150, 953, 959, 962, 970, 976, 1262, 1452, 2573, 3421, 4930, 4935
Conscription 5342, 5352, 5361
Conseil de l'Europe 5884
Conseil municipal 4963
Conseillers 759, 5699
Consensus 420, 1010, 1059, 4036
Consensus de groupe 1096, 4701
Conservateurs 2730
Conservation de la faune 3710, 3763
Conservation de la nature 257, 3747, 3822, 5237
Conservation des ressources 1093, 3804, 4047
Conservatisme 141, 860, 1207, 1971, 2140, 3012, 3322, 3365, 4111, 5286
Consolidation démocratique 4938
Consommateurs 519, 1268, 1710, 2650, 3059, 3799, 4284, 4315, 4319, 4321, 4326-4328, 4330, 4332, 4334, 4340, 4342, 4345, 4420, 5732
Consommation 342, 379, 395, 994, 1314, 1318, 1337, 1349, 1731, 1920, 2399, 2419, 2504, 2657, 2711, 3333, 3347, 3720, 3725, 3764, 3786, 3799, 3875, 4135, 4186, 4193, 4206, 4276, 4313, 4315, 4322, 4325, 4327, 4328, 4331-4335, 4337, 4340, 4342, 4345, 4410, 5956
Consommation alimentaire 1322
Consommation culturelle 1203
Consommation de masse 340, 3820
Consommation des ménages 4308, 4338
Constitution 3471, 4962, 5038, 5192, 5809
Constitutionalisme 4957
Construction de l'État 151, 3420, 3475, 4206, 4890
Construction de logement 3765, 3983, 4049, 5656
Construction nationale 162, 967, 983, 1772, 2153, 2723, 3242, 3430, 3510, 3789, 4914, 4930, 4966
Construction sociale 20, 109, 340, 358, 386, 387, 409, 671, 677, 968, 982, 1161, 1238, 1273, 1353, 1556, 1598, 1610, 1614, 1615, 1716, 1844, 2073, 2397, 2405, 2415, 2473, 2482, 2497, 2501, 2652, 2656, 2917, 2937, 3007, 3087, 3246, 3328, 3417, 3432, 3453, 3510, 3523, 3698, 3721, 3879, 3904, 4157, 4226, 4774, 4943, 4979, 5046, 5278, 5458, 5885
Constructivisme 358, 517, 643, 1563, 1615, 2209, 2219, 3700, 3744, 4636, 5310
Consultation mixte 3825
Consumérisme 1207, 1254, 1300, 1688, 1772, 2243, 2674, 3225, 3909, 4227, 4312,

INDEX DES MATIÈRES

4319, 4322, 4324, 4325, 4328, 4329, 4331-4333, 4336, 4340, 4342, 4345, 5971
Contact entre les cultures 1384, 2009, 2271, 2569, 3776, 4205, 4386, 5313, 5335
Contact linguistique 1182, 1798, 1804, 1812, 1813, 1825, 2523
Contes populaires 27
Contestation politique 4244, 4966, 4980, 5235, 5237, 5240, 5247, 5251, 5253, 5275
Contestation religieuse 1444
Contestation sociale 1976, 2339, 2567, 2634, 4244, 4980, 5236, 5240, 5257, 5275
Contraception 890, 2726, 2729, 2731, 2732, 2736, 2739, 2740, 2743, 2746, 2751, 2754, 2759, 2763, 2766, 2769-2771, 2774, 2779, 2797, 2804, 3079, 3279, 3296, 3299, 3312, 3332, 3337, 3350, 5200, 5851, 5943, 5945
Contrat de mariage 2917, 2978
Contrat de travail 5217
Contrat social 953, 2589, 2603, 2604, 2657, 4420
Contrats 13, 2288, 4220, 4380, 4465, 4520, 4552, 4627, 4829, 4846, 5217
voir aussi: Contrat de mariage, Contrat de travail, Contrat social
Contrats à terme 4352
Contremaîtres 1783, 4363, 5712
Contre-révolution 5238
Contrôle administratif 3869, 3871, 4406
Contrôle budgétaire 4975
Contrôle de qualité 1604, 1783, 2244, 5784, 5794, 5807, 5815
Contrôle financier 4310
Contrôle politique 42, 2340, 3457
Conurbation 4067
Convention européenne des droits de l'homme 5054
Conventions des Nations Unies 3813, 5601
Convergence 1697, 1798, 2034, 2518, 2560, 4221, 4818, 5622
Conversion religieuse 1397, 1446, 1489, 1492, 1493, 1496, 1526
Coopération 463, 656, 911, 927, 1019, 1021, 1027, 1040, 1068, 1151, 1638, 2088, 2289, 2307, 2345, 3480, 3517, 3834, 3838, 3840, 3850, 3919, 4032, 4100, 4163, 4322, 4356, 4497, 4820, 5220, 5780
Coopération économique 4198
Coopération internationale 2572, 2577, 3672, 5684, 5973
Coopération politique 3776
Coopération régionale 3671
Coopératives 3867, 3893, 5780
Coopératives de consommation 4316, 4330

Coopératives de logement 4117, 4232
Copte 1478
Coran 1089, 1518, 1525, 1542
Corporatisme 4467, 4642, 4820
Corps humain 199, 236, 239, 573, 669, 777, 791, 1189, 1214, 1232, 1277, 1325, 1347, 1358, 1368, 1497, 1559, 1861, 1970, 2597, 2651, 2755, 2809, 2880, 3045, 3092, 3108-3110, 3125, 3128, 3131, 3146, 3158, 3272, 3311, 3331, 3346, 4730, 4954, 5182, 5589, 5837, 5876
voir aussi: Anthropologie du corps, Organes
Corps législatif 4975
voir aussi: Législatures des États
Corrélation 452, 609, 890, 2821, 2831, 2839, 2924, 3476, 4792
Correspondance 162, 593
Corruption 931, 2535, 3827, 4204, 4427, 4683, 4877, 5055, 5091, 5094, 5219, 5267, 5282
Corruption politique 5219, 5282
Cortèges 3269
Cosmétique 1189, 1214, 1559, 3272, 3315
Cosmologie 259, 271, 1391, 3695, 3823
Cosmopolitisme 1424, 2348, 2546, 4902, 5311
Costume 1321, 1325, 1335, 3067, 3372
Côtes 3709
voir aussi: Littoraux
Couleur 1883, 3534
Couleur de la peau 3468, 3500, 4502
Cour 950, 3318, 5444, 5449, 5470
Cour de justice des Communautés européennes 4508, 5196
Cour Suprême 5034, 5038, 5154, 5155, 5160, 5171, 5183
Cours d'appel 5154
Cours d'eau 2777, 3728, 3822
Courses 4341, 4678
Courses de chevaux 1305
Coût 3784, 3832, 4068, 4497, 4767, 5401, 5565, 5581, 5748, 5754, 5760, 5931
Coût de l'éducation 2293
Coûts de la vie 3884
Coûts de l'enfant 2998, 4517, 4528
Coûts de main d'oeuvre 4449
Coûts sociaux 1442, 3752, 4065, 4251, 5057, 5622
Coutumes 992, 1174, 1291, 1322, 1325, 1835, 2429, 2504, 2992, 3303, 3468, 3954
Coutumes matrimoniales 2980, 3304
Coutumes sexuelles 522, 3303
Covariance 482
Création d'emplois 4447, 4450

SUBJECT INDEX IN FRENCH

Créativité 324, 374, 621, 634, 660, 672, 770, 1182, 1253, 1345, 1863, 2439, 2581, 3812, 4092, 4361, 5262
Crèches 4687, 5591
Crédit 4175, 4240, 4317, 4348
  voir aussi: Microfinancement, Monnaie et crédit
Crédit à la consommation 4317, 4341
Crédit rural 4284
Créole 1367, 3416
Crime 33, 161, 426, 471, 1442, 1921, 1991, 2119, 2400, 2535, 3036, 3121, 3287, 3338, 3498, 3781, 3849, 3986, 3995, 4007, 4013, 4390, 4949, 4979, 4980, 4982, 4984, 4989, 4992, 4995, 5000, 5001, 5003, 5006-5008, 5010, 5014, 5025, 5028, 5029, 5035, 5036, 5041, 5045, 5048, 5050, 5053, 5054, 5057-5062, 5064, 5066-5068, 5070, 5072, 5075, 5078, 5080-5082, 5085-5088, 5090, 5091, 5093-5095, 5099-5103, 5106, 5108-5116, 5119-5121, 5123, 5125, 5144-5146, 5172, 5176, 5194, 5282, 5312, 5365, 5367, 5370, 5392, 5401, 5428, 5429, 5438, 5440, 5441, 5450, 5451, 5453, 5455, 5456, 5467, 5471, 5544, 5558, 5617, 5899
  voir aussi Victimes de crime
Crime commerciale 5244
Crime organisée 2203, 5055, 5074, 5092, 5094, 5139, 5317
Crime violent 801, 1750, 2864, 2868, 4997, 5000, 5009, 5044, 5045, 5049-5051, 5070, 5079, 5097, 5102, 5113, 5120, 5440, 5441, 5448, 5453, 5455, 5456, 5471, 5474
Crimes contre l'humanité 1388, 5311, 5312, 5462
Crimes de guerre 1902, 1906, 5311, 5312
Crimes internationaux 3713, 5094
Criminalité 5015, 5027, 5045, 5047, 5052, 5059, 5061, 5064, 5066, 5067, 5076, 5078, 5082, 5088, 5091, 5092, 5099, 5103, 5105, 5113, 5117, 5119, 5121, 5365, 5445, 5634
Criminologie 426, 529, 2400, 2532, 2868, 3121, 3241, 4271, 4979, 4980, 4982, 5005, 5008, 5009, 5011, 5025, 5028, 5036, 5038, 5044, 5047-5049, 5051, 5055, 5057, 5059, 5062, 5064-5067, 5069-5071, 5073, 5074, 5076, 5077, 5080-5082, 5084-5088, 5092-5094, 5096, 5097, 5101, 5103, 5104, 5109-5113, 5117-5121, 5138, 5176, 5193, 5194, 5312, 5441, 5445, 5446, 5453, 5456, 5465, 5468, 5472
Crise de civilisation 3713
Crise de l'énergie 3713

Crise de l'enseignement 2251
Crise économique 1207, 2561, 2579, 2767, 2775, 3612, 3903, 3927, 4011, 4218, 4221, 4250
Crise financière 2579, 3085, 3609, 4055, 4250, 4256, 4347, 4935, 5622
Crise politique 1781, 5218, 5219
Crises internationales 1023, 1731, 2539, 3713
Critique 7, 52, 257, 303, 307, 333, 592, 1102, 1187, 1229, 1247, 1408, 1702, 1909, 1981, 1988, 3098, 3102, 3121, 3144, 3687, 4918, 5165, 5201, 5452
Critique littéraire 99, 241, 299, 1158, 1227, 1239, 1351, 1796, 1874, 1934, 1937, 1939, 1940, 1943, 1949, 1953, 1958, 3120, 3386
Croates 967, 1793, 1794, 3859
Croisement consanguin 2426, 3304
Croissance démographique 2638, 2686, 2693, 2697, 2706, 2710, 2711, 2714, 2715, 2721, 2747, 2752, 2774, 2792, 2793, 3608, 3713, 3818, 4083, 4170, 4606, 5780
Croissance économique 2266, 2434, 2561, 2574, 3661, 3815, 3817, 3893, 3986, 4046, 4177, 4203, 4228, 4261, 4264, 4278, 4287, 4289, 4357, 4407, 4558, 4824, 4935, 5626, 5642
  voir aussi: Théorie de la croissance
Croissance urbaine 3702, 3771, 3928, 3936, 3949, 3958, 4060, 4151, 4156, 4166, 4167, 4175
Croyance 8, 107, 136, 138, 141, 228, 230, 298, 352, 549, 580, 639, 650, 657, 694, 847, 857, 860, 880, 1052, 1300, 1374, 1375, 1383, 1421, 1490, 1606, 1846, 2035, 2198, 2209, 2360, 2655, 3145, 3406, 3724, 3726, 3758, 4221, 4408, 4421, 4425, 5128, 5529, 5962
Croyances médicales 5734, 5823, 5898, 5954
Croyances populaires 763, 1414, 1468, 3009
Croyances religieuses 145, 247, 295, 701, 1263, 1376, 1380, 1388, 1389, 1398, 1404, 1407, 1412, 1414, 1416, 1417, 1421, 1424, 1428, 1431, 1434-1436, 1438, 1441, 1447, 1451, 1454, 1457, 1463, 1469, 1470, 1476-1478, 1481, 1487-1491, 1500, 1501, 1503, 1504, 1508, 1511, 1515, 1523, 1526, 1527, 1538-1541, 1544, 1545, 1550, 2313, 2532, 2631, 2731, 2753, 2756, 3447, 3743, 3764
Cruse, Harold 4919
Culpabilité 3568, 5149, 5152, 5195, 5434
Culte 952, 1372, 1424, 2106
Culte des morts 1433
Cultes 1228, 1417, 3257

INDEX DES MATIÈRES

Culturalisme 597, 3507
Culture 7, 12, 33, 53, 122, 148, 164, 204, 268, 308, 326, 338, 343, 441, 569, 605, 643, 671, 677, 678, 681, 710, 822, 864, 955, 976, 981, 985, 992, 996, 1001, 1100, 1103, 1161, 1162, 1166-1170, 1175, 1177-1180, 1183, 1188, 1193, 1194, 1196, 1197, 1203, 1206-1208, 1211, 1212, 1218-1220, 1223, 1225, 1233, 1236, 1241, 1243, 1244, 1249, 1250, 1253, 1256, 1261, 1266, 1280, 1281, 1288, 1291, 1294, 1313, 1326, 1329, 1335, 1353, 1368, 1566, 1607, 1663, 1664, 1700-1702, 1709, 1713, 1724, 1735, 1743, 1756, 1764, 1811, 1813, 1824, 1837, 1851, 1855, 1856, 1888, 1890, 1892, 1898, 1907, 1908, 1911, 1947, 1959, 2009, 2113, 2252, 2255, 2298, 2328, 2394, 2477, 2502, 2522, 2526, 2543, 2547, 2549, 2552, 2557, 2563, 2663, 2909, 2953, 3067, 3090, 3092, 3115, 3157, 3216, 3253, 3273, 3278, 3306, 3315, 3322, 3388, 3400, 3427, 3440, 3465, 3507, 3540, 3591, 3646, 3683, 3689, 3712, 3756, 3789, 3848, 3933, 4017, 4121, 4126, 4138, 4202, 4212, 4227, 4336, 4359, 4381, 4417, 4567, 4916, 4943, 4994, 5065, 5067, 5232, 5246, 5253, 5277, 5347, 5356, 5363, 5386, 5458, 5529, 5907
voir aussi: Accès à la culture, Différence culturelle, Diversité des cultures, Sociologie de la culture, Subculture, Théorie de la culture
Culture de classe 1305
Culture de jeunes 1319, 1331, 1978, 1985, 1986, 2614, 2617, 2620, 2623, 2630, 2643, 5046, 5472
Culture de masse 1311, 1323, 1363, 1753, 1873, 1975
Culture d'entreprise 1134, 1157, 4370, 4379, 4381, 4386, 4389, 4413, 4420, 4544, 4624, 4644, 4658, 4769, 4798, 5252
Culture dominante 2530
Culture et personnalité 3427
Culture folklorique 1310, 2354, 3956
Culture indigène 3402, 4280, 4981, 5746
Culture juridique 5020, 5165, 5190, 5203
Culture locale 1363, 3723, 3894, 4287
Culture matérielle 1177, 1215, 1274, 1737, 1941, 3882, 4065, 4332, 4333
Culture minoritaire 1441, 3427, 3555
Culture musicale 3427
Culture nationale 150, 196, 662, 958, 962, 968, 989, 992, 996, 1103, 1167, 1181, 1182, 1186, 1188, 1291, 1308, 1329, 1480, 1845, 1881, 1885, 2335, 2573, 2576, 3445, 3595, 3888, 4644, 5259, 5308
Culture organisationnelle 1095, 1100, 1105, 1122, 1123, 1132, 4323, 4358, 5924
Culture politique 1004, 1159, 1169, 1226, 1679, 2439, 2649, 4203, 4898, 4939, 4955, 4966, 5293, 5294, 5301
Culture populaire 86, 104, 763, 835, 962, 976, 981, 1174, 1187, 1207, 1222, 1226, 1242, 1257, 1268, 1274, 1278, 1289, 1294, 1306, 1308-1312, 1319, 1320, 1325, 1328, 1333, 1336-1339, 1343, 1352, 1359-1361, 1363, 1365, 1370, 1371, 1668, 1724, 1728, 1738, 1740, 1745, 1746, 1753, 1758, 1761, 1770, 1771, 1780, 1859, 1879, 1882, 1889, 1899, 1903, 1907, 1908, 1921, 1974, 1976, 1985, 2504, 2522, 2617, 2618, 2630, 3113, 3141, 3157, 3216, 3305, 3355, 3919, 4332
Culture traditionnelle 58, 185, 992, 2575, 2733, 3776, 5320, 5746
Cultures agricoles 3708
Cultures fruitières 3912
Curie, Marie 1882
Curriculum 38, 1951, 1995, 2011, 2103, 2110, 2145, 2153, 2167, 2169-2171, 2177, 2180, 2186-2188, 2194, 2199, 2204, 2210, 2212, 2220, 2233, 2248, 2257, 2279, 2296, 2602, 5678, 5704
Custine Astolphe De 151
Cybernétique 1275
Cycle de vie 704, 1647, 2595, 2627, 2781, 2925, 4080
Cycles économiques 4213, 4233
Dalit 2394, 5269
Danse 1170, 1232, 1858, 1981, 3391
Danses traditionnelles 1346
Danseurs 1346, 1858
Darwin, Charles 571
Darwinisme 214, 390, 561, 898, 1558, 1583, 2426
Datation 3059, 3343, 5444, 5470
Davidson, Donald 114, 1231, 1846
Déboisement 2717
Début de l'époque moderne 237, 1160, 4263
Décentralisation 2120, 2258, 3410, 3771, 4150, 4152, 4550, 4797, 4836, 5629
Déchets 1277, 3715, 3750
Déchets dangereux 461, 1601, 3757
Décision 638, 1299, 4844, 5752
Décision d'emploi 4532, 4561
Décision statistique 638
Déclin économique 4066, 4273
Déclin urbain 4021
Décodage 1799

SUBJECT INDEX IN FRENCH

Décolonisation 951, 1880, 3945, 4935
Déconstruction 14, 124, 267, 328, 1556, 1621, 3117, 4621
Découvertes scientifiques 288, 1601, 1619
Dédommagement 3752
Déduction 1629, 1824
Déesse 3145
Defaut du marché 3806, 5522
Défense civile 3702
Degler, Carl 1431
Dégradation de l'environnement 2717, 3681, 3700, 3702, 3704, 3712-3714, 3717, 3722, 3731, 3733, 3757, 3759, 3761, 3811, 3813, 3814, 3853, 4216, 4246, 5686, 5700
Dégradation du sol 3733
Déités 1431
Deleuze, Gilles 218, 3788
Délinquance 2304, 2618, 3006, 4979, 4985, 4993, 5069, 5072, 5085, 5090, 5095, 5109, 5114, 5115, 5120
Délinquance juvénile 545, 2532, 2618, 4979, 4996, 5000, 5025, 5036, 5045, 5046, 5062, 5068, 5071, 5077, 5078, 5097, 5115, 5369, 5370, 5429, 5450, 5452, 5465, 5472, 5546
Délinquants 529, 1442, 1991, 3241, 4422, 4505, 4683, 4985, 4997, 5009, 5015, 5016, 5020, 5023, 5029, 5030, 5032, 5034-5036, 5041, 5042, 5047, 5056, 5064, 5065, 5068, 5071, 5078, 5083, 5086-5088, 5095, 5096, 5100, 5105, 5111, 5121, 5124, 5137, 5192, 5194, 5195, 5370, 5452, 5455, 5664, 5672, 5934
Demande 2043, 3909, 4791
Demande de main-d'oeuvre 4461
Demandeurs d'emploi 4504, 4582, 4588
Démilitarisation 5361
Démocratie 170, 173, 243, 955, 981, 1023, 1039, 1164, 1200, 1568, 1595, 1608, 1669, 1679, 1713, 1742, 1756, 2114, 2117, 2181, 2182, 2205, 2218, 2242, 2317, 2395, 2414, 2439, 3199, 3205, 3335, 3390, 3416, 3437, 3469, 3697, 3759, 3771, 3827, 3829, 3837, 3969, 4131, 4227, 4242, 4244, 4311, 4596, 4768, 4838, 4871, 4876, 4877, 4882, 4885, 4898, 4901, 4905-4907, 4913, 4927, 4928, 4933, 4934, 4938, 4943, 4944, 4947, 4951, 4957, 4966, 4968, 4969, 4972, 4975, 5139, 5180, 5201, 5218, 5226, 5233, 5248, 5250, 5261, 5284, 5303, 5352, 5361, 5363, 5973
voir aussi: Consolidation démocratique, Social-démocratie, Théorie de la démocratie

Démocratie industrielle 4823, 4838, 4839, 4877
Démocratie libérale 248, 1265, 4287, 4958
Démocratisation 52, 1568, 2025, 2111, 2115, 2388, 2513, 3828, 3869, 4055, 4095, 4227, 4281, 4368, 4823, 4836, 4864, 4890, 4893, 4955, 4957, 4965, 4966, 4974, 4976, 5189, 5233, 5250, 5258, 5261, 5282, 5288, 5301
Démographie 90, 451, 536, 1142, 1443, 1508, 1819, 2267, 2626, 2639, 2682, 2684, 2686, 2688-2692, 2694, 2703, 2705, 2706, 2709, 2710, 2713, 2714, 2716-2725, 2735, 2740, 2743, 2773, 2774, 2780, 2783, 2785, 2788, 2791, 2795, 2796, 2798, 2799, 2805, 2810-2812, 2814, 2815, 2819-2821, 2824, 2828, 2833, 2835-2837, 2846, 2857, 2904, 2942, 3211, 3423, 3518, 3528, 3603, 3615, 3639, 3715, 3725, 3758, 3764, 3778, 3795, 3951, 4024, 4252, 4276, 4367, 4408, 4615, 4641, 4697, 5626, 5720, 5728, 5757
Démographie ethnique 2811, 2812
Démonologie 1249
Densité de population 2686, 2714, 2736
Déontologie 43, 48, 539, 1420, 1942, 2218, 2366, 4709, 4772, 5192, 5679, 5690
Départements et territoires d'Outre-Mer 951
Dépendance 625, 723, 897, 1684, 2874, 2894, 4747, 5374, 5376-5379, 5381, 5382, 5384, 5385, 5387, 5389, 5391, 5395, 5396, 5398, 5399, 5402-5408, 5412, 5413, 5421, 5664, 5744, 5818, 5901
voir aussi: Toxicomanie
Dépendance économique 2945, 3625
Dépenses 3814, 5401
Dépenses alimentaires 2715
Dépenses de ménage 4276, 4342, 4561
Dépenses de santé 5524, 5744, 5756, 5761, 5781, 5785, 5787
Dépenses du secteur éducatif 2460
Dépenses publiques 4251, 4790, 5620, 5630
voir aussi: Subvention publique
Dépeuplement 2698, 2719, 2767, 4611
Dépositaire d'enjeux 411, 1097, 1127, 1146, 1308, 2110, 4417, 4420
Depression 741, 751, 755, 757, 764, 766, 776, 779, 781, 787, 800, 804, 807, 808, 811, 876, 897, 1670, 2583, 2659, 2874, 2885, 2960, 3015, 3055, 3591, 3901, 4710, 5192, 5405, 5433, 5434, 5710, 5838, 5935
Déréglementation 28, 2564, 3912, 4471, 4836, 4877
Déroulement de carrière 440, 2091, 2103, 3166, 3232, 4360, 4383, 4398, 4519,

INDEX DES MATIÈRES

4544, 4565, 4599, 4757, 4758, 4760-4762, 4766, 4780, 4781, 5663
Derrida, Jacques 12, 1609, 1621
Des gens d'un certain âge 1284, 2584, 2585, 2676
Désastres 767, 1146, 3615, 3690, 3699, 3751, 4265, 5464, 5910, 5911, 5923, 5964
    voir aussi: Catastrophes naturelles
Descartes, René 221
Description d'emploi 4689
Déségrégation 2110
Désert 5195
Désindustrialisation 3997, 4066
Désintégration de la famille 2917
Désirabilité sociale 1313
Désorganisation sociale 2536, 3858
Dessin 5592
Dessins humoristiques 586, 1257, 1320
Déterminants 2408, 2822, 5757
Déterminisme 136, 332, 341, 1412, 1636
Dette 2336, 4351, 5151
    voir aussi: Allègement de la dette
Dette extérieure 2502, 4287, 5363
Deuil 743, 767, 1751, 1937
Deuxième guerre mondiale 189, 976, 1004, 1218, 1888, 1902, 1976, 3495, 3502, 3518, 4898
Deuxième langue 2003, 2009
Dévaluation 847, 4223
Développement agricole 3889, 3922
Développement capitaliste 2534, 2540
Développement cognitif 553, 598, 600, 612, 619, 626, 633, 740, 2615, 2625, 3182, 4418, 5592
Développement culturel 57, 1219, 1797, 1855, 3940
Développement de la personnalité 553, 679, 698
Développement de l'éducation 2007, 2145, 2257
Développement de l'enfant 77, 544, 545, 551, 577, 607, 622, 623, 636, 660, 695, 743, 756, 792, 2301, 2453, 2596, 2598, 2599, 2601, 2606, 2608, 2646, 2685, 2738, 2893, 2898, 2903, 2921, 2928, 2935, 2946, 2988, 3004, 3009, 3013, 3016, 3027, 3029, 3046, 3047, 3049, 3050, 4469, 4777, 5050, 5097, 5447, 5550, 5551, 5571, 5589, 5591, 5633, 5912, 5969
Développement des collectivités 904, 1026, 1685, 2221, 2345, 3431, 3628, 3730, 3805, 3814, 3825, 3827-3832, 3834, 3836, 3838-3841, 3850, 3852, 3854, 3855, 3857, 3861-3863, 3865, 3907, 3911, 3967, 4044,

4052, 4070, 4071, 4117, 4258, 4299, 5107, 5716, 5969
Développement du curriculum 2179, 2180
Développement durable 1221, 1565, 2508, 2638, 3126, 3694, 3698, 3702, 3715, 3735, 3756, 3761, 3763, 3766, 3796, 3797, 3799-3805, 3807-3823, 3857, 3918, 3923, 3924, 3949, 4025, 4037, 4041, 4061, 4063, 4082, 4096, 4102, 4104, 4109, 4123, 4166, 4170, 5221
Développement économique 92, 1219, 1685, 2046, 2266, 2420, 2512, 2523, 2528, 2558, 2749, 2961, 3103, 3160, 3615, 3633, 3637, 3642, 3662, 3718, 3722, 3770, 3771, 3776, 3796, 3802, 3814, 3815, 3914, 3923, 3925, 3935, 3940, 3948, 3960, 3971, 4029, 4043, 4077, 4079, 4085, 4092, 4097, 4098, 4109, 4161, 4169, 4197, 4218, 4228, 4233, 4236, 4250, 4253, 4254, 4258, 4267, 4272, 4279, 4286, 4290, 4292, 4296, 4309, 4313, 4450, 4452, 4535, 4600, 4606, 4819, 4866, 5282, 5445, 5519, 5622, 5768
Développement humain 572, 575, 591, 726, 1161, 1994, 3160, 3173, 3809, 4260, 5675
Développement industriel 1756, 4162, 4323, 4458, 4748
Développement inégal 3927
Développement intellectuel 661
Développement minier 3827
Développement moral 46, 2615
Développement national 4115
Développement politique 57, 2795, 4392, 4885, 4970
Développement régional 1892, 2539, 3069, 3682, 3768, 3771, 3792, 3820, 3836, 3920, 3948, 4069, 4085, 4097, 4105, 4261, 4509, 4606, 4995, 5445
Développement rural 3535, 3612, 3813, 3852, 3866, 3867, 3871, 3876, 3895, 3914-3920, 3923-3925, 4240, 4458, 5261, 5968
Développement sectoriel 4385
Développement social 353, 598, 1107, 1301, 1368, 1415, 1542, 1729, 2046, 2364, 2503, 2511, 2519, 2528, 2535, 2609, 2685, 2898, 3016, 3041, 3067, 3174, 3203, 3528, 3615, 3642, 3836, 4040, 4097, 4254, 4267, 4286, 4290, 4392, 4481, 4560, 4571, 4970, 5519, 5629, 5683, 5688, 5694, 5695, 5700, 5701
Développement socioéconomique 982, 2514, 2568, 2606, 2740, 2767, 2833, 3086, 3275, 3624, 3801, 4066, 4189, 4195,

4197, 4203, 4261, 4279, 4337, 4347, 4495, 4606, 4793, 4890, 4948
Développement urbain 2024, 2138, 2571, 3755, 3813, 3868, 3927, 3928, 3935, 3936, 3940, 3941, 3947-3949, 3958, 3961, 3962, 3964, 3972, 3974, 3975, 3983, 3987, 3990, 3994, 3998, 4018, 4023-4025, 4031-4033, 4036, 4040, 4045, 4046, 4051, 4056, 4060, 4061, 4066, 4069, 4071, 4076, 4078, 4080, 4081, 4087, 4088, 4097, 4100, 4103-4105, 4108, 4109, 4113, 4115, 4117, 4120, 4127, 4136-4138, 4141, 4149, 4153, 4155, 4158, 4159, 4162, 4164, 4165, 4167, 4169, 4172-4175, 4178
Déviance 709, 2358, 2634, 3377, 3524, 4530, 4683, 5011, 5405
Devoir 1245, 2346, 3471
Dévolution 2529
Dewey, John 2117
Diabète 5970
Diable 1438
Dialectes 1793, 1798, 1801, 1840, 2523
Dialectes créoles 1801
Dialectes pidgin 1805
Dialectique 140, 218, 360, 362, 1210, 1650, 5166, 5677
Dialectologie 1798
Dialogue 31, 523, 901, 940, 1014, 1462, 1561, 1632, 1640, 1648, 1808, 1824, 1877, 4835
Dialogue entre les cultures 173, 4386
Diamant 3067
Diana [Princess of Wales] 1719, 1751
Diaspora 1263, 1836, 1880, 1978, 1985, 1990, 3445, 3497, 3557, 3636, 3646, 3650, 3654, 3668, 3676, 3680, 3778, 4118, 4125, 5328
Dictature 2567, 4095, 4973, 5266
Dictionnaires 81, 82, 84, 93, 96-98, 100, 103, 556, 1703
Dietrich, Marlene 1882
Dieux 221, 254, 293, 1374, 1375, 1389-1391, 1404, 1406, 1412, 1413, 1428, 1438, 1451, 1477, 1487, 1506
Différence 45, 368, 735, 1279, 2289, 2907, 2915, 3301, 3367, 3386, 3403, 3786, 3834, 4118, 4615
Différence culturelle 9, 134, 550, 676, 710, 806, 965, 1072, 1160, 1171, 1177, 1208, 1209, 1230, 1238, 1240, 1831, 2113, 2118, 2232, 2357, 2569, 2731, 3011, 3266, 3328, 3417, 3471, 3548, 4198, 4212, 4312, 4318, 4367, 4417, 4475, 4629, 4630, 5320, 5908
Différence d'âge 682, 4752, 5093

Différences de generations 2587, 2592, 4218, 4305, 4755, 5941
Différenciation culturelle 520, 1796, 4184, 4658
Différenciation raciale 2017, 2034, 2380, 4000, 4438, 5113, 5774
Différenciation sexuelle 689, 858, 1814, 2266, 3063, 3071, 3133, 3185, 3199, 3205, 3335, 4704
Différenciation sexuelle (culturelle) 20, 557, 583, 689, 708, 776, 914, 1290, 1321, 1544, 1760, 1814, 2025, 2041, 2072, 2076, 2198, 2472, 2561, 2608, 2658, 2743, 2754, 2888, 2894, 2915, 2976, 3005, 3038, 3048, 3064, 3065, 3069, 3070, 3074, 3079, 3087, 3088, 3115, 3131, 3158, 3165-3171, 3176, 3179, 3181-3183, 3187-3189, 3192, 3194-3198, 3200, 3201, 3203, 3206, 3208, 3209, 3216, 3217, 3222, 3226, 3231, 3243, 3244, 3261, 3281, 3306, 3307, 3372, 3592, 3623, 3665, 3677, 3749, 4371, 4377, 4383, 4415, 4477, 4480, 4506, 4519, 4520, 4526, 4533, 4534, 4536, 4537, 4539, 4540, 4543-4546, 4549, 4551, 4557, 4562, 4570, 4571, 4578, 4584, 4586, 4599, 4661, 4720, 4761, 4765, 4777, 4839, 4944, 5096, 5115, 5131, 5160, 5346, 5350, 5353, 5388, 5403, 5505, 5628, 5827, 5838, 5891
Différenciation sociale 1322, 2238, 2393, 2409, 2411, 2418, 2428, 2444, 2813, 2915, 3460, 3896, 4292, 5285
Différentiel de qualifications 4486
Difficulté de langue 622, 1653
  voir aussi: Dyslexie
Difficultés économiques 4606
Diffusion de la culture 1308, 1540, 2401
Diffusion de l'information 43, 923, 1200, 1732, 2748, 4933, 5169, 5407, 5965
Diffusion des innovations 484
Diffusion politique 1772
Dilemme du prisonnier 1073, 1638, 4388
Dilthey, Wilhelm 126
Dimension de la famille 653, 2032, 2741, 2756, 2818, 2904, 2927, 2948
Dimension de la ville 3929, 3948, 4033
Diplomatie 5333
Diplômes 2064, 2249, 4429, 4441, 4583, 4717, 4757, 4769
Diplômés d'université 1996, 2253, 2267, 2268, 2274, 3382, 4766, 4769, 5844
Directeurs 1013, 1104, 1119, 1147, 1718, 3281, 4421, 4512, 4565, 4569, 4599, 4627, 4629-4631, 4635, 4645, 4648, 4652,

INDEX DES MATIÈRES

4656, 4657, 4659, 4661-4663, 4738, 4759, 4774, 4786, 4809
Direction 684, 1010, 1065, 1068, 1093, 1153, 1336, 2118, 2151, 2240, 2257, 2321, 2398, 2405, 3067, 3115, 3163, 3911, 4253, 4417, 4543, 4615, 4620, 4622, 4624, 4630, 4632, 4637-4639, 4642, 4645, 4646, 4658, 4661, 4663, 4886, 5227, 5932
Direction de crise 724, 1018, 1097, 1146, 3713, 5141
Direction de l'entreprise 414, 582, 1151, 2571, 3069, 3791, 3885, 3927, 3942, 4209, 4239, 4273, 4311, 4369, 4371, 4372, 4393, 4394, 4407, 4415, 4651, 4665
Direction politique 1731, 2579, 4886, 4955, 5295
Dirigeant religieux 326
Discipline intellectuelle 5, 11, 38, 44, 53, 67, 167, 170, 183, 195, 339, 1491, 1556, 2207, 2216, 2255, 3115, 3232, 3545, 3788, 4413, 5206
Discipline parentale 5580
Discipline scolaire 2119
Discours 47, 117, 119, 126, 149, 233, 243, 261, 271, 367, 511, 593, 664, 916, 940, 1059, 1102-1104, 1108, 1127, 1139, 1165, 1208, 1313, 1345, 1361, 1428, 1531, 1561, 1567, 1642, 1648, 1650, 1668, 1685, 1727, 1748, 1752, 1772, 1789, 1790, 1792, 1808, 1830, 1832, 1833, 1839, 1844, 1852, 1960, 2208, 2354, 2402, 2468, 2496, 2579, 2588, 2643, 2730, 2940, 3005, 3037, 3061, 3062, 3102, 3117, 3258, 3259, 3266, 3272, 3273, 3317, 3339, 3354, 3365, 3497, 3499, 3500, 3508, 3697, 3700, 3717, 3723, 3727, 3788, 4016, 4065, 4137, 4138, 4265, 4361, 4362, 4515, 4618, 4666, 4912, 4918, 4952, 4966, 5061, 5162, 5165, 5184, 5254, 5299, 5315, 5589, 5603
Discrimination 349, 822, 858, 894, 1044, 1067, 1308, 1760, 2017, 2057, 2076, 2273, 2452, 2458, 2477, 2484, 2754, 3274, 3286, 3321, 3375, 3451, 3470, 3511, 3657, 3992, 3996, 4285, 4427, 4494, 4495, 4497, 4510, 4628, 5188, 5214, 5243, 5443, 5800, 5872, 5928, 5988
voir aussi: Âgisme
Discrimination dans l'emploi 2455, 2466, 4487-4489, 4491, 4496, 4498, 4500, 4507, 4509, 4690, 4691, 5203
Discrimination raciale 2060, 2232, 2266, 3451, 3466, 3478, 3483, 3497, 3505, 3507, 3517, 3521, 3529, 3599, 3654, 3981, 4000, 4015, 4416, 4491, 4501,
4502, 4511, 4690, 5031, 5129, 5142, 5160, 5171, 5490
Discrimination religieuse 3172, 4962
Discrimination salariale 2457, 4499, 4502, 4540, 4573
Discrimination sexuelle 20, 1613, 2041, 2076, 2783, 3105, 3171, 3180, 3275, 3284, 3285, 3290, 3352, 4488, 4504, 4508, 4511, 4512, 4540, 4562, 4576, 5358
Disparités régionales 2234, 2560, 2774, 3069, 3620, 3895, 3981
Dispensaires 5824
Disponibilités alimentaires 2706
Dissensus 1431, 5275
Dissidents 5148
Dissonance cognitive 652, 1075
Dissuasion 3849, 5007, 5029
Distance sociale 1083, 3164
Distribution 460, 491, 492, 1892, 2818, 4162
Divergence 1798, 2776
Diversification 6, 1010, 2363, 3401, 3919, 4234, 4243
Diversité des cultures 996, 1001, 1010, 1240, 1548, 1806, 1826, 2354, 2909, 2934, 3423, 3500, 3522, 4227, 4359, 4362, 5021, 5326, 5529
Divertissement 1187, 1318, 1320, 1708, 1731, 1753, 1756, 1765, 1772, 1882, 1977, 2486, 2618, 3353, 3391, 3644, 4060, 4787, 4954
Divination 1433
Divinités 1374
Division du travail 513, 1495, 2035, 2406, 2554, 2571, 2915, 3170, 3221, 3236, 3258, 3270, 3693, 4092, 4132, 4389, 4400, 4477, 4486, 4521, 4526, 4530, 4556, 4575, 4577, 4754
Division internationale du travail 3191, 4546
Divorce 2696, 2724, 2768, 2845-2859, 2911, 2923, 2924, 2962, 2968, 2975, 3022, 3054, 3056
Dizi 3531
Doctrines religieuses 132, 1498, 2870
Documentation 1884
Documents 104, 178, 1040, 3532
Dogmatisme 1552
Dogme 58, 141
Domestication animale 2342
Domination 245, 291, 799, 852, 1060, 2340, 2421, 3115, 3187, 3236, 3457, 3881, 4953, 4968, 5016, 5170, 5216, 5438
Dominicains 3398
Don 239, 931, 1839, 4194, 5860
Données d'enquête 500, 512, 518-520, 524, 525, 531, 535, 2157, 2759, 3633, 5891

SUBJECT INDEX IN FRENCH

Données statistiques 92, 478, 481, 512, 520, 2381
Dot 3265
Downsizing 4411, 4434, 4647, 4737
Droit 95, 426, 498, 1308, 1380, 1611, 1650, 1665, 1678, 1838, 1980, 2361, 2366, 2754, 3319, 3354, 3574, 4299, 4496, 4497, 4751, 4876, 4978, 4992, 5024, 5025, 5054, 5144, 5149, 5151, 5153, 5154, 5158-5163, 5165, 5167, 5171-5174, 5176, 5178-5183, 5185, 5189, 5191, 5193, 5194, 5198, 5199, 5206-5208, 5211, 5219, 5443, 5580, 5585, 5814, 5829, 5853, 5884, 5886, 5889
  voir aussi: Anthropologie du droit, Histoire du droit, Litige, Loi comparé, Loi environnementale, Loi islamique, Loi martiale, Loi sur l'immigration, Philosophie du droit, Sociologie du droit
Droit à la vie privée 1714, 4933, 4986, 4988
Droit à l'éducation 2014
Droit au travail 4870
Droit civil 2642, 2908, 5156, 5190, 5633
Droit commun 5055, 5167
Droit communautaire 3321, 4950, 5025, 5200
Droit constitutionnel 4933, 5889
Droit coutumier 2308, 3915, 5167, 5178
Droit criminel 311, 4998, 5000, 5005, 5007, 5009, 5018, 5025, 5027, 5028, 5034, 5036, 5038, 5041, 5054, 5056, 5098, 5150, 5166, 5175, 5176, 5192, 5858
  voir aussi: Droit pénal international
Droit d'asile 3680, 5637
Droit de la famille 2854, 2860, 2862, 2872, 2886, 2889, 2990, 5164, 5192, 5548
Droit du travail 1308, 2554, 4483, 4534, 4542, 4585, 4587, 4751, 4810, 4815, 4818, 4825, 4846, 4870, 5025
Droit économique 2196, 5025
Droit fiscal 2196
Droit international 2554, 3136, 4287, 5025, 5027, 5210, 5311, 5322
Droit international humanitaire 5025, 5312
Droit matrimonial 2917, 2992, 3471
Droit naturel 271, 360, 5161
Droit parlementaire 5025
Droit pénal international 5312
Droit public 5025, 5156
Droit traditionnel 5167, 5211
Droite 2361, 5883
  voir aussi: Extrême droite, Nouvelle droite
Droits 1466, 1484, 2346, 2461, 2495, 2734, 3205, 3335, 3675, 4324, 4915, 4933, 4950, 5161, 5196, 5247, 5271, 5326, 5854

Droits de la femme 2730, 2754, 2761, 2762, 2883, 3074, 3079, 3089, 3114, 3206, 3215, 3883, 4254, 4944, 5326
Droits de l'enfant 417, 2019, 2596, 2602-2604, 3813, 4482, 5068, 5192, 5209, 5560, 5576, 5580, 5585, 5601
Droits de l'homme 248, 349, 1466, 1482, 1650, 1713, 1731, 1781, 1995, 2019, 2030, 2344, 2361, 2460, 2498, 2554, 2754, 3074, 3115, 3327, 3375, 3469, 3542, 3582, 3615, 3624, 3651, 3754, 4254, 4268, 4287, 4299, 4360, 4417, 4423, 4482, 4682, 4903, 4949, 4971, 5021, 5025, 5139, 5159, 5161, 5200, 5244, 5309, 5312, 5320, 5322, 5326, 5361, 5601, 5605, 5700, 5805, 5809, 5853, 5884, 5887, 5889, 5915, 5929, 5930, 5952, 5972, 5988
  voir aussi: Convention européenne des droits de l'homme, Droits internationaux de l'homme
Droits de propriété 3755, 3891, 4220, 5881
Droits des animaux 1296, 1297, 2342, 5258
Droits des minorités 1531, 3419, 4628, 5021
Droits des travailleurs 4360, 4849
Droits du citoyen 349, 1531, 2454, 2492, 2498, 3115, 3389, 3391, 3431, 3669, 3749, 3777, 4950, 5002, 5048, 5136, 5139, 5159, 5242, 5258, 5273, 5280, 5320, 5357, 5609
  voir aussi: Droit à l'éducation, Droit au travail
Droits économiques 4268, 5809
Droits fondamentaux 2349, 2495, 2754, 4299, 4423, 4433, 4933, 4950, 5188, 5852, 5879, 5929, 5930, 5972
Droits indigènes 1620, 1769, 3526, 3771
Droits individuels 1620
Droits internationaux de l'homme 1730, 2354, 3681, 5322, 5326, 5576, 5805
Droits sociaux 3675, 4299, 4950, 4952, 5326, 5609, 5615, 5652, 5809, 5814
Du Bois, W.E.B. 3432, 3514
Dualisme 239, 1136, 2388, 5182
Duda-Gracz, Jerzy 1852
Dumézil, Georges 1395
Dummett, Michael 222
Dumont, Louis 2395
Durabilité 1093, 1152, 3697, 3705, 3749, 3759, 3765, 3771, 3796, 3801, 3805, 3808-3811, 3813, 3817, 3819-3822, 3827, 3924, 3961, 4028, 4037, 4061, 4163
Durée du chômage 4590, 4595, 4648
Durkheim, Émile 223, 330, 375, 801, 1245, 5158

INDEX DES MATIÈRES

Dynamique 643, 1265, 3971
Dynamique culturelle 868, 1395, 1566, 1682, 2908
Dynamique de groupe 655, 759, 829, 832, 844, 848, 852, 856, 858, 894, 999, 1011, 1029, 1033, 1037, 1040, 1043, 1046, 1051, 1053, 1057, 1058, 1060, 1061, 1063-1067, 1071, 1074-1077, 1079, 1080, 1083, 1084, 1086, 1095, 1130, 1143, 1639, 1684, 3517, 4366, 4384, 4607, 4632, 5437, 5672, 5831
Dynamique de la population 468, 2706, 2713, 2717, 2718, 2779, 3606, 3607, 4439, 5507
Dynamique économique 4132
Dynamique sociale 387, 1043, 1051, 1469, 2161, 2302, 2313, 2329, 2419, 2514, 2594, 2967, 3509, 3892, 4132, 5265
Dyslexie 2477
Earman, J. 1586
Eau 484, 2711
Écart des salaires 2023, 4305, 4464, 4495, 4498, 4499, 4502, 4503, 4509, 4525, 4538, 4539, 4547, 4551, 4556, 4573, 4878, 4880, 5891
Échange 303, 398, 466, 1062, 1163, 1648, 2341, 3353, 3902, 3907, 4187, 4193, 4351, 4380
Échange d'information 1084, 1113, 2580, 4395, 5954
Échange social 656, 1047, 1062, 1069, 4146
Echantillon 460, 525, 534, 2722, 2778, 2839, 2876, 2928, 3476, 3715, 4518, 4778, 5408
Échantillonnage 451, 468, 491, 504, 2595, 3182, 4262
Échec 4580
Échec scolaire 2020
Échelle d'attitude 890, 3749
Eckhart, Meister 220
Écoles 435, 459, 577, 862, 1875, 1990, 1993, 1998, 2000, 2014, 2017, 2024, 2029, 2034, 2036, 2038, 2044, 2051, 2059, 2062, 2065-2069, 2073, 2076, 2079, 2086, 2094, 2096, 2101, 2104, 2105, 2108-2111, 2114, 2116, 2121, 2122, 2124, 2125, 2131, 2135, 2138, 2142, 2143, 2146, 2151-2153, 2155, 2157, 2159, 2165, 2166, 2177, 2188, 2204, 2205, 2230, 2237, 2316, 2608, 2622, 2636, 2644, 2871, 2878, 3115, 3274, 3340, 3349, 3458, 3517, 3521, 3554, 4398, 5108, 5225, 5461, 5465, 5593, 5814, 5933, 5955
Écoles primaires 2212, 2218, 2231, 2234
Écoles privées 1998, 2077, 2126
Écoles publiques 2131, 4962

Écoles secondaires 2070, 2077, 2085, 2088, 2124, 2130, 2158, 2235, 2236, 2240, 2241, 5470, 5955
Écologie 22, 225, 558, 561, 1099, 1107, 1237, 1401, 1576, 2766, 2983, 3058, 3131, 3688, 3695, 3700, 3706, 3707, 3709, 3717-3720, 3725, 3730, 3732, 3737, 3740, 3742, 3747, 3751, 3753, 3758, 3759, 3761, 3762, 3766, 3774, 3797, 3798, 3811, 3816, 3820, 3925, 3949, 4114, 4132, 4155, 4293, 4346, 5252, 5911, 5958
Écologie culturelle 3531
Écologie humaine 2508, 3689, 3691, 3710, 3716, 3719, 3738, 3752, 3756, 3759, 3764, 3779, 3783, 3800, 3820
Écologie sociale 3720, 3740, 3741, 4468
Écologisme 3729, 3742, 3768, 3797, 4210
Économétrie 4503, 5832
Économie 6, 10, 1410, 1859, 2216, 2243, 3115, 4199, 4224, 4311, 4314, 5186, 5316
Économie agricole 3889
Économie capitaliste 1277
Economie comparative 4255, 5486
Économie de bien-être 4200, 5489
Économie de la distribution 4262
Économie de la population 1099, 2764, 3637
Économie de la santé 3039, 4304, 5507, 5728, 5732, 5740, 5750, 5754, 5756, 5760, 5761, 5770, 5772, 5777, 5785-5787, 5795, 5803, 5811, 5812, 5814, 5821, 5897, 5931, 5942, 5980
Économie de l'éducation 2167
Économie de l'entreprise 4370, 4425
Économie de l'environnement 2793, 3757, 3799, 3811, 3823
Économie de l'information 472, 5965
Économie de marché 1738, 2686, 3890, 4179, 4195, 4201, 4208, 4209, 4214, 4230, 4231, 4237, 4260, 4322, 4351, 4481, 4923, 5059
Économie des transports 4045, 4048, 4062
Économie domestique 1283
Économie du développement 2782, 2873, 3770, 3805, 3895, 4156, 4279, 5455
Économie du ménage 2035, 2676, 2858, 3054, 3190, 3619, 3924, 4184, 4263, 4273, 4310, 4317, 4338, 4486, 4556
Économie du sport 1357
Économie du travail 633, 2507, 4449, 4484, 4603, 4643, 4681, 4749, 4792
Économie expérimentale 3063
Économie financière 4256
Économie foncière 4047, 4156, 4164
Économie industrielle 4559
Économie internationale 3797

539

SUBJECT INDEX IN FRENCH

Économie locale 1733, 3069, 4280, 4439, 4579, 4589
Économie mathématique 2776, 4796, 5390
Économie mixte 2458
Économie mondiale 336, 379, 1131, 2128, 2446, 2554, 2559, 2562, 2567, 2571, 2572, 2578, 3663, 3693, 3750, 3797, 3851, 3927, 3952, 4202, 4205, 4206, 4212, 4233, 4486, 4558, 4825, 4850, 4863, 5187, 5622
Économie monétaire 4350
Économie néoclassique 4196, 4203, 4211, 4351, 4393
Économie politique 379, 1950, 2551, 3730, 3896, 3918, 4073, 4074, 4193, 4210, 4211, 4214, 4224, 4231, 4752, 4854, 4922, 5146, 5278, 5363
Économie publique 5620
Économie régionale 3927, 3997, 4058, 4069, 4833, 4935
Économie rurale 3852, 3868, 3884, 3897, 3898, 3903, 3915, 3916, 3923, 4248, 4264, 4486
Économie sociale 2496, 5057, 5475, 5786
Économie spatiale 3790
Économie urbaine 2571, 3927, 4045, 4070, 4103, 4124, 4162, 4174, 4245, 4264, 4327, 4453, 4490, 5475
Économies de transition 2593, 2686, 2712, 2833, 2961, 3455, 3870, 4168, 4209, 4241, 4255, 4292, 4429, 4573, 4790, 5003, 5773
Économies d'échelle 3893, 4151
Économisme 373
Économistes 375, 1859, 4191, 4255
Écossais 5213
Écosystèmes 3705, 3714, 3721, 3728, 3731, 3754, 3755, 3761
Écriture 17, 99, 151, 178, 198, 200, 415, 1140, 1637, 1711, 1763, 1858, 1907, 1914, 1915, 1919, 1922, 1924, 1925, 1936, 1938, 1944, 1959, 2005, 2040, 2206, 2268, 2314, 2588, 3079, 3112, 3230, 3931, 4807
Écrivains 249, 281, 283, 1901, 1918, 1922, 1925, 1936, 1937, 1939, 1945, 1948, 1956, 1959, 2439, 3107, 3120, 3122, 4898, 4935
voir aussi: Romancier
Édition 1323, 1557, 1726, 1754, 1952, 1955, 2269, 3112
Éducation 33, 252, 418, 437, 441, 448, 454, 459, 543, 545, 574, 587, 633, 647, 980, 984, 996, 1018, 1196, 1203, 1331, 1519, 1536, 1592, 1644, 1648, 1675, 1692, 1708, 1776, 1819, 1875, 1992, 1993, 1995, 1997-2003, 2005, 2006, 2011, 2012, 2015-2017, 2022, 2024, 2027, 2028, 2031-2033, 2039, 2041, 2042, 2045, 2046, 2048, 2050-2054, 2060, 2065-2068, 2071, 2073, 2074, 2076, 2078-2081, 2083-2087, 2090, 2092, 2094-2096, 2099, 2100, 2102-2108, 2112, 2115, 2117, 2119, 2122, 2125-2127, 2130, 2131, 2135-2137, 2141-2144, 2148, 2150-2152, 2154, 2156, 2160-2162, 2165-2168, 2172, 2175-2177, 2180, 2181, 2185, 2187-2189, 2191-2193, 2196, 2197, 2200-2203, 2206, 2211, 2214, 2217, 2218, 2220, 2221, 2224, 2229, 2230, 2232, 2233, 2237, 2247, 2254, 2258, 2259, 2265, 2270, 2279, 2324, 2361, 2378, 2383, 2391, 2414, 2430, 2434, 2453, 2454, 2464, 2482, 2517, 2602, 2607, 2632, 2636, 2677, 2736, 2749, 2786, 2787, 2803, 2822, 2825, 2871, 2974, 3016, 3019, 3026, 3057, 3067, 3075, 3112, 3115, 3177, 3203, 3237, 3265, 3282, 3414, 3435, 3509, 3517, 3571, 3582, 3604, 3643, 3653, 3671, 3715, 3723, 3724, 3854, 3965, 4040, 4077, 4176, 4268, 4301, 4367, 4393, 4398, 4435, 4441, 4453, 4481, 4506, 4523, 4538, 4586, 4598, 4605, 4762, 4771, 4772, 4779, 4807, 4869, 4900, 4915, 4947, 5072, 5139, 5225, 5266, 5269, 5287, 5335, 5465, 5538, 5569, 5583, 5591, 5593, 5612, 5634, 5642, 5663, 5678, 5684, 5686, 5688, 5694, 5697, 5703, 5704, 5709, 5711, 5713, 5723, 5969, 5976
voir aussi: Accès à l'éducation, Économie de l'éducation, Enseignement bilingue, Enseignement multiculturel, Enseignement obligatoire, Enseignement par correspondance, Enseignement post-scolaire, Enseignement post-secondaire, Enseignement primaire, Enseignement privé, Enseignement professionnel, Enseignement public, Enseignement secondaire, Enseignement supérieur, Enseignement technique, Histoire de l'éducation, Hygiène publique, Instruction civique, Pédagogie, Rendements d'éducation, Théorie de l'éducation
Éducation de base 1991, 2144
Éducation de masse 2129
Éducation des adultes 93, 1991, 2005, 2006, 2010, 2016, 2031, 2040, 2049, 2113, 2127, 2145, 2272
Éducation des femmes 2007, 2023, 2721, 5358
Éducation des minorités 2017, 2161

INDEX DES MATIÈRES

Éducation permanente 93, 2004, 2010, 2016, 2031, 2049, 2145
Éducation politique 2170, 2181
Éducation religieuse 225, 1396, 1400, 1419, 1422, 1445, 1542, 2126, 2169, 4962
Éducation sexuelle 2160, 2721, 3316, 3329, 3349, 5200, 5975, 5978
Éducation spéciale 2019, 2026, 2154, 2225
Éducation syndicale 4484
Effet 1308, 4347
Effet de serre 3711
Effet d'éviction 3979
Effets de groupe 1053
Effets psychologiques 755, 767, 883, 2893, 2895, 3471, 4324, 4347, 4626, 5838
Effets sur l'environnement 73, 559, 1567, 1601, 3718, 3760, 3783
Efficacité du marché 5615
Efficacité économique 4061, 4621
Efficacité organisationnelle 1114, 1128, 1132, 1133, 1154, 4618
Efficacité-coût 3895, 5486, 5656
Égalitarisme 657, 2414, 2439, 2708, 2972, 3237, 4201, 5225, 5262, 5296
Égalité 349, 389, 852, 2030, 2039, 2114, 2314, 2354, 2380, 2384, 2395, 2405, 2414, 2442, 2458, 2484, 3080, 3106, 3121, 3206, 3335, 3713, 3780, 3787, 4200, 4255, 4262, 4282, 4288, 4400, 4441, 4514, 4538, 4550, 4563, 4572, 4903, 4989, 5021, 5171, 5350, 5357
Égalité de chances 349, 2019, 2030, 2076, 2078, 2123, 2273, 2414, 3127, 4272, 4486, 4496, 4512, 4537, 4541, 4550, 4563, 4695, 5197, 5348
Égalité de rémunération 4496, 4552
Égalité des sexes 1369, 1626, 2786, 2939, 3104, 3136, 3155, 3169, 3174, 3180, 3185, 3204, 3205, 3267, 4254, 4526, 4534, 4538, 4541, 4542, 4549, 4552, 4569, 5358
Égalité économique 4242
Égalité sociale 2024, 2380, 2384, 2433, 3127, 3994, 4251, 5643
Egídio, Paulo 5098
Église catholique 1475, 1478, 1500, 1502, 1514, 3468, 5776
Eglise copte 1504
Église et État 1432, 1475, 1486, 2532, 3471, 4962
Église orthodox russe 1436, 1505
Église orthodoxe 1504, 1516, 1545
Églises 1035, 1375, 1378, 1415, 1429, 1436, 1460, 1474, 1479, 1485, 1490, 1494, 1496, 1508, 1511, 2655, 2890, 3692, 3843, 3967, 5481
Églises chrétiennes 1478, 1480, 1482, 3366
voir aussi: Anglicanisme, Hutterite, Luthéranisme
Ego 679, 780
Egocentrisme 905, 2938
Élaboration d'une politique 43, 71, 347, 866, 1023, 2702, 2745, 3121, 3319, 3352, 3486, 3649, 3705, 3808, 3830, 4041, 4497, 4587, 4611, 4789, 4858, 5024, 5212, 5221, 5225, 5317, 5471, 5604, 5627, 5641, 5647, 5814
Élargissement de l'UE 4913, 4966
Élasticité du revenu 5385
Électeurs 5219, 5300, 5301, 5305
Élections 1427, 1772, 2507, 2671, 3483, 4947, 5301, 5305, 5306, 5363
Élections à la Première Chambre 5219
Électorat 5303
Électricité 4788
Électronique 4134
Élevage 2342, 4142
Élèves 435, 479, 2014, 2044, 2047, 2058, 2065, 2097, 2102, 2163, 2198, 2218, 2229, 2235, 2608, 2621, 2644, 3274, 3458, 3517, 4062, 5470, 5955
Elias, Norbert 393, 4392, 5015
Éligibilité 5535, 5788
Élite 1608, 2223, 2321, 2391, 2397, 2398, 2401, 3803, 4204, 4292, 4897, 4898, 4951, 4965, 5060, 5284, 5335
Élite économique 3942, 4160, 5227
Élite politique 24, 3286, 3942, 4066, 4292, 4640, 4897, 5284, 5297
Élitisme 1369, 2290, 2391, 5024
Ellis, Ruth 1882
Émancipation 295, 1960, 2310, 3178, 3206, 3453, 3457
Émancipation de la femme 3132, 3134
Émeutes 2618, 5133, 5448, 5464
Émigrants 3631, 3638
Émigration 18, 1536, 2705, 3541, 3542, 3575, 3584, 3598, 3603, 3605, 3612, 3631, 3633, 3639, 3652, 3659, 3668, 3679, 3684, 3686, 3778, 3791
Émissions radiophoniques 1770
Émotion 226, 314, 388, 559, 565, 591, 596, 611, 650, 670, 671, 674, 676, 677, 682-690, 692, 696, 703-706, 708, 711, 713, 715, 718, 720, 723, 726-729, 731, 736, 739, 742, 777, 821, 823, 838, 850, 856, 863, 873, 892, 899, 907, 913, 920, 921, 933, 935, 943, 948, 955, 1013, 1047, 1057, 1075, 1109, 1112, 1210, 1334, 1359,

SUBJECT INDEX IN FRENCH

1573, 1647, 1666, 1844, 1927, 1967, 2733, 2809, 2847, 2850, 2916, 2931, 2977, 3017, 3030, 3034, 3048, 3052, 3057, 3282, 3318, 3724, 3827, 3873, 4106, 4140, 4345, 4697, 5015, 5034, 5040, 5277, 5303, 5434, 5447, 5477, 5680, 5856, 5925, 5939
voir aussi: Amour, Depression
Empathie 583, 747, 831, 905-907, 1075, 1551
Empire 188, 1195, 2553, 3510, 5360
Empire britannique 188
Empire français 5360
Empire ottoman 1522
Empire romain 1159
Empirisme 75, 133, 141, 292, 304, 369, 1181, 1581, 1611, 2209
Emploi 314, 414, 550, 768, 772, 1304, 1644, 2040, 2078, 2085, 2094, 2128, 2413, 2424, 2456, 2458, 2466, 2469, 2507, 2561, 2567, 2571, 2626, 2627, 2657, 2677, 2700, 2760, 2878, 3019, 3025, 3069, 3081, 3177, 3187, 3206, 3226, 3255, 3268, 3270, 3536, 3572, 3585, 3586, 3623, 3628, 3643, 3662, 3897, 4049, 4077, 4235, 4257, 4309, 4361, 4372, 4378, 4382, 4402, 4404, 4405, 4411, 4430, 4431, 4436, 4439, 4442-4445, 4453, 4455, 4457, 4459, 4463, 4472-4474, 4476, 4478, 4479, 4483, 4485, 4491, 4492, 4497, 4503, 4515, 4536, 4540, 4541, 4546, 4547, 4550, 4553-4555, 4557, 4568, 4571, 4576, 4577, 4583, 4594, 4596, 4597, 4600, 4614, 4627, 4644, 4647, 4664, 4673, 4676, 4685, 4686, 4688, 4694, 4724, 4732, 4738, 4740, 4753, 4755, 4758, 4760, 4761, 4763, 4769, 4777, 4786, 4793, 4814, 4827, 4828, 4835, 4836, 4842, 4866, 4872, 4881, 4915, 4949, 4983, 5121, 5217, 5265, 5365, 5567, 5624, 5625, 5633, 5642, 5654
voir aussi: Accès à l'emploi, Downsizing, Travail clandestin
Emploi à plein temps 2281
Emploi à temps partiel 2281, 2653, 4299, 4456, 4520, 4522, 4676, 4678
Emploi des femmes 2023, 2914, 2971, 2997, 3022, 3224, 3277, 3538, 4372, 4414, 4416, 4466, 4467, 4478, 4480, 4516, 4520, 4522, 4523, 4525, 4528-4532, 4543, 4549, 4552, 4553, 4559, 4567, 4569, 4573-4575, 4595, 5834
Emploi des jeunes 4435, 4447, 4449, 4454
Emploi rural 4516
Emploi temporaire 2741, 3229, 3791, 4299, 4447, 4456, 4676

Emploi urbain 4130, 4147, 4461, 4516, 4566
Employés 768, 1111, 1135, 1144, 1764, 1977, 2362, 3226, 3325, 3767, 4367, 4376, 4388, 4391, 4397, 4400, 4403, 4406, 4419, 4422, 4483, 4618, 4658, 4684, 4689, 4692, 4700, 4701, 4703, 4705-4707, 4712, 4718, 4722, 4723, 4728, 4729, 4732, 4745, 4746, 4748, 4760, 4779, 4803, 4808, 4809, 4812, 4822, 4827, 4830, 4831, 4844, 4846, 4861, 4862, 4866, 4876, 4880, 5607, 5794
Employés de bureau 3164, 4662
Employés de commerce 944, 4418
Employés des services publics 5214, 5220
Employeurs 1147, 3553, 4422, 4449, 4499, 4596, 4712, 4798, 4814, 4815, 4840, 4846, 4850, 4868
Enchère 1073
Encyclopédies 83, 86, 1178-1180, 2694, 3528
Endettement 2336
Endiguement 784
Endogamie 2701, 2984
Énergie 1623, 2508, 4637
Énergie non-renouvelable 3711
Énergie nucléaire 1597, 3734
Enfance 157, 554, 700, 756, 933, 1494, 1913, 2325, 2597, 2599-2602, 2605, 2607, 2610, 2618, 2635, 2780, 2912, 2916, 2922, 2932, 2951, 3004, 3041, 3056, 5051, 5209, 5461, 5557
Enfants 157, 225, 417, 419, 545, 577, 583, 586, 607, 608, 610, 622-624, 635, 636, 654, 754-756, 771, 782, 783, 1077, 1460, 1711, 1716, 1788, 1789, 1811, 2013, 2026, 2047, 2154, 2174, 2187, 2225, 2272, 2325, 2464, 2596-2598, 2600-2608, 2610, 2622, 2739, 2757, 2846-2848, 2851, 2853, 2854, 2859, 2871, 2884, 2899, 2904, 2923, 2927, 2931, 2934, 2935, 2946, 2950, 2975, 2988, 2994, 3001, 3003, 3004, 3010, 3012, 3014, 3016, 3017, 3019-3022, 3026, 3030-3032, 3034, 3039, 3040, 3042, 3047, 3048, 3050, 3054, 3055, 3169, 3216, 3239, 3260, 3338, 3446, 3651, 3901, 4257, 4430, 4442, 4452, 4469, 4531, 4548, 4765, 4900, 5078, 5132, 5409, 5427, 5428, 5430, 5447, 5461, 5528, 5544, 5546-5550, 5553, 5556-5559, 5561, 5562, 5564, 5565, 5571, 5572, 5579, 5580, 5583, 5586-5588, 5592-5594, 5596, 5598, 5601, 5608, 5612, 5661, 5671, 5675, 5680, 5696, 5721, 5757, 5768, 5769, 5792, 5820, 5838, 5906, 5912, 5918, 5925, 5933, 5936,

INDEX DES MATIÈRES

5949, 5959
voir aussi: Petits enfants
Enfants à la garde de l'État 5593
Enfants adoptés 2952, 3433
Enfants des migrants 2029
Enfants doués 660
Enfants handicapés 783, 2019, 2026, 2154, 2453, 2463, 2486, 2488, 5547, 5576
Engagement politique 3635
En-groupe 842, 843, 1044, 1058, 1063, 1083, 3446
Enlèvement 3471
Ennui 4710
Enquêtes 198, 424, 448, 501, 502, 509, 510, 512, 513, 519, 520, 522, 534-537, 751, 791, 1119, 1327, 1349, 1715, 1783, 1841, 2006, 2145, 2583, 2648, 2692, 2726, 2732, 2834, 2875, 2930, 2942, 3025, 3434, 3455, 3570, 3633, 3748, 3991, 3993, 3996, 4145, 4253, 4276, 4277, 4306, 4499, 4723, 4837, 4985, 5114, 5132, 5213, 5773, 5829, 5872
voir aussi: Sondages
Enquêtes économiques 4484
Enquêtes par correspondance 524, 527
Enquêtes par panel 811, 2636, 2803, 3835, 4014, 4881, 5307
Enquêtes sociales 477, 527, 2683, 3210, 3271, 3588, 4119, 5433, 5449
Enquêteurs 509, 4776
Enregistrement 1982
Enrichissement des tâches 4760
Enseignants 435, 523, 1654, 2014, 2024, 2044, 2079-2086, 2088, 2090, 2091, 2093-2106, 2112, 2118, 2121, 2146, 2173, 2184, 2187, 2189, 2195, 2198, 2200, 2202, 2215, 2218, 2225, 2235, 2237, 2241, 2246, 2316, 2453, 2592, 2602, 3031, 3260, 4494, 4735, 4772, 5213, 5465, 5550, 5642
Enseignement 47, 53, 1018, 1224, 1226, 1236, 1592, 1631, 1715, 1858, 1991, 1992, 2009, 2011, 2015, 2027, 2056, 2075, 2079, 2084-2087, 2091, 2092, 2094-2096, 2098, 2099, 2101-2104, 2114, 2116, 2121, 2148, 2164, 2169, 2174, 2176-2178, 2181-2183, 2185, 2187-2189, 2191, 2195, 2196, 2198, 2202, 2204, 2206-2208, 2212, 2215, 2216, 2218-2220, 2225, 2229, 2233, 2237, 2279, 2285, 2288, 2291, 2294, 2453, 2602, 3102, 3115, 4735, 4772, 4801, 5704
Enseignement bilingue 1785, 2050
Enseignement de la sociologie 38, 44, 2200
Enseignement des langues 1786, 2083, 2105, 2121, 2227, 2228

Enseignement multiculturel 2177, 3470
Enseignement obligatoire 4418
Enseignement par correspondance 2145
Enseignement post-scolaire 102, 2055, 2057, 2128, 2134, 2183, 2190, 2210, 2213, 2222, 2259, 2260, 2263, 2267, 2269, 2273, 2275, 2277, 2278, 2283-2287, 2290, 2291, 2293, 2296, 4794, 5703
Enseignement post-secondaire 2145
Enseignement primaire 1996, 2106, 2211, 2217, 2229, 2230, 2232, 3260, 5588
Enseignement privé 2029, 2141, 2251
Enseignement professionnel 2031, 2145, 4771, 4805, 4806
Enseignement public 2147, 2199, 2242, 2251, 2281, 2293, 2295
Enseignement religieux 3108
Enseignement secondaire 1257, 1419, 2072, 2082, 2087, 2091, 2092, 2109, 2124, 2130, 2149, 2159, 2178, 2179, 2210, 2237-2239, 2241, 3300, 3759, 4527, 4768, 4806
Enseignement supérieur 1, 44, 53, 78, 996, 1196, 1617, 1692, 1996, 2008, 2018, 2030, 2033, 2043, 2048, 2052, 2055-2057, 2072, 2108, 2128, 2129, 2132, 2134, 2139, 2145, 2147, 2159, 2190, 2195, 2196, 2202, 2210, 2213, 2242, 2243, 2247, 2249, 2253, 2254, 2256, 2257, 2259, 2262-2266, 2270-2280, 2283, 2285, 2287, 2289, 2292, 2294, 2297, 2299, 2383, 2454, 2624, 3232, 3292, 3477, 4040, 4454, 4514, 4564, 4655, 4762, 4791, 4794, 4805, 5705
Enseignement technique 2125, 4805, 4806
Enterrement 5890
Entre deux guerres 2117
Entreprises 49, 371, 1103, 1122, 1127, 1142, 1323, 2263, 2362, 3166, 3791, 3797, 3869, 4214, 4243, 4279, 4309, 4318, 4357, 4358, 4366, 4375, 4380, 4381, 4401, 4403, 4407, 4408, 4422, 4423, 4569, 4634, 4669, 4763, 4773, 4798, 4809, 4812, 4819, 4842, 4881, 4946, 5227, 5267, 5475, 5478, 5725
voir aussi: Petites et moyennes entreprises
Entreprises conjointes 1134
Entreprises étrangères 4633
Entreprises familiales 4218
Entreprises multinationales 2446, 2545, 3645, 3927, 4202, 4289, 4312, 4318, 4360, 4475, 4562, 4633, 4658, 4674, 4818, 5187, 5244
Entreprises privées 2514, 4657, 4748, 5591

SUBJECT INDEX IN FRENCH

Entretiens 20, 62, 186, 424, 469, 470, 503, 506, 508-511, 516, 518-521, 523, 527, 528, 532, 828, 1050, 1191, 1353, 1752, 1833, 2240, 2283, 2298, 2466, 2476, 2490, 2500, 2530, 2626, 2747, 2763, 2778, 3033, 3102, 3260, 3288, 3310, 3381, 3600, 3649, 3660, 3696, 4361, 4406, 4558, 4623, 4735, 5012, 5118, 5132, 5389, 5420, 5562, 5675, 5823, 5842, 5891, 5924
Environnement 225, 483, 558, 575, 641, 769, 2304, 2559, 2659, 2812, 2825, 3014, 3066, 3083, 3090, 3126, 3167, 3308, 3687, 3691, 3696, 3697, 3701, 3703, 3705, 3706, 3717, 3720-3728, 3731, 3734, 3737, 3742, 3746, 3750, 3753, 3758, 3761, 3762, 3765, 3766, 3803, 3815, 4108, 4114, 4146, 4246, 4313, 4358, 4420, 5067, 5244, 5337, 5517, 5529
 voir aussi: Milieu culturel, Milieu de travail, Milieu familial, Milieu rural, Milieu social, Milieu urbain
Environnement et politique 3681, 3718, 3759, 5221, 5255
Environnement humain 567, 2717, 2801, 3607, 3689, 3757, 3758, 4077, 5252
Environnement physique 559, 608, 1602, 3692, 3701, 3748, 3781, 3921, 4087
Environnementalisme 1093, 1152, 1297, 3705, 3710, 3717, 3729, 3732, 3742, 3743, 3749, 3759, 3797, 3818, 3838, 4062, 4084, 5252, 5254, 5255
Épargne 2676, 4184, 4326
Épidémiologie 709, 791, 3794, 5891, 5958, 5965, 5968, 5980
Épistémologie 8, 12, 20, 29, 30, 52, 107-110, 112-114, 118-120, 123, 125, 127-129, 131-133, 135-137, 140, 161, 254, 260, 261, 289, 300, 301, 309, 356, 363, 385, 409, 427, 494, 1216, 1234, 1396, 1400, 1404, 1422, 1428, 1445, 1552, 1568, 1570, 1573, 1582, 1592, 1606, 1610, 1628-1630, 1863, 1999, 2209, 2216, 2222, 2224, 2226, 2436, 2609, 2809, 3062, 3094, 3528, 3750, 4413, 4621, 4906, 5310
Époque victorienne 171, 5723
Épouses 2965, 2971, 3035, 3188, 4530, 5479
Époux 463, 900, 902, 908, 910, 916, 920, 926, 935, 936, 946, 1134, 2862, 2917, 2956, 2958, 2974, 2977, 2985, 3055, 3336, 4169, 4310, 4457, 4765, 5439, 5449
Équilibre 2447, 2782, 4124, 4351, 5455
Équilibre des forces 1030, 3210, 4354
Équilibre du marché 4124
Équilibre social 1920, 3404

Équité 461, 915, 1290, 3097, 3335, 3694, 3757, 3784, 4096, 4290, 4486, 5445
Équivalence 5763
Ergonomie 4776
Erotisme 3061, 3297, 3353
Erreur 27, 233, 498, 525, 624, 631, 666
Esclavage 1620, 2336, 2901, 3067, 3094
 voir aussi: Abolition de l'esclavage
Esclaves 263, 2901, 3528, 3793
Espace 39, 291, 313, 382, 572, 613, 641, 642, 976, 982, 1031, 1195, 1200, 1220, 1292, 1298, 1302, 1316, 1317, 1348, 1362, 1365, 1393, 1399, 1586, 1605, 1661, 1920, 1928, 1984, 2191, 2325, 2413, 2421, 2481, 2493, 2546, 2556, 2658, 3093, 3231, 3301, 3422, 3540, 3692, 3693, 3741, 3757, 3772, 3775, 3780, 3785-3788, 3790, 3860, 3864, 3876, 3907, 3945, 3969, 3996, 4048, 4065, 4082, 4102, 4120, 4124, 4127, 4129, 4131, 4134, 4140, 4144, 4149, 4168, 4219, 4315, 4329, 4346, 4350, 4489, 4521, 4939, 5240, 5418, 5424, 5845
 voir aussi: Analyse spatiale
Espace publique 1320, 1348, 1371, 1767, 2403, 2451, 2580, 2679, 3234, 3255, 3365, 3387, 3745, 3788, 3792, 3925, 4034, 4039, 4118, 4123, 4126, 4129, 4132-4134, 4140, 4146, 4851, 5248, 5361
Espace social 334, 1979, 2385, 3138, 3387, 3772, 3788, 4050, 4136, 4329
Espace urbain 1737, 2716, 3359, 3814, 3927, 3956, 4011, 4023, 4038, 4078, 4089, 4102, 4118, 4120, 4121, 4123, 4125-4128, 4131, 4132, 4134-4137, 4139-4142, 4144, 4146, 4147, 4155, 4156, 4941
Espacement des naissances 2822
Espagnols 710, 3575
Espèce 1558, 3755, 3759
Espérance de vie 2679, 2685, 2695, 2696, 2719, 2724, 2815, 2833, 2835, 2837, 4304, 5494, 5519, 5897
Esprit 12, 199, 221, 254, 293, 615, 654, 658, 760, 1423, 3108, 5182
Esprits 263, 2819
Essence 4223
Esthétique 2, 7, 30, 117, 241, 278, 300, 320, 340, 351, 573, 938, 1124, 1189, 1279, 1310, 1311, 1323, 1331, 1338, 1573, 1602, 1848, 1850, 1851, 1853, 1854, 1864, 1868, 1876, 1878, 1988, 2477, 2504, 3698, 4344, 4911
Esthétique urbaine 3941, 3970, 4026, 4054, 4075

INDEX DES MATIÈRES

Estimation 433, 453, 480, 482, 525, 2722, 2794, 4306, 4317, 5390
Estime de soi 576, 681, 693, 720, 725, 732, 843, 849, 852, 876, 881, 908, 933, 936, 972, 1064, 1076, 1156, 1198, 1666, 2885, 3021, 3049, 3052, 3055, 3183, 3591, 4187, 4615, 4719, 4750
Établissements de soins palliatifs 4667
Établissements d'enseignement 2014, 2048, 2253, 2291, 3290, 5678
Établissements humains 2505, 2511, 3655, 3771, 3774, 3813, 4102
Étalement urbain 3867
État 173, 351, 578, 1164, 2137, 2143, 2170, 2230, 2265, 2307, 2336, 2414, 2415, 2544, 2662, 3070, 3085, 3114, 3187, 3323, 3410, 3469, 3474, 3475, 3499, 3531, 3568, 3624, 3829, 3862, 3896, 3921, 3922, 4208, 4226, 4237, 4303, 4459, 4782, 4816, 4818, 4828, 4893, 4907, 4932, 4949, 4953, 4956, 4959, 4961, 4966, 4968, 4976, 4978, 5130, 5162, 5287, 5314, 5334, 5445, 5546, 5553, 5626, 5644
voir aussi: Chefs d'État, Église et État, Relations État-société, Théorie de l'État
État de droit 5192
État d'urgence 3611
État fédéral 1529, 5155
État socialiste 23, 1274, 5130
État-nation 306, 1192, 1220, 1246, 1519, 2386, 2446, 2461, 2532, 2565, 2568, 2570, 3420, 3468, 4227, 4892, 4910, 4939, 4953, 4959, 4966
État-providence 1480, 2320, 2455, 2554, 2567, 2682, 2945, 3065, 3169, 4018, 4192, 4231, 4247, 4259, 4271, 4520, 4596, 4922, 4945, 4987, 5482, 5484, 5506, 5602, 5604, 5606, 5613-5616, 5619, 5620, 5622, 5623, 5625, 5626, 5628, 5631, 5632, 5637, 5638, 5640-5645, 5648, 5650-5654, 5659-5662, 5766, 5814, 5819, 5982
voir aussi: Réforme de la sécurité sociale
États membres 2145, 5290
Éthique 16, 43, 46, 117, 131, 192, 201, 205, 206, 209, 216, 221, 227, 228, 232, 238, 243, 254, 255, 264, 268, 270, 274, 277, 288, 293, 302, 321, 328, 333, 340, 346, 362, 367, 378, 382, 417, 434, 444, 528, 539, 673, 733, 799, 909, 934, 1259, 1358, 1369, 1382, 1388, 1402, 1403, 1410, 1420, 1440, 1486, 1526, 1607, 1620, 1665, 1714, 1767, 1850, 2001, 2084, 2160, 2181, 2342, 2344, 2348-2350, 2354, 2355, 2362, 2365-2368, 2370, 2478, 2485, 2503, 2554, 2610, 2683, 2716, 2734, 2854, 3028, 3118, 3119, 3136, 3142, 3471, 3705, 3764, 3780, 3798-3801, 3919, 4293, 4307, 4359, 4417, 4421, 4422, 4424, 4427, 4497, 4658, 4684, 4772, 4917, 4984, 4988, 5161, 5169, 5174, 5180, 5181, 5208, 5316, 5327, 5330, 5355, 5371, 5400, 5442, 5679, 5704, 5730, 5770, 5817, 5850, 5853, 5854, 5861, 5863, 5865, 5868, 5869, 5871, 5875, 5876, 5883, 5884, 5886
voir aussi: Attitude moraliste envers le travail, Bioéthique, Code déontologique des affaires, Code déontologique médical, Déontologie
Éthique protestante 314, 370
Ethnicité 33, 681, 903, 952, 954, 964-967, 983, 985, 991, 997, 1000, 1011, 1171, 1195, 1315, 1373, 1392, 1397, 1431, 1452, 1513, 1529, 1551, 1769, 1775, 1777, 1786, 1801, 1811, 1813, 1815, 1823, 1834, 1912, 1978, 2003, 2011, 2014, 2068, 2077, 2083, 2143, 2290, 2359, 2376, 2392, 2431, 2436, 2441, 2470, 2525, 2530, 2532, 2550, 2552, 2608, 2612, 2751, 2760, 2770, 2834, 2841, 2842, 2917, 2950, 3024, 3043, 3061, 3067, 3073, 3076, 3115, 3126, 3222, 3242, 3259, 3263, 3271, 3317, 3323, 3383, 3390, 3392-3419, 3421, 3422, 3426-3429, 3432-3444, 3447-3450, 3461, 3467, 3471, 3472, 3474, 3475, 3478, 3483-3485, 3487, 3488, 3492, 3494, 3497, 3500, 3503, 3507, 3509, 3512, 3517, 3519, 3525, 3529, 3530, 3533-3535, 3537, 3544, 3545, 3548, 3556-3559, 3561, 3567, 3569, 3570, 3572, 3577, 3580, 3587, 3597, 3632, 3647, 3648, 3651, 3654, 3662, 3663, 3668, 3674, 3678, 3963, 3978, 4002, 4003, 4012, 4019, 4020, 4089, 4129, 4227, 4266, 4362, 4376, 4432, 4453, 4464, 4470, 4498, 4501, 4599, 4606, 5017, 5077, 5108, 5139, 5214, 5259, 5263, 5328, 5473, 5490, 5577, 5757, 5836, 5873, 5914, 5973
Ethnocentrisme 603, 837, 852, 1198, 1221
Ethnogéographie 4001
Ethnographes 1888
Ethnographie 8, 9, 20, 31, 355, 430, 462, 526, 536, 989, 1042, 1110, 1115, 1237, 1581, 1658, 1682, 1800, 1865, 1909, 2511, 2544, 2574, 2878, 3236, 3309, 3367, 3368, 3453, 3781, 4219, 4300, 4406, 5386
Ethnolinguistique 1823, 1834, 2584

545

SUBJECT INDEX IN FRENCH

Ethnologie 338, 801, 1002, 1170, 1509, 1870, 2902, 3530, 3635, 4212, 5314
Ethnologues 18
Ethnométhodologie 119, 312, 1561, 1870, 4636
Ethnomusicologie 1319, 1331, 1972, 1986
Ethnophilosophie 1166
Ethnopolitique 966
Ethnopsychologie 967
Ethnosociologie 9
Ethologie 596, 649, 656, 2744, 2912, 2973, 4143
Éthos 216, 2135, 5180
Étiologie 712, 723, 745, 755, 756, 2304, 4776
Étiquetage 859, 4265, 4472, 5419
Étiquette 2373
Étoiles 1217, 1228, 2618
Étrangers 960, 2313, 2376, 3467, 3496, 3605, 5335, 5452
Étude du travail 4702
Études africaines 71, 1482, 1976, 2121, 3326
Études américaines 1243
Études asiatiques 1483, 1506, 2992
Études commerciales 225
Études culturelles 7, 14, 159, 184, 292, 343, 369, 444, 590, 764, 817, 1001, 1018, 1109, 1158, 1166, 1174, 1176, 1178-1180, 1183, 1192-1196, 1199, 1211-1213, 1215-1228, 1231-1236, 1239-1242, 1244, 1245, 1252, 1261, 1272, 1276, 1278, 1288, 1305, 1311, 1314, 1316, 1318, 1321, 1329, 1336, 1337, 1339, 1358, 1360, 1361, 1364, 1365, 1409, 1566, 1609, 1614, 1668, 1669, 1688, 1693, 1695, 1698, 1707, 1726, 1729, 1738, 1740, 1741, 1744, 1746, 1756, 1758, 1771, 1772, 1775, 1777, 1799, 1859, 1862, 1864, 1874, 1880, 1894, 1895, 1920, 1933, 1940, 1955, 1958, 1986, 2211, 2214, 2252, 2298, 2327, 2349, 2504, 2524, 2547, 2565, 2607, 2992, 3072, 3155, 3157, 3225, 3245, 3250, 3311, 3316, 3350, 3355, 3357, 3409, 3415, 3435, 3443, 3465, 3490, 3494, 3569, 3571, 3676, 3683, 3730, 3756, 3766, 3887, 4192, 4202, 4290, 4398, 4477, 4772, 4965, 5259, 5289, 5333, 5343, 5745, 5943, 5966
Études de cas 2, 51, 454, 461, 555, 610, 750, 762, 780, 833, 890, 1010, 1016, 1091, 1140, 1152, 1153, 1338, 1471, 1673, 1702, 1705, 1708, 1984, 2139, 2158, 2218, 2249, 2255, 2299, 2338, 2473, 2649, 2838, 3037, 3068, 3238, 3390, 3473, 3674, 3752, 3760, 3762, 3807, 3827, 3886, 3921, 4023, 4035, 4044, 4083, 4117, 4147, 4152, 4160, 4176, 4200, 4246, 4348, 4358, 4379, 4393, 4397, 4409, 4462, 4472, 4486, 4568, 4616, 4618, 4645, 4653, 4707, 4713, 4849, 5012, 5125, 5133, 5221, 5670, 5707, 5719, 5751, 5759, 5891, 5924, 5932, 5970, 5973, 5975, 5977
Études de marché 519, 4341
Études de politique 426, 4673
Études des femmes 1970, 3078, 3079, 3107, 3115, 3122, 3123, 3234, 3248, 3363, 3376, 3379, 3665
Études post-soviétiques 1000, 1470, 3564, 3627
Études religieuses 56, 169, 1386, 1396, 1400, 1418, 1419, 1422, 1445, 1462, 1472, 2297
Études slaves 3427
Études soviétiques 166, 183
Études sur le développement 92, 2432, 2539, 3770, 3964, 4236, 4268, 4819, 5768
Études sur le paix 1995
Études sur les effets mésologiques 3708, 3709, 3767, 3815, 3819, 4025, 4084, 4108
Étudiantes 2299
Étudiants 11, 469, 541, 557, 588, 631, 710, 724, 751, 791, 942, 1014, 1024, 1058, 1083, 1203, 1626, 1654, 1993, 2002, 2008, 2009, 2021, 2028, 2033, 2045, 2052, 2055-2057, 2060, 2072, 2075, 2077, 2102, 2104, 2129, 2157, 2168, 2183, 2186, 2190, 2193-2195, 2206, 2223, 2238, 2239, 2245, 2246, 2248, 2253, 2268, 2276, 2277, 2288, 2290, 2444, 2454, 2482, 2523, 2585, 2913, 2945, 3232, 3274, 3282, 3291-3293, 3296, 3362, 3477, 3517, 3860, 4062, 4435, 4454, 4785, 5444, 5470, 5697, 5704, 5844, 5955, 5961
Étudiants étrangers 2274
Étymologie 2313
Européens 152, 1004, 3559, 3566
Euroscepticisme 5295
Euthanasie 5847, 5850, 5858, 5877, 5882, 5887, 5889
Évaluation 30, 111, 416, 419, 420, 428, 443, 454, 503, 518, 539, 774, 826, 843, 874, 877, 894, 1012, 1041, 1119, 2132, 2142, 2145, 2195, 2244, 2247, 2275, 2699, 3617, 3815, 3819, 3850, 4044, 4049, 4390, 4459, 4599, 4607, 4613, 4779, 4795, 5186, 5224, 5413, 5561, 5583, 5673, 5704, 5761, 5783, 5808, 5867, 5959
Évaluation de programme 411, 2281, 5958, 5960
Évaluation de projet 3807, 3813, 3839, 4075, 5977

INDEX DES MATIÈRES

Évaluation de soi 562, 639, 840, 871, 1143, 2086, 2378, 3281, 4607, 4615, 4703, 4719
Évangélisation 1493
Évangélisme 1431, 1433, 1442, 1485, 1498, 1503, 2890
Évolution 49, 390, 420, 463, 571, 573, 596, 601, 649, 773, 1121, 1558, 1578, 1583, 1636, 1638, 2329, 2508, 2744, 2973, 3018, 3797, 4502
  voir aussi: Darwinisme, Développement humain, Sélection naturelle
Évolution des emplois 4468
Évolution humaine 560, 1161, 1630, 2406, 2426, 2508, 3401, 3716, 3797
Évolutionnisme 185
Évolutionnisme culturel 3401
Examens 457, 2032, 2256, 3183, 5837
Exclusion sociale 576, 1666, 1687, 1991, 2037, 2073, 2119, 2332, 2375, 2385, 2386, 2399, 2400, 2403, 2423, 2432, 2448, 2451, 2456, 2459, 2461, 2469, 2474, 2479, 2548, 2577, 2634, 2653, 2737, 3370, 3381, 3416, 3460, 3537, 3579, 3594, 3605, 3656, 3781, 3802, 3902, 3982, 3989, 4056, 4169, 4247, 4283, 4299, 4368, 4445, 4587, 4590, 4950, 4952, 5016, 5367, 5418, 5420, 5422-5424, 5547, 5564, 5617, 5620, 5638, 5642, 5653, 5657, 5741, 5914, 5951
Exil politique 3598
Exilé 814, 1699, 1922, 3227, 3598, 3635, 3638, 3664, 3680
Existentialisme 145, 212, 311, 3129
Exode des compétences 1806, 3629, 3633
Exogamie 3304
Exotisme 1926
Expansionnisme 1004, 5319
Expectation 308, 657, 675, 853, 1285, 1622, 1725, 2640, 2677, 2775, 3055, 3613, 3622, 4246, 4484, 4582, 4723, 4964, 5154, 5503, 5919
  voir aussi: Anticipations du revenu
Expédition 567
Expérience du travail 4393
Expérience religieuse 1307, 1373, 1388, 1459
Expériences 45, 426, 433, 453, 462, 476, 515, 584, 643, 650, 656, 705, 716, 853, 865, 908, 1034, 1438, 1704, 4418, 5407
Expérimentation 870, 2344, 2581
Expérimentation d'animal 2342
Expertise 905, 4186, 4716
Experts 309, 348, 1294, 1565, 4346, 4613
Explication 137, 154, 830, 1570, 1629, 1630, 1633
Explication causale 193, 356

Exploitation 1308, 1620, 1903, 1950, 2384, 3115, 3338, 4201, 4442, 4935, 5869, 5871
Exploitation des ressources 3736
Exploration 58, 2179, 3143, 5325, 5335
Exportations 1359, 2561, 4206, 4450, 4458, 4658
Expositions 1851
Expression faciale 611, 683, 945
Extase 1347
Externalités 949, 3806, 4427, 5455
Extrême droite 2630, 3452, 5238, 5243
Extrémisme 1546, 5238
Extrémistes 5243
Fabrication industrielle 4212, 4278, 4450, 4682, 4748, 4840, 4845, 4854, 4882
Façon d'élever les enfants 3009
Facteurs culturels 35, 342, 409, 603, 797, 875, 888, 899, 1134, 1139, 1219, 1232, 1314, 1386, 1442, 1641, 1693, 1770, 1798, 1831, 1979, 2523, 2704, 2731, 2732, 2908, 3084, 3201, 4386, 4457, 4618, 5170, 5268, 5432, 5459, 5866, 5946
Facteurs de production 4833
Facteurs psychologiques 548, 550, 797, 875, 883, 1189, 1963, 3751, 5089, 5752
Facteurs sociaux 35, 64, 268, 548, 875, 899, 1189, 1309, 1322, 1340, 1385, 1564, 1589, 1693, 1694, 1827, 2155, 3084, 3334, 3704, 3820, 3827, 4122, 4267, 4618, 5064, 5186, 5254, 5386, 5468, 5866, 5944
Faible revenu 2746, 2841, 2991, 3019, 3027, 3625, 3757, 3813, 3984, 4010, 4022, 4087, 4116, 4169, 4299, 4302, 4587, 4593, 5475, 5543, 5565, 5567, 5611, 5627, 5649, 5656, 5669, 5788, 5969
Faillite
  voir: Insolvabilité
Faim 817, 3884
Faire un compromis 3987, 4451, 4475, 4724, 5766
Faits sociaux 387
Famille 402, 501, 545, 577, 769, 772, 900, 1050, 1170, 1227, 1267, 1275, 1290, 1495, 1695, 1927, 1936, 1991, 2034, 2036, 2043, 2066, 2070, 2071, 2074, 2372, 2425, 2456, 2463, 2489, 2497, 2501, 2542, 2583, 2590, 2591, 2600, 2602, 2608, 2626, 2635, 2636, 2639, 2644, 2647, 2656, 2662, 2683, 2685, 2725, 2756, 2784, 2786, 2803, 2848, 2849, 2855, 2858, 2866, 2871, 2876, 2891, 2897, 2900, 2901, 2904-2907, 2913, 2916, 2918-2921, 2923, 2925, 2929, 2931, 2932, 2934-2936, 2938, 2941-2943, 2946, 2947, 2950, 2952-2954, 2957, 2959, 2962, 2964-

SUBJECT INDEX IN FRENCH

2966, 2968, 2972, 2975, 2977, 2979,
2981-2983, 2985, 2986, 2989, 3008, 3010,
3019, 3020, 3026, 3030, 3032, 3041-3043,
3050, 3051, 3053, 3054, 3056, 3081, 3111,
3115, 3121, 3187, 3191, 3224, 3270, 3280,
3308, 3343, 3360, 3361, 3486, 3582,
3610, 3651, 3835, 3883, 3901, 4006,
4183, 4212, 4243, 4257, 4263, 4289,
4310, 4371, 4451, 4457, 4466, 4473,
4514, 4515, 4530, 4541, 4548, 4555,
4568, 4673, 4725, 4781, 4950, 5106,
5291, 5345, 5389, 5393, 5396, 5416,
5425, 5488, 5510, 5512, 5520, 5530,
5546, 5549, 5554, 5556, 5565, 5573,
5574, 5625, 5633, 5634, 5667, 5668,
5675, 5676, 5689, 5721, 5737, 5822,
5827, 5883, 5896, 5916, 5925, 5935, 5936
voir aussi Sociologie de la famille
Famille conjugale 1761, 2944, 3010
Famille étendue 771, 2899, 2932, 2944, 2948, 2949, 3010
Famille monoparentale 1687, 2858, 2878, 2881, 2915, 2923, 2991, 2993-2997, 3000, 3001, 3019, 3036, 3069, 4531, 5425, 5567, 5610, 5624, 5633, 5636, 5961
Famine 1923, 2714, 2747, 2827, 3887
Fanatisme 1081
Fascisme 2630
Fatalisme 2771, 3989
Fauset, Jessie Redmon 1227
Fécondité 2532, 2686, 2695, 2696, 2703, 2719, 2724-2726, 2728, 2729, 2736-2738, 2740, 2741, 2743, 2745, 2753, 2756, 2765-2769, 2771, 2773-2777, 2779-2788, 2790, 2791, 2794-2799, 2801, 2803-2805, 2902, 2927, 2971, 3000, 3075, 3203, 3279, 3337, 3716, 3795, 5528, 5610
voir aussi: Fertilité du sol
Fédéralisme 4072, 4949
Fédération 3493
Femelle 938, 1767, 1970, 2878, 3232, 3306, 3835, 4394, 4527, 5076, 5087, 5099, 5961
Fémininité 278, 669, 732, 1239, 1782, 1860, 1886, 1926, 1936, 1940, 1946, 1974, 2608, 2645, 2917, 3060, 3073, 3113, 3115, 3117, 3204, 3212, 3230, 3243, 3248, 3256, 3273, 3305, 3313, 3320, 3383, 3742, 4259
Féminisme 47, 117, 188, 204, 340, 369, 570, 669, 955, 1191, 1195, 1269, 1296, 1317, 1549, 1562, 1613, 1659, 1782, 1882, 1915, 1917, 1921, 1936, 1945, 2007, 2039, 2095, 2189, 2340, 2471, 2537, 2586, 2623, 2641, 2730, 2978, 3028, 3061, 3065, 3070, 3072, 3073, 3079, 3080, 3082, 3083, 3086, 3087, 3090,
3093-3102, 3105, 3107-3136, 3138, 3139, 3141-3159, 3161-3163, 3165, 3169, 3172, 3173, 3176, 3178, 3180, 3201, 3204, 3205, 3221, 3230, 3240, 3243, 3251, 3258, 3266, 3277, 3302, 3307, 3315, 3320, 3323, 3331, 3346, 3356, 3361, 3376, 3379, 3383, 3449, 3471, 3500, 3528, 3720, 3740, 4191, 4319, 4405, 4529, 4534, 4536, 4560, 4632, 4661, 4816, 4857, 4883, 4944, 4956, 5200, 5258, 5260, 5299, 5317, 5348, 5446, 5474, 5810, 5849, 5861
Femmes 5, 60, 104, 204, 278, 419, 469, 485, 570, 574, 581, 672, 722, 736, 777, 781, 797, 811, 824, 838, 1177, 1214, 1227, 1232, 1304, 1372, 1443, 1463, 1520, 1522, 1533, 1572, 1613, 1659, 1760, 1767, 1782, 1847, 1886, 1903, 1915, 1918, 1925, 1929, 1936, 1943, 1945, 1954, 1969, 2002, 2015, 2039, 2041, 2078, 2080, 2271, 2272, 2408, 2449, 2492, 2499, 2515, 2523, 2537, 2551, 2561, 2712, 2725, 2752, 2760, 2771, 2773, 2776, 2784, 2798, 2825, 2860, 2864, 2868, 2870, 2875, 2879, 2880, 2882, 2883, 2885, 2886, 2889, 2890, 2915, 2917, 2976, 3002, 3007, 3022, 3023, 3025, 3028, 3033, 3038, 3058, 3064, 3065, 3067, 3068, 3071, 3072, 3074-3078, 3080, 3085, 3088-3091, 3093, 3094, 3098, 3105-3107, 3110, 3112, 3114, 3115, 3118, 3125, 3128, 3135, 3138, 3141, 3143, 3145, 3148, 3149, 3151, 3152, 3154-3156, 3158, 3161-3163, 3169, 3172-3175, 3178-3180, 3184, 3189, 3193, 3195-3198, 3203, 3204, 3207-3209, 3214, 3227, 3245, 3247, 3250, 3252, 3254-3256, 3258, 3261, 3262, 3265, 3269, 3273, 3274, 3276, 3284, 3286, 3287, 3293, 3302, 3306-3308, 3315, 3317, 3318, 3332, 3352, 3374, 3384, 3392, 3500, 3518, 3538, 3549, 3557, 3565, 3582, 3599-3602, 3646, 3670, 3676, 3742, 3793, 3834, 3901, 3957, 4226, 4259, 4265, 4308, 4316, 4353, 4372, 4415, 4478, 4503, 4511, 4536, 4545-4548, 4555, 4558-4560, 4563, 4564, 4566, 4567, 4570-4572, 4574, 4576, 4694, 4765, 4857, 4882, 4883, 4944, 5002, 5011, 5012, 5026, 5070, 5076, 5099, 5112, 5144, 5155, 5223, 5244, 5260, 5318, 5326, 5346, 5348, 5353, 5362, 5363, 5382, 5386, 5388, 5409, 5439, 5443, 5446, 5451, 5467, 5469, 5474, 5480, 5483, 5516, 5521, 5546, 5600, 5628, 5633, 5685, 5823, 5843, 5857, 5915, 5917, 5959

548

Femmes au foyer 3280
Femmes et politique 3079, 3111, 3116, 3184, 3206, 3277, 4944, 5317
Femmes mariées 3210, 4524, 4532
Femmes rurales 2787, 3138, 3890, 4284
Femmes urbaines 4147
Féodalisme 185, 967
Ferme 3406, 3599, 3760, 3839
    voir aussi: Petites entreprises agricoles
Fermes familiales 4218, 4775, 5685
Fertilité du sol 3813
Fête nationale 58, 974, 996
Fêtes 1340, 1345, 1348, 1912
Fêtes foraines 3956
Fêtes religieuse 1534
Fétiche 303, 3305
Fétichisme 913, 4336
Fœtus 5873
Feu 4098
Fiabilité 433, 455, 501
Fiancée 2885
Fierté 862, 1358, 2667
Filiation
    voir: Filiation cognatique, Filiation matrilinéaire
Filiation cognatique 2930
Filiation matrilinéaire 3076
Fille 2910, 2927, 3023, 3033, 3093, 3202, 3229
Films 1332, 1365, 1699, 1879-1890, 1892-1911, 1978, 1983, 2665, 2677, 3157, 3305, 3355, 3384, 3391
Fils 2628, 2629, 2927, 2984, 3023, 3202
Fin de scolarité 2054
Finance 1323, 2137, 2259, 2271, 2571, 2713, 2909, 3804, 4317, 4348, 4350
Finance d'entreprise 4175
Financement de la recherche 43, 1618, 4805
Financement de la sécurité sociale 5605
Financement des partis 5219
Finances agricoles 3852
Finances internationales 2446
Finances locales 3852, 4169, 5635
Finances publiques 2196, 2259, 5475, 5514
Finno-Ougriens 3409, 3426, 3487, 3533
Fiscalité 4281, 5475
Fixation du prix 4767
Fixation du salaire 4842
Flexibilité du marché de l'emploi 4471
Flore 1313
Flusser, Vilém 4121
Flux de capitaux 4935
FMI 2561, 4250
Fodor, Jerry 231
Foi 1388, 1403, 1545, 1547, 2524, 2660, 2890

Foires
    voir: Fêtes foraines
Folie 5027, 5919, 5920
Folklore 801, 817, 981, 1310, 1343, 1912
Folklorisation 801
Folkloristes 1367
Fonction de coût 5760
Fonction publique 3290, 5215, 5223
Fonctionnaires 5223
Fonctionnalisme 267, 329, 398, 563, 1350, 1633, 4181, 4217, 4612, 4759
Fonctionnalisme structurel 400
Fonctionnement du groupe 1080, 4701
Fonctions d'utilité 1085, 4124
Fondamentalisme religieux 1394, 1411, 1505, 1523, 1541, 1543, 1546, 2520, 5083
Fondations de recherche 42, 2448
Football 969, 1305, 1306, 1315, 1341, 3680, 5448
Force du marché 1604, 3140, 4349
Forces armées 4549, 5339, 5342, 5344, 5346, 5347, 5352-5354, 5356, 5357, 5359, 5361, 5362
Forces politiques 1979, 4898, 5227
    voir aussi: Groupes de pression
Forces religieuses 1407, 1414, 1491
Forces sociales 2402
Fordisme 4520
    voir aussi: Post-fordisme
Foresterie 20, 3152, 3735
Forêt tropicale 3735, 3768, 3796
Forêts 2717, 3736, 3739, 3754, 5237
    voir aussi: Forêt tropicale
Forgerons 4781
Formalisation 563, 1106
Formation 105, 759, 775, 861, 1007, 1054, 1065, 2031, 2099, 2105, 2125, 2176, 2199, 2218, 2754, 3382, 3671, 4398, 4420, 4600, 4602, 4605, 4664, 4750, 4759, 4768, 4779, 4790, 4792-4800, 4802-4805, 4807, 4861, 4875, 5132, 5139, 5157, 5344, 5641, 5663, 5684, 5694, 5700, 5703, 5709, 5711, 5716, 5912, 5928
    voir aussi: Formation des enseignants, Formation en cours d'emploi, Formation professionnelle
Formation à la gestion 4628, 4671, 4759
Formation de classe 2446
Formation des attitudes 520, 676, 851
Formation des enseignants 2090, 2095, 2098, 2103, 4801, 5642
Formation d'identité 734, 954, 965, 967, 983, 987, 1020, 1161, 1300, 1409, 1990, 2047, 2436, 2501, 2530, 2608, 2618, 2878,

SUBJECT INDEX IN FRENCH

3059, 3227, 3362, 3382, 3410, 3411, 3441, 3445, 4125, 5293, 5334, 5430
Formation du lien affectif 1499
Formation en cours d'emploi 5713
Formation professionnelle 2037, 2626, 4448, 4792, 4797, 4799, 4803, 4804
Formule de Bayes 446, 451, 468, 2818, 2831
Fortifications 2451
Foucault, Michel 241, 243, 252, 277, 294, 340, 373, 374, 410, 1141, 1220, 1864, 2337, 3717, 4030, 4954, 4987, 5016, 5207
Foule 829, 1005, 1042, 5133
Foyer 2626, 2809, 3539, 5424, 5742
Fraassen, B.C. van 1630
Fragmentation de l'État 4892
Franc-maçonnerie 1453
Franco, Francisco 161
Fraternité 3362
Fratrie 769, 2070, 2071, 2613, 2839, 2901, 2912, 2930, 2952, 3052, 3053, 3213
Fraude 510, 4422, 4683, 5618
Frege, Gottlob 120
Freire, Paulo 2221
Fréquence 631
Fréquentation scolaire 2014
Freud, Sigmund 12, 579, 593, 599, 602, 632, 1621, 3342
Freyre, Gilberto 58, 1183, 1431
Friedlander, Saul 162
Frontières 173, 987, 1772, 2544, 2953, 3135, 3542, 3630, 3639, 3672, 4440, 4811, 4966
  voir aussi: Régions frontalières
Funèbres 1751
Funkenstein, Amos 145
Fusions d'entreprises 4876
Futurologie 1603, 2532
Gadamer, Hans-Georg 126
Gains 633, 2267, 2948, 2991, 4305, 4306, 4437, 4451, 4454, 4463, 4464, 4539, 4548, 4549, 4551, 4556, 4573, 4704, 4745, 4804, 4878, 5636, 5832
Galerie d'art 2573
Galileo Galilei 1555
Gaṅgeśa 233
Gaos, José 240
Garçons 2878, 3216, 3264
Garo 3530
GATT 4935
Gauche 4864, 4919
  voir aussi: Nouvelle gauche
Gellner, Ernest 968, 4288
Généalogie 1099, 1141, 2426, 5180
Généralisation 225, 455, 471, 474, 837, 1711
Génération 339, 771, 2089, 2360, 2401, 2517, 2532, 2537, 2546, 2589, 2590, 2592,
2594, 2618, 2657, 2735, 2876, 2926, 2943, 3026, 3523, 3543, 3568, 3588, 5302, 5403, 5520, 5602
Gènes 591, 712, 1620, 5730, 5864
Genet, Jean 1940
Génétique 596, 625, 712, 769, 773, 1567, 1576, 1595, 1825, 2304, 2701, 2742, 2755, 2757, 2812, 3014, 3308, 4933, 5390, 5730, 5848, 5854, 5863-5865, 5875, 5877, 5880, 5881, 5892
  voir aussi: ADN, Clonage
Génétique humaine 591, 1564, 1595, 1620, 2701, 3528, 5875
Génie génétique 1563, 1601, 2742, 5892
Génocide 192, 1388, 1896, 1902, 1906, 1990, 3070, 3518, 3611, 3640, 5312, 5462
Genre 5, 33, 35, 47, 104, 427, 460, 559, 570, 574, 576, 583, 681, 689, 722, 732, 734, 736, 776, 793, 803, 808, 811, 858, 948, 970, 972, 1227, 1239, 1290, 1303, 1317, 1321, 1339, 1352, 1356, 1369, 1433, 1522, 1532, 1533, 1551, 1562, 1572, 1613, 1654, 1684, 1695, 1759, 1761, 1802, 1814, 1822, 1839, 1847, 1860, 1915, 1917, 1918, 1928-1930, 1933, 1936, 1940, 1945, 1946, 1954, 1982, 2023, 2039, 2041, 2042, 2055, 2056, 2061, 2071, 2073, 2089, 2198, 2202, 2231, 2304, 2340, 2347, 2377, 2413, 2431, 2436, 2449, 2457, 2492, 2499, 2517, 2551, 2561, 2589, 2595, 2602, 2608, 2622, 2623, 2626, 2642, 2647, 2652, 2665, 2666, 2722, 2724, 2725, 2739, 2743, 2755, 2783, 2786, 2834, 2842, 2845, 2870, 2876, 2880, 2888, 2893, 2894, 2907, 2909, 2917, 2921, 2940, 2968, 2969, 2975, 3013, 3018, 3023, 3040, 3045, 3052, 3057, 3059, 3061-3063, 3066-3068, 3070-3074, 3076, 3079-3088, 3090-3094, 3096, 3097, 3099, 3104-3108, 3112, 3115, 3116, 3120, 3121, 3123-3127, 3130, 3135, 3137, 3138, 3142, 3152, 3153, 3158, 3159, 3161-3163, 3165-3167, 3169, 3171, 3173, 3175, 3179-3181, 3184-3188, 3190, 3192, 3194-3198, 3200, 3202-3204, 3207-3209, 3212-3219, 3221-3224, 3230, 3232-3235, 3238, 3242, 3244-3247, 3249, 3251, 3253, 3256, 3259, 3262, 3264, 3266, 3268, 3269, 3276, 3281-3283, 3285, 3288, 3302, 3305, 3307, 3308, 3315, 3320, 3323, 3324, 3327, 3330, 3340, 3341, 3345, 3352, 3356, 3363, 3368, 3376-3378, 3384, 3389, 3392, 3417, 3438, 3441, 3486, 3518, 3528, 3537, 3538, 3559, 3599, 3600, 3613, 3645,

INDEX DES MATIÈRES

3646, 3665, 3692, 3739, 3742, 3786, 3788, 3909, 3957, 4126, 4129, 4147, 4226, 4229, 4250, 4259, 4265, 4284, 4305, 4308, 4315, 4319, 4362, 4367, 4371, 4376, 4377, 4394, 4398, 4414-4416, 4440, 4443, 4464, 4467, 4477, 4478, 4480, 4499, 4503, 4504, 4507, 4513, 4514, 4519-4522, 4525, 4526, 4530, 4533, 4537-4542, 4544, 4545, 4547, 4548, 4552-4554, 4556, 4558, 4560, 4563, 4565, 4569, 4576, 4577, 4584, 4586, 4615, 4628, 4704, 4714, 4754, 4771, 4816, 4857, 4882, 4883, 4944, 4956, 4958, 5033, 5037, 5052, 5058, 5077, 5086, 5087, 5093, 5096, 5099, 5104, 5115, 5118, 5131, 5155, 5196, 5203, 5223, 5253, 5296, 5299, 5317, 5318, 5347, 5348, 5350, 5363, 5392, 5415, 5438, 5443, 5451, 5459, 5463, 5467, 5473, 5483, 5505, 5516, 5518, 5521, 5536, 5584, 5600, 5613, 5616, 5628, 5651, 5652, 5672, 5685, 5768, 5810, 5832, 5836, 5915, 5917, 5961, 5973, 5981
Genre de vie 1175, 2627, 2667, 3387, 3679, 3904, 5415, 5773
Genres littéraires 1332
Gens de maison 60, 3191, 3243, 3317, 4462, 4736
Géographie 91, 461, 500, 504, 528, 1328, 1399, 1597, 1661, 2348, 2367, 2716, 3073, 3121, 3179, 3553, 3688, 3693-3695, 3702, 3727, 3741, 3761, 3774, 3775, 3779, 3790, 3793, 3794, 3811, 3913, 3939, 3969, 3999, 4034, 4152, 4158, 4166, 4315, 4346, 4437, 5162, 5802, 5885, 5962
Géographie de la population 1252, 2752, 3606, 3795
Géographie économique 1314, 1892, 3770, 3773, 3927, 4135, 4175, 4247, 4486
Géographie historique 91, 94, 3958
Géographie humaine 84, 452, 507, 1232, 1657, 1661, 1917, 2367, 2403, 2658, 3073, 3301, 3537, 3540, 3691, 3756, 3767, 3769-3771, 3773-3775, 3778-3790, 3792, 3795, 3811, 3820, 3882, 3948, 3955, 4016, 4072, 4122, 4127, 4135, 4136, 4140, 4148, 4238, 4315, 4606, 5418, 5424
Géographie linguistique 1798, 1820
Géographie politique 1000, 3747
Géographie rurale 3879
Géographie urbaine 1657, 2473, 3745, 3928, 3932, 3948, 3958, 3997, 4000, 4001, 4034, 4072, 4074, 4092, 4122, 4135, 4139, 4154, 4158, 4460, 5426
Géométrie 1555

Géopolitique 1199, 2687, 3782, 3796, 4228
Gériatrie 2656, 5513
Gérontologie 2656, 2666, 2668, 2671, 2678, 2680, 5521, 5532-5534
Gestes 945, 1839, 1842
Gestion 47, 49, 416, 459, 684, 1033, 1049, 1080, 1090, 1094, 1097, 1100, 1103, 1104, 1108, 1110, 1117, 1119, 1121, 1144, 1146, 1157, 1323, 1622, 1660, 1701, 1718, 2104, 2133, 2159, 2241, 2243, 2274, 2279, 2335, 3180, 3246, 3281, 3821, 3824, 3861, 4056, 4064, 4232, 4354, 4360, 4363, 4364, 4370, 4400, 4402, 4406, 4422, 4492, 4510, 4521, 4543, 4562, 4604, 4608, 4612, 4619, 4620, 4622-4625, 4627, 4629, 4631, 4634-4637, 4639, 4642, 4646, 4648, 4650, 4652, 4654, 4655, 4657-4659, 4661, 4663, 4665-4667, 4669-4672, 4683, 4697, 4729, 4742, 4744, 4756, 4774, 4786, 4808, 4816, 4820, 4831, 4844, 4963, 5148, 5216, 5486, 5646, 5732, 5771, 5834
voir aussi: Aménagement hydraulique, Cadres moyens, Cadres supérieurs, Direction de crise, Sciences de gestion
Gestion administrative 4635, 5747
Gestion de commerce 416, 1101, 4355, 4364, 4645, 4651, 4653, 4654, 4665, 4666, 4668, 4707, 4748
Gestion de fonds 5629
Gestion de l'environnement 73, 3707, 3709, 3712, 3760, 3817, 3819, 3838, 4064, 4107, 4114, 4409, 5254
Gestion de produits 4322
Gestion de risque 43, 1660, 3702, 4346, 4348, 4727, 5951
Gestion des déchets 1190, 3813, 4025
Gestion des ressources 459, 3690, 3756, 3810, 3811, 3838, 3913, 4047, 4099, 4768
Gestion des universités 2251
Gestion des ventes 4658
Gestion du personnel 3290, 4356, 4403, 4512, 4544, 4601, 4603, 4605, 4610-4612, 4616, 4618, 4619, 4620, 4633, 4635, 4640, 4643, 4644, 4650, 4653, 4656, 4658, 4660, 4670, 4673, 4678, 4679, 4683, 4743, 4779, 4831
Gestion financière 4310, 4773
Gestion forestière 3705
Gestion hospitalière 4622, 5747, 5749, 5776, 5787, 5794
Gestion industrielle 73, 4651, 4668, 4727
Gestion sanitaire 5022, 5732, 5740, 5747, 5750, 5760, 5761, 5764, 5770, 5772, 5775, 5779, 5784-5786, 5790, 5794-5796,

SUBJECT INDEX IN FRENCH

5798, 5807, 5812, 5814, 5824, 5826, 5840, 5841, 5931, 5980
Gestion urbaine 3702, 3942, 3948, 4032, 4064, 4093
Ghetto 3518, 4001, 4009
Gibran, Gibran Khalil 1932
Gibson, William 1920
Giddens, Anthony 41, 75, 2300
Gide, André 1950, 2439
Gilligan, Carol 3182
Glossaires 99
Gnosticisme 1501
Godelier, Maurice 381
Goethe, Johann Wolfgang von 1161
Goffman, Erving 5016
Goldhagen, Daniel J. 410
Gonne, Maud 1227
González, Felipe 1839
Gorz, André 311
Goût 1745
Gouvernabilité 1994, 4949
Gouvernance 1308, 1608, 2134, 2151, 2532, 3759, 3808, 3814, 3922, 3942, 3947, 4041, 4058, 4066, 4085, 4113, 4163, 4169, 4178, 4427, 4608, 4876, 4877, 5140, 5162, 5202, 5216, 5282, 5749, 5771
Gouvernement 971, 1169, 1220, 1550, 1742, 2162, 2343, 2379, 2406, 3391, 4030, 4058, 4072, 4596, 4715, 4796, 4828, 4859, 4892, 4907, 4936, 4949, 4966, 4972, 5139, 5154, 5212, 5222, 5292
voir aussi: Administration coloniale, Administration locale, Administration régionale, Administration territoriale
Gouvernement d'entreprise 4417, 4641, 4642
voir aussi: Gestion de commerce
Gouvernement urbain 3947, 3959, 4066
Grabbe, Lester 169
Grahn, Judy 1969
Grammaire 1518, 1798, 1822, 2087, 2227, 4801
Gramsci, Antonio 1250
Grandes entreprises 4424, 4543, 5154
Grandes villes 471, 969, 1164, 1168, 1530, 1892, 1941, 2252, 2264, 2571, 2573, 2677, 2691, 2821, 3206, 3462, 3590, 3632, 3702, 3776, 3813, 3831, 3839, 3926-3929, 3931-3937, 3939, 3941-3943, 3946, 3948-3953, 3956, 3958, 3959, 3962, 3964, 3966, 3970-3972, 3987, 3992, 3994, 3995, 3999, 4001, 4005, 4007, 4010, 4012, 4029, 4031-4034, 4037, 4038, 4042, 4045, 4053, 4059, 4066, 4069, 4073, 4076-4078, 4081-4083, 4086, 4095, 4097, 4098, 4100, 4102, 4105, 4110, 4112, 4115, 4118, 4119, 4121, 4122, 4127, 4128, 4134, 4137, 4140, 4141, 4143, 4144, 4147, 4149, 4151, 4159-4161, 4168, 4169, 4171, 4173, 4233, 4436, 4439, 4492, 4579, 4941, 4991, 4995, 5049, 5085, 5087, 5119, 5215, 5426, 5526
voir aussi: Mégacité, Quartiers déshérités, Villes capitales
Grands-parents 771, 2582, 2588, 2667, 2680
Grecs 3566, 3592, 5089, 5304
Greffe 1039, 5826, 5878, 5883, 5891
Gregory, Augusta 1227
Grèves 1027, 2251, 4840, 4843, 4845-4847, 4850, 4874
Grossesse 551, 767, 800, 2074, 2638, 2734, 2738, 2740, 2743, 2745, 2763-2765, 2769, 2773, 2778, 2804, 2832, 2895, 2982, 2993, 3023, 3045, 3046, 3228, 3300, 3337, 3788, 4508, 5782, 5843, 5873, 5978
Groupement par aptitudes 2014
Groupements d'intérêt 2249, 3768, 4100, 4966, 5234
Groupements professionnels 842, 4501
Groupes de discussion 4726
Groupes de pression 2870, 3912, 5234, 5257
Groupes de travail 1111
Groupes d'égaux 577, 1068, 1639, 1654, 2028, 2059, 2174, 2206, 2218, 2643, 2753, 2897, 3509, 4401, 4608, 5369, 5450, 5933
Groupes ethniques 9, 581, 956, 1263, 1373, 1527, 1620, 1777, 1786, 1801, 2063, 2211, 2392, 2436, 2511, 2811, 2812, 2887, 2992, 3011, 3013, 3263, 3323, 3394, 3397, 3399, 3405, 3408, 3409, 3413-3415, 3419, 3421, 3424, 3425, 3428, 3429, 3436, 3440, 3442, 3447, 3450, 3451, 3454, 3456, 3459, 3460, 3475, 3482, 3483, 3487, 3492, 3496, 3501, 3504, 3511, 3512, 3519, 3520, 3525, 3530, 3533, 3545, 3552, 3558, 3567, 3568, 3577, 3583, 3640, 3647, 3685, 3730, 4001, 4009, 4118, 4129, 4249, 4445, 4460, 4479, 4492, 4495, 4498, 4500, 4575, 4776, 4966, 5102, 5226, 5386, 5436, 5441, 5563, 5621, 5791, 5832, 5900
Groupes informels 2127
Groupes majoritaires 903, 1052, 1067
Groupes minoritaires 1052, 1067, 1184, 1441, 1823, 2017, 3356, 3382, 3387, 3410, 3420, 3423-3425, 3515, 3548, 3568, 3576, 4005, 4249, 4500, 4501, 4628, 5062, 5089, 5304, 5527
Groupes religieux 1394, 1408, 1417, 1427, 1431, 1433, 1446, 1478, 1496, 1503,

INDEX DES MATIÈRES

1517, 1521, 2554, 3573, 3843, 3853, 3892, 3919
Groupes restreints 999
Groupes thérapeutiques 548
Guérillas 4864, 5233, 5445
Guérison 1442, 1520, 2660, 2663, 5349, 5821, 5839, 5859, 5874
Guérisseurs 1520, 5813
Guerre 162, 1195, 1731, 1732, 1906, 2205, 2348, 3315, 3485, 3624, 3631, 3859, 4095, 4482, 5318, 5323, 5327, 5329-5332, 5346, 5349, 5355, 5362, 5467, 5683, 5921, 5988
voir aussi: Art de la guerre
Guerre civile 162, 3465, 5466
Guerre civile américaine 1263
Guerre civile espagnole 1869
Guerre dans la Golfe 5345
Guerre de boer 957
Guerre froide 165, 1597
Guerre sainte 1380
Habermas, Jürgen 117, 126, 243, 359, 369, 2567, 4932
Habitants 3860, 5741
Habitat 3755
Habitudes 1288
Habitudes alimentaires 1300, 1303, 1322
Haider, Jörg 3452
Haine 3227, 5172
Hall, Stuart 1196, 2326
Hamburger, Sidney 1550
Hampâté Bâ, Amadou 1913
Handicap social 797, 2924, 2995, 3874, 4287, 4486, 4774, 5454
Handicapés 2454, 2456, 2458, 2460, 2462, 2466-2471, 2474-2476, 2478, 2480, 2481, 2485, 2487, 2489-2492, 2495, 2496, 2499, 2500, 4750, 5482, 5520, 5565, 5602, 5605, 5609
Handicapés mentaux 2456, 2485, 5927, 5930, 5938
Handicapés physiques 2456
Hanson, Pauline 1195, 3323
Harcèlement sexuel 777, 3282, 3284, 3287-3293, 3310, 4493, 4537, 5347
Hare Krishna 1384
Harris, Marvin 1431
Harvey, William 1591
Hassidisme 1545, 3450
Hausse de la fécondité 2796
Havel, Vaclav 4913
Hayek, Friedrich A. von 4181
Hébreu 1552, 1817, 1834, 1935, 3564
Hegel, Georg Wilhelm Friedrich 12, 117, 219, 235, 251

Hégémonie 328, 331, 368, 383, 1221, 1222, 1314, 1727, 1976, 2326, 2339, 2461, 2563, 3070, 3367, 3788, 4115, 4887, 5340
Heidegger, Martin 202, 236, 267, 1199, 1413
Heinich, Nathalie 1866
Heller, Agnes 1265
Hépatite 2824, 5968
Héritage 3112, 3619
Herméneutique 119, 122, 124, 126, 161, 266, 338, 376, 401, 1198, 1215, 1413, 1489, 1874, 2001, 5940
Héroïne 5374, 5375, 5378, 5379, 5385, 5386, 5395, 5401
Héros 961, 1332, 1735, 1887, 3218, 5683
Herzen, Alexander 224
Hétérogamie 2852
Hétérosexualité 596, 1821, 2608, 3199, 3201, 3218, 3299, 3301, 3307, 3321, 3345, 3352, 3365, 3383, 3386, 5837
Heures de travail 3025, 4305, 4551, 4708, 4712, 4724, 4745, 4747, 4749
voir aussi: Horaire variable de travail
Heuristique 63, 138, 595, 656, 863, 2179, 3705
Hiérarchie 879, 1038, 1039, 1074, 1100, 1217, 1835, 2301, 2303, 2341, 2395, 2406, 2434, 2441, 2447, 2536, 3180, 3231, 4391, 4657, 4733, 4737, 4761, 5168, 5267
Hindi 1818
Hindouisme 245, 246, 1376, 1398, 1399, 2346, 2394
Hindous 771, 1398, 1424, 2394, 3650
Hirner, Alexander 4, 144, 2302, 2411, 4930
Hispaniques 2017, 2036, 2692, 2936, 3336, 3396, 3398, 3413, 3498, 3515, 3521, 3565, 3570, 3996, 4000, 4019, 4453, 4470, 4492, 5244, 5873
Hispano-Américains 3396, 3563, 4440, 5171
Histoire 12, 15, 103, 110, 143, 146, 148, 150, 153-158, 160, 162-164, 167, 168, 170, 173, 175, 181, 184, 190-194, 196-198, 218, 235, 240, 241, 296, 319, 324, 343, 353, 362, 387, 593, 799, 870, 974, 975, 981, 984, 996, 1163, 1167, 1174, 1201, 1204, 1207, 1251, 1329, 1356, 1405, 1408, 1490, 1510, 1516, 1520, 1553, 1554, 1650, 1772, 1855, 1882, 1884, 1896, 1900, 1902, 1906, 1916, 1936, 1955, 1960, 1963, 1965, 1969, 1990, 2009, 2148, 2170, 2178, 2207, 2212, 2312, 2429, 2512, 2528, 2558, 3072, 3161, 3184, 3303, 3314, 3391, 3401, 3431, 3484, 3511, 3518, 3575, 3691, 3736, 3778, 3826, 3887, 3934, 3943, 3962, 4026, 4059, 4212, 4330, 4874, 4912,

553

SUBJECT INDEX IN FRENCH

4973, 5001, 5002, 5074, 5325, 5332, 5476, 5734, 5854
  voir aussi: Après-guerre, Début de l'époque moderne, Philosophie de l'histoire, Vie
Histoire agricole 2715, 3882, 3889
Histoire ancienne 151
Histoire coloniale 58, 164, 184, 188, 961, 1165, 1183, 1224, 1913, 1931, 2388, 2415, 2747, 3257, 3654, 3730, 3891, 4935, 4939, 5325, 5921, 5983
Histoire culturelle 171, 177, 188, 214, 1161, 1178, 1187, 1189, 1210, 1351, 1397, 1557, 1612, 1616, 1797, 1873, 1919, 1943, 1961, 3371, 3426, 3445, 3798, 3934, 5333
Histoire de la famille 2767, 2901, 3899, 4116, 5410
Histoire de la médicine 484, 779, 5734, 5857
Histoire de la musique 1979, 1981, 1982
Histoire de la philosophie 113, 120, 212, 214, 217, 224, 241, 242, 247, 254, 256, 262, 264, 267, 270-272, 278, 282, 357, 1591, 1611
Histoire de la religion 266, 1400, 1434
Histoire de la sociologie 1, 4, 5, 15, 23, 26, 36, 38, 40, 50, 58, 65, 144, 316, 318, 330, 339, 343, 354, 355, 365, 396, 408, 2411, 2435
Histoire de la technologie 154, 1554, 1588, 1597, 1598, 1621, 1674, 1851
Histoire de l'art 1853, 1854, 1863, 3342, 4752
Histoire de l'éducation 775, 2091, 2148, 2163, 2204, 2226
Histoire de l'Église 1475, 1478, 2169
Histoire des idées 106, 205, 208, 214, 217, 223, 232, 234, 237, 241, 242, 247, 251, 256, 262, 263, 265, 268, 271, 274, 288, 294, 296, 299, 315, 318, 361, 365, 377, 761, 775, 1248, 1250, 1271, 1478, 1588, 1591, 1854, 1876, 2540, 2604, 3078, 4239, 4894, 5098
Histoire des idées politiques 274, 307, 325, 2387, 4909, 4911, 4922, 4925, 4927
Histoire des langues 1797, 1798, 1805, 2227
Histoire des science sociales 4, 71, 144, 304, 564, 4897
Histoire des sciences 288, 1553, 1555, 1557, 1558, 1564, 1585, 1588, 1591, 1592, 1598, 1599, 1605, 1611, 1612, 1616, 1623-1625, 1630, 2226, 3719, 4030
Histoire des voyages 151, 5335
Histoire du capitalisme 4365
Histoire du droit 3891, 5025, 5181, 5211, 5324

Histoire du travail 3541, 4740, 4834, 4850, 4859, 4864
Histoire économique 1323, 2424, 2512, 2568, 4206, 4214, 4228, 4242, 4272, 4330
Histoire industrielle 2691, 3854, 4402
Histoire Littéraire 1913, 1919, 1941, 1956, 3098
Histoire médiévale 958
Histoire militaire 957, 5356, 5359
Histoire moderne 2, 143, 165, 177, 182, 186, 189, 1432
Histoire naturelle 284, 396, 1558, 3775
Histoire orale 179, 186, 194, 3371, 3496, 3854
Histoire politique 58, 143, 149, 151, 155, 159, 161, 177, 256, 1000, 1004, 1169, 1263, 1515, 1798, 1813, 1819, 2293, 2379, 2439, 3452, 3528, 3532, 3533, 3759, 3869, 4228, 4272, 4596, 4859, 4935, 4938, 4954, 5268
Histoire politique récente 1723
Histoire précolombien 2677
Histoire religieuse 145, 1405, 1432-1434, 1478, 1514, 1516, 1525, 1542
Histoire rurale 3886
Histoire sociale 1, 18, 149, 155, 157, 159, 166, 171, 174, 176-178, 180, 247, 288, 294, 322, 330, 355, 522, 660, 1226, 1260, 1263, 1305, 1307, 1311, 1312, 1323, 1326, 1432, 1480, 1522, 1557, 1873, 1916, 1946, 1973, 2091, 2264, 2277, 2306, 2356, 2386, 2424, 2426, 2434, 2439, 2504, 2528, 2530, 2542, 2691, 2901, 2915, 2994, 3210, 3232, 3295, 3338, 3371, 3396, 3459, 3882, 3934, 3983, 4192, 4206, 4242, 4263, 4330, 4731, 4767, 4768, 4898, 5042, 5254, 5268, 5298, 5335, 5357, 5546, 5723
Histoire urbaine 2901, 3371, 3926, 3928, 3935, 3941, 3947, 3950, 3980, 3983, 4026, 4030, 4042, 4057, 4128, 4132, 4137
Histoires 470, 1157, 1810, 1907, 1936, 1943, 2233, 3254, 3537, 5360
Histoires de vies 178, 194, 283, 376, 431, 490, 734, 2537, 2625, 3495, 4557, 5420, 5838
Historicisme 167, 169, 175, 365, 1390, 5246
Historiens 94, 123, 143, 145, 148, 151-153, 159-162, 174, 187, 192, 4935, 4980
Historiographie 34, 53, 54, 57, 123, 143-170, 172-176, 178-180, 182-198, 241, 958, 980, 986, 996, 1004, 1251, 1612, 1882, 1900, 1916, 1936, 1964, 2204, 2205, 2212, 2312, 2321, 2558, 3314, 3525, 4935
Højrup, Thomas 2230
Holisme 287, 376, 378, 676, 1401, 1579, 1839, 2508, 3514

INDEX DES MATIÈRES

Holocauste 145, 162, 165, 192, 410, 669, 814, 976, 985, 1388, 1547, 1896, 1902, 1906, 3502, 3518, 3532, 5312
Homer 241
Homicide 819, 4271, 5053, 5058, 5113, 5192, 5453, 5454
  voir aussi: Meurtre
Hommes 403, 722, 811, 1889, 1910, 2031, 2472, 2781, 2862, 3022, 3025, 3080, 3158, 3179, 3187, 3211, 3218, 3233, 3235, 3240, 3252, 3258-3260, 3272, 3274, 3275, 3307, 3308, 3346, 3350, 3391, 3457, 3670, 3673, 3996, 4437, 4459, 4470, 4548, 4554, 4765, 4794, 5155, 5388, 5404, 5411, 5432, 5457, 5460, 5584
Hommes de loi 1010, 3166, 4844, 5154, 5169, 5170, 5205
  voir aussi: Avocat
Hommes de métier 1616
Homo oeconomicus 4916
Homosexualité 786, 1227, 1488, 1691, 1811, 1882, 1950, 2688, 2867, 2990, 3061, 3082, 3137, 3199, 3218, 3264, 3308, 3313, 3314, 3321, 3323, 3324, 3340, 3345, 3352, 3354-3372, 3375-3383, 3385-3389, 4512, 5196, 5247, 5339, 5698, 5951
Honnêteté 568, 4697
Honneur et honte 388, 1358, 3115, 3891, 4187, 4581, 4990, 5141
Hôpitaux 757, 1040, 1078, 1857, 2773, 4568, 4770, 5016, 5690, 5726, 5743, 5747, 5749, 5755, 5765, 5782, 5789, 5790, 5796, 5799, 5834, 5879, 5899, 5942
Hôpitaux psychiatriques 95, 5016, 5056, 5192, 5420, 5914, 5920, 5924, 5927, 5930, 5932
Horaire variable de travail 2917, 4486, 4712, 4715
Hormones 3083
Hors-groupe 843, 2376
Horvat, Branko 4255
Hosain, Rokeya Sakhawat 3112
Hospitalisation 489, 5838
Hospitalité 2313, 3944
Hostilité 1009, 2966, 2987, 4711
Howard, Ebenezer 4051
Humanisme 29, 237, 241, 348, 374, 599, 1164, 1275, 1331, 1578, 1612, 3528, 4929, 5343, 5839
Humanité 209, 229, 241, 403, 1199, 1390, 1466, 1731, 3703, 3744, 3759, 4637
Humanités 28, 1224
Humeur 559, 680, 687, 709, 726, 850
Humour 244, 586, 686, 729, 921, 1181, 1642, 1710, 1784, 1839, 1887, 1967, 3404, 3467, 5293
  voir aussi: Plaisanteries
Hutcheson, Francis 12
Hutchins, Robert 225
Hutte
  voir: Élevage
Hutterite 1495
Hygiène publique 419, 2611, 3300, 3337, 5409, 5782, 5814, 5941, 5946, 5953, 5955, 5959, 5973, 5975, 5980, 5982, 5986
Hypnose 1963
Hypothèques 4000, 5286
Hypothèse 624, 1034, 1129, 1389, 1438, 1606, 2523, 2850, 4486
Idéalisme 125, 139, 232, 1243, 2667, 3701, 4207, 4361, 4420, 4785
Idées politiques 1199, 1879
  voir aussi: Histoire des idées politiques
Idées religieuses 1379
Identification 60, 872, 1897, 2301, 2436, 2543, 3394, 3407, 5194, 5618
Identification culturelle 1796
Identité 53, 57, 110, 118, 162, 240, 276, 282, 350, 362, 374, 379, 548, 569, 673, 684, 734, 770, 828, 834, 839, 894, 926, 951, 952, 955, 963-965, 971, 979, 982, 988-990, 999, 1000, 1002, 1004, 1066, 1077, 1090, 1100, 1120, 1159, 1163, 1167, 1176, 1181, 1185, 1188, 1195, 1197, 1208, 1209, 1214, 1234, 1252, 1261, 1269, 1272, 1288, 1300, 1303, 1328, 1331, 1384, 1392, 1397, 1409, 1424, 1447, 1474, 1488, 1512, 1513, 1519, 1532, 1548, 1549, 1609, 1662, 1684, 1685, 1744, 1758, 1772, 1789, 1811, 1813, 1815, 1816, 1834, 1862, 1881, 1931, 1935, 1960, 1974, 2002, 2003, 2060, 2191, 2218, 2255, 2314, 2325, 2346, 2361, 2381, 2394, 2415, 2436, 2449, 2480, 2497, 2529, 2530, 2543, 2548, 2549, 2552, 2600, 2616, 2618, 2622, 2645, 2646, 2757, 2880, 2890, 3045, 3061, 3070, 3072, 3092, 3095, 3096, 3123-3125, 3128, 3151, 3157, 3189, 3204, 3218, 3221, 3222, 3230, 3235, 3243, 3245, 3246, 3252, 3253, 3256, 3257, 3260, 3263, 3265, 3266, 3269, 3273, 3295, 3299, 3301, 3323, 3330, 3339-3341, 3345, 3347, 3353, 3354, 3358, 3361, 3374, 3377, 3382, 3392, 3393, 3398, 3402, 3403, 3406, 3408, 3415, 3418, 3423, 3425, 3429, 3430, 3432, 3438, 3439, 3441-3443, 3448, 3450, 3471, 3497, 3519, 3528, 3537, 3539, 3540, 3547, 3552, 3567, 3601, 3646, 3660, 3736, 3779, 3785,

555

3812, 3864, 3908, 3910, 3949, 3993,
4065, 4148, 4334, 4389, 4472, 4515,
4560, 4585, 4775, 4851, 4857, 4863,
4887, 4939, 4952, 4966, 4969, 4979,
4994, 5046, 5159, 5166, 5196, 5256,
5262, 5272, 5308, 5338, 5339, 5409,
5437, 5529, 5553, 5704, 5776, 5890, 5919
voir aussi: Formation d'identité, Politique d'identité
Identité culturelle 541, 966, 992, 997, 1184, 1192, 1198, 1202, 1205, 1207, 1230, 1242, 1318, 1331, 1668, 1758, 1880, 1899, 1936, 1949, 2047, 2178, 2394, 2549, 2575, 3355, 3392, 3406, 3422, 3441, 3554, 3589, 3595, 3676, 4141, 4205, 4924, 5156, 5259, 5328, 5409
Identité de groupe 837, 956, 972, 973, 988, 990, 999, 1036, 1044, 1058, 1082, 1252, 2552, 3362, 3386, 3410, 3421, 3545, 3554, 4366, 4472, 4924, 5159, 5328, 5437
Identité nationale 58, 147, 150, 159, 168, 187, 247, 669, 834, 953, 954, 958-965, 968-970, 977, 978, 981, 983-985, 987, 991, 995, 997, 998, 1000, 1003, 1167, 1182, 1192, 1193, 1227, 1315, 1499, 1798, 1813, 1816, 1819, 1845, 1881, 1885, 1973, 1981, 2153, 2177, 2204, 2532, 2538, 2573, 3070, 3214, 3250, 3251, 3355, 3400, 3421, 3441, 3445, 3468, 3487, 3532, 3534, 3548, 3557, 3595, 3634, 3635, 3646, 3676, 3789, 3945, 4221, 4227, 4913, 4914, 4924, 4930, 4959, 4962, 4966, 5218, 5295, 5308
Identité professionnelle 11, 4563, 4775, 5924
Identité régionale 963, 969, 1202, 1363, 1820
Identité sociale 548, 829, 834, 836, 848, 854, 859, 880, 881, 893, 973, 1020, 1034, 1042, 1044, 1057, 1076-1078, 1111, 1232, 1755, 1880, 1965, 2110, 2255, 2358, 2381, 2436, 2491, 2498, 2501, 2600, 3153, 3323, 3395, 3435, 3437, 3442, 3602, 3781, 4366, 4857, 5344
Idéologie 23, 34, 47, 149, 189, 295, 351, 929, 967, 968, 977, 1028, 1151, 1167, 1209, 1214, 1346, 1353, 1376, 1421, 1449, 1464, 1577, 1612, 1644, 1727, 1761, 1762, 1792, 1802, 1920, 1931, 1935, 1960, 1990, 2113, 2140, 2217, 2339, 2502, 2534, 2540, 2551, 2730, 2975, 3085, 3130, 3132, 3212, 3221, 3239, 3249, 3272, 3508, 3697, 3719, 3851, 3892, 4214, 4221, 4674, 4850, 4866, 4898, 4908, 4912, 4926, 4935, 4962, 4973, 4981, 5154, 5238, 5251, 5258, 5270,
5287, 5289, 5319, 5335, 5509, 5512, 5603, 5817, 5960
Idéologies politiques 187, 232, 968, 1221, 1263, 1351, 2280, 4925, 5258, 5285, 5309
Igbo 3868
Îles 982, 1811, 3621, 3776, 3913
Illégitimité 2791
Images 530, 630, 657, 1103, 1168, 1710, 1732, 1737, 1752, 1859, 1900, 1909, 2665, 2677, 3157, 3262, 3372, 3374, 3497, 4166, 4324, 5253, 5924
Imagination 12, 784, 994, 1110, 1711, 1975, 2047, 2664, 3322, 4900
Immigrants 414, 766, 805, 806, 954, 1319, 1384, 1427, 1521, 1698, 1737, 1777, 2029, 2033, 2038, 2083, 2232, 2313, 2376, 2612, 2624, 2680, 2732, 2784, 2870, 2936, 2950, 3336, 3413, 3434, 3461, 3511, 3523, 3536, 3538, 3545-3547, 3549, 3550, 3552-3554, 3558-3560, 3562-3565, 3567, 3570-3575, 3577, 3578, 3580-3583, 3585, 3588, 3590, 3591, 3593, 3594, 3596, 3599-3605, 3609, 3631, 3633, 3639, 3644, 3647, 3652, 3653, 3655, 3656, 3669, 3675, 3684, 3791, 3826, 3846, 3859, 4009, 4184, 4229, 4249, 4432, 4461-4463, 4473, 4821, 4856, 5081, 5089, 5144, 5292, 5441, 5529, 5632, 5791
Immigrants clandestins 3579, 5200
Immigration 414, 805, 954, 1834, 1949, 2420, 2532, 2559, 2691, 2784, 2922, 3394, 3398, 3459, 3497, 3541, 3542, 3544, 3545, 3556, 3558, 3564, 3565, 3567, 3569, 3573, 3574, 3578, 3579, 3587, 3591, 3593, 3597, 3599, 3601, 3602, 3604, 3617, 3630, 3632, 3633, 3647, 3648, 3651-3653, 3655, 3672, 3675, 3678, 3682-3684, 3686, 3778, 4002, 4184, 4252, 4479, 4552, 4596, 4821, 4856, 4939, 4952, 4983, 5275, 5632
Immigration clandestine 3630
Immunisation 5575, 5949
Immunité 5984
Impérialisme 134, 188, 710, 1165, 1392, 1819, 3782, 4196, 4935, 4944
Impérialisme culturel 248, 1733, 1931, 2545
Importations 1323, 1894, 4142
Impôt sur le revenu 2458
Impôts 5793
Incertitude 17, 357, 386, 668, 714, 730, 1098, 1261, 1766, 2222, 2309, 2536, 2640, 2794, 4346, 5236, 5484, 5690, 5945, 5970
Inceste 2912, 3304

INDEX DES MATIÈRES

Indépendance 995, 2317, 2318, 2502, 2626, 2667, 2878, 2996, 3024, 3229, 3776, 3891, 4218, 4275, 5511, 5639
Indicateurs 3800, 4486, 5433
Indicateurs démographiques 90, 5968
Indicateurs économiques 5756
    voir aussi: Clignotement des indicateurs économiques
Indicateurs sociaux 2408, 3294, 3590, 3752, 3874
Indiens 567, 3400, 3454, 3581, 3629, 4500, 5002
Individu et société 2214, 4904
Individualisme 28, 284, 287, 382, 578, 583, 801, 870, 1238, 1247, 1275, 1486, 2174, 2317, 2335, 3328, 3465, 3750, 3771, 3842, 3946, 4194, 4392, 4427, 4658, 4793, 4830, 4910, 4939, 5159, 5849
Individualité 17, 2214
Individus 103, 178, 181, 203, 219, 228, 241, 268, 277, 287, 306, 320, 323, 406, 428, 471, 577, 582, 594, 652, 691, 696, 715, 718, 726, 730, 763, 845, 867, 869, 896, 911, 1007, 1046, 1048, 1067, 1112, 1115, 1144, 1147, 1152, 1292, 1301, 1304, 1635, 2021, 2082, 2303, 2304, 2311, 2318, 2357, 2378, 2552, 2935, 2983, 3055, 3183, 3610, 3969, 4006, 4183, 4188, 4190, 4421, 4753, 4933, 5016, 5151, 5437, 5716
    voir aussi: Performance individuelle
Indonésiens 3655
Induction 162, 474, 476, 1824, 2099
Industrialisation 1200, 2420, 2434, 2537, 2691, 3919, 3949, 4007, 4055, 4108, 4152, 4179, 4287, 4296
Industrie 73, 1168, 2243, 2914, 3333, 3693, 3704, 3773, 3897, 4200, 4402, 4608, 4824, 4826, 4840
    voir aussi: Agroindustrie, Fabrication industrielle, Localisation industrielle, Secteur tertiaire
Industrie alimentaire 1286, 2545
Industrie automobile 1129, 4617, 4618, 4811
Industrie cinématographique 1100, 1699, 1891, 1894, 1895, 2677
Industrie culturelle 1100, 1194, 1856
Industrie de la construction 1565, 4420, 4572
Industrie de l'acier 4618
Industrie des communications 1754
Industrie du livre 1557
Industrie du vêtement 4694
Industrie hôtelière 4046, 4374
Industrie laitière 3893, 4142, 4226
Industrie minière 801, 3820, 3854, 4208, 4864
    voir aussi: Charbonnages

Industrie pétrolière 3711
Industrie pharmaceutique 5811, 5833
Inégalité 427, 454, 2014, 2025, 2030, 2064, 2115, 2116, 2123, 2141, 2336, 2384, 2386, 2402, 2409, 2424, 2428, 2440, 2442, 2448, 2532, 2813, 2844, 2999, 3286, 3307, 3475, 3671, 3771, 3996, 4169, 4216, 4227, 4269, 4282, 4309, 4460, 4464, 4491, 4495, 4587, 4628, 4696, 4793, 4941, 4949, 4950, 5057, 5154, 5244, 5445, 5465, 5756, 5811, 5988
    voir aussi: Inégalité économique, Inégalité sociale
Inégalité de revenu 2808, 2840, 3528, 3582, 4018, 4251, 4264, 4266, 4301, 4304, 4306, 4308, 4368, 4431, 4486, 4525, 4542, 5642, 5804
Inégalité de sexes 2561, 2870, 2875, 3076, 3087, 3165, 3177, 3178, 3186, 3200, 3203, 3207-3209, 3275, 3283, 3288, 3292, 4496, 4503, 4509, 4540, 4545, 4546, 4558, 4562, 4573, 4576, 5203, 5348, 5350, 5363, 5832, 5915
Inégalité économique 2371, 2384, 2521, 4274, 4285, 4497, 5057
Inégalité raciale 1431, 2036, 2062, 2212, 3454, 3482, 3491, 3514, 3528, 4505, 4509
Inégalité sociale 1, 824, 2048, 2064, 2073, 2115, 2116, 2324, 2378, 2384, 2386, 2396, 2402, 2407, 2409, 2413, 2430, 2431, 2442, 2498, 2602, 2605, 2714, 2838, 3488, 4004, 4271, 4274, 4290, 4291, 4293, 4304, 4486, 4983, 5190, 5244, 5445, 5475, 5516, 5603, 5642, 5665
Infanticide 2710, 5868
Inférence causale 497, 618
Infirmières 4439, 4711, 4784, 5508, 5651, 5746, 5799, 5826, 5832, 5834, 5839, 5843, 5846
Inflation 4347, 4949
Influence culturelle 1770, 1942, 2569, 2630, 2760, 2917, 2944, 3531, 5128
Influence du groupe 1059, 4090
Influence interculturelle 1770, 3653
Influence interpersonnelle 4620
Influence sociale 836, 845, 1036, 1038, 1494, 1567, 1770, 2756, 2778, 3167, 3178, 4620, 5154, 5306
Influences politiques 348, 1976, 2671, 5307
Influences religieuses 1438, 1480, 1512, 2753
Information 451, 481, 613, 639, 853, 867, 1015, 1055, 1088, 1116, 1200, 1261, 1554, 1565, 1634, 1646, 1648, 1656, 1658, 1687, 1704, 1717, 1731, 1749, 2337, 2554, 2829, 3724, 3734, 4056, 4179,

557

SUBJECT INDEX IN FRENCH

    4353, 4610, 4654, 4987, 5231, 5854, 5969, 5976
    voir aussi: Accès à l'information
Information du consommateur 4322, 4341
Information financière 4782
Information gouvernementale 3633
Information imparfaite 4763
Information juridique 95
Information sociale 3874
Informatique 2270, 4574
Informatisation 1040, 4179, 4406
Infrastructure de transport 4023
Infrastructure publique 3868, 3986, 4025, 4031, 4036, 4051, 4066, 4093, 4102, 4108, 4169, 4768
Infrastructure sociale 1817, 4042
Ingénierie 1554, 3765, 4571
Ingénieurs 4769, 4788
Initiation 4481
Injures 1347, 3201, 5967
Injustice 799, 4935
Innovation 1100, 1144, 1155, 1393, 1673, 2258, 2299, 2770, 3223, 3885, 3890, 3916, 3919, 4038, 4054, 4122, 4287, 4375, 4393, 4397, 4402, 4417, 4654, 4702, 4808, 5496, 5725
Inondations 767
Insectes 5968
Insolvabilité 5151
Instabilité économique 4299
Instabilité politique 3677
Institutionnalisation 1130, 1139, 1556, 2134, 4197, 4739, 4817, 5172, 5192, 5473, 5479, 5515, 5899
Institutionnalisme 1137, 1566, 2555, 3705, 4877, 4957, 4964, 5171, 5782, 5899
Institutions 68, 162, 802, 1028, 1120, 1133, 1149, 1155, 1156, 1162, 1190, 1464, 1568, 1608, 1619, 1626, 1826, 2113, 2125, 2289, 2291, 2317, 2345, 2361, 2443, 2679, 3238, 3734, 3775, 3855, 3867, 3918, 3922, 4097, 4178, 4181, 4190, 4280, 4301, 4310, 4380, 4699, 4790, 4791, 4793, 4817, 4845, 4881, 4936, 4946, 4961, 4966, 4971, 4978, 4992, 4993, 5020, 5147, 5202, 5213, 5220, 5225, 5265, 5287, 5358, 5593, 5638, 5641, 5793, 5942
    voir aussi: Établissements d'enseignement, Modification institutionnelle, Organismes d'aide, Réforme institutionnelle
Institutions financières 2561, 4284, 4317
Institutions politiques 4885, 4938, 4956, 4964, 4968, 5218, 5282
Institutions religieuses 1385, 1479, 3858

Instruction civique 2122, 2170, 2171, 2181, 2188, 2203, 2604
Intégration culturelle 1321, 1532, 1809, 1813, 1949, 2047, 2419, 2518, 3559, 3562, 3576, 3598, 3826, 5313
Intégration de la collectivité 1442, 1488, 5576
Intégration du groupe 4608
Intégration économique 2518, 4258, 4439, 4825, 4968
Intégration européenne 983, 1205, 1826, 2178, 2530, 3468, 4222, 4913, 4966, 5290, 5295, 5598, 5640
    voir aussi: Euroscepticisme
Intégration internationale 2507
Intégration politique 1826, 2518, 3576, 4966
Intégration régionale 2205, 2507, 2560, 3776
Intégration sociale 59, 388, 391, 709, 1026, 1321, 1494, 1532, 1685, 1809, 2033, 2047, 2073, 2136, 2312, 2375, 2403, 2404, 2409, 2429, 2433, 2459, 2469, 2474, 2475, 2483, 2530, 2585, 2618, 2664, 3439, 3444, 3471, 3537, 3554, 3562, 3568, 3577, 3582, 3594, 3602, 3607, 3611, 3635, 3802, 3826, 3833, 3902, 3983, 4001, 4005, 4091, 4287, 4585, 4722, 5033, 5420, 5432, 5436, 5638, 5702, 5741, 5904
Intellectuels 217, 224, 240, 281, 288, 299, 1158, 1187, 1268, 1336, 1363, 1411, 1553, 1608, 1707, 1924, 2294, 2298, 2383, 2412, 2439, 2534, 2554, 3222, 4897, 4898, 4914, 4935, 5281, 5298
Intelligence 621, 639, 653, 660, 661, 663, 715, 898, 1237, 2017, 2052, 2359, 2410, 2904, 3446, 5730
Intelligence artificielle 481, 1234, 1576
Intelligentsia 2412, 2439, 2529, 2534, 3407, 4914
Intensification agricole 3733
Intentions électorales 5303
Interaction conjugale 2761
Interaction culturelle 4207
Interaction en groupe 911, 1036, 1059, 1072, 1080
Interaction sociale 13, 20, 366, 406, 463, 540, 545, 573, 703, 828, 850, 875, 911, 917, 927, 935, 944, 945, 1026, 1082, 1098, 1113, 1120, 1208, 1298, 1573, 1632, 1647, 1649, 1655, 1708, 1755, 1788, 1831, 1846, 2135, 2198, 2252, 2308, 2318, 2323, 2329, 2373, 2402, 2482, 2489, 2491, 2493, 2619, 2661, 2782, 2931, 3318, 3432, 3505, 3517, 3565, 3585, 3741, 3798, 3839, 3910, 4389, 4404,

4416, 4701, 4741, 4774, 5170, 5267, 5313, 5337, 5414, 5607, 5954
Interaction symbolique 2645
Interactionnisme 312, 389
Interdépendance 939, 1022, 2070, 3759, 3771, 4618
Intérêt 4352, 4467
Intérêt personnel 382, 1073, 3493, 4181, 5077
Intérêt public 1734, 3759
Intermariage 2917
Internationalisation 1235, 1911, 2269, 2278, 2550, 3634, 4234, 4289, 4494, 4818, 5678, 5686
Internationalisme 3136, 4002
Internet 537, 1234, 1242, 1634, 1637, 1641, 1656, 1665-1668, 1670, 1671, 1674, 1676-1682, 1684, 1687, 1689-1693, 1713, 1756, 1822, 1920, 2129, 2197, 2201, 2223, 2325, 2581, 2667, 3253, 3392, 3463, 3505, 3797, 4056, 5230, 5241, 5288
Intervalles génésiques 2766
Intervention de l'État 3806, 4235
Intervention d'une troisième partie 1731, 5321, 5330, 5361
Intervention humanitaire 1730, 2704, 4287, 5319, 5321, 5330, 5362
Intervention militaire 1730, 1731, 5340
Interventionnisme 7
Intifada 5351
Intimité 69, 785, 916, 926, 935, 2313, 2983, 3344, 3380, 3383, 5919
Intolérance envers les homosexuels 1821, 3061, 3260, 3307, 3375, 3382, 5698, 5872
Intoxiqué 723, 5374, 5376, 5395, 5396, 5406
voir aussi: Toxicomanes
Invalidité 502, 555, 557, 716, 1898, 2019, 2044, 2431, 2452-2478, 2480-2484, 2487-2492, 2494-2496, 2498-2501, 2737, 2755, 2811, 2815, 3013, 3035, 3037, 3329, 4362, 4776, 5514, 5518, 5549, 5565, 5602-5604, 5606-5608, 5916
Inventaire des ressources 92
Inventions 965, 992, 4938
Investissements 3661, 4088, 4175, 5575, 5629
Investissements agricoles 3922
Investissements directs étrangers 2446, 2571, 4363
Investissements publics 5969
Investisseurs 4369
Iraniens 1427, 3680
Irrationalité 206
Islam 190, 980, 1089, 1126, 1263, 1380, 1389, 1422, 1517, 1519-1521, 1523-1534, 1537-1543, 1781, 1802, 1962, 2054, 2126, 2153, 2520, 2978, 3067, 3115, 3163, 3172, 3207, 3247, 3263, 3266, 3393, 3447, 3562, 3573, 3596, 4205, 4223, 4535, 4948, 4962, 5274, 5315, 5687
voir aussi: Coran, Soufisme
Islam et politique 1524, 3277, 5274
Islamisation 190, 1530, 1540, 4352
Isolement social 567, 2423, 2498, 4006, 5016, 5646, 5900
Italiens 567, 1180, 3422, 3566, 4229, 5304
Itinérants 1340, 5420
Jaïn 1424
Jalousie 821
James, William 12, 1472
Jameson, Fredric 1229
Japonais 567, 763, 1353, 2271, 2934, 3313, 3548
Jardins 1928, 4133
Jazz 1878, 1977, 1978, 1988, 4767
Jésuite 59
Jeu 782, 1350, 2608
Jeu de rôle 60
Jeûne 1504
Jeunes et politique 2617, 2638, 5243
Jeunes filles 681, 1928, 2041, 2074, 2449, 2608, 2623, 2632, 2645, 2667, 2727, 2878, 3115, 3156, 3212, 3216, 3254, 3352, 3509, 3793, 4129, 4482, 4527
Jeunesse 77, 155, 900, 921, 978, 1014, 1338, 1494, 1809, 1820, 1875, 1889, 1982, 2047, 2119, 2218, 2248, 2576, 2584, 2585, 2592, 2602, 2614, 2616, 2618, 2620-2623, 2626, 2627, 2634, 2635, 2637, 2639, 2640, 2648-2650, 2870, 2909, 2924, 2929, 2954, 3043, 3156, 3237, 3313, 3323, 3337, 3338, 3370, 3385, 3413, 3535, 3536, 3595, 3596, 3946, 3965, 4139, 4145, 4159, 4344, 4361, 4453, 4481, 4487, 4504, 4548, 4559, 4758, 4799, 4869, 4974, 4996, 5000, 5019, 5050, 5054, 5068, 5069, 5072, 5079, 5090, 5097, 5209, 5361, 5370, 5386, 5409, 5420, 5427, 5429, 5431, 5456, 5465, 5542, 5546, 5570, 5737, 5814, 5933, 5941, 5978
Jeunesse rurale 3894
Jeunesse urbaine 4435
Jeux 576, 656, 927, 949, 979, 2447
Jeux à deux personnes 949
Jeux d'argent 709, 1287, 5377, 5387, 5398, 5412
Jeux de stratégie 2308
Johnson, William 1462
Joie 831, 863
Jones, David 4980
Jouets 635

SUBJECT INDEX IN FRENCH

Journal 722
Journalisme 455, 1218, 1671, 1696, 1709, 1712, 1714, 1717, 1720, 1726, 1730, 1731, 1738, 1741, 1744, 1746, 1751, 1754, 1760, 1763, 1771, 2250, 3141, 3931, 4785, 4787, 5041, 5235
Journalistes 989, 996, 1351, 1714, 1720, 4935
Joyce, James 1937, 1941
Judaïsme 145, 169, 213, 235, 282, 1171, 1380, 1389, 1460, 1546-1549, 1551, 1817, 1896, 1912, 2177, 2842, 3518, 3743, 4535
  voir aussi: Hassidisme, Hébreu
Judiciaire 4983, 5183
Jugement 117, 120, 232, 300, 302, 498, 584, 631, 639, 706, 711, 833, 854, 855, 859, 867, 871, 890, 1049, 1437, 1856, 2352, 4613, 4911, 5850
Jugement social 823, 830, 856, 869, 878, 889
Juges 3891, 5155, 5157, 5170-5172
Juifs 145, 282, 669, 1001, 1014, 1026, 1187, 1442, 1544-1546, 1548-1550, 1786, 1791, 1902, 1912, 1916, 1935, 2177, 2419, 2551, 2619, 2753, 2760, 2842, 3418, 3448, 3450, 3455, 3462, 3477, 3483, 3502, 3518, 3532, 3566, 3600, 3636, 3647, 4919, 5304, 5529, 5907
Jumeaux 712, 2918, 3308
Jung, Carl 593, 1255, 2566
Jünger, Ernst 1199
Juridiction 4497, 5068
Juridiction criminelle 4982, 5001, 5004, 5005, 5014, 5018, 5028, 5032, 5083, 5101
Juridiction internationale 5311, 5322
Jurisprudence 2361, 4422, 4992, 5027, 5038, 5158, 5163, 5173, 5177, 5183, 5198, 5206, 5211
Jury 5160
Justice 124, 161, 186, 209, 270, 360, 674, 1008, 1019, 1442, 2352, 2361, 2439, 2448, 2589, 2603, 3042, 3780, 3787, 3816, 3891, 4293, 4306, 4483, 4599, 4626, 4660, 4702, 4723, 4905, 4909, 4937, 4958, 4971, 4983, 4990, 5010, 5019, 5020, 5032, 5034, 5072, 5110, 5125, 5135, 5147, 5154, 5161, 5174, 5180, 5192, 5197, 5244, 5318, 5332
  voir aussi: Administration de la justice
Justice distributive 2603, 4262, 4660, 4921, 4937
Justice économique 3705, 4242
Justice pénale 426, 1442, 2532, 2864, 4949, 4979, 4982, 4997-5010, 5013-5020, 5022-5026, 5028-5032, 5035-5038, 5041, 5043, 5059, 5064, 5068, 5098, 5101, 5116, 5119, 5126, 5129, 5132, 5135, 5145, 5150, 5174, 5175, 5193, 5195, 5205, 5364, 5370
Justice sociale 59, 1010, 1028, 2001, 2050, 2118, 2155, 2361, 2414, 2433, 2448, 2458, 2502, 2603, 3080, 3121, 3136, 3155, 3528, 3694, 3705, 3749, 3805, 3816, 3827, 3834, 3837, 4061, 4255, 4262, 4286, 4291, 4293, 4297, 4306, 4307, 4398, 4587, 4837, 4921, 4937, 4950, 4983, 4994, 5018, 5096, 5190, 5261, 5322, 5440
Kabyle 18, 3638, 4275
Kachin 2405
Kahlo, Frida 970
Kant, Immanuel 117, 121, 225, 242, 274, 279, 300, 343, 385, 1586
Kazakh 1527, 1539
Keynesianisme 4230
Khasi 3076
Khatemi, Mohammed 5315
Kibboutz 5351
Kierkegaard, Søren Aabye 244
King, Rodney 3506
King, Stephen 1927
Kouchner, B. 4287
Kristeva, Julia 4898
Kuhn, Thomas S. 1582
Kuki, Shūz 212
Kupka, František 1863
Laboratoire 433, 1610
Lacan, Jacques 3339
Laclau, Ernesto 368
Ladino 1817
Laïcisme 1386, 1535, 2346, 2439, 3853, 4929, 4962
Laissez-faire 3771
Langage 12, 76, 81, 82, 114, 119, 122, 156, 197, 202, 210, 244, 249, 297, 312, 340, 359, 378, 384, 470, 538, 547, 610, 623, 743, 836, 945, 979, 981, 1029, 1040, 1104, 1182, 1237, 1247, 1275, 1428, 1458, 1518, 1561, 1582, 1649, 1682, 1689, 1712, 1722, 1723, 1736, 1739, 1763, 1777, 1784-1786, 1788-1790, 1792-1794, 1797, 1798, 1801, 1802, 1804, 1806, 1807, 1809, 1811-1815, 1818-1820, 1825, 1828, 1830, 1832, 1834-1840, 1842, 1844-1847, 1865, 1872, 1877, 1894, 1935, 1957, 1990, 1991, 1997, 2003, 2025, 2107, 2121, 2188, 2190, 2227, 2523, 2909, 2936, 3005, 3061, 3133, 3139, 3227, 3363, 3409, 3415, 3426, 3432, 3561, 3564, 3580, 3598, 3931, 4137, 4179, 4421, 4801, 4959, 4969, 5021, 5132, 5153, 5177, 5410

INDEX DES MATIÈRES

voir aussi: Hindi, Langue nationale, Langue polonaise, Langues étrangères, Langues indo-européennes, Langues officielles, Langues vernaculaires, Philologie, Phrases, Portugais
Langage par signes 2461
Langue allemande 959, 1757, 1798, 1809, 1813, 1839, 2149
Langue anglaise 82, 97, 930, 1671, 1757, 1785, 1789, 1790, 1793, 1795, 1801, 1805, 1806, 1813, 1819, 1830, 1831, 1834, 1847, 1914, 1943, 1997, 2081, 2107, 2149, 2173, 3580, 4440, 4807, 5170
Langue arabe 1802, 1822, 1914, 1932, 1966, 2126
Langue catalane 1795, 1865
Langue espagnole 240, 1795, 1819, 1839, 1865, 4914
Langue française 168, 956, 979, 1182, 1789, 1795, 1798, 1822, 1914, 1931, 1942, 2082, 2126, 3423, 5239
Langue italienne 1789
Langue japonaise 1830
Langue maternelle 1786, 1811, 3407, 3595
Langue nationale 1777, 1794, 1798, 1825, 2025, 2121
Langue occitan 1986
Langue polonaise 2009
Langue russe 1834
Langues asiatiques et du pacifique 1805
Langues chinoises 1789, 1811, 1831, 1839, 2523
Langues étrangères 1654, 1793, 2083, 2149, 2227, 2228
Langues indo-européennes 1793, 1794, 1818, 1825
voir aussi: Sanscrit
Langues officielles 1838, 1843, 2121, 2523
Langues slavs 1793, 1794, 1825, 3595
Langues vernaculaires 31
Lao-tzu 200, 1382
Lau 3913
Lawrence, Stephen 5147
Leaders 1065, 1938, 3423, 3877, 4620, 4622, 4637, 4639, 4886, 4898, 5304
Leaders charismatiques 4886
Leaders politiques 326, 2266, 4935, 5284, 5288
Lecteurs 78
Lecture 1140, 1637, 1921, 2028, 2040
Légendes 3186
Législation 1030, 1734, 1980, 2458, 2702, 3290, 3630, 3745, 3810, 4133, 4396, 4488, 4496, 4695, 5153, 5164, 5173, 5176, 5200, 5204, 5221, 5492, 5560, 5706

Législation sociale 95
Législatures des États 4133
Légitimité 431, 895, 1013, 2243, 4351, 4640, 4767, 5040, 5213, 5216, 5218, 5282
Lenoir, Fréderic 1464
Lepsius, M. Rainer 2312
Lesbianisme 1488, 2492, 2688, 2915, 3061, 3125, 3134, 3340, 3352, 3356, 3361, 3363, 3364, 3369, 3373-3375, 3379, 3384, 3389, 5984
Levi, Primo 3518
Lévi Strauss, Claude 348
Levinas, Emmanuel 1382
Lévy, Bernard-Henri 281
Lexicologie 659
Libéralisation 4245, 4713, 4923, 4998, 5250, 5282, 5793
Libéralisme 170, 227, 320, 352, 382, 1188, 1197, 1361, 2143, 2361, 2734, 3365, 3419, 3471, 3816, 3849, 4224, 4230, 4898, 4915-4917, 4927, 4928, 4967, 5130, 5155, 5180, 5188, 5343, 5553, 5641, 5654
voir aussi: Néolibéralisme
Libération 295, 2310, 3133, 3134, 3172, 3295, 3298, 3349, 4935
Libéraux 4897, 4915
Libertariens 1412
Libertarisme 1412, 5238
Liberté 136, 220, 232, 245, 246, 343, 1141, 1164, 1412, 1569, 1867, 1987, 2303, 2317, 2361, 3740, 4288, 4297, 4497, 4898, 4900, 4903, 4910, 4911, 4915, 4920, 4926-4928, 4933, 4989, 5016, 5262, 5652, 5871
voir aussi: Libertés civiles
Liberté de la presse 1723, 1734
Liberté de l'enseignement 13, 225, 2280, 2295
Liberté de pensée 2295
Liberté d'expression 1679, 5162, 5298
Liberté d'information 4933, 5298
Liberté religieuse 1470, 1867, 3471
Liberté surveillée 3241, 5002, 5016, 5030, 5042, 5136, 5370, 5672
Libertés civiles 4935, 5153
Libre échange 4811
Licenciements 4483, 4508, 4737
Lieu de travail 1339, 2086, 3246, 3285, 3289, 3290, 3310, 3356, 3568, 4354, 4357, 4359, 4362, 4383, 4384, 4389, 4397, 4398, 4404, 4406, 4416, 4419, 4422, 4451, 4486, 4488, 4493, 4515, 4534, 4544, 4552, 4578, 4602, 4613, 4617, 4626, 4628, 4639, 4677, 4678, 4681, 4683, 4688, 4691, 4709, 4710, 4716, 4721, 4731, 4740, 4741, 4746, 4750,

SUBJECT INDEX IN FRENCH

4753, 4758, 4792, 4807, 4809, 4820, 4829, 4833, 4838, 4858, 4868, 4877, 4879, 5052, 5090
Ligne aérienne 3927
Liminalité 1912, 5262, 5462
Linguistes 1816
Linguistique 76, 138, 231, 359, 538, 547, 636, 729, 735, 1722, 1757, 1789, 1790, 1792-1795, 1797, 1802, 1804, 1807, 1813, 1815, 1817, 1818, 1822, 1823, 1829, 1830, 1838-1842, 1845, 1847, 1872, 1877, 2050, 2107, 3415, 4801
  voir aussi: Sociolinguistique
Litige 3891, 5039, 5041, 5154, 5184, 5189-5191, 5205
Littérature 57, 86, 99, 247, 281, 540, 975, 1158, 1181, 1187, 1207, 1227, 1243, 1279, 1307, 1323, 1789, 1796, 1865, 1877, 1882, 1901, 1913-1919, 1921, 1922, 1924-1940, 1942-1946, 1948, 1949, 1951, 1954-1970, 2047, 2298, 2314, 2439, 2522, 3051, 3079, 3098, 3120, 3122, 3225, 3245, 3262, 3386, 3539, 3635, 4030, 4056, 4144, 5152, 5356, 5976
  voir aussi: Histoire Littéraire, Poèmes, Poésie, Prose, Romans, Sociologie de la littérature
Littérature contemporaine 1930
Littérature épique 1920, 1934
Littérature orale 1913
Littoraux 1312, 3606, 3709, 3820
Livres 1323, 1557, 1924
Localisation 1268, 1755, 2545, 2568, 3355, 3802, 3851, 3864
Localisation géographique 528, 2633, 2748, 3767, 3820, 4046, 4249, 4291, 4833, 5844
Localisation industrielle 4315, 4346
Locataires 3824, 3979, 4220, 4232, 5286, 5491, 5611
Logement 608, 1283, 2313, 2407, 2424, 2626, 2661, 2683, 2716, 2809, 3231, 3460, 3582, 3587, 3620, 3655, 3765, 3845, 3949, 3961, 3966, 3972-3975, 3977, 3980, 3981, 3984-3987, 3990, 3992, 3994, 4003, 4010, 4011, 4014, 4020, 4049, 4058, 4083, 4091, 4110, 4111, 4113, 4116, 4126, 4136, 4161, 4225, 4229, 4302, 4774, 4950, 5063, 5417, 5476, 5491, 5494, 5496, 5509, 5511, 5523, 5611, 5612, 5615, 5621, 5631, 5637, 5645, 5646, 5655, 5656, 5741
Logement rural 3906
Logement urbain 3948, 3968, 3972, 3974, 3978, 3982, 3989, 4024, 4111, 4169, 5611
Logements sociaux 891, 3486, 3491, 3775, 3824, 3845, 3977, 3979, 3981-3983, 3985,
3988, 3989, 4087, 4111, 4117, 4225, 4232, 4774, 5102, 5491, 5509, 5611, 5612, 5617, 5621, 5627, 5631, 5637, 5645, 5646, 5649, 5655
Logiciel 1667, 2179, 4382
Logique 106, 113, 120, 128, 260, 286, 297, 380, 1265, 1391, 1610, 1640, 2508, 4385, 5179, 5201
Logique mathématique 370
Loi comparé 5165, 5178
Loi environnementale 3810, 5244
Loi islamique 1380, 1522, 3468, 4352
Loi martiale 3323
Loi sur l'immigration 3542, 3550, 3582, 3633
Loisir 469, 470, 1282, 1285, 1291, 1292, 1301, 1308, 1312, 1320, 1326, 1347, 1366, 2248, 2372, 2486, 2618, 2667, 2880, 2906, 3169, 3644, 4060, 4176, 4451, 4685, 4767
  voir aussi: Sociologie des loisirs
London, Jack 1323
Losev, Alexsei 249
Loterie 1287, 4262
Lotnik, Waldemar 3495
Louis XIV [King] 4954
Lowe, Adolph 4900
Loyauté 1439, 1794, 2986, 4601, 5168
Loyer 3845, 3985, 4486, 5491, 5612, 5649
Luhmann, Niklas 350, 359, 371, 372, 393, 394, 402, 403
Luthéranisme 1486
Lutte contre la crime 2203, 2532, 3036, 4390, 4986, 4989, 4997, 5008, 5014, 5024, 5059, 5063, 5088, 5107, 5112, 5124, 5140, 5143, 5448, 5472, 5474
Lutte de classes 2416, 4213
MacDonogh, Steve 1952
Machiavélisme 346, 5117
Machines 634, 1593
Macroanalyse 308, 471
Macroéconomie 4949
Macrosociologie 1183, 5388
Madia 1777
Mafia 2203, 5092, 5094, 5317
Magasins 4027, 4678
Magie 1622, 1905
Magyar 1816
Mahfouz, Najib 1966
Main d'œuvre 2551, 2561, 3180, 3626, 3630, 3633, 3658, 4437, 4454, 4490, 4506, 4518, 4532, 4582, 4600, 4737, 4803, 4823, 4836, 5520, 5845
  voir aussi: Cols bleus

Main-d'oeuvre féminine 4414, 4455, 4466, 4467, 4522, 4529, 4532, 4534, 4542, 4549, 4553, 4561
Maintien de l'ordre 2532, 2868, 4325, 4422, 4511, 4683, 4986, 4991, 4995, 5014, 5035, 5084, 5109, 5122-5124, 5126, 5128, 5130, 5131, 5133-5136, 5138-5141, 5143-5145, 5147, 5240, 5243, 5273, 5364, 5370, 5448
Maison 1283, 1284, 1288, 2421, 3620, 3695, 3786, 3953, 4310
Majorité politique 5248
Mal 293, 326, 1388, 1389, 1451, 1487, 5928
Malades 747, 748, 752, 761, 784, 794, 803, 809, 810, 813, 816, 5726, 5732, 5753, 5787, 5814, 5815, 5830, 5835-5837, 5852, 5854, 5879, 5882, 5883, 5889, 5893, 5896, 5899, 5904, 5919, 5929, 5930, 5976, 5982
Maladie 581, 694, 781, 887, 2044, 2470, 2655, 2660, 2809, 3037, 3040, 4692, 4696, 4703, 4708, 5502, 5507, 5518, 5534, 5594, 5727, 5813, 5842, 5847, 5850, 5856, 5866, 5891, 5893, 5898, 5928, 5950, 5960, 5970, 5980
Maladie d'Alzheimer 5529
Maladie mentale 95, 506, 738, 740, 743, 745, 750, 753, 762-764, 768, 772, 773, 779, 788, 789, 794, 804, 807, 808, 813, 816, 818, 820, 1947, 2334, 2478, 2659, 4950, 5016, 5027, 5056, 5078, 5137, 5192, 5377, 5420, 5479, 5529, 5604, 5736, 5738, 5891, 5904, 5906, 5907, 5909, 5912-5916, 5919, 5920, 5922, 5926-5930, 5934, 5938, 5939, 5941
Maladie sexuellement transmissible 2765, 2806, 3296, 3309, 3319, 3334, 3336, 5200, 5866, 5891, 5945, 5957, 5962, 5964, 5965, 5978, 5981
Maladies 386, 446, 453, 483, 484, 1620, 2719, 2762, 2808, 2844, 3309, 3332, 3334, 3794, 4611, 5363, 5534, 5735, 5773, 5838, 5857, 5866, 5891, 5942, 5944-5946, 5948, 5952, 5957, 5958, 5964, 5968, 5972, 5980, 5983, 5986
voir aussi: Anorexie, Hépatite, Malaria, SIDA, Trypanosomiase, Variole
Maladies de coeur 5968
Maladies professionnelles 4730
Malaise politique 4977, 5466
Malaise social 4977, 4993
Malaria 3708, 5980
Malcolm X 1882
Mâle 938, 1897, 3115, 3232, 3346, 3835, 3996, 4394, 4437, 4460, 5079
Malebranche, Nicolas 221

Malinowski, Bronislaw 12
Malthus, Thomas 2706
Malthusianisme 2715
Management de l'information 1088, 1645, 1667, 4395
Manifestations 1610, 4843, 5264
Manuels 89, 90, 102, 179, 438, 530, 566, 1617, 1694, 2274, 2282, 3831
Manuels scolaires 162, 318, 980, 2121, 2205, 2211, 2212, 2217, 3035
Maoïsme 4848
Maori 164
Marchands 4223
Marché 1508, 1873, 2243, 2244, 3272, 3907, 3966, 4124, 4132, 4192, 4193, 4215, 4237, 4314, 4322, 4355, 4363, 4459, 4715, 4976, 5287, 5740, 5777
voir aussi: Marchés étrangers
Marché de l'art 4219, 4752
Marché de l'immobilier 2571, 3927
Marché de viande bovine 5948
Marché du logement 2407, 3620, 3906, 3980, 3983, 3987, 4003, 4225, 5621, 5627, 5649, 5655, 5656
Marché du travail 633, 1123, 1305, 1892, 2014, 2037, 2043, 2457, 2554, 2602, 2647, 2712, 2914, 2929, 2999, 3188, 3189, 3559, 3565, 3604, 3620, 3623, 3626, 3633, 3658, 3881, 3996, 4322, 4398, 4415, 4429, 4431, 4436, 4439, 4442-4445, 4447, 4451-4453, 4458-4462, 4466, 4468-4470, 4473, 4476, 4479, 4481, 4482, 4485, 4486, 4490, 4498, 4501-4503, 4506, 4509, 4525, 4533, 4538, 4540, 4545, 4546, 4549, 4552, 4554, 4566, 4579, 4583-4585, 4587-4590, 4594-4596, 4598, 4613, 4634, 4677, 4681, 4714, 4742, 4760, 4771, 4778, 4780, 4784, 4793, 4804, 4810, 4815, 4825, 4835, 4837, 4856, 4869, 4985, 5223, 5365, 5392, 5633, 5642, 5651, 5658
voir aussi: Flexibilité du marché de l'emploi
Marché financier 4175, 4352
Marché financier international 4234, 4486
Marché foncier 3883, 4017, 4103
Marché mondial 2571
Marché noir 4373
Marchés étrangers 4363
Marginalité 331, 1985, 2073, 2423, 3227, 3579, 3771, 4283
Marginaux 1310, 2385, 2432, 2458, 3175, 3250, 3416, 3474, 3656, 3754, 4039, 4453, 5299, 5800, 5914

SUBJECT INDEX IN FRENCH

Mariage 910, 915, 936, 937, 946, 950, 1290, 1795, 2363, 2394, 2408, 2472, 2478, 2635, 2692, 2696, 2710, 2791, 2800, 2822, 2848, 2849, 2851, 2852, 2856-2858, 2861, 2891, 2897, 2901, 2905, 2911, 2915, 2917, 2919, 2925, 2926, 2933, 2944, 2949, 2955-2962, 2965, 2967-2970, 2972-2986, 2988-2992, 3000, 3001, 3015, 3020, 3026, 3046, 3051, 3055, 3170, 3203, 3211, 3221, 3237, 3343, 3360, 3471, 3550, 3557, 3623, 3835, 3846, 3873, 3883, 3901, 4432, 4451, 4531, 4551, 4556, 4575, 5345, 5538
  voir aussi: Âge au mariage, Intermariage, Remariage
Mariage consanguin 2822
Mariage prédeternimé 3265
Mariages interethniques 1812, 5538
Maris 2765, 2965, 2971, 3170, 3188, 4530, 5479
Marketing 1317, 1323, 1875, 1895, 3312, 3405, 3749, 3927, 3942, 3965, 4141, 4312, 4318, 4319, 4322, 4343, 4420
  voir aussi: Publicité
Markievicz, Constance 1936
Marque 1439, 4343
Martín-Barbero, Jesús 1158
Marx, Karl 67, 360-362, 4922, 4961
Marxisme 6, 23, 144, 252, 280, 284, 285, 299, 332, 342, 351, 360-363, 379, 381, 1194, 1218, 1221, 1229, 1233, 1250, 1444, 1478, 1879, 2384, 2406, 2416, 2440, 2445, 3137, 4179, 4201, 4336, 4373, 4570, 4864, 4865, 4904, 4919, 4925, 4934, 4961, 5286
Masai 2505, 2515
Masaryk, Thomas G. 4913
Masculinité 574, 732, 1191, 1339, 1341, 1503, 1562, 1744, 1782, 1910, 1927, 1940, 1946, 1974, 2608, 3070, 3115, 3189, 3217, 3218, 3222, 3225, 3230, 3233, 3235, 3236, 3240-3243, 3246, 3252, 3253, 3257, 3259, 3260, 3264, 3269, 3271, 3272, 3274, 3288, 3299, 3305, 3320, 3346, 3349, 3350, 3353, 3372, 3383, 4521, 4558, 5358, 5415, 5438
Masochisme 3121
Matérialisme 185, 252, 280, 477, 1390, 3720, 4188, 4296, 4315, 4336
Matérialisme culturel 1233
Matériaux de construction 3765, 4049
Maternité 792, 800, 1969, 2007, 2725, 2738, 2765, 2856, 2895, 2915, 2958, 2993, 3004, 3007, 3015, 3027, 3028, 3035, 3037, 3045, 3169, 3227, 3249, 3273, 3676, 4515, 4568, 5396, 5578, 5746, 5872, 5950
Mathématiques 225, 380, 440, 463, 465, 486, 496, 1581, 1585, 1602, 1605, 1610, 1623, 2015, 2179, 2288, 4124
Matriarcat 3060
Mauvais traitements infligés à un enfant 521, 3298, 5100, 5192, 5371, 5544, 5546, 5549, 5554, 5558, 5562, 5569, 5578, 5579, 5582, 5589, 5590, 5594, 5595, 5597, 5680
Maya 1170
McCarthyism 4897
McLuhan, Marshall 2522
Mécanisation 2715
Mécanismes du marché 1754
Médecine 2477, 3159, 3272, 4551, 4564, 5380, 5507, 5725, 5727, 5731, 5733, 5734, 5752, 5796, 5813, 5817, 5833, 5839, 5848, 5853, 5855, 5885, 5886, 5889, 5892, 5902, 5921, 5980, 5982
  voir aussi: Biomédicine, Chirurgie, Histoire de la médicine
Médecine alternative 5839, 5859, 5900
Médecine légal 473, 498, 521, 555, 1031, 5084, 5193
Médecine sociale 2344, 4730, 5724, 5727, 5728, 5731, 5733
Médecine traditionnelle 5813, 5821, 5823, 5962, 5980
Médecins 249, 794, 2532, 3629, 4770, 5675, 5726, 5753, 5760, 5765, 5772, 5788, 5824, 5827, 5830, 5833, 5835-5838, 5840, 5841, 5844, 5853, 5857, 5862, 5878, 5882, 5894, 5895, 5982
Médias 425, 590, 835, 989, 994, 996, 1024, 1100, 1190, 1200, 1215, 1226, 1227, 1242, 1252, 1269, 1309, 1318, 1320, 1337, 1351, 1368, 1409, 1431, 1622, 1637, 1649, 1660, 1664, 1669, 1671, 1681, 1683, 1687, 1691, 1693-1697, 1699, 1700, 1702-1709, 1711-1717, 1719-1723, 1726-1744, 1746-1749, 1751, 1753, 1754, 1756, 1758, 1760-1763, 1765-1769, 1771, 1773-1776, 1778, 1779, 1781-1783, 1882, 1887, 1920, 1924, 1955, 2250, 2324, 2507, 2522, 2526, 2548, 2554, 2581, 2596, 2645, 2667, 2748, 2942, 2993, 3061, 3112, 3121, 3127, 3141, 3156, 3159, 3228, 3341, 3358, 3365, 3375, 3384, 3391, 3393, 3498, 3506, 3508, 3517, 3601, 3699, 3775, 3931, 4095, 4134, 4296, 4354, 4640, 4847, 5041, 5235, 5264, 5279, 5288, 5289, 5307, 5329, 5398,

INDEX DES MATIÈRES

5408, 5435, 5704, 5866, 5872, 5960
  voir aussi: Multimédia, Presse
Médiation 925, 1006, 1007, 1009, 1010, 1016, 1019, 1024, 1025, 1030, 1215, 1647, 2850, 2854, 2908, 2928, 2947, 3053, 3635, 3891, 4064, 4985, 5020, 5184, 5337, 5361
Médicaments 1307, 1313, 1344, 1355, 2521, 2621, 3995, 4493, 5011, 5031, 5050, 5079, 5115, 5126, 5374, 5380, 5381, 5383, 5384, 5386, 5394, 5395, 5399, 5402, 5406, 5409, 5480, 5828, 5833, 5862, 5886, 5891, 5958
  voir aussi: Cannabis, Cocaïne, Héroïne, Opiat, Politique de la drogue, Trafic de la drogue, Usage de stupéfiants
Médicine du travail 4683, 4686, 4693, 4698, 4711, 4730, 4743, 4813, 5773, 5808
Mégacité 3702, 3947
Mehta, Deepa 3112
Melanchthon, Philipp 15
Membres de la Première Chambre 3286
Mémoire 161, 162, 181, 232, 501, 503, 579, 625, 629, 632, 640, 644, 654, 658, 670, 774, 785, 812, 975, 976, 986, 993, 994, 1008, 1384, 1433, 1434, 1621, 1735, 1758, 1822, 1896, 1906, 1965, 2174, 2625, 2679, 3094, 3422, 3532, 3638, 3777, 3782, 4183, 4343, 5349, 5579, 5671, 5831, 5921
Mémoire collective 147, 161, 162, 181, 223, 247, 951, 958, 974, 976, 982, 985, 986, 993-995, 1004, 1434, 1758, 1951, 2177, 2205, 3468, 4848, 4936
Mémoire nationale 150, 161, 957, 958, 974, 980, 1004, 1262
Mémoires 1913, 1938, 1964, 3518, 5423
Mémorials 957
Menace 173, 895, 2892, 5010
Ménages 513, 811, 1283, 1284, 2311, 2313, 2363, 2407, 2421, 2583, 2600, 2683, 2901, 2926, 2930, 2944, 2949, 2965, 3169, 3188, 3223, 3231, 3268, 3645, 3715, 3899, 3924, 4022, 4056, 4068, 4157, 4219, 4263, 4265, 4302, 4310, 4315, 4338, 4452, 4475, 4530, 4559, 4575, 5363, 5514, 5625, 5800
Mencius 266, 1423, 3108
Mendiant 5428
Menger, Carl 4181
Ménopause 2744, 2801
Mentalité 2396, 5285
Mer 3745
Mercosur 2507

Mère 695, 755, 771, 792, 796, 849, 2463, 2803, 2822, 2825, 2832, 2846, 2847, 2917, 2991, 2997, 3002, 3007, 3008, 3011, 3015, 3016, 3019, 3021, 3026, 3027, 3029, 3031-3035, 3040, 3045, 3057, 3093, 3228, 3239, 3270, 3280, 3434, 3676, 4531, 4553, 4568, 5200, 5425, 5480, 5589, 5636, 5757, 5792, 5935, 5950, 5969
Mères célibataires 2881, 2995, 2998-3001, 4531, 5119
Mères travailleuses 3169, 3270, 4517, 4528, 4534, 4555, 4557, 4568
Méritocratie 3491, 4507, 4551, 4615
Merleau-Ponty, Maurice 215, 225, 3146
Messages 1642, 1647, 1710, 1799
Messies 1478
Mesure 63, 419, 428, 433, 477, 494, 496, 498, 525, 711, 719, 1012, 1060, 1571, 1606, 2166, 2289, 2785, 3464, 3800, 3847, 4166, 4277, 4386, 4625, 4635, 4697, 5959
Mesure de la personnalité 1143, 4607
Mesure du bien-être 4251
Mesures protectionnistes 5010
Métaphore 12, 225, 642, 1473, 1682, 1780, 1872, 1928, 3719, 5890, 5932
Métaphysique 199, 207, 208, 218, 221, 222, 225, 233, 245, 246, 248, 250, 251, 258, 260, 267, 271, 272, 275, 276, 288-290, 303, 1413, 1574, 1586, 1868, 1871, 3142
Métayage 3896, 4220
Méthode expérimentale 45, 426, 584, 1161
Méthodes comptable 4310
Méthodes contraceptives 2753, 2761, 5200
Méthodes de formation 4671
Méthodes de planification 1030, 2676, 3624, 3821, 3831, 3872, 3876, 4029, 4047, 4055, 4057, 4064, 4069, 4073, 4082, 4083, 4086, 4099, 4101, 4104, 4108, 4112, 4118, 4167, 5521, 5758, 5936, 5977
Méthodes de recherche 20, 31, 88, 119, 163, 179, 180, 183, 411-418, 420-427, 429, 431, 432, 434, 436-438, 440, 442, 443, 450, 454, 456, 458, 472, 474, 475, 482, 487, 488, 490, 495, 497, 502, 505-508, 510, 514-516, 518, 520, 522, 526, 529, 531, 536, 537, 539, 591, 595, 603, 653, 713, 748, 841, 1293, 1445, 1590, 2012, 2282, 2465, 2610, 3666, 4625, 4982, 5073, 5367, 5557, 5709, 5720, 5818, 5898, 5979
  voir aussi: Travail sur le terrain
Méthodes d'exploitation agricole 20, 3760
Méthodes mathématiques 40, 413, 424, 452, 456, 464-467, 472, 476, 480, 485, 486,

SUBJECT INDEX IN FRENCH

491-493, 496, 635, 1043, 1045, 3838, 4756, 5154
Méthodes pédagogiques 2098, 2145, 2172, 2173, 2175, 2184, 2200, 2201
Méthodes statistiques 163, 421, 424, 445, 447, 453, 468, 475, 479-481, 491, 494, 495, 499
Méthodologie 2, 20, 41, 51, 63, 74, 88, 90, 112, 119, 123, 146, 164, 167, 176, 179, 182, 183, 194, 195, 301, 303, 309, 313, 321, 365, 374, 376, 392, 410, 412, 416, 418-420, 422, 424-426, 429, 430, 432, 435, 438, 439, 441, 444, 448, 457, 462, 480, 482, 484, 487, 488, 490, 497, 503, 509, 514-517, 526, 530, 533, 535, 587, 605, 629, 653, 713, 841, 870, 1102, 1104, 1113, 1244, 1396, 1408, 1552, 1570, 1580, 1582, 1631, 1711, 1800, 1870, 2012, 2224, 2476, 2681, 2699, 2700, 2726, 2785, 2985, 3063, 3118, 3121, 3178, 3406, 3775, 3794, 3795, 3830, 3993, 4025, 4030, 4044, 4265, 4266, 4276, 4312, 4604, 4625, 4659, 5073, 5135, 5173, 5199, 5224, 5329, 5399, 5442, 5452, 5688, 5867, 5876, 5959, 5968
Méthodologie anthropologique 526, 3143, 3545
  voir aussi: Observation participante
Méthodologie économique 515, 1140, 1377, 2723, 2943, 3063
Méthodologie sociologique 4, 34, 41, 50, 51, 55, 65, 112, 119, 312, 321, 330, 358, 364, 374, 377, 391, 392, 412, 413, 415, 423, 440, 474, 485, 491, 496, 510, 515, 526, 527, 921, 2315, 2411, 2583, 3194, 4930, 5435
Métier 1591, 4219, 4238
Métropole 3359, 3632, 3943, 3948, 3953
Meurtre 2719, 3520, 3944, 5058, 5113, 5147, 5323, 5441, 5453, 5454, 5468, 5472, 5858
Mexicains 536, 805, 2784, 3336, 4462
Mickiewicz, Adam 1934
Microanalyse 308, 431, 471, 799, 5170
Microéconomie 40, 4348
Microfinancement 4263
Migrateurs 953, 1987, 1990, 2590, 2691, 2790, 2940, 3085, 3263, 3537, 3539, 3540, 3543, 3548, 3549, 3566, 3592, 3614, 3641, 3643, 3649, 3669, 3680, 4099, 4257, 5200, 5823
Migration 18, 536, 814, 1174, 1263, 1362, 1528, 1532, 2038, 2047, 2232, 2429, 2574, 2590, 2693, 2697, 2701, 2704, 2722, 2741, 3135, 3214, 3229, 3391, 3489, 3537, 3539, 3540, 3543-3545, 3551, 3554, 3556, 3557, 3560, 3561, 3568, 3569, 3574, 3584, 3587, 3595, 3597, 3603, 3606-3610, 3613, 3614, 3616, 3618, 3620, 3622, 3623, 3625, 3627, 3630, 3633, 3637, 3639, 3642, 3643, 3645-3649, 3651, 3656, 3660-3665, 3667, 3668, 3670, 3671, 3673, 3674, 3678, 3679, 3682, 3685, 3686, 3789, 3791, 3795, 3859, 3866, 3997, 4197, 4227, 4257, 4443, 4446, 4463, 4606, 5232, 5791
Migration de retour 3558, 3592, 3603, 3618, 3621, 3641, 3662, 3859
Migration de travail 2559, 3191, 3229, 3396, 3544, 3552, 3556, 3557, 3569, 3587, 3597, 3609, 3618, 3619, 3628, 3644, 3645, 3648, 3651, 3655, 3657-3659, 3661, 3663, 3665, 3671, 3678, 3791, 3868, 4439, 4443-4445, 4458, 4529, 4784
Migration forcée 814, 3561, 3627, 3666
Migration internationale 805, 2530, 2689, 3541, 3543, 3551, 3568, 3575, 3598, 3629, 3634, 3635, 3637, 3641, 3644, 3648, 3650, 3652-3654, 3658, 3659, 3661, 3664, 3665, 3668, 3673, 3678, 3681, 3683, 3684, 3686, 3791, 4252, 5325, 5678
Migration interne 2944, 3229, 3541, 3557, 3607, 3610, 3614-3616, 3620, 3622, 3627, 3725, 3894, 4439
Migration rurale-urbaine 2689, 3551, 3608, 3619, 3626, 3813, 3868, 3894, 3903, 3964, 4162, 4177
Migration saisonnière 3791
Migration urbaine-rurale 2718, 3618, 3725, 3866, 3868, 3904, 4168
Migrations alternantes 3608, 3969, 4130, 4143
Milieu culturel 4990
Milieu de travail 2229, 4383, 4389, 4400, 4687, 4692, 4693, 4701, 4703, 4710, 4718, 4730, 5283, 5584, 5630
Milieu familial 2947
Milieu rural 3877, 3925
Milieu social 9, 649, 660, 827, 1324, 1480, 2995, 3701, 4506, 5447
Milieu urbain 608, 3807, 3813, 3926, 4028, 4037, 4096, 4102, 4106, 4114, 4123, 4145, 4166
Milieux d'affaires 4385
Militaires 5339, 5345, 5346, 5348, 5352, 5353, 5356, 5359, 5360, 5415
  voir aussi: Soldat
Militaires et politique 5341
Militarisation 3070, 3630, 5361, 5459
Militarisme 5343
Mill, John Stuart 45, 4922
Mines antipersonnel 5445, 5988

INDEX DES MATIÈRES

Mines de charbon 4725
Mineurs 2339, 4843
Ministères 42
Minorités 168, 173, 857, 877, 903, 1000, 1059, 1531, 1723, 1806, 1812, 2025, 2042, 2151, 2188, 2273, 2461, 3077, 3286, 3424, 3453, 3471, 3499, 3511, 3515, 3555, 3920, 4005, 4089, 4398, 4472, 4491, 4497, 4606, 4628, 4641, 5139
voir aussi Protection internationale des minorités
Minorités culturelles 1755, 3479
Minorités ethniques 771, 1319, 1532, 1620, 1698, 1721, 1736, 1748, 1777, 1786, 1985, 1986, 2017, 2024, 2026, 2042, 2050, 2051, 2062, 2067, 2069, 2077, 2080, 2089, 2143, 2188, 2376, 2470, 2523, 2866, 2934, 3397, 3407, 3409, 3413, 3414, 3419, 3423-3426, 3428, 3433, 3447, 3458, 3460, 3467-3469, 3474, 3479, 3484, 3507, 3515, 3533, 3563, 3576, 3577, 3631, 3656, 3668, 3978, 3981, 3988, 4009, 4497, 4500, 4507, 5017, 5081, 5089, 5147, 5214, 5292, 5304, 5527, 5621, 5713
Minorités linguistiques 979, 1723, 1786, 1793, 1795, 1816, 1823, 2050, 2523, 3423
Minorités nationales 1004, 1812, 1845, 3421, 3424
Minorités religieuses 1441, 1519, 1532, 1536, 2143, 3397
Mise en œuvre d'une politique 43, 1094, 3810, 4043, 4069, 4108, 4667, 5200, 5638
Missionnaires 1258, 1392, 1397, 1490, 1492
Missions religieuses 1433, 1492
Mobilisation politique 994, 3814, 4974, 5242
Mobilisation sociale 2730, 3766, 3814, 5240, 5263-5265, 5273, 5280, 5969
Mobilité ascendante 2383
Mobilité de la main d'œuvre 2790, 3541, 3545, 3627, 3633, 3636, 3639, 4437, 4444, 4468, 4626, 4780, 4798, 4811
Mobilité descendante 2591
Mobilité géographique 2790, 3613, 3634, 3767, 4521
Mobilité professionnelle 2047, 2089, 2532, 3643, 4245, 4438, 4440, 4468, 4755, 4762, 4780, 5281
Mobilité résidentielle 3085, 3622, 3628, 4004, 4014, 4130, 5415
Mobilité sociale 448, 2314, 2383, 2420, 2434, 2435, 2517, 2591, 2594, 2926, 3085, 3571, 4245, 4474, 4583, 5268, 5302
Mode 1254, 1274, 1316, 1325, 1335, 3256, 3315, 3372

Modèles 2, 90, 308, 396, 456, 461, 472, 541, 644, 657, 705, 710, 713, 719, 722, 735, 775, 1006, 1036, 1039, 1042, 1574, 2354, 2458, 2477, 2588, 2681, 2747, 2788, 2850, 2900, 2905, 2920, 3025, 3194, 3218, 3289, 3396, 3625, 3744, 3749, 3784, 4073, 4124, 4244, 4581, 4800, 4963, 5117, 5610, 5675, 5677, 5845
Modèles à émuler 3254, 3264
Modèles culturels 1395, 2917
Modèles de croissance 3771, 4166
Modèles de décision 638
Modèles de développement 3771, 3811, 4205, 4279
Modèles d'équilibre 467
Modèles d'équilibre général appliqués 4045
Modèles dynamiques 445, 466, 1085, 2967
Modèles économétriques 4264, 4752, 5956
Modèles économiques 10, 3923, 4305, 4427, 4791
Modèles input-output 1059
Modèles linéaires 500, 4733
Modèles mathématiques 452, 461, 463-465, 467, 476, 479, 485, 486, 489, 635, 1069, 2108, 2815, 4185, 4527, 4614, 5157, 5987
Modèles spatiaux 39
Modèles statistiques 446, 468, 478, 479, 482, 489, 2116, 4486, 4766
Modèles stochastiques 446
Modélisation 2, 141, 376, 483, 484, 500, 1055, 1605, 1623, 2014, 2048, 2053, 2213, 2690, 2818, 3310, 3620, 3741, 4049, 4670, 4860, 5384
Modernisation 58, 367, 977, 1190, 1204, 1264, 1267, 1336, 1494, 1533, 1675, 1685, 1724, 1729, 2100, 2137, 2163, 2242, 2364, 2505, 2516, 2517, 2537, 2567, 2691, 2733, 3390, 3541, 3716, 3718, 3776, 3803, 3890, 3963, 4033, 4069, 4108, 4155, 4228, 4243, 4258, 4261, 4287, 4373, 4575, 4866, 4890, 4899, 4904, 4963, 4990, 5189, 5245, 5294, 5512, 5622, 5639
Modernisation politique 4041
Modernisme 543, 1158, 1164, 1250, 1258, 1266, 1279, 1523, 1855, 1864, 1941, 1962, 1988, 2558, 3132, 3949, 4131, 4143, 4288, 4904, 4918, 5180
Modernité 19, 58, 86, 125, 214, 243, 253, 277, 291, 315, 324, 327, 335, 338, 367, 372, 397, 926, 973, 1127, 1160, 1162, 1166, 1194, 1197, 1199, 1200, 1215, 1246, 1248, 1249, 1251, 1253, 1254, 1256, 1257, 1260-1263, 1265, 1267, 1272-1274, 1276, 1277, 1280, 1281, 1361, 1366, 1368,

567

SUBJECT INDEX IN FRENCH

1405, 1431, 1464, 1589, 1595, 1609, 1706, 1728, 1746, 1780, 1860, 1864, 1951, 2309, 2333, 2388, 2400, 2440, 2505, 2516, 2532, 2602, 2605, 3064, 3086, 3247, 3367, 3537, 3722, 3753, 3869, 3946, 4138, 4216, 4217, 4227, 4332, 4337, 4351, 4365, 4885, 4899, 4904, 5180, 5246, 5294, 5309
Modes de vie 1371, 1645, 2503, 2593, 2615, 2642, 2650, 2664, 2711, 2814, 3462, 3679, 3791, 4119, 4295, 4334, 4410, 4593
Modification institutionnelle 1993, 2242, 2292, 2679, 4055, 4085, 4354, 4885, 5629
Mokken, R.J. 423
Monarchie 955, 4954
Monastères 1516
Mondialisation 52, 134, 159, 379, 393, 397, 931, 953, 977, 1158, 1184, 1199, 1218, 1220, 1221, 1240, 1257, 1265, 1268, 1308, 1363, 1393, 1397, 1409, 1427, 1637, 1645, 1671, 1713, 1729, 1755, 1756, 1777, 1804, 1806, 1895, 1994, 2009, 2191, 2252, 2261, 2263, 2271, 2278, 2294, 2355, 2364, 2386, 2399, 2446, 2461, 2496, 2507, 2519, 2521, 2532, 2543-2549, 2551-2581, 3068, 3070, 3073, 3154, 3155, 3355, 3634, 3659, 3663, 3669, 3672, 3684, 3688, 3693, 3697, 3722, 3727, 3760, 3776, 3791, 3797, 3802, 3827, 3837, 3851, 3903, 3912, 3922, 3923, 3927, 3936, 3943, 3952, 3956, 4119, 4127, 4160, 4192, 4198, 4202, 4221, 4222, 4227, 4234, 4250, 4252, 4258, 4260, 4261, 4278, 4293, 4312, 4313, 4378, 4410, 4430, 4434, 4486, 4546, 4624, 4674, 4682, 4713, 4818, 4819, 4850, 4863, 4884, 4892, 4902, 4910, 4923, 4935, 4967, 4968, 4976, 5187, 5229, 5236, 5241, 5252, 5256, 5259, 5265, 5272, 5313, 5315, 5325, 5335, 5363, 5622, 5640, 5684, 5686
Monnaie et crédit 4348
Monnaies 4192, 4347
Monogamie 4994
Monographies 1557
Monolinguisme 1789, 2523
Monopoles 5821
Monothéisme 1406
Montagnes 1353, 2152, 3733, 3820, 3925
Montesquieu, Charles Louis 4288
Monuments historiques 996, 4081
Moore, George Edward 2350
Morale 131, 201, 205, 208, 211, 216, 224, 225, 227, 229, 238, 241, 255, 264-266, 270, 273, 274, 302, 333, 389, 673, 702, 733, 1259, 1388, 1402, 1420, 1850, 1867, 2350, 2361, 2365-2367, 2370, 2373, 2485, 3119, 4427, 4933, 4937, 5174, 5177, 5180, 5197, 5865, 5876, 5888
Morales 48, 227, 241, 255, 276, 346, 1564, 1665, 1955, 2001, 2343, 2344, 2356, 2366, 2367, 2485, 2503, 2587, 2734, 3182, 3749, 3930, 4244, 4418, 4636, 5210, 5316, 5865, 5868, 5876, 5940
Moralité 3, 16, 46, 131, 192, 207, 211, 216, 227, 228, 238, 241, 255, 264-266, 270, 276, 300, 367, 583, 638, 650, 673, 674, 706, 717, 899, 906, 909, 929, 934, 1245, 1258, 1259, 1382, 1387, 1388, 1402, 1420, 1427, 1460, 1482, 1505, 1591, 1731, 1850, 1867, 2021, 2160, 2181, 2203, 2213, 2332, 2342, 2343, 2346, 2349, 2351, 2353, 2355, 2356, 2359, 2361, 2362, 2365, 2367-2369, 2373, 2932, 3085, 3301, 3320, 3366, 3534, 3747, 3780, 4229, 4293, 4358, 4417, 4420, 4427, 4428, 4497, 4898, 4916, 4917, 4984, 4990, 5016, 5117, 5149-5151, 5158, 5174, 5177, 5180, 5181, 5197, 5208, 5210, 5316, 5327, 5355, 5371, 5568, 5679, 5730, 5849, 5854, 5855, 5863, 5871, 5876, 5883, 5886
Morbidité 327, 694, 788, 2046, 2602, 2778, 2810, 2811, 2814, 2817, 5407, 5727, 5765, 5773, 5804, 5809, 5820, 5897, 5964, 5968
Moreno, Rafael 2294
Morgenthau, Hans Joachim 346
Morphologie 4046, 4143, 4158
Morrison, Toni 1965
Mort 327, 685, 724, 740, 809, 948, 1081, 1347, 1383, 1398, 1719, 1735, 1883, 1886, 1937, 2807, 2816, 2820, 2826, 2827, 2831, 2842, 2942, 5323, 5327, 5380, 5434, 5817, 5850, 5862, 5877, 5879, 5887, 5889, 5890, 5895, 5896
Mortalité 327, 478, 685, 1081, 1544, 2686, 2691, 2695, 2696, 2703, 2719, 2722, 2780, 2783, 2787, 2807, 2810, 2811, 2813-2815, 2817-2820, 2824, 2826, 2827, 2829-2835, 2837-2840, 2842-2844, 3202, 3622, 4304, 5756, 5773, 5838, 5897, 5956, 5968, 5983
Mortalité des enfants 2703, 2780, 2821-2823, 2825, 2828, 2839, 2994
Mortalité infantile 419, 2698, 2738, 2783, 2787, 2822, 2839, 2841, 3039, 5959
Motivation 276, 561, 648, 657, 665, 667, 684, 704, 725, 822, 946, 1021, 1022, 1061, 1066, 1071, 1084, 1157, 1285, 1293, 2059, 2141, 2285, 2368, 2788, 3042, 3183,

INDEX DES MATIÈRES

3667, 4180, 4391, 4597, 4707, 4709, 4768, 4794, 4802, 4886, 5397, 5406, 5460, 5470
Motivation au travail 4702, 4736
Motivation d'accomplissement
    voir: Réussite intellectuelle
Motocyclettes 1851
Mots 197, 210, 624, 659, 1757, 1822, 2313, 3205
Moulins 4446
Mounsi 1949
Mouvements agrariens 5245
Mouvements antinucléaires 5275
Mouvements contestataires 3777, 3827, 3954, 4039, 4848, 5235, 5236, 5265, 5266, 5274, 5275
Mouvements de libération 4864
Mouvements de résistance 2339, 2563
Mouvements écologiques 3729, 3749, 3827, 5244, 5252, 5255, 5272, 5275
Mouvements étudiants 1264, 2250, 2251, 2293, 2294, 2567, 3295, 5267, 5268
Mouvements féministes 1463, 1549, 2586, 2730, 2870, 2997, 3079, 3080, 3105, 3106, 3112, 3115, 3122, 3134, 3161, 3162, 4857, 5200, 5258, 5260
Mouvements indépendantistes 951
Mouvements littéraires 1932
Mouvements nationalistes 1935, 3425, 5263
Mouvements ouvriers 2339, 4834, 4879, 5261
Mouvements pacifistes 5275
Mouvements paysans 3891, 5245, 5261
Mouvements politiques 1010, 1453, 2573, 3162, 3391, 4558, 4960, 5226, 5233, 5234, 5241, 5242, 5247, 5258, 5265, 5266, 5269, 5270, 5275, 5276, 5280
    voir aussi: Mouvements antinucléaires
Mouvements pour les droits de l'homme 5805
Mouvements religieux 56, 1384, 1394, 1397, 1401, 1418, 1425, 1430, 1448, 1450, 1457, 1463, 1485, 1495, 1500, 1501, 1509, 1538, 1541, 1543, 3650, 5272, 5274
Mouvements sociaux 799, 1010, 1087, 2010, 2514, 2522, 2634, 2730, 3070, 3137, 3154, 3162, 3391, 3454, 3766, 3771, 3775, 3827, 3968, 4242, 4398, 4832, 4853, 4867, 4871, 4898, 4949, 4950, 4960, 4963, 4966, 4989, 5183, 5226, 5228, 5229, 5241, 5244, 5246-5260, 5262, 5264-5266, 5269-5273, 5275-5280, 5419, 5887
Mouvements travaillistes 2339, 2416, 2507, 2563, 2586, 4433, 4821, 4823, 4832, 4834, 4839, 4841, 4843, 4850, 4851, 4853, 4859, 4863, 4864, 4867, 4869, 4871, 4876, 5265
Mouvements urbains 3954, 3968, 5270, 5275
Moyen âge 1789
Moyens de transport 4062
Multiculturalisme 206, 322, 393, 395, 643, 806, 954, 996, 1164, 1174, 1226, 1483, 1535, 1592, 1721, 1865, 2212, 2240, 2326, 2380, 2399, 2433, 2436, 2480, 2532, 2550, 2554, 2917, 3155, 3397, 3401, 3405, 3430, 3435, 3444, 3460, 3488-3490, 3494, 3497, 3500, 3501, 3517, 3519, 3522, 3653, 3716, 3789, 4002, 4012, 4902, 4905, 4966, 5248, 5317, 5320, 5791, 5973
Multimédia 1634, 1658, 1688
Mumford, Lewis 1674
Murphy, Liam 4921
Musées 996, 1558, 2481
Musiciens 651, 1338, 1977, 1982, 1988, 4148, 4767
Musicologie 1972, 1982, 1989
Musique 835, 1309, 1310, 1319, 1331, 1338, 1348, 1745, 1856, 1865, 1878, 1971-1975, 1978-1980, 1982-1984, 1986, 1987, 2233, 3115, 3156, 3391, 3427, 4344
    voir aussi: Ethnomusicologie, Histoire de la musique, Sociologie de la musique
Musique folklorique 1973
Musique pop 1745, 1975, 1982, 1985
Musique populaire 1309, 1331, 1338, 1351, 1364, 1370, 1971, 1981, 1982, 1986, 4148
Musique religieuse 1975, 1983
Musique rock 1309, 1352, 1364
Musique traditionnelle 1973
Musulmans 280, 771, 1392, 1422, 1519, 1521, 1524, 1527-1535, 1537-1540, 1775, 1777, 2029, 2520, 2554, 2612, 2978, 3067, 3115, 3172, 3207, 3266, 3468, 3471, 3557, 3562, 4352
Mutilation génitale 3471
Mysticisme 256, 1308
Mythes 20, 155, 172, 249, 956, 961, 967, 980, 1167, 1576, 1965, 1969, 2317, 2328, 3115, 3186, 3638
Mythologie 977, 986, 1227, 1406
Naissance 551, 796, 800, 807, 2632, 2728, 2757, 2758, 2771, 2776, 2791, 2803, 2812, 2832, 2839, 2962, 2971, 2998, 3000, 3046, 5578, 5610, 5782, 5843
Nancy, Jean-Luc 205
Narcissisme 586, 803, 1699, 2327
Narration d'histoires 919, 1717, 2643
Natalité 2724

SUBJECT INDEX IN FRENCH

Nation 173, 965, 970, 971, 981, 987, 992, 1192, 1589, 1762, 1886, 1951, 2553, 2567, 3067, 3070, 3251, 3421, 3499, 3534, 3779, 4924, 4930, 4959
Nationalisme 187, 240, 966-968, 970, 971, 977, 980, 984, 985, 991, 992, 1000, 1193, 1195, 1227, 1330, 1358, 1359, 1369, 1607, 1731, 1736, 1762, 1794, 1813, 1819, 1845, 1934, 1936, 1951, 1979, 2177, 2218, 2306, 2326, 2532, 2557, 2567, 2630, 2795, 3067, 3070, 3112, 3242, 3269, 3383, 3419-3421, 3426, 3473, 3485, 3492, 3493, 3497, 3499, 4918, 4919, 4924, 4935, 4939, 4966, 5159, 5214, 5263, 5295
Nationalisme culturel 1188
Nationalité 18, 147, 981, 987, 1003, 1192, 1243, 1881, 2838, 3009, 3072, 3401, 3409, 3426, 3437, 3487, 3533, 3605
Nations Unies 1923, 2602, 3173, 4267, 5361
  voir aussi: Conventions des Nations Unies
Naturalisation 3563, 4964, 5535
Naturalisme 22, 257, 284, 285, 1558, 2368
Nature 22, 135, 199, 204, 221, 225, 257, 271, 284, 292, 362, 575, 608, 1176, 1225, 1563, 1567, 1574, 1591, 1621, 3014, 3131, 3152, 3306, 3696, 3698, 3700, 3703, 3710, 3721, 3744, 3748, 3749, 3753, 3783, 3839, 3851, 3926, 4108, 4138, 4227
Nature humaine 390, 1073, 1188, 2350, 3038, 3351, 3749, 5468
Navaho 5411
Navigation 58
Nazisme 165, 189, 326, 410, 1004, 1902, 2567, 3502, 3518, 3532, 3631, 4973, 5312
Nee, Victor 4241
Néerlandais 1798
Négociation 944, 999, 1006, 1010, 1012, 1015, 1017, 1018, 1021, 1022, 1024, 1040, 1049, 1055, 1084, 1345, 1704, 1829, 2079, 2908, 3472, 4690, 4751, 4837, 4868, 5184
Négociation collective 2079, 4537, 4550, 4751, 4815, 4824, 4828, 4829, 4841, 4842, 4850, 4855, 4870, 4876, 4880
Négociations salariales 4824, 4842
Négotiations de paix 5317
Négritude 1942
Néocolonialisme 1308, 3782, 4935
Néoinstitutionalisme 4346, 5641
Néolibéralisme 1994, 2018, 2263, 2292, 2507, 2513, 2558, 2563, 2564, 3140, 3537, 3750, 3880, 3912, 4206, 4208, 4211, 4227, 4230, 4250, 4269, 4373, 4817, 4867, 4892, 4910, 4949, 4952, 5232, 5261, 5630, 5971

Neurologie 589, 591, 596, 628, 630, 5406, 5410
Neutralité 683, 801, 1025, 5184
Névroses 593, 731, 743
New Deal 2459, 4097, 5624
Newcastle, T.M. 370
Nietzsche, Friedrich 241, 251, 263, 264, 267, 278, 298, 319
Nihilisme 241, 267, 1249
Nishida, Kitaro 265
Niveau de l'emploi 4505, 4881
Niveau de vie 1177, 2123, 2695, 2833, 3661, 3984, 4163, 4250, 4263, 4272, 4276, 4295, 4299, 4334, 4606, 4947, 5286, 5598
Niveau des salaires 4459, 4460, 4679, 4723
Niveau du chômage 4592, 4685
Niveaux d'enseignement 1494, 2031, 2037, 2041, 2072, 2333, 2756, 2760, 2852, 2948, 3279, 3670, 3671, 3748, 4447, 4583, 4595, 4717, 4755, 5578, 5757, 5838
Noblesse 263, 4954
Noguchi, Shika 3035
Noirs 53, 579, 710, 835, 1367, 1474, 1479, 1813, 1903, 1917, 2017, 2034, 2060, 2080, 2110, 2161, 2856, 3115, 3412, 3440, 3442, 3454, 3464, 3468, 3478, 3519, 3834, 3835, 3901, 3978, 3981, 3993, 4000, 4015, 4278, 4438, 4489, 4490, 4492, 4497, 4559, 4865, 5031, 5053, 5129, 5142, 5148, 5328, 5454, 5947
Nom de famille 3394
Nomades 1340, 3128, 3539
Nombre 619, 4346
Noms 118, 258
Non-violence 1025
Normal 5891
Normalisation 1794, 1826, 2214, 2448, 4601, 5763
Normes culturelles 888, 1508, 2021, 2134, 2349, 2821, 2929
Normes de qualité 2214, 2253, 2260, 2275, 5743
Normes sociales 243, 458, 650, 894, 1034, 1112, 1482, 1993, 2082, 2271, 2308, 2313, 2345, 2353, 2356, 2358, 2363-2365, 2369, 2373, 2375, 2421, 2661, 2755, 2799, 2880, 2920, 2929, 2990, 3199, 3307, 3806, 3847, 3946, 3969, 4180, 4240, 4295, 4457, 4581, 4793, 5122, 5128, 5164, 5335, 5368
Norvégien 3595
Nostalgie 814, 974, 3728
Nourriture 419, 941, 1293, 1297, 3546, 5494, 5959, 5961
Nouvelle droite 2100

Index des matières

Nouvelle gauche 4587, 5251
Nouvelles 1671, 1683, 1691, 1730, 1741, 1742, 1750, 1766, 1771, 3498, 5329
Nudité 2912
Nuptialité 2691, 2695, 2698, 2724, 2769, 2963
Nussbaum, Martha C. 5034
Nutrition 419, 2022, 2715, 5541, 5768, 5959, 5961, 5969
Objectifs de l'éducation 2139
Objection de conscience 5324, 5855
Objectivité 109, 126, 169, 215, 255, 261, 310, 399, 498, 605, 645, 1005, 1571, 1628, 1705, 2365, 5692
Objet 300, 406, 619, 1832
Obligation 4909, 4937
Obligation politique 4909, 5305
Obligations 3115, 4350
O'Brien, Edna 1936
Observation 45, 55, 194, 528, 617, 630, 2893, 5084
Observation participante 1005, 1912
Obstacles au développement 2539
Occidentalisation 1183, 1185, 1699, 1702, 2569
Occultisme 1416, 1511
OCDE 2679, 5514
Œuvre dramatique 171, 249, 1170, 1331, 1695, 1874, 1877, 1964, 2458
Œuvres d'art 1247, 1866, 1869, 1876
Œuvres littéraires 200, 1224, 1913, 1932, 1941, 3250
Offre 4136, 4380
  voir aussi: Approvisionnement en eau, Disponibilités alimentaires
Offre de main d'œuvre 4466, 4476, 4535, 4547, 4553, 4561
Offre et demande 4322
Oiseaux 3710, 4767
Oléoducs 3813
Oligarchie 4683, 4853
Ontogénie 1161
Ontologie 22, 29, 140, 213, 218, 225, 232, 250, 254, 266, 267, 284, 286, 360, 490, 563, 617, 847, 1216, 1270, 1391, 1571, 1628, 1871, 2300, 2609, 2809, 3744, 3750
Opéra 1318, 1971
Opérations bancaires 4705
Opérations sans bourse délier 929
Ophtalmologie 628
Opiat 5392, 5395, 5401
Opinion 470, 520, 1173, 1925, 2183, 2215, 2357, 2490, 2538, 2991, 3031, 3545, 3633, 4361, 4723, 5201, 5289, 5291, 5298, 5303, 5423, 5941

Opinion politique 2593, 3809, 4898, 5286, 5298
Opinion publique 455, 502, 519, 524, 534, 535, 537, 963, 978, 1004, 1327, 1658, 1705, 1719, 1731, 1747, 1752, 1781, 2311, 2396, 2401, 2857, 2922, 3352, 3522, 3527, 3706, 3734, 3983, 4090, 4094, 4145, 4847, 5083, 5135, 5143, 5186, 5186, 5200, 5213, 5214, 5218, 5219, 5255, 5289, 5290, 5329, 5426, 5783, 5891
Opposition politique 189, 4850, 4898, 5226, 5240, 5275, 5284, 5320
Optimisme 675, 1008, 3739
Options sur valeurs mobilières 4352
Orchestres 1100
Ordinateurs 37, 92, 458, 576, 634, 1036, 1339, 1634, 1660, 1664, 1667, 1669, 1676, 1678, 1681, 1688, 1692, 1693, 1779, 2056, 2172, 2197, 2201, 2210, 2223, 2314, 2554, 2581, 2667, 4387, 5228, 5230, 5288, 5901
Ordre mondial 2580, 3452
Ordre politique 28, 2140
Ordre public 2532, 4683, 4991, 4993, 4996, 5048, 5061, 5091
Ordre social 28, 458, 1047, 2140, 2315, 2634, 3512, 3833, 4255, 4933, 4976, 4990, 4995, 5009, 5130, 5151, 5343, 5445, 5451
Ordres 3886
Ordres chrétiens
  voir: Dominicains, Jésuite
Ordres religieux 1521
Organes 5871, 5878, 5883
Organisation 359, 396, 439, 1113, 1141, 1142, 1145, 1148, 1157, 1282, 1316, 1993, 2088, 3097, 4322, 4409, 4412, 4419, 4510, 4569, 4646, 4659, 4732, 4733, 4821, 4837, 4856, 4860, 4871, 5148, 5202, 5265, 5732, 5798, 5903
  voir aussi Organisations complexes, Organisme social, Sociologie des organisations
Organisation administrative 5758
Organisation communautaire 3431, 3827, 3836, 3858, 3861
Organisation du travail 397, 1040, 1091, 1117, 2125, 3062, 3568, 4357, 4362, 4365, 4389, 4395, 4398, 4401, 4544, 4618, 4634, 4643, 4647, 4650, 4652, 4838, 4872
Organisation industrielle 154, 4838, 4879
Organisation mondiale de la santé 2814, 3827, 5407, 5904, 5911
Organisation mondiale du commerce 2547, 3827, 4935, 5265

SUBJECT INDEX IN FRENCH

Organisations 49, 306, 386, 1008, 1029, 1033, 1040, 1064, 1068, 1076, 1080, 1088, 1090-1093, 1102-1104, 1109, 1110, 1112, 1114-1116, 1120-1124, 1126, 1127, 1137, 1138, 1144-1146, 1148, 1151-1156, 1200, 1384, 1635, 1660, 1701, 1718, 1957, 2307, 2450, 3062, 3097, 3154, 3246, 3416, 3775, 3803, 3828, 3853, 3863, 4100, 4355, 4386, 4397, 4402, 4422, 4468, 4483, 4622, 4628, 4640, 4644, 4648, 4654, 4657, 4669, 4672, 4673, 4680, 4718, 4728, 4729, 4734, 4767, 4847, 4861, 4876, 4940, 5276, 5279, 5283, 5400, 5478, 5732, 5767, 5794, 5798, 5799, 5854
  voir aussi: Culture organisationnelle
Organisations à but non-lucratif 61, 411, 931, 1035, 1100, 3877, 4235, 4512, 4667, 4768, 5478, 5484, 5486, 5491, 5775, 5816
Organisations africaines 4611
Organisations bénévoles 61, 1035, 1156, 1673, 2371, 2595, 2631, 3827, 3856, 4235, 4390, 4768, 4948, 5491, 5574, 5720, 5775
Organisations complexes 4622
Organisations de jeunesse 2614
Organisations féminines 3070, 4467
Organisations internationales 87, 2292, 3803, 4279
Organisations non-gouvernementales 1485, 3089, 3423, 3611, 3624, 3813, 3922, 3927, 4169, 4940, 4948, 4967, 5279, 5716, 5805
Organisations patronales 4814
Organisations professionnelles 4782
Organisations régionales
  voir: Organisations africaines
Organisme social 277, 893, 1238, 1324, 1415, 1469, 1481, 1500, 1656, 2302, 2309, 2364, 2395, 2426, 2462, 2917, 3171, 3368, 3518, 3528, 3783, 3858, 4195, 4313, 4373, 4511, 4979, 5016, 5085, 5091, 5231
Organismes d'aide 5330
Orientalisme 1165, 1209, 1566, 1699, 1978, 3094, 3497
Orientation aux valeurs 1203
Orientation professionnelle 48, 1726
Origine sociale 4229, 4781, 5284
Orphelinats 5576
Orphelins 2901
OTAN 1730, 1731, 5327, 5340
Ouvrages de référence 36, 81-83, 85-87, 90, 91, 93, 95-103, 105, 566, 1617, 1703, 2067
Ouvriers industriels 4618

Ouvriers qualifiés 1806, 2270, 3545, 3629, 3633, 3645, 3791, 4431, 4834, 5674
Ouvriers sexuels 2561, 3323, 3326, 3327, 3334, 3348, 4387, 4979, 5200, 5366, 5545, 5745, 5943
Pacification 5344, 5362
Pacifisme 5327
Paganisme 1392, 1421, 1539
Paiement 4539, 4676, 4679, 4704, 5217
  voir aussi: Égalité de rémunération
Paiements 927, 5552
Paix 57, 105, 161, 1007, 1008, 1014, 4931, 5465
  voir aussi: Accord de paix
Palestiniens 985, 1014, 1026, 1077, 1791, 2177, 2619, 3499
Panafricanisme 5328
Panique 731
Panislamisme 1543
Pantomime 1787
Paradigmes 27, 46, 54, 170, 182, 399, 821, 837, 858, 1025, 1150, 1194, 1197, 1431, 1489, 1607, 1625, 1630, 2502, 2508, 3090, 3497, 3749, 3952, 4360, 4612, 5244
Parapsychologie 540, 1780
Parcs nationaux 3754, 3763, 3822
Parenté 1267, 2426, 2582, 2802, 2901, 2902, 2930, 2938, 3646, 3791, 3899, 4212, 4253, 4725, 5168, 5390, 5536, 5573, 5587, 5590, 5962
Parents 900, 1494, 2029, 2054, 2065, 2155, 2230, 2236, 2347, 2360, 2425, 2463, 2464, 2488, 2592, 2593, 2603, 2757, 2847, 2859, 2872, 2894, 2896, 2899, 2916, 2929, 2934, 2974, 2994, 2996, 3000, 3001, 3006, 3009, 3012, 3017, 3022, 3024, 3037-3039, 3045, 3351, 3364, 4985, 5052, 5386, 5572, 5577, 5667, 5669, 5689, 5925, 5936
  voir aussi: Beaux-parents
Parents actifs 5624
Parlement 3286, 4975, 5213
Paroisse 1502
Parole 378, 703, 818, 901, 1639, 1642, 1647, 1650, 1653, 1788-1790, 1807, 1808, 1810, 1815, 1827, 1829, 1830, 1840, 1846, 1872, 1877, 2523, 2940, 3002, 5184, 5444
Parrainage 2901
Parsons, Talcott 373, 375, 400
Partage des risques 5931
Partage du travail 4685
Partenariat public-privé 2139, 3813, 4035, 4088, 4105, 4995, 5969
Parti pris 109, 460, 507, 512, 806, 832, 837, 881, 1005, 2250, 5235

INDEX DES MATIÈRES

Participation au groupe 1072, 2371
Participation au marché du travail 2399, 2624, 2677, 2971, 3127, 3168, 3169, 3224, 3237, 3279, 3549, 3553, 3568, 3582, 3643, 3677, 3996, 4368, 4437, 4438, 4452, 4454, 4466, 4480, 4481, 4487, 4500, 4504, 4505, 4517, 4518, 4522-4524, 4528, 4532, 4553, 4554, 4558, 4561, 4572, 4573, 4582, 4590, 4687, 4694, 4696, 5365, 5626, 5648
Participation de la citoyenneté 61, 1608, 2218, 2631, 3824, 3825, 3844, 3927, 3965, 4255, 4768, 5107, 5257
Participation de la collectivité 20, 2127, 2213, 2371, 2529, 3553, 3807, 3810, 3813, 3824, 3825, 3836, 3841, 3844, 3845, 3847, 3856, 3861, 3885, 4066, 4096, 4119, 4169, 4486, 4940, 5288, 5716, 5985
Participation des femmes 1925, 3160, 3193
Participation des travailleurs 4812, 4838, 4839
Participation électorale 472, 5304
Participation politique 71, 955, 1517, 1535, 1939, 2317, 2386, 2461, 2513, 2671, 2674, 3103, 3391, 3545, 3829, 3830, 3863, 3959, 4879, 4914, 4927, 4940, 4956, 4958, 4960, 4974, 5024, 5228, 5257, 5281, 5286, 5292, 5305, 5642
voir aussi: Activisme
Participation religieuse 1429, 1461, 1467, 1529, 3844, 4962
Participation sociale 71, 383, 687, 952, 1755, 1764, 2115, 2353, 2456, 2634, 2674, 2675, 2954, 3599, 3844, 3973, 4006, 4159, 4722, 4768, 4817, 5642
Partis chrétiens démocrates 5219
Partis communistes 1910, 4942
Partis conservateurs 3983
Partis de droite 3452, 5243, 5256
Partis de gauche 3137
Partis libéraux 5219
Partis politiques 3070, 4293, 4596, 5219, 5234, 5265, 5269
Partis socialistes 4293
Partis socio-démocrates 955, 4293, 4859
Partis travaillistes 1891, 2458, 3808, 3827, 4008, 5609
Parure 3315
Passage à la vie active 2626
Passé 148, 150, 158, 166, 182, 196, 222, 353, 549, 793, 799, 951, 963, 974, 975, 994, 1008, 1413, 1965, 4800
Passions 314, 897
Pastoralisme 2790
Paternalisme 5838, 5889

Paternité 2608, 2998, 3005, 3008, 3025, 3046, 3051, 5567
Paternité-maternité 77, 545, 756, 792, 849, 1761, 1998, 2035, 2488, 2608, 2854, 2884, 2897, 2898, 2901, 2911, 2915, 2916, 2932, 3004, 3005, 3007, 3011, 3013-3015, 3017, 3018, 3024-3026, 3030-3032, 3034, 3036, 3038-3040, 3043-3045, 3047-3051, 3054-3056, 3237, 3249, 3358, 3391, 4765, 5050, 5396, 5510, 5546, 5550, 5552, 5559, 5589, 5594, 5634, 5667, 5669, 5689, 5906
Pathologie 738, 739, 750, 2937, 5377, 5968
Patriarcat 967, 1277, 1296, 1549, 2880, 3089, 3096, 3138, 3173, 3186, 3187, 3240, 3251, 3262, 3313, 3793, 5058
Patrimoine culturel 280, 965, 974, 996, 1172, 1227, 1367, 1845, 1960, 1973, 3406, 3443, 3477, 3589, 3854, 4081, 4133, 5529, 5577
voir aussi: Préservation du patrimoine culturel
Patriotisme 962, 975, 2614, 5256
Patrizi, Francesco 156
Patronage 2314
Paupérisation 4277
Pauvres 608, 1747, 2375, 2397, 2746, 2878, 3667, 3992, 4020, 4246, 4263, 4299, 4300, 5082, 5279, 5366, 5565, 5653, 5971
Pauvreté 808, 1493, 1536, 1747, 1923, 1994, 2046, 2266, 2385, 2397, 2432, 2532, 2561, 2577, 2585, 2638, 2712, 2713, 2725, 2789, 2843, 2881, 3035, 3089, 3323, 3416, 3694, 3776, 3814, 3833, 3840, 3961, 3992, 4006-4009, 4021, 4157, 4189, 4191, 4216, 4217, 4227, 4246, 4247, 4249, 4251, 4252, 4257, 4259, 4263-4266, 4268-4270, 4277, 4280-4284, 4286, 4290, 4296, 4298-4300, 4307-4309, 4353, 4373, 4394, 4430, 4453, 4470, 4474, 4495, 4587, 4593, 4606, 4950, 4991, 5018, 5050, 5053, 5057, 5063, 5082, 5146, 5279, 5366, 5416, 5419, 5423, 5425, 5428, 5431, 5465, 5475, 5493, 5565, 5567, 5575, 5592, 5593, 5611, 5618, 5633, 5642, 5643, 5650, 5653, 5654, 5666, 5686, 5700, 5759, 5968
voir aussi: Réduction de pauvreté
Pauvreté rurale 2793, 3619, 3776, 3869, 3871, 3884, 3895, 3897, 3902, 3905, 4246, 4248, 4270, 4309, 5279
Pauvreté urbaine 58, 3842, 3927, 3967, 3989, 3992, 3997, 4006, 4007, 4011, 4087, 4169, 4246, 4470, 4991, 5053
Pays d'accueil 3567

SUBJECT INDEX IN FRENCH

Pays de l'Est 4631
Pays développés 1177, 2712, 3770, 5348, 5870
Pays en développement 92, 1177, 1195, 1620, 1702, 2078, 2112, 2113, 2144, 2186, 2432, 2483, 2513, 2712, 2747, 2750, 2763, 2767, 2770, 2771, 2793, 2820, 2836, 2963, 3067, 3085, 3090, 3103, 3148, 3160, 3211, 3238, 3378, 3610, 3637, 3702, 3714, 3759, 3770, 3802, 3804, 3815, 3961, 3964, 3972, 4102, 4116, 4161, 4163, 4169, 4172, 4205, 4258, 4267, 4276, 4280, 4287, 4430, 4571, 4644, 5057, 5229, 5260, 5282, 5363, 5445, 5655, 5684, 5768, 5802, 5813, 5870, 5980
Pays industrialisés 1620, 2113, 4618, 5819
Pays islamiques 4352
Pays moins développés 2397, 2432, 2638, 2786, 3629, 3637, 4170
Pays multiethniques 903, 2436, 2530, 3428, 3430, 3445
Pays nouvellement industrialisés 3671, 4228
Pays occidentaux 35, 191, 1384, 1464, 1486, 2930, 3084, 3117, 3452, 3949, 4631, 5005, 5968
Paysage 1362, 1589, 1936, 3689, 3719, 3728, 3753, 3777, 3779, 3851, 3879, 3882, 3941, 3970, 4059, 4141, 4145
Paysannerie 355, 3891, 4206
Paysans 1476, 2345, 2426, 3888, 3896, 3919, 3920, 4275
Péché 1460
Pêche côtière 3913
Pédagogie 15, 225, 574, 930, 1018, 1196, 1819, 1879, 1902, 2000, 2009, 2011, 2014, 2053, 2081, 2099, 2101, 2103, 2105, 2112, 2121, 2125, 2145, 2164, 2171-2173, 2175-2177, 2180-2182, 2184, 2185, 2188, 2189, 2191-2193, 2200-2202, 2206-2208, 2213, 2215-2217, 2220-2224, 2237, 2247, 2284, 2299, 3115, 3435, 3869
Peformance
 voir: Rendement du travail
Peine de mort 4999, 5001, 5043, 5152, 5155
Peinture 1852, 1861, 1869, 3139, 4767
Peirce, Charles Sanders 494
Pèlerinages 1399, 1433, 1499
Pénétration du marché 4407
Pensée des lumières 123, 242, 247, 248, 256, 315, 372, 1158, 1248, 1578, 1970
Pensée économique 3797, 4179, 4194, 4216, 4336, 4916
Pensée philosophique 12, 111, 114, 124-126, 133, 139, 142, 145, 201, 202, 204, 205, 207, 208, 211, 212, 215-218, 222, 224, 225, 230, 234-237, 240, 241, 244, 250, 257, 258, 262-267, 272, 273, 275, 279, 280, 282, 283, 288-290, 293, 295-298, 405, 563, 645, 1158, 1160, 1176, 1280, 1374, 1382, 1386, 1402, 1404, 1413, 1423, 1426, 1456, 1466, 1591, 1596, 1599, 1828, 1854, 1864, 1871, 1876, 2303, 2327, 2538, 3108, 3129, 3953, 4898, 4929, 5849
Pensée politique 224, 278, 335, 1199, 3144, 4210, 4884, 4888, 4894, 4898, 4899, 4902, 4905-4907, 4909, 4911, 4913, 4915, 4916, 4925, 4927, 4928, 4932, 4941, 4960, 5188, 5207
Pensée religieuse 145, 211, 233, 266, 272, 293, 1374, 1379, 1381, 1386, 1388, 1402, 1404, 1419, 1435, 1442, 1444, 1449, 1451, 1457, 1458, 1477, 1478, 1501, 1867
Pensée scientifique 214, 1391, 1555, 1569, 1580, 1589, 1600, 1619, 1627, 1630
Pensions de retraite 4353
Pentecôtisme 1431, 1474, 1482, 1507
Pénurie de main d'œuvre 2270, 3633
Perception 233, 327, 551, 573, 589, 611, 615, 620, 630, 634, 639, 643, 646, 654, 658, 714, 827, 849, 855, 859, 865, 866, 876, 884, 885, 891, 905, 918, 928, 942, 1086, 1096, 1105, 1112, 1144, 1177, 1606, 1719, 1819, 1820, 1859, 1871, 1942, 1989, 2008, 2055, 2195, 2218, 2360, 2397, 2473, 2628, 2629, 2670, 2755, 2836, 2913, 3021, 3042, 3287, 3462, 3478, 3496, 3727, 3748, 3930, 3970, 4145, 4351, 4484, 4487, 4631, 4673, 4701, 4702, 4717, 4785, 5283, 5308, 5426, 5542, 5543, 5690, 5830, 5894
Perception d'autrui 219, 552, 657, 840, 844, 851, 867, 878, 894, 937, 983, 1186, 1230, 1525, 1528, 1776, 2205, 2301, 2313, 3562, 3649
Perception de soi 142, 548, 549, 557, 562, 580, 609, 675, 679, 697, 801, 828, 874, 880, 896, 936, 960, 999, 1156, 1186, 1367, 1446, 2625, 2667, 2677, 3049, 3402, 3432, 4775, 5773
Perception sociale 607, 831, 850, 889, 895, 1173, 2393, 2755, 4111, 4188
Perception visuelle 444, 628, 645, 664, 1767, 1827, 2481, 3970
Père 1991, 2628, 2629, 2846, 2847, 2884, 3008, 3021, 3025, 3036, 3042, 3044, 3049, 3054, 3239, 5566, 5567
Performance du groupe 1056, 1072, 1096, 4670

INDEX DES MATIÈRES

Performance individuelle 651, 665, 725, 843, 1012, 2072, 4631, 4664
Périodiques 56, 1351, 1557, 1662, 1722, 1726, 1744, 2645, 3374, 3636, 3827, 3931
Permissivité sexuelle 3300
Personnalité 88, 241, 326, 561, 565, 569, 578, 586-589, 606, 673, 675, 678-680, 682, 684, 687, 690, 691, 694, 696-700, 702, 704, 707-714, 716, 719-721, 725-730, 733, 735, 742, 760, 787, 790, 827, 840, 842, 870, 873, 910, 914, 920, 928, 933, 937, 949, 1003, 1007, 1057, 1061, 1147, 1486, 1967, 2304, 2318, 2970, 3004, 3021, 3022, 3034, 3055, 3212, 3351, 4188, 4199, 4339, 4391, 4407, 4588, 4625, 4638, 4719, 4720, 4722, 4800, 5393, 5670, 5899
Personnel 411, 1010, 2240, 4662, 5919
Personnel hospitalier 5842
Personnel médical 907, 2487, 2497, 4999, 5651, 5690, 5726, 5736, 5762, 5771, 5772, 5825, 5826, 5835, 5840-5842, 5846, 5889, 5896, 5910, 5953, 5980
Personnes mariées 2969, 2990, 4457, 4557
Perspective mondiale 982, 2218, 2477, 2538, 3727, 3879, 4207, 4360, 4962
Persuasion 1730, 3749, 4199
Perte 716, 724, 815, 819, 948, 2910, 2942, 5721
Perte d'emploi 4439, 4484, 4579, 4594, 4737
Pessimisme 675, 691, 725, 1008, 4145
Pesticides 4674
Petite bourgeoisie 3164, 3973
Petite enfance 2641
Petites entreprises agricoles 2653, 3907
Petites et moyennes entreprises 1170, 3069, 3545, 3599, 4371, 4372, 4382, 4394, 4407, 4417, 4577, 4665, 4799
Petites villes 2841, 4119
Petits enfants 551, 659, 2609, 2828, 2895, 3002, 3020, 3027, 3034, 3622, 5872, 5947, 5950
Peur 591, 685, 752, 858, 1173, 2860, 2886, 3287, 3293, 3403, 3781, 3937, 3957, 5010, 5059-5061, 5070, 5080-5082, 5093, 5101, 5106, 5114, 5465, 5466, 5712
Phénoménologie 161, 215, 218, 224, 225, 228, 232, 236, 250, 310, 312, 599, 645, 746, 1419, 1682, 1725, 1953, 2422, 2609, 3129, 3146, 3695
Philanthropie 61, 996, 3844, 5476
Philippins 60, 1943, 2936, 3191, 3317, 3392, 3642, 3644, 4443, 4935
Phillips, D.Z. 1428
Philologie 241, 1798, 2009

Philosophes 12, 121, 126, 139, 145, 200, 201, 208, 211, 215, 218-220, 225, 230, 235, 240, 249, 251, 256, 262, 265, 266, 273, 282, 288, 296, 298, 299, 340, 344, 405, 1552, 1555, 2361, 3108, 5180
Philosophie 12, 21, 29, 54, 68, 83, 89, 106-108, 110-113, 118, 120, 121, 128-131, 133, 136, 138-142, 144-146, 151, 152, 156, 158, 160, 161, 193, 199-203, 208-224, 226, 228, 229, 231, 233-242, 244-248, 250-253, 257, 259-266, 268, 269, 272, 273, 275-278, 280-284, 286-289, 291, 292, 294, 296-298, 300, 301, 303-305, 311, 312, 315-318, 332, 333, 335, 340-342, 344, 351, 357, 367, 385, 403, 404, 407, 490, 568, 596, 617, 645, 701, 702, 728, 906, 909, 913, 934, 1028, 1124, 1176, 1188, 1195, 1204, 1206, 1216, 1231, 1239, 1247, 1248, 1250, 1253, 1256, 1259, 1266, 1271, 1276, 1289, 1292, 1379, 1382, 1387, 1388, 1420, 1423, 1426, 1449, 1456, 1458, 1464, 1466, 1473, 1552, 1563, 1569, 1578, 1579, 1583, 1586, 1593, 1596, 1599, 1600, 1602, 1611, 1615, 1638, 1655, 1706, 1828, 1832, 1848, 1853, 1854, 1864, 1868, 1876, 1988, 2298, 2300, 2303, 2319, 2327, 2350, 2362, 2368, 2400, 2503, 2531, 2609, 3101, 3108, 3129, 3130, 3133, 3142, 3449, 3492, 3703, 3790, 3801, 3851, 4192, 4194, 4216, 4350, 4405, 4894, 4904, 4920, 4926, 4937, 5153, 5158, 5179, 5180, 5201, 5673, 5716, 5850, 5865, 5866, 5884, 5888
voir aussi: Dualisme, Histoire de la philosophie, Morale
Philosophie analytique 114, 137, 258, 290, 1231
Philosophie de la religion 132, 200, 249, 266, 273, 1379, 1382, 1386, 1389, 1391, 1402, 1412, 1413, 1423, 1426, 1428, 1440, 1448, 1451, 1456, 1472, 1473, 1487
Philosophie de la science 5, 22, 135, 288, 1271, 1553, 1555, 1560, 1564, 1568, 1571, 1574, 1575, 1577, 1579, 1582-1586, 1592, 1593, 1599-1602, 1605, 1606, 1611, 1612, 1614, 1615, 1623-1625, 1627, 1628, 1630, 1871, 2209, 4360
Philosophie de langue 114, 1846
Philosophie de l'art 1850
Philosophie de l'éducation 225, 2004, 2082, 2117, 2145, 2177, 2181, 2193, 2226, 4900
Philosophie de l'histoire 152, 153, 156, 160, 193, 1201

SUBJECT INDEX IN FRENCH

Philosophie du droit 2313, 4917, 4933, 5149, 5152, 5153, 5158, 5161, 5163, 5167, 5173, 5177, 5179, 5181, 5182, 5188, 5192, 5195, 5198, 5208, 5210, 5311
Philosophie politique 129, 278, 281, 295, 307, 337, 366, 1194, 1251, 1466, 2117, 2369, 4230, 4894, 4898, 4900-4903, 4906, 4909, 4911, 4913, 4915-4917, 4920, 4921, 4923, 4924, 4926, 4928, 4929, 4931, 4933, 4934, 4937, 4938, 4969, 4972, 4973, 5188, 5207, 5305, 5311, 5327
Philosophie sociale 108, 121, 285, 295, 302, 353, 1553, 2313, 2498, 4898
Phonétique 1847
Phonologie 1798, 1847, 1989, 3002
Photographie 1346, 1737, 1870, 2188, 3375, 5037
Phrases 563, 617, 825, 5034
Phylogénie 1161
Physiologie 628, 630, 1593, 3110, 5406
Physiologie humaine 3109
Physique 1555, 1574, 1589, 1599, 1602, 1605, 1619, 1623, 1627
  voir aussi: Théorie des quanta
Picasso, Pablo 1869
Pidginisation 2523
Pinter, Harold 1877
Placement familial 2020, 2952, 3169, 5550, 5552, 5560, 5568-5570, 5587, 5597, 5721, 5925
Plaisanteries 1839, 3404, 3467
Plan d'expérience 5561
Planification de la famille 2721, 2728, 2729, 2731, 2732, 2735-2737, 2739-2741, 2745-2750, 2752, 2759-2764, 2769, 2771, 2792, 2799, 2800, 2804, 2939, 2971, 3337
Planification de la main-d'œuvre 4603
Planification de la santé 5523, 5724, 5758, 5770, 5777, 5807
Planification de l'entreprise 4035
Planification de l'environnement 3810
Planification des transports 3900
Planification du développement 3921, 4061, 4067, 4096, 4104, 4116, 4117, 4167, 4177
Planification financière 2676, 4310
Planification linguistique 1795, 1816, 1817, 1823, 1840, 1841, 2107, 2461
Planification régionale 1324, 3755, 3808, 3872, 3900, 3908, 4071, 4079, 4082, 4084, 4085, 4203, 5903
Planification rurale 2152, 3876, 3906
Planification sociale 3238, 4131
Planification stratégique 920, 1055, 1127, 2268, 3821, 3857, 3945, 4067, 4312,
4409, 4655, 4666-4668, 5271, 5337, 5740, 5977
Plantations 3882
Plato 270, 1650, 2370
Pluralisme 147, 199, 474, 964, 1002, 1201, 1216, 1455, 1548, 2083, 2181, 2365, 2380, 2443, 3441, 3489, 3490, 3501, 3522, 3789, 4012, 4195, 4494, 4905, 4928, 4951, 4972, 5167, 5185, 5859
Pluralisme ethnique 225, 3501, 3642
Pluralisme linguistique 1825, 2107
Pluralisme religieux 1377, 1424, 1425, 1440, 1448, 1525, 1547, 2532, 4962
Plurilinguisme 1000, 1838, 1843, 2523
Poèmes 1934
Poésie 186, 241, 1227, 1239, 1853, 1901, 1922, 1936, 1943, 1945-1947, 1959, 1969, 1989
Poésie épique 241
Police 705, 1009, 1844, 2860, 2868, 2888, 3284, 3325, 4683, 4980, 5006, 5010, 5109, 5122, 5123, 5125-5127, 5129-5148, 5243, 5364, 5448, 5765
Policiers 1009, 5135, 5142, 5192
Politiciens 348, 1550, 1553, 1725, 3323, 5222, 5281, 5301, 5363
Politique 6, 25, 47, 253, 268, 346, 799, 971, 1110, 1207, 1234, 1275, 1356, 1517, 1553, 1742, 1838, 1839, 1882, 1921, 1933, 1978, 2361, 2502, 2672, 3078, 3080, 3258, 3356, 3391, 3497, 3508, 3574, 3707, 3755, 3942, 3945, 4303, 4311, 4596, 4877, 4897, 4908, 5196, 5213, 5218, 5271, 5333
Politique à l'égard du consommateur 4317, 4341
Politique agricole 3760, 3878, 3880, 4142
Politique agricole commune 3878
Politique alimentaire 5969
Politique comparée 2, 2123, 2238, 3338, 4823, 5218
Politique culturelle 992, 1171, 1175, 1220, 1223, 1235, 1241, 1336, 1360, 1892, 2025, 3322
Politique de bien-être 2459, 3862, 4411, 4456, 5477, 5512, 5537, 5546, 5548, 5602, 5615, 5616, 5622, 5623, 5625, 5631-5633, 5636, 5637, 5639-5641, 5647, 5654, 5657, 5660
Politique de défense 5356, 5359
Politique de développement 1267, 1923, 3160, 3378, 3796, 3801, 3815, 3817, 3828, 3868, 3915, 3927, 4236, 4254, 4267, 4279, 4287, 5701
Politique de la drogue 2559, 5367, 5383

INDEX DES MATIÈRES

Politique de la jeunesse 4799
Politique de la recherche 2269
Politique de l'éducation 1991, 1992, 1994-1996, 2012, 2014, 2017, 2019, 2024, 2026, 2027, 2044, 2055, 2079, 2095, 2098, 2107, 2109, 2121, 2124, 2129-2133, 2136, 2138, 2144-2148, 2150, 2151, 2153, 2155, 2156, 2162-2164, 2166, 2167, 2169-2171, 2177, 2204, 2210, 2213, 2225, 2228, 2246, 2248, 2258, 2265, 2266, 2269, 2280, 2290, 2292, 2297, 3206, 3470, 3869, 4438, 4768, 4791, 4793, 4949, 4962, 5588, 5641, 5642
Politique de l'emploi 1891, 2455, 2459, 2554, 2702, 4267, 4438, 4447, 4476, 4489, 4490, 4507, 4516, 4552, 4589, 4598, 4696, 4795, 4797, 4799, 4810, 4824, 4835, 4837, 4872, 5624, 5641
Politique de l'environnement 64, 2513, 3688, 3705, 3706, 3711, 3718, 3738, 3755, 3759, 3796, 3800, 3803, 3804, 3806, 3808, 3810, 3818, 3819, 4063, 4107, 4246, 4358, 4486
Politique de libéralisation 2564
Politique de l'Union européenne 3878, 4541, 4966, 5295, 5640
Politique démographique 2712, 2721, 2728, 2752, 2763, 2770, 2792
Politique des médias 1733, 1734, 1763
Politique des pêches 3913
Politique des prix 3868
Politique des revenus 4542
Politique des salaires 3868
Politique des transports 4313
Politique d'identité 397, 966, 992, 1535, 1761, 2326, 2340, 3480, 5156, 5328
Politique d'immigration 954, 2693, 2870, 3468, 3542, 3545, 3555, 3584, 3586, 3602, 3605, 3630, 3649, 3658, 3662, 3669, 3673, 4939, 4964, 5222, 5632
Politique d'intégration active 2017, 2055, 2061, 2415, 3517
Politique du commerce international 5227
Politique du logement 3460, 3825, 3906, 3954, 3961, 3968, 3972, 3975-3978, 3980-3983, 3985, 3988-3990, 4010, 4022, 4024, 4080, 4110, 4232, 5416, 5509, 5611, 5627, 5631, 5637, 5646, 5655, 5656
Politique du travail 4456, 4471, 4552, 4576, 4587, 4596, 4696, 4749, 4809, 4810, 4815, 4818, 4829, 4837, 4842, 4850, 4851, 4867
Politique économique 64, 2496, 2561, 2571, 2707, 3615, 3804, 3817, 4052, 4063,
4185, 4189, 4206, 4236, 4248, 4281, 4587, 4817, 5605
Politique économique internationale 5316
Politique ethnique 3395, 3474
Politique étrangère 1023, 3654, 5316, 5317, 5336
Politique familiale 2922, 2997, 3169, 3220, 3312, 5164
Politique gouvernementale 386, 1442, 1891, 2098, 2403, 2442, 2513, 2657, 2707, 2792, 3114, 3312, 3542, 3602, 3640, 3702, 3814, 3817, 3827, 4054, 4078, 4133, 4248, 4354, 4486, 4491, 4497, 4907, 5002, 5243, 5416, 5426, 5497, 5548, 5567, 5600, 5624, 5635, 5664, 5788, 5882
Politique industrielle 3309, 3927, 4103, 4404, 4935
Politique intérieure 2704
Politique internationale 68, 2572, 3681, 4935, 5310
Politique linguistique 1000, 1785, 1809, 1816, 1817, 1819, 1823, 1838, 1841, 1843, 2107, 2228, 2461, 3555, 5021
Politique locale 1550, 2467, 3856, 5269
Politique macroéconomique 2561, 4596
Politique migratoire 3459, 3584, 3631, 3639, 3641, 3659, 3669, 3672, 3675, 5638
Politique mondiale 2541, 2553, 2572, 3723
Politique municipale 3927, 3950, 3959, 3968, 4100, 4169, 4941, 5229
Politique Noire 3506
Politique pénale 426, 4992, 5002, 5004-5008, 5018, 5024, 5026, 5032, 5083, 5114
Politique publique 426, 633, 1857, 2026, 2602, 2605, 2679, 3046, 3121, 3321, 3324, 3352, 3423, 3528, 3694, 3749, 3752, 3809, 4101, 4261, 4341, 4517, 4518, 4528, 4796, 4830, 4949, 4984, 4988, 5471, 5571
Politique régulatrice 4396
Politique rurale 3880, 3908, 3915, 4248
Politique sanitaire 2712, 2713, 3300, 4274, 4949, 5200, 5506, 5524, 5658, 5726, 5729, 5732, 5743, 5744, 5750, 5754, 5758, 5759, 5770, 5771, 5777, 5779, 5783, 5787, 5790, 5791, 5797, 5802, 5803, 5807, 5810, 5814, 5815, 5819, 5822, 5824, 5841, 5903, 5927, 5942, 5947, 5968, 5972-5974, 5980, 5982, 5986
Politique scientifique 1577, 1594, 1618
Politique sociale 43, 50, 64, 426, 852, 1991, 2385, 2390, 2397, 2423, 2433, 2442, 2458, 2461, 2467, 2496, 2498, 2521, 2532, 2539, 2602, 2677, 2688, 2707, 2745, 2763, 2804, 2870, 2873, 2997,

577

SUBJECT INDEX IN FRENCH

2999, 3091, 3114, 3220, 3261, 3312, 3491, 3809, 3869, 3895, 3981, 3989, 4008, 4044, 4052, 4063, 4111, 4185, 4259, 4274, 4283, 4298, 4299, 4497, 4563, 4580, 4686, 4789, 4835, 4862, 4872, 4945, 4949, 5004, 5017, 5023, 5126, 5146, 5225, 5367, 5371, 5414, 5416, 5463, 5471, 5477, 5482, 5496, 5498, 5504, 5509, 5512, 5513, 5532, 5537, 5541, 5547, 5548, 5569, 5571, 5574, 5588, 5591, 5602-5605, 5613, 5620, 5622-5624, 5627, 5629, 5630, 5633-5635, 5639, 5641-5643, 5647, 5649, 5650, 5654, 5661, 5665, 5666, 5716, 5786, 5927, 5929, 5958

Politique touristique 3820
Politique urbaine 2138, 3702, 3928, 3942, 3976, 3983, 4035, 4037, 4038, 4044, 4052, 4070, 4078, 4080, 4093, 4097, 4100, 4109, 4114, 4174, 4287, 4991
Politiques régionales 5221
Politisation 3149, 3365, 4974
Politologues 4897
Pollet, Jean-Daniel 1901
Pollution 1010, 3722, 3757, 3823, 4114, 4156
Pollution industrielle 73
Pollution transfrontière 3762
Polonais 960, 997, 1004, 1499, 1934, 3445, 3450
Polyandrie 2973
Polyarchie 4965
Polygynie 2406, 2939
Polysémie 1246, 1822
Polythéisme 1406
Pomme 3912
Ponge, Francis 1901
Population 447, 467, 473, 500, 963, 2532, 2683, 2687, 2689, 2690, 2693, 2694, 2700, 2701, 2705, 2709, 2714-2716, 2720, 2725, 2749, 2770, 2779, 2788, 2799, 2802, 2813, 2815, 2832, 2836, 2904, 2963, 2967, 3459, 3518, 3764, 3898, 3951, 4021, 4045, 4252, 5049, 5728
Population indigène 58, 198, 982, 1431, 1493, 1620, 1723, 1769, 1785, 1840, 2379, 2505, 2515, 2568, 3186, 3468, 3482, 3486, 3519, 3526, 3688, 3732, 3736, 3768, 3772, 3789, 3913, 3920, 4280, 4373, 4495, 5167, 5170, 5259, 5553, 5695, 5970
Population mondiale 2694, 2711
Population rurale 1476, 2832, 3170, 3608, 3748, 3866, 3905, 3915, 4103, 4218
Population urbaine 2797, 3170, 3585, 3948, 4053, 4068, 4156, 4176, 4245, 4470, 4490, 5229

Populisme 4897, 5024
Pornographie 1243, 1684, 3121, 3147, 3302, 3320, 3323, 3324, 3333, 3338, 3355, 4387, 5176
Ports 4090
Portugais 1865
Position socioéconomique 577, 710, 766, 1078, 2013, 2021, 2032, 2047, 2055, 2119, 2276, 2347, 2382, 2407, 2432, 2444, 2612, 2624, 2652, 2709, 2732, 2760, 2828, 2840, 2841, 2843, 2875, 2887, 2948, 3057, 3182, 3278, 3391, 3394, 3399, 3434, 3459, 3516, 3538, 3577, 3603, 3696, 3715, 3835, 3901, 3992, 4015, 4018, 4087, 4152, 4249, 4257, 4264, 4271, 4291, 4292, 4454, 4495, 4567, 5071, 5144, 5382, 5396, 5445, 5475, 5636, 5763, 5773, 5804, 5830, 5844, 5961
Positivisme 112, 126, 127, 304, 568, 1150, 2558, 4621, 5182
Possession 3471, 3570, 4827, 4984, 5030, 5816, 5898
Postcolonialisme 1165, 1213, 1913, 2148, 2705, 3072, 3230, 3392, 3782, 3869, 3871, 5483
Post-fordisme 397, 2100, 2532, 4234, 5644
Post-Guerre froide 1004, 1174, 3552, 4168, 4898, 5313
Post-matérialisme 477, 4296, 5238, 5270
Postmodernisme 14, 19, 30, 67, 109, 124, 127, 135, 158, 175, 184, 196, 261, 292, 305, 315, 335, 363, 369, 374, 382, 385, 393, 395, 543, 605, 922, 1141, 1150, 1158, 1194, 1221, 1222, 1225, 1229, 1247, 1250, 1252, 1255, 1258, 1259, 1261, 1266, 1268-1271, 1273, 1275, 1276, 1278, 1281, 1300, 1335, 1362, 1388, 1405, 1449, 1505, 1590, 1610, 1661, 1669, 1832, 1920, 1930, 1968, 2012, 2189, 2326, 2334, 2540, 2558, 3117, 3125, 3339, 3377, 3540, 3782, 3949, 3955, 4084, 4213, 4227, 4329, 4365, 4560, 4904, 4951, 4976, 5219, 5839
Post-structuralisme 197, 292, 328, 340, 344, 346, 1214, 3117, 3346, 4065
Potentiel de développement 2685
Pouvoir 37, 243, 319, 340, 374, 410, 476, 895, 912, 930, 982, 1013, 1029, 1060, 1069, 1070, 1151, 1196, 1197, 1200, 1220, 1235, 1253, 1427, 1499, 1532, 1562, 1576, 1685, 1743, 1792, 1897, 2006, 2050, 2221, 2314, 2322, 2336, 2337, 2339-2341, 2421, 2430, 2450, 2515, 2672, 2940, 2960, 3060, 3067, 3089, 3096, 3115, 3121,

578

INDEX DES MATIÈRES

3126, 3149, 3172, 3187, 3192, 3306, 3344, 3349, 3353, 3380, 3435, 3775, 3869, 3881, 3945, 4140, 4259, 4301, 4392, 4482, 4625, 4662, 4828, 4854, 4882, 4889, 4953, 4954, 4968, 5052, 5125, 5216, 5430, 5608, 5679, 5704, 5920
voir aussi: Pouvoir politique, Rapports de pouvoirs
Pouvoir d'achat 4193
Pouvoir de la collectivité 2338, 3836, 3852
Pouvoir exécutif 4949, 5732
Pouvoir judiciaire 3891, 5017, 5155
Pouvoir législatif 4949
Pouvoir local 3193
Pouvoir monopolistique 2502
Pouvoir personnel 4199
Pouvoir politique 2671, 4884, 4889, 4942, 4944, 4953, 4968, 5207, 5269
Pragmatique 266, 1789, 1807, 1808, 1829, 1830, 1833, 1839, 1872, 1877
Pragmatisme 248, 1472, 1650, 1957, 3827, 4084, 4207, 5854
Pratique 43, 60, 183, 301, 308, 376, 651, 775, 1010, 1115, 1253, 1565, 1610, 1878, 2004, 2082, 2189, 2218, 2413, 2428, 3153, 3274, 4287, 5246, 5254, 5557, 5673, 5676, 5677, 5709, 5714, 5829, 5940
Pratique commerciale 4425, 4636
Pratique de la pêche
  voir: Pêche côtière
Pratique religieuse 1001, 1263, 1376, 1429, 1431, 1435, 1436, 1467, 1504, 1507, 1511, 1515, 1518, 1527, 1539, 1544, 1545, 2842, 3202, 3468, 4535
Pratiques culturelles 952, 1353, 1527, 1804, 3009, 3266, 3315, 3471, 3750, 4120, 4280, 4955
Préférences 1038, 1733, 2256, 2739, 2967, 2984, 3026, 3345, 3705, 4013, 4106, 4130, 4284, 4305, 5154, 5529
Préférences du consommateur 1254, 4339
Préjugé 350, 657, 674, 822, 847, 857, 1052, 1075, 1748, 1781, 1821, 2417, 2452, 2464, 2477, 2484, 2497, 3283, 3319, 3455, 3461, 3518, 3562, 5928
Préjugé racial 844, 1431, 3461, 3463, 3467, 3468, 3476, 3494, 3504, 3508, 3514, 3515, 3517, 3528, 3529, 5703
Première Chambre 4975
  voir aussi: Membres de la Première Chambre
Préparation des aliments 3268
  voir aussi: Art culinaire
Prescription de rôle 1105

Préservation 3707, 3710, 3721, 3732, 3737, 3747, 3753, 3755, 3970, 3984, 4025, 4047, 4081, 4107, 4123, 4168
  voir aussi: Conservation de la nature, Conservation des ressources, Sauver de l'énergie
Préservation du patrimoine culturel 3744, 3820, 3984, 4081, 4133, 5237
Presse 455, 996, 1000, 1637, 1683, 1696, 1709, 1712, 1714, 1720, 1728, 1730, 1741, 1742, 1751, 1760, 1924, 2679, 3156, 3391, 3506, 3553, 5235, 5264, 5329, 5361
Pression démographique 3733
Prestation d'invalidité 5605
Prestige 2434, 2444
Preston, Ronald H. 1410
Prêts 1822, 4683
Prévention 791, 1010, 2817, 4731, 5146, 5409, 5467, 5554, 5566, 5814, 5950, 5964, 5967, 5968, 5981, 5983, 5986, 5987
Prévision technologique 1603, 2527
Prévisions 456, 500, 688, 722, 1112, 2038, 2700, 2805, 2825, 2837, 3270, 3801, 4276, 4721, 4796
Prévisions démographiques 2687, 2794
Prévisions économiques 2527
Prière 1428, 5687
Primates 619, 1161
Primatologie 2406
Principauté 2405
Priorités de recherche 415, 442
Prise de décision 129, 364, 370, 386, 561, 638, 674, 706, 833, 947, 1012, 1015, 1017, 1023, 1028, 1034, 1049, 1054, 1055, 1059, 1070, 1087, 1097, 1116, 1139, 1153, 1608, 1831, 1856, 2038, 2155, 2241, 2256, 2258, 2309, 2595, 2731, 2760, 2762, 2860, 2897, 3190, 3210, 3267, 3279, 3613, 3614, 3667, 3670, 3702, 3705, 3716, 3749, 3806, 3814, 3821, 3917, 3973, 4029, 4253, 4326, 4346, 4353, 4356, 4357, 4360, 4417, 4418, 4629, 4666, 4670, 4698, 4728, 4786, 4809, 4841, 4877, 4931, 5155, 5183, 5236, 5307, 5528, 5704, 5752, 5828, 5847, 5858, 5862, 5869, 5889, 5925, 5987
Prise de décision en groupe 1036, 1039, 1049, 1050, 1066, 1070, 1098, 1704, 4316, 4384, 4670
Prise en charge 104, 891, 1006, 2279, 2310, 2335, 2458, 2483, 2638, 3067, 3094, 3099, 3104, 3126, 3140, 3145, 3176, 3192, 3403, 3453, 3480, 3830, 3837,

SUBJECT INDEX IN FRENCH

3841, 3911, 4259, 4316, 4632, 4689, 4808, 4861, 4942, 4945, 5159, 5184, 5212, 5782
Prison 311, 426, 3391, 4979, 5005, 5011-5013, 5015, 5016, 5019, 5021, 5022, 5026, 5031, 5035, 5037, 5042, 5043, 5068, 5089, 5098, 5105, 5383, 5966
Prisonniers 1991, 4997, 4999, 5002, 5011-5013, 5022, 5026, 5033, 5037, 5042, 5068, 5100, 5192, 5664
  voir aussi: Réadaptation des prisonniers
Privation 819, 824, 2385, 2432, 2807, 2831, 3590, 3874, 3991, 4277, 4283
Privatisation 28, 2120, 2150, 2292, 2407, 2451, 3813, 4041, 4079, 4204, 4211, 4424, 4788, 5287, 5478, 5725
Prix de l'eau 3813
Prix du logement 2407, 3620, 5656
Prix du terrain 3986
Probabilité 473, 494, 525, 631, 833, 923, 2595, 2640, 2764, 2768, 2989, 4518, 5508
Problèmes sociaux 43, 50, 572, 574, 709, 717, 1173, 1199, 1349, 1976, 1991, 2104, 2119, 2162, 2332, 2358, 2400, 2404, 2473, 2521, 2524, 2535, 2618, 2636, 2804, 2861, 2865, 2871, 2873-2875, 2881, 2882, 2888, 3319, 3528, 3982, 3996, 4004, 4007, 4139, 4250, 4259, 4270, 4271, 4469, 4493, 4626, 4708, 4908, 4977, 4979, 5036, 5068, 5069, 5071, 5081, 5102, 5109, 5112, 5147, 5364, 5367, 5368, 5372, 5374, 5380-5382, 5384, 5396, 5400, 5403, 5407, 5411, 5414, 5418, 5419, 5421, 5424, 5425, 5427, 5429, 5431, 5435, 5436, 5440, 5445, 5450, 5455, 5464, 5471, 5472, 5534, 5546, 5570, 5596, 5670, 5702
Procès civil 4822
Processus judiciaire 5006, 5025, 5068, 5154, 5171, 5204, 5205
Processus markoviens 446, 492
Processus stochastiques 1638
Procréation 2912
Production 303, 379, 381, 1200, 1314, 2551, 3090, 3875, 4124, 4219, 4246, 4302, 4394, 4428, 4647, 5287, 5656
Production agricole 3731, 3760, 3875, 3889, 4206, 4240, 4243, 4674, 5948
Production alimentaire 1286, 3875
Production de masse 340, 1873
Production de viande bovine 5948
Productivité 2457, 3896, 3910, 4246, 4253, 4262, 4309, 4693, 4764, 5969
  voir aussi: Accroissement de la productivité
Productivité agricole 3890

Productivité du travail 4465, 4763
Produit agricole 4331
Produit d'origine animale 1293, 2342
Produits biologiques 4316
Produits chimiques 3083
Produits de base 303, 342, 4193, 4336
Produits ouvrés 2315
Produits pharmaceutiques 5380, 5801, 5833, 5864, 5980
Profane 1471
Professeurs 1631, 2089, 2444, 4935
Profession legale 5169, 5203
Professionnalisation 11, 1217, 4322, 4649, 4767, 4770, 4771, 4782, 4783, 5677
Professionnalisme 1354, 3411, 4767, 4773, 4954
Professions 478, 637, 705, 842, 1285, 1857, 2094, 2096, 2100, 2125, 2382, 2382, 2410, 2425, 2430, 2434, 2444, 3062, 3115, 3166, 3189, 3200, 3226, 3255, 3391, 4064, 4183, 4306, 4404, 4414, 4440, 4441, 4446, 4457, 4472, 4485, 4513, 4514, 4533, 4539, 4542, 4572, 4574, 4657, 4735, 4746, 4754, 4756-4758, 4762, 4764-4767, 4769, 4771, 4772, 4774-4778, 4781, 4783, 4785, 4787-4789, 4883, 5090, 5096, 5436, 5584, 5651, 5692, 5757, 5794, 5827, 5840, 5841, 5845
Professions médicales 4800, 5734, 5827
Professorat 1, 13, 28, 43, 47, 50, 53, 66, 67, 309, 438, 996, 1217, 1422, 1594, 1618, 2014, 2018, 2091, 2118, 2242, 2281, 2282, 2591, 3179, 3545, 3780, 4383, 4564, 4714, 4766, 5281, 5710
Profit 1015, 1894, 3797, 3823, 4668, 5816, 5871
Programmation 1749
Programme de gouvernement 42, 2748, 4251, 5629, 5969
Programmes de développement 2286, 3378, 3611, 5493, 5629
Programmes de recherche 1618
Programmes d'ordinateur 4667
Programmes électoraux 5307
Progrès scientifique 434, 1576, 1580, 1594, 1603, 1604, 1613, 2350, 2704
Progrès scientifique et technique 1608, 2120
Prohibition 3325
Projets de développement 2483, 2512, 3813, 3822, 3827, 3832, 3841, 5973
Projets de recherche 43, 60, 1620, 2397, 2465
Promotion professionnelle 4175, 4757, 4761, 4763, 4780, 5832
Propagande 1360, 1546, 1781
Prophètes 1525

INDEX DES MATIÈRES

Prophétie 1401
Propreté 3775, 4727, 4730, 5902, 5954
Propriétaires fonciers 3755, 3891
Propriété 258, 2571, 2926, 3940, 3990, 4060, 4097, 4109, 4204, 4220, 4226, 4233, 4474
  voir aussi: Biens culturels
Propriété collective 974
Propriété du domicile 2377, 3845, 3980, 3986, 4225, 4229, 5286, 5491
Propriété foncière 3451, 4080, 4156, 5649
  voir aussi: Marché de l'immobilier
Propriété intellectuelle 2261, 2580, 5870
Propriété privée 3471, 3755, 4113
Propriété publique 3927
Prose 1968
Prosodie 1810
Prospérité 2523
Prostitution 171, 1370, 1950, 3016, 3147, 3319, 3323, 3325-3327, 3332-3334, 3347, 3348, 3601, 4979, 5366, 5373, 5545, 5686, 5943
Protection de la vie privée 4933
Protection de l'enfance 1050, 5371, 5373, 5542, 5547, 5556, 5558-5560, 5569, 5572-5574, 5576, 5582, 5583, 5585, 5587-5589, 5596, 5597, 5633, 5667
Protection de l'environnement 73, 1010, 1093, 1152, 1601, 2513, 3706, 3711, 3717, 3723, 3724, 3728, 3732, 3739, 3744, 3749, 3754, 3762, 3763, 3765, 3796, 3797, 3803, 3804, 3806, 3810, 3819, 3820, 3914, 4025, 4058, 4062, 4081, 5254, 5255, 5330
Protection des données 2716
Protection des minorités 1531
Protection du consommateur 5732
Protection internationale des minorités 5340
Protection légale 4933, 5326, 5585
Protestantisme 208, 1431, 1481, 1498, 1510, 1513, 2357, 4239
Protestants 1343, 1484, 1495, 1512, 1513, 2439, 3012
Provinces 2254, 2529, 3606, 5571
Psychanalyse 12, 218, 340, 388, 558, 579, 584-586, 593, 599, 604, 632, 695, 699, 743, 744, 747, 748, 752, 761, 770, 779, 780, 782, 784, 801-803, 809, 810, 814, 816, 821, 897, 942, 1006, 1255, 1816, 1869, 1897, 1937, 1947, 2327, 2328, 2340, 2628, 2641, 2848, 3199, 3289, 3304, 3305, 3339, 3342, 5239, 5538, 5599, 5831, 5940
Psychiatre 555, 604, 615, 699, 754, 758, 762, 768, 772, 773, 775, 779, 788, 799, 801, 1053, 2877, 2946, 5016, 5056, 5089, 5137, 5387, 5405, 5420, 5460, 5473, 5899, 5907, 5909, 5913, 5920, 5921, 5930, 5932
Psychiatres 5056, 5683
Psychiatrie légal 5027, 5192, 5194, 5562, 5934
Psychiatrie sociale 753, 763, 765, 5736, 5900, 5919, 5922
Psychodrame 740
Psycholinguistique 547, 622, 1653
Psychologie 12, 25, 181, 199, 203, 215, 231, 289, 319, 326, 340, 388, 421, 422, 475, 503, 540, 541, 543, 544, 549-554, 556, 558-560, 562-567, 569, 570, 574, 575, 577-580, 582-592, 594, 596, 598, 600-602, 604-606, 608, 609, 613-617, 619-621, 625-629, 632, 635, 638, 640, 644, 646, 648-652, 654, 655, 658, 661, 663, 665-667, 670-672, 676, 678-682, 687, 689, 690, 693, 696, 699, 702, 707-710, 712, 713, 715, 717-721, 723, 725, 726, 729-733, 735-739, 741, 746, 750, 751, 755, 757, 759-762, 775, 777, 778, 782, 786, 787, 790, 794-796, 804, 806-810, 812, 813, 815, 818, 824, 829, 834, 838, 840, 845, 846, 849-851, 871-873, 879, 880, 883-885, 887, 892, 902, 905, 907, 914, 918-921, 928, 933, 936-939, 941, 943, 994, 1013, 1048, 1056, 1065, 1071, 1076, 1082, 1092, 1096, 1105, 1106, 1118, 1143, 1144, 1210, 1238, 1255, 1272, 1372, 1381, 1454, 1460, 1464, 1472, 1559, 1621, 1622, 1666, 1672, 1684, 1700, 1821, 1869, 1887, 1905, 1937, 1963, 1967, 2002, 2013, 2028, 2045, 2052, 2060, 2168, 2174, 2224, 2301, 2323, 2335, 2611, 2625, 2641, 2659, 2680, 2849, 2856, 2861, 2888, 2918, 2956, 2970, 2977, 2979, 3010, 3012, 3018, 3021, 3024, 3029, 3043, 3044, 3095, 3121, 3182, 3183, 3201, 3212, 3226, 3235, 3271, 3295, 3308, 3310, 3342, 3344, 3382, 3412, 3439, 3476, 3478, 3566, 3695, 3699, 3744, 3790, 4188, 4340, 4343, 4360, 4391, 4393, 4407, 4412, 4519, 4586, 4607, 4614, 4615, 4619, 4627, 4638, 4675, 4689, 4697, 4701, 4710, 4719, 4721, 4802, 4895, 5028, 5066, 5100, 5101, 5105, 5157, 5159, 5175, 5192-5194, 5331, 5377, 5397, 5409, 5410, 5434, 5453, 5457, 5516, 5687, 5752, 5773, 5798, 5856, 5893, 5901, 5902, 5936, 5939, 5957
  voir aussi: Psycotechnique

SUBJECT INDEX IN FRENCH

Psychologie clinique 545, 554, 565, 591, 603, 604, 680, 736, 738, 739, 741-745, 747-749, 751-757, 761, 764-766, 769-771, 773-777, 779, 781, 784, 787, 788, 792, 794, 796, 798, 800, 801, 803, 804, 807, 809, 810, 812, 813, 815, 816, 887, 1947, 2874, 2877, 2921, 3015, 3181, 3382, 5377, 5406, 5420, 5435, 5538, 5670, 5710, 5737, 5910, 5911, 5913, 5917, 5920, 5922, 5928
Psychologie de la forme 564
Psychologie de l'éducation 637, 647, 2028, 2168, 2197, 2206, 4671
Psychologie de l'enfant 417, 544-547, 554, 588, 598, 607, 619, 635, 654, 660, 743, 753, 754, 782, 819, 2599, 2607, 2610, 2847, 2892, 2893, 2903, 2946, 3004, 3014, 3029, 3032, 3034, 3044, 5097, 5579, 5918
Psychologie de l'environnement 442, 641, 839, 3749, 4106, 5529
Psychologie du développement 544, 547, 572, 575, 682, 731, 755, 1161
Psychologie économique 905, 4183, 4190, 4684
Psychologie évolutionniste 560, 561, 773, 3304, 3823, 5120
Psychologie expérimentale 606, 627, 631, 655, 658, 666, 720, 739, 760, 825, 870
Psychologie génétique 560
Psychologie industrielle 1092, 1118, 1138, 1143, 2335, 4607, 4619, 4638, 4671, 4675, 4802
Psychologie politique 3527, 4886, 4895, 5239, 5296, 5328, 5360
Psychologie sociale 45, 88, 442, 462, 548, 554, 556, 562, 565, 570, 575, 577, 588, 590, 601, 603, 604, 606, 620, 639, 650, 652, 676, 682, 683, 687-689, 700, 703, 707, 708, 712, 720, 722, 724, 727, 730, 732, 760, 776, 781, 821-841, 843-848, 850-870, 872-896, 898, 907, 908, 911, 914-917, 919, 925, 928, 930, 935, 939, 941, 942, 945, 946, 972, 973, 999, 1021, 1022, 1027, 1034, 1037, 1041, 1044, 1046, 1047, 1052, 1056-1058, 1061, 1063, 1067, 1071, 1076, 1081-1084, 1086, 1124, 1161, 1245, 1272, 1297, 1334, 1339, 1551, 1653, 1684, 1844, 1953, 2061, 2301, 2313, 2318, 2323, 2346, 2352, 2393, 2530, 2632, 2763, 2836, 2849, 2906, 2921, 3006, 3015, 3037, 3181, 3215, 3283, 3304, 3344, 3345, 3464, 3514, 3523, 3527, 3547, 3567, 3660, 3705, 3734, 3743, 3749, 3843, 4339, 4379, 4426, 4586, 4593, 4701, 4731, 4847, 4935, 5047, 5111, 5143, 5239, 5296, 5372, 5437, 5447, 5668, 5721, 5818, 5937, 5957, 5985
Psychologues 564, 592, 599, 604, 802, 868, 4731, 5084, 5192, 5209, 5412
Psychologues sociaux 870
Psychométrie 421, 475, 768, 3029
Psychopathologie 589, 591, 632, 709, 739, 750, 757, 765, 787, 790
Psychophysiologie 628
Psychoses 740, 758, 5460, 5681
Psychosociologie 693, 767, 5066, 5867, 5891
Psychothérapie 402, 591, 695, 737, 740, 746-748, 752, 778, 780, 782, 784-786, 793, 794, 803, 804, 812, 813, 816, 819, 820, 1442, 1464, 4895, 5192, 5349, 5406, 5420, 5595, 5599, 5670, 5682, 5683, 5714, 5907, 5938, 5940
Psycotechnique 546, 550, 556, 627, 661, 663, 798, 814, 886, 891, 1065, 1118, 2335, 4412, 4588, 4614, 4638, 4675, 4701, 4717, 4760, 4802, 5157, 5752
Public 425, 449, 1191, 1712, 1716, 1717, 1727, 1733, 1763, 1774, 1776, 1852, 1889, 1897
Publications scientifiques 1557
Publicité 1227, 1317, 1710, 1738, 1754, 1757, 1759, 1772, 1782, 2094, 2419, 2667, 3059, 3092, 3228, 3264, 3553, 4319, 4320, 4324, 4341, 4343, 5833, 5946, 5956
Puériculture 698, 2360, 2582, 2598, 2599, 2608, 2786, 2854, 2899, 2964, 2988, 2994, 2998, 3000, 3001, 3007, 3009, 3011, 3027, 3036, 4518, 5543, 5551, 5589
Purification ethnique 1730, 3070, 3420, 3485, 4966
Putnam, Robert D. 4203
Qualification requise pour l'emploi 550, 4726
Qualité de la vie 1923, 2480, 2680, 2711, 2814, 3370, 3581, 3793, 3857, 3904, 3991, 4123, 4247, 4296, 4297, 4693, 4724, 4740, 5372, 5531, 5532, 5607, 5738, 5838, 5889
Qualité de l'eau 2825, 3762
Qualité du service 1998, 2014, 2733, 3885, 4159, 4390, 5743, 5755, 5806, 5838, 5942
Qualité du travail 4702, 4740
Quartier 471, 577, 838, 849, 2935, 2995, 3577, 3833, 3835, 3840, 3845, 3853, 3858-3861, 3904, 3988, 4002, 4005-4008, 4010, 4013, 4014, 4022, 4028, 4034, 4056, 4070, 4080, 4086, 4091, 4119, 4155, 5049, 5063, 5071, 5102, 5582, 5612, 5742, 5963

INDEX DES MATIÈRES

Quartiers déshérités 3937, 3938, 3966, 3995, 4009, 4010, 4016, 4091, 4092, 4098, 4112, 4148, 4300, 4489, 4490, 5069, 5386
Questionnaires 460, 509, 520, 527, 532, 629, 711, 712, 742, 763, 768, 800, 833, 1798, 1820, 2157, 2183, 2530, 2775, 2913, 3292, 3739, 3749, 4119, 4618, 4698, 5221, 5403, 5691, 5710, 5792, 5829, 5891
Quine, W.V.O 1231
Race 33, 603, 669, 808, 814, 861, 964, 972, 1078, 1195, 1227, 1297, 1339, 1427, 1433, 1443, 1474, 1620, 1750, 1761, 1815, 1880, 1917, 1965, 1978, 2011, 2017, 2042, 2055, 2061, 2068, 2077, 2151, 2161, 2232, 2359, 2436, 2551, 2602, 2631, 2647, 2699, 2751, 2811, 2812, 2978, 2995, 3024, 3058, 3088, 3121, 3214, 3222, 3242, 3259, 3383, 3389, 3393, 3396, 3398, 3399, 3401, 3411, 3414, 3428-3430, 3432-3439, 3442, 3443, 3449, 3454, 3457, 3463, 3464, 3472, 3474, 3475, 3481, 3484, 3486, 3488, 3503-3506, 3510-3513, 3516, 3517, 3519, 3525, 3528, 3529, 3534, 3545, 3632, 3938, 4012-4014, 4020, 4089, 4291, 4376, 4416, 4431, 4435, 4464, 4472, 4473, 4479, 4496, 4497, 4502, 4505, 4507, 4510, 4559, 4615, 4628, 4733, 4865, 4939, 5017, 5031, 5053, 5081, 5102-5104, 5139, 5142, 5148, 5280, 5357, 5409, 5454, 5465, 5483, 5490, 5563, 5577, 5672, 5774, 5830, 5832, 5836, 5846, 5914
Races humaines 3759
Racisme 1620, 1748, 1917, 2011, 2063, 2163, 2630, 3172, 3433, 3437, 3449, 3452, 3456, 3458, 3461, 3463, 3464, 3466-3468, 3470, 3476, 3494, 3502-3504, 3507-3511, 3513, 3516-3518, 3522, 3523, 3529, 3534, 3542, 4919, 5147, 5171, 5243, 5319, 5713, 5872, 5928
Radicalisme 155, 1311, 1394, 1553, 2117, 3374, 4316, 4928, 5276
Radicaux 4865
Radio 1709, 1724, 1745, 1749, 1755, 1756, 1780, 2748
Radiodiffusion 1683, 1697, 1698, 1718, 1721, 1724, 1725, 1728, 1730, 1732, 1736, 1745, 1749, 1750, 1753, 1756, 1765, 1766, 1770, 1772, 1773, 1775, 1777, 1778, 1783, 4787
voir aussi: Diffusion politique
Raison 106, 107, 111-113, 121, 122, 126, 130, 131, 134, 136, 139, 141, 206, 226, 244, 268, 271, 360, 667, 1127, 1271, 1591, 2362, 2366, 3744, 4902, 4920

Raisonnement 30, 111, 129, 137, 583, 619, 664, 706, 823, 940, 1389, 1808, 1824, 2179, 2208, 2351, 2625, 3182, 5179
Rang de naissance 653, 698
Rapports de pouvoirs 444, 449, 528, 1151, 1823, 2250, 2337, 3193, 3267, 3410, 3911
Rareté 4179
Rassemblement des données 43, 424, 429, 432, 447, 455, 501, 504-513, 515, 516, 518-520, 522, 524-527, 529-536, 538, 585, 1137, 2006, 2053, 2213, 2276, 2476, 2683, 3213, 3381, 3397, 3428, 4270, 4276, 4277, 4737, 4747, 5555, 5582, 5662, 5891
Rationalisation 1139, 1860, 2548
Rationalisme 113, 212, 224, 256, 382, 1391, 1622, 2355, 3493, 4084, 4929, 5117
Rationalité 40, 106, 107, 116, 117, 121, 122, 129, 131, 133, 242, 261, 268, 272, 279, 314, 315, 324, 366, 370, 371, 465, 561, 602, 1020, 1127, 1197, 1198, 1247, 1271, 1277, 1280, 1570, 1630, 2311, 2351, 2575, 4030, 4065, 4180, 4275, 4326, 4388, 4428, 4739, 4778, 4920, 5162, 5303
Rationnement 5197, 5750, 5770
Rawls, John 2361, 2448, 2589, 4293
Réadaptation des handicapés 5604
Réadaptation des prisonniers 5030, 5032
Réadaptation sociale 5544
Réalisme 21, 55, 140, 207, 222, 258, 275, 285, 330, 341, 346, 360, 383, 391, 1136, 1235, 1270, 1428, 1570, 1578, 1596, 1610, 1752, 2319, 2809, 3687, 3700, 3701, 3775, 4361, 5310
Réalité virtuelle 641, 1656, 2772, 3820
Rébellion 986, 5239
Recensements 447, 451, 513, 2381, 2436, 2683, 2697, 2699, 2709, 2716, 2723, 2775, 2976, 3394, 3397, 3428, 3555, 3874, 4014, 4019, 4184, 5688
Recensements de population 3791
Récession 4007, 4828
Recettes fiscales 5620
Réchauffement de l'atmosphère 3711
voir aussi: Effet de serre
Recherche 49, 52, 54, 57, 71, 74, 76, 105, 168, 173, 195, 416, 430, 435-437, 454, 457, 517, 533, 538, 996, 1450, 1569, 1590, 1604, 1618, 1647, 1659, 1763, 1850, 1997, 1999, 2018, 2095, 2162, 2215, 2265, 2279, 2282, 2291, 2362, 2468, 2490, 2491, 2500, 2601, 2716, 2905, 2907, 2985, 3014, 3118, 3121, 3175, 3513, 3543, 3758, 3780, 4098, 4246, 4397, 4398, 4510, 5076, 5452, 5490, 5495,

SUBJECT INDEX IN FRENCH

5709, 5808, 5818, 5933
   voir aussi: Études de marché
Recherche action 427, 3118
Recherche agricole 4246
Recherche anthropologique 135, 3545
Recherche appliquée 90, 443
Recherche comptable 4310
Recherche de marketing 3312, 4324, 4345
Recherche démographique 90, 2687, 2704, 2752, 2792, 2820, 2828, 2868, 2976, 3047, 3607
Recherche d'emploi 4429, 4466, 4580, 4586, 4588, 4593
Recherche économique 54, 414, 436, 4744
Recherche empirique 55, 75, 339, 482, 540, 668, 711, 775, 1293, 1574, 2190, 3996, 4020, 4116, 4197, 4409, 4985, 5074, 5285, 5324, 5383, 5709
Recherche en cours 76
Recherche en science politique 4891, 5297
Recherche en sciences sociales 2, 13, 16, 25, 43, 45, 46, 54, 56, 70, 74, 167, 195, 356, 415, 418, 423, 424, 428, 431, 438, 439, 442, 445, 469, 470, 502, 514, 516, 520, 801, 890, 2809, 3182, 3396, 3545, 3666, 3978, 5038, 5880, 5960
Recherche et développement 42, 1604
Recherche ethnographique 31, 526, 1791, 2661, 3252, 3260, 3540, 5379
Recherche ethnologique 817
Recherche interdisciplinaire 61, 77, 186, 596, 1155, 2570, 3545, 4310, 4895, 4896, 5329
Recherche linguistique 76, 1798
Recherche médicale 795, 1620, 5406, 5502, 5853, 5869, 5870, 5875, 5880, 5891, 5942
Recherche opérationnelle 371, 5357
Recherche organisationnelle 1104, 1107, 1140, 1148, 4406
Recherche pédagogique 418, 437, 1992, 1999, 2089, 2182, 2924
Recherche scientifique 56, 73, 434, 1566, 1569, 1594, 1601, 1607, 1610, 1613, 1618, 1620, 1631, 2262, 2344, 5853, 5942
Recherche sociale 31, 42, 43, 48, 50, 52, 53, 59, 64, 101, 108, 116, 180, 310, 415, 417, 423, 428, 429, 436, 438, 443, 488, 495, 499, 502, 514, 520, 522, 529, 530, 537, 568, 653, 923, 1139, 1150, 1164, 1354, 1377, 2017, 2211, 2375, 2466, 2681, 2906, 2938, 3298, 3379, 3543, 3545, 4119, 4345, 4979, 5206, 5297, 5436, 5502, 5647, 5687, 5891
Recherche sociologique 1, 4, 5, 9, 20, 47, 50, 51, 54, 55, 62, 65, 66, 69, 75, 77, 81, 119, 166, 180, 321, 339, 347, 356, 412, 414,

416, 419, 423, 433, 440, 441, 444, 449, 450, 454, 456, 463, 466, 472, 474, 497, 511, 523, 710, 836, 1032, 1191, 1327, 1408, 1459, 1563, 2404, 2435, 2436, 2448, 2462, 2465, 2583, 2635, 2675, 2848, 2869, 2891, 2919, 2959, 2964, 2979, 3020, 3051, 3067, 3233, 3343, 3360, 3407, 3424, 3513, 3544, 3748, 4090, 4192, 4891, 4982, 5072, 5073, 5095, 5135, 5206, 5277, 5296, 5557, 5673, 5892, 5959, 5979
Recherche sur la communication 901, 1088, 1161, 1635, 1783
Recherche sur la gestion 4628
Recherche sur la paix 2619
Recherche sur le développement 553
Recherche sur les politiques gouvernementales 64, 426
Recherche sur l'opinion publique 509, 512, 520, 524, 535
Récidivisme 4997, 5121
Réciprocité 656, 1016, 1632, 2308, 2987, 3800, 3847, 4351, 4931, 5508
Récits 2, 127, 149, 156, 162, 175, 181, 435, 470, 508, 516, 677, 891, 919, 980, 984, 1104, 1127, 1157, 1161, 1176, 1258, 1270, 1275, 1739, 1766, 1824, 1839, 1882, 1920, 1937, 1957, 2581, 2622, 2625, 2643, 2651, 2664, 2878, 2932, 3214, 3250, 3371, 3495, 3496, 3539, 3640, 3697, 3777, 3864, 5034, 5424, 5430, 5495, 5896, 5898, 5946
Reconstitution de famille 5569
Récréation 1291, 1312, 2906, 3792, 3925, 4139
Recrutement 1446, 2092, 2256, 2274, 2631, 3286, 3665, 3673, 4429, 4439, 4489, 4490, 4569, 4603, 4613, 4615, 4732, 4784, 4875, 5352, 5845
Recyclage 3715
Redistribution du revenu 2406, 4209, 4299, 5662
Réduction de pauvreté 59, 1994, 2532, 3813, 3827, 3895, 3967, 3974, 4008, 4169, 4246, 4248, 4263, 4264, 4281, 4286, 4287, 4299, 4309, 4587, 4949, 5063, 5330, 5423, 5660, 5666, 5694, 5701, 5768
Réflexivité 18, 32, 183, 309, 359, 384, 386, 389, 401, 507, 1141, 1562, 1595, 2645, 2809, 4344, 4360, 5246, 5709
Réforme 419, 2132, 2294, 3325, 4818, 4848, 4876, 5139, 5212, 5361, 5622, 5810, 5903, 5959
Réforme administrative 4635, 4963, 5220
Réforme agraire 3918, 4248, 4949, 5245, 5363

INDEX DES MATIÈRES

Réforme constitutionnelle 2513
Réforme de la sécurité sociale 1991, 2455, 3976, 4439, 5618, 5633, 5639, 5643, 5654, 5658, 5661
Réforme de l'enseignement 68, 1224, 2024, 2069, 2079, 2103, 2117, 2122, 2133, 2137, 2138, 2140, 2145, 2146, 2148, 2154, 2156, 2158, 2164, 2210, 2238, 2292, 2513, 3869, 4598, 5225, 5642, 5703
Réforme économique 24, 2396, 2507, 2509, 2513, 2833, 3140, 3869, 3870, 3903, 3976, 4136, 4221, 4236, 4245, 4281, 4303, 4829, 4855, 4872, 4942, 5759
Réforme foncière 3867, 5261
Réforme institutionnelle 2513, 2961, 5282, 5904
Réforme légale 5039, 5041, 5054, 5154, 5187, 5200
Réforme politique 24, 1746, 2147, 2509, 2567, 3140, 3869, 4301, 4971, 5003, 5039, 5092, 5094, 5219, 5341
Réforme religieuse 145, 1433
Réforme sociale 2156, 2437, 2513, 2535, 2564, 3809, 4256, 4975
Réfugiés 814, 1536, 2218, 2530, 3354, 3586, 3611, 3624, 3660, 3664, 3666, 3674, 3677, 3680, 3681, 5585, 5637
Réfugiés politiques 1987, 3640, 3664
Régimes autoritaires 1467, 5266
Régimes fonciers 3768, 3883, 3887, 3975
Régimes politiques 1023, 1746, 2389, 3869, 4250, 4965, 4973, 5250, 5282, 5352
Régionalisation 2560, 2576, 3808
Régionalisme 969, 997, 1000, 1202, 1209, 2009, 2553, 2560, 2573, 3423, 4067, 4969, 5202, 5328, 5363
Régions 966, 1429, 2649, 2700, 2835, 2962, 3061, 3688, 3772, 4203, 4212, 4439, 4441, 4594, 4959, 5303, 5432, 5445, 5757
  voir aussi: Politiques régionales
Régions frontalières 987, 1798, 3468, 3768
Réglementation 220, 1133, 1190, 1756, 2100, 2280, 2356, 2580, 2741, 2816, 3325, 3672, 3673, 3734, 3814, 3880, 3922, 4153, 4235, 4352, 4396, 4587, 4617, 4683, 4751, 4782, 4818, 4976, 4989, 5125, 5402, 5407, 5524, 5777, 5870, 5880, 5881, 5884, 5888, 5942
Réglementation des prix 5649
Réglementation des salaires 4841
Réglementation du marché 3820, 4322
Régulation des naissances 2706, 2708, 2710, 2729, 2731, 2732, 2740, 2743, 2749, 2750, 2760, 2779, 3079, 3312

Régulation sociale 393, 409, 1070, 1707, 2321, 2322, 2356, 2364, 2421, 2516, 2741, 2891, 3524, 3775, 3858, 3891, 3945, 4074, 4131, 4187, 4396, 4683, 4718, 4908, 4912, 4933, 4973, 4975, 4977, 4979, 4981, 4985-4988, 4991, 4995, 5005, 5011, 5015, 5037, 5048, 5060, 5085-5087, 5098, 5099, 5103, 5104, 5107-5109, 5114, 5126, 5130, 5131, 5133, 5134, 5143, 5154, 5364, 5369, 5465, 5608, 5767, 5881
Réhabilitation de l'état de dépendance 5382, 5395, 5412, 5421, 5818
Réincarnation 1398
Relations bilatérales 2559
Relations centre-périphérie 3776, 4011, 4606
Relations civiles-militaires 957, 2502, 5340, 5341, 5352, 5360
Relations commerciales 3654, 4321
Relations culturelles 1072, 1231, 1244, 2592, 3479, 3527, 3684, 4198, 5333
Relations culturelles internationales 1421, 1942
Relations de classes 1305, 2377, 2426
Relations de dépendance 897, 2679, 5410
Relations des sexes 1110, 1317, 1352, 1782, 1928, 1930, 1974, 2377, 2708, 2939, 2969, 3060, 3066, 3070, 3076, 3079, 3081, 3097, 3112, 3165, 3170, 3176, 3184, 3186, 3208, 3209, 3220, 3225, 3231, 3234, 3236, 3238, 3240, 3241, 3244, 3252, 3275, 3277, 3283, 3292, 3320, 3330, 3356, 3670, 4126, 4416, 4544, 4552, 4558, 5058, 5317, 5318, 5350, 5442, 5908, 5962, 5975
Relations du travail 1117, 1122, 1123, 2559, 4250, 4357, 4363, 4400, 4402, 4415, 4420, 4455, 4465, 4537, 4550, 4602, 4623, 4633, 4634, 4648, 4650, 4663, 4677, 4689, 4691, 4695, 4712, 4713, 4725, 4727, 4728, 4742, 4792, 4798, 4803, 4809-4816, 4818-4826, 4828-4838, 4840-4847, 4849-4853, 4855, 4856, 4858, 4867-4869, 4872-4876, 4879, 4882, 4883, 4949, 5217, 5220
Relations école-collectivité 4486
Relations économiques 4104, 4322, 4380, 5536
Relations économiques internationales 2562, 2572, 3068, 3952, 4258, 4260, 5282
Relations enseignants-enseignés 2027, 2118, 3292, 3509
Relations entre générations 771, 1532, 1647, 1768, 2584-2589, 2591, 2593, 2594, 2672,

585

SUBJECT INDEX IN FRENCH

2682, 2872, 2917, 2927, 2934, 3237, 4755, 5536, 5634
Relations Est-Ouest 134, 989, 1186, 1230, 1268, 2518
Relations État-société 1199, 1467, 2576, 2752, 3106, 3474, 3922, 4169, 4774, 4823, 4832, 4945, 4951, 4969, 4970, 5048, 5148, 5162, 5214, 5222, 5237
Relations extérieures 1230, 3527, 5308
Relations familiales 402, 755, 1532, 1752, 1761, 2047, 2369, 2424, 2463, 2585, 2590, 2607, 2613, 2618, 2628, 2629, 2633, 2635, 2677, 2680, 2742, 2848, 2859, 2861, 2863, 2866, 2867, 2869, 2871, 2874, 2875, 2887, 2888, 2891, 2892, 2894, 2896, 2898-2900, 2903, 2908-2910, 2912, 2913, 2916-2921, 2925, 2927, 2933, 2935, 2937, 2939-2942, 2944-2949, 2951, 2952, 2954, 2959, 2960, 2964, 2969, 2977, 2979, 3013, 3020, 3032, 3033, 3037, 3047, 3050, 3051, 3053, 3219, 3220, 3229, 3239, 3267, 3343, 3360, 3382, 3385, 3524, 3645, 4218, 4555, 5118, 5192, 5345, 5382, 5492, 5505, 5510, 5525, 5528, 5530, 5537, 5541, 5552, 5566, 5569, 5577, 5594, 5668, 5671, 5681, 5687, 5693, 5916
Relations gouvernement central-local 4076
Relations gouvernementales 3526
Relations hommes-femmes 910, 922, 924, 932, 1810, 2761, 2977, 2985, 3066, 3124, 3149, 3201, 3288, 4310, 5449
  voir aussi: Époux
Relations humaines 680, 747, 870, 914, 921, 928, 934, 1016, 2369, 2667, 3126, 3352, 3550, 3775, 4363, 4608, 5439, 5461
Relations interdisciplinaires 3, 10, 16, 39, 603, 605, 1628, 2656, 3774, 3788, 4891, 4895, 5206, 5939, 5953
Relations interethniques 9, 57, 903, 1187, 1427, 1550, 1698, 1777, 1797, 1812, 1813, 1816, 2011, 2014, 2063, 2188, 2232, 2867, 2870, 3067, 3390, 3395, 3404, 3411, 3429, 3439, 3451, 3458, 3461, 3470, 3473, 3476, 3479, 3480, 3484, 3486-3490, 3492, 3501, 3507, 3508, 3515-3517, 3519, 3520, 3524, 3525, 3527, 3530, 3533, 3535, 3536, 3545, 3561, 3562, 3566, 3575, 3576, 3578, 3600, 3627, 3859, 4005, 4952, 5331, 5441, 5713
Relations intergroupes 72, 866, 879, 881, 894, 1005, 1041, 1042, 1051, 1052, 1058, 1075, 2110, 2240, 2619, 3464, 3515, 3517, 4285, 5343, 5687

Relations internationales 346, 1004, 1213, 2205, 2541, 2550, 2552, 2562, 2570-2572, 2577, 3762, 5025, 5257, 5308, 5314-5317, 5319, 5325, 5329, 5330, 5333-5335, 5363
  voir aussi: Relations Est-Ouest
Relations interpersonnelles 573, 574, 581, 591, 596, 697, 708, 709, 747, 822, 840, 853, 855, 874, 876, 898-900, 902-904, 906, 908, 910, 912-922, 924-928, 931-937, 939, 942, 943, 946, 950, 1004, 1021, 1027, 1036, 1051, 1057, 1061, 1064, 1071, 1078, 1084, 1110, 1119, 1142, 1651, 1660, 1677, 1681, 1810, 1945, 2363, 2667, 2862, 2867, 2879, 2889, 2891, 2918, 2956, 2958, 2959, 2966, 2970, 2989, 2990, 3310, 3343, 3347, 3352, 3411, 3746, 3892, 4240, 4367, 4374, 4383, 4675, 4689, 5012, 5434, 5461, 5468, 5568, 5607, 5668, 5753, 5849, 5954
Relations intragroupe 856, 2127, 3446
Relations médecin-malade 694, 740, 778, 897, 5828-5831, 5835, 5837, 5838, 5849, 5858, 5862, 5887, 5889, 5908
Relations parents-enfants 545, 695, 755, 819, 1647, 2613, 2626, 2628, 2629, 2667, 2682, 2847, 2853, 2859, 2893, 2895-2897, 2903, 2909, 2917, 2928, 2936, 2947, 2950, 2954, 3004, 3006, 3010, 3012, 3014, 3017, 3021, 3022, 3024, 3026, 3030-3032, 3034, 3037, 3041, 3043, 3044, 3047, 3049, 3052, 3053, 3056, 3057, 3228, 3364, 3385, 4777, 5538, 5539, 5546, 5575, 5578, 5692, 5693, 5848
Relations publique 4364, 4399
Relations raciales 835, 1075, 1431, 1442, 1926, 1949, 2011, 2060, 2240, 2530, 3077, 3088, 3099, 3395, 3412, 3429, 3431, 3436, 3439, 3441, 3444, 3449, 3452-3454, 3456, 3462, 3463, 3466, 3472, 3476, 3477, 3482, 3489, 3494, 3503-3507, 3509, 3511, 3512, 3515-3517, 3521, 3524-3526, 3529, 3534, 3599, 3641, 3769, 3950, 3988, 4002, 4013, 4015, 4089, 4472, 4491, 4865, 4919, 4971, 5050, 5142, 5147, 5713
Relations rurale-urbaine 2843, 3867-3869, 3871, 5279
Relations sexuelles 3311, 3350, 3351, 5449
Relations sociales 67, 321, 368, 388, 435, 517, 591, 700, 708, 728, 733, 843, 870, 872, 895, 904, 917, 923, 929, 939, 1051, 1060, 1079, 1244, 1277, 1372, 1568, 1610, 1642, 1677, 1878, 2011, 2313, 2321, 2322, 2332, 2369, 2372, 2384, 2465, 2565, 2609, 2901, 2953, 2993, 3149, 3176,

INDEX DES MATIÈRES

3241, 3301, 3503, 3747, 3791, 3845, 3865, 3904, 3908, 3956, 4126, 4137, 4212, 4215, 4272, 4321, 4333, 4349, 4376, 4389, 4401, 4833, 4893, 4922, 4939, 5033, 5090, 5272, 5313, 5328, 5536, 5564, 5568, 5607, 5677, 5891
Relativisme 135, 206, 241, 261, 268, 309, 405, 543, 1158, 1198, 1231, 1270, 1455, 1575, 1610, 1627, 2349, 4186, 4931, 5320
Religion 33, 56, 145, 169, 208, 221, 223, 230, 235, 237, 245, 246, 254, 270, 701, 880, 1171, 1199, 1372, 1373, 1375, 1378, 1379, 1381, 1385, 1386, 1388, 1392, 1393, 1395-1400, 1403, 1405, 1406, 1408, 1409, 1415, 1418, 1422, 1425, 1430, 1433-1435, 1437, 1439, 1441, 1444, 1445, 1448, 1450-1455, 1457, 1459-1461, 1463, 1465, 1466, 1469, 1470, 1474, 1478, 1481, 1483, 1485, 1486, 1490, 1493-1502, 1504-1509, 1511, 1513-1515, 1519, 1523, 1524, 1528, 1530, 1533, 1535, 1541, 1543, 1548, 1549, 1551, 1948, 1990, 2136, 2298, 2372, 2394, 2429, 2524, 2525, 2532, 2663, 2673, 2852, 2890, 2963, 2974, 2978, 3012, 3024, 3112, 3266, 3382, 3448, 3557, 3565, 3573, 3614, 3775, 3858, 3945, 4003, 4908, 4929, 4947, 5400, 5481, 5722, 5757, 5862, 5893, 5907
voir aussi: Anthropologie religieuse, Histoire de la religion, Monothéisme, Philosophie de la religion, Sociologie de la religion, Textes religieux
Religion comparée 1380, 1396, 1400, 1422, 1423, 1445, 1472
Religion et politique 1394, 1410, 1431, 1470, 1475, 1515, 1537, 1550, 3528, 4962
voir aussi: Islam et politique
Religion mondiale 1378
voir aussi: Christianisme, Hindouisme, Islam, Judaïsme
Religion populaire 1378, 1414, 1431
Religion traditionnelle 1431, 1464
Religiosité 880, 1372, 1375, 1383, 1433, 1437, 1438, 1461, 1469, 1481, 1500, 1509, 1512, 1544, 2239, 2655, 2732, 2753, 2982, 3448, 3614, 5238
Remariage 2910, 2924
Renaissance 237, 1436, 1859
Rendement du travail 707, 2084, 2096, 4412
Rendements d'éducation 2023, 2035, 2037, 2287, 4764
Renom 1217, 1228, 1318, 2383
Rénovation urbaine 3807, 3937, 3965, 3975, 3982, 4008, 4028, 4035, 4038-4040, 4043, 4044, 4052, 4056, 4066, 4070, 4071, 4076-4078, 4091, 4094, 4097, 4105, 4109-4113, 4154, 4159, 4174, 4995, 5063
Répartition de la population 2690, 2694, 2697, 2699, 2723, 3616
Répartition des pouvoirs 2321
Répartition du revenu 2430, 2830, 3249, 3731, 3805, 4201, 4242, 4281, 4294, 4306, 4921, 5628
Répartition en zones 4450
Répartition géographique 3877
Répartition par âge 2089, 2712, 2967
Répartition par sexe 2712
Répartition spatiale 452, 1362, 1657, 3625, 3773, 3879, 4046, 4092
Répertoires 79, 80, 85, 87, 105
Représentation 60, 627, 631, 633, 639, 655, 663, 666, 697, 833, 919, 990, 1041, 1046, 1061, 1064-1066, 1071, 1115, 1118, 1143, 1147, 1158, 1232, 1294, 1319, 1344-1346, 1598, 1839, 1868, 1964, 1992, 2022, 2096, 2099, 2166, 2920, 3146, 3153, 3230, 3301, 3368, 3788, 3819, 4161, 4187, 4363, 4408, 4412, 4600, 4602, 4607, 4625, 4634, 4638, 4646, 4668, 4673, 4689, 4760, 4779, 4802, 4954, 5410, 5760
Représentation des travailleurs 4819, 4853, 4855, 4863, 4871, 4873
Représentation du corps 1861, 3228, 3788
Représentation politique 2723, 4961, 5265, 5271, 5299
Représentations collectives 268
Représentations sociales 982, 1649, 1707, 1761, 2205, 2360, 3148, 3255, 3412, 3741, 5046, 5842, 5878
Représentations théâtrales 1862
Répression 632, 994, 3147, 3204, 3349, 4269, 4992, 5251, 5320
Reproduction culturelle 1873, 3676
Reproduction sexuelle 2692, 2706, 2726, 2744, 2747, 2754-2757, 2759, 2762, 2766, 2777, 2789, 2798, 2902, 2904, 2917, 2939, 2973, 3083, 3090, 3211, 3228, 3299, 3358, 5200
Reproduction sociale 383, 1074, 1727, 2300, 3080, 3150, 3786, 4462, 4552
Républicanisme 1970, 2439, 4969
Réseaux 32, 277, 486, 493, 662, 1040, 1045, 1069, 1100, 1115, 1146, 1155, 1594, 1660, 1672, 2088, 2110, 2210, 2213, 2333, 2334, 2337, 2501, 2802, 3078, 3463, 3673, 3847, 3867, 3881, 4031, 4056, 4108, 4240, 4369, 4371, 4376, 4429, 4588, 4641, 4654, 4732, 5242, 5306, 5510, 5747
Réseaux de communication 1632

SUBJECT INDEX IN FRENCH

Réseaux économiques 4369, 4380, 4381, 5227, 5237
Réseaux sociaux 54, 67, 379, 466, 493, 874, 948, 1035, 1038, 1043, 1045, 1060, 1062, 1069, 1074, 1085, 1087, 1146, 1512, 1610, 1632, 1636, 1680, 1681, 1686, 1990, 2314, 2315, 2333, 2334, 2357, 2456, 2494, 2646, 2666, 2667, 2747, 2759, 2782, 2836, 2901, 2948, 3585, 3670, 3843, 3848, 3865, 3875, 3910, 3938, 4004, 4006, 4197, 4374, 4383, 4460, 4507, 4690, 5092, 5111, 5237, 5244, 5282, 5300, 5306, 5517, 5533, 5590, 5709, 5962
Résidence 2901
Résidences secondaires 3791, 3906
Résistance 982, 1141, 1240, 1363, 1978, 2569, 2915, 3112, 3234, 3548, 4206, 4406, 4688, 4808, 5122, 5229, 5232, 5349, 5467, 5755, 5937
 voir aussi: Mouvements de résistance
Résistance à l'intégration 1442
Résistance au changement 2509
Résolution de problème 595, 705, 911, 947, 1604, 2053, 2061, 2179, 2850, 4074, 4395, 5699
Résolution des conflits 161, 517, 932, 1004, 1006, 1007, 1010, 1011, 1014-1016, 1019, 1024-1028, 1030, 1031, 2366, 3430, 3472, 3480, 3493, 3891, 4849, 5141, 5184, 5186, 5318, 5337, 5687
 voir aussi: Intervention d'une troisième partie
Respect mutuel des cultures 1198
Responsabilité 73, 111, 205, 407, 830, 896, 934, 1097, 1607, 1620, 2058, 2151, 2439, 2534, 2991, 3328, 3749, 3750, 4417, 4422, 4423, 4427, 4907, 4963, 5166, 5285, 5548, 5678, 5679, 5854, 5883, 5889
Responsabilité financière 411, 1029, 1030, 1742, 2097, 4310, 4621, 4906, 5139, 5749, 5854
 voir aussi: Transparence
Ressources économiques 1443
Ressources en eau 3690, 3707, 3798
Ressources financières 3877, 4369
Ressources forestières 3739
Ressources humaines 707, 1110, 1157, 2022, 2085, 2133, 2274, 2685, 3618, 3877, 4322, 4356, 4403, 4412, 4473, 4599-4606, 4610, 4613, 4616, 4618, 4619, 4621, 4633-4635, 4642, 4643, 4648, 4650, 4653, 4656, 4660, 4673, 4679, 4743, 4768, 5215, 5217

Ressources naturelles 58, 961, 2793, 3628, 3698, 3707, 3722, 3735, 3749, 3754, 3756, 3796, 3810, 3814, 3816, 3818, 4246
Ressources renouvelables 3810
Résultats économique 1153, 3996, 4207, 4249, 4374, 4592, 4602, 4633
Retard intellectuel 574, 783, 815, 878, 2019, 2026, 2028, 2206, 2225, 2468, 2469, 2482, 2485, 2486, 2489, 2497, 2499, 2500, 3329, 5682, 5720, 5926, 5934, 5938
Retrait 780, 4684
Retraite 1285, 2664, 2667, 2670, 2676, 2679, 2707, 2957, 3679, 3791, 5338, 5517, 5518
Retraites 2676, 2679, 2682, 2707, 2712, 4353, 4587, 4676, 5518, 5605, 5622
 voir aussi: Pensions de retraite
Retraités 3625
Réussite dans les études 2027, 2070, 2090, 2158, 2163, 2276, 2924, 3057, 3183, 4564, 4800
Réussite intellectuelle 479, 700, 862, 1626, 1992, 2005, 2008, 2014, 2017, 2020, 2024, 2027, 2032-2034, 2036, 2037, 2041, 2043, 2045, 2047, 2059-2061, 2063, 2068, 2070-2072, 2074, 2075, 2077, 2090, 2097, 2108, 2158, 2162, 2239, 2245, 2253, 2266, 2267, 2482, 2615, 2632, 2642, 2947, 3019, 3177, 3414, 3446, 3643, 4432, 4435, 4438, 4764, 4794, 4800, 5612, 5704
Réussite professionnelle 4752
Réussite sociale 2923, 3254
Réveil religieux 1467, 1470
Revendications foncières 5361
Revenu 441, 2410, 2457, 2590, 2700, 2787, 3042, 3715, 3835, 4011, 4014, 4020, 4277, 4295, 4301, 4303-4305, 4307, 4309, 4441, 4524, 4539, 4551, 4571, 4587, 5044, 5475, 5518, 5625, 5642
 voir aussi: Élasticité du revenu, Faible revenu, Salaire minimum
Revenu des ménages 2234, 2808, 2858, 3190, 4263, 4299, 4338, 4595, 5655
Revenu familial 2036, 4299
Revenu par tête 2855, 5621
Revenus d'investissement
 voir: Loyer
Rêves 212, 602, 961, 1426, 2641
Révisionnisme 1209, 4206
Révolte 1262, 2618, 5226, 5239
Révolution 1167, 1185, 1585, 1625, 1683, 2205, 2293, 2520, 2558, 2708, 3121, 4213, 4327, 5233, 5239, 5325
Révolution cubaine 1167
Révolution culturelle 185, 1264, 2567

Révolution française 2439
Révolution industrielle 2691
Rhétorique 12, 15, 106, 156, 346, 870, 1029, 1095, 1642, 1650, 1839, 1988, 2443, 3070, 3341, 4265, 4346, 4907, 4912, 5172, 5201, 5484
Rhodes, Cecil 1882
Ricœur, Paul 161
Rich, Adrienne 669
Richesse 1287, 1670, 2445, 2982, 3191, 3667, 3814, 4177, 4188, 4227, 4288, 4294, 4425, 4870, 5154, 5643
Rire 729, 1967, 5293
Risque 17, 386, 461, 467, 471, 483, 489, 561, 709, 714, 787, 838, 922, 923, 1349, 1563, 1595, 1609, 1660, 2309, 2320, 2636, 2640, 2773, 2808, 2836, 2838, 2845, 2933, 2962, 2981, 2995, 3067, 3309, 3316, 3326, 3351, 3624, 3700, 3702, 3704, 3734, 3752, 3759, 3930, 3979, 4260, 4353, 4416, 4417, 4552, 4580, 4984, 5009, 5061, 5071, 5080, 5081, 5140, 5383, 5386, 5387, 5407, 5433, 5468, 5485, 5554, 5570, 5578, 5773, 5838, 5867, 5891, 5942, 5948, 5957, 5964, 5970, 5978, 5984, 5987
   voir aussi: Partage des risques
Risque financier 4348, 4350, 4353
Risque moral 456, 909, 4756
Rites de passage 1321
Rites funéraires
   voir: Enterrement, Funèbres
Rituelle 245, 246, 952, 953, 976, 1074, 1348, 1433, 1442, 1534, 1964, 2330, 3092, 3418, 4315, 5338, 5368, 5932
Rivalité 2166
Robotique 1576
Rogers, Carl 599
Rokkan, Stein 4966
Rôle 1054, 1532, 2439, 2920, 4773, 5209
Rôle de sexes 485, 574, 1290, 1744, 1814, 1910, 1921, 1928, 1930, 1946, 1974, 2330, 2523, 2608, 2786, 2879, 2887, 2915, 2957, 2972, 3040, 3114, 3125, 3132, 3164, 3165, 3170, 3171, 3177, 3181, 3189, 3193, 3194, 3200, 3208, 3209, 3219-3221, 3223, 3228, 3232, 3233, 3235-3241, 3243-3245, 3248-3251, 3257, 3261, 3264, 3267, 3268, 3273-3275, 3281, 3307, 3339, 3358, 3372, 3592, 4324, 4400, 4416, 4521, 4526, 4527, 4544, 4545, 4554, 4558, 4567, 4584, 5131, 5200, 5203, 5350, 5388, 5505, 5584
Rôle des femmes 513, 1463, 2091, 2675, 2756, 2939, 3069, 3079, 3103, 3104, 3114, 3127, 3140, 3160, 3162, 3168, 3169, 3171, 3174, 3195, 3215, 3224, 3247, 3248, 3251, 3313, 3471, 4273, 4524, 4535, 5317, 5347, 5459, 5505
Rôle des hommes 1910, 3211, 3267, 5505
Rôles conjugaux 2761, 2980
Rôles professionnels 4618
Rôles sexuels 776, 3065, 3066, 3071, 3077, 3082, 3124, 3141, 3165, 3212, 3219, 3220, 3238, 3244, 3261, 3276, 3277, 3341, 3380, 5104, 5584, 5613
Rôles sociaux 734, 745, 1038, 1861, 1981, 2439, 2508, 2529, 2653, 2677, 2679, 2916, 2953, 3273, 3280, 3315, 3391, 4068, 5776
Rom 3520
Roman 1191, 1918, 1961, 1966, 1968, 5435
Romancier 1958, 1966
Romans 1191, 1243, 1917-1919, 1926, 1927, 1931, 1933, 1936, 1937, 1954, 1958, 1961, 1962, 1965, 1966, 1968, 1970, 3122, 3262, 3528
Romantisme 1197, 1968
Rorty, Richard 248
Rose, Gillian 253
Rosen, Robert 1606
Rotation de la main-d'œuvre 4517, 4684, 4720
Royaumes 172
Ruskin, John 1928
Russes 710, 1836, 2033, 2538, 3591, 5529
Saadawi, Nawal el 3122
Sacré 650, 1381, 1393, 1399, 1459, 1471, 1962
Sacrifice 239
Sage-femmes 5746
Said, Edward 1165, 1386
Saint-Martin, Louis Claude de 256
Saisonnalité 3745
Salaire minimum 4299
Salaires 2023, 2561, 2799, 4295, 4305, 4306, 4368, 4402, 4410, 4431, 4437, 4438, 4440, 4449, 4452, 4454, 4455, 4463, 4464, 4471, 4499, 4503, 4525, 4538, 4540, 4573, 4587, 4690, 4714, 4723, 4742, 4795, 4880, 5223
Salaires minimums 4307, 4486, 4587
Salariés 2679
Salles de classe 2027, 2102, 2229, 2231, 2608
Samba 1981
San 2379
Sanctions 5099
Sang 5860
Sans foyer 2334, 5271, 5414-5421, 5423-5431, 5558, 5592
Sans-abri 5414, 5416, 5419-5422, 5425, 5431

SUBJECT INDEX IN FRENCH

Sanscrit 132
Santayana, George 228
Santé 504, 541, 709, 780, 789, 887, 941, 1297, 1355, 2007, 2044, 2324, 2424, 2440, 2536, 2582, 2583, 2611, 2660, 2663, 2664, 2666, 2685, 2807-2809, 2811, 2812, 2814, 2815, 2824, 2830, 2833, 2845, 2999, 3159, 3226, 3311, 3316, 3325-3327, 3350, 3357, 3546, 3565, 3696, 4268, 4274, 4291, 4379, 4611, 4674, 4680, 4692, 4695, 4703, 4727, 4730, 4731, 5375, 5376, 5407, 5408, 5411, 5464, 5494, 5514, 5518, 5609, 5633, 5658, 5724, 5727, 5732, 5733, 5735, 5745, 5752, 5753, 5773, 5792, 5795, 5796, 5798, 5803, 5805, 5809, 5814, 5842, 5856, 5867, 5892, 5915, 5942, 5943, 5946, 5952, 5961, 5962, 5966, 5970, 5979, 5980, 5985, 5987
Santé de femmes 2726, 2750, 2751, 2754, 2758, 2765, 2777, 2779, 2792, 2798, 2801, 2817, 2832, 2834, 2999, 3083, 3095, 3115, 3210, 3231, 3280, 3373, 4291, 5200, 5746, 5782, 5838, 5902, 5917, 5947, 5960, 5962, 5980
Santé d'enfants 545, 753, 754, 783, 2007, 2022, 2703, 2738, 2823, 3039, 5200, 5575, 5757, 5873, 5947, 5949, 5954, 5969
Santé d'hommes 2472, 2829, 5411
Santé mentale 95, 545, 557, 574, 716, 742, 745, 751, 753, 755-758, 762, 764-768, 771, 776, 778, 780, 781, 783, 786, 788, 789, 792, 794, 795, 797, 800, 805, 807-809, 813, 816, 819, 876, 1053, 1898, 2020, 2154, 2478, 2499, 2602, 2647, 2655, 2660, 2664, 2856, 2877, 2885, 2893, 2895, 2906, 3044, 3048, 3226, 3382, 3666, 3696, 4698, 4699, 4731, 4735, 4746, 5016, 5022, 5033, 5137, 5381, 5393, 5394, 5406, 5420, 5434, 5464, 5488, 5516, 5633, 5658, 5665, 5683, 5710, 5720, 5735-5738, 5823, 5825, 5891, 5898-5901, 5903, 5905-5908, 5910-5912, 5915-5918, 5920, 5922, 5923, 5925-5929, 5931, 5935, 5937, 5939-5941, 5944, 5961
Santé publique 43, 709, 1349, 2602, 2719, 2726, 2762, 2817, 2823, 2830, 3115, 3300, 3311, 3326, 3327, 3757, 3827, 3961, 4087, 4274, 5386, 5397, 5445, 5471, 5525, 5658, 5731, 5744, 5745, 5754, 5759, 5781, 5788, 5789, 5791, 5801, 5813-5815, 5819, 5820, 5824, 5864, 5867, 5885, 5942, 5943, 5948, 5949, 5952, 5953, 5956, 5958, 5960, 5962-5964, 5966-5974, 5977, 5979-5982, 5986, 5988

Santé sexuelle 2160, 2638, 2726, 2754, 2765, 2777, 2789, 3294, 3296, 3331, 5200, 5981, 5985
Saro-Wiwa, Ken 1939
Sartre, Jean-Paul 215, 218, 281, 311
Satire 5293
Satisfaction 831, 946, 1285, 2495, 3462, 3973, 4183
Satisfaction au travail 715, 1111, 1118, 1131, 2093, 2267, 4618, 4662, 4677, 4679, 4680, 4684, 4689, 4697, 4699, 4704-4707, 4709-4711, 4714, 4717, 4719, 4720, 4722-4726, 4728, 4733, 4734, 4736, 4741-4744, 4746, 4758, 4827, 5283
Satisfaction conjugale 2913, 2960, 2966, 2968, 2970, 3382
Satisfaction de l'existence 482, 2004, 2666, 2668, 3581, 3679, 4725
Satisfaction de vie communautaire 3898
Satisfaction résidentielle 3824
Saussure, Ferdinand de 12
Sauver de l'énergie 1605, 1623
Savane 5968
Savimbi, Jonas 1756
Scandales 5219
Scepticisme 352, 358, 1404, 1552, 5265
Schatzki, Theodore 597
Schizophrénie 555, 758, 763, 765, 788, 5460, 5909, 5916, 5922
Schmitt, Carl 1199
Schön, D.A. 1095
Schopenhauer, Arthur 229
Schudson, Michael 1409
Schutz, Alfred 310
Science 13, 15, 22, 106, 126, 135, 225, 268, 279, 301, 334, 385, 396, 572, 775, 1150, 1234, 1271, 1286, 1401, 1416, 1558, 1560, 1563, 1566-1570, 1572-1574, 1577, 1579, 1580, 1582-1584, 1586, 1589, 1592, 1594, 1596-1598, 1600, 1603, 1605, 1607-1609, 1613-1615, 1618, 1619, 1623, 1626, 1628, 1629, 1631, 1633, 1871, 1996, 2015, 2209, 2237, 2262, 2288, 2309, 2350, 3115, 3719, 3759, 3823, 3837, 4571, 5201, 5839
voir aussi: Histoire des sciences, Informatique, Médecine légal, Philosophie de la science
Science du folklore 817
Science politique 2281, 3121, 3900, 4885, 4891, 4892, 4894, 4896, 4897, 4935, 5146
Sciences administrative 1037, 1087, 4623, 4641, 4670, 4690
Sciences de gestion 376, 416, 1090, 2335, 4355, 4413, 4610, 4627, 4630, 4636,

INDEX DES MATIÈRES

4649, 4651, 4652, 4659, 4663, 4666, 4668, 4669, 5224, 5790, 5834
Sciences de la communication 1635
Sciences de l'information 39, 4574
Sciences du comportement 42, 365, 422, 442, 549, 564, 572, 591, 609, 648, 699, 703, 737, 798, 870, 1089, 1125, 2877, 5094, 5799, 5891
Sciences du développement 572
Sciences juridiques 5154, 5166, 5204, 5211
Sciences naturelles 11, 22, 1574, 1624, 2314
Sciences sociales 2, 5, 6, 10, 13, 15, 21, 22, 24, 25, 27, 32, 38, 39, 41, 48, 56, 70, 74, 89, 100, 101, 112, 116, 174, 190, 268, 269, 301, 304, 309, 333, 334, 356, 369, 385, 396, 415, 418, 423, 429, 436, 439, 445, 447, 450, 457, 488, 495, 499, 507, 530, 533, 572, 801, 870, 912, 1089, 1102, 1216, 1224, 1231, 1244, 1245, 1289, 1366, 1610, 1628, 1870, 2182, 2227, 2281, 2284, 2462, 2716, 2907, 3063, 3700, 3774, 3790, 3795, 4181, 4205, 4351, 4889, 4901, 4948, 5075, 5206, 5297, 5310, 5357, 5704
Scientifiques 775, 1572, 1605, 1610, 1612, 1613, 1618, 1620, 1624, 1625, 3179
    voir aussi: Politologues, Spécialistes en sciences sociales
Scientologie 1378
Scolarité 225, 544, 980, 1331, 1809, 1991, 2011, 2017, 2022, 2023, 2034, 2041, 2042, 2047, 2054, 2058, 2064, 2066, 2068, 2074, 2095, 2097, 2109, 2120, 2121, 2124, 2130, 2131, 2133, 2141, 2142, 2152, 2155, 2156, 2159-2161, 2163, 2166, 2177, 2187, 2188, 2192, 2225, 2234, 2532, 2602, 2624, 2813, 2935, 3047, 3057, 3115, 3571, 4962
Script 671
Scrutin 5289
    voir aussi: Sondages d'opinion publique
Seacole, Mary 1960
Sécheresse 2827, 3690
Secours aux sinistrés 3699, 3751, 3813, 5321, 5330
Secret 5169
Sectarisme 1394, 1484, 1510
Sectes 56, 1498, 1536
Secteur agricole 3880
Secteur industriel 2139, 4847
Secteur informel 3190, 4099, 4116, 4373, 4429, 4596, 5380, 5492
Secteur privé 371, 1119, 1122, 1123, 3862, 4054, 4537, 4648, 4705, 4804, 4881, 4949, 5478, 5522, 5754, 5777, 5815

Secteur public 371, 1119, 1122, 1123, 3862, 4161, 4163, 4705, 4768, 4795, 4854, 4857, 4871, 4949, 5212, 5220, 5223, 5645, 5691, 5754, 5755
Secteur tertiaire 1977, 3927, 4092, 4179, 4235, 4237, 4321, 4416, 4459, 4736, 4831
Sécularisation 1175, 1228, 1375, 1386, 1508, 1514, 1529, 2025, 4962
Sécurité 1115, 1601, 2826, 2879, 3287, 3745, 3937, 3998, 4325, 4695, 4995, 5082, 5107, 5200, 5443, 5808, 5967
Sécurité alimentaire 2706, 3677, 3884
Sécurité de l'emploi 2085, 4388, 4411, 4471, 4484, 4692, 4703, 4714, 4729
Sécurité des produits 5200
Sécurité du travail 4433, 4683, 4727, 4730, 4813
Sécurité internationale 1995, 5314, 5325
Sécurité nationale 4949, 4993, 5314, 5353, 5363
Sécurité régionale 3776
Sécurité sociale 2458, 2657, 2677, 2712, 2846, 3001, 3169, 3588, 3619, 3985, 4191, 4247, 4293, 4299, 4411, 4439, 4456, 4479, 4580, 4594, 4595, 4862, 5475, 5487, 5504, 5506, 5507, 5535, 5551, 5581, 5603, 5606, 5610, 5617, 5620, 5622-5624, 5634, 5641, 5642, 5645, 5648, 5654, 5660, 5766, 5806
Segovia, Tomás 1922
Ségrégation 491, 2024, 2136, 2403, 2935, 3189, 3456, 3992, 3998, 4003, 4015, 4018, 4020, 4034, 4266, 4533, 5576
Ségrégation professionnelle 3285
Ségrégation raciale 1429, 2068, 3451, 3481, 3988, 4019, 4266
Ségrégation résidentielle 3383, 3451, 3481, 3994, 4003, 4019, 4020, 4034, 4125
Sélection du personnel 4569
Sélection naturelle 463, 898, 1583, 2329, 3401
Sellars, Wilfred 1871
Sémantique 139, 210, 231, 494, 563, 596, 617, 721, 729, 1638, 1804, 1822, 1828, 1842, 1989, 2250, 5177
Séminaires 1024
Sémiologie 1989
Sémiotique 326, 342, 1233, 1237, 1418, 1611, 1767, 1787, 1799, 1803, 1804, 1832, 1842, 1862, 1898, 2208, 3061, 3139, 3676, 4612
Sen, Amartya 1923, 5642
Sens 1984, 2493
    voir aussi: Audition, Goût, Vue
Sensation 551, 552, 1347

SUBJECT INDEX IN FRENCH

Sentiments 469, 686, 690, 696, 703, 713, 1666, 1947, 3038
Séparation maritale 2768, 2855, 2968, 2969, 2973
Séparatisme 1000, 3400, 3475, 4494
Sephardim 3483
Serbes 967, 991, 3859
Service chargé de faire respecter la loi 5006, 5048, 5124, 5128, 5134, 5136, 5139, 5140, 5145, 5154, 5204, 5282
Service clientèle 1127, 4416, 4544
Service militaire 3257, 5339, 5342, 5351
Services collectifs 3836, 4768, 5422, 5515, 5527, 5609, 5666, 5934
Services commerciales 4385
Services de santé 502, 525, 753, 797, 1923, 2470, 2679, 2751, 3381, 4032, 4087, 4304, 4433, 4439, 4682, 4784, 4831, 5019, 5197, 5200, 5407, 5420, 5497, 5499, 5522, 5561, 5609, 5726, 5731, 5732, 5735, 5738, 5739, 5741, 5747-5751, 5753, 5754, 5757, 5758, 5760-5763, 5765, 5769-5772, 5774-5777, 5779-5781, 5783-5786, 5790, 5791, 5794-5801, 5803-5812, 5814, 5816, 5818, 5819, 5821, 5822, 5824, 5825, 5834, 5835, 5838, 5840, 5841, 5843, 5846, 5852, 5860, 5894, 5896, 5903, 5905, 5909-5911, 5913, 5918, 5922, 5923, 5926, 5931, 5933, 5938, 5940, 5942, 5963, 5964, 5968, 5971, 5974, 5976, 5980
Services de voirie 2823, 3813
Services d'espionnage 5145
Services d'information 37, 78-80, 1646, 5669
Services financières 4284, 4782, 4831
Services publics 1745, 1778, 1849, 2873, 3784, 3885, 3960, 4032, 4159, 4169, 4768, 4818, 4832, 4950
Services sociaux 43, 767, 2463, 2469, 2477, 3630, 4152, 4169, 4585, 5373, 5422, 5478, 5480-5482, 5492, 5500, 5513, 5526, 5537, 5544, 5548, 5549, 5556, 5559, 5569, 5581, 5586, 5591, 5596, 5599, 5613, 5614, 5619, 5623, 5629, 5630, 5635, 5639, 5641, 5644, 5647, 5653, 5663, 5665, 5666, 5674, 5679, 5688, 5693, 5697, 5698, 5702, 5705-5708, 5711, 5712, 5715, 5716, 5718, 5719, 5739, 5780, 5820, 5903, 5904
Services urbains 4176
Sexe 709, 869, 913, 938, 1018, 1334, 1370, 1613, 2071, 2304, 2669, 2699, 2771, 2835, 2951, 2986, 3115, 3121, 3167, 3199, 3297, 3303, 3314, 3322, 3323, 3330-3333, 3335, 3344, 3347, 3348, 3353, 3374, 4387, 4551, 4733, 4761, 4777, 5470
Sexisme 1613, 1760, 1810, 1821, 3141, 3283, 3310, 4488, 4508, 4519, 5872
Sexologie 522, 3295, 3314
Sexualité 361, 593, 695, 769, 786, 926, 1258, 1317, 1352, 1358, 1488, 1761, 1821, 1882, 1897, 1929, 1940, 1950, 1969, 2160, 2478, 2608, 2641, 2652, 2708, 2737, 2817, 2880, 2907, 2986, 3018, 3028, 3061, 3085, 3090, 3115, 3121, 3137, 3149, 3199, 3225, 3242, 3248, 3253, 3294, 3295, 3297, 3298, 3301, 3303, 3305-3309, 3311, 3313-3317, 3321, 3323, 3324, 3328-3331, 3333, 3335, 3336, 3339-3343, 3345, 3346, 3349-3352, 3356, 3357, 3360, 3361, 3363, 3368, 3369, 3372, 3374, 3376-3379, 3382, 3383, 3385, 3386, 3389, 4512, 5100, 5196, 5371, 5438, 5459, 5698, 5745, 5837, 5943, 5946, 5966
 voir aussi: Bisexualité, Hétérosexualité, Homosexualité, Lesbianisme, Transsexualisme
Shan 5237
Shapiro, Francine 5721
She, Lao 3222
Shelley, Mary 1970
Shu-hsien, Liu 1477
SIDA 489, 581, 781, 1883, 2754, 2797, 2806, 2810, 2824, 3299, 3316, 3326, 3332, 3334, 3349, 3370, 4611, 5363, 5745, 5764, 5773, 5854, 5866, 5872, 5885, 5890, 5891, 5893, 5894, 5944-5946, 5952, 5957, 5965, 5966, 5968, 5974, 5980, 5982
Siegfried, André 4897
Signes 342, 1161, 1210, 1787, 1799, 1804
Sikhisme 1376, 1447
Sikhs 1376, 1447
Simmel, Georg 373, 4186, 4192
Simulation 458, 492, 620, 1085, 1623, 2231, 2693, 2722, 2802, 3741, 4317, 4486
Simulation de Monte Carlo 446, 483, 491, 492
Singhalese 1471
Sites historiques 1342
Situation de famille 2768, 2791, 2938, 2982, 5436, 5510
Skinner, Burrhus Frederic 599
Slaves 1816
Smart, Ninian 1419
Smith, Adam 12, 4288
Sobhuza, II [King] 12
Sociabilité 1680, 1686
Social-démocratie 3950, 4018, 4066, 4215, 4222, 4859

INDEX DES MATIÈRES

Socialisation 359, 573, 677, 1052, 1131, 1512, 1542, 1626, 1788, 2301, 2304, 2316, 2325, 2447, 2631, 2870, 2897, 2898, 2909, 3011, 3026, 3173, 3216, 3271, 3568, 4320, 4427, 4481, 4543, 4608, 4622, 4722, 4900, 5050, 5108, 5266, 5344, 5534, 5538, 5563
Socialisation politique 1827, 2181, 2614, 2671, 3206, 3869, 4956
Socialisme 284, 1936, 1979, 2416, 2563, 3100, 4210, 4213, 4215, 4222, 4864, 4898, 4922, 4934, 4942, 4946
Socialisme d'État 746
Socialisme du marché 4215, 4241, 4829
Société 6, 7, 17, 279, 284, 301, 329, 394, 397, 403, 405, 406, 408, 439, 441, 763, 1195, 1200, 1333, 1417, 1432, 1461, 1483, 1493, 1495, 1524, 1590, 1609, 1646, 1729, 1756, 1790, 1815, 1837, 1852, 1933, 1961, 2305, 2310, 2322, 2324, 2327, 2328, 2337, 2343, 2392, 2414, 2437, 2438, 2440, 2451, 2463, 2507, 2527, 2556, 2563, 2567, 2600, 2614, 2662, 2942, 2961, 2983, 3071, 3092, 3111, 3262, 3552, 3707, 3712, 3723, 3753, 3783, 3861, 3998, 4196, 4200, 4206, 4256, 4307, 4349, 4351, 4444, 4458, 4469, 4983, 5047, 5058, 5159, 5246, 5294, 5332, 5338
    voir aussi: Individu et société
Société agraire 3889
Société civile 54, 58, 243, 405, 904, 1442, 1479, 1517, 1643, 1675, 1756, 1764, 2088, 2134, 2181, 2203, 2371, 2387, 2506, 3403, 3416, 3423, 3468, 3506, 3683, 3694, 3702, 3802, 3810, 3828, 3917, 3927, 4095, 4119, 4169, 4192, 4215, 4272, 4467, 4768, 4890, 4901, 4916, 4932, 4940, 4948, 4950, 4955, 4960, 4967, 4974, 4976, 4978, 5015, 5125, 5139, 5200, 5213, 5241, 5285, 5294, 5330
Société contemporaine 28, 32, 243, 386, 801, 1164, 1190, 1199, 1254, 1263, 1383, 1447, 1644, 1679, 1690, 1855, 1964, 2140, 2307, 2331, 2410, 2413, 2438, 2556, 2617, 2980, 3168, 3448, 4298, 4967, 4972, 4976, 4980, 5278
Société de consommation 4328, 4329, 4333, 4342
Société de l'information 37, 379, 1199, 1636, 1643-1646, 1657, 1658, 1674-1676, 1678, 1683, 1685, 2006, 2210, 2309, 2412, 2477, 2519, 2532, 2548, 4570
Société de masse 1323, 1719, 4119, 5248
Société future 2540

Société industrielle 2420, 5238, 5630
Société internationale 336, 393, 1919, 2191, 2521, 2546, 2550, 2555, 2557, 2570, 2572, 2576, 3659, 3669, 5317
Société politique 1245
Société post-apartheid 957, 964, 1507, 1880, 1942, 2436, 3171, 3395, 3430, 3438, 3471, 3599, 3769, 4096, 4101, 4282, 4971, 5703
Société post-industrielle 2412, 2519, 2540, 3396, 3956, 4227, 4298, 4365, 4436, 4459, 5630
Société pré-industrielle 2542
Société primitive 1964
Société rurale 3891, 3916
Société urbaine 50, 3842, 3939, 3959, 4027, 4092, 4128
Sociétés complexes 3832, 5248
Sociétés postcoloniales 184, 951, 995, 1158, 1195, 1213, 1224, 1227, 1268, 1589, 1880, 1962, 2388, 2415, 3148, 3227, 3417, 3445, 3641, 3642, 3782, 4975, 5007, 5187, 5328
Sociétés post-communistes 24, 477, 992, 993, 1000, 1328, 1470, 1505, 1511, 1746, 1816, 2088, 2156, 2217, 2228, 2333, 2407, 2437, 2438, 2533-2536, 2538, 2593, 2606, 2637, 2649, 2689, 2695, 2837, 3081, 3105, 3227, 3455, 3469, 3627, 4079, 4168, 4209, 4227, 4273, 4349, 4429, 4474, 4486, 4606, 4790, 4820, 4836, 4898, 4925, 4974, 5003, 5039, 5060, 5116, 5134, 5214, 5263, 5281, 5284, 5294, 5297, 5356, 5489
Sociétés socialistes 1295
Sociobiologie 27, 596, 649, 656, 1567, 2744, 2912, 2973, 2983, 3304, 3318
Sociographie 24
Sociolinguistique 76, 538, 571, 610, 622, 853, 916, 930, 940, 945, 959, 979, 1120, 1689, 1722, 1784, 1788, 1790, 1791, 1793-1796, 1799, 1801-1803, 1805, 1807, 1808, 1810, 1811, 1813-1821, 1825-1827, 1832, 1833, 1835, 1837, 1838, 1843, 1846, 1847, 2121, 2208, 2523, 2936, 2940, 3358, 3363, 5170
Sociologie 3, 5, 10, 11, 16-18, 23, 25, 26, 28, 31, 32, 36, 38, 40, 41, 44, 51, 55, 58, 62, 66, 67, 72, 77, 81, 100, 130, 166, 269, 288, 318, 319, 329, 330, 334, 338, 343, 348, 354, 359, 371, 385, 392, 395, 396, 398, 401, 404, 407, 450, 801, 912, 1002, 1047, 1107, 1553, 1858, 1870, 1944, 2331, 2393, 2462, 2853, 2918, 2930, 3158, 3513, 3693, 3699, 3704, 3900, 4131,

SUBJECT INDEX IN FRENCH

4314, 4323, 4413, 4507, 4754, 4762, 4783, 4978, 5106, 5166, 5204, 5332, 5485, 5523, 5665, 5817
voir aussi: Enseignement de la sociologie, Histoire de la sociologie
Sociologie appliquée 67
Sociologie criminelle 5013, 5051, 5064, 5096, 5098, 5102, 5106, 5110, 5120
Sociologie de la connaissance 5, 70, 127, 130, 746, 1115, 1116, 1411, 1556, 1575, 1587, 1595, 1610, 1614, 1617, 1629, 2565, 3176, 4610, 5885
Sociologie de la culture 1192, 1855, 2443
Sociologie de la famille 50, 2899, 2903, 2906, 2917, 2948, 2971, 3047
Sociologie de la littérature 1927, 1953
Sociologie de la musique 1309, 1972, 1982, 1987, 1988
Sociologie de la profession 4533
Sociologie de la religion 56, 400, 1228, 1377, 1381, 1385, 1401, 1403, 1406, 1410, 1411, 1415, 1418, 1425, 1430, 1431, 1433-1435, 1437, 1446, 1448-1450, 1461, 1464, 1475, 1492, 1508, 1521, 3919, 5722
Sociologie de la science 29, 498, 537, 1556, 1561, 1562, 1575, 1577, 1579, 1584, 1596, 1610, 1614, 1616, 1617, 1619, 5885
Sociologie de l'art 1852, 1855, 1866
Sociologie de l'éducation 50, 77, 1991, 2000, 2002, 2003, 2014, 2024, 2030, 2051, 2054, 2062, 2064, 2069, 2071, 2080, 2090, 2097, 2104, 2108, 2110, 2146, 2158, 2164, 2192, 2202, 2225, 2240, 2284, 2532, 3176, 3340, 4772
Sociologie des loisirs 1301, 2906
Sociologie des organisations 416, 1064, 1090, 1109, 1115, 1132, 1142, 1145, 1385, 4355, 4392, 4403, 4409, 4413, 4622, 4627, 4731
Sociologie du droit 3284, 4511, 4998, 5025, 5124, 5150, 5151, 5153, 5154, 5158, 5166, 5168, 5172, 5183, 5185, 5187-5189, 5192, 5199, 5204, 5206, 5211
Sociologie du milieu 3687, 3698, 3700, 3706, 3712, 3730, 3783, 4086
Sociologie du sport 962, 1305, 1306, 1326, 1330, 1341, 1355-1358, 1369, 3217
Sociologie du théâtre 1862
Sociologie du travail 412, 440, 715, 2953, 3062, 3347, 4289, 4365, 4368, 4373, 4377, 4378, 4382, 4389, 4395, 4398, 4401, 4403-4405, 4411, 4416, 4448, 4456, 4461, 4468, 4469, 4471, 4477, 4488, 4616, 4700, 4702, 4704, 4715, 4718, 4732, 4740, 4745, 4758, 4761, 4771, 4821, 4832, 4856, 4867

Sociologie économique 67, 336, 408, 1324, 2526, 3164, 3169, 3907, 4179, 4180, 4182, 4190, 4191, 4194, 4195, 4224, 4235, 4237, 4241, 4263, 4285, 4323, 4326, 4374, 4380, 4403, 4405, 4423, 5365
Sociologie industrielle 1138, 4323, 4389, 4392, 4400, 4403-4405, 4811
Sociologie médicale 400, 2440, 2487, 3900, 4696, 4703, 4800, 4999, 5400, 5731, 5733-5735, 5773, 5804, 5811, 5826, 5852, 5856, 5857, 5859, 5861, 5863, 5864, 5867, 5868, 5875, 5877, 5878, 5880, 5892, 5893, 5896, 5897, 5900
Sociologie militaire 5338-5340, 5342, 5344-5346, 5350, 5351, 5353, 5354, 5356, 5359-5362
Sociologie politique 16, 307, 325, 335, 368, 400, 1360, 1364, 2312, 4884, 4885, 4887-4891, 4894-4899, 4901, 4915, 4921, 4932, 4936, 4943, 4951, 4953, 4961, 4974, 5227, 5233, 5235, 5238, 5277, 5281, 5289, 5297, 5300, 5302, 5307, 5466
Sociologie rurale 20, 788, 1632, 2022, 2152, 2532, 3619, 3729, 3742, 3870, 3872-3875, 3878, 3881, 3884, 3892, 3894, 3897-3899, 3902, 3910, 3912, 3917, 3920, 4270, 4591, 4981, 5374, 5418
Sociologie urbaine 32, 50, 788, 1168, 1365, 1530, 1991, 2024, 2062, 2069, 2104, 2146, 2532, 2972, 3340, 3413, 3610, 3632, 3725, 3729, 3842, 3860, 3870, 3872, 3926, 3929-3933, 3937, 3938, 3944-3946, 3950-3952, 3954, 3957, 3959-3961, 3963, 3966-3969, 3971, 3972, 3974, 3978, 3982, 3983, 3987, 3991, 3994, 3995, 3998-4000, 4005, 4012, 4013, 4015-4017, 4021, 4029, 4031, 4043, 4051, 4056, 4059, 4073, 4076, 4108, 4111, 4121, 4127, 4128, 4139, 4143, 4144, 4149, 4151, 4154, 4159-4161, 4165, 4168, 4172, 4173, 4233, 4327, 4431, 4436, 4445, 4892, 5079, 5119, 5270, 5274, 5275, 5279, 5374, 5424, 5900
Sociologues 1, 4, 11, 23, 36, 44, 50, 58, 62, 65-68, 72, 75, 144, 288, 316, 330, 341, 343, 347, 373-375, 377, 388, 395, 398, 400, 402, 403, 423, 801, 1212, 1431, 1866, 2302, 2411, 4195, 4241, 4766, 4888, 4898, 4930, 5098, 5225
Socrates 270
Sœur 769
Soi 69, 106, 199, 207, 219, 220, 236, 245, 246, 266, 276, 283, 340, 541, 543, 558, 569, 601, 602, 657, 679, 699, 702, 718, 732, 734, 737, 744, 785, 803, 809, 814,

825, 839, 840, 851, 871, 873, 874, 878, 894, 915, 933, 937, 991, 1063, 1147, 1161, 1214, 1251, 1361, 1426, 1454, 1551, 1937, 1947, 1949, 1960, 1964, 2021, 2303, 2566, 3033, 3045, 3059, 3108, 3115, 3135, 3227, 3256, 3263, 3395, 3418, 4349, 4392, 4967, 5073, 5095, 5159, 5697, 5944

Soins 749, 1050, 2927, 3037, 3108, 3169, 3219, 3740, 4486, 4687, 5479, 5486, 5488, 5501, 5503, 5520, 5525, 5527, 5543, 5613, 5660, 5707, 5708, 5715, 5719, 5739, 5753, 5764, 5843, 5856, 5916

Soins à long terme 5504, 5506, 5513, 5515, 5519, 5536

Soins en dehors du milieu hospitalier 758, 792, 2458, 2470, 2489, 2497, 2712, 3751, 5137, 5363, 5397, 5400, 5421, 5422, 5490, 5492, 5496, 5497, 5501, 5511, 5533, 5693, 5718, 5736-5742, 5749, 5771, 5787, 5800, 5900, 5904, 5909, 5913, 5919, 5922, 5927, 5934, 5940, 5982

Soins médicaux 1564, 2470, 2751, 3185, 5197, 5497, 5524, 5534, 5698, 5734, 5743, 5748, 5750, 5759, 5764, 5778, 5781, 5784, 5797, 5806, 5808, 5812, 5819, 5822-5824, 5835, 5859, 5902, 5971

Soins médicaux généraux 43, 371, 419, 525, 764-766, 789, 800, 887, 2456, 2602, 2750, 2780, 2814, 2817, 2821, 2838, 3007, 3039, 3185, 3311, 3327, 3373, 3382, 4032, 4087, 4304, 4711, 4949, 4999, 5022, 5197, 5392, 5420, 5421, 5479, 5494, 5497-5499, 5502, 5504, 5505, 5507, 5508, 5513, 5521, 5525, 5526, 5530, 5541, 5583, 5614, 5651, 5690, 5698, 5725, 5727-5729, 5731-5733, 5735-5738, 5742, 5745-5747, 5749-5754, 5757, 5760-5767, 5770-5772, 5776-5781, 5784-5787, 5789, 5790, 5793-5798, 5802-5814, 5816-5821, 5825, 5826, 5833, 5835, 5837, 5840, 5841, 5845, 5846, 5852, 5864, 5869, 5873, 5874, 5877, 5879, 5891, 5896, 5897, 5901, 5903, 5905, 5906, 5910, 5911, 5913-5916, 5918, 5922, 5923, 5926, 5927, 5929, 5931, 5937, 5939, 5942, 5947, 5949, 5950, 5952, 5959, 5963, 5972, 5976, 5980-5982, 5986
voir aussi: Soins à long terme

Soins médicaux primaires 5751, 5758, 5759, 5762, 5778, 5822, 5824, 5905, 5953

Soins médicaux privée 5754, 5776

Soins résidentiels 2674, 2679, 5016, 5479, 5496, 5499, 5501, 5504, 5513, 5522, 5530, 5542, 5569, 5570, 5596, 5607, 5608, 5740, 5741, 5978

Sokal, Alan 135

Soldat 5606

Solidarité 371, 923, 929, 931, 1151, 1499, 2313, 2332, 2590, 2682, 3155, 3730, 3842, 3892, 4250, 4299, 4834, 4850, 4945, 4970, 5151

Solidarité de groupe 1047

Solitude 578, 701, 1670, 2311, 5893

Sollicitations 3535, 3912, 4966

Solzhenitsyn, Aleksandr 4898

Sommeil 4698

Sondages 705, 3617, 3853

Sondages d'opinion publique 512

Songhay 1888

Sorcellerie 303, 3186

Sorciers 3186

Soufisme 1521

Sources d'information 78-80, 92, 101, 102, 447, 3853, 3874, 4686

Sous-alimentation 3759, 5541, 5969

Sous-classe 3656, 3775, 3989

Sous-développement 3702, 3798, 4205, 4261

Sous-traitance 4448

Soutien social 767, 771, 793, 935, 948, 1054, 1691, 2299, 2494, 2585, 2712, 2852, 2881, 2890, 2934, 2979, 3015, 3048, 3293, 3370, 3381, 3586, 3619, 3846, 4448, 4741, 5033, 5116, 5244, 5400, 5413, 5463, 5475, 5488, 5492, 5517, 5521, 5525, 5531-5533, 5552, 5566, 5572, 5574, 5590, 5669, 5687, 5693, 5716, 5736, 5742

Souveraineté 2547, 2553, 3672, 4287, 4939, 4957, 5207, 5232, 5256, 5334

Spark, Muriel 3262

Spécialisation de la production 2406

Spécialistes en sciences sociales 48, 1620

Spécificité culturelle 1240, 3888, 4426, 4624, 5908

Spectateurs 1327, 1725, 1774, 5448

Spéculation en bourse 4352

Spencer-Brown, G. 380

Sphère privée 110, 371, 1371, 1659, 1662, 1751, 1938, 2313, 2451, 2941, 3060, 3365, 3946, 4171, 4933, 4984, 4988, 5299, 5982

Sphère publique 44, 106, 110, 196, 371, 955, 1190, 1196, 1199, 1659, 1751, 1782, 1826, 1889, 1938, 2434, 2439, 3060, 3134, 3365, 3946, 4171, 4851, 4932, 4933, 4966, 5162, 5263, 5279, 5299, 5982

Spielberg, Steven 1882

Spinoza, Benedictus de 254

Spiritualité 225, 581, 719, 998, 1249, 1372, 1381, 1384, 1416, 1421, 1424, 1427, 1444, 1446, 1454, 1457, 1477, 1501, 1549, 1551, 1975, 1983, 2106, 2673, 2890, 3145, 3382, 4360, 5409
Sport 951, 962, 979, 1081, 1305, 1306, 1308, 1315, 1326, 1327, 1330, 1341, 1344, 1347, 1350, 1353-1358, 1368, 1369, 2321, 2618, 3217, 3252, 4767, 5448
  voir aussi: Anthropologie du sport, Baseball, Football, Sociologie du sport
Squatters 3961, 3974, 4169, 4302
Stabilité conjugale 2966, 2969
Stabilité d'emploi 4738
Stabilité économique 4949
Stalinisme 4973
Statique 1555
Statistique 101, 116, 421, 433, 434, 451, 468, 475, 478, 480, 494-496, 499, 502, 631, 1059, 1431, 1442, 1610, 2089, 2101, 2234, 2533, 2626, 2688, 2716, 2776, 2794, 2808, 2823, 2829, 2840, 2852, 3408, 4175, 4266, 4582, 4646, 4723, 4780, 4796, 5324, 5389, 5728, 5744
Statistiques de population 2690, 2694, 2712, 2805, 2835, 3773
Statut de la femme 2449, 2873, 2891, 2955, 3079, 3081, 3087, 3091, 3103, 3104, 3111, 3112, 3131, 3140, 3160, 3168, 3169, 3174, 3184, 3192, 3193, 3196-3198, 3203, 3206, 3215, 3224, 3234, 3247, 3251, 3262, 3277-3279, 3290, 3549, 3767, 3793, 4535, 4537, 4564, 5969
Statut économique 2748, 3996, 4530, 5519
Statut international 5308
Statut juridique 1520, 1522, 3290, 3471, 3585, 5156, 5580, 5585
Statut professionnel 842, 2382, 2434, 4765, 4776
Statut social 710, 1686, 1835, 1861, 2078, 2376, 2378, 2386, 2393, 2408, 2410, 2430, 2444, 2449, 2474, 2545, 2591, 2631, 2677, 2679, 2917, 3013, 3192, 3215, 3407, 3410, 3563, 3996, 4187, 4376, 4567, 4781, 5168, 5296, 5300, 5436
Stéréotypes 20, 574, 657, 822, 824, 826, 832, 834, 835, 843, 846, 853, 854, 857, 859, 861, 863, 865, 866, 877, 880, 881, 891, 895, 1014, 1310, 1339, 1768, 1899, 1909, 1946, 2009, 2061, 2584, 2657, 2665, 2677, 2900, 2950, 3181, 3229, 3245, 3248, 3257, 3281, 3372, 3382, 3404, 3414, 3416, 3457, 3527, 3562, 3649, 3894, 4265, 4472, 4521, 4543, 4661, 5253, 5717, 5837

Stéréotypes nationaux 3527
Stéréotypes raciaux 1308, 3517
Stéréotypes sociaux 832, 5842
Stérilisation 2726, 2752
Stérilisation féminine 2729, 2733, 5200
Stérilisation masculine 2729
Stérilité 2735, 2772, 2789, 5200
Stimulants du travail 4587
Stimulants économiques 4180
Stimulants financiers 2092, 3814, 4438
Stimulus 594, 643, 667, 686
Stratégie de développement 1221, 2286, 2483, 3104, 3174, 3822, 3832, 4252, 4290
Stratégie de recherche 60, 415, 1005, 2344, 4181
Stratégie de survie 596, 1995, 3574, 3902, 4273, 5229, 5430
Stratégie économique 5445
Stratégies d'entreprises 4420, 4672, 4786, 4791
Stratemeyer, Edward 3225
Stratification professionnelle 4376, 4755
Stratification sociale 33, 65, 285, 308, 879, 1205, 1227, 1376, 1513, 2035, 2063, 2223, 2324, 2374-2377, 2381, 2382, 2384, 2385, 2387-2391, 2393-2395, 2398, 2405, 2410-2412, 2417, 2418, 2420, 2422, 2427, 2430-2438, 2440, 2441, 2444, 2445, 2447, 2449, 2466, 2468, 2476, 2487, 2499, 2524, 2548, 2591, 3076, 3171, 3436, 3443, 3512, 3820, 3992, 3996, 4065, 4187, 4209, 4271, 4294, 4474, 4533, 4921, 4983, 5016, 5077, 5215, 5296, 5423, 5430, 5487, 5625
Strike, Kenneth A. 2218
Structuralisme 14, 1068, 1221, 2384, 3117, 3775, 4612, 5245
Structure de classe 2390, 2445, 2578, 2870, 3528, 4436
Structure de la famille 50, 771, 1752, 1761, 2035, 2472, 2635, 2642, 2703, 2712, 2742, 2848, 2853, 2858, 2891, 2896, 2899, 2903, 2910, 2913, 2914, 2917, 2919, 2923, 2924, 2926, 2927, 2929, 2933, 2937, 2938, 2941, 2943-2945, 2949, 2951, 2955, 2959, 2964, 2979, 2988, 2989, 2994, 2996, 3020, 3026, 3051, 3115, 3169, 3236, 3343, 3360, 3382, 3434, 3897, 4192, 5528, 5538, 5540, 5552, 5590
Structure de l'État 5227
Structure de l'organisation 1087, 1094, 1096-1100, 1105-1107, 1114, 1125, 1132, 1133, 1140, 1149, 1153, 1154, 1384, 1385, 1443, 1660, 1718, 2133, 2250, 2251, 3097, 3362, 3813, 4356, 4395, 4424, 4609,

INDEX DES MATIÈRES

4623, 4632, 4656, 4660, 4680, 4734, 4737, 4773, 4787, 4788, 5154, 5267, 5799
Structure des salaires 4763
Structure du marché 4003, 4778
Structure du marché du travail 2434, 2455, 3549, 3594, 3677, 4382, 4429, 4434, 4480, 4516, 4547, 4552, 4554, 4582, 4790, 4856, 4985
Structure économique 4942, 5821
Structure politique 3418, 4966, 4973, 5249
Structure professionnelle 2532, 4414, 4434, 4771
Structure sociale 40, 41, 65, 285, 326, 329, 347, 368, 372, 394, 837, 1002, 1062, 1074, 1079, 1087, 1222, 1800, 1878, 1974, 2064, 2300, 2305, 2312, 2319, 2320, 2322, 2326, 2327, 2334, 2338, 2384, 2391-2394, 2398, 2400, 2427, 2430, 2434, 2435, 2437, 2438, 2441, 2445, 2494, 2532, 2535, 2536, 2555, 2564, 2578, 2591, 2597, 2657, 2675, 2701, 2870, 2923, 3087, 3418, 3668, 3899, 3909, 3917, 3927, 4314, 4441, 4746, 4921, 4942, 4977, 5092, 5104, 5245, 5302
Structure urbaine 3948, 4053, 4103
Stupéfiants 1307, 5386, 5828
Subalterne 1978, 3148, 5162, 5229
Subculture 155, 1331, 1335, 1340, 1352, 1370, 1974, 1986, 2630, 3156, 3387, 4007, 5108, 5429
Subjectivité 20, 109, 148, 162, 204, 226, 300, 320, 391, 399, 428, 507, 645, 744, 801, 839, 892, 1137, 1161, 1195, 1232, 1289, 1876, 1917, 3130, 3153, 3293, 3350, 3438, 3537, 3788, 3953, 4392, 4808, 5084, 5166, 5430, 5692
Subvention publique 2287
Subventions 3169, 3590, 3979, 3988, 4587, 4756
Subversion 3368, 5165
Succession 2398, 4625
Suffrage 3146
Suicide 793, 2719, 2831, 2844, 4994, 5432-5436, 5773, 5838, 5849, 5858, 5882, 5887, 5889, 5895
Sujet 406, 744, 2322, 3151
Sullivan, Louis 4131
Sunnites 1537
Supermarchés 4678
Suprématie du droit 4909, 4955, 4989, 5154, 5181, 5187
Surabondance de main d'oeuvre 4483
Surdité 1827, 2453, 2479
Suri 3531
Surnaturel 1438

Surpeuplement 5417
Surveillance 178, 2709, 4140, 4683, 4954, 4986-4988, 4995, 5016, 5881, 5885
Swahili 1709
Symboles 8, 122, 348, 810, 961, 963, 1000, 1100, 1161, 1238, 1899, 3701, 4192
Symbolisme 331, 342, 380, 955, 982, 1258, 1308, 1343, 1347, 1383, 1418, 1799, 1868, 1928, 3093, 3128, 3367, 3418, 4065, 4115, 4349, 4759
Symbolisme religieux 1418
Syncrétisme religieux 1539
Syndicalisme 2507, 4417, 4813, 4854, 4864, 4874, 4875, 4880, 4949, 5220
Syndicats 1891, 2079, 2450, 3127, 4208, 4250, 4354, 4537, 4587, 4596, 4618, 4650, 4679, 4682, 4813, 4815, 4816, 4819-4822, 4824, 4829, 4832, 4835, 4836, 4843, 4847, 4850-4883, 5148, 5243, 5265
Syndiqués 4875, 4878, 4880
Syntaxe 623, 5170
Systématisation 121
Système de jugement par jury 5157
Système financier 3927
Système international 336, 1995, 2541, 2562, 2568, 3672
Système monétaire international 2446
Système pénitentiaire 5192
Système pileux 3272
Systèmes agricoles 3879, 4775
Systemes culturels 2566, 3417
Systèmes de communication 1108
Systèmes de paiement 4402, 5789, 5931
Systèmes de parenté 3164
  voir aussi: Endogamie, Exogamie
Systèmes de planification 1030, 3921
Systèmes de prévoyance 4293
Systèmes de production 308, 1892, 2627, 3893, 4243, 4818, 4838, 4934
Systèmes de valeur 524, 1205
Systèmes d'enseignement 50, 93, 437, 1223, 1715, 1991, 1994, 1996, 2010, 2011, 2014, 2016, 2017, 2021, 2024, 2047, 2049, 2054, 2058, 2059, 2063-2065, 2068, 2076, 2077, 2081, 2084, 2085, 2093, 2094, 2108, 2109, 2111-2116, 2120, 2122-2124, 2126, 2128-2131, 2133, 2135-2138, 2140, 2142, 2144-2148, 2150, 2151, 2153, 2155, 2158, 2159, 2161, 2163-2165, 2167, 2169, 2171, 2173, 2176, 2177, 2180, 2181, 2184, 2192, 2204, 2218-2220, 2226, 2230, 2236, 2238, 2245-2247, 2256, 2259, 2260, 2265, 2266, 2275, 2277, 2283-2285, 2296, 2316, 2378, 2460, 3491, 3521, 3869, 4598, 4640, 4805, 4806, 4949, 5678

SUBJECT INDEX IN FRENCH

Systèmes d'information 376, 1040, 1113
Systèmes d'information géographique 3813, 3820, 4102, 4166, 5582, 5802, 5838, 5968
Systèmes économiques 336, 1200, 2320, 3766, 3823, 3869, 4195, 4208, 4215, 4221, 4223, 4224, 4231, 4236, 4946
Systèmes juridiques 1010, 1734, 3136, 3891, 4422, 4823, 4999, 5020, 5025, 5038, 5043, 5054, 5139, 5150, 5154, 5157, 5160, 5163-5165, 5167, 5168, 5173, 5183, 5189-5191, 5193, 5198, 5204, 5207, 5211, 5282, 5546
  voir aussi: Culture juridique
Systèmes monétaires
  voir: Système monétaire international
Systèmes politiques 1195, 1200, 2389, 2502, 2507, 2559, 3323, 4201, 4938, 4956, 4966, 4970, 5207, 5219, 5282, 5325
Systèmes sociales 65, 279, 287, 306, 318, 336, 359, 368, 369, 372, 380, 381, 391, 392, 394, 402, 403, 408, 439, 821, 1054, 1121, 1282, 1545, 2140, 2300, 2302, 2305, 2310, 2312, 2320, 2322, 2329, 2384, 2391, 2394, 2395, 2405, 2411, 2420, 2427, 2435, 2436, 2445, 2532, 2758, 2955, 2984, 2990, 3800, 3865, 4050, 4228, 4837, 4970, 5306, 5821
Tabac 2824, 5407, 5956
Tabou 650, 1822, 2394, 3304
Tâche du groupe 1704
Tamouls 5331
Taoïsme 200, 1382, 1456, 1458, 1473
Tarde, Gabriel 67
Tatar 1392
Taux de fécondité 2698, 2702, 2721, 2735, 2743, 2775, 2784, 2788, 2793, 2795, 2799, 2802, 2805, 2822
Taux de mortalité 2689, 2819, 2837
Taux de natalité 2686, 2689, 2705, 2706, 2714, 2719, 2728, 2777, 2779, 2784, 2785, 2795, 2798, 2800, 2805
Taux de profit 4234
Taux de rendement 662
Taux d'inflation 4347
Taxonomie 650, 1408, 1999, 2308, 3345
Taylor, Charles 206, 207, 266
Tchèques 1004, 1816
Techniciens 4563, 4769
Techniques de fabrication 4617
Techniques de gestion 662, 1094, 1111, 4399, 4420, 4621, 4623, 4625, 4633, 4640, 4647, 4650, 4656, 4667, 4671, 4808, 5128
Techniques de prévision 4486
Techniques de vente 4418
Techniques du corps 3272

Technocratie 340, 2219
Technologie 37, 39, 291, 634, 1054, 1113, 1154, 1275, 1286, 1554, 1559, 1562, 1563, 1566, 1568, 1588, 1595, 1598, 1609, 1616, 1621, 1622, 1626, 1656, 1663, 1679, 1690, 1697, 1759, 1822, 1851, 1996, 2039, 2176, 2262, 2266, 2286, 2328, 2508, 2563, 2731, 2758, 3127, 3206, 3223, 3700, 3704, 4030, 4049, 4056, 4179, 4417, 4428, 4570, 4571, 4574, 4649, 4658, 4715, 4738, 4744, 4763, 4786, 5790, 5864, 5879
  voir aussi: Biotechnologie, Histoire de la technologie, Technologies nouvelles
Technologie de l'éducation 2172, 2175, 2201
Technologie de l'information 37, 1200, 1302, 1554, 1634, 1636, 1643-1645, 1659-1665, 1667, 1671-1678, 1680, 1688, 1689, 1692, 1713, 1774, 1779, 2006, 2039, 2056, 2172, 2175, 2176, 2197, 2201, 2210, 2223, 2270, 2325, 2337, 2519, 2526, 2532, 2571, 2578, 2608, 3156, 3253, 3505, 3797, 4056, 4095, 4102, 4213, 4346, 4377, 4382, 4434, 4574, 5228, 5230
  voir aussi: Réalité virtuelle
Technologie de pointe 4213, 4690
Technologie des communications 537, 1015, 1036, 1242, 1634, 1636, 1641, 1643, 1657, 1659, 1660, 1663-1666, 1668, 1670, 1672-1675, 1677, 1679-1681, 1683-1685, 1687, 1689, 1690, 1704, 1732, 2526, 2532, 2571, 4056, 5228, 5901
Technologie numérique 1661, 1667, 1669, 1779, 2596
Technologie reproductive 2735, 2902, 5785, 5851, 5863
Technologies nouvelles 511, 1234, 1242, 1593, 1595, 1603, 1662, 1672, 1756, 2129, 2272, 2519, 2532, 2559, 2596, 2667, 4031, 4243, 4315, 4377, 4382, 4400, 4647, 4688, 4786, 4933, 4988, 5880
Télécommunications 1298, 1302, 1634, 1637, 1641, 1657, 1660, 1661, 1663, 1678, 1686, 1688, 1732, 1780, 2554, 3927, 4095, 4122, 4124, 4167, 4688, 4738
Télématique 1688, 2201
Téléphone 518, 532, 1686, 1687, 2588, 4732
Télétravail 4738
Télévision 449, 1100, 1191, 1223, 1227, 1333, 1334, 1336, 1337, 1359-1361, 1641, 1687, 1690, 1695, 1698, 1701, 1707, 1709-1711, 1716, 1717, 1719, 1725, 1729, 1731, 1732, 1737, 1738, 1740, 1748, 1750, 1752, 1753, 1758, 1764-1768, 1770-1778,

INDEX DES MATIÈRES

1783, 1882, 1908, 2419, 2507, 2522, 2554, 2667, 2748, 3127, 3498, 3517, 3775
Témoinage 137, 179, 963, 1389, 1629, 4984, 5084, 5132, 5194, 5205, 5680
Temples 1384
Temporal dimension 32, 223, 236, 290, 297, 490, 552, 562, 639, 642, 1298, 1571, 2408, 2651, 2772, 3169, 3188, 3200, 3540, 3767, 3848, 3860, 3907, 4350
Temps 212, 222, 254, 290, 291, 313, 387, 409, 441, 572, 1031, 1055, 1161, 1200, 1282, 1292, 1301, 1365, 1413, 1586, 1627, 1966, 2533, 2546, 2575, 2581, 3820, 3864, 3956, 4137, 4751, 5240, 5604, 5946
Temps 767
  voir aussi: Changement de climat, Climat
Temps de loisir 1301, 3200, 4475
Temps de travail 3169, 4305, 4475, 4524, 4685, 4712, 4724, 4751, 4810
Tendances de recherche 4, 25, 50, 56, 66, 67, 75, 174, 182, 191, 339, 1218, 3067, 3233, 5673
Tension mentale 545, 550, 581, 716, 721, 722, 741, 742, 751, 764, 766, 767, 795, 796, 805, 807, 819, 820, 887, 1347, 2096, 2855, 2874, 2895, 2921, 2965, 3181, 3478, 3751, 3873, 4291, 4377, 4680, 4686, 4692, 4693, 4698, 4699, 4703, 4705, 4706, 4711, 4713, 4724, 4726, 4731, 4734, 4735, 4743, 4746, 4773, 5033, 5349, 5369, 5488, 5710, 5721, 5838, 5921, 5928, 5935
Terminologie 81, 100, 300, 408, 1822, 2374, 2375, 4960
Terrain 998, 2711, 3732, 3883, 3887, 3896, 3966, 4145, 4232, 5363
Terreur 685, 752, 1081, 1781, 3457, 4973, 5466
Territoire 966, 987, 1000, 1288, 1362, 3684, 3693, 3869, 3871, 3953
  voir aussi: Départements et territoires d'Outre-Mer
Territorialité 58, 1000, 1806
Test d'aptitude 2214
Tests d'aptitude 1787
Tests de personnalité 587
Tests empiriques 477, 2214, 4298, 5073, 5075
Textes 138, 151, 169, 530, 666, 984, 1353, 1757, 1796, 1832, 1874, 1924, 1944, 2190, 3775
Textes religieux 200, 233, 266, 1382, 1402, 1426, 1458, 1473, 1478, 1518, 1534, 1552
Textiles 3881, 4219, 4446
Thai 3479
Thanatologie 1383

Théâtre 171, 1100, 1862, 1868, 1872, 1874, 1875, 3112, 3391
  voir aussi: Sociologie du théâtre
Théologie 3, 15, 145, 220, 221, 239, 267, 272, 1379, 1388, 1390, 1391, 1410, 1413, 1452, 1455, 1462, 1477, 1478, 1483, 1487, 1491, 1497, 1506, 1526, 1547, 1564, 3028, 5687, 5722
Théologie chrétienne 266, 1388
Théologie de libération 1478, 1514
Théorie anthropologique 14, 109, 381, 449, 929, 1395, 2544
Théorie artistiques 1848, 1866, 1869
Théorie critique 213, 253, 274, 285, 303, 307, 315, 317, 325, 337, 354, 365, 366, 369, 398, 1221, 1233, 1265, 1278, 1296, 1314, 1566, 1713, 1792, 1848, 1878, 3102, 3144, 3453, 4911, 5166, 5704
Théorie de chaos 292, 2323, 5091
Théorie de la croissance 2793
Théorie de la culture 1395
Théorie de la décision 115, 364, 366, 464, 515, 606, 638, 1049, 1050, 1085, 4391, 5752
Théorie de la démocratie 3437, 4906, 4907, 4928, 4947
Théorie de la firme 4407, 4753
Théorie de la planification 3814, 4030, 4036, 4041, 4073, 4084, 4118
Théorie de la valeur 288, 4186
Théorie de l'action 363, 371, 373
Théorie de l'éducation 647, 2004, 2011, 2164, 2168, 2170, 2171, 2177, 2181, 2224, 2280
Théorie de l'emploi 4588, 4597
Théorie de l'État 4961
Théorie de l'information 1587
Théorie de l'intégration 1494
Théorie de l'organisation 396, 1019, 1032, 1033, 1089-1094, 1098, 1100, 1101, 1104-1111, 1114, 1115, 1117, 1118, 1120-1123, 1125, 1127-1130, 1132, 1133, 1136-1138, 1140-1143, 1145, 1148, 1150, 1154, 1157, 1672, 1701, 1957, 2555, 3097, 3705, 3775, 4346, 4360, 4408, 4409, 4412, 4424, 4427, 4428, 4468, 4607, 4609, 4612, 4617, 4618, 4622, 4627, 4632, 4638, 4648, 4649, 4669, 4672, 4770, 4802, 5216, 5555, 5799, 5932
Théorie de l'utilité 342, 464, 3705
Théorie de mandant et mandataire 4416
Théorie de systèmes 345, 350, 359, 371, 372, 376, 380, 386, 402, 552, 1006, 1115, 1652, 1705, 1999, 2323, 2409, 2411, 2508, 3037, 3705, 4833, 4970, 5236, 5668, 5735

SUBJECT INDEX IN FRENCH

Théorie des jeux 366, 420, 463, 467, 486, 1079, 1638, 2308, 4388, 5154, 5231
Théorie des quanta 1602, 1614, 1623
Théorie des relations internationales 4818, 5315, 5317, 5319, 5336
Théorie des systèmes généraux 1270
Théorie du change 1062, 2341
Théorie du conflit 399, 1011, 1020, 1025, 1028, 2850, 4217, 4378
Théorie du développement 585, 1221, 2528, 2539, 2774, 3160, 3770, 3771, 3803, 4177, 4279, 4287
Théorie du groupe 947, 1029, 1037, 1061, 1074, 1076, 1081
Théorie du marché 2967
Théorie du rôle 4416
Théorie économique 381, 1098, 1377, 1570, 2447, 2706, 3000, 3705, 3927, 4181, 4196, 4211, 4230, 4351, 4405, 4739
Théorie feministe 20, 449, 570, 600, 674, 1195, 1234, 1269, 1296, 1449, 1882, 1913, 1915, 2347, 2471, 2589, 2623, 2917, 2978, 3079, 3086, 3087, 3095-3097, 3099-3101, 3107-3113, 3115-3121, 3123-3125, 3129-3131, 3135, 3137-3139, 3141-3144, 3146-3148, 3150-3153, 3155, 3158, 3159, 3162, 3169, 3205, 3228, 3243, 3261, 3282, 3288, 3299, 3302, 3324, 3339, 3377, 3449, 4191, 4839, 4958, 5299, 5474, 5544, 5861
Théorie générale 258, 409, 1210, 5108
Théorie juridique 1566, 4907, 5025, 5149, 5150, 5152, 5158, 5160, 5161, 5163, 5165, 5166, 5173, 5177, 5179-5181, 5185, 5188, 5197-5199, 5201, 5207, 5208, 5210, 5311, 5322
Théorie linguistique 1239, 1722, 1989
Théorie littéraire 99, 669, 1789, 1919, 3102
Théorie militaire 5348, 5355
Théorie monétaire 4193
Théorie politique 307, 325, 352, 368, 393, 1039, 1194, 1221, 1250, 1265, 2546, 3144, 4889, 4890, 4897, 4901, 4902, 4907, 4918, 4922, 4924, 4925, 4932, 4936, 4941, 4953, 4972, 5055, 5201, 5336, 5886
Théorie sociale 6, 10, 14, 21, 26, 32, 34, 35, 41, 53, 68, 75, 89, 108, 121, 158, 214, 217, 243, 253, 268, 269, 275, 277, 285, 287, 294, 296, 307-309, 311, 315-318, 320, 322, 325, 326, 328-330, 332, 334, 335, 337, 340, 341, 343, 345, 348, 351-354, 357, 358, 361-363, 366-368, 371, 372, 375, 377, 378, 381, 383-385, 387, 390, 392, 393, 395, 397, 401, 403-407, 410, 430, 439, 463, 474, 575, 825, 875, 881, 922, 968, 990, 1011, 1031, 1039, 1053, 1074, 1081, 1115, 1130, 1139, 1158, 1166, 1194, 1199, 1210, 1214, 1215, 1221, 1235, 1238, 1245, 1250, 1253, 1263, 1272, 1273, 1276, 1278, 1280, 1281, 1289, 1325, 1351, 1366, 1390, 1403, 1598, 1614, 1647, 1651, 1706, 1792, 1848, 1879, 1921, 2211, 2217, 2300, 2302, 2310, 2317, 2319, 2330, 2331, 2346, 2349, 2384, 2395, 2402, 2413, 2417, 2428, 2433, 2465, 2477, 2528, 2531, 2546, 2568, 2589, 2622, 2742, 3084, 3086, 3100, 3101, 3124, 3130, 3139, 3142, 3144, 3151, 3339, 3368, 3376, 3444, 3453, 3504, 3629, 3693, 3698, 3721, 3788, 3802, 4180, 4181, 4186, 4193, 4196, 4360, 4419, 4837, 4865, 4889, 4893, 4894, 4898, 4911, 4918, 4920-4922, 4925, 4987, 5049, 5074, 5086, 5122, 5130, 5246, 5273, 5309, 5369, 5372, 5603, 5619, 5650, 5652
voir aussi: Analyse post-structurale
Théorie sociologique 5, 7, 14-16, 21, 23, 26, 27, 29-31, 33, 34, 41, 44, 51, 55, 65-67, 69, 72, 75, 115, 119, 122, 143, 197, 223, 243, 248, 269, 275, 287, 288, 292, 294, 304, 306, 307, 312-314, 316-319, 321, 323, 324, 327, 328, 330, 332, 334-337, 339, 341, 345, 347, 350-352, 354-357, 361, 363, 364, 369-374, 377, 378, 381, 383, 386-390, 394-396, 398-400, 402-404, 406, 408, 474, 563, 567, 745, 759, 875, 943, 1062, 1110, 1120, 1152, 1194, 1196, 1201, 1211, 1212, 1229, 1233, 1251, 1263-1266, 1273, 1350, 1352, 1395, 1403, 1406, 1446, 1449, 1570, 1575, 1581, 1621, 1633, 1640, 1649, 1651, 1693, 1705, 1706, 1715, 1800, 1842, 1858, 1866, 1944, 2117, 2300, 2302, 2312, 2315, 2319, 2322, 2329, 2341, 2384, 2397, 2430, 2435, 2436, 2440, 2448, 2510, 2519, 2531, 2540, 2555, 2568, 2953, 3057, 3086, 3100, 3101, 3142, 3151, 3194, 3514, 3528, 3632, 3701, 3705, 3712, 3946, 4187, 4196, 4239, 4329, 4404, 4616, 4888, 4953, 4987, 5073, 5075, 5095, 5120, 5270, 5276, 5277, 5319, 5332, 5336, 5668, 5709, 5817, 5878
Thérapeutique 5721
Thérapie 705, 737, 742, 746, 747, 749, 767, 770, 772, 782, 794, 799, 813, 2628, 3093, 5175, 5391, 5406, 5412, 5413, 5538, 5668, 5675, 5699, 5721, 5737, 5742, 5839, 5847, 5870, 5874, 5884, 5925, 5928, 5936, 5938

Thérapie familiale 402, 1270, 1275, 2613, 2900, 2905, 2910, 2911, 2920, 2937, 2946, 2960, 2987, 3037, 3382, 5566, 5595, 5599, 5668, 5671, 5675, 5680-5682, 5717, 5721
Thérapie professionnelle 1053, 5420, 5939
Thesaurus 82, 97
Thèses 457, 2282
Thomasius, Christian 208
Tilly, Charles 2384
Tissage 4568
Tocqueville, Alexis de 4288
Tolérance 350, 352, 1058, 1547, 1995, 2380, 2990, 3420, 3462, 3470, 4422, 4962, 4996, 5208, 5662
Tolstoy, Leo 5356
Topologie 1605, 3358
Totalitarisme 410, 1253, 2567, 4973
Tourisme 1170, 1257, 1314, 1317, 1324, 1328, 1329, 1342, 1346, 1362, 1366, 1367, 1950, 2545, 3143, 3334, 3348, 3375, 3443, 3709, 3735, 3745, 3754, 3761, 3763, 3771, 3772, 3776, 3777, 3785, 3791, 3792, 3820-3822, 3854, 3908, 3914, 3925, 3944, 3970, 4113, 4219, 4238, 5080, 5335
Tourisme international 1342, 1366, 3792, 4046, 4238, 5335
Toxicomanes 5375, 5376, 5378, 5401, 5801
Toxicomanie 5367, 5375, 5376, 5379, 5386, 5406, 5664, 5801
Tradition 134, 892, 965, 975, 992, 1002, 1183, 1257, 1343, 1408, 1533, 1549, 2388, 2516, 2915, 3064, 3221, 3265, 3266, 3268, 3362, 3646, 3723, 3736, 3869, 3949, 4128, 4141, 4201, 4243, 4367, 4577, 4864, 5317, 5529
Tradition culturelle 561, 1170, 1175, 1267, 1343, 1364, 1367, 2575, 2866
Tradition orale 986, 1433, 1913
Traditionalisme 992, 1222, 1363, 4217
Traditions artistiques 1861
Traditions populaires 1973
Traditions religieuses 1408, 1442, 1444, 1456, 1504
Traduction 132, 1231, 1534, 1557, 1582, 1689, 1822, 1915, 1978, 2227, 2461
Trafic de la drogue 2559
Trains 2826
Traitement de l'information 552, 580, 623, 625, 642, 655, 658, 662, 663, 666, 823, 827, 865, 920, 1084, 5579
Traitement des données 2201
Traitement hospitalier 5788

Traitement médical 705, 747-749, 765, 766, 772, 813, 816, 2905, 3010, 5375, 5391, 5395, 5398, 5401, 5406, 5407, 5413, 5420, 5480, 5502, 5670, 5680, 5737, 5743, 5744, 5764, 5766, 5806, 5818, 5847, 5874, 5877, 5879, 5882, 5889-5892, 5902, 5906, 5912, 5913, 5918, 5928, 5936, 5952, 5968, 5971, 5982, 5986
Traités 3526
Traits de personnalité 678, 694, 698, 710, 727, 735, 855
Tranche d'âge 534, 1768, 2587, 2597, 2616, 2618, 2620, 2648, 2681, 2724, 2827, 2835, 2852, 2893, 3606, 3620, 3625, 4362, 4581, 4752, 4852, 5432, 5610
Transfert 846
Transfert de technologie 2580
Transition de régime 746, 1942, 2533, 2534, 4292, 4971, 5003, 5341
Transnationalisme 52, 983, 1240, 1263, 1268, 1363, 1467, 1737, 2446, 2545, 2553, 2562, 2571, 3148, 3499, 3540, 3599, 3632, 3645, 3683, 3826, 4032, 4768, 4957, 5241, 5242, 5252, 5313, 5335
Transparence 1608, 3807, 4227, 4955, 4963
Transport 291, 1299, 1302, 3877, 4045, 4051, 4062, 4068, 4083, 4124, 5225, 5335
voir aussi: Moyens de transport
Transport ferroviaire 2826, 4048, 4076
Transport public 1299, 2716, 3994, 4023, 4068, 5093
Transport urbain 3982, 4037, 4053, 4062, 4074, 4087
Transsexualisme 786, 803
Traumatisme 742, 764, 767, 779, 785, 795, 796, 812, 814, 815, 819, 820, 1004, 1844, 2510, 2536, 2874, 5349, 5458, 5683, 5721, 5910, 5917, 5921, 5923
Travail 291, 311, 314, 707, 1282, 1290, 1672, 2372, 2399, 2421, 2457, 2507, 3121, 3188, 3268, 3545, 3633, 3909, 4206, 4231, 4263, 4368, 4395, 4411, 4442, 4444, 4446, 4448, 4453, 4456, 4458, 4467, 4478, 4479, 4485, 4524, 4539, 4558, 4560, 4576, 4591, 4616, 4643, 4649, 4677, 4681, 4715, 4740, 4811, 4812, 4819, 4820, 4825, 4826, 4832, 4853, 4859, 4863, 4864, 4873, 4875
voir aussi: Anthropologie du travail, Division du travail, Main-d'œuvre féminine
Travail à domicile 1283, 2141, 4302
Travail agricole 513

Subject Index in French

Travail bénévole 59, 61, 734, 1035, 1156, 1285, 1512, 2371, 3843, 3844, 3862, 4768, 5484, 5586, 5615, 5719, 5723
Travail clandestin 4449
Travail de classe 2027
Travail d'équipe 463, 655, 1033, 1048, 1056, 1065, 1071, 1072, 1080, 1091, 1135, 1660, 4356, 4384, 4408, 4428, 4607, 4608, 4617, 4618, 4670, 4741, 5715, 5846, 5934
Travail des enfants 2035, 4430, 4442, 4449, 4452, 4455, 4469, 4482, 5366, 5686
Travail des femmes 3194, 3206, 3281, 3677, 4480, 4525, 4536, 4544, 4560, 5969
Travail intellectuel 4199
Travail ménager 1290, 2272, 2957, 3121, 3170, 3188, 3221, 3267, 3307, 4337, 4452, 4462, 4529
Travail par roulement 2975
Travail social 764, 1053, 2423, 2456, 2582, 2602, 2859, 2865, 2869, 2884, 2887, 2952, 3586, 4585, 5016, 5023, 5373, 5427, 5464, 5481, 5483, 5488, 5490, 5495, 5527, 5530, 5533, 5540, 5542-5545, 5549, 5550, 5554, 5556, 5557, 5559, 5566, 5569, 5570, 5572, 5574, 5578, 5586, 5589, 5599, 5635, 5647, 5657, 5663-5667, 5669, 5670, 5672-5674, 5676-5679, 5683-5689, 5692-5716, 5719, 5720, 5722, 5723, 5739, 5764, 5904, 5908, 5910, 5911, 5917, 5923
Travail social des groupes 2199, 5030
Travail sur le terrain 9, 76, 538, 716, 1110, 1130, 1353, 1581
Travailleurs 1111, 1927, 3553, 3633, 3663, 3671, 3673, 4263, 4275, 4403, 4416, 4433, 4441, 4444, 4448, 4471, 4485, 4558, 4591, 4599, 4698, 4700, 4702, 4726, 4729, 4739, 4741, 4745, 4803, 4809, 4813, 4815, 4817, 4821, 4822, 4826, 4840, 4849, 4850, 4855, 4858, 4869 *voir aussi:* Chercheurs, Cols blancs, Employés de bureau, Employés de commerce, Gens de maison, Ouvriers industriels, Ouvriers qualifiés, Travailleuses
Travailleurs âgés 4465
Travailleurs agricoles 1359, 2886, 3889, 4558, 4674, 4775
Travailleurs étrangers 2574, 3572, 3587, 3594, 3597, 3642, 3657, 4363, 4463, 4529, 4856
Travailleurs handicapés 2455, 2468, 2489, 5215
Travailleurs indépendants 3594, 4432, 4456, 4459, 4461, 4473, 4474, 4479, 4556, 4598, 4665, 4676, 4780

Travailleurs migrants 58, 2550, 2886, 3556, 3568, 3597, 3609, 3662, 3665, 4443, 4552, 5638
Travailleurs professionnels 799, 802, 1285, 1305, 1977, 2082, 3175, 4383, 4457, 4518, 4555, 4601, 4738, 4770, 4779, 4782, 4788, 4789, 4793, 4876, 5709, 5845, 5925, 5953
Travailleurs saisonniers 3661
Travailleurs sociaux 2464, 2882, 4789, 5023, 5483, 5488, 5501, 5527, 5530, 5540, 5545, 5549, 5556, 5569, 5572, 5595, 5630, 5663, 5666, 5667, 5672, 5674, 5676, 5685, 5687, 5689, 5690, 5692, 5694, 5695, 5697, 5700, 5701, 5705-5714, 5716, 5718, 5719, 5722
Travailleuses 513, 2091, 3040, 3075, 3127, 3229, 3232, 3267, 3270, 3280, 3325, 3557, 3670, 4415, 4443, 4462, 4478, 4480, 4488, 4504, 4508, 4513, 4516, 4517, 4523, 4524, 4536, 4557, 4558, 4565, 4566, 4568, 4570, 4575, 4632, 4694, 4839, 4883, 5131, 5203, 5651, 5838
Travaux publics 1849
Travestisme 3276
Tremblements de terre 3702, 5923
Tribalisme 3417, 5363
Tribunaux 1010, 3891, 5017, 5054, 5056, 5072, 5132, 5137, 5139, 5154, 5157, 5170, 5172, 5184, 5191, 5205, 5209 *voir aussi:* Cour Suprême
Tribunaux militaires 5139
Tribunaux pour enfants 5036, 5068, 5192, 5209, 5583
Tribus 2379, 2505, 2515, 2783, 3736, 3776, 3920, 5553
Tristesse 683, 690, 863, 948
Troisième Reich 173, 189, 3532
Tromperie 949, 2986
Troubles de comportement 545, 591, 756, 2892, 3032, 3050, 5405, 5468, 5901, 5906, 5918
Troubles de la personnalité 695, 731, 788, 790, 820
Troubles du comportement alimentaire 506, 744, 777, 791, 817, 2667, 5182, 5847
Trypanosomiase 5968
Tsung-hsi, Huang 1423
Turcs 1985, 2227, 2940, 3536, 3596, 3605, 5823
Turing, Alan 1593
Turner, Stephen 597
Types de consommation 3799, 4335

INDEX DES MATIÈRES

Typologie 399, 1459, 1569, 1999, 2111, 2363, 2646, 3192, 3625, 3930, 4407, 4582, 4584, 4623, 4994, 5460, 5771
UNHCR 3611, 3674
UNICEF 5973
Unification d'Allemagne 165, 2124, 2567, 2922, 3455, 3532, 4066, 4297, 4795
Union européenne 64, 969, 1000, 2423, 2518, 2530, 2684, 2720, 3069, 3220, 3321, 3468, 3878, 3890, 4203, 4439, 4541, 4589, 4783, 4813, 4835, 4837, 4872, 4952, 4957, 4966, 5025, 5290, 5295, 5598, 5622, 5623, 5793
  voir aussi: Élargissement de l'UE, Politique agricole commune
Unionisme 2079, 3269, 4832, 4852, 4861, 4862, 4867, 4868
Unions monétaires 4185
Universalisme 255, 340, 382, 405, 888, 1198, 1208, 1240, 1267, 1269, 2212, 2348, 2349, 2563, 3335, 4923, 4931, 5320
Universités 47, 50, 85, 102, 191, 225, 339, 376, 775, 996, 1155, 1158, 1203, 1217, 1604, 1617, 1631, 1715, 2009, 2018, 2033, 2045, 2052, 2057, 2075, 2089, 2118, 2129, 2139, 2145, 2147, 2183, 2188, 2195, 2196, 2200, 2207, 2213, 2222, 2223, 2226, 2242-2245, 2248, 2249, 2251-2264, 2266-2269, 2274, 2277, 2278, 2280, 2281, 2283-2286, 2290, 2291, 2293-2296, 2298, 2299, 2361, 2383, 2454, 3067, 3078, 3115, 3175, 3183, 3291, 3293, 3296, 3439, 3398, 4494, 4514, 4563, 4564, 4655, 4714, 4733, 4935, 4949, 5267, 5268
Urbanisation 1540, 2561, 2718, 2733, 3010, 3486, 3612, 3616, 3702, 3755, 3813, 3867, 3927, 3932, 3947-3949, 3955, 3960, 3962, 3964, 4011, 4142, 4149-4152, 4156, 4158, 4160, 4162-4166, 4168, 4170-4173, 4175-4178, 4197, 5055, 5686
Urbanisme 3929, 3955, 4010, 4023, 4033
Usage de stupéfiants 5115, 5392, 5409, 5664, 5958, 5966
Usage de substances toxiques 5409
Usage du tabac 625, 709, 890, 2738, 2845, 5389, 5407, 5433, 5956, 5968, 5986
Usines 4430, 4617
Utilisation des ressources 3713, 3735, 4246
Utilisation des terres 3152, 3611, 3696, 3876, 3914, 4035, 4047, 4058, 4059, 4074, 4082, 4088, 4099, 4108, 4145, 4170, 4189, 5363, 5838, 5968
Utilitarisme 276, 346, 373, 375, 2445, 5886
Utopie 295, 801, 1229, 3697, 3787, 4210, 4917

Utopisme 1622, 1941
Vacances 1312, 2330, 3679, 4751, 5080
Vache 5948
Valeur 2, 472, 638, 1246, 1716, 1859, 2018, 2341, 2412, 2639, 3402, 3703, 3705, 3744, 3763, 4186, 4351, 4390
Valeurs 11, 48, 170, 206, 226, 241, 264, 319, 393, 524, 650, 737, 892, 986, 1012, 1073, 1095, 1112, 1156, 1183, 1247, 1285, 1359, 1369, 1387, 1388, 1406, 1421, 1440, 1642, 2084, 2186, 2218, 2347, 2351-2353, 2357, 2359, 2361, 2362, 2365, 2366, 2372, 2373, 2502, 2587, 2646, 2675, 2920, 2945, 3013, 3178, 3202, 3324, 3486, 3547, 3726, 3818, 3914, 4148, 4229, 4296, 4307, 4417, 4422, 4497, 4644, 4658, 4910, 4962, 5208, 5409, 5529, 5630, 5704, 5783, 5829
Valeurs culturelles 996, 1176, 1203, 1609, 1864, 2505, 2566, 3009, 3660, 4253, 4359, 4823, 5397
Valeurs sociales 160, 1292, 2283, 2313, 2343, 3081, 3589, 3806, 4318, 4642
Validité 4599, 5179
Vampires 1239
Vandalisme 5369
Vandelisme 1341
Vargas, Fred 1958
Variance 496, 668, 866, 2304
Variation régionale 1209, 2701, 2844, 2944, 3113, 4281, 4587, 5454, 5494, 5537, 5968
Variations saisonnières 445, 2800, 2819, 3767, 5324, 5636, 5756
Variole 5983
Veblen, Thorstein Bunde 1848
Védisme 1384
Végétarisme 1296
Vengeance 263, 5040
Ventes 4320, 4420
Vérification comptable 3195-3198, 4355, 4773, 5023
Verité 106, 120, 140, 146, 202, 209, 213, 224, 256, 261, 277, 296, 297, 455, 494, 568, 579, 926, 1008, 1018, 1110, 1403, 1472, 1578, 1581, 1731, 1878, 3354
Vêtements 1316, 2399, 3067, 3256, 4344
Veuvage 2910
Veuve 186, 2652, 2923
Viande bovine 5948
Viande de porc 3447
Victime de viol 5457
Victime de violence 2878, 5192, 5321, 5457, 5470
Victimes 471, 767, 814, 1719, 2235, 2863, 3289, 3458, 3624, 5020, 5044, 5112, 5116,

SUBJECT INDEX IN FRENCH

5123, 5175, 5321, 5440, 5457, 5458, 5683
voir aussi: Aide aux victimes de crime
Victimes de crime 5040, 5061, 5080, 5101, 5106
Vidéo 444, 686, 1018, 1711, 1779, 1889, 1909, 2175
Vidyālankāra, Raghunātha 132
Vie 179, 431, 490, 2020, 3094, 3268, 5438, 5573
Vie active 1304, 1645, 3255, 4738, 4739, 4757
Vie communautaire 2371, 3845, 3902
Vie conjugale 2861, 2911
Vie culturelle 86, 331, 1175, 1476, 1527, 1889, 2534, 4981
Vie économique 1298, 4322
Vie familiale 792, 1284, 1371, 1690, 1809, 2574, 2633, 2898, 2903, 2915, 2921, 2925, 2950, 3050, 3255, 3328, 4557, 5633, 5693
Vie internationale 2570
Vie politique 1298, 1889, 4895, 5299
Vie privée 69, 1361, 2941, 4988
voir aussi: Droit à la vie privée
Vie quotidienne 30, 469, 711, 722, 802, 1211, 1278, 1282, 1283, 1287, 1288, 1291, 1292, 1294, 1295, 1303, 1304, 1316, 1359, 1371, 1728, 1978, 1984, 2157, 2352, 2456, 2606, 2649, 2677, 2679, 2830, 3091, 3255, 3256, 3297, 3387, 3484, 3767, 3845, 4011, 4115, 4295, 5428, 5891, 5894
Vie religieuse 998, 1407, 1433, 1520, 2673
Vie rurale 1363, 3886-3888, 3895, 3904, 3916
Vie sociale 268, 284, 310, 320, 331, 334, 369, 387, 406, 1174, 1200, 1219, 1238, 1245, 1291, 1292, 1294, 1298, 1304, 1322, 1333, 1340, 1442, 1590, 1686, 1728, 2003, 2217, 2301, 2334, 2337, 2373, 2429, 2504, 2555, 2683, 3383, 3514, 3596, 3785, 3864, 3888, 3949, 3954, 4125, 4262, 4298, 4768, 4977, 5123, 5215, 5308, 5716
Vie urbaine 2377, 2633, 2679, 3359, 3387, 3848, 3928, 3929, 3933, 3934, 3939, 3948, 3949, 3953, 3955, 3993, 3996, 4021, 4027, 4065, 4119, 4132, 4135, 4144, 4147, 4148, 4155, 5429
Vieillesse 612, 2651, 2658, 2668, 2671, 2678, 5016, 5510, 5511, 5515, 5523, 5526, 5536, 5738
Vieillissement 612, 716, 1647, 2532, 2583, 2584, 2588, 2590, 2651, 2652, 2654, 2659, 2664-2668, 2670, 2672-2674, 2676, 2678-2680, 2707, 2801, 3272, 4558, 4581, 5479, 5492-5494, 5498, 5502, 5503, 5507,

5508, 5510, 5516, 5518-5520, 5525, 5531, 5532, 5602, 5738, 5740
Vieillissement de la population 2654, 2656, 2657, 2669, 2677, 2679, 2693, 2702, 2707, 2712, 2713, 2802, 2805, 2934, 3951, 5498, 5512, 5514, 5519
Vietnamiens 975
VIH 427, 581, 781, 1883, 2726, 2754, 2806, 2810, 3037, 3309, 3311, 3316, 3326, 3327, 3329, 3332, 3370, 3380, 3381, 4611, 5200, 5363, 5386, 5387, 5745, 5764, 5773, 5838, 5854, 5856, 5872, 5874, 5885, 5890, 5891, 5894, 5942, 5944, 5945, 5951, 5952, 5957, 5958, 5964-5966, 5968, 5974, 5975, 5980-5982, 5984, 5987
Villages 1295, 1707, 2152, 2338, 3644, 3739, 3776, 3831, 3855, 3885, 3886, 3890, 3892, 3899, 3916, 3917, 4477, 5279
Villes 2338, 3447, 3831, 3932, 3941, 3945, 3946, 3953, 3964, 3969, 3971, 3992, 4021, 4029, 4051, 4060, 4078, 4122, 4152, 4154, 4161, 4165, 4171, 4233
voir aussi: Bidonville, Petites villes
Villes capitales 3940, 3947, 3949, 3963, 4048, 4057, 4066, 4099, 4113, 4136
Villes nouvelles 3983, 4070, 4172
Viol 3070, 3112, 3298, 3534, 5191, 5449, 5457-5459, 5462, 5546
Violence 801, 835, 872, 908, 1199, 1341, 1887, 1889, 2119, 2321, 2340, 2369, 2521, 2643, 2754, 2860-2863, 2865-2867, 2871, 2872, 2874, 2875, 2877, 2882, 2883, 2886-2890, 2892, 2894, 2951, 2979, 3138, 3201, 3438, 3457, 3468, 3485, 3492, 3520, 3531, 3930, 3938, 3944, 3957, 4269, 4482, 4691, 4977, 4984, 4993, 4997, 5044, 5050, 5058, 5062, 5068, 5069, 5097, 5114, 5133, 5138, 5139, 5251, 5256, 5327, 5331, 5349, 5361, 5368, 5430, 5437-5440, 5442-5452, 5454, 5456, 5461-5473, 5580, 5594, 5838, 5914, 5917, 5934
Violence dans la famille 2860-2876, 2878-2889, 2891-2893, 2895, 2991, 5144, 5382, 5439, 5444, 5451, 5459, 5463, 5469, 5594
Violence politique 186, 1000, 1262, 1546, 1707, 1781, 2340, 5233, 5466
Vocabulaire 100, 4179
Voile 3172, 3266
Vol 471, 5067, 5085, 5367, 5369
Volcans 3702, 3776
Volonté à payer 3705
Voyages 65, 1176, 1329, 1393, 1528, 2826, 3143, 3230, 3245, 3443, 4053, 5313,

5335, 5415
voir aussi: Histoire des voyages
Voyages internationaux 3348
Vraciu, Ioan 3354
Vue 628, 1897
Vygotsky, Lev 162, 1161, 2224
Walder, Andrew 4241
Walser, Martin 3532
Walzer, Michael 2448
Wampar 3776
Washington, Booker T. 3528
Weber, Max 314, 318, 343, 364, 365, 370, 373, 408, 409, 801, 1406, 4239, 5211
Weil, Eric 225
Wendt, Alex 5310
Weor, Samael Aun 1501
Whitehead, Alfred North 225
Wilde, Oscar 1882
Winch, Peter 268, 303, 304
Winfrey, Oprah 1361
Wittgenstein, Ludwig 225, 262, 268, 282, 303, 304, 1846
Wolof 3907
Woolf, Virginia 1941
Xénophobie 1705, 3452, 3455, 3466, 3485, 3502, 3599
Xhosa 1841, 2523
Yeats, William Butler 1227
Yi, Cheng 266
Yoruba 1431, 2761
Yougoslaves 4255
Yukagir 3425
Zen 202, 250, 1464

Zionisme 985, 991, 1380, 1546, 2177, 3420, 3450
Zone agricole 3813
Zone tropicale 5980
Zones industrielles 3206, 4848
Zones piétonnières 4146
Zones résidentielles 3481, 3899, 3970, 3987, 4022, 4054, 4098, 4130, 4136, 4153, 4165
Zones rurales 1343, 1468, 2186, 2234, 2655, 2660, 2663, 2675, 2712, 2718, 2739, 2800, 2843, 2886, 2939, 2961, 3010, 3043, 3612, 3626, 3767, 3776, 3841, 3866, 3876, 3884, 3886, 3897, 3900, 3901, 3905, 3908, 3915, 3924, 4108, 4292, 4558, 5417, 5757, 5838, 5954, 5962, 5975
Zones suburbaines 2451, 2633, 3725, 3983, 3993, 4026, 4077, 4112, 4119, 4150, 4164, 4175, 4176, 4489, 4490, 5426, 5526
Zones urbaines 471, 2104, 2151, 2234, 2451, 2789, 2841, 2843, 2889, 2998, 3010, 3300, 3359, 3612, 3696, 3784, 3848, 3933, 3939-3942, 3946, 3948, 3949, 3951, 3953, 3957, 3958, 3960, 3963, 3966, 3971, 3976, 3995, 3999-4001, 4016, 4021, 4025, 4029, 4031, 4042, 4048, 4050, 4057, 4058, 4060, 4065, 4072, 4075, 4077, 4093, 4099, 4101, 4107, 4120, 4128, 4139, 4142, 4149, 4151, 4153, 4157, 4159, 4161, 4163, 4165, 4168, 4174, 4175, 4182, 4233, 4301, 4303, 4492, 4511, 4558, 4566, 5053, 5119, 5271, 5386, 5815, 5962